Legal Research and Writing for Paralegals

Chapter 9 & 10 final

The McGraw-Hill Paralegal List

WHERE EDUCATIONAL SUPPORT GOES BEYOND EXPECTATIONS.

Introduction to Law & Paralegal Studies
Connie Farrell Scuderi
ISBN: 0073524638
© 2008

Introduction to Law for Paralegals
Deborah Benton
ISBN: 007351179X
© 2008

Basic Legal Research, Second Edition
Edward Nolfi
ISBN: 0073520519
© 2008

Basic Legal Writing, Second Edition
Pamela Tepper
ISBN: 0073403032
© 2008

Contract Law for Paralegals
Linda Spagnola
ISBN: 0073511765
© 2008

Civil Law and Litigation for Paralegals
Neal Bevans
ISBN: 0073524611
© 2008

Wills, Trusts, and Estates for Paralegals
George Kent
ISBN: 0073403067
© 2008

The Law Office Reference Manual
Jo Ann Lee
ISBN: 0073511838
© 2008

The Paralegal Reference Manual
Charles Nemeth
ISBN: 0073403075
© 2008

The Professional Paralegal
Allan Tow
ISBN: 0073403091
© 2009

Ethics for Paralegals
Linda Spagnola and Vivian Batts
ISBN: 0073376981
© 2009

Family Law for Paralegals
George Kent
ISBN: 0073376973
© 2009

McGraw-Hill's Torts for Paralegals
ISBN: 0073376930
© 2009

McGraw-Hill's Real Estate Law for Paralegals
ISBN: 0073376957
© 2009

Legal Research and Writing for Paralegals
Pamela Tepper and Neal Bevans
ISBN: 007352462X
© 2009

McGraw-Hill's Criminal Law for Paralegals
ISBN: 0073376965
© 2009

McGraw-Hill's Law Office Management for Paralegals
ISBN: 0073376949
© 2009

Legal Terminology Explained
Edward Nolfi
ISBN: 0073511846
© 2009

For more information or to receive desk copies, please contact your McGraw-Hill Sales Representative.

Legal Research and Writing for Paralegals

Pamela R. Tepper
University of the Virgin Islands

Neal R. Bevans
Western Piedmont Community College

McGraw-Hill Higher Education

Boston Burr Ridge, IL Dubuque, IA New York San Francisco St. Louis
Bangkok Bogotá Caracas Kuala Lumpur Lisbon London Madrid Mexico City
Milan Montreal New Delhi Santiago Seoul Singapore Sydney Taipei Toronto

The McGraw·Hill Companies

LEGAL RESEARCH AND WRITING FOR PARALEGALS

This book is printed on acid-free paper.

3 4 5 6 7 8 9 0 VNH/VNH 1 5 4 3 2

ISBN 978-0-07-352462-7
MHID 0-07-352462-X

Vice President/Editor in Chief: *Elizabeth Haefele*
Vice President/Director of Marketing: *John E. Biernat*
Sponsoring editor: *Natalie Ruffatto*
Developmental editor: *Alaina Grayson*
Freelance developmental editor: *Beth Baugh*
Marketing manager: *Keari Bedford*
Lead media producer: *Damian Moshak*
Media developmental editor: *William Mulford*
Director, Editing/Design/Production: *Jess Ann Kosic*
Project manager: *Jean Starr*
Production supervisor: *Janean Utley*
Designer: *Marianna Kinigakis*
Media project manager: *Mark Dierker*
Cover design: *Studio Montage*
Interior design: *Jenny El-Shamy*
Typeface: *10.5/13 Times New Roman*
Compositor: *Aptara, Inc.*
Printer: *RR Donnelley*
Cover credit: © *Royalty-Free/CORBIS*

Library of Congress Cataloging-in-Publication Data

Tepper, Pamela R., 1957-
Legal research and writing for paralegals / Pamela R. Tepper, Neal R. Bevans. — 1st ed.
p. cm.—(The McGraw-Hill paralegal list)
Includes bibliographical references and indexes.
ISBN-13: 978-0-07-352462-7 (alk. paper)
ISBN-10: 0-07-352462-X (alk. paper)
1. Legal research—United States. 2. Legal composition. I. Bevans, Neal R., 1961- II. Title.
KF240.T47 2009
340.072'073—dc22

2008004076

The Internet addresses listed in the text were accurate at the time of publication. The inclusion of a Web site does not indicate an endorsement by the authors or McGraw-Hill, and McGraw-Hill does not guarantee the accuracy of the information presented at these sites.

www.mhhe.com

Dedication

To my mom, Irene Tepper—this one's just for you and only you. Your support in this massive project never went unnoticed. Much love.

Pamela Tepper

About the Authors

Pamela R. Tepper is general counsel and vice president of Legal Affairs at the Gov. Juan F. Luis Hospital, St. Croix, U.S. Virgin Islands. Tepper worked in the Virgin Islands' Department of Justice as the deputy solicitor general, managing government contracts for the territory and special projects. She has taught paralegal studies at Southeastern Paralegal Institute, Southern Methodist University, and the University of Texas, Arlington campus. She continues her teaching at the University of the Virgin Islands, where she teaches Legal Research and Writing in the certificate and associates degree programs. *Basic Legal Writing,* 2d edition, is one of a number of books written by Tepper, which include *Contracts and the Uniform Commercial Code, Texas Legal Research,* and *Basic Legal Research and Writing.* Tepper graduated from Hamilton College with a B.A. and New England School of Law with a J.D. She is licensed to practice in Texas and the Virgin Islands.

Neal R. Bevans, is a former assistant district attorney and private attorney. A veteran of over 150 trials, Bevans has tried every major felony from rape, murder, and narcotics to armed robbery. One of his cases was televised nationally on Court TV. He has had extensive civil litigation experience while working as an insurance defense attorney. He has a J.D. degree from the University of Georgia (Order of the Barrister) and has been a college instructor for more than ten years. A multiple-year honoree in *Who's Who among America's Teachers,* Bevans is the author of numerous magazine articles and textbooks, including *Civil Law and Litigation for Paralegals.*

Preface

Mastering legal research and legal writing is like mastering a new language. It takes time until all the pieces come together. That's why this text is designed for you, the paralegal. Today, more than ever, paralegals are integral to the practice of law. Researching the law and drafting legal documents are some of the tasks paralegals must perform in a landscape that is ever changing because of the development of new technologies. This textbook takes these changes into account.

The textbook focuses on the critical areas that a paralegal will encounter in his or her daily practice. What is the law and how do I find it? How does the Internet affect what I do? Where can I locate examples of legal documents to assist in the drafting process? How do I integrate legal research into my legal writing? These are some of the questions that paralegals confront—questions that are answered in this textbook.

There are common threads to all the chapters, which are designed to provoke thought, illustrate practical application, and assist in developing assignments. Each chapter has cases that relate to the topics covered, called You Be the Judge. Some may even be familiar. The point of the cases chosen is twofold: (1) to show how the law relates to the topics discussed in the chapter, and (2) to show cases of situations that are happening today. The law is always changing. It should not be thought of as something remote. That is why cases involving the Iraq War, the Internet, and employment discrimination are showcased throughout the chapters.

Ethics is integral to the practice of law for both attorneys and paralegals. Yet, ethical issues involving paralegals are unique. Each chapter has a section titled Ethics Alert, which is devoted to some of the ethical issues a paralegal may face in the workplace. These issues are compounded because of today's technology and the Internet. As such, in each chapter there is a section devoted to the discussion of everything technology-related, called the The E-Factor. Here, technology is discussed from the use of e-mail and cellular telephones to participating in blogs and list servers. There are no limitations. Both the Ethics Alert and The E-Factor sections present issues that are relevant to how the paralegal practices today.

So much of the practice of law seems arcane and distant. Often we wonder why we are learning about a particular area and really just want to know how it all applies to real life. That is why each chapter contains a section called A Day in the Life of a Paralegal. This section offers real-life scenarios that a paralegal will confront. Hopefully, the fact scenarios will take some of the mystery out of the practice of law and show the human side of law practice.

To assist your understanding of the topics covered, extensive checklists and diagrams are provided. They act as a summary of the topics within each chapter. Use them as you begin a legal research or writing project.

Within each chapter, there are Practice Tips that identify some of the practical pointers used in the everyday practice. They are meant to compliment the text and continue the practical approach. Another new chapter feature is the Quick Quizzes. They consist of five true/false questions related the different sections of the chapter. For convenience, answers to the questions are located at the end of each chapter.

And finally, numerous practical exercises are contained within each chapter. Since the Internet is integral not only to the practice of law but to our daily lives, Internet exercises are highlighted throughout each chapter in the Cyber Trips. These are hands-on exercises that use the Internet exclusively. In today's day and age, technology and the Internet cannot be avoided. That is why familiarizing yourself with all types of technology and gaining a comfort level on the Internet is critical to your success as a paralegal. These Internet exercises are complemented by exercises at the end of each chapter, with one comprehensive project at the end of the chapter titled Portfolio Assignment. The Portfolio Assignments are designed as skill builders. However, they are also meant to create a "portfolio" for job interviews to showcase your work.

Since this text combines both legal research and legal writing, it will become a constant reference point even after you have completed your paralegal program. That is what makes this textbook unique from others—it is practical in its scope and practice.

ORGANIZATION OF THE TEXT

The text is composed of nineteen chapters and is divided into two main sections; the first section (Parts One through Three) focuses on legal research, both print and electronic, while the second section (Parts Four through Six) focuses on all aspects of legal writing. The first five chapters (Part One) focus on the court system and the sources of the law—primary and secondary. The student is introduced to legal citation and electronic research, which is discussed in more detail in later chapters. Once the basic sources of the law are understood, the text details the legal research "process" through "finding tools" such as digests and encyclopedias. This is followed by an entire chapter on Shepard's Citations and KeyCite, the two main legal tools for validating and updating. The remaining chapters in the first half of the text illustrate the dynamics of electronic research, introducing the student to the primary styles of searching—terms and connectors (Boolean) and natural language. Internet search techniques are coupled with an overview of the general sources available on the Internet. The last chapter of the legal research part culminates with a roadmap for students to use in all aspects of their legal research.

Once the legal research is concluded, the student is introduced to the intricacies of legal writing. Beginning with an overview of writing "do's" and "don'ts" in Chapters 11 through 13, the text details the importance of understanding one's purpose, audience, and other variables such as court rules and time constraints. Chapter 14 is devoted to learning how to properly cite legal authority as well as integrating legal citations into a legal document.

The rest of the legal writing section is dedicated to drafting of typical documents a paralegal will encounter in practice—hence a practical approach to legal writing. Thus, Chapter 15 introduces the student to all aspects of legal correspondence; Chapter 16 introduces the internal office memorandum; Chapter 17 is a brief overview of many of the documents a paralegal will draft in the litigation and discovery process; and Chapters 18 and 19 conclude with typical persuasive documents: the memorandum of law to the trial court and the appellate brief.

TEXT DESIGN

Each chapter begins with chapter objectives, followed by a Case Fact Pattern that was created to illustrate the application of legal writing concepts to the practice of law. Some may sound familiar, but any reference to names and places existing in either the past or present is purely coincidental. The list of objectives is a guide to the chapter and provides a focus for understanding the concepts presented in that chapter. The chapters build on one another; therefore, it is important to master the tasks and objectives in each chapter.

Although each chapter discusses the substantive points of legal research and legal writing, special features are included as mentioned earlier, such as You Be the Judge, Ethics Alert, and The E-Factor as well as Practice Tips, Key Terms and Practical Considerations. These sections combine practice, technology, and ethical issues that paralegals will face as they practice in real life. The section titled Practical Considerations offers helpful pointers from the paralegal's perspective rather than the attorney's. Often checklists are located in this section, but can also be found throughout the chapters.

For convenience and review, each chapter concludes with chapter summaries and exercises. These summaries and review activities provide an overview of the general points discussed in the chapter and act as a study guide and quick reference. The exercises offer practical approaches to the material contained in the chapter. At the end of each chapter exercise is a comprehensive practical exercise called Portfolio Assignment. This exercise is designed to use the skills mastered in the chapter and apply them to a practical assignment. The assignments in the legal writing part are designed for the students to use as samples of their work as they begin the interview process.

The approach and the design of this text are user-friendly. Key terms are shown in bold and defined in the margins at first use, with a list of these terms appearing at the end of each chapter. Students are encouraged to write in the books, to complete the activities, and to keep this text at home or in the office as a handy reference guide. Also included in the book, promoting the user-friendly approach, are comic strips from many of our favorite illustrators from the daily newspapers. The comic strips provide a backdrop for many of the concepts discussed in the chapter, including many of the ethical issues that arise in everyday practice.

This book will engage the students and teach them about the world of legal research and writing in a practical, accessible manner. Hopefully, while the students are learning the concepts, they will have some fun in the process.

OTHER LEARNING AND TEACHING RESOURCES

The **Online Learning Center (OLC)** is a Web site that follows the text chapter by chapter. OLC content is ancillary and supplementary material germane to the textbook—as students read the book, they can go online to review material or link to relevant Web sites. Students and instructors can access the Web sites for each of the McGraw-Hill paralegal texts from the main page of the Paralegal Super Site, www.mhhe.com/paralegal. Each OLC has a similar organization. An Information Center features an overview of the text, background on the author, and the Preface and Table of Contents from the book. Instructors can access the instructor's manual and PowerPoint presentations from the Instructor's Resource CD (IRCD). Students see the Key Terms list from the text as flashcards, as well as additional quizzes and exercises.

Acknowledgments

To complete a project of this complexity, you must have the support of many people—and I did. To the phenomenal team at McGraw-Hill, I say thank you—Keari Bedford, Margaret Berson, Sharon O'Donnell, Jean Starr, and Natalie Ruffatto. But I must single out one person on the team who was "my rock" throughout the entire process, Natalie Ruffatto. As my sponsoring editor, you were supportive and insightful when I needed it. You always were available to answer any question and offer counsel when necessary. At times, this project was a challenge, but you really made it easy for me to shine. I truly do not know what I would have done without your leadership and friendship. So, Natalie, a thousand "thank you's" are extended to you. This book is a better product because of you and your hard work.

Projects such as this have many professionals who review the manuscript offering valued suggestions. I cannot thank the reviewers enough for their thoughtful comments. There is no doubt in my mind that this book is a better product because of all of you. Therefore, thank you to:

Eric Allen Cooper
Montclair State University

Elizabeth Dibble
Southwestern Illinois College

Julie Falcone
Academy of Court Reporting

Erma Hart
Wharton County Junior College

Linda Wilke Heil
Central Community College, Nebraska

Robin Jefferson Higgins
Webster University

Patricia Minikon
University of Maryland University College

Nina Neal
Central Piedmont Community College, North Carolina

Carole Olson
El Centro College

Emil A. Radosevich
Central New Mexico Community College

Lorri Ambrose Scott
Roosevelt University

Heather Tucker
McCann School of Business and Technology

Cathy Underwood
Pulaski Technical College

Deb Vinecour
SUNY Rockland Community College

Bobby Wheeler
Highline Community College

On the home front, I am one of the lucky ones surrounded by wonderful friends and family. Some days were tougher than others when deadlines loomed and my editors wanted the next chapter. But my friends and family kept me sane and grounded. To my friend and colleague, Pam Colon, your suggestions for some of the litigation chapters were welcomed. You were there for me when I needed someone I could trust to review the manuscript for accuracy and content. I am indebted to you. And to my dear friends Darice Plaskett and Xaulanda Simmonds Emmanuel—the girls—you both offered words of encouragement when I needed them. Thank you. But I must single out my "artist" friend, Xaulanda, who helped me with the graphics. I am in awe of your talent and creativity. You added a layer to this book that I could not have done without you. And of course, my legal assistant, Paula Henderson; you are always there to assist me with whatever I need—a special thank you.

There is no doubt that my family is glad that this book is completed. My niece, Samantha, and nephews, Matthew, Drew and Mason, were my welcomed breaks. You guys always made me laugh and forget my deadlines for a few minutes. Thank you for making me feel special all the time. You guys are the best. Mom, Marc, Andy, Donna, and Michele, thanks for listening and putting up with me during the past year. It did not go unnoticed. But most importantly, thanks to my brother Marc, who offered me assistance with suggestions when the "well was running dry."

And I save the best for last, Beth Baugh, my developmental editor. For once I am at a loss for words. It is difficult to express the absolute gratitude and respect I have for you. You always go above and beyond to make me "look good." You are always, always there for me. No question is too small or trite. It is appreciated that you have so much confidence in me when I feel as though I am losing focus. You keep me on track. What would I do without you! You are just the best. Thank you.

Pamela R. Tepper

Postscript

When I originally wrote the acknowledgments, Jean Starr, my project manager, was just a name to me. After the book was turned in, she went to work—and boy, did she. Had it not been for her diligence and expertise, I do not know what the final product wold have looked like. She is amazing and one of the best McGraw-Hill has to offer.

Guided Tour

Legal Research and Writing for Paralegals takes students on a step-by-step journey through the intricacies of researching legal issues and creating legal documents. The focus is on critical areas paralegals deal with daily: what law is and how to find it, what role the Internet plays in legal research, how to incorporate legal research into writing, and how to create an array of legal documents. Ethics are integral to the practice of law, and each chapter addresses issues particularly relevant to paralegals. The many practical assignments throughout and at the end of each chapter allow students to put into practice what they are learning about research and writing. The pedagogy of the book focuses on three main goals:

- Learning outcomes (critical thinking, vocabulary building, skill development, issues analysis, writing practice)
- Relevance of topics without sacrificing theory (ethical challenges, current law practices, technology application)
- Practical application (real-world exercises, practical advice, portfolio creation)

After completing this chapter, you will be able to:

- Understand how the American legal system developed.
- Differentiate between the different branches of government.
- Compare the organization of the federal and state court systems.
- Explain the role of the U.S. Supreme Court in the court system.
- Discuss the importance of the appellate process.
- Illustrate differences between state court systems.
- Comprehend the significance of researching a court's jurisdiction.
- Learn the different labels of the parties in the court system.
- Understand the importance of the court rules.
- Identify the responsibilities of a paralegal in the court process.

Chapter Objectives

Provides a roadmap of the issues covered in each chapter and highlights the concepts students should understand after reading each chapter.

Case Fact Pattern

Presents a hypothetical situation to illustrate how legal research and writing are applied in the practice of law.

CASE FACT PATTERN

An unusual case has just come into your law office. A teacher has been fired from her job. Apparently while she was teaching her class, one of her elementary school students asked questions about the war in Iraq. The student inquired as to whether the teacher participated in political activities involving the war. The teacher responded by stating that she saw a placard saying "Honk for Peace." To show her support, she honked her horn. Days later, the teacher was terminated as parents complained about her expressing her opinion about the war. There was a district school policy that teachers were not to express their personal political views to students. The teacher believes her First Amendment rights were violated and that she was discriminated against for being over the age of fifty. Your supervising attorney has a hearing on the matter in a week and asks you to research the issue. Knowing where to begin and where to look for legal support is crucial.

A Day in the Life of a Paralegal

Describes real-life scenarios paralegals encounter on a daily basis and puts a "human" face on the practice of law.

A DAY IN THE LIFE OF A PARALEGAL

Attorneys are notorious for long, convoluted sentences. Most attorneys subscribe to the writing technique that more is better. Once again, you are presented with a legal document to review. It is a brief in support of a motion that your attorney has prepared. Although you have just been asked to proofread the document for typographical errors and citation form, you notice a number of sentences that are run-ons. They really detract from the argument, but you know your attorney hates to have his writing corrected or edited, especially by a paralegal. You are not sure what to do and how to handle the matter.

There are a number of ways to handle this situation. One is to do nothing and perform the tasks requested. (This should be unacceptable to you.) Another possibility is to offer suggested changes in a separate draft and let the attorney decide which language is preferred. Let the attorney know, through some method of highlighting the rewritten sentences, subtly offering alternative choices. And, there is the direct method. Discuss your suggested changes with your attorney. Any attorney who truly cares about the final work product should appreciate the suggestions especially if the changes enhance the quality of the legal document. Always use your best judgment!

Practice Tip

Presents different nuances of research and writing to help students navigate the legal terrain.

PRACTICE TIP

The Defendant/Plaintiff Table Index has been replaced in a number of digests by the Table of Cases, which lists each party's name regardless of whether they were the plaintiff or the defendant. However, some jurisdictions or older digests still may have a Defendant/Plaintiff Table. Simply be aware that both volumes exist and check the digest set you are using to determine what corresponding indexes are used.

ETHICS ALERT

Writing counts. How you communicate counts. If you produce a substandard product, it is a reflection on you, your supervising attorney, and your firm. Judges pay close attention to the written documents submitted to their courts. Although as a paralegal you may not be directly responsible for the legal documents submitted, the case law is growing on the subject of attorneys and "poor legal writing." Courts are now holding that poor legal writing is a direct reflection on one's competency. The rules of professional responsibility for lawyers, Canon 6 of the Model Code, require that a "lawyer should represent the client competently." Although competency is a standard that we are striving to achieve, it is often undefined. As U.S. Supreme Court Justice Potter Stewart in a case involving the pornography standard stated, "I know it when I see it." *Jacobellis v. Ohio,* 378 U.S. 184, 197 (1964). That has essentially become the standard for judging competency in legal writing. A recent judge in the U.S. District Court for the District of New Jersey sanctioned and admonished a repeat offender for filing sloppy, incomprehensible legal documents. In expressing his disgust with the attorney, Judge Orlofsky observed that "[a]ttorneys may not, consistent with their professional obligations, substitute the 'cut and paste' function of their word processor for the research, contemplation, and draftsmanship that are the necessary elements of responsible legal representation." He further said that an attorney cannot substitute "mouse clicks" for legal judgments. *Mendez v. Draham,* 182 F. Supp. 2d 430, 431 (D. N.J. 2002). This attorney had been admonished three times in eighteen months, and one of his sanctions was to take a class on professional responsibility. As a paralegal you must decide the level of your competency and not be pushed into areas for which you are not competent. Too often attorneys rely, quite heavily, on their paralegals to do their work. Do not get caught in that trap. You should strive for the highest of standards, but you are not the attorney. You did not attend law school or take the bar exam. Paralegals are easy scapegoats. Be mindful that competent and quality representation is the attorney's ethical obligation—that includes competent legal writing as well.

Ethics Alert

Highlights ethical issues and situations paralegals and attorneys face in the day-to-day practice of law.

Quick Quiz True/False Questions

1. Shepard's Citations Service online and KeyCite have the same system of identifying the treatment of a case.
2. KeyCite uses a flagging system to alert the researcher about negative treatment in a case.
3. KeyCite provides a detailed schematic of the appeals history of a case.
4. Shepard's online can be used only as a validation and not as a research tool.
5. Shepard's Citations Service online and KeyCite provide a method of verifying the status of a federal or state statute.

Quick Quiz True/False Questions

Tests students' knowledge of key concepts after each major section in the chapter.

THE E-FACTOR

Electronic filing of briefs presents unique issues for the paralegal and attorney. Many courts have limitations on the size of the electronic file. If your brief and supporting documents exceed the megabytes requirement, then the document must be filed manually. Often you will need to file a notice of manual filing when you file a document manually. Most courts provide an example of this document. Figure 18.14 is a sample notice of manual filing. The courts make it quite clear that a document filed manually does not excuse untimely filing of the entire submission. Since e-filing is becoming mandatory in most federal courts, stay current on your jurisdiction's requirements.

Another e-filing issue requiring attention is privacy. As so many individuals have been victims of identity theft, personal information about parties to a case should be **redacted,** when possible. Redacted is the fancy way of saying "taken out." Balancing the public's rights to know against the privacy and security of litigants is a fine line. Courts warn attorneys not to include sensitive information in documents filed with the court. Courts suggest redacting "personal data identifiers" such as

- Social Security numbers;
- financial account numbers;
- dates of birth;
- names of minor children; and
- (in criminal cases only) home addresses.

(See U.S. District Court Northern District of Ohio Electronic Filing Policies and Procedures Manual, January 1, 2006.)

Although e-filing has many attributes, such as twenty-four-hour, seven-day-a-week filing capabilities, reduced use of paper clutter in court files, and instantaneous access to court documents, the technical glitches we all experience are not eliminated. There are help desks and trainings for use of the "new" e-filing systems. Understanding the process and how that process interacts with the rules of court will take time for those just introduced to the world of law and legalese. Do not get frustrated. Ask questions, review the court Web sites, and get trained. E-filings are here to stay, so learn the process and rules.

The E-Factor

Discusses how technology affects all facets of legal research and writing—from cell phones to e-mails to blogs. Both the possibilities and limitations of technology are considered.

You Be the Judge

Shows how the topics discussed in the chapter relate to the law and highlights currents cases and situations.

YOU BE THE JUDGE

A man convicted on drug charges wants to challenge his conviction. He has located a case that may be persuasive on the issue. The problem is the case is unpublished and the state of Arkansas has a prohibition against citing unpublished cases. Because he cannot use the unpublished case, he believes his due process rights have been violated. In *Weatherford v. State,* 352 Ark. 324, 101 S.W.3d 227 (2003), the court analyzed the debate over citing unpublished cases. As the court noted, in adopting its case publication rule, it "sought to achieve two goals—a reduction in the volume of published opinions and a reduction in the amount of time devoted to opinion writing. The justification for the first goal lies simply in the undeniable truth that many appellate court opinions are of no precedential value. Of course, like snowflakes, no two cases are exactly alike. But, for the purpose of selective publication, the question is whether the factual differences between one case and another are of precedential value." *Id.* at 233. As the debate continues, review the *Weatherford* case. What are the leading cases on the issue? What circuits have led the debate on the issue? What rule did the court rely upon in reaching its result and why?

Cyber Trip

Encourages students to go to the Internet to learn more about a wide array of legal issues.

CYBER TRIP

Using either www.nala.org or www.usdol.gov, find a legal opinion regarding paralegals and the application of Section 13(a)(1) of the Fair Labor Standards Act (FLSA). (Hint: The opinion was issued in 2006.)

Practical Considerations

Focuses on the practical aspects faced by paralegals conducting legal research and creating legal documents.

PRACTICAL CONSIDERATIONS: PRACTICE MAKES PERFECT . . . ALMOST

A novice writes a paragraph. He rereads it. It isn't good. It fails to make the point he wanted to make. The logic doesn't follow from beginning to end. Is he a bad writer?

He might think he is—but he isn't.

He isn't, at least, if he recognized the cardinal rule of writing: almost no one gets it right on the first try.

He isn't a bad writer if he recognizes the weaknesses in his paragraph and then takes out the tools of an editor—a pencil, eraser, scissors, and tape (or their word-processing equivalents)—to begin the task of improving it. Rereading, editing, revising, reworking, shifting paragraphs, substituting words, inserting explanations, deleting redundant elements, eliminating grammatical errors, crossing out, inserting, rereading, rereading, *rereading*—these are the elements that go into good writing.

Nothing you've learned about rules, style, design, and persuasiveness will be of any use if you fail to understand that writing is reading.

Nor is the process easy. "A writer is someone for whom writing is more difficult than it is for other people," said Thomas Mann. Writing is hard work—designed, ironically, to create the appearance of effortlessness and, in the case of legal writing, to persuade.

Since 1926, *The Bluebook* has been the authority for citation form. The *ALWD Manual* is another accepted authority for citation form. *ALWD* has a more user-friendly approach to understanding citation form. Another citation approach is the *Universal Citation Guide,* formulating a neutral citation format. Each jurisdiction follows different guides; local rules provide guidance on which format to use.

Case citations fall into a basic format. Cite the name of the case, the volume, the reporter, the page where the case begins, and the date of the decision. Unless dictated by citation form, often information about the court is inserted into the parenthetical with the date of the case. Statutes are cited by identifying the title, code, code section, and the date. This basic format is followed for administrative rules and regulations as well. Whether a primary or secondary source, all legal authority cited must be properly identified according to the rules of citation.

Legal authority must be integrated into legal documents. Citations are placed in sentences to direct a reader as to the basis of the authority relied upon. Short form citations may be used after a complete citation is identified in the text. Signals and string citing provide a method of listing additional authorities in a text. Additionally, when used properly, quotations are a vehicle to cite legal authority.

Summary

Chapter Summary

Provides a quick review of the key concepts covered in the chapter.

Key Terms

affirmative defenses
allegations
amended pleading
answer
caption
certificate of service
complaint
count
counterclaim
cross-claim lawsuit
deponent
deposition on written questions
discovery
duces tecum
equitable relief
fact pleading
form books
general defenses
instructions and definitions
interrogatory
legal remedy
models
motion for more definite statement
motion for protective order
motion for sanctions
motion for summary judgment
motion to compel discovery
motion to dismiss
notice pleading
oral deposition
pleadings
prayer for relief
process server
request for admission
request for production of documents and things
service of process
special defenses
subpoena
summons
supplemental pleading
verification
video deposition

Key Terms

Introduce students to basic legal terminology. Key terms are used throughout the chapters, defined in the margins, and listed at the end of each chapter. A common set of definitions is used consistently across the McGraw-Hill paralegal titles.

Review Questions

1. What is the difference between primary authorities and secondary authorities?
2. Explain the differences between mandatory authority and persuasive authority.
3. Identify the primary sources of the law.
4. What source of law is considered the supreme law of the land?
5. What is the purpose of administrative rules and regulations?
6. What is the difference between a slip law and secession law?
7. List the different types of court rules.
8. Explain the difference between a treatise and *American Law Reports.*
9. How does a law review article compare to a legal encyclopedia?
10. Why are attorney general opinions important to governmental entities?

Review Questions and Exercises

Ask students to apply critical thinking skills to the concepts learned in each chapter and test the students' retention and understanding of the chapter materials.

Portfolio Assignments

Ask students to use the skills mastered in each chapter to reflect on major legal issues and create documents that become part of the paralegal's portfolio of legal research. The Portfolio Assignments are useful as both reference tools and as samples of work product.

PORTFOLIO ASSIGNMENT

Your supervising attorney has been a bit overzealous lately in his representation of some of his clients. To put it bluntly, he insulted a judge one too many times. He's concerned. What bothers him most is that he was just doing his job—he's just too good. He has never been sanctioned by a court nor had any disciplinary action. This is the first time he may have crossed the line. He heard about a recent case from Puerto Rico and wants you to get a copy. You first think "Puerto Rico; I didn't know their laws applied in New York." The citation for the case is *In Re Alexander Zeno,* 504 F.3d 64 (1st Cir. 2007). Your attorney first wants you to brief the case and answer the following questions:

a. Can the case be used in your jurisdiction? (Explain your answer.)
b. Why does your attorney need to worry about this case?
c. Can your attorney argue any First Amendment rights? Are there any cases in the *Zeno* case that address that issue? If so, review them for your attorney.
d. Are there any cases cited by the court that can be distinguished?
e. Can *In Re Alexander Zeno* be distinguished?

Brief Contents

Contents

Chapter 19
The Appellate Brief 567

Legal Research and Writing for Paralegals

Part One

Mastering the Law

Chapter 1

The American Legal System: Navigating through the Process

After completing this chapter, you will be able to:

- Understand how the American legal system developed.
- Differentiate between the different branches of government.
- Compare the organization of the federal and state court systems.
- Explain the role of the U.S. Supreme Court in the court system.
- Discuss the importance of the appellate process.
- Illustrate differences between state court systems.
- Comprehend the significance of researching a court's jurisdiction.
- Learn the different labels of the parties in the court system.
- Understand the importance of the court rules.
- Identify the responsibilities of a paralegal in the court process.

Legal research is more than just finding cases in a library or on the Internet. The American legal system is one of the most important basic concepts to understand before you approach any projects in legal research. Think back to those days of your civics classes when you had to learn about the three branches of government and the relationship they have to each other. You probably never thought that you would have to revisit the eighth grade again. At least this time, you can quickly refresh your memories and focus on what you need to know as you embark on your paralegal career. In this chapter, we will revisit the past as a framework for the future. Keep in mind that the concepts you learn in this chapter build the foundation for the other chapters. Let's understand why understanding the American legal system is important to legal research.

THE AMERICAN LEGAL SYSTEM: A REFRESHER

The basis of the American legal system is the distribution of authority between the federal and state governments. Under the **U.S. Constitution**, the federal government was created consisting of three branches of government: the executive, the legislative,

U.S. Constitution
The fundamental law of the United States of America, which became the law of the land in March of 1789.

CASE FACT PATTERN

A new client, Dave Landry, has scheduled an appointment to meet with your supervising attorney. Based on your brief telephone call with him, it appears he wants to sue some credit card companies for sending advertisements based on his belief that fraud and misrepresentation are being committed. Dave has recently received a flood of mail from credit card lenders, promising him that he is preapproved for a credit card for $5,000. Some days, he receives two or three of these offers. Dave has had some problems with his credit in the past, so he welcomes a preapproved credit card. However, when he called to get his preapproved credit card, he learned there are application and other fees and, even if he pays these fees, he is not guaranteed to receive a credit card. Dave wants to sue the credit card companies, but runs into a practical problem. He doesn't know where to file his case. Some of the companies that have sent him these offers are based in his own state of Wisconsin, but others are based in states scattered across the country. Dave does not understand the differences between federal and state courts and the significance of jurisdictional questions involved. That's why he has contacted your supervising attorney's law firm to represent him. Dave wants to stop these companies' practices now.

and the judicial. Each branch has its own function derived from the U.S. Constitution, creating a "separation of power" between those three branches. Likewise, each branch of government acts as a "check and balance" on the other so that no one branch oversteps its authority. Within the U.S. Constitution are articles and amendments that set forth not only the branches of government but many of our basic rights as citizens. The ways in which the branches interact with each other and protect our basic rights are the cornerstones of our system of government.

Moreover, while the U.S. Constitution created three branches of the federal government, it also provided for delegated authority to the states under the Tenth Amendment. The caveat to this delegation of authority was that no state could create any act in contravention of the U.S. Constitution. Thus, as long as a state acted within the bounds of the U.S. Constitution, its power and authority would be respected. As you will learn, that may be a concept that is easier said than done.

THE U.S. CONSTITUTION AND ITS AMENDMENTS: THE FOUNDATION OF GOVERNMENT

Adopted in 1787 and effective on March 4, 1789, the U.S. Constitution created our American legal system—a delicate balance between the federal and state government. For our purpose, it is important to remember that the first three articles of the U.S. Constitution establish the three branches of government.

Article I establishes the Congress of the United States, which consists of the Senate and the House of Representatives. Empowered to Congress is the right to create laws, which is supported in Article I, section 8 delineating those powers and others within that article. Essentially, the U.S. Congress has the responsibility to propose and pass legislation (bills), which, for the most part, must be signed by the president of the United States to be effective. The exception is when the president vetoes a bill and Congress overrides the veto; in that instance, the bill becomes law. Chapter 5 details the legislative process.

CYBER TRIP

Locate a copy of the U.S. Constitution on the Internet and find the sections that set forth the powers of Congress and the limitations to those powers.

This leads us to Article II of the U.S. Constitution, which establishes the executive branch of government. Under Article II, the U.S. Constitution designates the executive power to the president and sets forth the process of electing a president. Among some of the responsibilities assigned to the president is that of commander in chief of the military as well as the authority to grant pardons and reprieves to individuals convicted of offenses. Some of the president's powers require the advice and consent of the Senate, such as entering into treaties, nominating ambassadors and administrators (the president's cabinet), and appointing federal judges, including the justices of the U.S. Supreme Court.

Within the executive branch, numerous executive departments and agencies exist, which answer to the chief executive—the president. These executive agencies are considered administrative agencies, some of whom gain their authority directly from the president or, in some instances, from a legislative grant of authority from Congress.

Although the both the president and Congress have some degree of autonomy, the U.S. Constitution rests the power to review acts of Congress and the president with the third branch of government—the judicial branch. Of course, the president has the power to appoint federal judges with the advice and consent of Congress. But the branch of government that has the ultimate responsibility to review and even declare acts of Congress and the president unconstitutional is the judicial branch. Under Article III, the U.S. Supreme Court was created. With its creation, only one court is vested with the authority to be the final arbiter of American law. But the power to create other "inferior" courts (the lower courts) is vested with the U.S. Congress. Notice how the check and balance system under the Constitution works. The president appoints federal judges and justices; Congress confirms the appointment and also creates additional "inferior" courts; yet the judicial branch reviews decisions regarding the actions of both. This is the basis of our federal court system.

For example, when the president makes an appointment to the U.S. Supreme Court, that appointee must be approved by Congress. Think back to the confirmation proceedings of Justice Clarence Thomas. Congress convened in-depth hearings prior to giving consent to the appointment. In the case of Judge Robert Bork, who was nominated by President Reagan in 1987, Congress convened hearings but did not approve his appointment. And more recently, in 2005, President Bush appointed then White House counsel Harriet Miers to the U.S. Supreme Court. Because of outside political pressure, Miers withdrew her nomination and congressional hearings never ensued.

Perhaps one of the most poignant and historically significant examples of our federal system's checks and balances is the impeachment proceedings of then president Richard Nixon. (You may recall hearing or reading about the Watergate scandal.) In that instance, Congress convened impeachment hearings to determine whether President Nixon acted improperly while in office. Congress had oversight to investigate the actions of the president. As part of the investigative process, Congress had requested documents, including tape recordings of conversations between the president and his staff. The president refused. The courts stepped in and ordered the president to produce the tapes for review by Congress. The end result was that the president was not above the law and, as history shows, resigned his office. The Watergate matter is a clear example that the document passed in 1788 remains not only vital, but the standard by which *all* citizens continue to be judged against to this day. Figure 1.1 provides a listing of the articles of the U.S. Constitution.

Quite possibly one of the most significant concepts that underlies our American legal system is that the U.S. Constitution is "the supreme Law of the Land." In Article VI of

FIGURE 1.1
The Articles of the U.S. Constitution

The Constitution

Preamble
Article I. Legislative Department
Article II. Executive Department
Article III. Judicial Department
Article IV. States' Relations
Article V. Mode of Amendment
Article VI. Prior Debts, National Supremacy, Oaths of Office
Article VII. Ratification

YOU BE THE JUDGE

In 1974, the president of the United States was requested to produce tape recordings by the U.S. Congress. These tapes contained conversations between the president and his aides that incriminated the White House in some criminal activity at the Watergate hotel and office complex. After many legal maneuvers by the president's representatives, the case made its way to the U.S. Supreme Court. Arguing that a "dispute" regarding the executive branch was privileged, the president refused to release the complete unedited versions of the tapes. The **special prosecutor** in the case argued that no **executive privilege** is absolute especially when criminal activities are implicated. Review *United States v. Nixon*, 418 U.S. 683, 94 S. Ct. 3090, 41 L. Ed. 2d 1039 (1974). What was the basis of the U.S. Supreme Court's decision to require production of the tapes? Did the Court accept the president's argument regarding the need for "separation of powers" between the branches of government? What interests did the Court have to balance in reaching its conclusion?

special prosecutor
Specially appointed government attorney.

executive privilege
Special protection afforded communications of the president.

the Constitution, no law, federal or state, can contradict, challenge, or oppose the principles stated in that document. In the words of Article VI of the U.S. Constitution:

> *This Constitution, and the Laws of the United States which shall be made in Pursuance thereof; and all Treaties made, or which shall be made, under the authority of the United States, shall be the supreme Law of the Land; and the Judges in every State shall be bound thereby, any Thing in the Constitution or Laws of any State to the Contrary notwithstanding.*

This passage leaves no question as to the intent of the founders.

No one really knows what they would think if they saw the complexity of our legal system today. But to think that the articles of our Constitution, a document drafted over 230 years ago, remain unchanged and fully functional is a credit to the strength of all its components. Think about it. The U.S Constitution provides for a system of government that operates and governs our entire country today. That basic arrangement remains the foundation of the American legal system. Figure 1.2 provides a chart of the three branches of the federal government.

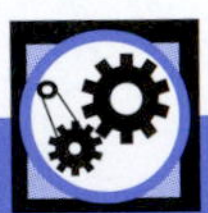

PRACTICE TIP

You can locate the *Nixon* case by its citation. The citation consists of the numbers and abbreviations that follow the name of the case. The first group of numbers is the volume, followed by an abbreviation, which is the case reporter; and finally, the last group of numbers represents the page where the case begins. (Citations and reporters are discussed more fully in later chapters.)

THE AMENDMENTS TO THE CONSTITUTION: THE BILL OF RIGHTS

In addition to the main articles of the U.S. Constitution, the founders created some basic rights in the form of amendments. The first ten amendments to the Constitution are known as the **Bill of Rights.** These rights are delineated in Figure 1.3.

Bill of Rights
Set forth the fundamental individual rights government and law function to preserve and protect; the first ten amendments to the Constitution of the United States.

Additional amendments were passed over the years, which expanded some of our basic rights. For example, the Fourteenth Amendment provided for equal protection of all U.S. citizens; the Nineteenth Amendment gave women the right to vote; and the Twenty-Sixth Amendment reduced the minimum age of voting from twenty-one to eighteen years Amending the Constitution is not an easy task. For a new amendment to pass, three-fourths of the states must vote to add the amendment. That is not an easy undertaking.

Now that we have a refresher in the creation of the basic federal government structure, we will examine the third branch of government, the judicial system, to understand the components of the federal and state court systems.

Quick Quiz True/False Questions

1. The three branches of government set forth in the U.S. Constitution are the legislative, judicial, and administrative branches of government.
2. The U.S. Constitution establishes the U.S. Supreme Court.

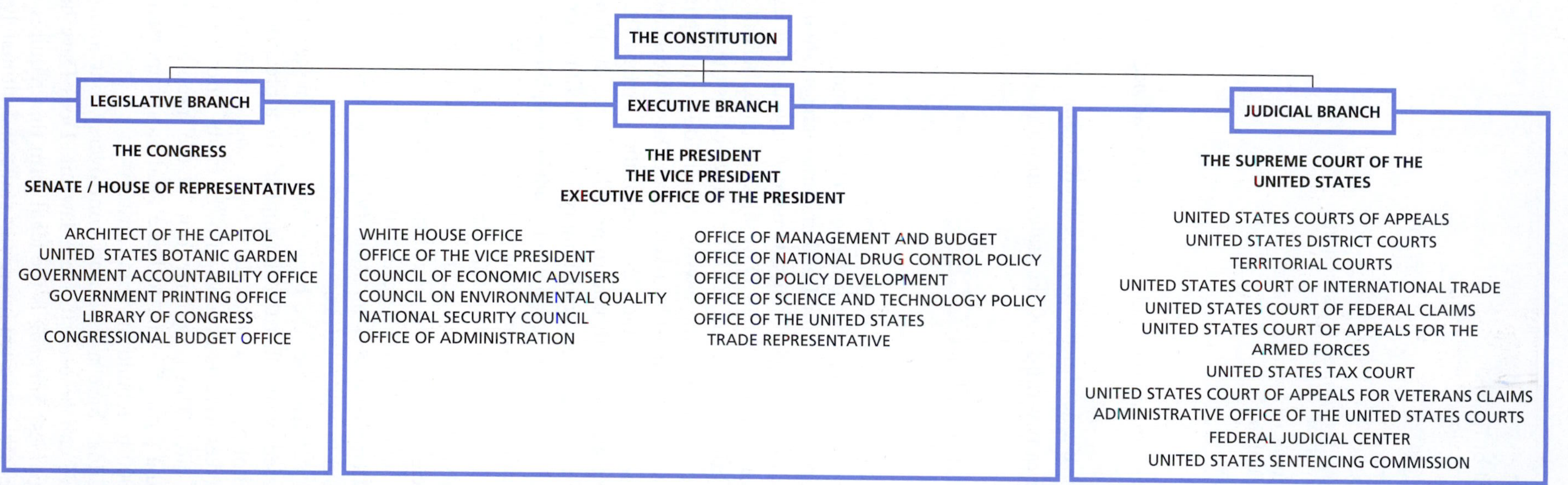

FIGURE 1.2 **Chart of the Three Branches of the Federal Government**

Source: Adapted from http://bensguide.gpo.gov/files/gov_chart.pdf (accessed November 26, 2007).

FIGURE 1.3
The Bill of Rights to the Constitution

Amendments to the Constitution

First through Tenth Amendments: Bill of Rights
First Amendment—Religion and Expression
Second Amendment—Bearing Arms
Third Amendment—Quartering Soldiers
Fourth Amendment—Search and Seizure
Fifth Amendment—Rights of Persons
Sixth Amendment—Rights of Accused in Criminal Prosecutions
Seventh Amendment—Civil Trials
Eighth Amendment—Further Guarantees in Criminal Cases
Ninth Amendment—Unenumerated Rights
Tenth Amendment—Reserved Powers

fraud
A knowing and intentional misstatement of the truth in order to induce a desired action from another person.

misrepresentation
A reckless disregard for the truth in making a statement to another in order to induce a desired action.

lawsuit
Legal mechanism to resolve disputes between parties.

plaintiff
The party initiating legal action.

defendant
The party against whom a lawsuit is brought.

advisory opinion
Statement of potential interpretation of law in a future opinion made without real case facts at issue.

standing
Legally sufficient reason and right to object.

3. The president of the United States can appoint judges without the advice and consent of the U.S. Congress.
4. The Bill of Rights is the first twelve amendments to the Constitution.
5. Amending the Constitution requires two-thirds of the states' approval.

AN OVERVIEW OF THE COURT PROCESS: WHERE CAN I SUE?

Using the Case Fact Pattern from the beginning of the chapter as a backdrop, we will weave our way through the court process. Remember our client Dave Landry who is angry and wants to sue the credit card companies for **fraud** and **misrepresentation** for sending him sham credit offers in the mail? He will bring a **lawsuit.** A lawsuit is a legal mechanism to resolve disputes between parties. When Dave files his case, he will be known as the **plaintiff**, the party that brings the lawsuit, and the party he files the lawsuit against is the **defendant**, the party responding to the lawsuit. Where does he begin?

Before Dave can sue anyone, certain questions must be asked. Does Dave have a claim, or in legal jargon "a case and controversy"? Under the U.S. Constitution, Article III, in order for a court to act, there must be an actual problem to remedy—hence the phrase "case and controversy." The Constitution requires an actual injury, not a "fictitious one," before a court can hear a matter. Courts generally cannot offer **advisory opinions** as to what may happen if a controversy occurs. An advisory opinion is usually in the form of a request of interested parties as to how a court may rule should a claim or dispute develop. Advisory opinions are prohibited by courts. The theory behind this prohibition is that since the U.S. Constitution clearly states that courts can only hear cases and controversies, a court cannot render an opinion on an event that has not occurred. In fact, President George Washington attempted to seek an advisory opinion from the U.S. Supreme Court, but the court declined to render advice.

We now return to our Case Fact Pattern from the beginning of the chapter. Dave does have a case and controversy based on the fact that he applied for a preapproved credit card and learned that he was not preapproved at all. He also was injured by the fact that the offer did not state that fees were associated with the credit card when he attempted to accept the credit card offer. This is another form of the fraud and misrepresentation by the companies and a form of injury to Dave. And most importantly, Dave would have had to spend $5,000 to rebuild his credit history.

We have established that Dave does have a case and controversy, but another question must be asked before Dave can proceed to file a lawsuit. Does Dave have **standing** to sue the credit card companies? *Standing* is the legal term that requires the party bringing a lawsuit to have a legally protected interest at stake and ultimately an

PRACTICE TIP

Although the U.S. Constitution prohibits advisory opinions at the federal level, some state constitutions permit advisory opinions in limited circumstances.

interest in the outcome. In its simplest terms, has Dave suffered an injury for which the court can grant relief? The answer is yes. Dave was preapproved for a credit card. When he called for the credit card, he was told he had to pay fees and qualify. He was not preapproved at all. Dave was injured because he did not receive his preapproved credit card as promised by the credit card companies. On the other hand, an individual who did not receive the credit card offers in the mail would not have standing to bring a lawsuit. No injury occurred and no protected interest was at stake; therefore the court could not grant any relief. We agree that Dave has standing to bring a lawsuit.

One more issue that we must consider before Dave brings his lawsuit is whether he waited too long to bring his claims. The time period in which a party must file a lawsuit is called the **statute of limitations.** Statutes of limitations vary according to the **cause of action** or claim of the injured party. For our purpose, we'll assume that Dave has contacted the law firm within the statute of limitations for filing a fraud and misrepresentation case.

Now that we know Dave has standing and his case is within the statute of limitations, where does he go to have his problem heard? A court of law, of course! A **court** is a place where a party or parties can go to have their problems resolved by a **judge** or **jury. Trial courts** are where witnesses testify, juries are impaneled, evidence is admitted, and the drama of a trial is played out. These are the courts with which most people are familiar through television dramas that feature the work of trial courts. A court, through either a judge or a jury, decides ultimately which party wins or loses its case. It is said that these courts have **jurisdiction** to hear a case. When we use the term *jurisdiction,* we refer to a court's power to make rulings on issues. Therefore courts can hear a wide variety of cases, including both civil and criminal matters, as long as they have jurisdiction.

We digress from our discussion of jurisdiction to define the difference between civil and criminal law. This becomes important as some courts only have the authority to hear one or the other. **Civil law** encompasses disputes that arise between private parties. In a civil case the remedy for a dispute can be **monetary** or **equitable** in nature. Monetary relief can be in the form of money, known as **compensatory damages.** These are the most common type of civil damages. Another kind of civil remedy is punitive damages.

Punitive damages are awarded in a limited number of cases and only when the conduct of a party is so offensive and heinous that the court wants to send a message and make an example of the wrongdoer. Punitive damages are often awarded in cases involving fraud when it is shown that the conduct of a party was intentional and deliberate.

Another form of civil remedy is **equitable relief.** When monetary compensation is inappropriate or cannot be determined, the court may award equitable relief. A common type of equitable relief is an **injunction.** Injunctions are an appropriate remedy when a party wants another party to refrain from doing something or in the converse, direct a party to do something. In our case, Dave could try to seek an injunction from the credit card companies from sending offers in the mail that are not truthful.

On the other hand, **criminal law** regulates the conduct of persons who commit acts against society. Statutes define the type of behavior that is considered criminal and impose penalties for violation of those statutes. Penalties range from fines, imprisonment, or in extreme cases, death. Only a government, through a **prosecutor**, can file a criminal lawsuit against a party; therefore, Dave can only file a civil case.

The next question is: Can Dave file his case in any court? The answer to that question is "no." As we noted previously, in order to file a case in a court, the court must have jurisdiction to hear the case. For a court to hear a case, it must have both **personal jurisdiction** over the parties and **subject matter jurisdiction** over the disputes before it.

statute of limitations
Establishes the applicable time limits for filing and responding to certain claims or legal actions.

cause of action
A personal, financial, or other injury for which the law gives a person the right to receive compensation.

court
Place where parties have problems resolved.

judge
Trier of law.

jury
Trier of fact.

trial courts
Courts that hear all cases and are courts of general jurisdiction.

jurisdiction
The power or authority of the court to hear a particular classification of case. Also, the place or court that may hear a case, based on subject matter and/or geographic area.

civil law
The legal rules regarding offenses committed against the person.

monetary remedy
Money damages.

equitable remedy
Nonmonetary damages, such as an injunction.

compensatory damages
A payment to make up for a wrong committed and return the nonbreaching party to a position where the effect or the breach has been neutralized.

punitive damages
An amount of money awarded to a nonbreaching party that is not based on the actual losses incurred by that party, but as a punishment to the breaching party for the commission of an intentional wrong.

equitable relief
A remedy that is other than money damages, such as refraining from or performing a certain act; nonmonetary remedies fashioned by the court using standards of fairness and justice. Injunction and specific performance are types of equitable relief.

injunction
A court order that requires a party to refrain from acting in a certain way to prevent harm to the requesting party.

criminal law
Law that regulates acts against society.

prosecutor
Attorney representing the people or plaintiff in criminal matters.

personal jurisdiction
A court's power over the individuals involved in the case; when a court has personal jurisdiction, it can compel attendance at court hearings and enter judgments against the parties.

subject matter jurisdiction
A court's authority over the res, the subject of the case.

Personal jurisdiction concerns the authority or power of a court to decide a case between the parties involved. It includes the power not only to make decisions regarding those parties but also to have those decisions enforced. Personal jurisdiction is linked to a party's residence or domicile. No court can adjudicate a case unless the parties live in the state or federal district where the court sits. However, the parties can agree to have a court hear a case, which in turn provides the court with personal jurisdiction. A more complex method of gaining personal jurisdiction over parties is determining whether there are sufficient contacts with the state so that it's reasonable to make them appear in that court. Courts have determined that doing business in a state, as the credit card companies in our example were doing, is sufficient contact to constitute personal jurisdiction over the party. Owning property in a state also is considered sufficient contact for a court to have personal jurisdiction. These types of issues are usually dealt with by your supervising attorney.

But let's see how it works. Dave lives in Wisconsin and one of the credit card companies has a place of business in Wisconsin. Since both parties reside in the state, a Wisconsin court would have personal jurisdiction over the parties. When parties are from different states, personal jurisdiction usually involves the power of a court over the defendant. Normally, a court cannot adjudicate claims of a party for which there is no personal jurisdiction. We continue our analysis of Dave's case. Suppose the credit card company does not have any place of business in Wisconsin, but has offices all over the northeast. Would the Wisconsin court have jurisdiction? That's a difficult question. On its face, it appears that the court would not have personal jurisdiction, but if the credit card company mailed information to Dave and other Wisconsin residents, could the court have personal jurisdiction? It is quite possible but that would be an argument for your supervising attorney and one that probably would require legal research. Undoubtedly, you now understand the significance and importance of personal jurisdiction.

Not only must the court have personal jurisdiction over the parties but subject matter jurisdiction as well. Subject matter jurisdiction involves the authority of a court to hear certain types of cases based upon the powers conferred by the Constitution or a statute. Simply stated, subject matter jurisdiction deals with the court's authority to decide the "issues" or "subject" of the lawsuit.

For example, if the U.S. Constitution states that a court can hear cases involving a federal statute, that is considered its subject matter jurisdiction. A case that deals with a state statute cannot be filed in a federal court, because the court does not have subject matter jurisdiction.

Consequently, Dave must file his case in a court that has personal and subject matter jurisdiction over the party *and* the subject of his lawsuit. This is not an easy situation because Dave has claims against credit card companies in his home state and claims against credit card companies in other states as well. The decision that the supervising attorney must make is "in which court should I file the lawsuit? Will I file the lawsuit in a federal court or a state court?" This is where the question of jurisdiction becomes critical not only to the decision as to where to file a case, but to what law applies to the case when filed. Before we continue with Dave's lawsuit, we must understand the federal and state court systems to determine in which court to file "our" lawsuit.

Quick Quiz True/False Questions

1. Jurisdiction is the power of a court to hear a case.
2. A statute of limitations is the time period in which a lawsuit must be filed.
3. The plaintiff is the party that responds to a lawsuit.
4. Criminal law regulates the conduct of persons who commit acts against society.
5. Personal jurisdiction and subject matter jurisdiction are the same.

THE FEDERAL COURT SYSTEM

Returning to our discussion of the Constitution, the founders clearly established a high court, the U.S. Supreme Court, and other "inferior courts." The premise of that court system is straightforward: The actions of one court can be reviewed (and changed) by another, higher court. Seen this way, the court system, whether on the state or federal level, is arranged as a pyramid. At the base of the pyramid are the various trial courts, followed by the appellate courts and at the top of the pyramid a U.S. Supreme Court. The federal trial courts are the U.S. district courts; the appellate courts are the U.S. courts of appeal; and of course, the highest appellate court is the U.S. Supreme Court. Starting with the trial courts, we will now examine the federal court system as it exists today.

PRACTICE TIP

In addition to many U.S. courts being divided into additional districts, many districts have divisions within those districts that hear cases. For example, the Northern District in Georgia encompasses the Atlanta Division, Gainesville Division, Newnan Division, and Rome Division. Always check to see whether there are divisions within a federal district court.

The Structure of the United States District Courts

We now know the federal trial courts are called **U.S. district courts.** These are the courts where federal cases begin. There are ninety-four district courts within the United States and its territories: Eighty-nine district courts are scattered throughout the United States, with additional district courts in Puerto Rico, the U.S. Virgin Islands, the District of Columbia, Guam, and the North Mariana Islands. The assignment of districts is not based on geographic area, but on population statistics, accounting for the fact that Alaska, though the largest state, has only a single judicial district, while smaller but more populous states, such as California, Texas, and New York, have several districts. The federal districts are divided into subdistricts, such as the Middle District, Central District, Northern District, Southern District, Eastern District, or Western District. Each court hears the cases filed within its district. See Figure 1.4 for a list of the U.S. district courts.

As is evident from the chart in Figure 1.4, there are quite a large number of district courts around the country. The questions on your mind must be: "Do all federal trial courts hear all cases?" and "How does the attorney know where to file a case?" You already know that a court has to have jurisdiction to hear a case. And, you already know that jurisdiction is granted by either the U.S. Constitution or a legislature (in this case the legislature being the U.S. Congress since we are dealing with the federal courts).

U.S. district courts
Federal trial courts.

federal question jurisdiction
The jurisdiction given to federal courts in cases involving the interpretation and application of the U.S. Constitution or acts of Congress.

diversity of citizenship jurisdiction
Authority of the federal court to hear a case if the parties are citizens of different states and the amount at issue is over $75,000.

limited jurisdiction
Jurisdiction of a court that is constrained by statute or constitutional provision and is prohibited from hearing cases not specifically authorized.

There are two types of federal court jurisdiction: **federal question** and **diversity of citizenship jurisdiction.** In order to qualify for federal jurisdiction, a party must show that the case involves one of these types of jurisdiction; otherwise, the action must be brought in another venue.

Because federal courts are only empowered to hear these types of cases, they are all courts of limited subject matter jurisdiction. **Limited jurisdiction** is exactly what the name implies: Only particular types of cases can be heard by courts of limited jurisdiction. Jurisdiction can be limited by subject matter or the amount in controversy. For federal courts, those limitations are designated either by Congress or the U.S. Constitution. Likewise, state courts have courts of limited jurisdiction with those limits designated by the respective states' constitution and legislature. Later in the chapter we will examine the jurisdiction of state courts, but for now we will continue our focus on federal jurisdiction.

Federal Question Jurisdiction

Federal courts are specifically authorized to consider questions involving the application of the U.S. Constitution or a federal statute. Federal question jurisdiction involves not only the U.S. Constitution or a federal law, but also cases involving the U.S. government. Depending on the "subject matter" of the lawsuit, states and foreign governments may be sued in federal court. For example, if a party has a claim under the First Amendment, right to free speech, that case would be filed in the federal

FIGURE 1.4
List of U.S. District Courts

State	Districts within State	Name of District(s)
Alabama	3	Northern, Middle, and Middle
Alaska	1	None*
Arizona	1	None
Arkansas	2	Eastern and Western
California	4	Northern, Eastern, Central, and Southern
Colorado	1	None
Connecticut	1	None
Delaware	1	None
District of Columbia	1	None
Florida	3	Northern, Middle, and Southern
Georgia	3	Northern, Middle, and Southern
Guam	1	None
Hawaii	1	None
Idaho	1	None
Illinois	3	Northern, Southern, and Central
Indiana	2	Northern and Southern
Iowa	2	Northern and Southern
Kansas	1	None
Kentucky	2	Eastern and Western
Louisiana	3	Eastern, Middle, and Western
Maine	1	None
Maryland	1	None
Massachusetts	1	None
Michigan	2	Eastern and Western
Minnesota	1	None
Mississippi	2	Eastern and Western
Missouri	2	Eastern and Western
Montana	1	None
Nebraska	1	None
Nevada	1	None
New Hampshire	1	None
New Jersey	1	None
New Mexico	1	None
New York	4	Northern, Eastern, Southern, and Western
North Carolina	3	Eastern, Middle, and Western
North Dakota	1	None
N. Mariana Islands	1	None
Ohio	2	Northern and Southern
Oklahoma	3	Northern, Eastern, and Western
Oregon	1	None
Pennsylvania	3	Eastern, Middle, and Western
Puerto Rico	1	None
Rhode Island	1	None
South Carolina	1	None
South Dakota	1	None
Tennessee	3	Eastern, Middle, and Western
Texas	4	Northern, Southern, Eastern, and Western
Utah	1	None
Vermont	1	None
Virgin Islands	1	None
Virginia	2	Eastern and Western
Washington	2	Eastern and Western
West Virginia	2	Northern and Southern
Wisconsin	2	Eastern and Western
Wyoming	1	None

*Those with only one district have divisions within the district as do states with multiple districts.

YOU BE THE JUDGE

Recent debate over the detainees (prisoners) being held in Guantanamo Bay, Cuba, has sparked issues over federal jurisdiction. The recent case of *Rasul v. Bush*, 542 U.S. 466, 124 S. Ct. 2686, 159 L. Ed. 2d 548 (2004), addressed the issue as to whether a federal court had jurisdiction to hear cases of those being detained, but never charged with an offense, at Guantanamo Bay. The detainees raised a number of constitutional and federal statutory issues. Specifically, the detainees applied for a writ of **habeas corpus** (Latin for "you have the body") because they claimed unlawful detention by the federal government. This case also raised the issue of the extent of presidential authority. Review the *Rasul* case. What are the facts surrounding the case? Did the Court find that the federal district court had jurisdiction to hear Rasul's claims? What authority did the executive branch rely upon to justify its actions? Did the Court uphold the executive branch's actions? Why or why not? This case is another example of the checks and balances set forth under the U.S. Constitution.

district court. A federal court would hear a case concerning violations of the Medicare Prescription Drug, Improvement and Modernization Act. The reason is that Medicare is a federal program authorized under a federal statute. Similarly, when a case involves combatants of war (such as those from the Iraqi and Afghan conflicts) held in violation of the Constitution and federal statutes, a federal district court hears the case. A federal court could not hear a case involving evasion of state taxes, although it can hear a case regarding evasion of federal taxes.

habeas corpus
A writ employed to bring a person before a court, most frequently to ensure that the party's imprisonment or detention is not illegal.

Diversity Jurisdiction

Diversity jurisdiction is more complex. Diversity involves parties from different states or a U.S. citizen and a party or parties from another country. The rules establishing citizenship are actually based on the rules we previously discussed concerning personal jurisdiction. Recall that personal jurisdiction is based upon where a party resides or is domiciled. If a plaintiff resides in one state and the defendant is domiciled in another, that will satisfy the first requirement of diversity jurisdiction. However, diversity of citizenship does not always guarantee that a federal court will accept a particular case. There is an additional requirement before federal court jurisdiction is invoked. The caveat to diversity jurisdiction is that the amount in controversy between the parties must exceed $75,000. That means that if the damages in the case are less than $75,000, the case cannot be heard by a federal district court.

The logic of diversity of citizenship jurisdiction is one of fairness. The theory is that a state court favors citizens from that state while federal courts are more "neutral." Diversity cases are not exclusive to federal court jurisdiction. Cases involving parties from different states with more than $75,000 in controversy also can be brought in a state court. (This will be discussed later in the chapter.)

There are instances where the federal district courts have **exclusive jurisdiction** to hear certain cases. When a court has exclusive jurisdiction, *only* that court can hear the type of case before it. Legislatively, Congress has granted the federal courts exclusive jurisdiction to hear bankruptcy cases, which are heard by **bankruptcy courts.** A bankruptcy case involves the judicial relief from debts created by a **debtor.** In a bankruptcy case, a debtor can seek the court's protection from its creditors, create a plan of repayment to those creditors if assets are available, or request liquidation of the assets. Regardless of the process, only a federal bankruptcy court can hear matters involving a bankruptcy action.

Similarly, there are two additional federal trial courts that have exclusive jurisdiction: the **Court of International Trade** and the **U.S. Court of Federal Claims.** The Court of International Trade hears cases involving international trade and customs issues. Conversely, the U.S. Court of Federal Claims only hears cases centered on federal contract

exclusive jurisdiction
Only one court has the authority to hear the specific case; for example, only a federal court can decide a bankruptcy case. Jurisdiction of a court that limits that type of cases it hears to only that court.

bankruptcy courts
Federal courts of exclusive jurisdiction to hear cases regarding debtors.

debtor
One of the parties in a bankruptcy action who owes money to creditors.

Court of International Trade
Part of the federal lower-court level authorized to hear matters related to international trade agreements and disputes.

U.S. Court of Federal Claims
Part of the lower or trial court level of the federal court system in which disputes with the U.S. government are heard.

disputes, money disputes against the United Stated, property disputes (unlawful "takings" of private property), and general claims filed against the United States. Therefore, these courts have both limited and exclusive federal jurisdiction.

The Magistrate System: A Helping Hand for Federal Trial Judges

docket
A court's caseload.

magistrate judge
A public civil officer, possessing such power—legislative, executive, or judicial—as the government appointing him or her may ordain.

Due to the sheer volume of federal cases, a system was developed to assist federal trial court judges in disposing of their **dockets**—the court's caseload. Beginning in 1968, Congress authorized the creation of a magistrate system. Under the magistrate system, district court judges may appoint a **magistrate judge** to assist them with managing their cases. As long as the parties to the case consent, magistrate judges hear and decide motions, conduct settlement and pretrial conferences, and try civil and criminal cases (except for criminal felony cases). These magistrate judges offer much needed assistance to a clogged court system. Over the course of a year, a magistrate judge within a federal district court hears hundreds of legal matters, and without them cases would linger in the system indefinitely. Think of the magistrate judge system as a trial court within a trial court.

PRACTICE TIP

Many state courts use magistrate judges to move cases within a docket more quickly. The state court magistrate systems are created by state statute.

The Federal Circuit Courts of Appeals: Intermediate Appellate Courts

appellate jurisdiction
Power of a court to hear challenges from a lower court.

appellant
The party filing the appeal; that is, bringing the case to the appeals court.

appellee
The prevailing party in the lower court, who will respond to the appellant's argument.

U.S. circuit courts of appeals
Appeals courts in the federal system.

en banc
Appellate review by the entire circuit appeals judiciary after review by the intermediate panel.

Oftentimes the losing party in a trial wants to appeal the decision of the trial judge. This is possible by filing an appeal in the appropriate court. Along with trial courts, jurisdiction is an important concept. Appeals courts have **appellate jurisdiction.** Appellate jurisdiction is the authority of an appeals court to hear challenges (appeals) from a lower court. As a general rule, the circuit courts of appeals do not have the discretion to accept or reject a request for appeal as long as it is properly filed. The party filing an appeal is called the **appellant**, while the party responding to an appeal is called the **appellee.**

Both civil and criminal cases may be appealed to the respective federal appeals court, but the government cannot file an appeal if a defendant is found not guilty. Additionally, either party in a criminal case may appeal the imposition of a sentence by a judge after a guilty verdict.

Thus, the ninety-four federal judicial districts are organized into twelve regional circuits, including the District of Columbia, each of which has an appellate court to oversee it. These courts are referred to as the **U.S. circuit courts of appeals** and they hear all appeals from courts located within their circuits. There is a thirteenth circuit that hears all appeals from the Federal Circuit, including appeals from the U.S. Court of International Trade, the U.S. Court of Federal Claims, and various patent and trademark offices. Figure 1.5 is a map chart of the states and territories located in the respective circuit courts of appeals.

Unlike a federal trial court, appeals cases are heard by a panel of judges. Normally, a panel consists of three judges. On rare occasions the entire court may hear a case, which is known as **en banc.** (*En banc* is French for "in the bench.") Only when an issue has unusual significance or when a decision of the court appears to conflict with a previous decision of that court will an entire appeals court hear a case. Additionally, en banc decisions may be dictated by the practices (or rules) of the court. Consequently, en banc decisions are rare.

Recall that bankruptcy courts are specialized trial courts within the federal district court system. The process of appealing a bankruptcy case is a little different. Bankruptcy cases are appealed to the U.S. district court within their district. However, due to the increased number of appeals from the bankruptcy courts, many courts of appeals have established an additional intermediate court of appeals, known as the

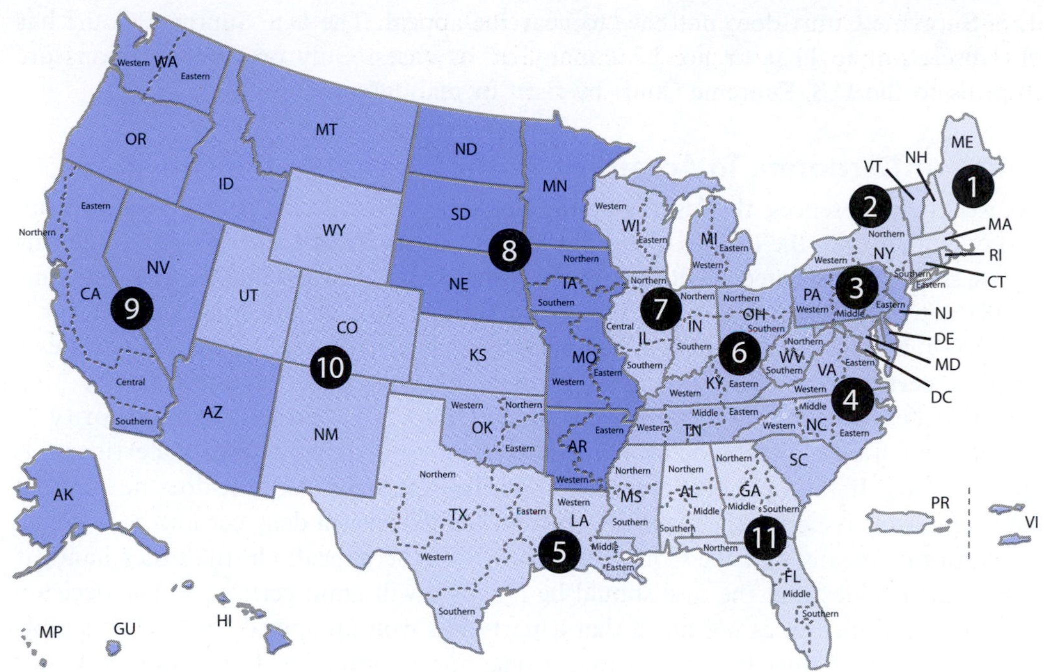

FIGURE 1.5
Map of the Federal Circuit Courts and District Courts
Source: Map from U.S. Courts, available at www.uscourts.gov.

bankruptcy appellate panel. These panels consist of three bankruptcy judges who hear the initial appeal. Because of these panels, fewer cases are appealed to the appropriate federal court of appeals. Although the bankruptcy appellate panels have made great strides, a party still has the right to appeal a decision from a panel to the federal circuit court of appeals.

bankruptcy appellate panel
Panel that hears an initial bankruptcy appeal.

Now that's an overview of the federal circuit courts of appeals. But that is not the end of the federal appeals process. When parties are dissatisfied with the decision of a federal court of appeals, they have one more place to challenge the result—the U.S. Supreme Court.

CYBER TRIP

Locate an example of the en banc rule from the First Circuit Court of Appeals at www.ca1.uscourts.gov/rules/ rule 12-3.pdf.

THE U.S. SUPREME COURT: THE FINAL WORD

Make no mistake about it—the U.S. Supreme Court is the highest court in the American judicial system. It has the final word not only on all federal cases, but cases from all fifty states and the territories. But, unlike the federal circuit courts of appeals, the

Frank and Ernest

Source: © 2005 Thaves. Reprinted with permission. Newspaper dist. by NEA, Inc.

U.S. Supreme Court does not have to hear the appeal. The U.S. Supreme Court has the discretion to hear or not hear many of its cases. Only on rare occasions are appeals to the U.S. Supreme Court by right or mandatory.

Writs of Certiorari: To Accept or Deny . . . That Is the Question

At weekly conferences, the justices of the Supreme Court decide which cases to hear. No one other than the justices of the Supreme Court is present. No one can argue why a case should be accepted. In fact, there are no hard and fast rules that the U.S. Supreme Court is required to follow in accepting or denying a case for full consideration.

writ of certiorari
Granting of petition, by the U.S. Supreme Court, to review a case; request for appeal where the Court has the discretion to grant or deny it.

To request the U.S. Supreme Court hear an appeal on a case, the appellant files a **writ of certiorari.** A writ of certiorari is a legal document requesting the high court to hear the appeal. The U.S. Supreme Court is vested with the authority to decide which cases it will hear. Thus, accepting or denying a writ of certiorari is discretionary. If the Court believes that a specific case lacks merit, or does not present any significant issue for the justices to review, the Court will deny certiorari. A denial of certiorari means that the Court refuses to hear the appeal. On the other hand, if the Court decides that the case should be heard, it will grant certiorari. The decision to grant certiorari does not mean that a party has won on appeal. Instead, it simply means that the Court has agreed to consider the appeal. The U.S. Supreme Court often grants certiorari in three primary areas: (1) matters where the issues have significant social or political application in other areas of law, (2) matters involving an interpretation of the U.S. Constitution, or (3) matters where conflicts among the circuit courts of appeals have caused different legal interpretation of a federal law.

PRACTICE TIP

Attorneys refer colloquially to a writ of certiorari as "cert."

The unwritten rule, known as the "Rule of Four," has governed which cases are heard by the high court. If four justices favor the granting of the writ of certiorari, then the case is heard. Consequently, when the announcement is made that a case has been granted certiorari, no reason is given. Likewise, when a case is denied certiorari, no reason is given. Many attempt to interpret the significance of the "denial" of certiorari, but caution should be taken not to overemphasize the meaning of a denial of certiorari. It does not mean the Court agrees with the lower court's decision. To place this all in perspective, review the graph in Figure 1.6, which shows the number of cases acted upon under a writ of certiorari.

In the modern era, there are nine justices who serve on the U.S. Supreme Court, one of whom serves as the chief justice. These justices make decisions that affect every citizen of the United States, and their decisions are final. When a party loses an appeal at the U.S. Supreme Court, there is no other court with whom to file an appeal.

CYBER TRIP

Locate a case on the U.S. Supreme Court Web site, www.supremecourtus.gov, that either deals with or has dealt with how judges are selected. (Hint: The state of New York may have been involved.)

Therefore, in reviewing the federal court process, we return to our characterization of the court systems as a pyramid, with U.S. district courts forming the base of the pyramid; a party who loses at the district court level can file an appeal and effectively move higher up in the pyramid. For instance, the U.S. circuit court of appeals for a particular district hears cases from that district located within that judicial circuit because it has appellate jurisdiction. Similarly, decisions from a particular U.S. court of appeal would go to the U.S. Supreme Court because that court has appellate jurisdiction over all U.S. circuit courts of appeals. No court has appellate jurisdiction to review the decisions of the U.S. Supreme Court—the final word.

Quick Quiz True/False Questions

1. All states have at least one federal district court.
2. Federal district courts can only hear cases involving a federal question.

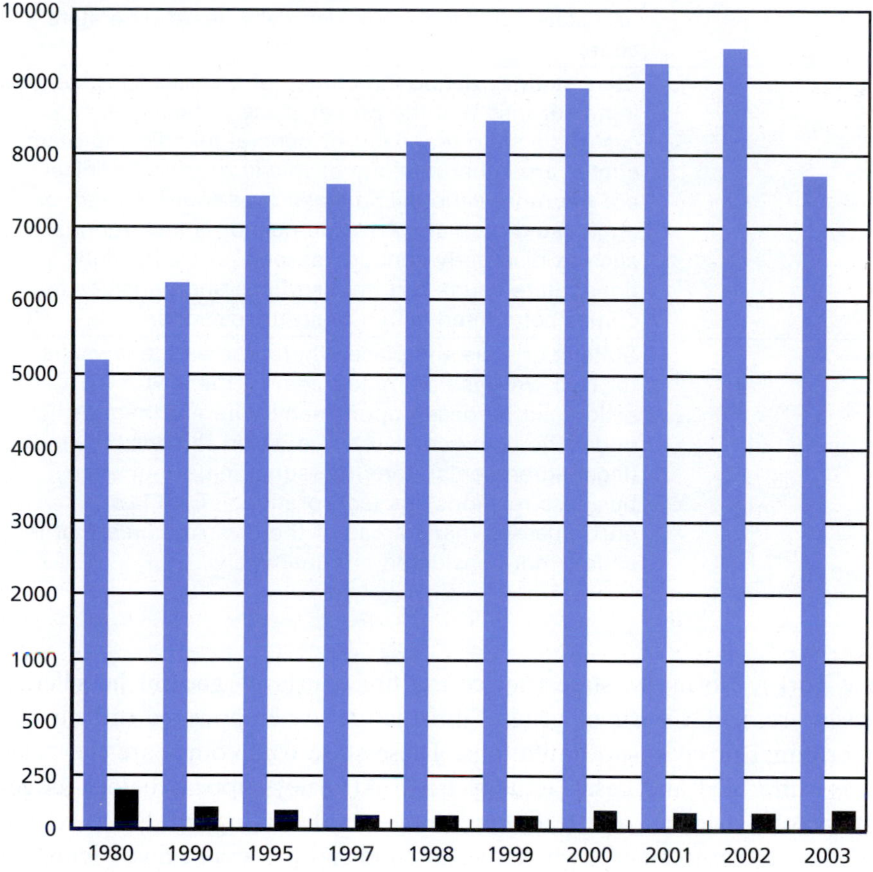

FIGURE 1.6
Number of Cases Accepted for Hearing under a Writ of Certiorari

Source: Peter J. Messitte, "The Writ of *Certiorari:* Deciding Which Cases to Review," *eJournalUSA,* April 2005. Retrieved from http://usinfo.state.gov/journals/itdhr/0405/ijde/messitte.htm (accessed November 26, 2007).

3. Both bankruptcy and federal district courts are courts of limited jurisdiction.
4. There are twelve federal circuit courts of appeals.
5. State supreme courts can review the U.S. Supreme Court.

THE STATE COURT SYSTEMS: COMMON THREADS

In many ways, the state court systems are a mirror of the federal system. However, state courts are limited to the geographic limits of the state and are created by the respective state constitutions and legislatures. As you will learn, each state determines its court system. Most states have a three-tiered court system—a trial court, an intermediate appellate court, and a state supreme court—while the remaining states have a two-tiered system. Learning and knowing your state's court system is essential to any research project. Therefore, just as we did with the federal system, we will begin our discussion of the state court system with the trial courts, where the legal process begins.

State Trial Courts: What's in a Name?

Unlike the federal district courts, whose name is the same in all the federal districts, state trial courts' names are as unique as the state in which they preside. Some examples of state trial court names are Superior Court, Chancery Court, District Court, Court of Common Pleas, and even the Supreme Court (which is the name of the trial

PRACTICE TIP

In very limited circumstances, the Supreme Court acts as a trial court and has **original jurisdiction.** For instance, Article III, section 2 of the U.S. Constitution provides that the Supreme Court has original jurisdiction in cases "affecting ambassadors, other public ministers and counsels." However, the majority of the Court's work focuses on its appellate jurisdiction.

original jurisdiction
Authority of a court to review and try a case first.

FIGURE 1.7
Sampling of Types of State Court Actions

Type of Action	Description of Action
State constitutional questions	Just as cases involving the U.S. Constitution are heard in a federal court, cases concerning the interpretation of a state constitution are generally heard by a state court.
State crimes	State statutes define the crimes of a particular state. It is no surprise that the proper place to hear these cases is a state trial court of general jurisdiction. State crimes are either a felony or misdemeanor. Felonies are the more serious crimes such as murder, rape, or aggravated burglary. A misdemeanor is less serious such as disorderly conduct, assault, or traffic violations. State courts can impose fines and penalties for crimes committed within their jurisdictions.
Civil actions	State courts are the place where parties file lawsuits for civil wrongs committed against them. A civil action can be based upon many different theories under the law. Actions can be based in contract (legal agreements), torts (personal injury), or even business relationships (corporations). Civil law encompasses many areas of the law. Any area that is usually not considered criminal is civil.

general jurisdiction
The court is empowered to hear any civil or criminal case.

probate court
The court process of determining will validity, settling estate debts, and distributing assets.

family court
Court of limited jurisdiction that hears cases such as divorce, custody, and child support.

juvenile court
Court of limited jurisdiction that hears cases involving minors.

small claims court
Court whose jurisdiction is generally limited by monetary ceilings.

courts in New York). Normally, state trial courts are courts of **general jurisdiction** where most cases are filed. Courts of general jurisdiction are empowered to hear any kind of case, criminal or civil—no limitations. These state trial courts are the place where most cases are filed and cases actually tried. Attorneys appear before judges and juries and present evidence and testimony. Judges make rulings on evidence and juries reach verdicts in cases. Here is where the state judicial process begins. Figure 1.7 presents a sampling of the types of cases a state court entertains.

Most trial court jurisdictions are confined to a district or county in which they are located. These limitations define the boundaries or the powers of the court. For instance, a court of one county does not have the authority to make decisions for another county. This would not be within its jurisdiction.

PRACTICE TIP

Do not assume the name of a court implies its level of authority. Normally, the term "supreme court" implies highest court of a jurisdiction. But in the state of New York that is not the case. Pay close attention to the names of the courts in the jurisdiction you are practicing and the jurisdiction in which a case is filed if outside your attorney's scope of practice.

Specialized State Trial Courts

Many states create specialized trial courts by carving out specialized areas of jurisdiction giving that court limited jurisdiction. These specialized trial courts may range from a probate court to a family court to a small claims court. Each has a designated area of concentration either by subject matter or amount in controversy. For example, a **probate court** handles all matters relating to wills and other estate matters. When an individual needs to determine the allocation of a deceased family member's estate, in many states that case would be filed in a probate court. Similarly, in matters of divorce, paternity, or custody, many states designate a particular trial court to hear only matters relating to "family law" issues, known as a **family court.**

Family issues also encompass juvenile matters. With the increase in juvenile matters, many states have created specializing courts known simply as **juvenile courts.** These courts ordinarily hear cases ranging from such serious matters as felony crimes, such as murder, to lesser offenses, such as school delinquency. You must check your state court system to determine whether a specialized trial court exists for juvenile cases.

Additionally, trial courts are created to hear cases involving small amounts in controversy. Usually these courts are referred to as **small claims courts.** Small claims courts generally will hear cases involving less than $7,500. Another type of specialized trial court is a **municipal court.** These courts usually hear cases regarding traffic tickets or matters involving city ordinances. Figure 1.8 provides examples of specialized state courts of limited jurisdiction.

municipal court
City court of limited jurisdiction that hears cases such as traffic violations and violations of city ordinances.

In many instances, the jurisdiction of a general trial court and a specialized trial court overlap. When this occurs, **concurrent jurisdiction** exists. Concurrent jurisdiction exists where two or more courts can hear a particular case. Concurrent jurisdiction can exist between the federal and state court systems or between different trial courts within the same state. When concurrent jurisdiction exists the supervising attorney decides where a case will be filed. As you may guess, determining where to file a case may be a strategic decision on the part of the responsible attorney.

concurrent jurisdiction
Jurisdiction over the subject matter exists in both state and federal court, unless statutorily prohibited.

Let's see how this concept works using Texas as an example. Texas has two types of basic trial courts: district courts and county courts. District courts can hear cases where the amount in controversy is at least $500 with no upper limit. These are courts of general jurisdiction. A county court can hear cases, for purposes of our example, where the amount in controversy exceeds $200 but is less than $5,000. That means that either a district court or a county court can hear a case involving $3,000 in controversy. The courts have concurrent jurisdiction in this matter.

FIGURE 1.8
Examples of Specialized State Courts of Limited Jurisdiction

Type of Specialized State Court	Description
Probate court	This court handles issues regarding a person's estate, specifically wills. The court monitors the distribution of a person's estate. These courts also hear disputes involving the distribution of a person's estate. Additionally, many probate courts hear matters concerning guardianships as well. A guardianship is a when a court orders another party to legally make decisions on behalf of another party. A guardianship may occur because the party is a minor, or in the case of an elderly person, a guardian may be appointed because the person is mentally incompetent.
Family court	Most matters concerning divorce, custody, and child support are heard in a family court. Here the court determines the division of marital property, such as alimony and palimony. It also determines custody rights of parents including visitation. Sometimes adoption and paternity cases fall under a family court's jurisdiction or a juvenile court.
Juvenile court	In today's world, juvenile courts perform many functions. They handle cases ranging from termination of parental rights to child delinquency. One jurisdictional limitation is the age of the person who appears before this court; depending on a state's definition of majority, a juvenile court could hear cases involving persons up to the age of twenty-one. Extremely heinous acts of a child may ultimately be heard by an adult court regardless of the age, however.
Municipal court	Many jurisdictions combine municipal and traffic courts into one municipal court. Usually a municipal court hears cases involving violations of city ordinances (city statutes). That is why traffic courts often fall within the jurisdiction of a municipal court, because traffic violations are often local in nature.
Small claims court	To alleviate the number of cases in trial courts of general jurisdiction, small claims courts hear matters involving amounts usually less than $7,500. Typically private citizens handle these matters without an attorney. In fact, some small claims courts do not allow attorneys in the court. Another area often under the jurisdiction of small claims courts is matters concerning landlords and tenants, specifically evictions. Again, the reasoning is that the amounts in controversy are relatively low and will not involve an attorney.

Assume that a couple in Texas wants to divorce and their combined estate is only $4,000. Can either a district court or the county court hear the case? On its face the question seems to suggest the answer yes. However, as you will learn throughout this text, legal research is important. If we had performed research on the jurisdictional and subject matter limits of these courts, we would have learned that only a district court can hear matters involving divorce regardless of the amount in controversy. (By researching the statute, you would have learned this fact. Once again, the important point is not to assume; you should be thorough with your legal research. A complete discussion of statutory research is found in Chapter 5.) See Figure 1.9 for a diagram of concurrent jurisdiction using our Texas court example.

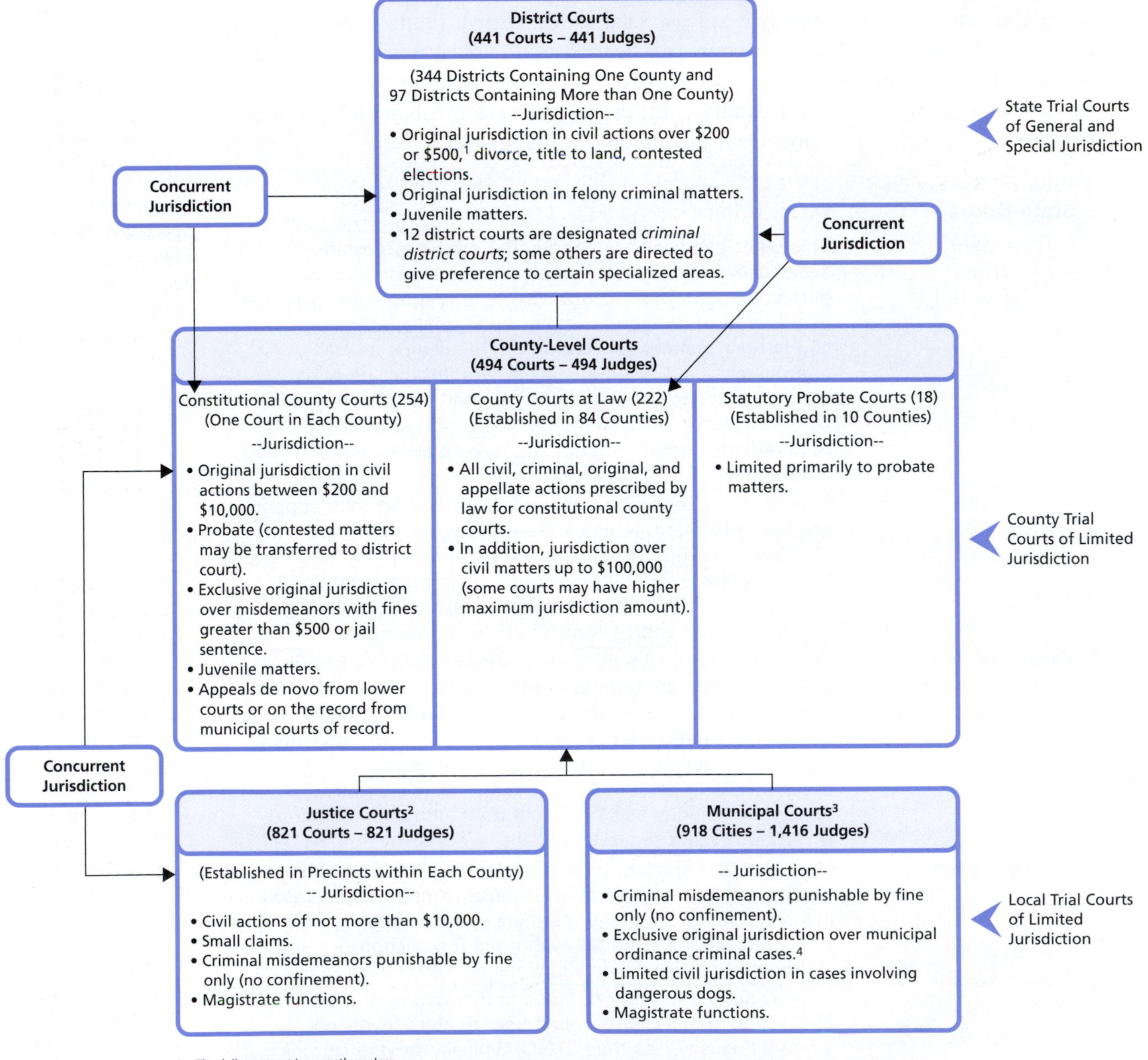

FIGURE 1.9 Diagram of Concurrent Jurisdiction within the Texas Trial Court System

Source: Adapted from "Court Structure of Texas," www.courts.state.tx.us/oca/pdf/Court_Structure_Chart.pdf (accessed November 26, 2007).

Intermediate State Appellate Courts: Appeals as of Right

Many states have an intermediate appellate court that hears appeals from state trial courts. In most cases, appellate courts must hear all cases brought before them. The right of a losing party to bring an appeal to these courts is referred to as "appeal as of right," meaning that a party usually has the right to at least one appellate hearing.

For those states with a three-tiered system, the intermediate state court of appeals is the first level of appellate review. It is where most parties bring their appeals when they lose in the trial court.

In essence, the party bringing the appeals believes that the judge or jury's decision at the trial court is wrong. It is important to remember that courts of appeals do not retry cases; the losing party is not given the opportunity of presenting new witnesses and evidence that was not heard in the original case. More importantly, appellate courts are not empowered to hear new testimony or consider newly discovered evidence. They focus on what happened in the trial court. These judges consider only the written record, such as the transcript of a trial, in making their decision. If they believe that an error occurred, they are empowered to change the court's decision or jury verdict or if the judges agree with the trial court's action, do nothing by leaving the lower court's decision intact. Of course, the judges of an appellate court weigh the written record presented against the law.

PRACTICE TIP

Approximately ten states have a single appellate court, which is the court of last resort.

Courts of appeals have panels of judges who listen to the presentation of arguments by attorneys as to why the decision of the trial court should be changed. Most panels consist of three judges. However, the total numbers of judges who sit on state courts of appeals vary. Some states, such as Idaho, have as few as three judges who hear all appeals; larger states, such as Michigan, have twenty-eight appeals court judges sitting in groups of three panels for four districts.

For those states with a three-tiered court system, a party who is dissatisfied with the decision of the intermediate appellate court may appeal the decision to the highest appellate court, often called the state supreme court.

PRACTICE TIP

The states of Texas and Oklahoma have two high courts of last resort. The Texas and Oklahoma supreme courts hear appeals on civil matters while the Texas and Oklahoma courts of criminal appeals hear cases involving criminal matters. These are the only states that have two high courts of appeals. Neither court of last resort can review the other's decisions. Only the U.S. Supreme Court can review decisions of these courts.

The Highest State Appellate Courts: A State's Court of Last Resort

All states have a high court that, like the U.S. Supreme Court, is the final authority on appellate issues. Although this court is usually referred to as the state supreme court, this is not always the case. For example, in New York, the state's highest court is referred to as New York Court of Appeals. Likewise, in Massachusetts the highest court is referred to as the Supreme Judicial Court of the Commonwealth of Massachusetts, the SJC for short. State high courts share many similarities with the U.S. Supreme Court. For instance, many of these courts have certiorari authority—the right to decide to hear or not hear a case—while others do not. This highest appellate court serves the same role on the state level as the U.S. Supreme Court serves on the federal level: It is the final authority on appellate issues in that jurisdiction.

In most states, the state highest appellate court consists of as few as five justices or as many as nine. Some states appoint new members to their highest court, while others elect them. As with any appellate judge, including the intermediate appellate-level judges, no witnesses or evidence is presented. The judges base their decisions on the briefs filed, the oral arguments presented, and, of course, the law. Most importantly, except for the U.S. Supreme Court, a state's highest appellate court is the final judicial authority for that state law.

We have completed our review of both the federal and state court systems. Now we need to revisit Dave from our Case Fact Pattern and determine in which court Dave can file his lawsuit. Although Dave may have defendants from different states, federal diversity jurisdiction is ruled out for two reasons. Dave's damages will not exceed $75,000 and both he and one of the credit card companies are in his home state, destroying diversity jurisdiction. Even if there were diversity between the parties, it

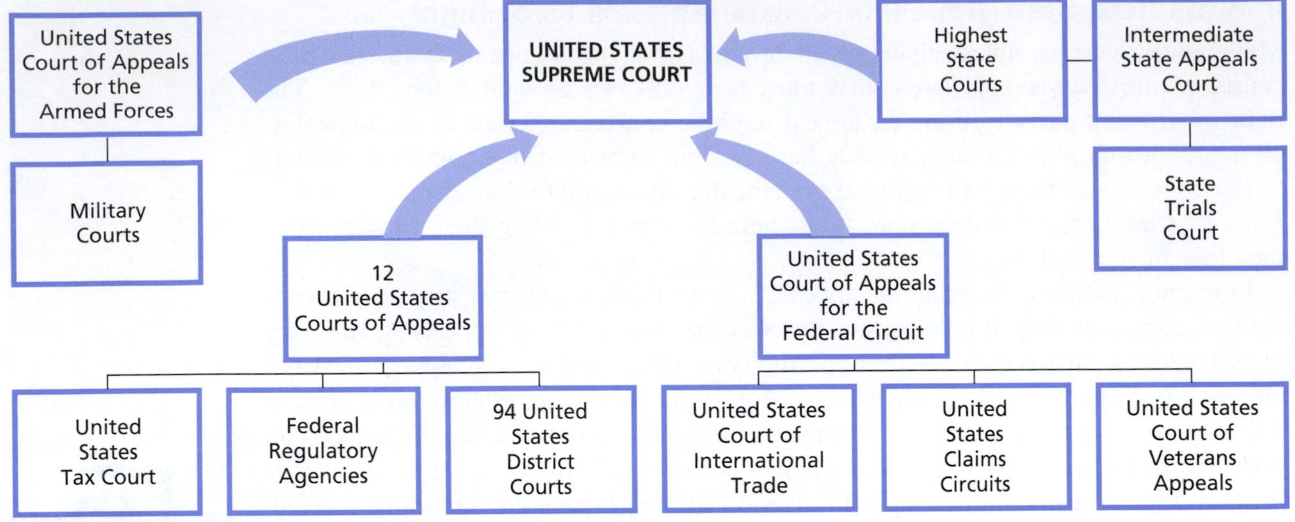

FIGURE 1.10 **Chart Showing a Case Moving through the Court System**

Source: Obtained from www.uscourts.gov/outreach/resources/pathsupremect.gif (accessed November 26, 2007).

appears that Dave's damages are not nearly enough to meet the minimum threshold of $75,000. Therefore, it is safe to say that Dave's lawsuit will be filed in a state court. Probably because of the possible complexity of the issues, the lawsuit would be filed in a state court of general jurisdiction, such as a superior or district court. Figure 1.10 is a chart of the path a case follows through the federal and state court systems.

CYBER TRIP

Using www.ncsconline.org, locate a chart of your state court. Compare the chart with your state's official court Web site. Additionally, choose three states and compare their court systems with your home state. See also the McGraw-Hill portal, www.mhhe.com/paralegal, for additional information on the state court system.

Quick Quiz True/False Questions

1. All state court systems have trial courts, an intermediate court of appeals, and a state supreme court.
2. Trial courts can be courts of general and limited jurisdiction.

ETHICS ALERT

Legal professionals have a code of ethics and ethical responsibilities. Judges are no different. Federal judges must abide by the Code of Conduct for United States Judges with each state having a judicial code of conduct as well. Judicial codes of conduct provide guidance on a number of issues from impartiality to judicial integrity, and from permissible out-of-court activities to avoiding any form of impropriety or even its appearance.

The last ethical standard, the appearance of an impropriety, is important. As a paralegal, this is an area where your supervising attorney may request your assistance. Under this ethical standard, judges cannot participate in cases where they have a personal bias, a financial interest, prior involvement in the case, or personal knowledge of the disputed facts. In the legal world, these situations create conflicts of interest. A conflict of interest may be real or perceived. It may not make a difference, however. Even the appearance of an impropriety may create a conflict of interest and an ethical violation.

Therefore, you need to pay attention to the judges your firm or company practices before and do your homework. Often judges don't even know a problem exists until the case commences or is well into the process. Most judges will immediately recuse themselves as soon as they realize a problem exists or may exist. The term *recuse* simply means to excuse oneself from the legal process. Even if the judge believes objectivity is possible, judicial standards of conduct require the judge to remove himself or herself from hearing the appeal.

Be aware that ethical standards of conduct apply not only to you and your attorney, but also to those who make the legal decisions—judges.

3. State courts and federal courts share concurrent jurisdiction on some matters.
4. Generally, state intermediate courts of appeals have the discretion to accept or deny a properly filed appeal.
5. All states have one court of last resort.

THE COURT RULES: CODES OF DIFFERENT COLORS

All courts have rules. The U.S. Supreme Court has rules. All the federal circuit courts of appeals and district courts have rules. To add to the mix, all state courts have rules as well. Sometimes the rules are the same; sometimes they are not. Some courts have rules that apply only to those courts and, believe it or not, some judges have rules just for their court. That is why it is so important to learn about the process and rules of the court in which you will practice. We will briefly examine the primary rules that govern the court process.

Trial Court Rules: The Federal Rules of Procedure—Civil and Criminal

Unless there were rules governing the court process, it would be quite chaotic. The basic rules that govern the litigation procedure in federal courts are the **Federal Rules of Civil Procedure.** The rules cover procedure from filing a lawsuit to conducting a trial. Any attorney remotely involved in the litigation process has to be familiar with the rules of civil procedure. The Federal Rules of Civil Procedure are relatively easy to locate as virtually all the federal court Web sites have a copy of the rules posted. As part of your job as a paralegal, you need to familiarize yourself with the rules of civil procedure. As noted in Figure 1.11, the Federal Rules of Civil Procedure guide legal professionals through the entire litigation process.

Federal Rules of Civil Procedure
Federal civil rules of court.

In addition to the general federal rules of civil procedure are local rules of civil procedure. These rules are of particular importance because they govern the process in a particular jurisdiction, district, or court. Most courts have some form of local rules that apply to their court. These rules may dictate the length of a legal document or how attorneys are required to communicate with each other. Whatever those rules may be, the local rules of the federal district courts need to be reviewed in conjunction with the universal federal rules of civil procedure.

The process for civil trials differs from that of criminal trials. As a result, there are separate **Federal Rules of Criminal Procedure.** These rules govern how federal criminal cases are prosecuted. Although these rules are beyond the scope of this text, it is important to note that the criminal trial process and the civil trial process are quite

Federal Rules of Criminal Procedure
Federal criminal rules of court.

FIGURE 1.11
General Content of the Federal Rules of Civil Procedure

Federal Rules of Civil Procedure

I. Scope of Rules—One Form of Action
II. Commencement of Action; Service of Process, Pleadings, Motions, and Orders
III. Pleadings and Motions
IV. Parties
V. Depositions and Discovery
VI. Trials
VII. Judgment
VIII. Provisional and Final Remedies
IX. Special Proceedings
X. District Courts and Clerks
XI. General Provisions
XII. Appendix of Forms
XIII. Supplemental Rules for Certain Admiralty and Maritime Claims

A DAY IN THE LIFE OF A PARALEGAL

You are at the courthouse filing some legal documents in a divorce case. You decide to take a look at the file and notice an order you never saw before. As you leaf through the file, you notice a letter requesting the court to issue an order freezing the bank accounts of your client. You are shocked. The letter was written to the judge directly without a copy being sent to your firm. The order was signed yesterday and takes effect tomorrow. The action of the opposing counsel is improper and constitutes an **ex parte communication.** You remember your attorney telling you that contacts with a judge without both counsel present are not permitted. She also told you that sometimes attorneys do things to get the upper hand, and that you should watch out. You immediately make a copy of the order and letter for your attorney and rush back to the office. When you get back, you show your attorney the documents; she immediately calls the bank to let them know that she will be filing a motion to stop the order from going into effect. No damage has been done to the client yet and your quick response made what could have been a catastrophic situation manageable. The moral of the story is that no communication, oral or written—except in very limited situations—should be made to a judge without all counsel present.

ex parte communication
A communication between one party in a lawsuit and the judge.

Federal Rules of Evidence
The procedure for the introduction of evidence in a federal legal proceeding.

different. Therefore, it is important to review independently the criminal rules of procedure if you and your supervising attorney are involved in a criminal prosecution.

There is another set of court rules that govern the admission of evidence in federal trials. The rules are the **Federal Rules of Evidence.** Under these rules, judges admit evidence and rule on objections. The rules are divided into eleven articles, which include specific rules that guide attorneys and judges on the relevancy and admissibility of evidence. In many respects, these are probably the most visible rules in the courtroom, as television and film dramatize daily. We all have seen the lawyer jump to his feet and say "Objection, Your Honor, hearsay evidence." That's the rules of evidence in action.

PRACTICE TIP

All the federal rules of civil and criminal procedure can be located at www.uscourts.gov. Each court has a separate website with its local rules. Simply follow the links from the general federal courts website.

Federal Appellate Court Rules: Circuit Courts of Appeals

It will come as no surprise that there are appellate court rules for the federal circuit courts of appeals. Similar to the Federal Rules of Civil Procedure, there are general federal appellate rules as well as local court rules for the various circuits. The local rules will identify any special rules for a particular area. If you become involved in an appellate case, be sure to retain a copy of both sets of rules. Each court posts its rules and any amendments on its sites, but the general Web site for the federal circuit courts of appeals is www.uscourts.gov.

U.S. Supreme Court Rules of Procedure

The U.S. Supreme Court has its own rules. These rules dictate the presentation of briefs, including the color of the cover sheets, font size, and width of margins within the brief. Unlike any court before which legal professionals have practiced, errors of form in the U.S. Supreme Court may cause a document to be rejected for filing. The U.S. Supreme Court Web site at www.supremecourtus.gov posts its rules and any amendments to those rules.

PRACTICE TIP

Don't be fooled into thinking that the local rule of one court is the same for another court. Always check to determine whether a court, regardless of the level, has local rules.

State Court Rules

State courts have rules of court as well. Many states have a mirror of the federal rules of procedure, while others such as Texas and California have significantly different rules of procedure. Do not think that knowing the federal rules of court automatically means that you know your state rules of court. In fact, assume that your state rules of civil and criminal procedure are completely different from the federal rules—review them before you proceed with an assignment.

Texas Local Rule of Court for Montgomery County

Rule 3.16 Filing of Pleadings

All pleadings, motions, orders and other papers, including exhibits attached thereto, when offered for filing or entry, shall be descriptively titled and punched at the top of the page to accommodate clerk's 2.75" center-to-center flat-filing system. Each page of each instrument shall on the lower right-hand margin thereof be numbered and titled, i.e. "Plaintiff's Original Petition Page 2." Orders and Judgments shall be separate documents completely separated from all other papers. If documents not conforming to this rule are offered, the clerk shall return the documents to the counsel or party unfiled. Counsel shall furnish the clerk with sufficient copies to perfect service or notice.

Arizona Rule of Civil Procedure for the Superior Courts

(d). Method of preparation and filing All pleadings and other papers filed in any action or proceeding shall be on white, opaque, unglazed paper measuring 8½ inches × 11 inches, with a margin at the top of the first page of not less than 2 inches; a margin at the top of each subsequent page of not less than 1½ inches; a left-hand margin of not less than 1 inch; a right-hand margin of not less than ½ inch; and a margin at the bottom of the page of not less than ½ inch.

FIGURE 1.12
Examples of Local Rules of Court

State appeals courts have separate and distinct rules to follow. If your state has a three-tiered court system, be sure not to confuse the intermediate court of appeals rules with the highest court of appeals in your state. Like the federal courts, state courts have local rules of court. These local rules appear at all levels of court from the trial courts to the courts of last resort. And don't assume that each trial court has the same local rules. A probate court may have different rules than the family court. Figure 1.12 is an example of a local rule of court for the district courts in Montgomery County, Texas, followed by a different rule of filing in Arizona.

An important point to remember is that many of the state courts, especially the smaller trial courts such as small claims courts, may not have Web sites. You may have to request the local rules through the clerk's office of that court. Just stay alert to the subtle nuances of court rules.

Throughout this text, emphasis will be placed on learning the court rules. The reason for the emphasis is that not only are the rules important, but your role as a paralegal in relationship to those rules is important. It may seem a bit daunting now,

PACER
Federal court online document system.

THE E-FACTOR

Public Access to Court Electronic Records, commonly known as **PACER**, is the federal court document system, which allows public access to all docket and case information. This system is available in all the federal courts. To access the database, locate the specific court Web site of the jurisdiction from which you want information. Information such as newly filed cases, status of cases, court orders, opinions, and other information regarding cases can be found. Some courts even provide image copies of filed documents.

As part of the PACER system, there is a U.S. Party/Case Index. This index is a national locator index of all federal court cases, trial and appellate. By entering a party's name in the text box, you can locate all federal cases in which that party is involved—that means you can conduct a nationwide search of a party with the click of a button. If you locate relevant information on a party, you can visit the specific PACER site for the court where the case is filed.

An important note about PACER is that it is not free and is not modeled after a typical Web page. You must register with PACER and will be charged according to its rules of usage. For people used to surfing the Internet, it can be surprising to learn that PACER charges for access to each document. Bouncing from document to document in PACER can incur some pretty hefty costs, whether you actually print or even read the document on the page you are accessing. Consequently, review the charges section of the PACER registry so you have a clear understanding as to how and under what circumstances you will be charged. The good news is that PACER can be accessed anytime, day or night, without running to the courthouse to review a file.

FIGURE 1.13
Checklist of Preliminary Considerations to Filing a Lawsuit

Court Checklist

- Gather facts to determine whether there is an actual dispute—case and controversy. Coupled with this concept is whether the client has standing to bring the lawsuit.
- Identify the applicable statute of limitations involved in the matter.
- Determine whether the case involves federal or state claims.
- Commence legal research as needed.
- Establish whether any court has exclusive jurisdiction to hear the case based on the facts presented.
- If federal claims exist, is the case based upon a federal question or diversity of citizenship?
- Evaluate which federal district court is proper to file the lawsuit. Be sure to check whether the district has subdistricts and whether within the subdistricts, divisions exist.
- Review the facts to determine whether personal and subject matter jurisdiction over the parties exists.
- Peruse the federal civil rules of procedure, including any local rules of court.
- If a state claim exists, along with your supervising attorney, decide in which court the case should be filed. Does a specialized state court exist for the facts of the case?
- Examine the facts to determine which state has personal and subject matter jurisdiction over the parties and the claims.
- Review the state rules of civil procedure and any local court rules that may apply to the case.
- Alternatively, if concurrent jurisdiction exists for the case, consider the possible courts and the strategic advantages of those courts with your supervising attorney.
- File the lawsuit in the appropriate trial court.

Each of the elements in this checklist should be done in consultation with your supervising attorney.

but as you begin to learn the process, you will also understand what is required by the court and its personnel. Therefore, Figure 1.13 provides a checklist of some preliminary considerations prior to filing a lawsuit.

PRACTICAL CONSIDERATIONS: THE PARALEGAL IN THE COURT PROCESS, OR WHY SHOULD I CARE?

Paralegals are an essential part of the court process. That is why you need a working understanding not only of your state and federal court system, but also the location of those courts, hours of operation, and names of court personnel. You will be the link to the day-to-day "comings and goings" in the courthouse.

Assume at this juncture that you have mastered the court system of your jurisdiction. You know the types of courts within the court system, especially the different types of trial courts. You know whether your state has a two-tiered or three-tiered court system. And you know each court's basic jurisdiction. Now, the next step is mastering some practical information about your state court.

Location of the Courts

Many state courts have not converted to electronic filings of court documents. This means that you have to physically go down to the courthouse and file legal documents. Be sure you know in which court to file your documents. Do you file the documents directly with the court? Do you file the documents with the court clerk? Is there a difference between the court clerks of the various trial courts in your state? You need to know the answers to these questions to be effective.

Most courts have Web sites. For those that do not, there are pamphlets, guides, and written material that provide the addresses of courts, names of the court clerks, and the names of the judges of the respective courts. Learn this information. Keep this information on your desk or at least in a place that is easily accessible. You are probably the one who will be sent to the courthouse to file that eleventh-hour legal document, and you need to know how to get there quickly and efficiently.

Hours of Operation

Coupled with knowing where to go is knowing the hours of operation of the various courts. Do all the courts open at 8:00 a.m. and close at 5:00 p.m.? Does the court have special hours for filing certain types of legal documents? Do your local or state courts close on all federal holidays? Are there state holidays on which a court may be closed? Learn the answers to these questions by paying attention to what's going on in your court.

Filing Fees

Most lawsuits, especially complaints and petitions, have filing fees associated with them. Find out the costs of filing fees for the matter you are filing. Don't get caught with a court clerk rejecting your legal document because your check was incorrect. Having a court reject the filing of a legal document could be malpractice, especially if statute of limitations and court deadlines are involved.

Sometimes you may practice in courts that are unfamiliar to you. You must learn how those courts work as well. Do not assume that a court system in another jurisdiction operates under the same rules and conditions as the court you are familiar with practicing in. Don't assume that a court operates on the same notions even if it is located in the next county, let alone another state. Always pay attention to the finer details of the operations of a court.

Court Personnel

Learn the names of court personnel. You need to know the difference between the clerk of the court and a clerk who works in the court. When you prepare correspondence, as you invariably will, know to whom you will be directing that correspondence. (Chapter 15 will focus on legal correspondence.) Don't insult court personnel by addressing a letter to the wrong individual.

Get to know the court personnel with whom you will work. They are an invaluable asset. Most court personnel have been on the job for quite some time and know all the nuances and subtleties required in the court process. Ask questions. They will help you. In fact, most court personnel are eager to help you. Paralegals and court personnel work hand in hand.

With all this said, now you understand why the court system is important to master and how important you are to the process. Understanding the court system is only the beginning; in the chapters that follow you will learn about all the sources of the law and how to use them. Each source builds on the other. Master them.

YOU BE THE JUDGE

Correct filing fees are essential when filing a lawsuit—even when the fee is only $3 short. As a lawyer and his assistant learned in *Duran v. St. Luke's Hospital*, 114 Cal. App. 4th 459, 8 Cal. Rptr. 3d 1 (Cal. App. 1 Dist. 2003), following up with a court clerk is critical to the process. In this case, the law firm attempted to file a medical malpractice case with only three days until the statute of limitations ran out. The law firm sent the case to the court by Federal Express as the case was not in their home jurisdiction. Unknown to the firm, the filing fee was incorrect. The court clerk rejected the filing of the complaint and the law firm did not learn of the problem until *after* the statute of limitations had run out. Even though the court was sympathetic to the plaintiffs and the law firm's plight, the court had no choice but to deny the filing of the complaint. Review *Duran v. St. Luke's Hospital.* What are the facts of the case? Why did the court rule in favor of St. Luke's Hospital? What important issue do a paralegal and an attorney learn from this case? (Note: The plaintiffs filed a medical malpractice case against the hospital. Quite possibly, the case turned into a legal malpractice case against the law firm.)

Summary

The U.S. Constitution is the foundation of the American legal system, which encompasses three branches of government: legislative, executive, and judicial. Each branch is a check and balance on the other. Along with the U.S. Constitution, basic rights are created through the Bill of Rights, the first ten amendments, and the remaining sixteen amendments. For a new amendment to be passed, three-fourths of the states must approve.

When parties have a dispute, they will file a lawsuit. A party must have standing to bring the lawsuit and comply with the applicable statute of limitations. In order for a court to hear a lawsuit, it must have both personal and subject matter jurisdiction. Courts can hear civil matters and award monetary and equitable remedies; in criminal lawsuits, courts can assess fines and penalties as well as sentence defendants to imprisonment.

There are two basic court systems: federal and state. The federal system is a three-tiered system. The trial courts are called district courts, of which there are ninety-four. The two types of federal jurisdiction are federal question and diversity of citizenship. Specialized district courts are bankruptcy courts, Court of International Trade, and U.S. Court of Federal Claims. Decisions from a federal district court may be appealed to one of thirteen circuit courts of appeals. The court of last resort is the U.S. Supreme Court, which usually hears cases based upon an application for a writ of certiorari. All decisions of the U.S. Supreme Court are final.

State court systems vary. Some states have a two-tiered system while others have a three-tiered system. Not only are the state court systems varied, but the names of the courts within states are often varied. Most states have general and specialized trial courts, which hear cases bases upon their jurisdictional constraints. Some courts have overlapping or concurrent jurisdiction, which means that the same case may be filed in a number of courts. Each state has a court of last resort, often called a state supreme court. Decisions of a state supreme court can be appealed to the U.S. Supreme Court.

Both the federal and state courts have rules of court. The federal trial rules are known as the Federal Rules of Civil Procedure and Federal Rules of Criminal Procedure. Most federal district courts have local rules to supplement the rules of civil and criminal procedure. Federal appellate courts, including the U.S. Supreme Court, have rules as well. Each federal circuit court of appeals has additional local rules to follow.

State courts have rules of court. There usually are general rules of procedure with each court promulgating rules for their respective courts. Coupled with the trial courts, all the appellate state courts have rules of procedure often followed by local rules of court as well.

Paralegals are integral to the court system. Not only should paralegals master the various rules of court within their jurisdiction, but they should also learn the location of the courts, filing fees, hours of operation, and names of court personal. Paralegals often are the links to the day-to-day business within the court system.

Key Terms

advisory opinion
appellant
appellate jurisdiction
appellee
bankruptcy appellate panel
bankruptcy courts
Bill of Rights
cause of action
civil law
compensatory damages
concurrent jurisdiction
court
Court of International Trade
criminal law
debtor
defendant
diversity of citizenship jurisdiction
docket
en banc
equitable relief
equitable remedy
ex parte communication

exclusive jurisdiction
executive privilege
family court
federal question jurisdiction
Federal Rules of Civil Procedure
Federal Rules of Criminal Procedure
Federal Rules of Evidence
fraud
general jurisdiction
habeas corpus
jurisdiction
judge
jury
juvenile court
injunction
lawsuit
limited jurisdiction
magistrate judge
misrepresentation
monetary remedy
municipal court
original jurisdiction
PACER
personal jurisdiction
plaintiff
probate court
prosecutor
punitive damages
small claims court
special prosecutor
standing
statute of limitations
subject matter jurisdiction
trial court
U.S. circuit courts of appeals
U.S. Constitution
U.S. Court of Federal Claims
U.S. district courts
writ of certiorari

Review Questions

1. How is the U.S. Constitution organized?
2. Describe the concept of "separation of powers" under the U.S. Constitution.
3. Define the term *standing* and explain why it is important in the legal process.
4. What is the jurisdiction of the U.S. district courts?
5. Compare and contrast exclusive jurisdiction and limited jurisdiction.
6. What is a writ of certiorari?
7. Identify the structure of the federal court system.
8. What is the general composition of most state court systems? Distinguish some possible differences.
9. What are court rules and why are they important?
10. Identify what role a paralegal may play in the court process.

Exercises

1. Governor Greaux is the governor of the state of Louisiana. He was born in Lyon, France, and wants to run for president of the United States. What provision of the U.S. Constitution determines whether he can run or not?
2. Using your federal court circuit as a guide, chart the organization of that court system, beginning with the trial court and proceeding to the highest appellate court.
3. Prepare a diagram of your state's court system showing the relationship of trial courts to appellate courts.
4. Prepare a complete summary of all the courts in your area, beginning with the smallest courts—including magistrate, small claims, traffic, city, and other courts—and then progressing through to higher courts, whether called state court, superior court, or some other name. As you prepare your summary, list the powers and responsibilities of each of these courts, as well as where they are located and Web site and telephone contact information.
5. Locate a copy of your state's constitution. Compare the provisions of your state constitution with the federal Constitution? Identify the similarities and significant differences.

6. Determine how many judges preside in your state's highest court and identify who is the chief judge.
7. Choose a state other than your own, and compare and contrast the differences and similarities in the court systems.
8. Compare and contrast your state court system with the federal court system in your state.
9. Margaret Millhouse is from Nevada. Prices for cars are high, so she decided to buy a car in the neighboring state of California. She thought she wanted an SUV, but saw the new Mercedes sports coupe and just had to have it. On the way home, some teenagers were trying to pass her on an open highway. They tried one time, but oncoming traffic forced them to retreat. A mile down the road, the teenagers attempted again, but didn't notice that Margaret was stopped at a red light and hit the rear of her car, smashing the entire back end. The accident occurred in Nevada, but the teenagers were all from California. The value of the car was $50,000. Margaret was injured from the accident. Her medical bills are $25,000 and climbing. Margaret wants to sue the teenagers. In what court could Margaret file her lawsuit and why?
10. Five soccer players from State College were wrongfully accused of sexually assaulting three women. After a thorough investigation, it was determined that the prosecutor and the police withheld critical information that exonerated the five players. Although the criminal charges were dismissed against the players, their reputations in the communities where they live will never be the same. The five players, who all reside in North Carolina, decided they will file a civil rights lawsuit that includes allegations of invasion of privacy, libel, and slander. The players intend to sue the college, the prosecutor, and the Collegetown police force. Identify the court(s) where the players may file their lawsuit. Support your response with a detailed explanation as to why a particular court was chosen over another.

PORTFOLIO ASSIGNMENT

Kimmie Simmone is an avid art lover from Paris, Texas. This year Kimmie decided to spend her vacation in the "Big Apple," New York City, wandering through art galleries. One of the galleries Kimmie visited had a modern art exhibit featuring abstract American artist Cy Twombly, who was originally from Virginia, but presently resides in Europe. While viewing one of his most famous works, an all-white canvas painting, Kimmie was overcome with emotion and placed a red lipstick-laden kiss right in the center. She was immediately arrested for destruction of property and a host of other offenses. The owner, Laurence Avignon, who resides in Seattle, Washington, claims the painting is estimated to be worth close to $3 million. Restorers have tried countless products to remove the lipstick stain, but have been unsuccessful. Not only is Kimmie being prosecuted criminally but the owner of the painting wants to file a civil lawsuit. Based on the facts, in which courts could a civil case be filed? In which court would the criminal case be filed? Detail your response with an explanation of why a particular court was chosen. (Explore all possibilities.)

Quick Quiz True/False Answers

Page 6	Page 10	Page 16	Page 22
1. False	1. True	1. True	1. False
2. True	2. True	2. False	2. True
3. False	3. False	3. True	3. True
4. False	4. True	4. False	4. False
5. False	5. False	5. False	5. False

Chapter 2

The Sources of the Law: What's in a Law Library

After completing this chapter, you will be able to:

- Understand the difference between primary and secondary sources of the law.
- Describe the difference between reporters and codes.
- Differentiate between slip laws, session laws, and codes.
- Distinguish the sources of administrative regulation.
- Use secondary sources such as legal encyclopedias and treatises.
- Explain the hierarchy of the law.
- Understand the concepts of mandatory authority and persuasive authority.
- Compare and contrast encyclopedias and legal treatises.
- List the various types of secondary authority.
- Identify differences between a legal encyclopedia and American Law Reports.

Learning the law is like learning a new language. You will have to learn new words and new concepts, and face new challenges. This chapter introduces you to the "language of the law," its sources, and how it developed. You will be introduced to primary and secondary sources of the law, such as cases and encyclopedias. Building on each concept, you will begin the process of learning what the law is and how to "find" it. The process takes time and patience, but once you master the basics you will approach each concept and assignment like a puzzle whose clues need to be unraveled. Embrace it and attack it like any other task you have studied. The most important point to remember is patience. Rome wasn't built in a day! Now, let's get started.

The field of law is complex, with the American legal system generating over 100,000 published opinions each year, volumes upon volumes of new and existing statutory materials, and thousands of treatises and articles analyzing the evolution and application of the law. No one individual can ever hope to master every element, angle, and detail in the law library. With practice, the process does get easier. So, whenever a new situation arises requiring the application of legal principles, you will be faced once again with that question—what is the law? In this chapter and the chapters that follow, you'll learn how to find answers.

CASE FACT PATTERN

Catherine Thacker is a paralegal who recently has been given an assignment by her supervising attorney in her department. The attorney wants Catherine to locate legal authority to support the client's position in a pending lawsuit. Catherine has found several references, including a legal periodical, a section from a legal encyclopedia, and an opinion from a neighboring state. All of these sources support the client's position. But Catherine also has located an opinion from her own state's court of appeals that is contrary to all of these other sources. Catherine is in a dilemma. Can she use the other sources as authority in this case? Can she ignore the case from the court of appeals or, if she decides not to ignore it, what are the consequences? Will she be required to ignore the authorities? These are some of the questions that attorneys and paralegals ask every day when performing legal research.

LEGAL RESEARCH IN GENERAL

Congress, the fifty state legislatures, and the thousands of local legislatures all generate legislation in the form of statutes and ordinances. The federal court system, the fifty state court systems, and the local court systems all churn out written opinions. The many executive agencies and departments release regulations and quasi-judicial decisions. Moreover, these activities have been going on for years, decades, centuries! As a result, an enormous quantity of law has been produced and, theoretically, must be sorted through when addressing a legal research problem.

A comprehensive law library, the storehouse for all these materials, is indeed an impressive sight. With rows and rows of uniform volumes, shelves of multivolume treatises and statutory codes, looseleaf binders with up-to-the-minute pronouncements, computers and the Internet, the available resources are vast.

Although the volume of material that might apply to a given research problem is truly staggering, you should not throw up your hands and say "Impossible!" before you even start. Fortunately, there is help. Over the years a logical, thorough, and even ingenious system of research aids has been developed that enables you to focus on the heart of your research problem. We will touch on those research aids in this chapter with more detail in Chapter 6.

However, there are a few basic concepts to keep in mind as you begin your study of this system. First, when faced with a specific research project, you need to understand your goal before you start. Are you interested in finding out what the current law is? Are you interested in tracing the development of the law? Do you need to determine precisely what the law was at some specific time when events critical to the resolution of your client's problem occurred? Or are you simply interested in a general understanding of a new area of the law? Your approach will differ depending upon your goal.

Second, you should consciously devise an approach that is both thorough and efficient. It would be unwise to simply plunge in. The complexity of the subject matter and the potential for getting lost and confused in a mass of materials require that you think before you act.

Finally, if you do become stumped or confused, as you inevitably will, get help. Consult with your supervising attorney. Ask another paralegal. Talk to the librarian (law librarians are helpful and often extremely knowledgeable about both research in general and the peculiarities of their specific law library). Don't give up your solo efforts too quickly, but don't waste time floundering, either. Sometimes a brief tip from someone with experience can save you hours of frustration.

As your skills develop, you will begin to understand that mastering legal research is a continuing process in which new ideas and information enable you to refine and perfect your own personal approach. The following sections introduce you to the primary and secondary sources of the law available to assist in the legal research process along with some of the legal concepts associated with those sources.

PRECEDENTIAL VALUE: PRIMARY AUTHORITY VERSUS SECONDARY AUTHORITY

Before we discuss the many available resources, let's consider an important and basic principle that underlies all legal research.

Imagine for a moment an appellate judge sitting in her chambers, having just left the courtroom where opposing sides in an appeal have concluded oral argument. On her desk are the competing briefs, each filled with references to cases, statutes, treatises, and other sources, each presenting a compelling rationale. How does the judge weigh the relative merits of the differing points of view? How does she decide who wins and who loses?

Although every judge has a characteristic style and every case its own peculiar twist, there is in fact a pattern to the manner in which judicial decision making proceeds. That pattern is steeped in legal history and is the doctrine of ***stare decisis***. *Stare decisis* means that decisions from a court with substantially the same set of facts should be followed by that court and all lower courts under it. Chapter 1 provided a general understanding of the court system, but let's put the concepts from our study of the court system into practice for understanding how the principle of *stare decisis* works. Recall that the courts where most controversies are filed are known as trial courts. Trial courts usually have the power to hear all types of cases depending upon the extent of their jurisdiction.

stare decisis
(Latin) "Stand by the decision." Decisions from a court with substantially the same set of facts should be followed by that court and all lower courts under it; the judicial process of adhering to prior case decisions; the doctrine of precedent whereby once a court has decided a specific issue one way in the past, it and other courts in the same jurisdiction are obligated to follow that earlier decision in deciding cases with similar issues in the future.

When a party from the trial court is dissatisfied with the decision of that court, an appeal may be filed. We already know that appellate courts review the decisions of

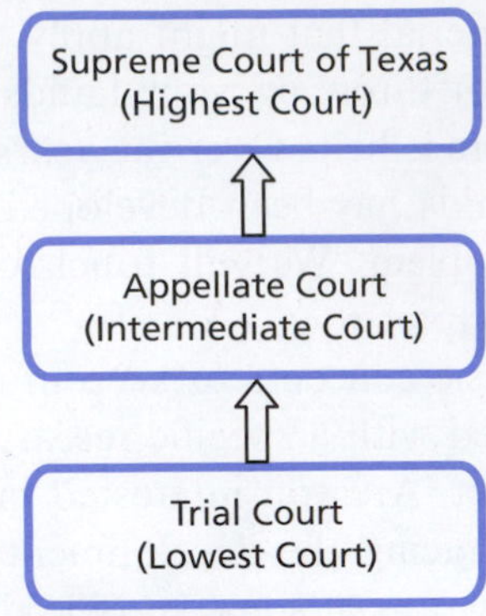

FIGURE 2.1 Texas Civil Court System

trial courts and often consist of panels of three judges who render a decision based upon the existing law of that court. The final and highest court in many states is the state supreme court. Often the state supreme courts are the court of last resort for most litigants unless the case presents a constitutional or federal issue. In those very limited instances, a state court decision may be appealed to the highest court in the United States: the U.S. Supreme Court. Let's see how these legal principles work. Suppose you live in Texas. The civil court system generally appears as in Figure 2.1.

A decision is handed down by the Dallas Appeals Court. Who must follow that decision? All trial courts under the Dallas Appeals Court and that appeals court. What about a decision from the San Antonio Appeals Court? Does that court have to follow the Dallas Appeals Court? The answer is no. However, if the case is appealed to the Texas Supreme Court, must the San Antonio Appeals Court follow that court's decision? The answer is yes. That is how the doctrine of *stare decisis* works. You will search for cases from the highest applicable court that most closely follow your legal proposition. This search leads you to cases that set the **precedent** for your research problem.

precedent
The holding of past court decisions that are followed in future judicial cases where similar facts and legal issues are present.

As a general proposition, decisions are based upon the precedential value of the competing sources cited by the parties. Legal research thus becomes a search for those authorities with the most powerful precedential value. **Precedential value** is the force that a cited authority exerts upon the judge's reasoning. In order to determine the degree of precedential value of a given authority, the judge determines whether it is primary or secondary; if it is primary, he or she must determine whether it is mandatory or merely persuasive.

precedential value
The force that a cited authority exerts upon the judge's reasoning.

Primary authority is composed of the original text of the sources of law—the language of court opinions, the provisions of constitutions, the requirements of statutes, the guidelines of agency regulations. Primary authority is, in effect, the law itself.

primary authority
The original text of the sources of law, such as constitutions, court opinions, statutes, and administrative rules and regulations.

Primary authority can be either mandatory or persuasive. **Mandatory authority** is binding upon the court considering the issue—a statute or regulation from the relevant jurisdiction that applies directly; a case from a higher court in the same jurisdiction that is directly on point; or a constitutional provision that is applicable and controlling. It is best to rely upon mandatory authority in your research, because the court is compelled to follow it. If two primary authorities conflict (as where a statute has been passed to counteract a court opinion, or where principles embedded in the applicable constitution render a statute unconstitutional), the court is compelled to follow the mandatory authority.

mandatory authority
A source of law that a court must follow in deciding a case, such as a statute or federal regulations.

All nonmandatory primary authority is **persuasive authority.** A case on point, but from a different jurisdiction, or from a lower or equivalent court in the same jurisdiction, would constitute persuasive authority, as would a statute on point but from a different state.

persuasive authority
A source of law or legal authority that is not binding on the court in deciding a case but may be used by the court for guidance, such as law review articles; all nonmandatory primary authority.

Let's revisit our Case Fact Pattern and determine whether our paralegal, Catherine, must follow the unfavorable case decision from her state or the favorable authority

YOU BE THE JUDGE

Determining which precedent must be followed was the issue before the U.S. Court of Appeals for the Ninth Circuit in *Ryman v. Sears, Roebuck and Co.*, 505 F.3d 993 (9th Cir. 2007). A federal court was faced with deciding which law to follow when the highest court decision in a jurisdiction to opine on an issue was an intermediate state appellate court. As the court observed in its opinion, "[w]here there is not convincing evidence that the state supreme court would decide differently, a federal court is obligated to follow the decisions of the state intermediate appellate courts." *Id.* at 995. Read the *Ryman* case. What are the facts of the case? What critical fact was important to the court's decision? What state opinions within the Ninth Circuit Court of Appeals was the court examining?

from another state. The answer is straightforward. Although the favorable authority from another state would yield a better outcome for the client, Catherine's supervising attorney must follow the case law from her jurisdiction because it is mandatory authority. In fact, there is not only a legal obligation to follow the mandatory authority, but an ethical obligation to disclose this authority to the court.

Secondary authority, on the other hand, is a step removed from the original text. It may consist of the comments of an expert expressed in a treatise. It may be found in the pages of a legal encyclopedia, or in articles in a law review, or in analysis set forth in a looseleaf service. It may include the unofficial provisions of a "Restatement" of the law. Whatever the source, however, all forms of secondary authority have one thing in common—they are not the law itself, but rather analyses of the law.

secondary authority
Authority that analyzes the law such as a treatise, encyclopedia, or law review article.

Apply these concepts with a simple example. Assume you are writing a brief to be considered by an intermediate appellate court in California. A case on point decided by the California Supreme Court would constitute mandatory authority. If such a case existed and was the only applicable mandatory authority, you might not have to go further in your research. If no such case existed, and no other mandatory authority existed, then a case on point decided by the Nevada Supreme Court would constitute persuasive primary authority—which means that your California intermediate appellate court, although not bound by the Nevada decision, might at least be persuaded by its logic. Finally, in addition to citing primary authorities, you might also want to cite to the principles enunciated in a respected treatise in the applicable field. The treatise, though only a secondary authority, might be held in such esteem by the court that it, too, has substantial persuasive value. Indeed, a secondary authority might be given more persuasive weight by a court than a nonmandatory primary authority.

In the pages that follow, we will be considering numerous different authorities. As you read these pages, and later in your research, you should always keep in mind the concepts of primary and secondary authority. In the context of a specific research project, you should also consider whether a given primary authority is mandatory or merely persuasive.

PRACTICE TIP

One way of evaluating whether a particular law is mandatory or not is to ask this simple question: Is the judge in this case bound to follow it? If the answer is yes, then it is mandatory authority.

Quick Quiz True/False Questions

1. *Stare decisis* is a legal doctrine that states that courts should follow only the decisions of intermediate appellate courts.
2. The process of legal research is the search for the most powerful legal precedents.
3. Primary authority consists only of cases, constitutions, and statutes.
4. Authority from another jurisdiction is considered mandatory authority.
5. Secondary authority interprets or explains primary authority.

CYBER TRIP

Using the Internet, find a copy of your state's constitution. Determine which provisions of that state constitution establish the three branches of government within your state.

THE PRIMARY SOURCES OF THE LAW

Without question, when beginning a legal research project, you always want to search for the primary sources of the law—a constitution, statutes, case law, administrative rules and regulations, and court rules. We will examine each more closely.

Constitutions: A Map for Governing

In Chapter 1, we examined the U.S. Constitution as the foundation of the American legal system. Recall the U.S. Constitution is divided into articles and amendments with the first ten amendments constituting the Bill of Rights. It defines the three branches of the federal government and creates a check and balance system on those branches of government. From a research perspective, that document is a primary source of the law and perhaps the most important primary source. All primary sources of the law must be consistent with the principles set forth in the U.S. Constitution.

Similarly, each state has a constitution, which sets the framework of government, establishes a system of checks and balances, and sets the powers and limitations for that particular state's government. State constitutions are a primary source of the law as well. No two state constitutions are exactly alike, but all state constitutions are measured against the U.S. Constitution. No provision of a state constitution can conflict or contradict the provisions of the U.S. Constitution. For legal research purposes, a state's constitution is an important reference for all state law issues.

Therefore, when we discuss the implications of the U.S. Constitution not only as a primary source but in terms of mandatory authority, it should come as no surprise that it has precedence over any other state or federal law. In terms of mandatory authority, the provisions of the U.S. Constitution are binding on all federal and state jurisdictions. It is the ultimate source of mandatory authority.

bill
Law proposed by a legislature.

statute
Written law enacted by the legislative branches of both federal and state governments.

slip law
The first format in which a newly signed statute appears; a copy of a particular law passed during a session of legislature.

session laws
The second format in which new statutes appear as a compilation of the slip laws; a bill or joint resolution that has become law during a particular session of the legislature.

statutes at large
Federal session laws.

code
A multivolume compilation that groups statutes by subject matter and is well indexed, in order to make the statutes more accessible for research purposes.

Statutory Law: Federal and State

The U.S. Congress and the fifty state legislatures pass many **bills** each year. These bills become statutes with the signature of the president or governor.

Statutes are primary sources of law passed by a legislature. As you recall from the previous chapter, the federal legislative branch is the U.S. Congress, composed of the Senate and House. For the legislative process to begin, a bill must be introduced by one of the houses of Congress. After much scrutiny, if a bill passes both houses of Congress, it is presented to the president for signature. If the president signs the bill it becomes law.

The first format in which a newly signed statute appears is called a **slip law.** A slip law contains a single enactment only. A slip law is an official publication of a single statute or *act* (a group of related statutes). It usually identifies a public act number or other official designation associated with this single statute or act. Figure 2.2 shows an act of the U.S. Congress in a slip law form.

The second format in which newly passed statutes appear is **session laws.** Session laws are the compilation of all the slip laws from a legislative session. Session laws are permanent collections of the statutes of one jurisdiction, printed periodically in chronological order of issuance, and with each new edition including only those laws passed since the previous edition. The federal session laws are referred to as the **statutes at large.** Statutes concerning diverse subjects are generated in each legislative session, with no particular order to their issuance. Session laws are useful for checking recent legislation, but they are often inadequately indexed and difficult to use for comprehensive research.

The final, and most comprehensive, form in which you will find a statute is a code. Each year all of the current statutes are gathered together and published in a **code.** A code is a multivolume compilation of all the statutes from a particular legislature. Figure 2.3 diagrams the different forms of a statute.

Public Law 110–96
110th Congress

An Act

To amend the penalty provisions in the International Emergency Economic Powers Act, and for other purposes.

Oct. 16, 2007
[S. 1612]

Be it enacted by the Senate and House of Representatives of the United States of America in Congress assembled,

International Emergency Economic Powers Enhancement Act.
50 USC 1701 note.

SECTION 1. SHORT TITLE.

This Act may be cited as the "International Emergency Economic Powers Enhancement Act".

SEC. 2. INCREASED PENALTIES FOR VIOLATIONS OF IEEPA.

(a) IN GENERAL.—Section 206 of the International Emergency Economic Powers Act (50 U.S.C. 1705) is amended to read as follows:

"SEC. 206. PENALTIES.

"(a) UNLAWFUL ACTS.—It shall be unlawful for a person to violate, attempt to violate, conspire to violate, or cause a violation of any license, order, regulation, or prohibition issued under this title.

"(b) CIVIL PENALTY.—A civil penalty may be imposed on any person who commits an unlawful act described in subsection (a) in an amount not to exceed the greater of—

"(1) $250,000; or

"(2) an amount that is twice the amount of the transaction that is the basis of the violation with respect to which the penalty is imposed.

"(c) CRIMINAL PENALTY.—A person who willfully commits, willfully attempts to commit, or willfully conspires to commit, or aids or abets in the commission of, an unlawful act described in subsection (a) shall, upon conviction, be fined not more than $1,000,000, or if a natural person, may be imprisoned for not more than 20 years, or both."

(b) EFFECTIVE DATE.—

Applicability.
50 USC 1705 note.

(1) CIVIL PENALTIES.—Section 206(b) of the International Emergency Economic Powers Act, as amended by subsection (a), shall apply to violations described in section 206(a) of such Act with respect to which enforcement action is pending or commenced on or after the date of the enactment of this Act.

(2) CRIMINAL PENALTIES.—Section 206(c) of the International Emergency Economic Powers Act, as amended by subsection (a), shall apply to violations described in section 206(a) of such Act with respect to which enforcement action is commenced on or after the date of the enactment of this Act.

Approved October 16, 2007.

LEGISLATIVE HISTORY–S. 1612:
SENATE REPORTS: No. 110–82 (Comm. on Banking, Housing, and Urban Affairs).
CONGRESSIONAL RECORD, Vol. 153 (2007):
June 26, considered and passed Senate.
Oct. 2, considered and passed House.

FIGURE 2.2 Example of a Slip Law Passed by the U.S. Congress

Source: International Emergency Economic Powers Act. Obtained from GPOAccess, http://frwebgate.access.gpo.gov/cgi-bin/useftp.cgi?IPaddress=162.140.64.183&filename=publ096.pdf&directory=/diska/wais/data/110_cong_public_laws (accessed November 27, 2007).

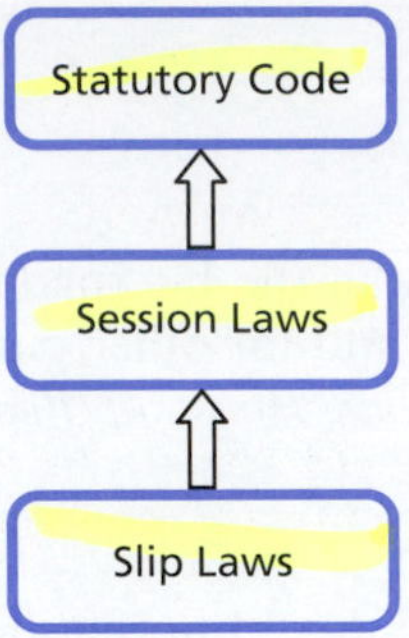

FIGURE 2.3 Different Forms of a Statute

PRACTICE TIP

The federal government and most states issue slip laws, but they are rarely used for research purposes because there are other, more comprehensive formats in which the new statute will shortly appear, such as a code.

Statutory Codes

The solution to the problem of researching statutes is provided by codes. A code is a set of volumes, issued by order of the legislature, that groups statutes by subject matter and is well indexed, in order to make the statutes more accessible for research purposes. Federal statutes are contained in the ***United States Code.***

United States Code Federal statutes currently in force in the United States.

United States Code Annotated Federal code published by ThomsonWest that contains "finding tools."

United States Code Service Federal code published by LexisNexis that contains "finding tools."

ordinance A law passed by a local government, such as a town council or city government.

The *United States Code* contains all of the federal laws that are currently in force and binding on the United States; presently, there are fifty titles in the *United States Code*. As you will learn in more detail in Chapter 5, there are different versions of the *United States Code*—annotated and unannotated. For research purposes, the distinction is significant as the annotated codes contain valuable legal research "finding tools." These are the tools you will need to locate supporting primary sources for your legal research assignments. The *United States Code* is the unannotated version of federal statutes, while the ***United States Code Annotated*** and the ***United States Code Service*** are the annotated versions of the federal statutes.

States have statutory codes containing all the laws passed by a state legislature. They, too, have slip laws, session laws, and statutory codes. What should not come as a surprise is that names of the state statutory codes vary significantly among the states. Some are simply known by their state name, while others have names that appear to have no relationship to the statutes at all. Regardless of the name of your state statutes, they are a primary source of the law. Like the federal statutes, states have official and unofficial versions of their statutes. You should check your own jurisdiction to verify which version of its statutes is the official one. Knowing which version of a statute is official and unofficial will become important for referencing purposes.

Consequently, there is a federal code that contains all of the federal statutes, and there are individual state codes containing each state's statutes. Most public libraries contain a complete set of the state's code. Law libraries usually have not only state codes, but also a complete set of the *United States Code.* And of course, the Internet provides a source to locate federal and state statutes.

Local Ordinances: City and County Statutes

Many municipalities, and some counties, have a code of **ordinances** analogous to a statutory code. These ordinances govern the conduct of individuals and businesses within the jurisdiction of that city or county. They are considered a primary source of the law. You may not realize it, but we are affected by local ordinances each day. Ordinances govern such matters as public drinking, jaywalking, and smoking in restaurants. As such, ordinances may have far-reaching effects, often with constitutional implications. Check your local library or the Internet for more information about the system in your community. Figure 2.4 shows sections of city ordinances from the city of Boston. A city council has a wide degree of latitude in its ability to regulate city issues from "firing cannons" (yes, that's right!) to defining what constitutes disorderly

16-5 FIREARMS.

16-5.1 Firing of Cannons and Guns.

No person shall fire or discharge a cannon, gun, fowling-piece, or firearm, within the limits of the City, except at a military exercise or review authorized by the military authority of the Commonwealth or by the City Council or Mayor of the City, or in the lawful defense of the person, family, or property of a citizen; provided, however, that this prohibition shall not apply to persons engaged in target practice on a range or other premises licensed to be used for such purpose by the City Council.
(CBC 1975 Ord. T14 § 274)

16-10.4 Disorderly Conduct.

No person shall, within any market limits, play any game, lie down, sleep, or behave in a noisy, or riotous manner, or scuffle, or throw any missile or thing whatsoever.
(CBC 1975 Ord. T14 § 282; Ord. 1991 c. 5 § 23; Ord. 1992 c. 7 § 4)

16-25 OBSCENE AND PORNOGRAPHIC MATERIAL.

16-25.1 Fine for Selling.

Whoever sells or distributes, or imports, or loans, or possesses with the intent to sell, or exhibits, prints, or publishes for the purpose of selling or distributing a book, pamphlet, ballad, printed paper, phonographic record, print, picture, figure, image, or description which depicts or describes:

a. Patently offensive representations or descriptions of ultimate sexual acts, normal or perverted, actual or simulated, or

b. Patently offensive representations or descriptions of masturbation, excretory functions, lewd exhibition of the genitals, shall be subject to a fine of fifty ($50.00) dollars for each day on which such violation occurs or during which such violation continues.

[This ordinance was passed in 1973, under the guidelines established in **Miller v. California,** 441 U.S. 925, 37 L. Ed. 2d 419 (June 21, 1973).]
(CBC 1975 Ord. T14 § 353)

FIGURE 2.4 **Different City Ordinances from the City of Boston**

PRACTICE TIP

Some states, such as Texas and New York, have individual names in the titles of their statutes. The Texas statutes are called "Vernon's Annotated Texas Statutes," whereas the New York statutes are called "McKinney's Consolidated Laws of New York Annotated." These were former publishers of the respective state statutes and the names simply were retained. Many state statutes reference the state within the name, such as the Colorado Revised States or Massachusetts General Laws.

conduct. The third example of a Boston city ordinance is in response to a U.S. Supreme Court ruling on pornography. Here we see the judicial and "city" legislative branches of government responding to each other.

Court Rules

We discovered in Chapter 1 that court rules govern the litigation process in civil and criminal proceedings. The rules used to guide the civil process in the federal courts are the Federal Rules of Civil Procedure, and for criminal cases, the Federal Rules of Criminal Procedure. These rules control the court process and are the guide for judges and attorneys in litigating or prosecuting a case.

We also addressed other types of court rules such as the Rules of Evidence, governing the admission of evidence at a trial, and Rules of Appellate Procedure, governing the parties on an appeal. The complexity of the rules of court is compounded even further because many courts have their own local rules for their individual courts. These rules supplement the existing rules and also must be consulted when practicing in any court, whether state or federal. What we did not address in that chapter was that court rules are a primary source of the law. Likewise, court rules can be both mandatory and persuasive. They are mandatory for a court of the jurisdiction in which they are being enforced, and are primary persuasive authority for jurisdictions outside the boundaries of the court. Figure 2.5 illustrates the components of a federal court rule—the Federal Rule of Evidence for hearsay.

CYBER TRIP

Locate a copy of the city ordinance in Chicago that banned restaurants from serving the French delicacy *foie gras.* Determine what state has banned the production of *foie gras* by 2012 as well.

FIGURE 2.5
Federal Rule of Evidence on Hearsay

Rule 801. Definitions

The following definitions apply under this article:
(a) Statement.—A "statement" is (1) an oral or written assertion or (2) nonverbal conduct of a person, if it is intended by the person as an assertion.
(b) Declarant.—A "declarant" is a person who makes a statement.
(c) Hearsay.—"Hearsay" is a statement, other than one made by the declarant while testifying at the trial or hearing, offered in evidence to prove the truth of the matter asserted.
(d) Statements which are not hearsay.—A statement is not hearsay if—
(1) Prior statement by witness.—The declarant testifies at the trial or hearing and is subject to cross-examination concerning the statement, and the statement is (A) inconsistent with the declarant's testimony, and was given under oath subject to the penalty of perjury at a trial, hearing, or other proceeding, or in a deposition, or (B) consistent with the declarant's testimony and is offered to rebut an express or implied charge against the declarant of recent fabrication or improper influence or motive, or (C) one of identification of a person made after perceiving the person; or
(2) Admission by party-opponent.—The statement is offered against a party and is (A) the party's own statement, in either an individual or a representative capacity or (B) a statement of which the party has manifested an adoption or belief in its truth, or (C) a statement by a person authorized by the party to make a statement concerning the subject, or (D) a statement by the party's agent or servant concerning a matter within the scope of the agency or employment, made during the existence of the relationship, or (E) a statement by a coconspirator of a party during the course and in furtherance of the conspiracy. The contents of the statement shall be considered but are not alone sufficient to establish the declarant's authority under subdivision (C), the agency or employment relationship and scope thereof under subdivision (D), or the existence of the conspiracy and the participation therein of the declarant and the party against whom the statement is offered under subdivision (E).
(Pub. L. 93-595, § 1, Jan. 2, 1975, 88 Stat. 1938; Pub. L. 94-113, § 1, Oct. 16, 1975, 89 Stat. 576; Mar. 2, 1987, eff. Oct. 1, 1987; Apr. 11, 1997, eff. Dec. 1, 1997.)

NOTES OF ADVISORY COMMITTEE ON PROPOSED RULES

[text omitted]

Rule 802. Hearsay Rule

Hearsay is not admissible except as provided by these roles or by other rules prescribed by the Supreme Court pursuant to statutory authority or by Act of Congress.
(Pub. L. 93-595, § 1, Jan. 2, 1975, 88 Stat. 1939.)

case law
Body of decisions published by courts.

reporters
Volumes that contain case decisions.

Case Law: Decisions, Decisions, and More Decisions

Perhaps one of the most familiar sources of the law is **case law.** Case law is the body of published decisions by courts. When a court reaches a decision in a case both at the trial and appellate levels, the reasons for the decision are explained in a written opinion. This opinion discusses not only the facts of the particular case but also the law that applies to those facts. These are the decisions that guide judges in making their decisions on cases before them. Using the principles of *stare decisis* and precedent, judges review the case law of the past and apply it to present situations.

Case law is primarily located in a **reporter.** A reporter is a book or volume that contains cases. In the past, case decisions with precedential value were the only ones published. However, with the advent of the E-Government Act of 2002 and the Internet, more and more unpublished cases are available for review. The big debate is: to what extent can unpublished cases be used in legal research? This is a debate that crosses both federal and state lines, often with no easy answer. Consequently, you and your supervising attorney will have to study the rules of the jurisdiction for which you want to cite an unpublished case.

PRACTICE TIP

Rules of court are often located in either the federal statutory codes or, at the local level, in state statutory codes.

FIGURE 2.6
Hierarchy of Case Law

The Federal and State Court Systems Connected

U.S. Supreme Court Decisions: Cases from both state supreme courts and federal circuit courts of appeals are appealed to the U.S. Supreme Court. Since the U.S. Supreme Court is the highest court in the United States, the decisions of the Court are mandatory authority for all courts—federal and state—in the United States.

State Court System

State Supreme Court Decisions: All states have a court vested with authority to make final adjudications on state law issues. Although many states refer to this court as the state supreme court, this terminology is, by no means, universal. By whatever name, this court is empowered to make final decisions about questions of state law, including interpretations of the state constitution and the application of state statutes. Decisions from this court are mandatory authority for all lower courts in the state, including the state court of appeals and all trial courts.

State Court of Appeals Decisions: Most states have at least one intermediate court of appeals. In states that have one, it is the first tier of appeal for litigants dissatisfied with the decision from a trial court in the state. Decisions from this court are mandatory authority for all lower courts in the state, including trial courts, small claims courts, and others. However, decisions from this court have no binding effect on the state supreme court because that court has a more powerful position in the state court hierarchy.

Federal Court System

U.S. Circuit Courts of Appeals Decisions: In Chapter 1, we saw that the United States is divided into thirteen federal circuits and that each of these circuits has its own court of appeals. These courts are the highest appellate courts in their circuits, but their decisions have no precedential value for other circuits. A decision by the First Circuit Court of Appeals, for example, is not mandatory authority for a court in the Third Circuit. These circuits operate independently of one another, although courts in one circuit often look to decisions from other circuits as examples of persuasive authority.

U.S. District Court Decisions: U.S. district courts are the trial courts located within specific federal circuits. Decisions from the appellate court in its circuit are mandatory authority for these courts, but decisions made by appellate courts in other circuits are not. A U.S. district court must follow the decisions of its own circuit court of appeals, but may use decisions from other circuits as persuasive authority. Further, decisions from the respective trial courts in that district must be followed by that trial court within that district but not necessarily another trial court from a different district from that same state.

Because case law is a primary source of the law, it is mandatory authority. However, case law can also be primary persuasive authority as well. Thus, attention must be paid not only to the type of authority but its origin. Using the principles from Chapter 1, case law has a hierarchy, as identified in Figure 2.6.

PRACTICE TIP

Recall that Texas and Oklahoma have two high courts of equal authority. Matters involving criminal issues are governed by the respective court of criminal appeals and matters involving civil matters are governed by the respective state's supreme court.

Administrative Rules, Regulations, and Decisions

The final primary source of the law comes from administrative agencies. Administrative agencies derive their authority from the executive and legislative branches of government to monitor a wide range of governmental activities. Under their authority, they can generate rules and regulations that citizens and business entities must follow. Examples of administrative agencies that promulgate rules and regulations are the Internal Revenue Service (IRS), which is authorized to collect taxes, while the Federal Aviation Agency (FAA) is tasked with maintaining and monitoring the aviation industry. Almost all agencies work under the direct authority of the executive branch, making them responsible to the president on the federal level and to individual state governors on the state level. One of the basic principles involved in the creation of any administrative agency is the right of that agency to create its own

YOU BE THE JUDGE

At issue in *Jorgenson v. County of Volusia,* 846 F.2d 1350 (11th Cir. 1988), was a county ordinance prohibiting nude or seminude entertainment where alcoholic beverages are sold and consumed. Specifically, had the state delegated the authority to regulate the sale or consumption of alcohol to local governments? The case also addresses the issue of constitutional delegation of authority, the autonomy of local statutes, and the review of those issues by a court. The court hearing the case had been waiting for the Supreme Court of Florida to rule on the issue. Unknown to the lower court, the supreme court had ruled on the issue, but the plaintiffs' attorney failed to apprise the court of the decision. Adding insult to injury, the plaintiffs' attorney had been involved in the Florida Supreme Court case and withheld the information from the court—not a good idea. Review the *Jorgenson* case. Identify some of the concerns of the court in rendering the decision. What remedy did the court impose on the appellants' attorney, if any? What cases were dispositive on the issues before the court? What ethical issues are raised by the case?

rules to govern its day-to-day activities. Further discussion of the process of creating administrative rules and regulations is presented in later chapters.

Federal Administrative Rules and Regulations

Federal Register
Pamphlet service that records the daily activity of Congress.

Code of Federal Regulations
Federal statutory law collection.

Federal regulations are printed in the ***Federal Register:*** this daily journal contains regulations (as well as proclamations, orders, and notices) issued by federal agencies. There is an annual compilation of all effective regulations arranged by subject, however, called the ***Code of Federal Regulations.***

Administrative agencies also render quasi-judicial decisions. Unlike case reporters, no one publication compiles all administrative decisions in a single place. Unfortunately, every agency publishes its own decisions. For example, the Federal Trade Commission not only publishes its decisions from 1996 on its Web site (www.ftc.gov); they also can be found in CCH Trade Regulation Reporter, a looseleaf service. This service also includes legislation and regulations as part of its coverage of the topic. Thus, it can be quite a challenge to locate administrative decisions.

State and Local Administrative Agencies

The systems employed by the states and municipalities to compile administrative regulations and decisions vary widely, although many are based loosely on the federal format already described. Some jurisdictions update their publication of regulations fairly frequently, others only occasionally. In many instances you must contact the relevant agency directly in order to identify the current effective regulations. You should learn the system that applies in your state and in any local jurisdiction in which you will be working.

However, regardless of the name or form administrative rules, regulations, and decisions take, they are a primary source of the law. Federal and state administrative regulations and decisions can be mandatory or persuasive authority depending on the jurisdictional issue that may arise. As a summation, Figure 2.7 is a chart of the primary sources of the law.

THE HIERARCHY OF THE LAW

This chapter illustrated the types of primary legal source material found in legal research. They are generally constitutions, statutes, cases, court rules, and administrative rules and regulations. Remember, a primary source is the law itself. When researching, how do you know if one primary source is more authoritative than another? Which one should be used and how?

The U.S. Constitution is the supreme law of the land. When you are researching a problem, bear in mind that the U.S. Constitution prevails over all other primary sources of the law. Similarly, state constitutions set out the rights of its citizens. Those rights may not

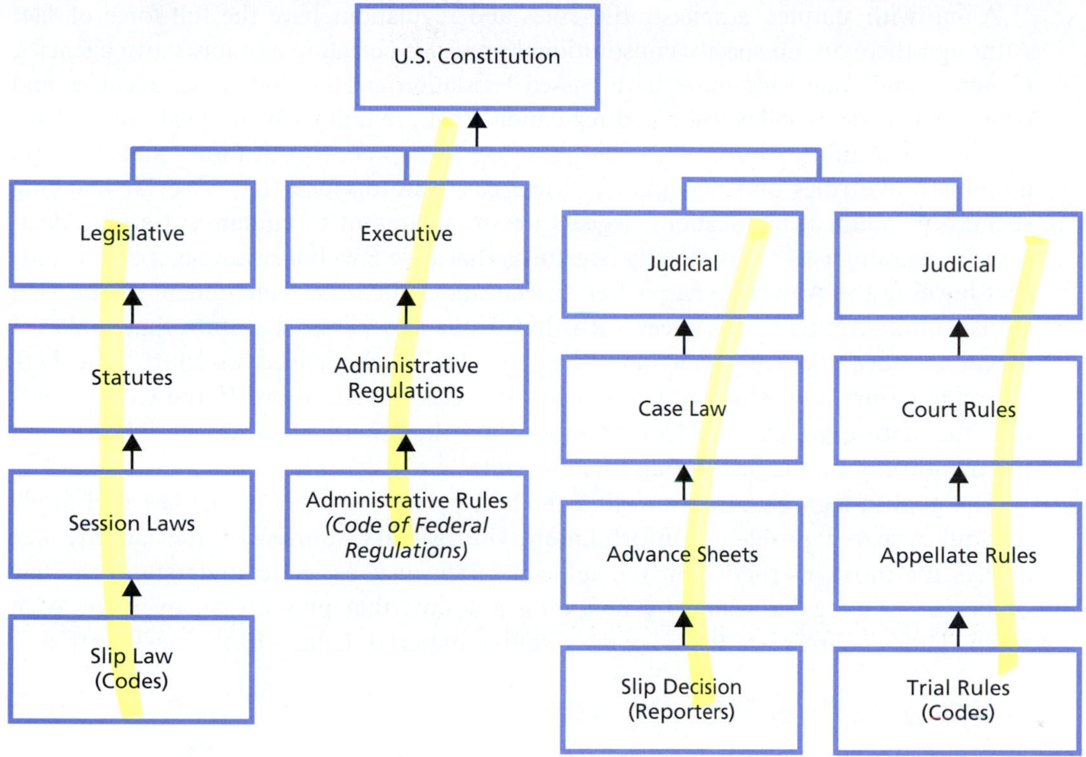

FIGURE 2.7 **Primary Sources of the Law**

conflict, limit, or decrease the rights granted by the U.S. Constitution, although some state constitutions have extended rights afforded under our Constitution. That is permissible.

The next tier of primary authority is a statute. The U.S. Congress passes legislation subject to signing or veto by the president. Similarly, states have legislatures, which pass legislation signed or vetoed by their respective governors. Any statute passed must not conflict with the U.S. Constitution. And notably, state statutes may not conflict with federal statutes. Federal law preempts state law, which means that states cannot pass laws that conflict with federal law. Think about when you pass through security to board an airplane. The security check is governed by federal law, and as such, states cannot pass laws that interfere or conflict with the process.

A DAY IN THE LIFE OF A PARALEGAL

Three days to complete your research project is just not enough. You have lots of other work from other partners in the firm and you just don't have time to get to the library. Since you are working at a small law firm, access to the fee-based Web sites is reserved for the partners and associates. Pressed for time, you attempt to use some of the free law-based Web sites to conduct your research. The issue involves a *Terry* stop, which you know was decided by the U.S. Supreme Court in *Terry v. Ohio,* 392 U.S. 1 (1968). The problem is that you are unable to access the case and you can't understand why. Then you realize that the databases from the Web sites you are using do not go back far enough. You realize the limitations of the Internet—many sites offer only a limited inventory of cases and statutes. The sites you found offer case law dating back only twenty years. It wouldn't be a problem, but the cases you need predate the database. Without a comprehensive collection of cases, you would be hard-pressed to say that a thorough examination of the assignment was done. It looks as if you will be visiting the library after all. Although most fee-based legal research sites offer a more comprehensive collection of cases, if you only have access to general Internet Web sites, be aware of its limitations. Use your best judgment in determining whether the Internet is sufficient as your sole source for a legal research project. As you will learn, no one project is exactly the same and each will have different legal resource requirements.

Along with statutes, administrative rules and regulations have the full force of law. Although there are no specific constitutional provisions creating administrative agencies, Congress and state legislatures have passed legislation creating individual agencies and defining their powers. The rules and regulations that are ultimately adopted are the law.

Albeit a primary source of the law, case law interprets constitutions, statutes, and administrative rules and regulations. When cases are decided that have far-reaching social and political implications, legislatures may attempt to circumvent a case decision by passing a law that directly overturns that case law. For example, a court finds that burning the American flag is free speech under the First Amendment of the U.S. Constitution. Congress disagrees with that result and passes a statute that makes it illegal to burn the American flag. Now, the law is challenged in court. The U.S. Supreme Court finds that the law violates the U.S. Constitution. If the Court holds that the statute violates the Constitution, then the law is struck down. Therein lies the dichotomy of the law through its hierarchy.

The goal in legal research is to find the best primary sources of the law that apply to your research problem. Unfortunately, the primary sources of the law are not always the most instructive on the subject. Often, it is easier to understand the law or begin your legal research by reviewing a source that presents an overview of a topic. Those sources are the secondary source material defined in the next section.

Quick Quiz True/False Questions

1. Session laws are the chronological compilation of the slip laws.
2. City ordinances are analogous to a state statute except they govern cities and towns.
3. Case decisions can be found only in a case reporter.
4. Sources that contain administrative rules and regulations are the *Federal Register* and the *Code of Federal Regulations.*
5. Within the hierarchy of the law, case law is the highest authority.

SECONDARY SOURCES

All the materials we've discussed in this chapter thus far have been primary sources. There are a variety of secondary sources as well—sources a step removed from the primary authority, but valuable for their analytic insights and useful explanations. Those sources consist of legal encyclopedias, *American Law Reports,* uniform laws and restatements, treatises and texts, law reviews and periodicals, attorney general opinions, looseleaf services, and legal dictionaries. Since most of these sources are discussed in greater detail in the chapters that follow, only a brief introduction is warranted.

Legal Encyclopedias

legal encyclopedia
A multivolume compilation that provides in-depth coverage of every area of the law.

pocket parts
Annual supplements to digests.

supplement
Stand-alone softbound volume that provides updates of the law.

A **legal encyclopedia** is a multivolume compilation that provides in-depth coverage of every area of the law. As a secondary source, encyclopedias are valuable, especially for gaining insight into areas of the law with which there is little familiarity. Virtually all conceivable legal topics are covered in an encyclopedia, making them an excellent source if you need a quick "broad brushstroke" of an area. They also provide references to cases and other legal sources in their footnotes. Always consult the footnotes as you are reading a legal encyclopedia.

Corpus Juris Secundum (commonly known as *C.J.S.*) and *American Jurisprudence, 2d* (commonly known as *Am. Jur. 2d*) are the leading legal encyclopedias. Since both encyclopedias now are owned by the same publishing house, many of the features within the volumes are the same. Additions to topics are provided in a **pocket part**, which is a softbound paper supplement in the back of a volume, or in a stand-alone bound **supplement.**

Malpractice
Romualdo P. Eclavea, LL.B., LL.M.

Scope
This article treats the professional liability of accountants, architects, attorneys, medical practitioners, and hospitals, broadly classified as malpractice. It discusses what is malpractice, malpractice distinguished from "simple" or "ordinary" negligence, bases of professional liability in tort and contract, the applicable standard of care, defenses, vicarious liability, malpractice actions, countersuits, and malpractice (professional liability) insurance. Legislative reactions to the perceived medical malpractice insurance crisis are also covered.

Federal Aspects
Federal cases that apply the New York law of malpractice are cited in this article. These include cases brought under the Federal Tort Claims Act, since the liability of the federal government is determined in accordance with state substantive law. The difference in an accountant's duties owed to third persons under state common law and federal securities law is mentioned. New York also takes income tax consequences into consideration when making an award of damages in a medical malpractice case.

Treated Elsewhere
Regulation of attorneys, and attorney–client relationship, generally see Attorneys at Law
Regulation of accountants and architects, generally see Businesses and Occupations
Regulation of hospitals and other health care facilities, generally see Hospitals, and Related Health Care Facilities
Regulation of physicians and other health care professionals, physician–patient relationship, and malpractice as a defense to a collection action brought by a doctor, see Physicians, Surgeons, and Other Healers
Overview of general rules of damages and the collateral source rule, see Damages §§ 128 et seq.
Evidentiary privilege for patient–physician communications, see Evidence and Witnesses §§ 881 et seq.
Structured judgments, see Judgments
General principles of negligence, standard of care, comparative negligence, and assumption of risk, see Negligence
Effect of Workers' Compensation Law on commonlaw remedy for malpractice, see Workers' Compensation § 110

sets forth parameters of article

addresses federal aspects of subject in article

areas of law excluded from article

FIGURE 2.8
Page from New York's State-Specific Encyclopedia
Source: From *New York Jurisprudence 2d,* 76, Malpractice 2003. Reprinted with permission from ThomsonWest.

Although encyclopedias are considered a secondary source, they also are a **finding tool.** A finding tool is a legal resource that assists legal professionals in locating both primary and secondary sources of the law. Many secondary sources perform a dual function. Thus, encyclopedias are a secondary source when used as a general guide to the law through their extensive commentaries and as a finding tool to locate various primary sources of law.

Many states have encyclopedias as well. Often state encyclopedias are more informative as they focus on the law of the jurisdiction for which they are written. When there is a choice between a general legal encyclopedia and a state-specific encyclopedia, choose the state encyclopedia as your reference. Figure 2.8 is a page from a state-specific encyclopedia from New York. Observe that in the explanation sections the references are to New York law only.

PRACTICE TIP

Since the earlier volumes of *American Jurisprudence* were produced by a publisher other than ThomsonWest, some of the finding tools will be different in the earlier volumes from the later ones.

finding tool
Legal resource that assists in locating primary and secondary sources of the law.

American Law Reports: A Source of Many Possibilities

Some may say that ***American Law Reports*** are books with multiple personalities. *American Law Reports—A.L.R*—is primarily known for its thoughtful and extensive commentaries

American Law Reports
Set of books known for its annotations, which contain both primary and secondary sources of the law.

annotation
An in-depth analysis of a specific and important legal issue raised in the accompanying decision, together with an extensive survey of the way the issue is treated in various jurisdictions.

uniform laws
Proposed standardized statutes that may be adopted by a state.

statement
A recitation of the common law in a particular legal subject; a series of volumes authored by the American Law Institute that tell what the law in a general area is, how it is changing, and in what direction the authors think this change is headed.

common law
Judge-made law, the ruling in a judicial opinion.

PRACTICE TIP

A.L.R. is now published by Thomson-West. As of January 1, 2008, *A.L.R.* will be found only on Westlaw, the ThomsonWest fee-based assisted legal research Web site.

called **annotations.** These annotations completely analyze a subject from every angle and every jurisdiction referencing the constitution, cases, statutes, and administrative regulations as necessary. The basis of each annotation is a case that it deems important or whose subject is noteworthy. The entire case is reported in *A.L.R.* just as it would appear in a case reporter. Thus, this legal source serves as a primary, secondary, and finding tool all wrapped into one, hence its multiple personalities. At first blush that combination sounds heavenly—all legal sources in one set of books. But, of course, like most things, it is too good to be true. *American Law Reports* is selective in the primary sources it reports, the subject of its annotations, and the extent of its finding tools. Therefore, unless you find an annotation on your research assignment, you will not use *A.L.R.*

A.L.R. is published in six series with a separate series dealing with federal issues, *A.L.R. Federal.* Indexes provide access to the various series, so they definitely are worth reviewing. Chapter 6 further defines the content and uses of *A.L.R.*

Uniform Laws and Restatements

The **uniform laws** are a secondary source unless adopted by a state as law. Essentially, legal professionals participate in the National Conference of Commissioners on Uniform State Laws. As appointees by their respective states and territories, these individuals draft laws that, if adopted, provide standardization in certain areas of state law. Acts such as the Uniform Commercial Code, which has been adopted in some form in virtually all the states, had their origins under the Commission.

The **Restatements** were conceived to perform a similar purpose for the **common law.** In the 1920s a group of distinguished legal experts formed the American Law Institute for the purpose of drafting organized and detailed studies of common law in certain areas. They feared that the growing complexity and inconsistency of common law would undermine our legal system; their solution was to create a body of law approved by an independent committee of distinguished legal scholars and available to all who wished to cite to it. *Restatements* have been issued in several areas of the law (including contracts, property law, torts, and conflict of laws, among others). Subsequent developments have resulted in the issuance of second and third editions in several areas, for example, the *Restatement of the Law of Torts, 2d.*

The courts have been receptive to the law as expressed in the Restatements, which now carry more authoritative weight than the legal encyclopedias. However, you should keep in mind that the Restatements, as a secondary authority, do not overrule existing case precedent in a jurisdiction. They might persuade a court, but they can never mandate a particular result unless adopted by the state.

The text of the restatements may provide useful support if you are attempting to overturn a precedent in your jurisdiction that goes against generally accepted Restatement doctrine. In addition to the text, you may also find that the cross-references to cases are useful. Figure 2.9 is a page from the *Restatement of Agency, 3d.* The Restatement is structured so that it provides a basic statement of the law, followed by comments by its authors and illustrations as to how the principles set forth in the statement of the law should be interpreted.

Treatises and Texts

treatise
A scholarly study of one area of the law.

A **treatise** is a scholarly study of one area of the law. Treatises differ from Restatements in that they are usually the work of one author or group of authors, rather than the result of a collective effort such as that expended to make the Restatements so broadly accepted.

Treatises vary with regard to the force of their persuasiveness. Some, like William Prosser's classic text on tort law, currently published by West as *Prosser and Keeton on the Law of Torts,* 5th ed. (West 1984), is widely recognized as authoritative and often cited by the courts. Others are less widely accepted.

Treatises also vary with regard to depth of treatment. Some are multivolume, some a single volume. A one-volume treatise is commonly referred to as a *text.* ThomsonWest

§ 4.05 AGENCY Ch.

[text omitted] applicable statute of limitation has run). For English authority on the impact of ratification, see Presenta-diones Musicales SA v. Secunda, [1994] Ch. 271 (ratification of issue of writ after limitation period had run was effective and related back to date on which writ issued).

§ 4.06 Knowledge Requisite to Ratification

A person is not bound by a ratification made without knowledge of material facts involved in the original act when the person was unaware of such lack of knowledge.

Comment:

a. *Cross-references.* Section 4.01(2) states the circumstances that constitute a ratification. Section 4.02 states the effects of ratification.

b. *Effect of lack of knowledge.* A person who has ratified is not bound by the ratification if it was made without knowledge of material facts about the act of the agent or other actor. Thus, ratification concerns actions that have already taken place, of which the person is aware, not actions or events that may occur in the future. The burden of establishing that a ratification was made with knowledge is on the party attempting to establish that ratification occurred. This is consistent with how the burden of establishing the existence of a relationship of agency is allocated. See § 1.02, Comment *d.* A person may be estopped to deny ratification as stated in § 4.08.

Ratification requires that the principal have actual knowledge of material facts, not notice as defined in § 1.04(4). A principal may choose to affirm without knowing the material facts. The fact that the principal had knowledge may be inferred, as may the principal's assumption of risk of lack of knowledge. See Comment *d.*

This doctrine alternatively, has been characterized as creating an election to avoid a ratification. See Restatement Second, Agency § 91. Many contemporary cases, however, allocate the burden of showing that a ratification was made with knowledge to the party seeking to hold a person liable on the basis that the person ratified another's act. However characterized, this doctrine is analogous in effect to the contract-law doctrine that permits a party to avoid a contract when a material misrepresentation induced the party's assent to the contract. See Restatement Second, Contracts § 164. The power of evidence is lost if the party, after knowing of the misrepresentation, manifests affirmance of the transaction to the other party or acts inconsistently with disaffirmance with regard to anything received through the transaction. Id. § 380(2). Contract-law doctrine also permits a party to avoid a transaction on the basis of unilateral mistake, but only when the effect of enforcing the contract would be unconscionable, or the 386 [text omitted]

FIGURE 2.9
Page from the *Restatement of Agency, 3d*

Source: Restatement, Third, Agency, copyright 2006 by the American Law Institute. Reprinted with permission.

publishes a series of one-volume scholarly **texts** known collectively as **hornbooks** (the Prosser work is part of this series), as well as much less thorough paperback treatments known collectively as the **nutshell** series. Nutshells generally provide good introductions to areas with which you are not familiar, whereas hornbooks fill in many more of the gaps. Neither hornbooks nor nutshells are often cited in legal briefs on disputed points (Prosser being a notable exception), although generally accepted legal principles are sometimes informally categorized as "hornbook law."

Some treatises are multivolume works covering a subject area in extraordinary detail, and some of these have had wide acceptance by the courts over the years (*Wigmore on Evidence* is a good example). Whether or not they are persuasive when cited to the court, such comprehensive treatises are usually useful for the purpose of learning about an area of law or finding cases on point.

When using a treatise or text, there is one important consideration to keep in mind. You must determine whether the scholarly purpose of the author(s) was to state the law as it *is* or as it *should be.* If the text is presenting the law as it is, it will be valuable

texts
One-volume treatises.

hornbooks
Scholarly texts; a series of textbooks that review various fields of law in summary narrative form, as opposed to casebooks, which are designed as primary teaching tools and include many reprints of court opinions.

nutshell
A paperback series of the law; condensed versions of hornbooks.

FIGURE 2.10
Introductory Material from a Legal Treatise on Constitutional Law

Source: From Ronald D. Rotunda and John E. Nowack. *Treatsie on Constitutional Law: Vol. 1, Substance and Procedure,* 3e. Reprinted with permission from ThomsonWest.

table of contents for section

text of article

footnotes with supporting legal authority

FEDERAL JURISDICTION Ch. 2

[text omitted] Page

I. A BRIEF INTRODUCTION TO THE DEVELOPMENT OF FEDERAL JURISDICTION: CONSTITUTIONAL AND STATUTORY

§ 2.1 **Overview of the Present Jurisdictional Framework of the Supreme Court**

The Supreme Court is the only federal court created directly by the Constitution. Article III mandates that the judicial power be vested in "one Supreme Court": As to the inferior courts, the judicial power is vested only as the Congress "may from time to time ordain and establish" such lower courts.[1]

§ 2.1

1. U.S. Const. art. III, § 1.

See generally S. Law, The Jurisdiction and Powers of the United States Supreme Court (1852); A. Conkling, Treatise on the Organization, Jurisdiction, and Practice of the Courts of the United States (4th ed. 1864); P. Phillips, The Statutory Jurisdiction and Practice of the Supreme court of the United States (1872); B. Curtis, Jurisdiction, Practice, and Peculiar Jurisprudence of the Courts of the United States (1880); J.F. Jameson, The Predecessor of the Supreme Court, In J.F. Jameson, Essays in the Constitutional History of the United States 8 (1889); H. Taylor, Jurisdiction and Procedure of the Supreme Court of the United States (1905); Brown, The New Federal Judicial Code, 36 Rept. A.B.A. 389 (1911); Warren, New Light on the History of the Federal Judiciary Act of 1789, 37 Harv.L.Rev. 49 (1923); J. Hopkins, The New Federal Equity Rules (4th ed. 1924); Putnam, How the Federal Courts Were Given Admiralty Jurisdiction, 10 Corn. L.Q. [text omitted]

as a tool to find primary sources. If the text is presenting the law as it should be, the persuasive value of the conclusions will be affected by their relationships to existing precedent, in conjunction with the logic of the argument presented and the prestige of the author(s). Figure 2.10 provides the introductory material from a noted legal treatise on constitutional law. Notice how the treatise cites numerous authorities in its footnotes. As you will learn, footnotes often are just as important as the text, whether from a primary or secondary authority.

Law Reviews and Periodicals

In addition to multivolume or book-length treatises, there are also legal publications that print articles of interest. **Law reviews** are periodicals edited by the top students at each law school, featuring scholarly articles by leading authorities and notes on various topics written by the law students themselves. A law review usually carries the name of its law school as part of its title (for example, the *Harvard Law Review* or the *University of Pennsylvania Law Review*). Like many other secondary sources, these articles are most valuable as learning tools or sources to relevant primary authorities, and are not often cited in briefs. Nevertheless, an article in a leading law review by a top scholar can have a substantial impact on the profession.

law reviews
Periodicals edited by the top students at each law school, featuring scholarly articles by leading authorities and notes on various topics written by the law students themselves.

There are also numerous legal periodicals published by bar associations or private publishers. These periodicals vary in quality from scholarly journals to newsletters. Some are useful as research tools for the profession as a whole; others provide limited information to defined segments of the bar.

Attorney General Opinions

Whether at the federal or state level, the attorney general is the highest-ranking legal officer in either the federal or a state government. The attorney general is the government's lawyer and represents the various agencies and departments within its jurisdiction. Each state has an attorney general; and the federal government has only one attorney general. The function of any attorney general is to oversee both criminal and civil matters affecting a government.

attorney general opinions
Legal opinions given by the highest-ranking legal officer in the federal government or a state.

However, as one of their many duties, attorney generals respond to inquires from the public entities they represent. Oftentimes government agencies and departments have significant legal questions for which an answer is needed. In essence, these governmental entities are seeking the guidance of the attorney general before they act inappropriately. The guidance may be as informal as a letter or, if legally significant, in the form of an **attorney general opinion.** Since these documents are a learned opinion of the attorney general, they are a secondary source of law. Many attorney general opinions are published or posted on the respective Web sites. Sometimes, an attorney general opinion is the only guidance in an area of law when a court has not rendered a decision on the issues presented. If a court issues a case decision, that decision supersedes the attorney general opinion because that decision is primary authority.

looseleaf service
A service that publishes recently decided court decisions in looseleaf binders, such as *U.S. Law Week;* provides for information to be easily updated. The loose pages are used to replace the existing pages in the notebook to ensure that the most current information is available.

Looseleaf Services

The textual treatment that **looseleaf services** provide is a valuable secondary resource. As the name suggests, looseleaf services consist of pages or pamphlets inserted into looseleaf binders. The logic behind the system is that pages can easily be removed and replaced by new and current updates of the law. Many publishing companies provide looseleaf services for a myriad of topics. Thus, looseleaf services bring together in one topical reporter applicable case texts, statutes, regulations, and independent analyse. The result is looseleaf services can provide both primary and secondary sources and, in some instances, finding tools.

PRACTICE TIP

Only governmental entities can seek an opinion from an attorney general. A private citizen cannot request the attorney general to render an opinion on a legal matter.

Legal Dictionaries

An important secondary source for all legal professionals is a legal dictionary, especially in the beginning when legal terminology is so unfamiliar. Legal dictionaries have limited use as they will assist only in understanding legal terminology. That means you shouldn't throw away your standard dictionary. Courts reference a legal dictionary

FIGURE 2.11
Secondary Sources of the Law: A Summary

Legal Encyclopedias *Corpus Juris Secundum (C.J.S.)* *American Jurisprudence (Am. Jur.)* State specific	Overview of the law. Use of footnotes for locating primary sources of the law.
American Law Reports (A.L.R.) Six series	Detailed annotations. Selective treatment of a topic based upon case.
A.L.R. Federal	Complete assessment of all jurisdictions. Caveat: Not all legal subjects covered.
Uniform Laws	Standardization of statutes from legal professionals. If proposed statute adopted becomes primary law.
Restatements	Standardization of the common law in various areas of the law.
Treatises Hornbooks Texts Nutshells	Scholarly study of the law. Range from a single volume to multivolume series. Usually found only as print sources. Hornbooks are one-volume treatises.
Law Review Journals and Legal Periodicals	(1) Legal publication from a law school. Contains articles from legal scholars and students. Note: Extensive footnotes contain primary sources and additional secondary sources. (2) Published by bar associations or private publishers. Articles usually written by lawyers. Quality of articles varies.
Attorney General Opinions Federal State	Opinions rendered by the head of the U.S. or state Department of Justice. Only government agencies can request an opinion. Opinions are only advisory. Case law can consist of opinions rendered by the head of the U.S. or state Department of Justice. Opinions are only advisory. Case law can supersede opinion.
Looseleaf Services	Consist of commentaries, articles, and primary sources on a specific subject of the law. Pages or pamphlets are easily replaced for updating.
Legal Dictionaries	Assist in defining and understanding legal terminology.

when they are looking for a precise definition of a legal term. Consequently, it is not uncommon to see this secondary source referenced in a court decision.

As a review, Figure 2.11 provides a chart of secondary sources of the law discussed in this chapter.

DIGESTS AND CITATORS: NEITHER PRIMARY NOR SECONDARY SOURCES

To complete our discussion of the sources of the law, mention must be made of the sources that are used strictly to locate the primary and secondary sources. The main finding tools are digests and citators. A **digest** is a multivolume set containing summaries of the law extracted from cases. Legal digests provide encapsulated or summarized versions of law that help legal researchers begin the process of narrowing their focus on a particular issue. Digests can be extremely helpful in beginning a legal research project. A digest can present, for example, both a broad overview of a legal topic and precise information on a narrowly tailored issue within a topic. Digests are prepared by private publishers, who hire legal professionals to review opinions, extrapolate the legal

digest
A collection of all the headnotes from an associated series of volumes, arranged alphabetically by topic and by key number or summary of testimony with indexed references of a deposition.

ETHICS ALERT

Legal research can be a sticky subject, especially for the inexperienced. Quite often lawyers will take cases to simply pay the bills without thinking about their level of experience on the matter. That can be a disaster waiting to happen for both the attorney and the paralegal. Suppose you are working for a solo practitioner and a client wants to file a bankruptcy case. Your supervising attorney believes that between the two of you, you can learn all you need to know about the subject. Actually, you are both entering into the "danger zone." Although the rules of ethics require attorneys to perform adequate research, that term is vague. All the research in the world often does not suffice. To illustrate this point, *In re Farmer,* 950 P.2d 713 (Kan. 1997) involved a disciplinary action of an attorney. Among some of the complaints raised against Farmer is that he failed to properly represent his client in a bankruptcy case; he failed to adequately supervise his staff, including nonlawyer assistants. As the evidence in the case showed, Farmer blamed his problems on his staff—an all-too-common excuse used by some attorneys. Ultimately, the court determined Farmer's behavior was egregious and suspended him indefinitely from the practice of law—thank goodness!

The important point to remember is "know your limitations" even if your attorney does not know his. Ethically, it is the attorney who is representing the client and whose license is on the line. However, the sad reality is that many attorneys rely too heavily on either inexperienced lawyers or paralegals to perform their work. Know when to say "no" not only for your sake but the sake of the client's case.

PRACTICE TIP

Never reference a digest or a citator in any legal assignment. It is neither a secondary nor a primary source.

points from that opinion, and then prepare short paragraph summaries of those points of law from that case. Digests cover all jurisdictions, both federal and state.

Perhaps the most significant feature of the digest system is the **Key Number System.** Every case decision is reviewed by the publisher's team of legal experts. The reviewers determine the points of law in the case and assign a legal topic from a list of approximately 400; they then assign a key number, which represents a subtopic under the main topic. All these summaries are indexed in the digests. They are one of the most important finding tools in legal research. Chapter 6 covers finding tools and discusses the significance of the digest system in the legal research process.

Key Number System
A detailed system of classification that currently divides the law into more than 400 separate categories or topics.

As significant as digests are to the process, so too are **citators.** Citators not only assist with legal research but also are the tools that validate whether a legal source is still considered good law. Until recently, there was only one recognized citator in legal research: Shepard's Citations. Shepard's is now in both print and electronic form. Under the Shepard's system, you can verify how a court treated a case you are reviewing, determine if the case has been overruled, and find sources that have referenced the case you are validating.

citators
A series of books that both update the law and act as finding tools.

Shepard's now has competition from West's KeyCite, which is the Westlaw version of its citator. Using the same principles as Shepard's, KeyCite allows a researcher to review the significance a court placed on a particular case, find other legal sources that have cited the case and, of course, determine whether the case is still good law. Both digests and citators are critical resources in the research process and, as such, we devote entire chapters to their topics.

Quick Quiz True/False Questions

1. Legal encyclopedias contain pocket parts and supplements with updates. True
2. Annotations are located in *American Law Reports,* which is both a primary and secondary source. True
3. Restatements interpret statutory law and the uniform laws interpret the common law. False
4. Scholarly texts include legal treatises and attorney general opinions. False
5. Digests and citators are the most important primary source of the law. False

THE E-FACTOR

Locating legal sources on the Internet can be challenging. The real question is the authenticity and reliability of the Web site. In simple terms, be familiar with the source of the sites you are using. It is generally safe to rely on government Web sites, which verify the information before it is posted. Simply search for sites with Web addresses that end in ".gov" for information pertaining to the U.S. Constitution, statutes, cases, court rules, and administrative rules and regulations. These sites have material in their official form and also have many secondary sources that explain the primary sources of the law.

Equally reliable are the official state Web sites. States often post their primary sources of law along with a host of explanatory material to supplement them. The scope of state Web sites varies, but at least you can rely on the accuracy of the material presented.

Many of the law schools have extensive online libraries, which are usually free. Along with most primary sources, law schools have secondary sources, such as law review journal articles. You also will find many student-based "tutorials" posted, which offer considerable insight to legal research materials; suggested Web sites to visit are posted as well.

The problems arise when using a site whose material cannot be verified. Because of user complaints, many of these sites are posting disclaimers as to the accuracy of the material cited. The Internet is vast and growing more expansive every day. No one can imagine the world without the Internet, but as you embark on your career as a paralegal, you must pay closer attention to the Web sites you use when performing legal research—accuracy counts.

CITATIONS: LOCATING LEGAL SOURCES

Do you think you can walk into a library and miraculously begin pulling books off the shelves in the hope that you will find the legal sources you need? Of course not! With the number of primary and secondary sources in a library or on the Internet, there has to be a method to logically locate legal sources. That method is through a **legal citation.** Every legal source has this unique identifier, which combines abbreviations and numbers creating the legal citation. By using legal citations you can find precisely the legal source needed, whether primary or secondary, moving effortlessly through a library or the Internet to locate the sources needed.

legal citation
Unique identifier of all legal sources.

As we will learn in the coming chapters, the main guides for understanding and learning legal citations are *The Bluebook: A Uniform System of Citation* and the *ALWD Manual of Style.* From these guides you will learn about the many forms and nuances of citations. In Chapters 3 and 5, you will be introduced to citations for the primary sources of the law. This is followed by a detailed discussion of citations and how to incorporate legal citations into a legal document in Chapter 14. But let's not get ahead of ourselves; we will approach the process in a step-by-step manner as we discover the world of legal research and writing.

PRACTICAL CONSIDERATIONS: ONE QUESTION AT A TIME

Let's face it; none of us can just jump into a legal research project without knowing something about the subject we are researching. Unless you have some experience in a particular field, rushing to review a primary source of the law might be futile. Although you should not cite secondary sources, they should always be your starting point—especially in the beginning. Educate yourself on the law. That will help you distinguish good information from bad.

And, ask questions. Ask questions of your supervising attorney, associates, other paralegals, and staff. That is part of the process. In fact, when you don't ask questions, that's when the trouble begins. Find out which sources are best for the project you are assigned. Remember, attorneys and paralegals who have been practicing for a while can guide you to the best legal sources to review.

The beginning admonishment to you in this chapter was that "Rome wasn't built in a day!" So, don't expect to know all the answers to the questions posed the first day on the job. No one expects it, so why should you? Gaining legal knowledge will be a gradual process. Each day you will learn more and more, building on that knowledge base. Research is a step-by-step approach, but most importantly, you cannot be a team of one.

Summary

It is important for paralegals to understand the sources of the law. Primary authorities consist of constitutions, statutes, case law, court rules, and administrative rules and regulations. There are two types of primary authority: mandatory and persuasive. Mandatory primary authority is the original text of the law and is binding on all participants in a particular jurisdiction. Persuasive primary authority consists of judicial decisions, statutes, or constitutional provisions from different jurisdictions, such as another state or different federal district.

Secondary authority consists of a wide variety of publications that are devoted to explaining or interpreting primary authorities. Secondary authorities cannot be cited in most legal work, but they do provide an excellent way to locate primary authorities. Secondary authorities include legal encyclopedias, *American Law Reports,* uniform laws and restatements, treatises and texts, law reviews and periodicals, attorney general opinions, looseleaf services, and legal dictionaries. Many secondary sources have a dual function. They are a secondary source as well as a finding tool. A finding tool assists in locating applicable primary sources.

And finally, although neither a primary nor a secondary source, digests and citators are critical to any legal research project. With all these legal sources, the method used to locate them is by its legal citation.

Key Terms

American Law Reports
annotation
attorney general opinions
bill
case law
citators
Code of Federal Regulations
code
common law
digest
Federal Register
finding tool
hornbooks
Key Number System
law reviews
legal citation
legal encyclopedia
looseleaf service
mandatory authority
nutshell
ordinance
persuasive authority
pocket parts
precedent
precedential value
primary authority
reporters
restatement
secondary authority
session laws
slip law
stare decisis
statute
statutes at large
supplement
texts
treatise
uniform laws
United States Code
United States Code Annotated
United States Code Service

Review Questions

1. What is the difference between primary authorities and secondary authorities?
2. Explain the differences between mandatory authority and persuasive authority.
3. Identify the primary sources of the law.
4. What source of law is considered the supreme law of the land?
5. What is the purpose of administrative rules and regulations?
6. What is the difference between a slip law and secession law?
7. List the different types of court rules.
8. Explain the difference between a treatise and *American Law Reports.*
9. How does a law review article compare to a legal encyclopedia?
10. Why are attorney general opinions important to governmental entities?

Exercises

1. Determine the name of your state's official case reporter and statutory code. Prepare a list of state-specific secondary sources in your jurisdiction as well.
2. Using your state as a guide, determine whether your state has Web sites for any of its courts. Review the sites and determine whether the rules of court are located on the site and whether any local rules exist for the various courts. (There should be, at least, a Web site for your state's court of last resort. If an intermediate court of appeals exists, review the site[s] as well.)
3. You have been asked to review several different primary authorities for an assignment. However, in order to properly complete the assignment, you must be able to rank these sources by their precedential value. Rank the following legal sources according to the hierarchy of the law discussed in the chapter:
   a. State constitution
   b. State supreme court decision
   c. U.S. Supreme Court decision
   d. Legal encyclopedia
   e. Intermediate state court of appeals decision
4. Which of the following qualifies as mandatory authority?
   - State statute
   - U.S. Constitution
   - Your textbook
   - A scholarly article on federal law
   - Restatement of Contracts
   - Attorney general opinion
   - Federal case decision
   - Regulation from the Environmental Protection Agency
5. Determine the name of your state's attorney general and locate three opinions covering any topic that were rendered by him or her within the past three years.
6. Visit a local law library and find the following sources:
   a. *Corpus Juris Secundum—C.J.S.*
   b. *American Jurisprudence 2d—Am. Jur. 2d*
   c. *United States Code,* either annotated or unannotated
   d. *Code of Federal Regulations*
   e. Your state's encyclopedia
   f. Your state's statutory code
   g. Your state's case reporters

7. Locate a copy of the U.S. Constitution and your state constitution. Compare and contrast the provisions in both documents. Prepare a list of those provisions in your state constitution that are different from the U.S. Constitution.
8. In your local law library, find legal treatises on the following subjects. Identify the author(s) and the name of the treatise. (Texts and nutshells are excluded.)
   a. Contracts
   b. Torts
   c. Constitutional law
   d. Real property
   e. Civil procedure
   f. Evidence
   g. Family law

PORTFOLIO ASSIGNMENT

Carrie was just given a legal research assignment by her supervising attorney. A client was fined for using her cell phone while she was driving. The client doesn't recall any law being passed that prohibited the use of cell phones while driving. She wants to fight the citation. Carrie knows this is a relatively new area of the law and is not sure where to start. Prepare a possible research plan for Carrie using both primary and secondary sources of the law. Support your research plan by explaining the basis behind your choices.

Quick Quiz True/False Answers

Page 35

1. False
2. True
3. False
4. False
5. True

Page 44

1. True
2. True
3. False
4. True
5. False

Page 51

1. True
2. True
3. False
4. False
5. False

Chapter 3

Case Law and Reporters: Finding Judges' Opinions

After completing this chapter, you will be able to:

- Understand the origins of the common law and its impact on case law.
- Discuss the development of case law.
- Locate a case in a library from its citation.
- Differentiate between an official reporter and an unofficial reporter.
- Define a parallel citation and its use.
- Find the different reporters in the national reporter system.
- Compare the components of the different U.S. Supreme Court reporters.
- Use the star-paging system found in unofficial case reporters.
- Identify the basic components of a reporter.
- Discover cases from various print and electronic sources.

With a general understanding of the court system and the different sources of the law, we begin to focus on the individual sources. Of all the sources of law, case law is the backbone of the system. It is the "interpreter" of all the sources of law. Although we know that the supreme law of the land is the U.S. Constitution, judges are the ones who ultimately decide how the Constitution is interpreted and applied to a specific set of facts. In this chapter, we review the history of case law through the common law and how a system for organizing all case law developed.

CASE FACT PATTERN

Your attorney was appointed to represent a criminal defendant in federal court. The defendant has his sentencing hearing tomorrow, and you read on the CNN Web site that the U.S. Supreme Court just handed down a decision that may affect the outcome of your attorney's hearing. You hope the case has been posted on the U.S. Supreme Court Web site so that you can review it. Since you know the name of the case, you check the site to see if the case is available. It is! After reviewing it, you immediately bring the case to your attorney's attention. Can you use the case in the legal brief you are assisting your attorney to prepare for his court case? Does your attorney have to tell the prosecutor about the case? These are just some of the issues that arise when preparing an assignment. Legal research involves not only finding the law, but also determining the ethical boundaries in presenting it.

THE DEVELOPMENT OF CASE LAW: UNLOCKING OUR COMMON LAW ROOTS

common law
Judge-made law; the ruling in a judicial opinion.

case law
Published court opinions of federal and state appellate courts; judge-created law in deciding cases, set forth in court opinions.

Formal statutory laws are created by a legislature. We know these laws guide how society judges the behavior of individuals. Violation of statutory law often results in some type of fine, penalty, or disposition. However, not all behavior is governed by a statute. What happens when parties have claims for which there is no statute? How does society adjudicate those claims? The basis for deciding disputes where there is no statutory mandate is the **common law.** Since the American colonies had no basis for guidance other than the English legal system, they adopted that system. That system focuses on the customs and practices of a society. In the American legal system, judges apply the principles of common law when they make decisions. When those decisions are reduced to writing, **case law** is created. Although common law is sometimes referred to as "unwritten law," the huge body of cases recording the decisions of judges refutes that misnomer. To say it simply, common law is the written law—that law which has not been enacted by a legislature or signed into existence by the executive branch.

PRACTICE TIP

The states that recognize common law marriage in some form are Alabama, Colorado, District of Columbia, Georgia, Idaho, Iowa, Kansas, Montana, New Hampshire, Ohio, Oklahoma, Pennsylvania, Rhode Island, South Carolina, Texas, and Utah.

The Importance of Common Law Today

Although many states have either abolished or severely limited the application of common law principles, some common law principles continue today. One noted exception is marriage. At least ten states and the District of Columbia recognize common law marriage, which means that, in some cases, a marriage may be valid without a formal ceremony or state license. (Now, don't get too nervous; just living together does not constitute a common law marriage in any state.) There are common factors that a couple must show to be considered married under the common law. These factors include such things as agreeing to be married, cohabitating, and telling others you are married. Filing joint tax returns in some states that recognize common law marriage is another means of evidencing the relationship.

Therefore, principles of custom and past practice do play a role in today's society. Their importance should not be overlooked, which is why the common law continues to guide court decisions, provide assistance with new issues, provide a framework for statutes created under common law principles, and reflect the importance of *stare decisis*—a principle discussed in Chapter 2. We examine the concept of *stare decisis* in more detail and its impact on case law in the following section.

preemption
Right of the federal government to exclusive governance over a state in certain matters.

YOU BE THE JUDGE

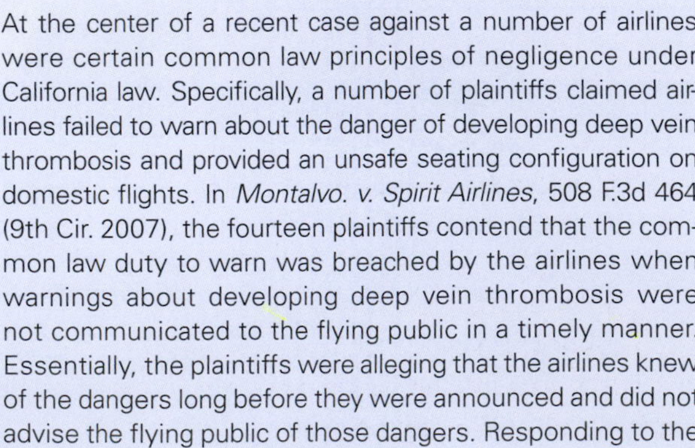

At the center of a recent case against a number of airlines were certain common law principles of negligence under California law. Specifically, a number of plaintiffs claimed airlines failed to warn about the danger of developing deep vein thrombosis and provided an unsafe seating configuration on domestic flights. In *Montalvo. v. Spirit Airlines*, 508 F.3d 464 (9th Cir. 2007), the fourteen plaintiffs contend that the common law duty to warn was breached by the airlines when warnings about developing deep vein thrombosis were not communicated to the flying public in a timely manner. Essentially, the plaintiffs were alleging that the airlines knew of the dangers long before they were announced and did not advise the flying public of those dangers. Responding to the allegations, the airlines involved raised issues of federal **preemption** stating that federal law superseded any law or regulation from a state when faced with airline or passenger safety. The Ninth Circuit Court of Appeals examined and dismissed the common law claims of "failure to warn" based on the preemption issue. However, the court was not completely convinced that plaintiffs' claims lacked merit on the unsafe seating configuration issue. Examine the *Montalvo* case. What were the facts surrounding the plaintiffs' claims? What principles of law did the court discuss in reaching its conclusion? What is the court's result in the case? As the *Montalvo* case illustrated, common law principles still play an important role in case law decisions today.

The Rule of Precedent or *Stare Decisis*

In Chapter 2, we touched on the concept of *stare decisis*. We learned that it is one of the most important legal principles in legal research. Recall that the basic idea behind *stare decisis* is that when judges are presented with cases involving similar issues and facts as other cases, they will reach similar results. To illustrate this principle, we will begin with a nonlegal issue and then gradually expand the discussion into the realm of law.

Consider two brothers, John and Carl. John has just turned sixteen. His older brother, Carl, is eighteen. When Carl turned sixteen he was allowed to drive the family car on dates. He was also allowed to stay out until midnight on Fridays and Saturdays. John approaches his parents and makes the following argument:

> *I'm sixteen now, and I want the same privileges that you gave Carl. I want to drive the family car on dates and I want to stay out until midnight on weekends.*

John's argument is that his "case" involves similar issues and similar facts as a previous decision. He argues that Carl's situation is a precedent for how his parents should act in his situation.

When attorneys ask judges to rule in cases, they are doing exactly the same thing that John is doing with his parents. They are basing their argument on prior cases and statutes. However, the only way to know what those prior cases and statutes are is to research them and be ready to discuss them with the judge. As you are already aware, the rule of precedent is closely tied in with the critically important principle of *stare decisis*. Stated simply, judges believe that predictability is an important consideration for a legal system and implicitly agree to be bound by precedents.

This system is based upon basic fairness and promotes the concept that similar facts and similar issues should dictate a similar result. To create a system that runs counter to this basic principle would create instability in the foundation of the legal system. Thus, the rule of precedent is not simply a rule of practice; it actually helps maintain the faith of the American people in their legal system.

We continue with our example of John's request to drive the family car and stay out later on Fridays and Saturdays. As you recall, his argument was based on fairness. After all, his brother, Carl, received those privileges when he reached the age of sixteen.

The response of John's parents was: "Yes, that's true. We did give Carl those privileges, but, unlike you, he hadn't been caught smoking pot in his room. You haven't demonstrated the same level of maturity as Carl, therefore you won't get the same privileges."

In the situation outlined in our example, John's parents have ruled that his case is not the same as the previous situation. The facts are different and this justifies a different result. This is exactly how a court rules on issues presented by attorneys. The attorneys will argue that their case is either exactly like a previously decided case (and that the judge should rule the same way) or that their case is somehow different (and that the judge should rule in a different way). Under *stare decisis,* a judge is bound by the precedent set in another case, even if the judge doesn't like the ruling, which explains why one of the most controversial decisions in American legal history, *Roe v. Wade,* has not been overturned.

The interesting aspect of *stare decisis* is that there is no statute that requires courts to follow it. You will not find a *stare decisis* rule or statute stating that all judges must follow it. Why then would judges almost always follow the principle of *stare decisis*? Why can't a judge simply ignore *stare decisis* and make any decision that she sees fit? The most practical explanation for judges to follow *stare decisis* is that her decisions would be overturned on appeal. Although that might not seem like much of a burden, judges do not like having their decisions overruled by higher courts. They attempt to follow the law as they understand it, and by following *stare decisis* they ensure that the majority of their decisions will be upheld on appeal.

Judicial Review: The Importance of Case Law

judicial review
The power of a court to determine the constitutionality of actions of the executive and legislative branches of government.

Linked with the principles of *stare decisis* and precedent is the principle of **judicial review.** This principle was created in the landmark case of *Marbury v. Madison,* when the U.S. Supreme Court declared that the judicial branch had the power to review and declare acts of Congress unconstitutional. This case set one of the most important precedents in American history and paved the way for courts to review other kinds of actions as well. Under the guise of judicial review, the Supreme Court invalidated state laws, voided administrative rules and regulations, and determined the constitutionality of the conduct of the president of the United States. As a result, this constitutional doctrine affords all courts, federal and state, the power to invalidate acts of the legislative and executive branches of government by pronouncing them unconstitutional. Courts have the final word, for better or worse. Are judges always right? Of course not. As former Supreme Court justice Robert H. Jackson observed in *Brown v. Allen,* 344 U.S. 443 (1953), about the powers of the U.S. Supreme Court: "We are not final because we are infallible, but we are infallible only because we are final." That truly places the concept of judicial review in context.

Now that we have an understanding of how case law developed, you must be eager to know where to find it. We open the door to the world of case reporters.

Quick Quiz True/False Questions

1. The common law is based upon statutes passed by the British.
2. Case law is the common law in written form.
3. When applying the principles of *stare decisis,* judges will not review how other courts decided a particular set of facts.

YOU BE THE JUDGE

A district court in Oregon recently exercised the principle of judicial review in a high-profile case. In *Mayfield v. United States of America,* 504 F. Supp. 2d 1023 (D. Or. 2007), Brandon Mayfield was investigated by the U.S. government for his alleged participation in the Madrid commuter train bombings of 2004. Under the Foreign Intelligence Surveillance Act (FISA) as amended by the Patriot Act, the government's authority to investigate persons suspected of a crime was expanded. Rather than the Fourth Amendment requirement of probable cause, the requirement under the Act was relaxed. Mayfield argued throughout the process that his Fourth Amendment rights were being violated. And, he continued to argue that the driving force behind the government's investigation was his Muslim faith, even though Spanish authorities had arrested a Moroccan suspect based on the evidence at the scene. After it was determined that Mayfield had no involvement in the Madrid bombings, he filed a case against the U.S. government stating that sections of the FISA as amended by the Patriot Act violated the Fourth Amendment. The U.S. district court agreed. After a detailed analysis of the history of Fourth Amendment case law, weighing all sides and all interests, the Court stated "[f]or over 200 years, this Nation has adhered to the rule of law—with unparalleled success. A shift to a Nation based on extra-constitutional authority is prohibited, as well as ill-advised." *Id.* at 1042. What language was amended in the statute and what effect did it have for government intelligence surveillance? What critical facts did the court find significant in determining that the government's behavior violated the Fourth Amendment? Did the court find Mayfield had standing and a "case and controversy?" Why or why not?

4. Using principles of judicial review, courts can declare statutes unconstitutional.
5. Common law principles are not recognized by our courts any longer.

FINDING CASE LAW

Judicial opinions, which are often simply referred to as *cases,* are a primary source of the law and are published in a continuing series of hardbound volumes called **reporters.** Reporters are organized not by topic but chronologically. This poses the problem of how to find those cases relevant to a given research topic without sifting through every case in every volume.

judicial opinions
Analysis of a decision issued by an appellate court panel.

reporters
Hardbound volumes containing judicial decisions.

In this section and succeeding sections, we discuss methods of dealing with this obstacle. A logical starting point is the citation concept.

Citations: What Do All Those Letters and Numbers Mean?

Citations are the keys that unlock the information in a law library. Your understanding of the citation concept will improve as you work your way through the following sections, and especially as you do your own research. So, what is a citation? A citation is the formal reference to a legal source. This legal source may be primary or secondary. It contains specific information that allows you to locate the legal source with relative ease. The components of a citation differ depending upon its source. Thus, a case citation has different components than a statute, and a statute has different components than a constitution. Throughout this text, you will learn how to use the citations for many legal sources, with Chapter 14 teaching you how to incorporate legal citations into your legal writing. But, let's not get ahead of ourselves.

We will begin by focusing on the components of a citation with a case. The case is a famous one decided by the United States Supreme Court—*Miranda v. Arizona,* 384 U.S. 436, 86 S. Ct. 1602, 16 L. Ed. 2d 694 (1966). (You know the case. In almost every episode of television shows like *Law and Order,* people are arrested and read their rights: "You have the right to remain silent . . ."; this is the case that set forth those requirements.) But have you ever wondered where those lists of rights originated, or better yet, how to find the case? You might first ask yourself, "Why all those numbers and letters after the name of the case?" The letters and numbers, together with the name *Miranda v. Arizona,* constitute the citation for the reporter opinion. In this context, a case **citation** (also called a cite) provides information that directs you to the exact page in the exact volume of each reporter in which the text of this case appears. We will analyze each component of the citation, but first a word about consistency in citation form.

citation
Information about a legal source directing you to the volume and page in which the legal source appears.

PRACTICE TIP

A citation is also referred to as a cite.

As you can imagine, with the large number of courts in the American system, there are different reporters that publish judicial opinions, each requiring a unique citation. There is also a need for citations associated with statutes, regulations, municipal codes, treatises, law review articles, and other legal publications and materials. In order to minimize inconsistency in practice, standard systems of citation were developed. The leading authority for the rules on citations is *The Bluebook: A Uniform System of Citation,* published in book format by the law reviews of several leading law schools. This citation system became the universal model until the publication in 2000 of the *ALWD Citation Manual. The Bluebook* has been known to be difficult to use and master, resulting in the ever-increasing adoption of the *ALWD* system. Published by Aspen Publishers, the *ALWD Citation Manual* is considered easier to use.

PRACTICE TIP

Because *The Bluebook: A Uniform System of Citation* has a bright blue cover, the citation system is known informally as the "bluebook system" or "bluebook format."

Although both systems are recognized, the *ALWD Citation Manual* is becoming an acceptable alternative. The trend for many courts, however, is toward a universal system of citation, erasing the mystery of proper citation once and for all. The *Universal Citation Guide,* published by the American Association of Law Libraries in 1999, offers an alternative form for standardized citation form. Whether this system will become the ultimate "bible" for citation form is anyone's guess. Your attorney will guide you as to the proper form to use in your jurisdiction. More detail on proper citation format and integrating it into legal writing is addressed in Chapter 14.

Now, let's return to our consideration of the citation for *Miranda v. Arizona.* First, let's take the name of the case. There are literally pages of rules on proper identification of parties in the name portion of the citation. You should check either *The Bluebook* or *ALWD Citation Manual* to review some of the trickier aspects for most cases; however, it is sufficient to remember that the name of a lawsuit (for citation purposes) will contain the last name of the parties to the lawsuit, generally the full name for a business entity (for example, "Computer Technologies, Inc."). The names of the parties in the case are either underlined or italicized. For example:

PRACTICE TIP

Case reporters capitalize the names of the parties you will use in your citation. If the names in the case are not capitalized, they will not appear as part of the citation. This is particularly important when multiple parties are listed in the case.

Miranda v. Arizona
Miranda v. Arizona

The "v" in the middle stands for "versus." The "v" is always lowercase followed by a period (.). The "v." is also underlined or italicized as part of the citation.

Now we turn to the remaining components of the citation. We will analyze each group of letters and numbers, one at a time.

First, 384 U.S. 436 represents that the case appears in Volume 384 of the *United States Reports* at page 436. Reporters are designated as either an **official reporter** or **unofficial reporter.** The official reporter for the United States Supreme Court is *U.S. Reports.*

Two basic rules can be drawn from the citation 364 U.S. 436. First, the volume number always appears before the reporter's abbreviation. Second, the page number always appears after the abbreviation.

The next group of letters and number in our example is "86 S. Ct. 1602." This group refers to another reporter, published by ThomsonWest, called the *Supreme Court Reporter,* which also publishes Supreme Court cases. For citation purposes, it is abbreviated as *S. Ct.* Thus, the case of *Miranda v. Arizona* also appears in volume 86 of the *Supreme Court Reporter* at page 1602. (Remember our rule: volume number before abbreviation, page number after.)

official reporters
Government publications of court decisions (for example, 325 Ill.3d 50).

unofficial reporters
A private case reporter not designated by a court as an official publication of court decisions (for example, 525 N.E.2d 90).

And the final group of letters and numbers in our example is "16 L. Ed. 2d 694." As with the *Supreme Court Reporter,* this group refers to yet another reporter that publishes United States Supreme Court cases, called *United States Supreme Court Reports, Lawyers' Edition,* published by LexisNexis. It is abbreviated as "L. Ed." and since the case is found in the second series of that reporter, "2d" is added to the citation. Therefore, *Miranda v. Arizona* also appears in volume 16 of the second series of *Lawyers' Edition* on page 694. Both the *Supreme Court Reporter* and *Lawyers' Edition* are considered unofficial reporters. You will learn more about the need for and great usefulness of such reporters in succeeding sections of this chapter.

PRACTICE TIP

To remember the important pieces of information to retrieve a case, just keep saying to yourself "volume, reporter, page."

It is important to note that recently there was a major change in legal publishing. For years, the leading legal publishers were West Publishing Company and Lawyers Cooperative Publishing Company. Both companies are now under the umbrella of the Thomson Corporation publishing under the name ThomsonWest.

The other leading legal publisher is Reed Elsevier, which now owns LexisNexis. You will see some legal publications under the LexisNexis brand that were previously under another publisher. You can use either set of publications; it is simply a matter of preference and availability.

When a case text is found in two or more reporters, the citations for that case are known as **parallel citations** (see Figure 3.1). When parallel citations exist, the official reporter is always listed first. Thus for *Miranda v. Arizona* the official citation, "384 U.S. 436," precedes the parallel citations "86 S. Ct. 1602, 16 L. Ed. 2d 694." We discuss official and unofficial reporters in more detail in later sections of this chapter.

parallel citation
Case found in more than one reporter.

The final reference in the citation is (1966). This is, as you might have guessed, the year in which *Miranda v. Arizona* was decided. The year of decision, in parentheses, is always included at the end of the citation. Sometimes the name of the court that decided the case will also appear within these final parentheses. Since some reporters publish decisions from several courts and even several states, it is sometimes impossible to discern the court by simply identifying the reporters; hence, proper citation for a case appearing in such a reporter must include identification of the specific court that decided the case.

PRACTICE TIP

Parallel citations can be located in the *National Reporter Blue Book,* which has a conversion table giving the parallel citations to cases. There are state "blue and white" books for those states with an official and unofficial reporter. *Shepard's Citations* provides parallel citations as well.

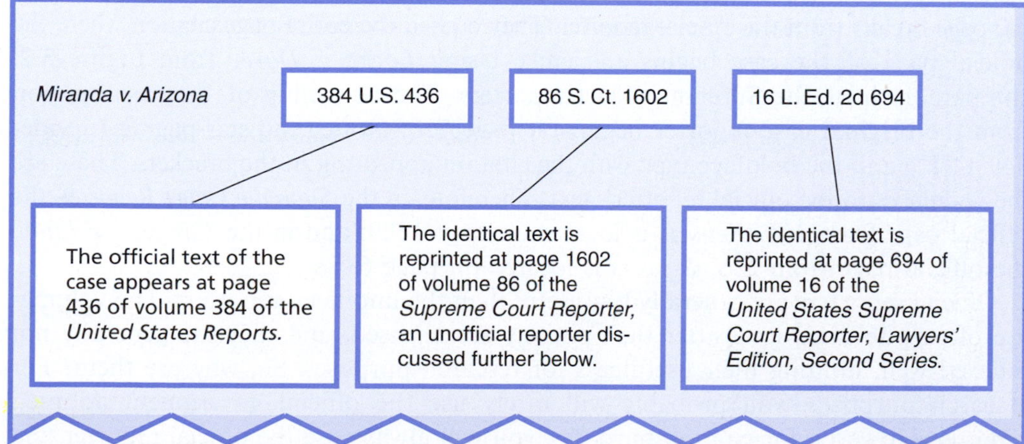

Miranda v. Arizona
384 U.S. 436
86 S. Ct. 1602
16 L. Ed. 2d 694
The official text of the case appears at page 436 of volume 384 of the United States Reports.
The identical text is reprinted at page 1602 of volume 86 of the Supreme Court Reporter, an unofficial reporter discussed further below.
The identical text is reprinted at page 694 of volume 16 of the United States Supreme Court Reporter, Lawyers' Edition, Second Series.

FIGURE 3.1 Case Citation with Parallel Citations

Your understanding of the citation concept will improve as you work your way through the following sections, and especially as you do your own research. Several citation exercises appear at the end of this chapter.

We have mentioned that differentiating between official and unofficial reporters is important for citation purposes. The next section discusses why knowing the differences is important.

Official Reporters versus Unofficial Reporters

An official reporter is one sanctioned by the court generating the opinions contained within its pages. The *United States Reports,* for example, is the official reporter for Supreme Court decisions, and is published by the U.S. government. Most of the states have one or more official reporters for the decisions of their various courts. Many of these are published by the respective state governments; for some states, however, the reporter designated as official is one of the unofficial reporters from the National Reporter System (to be discussed further) or some other unofficial reporter.

The citation of a case from a state that has an official reporter will list the official reporter first, generally followed by parallel citations to the National Reporter System. Check your citation manual and find the rule that establishes the appropriate order. But what happens when you do not have access to an official reporter? Worse yet, you will probably only have access to an unofficial reporter, and for citing purposes, you must cite the official reporter. Starting to see a problem? There has to be a system that addresses this issue. The answer is, of course, such a system exists. The system is known as star-paging.

star-paging
A practice that enables the reader to identify the page breaks in one reporter by reviewing the decision as reprinted in another reporter.

Star-Paging

Pagination as it appears in the official reporter is reflected in an unofficial reporter through the use of **star-paging.** The symbol used to identify star-paging is an upside-down "T" with the page noted at the bottom. It looks like this: "⊥." Star-paging is a practice that enables us to identify the page breaks in one reporter by reviewing the decision as reprinted in another reporter. By utilizing these star-paging notations when writing a legal document, the drafter can reference the page and volume of important language as it appears in both ThomsonWest's *regional reporter* and the official *reporter from that jurisdiction,* even though she only has the regional reporter at hand. Star-paging is often (but not always) found in unofficial reporters; it is never found in official reporters, and thus constitutes an additional reason why unofficial reporters can be superior to official reporters as research tools.

PRACTICE TIP

The official citation is usually the one required for citation purposes. However, more than likely you will use the unofficial reporter for research and citation purposes.

ThomsonWest is not the only publisher that uses star-paging. LexisNexis, the publisher of the *Supreme Court Reports, Lawyers' Edition,* uses a different method to show the page breaks from the official reporter. They embed the entire page citation where the official page of the case begins and ends. Using *Locke v. Davey* from Figure 3.2, compare each of the Supreme Court reporters. The beginning of the case opinion from the original case reporter begins on page 715. Notice the star-paging (upside-down "T") and the boldface type with the citation appearing in the brackets. These are the references to the official reporter's text. Therefore, in the *Supreme Court Reporter,* the official page from *U.S. Reports* is located on page 1309; and in the *Lawyers' Edition,* the official page from *U.S. Reports* is located on page 6.

PRACTICE TIP

Think of star-paging symbols as an imaginary page turner. Each time you see a star-paging reference, the page in the official reporter is being turned.

Official reporters are generally less useful than the unofficial reporters. The volumes are often published long after the opinions are released, and they are generally not indexed well, limiting their usefulness for research purposes. So, why use them? For research purposes, you probably will rarely use the official government adopted reporter. However, for citation purposes, you will always use the official reporter and that is one of the main reasons why you need to be familiar with official reporters and why understanding star-paging is so important.

A

Cite as: 540 U.S. 712 (2004) 715

Opinion of the Court

CHIEF JUSTICE REHNQUIST delivered the opinion of the Court.

The State of Washington established the Promise Scholarship Program to assist academically gifted students with postsecondary education expenses. In accordance with the State Constitution, students may not use the scholarship at an institution where they are pursuing a degree in devotional theology. We hold that such an exclusion from an otherwise inclusive aid program does not violate the Free Exercise Clause of the First Amendment.

The Washington State Legislature found that "[s]tudents who work hard

…nplete high school with high acade…

…ttend college because they canno…

…ficient." Wash. Rev. Code Ann. §…

… those high-achieving students, t…

B

U.S. 715 **LOCKE v. DAVEY** **1309**

Cite as 124 S. Ct. 1307 (2004)

[text omitted]

suggests animus toward religion. In the historic and substantial state test at issue, it cannot be concluded the denial of funding for vocational religious instruction alone is inherently constitutionally suspect. Without a presumption of un-constitutionality, Davey's petition must fail. The State's interest is not funding the pursuit of devotional degrees is substantial, and the exclusion of such funding places a relatively minor burden on Promise Scholars. If any room exists between the two Religion Clauses, it must be here. Pp. 1311–1315.

§ 299 F.3d 745 reversed.

REHNQUIST, C.J., delivered the opinion of the Court, in which STEVENS, O'CONNOR, KENNEDY, SOUTER, GINSBURG, AND BREYER, JJ., joined. SCALIA, J., filed a dissenting opinion in

For U.S. Supreme Court briefs, see:
2003 WL 21715040 (Pet.Brief)
2003 WL 22137308 (Resp.Brief)
2003 WL 22439887 (Reply.Brief)

Chief Justice REHNQUIST delivered the opinion of the Court.

$\perp_{715}$The State of Washington established the Promise Scholarship Program to assist academically gifted students with postsecondary education expenses. In accordance with the State Constitution, students may not use the scholarship at an institution where they are pursuing a degree in devotional theology. We hold that such an exclusion from an otherwise inclusive aid program does not violate the Free Exercise Clause of the First Amendment.

The Washington State Legislature found that "[s]tudents who work hard . . . and [text omitted]

C

U.S. SUPREME COURT REPORTS **158 L Ed 299**

[text omitted]

OPINION OF THE COURT

[540 US 715]

Chief Justice **Rehnquist** delivered the opinion of the Court.

[1a] The State of Washington established the Promise Scholarship Program to assist academically gifted students with postsecondary education expenses. In accordance with the State Constitution, students may not use the scholar-ship at an institution where they are pursuing a degree in devotional theology. We hold that such an exclusion from an otherwise inclusive aid program does not violate the Free Exercise Clause of the First Amendment.

The Washington State Legislature found that "[s]tudents who work hard . . . and successfully complete high school with high academic marks, may not have the financial ability to attend college because they cannot obtain financial aid or the financial aid is insufficient." Wash. Rev. Code Ann. § 28B.119.005 (Supp. 2004). In 1999, to assist these high achieving students, the legislature created the

[540 US 716]

Promise Scholarship Program, which provides a scholarship, renewable for one year, to eligible students for post-secondary education expenses. Students may spend their funds on any education-related expense, including room and board. The scholarships are funded through the State's general fund, and their amount varies each year depending on the annual appropriation, which is evenly prorated among the eligible students. Wash. Admin. Code § 250-80-050(2) (2003). The scholarship was worth $1,125 for academic year 1999–2000 and $1,542 for 2000–2001.

To be eligible for the scholarship, a student must meet academic, income, and enrollment requirements. A student must graduate from a Washington public or private high school and either graduate in the top 15% of his graduating class, or attain on the first attempt a cumulative score of 1,200 or better on the Scholastic Assessment Test I or a score of [text omitted]

FIGURE 3.2 Comparison of the Different Sources of Star-Paging

Note: A: *U.S. Reports,* (original text); B: *U.S. Supreme Court Reporter* (ThomsonWest); C: *U.S. Supreme Court Reports, Lawyer's Edition.*

Source: B. From the Supreme Court Reporter. Reprinted with permission from ThomsonWest. C: Reprinted with permission of LexisNexis.

PRACTICE TIP

The official citation is always before any unofficial parallel citation.

On the other hand, unofficial reporters are exactly what the name suggests. These reporters are not sanctioned by the court and usually published by private publishers. The decision is the same in an official and unofficial reporter. What distinguishes most unofficial reporters from an official reporter is the "additional" information the unofficial reporter provides about the case. For example, unofficial reporters provide a brief summary of the case, which includes the ruling of the court. They also provide valuable finding tools so you can easily locate other cases either dealing with or associated with the points of law addressed in the case. Are you starting to get the picture—shortcuts for the researcher! Thus, when an attorney or paralegal has a choice, she will lean toward using the unofficial reporter.

Today the most popular venue for reporting cases is in the National Reporter System published by ThomsonWest. Along with other unofficial reporting systems, valuable information is provided that will assist you in your legal research efforts. We turn to the ThomsonWest National Reporter System first.

PRACTICE TIP

The early U.S. Supreme Court case volumes were published by private individuals (and not the U.S. government) bearing their name. You may see a citation such as *Marbury v. Madison*, 5 U.S. (1 Cranch) 137 (1803). Private reporter names appear for the first ninety volumes of the *U.S. Reports.* Do not cite the private reporter. Use a citation manual for proper citation form.

Quick Quiz True/False Questions

F 1. A citation is used only for primary sources of the law.
T 2. The two most prominent manuals for citation rules are *The Bluebook* and *ALWD Manual.*
T 3. A parallel citation indicates that a case can be located in at least two different reporters.
F 4. Star-paging is located in official reporters.
T 5. When citing a case, always use the official reporter citation.

National Reporter System: A Systematic Approach

By the end of the 1880s, the West Publishing Company of St. Paul, Minnesota (now ThomsonWest) had developed a reporter system covering the decisions of all the states. Called the National Reporter System, it contained seven **regional reporters** corresponding to geographic areas of the country. This system is still in use today. The names of the seven regional reporters, with their abbreviations for citation purposes, are provided in Table 3.1.

regional reporters
Reporters that contain the cases of all the states in a particular geographic area.

Each of these reporters contains the decisions of the courts of several states. Table 3.2 shows the states currently covered by each reporter. Each regional reporter contains all of the decisions of the highest court, and often many of the decisions of one or more lower courts of these states, for the time period covered.

As the number of volumes in each of these regional reporters reached 200 or 300, a second series was initiated, with the numbering starting over again at volume 1. The second series is designated in a citation by the indicia "2d" appearing after the abbreviation. And now, as volumes in the second series reach 999, a third series, denoted as "3d," exists. Whereas a case in the first series of *Pacific Reporter,* for example, might have the citation "197 P. 32" (meaning the text appears at page 32 of volume 197 of the first series), a case in the second series might have the citation "5 P.2d 17" (meaning the text appears on page 17 of volume 5 of the second series); and a later

TABLE 3.1
Seven Regional Reporters

Atlantic Reporter	A.
North Eastern Reporter	N.E.
North Western Reporter	N.W.
Pacific Reporter	P.
South Eastern Reporter	S.E.
South Western Reporter	S.W.
Southern Reporter	So.

Regional Case Reporter	States Covered
Atlantic	Connecticut, Delaware, D.C., Maine, Maryland, New Hampshire, New Jersey, Pennsylvania, Rhode Island, Vermont
North Eastern	Illinois, Indiana, Massachusetts, New York, Ohio
North Western	Iowa, Michigan, Minnesota, Nebraska, North Dakota, South Dakota, Wisconsin
Pacific	Alaska, Arizona, California, Colorado, Hawaii, Idaho, Kansas, Montana, Nevada, New Mexico, Oklahoma, Oregon, Utah, Washington, Wyoming
South Eastern	Georgia, North Carolina, South Carolina, Virginia, West Virginia
South Western	Arkansas, Kentucky, Missouri, Tennessee, Texas
Southern	Alabama, Florida, Louisiana, Mississippi

TABLE 3.2
States Covered in Specific Regional Reporters

case in the third series might have the citation "117 P.3d 365" (meaning the text appears at page 365 of volume 117 of the third series).

Because the number of cases generated by the courts of California and New York is extensive, West established two separate reporters, the *California Reporter* and the *New York Supplement,* to handle the volume of opinions. Although the decisions of the highest courts of these states continue to be published in their respective regional reporters (California's in the *Pacific Reporter;* New York's in the *Northeastern Reporter*), the separate supplementary reporters publish the significant lower court decisions as well. The citation abbreviation for the *California Reporter* is Cal. Rptr., Cal. Rptr. 2d, or Cal. Rptr. 3d; for *New York Supplement* it is N.Y.S. or N.Y.S.2d.

PRACTICE TIP

The *Southern Reporter* is cited as So. (not S.).

The National Reporter System remains current not only through the frequent publication of bound volumes, but also by issuance of **advance sheets,** which are softcover pamphlets containing the most recent cases (and paged exactly as they will later appear in the permanent bound volumes). Cases may appear in these advance sheets many months or even more than a year before they appear in an official reporter, making the regional reporters significantly more current, hence more useful, than the official reporters of most states.

advance sheets
Softcover pamphlets containing the most recent cases.

A DAY IN THE LIFE OF A PARALEGAL

You are busy researching an assignment, running around the library retrieving cases. As part of your research plan, you methodically list all the cases you want to review. Pulling all the appropriate reporters from the shelves, you begin to review the cases, opening up to the page where the case begins. While you begin reading one of the cases, you notice that the page where the case begins is in the middle of the case. That just can't be. You look at your list of citations. You pulled the correct volume and reporter. You don't understand what happened. Upon closer examination you realize that the citation for the case was the third series of the case reporter, not the second. In your haste, you simply missed that. When you return to the shelves and pull the correct reporter and series, you look up the citation in the third series of that reporter. And yes, there is the case you are looking for. This mix-up has happened to everyone at one time or another. We often forget about the different series of reporters and mistakenly retrieve the wrong series of a reporter from the shelf. Of course, this is not earth-shattering, but it does illustrate the importance of precision not only in retrieving a reporter, but in writing down the citation. It is critical to delineate the series of a reporter as they all contain different cases. Volume 358 of the *Pacific Reporter second series* has a completely different listing of cases than volume 358 of the *Pacific Reporter third series*. Pay attention to the subtle nuances of citation form and it will save you from one of those "ah ha" moments.

slip opinion
The first format in which a judicial opinion appears.

Another form of a recently handed-down court opinion is a slip opinion. A **slip opinion** is the first format in which a judicial opinion appears. It is individually paginated (beginning with page one) and is often simply the typewritten text generated by the court's own clerical staff. In some states, slip opinions are gathered together informally in a binder or folder at the law library or the courthouse. In other states, slip opinions are published, but their high expense and delayed availability make them impractical research tools. The published slip opinion may even appear after the advance sheet version is available. However, with the advent of the Internet and computer-assisted research such as Westlaw and LexisNexis, case decisions can be retrieved virtually the day they are handed down by the court. Although electronic research will be discussed in more detail in later chapters, a brief mention is important at this juncture.

There is no denying the fact that many courts post copies of their cases on their Web sites within hours of a decision being released. Part of this phenomenon is due to a 2002 federal statute, the E-Government Act. This statute required all federal courts to post all decisions from their courts. Access to court decisions has never been easier and more voluminous. The impact of the Internet cannot be understated regarding access to the most current cases. Even many state courts post their case decisions on the Internet within hours of release. The cries of attorneys stating they did not know of a court decision are falling on deaf ears of judges. More now than ever, our access to information is virtually instantaneous. The excuses of the past are just a faint whisper. Therefore, although cases appear in numerous print forms relatively quickly, often the Internet is the fastest way to learn and retrieve case information.

However, there is a huge caveat. Often the decisions posted by a court on the Internet are not final. Sometimes parties have further procedural rights, such as requesting a rehearing or after review; as such, the court may make changes. Many courts post warnings on slip opinions alerting attorneys and the public that the posted opinions are not final. Alert your attorney if you are using a slip opinion in your research. There may be some procedural requirements under the court rules of your jurisdiction for using a slip opinion. Figure 3.3 is an example of a slip opinion from the Supreme Court

FIGURE 3.3 Slip Opinion from the Missouri Supreme Court

Source: Your Missouri Courts: The Judicial Branch of State Government, www.courts.mo.gov (accessed November 11, 2007).

This slip opinion is subject to revision and may not reflect the final opinion adopted by the Court.

Opinion
Supreme Court of Missouri

Case Style: Dr. Gary Edwards, Appellant v. Lawrence M. Gerstein, et al., Respondents.

Case Number: SC88313

Handdown Date: 10/30/2007

Appeal From: Circuit Court of Cole County, Hon. Thomas J. Brown III

Counsel for Appellant: J. Dale Wiley

Counsel for Respondent: Matthew B. Briesacher

Opinion Summary:

This summary is not part of the opinion of the Court. It has been prepared by the Communications Counsel for the convenience of the reader. It has been neither reviewed nor approved by the Supreme Court and should not be quoted or cited. The opinion of the Court, which may be quoted, follows the summary.

Overview: This case involves the question of whether members and an employee of the Missouri Board of Chiropractic Examiners are immune from suit by a chiropractor for alleged gross negligence during the board's disciplinary investigation of him. On appeal, the Supreme Court holds unanimously that the trial court properly dismissed the chiropractor's malicious prosecution claims against the board employee because the chiropractor failed to state a

Cont.

FIGURE 3.3 **Slip Opinion from the Missouri Supreme Court** *Cont.*

claim. The Supreme Court further holds, by a 6-1 vote, that the trial court should not have dismissed the chiropractor's gross negligence claims against the board members under the doctrines of official immunity and public duty, or quasi-judicial immunity because section 331.100.5, RSMo, states that board members shall not be personally liable *except for gross negligence.*

[text omitted]

Facts: Dr. Gary Edwards filed a lawsuit alleging that certain members of the Missouri Board of Chiropractic Examiners acted with gross negligence during the board's disciplinary proceedings against him and alleging that a board employee engaged in malicious prosecution during her investigation of claims against Edwards. After venue in the case was moved from Jackson County to Cole County, the circuit court ultimately dismissed Edwards' suit, finding the board members were entitled to quasi-judicial immunity and that the board employee was immune from suit under the official immunity and public duty doctrines. Edwards appeals.

AFFIRMED IN PART; REVERSED IN PART; REMANDED.

Court en banc holds: (1) The circuit court erred in sustaining the board's motion to dismiss on the ground that its members were entitled to quasi-judicial immunity. Section 331.100.5, RSMo, provides that board members "shall not be personally liable either jointly or separately" for any acts they commit in performing their official duties as board members "except gross negligence." By its plain language, the statute supersedes the board's common law immunity if board members are grossly negligent in performing their duties. This analysis is consistent with *State ex rel. Golden v. Crawford,* 165 S.W.3d 147 (Mo. banc 2005), which held that section 190.307, RSMo, superseded common law official immunity in instances where gross negligence can be established. Although *Golden* dealt only with official immunity and this case involves quasi-judicial immunity, the distinction is without difference because both were common law immunities subject to legislative modification. Here, section 331.100.5 permits suits against the board for gross negligence.

[text omitted]

Opinion concurring in part and dissenting in part by Chief Justice Smith: The author agrees with the principal opinion that section 331.100.5, RSMo, waives the board members' immunity under the official immunity and public duty doctrines. Those two doctrines exist primarily to protect the government and its agents from liability for acts performed on behalf of citizens. Quasi-judicial immunity, however, is different in kind than official immunity or the public duty doctrine. Its purpose is to protect the integrity of the investigatory and judicial processes from unwarranted intrusions. This immunity clearly applies to judicial decisions and cannot be waived by statute. The United States Supreme Court has held that quasi-judicial immunity applies to administrative personnel who are performing quasi-judicial or quasi-prosecutorial functions as well, however. This is true because immunity "is justified and defined by the functions it protects and serves, not by the person to whom it attaches." *Forrester v. White,* 484 U.S. 219, 227 (1988).

[text omitted]

Citation:

Opinion Author: Richard B. Teitelman

Opinion Vote: AFFIRMED IN PART; REVERSED IN PART; REMANDED. Price, Limbaugh, Russell, and Wolff, J.J., and Barney, Sp.J., concur; Smith, C.J., concurs in part and dissents in part in separate opinion filed. Breckenridge, J., not participating.

Opinion:

This slip opinion is subject to modification until the Court has ruled on the parties' motions for rehearing, if any, and will become final only after the Court issues its mandate. To see when the Court issues its mandate, please check the docket entries for the case on Case.net.

Dr. Gary Edwards filed suit in Jackson County alleging that several members of the Missouri Board of Chiropractic Examiners acted with gross negligence during the Board's disciplinary proceedings against him. Dr. Edwards' petition also alleged that a Board employee engaged in malicious prosecution during her investigation of the claims against Dr. Edwards. The Board members and the employee filed a motion to dismiss, or in the alternative to transfer the case to the circuit court of Cole County. The case was transferred to Cole County. The circuit court dismissed Dr. Edwards' suit after concluding that the Board members were entitled to quasi-judicial immunity and that the Board employee was immune from suit under the official immunity and public duty doctrines.

Dr. Edwards appeals. He asserts that neither the Board members nor the Board employee are immune from suit and, further, that venue is proper in Jackson County. The judgment dismissing Dr. Edwards' claims against the Board members is reversed. The judgment dismissing Dr. Edwards' malicious prosecution claims against the Board employee is remanded with directions to dismiss those claims without prejudice. Finally, the trial correctly determined that venue was proper in Cole County.

[text omitted]

FIGURE 3.4
Notice of Filings of Opinions of the Iowa Supreme Court

Source: Iowa Judicial Branch, www.judicial.state.ia.us (accessed November 11, 2007).

Opinions of the Supreme Court will be filed at 8:15 a.m. on Fridays except on holidays. For your convenience, the Judicial Branch offers a *free e-mail notification* service for Supreme Court opinions, Court of Appeals opinions, press releases and orders.

Opinions Expected Next Filing Date

A list of cases on which the Supreme Court is expected to rule will be filed at 8:30 a.m. on the Thursday preceding each opinion filing day.

Most Recent Opinions

Notice: The opinions posted on this site are slip opinions only. Under the Rules of Appellate Procedure a party has a limited number of days to request a rehearing after the filing of an opinion. Also, all slip opinions are subject to modification or correction by the court. Therefore, opinions on this site are not to be considered the final decisions of the court. The official published opinions of the Iowa Supreme Court are those published in the North Western Reporter published by the West Publishing Company.

PRACTICE TIP

Many services, both free and fee-based, offer Web alerts when decisions are reported by courts that may be of particular interest to a legal professional. Signing up for the services is easy, with the alerts being sent to an e-mail address. If you are working in a specific area of the law, such as labor relations, personal injury or health care, you can have any new case sent to you by e-mail and always be up-to-date. With these services, you can add or delete areas of interest.

of Missouri. Observe the warnings within the opinion. This is followed by Figure 3.4, which is an example of the Iowa Supreme Court advising the public of its procedures for posting cases as well as a warning as to the use of a slip opinion.

Returning to our discussion of the National Reporter System, each volume contains a table of cases in the front, listing alphabetically by state all those cases whose full text appears in that volume. Each volume also contains subject indexes in the rear of the volume (the subject indexes appear near the front of the advance sheets). The foundation for these indexes is the Key Number System, which is perhaps the single most important element in American legal research. Mastering this system is essential to mastering legal research. This system was briefly discussed in the previous chapter, and later in Chapter 6, you will learn the details of this system and have a clearer understanding of the interrelationship between the sources of the law and finding them in the law library or online.

Finding U.S. Supreme Court Decisions

The regional reporters of the National Reporter System collect cases from the fifty state court systems and territories. What about the federal courts? Where are federal decisions collected, and how do we go about finding the federal cases we need for our research? Let's start with the Supreme Court.

There are four principal print sources of the decisions of the U.S. Supreme Court. You already know the three primary reporters from our discussion of the *Miranda v. Arizona* citation—*United States Reports, Supreme Court Reporter,* and *United States Supreme Court Reports, Lawyers' Edition.* These sources consist of bound volumes and advance sheets. There is also an important source published in looseleaf format—*The United States Law Week*.

The *United States Reports* series, as you recall, is the official series, and its publication (even the advance sheets) lags far behind the issuance of opinions, making it less useful than the other sources for research purposes. In addition, *U.S. Reports* also lacks research aids such as effective indexing by topic, available in the other sources. Perhaps the most useful contribution of *U.S. Reports* is its presentation of a syllabus (a relatively detailed summary) of each decision, prepared by the official court reporter. These syllabi, however, appear in the unofficial sources as well.

The *Lawyers' Edition* series is an unofficial reporter (formerly published by the Lawyers Cooperative Publishing Company) and now part of LexisNexis. These volumes are now in their second series, abbreviated for citation purposes as *L. Ed. 2d.* They are indexed according to a system that categorizes points of law utilizing a case headnote system. This case headnote system is a research "finding tool" and will be

CYBER TRIP

Locate sites in your state that provide access to case law for your state's highest court. How far back can you research cases? Do the sites also provide access to state statutes and courts of appeals cases?

addressed in detail in Chapter 6. There are two features of the *Lawyers' Edition* volumes, in addition to their timely publication, that make them useful research tools. First, they often provide summaries of the briefs of the opposing attorneys, which are not found in *U.S. Reports* or the *Supreme Court Reporter*. Second, each volume presently contains *A.L.R.* annotations, which you will recall are in-depth articles that analyze selected issues raised in some of the more important cases appearing in that volume, and identify additional relevant cases.

PRACTICE TIP

Effective January 1, 2008, *American Law Reports* is exclusive to WestLaw. It will no longer be a part of LexisNexis information.

The *Supreme Court Reporter* (citation abbreviation *S. Ct.*) is a publication of Thomson-West. It utilizes the key number/digest system seen in the National Reporter System, making it a useful resource for cross-referencing decisions in the state courts and the lower federal courts. As mentioned earlier, this system is the foundation for all legal research.

Although both the *Lawyers' Edition* and the *Supreme Court Reporter* issue advance sheets much sooner than does *U.S. Reports,* preparation of head notes and annotations (and other production realities) still produces a lag time between issuance of the opinions and their appearance in print. To meet the immediate needs of the legal community, *The United States Law Week* publishes full texts of the decisions almost immediately upon their issuance by the Supreme Court. The *U.S. Law Week* publication is a **looseleaf service,** publishing pages with prepunched holes for insertion into looseleaf binders. In addition to the Supreme Court decisions, it contains sections on other recent legal developments. You should cite to *U.S. Law Week* only when the Supreme Court decision has not yet appeared in one of the other advance sheets (citation abbreviation *U.S.L.W.*). The *U.S. Law Week* is published weekly, with special editions when the Supreme Court is releasing substantial volumes of opinions.

looseleaf service
A service that publishes recently decided court decisions in looseleaf binders, such as *U.S. Law Week;* provides for information to be easily updated. The loose pages are used to replace the existing pages in the notebook to ensure that the most current information is available.

There are other sources of Supreme Court decisions, as well. These include other looseleaf services (such as the *U.S. Supreme Court Bulletin*), newspapers (which are never cited as a source for the text of an opinion), and the various online computer services.

However, perhaps the most important source for U.S. Supreme Court cases in electronic form is its Web site, www.supremecourtus.gov. Within hours of a public announcement of a case decision, the actual opinion is posted on the site. Although it is not the final version, it is pretty close. The case does not have the finding tools or even a citation, but is still available for immediate review.

ETHICS ALERT

You have found a great case that may help your attorney win a case. The case was just handed down today by the U.S. Supreme Court and you plan on citing it in the brief you are preparing for tomorrow's hearing. You don't tell your attorney about the case; you just cite it in the brief. Of course you make a copy for yourself and your attorney to review, but not for opposing counsel (who you know is returning from his European holiday today). Can you cite the case in the brief, and what ethical responsibilities, if any, do you have in this circumstance?

The answer is probably yes if you provide a copy of the case to all parties and the opposing counsel has an opportunity to review the case. Not only may the court rules guide this hypothetical situation but also the rules of ethics, more formally known as the Rules of Professional Responsibility. As a paralegal, you can be held to the same ethical standards as attorneys because of the substantive legal work you perform under their supervision. Having a sufficient understanding of the professional conduct expected not only of the attorney, but indirectly of the paralegal, is critical since attorneys *are* responsible for and will be held accountable for the unprofessional misconduct of their staff. Become familiar with the Model Rules of Professional Conduct. Check the American Bar Association (ABA) Web site, www.abanet.org, for the current professional ethical standards. Additionally, paralegal associations, such as the National Federation of Paralegal Associations and the National Association of Legal Assistants, offer a framework for paralegals and their supervising attorney to follow. This is another ethical scenario that should provoke thought, alert you, and provide awareness of some of the ethical issues that are present in the paralegal profession.

PRACTICE TIP

When using sources that can only be located on the Internet, print hard copies of the law or case for the court and all parties involved in the case. Do not risk having the court exclude the information by not having copies available.

COMPARING THE DIFFERENT REPORTERS

CYBER TRIP

Log on to the U.S. Supreme Court Web site and locate a case decided within the past six months and review it. Also, find on the Web site the corresponding briefs filed by all the parties in the case.

Publishers provide different information for the cases they report. Some reporters provide more helpful information than others. Although you should cite to the official reporter, the reality is that the case you review is probably located in one of the unofficial reporters. Let's compare the different versions of a U.S. Supreme Court case, using *Locke v. Davey,* 540 U.S. 712, 124 S. Ct. 1307, 158 L. Ed. 2d 1 (2003). (See Figure 3.5 for a comparison of the U.S. Supreme Court Reporters.) We will review only the beginning material of the case. Let's start with the *U.S. Reports* version:

U.S. Reports

1. The *U.S. Reports* case gives a "syllabus" of the case only. In the syllabus a brief synopsis of the case is presented with the prior proceedings. Included in the syllabus is the U.S. Supreme Court's holding with the page references as to where the basis of the holding is discussed.
2. A reference to the lower court opinion is noted with the disposition of the U.S. Supreme Court; in this case, it reversed and remanded the case.
3. The syllabus notes each justice's opinion in the case. In the syllabus for the *Locke* case, Justice Rehnquist wrote the majority opinion for the court, while Justice Scalia wrote the dissenting opinion.
4. The syllabus also identifies who argued the case for the parties. In a footnote to the syllabus, it is noted that a number of *amicus* briefs were filed by a number of organizations. No additional information is provided to the reader, such as headnotes, key numbers, or other research sources.

Supreme Court Reporter (ThomsonWest publication)

1. At the top of the case are the official citation from *U.S. Reports* and the parallel citation to the *Lawyers' Edition.*
2. A brief synopsis of the case and holding is presented. This is the publisher's added editorial comments. Following the holding is the disposition of the court along with a notation as to which justices filed dissenting opinions.
3. Following the synopsis are the headnotes with West key numbers and topics. There are three headnotes dealing with the topics Constitutional Law and Colleges and Universities. The key numbers, representing the subtopics, address four different key numbers under three headnotes.
4. A new feature is the West Codenotes. Here West is referencing the state statute that was at issue. Other cases may reference one or more state statutes if relevant to the decision.
5. The "official" syllabus is reprinted. It is exactly as it appears in *U.S. Reports* with the star-paging references.
6. The briefs that were submitted by the parties are given with the Westlaw reference. In the original opinion from *U.S. Reports,* all the amicus curiae are listed. However, in the *Supreme Court Reporter* edition, they are omitted. The official opinion begins and continues to cite the star-paging references to *U.S Reports.*

United States Supreme Court Reports, Lawyers' Edition (LexisNexis)

1. The official citation from *U.S. Reports* and the parallel citations are noted in the caption of the case.
2. The holding, or as it is referenced—Decision—is the first piece of "unofficial publisher" information introduced in the *Lawyers' Edition.*

3. The next section is the "summary" of the case with some basic facts, prior history of the case, disposition, and the holding of the case. Note that in the summary section there are summaries of the briefs submitted, which are located at the end of the volume.
4. A headnote section is identified but it is "classified" to the *United States Supreme Court Digest, Lawyers' Edition* only. What this means is that these headnotes can only be keyed to its publisher's legal research sources. In this case, LexisNexis publishes the *Lawyers' Edition. Only* LexisNexis sources will be referenced.
5. Unlike the *Supreme Court Reporter*'s edition, there are five headnotes all under the topic Constitutional Law with different section number references (the equivalent to a key number).
6. The research references are *American Jurisprudence* (encyclopedia), *United States Code Service* (federal statutes), and *American Law Reports,* to name a few cited. Reference also is made to Shepard's Citators.
7. The attorneys who argued the case are listed followed by the official syllabus from *U.S. Reports.*
8. The star-paging references are noted throughout the case. Observe the different way the *Lawyers' Edition* identifies the star-paging using the entire citation within brackets.

This comparative exercise shows the clear differences in the information each reporter provides. All the differences should be a blessing and a warning to you. The blessing is the obvious abundance of resource materials revealed by the various publishers of the opinions. The warning is that virtually everything mentioned in the preceding description of the reporters cannot and should not be referenced when citing your research authority. Of course, use it to guide you to your legal research sources, but do not use it as the "source" of your legal authority.

Quick Quiz True/False Questions

1. The National Reporter System contains only the official version of cases.
2. Some regional reporters are the only place where certain state cases are printed.
3. The official reporter for U.S. Supreme Court cases is the *Supreme Court Reporter.*
4. The unofficial Supreme Court reporters provide a number of finding tools.
5. A slip opinion is the first format available to review a case decision.

Federal Court Decisions

With the importance attached to decisions of the federal courts in the American legal system, it is odd to note that there is no official government reporter of federal decisions below the level of the Supreme Court. The reporters prepared by West for federal decisions are the *Federal Supplement* (publishing decisions of the United States district courts and certain other courts since 1932) and the *Federal Reporter* (dating back to 1880 and currently publishing decisions of the appellate circuits; prior to 1932 the *Federal Reporter* published U.S. district court cases as well). These are the standard sources for federal case law, cited respectively as *F. Supp.* or *F. Supp. 2d* and *F., F.2d, or F.3d.* Federal cases prior to 1880 are collected in the West set *Federal Cases.*

When reviewing cases from the federal courts, be alert to the circuit in which your legal problem originates. As you will recall from Chapter 1, there are twelve federal

FIGURE 3.5 Comparison of the U.S. Supreme Court Reporters

Note: A: Original case; B: *U.S. Supreme Court Reports, Lawyers' Edition;* C: *U.S. Supreme Court Reporter* (ThomsonWest).

Source: B. Reprinted with permission of LexisNexis. C. Reprinted with permission from ThomsonWest.

712 **OCTOBER TERM, 2003** 

Syllabus

LOCKE, GOVERNOR OF WASHINGTON, ET AL. *v.* DAVEY

CERTIORARI TO THE UNITED STATES COURT OF APPEALS FOR THE NINTH CIRCUIT

No. 02-1315. Argued December 2, 2000—Decided February 25, 2004

Washington State established its Promise Scholarship Program to assist academically gifted students with post-secondary educational expenses. In accordance with the State Constitution, students may not use such a scholarship to pursue a devotional theology degree. Respondent Davey was awarded a Promise Scholarship and chose to attend Northwest College, a private, church-affiliated institution that is eligible under the program. When he enrolled, Davey chose a double major in pastoral ministries and business management/administration. It is undisputed that the pastoral ministries degree is devotional. After learning that he could not use his scholarship to pursue that degree, Davey brought this action under 42 U. S. C. § 1983 for an injunction and damages, arguing that the denial of his scholarship violated, *inter alia,* the First Amendment's Free Exercise and Establishment Clauses. The District Court rejected Davey's constitutional claims and granted the State summary judgment. The Ninth Circuit reversed, concluding that, because the State had singled out religion for unfavorable treatment, its exclusion of theology majors had to be narrowly tailored to achieve a compelling state interest under *Church of Lukumi Babalu Aye, Inc. v. Hialeah,* 568 U. S. 520. Finding that the State's antiestablishment concerns were not compelling, the court declared the program unconstitutional.

Held: Washington's exclusion of the pursuit of a devotional theology degree from its otherwise-inclusive scholarship aid program does not violate the Free Exercise Clause. This case involves the "play in the joints" between the Establishment and Free Exercise Clauses. *Walz v. Tax Comm'n of City of New York,* 397 U. S. 664, 669. That is, it concerns state action that is permitted by the former but not required by the latter. The Court rejects Davey's contention that, under *Lukumi, supra,* the program is presumptively unconstitutional because it is not facially neutral with respect to religion. To accept this claim would extend the *Lukumi* line of cases well beyond not only their facts but their reasoning. Here, the State's disfavor of religion (if it can be called that) is of a far milder kind than in *Lukumi,* where the ordinance criminalized the ritualistic animal sacrifices of the Santeria religion. Washington's program imposes neither criminal nor civil sanctions on

---

Cite as: 540 U.S. 712 (2004) 713

Syllabus

any type of religious service or rite. It neither denies to ministers the right to participate in community political affairs, see *McDaniel v. Paty,* 435 U. S. 618, nor requires students to choose between their religious beliefs and receiving a government benefit, see, e.g., *Hobbie v. Unemployment Appeals Comm'n of Fla.,* 480 U. S. 136. The State has merely chosen not to fund a distinct category of instruction. Even though the differently worded Washington Constitution draws a more stringent line than does the Federal Constitution, the interest it seeks to further is scarcely novel. In fact, there few areas in which a State's antiestablishment interests come more into play. Since this country's founding, there have been popular uprisings against procuring taxpayer funds to support church leaders, which was one of the hall marks of an "established" religion. Most States that sought to avoid such an establishment around the time of the founding placed in their constitutions formal prohibitions against using tax funds to support the ministry. That early state constitutions saw no pro blem in explicitly excluding *only* the ministry from receiving state dollars reinforces the conclusion that religious instruction is of a different ilk from other professions. Moreover, the entirety of the Promise Scholarship Program goes a long way toward including religion in its benefits, since it permits students to attend pervasively religious schools so long as they are accredited, and student are still eligible to take devotional theology courses under the program's current guidelines. Nothing in the Washington Constitution's history or text or in the program's operation suggests animus toward religion. Given the historic and substantial state interest at issue, it cannot be concluded that the denial of funding for vocational religious instruction alone is inherently constitutionally suspect. Without a presumption of unconstitutionality, Davey's claim must fail. The State's interest in not funding the pursuit of devotional degrees is substantial, and the exclusion of such funding places a relatively minor burden on Promise Scholars. If any room exists between the two Religion Clauses, it must be here. Pp. 718–725.

299 F. 3d 748, reversed.

REHNQUIST, C. J., delivered the opinion of the Court, in which STEVENS, O'CONNOR, KENNEDY, SOUTER, GINSBURG, and BREYER, JJ., joined. SCALIA, J., filed a dissenting opinion, in which THOMAS, J., joined, *post,* p. 726. THOMAS, J., filed a dissenting opinion, *post,* p. 734.

Cont.

FIGURE 3.5 **Comparison of the U.S. Supreme Court Reporters** *Cont.*

Narda Pierce, Solicitor General of Washington, argued the cause for petitioners. With her on the briefs were *Christine O. Gregoire,* Attorney General, *William Berggren Collins,*

Ⓑ

[text omitted] [540 US 712]

GARY LOCKE, GOVERNOR OF WASHINGTON, et al., Petitioners

v

JOSHUA DAVEY

540 US 712, 158 L Ed 2d 1, 124 S Ct 1307

[No. 02-1315]

Argued December 2, 2003. Concluded February 25, 2004.

Decision: Washington state's postsecondary education scholarship program, under which students were not permitted to use scholarship to pursue degree in devotional theology, held not to violate First Amendment's free exercise clause.

SUMMARY

The state of Washington established a scholarship program in order to assist students from low- and middle-income families with the cost of postsecondary education. In accordance with Washington's state constitution—which included a provision that no public money or property was to be appropriated for or applied to any religious worship, exercise, or instruction—the scholarship program did not permit students to use the scholarship to pursue "a degree in theology."

[text omitted]

On certiorari, the United States Supreme Court reversed. In an opinion by REHNQUIST, CH. J., joined by STEVENS, O'CONNOR, KENNEDY, SOUTER, GINSBURG, AND BREYER, JJ., it was held that the scholarship program's exclusion with respect to students pursuing n degree in devotional theology did not violate the First Amendment's free exercise clause, for:

(1) The scholarship program was not presumptively unconstitutional.

(2) It was not true that because the scholarship program funded training for all secular professions, the state had to fund training for religious professions.

(3) There was nothing in the history or text of the relevant provision of the state constitution, or in the operation of the scholarship program, that suggested animus towards religion.

(4) The state's interest in not funding the pursuit of devotional degrees was substantial.

(5) The exclusion of such funding placed a relatively minor burden on scholarship recipients.

SCALIA, J., joined by THOMAS, J., dissenting, expressed the view that (1) when a state makes a public benefit generally available, that benefit becomes part of the baseline against which burdens on religion are measured; (2) when the state withholds that benefit from some individuals solely on the basis of religion, the state violates the free exercise clause; and (3) in the case at hand, (a) no field of study but religion was singled out for disfavor, and (b) the student was seeking not a special benefit to which others were not entitled, but only the right to direct his scholarship to his chosen course of study, a right that every other scholarship recipient enjoyed.

THOMAS, J., dissenting, expressed the view that (1) the study of theology did not necessarily implicate religious devotion or faith, and (2) on the assumption that the state of Washington denied scholarships to only students who pursued a degree in devotional theology, the dissenting opinion of SCALIA, J., was correct in the case at hand.

HEADNOTES

Classified to United States Supreme Court Digest, Lawyers' Edition

Constitutional Law § 983—religious freedom—state scholarship program—exclusion for theology degree

1a-1d. With respect to a state that maintained a postsecondary-education scholarship program, but—in accordance with a provision in the state's constitution that no public money or properly was to be appropriated for or applied to any religious worship, exercise, or instruction—did not permit students to use the scholarship to pursue a degree in devotional theology, such an exclusion from the otherwise inclusive program did not violate the free exercise clause of the Federal Constitution's First Amendment, for: (1) The scholarship program was not

[text omitted]

Cont.

FIGURE 3.5 **Comparison of the U.S. Supreme Court Reporters** *Cont.*

RESEARCH REFERENCES

15A Am Jur 2d, Colleges and Universities § 40; 16A Am Jur 2d, Constitutional Law § 434
USCS, Constitution, Amendment 1
L Ed Digest, Constitutional Law § 983
L Ed Index, Private or Parochial Schools; Religious Freedom; Scholarships; Theological Students

Annotations:

Establishment and free exercise of religion clauses of Federal Constitution's First Amendment as applied to public aid to sectarian schools or students at such schools---Supreme Court cases. 153 L Ed 2d 991.

Supreme Court cases involving establishment and freedom of religion clauses of Federal Constitution. 37 L Ed 2d 1147.

The Supreme Court and the right of free speech and press. 93 L Ed 1151, 2 L Ed 2d 1706, 11 L Ed 2d 1116, 16 L Ed 2d 1053, 21 L Ed 2d 976.

SHEPARD'S® Citations Service. For further research of authorities referenced here, use SHEPARD'S to be sure your case or statute is still good law and to find additional authorities that support your position. SHEPARD'S is available exclusively from LexisNexis®.

APPEARANCES OF COUNSEL ARGUING CASE

Narda Pierce argued the cause for petitioners.
Jay A. Sekulow argued the cause for respondent.
Theodore B. Olson argued the cause for the United States, as amicus curiae, by special leave of court.
Summaries of Briefs; Names of Participating Attorneys, p 1005, infra.

SYLLABUS BY REPORTER OF DECISIONS

Washington State established its Promise Scholarship Program to assist academically gifted students with post-secondary education expenses. In accordance with the State Constitution, students may not use such a scholarship to pursue a devotional theology degree. Respondent [text omitted]

Ⓒ

540 U.S. 712, 158 L.Ed.2d 1
Gary LOCKE, Governor of Washington;
et al., Petitioners,
v.
Joshua DAVEY.
No. 02-1315.
Argued Dec. 2, 2003.
Decided Feb. 25, 2004.

Background: College student sued governor and officials of state's higher education coordinating board alleging that statute prohibiting state aid to any post-secondary student pursuing degree in theology, and board's implementing policy, violated Free Exercise Clause. The United States District Court for the Western District of Washington, Barbara J. Rothstein, Chief Judge, granted summary judgment for defendants, and the United States Court of Appeals for the Ninth Circuit, Rymer, Circuit Judge, 299 F.3d 748, reversed. Defendants appealed.

Holding: The Supreme Court, Chief Justice Rehnquist, held that state did not violate Free Exercise Clause by refusing to fund devotional theology instruction.

Judgment of Court of Appeals reversed.

Justice Scalia filed a dissenting opinion in which Justice Thomas joined.

Justice Thomas filed a dissenting opinion.

1. Constitutional Law ⚿84.1

There are some state actions permitted by the Establishment. Clause but not required by the Free Exercise Clause. U.S.C.A. Const.Amend.1.

2. Colleges and Universities ⚿2
Constitutional Law ⚿84.5(6)

State did not violate Free Exercise Clause by denying scholarship to student pursuing devotional theology degree at private college, pursuant to state statute prohibiting state aid to any post-secondary student pursuing degree in theology, and higher education coordinating board's implementing policy; state's refusal to fund theological instruction, although it funded training for secular professions, was not presumptively unconstitutional, since state's interest in not funding theological instruction was not based on hostility to religion, but rather was to avoid establishment of religion, and it placed relatively minor burden on students. U.S.C.A. Const.Amend. 1; West's RCWA Const. Art. 1, § 11; West's RCWA 2SB.10.814; Wash. Admin. Code § 250-80-020(12)(f).

3. Constitutional Law ⚿84.6(2)

For purposes of the Establishment Clause, the link between government funds and religious training is

Cont.

FIGURE 3.5 **Comparison of the U.S. Supreme Court Reporters** *Cont.*

broken by the independent and private choice of recipients. U.S.C.A. Const.Amend. 1.

West Codenotes

Negative Treatment Reconsidered
West's RCWA 28B.10.814.

*Syllabus**

Washington State established its Promise Scholarship Program to assist academically gifted students with postsecondary education expenses. In accordance with the State Constitution, Students may not use such a scholarship to pursue a devotional theology degree. Respondent Davey was awarded a Promise Scholarship and chose to attend Northwest College, a

[text omitted]

299 F.3d 748, reversed.

REHNQUIST, C.J., delivered the opinion of the Court, in which STEVENS, O'CONNOR, KENNEDY, SOUTER, GINSBURG, and BREYER, JJ., joined. SCALIA, J., Filed a dissenting opinion, in which THOMAS, J., joined, *post,* p. 1315. THOMAS, J., filed a dissention opinion, *post,* p. 1820

Narda Pierce, Olympia, WA for Petitioners.

Jay A. Sekulow, Virginia Beach, VA, for Respondent.

Theodore B. Olson for United States as amicus curiae, by special leave of the Court, Washington D.C., supporting the respondent.

[text omitted]

For U.S. Supreme Court Briefs, see:

2003 WL 21715040 (Pet.Brief)

2003 WL 22187308 (Resp.Brief)

2003 WL 22489887 (Reply.Brief)

Chief Justice REHNQUIST delivered the opinion of the Court.

⊥715The State of Washington established the promise Scholarship Program to assist academically gifted students with postsecondary education expenses. In accordance

[text omitted]

circuits and one federal circuit court (in the District of Columbia). Many of the states' federal trial courts are divided into districts as well. (See Figure 1.5 for a map of the federal circuits and district courts.)

Because of the E-Government Act of 2008, all cases are published whether they are considered precedential or not. In the past, the only cases published were the ones the court deemed to have precedential value. However, that has changed with the E-Government Act. Now all cases are available for review, spurring a debate among jurists, attorneys, and legal professionals as to the use of these so-called unpublished cases. ThomsonWest's immediate response to the issue was to create a new reporter known as the *Federal Appendix (Fed. Appx.)* in 2001. This reporter contains only unpublished federal cases. Treatment of these cases is determined by the individual court or the persuasive talents of an attorney.

PRACTICE TIP

Citing the *Federal Appendix* reporter in an assignment may be prohibited by the rules of the court. However, if you do find an unpublished case that may be an important precedent for a client, bring the case to your supervising attorney's attention.

A New Debate: Published versus Unpublished Cases—What's a Legal Professional to Do?

A turning point for case publication was 2001 with the E-Commerce Act. Now all federal courts are required to publish all cases regardless of the precedential value of the case. For the first time, case decisions that were exchanged between only the parties involved were suddenly accessible to the public. Published cases often retain such words as "precedential" or "published" on the top of the first page of the case. This is distinguished from a case that is not considered precedent setting, which will have the notation "unpublished" or "nonprecedential" on the front pages.

The debate arises on a number of fronts. First, the fact that the case is now published and available although it is "technically" unpublished poses some interesting ethical issues for attorneys. Some would argue that even though a case is considered nonprecedential, if it supports a client's case an attorney should be able to use it. The rules of professional responsibility require attorneys to zealously represent their client and perform adequate legal research in furtherance of the client's position. If an attorney cannot use or cite a case because it is unprecedential and considered unpublished, a major dilemma arises. Is this a violation of the rules of professional responsibility? What are the limits of that responsibility?

Even the federal circuit courts of appeals have differing views of the use of unpublished cases. A new federal rule of appellate procedure, Rule 32.1, offers specific circumstances when unpublished cases can be used. Figure 3.6 provides the text and

FIGURE 3.6 **Federal Appellate Rule 32.1 Addressing Citation of Unpublished Opinions**

Source: Reprinted with permission of ThomsonWest.

Federal Rules of Appellate Procedure Rule 32.1, 28 U.S.C.A.

United States Code Annotated Currentness
Federal Rules of Appellate Procedure (Refs & Annos)
Title VII. General Provisions
Rule 32.1, Citing Judicial Dispositions

(a) **Citation Permitted.** A court may not prohibit or restrict the citation of federal judicial opinions, orders, judgments, or other written dispositions that have been:

(i) designated as "unpublished," "not for publication," "non-precedential," "not precedent," or the like; and

(ii) issued on or after January 1, 2007.

(b) **Copies Required.** If a party cites a federal judicial opinion, order, judgment, or other written disposition that is not available in a publicly accessible electronic database, the party must file and serve a copy of that opinion, order, judgment, or disposition with the brief or other paper in which it is cited.

CREDIT(S)

(Added Apr. 12, 2006, eff. Dec. 1, 2006.)

ADVISORY COMMITTEE NOTES

2006 Adoption

Rule 32.1 is a new rule addressing the citation of judicial opinions, orders, judgments, or other written dispositions that have been designated by a federal court as "unpublished," "not for publication," "non-precedential," "not precedent," or the like. This Committee Note will refer to these dispositions collectively as "unpublished" opinions.

Rule 32.1 is extremely limited. It does not require any court to issue an unpublished opinion or forbid any court from doing so. It does not dictate the circumstances under which a court may choose to designate an opinion as "unpublished" or specify the procedure that a court must follow in making that determination. It says nothing about what effect a court must give to one of its unpublished opinions or to the unpublished opinions of another court. Rule 32.1 addresses only the *citation* of federal judicial dispositions that have been *designated* as "unpublished" or "non-precedential"—whether or not those dispositions have been published in some way or are precedential in some sense.

Subdivision (a). Every court of appeals has allowed unpublished opinions to be cited in some circumstances, such as to support a contention of issue preclusion. But the circuits have differed dramatically with respect to the restrictions that they have placed on the citation of unpublished opinions for their persuasive value. Some circuits have freely permitted such citation, others have discouraged it but permitted it in limited circumstances, and still others have forbidden it altogether.

Rule 32.1(a) is intended to replace these inconsistent standards with one uniform role. Under Rule 32.1(a), a court of appeals may not prohibit a party from citing an unpublished opinion of a federal court for its persuasive value or for any other reason. In addition, under Rule 32.1(a), a court may not place any restriction on the citation of such opinions. For example, a court may not instruct parties that the citation of unpublished opinions is discouraged, nor may a court forbid parties to cite unpublished opinions when a published opinion addresses the same issue.

Rule 32.l(a) applies only to unpublished opinions issued on or after January 1, 2007. The citation of unpublished opinions issued before January 1, 2007, will continue to be governed by the local rules of the circuits.

Subdivision (b). Under Rule 32.1(b), a party who cites an opinion of a federal court must provide a copy of that opinion to the court of appeals and to the other parties, unless that opinion is available in a publicly accessible electronic database—such as a commercial database maintained by a legal research service or a database maintained by a court. A party who is required under Rule 32.1(b) to provide a copy of an opinion must file and serve the copy with the brief or other paper in which the opinion is cited. Rule 32.1(b) applies to all unpublished opinions, regardless of when they were issued.

F. R. A. P. Rule 32.1, 28 U.S.C.A., FRAP Rule 32.1

Amendments received to 08-01-07

YOU BE THE JUDGE

A man convicted on drug charges wants to challenge his conviction. He has located a case that may be persuasive on the issue. The problem is the case is unpublished and the state of Arkansas has a prohibition against citing unpublished cases. Because he cannot use the unpublished case, he believes his due process rights have been violated. In *Weatherford v. State,* 352 Ark. 324, 101 S.W.3d 227 (2003), the court analyzed the debate over citing unpublished cases. As the court noted, in adopting its case publication rule, it "sought to achieve two goals—a reduction in the volume of published opinions and a reduction in the amount of time devoted to opinion writing. The justification for the first goal lies simply in the undeniable truth that many appellate court opinions are of no precedential value. Of course, like snowflakes, no two cases are exactly alike. But, for the purpose of selective publication, the question is whether the factual differences between one case and another are of precedential value." *Id.* at 233. As the debate continues, review the *Weatherford* case. What are the leading cases on the issue? What circuits have led the debate on the issue? What rule did the court rely upon in reaching its result and why?

advisory committee notes of this rule. Little guidance is given as to the precedential value of unpublished opinions, only that they may be cited.

But this is only a federal court rule of procedure. It does not address the issue for state courts. Many states, such as California, prohibit the use of unpublished cases, while others are still on the fence. Be mindful when you locate an unpublished case that would help promote a client's interest. Bring the case to your attorney's attention. She will have to decide how to use the case and reconcile it not only with the rules of court but the state's rules of professional responsibility. For your part, be sure to always conduct thorough and adequate research even if that research produces some challenging professional and ethical issues.

Subject-Specific Reporters

There are also several reporters in the West system that print only those federal decisions relating to a specific topic. The *Federal Rules Decisions* (cited as *F.R.D.*) contains decisions relating to the *Federal Rules of Civil Procedure, Federal Rules of Criminal Procedure,* and other rule-related cases. Due to the wealth of cases being decided on procedural issues, ThomsonWest in 1938 began publishing these cases separately.

West's *Bankruptcy Reporter* (cited as *B.R.*) contains decisions of the federal bankruptcy courts and other courts that relate to bankruptcy matters from 1980. Even cases from all the federal appellate courts, including the U.S. Supreme Court, are reprinted in this reporter.

Since 1983, cases from the Federal Court of Claims are printed in ThomsonWest's *Federal Claims Reporter* (formerly the *United States Claims Court Reporter*). Like the *Bankruptcy Reporter,* cases from all the federal appellate courts are reprinted in this reporter.

A reporter that contains both cases and other primary sources of law is West's *Social Security Reporting Service.* This reporter contains cases involving social security issues from all the federal courts, including the U.S. Supreme Court. Cases from state appellate courts dealing with a social security issue also are reported. A unique feature of this reporter is that it provides in separate bound volumes administrative rules and regulations along with any changes as well as statutes relating to social security.

Since the area of education produces a high volume of cases, West began publishing in 1982 the *Education Law Reporter*. This reporter covers only selected case decisions from both the federal and state courts. Unique to this reporter is that it does provide articles on education—a secondary source.

Starting in 1992, West began collecting cases from the U.S. Court of Veterans Appeals in one reporter. This reporter is the *Veterans Appeals Reporter* where only federal cases involving U.S. veterans are provided.

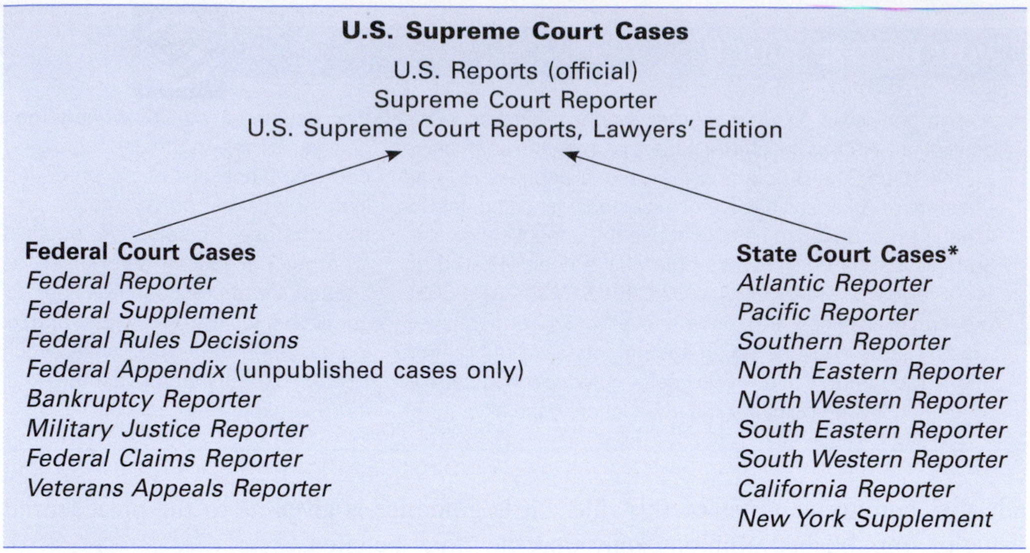

FIGURE 3.7
Diagram of the National Reporter System

U.S. Supreme Court Cases
U.S. Reports (official)
Supreme Court Reporter
U.S. Supreme Court Reports, Lawyers' Edition

Federal Court Cases
Federal Reporter
Federal Supplement
Federal Rules Decisions
Federal Appendix (unpublished cases only)
Bankruptcy Reporter
Military Justice Reporter
Federal Claims Reporter
Veterans Appeals Reporter

State Court Cases*
Atlantic Reporter
Pacific Reporter
Southern Reporter
North Eastern Reporter
North Western Reporter
South Eastern Reporter
South Western Reporter
California Reporter
New York Supplement

*Regional reporters: Many states have official reporters separate from regional reporters. Verify state rules.

The final specialized reporter is the *Military Justice Reporter.* This reporter contains cases from the U.S. Court of Appeals for the Armed Services from 1978 to the present. That court of appeals reviews military courts-martial proceedings. The U.S. military justice system is a completely separate system with its own rules and regulations primarily governed by the Uniform Code of Military Justice.

All these West reporters utilize the key number/digest system. They also provide brief summaries of the cases as do all the other reporters in the National Reporter System. Figure 3.7 is a diagram of some of the National Reporter System.

American Law Reports (*A.L.R.*) as a Reporter

In the previous chapter we mentioned that *American Law Reports* also acts as a reporter. The *A.L.R.* series publishes full texts of selective state and federal court decisions. These case decisions are presently located at the end of the volume and since *A.L.R.* is published by ThomsonWest, all finding tools related to the case are cited as well.

Other Unofficial Reporters

Although the West and *A.L.R.* systems are by far the most important unofficial reporters, there are other unofficial reporters that exist or have existed in the past in various jurisdictions. When doing research you must make sure that you have accounted for all potential sources of cases, including other reporter systems. This can be accomplished by conferring with your local legal librarian or your supervising attorney, by referring to your citation manual, which lists reporters for each jurisdiction, or by conducting your own thorough library search for potential sources. The latter method, although more difficult, will provide you with useful exposure to the law library.

Looseleaf Services

Yet another source of case law is found in the looseleaf services, introduced in the discussion of *U.S. Law Week* in the section on Supreme Court cases. There are a large number of looseleaf services covering a wide variety of topics. Some of the major publishers are the Bureau of National Affairs (BNA); Commerce Clearing House (CCH), a Wolters Kluwer business; and Aspen Publishers. The specific format of each depends upon the publisher, the nature of the material covered, and the scope of the service.

A few generalizations apply to most looseleaf services. Each usually applies to only one topic; for example, the *Federal Securities Law Reporter* published by CCH relates only to laws regulating securities issuance and transactions. Weekly updates are usually provided in the form of prepunched supplement or replacement pages to be inserted into the binder in which the service is maintained. Coverage often extends to both state and federal cases relating to the topic, as well as applicable statutes and textual analysis. Looseleaf services are often organized in a complex but extremely effective manner, with numbered paragraphs and topical indexes. For a detailed explanation, refer to the explanatory materials that are included with each service. Often cases are summarized in the text but reprinted in full in companion looseleaf volumes; these companion volumes are organized in a manner similar to reporters, and some looseleaf services ultimately reissue them in permanent bound volumes.

Many of the cases in the looseleaf services are reprinted nowhere else, not even in the reporters of the West system. For this reason, the looseleaf services can be a valuable resource. It is convenient to have textual materials and cases and statutes from many jurisdictions all in one location and with one common system of indexing. Finally, the weekly updates often make the looseleaf services the most current source of information available.

Quick Quiz True/False Questions

1. The federal reporter that contains district court decisions is the *Federal Supplement*.
2. The *Federal Rules Decisions* and *Bankruptcy Reporter* are subject-specific reporters.
3. Looseleaf services and *American Law Reports* contain both primary and secondary sources within their pages.
4. Unpublished federal cases are located in the *Federal Reporter* as well as the *Federal Appendix*.
5. Cases from the Federal Court of Claims can be located in both the *Federal Claims Reporter* and the *Military Justice Reporter*.

THE CONTENTS OF A CASE REPORTER: WHAT'S INSIDE

Before you venture inside the library searching for case opinions, you need to have a working knowledge of the information contained within a reporter. Because ThomsonWest's National Reporter System is the most extensive, we review the contents of a reporter from one of its series—the *Federal Reporter*. Regardless of the specific jurisdiction in which a reporter is found, all ThomsonWest reporters have some common characteristics.

Name of Reporter and its Table of Contents: When you first open a reporter, you will notice the name of the reporter, its volume number, and a designation of the court(s) from which the cases within it pages were argued. Following the introductory page is a brief table of contents. In that table, the judges of the court(s) are identified, the table of cases reported, and a subsequent table showing the table of cases organized by circuit or jurisdiction, words and phrases (associated with the finding tool), texts of the opinions, and the associated key number digest references (another finding tool).

Judges of the Court: The reporter lists all the judges within the jurisdictions covered in the reporter with the date of their appointment to the bench. The section also lists where the judges are from.

Cases Reported: An alphabetical listing of all the cases reported in that volume is provided next. Each case is listed twice by the name of the plaintiff and the defendant. This affords you the opportunity to look up a case by either party. This is especially helpful when you only know the name of one party to a case. Along with the name of the case, this section provides the name of the jurisdiction from where the case originated. For example, if a case originated in Nebraska from the Eighth Circuit, you will see in a parenthetical next to the name of the case "C.A.8 (Neb.)." The page where the case appears in that volume follows the name.

A second section also entitled "Cases Reported" groups the cases located in that volume of the reporter by specific jurisdiction. For example, all the cases from the second circuit will be listed together with case name and page where the case begins within that volume.

Words and Phrases: Courts often interpret or construe words within a case, giving them a specific judicial meaning. There is a separate set of books known as *Words and Phrases* that index cases from courts that have judicially defined a particular word or phrase within a case. In this section, the words and phrases interpreted in that volume are listed with the cases, jurisdiction, and citation for ready access.

The Reported Cases: The bulk of the reporter volume contains the cases themselves. Each case is fully reported commencing with the complete name of the case, its editorial supplements, finding tools (headnotes and topic and keys from the digests), and the actual opinion as reported by the court that authored it. Each case ends with the symbol of a West key, the symbol used in the West Key Number Digest, separating it from the next case.

Key Number Digest: At the end of the reporter volume is a specialized version of the West digest topics and related keys of those cases reported in that volume. Although the West Key Number Digest is covered in later chapters, you need to be aware that reporters do contain this information. Each case reported in that volume is reduced to the particular points of law contained within the case and assigned its relevant topic and associated key number to assist with legal research.

CYBER TRIP

Go to your federal circuit court of appeals Web site. What is the location of the clerk's office? Now, proceed to the site for your state's district courts. What is the location of the district courts for your state? Which district is the "main" location for that district?

Additional Features in the *Supreme Court Reporter*: The *Supreme Court Reporter* has some important features. The parallel citation to the official *U.S. Reports* Supreme Court reporter that corresponds to the cases identified in that reporter is listed. Within its pages are all the memorandum opinions from the court. These decisions usually are simply one line, mostly denying a petition for writ of certiorari or reporting the action of the U.S. Supreme Court.

Quick Quiz True/False Questions

1. Reporters provide a list of all cases located in that particular volume.
2. Finding tools, such as *Words and Phrases* and Key Number Digest references, are provided in many reporters.
3. Some reporters, such as the *Supreme Court Reporter,* provide memorandum decisions.
4. All jurisdictions allow unpublished cases to be cited.
5. There are no uniform rules for presenting or citing unpublished decisions in federal and state courts.

CYBER TRIP

Locate your state's highest appellate court Web site and locate a decision from the last year that addressed a contract or tort issue.

PRACTICAL CONSIDERATIONS: CITATIONS AND THE INTERNET

Cases are posted so quickly on the Internet that they do not have citations. This means that for many "hot off the press" cases, no volume and page have been assigned. Until the court issues its *final* edited version of the case, a month or two could pass without the ability to formulate a formal citation. In this instance, *The Bluebook* and *ALWD Manual* will be the guide. Usually in these instances information such as the name of the case, the court, and the date the case was decided is sufficient until the specific volume and page numbers are determined. Westlaw and

THE E-FACTOR

Most state and federal courts maintain websites where they publish recently decided cases, as well as court rules and other important information. Many of these web sites offer direct access to case decisions within minutes of their publication. We have already mentioned the United States Supreme Court website www.supremecourtus.gov/, which provides case information in PDF format along with the rules of court and briefs of parties.

However, the U.S. federal courts have a general website, which links all the federal courts. The site is located at www.uscourts.gov/courtlinks. On the general website is a directory to narrow your search to a particular court. Once you have located the appropriate court, click the Enter button and you will be directed to that court's website. Each of the United States circuit courts of appeals have their own web sites. You can also directly access a particular court by searching for it using an Internet search engine. For example, www.ca3.uscourts.gov provides access to the Third Circuit Court of Appeals. You could access its court decisions, the rules of court, including newly posted amendments to the Third Circuit Local Appellate Rules, brief requirements, orders of the court, and many other important sources of information.

Similarly, federal districts have websites that can be accessed either from www.uscourts.gov or the court's direct website. For instance, if you wanted to locate the Northern District of Georgia United States District Court, you would enter www.gand.uscourts.gov and all the information pertaining to that federal district court would be listed. Try a search engine, such as Google, Yahoo! or any of the many others to locate information on a federal court.

Although not as advanced as the federal court system, many state courts post information on Web sites as well. Information from a state's highest court and intermediate courts of appeals is often available. Decisions are often updated daily with corresponding rules of court listed as well. A feature of many of the state court sites, especially the state Supreme Court Web sites, is a chart of that state's court system. Take the time to see what's on them.

LexisNexis provide citations to new case decisions and if access is possible, cite to one of those Web sites. Citations to Westlaw and LexisNexis include the following information:

Westlaw: Name of the case, docket number, year case decided, the abbreviation for Westlaw—WL—followed by the Westlaw law case report number and a parenthetical with the court, complete date, including the year. *Doe v. Doe,* No. 07-1111, 2007, WL 576749 (D. N.J. December 21, 2007).

LexisNexis: Include the same information as Westlaw except use the corresponding information from LexisNexis along with the reference LEXIS rather than WL. The citation is *Doe v. Doe,* No. 07-1111, 2007 LEXIS 35891 (D. N.J. December 21, 2007). (Note: This is a fictitious citation.)

When using a new case that does not have citation information, prepare sufficient copies of the case for the judge and opposing counsel, as suggested in the Ethics Alert.

Additionally, courts also may have rules for presenting cases that have been published only in electronic format. Review your local rules of court for guidance. A court decision may be dispositive of your case, but if you are the only one who can find or has access to it, the court may prohibit using the case out of fairness to all the parties.

PRACTICE TIP

Slip decisions are posted on Westlaw and LexisNexis with a citation corresponding to that fee-based service. When you see a case cite with the reporter designation as "WL" that means it is from Westlaw; when you see a case cite with the designation "LEXIS" or "LX," that is the LexisNexis citation. Review a citation manual for proper citation form.

Summary

The common law is based upon the English legal system, which is steeped in the customs and practices of society. Case decisions are created from the common law and in their written form, common law is case law. Common law is important as it guides judges in making their decisions. An important doctrine that is the fabric of the American legal system is the principle of *stare decisis. Stare decisis* stands for the principle that previously decided cases should be followed by other courts creating a precedent. These principles provide stability in both our legal and court systems.

Equally important is the principle of judicial review. Created in *Marbury v. Madison,* this principle allows courts to review and declare acts of Congress, acts of the executive, and acts of states unconstitutional. Courts have the ultimate final review.

Cases are contained in reporters and located through their citation. The two main guides for citation rules are *The Bluebook* and *ALWD Manual*. Each provides detailed information on the rules of citation.

There are reporters for all the courts. The Supreme Court reporters are *U.S. Reports, Supreme Court Reporter,* and the *Lawyers' Edition* of the *U.S. Supreme Court Reports.* These reporters are followed by the federal case reporters, which are the *Federal Reporter, Federal Supplement, Federal Rules Decisions, Federal Appendix,* and a number of specialized reporters.

State reporters are located in a regional reporter or a state official reporter or both. The regional reporters are part of the National Reporter System published by ThomsonWest. The regional reporters are the *Southern, South Eastern, South Western, North Eastern, North Western, Pacific,* and *Atlantic*. Two states have reporters only containing their cases: *New York Supplement* and the *California Reporter.*

Regardless of the name of the reporter, when citing a case, the official reporter citation must be used. When the official reporter is unavailable, star-paging enables a researcher to cite from the unofficial reporter. Symbols, such as an upside-down "T" or brackets with page designations, are integrated within the unofficial cases, allowing the researcher to identify the exact pages from the official reporter. The same case from a different reporter is known as parallel citation.

Cases can be found in numerous other places. *American Law Reports* and looseleaf services provide alternatives to the West system. Other reporters exist that should be examined for complete research results.

Key Terms

advance sheets
case law
citation
common law
judicial opinions
judicial review
looseleaf service
official reporters
parallel citation
preemption
regional reporters
reporters
slip opinion
star-paging
unofficial reporters

Review Questions

1. Explain the significance of the common law and its relationship to case law.
2. Why is judicial review an important concept in the law?
3. What are the basic components of a case citation?
4. What is a parallel citation?
5. Why are there are three reporters for the U.S. Supreme Court?
6. What is the significance of the National Reporter System?
7. Define the difference between an official reporter and an unofficial reporter.
8. List the regional reporters from the National Reporter System.
9. Other than reporters from the National Reporter System, where can case decisions be located?
10. Identify the type of information that is contained in a case reporter?

Exercises

1. Identify the abbreviations for the following reporters.
   a. *Supreme Court Reporter*
   b. *Federal Supplement*
   c. *New York Supplement*

   d. *Bankruptcy Reporter*
   e. *Southern Reporter*
   f. *North Western Reporter*
   g. *U.S. Supreme Court Reports, Lawyers' Edition*

2. Locate the cases cited in the following list and identify the name of the case and the year the case was decided.
   a. 403 U.S. 388
   b. 180 F.3d 1022
   c. 119 N.E.2d 351
   d. 760 S.W.2d 242
   e. 127 S. Ct. 2553
   f. 245 Cal. Rptr. 449
   g. 473 S.E.2d 415
3. Identify the name of the case and the reporter in which the following cases appear.
   a. 398 F. Supp. 917
   b. 164 L. Ed. 2d 349
   c. 644 N.W.2d 354
   d. 941 S.W.2d 663
   e. 160 S.E.2d 528
   f. 402 F.3d 1039
   g. 658 A.2d 1065
4. The following cases have famous quotes associated with them. Locate the case, the justice attributed with the quote, and the page where the quote appears within the case.
   a. *Brown v. Allen,* 344 U.S. 443, 73 S. Ct. 397, 97 L. Ed. 469 (1953): "We are not final because we are infallible, but we are infallible only because we are final. That truly places the concept of judicial review in context."
   b. *Graves v. New York ex. rel. O'Keefe,* 306 U.S. 466, 59 S. Ct. 595, 83 L. Ed. 927 (1939): "[T]he ultimate touchstone of constitutionality is the Constitution itself, and not what we have said about it."
   c. *Jacobellis v. Ohio,* 378 U.S. 184, 84 S. Ct. 1676, 12 L. Ed. 2d 793 (1964): "I know it when I see it."
   d. *Reynolds v. Sims,* 377 U.S. 533, 84 S. Ct. 1362, 12 L. Ed. 2d 506 (1964): "Legislators represent people, not trees or acres. Legislators are elected by voters, not farms or cities or economic interests."
   e. *Jones v. Barnes,* 463 U.S. 745, 103 S. Ct. 3308, 77 L. Ed. 2d 987 (1983): "I cannot accept the notion that lawyers are one of the punishments a person receives merely for being accused of a crime."
   f. *Planned Parenthood v. Casey,* 505 U.S. 833, 112 S. Ct. 2791, 120 L. Ed. 2d 674 (1992): "I am 83 years old. I cannot remain on this Court forever, and when I do step down, the confirmation process for my successor well may focus on the issue before us today. That, I regret, may be exactly where the choice between two worlds will be made."
5. Identify the judge and name of the case from the following citations:
   a. 303 F. Supp. 2d 596
   b. 144 N.E.2d 530
   c. 197 S.E. 566
   d. 523 S.E.2d 651
   e. 931 S.W.2d 760
   f. 190 Cal. Rptr. 335

6. Using your state, determine the following:
   a. Does your state have a separate official reporter?
   b. What is the regional reporter for your state?
   c. What states are located in your regional reporter?
   d. Do all the states in your regional reporter have official reporters? If so, identify the state and the name of the official reporter.
7. Choose a state, other than your own, from your federal circuit court of appeals and determine whether that state has an official state reporter. If so, identify the reporter, or if it does not, identify the reporter that publishes its case decisions.
8. The firm with whom you are employed has been presented with an unusual case. During a brief period when same-sex marriages were considered to be legal in another state, Mario and his life partner, Greg, drove to that state and were married in that state. We will assume they have a valid marriage certificate, but our state does not recognize same-sex marriages. As sometimes happens, their relationship disintegrated and they are now seeking a divorce. Because of our state's position on same-sex marriage, there is no provision for a divorce action in this situation. There is certainly no statutory guidance on this question. How do you research this question? Discuss all aspects of the issue including all available legal sources, such as the type of legal sources you would use and possible jurisdictions for filing an action. Identify the reporters in your jurisdiction where the cases may be found on the topic.

PORTFOLIO ASSIGNMENT

A unique case has just landed on your desk. Your firm's client, Roland Gilbert, is from your home state of Mississippi. He states that he fathered a child, but was told by his ex-girlfriend, Serena Fox, that she could not have children. So it was a big surprise when she called him and told him he had a son. Of course, he doesn't want to pay child support. Your attorney has been following the law on this issue and has provided you with two cases from the Federal Circuit Court of Appeals for the Sixth Circuit: *Dubay v. Wells*, 506 F.3d 422 (6th Cir. 2007) and *N.E. v. Hedges*, 391 F.3d 832 (6th Cir. 2004). These cases raise some interesting arguments about *Roe v. Wade*. "If a woman has the right to choose, so should a man." Your attorney wants you to review *Dubay* and *N.E. v. Hedges*. After you retrieve copies of the cases, he wants you to highlight some of the issues and arguments raised by all the parties. On a separate sheet of paper using the headings provided below, write down all the possible issues involved. By each issue identify whether it involves a state or federal constitutional issue; a state or federal statute; or state or federal case law.

Highlights of Roland Gilbert Case Issues and Arguments

Source of Law for Client	Sources of Law against Client

Quick Quiz True/False Answers

Page 60	Page 66	Page 73	Page 81	Page 82
1. False	1. False	1. False	1. True	1. True
2. True	2. True	2. True	2. True	2. True
3. False	3. True	3. True	3. True	3. True
4. True	4. False	4. False	4. False	4. False
5. False	5. True	5. True	5. False	5. True

Chapter 4

Understanding and Briefing of Case Decisions

After completing this chapter, you will be able to:

- Distinguish between a case brief and a trial or appellate brief.
- Describe the components of a printed opinion.
- Explain the usefulness of star-paging.
- Differentiate between a majority opinion and a dissent.
- Describe the components of a case brief.
- Identify the relevant facts in an opinion.
- State the issues presented by a written opinion.
- Trace the procedural history of a case as set forth in the opinion.
- Identify the holding of the court and the disposition of the case.
- Analyze and summarize the reasoning behind an opinion.

We all know how to read. Right! But learning how to read the law requires "new" reading skills. You must learn the difference between the court's holding (rule of the case), and its reasoning (the legal resources used to support the holding). And you must learn how to summarize cases succinctly, providing the key points and highlights. Determining what's important and what's not is a skill learned over time. You will begin the process of case briefing in this chapter, building on the skills from the previous chapters.

CASE FACT PATTERN

Your supervising attorney has been retained by a major network. The network wants to televise an upcoming trial about a custody dispute between the "alleged" father of a child whose mother is a well-known political figure. The network believes it has a First Amendment right to televise the trial and files a court action against the state of New York, where the trial is to commence. Your research has revealed a recent case, *Courtroom Television Network LLC v. State,* 5 N.Y.3d 222, 833 N.E.2d 1197 (2005). After a quick review of the case, you believe this case may have significant implications in your situation. You have been provided with a copy of the case and your supervising attorney has asked you to highlight the important points for her review. She wants the opinion crystallized into a straightforward summary.

THE CASE BRIEF DISTINGUISHED

The word *brief* has two separate and distinct connotations in legal practice. First, it can refer to a document filed with a court to present the legal argument of one party in a lawsuit, citing as many cases, statutes, and other sources of law as are deemed necessary to support the argument. Such a brief is usually further identified by including the level of the court in which the brief is filed: if in the trial court, it is a *trial brief;* if an appellate court, it is an *appellate brief.* These briefs do not provide an objective discussion of the law, but rather a one-sided argument intended to persuade the court of the validity of the party's position. We discuss such briefs in some detail in later chapters.

case brief
An objective summary of the important points of a single case; a summary of a court opinion.

The word *brief* also appears in the term *case brief.* A **case brief** is an objective summary of the important points of a single case. If properly prepared, it will provide the reader with a concise abstract of the reasoning of the opinion, as well as important collateral information such as case name, citation, and identity of the parties. The key word is *objective*—the case brief should accurately reflect the meaning of the case, whether that meaning is helpful to your client or harmful.

As you might have guessed, the case brief is not a document prepared for the eyes of the court, nor is it shared with opposing parties. It is an internal document, designed to help attorneys develop an objective understanding of the impact of existing case law on the viability of their client's position. Only when such an understanding is reached can persuasive strategies be developed.

THE COMPONENTS OF A PRINTED OPINION

As you have learned, reporters are collections of printed opinions, or cases. A case brief is a summary of one of these cases. In order to understand the method of briefing a case, then, it is necessary to learn about the components of a printed opinion. You are already familiar with some of these components from the previous chapter.

Figure 4.1 reprints a full page from volume 833 of the *North Eastern 3d* (which, as you recall, is the ThomsonWest publication for some New York decisions), page 1197. For additional decisions beyond those already appearing in the *North Eastern Reporter,* the *New York Supplement* is a suggested resource. The page shown (page 1197) is the first page of our subject case, *Courtroom Television Network, LLC v. State of New York,* and it contains a wealth of information.

PRACTICE TIP

Recall that cases appear in many sources. The official reporter is designated by the state whereas the unofficial reporter is not and is a product of a particular publisher. Cases may appear in a number of unofficial reporters. The various reporters offer different research sources depending upon the publisher.

Let's start with the top line above the name of the case, identified as *A* in Figure 4.1. The notation "5 N.Y.3d 222" is a reference to the official reporter, *New York Reports,* where *Courtroom Television Network* also appears. Unofficial reporters often provide information as to the pagination in the official reporter.

Star-Paging

Recall from our discussion of reporters that star-paging appears in an unofficial reporter and is identified either by an upside-down "T" with the page noted at the bottom or embedded within the case in bracketed boldface citations. In a ThomsonWest publication, it looks like this: "⊥"; in a LexisNexis publication existed for our case, it would look like this: **[5 N.Y. 222]** The star-paging notations identified as *B* in Figure 4.1 identify the page breaks for pages 228 and 229 as they appear in the *New York Reports.* (Note: The original case from *New York Reports* had pages listing the attorneys and interested parties involved in the case. That is why there is a succession of star-paging notations on the second page of the case.) By utilizing these star-paging notations when writing a brief, the drafter can reference the page and volume of

FIGURE 4.1 A Sample Page from the *North Eastern Reporter*

Note: A: Reference to official reporter; B: Star-paging notations; C: Short-form case name with citation; D: Parallel citation; E: Full case name; F: Docket number would appear here (the case in this figure does not have a docket number); G: Court and date of decision; H: Case synopsis; I: Headnote; J: Attorneys; K: Judge.

Source: From the *North Eastern Reporter.* Reprinted with permission from ThomsonWest.

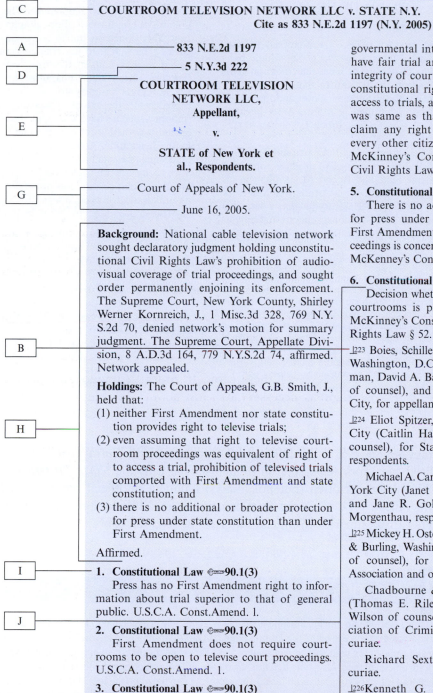

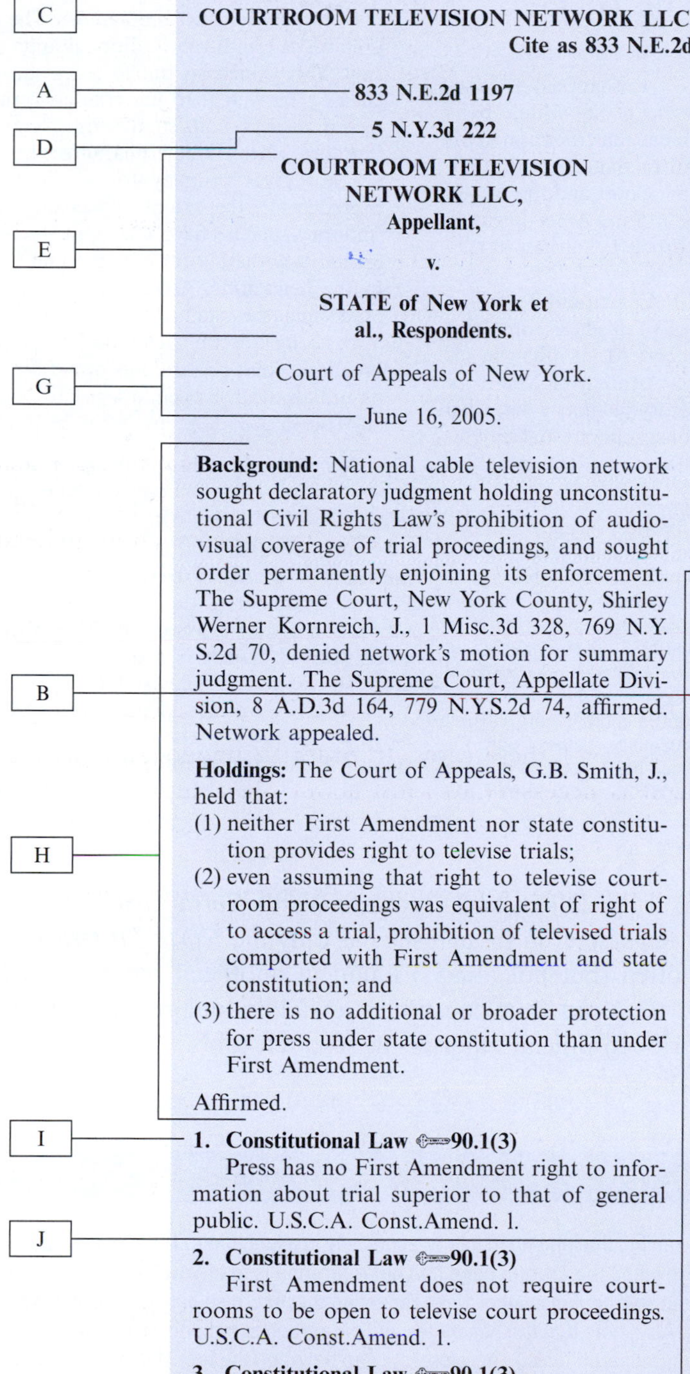

COURTROOM TELEVISION NETWORK LLC v. STATE N.Y. **1197**

Cite as 833 N.E.2d 1197 (N.Y. 2005)

833 N.E.2d 1197

5 N.Y.3d 222

COURTROOM TELEVISION NETWORK LLC,
Appellant,

v.

STATE of New York et al., Respondents.

Court of Appeals of New York.

June 16, 2005.

Background: National cable television network sought declaratory judgment holding unconstitutional Civil Rights Law's prohibition of audio-visual coverage of trial proceedings, and sought order permanently enjoining its enforcement. The Supreme Court, New York County, Shirley Werner Kornreich, J., 1 Misc.3d 328, 769 N.Y. S.2d 70, denied network's motion for summary judgment. The Supreme Court, Appellate Division, 8 A.D.3d 164, 779 N.Y.S.2d 74, affirmed. Network appealed.

Holdings: The Court of Appeals, G.B. Smith, J., held that:

(1) neither First Amendment nor state constitution provides right to televise trials;

(2) even assuming that right to televise courtroom proceedings was equivalent of right of to access a trial, prohibition of televised trials comported with First Amendment and state constitution; and

(3) there is no additional or broader protection for press under state constitution than under First Amendment.

Affirmed.

1. Constitutional Law 🔑90.1(3)

Press has no First Amendment right to information about trial superior to that of general public. U.S.C.A. Const.Amend. 1.

2. Constitutional Law 🔑90.1(3)

First Amendment does not require courtrooms to be open to televise court proceedings. U.S.C.A. Const.Amend. 1.

3. Constitutional Law 🔑90.1(3)

State constitution's free speech provision does not provide right to televise trials. McKinney's Const. Art. 1, § 8.

4. Constitutional Law 🔑90.1(3)
Trial 🔑20

Even assuming that right to televise courtroom proceedings was equivalent of right of access to trial, Civil Rights Law's prohibition of televised trials comported with First Amendment's and state constitution's free speech provisions; governmental interests in right of defendant to have fair trial and in trial court's maintaining integrity of courtroom outweighed any absolute constitutional right of press or public to have access to trials, and, since press's right of access was same as that of public, press could not claim any right or privilege not common to every other citizen. U.S.C.A. Const.Amend. 1; McKinney's Const. Art. 1, § 8; McKinney's Civil Rights Law § 52.

5. Constitutional Law 🔑90.1(3)

There is no additional or broader protection for press under state constitution than under First Amendment insofar as access to court proceedings is concerned. U.S.C.A. Const.Amend. 1; McKenney's Const. Art. 1. § 8.

6. Constitutional Law 🔑50

Decision whether or not to permit cameras in courtrooms is prerogative of state legislature. McKinney's Const. Art. 1, § 8; McKinney's Civil Rights Law § 52.

⊥223 Boies, Schiller & Flexner LLP, Armonk and Washington, D.C. (David Boies, Jonathan Sherman, David A. Barrett and George F. Carpinello of counsel), and Douglas P. Jacobs, New York City, for appellant.

⊥224 Eliot Spitzer, Attorney General, New York City (Caitlin Halligan and Gregory Silbert of counsel), for State of New York and others, respondents.

Michael A. Cardozo, Corporation Counsel, New York City (Janet L. Zaleon, Kristin M. Helmers and Jane R. Goldberg of counsel), for Robert Morgenthau, respondent.

⊥225 Mickey H. Osterreicher, Buffalo, and Covington & Burling, Washington, D.C. (Timothy L. Jucovy of counsel), for National Press Photographers Association and others, amici curiae.

Chadbourne & Parke LLP, New York City (Thomas E. Riley, Philip Pfeffer and Jennifer Wilson of counsel), for New York State Association of Criminal Defense Lawyers, amicus curiae.

Richard Sexton, New York City, amicus curiae.

⊥226 Kenneth G. Standard, Albany, Slade R. Metcalf, Kevin W. Goering, Edward J. Klaris and Aimee E. Saginaw for New York State Bar Association, amicus curiae.

Jonathan E. Gradess, Albany, and Stephanie J. Batcheller for New York State Defenders Association, amicus curiae.

McNamee, Lochner, Titus & Williams, P.C., Albany (Michael J. Grygiel and Morgan A. Costello of counsel), for Clear Channel Communications, Inc., amicus curiae.

Cont.

FIGURE 4.1 A Sample Page from the *North Eastern Reporter* *Cont.*

J

⊥227 Patterson, Belknap, Webb & Tyler LLP, New York City (Saul B. Shapiro of counsel), for ABC, Inc. and others, amici curiae.

OPINION OF THE COURT

K

G.B. SMITH, J.

The primary issue on this appeal is whether Civil Rights Law ⊥228 § 52, which bans audiovisual coverage of most courtroom proceedings,[1] violates the Federal or State Constitution. We agree with the Supreme Court and the Appellate Division that there is no First Amendment or New York Constitution, article I, § 8 right to televise a trial.

On September 5, 2001, Courtroom Television Network LLC (Court TV) filed a complaint against the State and Robert Morgenthau in his official capacity as District Attorney of New York County seeking a declaratory judgment that Civil Rights Law § 52 is unconstitutional and enjoining the prosecutor's office from enforcing it.[2]

1. Civil Rights Law § 52 provides in part: "No person, firm, association or corporation shall televise, broadcast, take motion pictures within this state of proceedings, in which the testimony of witnesses by subpoena or other compulsory process is or may be taken, conducted by a court, commission, committee, administrative agency or other tribunal in this state . . . ."
2. Since there is no pending action by the District Attorney of New York County against Court TV, there is no justiciable issue before us, and the case against the District Attorney should be dismissed.

On July 15, 2003, Supreme Court granted summary judgment to defendants stating:

> "the court declines to establish a constitutional rule in New York granting the media a right to televise court proceedings. The record is consistent with the traditional approach of New York courts to public access questions, giving great weight to fair trial concerns. The record also is consistent with New York's statutory scheme which guarantees public trials, but gives primacy to fair trial rights. Moreover, to the extent any changes to the statutory scheme have been put into experimental use, these were initiated and reviewed by the Legislature. A state constitutional rule expanding the rights of the media in New York to include the right to photograph and broadcast court proceedings would derail what is, and always has been, a legislative process." (1 Misc.3d 328, 375, 769 N.Y.S.2d 70 [2003].)

The Appellate Division affirmed. Court TV appeals as of right on constitutional grounds pursuant to CPLR 5601(b)(1).

Court TV asserts that section 52 denies it the right of access to trials guaranteed by the First Amendment to the United States Constitution and article I, § 8 of the New York State Constitution. Court TV argues further that most states permit televised trials; that New York stands alone in having an ⊥229 "absolute ban" on televised trials and that the evidence supporting access to information for the gen- [text omitted]

important language as it appears in both ThomsonWest's *North Eastern Reporter* and the official *New York Reports,* even though she has only the *North Eastern Reporter* at hand. Star-paging is often (but not always) found in unofficial reporters; it is never found in official reporters, and thus constitutes an additional reason why unofficial reporters can be superior to official reporters as research tools.

PRACTICE TIP

Sometimes star-paging can be challenging to follow, especially in a long case. The easiest way to assure yourself that you are citing the correct page for your reference is to always start at the top of the case and pinpoint the next star-paging symbol. Keep repeating that exercise and you will always have accurate official paging. Also, note that the headnotes and paragraph summaries are from the unofficial publishers. (They are your research tools.) Therefore, the gap between the first star-paging symbol and the second may be extensive. That is simply material that was not contained in the official reporter.

Shorthand Case Name

We next turn to the section we have labeled *C* in Figure 4.1. This is the shorthand form of the case name, with an instruction as to the appropriate citation. These instructions do not always conform to the rules set down in *The Bluebook, ALWD*

Manual, or the rules of the court; where there is a discrepancy, you should follow the appropriate citation manual. Plainly stated, the direction by the unofficial reporter may be "wrong," which is the case here. For example, the court rules in New York State where New York authorities are cited use the official *New York Reports* citations and not the unofficial reporter, if available. (Check with your attorney for which form to use.) In any event, this citation will appear on alternate pages.

Parallel Citation

The *D* label in Figure 4.1 shows the correct parallel citation for the case in *New York Reports, 5 N.Y.3d 222 (2005)*. Just as a reminder, this means that the case begins on page 222 of volume 5 of the third series of that reporter.

When you review the case online, you may have a number of parallel citations. If you retrieved the *Courtroom Television Network* case from Westlaw or LexisNexis, some of the parallel citations may be different as well as the star-paging formatting within the case. Let's compare each online citation source.

Westlaw: *Courtroom Television Network LLC v. State,* 5 N.Y.3d 222, 833 N.E.2d 1197, 800 N.Y.S.2d 522, 33 Media L. Rep. 1887, 2005 N.Y. Slip Op. 05120

LexisNexis: *Courtroom Television Network LLC v. State,* 5 N.Y.3d 222, 833 N.E.2d 1197, 800 N.Y.S.2d 522, 2005 N.Y. LEXIS 1260, 33 Media L. Rep. 1887.

The case can be found in *New York Reports,* the official New York reporter; the case also can be located in the *Northeastern Reporter,* the *New York Supplement,* and the *Media Law Reporter,* a looseleaf reporter service. Westlaw offers the original slip opinion citation and LexisNexis offers a citation to its online service. You are wondering which one to cite. Check your local rules of court, *The Bluebook,* or *ALWD Manual.* The point is that different legal sources offer different information.

Another important point to note is that the star-paging system within online legal sources is different. The online version of the case provides multiple star-paging references. It denotes one star * for the first legal source, two stars ** for the second source, three stars *** for the third source, and so on. In Figure 4.2 notice the Westlaw page with the different numbered star sources. The first represents the *New York Reports,* followed by the *Northeastern Reporter* and finally, the *New York Supplement* source. The same holds true in Figure 4.3 using the LexisNexis source.

PRACTICE TIP

Familiarize yourself with the different legal reporting sources, including the online legal research sources. You never know what sources will be available to you on the job. Be flexible.

caption
The full name of the case, together with the docket number, court, and date of the decision.

Full Name of Case

E in Figure 4.1 is the full name of the case, identifying all the parties and their roles (that is, Plaintiff or Defendant; Appellant or Respondent). The full name, together with the docket number, court, and date of the decision, is called the **caption** (labels *E, F,* and *G* combined). Notice the names of the parties. The name of the Plaintiff/Appellant is Courtroom Television Network LLC. The name is in capital letters. That signals to the reader to use only that name when using the citation of the case. However, the name of the Defendant/Appellee, State of New York, is a bit different. Only the word "State" is in capital letters. The case guides you on how to cite the name of the case. The general rule is that if the court of the state decides the opinion, then only use the word "State" (or any other reference such as Commonwealth) to refer to the named state. If a case is decided by another court, state or federal, refer specifically to the name of the state. Therefore, if the state of New Jersey decided our case, the citation would be *Courtroom Television Network LLC v. New York*. However, consult your citation manual for the proper form.

PRACTICE TIP

The names of the party designations often change during the appeal process. The individual or entity bringing the appeal may be called the Appellant or Petitioner. Conversely, the party responding to the appeal may be called the Appellee or Respondent. Your jurisdiction establishes the appropriate party designations.

FIGURE 4.2 **Westlaw Page of *Courtroom Television Network LLC v. State***

Source: From the Westlaw Page of *Courtroom Television Network LLC v. State.* Reprinted with permission from ThomsonWest.

833 N.E.2d 1197
5 N.Y.3d 222, 833 N.E.2d 1197, 800 N.Y.S.2d 522, 33 Media L. Rep. 1887, 2005 N.Y. Slip Op. 05120
(Cite as: 5 N.Y.3d 222, 833 N.E.2d 1197)

Courtroom Television Network LLC v. State N.Y., 2005.
Court of Appeals of New York.
COURTROOM TELEVISION NETWORK LLC,
Appellant,
v.
STATE of New York et al., Respondents.
June 16, 2005.

Background: National cable television network sought declaratory judgment holding unconstitutional Civil Rights Law's prohibition of audiovisual coverage of trial proceedings, and sought order permanently enjoining its enforcement. The Supreme Court, New York County, Shirley Werner Kornreich, J., 1 Misc.3d 328, 769 N.Y.S.2d 70, denied network's motion for summary judgment. The Supreme Court, Appellate Division, 8 A.D.3d 164, 779 N.Y.S.2d 74, affirmed. Network appealed.

Holdings: The Court of Appeals, G.B. Smith, J., held that:

(1) neither First Amendment nor state constitution provides right to televise trials;
(2) even assuming that right to televise courtroom proceedings was equivalent of right of access to trial, prohibition of televised trials comported with First Amendment and state constitution; and
(3) there is no additional or broader protection for press under state constitution than under First Amendment.

Affirmed.
West Headnotes
[1] Constitutional Law 92 ⚿90.1(3)

⚿92 Constitutional Law
⚿92V Personal, Civil and Political Rights
⚿92k90 Freedom of Speech and of the Press
⚿92k90.1 Particular Expressions and Limitations
⚿92k90.1(3) k. Interference with Judicial Proceedings; Contempt; Publicity. Most Cited Cases

Press has no First Amendment right to information about trial superior to that of general public. U.S.C.A. Const.Amend. 1.

[2] Constitutional Law 92 ⚿90.1(3)

⚿92 Constitutional Law
⚿92V Personal, Civil and Political Rights
⚿92K90 Freedom of Speech and of the Press
⚿92k90.1 Particular Expressions and Limitations
⚿92K90.1(3) k. Interference with Judicial Proceedings; Contempt; Publicity. Most Cited Cases

First Amendment does not require courtrooms to be open to televise court proceedings. U.S.C.A. Const.Amend. 1.

[3] Constitutional Law 92 ⚿90.1(3)

⚿92 Constitutional Law
⚿92V Personal, Civil and Political Rights
⚿92k90 Freedom of Speech and of the Press
⚿92k90.1 Particular Expressions and Limitations
⚿92k90.1(3) k. Interference with Judicial Proceedings; Contempt; Publicity. Most Cited Cases

State constitution's free speech provision does not provide right to televise trials. McKinney's Const. Art. 1, § 8.

[4] Constitutional Law 92 ⚿90.1(3)

⚿92 Constitutional Law
⚿92V Personal, Civil and Political Rights
⚿92k90 Freedom of Speech and of the Press
⚿92k90.1 Particular Expressions and Limitations
⚿92k90.1(3) k. Interference with Judicial Proceedings; Contempt; Publicity. Most Cited Cases

Even assuming that right to televise courtroom proceedings was equivalent of right of access to trial, Civil Rights Law's prohibition of televised trials comported with First Amendment's and state constitution's free speech provisions; governmental interests in right of defendant to have fair trial and in trial court's maintaining integrity of courtroom outweighed any absolute constitutional right of press or public to have access to trials, and, since press's right of access was same as that of public, press could not claim any right or privilege not common to every other citizen. U.S.C.A. Const. Amend. 1; McKinney's Const. Art. 1, § 8; McKinney's Civil Rights Law § 52.

Trial 388 ⚿20

⚿388 Trial
⚿388III Course and Conduct of Trial in General
⚿388k20 k. Publicity of Proceedings. Most Cited Cases.

[5] Constitutional Law 92 ⚿90.1(3)

⚿92 Constitutional Law
⚿92V Personal, Civil and Political Rights
⚿92k90 Freedom of Speech and of the Press
⚿92k90.1 Particular Expressions and Limitations
⚿92k90.1(3) k. Interference with Judicial Proceedings; Contempt; Publicity. Most Cited Cases

There is no additional or broader protection for press under state constitution than under First Amendment insofar as access to court proceedings is concerned. U.S.C.A. Const.Amend. 1; McKinney's Const. Art. 1, § 8.

[6] Constitutional Law 92 ⚿50

⚿92 Constitutional Law
⚿92III Distribution of Governmental Powers and Functions
⚿92III(A) Legislative Powers and Delegation Thereof
⚿92k50 k. Nature and Scope in General. Most Cited Cases

Decision whether or not to permit cameras in courtrooms is prerogative of state legislature. McKinney's Const. Art. 1, § 8; McKinney's Civil Rights Law § 52.

*****523** Boies, Schiller & Flexner LLP, Armonk and Washington, D.C. (David Boies, Jonathan Sherman, David A. Barrett and George F. Carpinello of counsel), and Douglas P. Jacobs, New York City, for appellant.

Eliot Spitzer, Attorney General, New York City (Caitlin Halligan and Gregory Silbert of counsel), for State of New York and others, respondents.

Michael A. Cardozo, Corporation Counsel, New York City (Janet L. Zaleon, Kristin M. Helmers and Jane R. Goldberg of counsel), for Robert Morgenthau, respondent.

*****524** Mickey H. Osterreicher, Buffalo, and Covington & Burling, Washington, D.C. (Timothy L. Jucovy of counsel), for National Press Photographers Association and others, amici curiae. Chadbourne & Parke LLP, New York City (Thomas E. Riley, Philip Pfeffer and Jennifer Wilson of counsel), for New York State Association of Criminal Defense Lawyers, amicus curiae.

Richard Sexton, New York City, amicus curiae.

Kenneth G. Standard, Albany, Slade R. Metcalf, Kevin W. Goering, Edward J. Klaris and Aimee E. Saginaw for New York State Bar Association, amicus curiae.

Jonathan E. Gradess, Albany, and Stephanie J. Batcheller for New York State Defenders Association, amicus curiae.

McNamee, Lochner, Titus & Williams, P.C., Albany (Michael J. Grygiel and Morgan A. Costello of counsel), for Clear Channel Communications, Inc., amicus curiae.

Patterson, Belknap, Webb & Tyler LLP, New York City (Saul B. Shapiro of counsel), for ABC, Inc. and others, amici curiae.

***227 **1199 OPINION OF THE COURT**

G.B. SMITH, J.

The primary issue on this appeal is whether ***228** Civil Rights Law § 52, which bans audiovisual

[text omitted]

FIGURE 4.3 **Lexis Page of *Courtroom Television Network LLC v. State***

Source: Reprinted with permission of LexisNexis.

Courtroom Television Network LLC, Appellant, v. State of New York et al., Respondents.

No. 88

COURT OF APPEALS OF NEW YORK

5 N.Y.3d 222; **833 N.E.2d 1197;** 800 N.Y.S.2d 522; 2005 N.Y. LEXIS 1260; 33 Media L. Rep. 1887

April 27, 2005, Argued;
June 16, 2005, Decided

PRIOR HISTORY: Appeal, on constitutional grounds, from an order of the Appellate Division of the Supreme Court in the First Judicial Department, entered June 22, 2004. The Appellate Division affirmed an order and judgment (one paper) of the Supreme Court, New York County (Shirley Werner Kornreich, J.; op 1 Misc. 3d 328, 769 N.Y.S.2d 70), which had denied plaintiff's motion for partial summary judgment, granted the motions by defendants State of New York, George E. Pataki, and Eliot Spitzer for summary judgment, searched the record and granted summary judgment to defendant Robert Morgenthau, declared that Civil Rights Law § 52, on its face, is not unconstitutional under the United States Constitution First Amendment, and declared that Civil Rights Law § 52, on its face, is not unconstitutional under New York Constitution, article I, § 8.

Courtroom Tel. Network LLC v State of New York, 8 A.D.3d 164, 779 N.Y.S.2d 74, 2004 N.Y. App. Div. LEXIS 8662 (N.Y. App. Div. 1st Dep't, 2004), affirmed.

DISPOSITION: Order affirmed, with costs.

HEADNOTES: Courts—Audiovisual Coverage of Judicial Proceedings—Ban against Coverage Not Unconstitutional

Civil Rights Law § 52, which bans audiovisual coverage of most courtroom proceedings, does not violate either United States Constitution First Amendment or New York Constitution, article I, § 8. The First Amendment guarantees the press and the public a right of access to trial proceedings, but not the right to televise those proceedings. Although the public acquires information about trials chiefly through the press and electronic media, the press is not imbued with any special right of access. Civil Rights Law § 52 does not prevent the press, including television journalists, from attending trials and reporting on the proceedings; it merely restricts the means that can be used in order to gather news. Nor is there any additional or broader protection under New York Constitution, article I, § 8, than under the First Amendment insofar as access to court proceedings is concerned. Rather, the authority to decide whether or not to permit cameras in the courtroom has been constitutionally delegated to the Legislature.

JUDGES: Opinion by Judge G.B. Smith. Chief Judge Kaye and Judges Ciparick, Rosenblatt, Graffeo, Read and R.S. Smith concur.

OPINION BY: G.B. SMITH

OPINION: [**1199] [***524] [*227]

G.B. Smith, J.

"the court declines to establish a constitutional rule in New York granting the media a right to televise court proceedings. The record is consistent with the traditional approach of New York courts to public access questions, giving great weight to fair trial concerns. The record also is consistent with New York's statutory scheme which guarantees public trials, but gives primacy to fair trial rights. Moreover, to the extent any changes to the statutory scheme have been put into experimental use, these were initiated and reviewed by the legislature, A state constitutional rule expanding the rights of the media in New York to include the right to photograph and broadcast court proceedings would derail what is, and always has been, a legislative process." (1 Misc. 3d 328, 375, 769 N.Y.S.2d 70 [2003].)

The Appellate Division affirmed. Court TV appeals as of right on constitutional grounds pursuant to CPLR 5601 (b) (1).

[***525] Court TV asserts that section 52 denies it the right of access to trials guaranteed by the First Amendment to the United States Constitution and article I, § 8 of the New York State Constitution. Court TV argues further that most states permit televised trials, that New York stands alone in having an [*229] "absolute ban" on televised trials and that the evidence supporting access to information for the general [**1200] public far outweighs any attendant problems of having cameras in the courtroom. New York State counters that there is no First Amendment right to televised trials, and that the concerns of Court TV are more appropriately directed to the legislature than to the courts. The State additionally argues that allowing cameras in the courtroom is a discretionary policy determination that may be made by the Legislature.

I. First Amendment

The First Amendment to the United States Constitution guarantees the press and the public a right of access to trial proceedings, Without the right to attend trials, "which people have exercised for centuries, important aspects

Cont.

FIGURE 4.3 Lexis Page of *Courtroom Television Network LLC v. State Cont.*

of freedom of speech and 'of the press could be eviscerated'" (*Richmond Newspapers, Inc. v Virginia,* 448 U.S. 555, 580, 65 L. Ed. 2d 973, 100 S. Ct. 2814 [1980]; *see also Globe Newspaper Co. v Superior Court, County of Norfolk,* 457 U.S. 596, 605, 73 L. Ed. 2d 248, 102 S. Ct. 2613 [1982]; *Press-Enterprise Co. v Superior Court of Cal., Riverside Cty.,* 464 U.S. 501, 510, 78 L. Ed. 2d 629, 104 S. Ct. 819 [1984] [*Press Enterprise I*]; *Press-Enterprise Co. v Superior Court of Cal. County of Riverside,* 478 U.S. 1, 9, 92 L. Ed. 2d 1, 106 S. Ct. 2735 [1986] [*Press Enterprise II*]).

Though the public acquires information about trials chiefly through the press and electronic media, the press is not imbued with any special right of access. Rather, the media possesses "the same right of access as the public . . . so that they may report what people in attendance have seen and heard" (*Richmond Newspapers,* 448 U.S. at 573). Thus, the press has "no right to information about a trial superior to that of the general public" (*Nixon v Wilmer Communications Inc.,* 435 U.S. 589, 609, 55 L. Ed. 2d 570, 98 S. Ct. 1306 [1978]), nor any right to information greater than the public (see *Houchins v KQED, Inc.,* 438 U.S. 1, 15, 57 L. Ed. 2d 553, 98 S. Ct. 2588 [1978]).

Civil Rights law § 52 does not prevent the press, including television journalists, from attending trials and reporting on the proceedings. What they cannot do under the statute is bring cameras into the courtroom. This is not a restriction on the openness of court proceedings but rather on what means can be used in order to gather news. The media's access is thus guaranteed. But it does not extend to a right to televise those proceedings (*Westmoreland v Columbia Broadcasting Sys., Inc.,* 752 F.2d 16, 23 (2d Cir 1984]). "There is a long leap . . . between a public right under the First Amendment to attend trials and a public right under the First Amendment to see a given trial televised" (*id.*).

[*230] *Estes v Texas* (381 U.S. 532, 14 L. Ed. 2d 543, 85 S. Ct. 1628 [1965]) is the seminal case on televising a trial. Five Justices concurred in the Court's holding that the petitioner had been denied due process because of the televising and broadcasting of his trial and held there was no constitutional right of the press to

[text omitted]

PRACTICE TIP

When cases have multiple parties, the name in capital letters designates which party to use in the case name of the citation.

PRACTICE TIP

Often Latin references are used in cases. In the *Courtroom Television* case, the caption uses the term *et al.*; this term means "and others" and is frequently used when omitting the names of the parties in a case because it is unnecessary or too cumbersome. Never use *et al.* in a case citation.

Another issue you may encounter in case names is abbreviations. There are rules as to when and how to abbreviate certain words. For example, if your case had the name "Hospital" in it, some court rules and manuals would allow the abbreviation "Hosp." Or, if the name of one of the parties contained the word "corporation," abbreviating the word as "corp." may be appropriate. Under both *The Bluebook* and the *ALWD Manual,* a listing of permissible abbreviations is noted. Review a citator manual for the correct use of any abbreviation in a case name.

Party designations differ depending upon the type of case. You may observe a caption with the words "In Re," which is a typical designation in a bankruptcy case. "In Re" means "regarding" and is used to denote "in the matter of" that particular party, such as a bankruptcy case. Other party designations include "Ex Rel," which is the Latin abbreviation for "ex relatione." You will see this abbreviation in a caption when one party acts as a representative of another. Additionally, you may see a caption that only identifies the parties by initials. This practice is common in juvenile cases or other sensitive matters when the court or the parties determine that revealing a party's name may cause legal, psychological, or even physical consequences.

Another practice that is common when parties do not want to be identified is to use a pseudonym, such as in the case of *Roe v. Wade.* The person who brought the case was not named "Roe." Because of the sensitive nature of the issues brought before the court, the individual's identity was protected. Similarly, you may see the party designation of "Doe," which is also a way to protect a party's identity or designate a party unknown to a litigant. This is used to protect a **statute of limitations** problem when all the parties to an action are unknown. If you see a party designation in a case that is unfamiliar to you, either look it up in a law dictionary or ask your supervising attorney for guidance. Figure 4.4 identifies examples of different types of captions you may encounter.

Docket Number, Court, and Date

The *G* label provides the full name of the court that rendered the opinion, and the date of rendering. In this case the Court of Appeals of New York, its highest court, handed down its decision on June 16, 2005.

FIGURE 4.4
Examples of Different Caption Styles

IN THE SUPREME COURT OF TEXAS

No. 05-0249

IN RE DISCOUNT RENTAL, INC., RELATOR

ON PETITION FOR WRIT OF MANDAMUS

IN THE UNITED STATES BANKRUPTCY COURT
FOR THE DISTRICT OF DELAWARE

IN RE:	)	Chapter 11
	)	
PLANET HOLLYWOOD	)	Case Nos. 99-3612 (MFW)
INTERNATIONAL, et al.	)	through 99-3637 (MFW)
	)	
Debtors.	)	(Jointly Administered Under
	)	Case No. 99-3612 (MFW))
	)	

STATE of Utah, Plaintiff and Appellee,
v.
Troy LABRUM, Defendant and Appellant.
No. 970099–CA.
Court of Appeals of Utah.
May 7, 1998
Rehearing Denied July 15, 1998.

IN THE SUPREME COURT OF TEXAS

NO. 06-0686

JANE DOE 1, INDIVIDUALLY AND AS NEXT FRIEND OF
JANE DOE 2, A MINOR CHILD, PETITIONER,
V.
PILGRIM REST BAPTIST CHURCH, RESPONDENT

ON PETITION FOR REVIEW FROM THE
COURT OF APPEALS FOR THE FIFTH DISTRICT OF TEXAS

PRACTICE TIP

New York is one of the few states, if not the only one, that designates its trial court as the "supreme court." Do not confuse this court with the U.S. Supreme Court. They are entirely different, with New York's Supreme Court cases having limited precedential value, unlike cases of the U.S. Supreme Court.

statute of limitations
Establishes the applicable time limits for filing and responding to certain claims or legal actions.

Many cases identify the docket number of the case. A **docket number** is assigned by the court to the case for its own administrative purposes. If you visited the appropriate courthouse and asked to see the file for this case, some courts require the docket number so that they could locate it in their files. This case does not identify a docket number, but the case in Figure 4.5 provides an example of a case with a docket number.

docket number
The number assigned by the court to the case for its own administrative purposes.

FIGURE 4.5
Example of a Case Caption with a Docket Number

Source: From the *Supreme Court Reporter.* Reprinted with permission from ThomsonWest.

541 U.S. 246, 158 L.Ed.2d 529
ENGINE MANUFACTURERS ASSOCIATION and Western States Petroleum Association, Petitioners,
v.
SOUTH COAST AIR QUALITY MANAGEMENT DISTRICT, et al.
No. 02–1343.
Argued Jan.14, 2004.
Decided April 28, 2004.

docket number

Synopsis

synopsis
A short paragraph summary prepared by the publisher in unofficial reporters that identifies the issue, the procedural history, and the ruling of the court in the instant case.

syllabus
A short paragraph summary in the official reporter identifying issue, procedural history, and ruling of the court; an editorial feature in unofficial reporters that summarizes the court's decision.

Item *H* in Figure 4.1 is called the **synopsis** of the case. It is an extremely short summary, prepared not by the court but by the publisher. It identifies the issue, the procedural history, and the ruling of the court in the instant case ("instant" is used in legal documents to mean *present* or *current;* this instant case is *Courtroom Television Network v. State*). The synopsis is in a sense a preview; since it is an unofficial editorial addition, it should never be formally cited, but only informally reviewed.

Sometimes a synopsis is prepared by the official reporter of decisions. Such an "official" synopsis is called a **syllabus,** as you learned in the Chapter 3 discussion of *United States Reports* (where each U.S. Supreme Court case is given a syllabus). Although "official," a syllabus is not part of the court's opinion and, like the synopsis, should never be formally relied upon or cited.

West Key Number and Headnote

PRACTICE TIP

The information identified in the case prior to the name of the judge is usually created by the publishers and is not considered the law. Everything that follows the name of the judge who wrote the opinion is the law. That's what you will use when researching an assignment.

I in Figure 4.1 identifies the West key number and headnote. You may recall that a case headnote is a paragraph summary of a point of law contained within the case. The headnote also has a topic and key number assigned by the publisher, ThomsonWest. These topics and keys are the centerpiece for the West Digest System, which is discussed in more detail in Chapter 6. The *Courtroom Television Network* case contains six headnotes, referencing the points of law discussed within the case. Notice each is numbered individually and is referenced within the case. These headnotes can be used to locate other cases that may be relevant to your research. As with the synopsis, the case headnote is used as a quick reference and is not cited as legal authority.

Although it seems as if the only publisher of cases is ThomsonWest, there are a number of publishers that do not use the West key number and headnote system. Cases published by LexisNexis sometimes refer to their headnotes as annotations, although the term *headnote* is now more of a generic term for the short paragraph summaries of the law at the beginning of a case. As a new paralegal, don't get confused with the features from all the different publishers. Virtually all have the same basic features simply with different names.

Attorneys and Judge

amicus brief
Brief filed by a nonparty to an appeal who has an interest, whether political, social, or otherwise, in the outcome of the case.

amicus curiae
Ttranslated from the Latin as a "friend of the court."

J identifies the attorneys for the parties. The plaintiff has counsel and both defendants have separate counsel representing them. However, since this case could affect many entities and have widespread implications, **amicus briefs** were filed on behalf of a number of groups that had an interest in the outcome. **Amicus curiae** means "friend of the court." In cases where there is a significant political or social issue, it is common for interested parties to file an amicus brief. Often, an amicus brief is filed in U.S. Supreme Court cases. Amicus briefs are not as common in state cases.

K in Figure 4.1 identifies the judge who was assigned to write the opinion of the court, Justice G.B. Smith. The decision as to who is assigned to write the decision is an internal court matter. Usually the more significant decisions are written by the chief justice of that court.

Text and Disposition

disposition
Appears at the end of the opinion and tells the reader how the court handled the lower court decision.

The name of the judge who wrote the opinion is followed by the text of his or her opinion. The text or body of the decision contains the detailed reasoning by which the court reached its result. That result, which appears at the end of the opinion and is often simply a word or two telling the reader who won the lawsuit and any instructions by the appellant court to the lower court as to how to handle or revise its decision, is called the court's **disposition.** The disposition in this case was that the lower court's decision was affirmed. (For full text and disposition, see Figure 4.6.)

FIGURE 4.6 **Full Text of Courtroom RV Decision**

Source: From the *North Western Reporter*. Reprinted with permission from ThomsonWest.

COURTROOM TELEVISION NETWORK LLC v. STATE N.Y. **1197**
Cite as 833 N.E.2d 1197 (N.Y. 2005)

833 N.E.2d 1197
5 N.Y.3d 222

COURTROOM TELEVISION NETWORK LLC, Appellant,

v.

STATE of New York et al., Respondents.

Court of Appeals of New York.

June 16, 2005.

Background: National cable television network sought declaratory judgment holding unconstitutional Civil Rights Law's prohibition of audio-visual coverage of trial proceedings, and sought order permanently enjoining its enforcement. The Supreme Court, New York County, Shirley Werner Kornreich, J., 1 Misc.3d 328, 769 NY. S.2d 70, denied network's motion for summary judgment. The Supreme Court, Appellate Division, 8 A.D.3d 164, 779 N.Y.S.2d 74, affirmed. Network appealed.

Holdings: The Court of Appeals, G.B. Smith, J., held that:

(1) neither First Amendment nor state constitution provides right to televise trials;

(2) even assuming that right to televise courtroom proceedings was equivalent of right of to access a trial, prohibition of televised trials comported with First Amendment and state constitution; and

(3) there is no additional or broader protection for press under state constitution than under First Amendment.

Affirmed.

1. Constitutional Law ⚷90.1(3)

Press has no First Amendment right to information about trial superior to that of general public. U.S.C.A. Const.Amend. 1.

2. Constitutional Law ⚷90.1(3)

First Amendment does not require courtrooms to be open to televise court proceedings. U.S.C.A. Const.Amend. 1.

3. Constitutional Law ⚷90.1(3)

State constitution's free speech provision does not provide right to televise trials. McKinney's Const. Art. 1, § 8.

4. Constitutional Law ⚷90.1(3)
Trial ⚷20

Even assuming that right to televise courtroom proceedings was equivalent of right of access to trial, Civil Rights Law's prohibition of televised trials comported with First Amendment's and state constitution's free speech provisions; governmental interests in right of defendant to have fair trial and in trial court's maintaining integrity of courtroom outweighed any absolute constitutional right of press or public to have access to trials, and, since press's right of access was same as that of public, press could not claim any right or privilege not common to every other citizen. U.S.C.A. Const.Amend. 1; McKinney's Const. Art. 1, § 8; McKinney's Civil Rights Law § 52.

5. Constitutional Law ⚷90.1(3)

There is no additional or broader protection for press under state constitution than under First Amendment insofar as access to court proceedings is concerned. U.S.C.A. Const.Amend. 1; McKenney's Const. Art. 1. § 8.

6. Constitutional Law ⚷50

Decision whether or not to permit cameras in courtrooms is prerogative of state legislature. McKinney's Const. Art. 1, § 8; McKinney's Civil Rights Law § 52.

⊥223 Boies, Schiller & Flexner LLP, Armonk and Washington, D.C. (David Boies, Jonathan Sherman, David A. Barrett and George F. Carpinello of counsel), and Douglas P. Jacobs, New York City, for appellant.

⊥224 Eliot Spitzer, Attorney General, New York City (Caitlin Halligan and Gregory Silbert of counsel), for State of New York and others, respondents.

Michael A. Cardozo, Corporation Counsel, New York City (Janet L. Zaleon, Kristin M. Helmers and Jane R. Goldberg of counsel), for Robert Morgenthau, respondent.

⊥225 Mickey H. Osterreicher, Buffalo, and Covington & Burling, Washington, D.C. (Timothy L. Jucovy of counsel), for National Press Photographers Association and others, amici curiae.

Chadbourne & Parke LLP, New York City (Thomas E. Riley, Philip Pfeffer and Jennifer Wilson of counsel), for New York State Association of Criminal Defense Lawyers, amicus curiae.

Richard Sexton, New York City, amicus curiae.

⊥226Kenneth G. Standard, Albany, Slade R. Metcalf, Kevin W. Goering, Edward J. Klaris and Aimee E. Saginaw for New York State Bar Association, amicus curiae.

Jonathan E. Gradess, Albany, and Stephanie J. Batcheller for New York State Defenders Association, amicus curiae.

McNamee, Lochner, Titus & Williams, P.C., Albany (Michael J. Grygiel and Morgan A. Costello of counsel), for Clear Channel Communications, Inc., amicus curiae.

⊥227 Patterson, Belknap, Webb & Tyler LLP, New York City (Saul B. Shapiro of counsel), for ABC, Inc. and others, amici curiae.

OPINION OF THE COURT

G.B. SMITH, J.

The primary issue on this appeal is whether Civil Rights Law ⊥228 § 52, which bans

Cont.

FIGURE 4.6 **The Court's Decision with Disposition** *Cont.*

prior proceedings

facts

audiovisual coverage of most courtroom proceedings,[1] violates the Federal or State Constitution. We agree with the Supreme Court and the Appellate Division that there is no First Amendment or New York Constitution, article I, § 8 right to televise a trial.

On September 5, 2001, Courtroom Television Network LLC (Court TV) filed a complaint against the State and Robert Morgenthau in his official capacity as District Attorney of New York County seeking a declaratory judgment that Civil Rights Law § 52 is unconstitutional and enjoining the prosecutor's office from enforcing it.[2] On July 15, 2003, Supreme Court granted summary judgment to defendants stating:

> "the court declines to establish a constitutional rule in New York granting the media a right to televise court proceedings. The record is consistent with the traditional approach of New York courts to public access questions, giving great weight to fair trial concerns. The record also is consistent with New York's statutory scheme which guarantees public trials, but gives primacy to fair trial rights. Moreover, to the extent any changes to the statutory scheme have been put into experimental use, these were initiated and reviewed by the Legislature. A state constitutional rule expanding the rights of the media in New York to include the right to photograph and broadcast court proceedings would derail what is, and always has been, a legislative process." (1 Misc.3d 328, 375, 769 N.Y.S.2d 70 [2003].)

The Appellate Division affirmed. Court TV appeals as of right on constitutional grounds pursuant to CPLR 5601(b)(1).

Court TV asserts that section 52 denies it the right of access to trials guaranteed by the First Amendment to the United States Constitution and article I, § 8 of the New York State Constitution. Court TV argues further that most states permit televised trials; that New York stands alone in having an ⊥229 "absolute ban" on televised trials and that the evidence supporting access to information for the general public far outweighs any attendant problems of having cameras in the courtroom. New York State counters that there is no First Amendment right to televised trials, and that the concerns of Court TV are more appropriately directed to the Legislature than to the courts. The State additionally argues that allowing cameras in the courtroom is a discretionary policy determination that may be made by the Legislature.

1. Civil Rights Law § 52 provides in part: "No person, firm, association or corporation shall televise, broadcast, take motion pictures within this state of proceedings, in which the testimony of witnesses by subpoena or other compulsory process is or may be taken, conducted by a court, commission, committee, administrative agency or other tribunal in this state . . . ."
2. Since there is no pending action by the District Attorney of New York County against Court TV, there is no justiciable issue before us, and the case against the District Attorney should be dismissed.

I. *First Amendment*

The First Amendment to the United States Constitution guarantees the press and the public a right of access to trial proceedings. Without the right to attend trials, "which people have exercised for centuries, important aspects of freedom of speech and 'of the press could be eviscerated'" (*Richmond Newspapers, Inc. v. Virginia,*. 448 U.S. 555, 580, 100 S.Ct. 2814, 65 L.Ed.2d 973 [1980]; see also *Globe Newspaper Co. v. Superior Court, County of Norfolk,* 457 U.S. 596, 605, 102 S.Ct. 2613, 73 L.Ed.2d 248 [1982]; *Press–Enterprise Co. v. Superior Court of Cal., Riverside Cty.,* 464 U.S. 501, 510, 104 S.Ct. 819, 78 L.Ed.2d 629 [1984] [*Press Enterprise I*]; *Press–Enterprise Co. v. Superior Court of Cal., County of Riverside,* 478 U.S. 1, 9, 106 S.Ct. 2735, 92 L.Ed.2d 1 [1986] [*Press Enterprise II*]).

[l] Though the public acquires information about trials chiefly through the press and electronic media, the press is not imbued with any special right of access. Rather, the media possesses "the same right of access as the public . . . so that they may report what people in attendance have seen and heard" (*Richmond Newspapers,* 448 U.S. at 573, 100 S.Ct. 2814). Thus, the press has "no right to information about a trial superior to that of the general public" (*Nixon v. Warner Comrnunications, Inc.,* 435 U.S. 589, 609, 98 S.Ct, 1306, 55 L.Ed.2d 570 [1978]), nor any right to information greater than that of the public (see *Houchins v. KQED, Inc.,* 43 U.S. 1, 15, 98 S.Ct. 2588, 57 L.Ed.2d 55: [1978]).

[2] Civil Rights Law § 52 does not prevent the press, including television journalists, from attending trials and reporting on the proceedings. What they cannot do under the statute is bring cameras into the courtroom. This is not a restriction on the openness of court proceedings but rather on what means can be used in order to gather news. The media's access is thus guaranteed. But it does not extend to a right to televise those proceedings (*Westmoreland v. Columbia Broadcasting Sys., Inc.,* 752 F.2d 16, 23 [2d Cir. 1984]). "There is a long leap . . . between a public right under the First Amendment to attend trials and a public right under the First Amendment to see a given trial televised" (*id.*).

⊥230*Estes v. Texas*, 381 U.S. 532, 85 S.Ct. 1628, 14 L.Ed.2d 543 [1965] is the seminal case on televising a trial. Five Justices concurred in the Court's holding that the petitioner had been denied due process because of the televising and broadcasting of his trial and held there was no constitutional right of the press to have access to the courtroom during a trial. The Court listed a number of concerns about the presence of cameras at the trial, including the prejudicial impact of pretrial publicity on the jurors, the impact on the truthfulness of the witnesses, responsibilities placed on the trial judge to assure a fair trial and the impact on the petitioner. The Court wrote, "A defendant on trial for a specific crime is entitled to his day in court, not in a stadium, or a city or nationwide arena" (381 U.S. at 549, 85 S.Ct. 1628; see also *Sheppard v. Maxwell,* 884

Cont.

FIGURE 4.6 **The Court's Decision with Disposition** *Cont.*

U.S. 333, 355, 86 S.Ct. 1507, 16 L.Ed.2d 600 [1966]). The Court did acknowledge that "the ever-advancing techniques of public communication and the adjustrnent of the public to its presence may bring about a change in the effect of telecasting upon the fairness of criminal trials" (381 U.S. at 551–552, 85 S.Ct. 1628).

Today, television has become a "commonplace . . . affair in the daily life of the average person" (*id.* at 595, 85 S.Ct. 1628 [Harlan, J., concurring]). While the Supreme Court has revisited the effects of televised coverage of trials, concluding that such broadcasts are not a per se violation of fair trial rights, it has never deviated from its holding that " 'there is no constitutional right to have (live witness) testimony recorded and broadcast'" (*Chandler v. Florida,* 449 U.S. 560, 569, 101 S.Ct. 802, 66 L. Ed.2d 740 [1981], quoting *Nixon v. Warner Communications, Inc.,* 435 U.S. 589, 610, 98 S. Ct. 1306, 55 L.Ed.2d 570 [1978]).[3]

⊥231Thus, it is dear that the Federal Constitution does not require courtrooms to be open to televise court proceedings.

II. *The New York State Constitution*

[3] The New York State Constitution, similarly, does not provide a right to televise trials. Article I, § 8 states, "Every citizen may freely speak, write and publish his or her sentiments on all subjects, being responsible for the abuse of that right; and no law shall be passed to restrain or abridge the liberty of speech or of the press." Court TV argues that Civil Rights Law § 52 is an unlawful "restraint on the press." It concedes, however, that this Court has not "explicitly" recognized "a state constitutional right to public and press access to trial court proceedings," While we have in certain circumstances interpreted article I, § 8 more broadly than its federal counterpart (*see O'Neill v. Oakgrove Constr.,* 71 N.Y.2d 521, 530–532, 528 N.Y.S.2d 1, 523 N.E.2d 277 [1988] [then Judge Kaye concurring]), we decline to do so here.

In New York, the press, like the public, has a right of access to criminal proceedings (*see Matter of Westchester Rockland Newspapers v. Leggett,* 48 N.Y.2d 430, 437–438, 423 N.Y.S.2d 630, 399 N.E.2d 518 [1979]; *Matter of Gannett Co. v. De Pasquale,* 43 N.Y.2d 370, 376, 401 N. Y.S.2d 756, 372 N.E.2d 544 [1977]; *Matter of Associated Press v. Bell,* 70 N.Y.2d 32, 38, 517 N.Y.S.2d 444, 510 N.E.2d 313 [1987]). This includes access to pretrial hearings (*id.* ["We conclude, therefore, that the public and the press may have a First Amendment right of access to pretrial suppression hearings"]). Any exception to a public trial should be narrowly construed (Westchester Rockland Newspapers v. Leggett, 48 N.Y.2d at 443, 423 N.Y.S.2d 630, § 218[9][c], as amended by L. 1995, ch. 8). After each experiment, lasting approximately two to three years, the Legislature reviewed the findings and reports on audiovisual equipment in the courtroom, all of which recommended cameras in the courtroom, and, after each review, rejected the recommendation. On June 30, 1997, the Legislature and Governor allowed Judiciary Law § 218 to sunset. Thus, the ban on televised trials contained in Civil Rights Law § 52 resumed as of July 1, 1997, a ban which continues to the present. Despite the technological improvements to audiovisual equipment, which renders its presence in courtrooms less obtrusive, the Legislature has not seen fit since 1997 to amend section 52 or reenact section 218.

We will not circumscribe the authority constitutionally delegated to the Legislature to determine whether audiovisual coverage of courtroom proceedings is in the best interest of the citizens of this state. "A state constitutional rule expanding the rights of the media in New York to include the right to photograph and broadcast court proceedings would derail what is, and always has been, a legislative process" (1 Misc.3d 328, 375, 769 N.Y.S.2d 70 [2003], *supra*).

holding

For all of the foregoing reasons, we hold that Civil Rights Law § 52 is constitutional under both the First amendment to the United States Constitution and article I, § 8 of the New York State Constitution.

court's disposition

⊥235Accordingly, the order of the Appellate Division should be affirmed, with costs.

Chief Judge KAYE and Judges CIPARICK, ROSENBLATT, GRAFFEO, READ and R.S. Smith concur.

Order affirmed, with costs.

3. We note that after *Chandler,* no Federal Circuit Court has opined that the Federal Constitution guarantees the media a right to televise trials (*see e.g. Westmoreland v. Columbia Broadcasting Sys., Inc.,* 752 F.2d 16, 24 [1984]; *Whiteland Woods, L.P. v. Township of W. Whiteland,* 193 F.3d 177, 181 [3d Cir.1999] [press has no absolute light of access to a criminal trial]; *U.S. v. Edwards,* 785 F.2d 1293, 1295 [5th Cir. 1986], [First Amendment does not guarantee a positive right to televise or broadcast criminal trials]; *Conway v. United States,* 852 F.2d 187, 188–189 [6th Cir.1988] [no First Amendment right to televise judicial proceedings]; *United States v. Kerley,* 753 F.2d 617, 621 [7th Cir.1985] ["exclusion of cameras from federal courtrooms is constitutional"]; *Rice v. Kempker* 374 F.3d 675, 678 (8th Cir.2004) ["the First Amendment does not protect the use of video cameras or any other cameras or, for that matter, audio recorders in the execution chamber"]; *California First Amendment Coalition v. Woodford,* 299 F.3d 868, 877 [9th Cir.2002] [reaffirms First Amendment right of access to attend executions]; *Combined Communications Corp. v. Pinesilver,* 672 F.2d 818, 821 [10th Cir.1982] ["The First Amendment does not guarantee the media a constitutional right to televise inside a courthouse"]; *United States v. Hastings,* 695 F.2d 1278, 1280 [11th Cir.1983] [right of access does not extend to "the right to televise, photograph, record, and broadcast federal criminal trials"]).

The text of an opinion generally sets forth the facts of the case and the procedural history. It then analyzes the issues presented and, citing precedent and drawing upon applicable legal principles and logic, reaches a conclusion. The text is the heart of a case; it is from the text that analogies can be drawn to pending controversies. In *Courtroom Television Network,* the court carefully analyzes the history of the law, both federal and state, regarding the constitutional implications of the First Amendment and the rights of an accused individual to a fair trial; the court was quite clear that the law and history on this matter in New York are very settled and deliberate. The court spends a considerable amount of time carefully reviewing the case law and legislation from all angles. The law and rights involved had a detailed history with the legislature experimenting previously with "rules regarding audiovisual broadcasts of trial proceedings."

holding
That aspect of a court opinion which directly affects the outcome of the case; it is composed of the reasoning necessary and sufficient to reach the disposition.

reasoning
The court's rationale that sets forth the legal principles the court relied upon in reaching its decision.

dictum
A statement made by the court in a case that is beyond what is necessary to reach the final decision.

In analyzing the text, you should keep in mind the concepts of **holding, reasoning,** and **dictum** (plural *dicta*). Although discussed in more detail later in this chapter, these concepts are worth noting here as we analyze the information contained within a court opinion. The court's holding is that aspect of the decision which directly affects the outcome of the case; it is composed of the reasoning necessary to reach the disposition. The reasoning or rationale sets forth the legal principles the court relied upon to reach its decision or holding. Here, the court may cite the Constitution, a statute, a case opinion, or a rule or regulation to support its decision. The reasoning, in effect, is the court's legal justification for "how" and "why" it reached its conclusion. Dicta, on the other hand, are statements made by the court that are beyond what is necessary to reach the disposition. For example, if a court suggests that a different result might have been reached if certain facts had been different, such a statement is dictum; or when, as in *Courtroom Television Network,* a discussion of technological changes of public communications occurred, this is dictum (as you read *Courtroom Television Network,* you will see an example of dictum). The difference between holding and dictum is important: a holding carries the precedential force of *stare decisis,* whereas dictum serves as a nonbinding comment having no future effect on a court.

affirmed
Disposition in which the appellate court agrees with the trial court.

reversed
Disposition in which the appellate court disagrees with the trial court.

remanded
Disposition in which the appellate court sends the case back to the lower court for further action.

vacated
Disposition in which an appellate court voids the decision of the lower court.

***per curiam* decision**
A decision that reflects agreement of all the judges on the correct disposition of the case.

Turning to the end of the opinion, you will see the disposition. The disposition identifies whether the appellate court agreed or disagreed with the lower court's decision. Words such as "affirmed" or "reversed" signal how the appellate court treated the lower court decision. A case is **affirmed** when the appellate court agrees with the lower court's decision. By affirming the court's decision, the appellate court is giving its "stamp of approval" to the lower court. The decision of the lower court in *Courtroom Television Network* was affirmed, meaning that the appellate court agreed with the trial court. If the appellate court had disagreed, the decision of the lower court would have been **reversed.** Since an appellate court has the authority to change the decision of the lower court, the court must follow the directive of the appellate court whether they are in agreement with the decision or not. Sometimes an appellate court agrees with some parts of an appealed decision but disagrees with other parts, resulting in a disposition in which the decision is "affirmed in part and reversed in part." See Figure 4.7 for excerpts of differing opinions of justices in the same case, *U.S. v. Leahy.* Sometimes the disposition requires that the case be sent back to the lower court for further consideration, as would have been the case if the appellate court had reversed the trial court in *Courtroom Television Network.* Such decision has been reversed and **remanded.** When a case is remanded to the lower court, the appellate court instructs the lower court to change its decision, reform it, or have a new hearing.

Sometimes an appellate court simply voids the decision of the lower court. The disposition under these circumstances uses the term **vacated.**

Most appellate cases are decided by a panel of several judges. If all the judges agree on the correct disposition of the case, the decision is rendered ***per curiam.*** (This phrase means the court as one body.) No particular judge is designated to

FIGURE 4.7
Excerpts from *U.S. v. Leahy*
Source: From Third Circuit Court of Appeals Web site, www.ca3uscourts.gov.

SLOVITER, Circuit Judge, concurring.

I approve and join Parts I. and II. of the majority opinion. I join in the judgment of Parts III. and IV. While I believe that Judge McKee's dissent has much to commend it, in the last analysis, I join the majority because the majority opinion persuades me that restitution is not a punishment governed by the Sixth Amendment.

FISHER, Circuit Judge, with whom Judge BARRY joins, concurring in part in the judgment.

I approve and join in Parts I, II, and III of the majority opinion. I concur only in the judgment as to Part IV. I would base our holding that the imposition of restitution did not violate the Sixth Amendment right to a jury trial solely on the conclusion that restitution is not the type of criminal penalty to which the right to a jury trial attaches. As the majority opinion correctly notes, "orders of restitution have little in common with the prison sentences challenged by the defendants in Jones, Apprendi, Blakely and Booker." Maj. Op. at 19. The issue of restitution was not before the United States Supreme Court in any of those decisions, and the Supreme Court gave no indication in those decisions that the right to a jury trial applies to any form of criminal penalty other than imprisonment. Accordingly, I would not reach – and do not join – the majority's conclusion that restitution orders do not constitute an increase in punishment beyond the "statutory maximum" for the offense.

McKEE, Circuit Judge. Concurring in part and dissenting in part with Judges RENDELL, AMBRO, SMITH, and BECKER joining.

Given the Supreme Court's holding in *Libretti v. United States,* 516 U.S. 29 (1995), I agree that a judicial determination of the amount of forfeiture when imposing a criminal sentence does not violate the Sixth Amendment right to a jury trial. Although I find it difficult to reconcile *Libretti* with the Court's subsequent decisions in *Blakely v. Washington,* 542 U.S. 296 (2004), and *United States v. Booker,* 125 S. Ct. 738 (2005), any tension between *Libretti* and those cases must be resolved by the Supreme Court, as the majority explains. *See* Maj. Op. at 9 (citing *United States v. Ordaz,* 398 F.3d 236, 241 (3d Cir. 2005)). I therefore join Section II of the majority opinion. However, for the reasons set forth below, I do not agree that a judge can determine the amount of restitution under either the Mandatory Victims Restitution Act ("MVRA"), 18 U.S.C. § 3663A, or the Victim Witness Protection Act ("VWPA"), 18 U.S.C. § 3663, without violating the Sixth Amendment. Accordingly, I respectfully dissent from Section IV of the majority opinion (captioned, "Restitution and *Booker*").

Frank and Ernest

write the opinion of the court. *Per curiam* opinions are used when the principles of law are so firmly established as not to warrant further explanation or in areas of the law where the court does not seek to draw particular attention to the case. See Figure 4.8 for an example of a *per curiam* opinion. Notice the disposition in the case—reversed and remanded.

en banc decisions
Decisions made by the court as a whole because of their legal significance.

On the other hand, a court may render a decision **en banc.** This type of decision refers to a case where the entire court participates in the decision rather than a select panel. Usually courts decide cases en banc because of the legal significance of the case. The case *U.S. v. Leahy* was decided en banc by the Third Circuit Court of Appeals. See Figure 4.9.

majority opinion
An opinion where more than half of the justices agree with the decision. This opinion is precedent.

concur
To agree with the majority opinion.

concurring opinion
An opinion in which a judge who agrees with the ultimate result wishes to apply different reasoning from that in the majority opinion.

Occasionally the judges on the panel disagree about the proper disposition. In such a case the majority rules, hence the majority judges issue the binding decision of the court, written as a **majority opinion.** A judge who agrees with the majority opinion is said to **concur.** A judge who agrees with the ultimate result but wishes to apply different reasoning from that in the majority opinion can file a **concurring opinion,** which sets forth the alternative reasoning (in *Courtroom Television Network,* Chief Judge Kaye and Judges Ciparick, Rosenblatt, Graffeo, Read, and R.S. Smith concurred; since they wrote no separate opinion, they presumably agreed with the reasoning of Justice G.B. Smith's opinion).

dissent
Opinion in which a judge disagrees with the result reached by the majority.

dissenting opinion
An opinion outlining the reasons for the dissent, which often critiques the majority and any concurring opinions.

If a judge disagrees with the result reached by the majority, he or she is said to **dissent.** An opinion outlining the reasons for the dissent often critiques the majority and concurring opinions, and is known as a **dissenting opinion.** Figure 4.10 is the full opinion from *Tory v. Cochran.* In that opinion, both majority and dissenting opinions were written. Review the case to understand the reasoning behind the majority opinion and the counterviewpoint of the dissenting justices.

It is possible that an individual judge may agree with part of the majority decision and disagree with part. He or she is then said to "concur in part and dissent in part," and this judge, too, can set forth his or her reasoning in a separate opinion.

FIGURE 4.8 **A *Per Curiam* Opinion**

Source: From the U.S. Supreme Court Web site, www.supremecourtus.gov.

Cite as: 546 U. S. _____ (2005) 1

Per Curiam

SUPREME COURT OF THE UNITED STATES

ANTHONY KANE, WARDEN v. JOE GARCIA ESPITIA

ON PETITION FOR WRIT OF CERTIORARI TO THE UNITED STATES COURT OF APPEALS FOR THE NINTH CIRCUIT

No. 04–1538. Decided October 31, 2005

court opinion *per curiam*

PER CURIAM.

Respondent Garcia Espitia, a criminal defendant who chose to proceed *pro se,* was convicted in California state court of carjacking and other offenses. He had received no law library access while in jail before trial—despite his repeated requests and court orders to the contrary—and only about four hours of access during trial, just before closing arguments. (Of course, he had declined, as was his right, to be represented by a lawyer with unlimited access to legal materials.) The California courts rejected his argument that his restricted library access violated his Sixth Amendment rights. Once his sentence became final, he petitioned in Federal District Court for a writ of habeas corpus under 28 U. S. C. §2254. The District Court denied relief, but the Court of Appeals for the Ninth Circuit reversed, holding that "the lack of any pretrial access to lawbooks violated Espitia's constitutional right to represent himself as established by the Supreme Court in *Faretta* [v. *California,* 422 U. S. 806 (1975)]." *Garcia Espitia v. Ortiz,* 113 Fed. Appx. 802, 804 (2004). The warden's petition for certiorari and respondent's motion for leave to proceed *in forma pauperis* are granted, the judgment below reversed, and the case remanded.

A necessary condition for federal habeas relief here is that the state court's decision be "contrary to, or involv[e] an unreasonable application of, clearly established Federal law, as determined by the Supreme Court of the United States." 28 U. S. C. §2254(d)(1). Neither the opinion below, nor any of the appellate cases it relies on, identifies

Cont.

FIGURE 4.8 **A *Per Curiam* Opinion** *Cont.*

a source in our case law for the law library access right other than *Faretta.* See 113 Fed. Appx., at 804 (relying on *Bribiesca v. Galaza,* 215 F. 3d 1015, 1020 (CA9 2000) (quoting *Milton v. Morris,* 767 F. 2d 1443, 1446 (CA9 1985)); *ibid.* ("*Faretta* controls this case").

The federal appellate courts have split on whether *Faretta,* which establishes a Sixth Amendment right to self-representation, implies a right of the *pro se* defendant to have access to a law library. Compare *Milton, supra,* with *United States* v. *Smith,* 907 F. 2d 42, 45 (CA6 1990) ("[B]y knowingly and intelligently waiving his right to counsel, the appellant also relinquished his access to a law library"); *United States ex rel. George v. Lane,* 718 F. 2d 226, 231 (CA7 1983) (similar). That question cannot be resolved here, however, as it is clear that *Faretta* does not, as §2254(d)(1) requires, "clearly establis[h]" the law library access right. In fact, *Faretta* says nothing about any specific legal aid that the State owes a *pro se* criminal defendant. The *Bribiesca* court and the court below therefore erred in holding, based on *Faretta,* that a violation of a law library access right is a basis for federal habeas relief.

The judgment below is reversed, and the case is remanded for further proceedings consistent with this opinion.

It is so ordered.

FIGURE 4.9 ***U.S. v. Leahy* En Banc Opinion**

Source: From Third Circuit Court of Appeals Web site, www.ca3uscourts.gov.

OPINION OF THE COURT

FUENTES, Circuit Judge.

en banc decision of court

We ordered rehearing en banc in three separate appeals to determine whether the District Courts' orders of restitution and forfeiture violated defendants' Sixth Amendment right to trial by jury.

1. Background

In United States v. Paul J. Leahy, No. 03-4490, following trial, a jury found defendant Dantone, Inc. ("Dantone"), and its two senior managers, defendants Paul Leahy and Timothy Smith, guilty of engaging in, and aiding and abetting, bank fraud in violation of 18 U.S.C. § 1344.[1] Defendants' convictions stemmed from their defrauding various banks out of profits derived from Dantone's auctioning of 311 repossessed and after-lease cars on behalf of the banks. At sentencing, the District Court imposed prison sentences upon Leahy and Smith and entered orders of forfeiture in the sum of $418,657 and restitution in the sum of $408,970, jointly and

---

[1]This case was tried together with United States v. Dantone, Inc., No. 03-4560, and United States v. Timothy Smith, No. 03-4542.

Cont.

FIGURE 4.9 *U.S. v. Leahy* **En Banc Opinion** *Cont.*

severally, against all three defendants. Dantone, Leahy and Smith appeal both their convictions and the orders of forfeiture and restitution.[2]

In United States v. Kennard Gregg, No. 04-2912, after being arrested and charged for twice attempting to sell counterfeit money to a government informant, defendant Gregg pled guilty to two counts of dealing in counterfeit obligations in violation of 18 U.S.C. § 473. Gregg was sentenced to six months in prison and three years of supervised release, and ordered to pay restitution to the federal government in the amount of $350. He appeals only the restitution order.

In United States v. James C. Fallon, No. 03-4184, a jury convicted defendant Fallon of one count of wire fraud in violation of 18 U.S.C. § 1341, and three counts of mail fraud in violation of 18 U.S.C. § 1343 in connection with marketing his company's Derma Peel skin treatment without FDA approval. Fallon was sentenced to 12 months in prison and ordered to pay restitution in the amount of $55,235. Fallon appeals both his conviction and the District Court's restitution order.

In these appeals, all five of the defendants – Dantone, Leahy, Smith, Gregg and Fallon – challenge their respective restitution orders on Sixth Amendment grounds, arguing that, in accordance with United States v. Booker, 125 S. Ct. 738 (2005), the facts underlying the orders should have been submitted to a jury and established by proof beyond a reasonable doubt. Additionally, on the same grounds, Dantone, Leahy and Smith challenge their orders of forfeiture. We called for rehearing en banc to consider three sentencing issues:

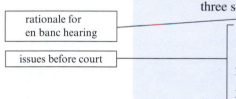

rationale for en banc hearing

issues before court

1. Whether the decision of the Supreme Court in Booker applies to forefeiture;
2. Whether orders of restitution are a criminal penalty;
3. Whether Booker applies to orders of restitution under the Victim and Witness Protection Act (the

[2]Defendants' appeal of their criminal convictions in this case, as well as in United States v. Fallon, infra will be addressed in separate opinions.

Some decisions, particularly those of the U.S. Supreme Court, may have several written opinions, with various coalitions of judges concurring and dissenting on different points. It sometimes requires a fair amount of analysis to unravel the meaning of the court's disposition in such a case. In any event, a written opinion always identifies which judges concurred and which dissented. (See Figure 4.7.)

Although most of this analysis relates to appellate opinions, trial court opinions can also be published in reporters. If a trial court opinion relates to a decision on a pending motion, the disposition will either "grant" or "deny" the motion. If the opinion is a final decision after trial, the disposition will indicate that judgment was entered for either plaintiff or defendant.

FIGURE 4.10 **Opinion from *Tory v. Cochran***

Source: From the U.S. Supreme Court Web site, www.supremecourtus.gov.

SUPREME COURT OF THE UNITED STATES

No. 03–1488

ULYSSES TORY, ET AL., PETITIONERS v. JOHNNIE L. COCHRAN, JR.

ON WRIT OF CERTIORARI TO THE COURT OF APPEAL OF CALIFORNIA, SECOND APPELLATE DISTRICT

[May 31, 2005]

JUSTICE BREYER delivered the opinion of the Court.

Johnnie Cochran brought a state-law defamation action against petitioner Ulysses Tory. The state trial court determined that Tory (with the help of petitioner Ruth Craft and others) had engaged in unlawful defamatory activity. It found, for example, that Tory, while claiming falsely that Cochran owed him money, had complained to the local bar association, had written Cochran threatening letters demanding $10 million, had picketed Cochran's office holding up signs containing various insults and obscenities; and, with a group of associates, had pursued Cochran while chanting similar threats and insults. App.38, 40–41. The court concluded that Tory's claim that Cochran owed him money was without foundation, that Tory engaged in a continuous pattern of libelous and slanderous activity, and that Tory had used false and defamatory speech to "coerce" Cochran into paying "amounts of money to which Tory was not entitled" as a "tribute" or a "premium" for "desisting" from this libelous and slanderous activity. Id., at 39, 42–43.

After noting that Tory had indicated that he would continue to engage in this activity in the absence of a court order, the Superior Court issued a permanent injunction. The injunction, among other things, prohibited Tory, Craft, and their "agents" or "representatives" from "picketing," from "displaying signs, placards or other written or printed material," and from "orally uttering statements" about Johnnie L. Cochran, Jr., and about Cochran's law firm in "any public forum." *Id.,* at 34.

Tory and Craft appealed. The California Court of Appeal affirmed. Tory and Craft then filed a petition for a writ of certiorari, raising the following question:

> "Whether a permanent injunction as a remedy in a defamation action, preventing all future speech about an admitted public figure, violates the First Amendment." Pet. for Cert. i.

We granted the petition. 542 U. S. ___ (2004).

After oral argument, Cochran's counsel informed the Court of Johnnie Cochran's recent death. Counsel also moved to substitute Johnnie Cochran's widow, Sylvia Dale Mason Cochran, as respondent, and suggested that we dismiss the case as moot. Tory and Craft filed a response agreeing to the substitution of Ms. Cochran. But they denied that the case was moot.

We agree with Tory and Craft that the case is not moot. Despite Johnnie Cochran's death, the injunction remains in effect. Nothing in its language says to the contrary. Cochran's counsel tells us that California law does not recognize a "cause of action for an injury to the memory of a deceased person's reputation," see Kelly v. Johnson Pub. Co., 160 Cal. App. 2d 718, 325 P. 2d 659 (1958), which circumstance, counsel believes, "moots" a "portion" of the injunction (the portion "personal to Cochran"). Respondent's Suggestion of Death, etc., 4 (emphasis added). But counsel adds that "[t]he [i]njunction continues to be necessary, valid and enforceable." Id., at 9. The parties have not identified, nor have we found, any source of California law that says the injunction here *automatically* becomes invalid upon Cochran's death, not even the portion personal to Cochran. Counsel also points to the "value of" Cochran's "law practice" and adds that his widow has an interest in enforcing the injunction. Id., at 11–12. And, as we understand California law, a person cannot definitively know whether an injunction is legally void until a court has ruled that it is. See *Mason v. United States Fidelity & Guaranty Co.,* 60 Cal. App. 2d 587, 591, 141 P. 2d 475, 477–478 (1943) ("[W]here the party served believes" a court order "invalid he should take the proper steps to have it dissolved"); *People v. Gonzalez,* 12 Cal. 4th 804, 818, 910 P. 2d 1366, 1375 (1996) ("[A] person subject to a court's injunction may elect whether to challenge the constitutional validity of the injunction when it is issued, or to reserve that claim until a violation of the injunction is charged as a contempt of court"). Given the uncertainty of California law, we take it as a given that the injunction here continues significantly to restrain petitioners' speech, presenting an ongoing federal controversy. See, *e.g., Dombrowski v. Pfister,* 380 U. S. 479, 486–487 (1965); *NAACP v. Button,* 371 U. S. 415, 432–433 (1963). Consequently, we need not, and we do not, dismiss this case as moot. Cf. *Firefighters v. Stotts,* 467 U. S. 561, 569 (1984) (case not moot in part because it appears from "terms" of the injunction that it is "still in force" and "unless set aside must be complied with").

Cont.

FIGURE 4.10 **Opinion from *Tory v. Cochran* *Cont.***

At the same time, Johnnie Cochran's death makes it unnecessary, indeed unwarranted, for us to explore petitioners' basic claims, namely (1) that the First Amendment forbids the issuance of a permanent injunction in a defamation case, at least when the plaintiff is a public figure, and (2) that the injunction (considered prior to Cochran's death) was not properly tailored and consequently violated the First Amendment. See Brief for Petitioners ii, iii. Rather, we need only point out that the injunction, as written, has now lost its underlying rationale. Since picketing Cochran and his law offices while engaging in injunction-forbidden speech could no longer achieve the objectives that the trial court had in mind (i.e., coercing Cochran to pay a "tribute" for desisting in this activity), the grounds for the injunction are much diminished, if they have not disappeared altogether. Consequently the injunction, as written, now amounts to an overly broad prior restraint upon speech, lacking plausible justification. See *Nebraska Press Assn. v. Stuart,* 427 U. S. 539, 559 (1976) ("[P]rior restraints on speech and publication are the most serious and the least tolerable infringement on First Amendment rights"); *Pittsburgh Press Co. v. Pittsburgh Comm'n on Human Relations,* 413 U. S. 376, 390 (1973) (a prior restraint should not "swee[p]" any "more broadly than necessary"). As such, the Constitution forbids it. *See Carroll v. President and Comm'rs of Princess Anne,* 393 U. S. 175, 183–184 (1968) (An "order" issued in "the area of First Amendment rights" must be "precis[e]" and narrowly "tailored" to achieve the "pin-pointed objective" of the "needs of the case"); see also *Board of Airport Comm'rs of Los Angeles v. Jews for Jesus, Inc.,* 482 U. S. 569, 575, 577 (1987) (regulation prohibiting "all 'First Amendment activities' " substantially overbroad).

We consequently grant the motion to substitute Sylvia Dale Mason Cochran for Johnnie Cochran as respondent. We vacate the judgment of the California Court of Appeal,and we remand the case for proceedings not inconsistent with this opinion. If, as the Cochran supplemental brief suggests, injunctive relief may still be warranted, any appropriate party remains free to ask for such relief. We express no view on the constitutional validity of any such new relief, tailored to these changed circumstances, should it be entered.

It is so ordered.

JUSTICE THOMAS, with whom JUSTICE SCALIA joins, dissenting.

I would dismiss the writ of certiorari as improvidently granted. We granted the writ, as the Court notes, to decide

> "[w]hether a permanent injunction as a remedy in a defamation action, preventing all future speech about an admitted public figure, violates the First Amendment." Pet. for Cert. i; *ante,* at 2.

Whether or not Johnnie Cochran's death moots this case, it certainly renders the case an inappropriate vehicle for resolving the question presented. The Court recognizes this, ante, at 3, but nevertheless vacates the judgment below, ante, at 4. It does so only after deciding, as it must to exercise jurisdiction, that in light of the uncertainty in California law, the case is not moot. Ante, at 2–3; *ASARCO Inc. v. Kadish,* 490 U. S. 605, 621, n. 1 (1989) (when a case coming from a state court becomes moot, this Court "lack[s] jurisdiction and thus also the power to disturb the state court's judgment"); see also *City News & Novelty, Inc. v. Waukesha,* 531 U. S. 278, 283–284 (2001).

In deciding the threshold mootness issue, a complicated problem in its own right, the Court strains to reach the validity of the injunction after Cochran's death. Whether the injunction remains valid in these changed circumstances is neither the reason we took this case nor an important question, but merely a matter of case-specific error correction. Petitioners remain free to seek relief on both constitutional and state-law grounds in the California courts. And, if the injunction is invalid, they need not obey it: California does not recognize the "collateral bar" rule, and thus permits collateral challenges to injunctions in contempt proceedings. *People v. Gonzalez,* 12 Cal. 4th 804, 818, 910 P. 2d 1366, 1375 (1996) (a person subject to an injunction may challenge "the constitutional validity of the injunction when it is issued, or . . . reserve that claim until a violation of the injunction is charged as a contempt of court"). The California courts can resolve the matter and, given the new state of affairs, might very well adjudge the case moot or the injunction invalid on state-law grounds rather than the constitutional grounds the Court rushes to embrace. As a prudential matter, the better course is to avoid passing unnecessarily on the constitutional question. See *Ashwander v. TVA,* 297 U. S. 288, 345–348 (1936) (Brandeis, J., concurring).

The Court purports to save petitioners the uncertainty of possible enforcement of the injunction, and thereby to prevent any chill on their First Amendment rights, by vacating the decision below. But what the Court gives with the left hand it takes with the right, for it only invites further litigation by pronouncing that "injunctive relief may still be warranted," conceding that "any appropriate party remains free to ask for such relief," and "ex-press[ing] no view on the constitutional validity of any such new relief." Ante, at 4. What the Court means by "any appropriate party" is unclear. Perhaps the Court means Sylvia Dale Mason Cochran, Cochran's widow, who has taken his place in this suit. Or perhaps it means the Cochran firm, which has never been a party to this case, but may now (if "appropriate") intervene and attempt to enjoin the defamation of a now-deceased third party. The Court's decision invites the doubts it seeks to avoid. Its decision is unnecessary and potentially self-defeating. The more prudent course is to dismiss the writ as improvidently granted. I respectfully dissent.

CYBER TRIP

Locate a case decided within the past year from your federal circuit court of appeals and identify all the components of the case; now locate the same case on Westlaw or LexisNexis and compare the different components of the case.

PRACTICE TIP

Your attorney(s) will always want to know whether the case is still good law. Attach a copy of the citator page to the case you are briefing to your supervising attorney. Let him have the opportunity to review the case for himself, especially if something in the citator page warrants further investigation. This practice will exhibit your thoroughness and show your professionalism.

A Quick Note: Universal Citation Paragraph Notations and Headnote Notations

Within some case opinions, you will notice paragraph designations similar to the ones noted in Figure 4.11. These designations are in those state cases which use the universal citation format. A universal citation is a form used by a number of jurisdictions that identifies the name of the case, year of the decision, court abbreviation, sequentially assigned opinion number, and the notation "U" if the opinion is unpublished. The format is the same, regardless of the jurisdiction, hence the term *universal citation.* In the universal citation format, the paragraph of your legal reference must be cited in your legal document. States such as North Dakota, Vermont, Wyoming, and New Mexico use a universal citation format. If you practice in or are involved in a case that uses the universal citation format, be sure you properly cite your legal authorities to the court. Many jurisdictions are adopting this citation format. (For more thorough discussion of universal citations, consult Chapter 14.)

Additionally, you will also observe a bracket number before a number of paragraphs within the case. (See Figure 4.6) These are the headnote paragraph references. Using the *Courtroom Television Network* case as our guide, notice headnotes 1 and 2 begin on page 1200. Headnote 3 begins on page 1201. Sometimes you will see more than one headnote number associated with a paragraph in a case. This means that a "group" of headnotes are discussed in the section of the case. So, if you are only interested in the point of law contained in headnote 3, you can immediately review that section of the case with a bracketed number [3] to determine whether that point of law is what you need for your research. Use caution when jumping to the relevant headnote section within the case. Do not use this shortcut method as a means to avoid reading the case. Remember, it is a helping tool and should be used to determine relevancy and not as a means to sidestep your work.

Quick Quiz True/False Questions

1. All case opinions have star-paging in them.
2. Party designations change throughout the appellate process.
3. A *per curiam* opinion is written on behalf of the entire court with no particular judge assigned to the case.
4. Headnotes are part of the official text of a court opinion.
5. The procedural history and disposition in a case are the same.

THE COMPONENTS OF A CASE BRIEF

Rather than simply recite and define the components of a case brief, in this section we take you step by step through the preparation of a comprehensive case brief form, *Courtroom Television Network v. State* (the finished product appears as Figure 4.13 at the end of this chapter).

Updating the Case

Before you begin any case brief, you must verify that the case or cases you are briefing are still good law. You wouldn't want to spend your time briefing a case only to learn that it is "overruled." A good practice is to update all your cases either through Shepard's Citator or KeyCite before you begin reading or briefing your case. Both Shepard's and KeyCite provide a mechanism to determine whether the case you are reviewing is still good law. Simply stated, has the case you have chosen been overruled by a court? The usefulness of the citator services cannot be overstated. This concept is discussed in detail in Chapter 7, but it is worth noting as it will become an integral part of what you will do when you brief a case.

FIGURE 4.11 **Paragraph Designations for Universal Citation Formats**

Source: From *Atlantic Digest, 2nd Series.* Reprinted with permission from ThomsonWest.

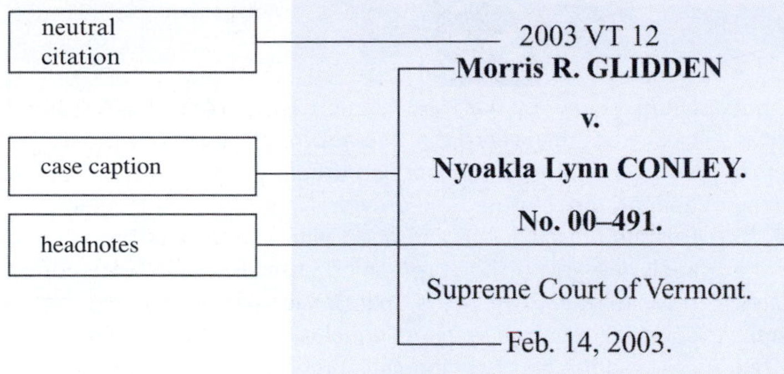

2003 VT 12

Morris R. GLIDDEN

v.

Nyoakla Lynn CONLEY.

No. 00–491.

Supreme Court of Vermont.

Feb. 14, 2003.

Maternal grandmother filed request for visitation. The Windham Family Court, Mary Miles Teachout, J., granted temporary visitation and subsequently denied father's motion for reconsideration of visitation award. Father appealed. The Supreme Court, Skoglund, J., held that: (1) statutory provision governing grandparent visitation was not in violation of a parent's due process rights by not having any absence or consideration to a parent's decision regarding child-grandparent contact, and (2) trial court, in applying statutory provision governing grandparent visitation, impermissibly infringed on father's right to decide what visitation was in his child's best interests by not giving due deference to father's decision regarding grandparent-child contact, and this violated father's right to due process.

Reversed.

1. Child Custody 🔑921(3)

An appellate court reviews an order granting visitation to determine whether the court exercised its discretion on grounds that are clearly unreasonable or untenable.

2. Constitutional Law 🔑48(1)

When considering the constitutionality of a statute, a court begins by presuming that the legislative enactment is constitutional.

3. Constitutional Law 🔑48(1)

In the absence of clear and irrefragable evidence that a statute infringes the paramount law, a court will not strike down a statute as unconstitutional.

4. Constitutional Law 🔑48(1)

If a court can construe the statute in a manner that meets constitutional requirements, it will do so unless the statute's plain language precludes it. [text omitted]

[1–4]. ¶-11. We review an order granting visitation to determine whether the court exercised its discretion on grounds that are clearly unreasonable or untenable. *Cleverly v. Cleverly*, 151 Vt. 351, 355–56, 561 A.2d.99, 102 (1989). When considering the constitutionality of a statute we begin by presuming that the legislative enactment is constitutional. *In re Proceedings Concerning a Neglected Child*, 129 Vt. 234, 240–41, 276 A.2d 14, 18 (1971). In the absence of "clear and irrefragable evidence that [the statute] infringes the paramount law," we will not strike down a statute as unconstitutional. *Id.* Moreover, if we can construe the statute in a manner that meets constitutional requirements, we will do so unless the statute's plain language precludes it. *In re Montpelier & Barre R.R.* 135 Vt. 102, 103–04, 369 A.2d 1379, 1380 (1977). Therefore, we examine Vermont's grandparent visitation statute in the context of the visitation order at issue in this appeal to determine whether the court abused its discretion by applying the statute in a manner that infringes on Glidden's right to raise Amanda without interference by the state.

[5–8] ¶-12. The United States Supreme Court has "long recognized that freedom of personal choice in matters of marriage and family life is one of the liberties protected by the Due Process Clause of the Fourteenth Amendment." *Cleveland Bd. of Educ. v. LaFleur,* 414 U.S. 632, 639–40, 94 S.Ct. 791, 39 L.Ed.2d 52 (1974). The interest of a parent in the custody, care, and control of his child may be the oldest of the fundamental liberty interests our federal constitution protects. *Troxel,* 530 U.S. at 65, 120 S.Ct. 2054; *In re S.B.L.,* 150 Vt. 294, 303, 553 A.2d 1078, 1084 (1988). The state must generally show a compelling interest "before it encroaches upon the private realm of family life." *In re Proceedings Concerning a Neglected Child,* 130 Vt. 525, 530, 296 A.2d 250, 253 (1972). Indeed, there is a "presumption that fit parents act in the best interests of their children." *Troxel,* 530 U.S. at 68, 120 S.Ct. 2054. "[S]o long as a parent adequately cares for his or her children (i.e., is fit), there will normally, be no reason for the State to inject itself into the private realm of the family to further question the ability of that parent to make the best decisions concerning the rearing of that parent's children." *Id.* at 68–69, 120 S.Ct. 2054. [text omitted]

YOU BE THE JUDGE

Not only is updating the validity of a case important, but performing your own research adequately is critical as well. Do not rely upon the opinion of others as the sole source of your research. A young assistant U.S. attorney learned this the hard way in *United States v. Vastola*, 25 F.3d 164 (3d Cir. 1994). At issue was the interpretation of a wiretapping statute and at what point the statute required information to be sealed in an investigation. The assistant U.S. attorney conducted extensive legal research, but reached a "mistaken" conclusion as to the status of the law, causing a critical misstatement of the law to the court. Under review by the Third Circuit Court of Appeals, it was clear from the record that the attorney had sought the assistance of her supervisor and others as to the interpretation of the statute. All provided incorrect information. Despite her diligence and good faith attempts to properly apply the law in the wiretapping case, the court was not sympathetic. Review the *Vastola* case. What facts did the court rely upon to reach its conclusion? What Third Circuit case did the court distinguish and why? Was the result affected by the conduct of the attorney's supervisors? Is the result just? Why or why not?

PRACTICE TIP

Invest in a law dictionary. Many of the legal terms in a case are new and unfamiliar. You will need a dictionary by your side, at least in the beginning, until you have mastered basic legal language.

Reading the Case

Updating of the case is complete, and now you must begin the process of case briefing. You cannot brief a case until you understand it, and you cannot understand it until you read it. Furthermore, when you read it, you should read the entire case, from start to finish. This might seem obvious, and indeed it should be, but it is a basic rule too often honored in the breach. Resist the temptation to skim, to rely on the editor's synopsis, to rely on the headnotes, or to search for the disposition without reading the court's underlying reasoning. There are problems ahead for those who think that they don't have the time to read the whole case or can get everything they need from the first and last page. Indeed, as we discuss, in *Courtroom Television Network*, you will see excellent examples of what a close reading can reveal.

Remember also that one reading is rarely enough for anyone and certainly not enough for a beginning paralegal. At a minimum, you should read the case once to develop a general understanding of the obvious points and a second time to pick out the more subtle points. You should probably read it a third time to verify the points you found in the first two readings; constantly refer back to the case for specifics as you prepare your case brief. Before proceeding with this chapter, read *Courtroom Television Network v. State* with care. Now, read it again!

Identification of the Case

The first component of a case brief is, of course, to identify the case. This is done in our case brief both at the top of the page and in the citation section:

Case Brief—Courtroom Television Network LLC v. State

Citation:

Courtroom Television Network LLC v. State, 5 N.Y.3d 833 (2005)

Courtroom Television Network LLC v. State, 5 N.Y.3d 833 N.E.2d 1197, 800 N.Y.S.2d 522 (2005) (Depending on the citation rules or the state in which you are citing the case, a parallel citation format may be appropriate.)

PRACTICE TIP

Copy all cases you intend to brief or give to your attorney. Some attorneys do not want to rely on anyone else's interpretation of a case without at least the opportunity, if they choose, to review the case as well. They might not brief it; they might only review salient points in the case. The case you forget to copy invariably is the case your attorney asks to review. Therefore, simply copy all the cases you intend to present to your supervising attorney.

Parties

The parties section of our case brief identifies who brought the case, to whom it was brought against, and who appealed it. The parties are as follows:

> **Parties:**
>
> *Courtroom Television Network LLC* (plaintiff/appellant); State of New York (defendant/respondent); Robert Morgenthau as the New York County District Attorney (defendant/respondent). [Note: The identities of the respondents are not readily apparent from the citation. The listing of the attorneys section for the case does reference representation for the New York County District Attorney. The case only mentions the District Attorney as a party respondent in the introduction in the formal opinion.]

The identity of the plaintiff is clear and also the appellant.

It is not clear, however, exactly who are the defendants. First look at the caption of the case. It would seem that the State of New York is the defendant/appellant. However, the caption refers to the defendants and uses the term *et al.;* the only hint is in the section listing the attorneys and who they represent at the beginning of the case. Consequently, there appear to be two other named defendants in this case.

As it turns out, these issues do not have any impact on the court's decision. Nevertheless, two lessons should be learned. First, as we emphasize at great length in later chapters, it is extremely important to express yourself clearly in every legal document you draft. Second, you have to read with great attention to detail. Any discrepancy or vagueness in a case opinion can give you an opening to distinguish a case cited by your opponent; conversely, it could be used by your opponent to discredit a case cited by you. You must analyze opinions with great care.

PRACTICE TIP

A shorthand notation of a party's name is appropriate as long as you include the notation in a parenthetical reference next to the name you are abbreviating.

Facts

The **facts** that should be included in a case brief are those which are relevant and necessary to gain a full and accurate understanding of the impact of the court's decision. Our case brief reads as follows:

> **Facts:**
>
> On September 5, 2001, Court Television (Court TV) filed a complaint against the State of New York and the District Attorney for New York County, Robert Morgenthau. The plaintiff was seeking a declaratory judgment that the New York's Civil Rights Law, specifically, section 52, is unconstitutional. The basis for the challenge was that New York State prevents cameras, audiovisual, broadcasting, and other forms of media communication in the courtroom when testimony of witnesses by subpoena or any other compulsory process is being taken by a court or court-like tribunal. Court TV asserts that the ban on televised trials violates its right to access in accordance with the First Amendment and New York State Constitution. The State of New York responded by asserting that no constitutional right to televised trials, under either the U.S. Constitution or New York State Constitution, exists. They further assert that the issue of cameras in the courtroom is legislative, not constitutional.

The key facts in this decision are clear and straightforward. Most cases are not so easy. Often, you will have to extrapolate from the case the "key" facts and disregard those facts that are merely incidental to the case and do not have a direct correlation to the result. For example, the court spends a few paragraphs discussing the arguments of the plaintiffs. Sometimes these points are not important to the result of the case and are absent from the case brief. However, since in this case the facts are mainly legal issues, they are essential to the court's review. Important facts affecting the decision of the court are considered to be **relevant** and **material**. Material facts are pivotal in the court's weighing of their relevance to the case. If the fact was omitted, what effect would it have on the outcome? Is the fact essential to the court's conclusion? If a fact is unimportant, it is considered **immaterial** or incidental; if unnecessary to understand the court's decision, it is considered irrelevant. The concepts of relevancy and materiality are not entirely distinct; there is a certain amount of overlap in meaning and usage.

facts
Significant objective information in a case.

relevant fact
A fact that is significant to a case and its holding.

material fact
A fact that is essential to the case and its holding; a fact that, if different, might alter the entire outcome of the case.

immaterial fact
A fact that is unimportant to the case and its holding.

PRACTICE TIP

Always italicize any reference to a case name, whether a shorthand version or the complete formal citation.

Prior Proceedings

prior proceedings
The procedural history of a case before the case reached the present court.

In order to understand the meaning of an opinion, the reader must first understand the procedural history of the case. Often the procedural setting is a crucial consideration in evaluating the extent to which the opinion can be applied to your client's case. The **prior proceedings** section of our case brief for *Courtroom Television Network* reads as follows:

> **Prior proceedings:**
> Plaintiff filed an action for declaratory judgment seeking section 52 of the New York Civil Rights Law unconstitutional against the State of New York and the District Attorney of New York County. Defendants filed a Motion for Summary Judgment to declare that no constitutional right existed to televise court proceedings. A summary judgment was granted by the trial court. Plaintiff appealed the summary judgment and dismissal of the complaint. The Appellate Division of the Supreme Court affirmed the trial court's decision. Plaintiff appeals.

Thus the plaintiff brought suit against the two government defendants to declare a New York state statute unconstitutional. The plaintiff also wanted to enjoin the defendants from enforcing the civil rights law banning television in the courtroom. The defendants responded by filing a motion for summary judgment, presumably arguing the constitutionality of the state statute and that the U.S. Constitution and New York State Constitution do not provide nor guarantee the right to televise court proceedings. The court agreed with the defendants and dismissed the case. The plaintiffs filed an appeal with the Appellate Division of the Supreme Court of New York.

All prior proceedings are not as direct as the *Court Television Network* case. Review the diagram of *U.S. v. Booker* in Figure 4.12 and see how complex prior proceedings can be.

Issues

issue
The legal problem presented or point of law or fact on which the appeal is based; questions presented; a section that identifies the legal issues presented in the memorandum of law to the trial court.

declaratory judgment
The court's determination of the rights and responsibilities of a party with respect to the subject matter of the controversy.

motion for a summary judgment
A motion by either party for judgment based on all court documents.

The **issue** in the appeal is that point or points, if more than one issue is appealed, on which the appeal was based. Our case brief identifies the issue as follows:

> **Issue:**
> Is New York's Civil Rights Law section 52, which prohibits audiovisual coverage of most courtroom proceedings, constitutional under both the federal and state constitutions?

The derivation of this issue is straightforward. The plaintiff asserts that the trial court was wrong in denying its **declaratory judgment** and granting the defendants a **motion for a summary judgment** finding that the statutory and constitutional law for the state of New York did not provide a right to televise courtroom proceedings. The court must address and decide this issue. Many judges make it easy to find the issue in a case. They often state "the issue before us is . . ." or "we are asked to decide. . . ." Pay close attention to the language in the case as it will be helpful in formulating the issue. In this case, the very first line of the opinion tells the reader what the issue is. The court states: "The primary issue on this appeal is whether Civil Rights Law section 52, which bans audiovisual coverage of most courtroom proceedings, violates the federal or state constitution."

One quick and easy method of drafting the issues section is to determine the holding, and then turn the holding into a question. This method is not recommended, however, because it requires working backward.

You will often observe an issue couched in terms such as "whether" (as in this case), "does," "to the extent that . . . ," and other forms of a question. Crafting an issue can be an art, especially in an appellate brief. This concept will be discussed in greater detail in the chapters addressing the legal memoranda and appellate briefs.

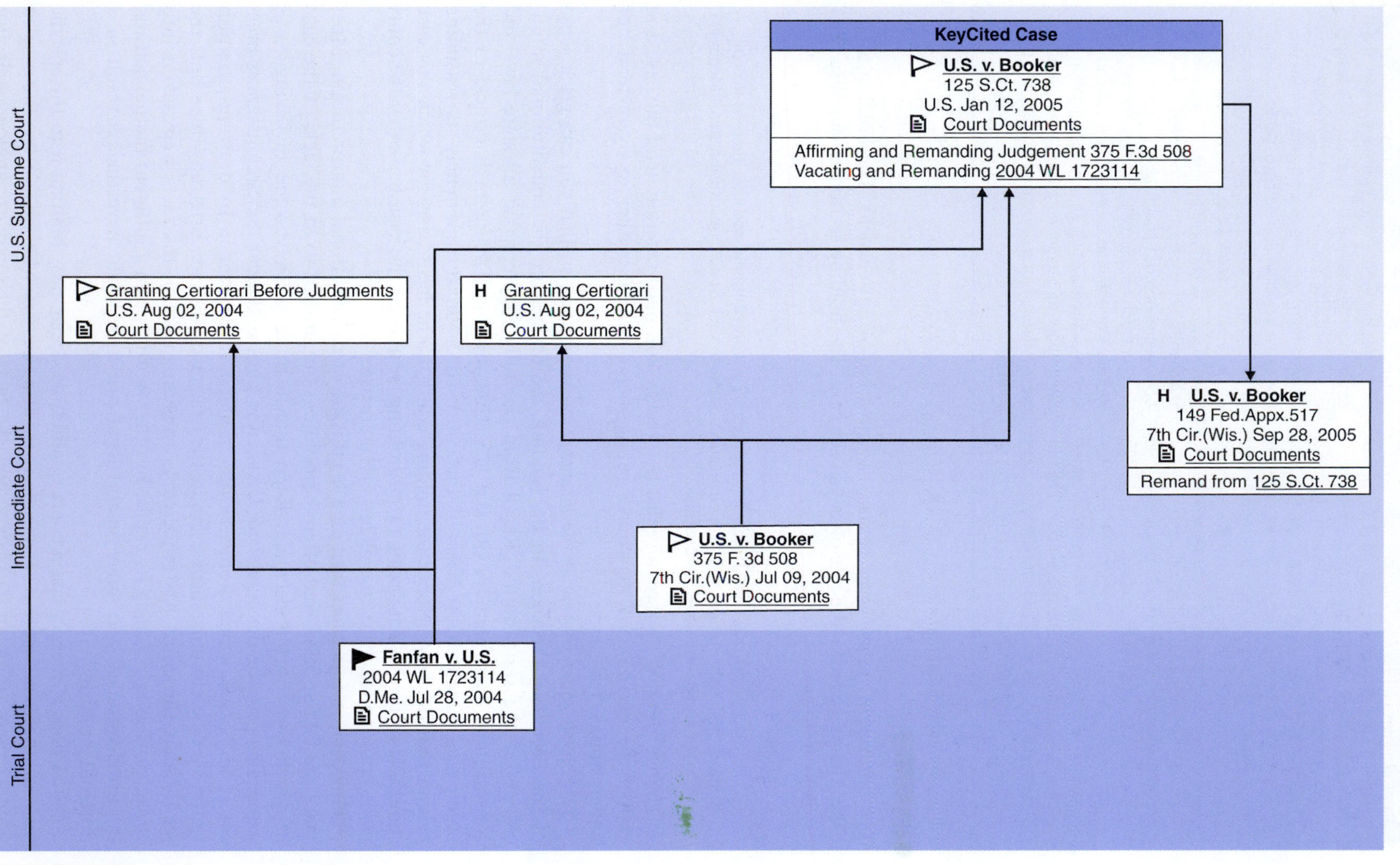

FIGURE 4.12 **Diagram of Prior Proceedings of *U.S. v. Booker***

Source: From Westlaw. Used with permission from ThomsonWest.

ETHICS ALERT

As painful as it may seem, under the rules of professional responsibility, an attorney must bring adverse legal authority to the attention of a court. You cannot ignore or bury a case in the fine print when the precedent it sets is contrary to the client's interest. Courts will sanction the attorney for such behavior. The reality is that the opposing counsel will probably find the case anyway—and you can rest assured that it will bring it to the court's attention. When you locate a case that "appears" to be adverse, immediately bring it to your attorney's attention. Sometimes your interpretation of a case may be different than the attorney's. Additionally, attorneys know how to "distinguish" cases based on facts or legal principles. Recall in Chapter 3 our discussion of *stare decisis* where one brother wanted the same privileges as his older brother. His parents said no because the facts were distinguishable, allowing them to come to a different conclusion. The same principle applies here. What appears on its face to be adverse actually may be turned into a possible result. Of course, sometimes an adverse case is, and will continue to be, adverse to a client's interest no matter how the facts and law are presented. Regardless of the result for the client, you have an obligation to bring to your attorney's attention all case law, good or bad. In turn, the attorney has an ethical obligation to decide how to handle the adverse case, and at the very least, has an obligation to bring it to the court's attention.

PRACTICE TIP

Only examine and cite the facts relevant to the litigation about which the court is asked to decide. Do not confuse those facts with a court's discussion of the facts in a precedent-setting case.

Holding

The holding of a case is, of course, the most important element. The holding establishes the precedent—the rule of law in the case. The holding section of our case brief reads as follows:

> **Holding:**
> The Court held that Civil Rights Law section 52 is constitutional and that there is no constitutional right under the U.S. Constitution or New York State Constitution guaranteeing a right to televise court proceedings.

The wording of this section must be precise. You must carefully read the case and extract the meaning of the court's ruling, being careful neither to overextend nor underestimate the scope.

Let's look more closely at the language we've chosen, so that you can get a sense of the necessary precision. In the holding, we underscore the constitutional implications of the state statute. Recall from previous chapters that all state laws and constitutions must comply with the U.S. Constitution. This point is critical to the holding as it defines the basis of the court's decision and ultimately its reasoning behind that decision. Notice the holding contains the legal basis for which this case stands. Therefore, when drafting your holding, search for the legal basis that the court relies upon to reach its rule of law for that case.

However, not all cases turn on a legal issue or constitutional interpretation. Most cases are fact-specific, and often the holdings are drafted to fit the facts of the case in which the court is deciding. Keep this in mind when you are reviewing cases whose facts can be distinguished. Utilize the phrase "Under the circumstances present in this case," which should set off an alarm in the reader. By drawing attention to the specific circumstances present, the drafter of the case brief has tipped off the reader that the court has rendered a decision in which the facts were taken into consideration in reaching its result. In other words, given a different factual setting, the application of the same general legal principle might nevertheless result in a different holding.

What does it mean when a court qualifies its decision by limiting it to the specific facts of the case before it? It means that future parties who seek to use the case to support their argument must show how the facts of their case are analogous. It also presents an opportunity for a party seeking to discredit the precedential value of the case to distinguish it based upon the facts. Consequently, word choice is critical in drafting a holding in a case.

Reasoning

In the **reasoning** section of our case brief, we analyze the rationale behind the court's holding.

> **Reasoning:**
>
> The case law is well settled in this area of law. Relying on a U.S. Supreme Court case, *Estes v. Texas,* 381 U.S. 532 (1965), the New York Court of Appeals opined that access to a court proceeding is different than the right to televise it. No one's right to access to the courtroom was denied or violated. Noting what may be considered the intrusive factor of televised court proceedings, the court had to balance the rights of the parties involved, including the jurors, judge, and witnesses. The court ultimately recognized that the most important right involved is that of the accused right to a fair trial.
>
> Neither the First Amendment, New York State Constitution, nor the Civil Rights Law section 52 deprives the media from attending the proceedings itself. They only limit the broadcast of the trial, which the court clearly had the right to do. The court reviewed the history of the law in New York and indicated that the law was well settled. The conclusion was that there was no constitutional guarantee to televise a court proceeding and that Court TV's rights had not been violated.
>
> There is *dictum* that discusses how the federal courts handle the issue. As the court points out, the federal courts take the same approach as the New York state courts barring telecasting trials. Again noting the balancing test, the court focused on the rights of the accused and the governmental interests involved. The end result is the rights of the accused are the main concerns of the courts.

The first paragraph of the reasoning clearly states the issue that is to be addressed. The laws in New York and the U.S. Supreme Court are well established and the court's reasoning makes this abundantly clear throughout its decision. Analyzing the statutes and case law, the court is balanced in its approach. Notice that the court addresses the arguments of both the plaintiff and defendants, methodically applying the case precedents to each.

The second paragraph of the reasoning section analyzes the appellant's attempt to argue that New York is one of the only states to bar television in the courtroom, to no avail. In the court's opinion, it deliberately reviews the case law, ultimately arriving at the same conclusion as the trial court and appellate division that there is no constitutional right to televise court proceedings. Thus, the dismissal of the action at the trial court was appropriate.

The final lines of the reasoning section allude to the court's dictum. Here, the dictum refers to other courts' treatment of the issue, noting that federal courts do not permit legal proceedings to be televised as well.

This court's reasoning is relatively straightforward. As you will experience, not all cases present such a succinct, direct evaluation of the legal principles that support the

YOU BE THE JUDGE

A case for disciplinary action against an attorney is serious. *In Re Fletcher,* 424 F.3d 783 (8th Cir. 2005), involves an attorney who violated numerous codes of conduct. This case was reviewed by a number of courts; all ultimately found that the attorney's conduct constituted malpractice. Read the case and learn the importance of understanding the lower and appellate review process. What actions did the attorney commit that warranted the disciplinary action? What was the appeals court disposition in the case? Identify the court's reasoning in the case. What were the pivotal facts resulting in the court's holding?

CYBER TRIP

Using www.supremecourtus.gov, locate a criminal case decided within the past two years that deals with an issue of search and seizure and prepare the case brief.

court's reasoning. Therefore, remember to review each case slowly and critically. The longer the case, often the more complex it will be to brief. Get in the habit of copying the cases needed, taking notes on the case itself and on a notepad. These practices will help you present a more thorough and comprehensive case brief for your supervising attorney to review.

Disposition

The purpose of the disposition section of the case brief is to alert the reader to the outcome of the case. The key to drafting it is to be concise. In *Courtroom Television Network,* where the appeals court found that the Appellate Division of the Supreme Court was correct in affirming the trial court's granting the summary judgment for the Defendants, the disposition can be relayed in one word: "Affirmed." For a more complex disposition, see Figure 4.10, *Tory v. Cochran.* Review the last paragraph of the majority opinion.

PRACTICE TIP

Every attorney has his or her own style for case briefing. Some want more information, some less. Check with your supervising attorney for the format to use, especially if the brief is reviewed by that attorney. The basic components of this chapter will always be your guide.

DEVELOPING THE CASE BRIEF

Case briefs are a specialized form of note taking. As you become more familiar with the format and language of a case, your note taking will become more precise and developed. There are no hard and fast rules for case briefing; some attorneys prefer more detail—a long form brief; others prefer a condensed version that identifies the facts, issue, holding, and reasoning—the short form. Whatever form your brief takes, long or short, there are some common practical tips that can be established from the process. The following checklist is a guide:

Checklist for a Case Brief

- ☐ Identify the case brief components on a sheet of paper.
- ☐ Read the case and take notes by filling in the designated sections of a case brief—the facts, issue, holding, and reasoning (or the format designated by your supervising attorney). That is your rough first draft.
- ☐ Review your notes. Read the case again. See if you agree with your original notes or need to add or change some of your notes.

A DAY IN THE LIFE OF A PARALEGAL

As you are researching, you find an unpublished case in your jurisdiction that is on point and will be dispositive of the issues in a case on which you are working. The case was published in June 2005 and you know you have hit the jackpot. You bring the case to your attorney's attention. She is ecstatic. When both of you check the rules of court in your jurisdiction for citing unpublished cases, the rules are quite clear—it is forbidden. Your attorney suggests a number of possibilities. First, you can keep researching and see if you can find a published case that presents the same or similar legal principles in your jurisdiction. Second, you could see if other jurisdictions have addressed the same issue. Although the precedential value would only be persuasive, at least it would be a reported published case. And finally, your attorney could bring the case to the court's attention, supplying both the court and opposing counsel with a copy of the case, and argue how the rights of the client are affected by not considering the case. If the court refuses to use the unpublished case, citing its rules of court, this may be one of those instances where your attorney appeals because of the issues it presents. As a paralegal, you will face this issue regularly especially as access to unpublished cases on the Internet expands. What you need to be acutely aware of are the unethical attorneys who may attempt to pass off the case as something other than unpublished, compromising both you and the attorney's credibility. This is one of those instances when you must "play by the rules." Challenges must be made through the appropriate judicial process, if necessary.

THE E-FACTOR

The electronic age has made it easier to find cases as well as to verify their validity. Because of that, it is inexcusable not to take the time to be thorough in a case briefing assignment. Although the Internet cannot provide the case brief and analysis for you, LexisNexis and Westlaw have tools that make the process more comprehensive. For example, Westlaw provides a feature that graphs the history of the prior proceedings of a case. *U.S. v. Booker*, Figure 4.12, illustrates the appellate history of the case.

LexisNexis provides an appellate history feature as well. Your attorney expects that your case brief will be complete, which includes the updating process.

New cases are decided every day; these case decisions may affect a client's case. Subscribe to case alerts. Case alerts provide information about newly decided cases as well as important developments in a case. They are subject- and jurisdiction-specific. If the practice your firm or company focuses on, for example, is securities law or intellectual property law, you can sign up on many legal Web sites for up-to-the-minute information on changes or newsworthy information about an area of interest. Or, if you are interested in all cases from the Tenth Circuit Court of Appeals, alerts can be tailored just for that court. Many of these Web sites, such as www.findlaw.com, are free. LexisNexis and Westlaw offer case alerts, but you must be a subscriber to their services. Don't be left behind. Sign up for alerts whenever possible to stay current on a subject.

- □ Begin transforming your notes into sentences for each section identified in the brief.
- □ Review your draft.
- □ Read the case one more time.
- □ Review and edit the case brief for comprehensiveness and clarity.
- □ Add a section at the end of the brief entitled "Comments or Notes." Here, you can write down your impressions of the case, such as "case on point," "facts distinguishable," "court applied this type of analysis, where our case facts requires . . . ," "case favors opposing position," "good alternative view," or "bad case, not on point." Use this section to jog your memory when you meet with your supervising attorney to discuss the case briefs.

Remember, briefs can be as long or as short as you need. Practice and time constraints may establish your needs. And most importantly, it does get easier with practice.

Quick Quiz True/False Questions

1. When briefing a case, rely on the syllabus or synopsis prepared by the publisher.
2. The fact section of a brief should contain relevant and material facts.
3. The holding is equivalent to the rule of law in the case.
4. Reasoning and dicta of a case are the same.
5. A typical disposition in a case is reversed and remanded.

PRACTICAL CONSIDERATIONS: PRACTICE, PRACTICE, PRACTICE

There you have it—a complete and concise case brief for *Courtroom Television Network LLC v. State of New York*. Having followed the step-by-step logic behind that case brief, you have now gained the raw skills necessary to unravel the law that lurks within the thousands, indeed millions, of opinions that fill every law library and the Internet.

Of course, you will need much practice to refine those skills, and you will learn much about the law along the way. Some things that you learn will surprise you—such as the fact that not all judges write with clarity. You will also learn that opinions are written assuming that readers are trained to understand legal concepts and decipher

FIGURE 4.13 **Sample Case Brief**

Case Brief—Courtroom Television Network LLC v. State

Citation:
Courtroom Television Network LLC v. State, 5 N.Y.3d 833 (2005) or
Courtroom Television Network LLC v. State, 5 N.Y.3d 833 N.E.2d 1197, 800 N.Y.S.2d 522 (2005)

Parties:
Courtroom Television Network LLC (plaintiff/appellant); State of New York (defendant/respondent); Robert Morgenthau as the New York County District Attorney (defendant/respondent).

Facts:
The facts in this case are undisputed. On September 5, 2001, Court Television (Court TV) filed a complaint against the State of New York and the District Attorney for New York County, Robert Morgenthau. The plaintiff was seeking a declaratory judgment that the New York's Civil Rights Law, specifically, section 52, is unconstitutional. The basis for the challenge was that New York [per p. 111] State prevents cameras, audiovisual, broadcasting and other forms of media communication in the courtroom when testimony of witnesses by subpoena or any other compulsory process is being taken by a court or court-like tribunal. Court TV asserts that the ban on televised trials violates its right to access in accordance with the First Amendment and New York State Constitution. The State of New York responded by asserting that no constitutional right to televised trials, under either the U.S. Constitution or New York State Constitution, exists. They further assert that the issue of cameras in the courtroom is legislative, not constitutional.

Prior proceedings:
Plaintiff filed an action for declaratory judgment seeking section 52 of the New York Civil Rights Law unconstitutional against the State of New York and the District Attorney of New York County. Defendants filed a Motion for Summary Judgment to declare that no constitutional right existed to televise court proceedings. A summary judgment was granted by the trial court. Plaintiff appealed the summary judgment and dismissal of the complaint. The Appellate Division of the Supreme Court affirmed the trial court's decision. Plaintiff appeals.

Issue:
Is New York's Civil Rights Law section 52, which prohibits audiovisual coverage of most courtroom proceedings, constitutional under both the federal and state constitutions?

Holding:
The Court held that Civil Rights Law section 52 is constitutional and that there is no constitutional right under the U.S. Constitution or New York State Constitution guaranteeing a right to televise court proceedings.

Reasoning:
The case law is well settled in this area of law. Relying on a U.S. Supreme Court case, *Estes v. Texas,* 381 U.S. 532 (1965), the New York Court of Appeals opined that access to a court proceeding is different than the right to televise it. No one's right to access to the courtroom was denied or violated. Noting what may be considered the intrusive factor of televised court proceedings, the court had to balance the rights of the parties involved, including the jurors, judge and witnesses. The court ultimately recognized that the most important right involved is that of the accused right to a fair trial.

Neither the First Amendment, New York State Constitution, nor the Civil Rights Law section 52 deprives the media from attending the proceedings itself. They only limit the broadcast of the trial, which the court clearly had the right to do. The court reviewed the history of the law in New York and indicated that the law was well settled. The conclusion was that no constitutional guarantees to televise a court proceeding existed and that Court TV's rights had not been violated.

There is dictum that discusses how the federal courts handle the issue. As the court points out, the federal courts take the same approach as the New York state courts barring telecasting trials. Again noting the balancing test, the court focused on the rights of the accused and the governmental interests involved. The end result is the rights of the accused are the main concerns of the courts.

Disposition:
Affirmed.

legalese. You must be prepared to overcome these obstacles. Keep your legal dictionary at hand, learn as much as you can about the substantive law, learn where to find the answers to questions that arise, persevere until you understand the problem at hand, and don't be afraid to ask for help.

As you gain experience in case briefing, you will develop your own techniques, or learn techniques preferred by your supervising attorney. For example, in order to conserve space, some firms prefer case briefs that identify the litigants (parties to a lawsuit) as *P* and *D* rather than as plaintiff and defendant, or sometimes by the Greek letters π (pi) for plaintiff and Δ (delta) for defendant. Another shorthand notation is the letter *K* for contract. No one technique is preferable; but whatever format or style you choose, remember that your brief must be thorough, accurate, and understandable to those who need to read and rely upon it.

Finally, in preparing a case brief you should always keep in mind the goal of the attorney for whom you are working. For some cases an extensive and detailed analysis will be necessary; for other cases, little more will be needed than a brief statement of the facts and holding. Some case briefs are thus long and formalized; others short. You and your supervising attorney are a team, and to function well as a team you must coordinate your goals.

Summary

A case brief is an objective summary of the important points of a case. This is different from a trial brief or appellate brief, each of which is drafted not to be objective, but rather to persuade.

The typical printed opinion appearing in a reporter contains several characteristic components. Star-paging enables the reader to identify page references from other reporters. The shorthand case name identifies the case at the top of the page. The parallel citation provides references to other reporters in which the case text appears. The full name of the case identifies all the parties and their position in the litigation (for example, plaintiff or defendant). The docket number is assigned to the case by the court for administrative purposes, and is usually included along with the date the decision was rendered and the full name of the court. The synopsis is an extremely short summary of the case prepared not by the court, but by the publisher of the reporter. A syllabus is a summary prepared by the court. Key numbers and headnotes are included, as well as the names of the attorneys and judges involved in the matter and, of course, the text and disposition of the case. Decisions can be affirmed or reversed or subject to some other disposition. There can be majority opinions, dissenting opinions, and concurring opinions. The holding of a court is that aspect of the decision which directly affects the outcome of the case; dictum is a statement made by the court that goes beyond what is necessary to reach the disposition.

When preparing a case brief, you must first read the relevant case, and then follow several steps to produce a document with several components. First, identify the case. Second, describe the parties. Third, identify the issues that were before the court for decision. Fourth, set out the relevant facts. Fifth, trace the procedural history of the case. Sixth, identify the holding of the court, taking great care to reflect accurately the precise parameters of the court's decision. Seventh, analyze the court's reasoning, again taking great care to restate and summarize the court's rationale. Eighth, alert the reader to the outcome of the case with a concise, shorthand statement of the court's disposition.

In drafting case briefs, you must overcome obstacles such as poorly drafted or highly technical judicial opinions. Over time you will develop your own style or learn the characteristic style preferred by your firm. Always keep in mind the goal that you and your supervising attorney are attempting to accomplish with the drafting of the case brief. This goal will influence length, formality, and general content.

Key Terms

affirmed
amicus brief
amicus curiae
caption
case brief
concur
concurring opinion
declaratory judgment
dictum
disposition
dissent
dissenting opinion
docket number
en banc decisions
facts
holding
immaterial fact
issue
majority opinion
material fact
motion for a summary judgment
per curiam decision
prior proceedings
reasoning
relevant fact
remanded
reversed
statute of limitations
syllabus
synopsis
vacated

Review Questions

1. What is the difference between a case brief and a brief written for a trial or appellate court?
2. What are the components of a printed opinion?
3. Why is star-paging useful?
4. What is the difference between a majority opinion and a dissent?
5. What are the components of a case brief?
6. Identify two components of a printed opinion in an unofficial reporter not found in the official reporter.
7. How do you identify the issues presented by a written opinion?
8. How do you locate the procedural history of a case as set forth in the opinion?
9. What is a holding? What is a disposition?
10. What is the reasoning of an opinion?

Exercises

1. Read *Condit v. National Enquirer, Inc.,* 248 F. Supp. 2d 945 (E.D. Cal. 2002), and answer the following questions:
   a. What are the facts in *Condit*?
   b. Identify the holding in the case.
   c. What is the reasoning in the case?
   d. Was this cased appealed? Provide an explanation for your answer.
2. In your law library, find *Trump v. Chicago Tribune,* 616 F. Supp. 1434 (S.D. N.Y. 1985), and perform the following tasks:
   a. Name the parties to the case.
   b. Identify the court and the case reporter.
   c. List the West topics and keys in the case.
   d. Identify the objectives of the parties.
   e. List the prior proceedings.
3. Locate *Bed, Bath & Beyond, Inc. v. Urista,* 211 S.W.3d 753 (Tex. 2006), and answer the following questions:
   a. What is the holding?
   b. What are the prior proceedings?
   c. What is the court's reasoning behind its holding?

4. Your attorney has asked you to brief *Elvis Presley Enterprises v. Capece,* 141 F.3d 188 (5th Cir. 1998). Prepare the case brief.
5. Define the following terms:
   a. star-paging
   b. holding
   c. dictum
   d. concurring opinion
   e. en banc
   f. appellee
6. Check the U.S. Supreme Court Web site, www.supremecourtus.gov, and determine whether any new cases have been reported in the last six months. Choose one case and prepare a case brief. Hint: Check recent slip opinions.
7. Determine the federal court of appeals in your jurisdiction. Search on the Web site and locate a criminal case that was decided in the last year. Brief one of the cases and answer the following questions:
   a. Identify the parties to the case.
   b. Who is the appellant? The appellee?
   c. What is the holding and disposition in the case?
8. Brief *Clay v. U.S.*, 537 U.S. 522 (2003), and answer the following questions:
   a. What are the parallel citations for the case?
   b. Who wrote the opinion for the court?
   c. Identify the number of the headnotes with their associated topic and keys.
   d. What is the disposition of the case?

PORTFOLIO ASSIGNMENT

Your supervising attorney has been a bit overzealous lately in his representation of some of his clients. To put it bluntly, he insulted a judge one too many times. He's concerned. What bothers him most is that he was just doing his job—he's just too good. He has never been sanctioned by a court nor had any disciplinary action. This is the first time he may have crossed the line. He heard about a recent case from Puerto Rico and wants you to get a copy. You first think "Puerto Rico; I didn't know their laws applied in New York." The citation for the case is *In Re Alexander Zeno,* 504 F.3d 64 (1st Cir. 2007). Your attorney first wants you to brief the case and answer the following questions:

a. Can the case be used in your jurisdiction? (Explain your answer.)
b. Why does your attorney need to worry about this case?
c. Can your attorney argue any First Amendment rights? Are there any cases in the *Zeno* case that address that issue? If so, review them for your attorney.
d. Are there any cases cited by the court that can be distinguished?
e. Can *In Re Alexander Zeno* be distinguished?

Quick Quiz True/False Answers

Page 108

1. False
2. True
3. True
4. False
5. False

Page 117

1. False
2. True
3. True
4. False
5. True

Chapter 5

Researching Constitutions, Statutes, and Administrative Rules and Regulations

After completing this chapter, you will be able to:

- Determine what primary source is the supreme law of the land.
- Understand the differences between the U.S. Constitution and state constitutions.
- Learn where to find federal statutes.
- Distinguish between the official and unofficial codes.
- Locate the legislative history of a statute.
- Identify the "fourth" branch of government.
- Discuss the process of formulating and enacting an administrative rule.
- Find administrative rules, regulations, and decisions.

One concept should be clear: All laws, statutory or administrative, must comply with the requirements of the U.S. Constitution. Often Congress, administrative agencies, and sometimes even the president of the United States believe they are above the law. What is abundantly clear is that we are all governed by the same piece of paper that was drafted in the 1700s. Now, more than ever, we know that the U.S. Constitution is the document that guides our daily lives and no branch of government is immune from its requirements. Let's understand why.

CASE FACT PATTERN

An unusual case has just come into your law office. A teacher has been fired from her job. Apparently while she was teaching her class, one of her elementary school students asked questions about the war in Iraq. The student inquired as to whether the teacher participated in political activities involving the war. The teacher responded by stating that she saw a placard saying "Honk for Peace." To show her support, she honked her horn. Days later, the teacher was terminated as parents complained about her expressing her opinion about the war. There was a district school policy that teachers were not to express their personal political views to students. The teacher believes her First Amendment rights were violated and that she was discriminated against for being over the age of fifty. Your supervising attorney has a hearing on the matter in a week and asks you to research the issue. Knowing where to begin and where to look for legal support is crucial.

Source: NON SEQUITOR © Wiley Miller. Dist. By UNIVERSAL PRESS SYNDICATE. Reprinted with permission. All rights reserved.

THE SUPREME LAW OF THE LAND—THE U.S. CONSTITUTION

constitution
The organic and fundamental law of a nation or state, which may be written or unwritten, establishing the character and conception of its government, laying down the basic principles to which its internal life is to be conformed, organizing the government, regulating functions of departments, and prescribing the extent to which a nation or state can exercise its powers.

In Chapter 1, this book presented an overview of the American legal system. As the basis of "our" democracy, **constitutions** govern how we live and interpret the principles by which we live.

The U.S. Constitution consists of seven articles and twenty-six amendments. These articles and amendments establish the framework of our federal government. The first ten amendments created our basic rights, known as the Bill of Rights. As we now know, it is the supreme law of the land.

Interpreting the U.S. Constitution

Since the U.S. Constitution is the supreme law of the land, all primary law is interpreted in accordance with the U.S. Constitution. This means that all laws are measured against the U.S. Constitution. When researching a project assigned by your supervising attorney, you should always ask yourself, "Do the actions of the parties have constitutional implications?" Review a case in "You Be the Judge" that had constitutional implications.

Don't fool yourself into believing that statutes and case law are the most important primary source of the law. All primary sources of the law must comport with the ultimate law of the land—the U.S. Constitution.

injunction proceeding
A judicial proceeding where an order may be issued requiring a party to cease an act or perform an act.

State Constitutions

As part of our constitution's delegation of powers, each state, and territory for that matter, has the right to create its own state constitution to govern its citizens.

YOU BE THE JUDGE

Journalists epitomize First Amendment rights. Freedom of speech is one of our most basic rights. It is not a surprise that one of the major networks uncovered some questionable practices in a meat-packing plant in South Dakota. The network and its newscaster wanted to air footage of the meat-packing plant's interior, exhibiting some of its practices. The company sought to block the telecast through an **injunction proceeding.** Various state courts barred the telecast from airing, which the network appealed. The issue before the U.S. Supreme Court was whether the actions of the state courts infringed on the network's and newscaster's First Amendment rights to freedom of expression. The U.S. Supreme Court noted "any prior restraint on expression comes to this Court with a 'heavy presumption' against its constitutional validity." *CBS, Inc. v. Davis,* 510 U.S. 1315 (1994). In reviewing the case, the U.S. Supreme Court determined a First Amendment violation occurred. Along with so many other cases, this case represents our Constitution protecting one of our most basic rights—free speech. Review *CBS, Inc. v. Davis* and determine why only one justice decided this case. What was the holding in the case? What are the prior proceedings of the case?

Virtually all the states have their own constitutions. A state cannot create a constitution that conflicts with the U.S. Constitution, although it can grant more rights to its citizens but not fewer. For example, the Washington State Constitution, section 35, grants victims of crimes certain rights. This right is not one specifically enumerated under the U.S. Constitution but does not conflict with it, either.

All the state constitutions are worded differently and structured differently. Compare the introductory preambles and contents of the constitutions of New York and Washington State in Figure 5.1. Notice the choice of words. Can they be reconciled with the First Amendment to the U.S. Constitution?

FIGURE 5.1
Preamble and Bill of Rights for (A) State of Washington and (B) State of New York

Source: From *Revised Code of Washington Annotated.* Reprinted with permission from ThomsonWest.

Ⓐ CONSTITUTION OF THE STATE OF WASHINGTON

PREAMBLE

We the people of the State of Washington, grateful to the Supreme Ruler of the Universe for our liberties, do ordain this constitution.

ARTICLE 1

DECLARATION OF RIGHTS

§§ 1 to 11 appear in this volume.

Section

1. Political Power.
2. Supreme Law of the Land.
3. Personal Rights.
4. Right of Petition and Assemblage.
5. Freedom of Speech.
6. Oaths—Mode of Administering.
7. Invasion of Private Affairs or Home Prohibited.
8. Irrevocable Privilege, Franchise or Immunity Prohibited.
9. Rights of Accused Persons.
10. Administration of Justice.
11. Religious Freedom.
12. Special Privileges and Immunities Prohibited.
13. Habeas Corpus.
14. Excessive Bail, Fines and Punishments.
15. Convictions, Effect of.
16. Eminent Domain.
17. Imprisonment for Debt.
18. Military Power, Limitation of.
19. Freedom of Elections.
20. Bail, When Authorized.
21. Trial by Jury.
22. Rights of the Accused.
23. Bill of Attainder, Ex Post Facto Law, Etc.
24. Right to Bear Arms.
25. Prosecution by Information.
26. Grand Jury.
27. Treason, Defined, Etc.
28. Hereditary Privileges Abolished.
29. Constitution Mandatory.
30. Rights Reserved.
31. Standing Army.
32. Fundamental Principles.
33. Recall of Elective Officers.
34. Same.
35. Victims of Crimes—Rights.

Cont.

FIGURE 5.1
Cont.

Ⓑ CONSTITUTION OF THE STATE OF NEW YORK
Preamble

WE, THE PEOPLE of the State of New York, grateful to Almighty God for our Freedom, in order to secure its blessings, DO ESTABLISH THIS CONSTITUTION.

ARTICLE I—BILL OF RIGHTS

Section
1. [Rights and privileges secured; uncontested primary elections.]
2. [Trial by jury; how waived.]
3. [Freedom of worship; religious liberty.]
4. [Habeas corpus.]
5. [Bail; fines; punishments; detention of witnesses.]
6. [Grand jury; waiver of indictment; right to counsel; informing accused; double jeopardy; self-incrimination; waiver of immunity by public officers; due process of law.]
7. [Just compensation for taking private property; private roads; drainage of agricultural lands.]
8. [Freedom of speech and press; criminal prosecutions for libel.]
9. [Right to assemble and petition; judicial divorces; gambling, except pari-mutuel betting, prohibited.]
10. [Repealed.]
11. [Equal protection of laws; discrimination in civil rights prohibited.]
12. [Security against unreasonable searches, seizures and interceptions.]
13. [Repealed.]
14. [Common law and acts of the state legislatures.]
15. [Repealed.]
16. [Damages for injuries causing death.]
17. [Labor not a commodity; hours and wages in public work; right to organize and bargain collectively.]
18. [Workers' compensation.]

As with all legal research sources, do not assume anything. Check your state constitution to understand the backdrop of how it was developed.

Quick Quiz True/False Questions

1. The first fifteen amendments to the U.S. Constitution are known as the Bill of Rights.
2. All state constitutions must comport with the U.S. Constitution.
3. The U.S. Constitution is not the supreme law of the United States.
4. Some state constitutions grant their citizens more rights than the U.S. Constitution.
5. Constitutions govern how we live and are a primary source of the law.

UNDERSTANDING STATUTES AND CODES

conference committee
A committee made up of members of both houses of Congress who review a bill, iron out the differences, and present it for approval to their respective bodies.

veto
Rejection of a bill by the president or governor.

We all remember sitting in school learning about "how a bill becomes law." It did not seem very important then and probably made you want to fall asleep. But the lessons of the past have a funny way of resurfacing, and it's time again to clear out the cobwebs, dig deep, and recall the process once more. This time the significance is clear and the importance understood. Let's review the legislative process and relate it to being a paralegal in the law office.

Initiating the Legislative Process

The legislative process often can be a long, arduous, and even contentious one. With so many personal and political interests at stake, the legislative process is an important one. In the federal context, bills are introduced by a representative of Congress and assigned a legislative number: HR for bills in the House of Representatives and S for bills in the Senate. A bill is simply the formal introduction of a piece of legislation. After the assignment of the bill's number, the bill is then assigned to the appropriate congressional committee for review and debate. Often a bill introduced in committee changes. The bill may be rewritten completely or amended by the committee. The committee has the right to conduct hearings, to investigate, or to clarify any issues that are related to the bill. If the bill passes a vote of the assigned committee, the bill is "reported out" and awaits debate or review by the entire body, either the House or the Senate. Depending on which house of Congress originates the bill, if passed, the bill then moves to the other respective congressional body for approval.

All bills must be passed by a majority of that body's membership: A Senate bill requires 51 votes and the House requires 218 (of 435). (Note the House number changes based upon the number of House representatives. It is always a simple majority.) If both houses of Congress pass the bill, then the bill works its way to a **conference committee.** The conference committee is a committee made up of members from both houses who review the bill, iron out the differences in the respective versions, and send it back to the respective bodies for their final approval. After being printed and signed by the presiding officers of the respective houses of Congress, the bill is sent to the president for review and consideration.

Once the bill is received, the president has ten days to sign it, veto it, or do nothing. A **veto** is the constitutional procedure wherein the president refuses to sign a bill sent by Congress into law. If the president vetoes the bill, the bill is not dead. If two-thirds of each house of Congress votes to "override" the president's decision, then the bill will become law. (Yes, that means over the objection of the president. Overriding a veto is a rare occurrence.) There is a caveat, however, regarding passing a bill when the president "does nothing." A bill becomes law without the president's signature only if Congress is in session. If Congress is not in session, or has adjourned before the expiration of the ten-day time limit, the bill will not become law. This process is known as the pocket veto. A **pocket veto** is the "indirect rejection" of a bill by a president. The pocket veto automatically defeats the bill from becoming law.

When a bill passes both houses of Congress and is signed into law by the president, a **public law number** is assigned and the legislation is **enacted.** Enacted in this context means the bill, or now the new law, "goes into effect." The public law number signifies that the bill is now law. What happens after the bill becomes a public law is the next phase in understanding the legislative process.

This basic process is followed also by states. Most states may have a **bicameral process,** that being two legislative bodies, or a **unicameral process,** with only one legislative body, such as Nebraska and some of the U.S. territories. When a bill is passed, the chief executive of the state, the governor, signs the bill into law or vetoes it, like the president. Figure 5.2 is a diagram of how a bill becomes law using the state of Colorado as an example.

Slip Laws and Session Laws

As discussed in the previous section, the U.S. Congress and the fifty state legislatures pass many bills. These bills become statutes with the signature of the president or governor.

Recall from earlier chapters that the first format in which a newly signed statute appears is called a **slip law.** A slip law is an official publication of a single statute or *act* (a group of related statutes). A slip law usually identifies a public act number or other official designation associated with this single statute or act. Slip laws also

pocket veto
A veto of a bill when Congress or state legislature is not in session or has adjourned before the expiration of the ten-day time limit. An indirect rejection of a bill as no action occurs by the president or governor.

public law number
The number assigned a bill after it is signed into law.

enacted
A bill that is in effect.

bicameral process
One of the types of legislative bodies that has two separate houses required to pass a bill, such as the House and Senate of the U.S. Congress.

unicameral process
A legislature that has only one body required to pass a bill, such as Nebraska.

PRACTICE TIP

Public laws are categorized by the congressional session, such as the 107th Congress, followed by the number in which that law was enacted during that session. For example, the USA PATRIOT Improvement and Reauthorization Act of 2005 was passed by the 109th Congress and was the 177th act that was passed—Public Law 109–177.

slip law
The first format in which a newly signed statute appears; a copy of a particular law passed during a session of legislature.

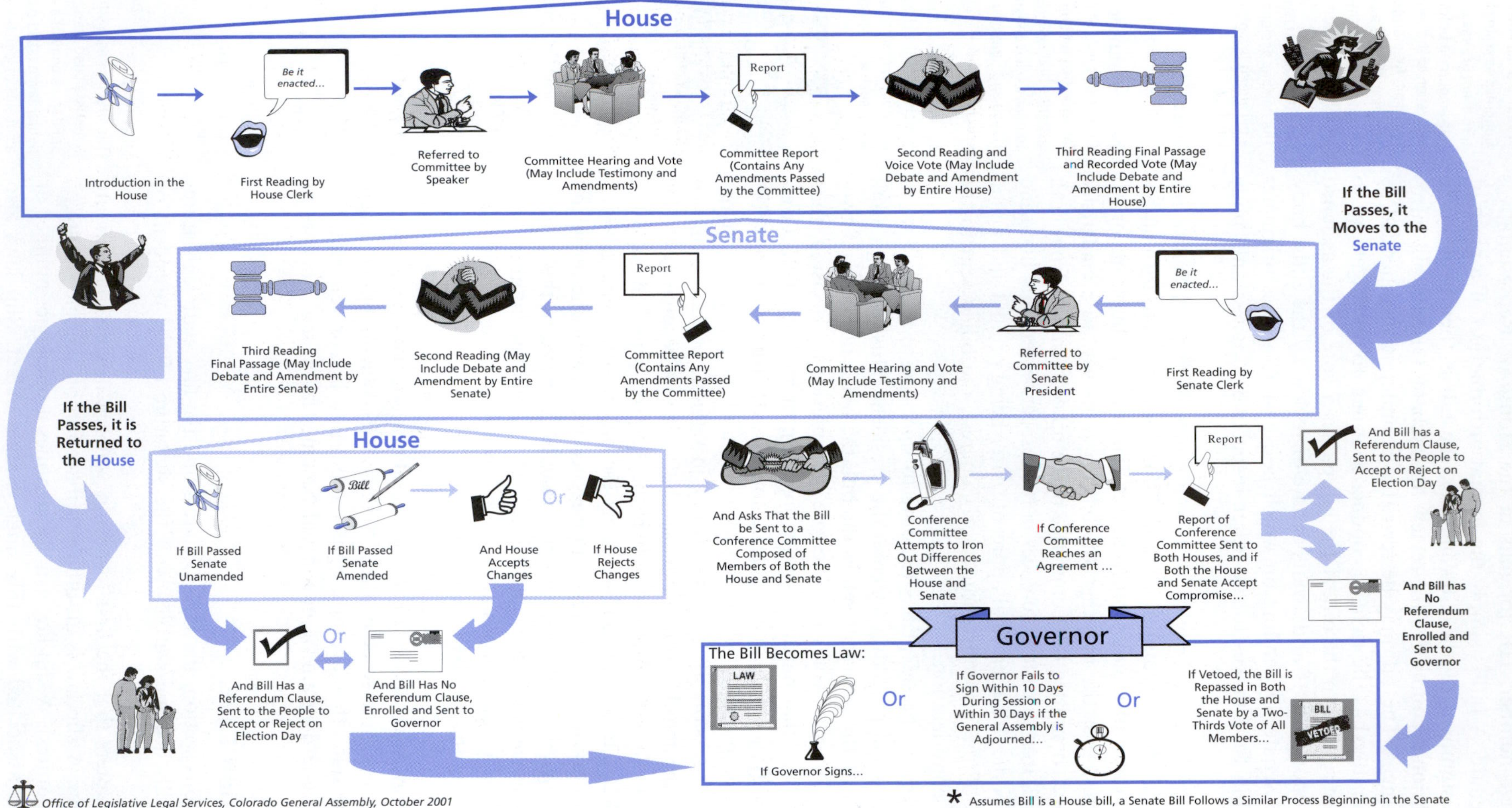

FIGURE 5.2 **Diagram of How a Bill Becomes Law Using the State of Colorado as a Guide**

Source: Office of Legislative Legal Services, Colorado General Assembly, October 2001, www.state.co.us/gov_dir/leg_dir/olls/PDF/Bill%20becomes%20law%20chart.pdf (accessed December 10, 2007).

PRACTICE TIP

To use the *Statutes at Large,* identify the law you need. The *Statutes at Large* are categorized by volume and page where the statute begins. (Remember, each volume represents only statutes from a specific legislative session.) Using the PATRIOT Improvement Act again, if the citation is 120 Stat. 192, this means that your statute appears in volume 120 with the text beginning on page 192.

include guides to the legislative history of the law, such as the committee where the law originated with a corresponding committee report number and reference to the *Congressional Record* in which that law appeared. The federal government and most states issue slip laws, but they are rarely used for research purposes because there are other, more comprehensive formats in which the new statute will shortly appear.

The second format in which new statutes appear is a compilation called the **session laws.** Session laws are permanent collections of the statutes of one jurisdiction and compiled chronologically. They are generally printed after a legislative session by order of issuance. The federal session laws are the ***Statutes at Large.*** The *Statutes at Large* are the official permanent collection of the laws passed by each session of Congress. Each volume contains a table of contents and index with a legislative history appearing at the end of each law. Figure 5.3 is an example of the PATRIOT Improvement Act, which was enacted into law by the president. It appears in its slip law format.

session laws
The second format in which new statutes appear as a compilation of the slip laws; a bill or joint resolution that has become law during a particular session of the legislature.

Statutes at Large
Official permanent collection of the laws passed by each session of Congress.

Statutes concerning diverse subjects are generated in each legislative session, with no particular order to their issuance. Session laws are useful for checking recent legislation, but they are often inadequately indexed and difficult to use for comprehensive research.

Statutory Codes: The Final Comprehensive Source

The final and permanent source for statutes is a **code.** A code is a multivolume compilation that groups statutes by subject matter. It is indexed, making statutes more

code
A multivolume compilation that groups statutes by subject matter and is well indexed, in order to make the statutes more accessible for research purposes.

FIGURE 5.3 **Slip Law Version of the PATRIOT Improvement Act**

Public Law 109–177
109th Congress

Mar. 9, 2006
[H.R. 3199]

An Act

To extend and modify authorities needed to combat terrorism, and for other purposes.

Be it enacted by the Senate and House of Representatives of the United States of America in Congress assembled,

USA PATRIOT Improvement and Reauthorization Act of 2005. 18 USC 1801 note.

SECTION 1. SHORT TITLE; TABLE OF CONTENTS.

(a) Short Title.—This Act may be cited as the "USA PATRIOT Improvement and Reauthorization Act of 2005".

(b) Table of Contents.—The table of contents for this Act is as follows:

Sec. 1. Short title; table of contents.

TITLE I—USA PATRIOT IMPROVEMENT AND REAUTHORIZATION ACT

Sec. 101. References to, and modification of short title for, USA PATRIOT Act.
Sec. 102. USA PATRIOT Act sunset provisions.
Sec. 103. Extension of sunset relating to individual terrorists as agents of foreign powers.

Cont.

FIGURE 5.3 **Slip Law Version of the PATRIOT Improvement Act** *Cont.*

[text omitted]

TITLE I—USA PATRIOT IMPROVEMENT AND REAUTHORIZATION ACT

SEC. 101. REFERENCES TO, AND MODIFICATION OF SHORT TITLE FOR, USA PATRIOT ACT.

(a) REFERENCES TO USA PATRIOT ACT.—A reference in this Act to the USA PATRIOT Act shall be deemed a reference to the Uniting and Strengthening America by Providing Appropriate Tools Required to Intercept and Obstruct Terrorism Act (USA PATRIOT Act) of 2001.

18 USC 1 note.

(b) MODIFICATION OF SHORT TITLE OF USA PATRIOT ACT.—Section 1(a) of the USA PATRIOT Act is amended to read as follows:

"(a) SHORT TITLE.—This Act may be cited as the 'Uniting and Strengthening America by Providing Appropriate Tools Required to Intercept and Obstruct Terrorism Act of 2001' or the 'USA PATRIOT Act'."

SEC. 102. USA PATRIOT ACT SUNSET PROVISIONS.

18 USC 2510 note.

(a) IN GENERAL.—Section 224 of the USA PATRIOT Act is repealed.

[text omitted]

TITLES OF
UNITED STATES CODE
AND
UNITED STATES CODE ANNOTATED

1. General Provisions.
2. The Congress.
3. The President.
4. Flag and Seal, Seat of Government, and the States.
5. Government Organization and Employees.
6. Domestic Security.
7. Agriculture.
8. Aliens and Nationality.
9. Arbitration.
10. Armed Forces.
11. Bankruptcy.
12. Banks and Banking.
13. Census.
14. Coast Guard.
15. Commerce and Trade.
16. Conservation.
17. Copyrights.
18. Crimes and Criminal Procedure.
19. Customs Duties.
20. Education.
21. Food and Drugs.
22. Foreign Relations and Intercourse.
23. Highways.
24. Hospitals and Asylums.
25. Indians.
26. Internal Revenue Code.
27. Intoxicating Liquors.
28. Judiciary and Judicial Procedure.
29. Labor.
30. Mineral Lands and Mining.
31. Money and Finance.
32. National Guard.
33. Navigation and Navigable Waters.
34. Navy (*See Title 10, Armed Forces*).
35. Patents.
36. Patriotic and National Observances, Ceremonies, and Organizations.
37. Pay and Allowances of the Uniformed Services.
38. Veterans' Benefits.
39. Postal Service.
40. Public Buildings, Property, and Works.
41. Public Contracts.
42. The Public Health and Welfare.
43. Public Lands.
44. Public Printing and Documents.
45. Railroads.
46. Shipping.
47. Telegraphs, Telephones, and Radiotelegraphs.
48. Territories and Insular Possessions.
49. Transportation.
50. War and National Defense.

FIGURE 5.4
The Titles under the *United States Code*

Source: From *United States Code Annotated.* Reprinted with permission from ThomsonWest.

accessible for research purposes. Federal statutes are contained in the volumes known as the *United States Code* (cited as *U.S.C.*); it presently has fifty titles. (See Figure 5.4.)

A code is sometimes deemed the official text of some or all of the statutes it contains. It is important to consider, for a moment, this concept of "official" as it applies to statutes. As a practical matter, if one assumes that each version of a text accurately reproduces the true text, it doesn't matter which is official. On occasion, however, the text of one version may contain an error, creating a situation where different versions of the same statute exist. Under such circumstances it becomes important to know which version—slip or session or code—is deemed by the legislature to be the official version. For the federal government, portions of the *United States Code* have been officially adopted, making the code version official for those portions; for other federal statutes, the official version is found in the *Statutes at Large.*

Organization of the *United States Code*

As previously mentioned, the *United States Code* is divided into fifty titles. Each title represents a subject within the code. For example, Title 20 deals with education laws, Title 26 deals with laws governing the Internal Revenue Service, and Title 42 deals with laws relating to Public Health and Welfare. Each title can be subdivided into subtitles, chapters, subchapters, parts, and subparts. What is common to each title is the use of individual sections, representing specific areas of the law of that title.

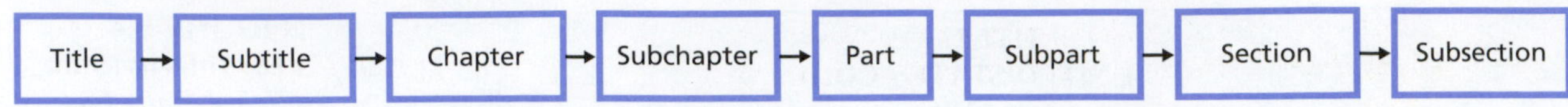

FIGURE 5.5 Structure of a Title within the *United States Code*

Consequently, you may hear someone refer to Title IX, which is a subtitle of Title 20, Education, dealing with discrimination based on sex or blindness. In one context, we know it as the title that establishes equality for women in sports. However, Title IX is a subtitle of the main title—Title 20.

Generally, you will focus on the overall title and its corresponding section. Citing Title IX of the Education Act is 20 U.S.C. §§ 1681–1688. Figure 5.5 shows possible subdivisions for a general title of the *United States Code.*

Pay close attention to the labels given a statute and its subparts. The easiest way to alleviate any confusion is to simply focus on the proper citation of the statute. That will lead you to the correct section of the statute referenced.

annotated code
A code that provides, in addition to the text of the codified statutes, such information as cases that have construed the statute; law review articles that have discussed it; the procedural history of the statute (amendments or antecedents); cross-references to superseded codifications; cross-references to related statutes; and other information.

pocket parts
Annual supplements to digests.

supplements
Individual stand-alone paperbound volume that provides updates of the law.

Annotated Codes

Although the *United States Code* is considered the official version of most U.S. statutes, most attorneys and paralegals use one of the unofficial versions of the code: *United States Code Annotated* (cited as *U.S.C.A.*) or *United States Code Service* (cited as *U.S.C.S.*). The *United States Code Annotated* is published by ThomsonWest and the *United States Code Service* is published by LexisNexis. The burning question on your mind is "who cares?" Actually, you should care because *U.S.C.A.* and *U.S.C.S.* contain all the associated research material you need to begin a research project, unlike *U.S.C.* Both annotated codes provide summaries of case law interpreting the statutory section you are researching and references to any corresponding research material that may be relevant, such as an encyclopedia or law review article. In short, the abundance of information provided by the **annotated codes** makes them not only invaluable reference tools but essential. An annotated code provides the text of all statutes along with research aids that analyze the statutory code section referenced. A passage from *United States Code Annotated* appears in Figure 5.6.

Pocket Parts and Supplements: Checking for Updates in the Law

PRACTICE TIP

Always check the pocket parts and supplements to determine whether a statute has been amended or repealed. The lack of a reference to your statute means that your statute has not been amended or repealed during the time period of the pocket part or supplement.

An integral part of any code, official or unofficial, is the **pocket parts** and **supplements.** The pocket parts are the softbound supplements that are inserted in the back of each code volume. Normally, they are issued annually. When a pocket part becomes too large to be inserted in the back of the volume itself, a stand-alone supplement is added. The pocket parts and supplements *must* be read in conjunction with the text to the main volume. Often the main volumes contain statutory sections that have been repealed or heavily amended by pocket parts and supplements. Your research is never complete unless these supplements are consulted.

The problem with pocket parts and supplements is that they are generally updated annually. What happens if a statute is amended or repealed? The answer is that in today's world, with the accessibility of the Internet, you must check either a fee-based Web site, such as Westlaw or LexisNexis, to determine the status of a statute or a government Web site. There is no way to avoid a computer in today's Internet age. Suggested free Web sites to consult are listed in this chapter's section titled "Practical Considerations."

Therefore, unlike the unannotated versions of a code, the annotated version has all the useful research tools to make your job easier. Understanding the information contained in a statute with its corresponding research sources is important. Consequently, let's learn about all the components of an annotated version of a statute.

FIGURE 5.6 **Passage from the *United States Code Annotated***

Source: From *United States Code Annotated.* Reprinted with permission of ThomsonWest.

§ 154. Regulations for preparation and sale; licenses

text of statue

The Secretary of Agriculture is hereby authorized to make and promulgate from time to time such rules and regulations as may be necessary to prevent the preparation, sale, barter, exchange, or shipment as aforesaid of any worthless, contaminated, dangerous, or harmful virus, serum, toxin, or analogous product for use in the treatment of domestic animals, or otherwise to carry out this chapter, and to issue, suspend, and revoke licenses for the maintenance of establishments for the preparation of viruses, serums, toxins, and analogous products, for use in the treatment of domestic animals, intended for sale, barter, exchange, or shipment as aforesaid.

session reference

(Mar. 4, 1913, c. 145, § 1 [part], 37 Stat. 832; Dec. 23, 1985, Pub.L. 99–198, Title XVII, § 1768(b), 99 Stat. 1654.)

HISTORICAL AND STATUTORY NOTES

statutory history and amendments

Revision Notes and Legislative Reports

1985 Acts. House Report No. 99–271(Parts I and II), Senate Report No. 99–145, and House Conference Report No. 99–447, see 1985 U.S. Code Cong. and Adm. News, p. 1103.

Codifications

Another section 1768 of Pub.L. 99–198 amended section 136y of Title 7, Agriculture.

Amendments

1985 Amendments. Pub.L. 99–198, § 1768(b), inserted "or otherwise to carry out this section".

FEDERAL SENTENCING GUIDELINES

Violations of statutes and regulations dealing with any food, drug, biological product, device, cosmetic, or agricultural product, see § 2N2.1, 18 USCA.

general research sources

LIBRARY REFERENCES

applicable *Code of Federal Regulations*

Administrative Law

Licensing and permits for use of biological products, see 9 CFR § 101.1 et seq.

secondary source explanation of statute topic

Encyclopedias

25 Am Jur 2d, Drugs and Controlled Substances § 129.

Forms

10 Federal Procedural Forms L Ed, Foreign Trade and Commerce § 33:1.

Cont.

FIGURE 5.6 Passage from the *United States Code Annotated Cont.*

secondary source material

caselaw on topic

21 § 154 **FOOD AND DRUGS Ch. 5**

Law Review and Journal Commentaries

Federal regulation of agricultural biotechnologies. Thomas O. McGarity, U.Mich.J.L.Ref. 1089 (1987).

Texts and Treatises

Food, Drugs, and Cosmetics, 13 Fed Proc L Ed § 35:491.

WESTLAW ELECTRONIC RESEARCH

See WESTLAW guide following the Explanation pages of this volume.

Notes of Decisions

State regulation and control 1

---

1. State regulation and control

Animal and Plant Health Inspection Service's (APHIS) preemption of state laws that "impose requirements which are different from, or in addition to, those imposed by [United States Department of Agriculture (USDA)]" regarding the safety, efficacy, potency, purity, or labeling of licensed vaccines preempts inconsistent substantive state law "requirement," but not state common law remedies, and thus, common-law claims are not preempted to the extent that they seek relief for alleged violations of the federal substantive standards. Symens v. Smith Kline Beecham Corp., C.A.8 (S.D.) 1998, 152 F.3d 1050.

Dissecting a Statute

Most statutes follow the same basic format. For this task, we will use the federal statute from the *United States Code Annotated* (*U.S.C.A.*) from Figure 5.6. Beginning from the top:

a. Title number—At the top of the page, the title of the statute is identified. In the citation, which helps you locate the statute, the title is usually first.

b. Section number—This number is the specific section of the portion of the statute you are reviewing.

c. Section name—The section name is simply the title of the statutory section you are reviewing. This section gives you a general idea what the section is about.

d. Text of statute—The text of the statute is the law itself. This section is the exact text passed by the U.S. Congress and signed into law by the president. Reviewing the text is critical to understanding your research problem and what principles will guide your research.

e. Session law reference—Located right after the statutory section, this section provides information as to the volume number in which the original text of the statute appeared.

f. Historical note—The historical note provides a history of the statute, from enactment through the amendment process. Often, a statute has been amended numerous times. It is important to pay attention to the information in this section, as subtle word changes are noted that would affect your research. Changes, such as time limits, are important.

g. Cross-references—The cross-reference section provides other related or relevant statutes on the subject covered in the statute or administrative code sections from the *Code of Federal Regulations* (discussed later in the chapter). This section is important as it may lead you to other applicable statutory or regulatory sections. In Figure 5.6, the federal sentencing guidelines are referenced as part of this section as well.

h. Library references—Consider this your shortcut to researching the topic. Relevant topics and keys are cited as well as corresponding encyclopedia references. (Note that this section corresponds to the reference books published by that company. For example, since *U.S.C.A.* is published by ThomsonWest, only ThomsonWest books will be noted here. If we used *U.S.C.S.* as the example, there would not be a West topic and keys, but LexisNexis annotations and references to its publications.) Additional secondary sources are referenced, such as law review articles and treaties. More on the reference guides and finding tools can be found in Chapter 6.

i. Notes of decisions—This section presents the case law related to the code section. Cases that have interpreted this section are summarized in a "headnote" style text. Read this section carefully as it will lead you to case decisions involving your statutory section. Pay close attention to the jurisdiction-specific notations. If your fact situation is in Illinois, then you want to look for cases in either the Seventh Circuit Court of Appeals or cases in the U.S. district courts in Illinois. Those cases will be the "mandatory authority" with cases from other jurisdictions being persuasive. (Don't forget what you learned in earlier chapters of this text. All chapters build on one other.) The notes of decisions section is structured with U.S. Supreme Court cases referenced first, followed by federal court of appeals cases and then the U.S. district court cases. States are listed alphabetically within the section. Some code sections have numerous cases identified continuing for many pages. To organize the volume of cases, section topics are shown in bold to guide the researcher to the areas of the law that are of interest. These subsections will assist you in narrowing your search.

j. Pocket parts and supplements—As mentioned in the previous section, for newer information regarding the statute, check the pocket parts and supplements. Your research is not complete until the pocket parts and coordinating supplements are reviewed. Often the pocket parts and supplements contain recent changes to the statute, such as an amendment, and more importantly, repeals. Before you proceed to analyzing the relevant statutory section, *do not overlook the pocket parts and supplements.* If your section has been repealed, your research may lead in a different direction. Or worse, it may be obsolete and inaccurate. Plainly stated, you may be wasting time on something that is no longer valid law! The pocket parts and supplements will contain new cases and new related research entries as well.

CYBER TRIP

Choose a federal statute (of interest to you) and determine whether it has been amended or repealed by the current U.S. Congress. Suggested statutes are the USA PATRIOT Act, Freedom of Information Act, Megan's Law, Amber Alert Law, Brady Law, or any federal criminal statute.

YOU BE THE JUDGE

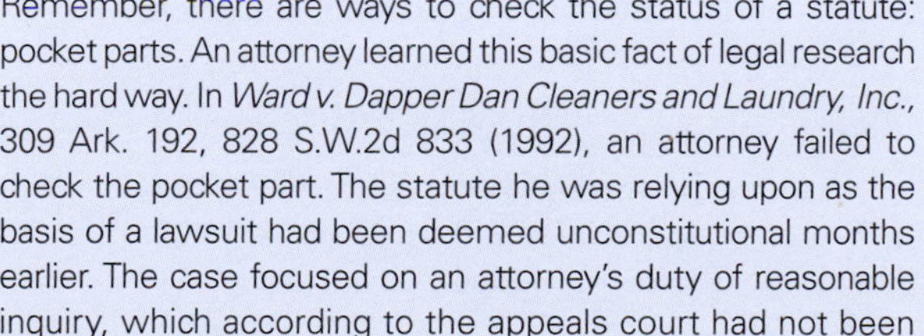

Remember, there are ways to check the status of a statute: pocket parts. An attorney learned this basic fact of legal research the hard way. In *Ward v. Dapper Dan Cleaners and Laundry, Inc.*, 309 Ark. 192, 828 S.W.2d 833 (1992), an attorney failed to check the pocket part. The statute he was relying upon as the basis of a lawsuit had been deemed unconstitutional months earlier. The case focused on an attorney's duty of reasonable inquiry, which according to the appeals court had not been fulfilled. As the court pointedly noted, "appellee's counsel need only to have checked the pocket part of volume 16 of the Arkansas Code to discover under the case notes designation in the cumulative supplement that the prejudgment attachment provisions, §16-110-104 to -111, had been ruled unconstitutional. If counsel had made such a reasonable inquiry into the applicable law prior to signing appellee's petition for prejudgment attachment, he obviously would never have filed it." *Id.* at 836. Clearly, a lesson learned is a lesson not forgotten. Read the case. What are the critical facts of the case? What was the court's disposition in the case? What professional rules of responsibility did the judge cite in the reasoning?

Using an Annotated Code: The General Index

general index
The index at the end of the statutes that provides a guide to locating relevant statutes.

To assist the researcher in locating relevant statutes, there must be a mechanism to find a statute, short of pulling each book off the shelf. The mechanism in the annotated codes is its indexes. At the end of all the code volumes are **general** or **subject indexes.** General or subject indexes provide the guide to locating relevant statutes. But let's get something out of the way now; what you think is a logical way to index a subject may not be the way the index is organized. Often words that appear to be a logical way to find a particular statute are not the way at all. All you can do is keep trying different synonyms. Sometimes the index will offer alternative words that lead you to closer to the answer. And sometimes, the words you choose are right on target. It would be wonderful to offer words of wisdom. What can be stated is that as you become more familiar with using the general and subject indexes of a statutory code, you will become more familiar with the type of words used by the compilers of the indexes.

When you find words or phrases that work, you will find a corresponding title and section number of the code. This will lead you to applicable statutory sections that govern your research topic. Remember that once you have the applicable statutory section, you should review both the main volume of the code *and* the pocket part. Using Figure 5.7 as your reference, you want to find information on the Amber Alert

FIGURE 5.7 **General Index for the *United States Code Annotated***
Source: From *United States Code Annotated.* Reprinted with permission from ThomsonWest.

CHILDREN AND MINORS
See, also, Dependents, generally, this index
Abandonment, [words and phrases]
AIDS, assistance, **42 § 670 nt**
Drug addicts, assistance, **42 § 670 nt**
Servicemembers group life insurance, **38 § 1965**
Abduction. Kidnapping, generally, post
Abuse. Child Abuse and Neglect, generally, this index
Acquired Immune Deficiency Syndrome (AIDS), this index
Actions and proceedings,
Big Brothers Big Sisters of America, **36 § 30105**
Internet, information, collection, **15 § 6504**
Sexual exploitation, **18 §§ 2252A, 2255**
Actual sexually explicit conduct, definitions, **18 § 2257**
Address, Internet, information, collection, **15 § 6501 et seq.**
Administration On Children, Youth, and Families, generally, this index
Adolescent Family Life, generally, this index
Adoption, generally, this index
Adult Education, generally, this index
Advertisements, this index
Advisory committees,
Children and Terrorism National Advisory Committee, **42 § 247d–6**
Pediatric pharmacology, **42 § 284m nt**
Advocacy, crime victims, **42 § 14043c**
Afghanistan, foreign assistance, **22 § 2374 nt**
After-Born Children, generally, this index
Age, Internet, control, protection, **47 §§ 230, 231**
Airbags, studies, **49 § 30127 nt**
Alaska, grants, demonstration projects or programs, **42 § 3121 nt**
Alcoholic beverages, prenatal and postnatal care, **42 § 247b–13**
Alcoholics and alcoholism,
Early intervention, **42 § 290bb–8**
Federal aid highways, **23 § 161**
High risk families, services, **42 § 290bb–25a**
Reduction, **42 § 290bb–25b**
Research, **42 § 290bb–34**
Services, **42 § 290bb–7**
Technical assistance and cooperation, **42 § 290bb–34**
Training, **42 § 290bb–34**
Violence, **42 § 290bhh**
Alerts,
AMBER Alert, 42 § 5791 et seq.
Code Adam Alert, **42 §§ 5601 nt, 5792, 5792a**
Aliens, this index
AMBER Alert, **42 § 5791 et seq.**
American Conservation and Youth Service Corps. National and Community Service, this index
American War Mothers, **36 § 22501 et seq.**
Amicus curiae, Internet, information, collection, **15 § 6504**
Ammunition,
Crimes and offenses, **18 § 924**
Weapons, possession, sales, delivery, transfers, exemptions, crimes and offenses, **18 § 922**
Annuities, justices and judges, payments, **28 § 376**

Cont.

FIGURE 5.7 General Index for the *United States Code Annotated* Cont.

statute. You know that the statute involves missing children. Look up the most obvious words such as *children, child,* or *minors.* In this index, the entry "children and minors" appears to be relevant. When scanning the page, there is a clear entry for Amber Alert under children and minors. Notice it's also listed under "kidnapping." The code section you are researching may have multiple entries and multiple ways to locate it.

Popular Name Index

Popular Name Index
An index located at the end of the statutes that provides the common name for a statute.

When you do not know the formal or proper name of the statute and know only its colloquial name, initials, bill title, or an acronym, use the **Popular Name Index.** The Popular Name Index contains the commonly used name and gives the "formal" title and code section reference. It also gives the public law number and the *Statutes at Large* citation. For example, you want to find information on the federal requirements for registration of sex offenders. All you know is that the commonly used reference is "Megan's Law." You would look up Megan's law in the Popular Name Index and the common usage should lead you to the formal code section. In Figure 5.8, a sample from the Popular Name Index is provided using Megan's law. Notice that the reference provides other related statutes. At the end of the section, the public law number is identified and the *United States Code* reference.

Or, if you wanted to know the reference and formal name for the USA PATRIOT Act, the Popular Name Index would give you the following: United and Strengthening America by Providing Appropriate Tools Required to Intercept and Obstruct Terrorism Act of 2001, Public Law No. 107, 115, Stat. 272 (2001). (Bet you didn't know that's what it stood for!) The Sarbanes-Oxley Act, SOX for short, is the act that was passed because of the Enron scandal. This act focuses on corporate integrity and accountability. It begins at 15 U.S.C. section 7201 and is formally known as the Public Company Accounting Reform and Corporate Responsibility Act. And finally, the NLRA, which is the National Labor Relations Act and deals with relationships between employers and employees, is located in 29 U.S.C. section 151 (2000) as amended. These are some examples of popular name references you may find in the Popular Name Index.

A DAY IN THE LIFE OF A PARALEGAL

Finding recently passed or amended statutes is not always easy. Your supervising attorney gives you a research assignment. You check what you believe is the current version of the statute in the *United States Code Annotated.* Of course you check the latest version of the pocket part where there are no recent changes to the statute. What you don't realize is that the pocket part is a year old and the statute you are researching had significant changes within the past two months. (Remember, the pocket parts are published annually and any new changes will generally not appear until the following year.) If you do not have the most recent version of the statute, your research is not only incomplete, but faulty. What should you do to assure yourself that you have left no stone unturned and you are presenting your attorney with the most current status of the law?

As a paralegal you have a few options. Checking the *Congressional Record* for the most recent versions of all recently passed statutes is a start. The *Record* is printed daily and is found either online or in law libraries. Another approach would be to contact the legislature you are researching directly. All legislatures, both the federal and states, have offices that can help you gain access to the most up-to-date versions of the law. Sometimes they can fax or e-mail any recent changes or direct you to where you can find the current listing of the law you are researching. Many legislatures have Web sites that post laws as they are passed (just like the posting of court decisions). Check the Web sites of the origin of the statute for assistance. Additionally, Shepard's citators (discussed in detail in Chapter 7) provide an updating mechanism for statutes. The federal version is more complete than state versions, however. The lesson here is: "do not assume" that the pocket parts will give the most recent and current status of the law. Go that extra mile and be sure you have reviewed all the available avenues!

POPULAR NAME TABLE 46

AMBER Alert Act (America's Missing—Broadcast Emergency Response Alert Act)
See, also, Amber Hagerman Child Protection Act of 1996
See, also, Code Adam Act of 2003
See, also, International Parental Kidnapping Crime Act of 1993
See, also, Jacob Wetterling Crimes Against Children and Sexually Violent Offender Registration Act
See, also, Megan's Law
See, also, National Child Search Assistance Act of 1990
See, also, Parental Kidnapping Prevention Act of 1980 (PKPA)
See, also, Prosecutorial Remedies and Other Tools to end the Exploitation of Children Today Act of 2003 (PROTECT Act)
See, also, Suzanne's Law
Pub.L. 108–21, Title III, Subtitle A (§§ 301 to 305) April 30, 2003, 117 Stat. 660 (42 §§ 5791, 5791a to 5791d)
[text omitted]

Medicine Equity and Drug Safety Act of 2000 (MEDS Act)
See, also, Agriculture, Rural Development, Food and Drug Administration, and Related Agencies Appropriations Act, 2001
Short title, see 21 USCA § 301 note
Pub.L. 106–387, § 1(a) [Title VII, § 745], Oct. 28, 2000, 114 Stat. 1549, 1549A–35 (21 §§ 301 note, 331, 333, 381, 384)

MEDS Act
See Medicine Equity and Drug Safety Act of 2000

Megan's Law
See, also, AMBER Alert Act (America's Missing—Broadcast Emergency Response Alert Act)
See, also, Amber Hagerman Child Protection Act of 1996
See, also, Code Adam Act of 2003
See, also, International Parental Kidnapping Crime Act of 1993
See, also, Jacob Wetterling Crimes Against Children and Sexually Violent Offender Registration Act
See, also, National Child Search Assistance Act of 1990
See, also, Parental Kidnapping Prevention Act of 1980 (PKPA)
See, also, Prosecutorial Remedies and Other Tools to end the Exploitation of Children Today Act of 2003 (PROTECT Act)
See, also, Suzanne's Law
Short title, see 42 USCA § 13701 note
Pub.L. 104–145, May 17, 1996, 110 Stat. 1345 (42 §§ 13701 note, 14071)

Mellon Art Gallery Act
Mar. 24, 1937, ch. 50, 50 Stat. 51 (20 §§ 71 to 75)

Membrane Processes Research Act of 1992
Short title, see 42 USCA § 10341 note
Pub.L. 102–490, Oct. 24, 1992, 106 Stat. 3142 (42 § 10341, 10341 note, 10342 to 10345)

Menominee Restoration Act
Short title, see 25 USCA § 903 note
Pub.L. 93–197, Dec. 22, 1973, 87 Stat. 770 (25 §§ 903 to 903f)

FIGURE 5.8
Popular Name Index from the *United States Code Annotated*
Source: From *United States Code Annotated.* Reprinted with permission from ThomsonWest.

The Conversion Table

The conversion table is also part of the code's indexing system. Located in a separate volume, this index allows you to locate and convert a public law number into the *Statutes at Large* reference as well as to find the actual title and section of the codified statute.

State Statutes

All states have at least one annotated code, and in some large states, such as California, publishers issue competing versions. Most state annotated codes are published in hardbound volumes updated with advance sheets and pocket parts. When a pocket part becomes too large to fit in the back of the volume, either a supplementary pamphlet is added or a new volume created to replace the old one. Not all state statutes are published in hardbound volumes; some are published in looseleaf format, such as New Mexico and one of Kentucky's versions of its statutes. Provision is generally made for publication of some version of the session laws (usually without annotation, but including an index and possibly a table of codified statutes affected), which may appear even before the government's version of the session laws. Most states also have a general index keyed to their statutes. Use the same technique you learned for locating federal statutes to find a state statute; look up applicable words and phrases until (hopefully) you find what you need. Some state statutes have a Popular Name Index, but they are not nearly as extensive and useful as the federal code's Popular Name Index. You should check your law library to learn more about the annotated code and session law volumes in your state.

Finding and Dissecting a State Statute

Similar to an annotated federal statute, state statutes have many of the same components. However, state statutes are not codified the same way. Some are cataloged by subject, others simply by a numerical system. Learning how your state statute is assembled is an important exercise for any paralegal. Let's compare Colorado's and Oregon's Amber Alert statutes using the general indexes to locate the statute. In Figure 5.9 a page from the general index of *Colorado Revised Statutes Annotated* is identified.

FIGURE 5.9
Page from the General Index of *Colorado Revised Statutes Annotated*

Source: From *Colorado Revised Statutes Annotated.* Reprinted with permission from ThomsonWest.

CHILDREN AND MINORS—Cont'd
Medical care and treatment—Cont'd
Emergencies, ex parte emergency orders, **19–1–104**
Handicapped persons, **25–1.5–101**
Immunization, infants, **25–4–1701 et seq.**
Marijuana, **Const. Art. 18, § 14**
Nurse home visitor program, **25–31–101 et seq.**
Orders of court, emergencies, **19–1–104**
Pregnancy, consent, **13–22–103.5**
Sex offenses, examination, **13–22–106**
Medical information, metabolic defects, distribution, **25–4–803**
Medical records. Custody of children, ante
Medicine. Drugs and medicine, generally, ante
Mental health professionals, custody, evaluations and reports, **14–10–127**
Mentally ill persons, **27–10.3–101 et seq.**
Adoption of children, social services, subsidies, **26–7–101 et seq.**
Appeal and review, residential services, denied, **27–10.3–104**
Diagnostic center, University of Colorado, **23–23–101 et seq.**
Dispute resolution, treatment, **27–10.3–107**
Funds, treatment, **27–10.3–106**
Medical assistance, **25.5–5–307**
Repeal, **27–10.3–108**
Reports, residential services, denied, **27–10.3–105**
Residential care facilities, rates and charges, **26–1–132**
Mentally Retarded and Developmentally Disabled Persons, this index
Mentors and mentoring, **25–20.5–203**
Family resource center programs, **26–18–104**
Metabolic defects. Newborns, post
Migrant children, Schools and School Districts, this index
Mines and minerals, employment, **Const. Art. 16, § 2**
Missing persons,
Amber alert program, 24–33.5–415.7
Definitions, **24–33.5–415.1**
Lists, investigation bureau, **24–33.5–415.1**
Notice, amber alert program, **24–33.5–415.7**
Reports, crimes and offenses, **16–2.7–101 et seq.**
Mitigating factors, alcoholic beverages, training, **12–47–601**
Modification. Custody of children, ante
Motion pictures,
Obscenity, generally, post
Sexual exploitation of children, **18–6–403, 18–6–404**
Sexually explicit materials harmful to children, admission, **18–7–501 et seq.**
Violence, dispensing violent films to minors, **18–7–601**

FIGURE 5.10 Partial Test of the Statue Showing the Section Number from the Colorado Statute

Source: From *Colorado Revised Statutes Annotated.* Used with permission from ThomsonWest.

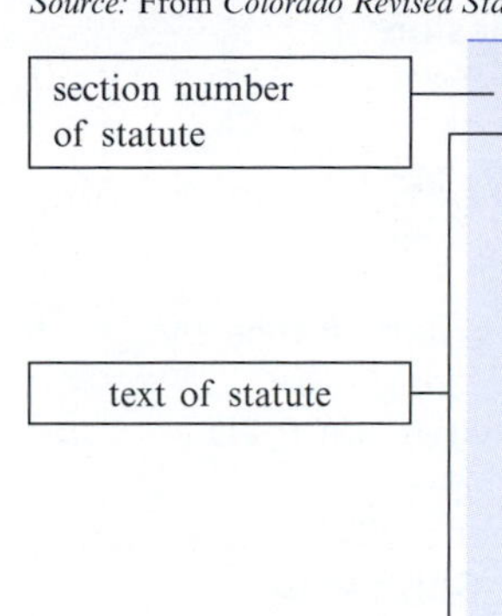

§ 24-33.5—415.7. Amber alert program

(1) The general assembly hereby finds that, in the case of an abducted child, the first few hours are critical in finding the child. To aid in the identification and location of abducted children, there is hereby created the Amber alert program, referred to in this section as the "program," to be implemented by the bureau. The program shall be a coordinated effort among the bureau, local law enforcement agencies, and the state's public and commercial television and radio broadcasters.

(2) For the purposes of this section, "abducted child" means a child:

(a) Whose whereabouts are unknown:

(b)(I) Whose domicile at the time he or she was reported missing was Colorado; or

(II) About whom credible information is received from a law enforcement agency located in another state that the abducted child is traveling to or in the state of Colorado;

(c) Whose age at the time he or she was first reported missing was seventeen years of age or younger, including a newborn; and

(d) Whose disappearance poses a credible threat as determined by local law enforcement to the safety and health of the child.

Since we know that an Amber Alert has to do with "missing or kidnapped children," words such as *children, minors, missing children,* or *kidnapped children* should be looked up in the index. Notice the general entry in Colorado's statutory index is "children and minors." If you review the entries under that heading, you will find an entry for "missing persons." Under that entry is a specific notation to the Amber Alert program. The entry sends you to 24-33.5—415.7 of the revised statutes annotated (see Figure 5.10). If you checked the main volume first (at least at this printing), no entry for the statute is found. Therefore, immediately check the pocket part. In the pocket part, you will find the above entry, titled Amber Alert program. In reviewing the statute you will observe:

a. The statutory reference—This is the official statutory section.
b. Name of the section—The name of the statutory section is identified.
c. General statute—Each section of the statute is delineated section by section and part by part. The legal requirements are set forth in this part for which review and analysis is required.
d. Additions and amendments—At the end of the code section itself, reference is made to how the law evolved.
e. Historical and statutory notes—Changes to the law are noted in this section such as word changes, new sections, and deletions.
f. Code of regulations references—The corresponding administrative rules and regulations may be listed here for that state.
g. Library reference—Any additional research material, such as West's topics and keys, encyclopedia references, or other finding tools would be referenced here.
h. Notes of decision (or similar title)—Any cases that have interpreted or construed the statute would be located in this section. Since you are in a state-specific book, usually only cases from that state will be listed including decisions from that state's federal courts.

PRACTICE TIP

The structure of state codes varies significantly. Become familiar with code content and structure for the state in which you are conducting research. The introductory material in the state codes provides guidance on how to use that particular state code and its references.

Now compare the Amber Alert statute in Oregon. Let's use the general index found in Figure 5.11. Using the same words as before, see if we can find the Amber Alert

FIGURE 5.11 General Index from the *Oregon Statutes*

CHILDBIRTH
See PREGNANCY AND CHILDBIRTH, generally

CHILDREN
See MINORS, generally

first reference sends you to another reference

CHILDREN AND FAMILIES, STATE COMMISSION ON
(Generally), 417.705 et seq.
Account, 417.733
Duties, 417.735
Establishment, 417.730
Evidence-based programs, expenditures, 182.515, 182.525
Juvenile Crime Prevention Advisory Committee, 417.845, 417.850
Officers, 417.740
Rules, 417.735, 417.745

CHILDREN AND FAMILY SERVICES
See also CHILD WELFARE SERVICES
(Generally), 417.705 et seq., 417.735
Advisory committees, 417.750
Characteristics of service system, 417.720
Community learning centers, see **COMMUNITY LEARNING CENTERS, generally**
Community level delivery systems, including education, information and referral services, 417.360
County authority, limitation, 417.839
Definitions, 417.705
Deschutes County, demonstration project, providing services, 417.830
Duties, state agencies, 417.707
Early childhood programs
Administrative rules, 417.728
Components, 417.728
Findings, legislature, 417.708
Goals, Oregon Early Childhood System, 417.727
Interagency coordination, 417.728
Legislative findings, 417.708
Local commissions, 417.777
Oregon Early Childhood System, goals, 417.727
Parents-as-teachers programs, 417.793
[text omitted]

MINORS (Cont.)
Jurisdiction, see **JUVENILE COURTS AND PROCEEDINGS**
Jurors, 10.030
Juvenile courts and proceedings, see **JUVENILE COURTS AND PROCEEDINGS,** generally
Juvenile delinquents and dependents, see **JUVENILE DELINQUENTS AND DEPENDENTS,** generally
Labor, see **LABOR AND EMPLOYMENT**
Liability of parent, see **PARENT AND CHILD**
Limitation of actions, suspension, 12.160, 12.170
Litter cleanup program, 366.157
Loans to, education, validity, 348.105
Lottery, State, see **LOTTERY, STATE**
Mail
Guardians or conservators, appearance by, ORCP 27, ORCP 27A
Summons, manner of service, ORCP 7D
Majority, 109.510, 109.520
Marriage, see **MARRIAGE,** generally
Medical care, see **MEDICAL CARE AND TREATMENT**
Mental disease or defect, see **JUVENILE COURTS AND PROCEEDINGS**
Mental illness and health, see **MENTAL ILLNESS AND MENTAL HEALTH**
Military Department programs, at-risk youth, policies and procedures, 396.360
Minimum wages, see **COMPENSATION AND SALARIES**
Misrepresentation of age, 471.135
Missing children, see **MISSING PERSONS**
Money to, without conservatorship, 126.700
Mothers, majority presumed, 109.090, 109.326
Motor vehicles, see **MOTOR VEHICLES**
Name, change, see **NAMES**
Neglect, see **CHILD NEGLECT,** generally
Nonsupport, criminal, 163.555
[text omitted]

second reference sends you to another part of the index

MISCONDUCT (Cont.)
School personnel, administering medication, 339.870
Sexual misconduct, 163.445
Signaling device, electronic, exceptions to liability exemption, 401.627
Trials
New, grounds for, ORCP 64B
Relief from judgment, ORCP 71B
Veterinarians, farriers, written release, 30.695
Waste tires, disposal, state or local government liability, 459.780

MISCONDUCT IN OFFICE
See OFFICIAL MISCONDUCT, generally

MISDEMEANORS
Crimes and offenses, see **CRIMES AND OFFENSES**
Fines and penalties, see **FINES AND PENALTIES**
Sentence and punishment, see **SENTENCE AND PUNISHMENT**

MISJOINDER
Parties, ORCP 30

Cont.

FIGURE 5.11 General Index from the *Oregon Statutes Cont.*

final reference

statute. If we looked under "children" as we did in Colorado, notice that the index sends you to a section titled "Minors." (Remember, different books and different publishers catalog things differently.) If we look up the word "minors" we see a section titled "Missing Persons." Still, we have not found the correct entry. If you look under the words "missing persons," you see an entry "Children" and under that entry there is an entry titled "Amber Plan, abducted children." That appears to be "our" section. The entry references section 181.035. In the entry, you find a general statement as to the procedure for an Amber Alert situation. Notice the note at the end, however. The note states "181.035 was enacted into law by the Legislative Assembly but was not added to or made a part of ORS chapter 181 or any series therein by legislative action. See Preface to *Oregon Revised Statutes* for further explanation." What you should do now is locate the Preface to the *Oregon Revised Statutes* and see what it says. Figure 5.12 is a copy of the preface and there is a section titled "Not

FIGURE 5.12 Preface to the *Oregon Revised Statutes*

PREFACE

2005 EDITION

Publication of Oregon Revised Statutes. The Legislative Counsel Committee, pursuant to ORS 171.275, publishes *Oregon Revised Statutes* and distributes the up-to-date statute text, index, comparative section tables and annotations.

The statute text of the first official edition of *Oregon Revised Statutes,* published in 1953, was bound in "loose-part" form with each chapter constituting a part that could be removed from the binder.

Until 1989, replacement parts were identified by the words REPLACEMENT PART, preceded by the year of publication on the first page of each part. Those chapters that were reprinted, but were not replacement parts because they contained no new material, were identified by the designation, "(19 __ reprint)," indicating the year in which they were reprinted.

The first softcover edition of *Oregon Revised Statutes* was published in 1989. The 2005 edition of *Oregon Revised Statutes* consists of 21 softbound volumes.

A Table of Titles and a Table of Titles and Chapters, covering all 17 volumes of the statute text, follow this Preface. Each volume is preceded by a Table of Titles and Chapters of the statutes contained in that volume. A

Cont.

FIGURE 5.12 **Preface to the *Oregon Revised Statutes* Cont.**

chapter outline precedes each chapter and lists the ORS sections and certain temporary provisions compiled in that chapter.

Chapters that have been entirely repealed or renumbered are no longer listed in the Tables of Titles and Chapters, but a page identifying each of those chapters and indicating the disposition of the former content of the chapter is in the appropriate place in the statute text.

In addition to the statutes, *Oregon Revised Statutes* contains the Oregon Rules of Civil Procedure, printed pursuant to ORS 1.750. The rules appear in Volume 1 immediately preceding ORS chapter 12.

[text omitted]

Changes in text of Acts. A number of the types of changes made in the text of enrolled Acts for publication in *Oregon Revised Statutes* are explained and illustrated below.

(1) Changes made pursuant to general authority granted by ORS 173.160:

(a) ORS numbers are assigned to codified session law sections. For example, section 210, chapter 459, Oregon Laws 1991, is compiled as ORS 310.140.

(b) Long sections of session laws may be divided into several shorter ORS sections. For example, section 240, chapter 16, Oregon Laws 1985, is compiled as the series ORS 816.040 to 816.290.

(c) Several sections of session laws may be combined in one ORS section. For example, sections 1, 2, 3 and 3a, chapter 690, Oregon Laws 1991, are compiled as ORS 475.996.

(d) Existing ORS sections are assigned new ORS numbers if reorganization of the material is warranted. For example, ORS 411.450 was renumbered as ORS 411.434 and then renumbered again as ORS 416.090.

(e) Actual effective dates· are inserted in place of "the effective date of this Act." For example, "the effective date of this 1993 Act" was replaced by "November 4, 1993" in section 3, chapter 792, Oregon Laws 1993, compiled as ORS 215.710.

(f) References in session laws to "this (year) Act" or to a section of the session laws are replaced by specific ORS references. For example, in section 4, chapter 733, Oregon Laws 2003, compiled as ORS 238A.070, the words "sections 5 to 26 of this 2003 Act" are replaced by "ORS 238A.100 to 238A.245." Also, in the amendments to ORS 128.826 by section 3, chapter 532, Oregon Laws 1991, the words "section 6 of this 1991 Act" are replaced by "ORS 128.824."

(g) Alterations are made in unamended ORS sections containing references to a specific series of ORS sections when new session law sections were "added to and made a part of" that ORS series. For example, "ORS 517.910 to ***517.950***" (emphasis added) cited in ORS 517.905 in the 1989 edition was expanded to "ORS 517.910 to ***517.987***" (emphasis added) in the 1991 edition to accommodate sections 2 to 24a, chapter 735, Oregon Laws 1991, which were added to and made a part of ORS 517.910 to 517.950, but which could not be accommodated numerically within the existing series.

(2) Changes made pursuant to specific statutes. Alterations are made in unamended ORS sections pursuant to specific statutes directing the substitution of new words or phrases for existing words or phrases. For example, section 3, chapter 380, Oregon Laws 1991, authorized the substitution of "Board on Public Safety Standards and Training" for "Board on Police Standards and Training" in *Oregon Revised Statutes.* A complete list of statutes authorizing substitutions of this nature appears as a note at the end of this Preface.

"Not added to and made a part of." Notes may indicate that a particular ORS section was not added to and made a part of the ORS chapter or series in which the section appears. These notes mean that the placement of the section was editorial and not by legislative action. Notes also are used when the series references are either too numerous or too complex to bear further adjustment. However, the note does ***not*** mean that the section not added to a series or a chapter is any less the law. The note is intended ***only*** to remind the user that definitions, penalties and other references to the series should be examined carefully to determine whether they apply to the noted section.

For example, *Oregon Revised Statutes* contains chapter 137 relating to judgment, execution, parole and probation. A law relating to any of those subjects may be enacted but not legislatively added to ORS chapter 137, even though the section clearly belongs with the related materials found in that chapter. The Legislative Counsel compiles the section where it logically belongs and provides the "not added to" note.

[text omitted]

actual Amber alert statute in Oregon

181.035 Amber Plan; rules. (1) The Department of State Police shall work with Oregon law enforcement agencies, the Department of Transportation, local media and broadcasters and others to fully implement a state Amber Plan.

(2) The Department of State Police shall adopt rules establishing the criteria to be applied in determining whether to issue an alert under the Amber Plan.

(3) A broadcaster participating in an Amber Plan implemented under this section is immune from civil liability for any act or omission of the broadcaster in the course and scope of that participation. The immunity provided under this subsection:

(a) Applies regardless of the method of transmission used by the broadcaster.

(b) Does not apply to intentional misconduct or to conduct that was grossly negligent. [2003 c.314 §1; 2005 c.441 §1]

Note: 181.035 was enacted into law by the Legislative Assembly but was not added to or made a part of ORS chapter 181 or any series therein by legislative action. See Preface to Oregon Revised Statutes for further explanation.

added to and made a part of." The reference makes it clear that the section is still considered law. The lesson learned here is to read the statute you are reviewing carefully and completely to understand its effect and composition.

PRACTICE TIP

The legislative branch, whether federal or state, has the primary responsibility to make laws. When researching, always check to determine if there is a relevant statute that applies to your fact situation. However, to be thorough, always review applicable cases and other primary authorities.

Conflicts between Federal and State Statutes—Who Rules?

When there is a conflict between state laws and the U.S. Constitution, the U.S. Constitution always wins. Conceptually this is known as **preemption.** Preemption is a concept based upon a judicial doctrine that interpreted the supremacy clause of the U.S. Constitution. Under the doctrine of preemption, if a federal and state law conflict, federal law and the U.S. Constitution always take precedence over the state law. You may ask yourself, "how does this work?" Let's use a recent case from the Fifth Circuit Court of Appeals. In *Brown v. Brown & Williamson Tobacco Corporation,* 479 F.3d 383 (5th Cir. 2007), the federal statute involved is the Cigarette Labeling and Advertising Act and the labeling of "light" cigarettes. The plaintiffs in the case claim that a Louisiana state statute and common law claims are not preempted (meaning superseded) by the federal statute. In this instance, the court pointed out that the federal government had a long history of regulating cigarette advertising. Federal regulations through the Federal Trade Commission (FTC) set the standards for the use of descriptive terms in advertising, such as "light" or "low-tar" in describing the nicotine and tar content in cigarettes. Because of the history and extensive involvement of the FTC in regulating cigarette labeling and advertising, the court held that the state claims were preempted by federal law. There are instances where state statutes appear to conflict with federal law but are not preempted; remember, case law must be reviewed to understand the legal arguments for those exceptions.

preemption
Right of the federal government to exclusive governance in matters concerning all citizens equally.

A Quick Note about Locating Constitutions

The U.S. Constitution is reprinted and annotated in both the *U.S.C.A.* and *U.S.C.S.* It is also printed by the federal government in a separate pamphlet, and can be found as an appendix in a wide variety of sources. The availability of annotated information is as important (perhaps even more important) when researching the Constitution as when researching statutes, in that the impact and accepted meaning of the broad provisions of the Constitution can only be gauged through an analysis of court interpretations. Therefore, to determine how sections of the U.S. Constitution have been interpreted, review one of the annotated codes (or, as will be discussed in later chapters, a fee-based service). There you will find cases interpreting the constitutional issues.

The text of state constitutions is likewise found in annotated state codes (and unannotated versions as well). State constitutions vary widely in terms of length and depth of coverage, with some going into great detail about the workings of state government. State cases and cross-references are found in the annotation sections of the respective state codes and are an important source to review.

There are many other resources relating to the Constitution and state constitutions. However, for most of your assignments as a paralegal, the constitutional texts found in the annotated codes, federal and state, will adequately fulfill your requirements.

A Checklist for Locating Statutes

Developing a plan to tackle statutory research is critical to your successful completion of an assignment. Some suggestions for a checklist are as follows:

- Determine whether your issue involves federal or state law.
- Write down applicable words and phrases that apply to your fact situation.
- Locate the general or subject index at the end of the codes. Begin looking up the words and phrases until you find an applicable code section.

- In conjunction with the general index, if you believe you know the common name or popular name of the statute, look up the name in the Popular Name Index. Remember, some state statutes have Popular Name Indexes, but not all. If you locate the statute through the popular name, identify the code title and section where the statute appears.
- Retrieve the appropriate volume of the statutory code, and locate the applicable code section. Before reading the code section, check the pocket parts or supplements to determine whether any amendments or changes occurred in the statute. If the statute has not been repealed, begin reading the code section in its entirety, including the pocket part sections, if revised.
- Review the cross-references to determine whether other statutes may apply.
- Review the library references for additional primary and secondary sources that may be helpful.
- Review the notes of decisions section, which contains cases that have interpreted the statutory section.
- Check the session laws to determine whether there are any recent changes in the statute.
- Check the legislative Web sites for any changes in the statute.

All that you can ask of yourself is to be thorough. If you follow the trail, you will not leave a stone unturned.

Using the Internet for Statutory Research: The Unavoidable

With updates often issued annually, there is no way to avoid using the Internet to gain access to the most current statutory information. Whether you use a fee-based site or a government Web site, you must check the Internet for current information. Usually the lag time between a statutory change and its update on the Internet is often just twenty-four to forty-eight hours. That is a huge difference from the print-based sources, both federal and state, which are updated annually. Therefore, review your state legislative and federal government Web sites for the most complete and up-to-date information on statutes.

Citing a Statute

In previous chapters, we discussed how to cite a case. Statutes also have a specific format for citation. Since federal statutes are identified by their titles, rather than their volume, the first group of numbers is the title where the statute can be found. Consequently, when you search for a statute, look on the binding for the beginning of the title for which you are interested. The next item of information is the name of the

YOU BE THE JUDGE

A man protests on a street corner in Dallas, Texas, by burning the American flag. He is arrested on the grounds that he violated a state statute that prohibited the desecration of a state or national flag. The U.S. Supreme Court held that the state statute is unconstitutional as it violates the First Amendment's right to free speech. The U.S. Congress is incensed by the Court's ruling and passes the Flag Protection Act of 1989, which made it a criminal act when a person knowingly "mutilates, defaces, physically defiles, burns, maintains upon the floor or ground, or tramples upon" a flag of the United States. Review *United States v. Eichman,* 496 U.S. 310, 313 (1990). Compare *Texas v. Johnson,* 491 U.S. 397, 109 S. Ct. 2533, 105 L. Ed. 2d 342 (1989) and *United States v. Eichman,* 496 U.S. 310, 110 S. Ct. 2404, 110 L. Ed. 2d 287 (1990), both of which dealt with the flag-burning issue. Contrast the facts of both cases. What is the significant difference in the cases? What were the holdings of the U.S. Supreme Court? Are these holdings different? Can they be reconciled?

code. For federal statutes, the code is the *U.S. Code.* It is abbreviated as *U.S.C.* You must always cite to the official code. Unlike reporters with their star-paging system, the federal statutes do not have an elaborate referencing system. Since you will most likely have either the *U.S. Code Annotated* or the *U.S. Code Service* as a reference tool, simply drop the "A" from Annotated or the "S" from Service and voilà, you have the proper citation for a federal code. Seems a bit simplistic, but that's it.

The next part of the citation contains the symbol for section: "§." This symbol is followed by the actual section of the statute referenced. Therefore, a citation for a statute is 42 U.S.C. § 2401. That means you are searching for Title 42 in the *United States Code* and specifically section 2401.

State statutes vary significantly as to composition. This is particularly important as all the state statutory code names vary as well as the arrangement of those codes. Some codes are divided into titles; others are divided into subject codes, while others are listed numerically. Check a citation manual for guidance on the specific rules for citing a state statute.

PRACTICE TIP

Two section §§ symbols together indicates more than one section, such as 42 U.S.C. §§ 1–10. When you see a statute cited using the words *et seq.*, it means "and what follows." This suggests that the statute is being cited for its general contents and appears as follows: 42 U.S.C. § 1 *et seq.*

Local Governments: Charters and Ordinances

We know that ordinances and charters are primary sources of the law. As a general rule, most cities and towns are created by state statute. These statutes delegate the authority upon which the city or town may act. To govern, these municipalities create local constitutions known as **charters.** Charters identify how the municipal government is organized and the authority of the departments and agencies within the municipality. Many municipalities have a code of **ordinances** analogous to a statutory code. These ordinances are passed by the local legislative bodies, such as a city council. As a result, ordinances affect only the town or city that enacted the local law. Municipal codes rarely have case citations, although there is some coverage in the individual state editions of Shepard's. Check your local library for more information about the system in your community.

charter
Local constitution.

ordinance
A law passed by a local government, such as a town council or city government.

Finding Municipal or Local Ordinances

Most municipal or local ordinances can be found at city hall, the city clerk's office, or some other official office of a city or town. Usually these offices maintain copies of the ordinances for that city or town only. Copies of municipal ordinances also are found in most local public libraries.

As many cities and towns advance into the electronic age, Web sites are being developed, which often have current ordinances available. Updating on the Internet may be problematic, so as a precaution always verify the status of a municipal ordinance through a hard copy from the city hall or city clerk's office. Chances are that the larger cities and towns have extensive Web sites. Check to see when a Web site has last been updated to determine whether additional research is necessary. Some city Web sites offer step-by-step instruction in locating an ordinance for that town.

Unfortunately, researching a municipal ordinance may be "hit or miss" depending on the financial resources and available personnel of the city or town. But do check the Internet, local government offices, and libraries for the best sources for municipal information.

CYBER TRIP

Determine whether your city or town has a Web site with its municipal ordinances and local charters. Peruse the site and observe its contents. If your town does not have a Web site, choose the closest metropolitan area.

Court Rules: A Guide to the Court Process

Annotated in the *U.S.C.A.* and *U.S.C.S.* and reprinted under separate cover are the **rules of court.** The court rules govern the litigation process in civil and criminal proceedings. (*Civil law* resolves disputes between parties and often involves some type of monetary compensation for the wrongful acts of another party. On the other hand,

rules of court
The rules that govern the litigation process in civil and criminal proceedings.

ETHICS ALERT

In this chapter, one of the primary sources of the law, court rules, was discussed. Court rules govern the judicial and litigation process. One of the most important court rules is Rule 11 of the Federal Rules of Civil Procedure, which provides that attorneys must have adequate legal basis in promoting a client's position. That means an attorney cannot misrepresent a client's position and expect the court to overlook the infraction. In *Jenkins v. Methodist Hospital of Dallas, Inc.*, 478 F.3d 255 (5th Cir. 2007), a court, ***sua sponte*** (Latin for "of one's own accord"), admonished an attorney for misrepresenting the language in an affidavit of his client, which, if accepted, would have changed the meaning of the statement and possibly the outcome of the case. The attorney claimed that the misstatement was not intentional; but when pressed, he blamed the error in the statement on an associate attorney's failure to "catch" the error. In relying on Rule 11, the Court reviewed the advisory notes to assist in determining whether sanctions were proper. The advisory committee note stated that a lawyer must "stop-and-think' before . . . making legal or factual contentions." *Id.* at 265 citing Advisory Committee Notes on Fed. R. Civ. p. 11 (1993 Amendments). The lower court concluded that "for his unprofessional conduct in not verifying the accuracy of the alleged quotation and in not promptly withdrawing it when the error was pointed out in Defendants' Reply Brief," the court gave the attorney a public reprimand. *Id.* at 266. The appeals court agreed with the lower court's handling of the matter and affirmed the public reprimand.

sua sponte
On his or her own motion; rarely exercised right of the judge to make a motion and ruling without an underlying request from either party.

PRACTICE TIP

Pay close attention to the local rules of courts. Often documents that you file may be rejected because you didn't follow a local rule. (Worse yet, malpractice or ethical violations could occur, such as the dismissal of a client's claim.) If you and your attorney are practicing in a new court, *always* check the local rules of court for that court's nuances. Doing so could mean the difference between success and failure on a case; or worse, could cost you your job.

criminal law involves the wrongful acts committed by an individual against society. Normally, state and federal legislatures define those acts that violate society's standards imposing a punishment, such as imprisonment, fines, or in extreme cases, death, for violation of those standards.) The rules used to guide the civil process in the federal courts are the Federal Rules of Civil Procedure, and for criminal cases, the Federal Rules of Criminal Procedure. These rules control the court process and are the guide for judges and attorneys in litigating or prosecuting a case.

Other types of court rules are the Rules of Evidence, governing the admission of evidence at a trial, and Rules of Appellate Procedure, governing the parties on an appeal. These rules are often located in either the federal codes or, at the local level, in state codes. The complexity of the rules of court is compounded even further because many courts have their own rules for their individual courts, known as **local rules.** These rules supplement the existing rules of court and also must be consulted when practicing in any court, whether state or federal.

local rules
Individual rules for a particular court that supplement the other rules of court.

This case presents a number of ethical and practical issues to consider. First, do not misrepresent your client's position (and think you or your attorney will get away with it). Present the facts of a client's case accurately and honestly. Second, Rule 11 sanctions should not be taken lightly; they reflect on your attorney as well as those associated with him or her. Review the case and notice how quick the attorney was to blame "an associate" for the error. Don't think this could not happen to you. All too often when a case is going "downhill," attorneys search for scapegoats. Usually, judges are quick to recognize this behavior for what it is: causing more harm. The moral of the story is: perform your job with integrity and don't get caught being the "fall guy" for anyone's bad behavior. Pay attention to what's going on around you. Third, the case teaches us to carefully proofread documents submitted to a court. Do not underestimate the importance of proofreading any document submitted to your attorney. Be thorough. And finally, in this case the attorney was given two months to correct his error or misstatement of fact. He ignored the court and was sanctioned. Deadlines are important, and had the attorney in the *Jenkins* case respected the deadlines given by the court, his actions might have been mitigated.

Quick Quiz True/False Questions

1. The *United States Code* is the unofficial version of federal statutes.
2. Annotated codes have a section that analyzes cases called notes of decisions.
3. Preemption means that a state statute supersedes a federal statute.
4. Court rules cannot be found in the *United States Code Annotated* or *U.S. Code Service.*
5. All state codes are cataloged the same way.

LEGISLATIVE HISTORY: FINDING THE "TRUE" MEANING OF THE WORDS

Sometimes the language of a statute may not be entirely clear, and a dispute may arise over its meaning. In such a case the **legislative history** can be consulted. For some bills the legislative history can be extensive. Legislative histories for federal statutes are generally on file at the more comprehensive law libraries; however, some suggested places to review a bill's legislative history are:

legislative history
The transcripts of the legislative debates leading up to the passage of the bill that became the law or statute.

a. Committee Hearings: Both the House and Senate hold hearings on proposed legislation. When a hearing occurs, a transcript of the testimony is taken. This transcript may offer insight as to the legislative intent. The best place to locate committee hearing reports is a government-sponsored Web site such as www.access.gpo.gov.
b. Committee Reports: When a bill is reported out of committee, the committee produces a report with an analysis of the bill and the basis for the committee's recommendations. This may be the best place to locate a legislative history. Again, the best place to find a committee report is www.access.gpo.gov.
c. Floor Debates: The official record of all House and Senate debates is the ***Congressional Record.*** The *Record* is printed daily and can be helpful in determining legislative history of a law. In addition to the previously referenced government Web site, another helpful government Web site is www.thomas.gov.

Congressional Record
Contains the official records of proceedings and debates of Congress.

Finding legislative histories may be a challenge. Some common places for guidance are:

a. *CCH Congressional Index:* This set of books contains digests of bills, voting records of members of Congress, and current news.
b. Congressional Information Service (CIS): This service includes a number of sources such as the *CIS Index, CIS Annual,* and *CIS Legislative Histories.* Each source is printed annually.
c. *U.S. Code Congressional and Administrative News:* This legislative source publishes by year the statutes passed in that congressional session, some committee reports and, most importantly, West research references.

Some books are known for being authorities on legislative histories. The two best-known books are *Sources of Compiled Legislative Histories* by Nancy P. Johnson and *Federal Legislative Histories: An Annotated Bibliography and Index to Officially Published Sources* by Bernard Reams. These treatises may be a good starting point for locating information on a statute's legislative history.

The question on your mind is, "why should I care about a statute's legislative history?" Generally, you don't. When your research hinges on an interpretation of a word or why a particular word was used over another, the legislative history can be very beneficial. Congressional debates may identify the intent surrounding words, which may guide a

PRACTICE TIP

Some states, such as Arizona, do not maintain legislative histories for publication.

CYBER TRIP

Determine whether your state posts electronic versions of its legislative histories and from what date those electronic histories begin.

court in making a decision on that case, especially when case law does not exist on the matter. In the *Brown v. Brown & Williamson Tobacco Corporation* case noted earlier in the chapter, the tobacco company prepared an extensive legislative history of federal oversight of the tobacco industry in support of its position before the court. The court utilized this history in deciding the case. Consequently, the legislative history was not only relevant but persuasive in presenting the position of the defendants in the case.

State Legislative History

For state legislative histories pertaining to state statutes, you may have to dig a little deeper. Go to the state library at your state's capital or the legislative archives; check the location of these records for your own state. To obtain the legislative history of an out-of-state statute, you will almost certainly have to contact a library in that state or that state legislature. Most states now have Web sites devoted to the actions of the respective state legislature. How extensively the legislative histories date back varies from state to state. Most have archive histories, which may only be accessible in person through the use of microfilm or microfiche. You will have better luck with newer statutes as many of those legislative histories are computerized.

A Checklist for Locating Legislative Histories

There are no hard and fast rules for researching a state's legislative history. However, here are some suggestions:

- The best place to begin examining a legislative history is in the historical notes at the end of the statute itself.
- Review the historical notes section of the statute for amendments.
- The *Congressional Record* may offer insight into the history of the statute along with the respective congressional committee reports.
- Check printed material such as the *U.S. Congressional and Administrative News* or a source by the Congressional Information Service (CIS).
- Check the books by Nancy P. Johnson and Bernard Reams; these publications are known for their extensive treatment of legislative histories.
- With legislative histories, the best places to locate information are on the Internet on government-sponsored Web sites, including those by the U.S. Congress and Library of Congress.
- Contact the legislatures, either federal or state, directly and locate personnel who can assist you with your inquiry.

Quick Quiz True/False Questions

1. Legislative histories help provide the intent of a particular statute.
2. The committee reports from Congress are the only place to locate a legislative history.
3. The historical notes section of a statute provides insight into the legislative history.
4. State legislative histories can be found only in a state library.
5. Government Web sites provide the best places to locate legislative histories.

ADMINISTRATIVE REGULATIONS AND DECISIONS: IS THERE A NEEDLE IN THE HAYSTACK?

Often known as the "fourth" branch of government, administrative agencies govern the regulatory process. Created by federal or state statutes, administrative agencies govern the processes of a particular area by enacting rules and regulations, and adjudicating cases involving those agencies. Before learning where to find administrative rules, regulations, and cases, a general overview of the functions of an administrative agency is in order.

The Development of Administrative Agencies

As we are all aware, the U.S. Constitution created three branches of government: legislative, executive, and judicial. As the population of the United States grew, it became apparent that more specialized oversight of various areas was needed. In the early 1940s, regulation of industry became too much for Congress. To unburden some of the oversight authority, Congress statutorily created **administrative agencies** by "delegating" certain limited and defined authority to legislate, adjudicate, and investigate. Although considered questionable then, the delegation of these oversight powers is quite commonplace in today's world.

administrative agencies
Statutorily created departments that have the authority to legislate, adjudicate, and investigate matters between parties or violations of rules or regulations.

Through legislation, Congress (or a state legislature) passes a statute creating the specific administrative agency. Within that statute, parameters of the authority are set in place. The administrative agency must act within the confines of the legislative enactment or risk its actions being deemed unconstitutional by a court. Additionally, Congress set forth checks and balances by passing the **Administrative Procedure Act** (APA; 5 U.S.C. §§ 551–707). This act lays the groundwork for how federal administrative agencies work and how they create rules and regulations and adjudicate violations of those rules and regulations. States have similar enabling statutes that govern how an agency functions.

Administrative Procedure Act (APA)
A statute that lays the foundation as to how administrative agencies function, create rules and regulations, and adjudicate violations of those regulations.

Administrative agencies are a part of our everyday life. You might not think about it, but every time you step on an airplane, breathe clean air, or watch television, administrative agencies have set forth rules and regulations that govern related behavior. For example, recall Janet Jackson's wardrobe malfunction at the 2004 Super Bowl game. The network that aired the Super Bowl half-time program was fined by the Federal Communications Commission (FCC) for indecent acts and violating the FCC rule on indecency in the media. After September 11, 2001, higher constraints were placed on passengers traveling by air through the creation of the Transportation Security Administration, commonly known as the TSA. Screening all liquids prior to boarding an airplane or eliminating sharp objects in carry-on luggage are just a few examples of this administrative agency's oversight. Examples of administrative rules and regulations affecting your daily life are numerous; you just never realized it.

rule or regulation
Similar to a statute, the agency's protocols that govern the behavior of citizens and businesses.

rulemaking
The agency process of developing its rules and regulations.

Rulemaking Authority: How Agencies Create Their Rules and Regulations

Through the delegation of the legislative authority, administrative agencies create rules and regulations by using their "rulemaking" authority. Similar to a statute, a **rule** or **regulation** governs the behavior of citizens and businesses. Rules and regulations have the same effect as a statute with fines and penalties levied for their violation. There are three basic types of **rulemaking**: formal rulemaking, informal rulemaking, and hybrid rulemaking. Although the most common is informal rulemaking, understanding the differences is critical to learning the process.

CYBER TRIP

To see how the informal rulemaking process works, go to the ICF Consulting Web site at www.icfi.com/Services/Regulatory_Support/doc_files/noprint_Flowchart.pdf. It will assist you in understanding the administrative process more thoroughly.

- **Formal Rulemaking:** Formal rulemaking, or rulemaking on the record, is a trial-type proceeding. When this type of rulemaking takes place, formal public hearings are convened with witnesses and evidence presented. Additionally, the proposed rule must be published so the public can either comment or present testimony. It is a very structured, long process and rarely used.
- **Informal Rulemaking:** Informal rulemaking is also known as "notice and comment" rulemaking. In this process, a rule is published and the public is given an opportunity to comment on the proposed rule. Sometimes the comments

are incorporated into the rule, and other the times the rule will go into effect without regard to the public's comments. This process is the most common way for promulgating agency rules and regulations.

- **Hybrid Rulemaking:** A combination of formal and informal rulemaking, hybrid rulemaking occurs when required by statute. Under hybrid rulemaking, a record is created justifying the rule or regulation that is affected.

Agencies cannot make their rules and regulations in a vacuum. Under the APA, procedures are set forth for agencies to follow when creating or amending rules and regulations. To promulgate a new or amended rule or regulation, an agency often has to take part in a three-step process. The agency must notify the public of a proposed rule or regulation or a change in an existing one. The public has an opportunity to make comments on the proposed rule or change. Rules and regulations generally cannot become final unless the public has the opportunity to comment. A published time period for the notice and comment occurs. Sometimes the comments evoke change in the original proposed rule. After a final rule is drafted it is then published so those affected will become aware of the rule. There are a wide variety of federal, state, and municipal agencies that issue rules and regulations. The ability to find these regulations and the administrative decisions construing them is an important element of your skills as a paralegal. The challenge, for all of us, is locating administrative rules and regulations. As you will learn, administrative rules and regulations, whether federal or state, are not always organized in the most logical fashion. Sometimes you feel as though you are looking for a needle in a haystack! However, we must push on and do our best to find it.

Judicial Authority: Administrative Agencies Acting like a Court

Along with their authority to create rules and regulations, administrative agencies also can adjudicate controversies between parties. When an agency acts as a court, it renders judicial decisions called **administrative decisions or orders.** These decisions have the same effect as a decision of a court but may be reviewed by a federal court for very limited purposes, if necessary. Before an administrative decision can be reviewed by a court, all the administrative remedies must be exhausted. This is known as the doctrine of **exhaustion of administrative remedies.** What this means is: if an administrative agency provides a means to challenge a decision of an administrative hearing officer or judge, the administrative process must be exhausted before filing a challenge in a federal or state court. Normally the review of an administrative decision is limited.

administrative decisions or orders
The judicial-like decisions of an administrative agency.

exhaustion of administrative remedies
Provision that a nonlitigation process to informally resolve disputes must be attempted prior to filing a complaint.

The question you should be asking yourself is, "where can I find these rules and regulations that may govern a client or me?" The answer is in the *Federal Register* and *Code of Federal Regulations.*

Finding Federal Administrative Rules and Regulations

There are two main sources for finding hardbound sources of administrative rules and regulations: the *Federal Register* and the *Code of Federal Regulations.* Each is discussed in this section.

The Federal Register

Federal regulations have been printed for over fifty years in the *Federal Register,* a daily journal of all regulations (as well as proclamations, orders, and notices) issued by federal agencies. It is the official publication of rules and regulations and notices of executive actions by federal agencies. The *Federal Register* (cited as *Fed. Reg.*) is analogous to the *Statutes at Large* in that it publishes regulations chronologically, rather than by subject, and thus is unwieldy for comprehensive research. The types of information found in the *Federal Register* vary, but the following are representative of the documents published:

- Proposed and Final Rules and Regulations: Any rule or regulation that an agency intends to pass must be published first in the *Federal Register*. For proposed rules, the rule is set forth within the time period in which interested parties have to comment on the rule. Relating to the proposed rule may be announcements of public hearings, corrections to the proposed rule, or any other action affecting the rule. Similarly, when the final rule is passed, the complete text of the final rule will appear with commentary on the purpose behind the rule.
- Presidential Documents: Any documents relating to the president, such as proclamations, executive orders, or important letters, may be published in the *Federal Register*. Figure 5.13 is an example of a presidential document printed in the *Federal Register*.
- Notices and Meetings: Any meetings that affect the public as well as hearings are published in the *Federal Register*. Coupled with these notices is information pertaining to reports or studies that may be available to the public for review, such as reports on employee safety under the Occupational Safety and Health Administration (OSHA).

CYBER TRIP

Locate an administrative decision from the U.S Environmental Protection Agency (EPA) and the National Labor Relations Board (NLRB).

Presidential Documents

Memorandum of December 22, 2005

Order of Succession of Officers to Act as Secretary of Defense

Memorandum for the Secretary of Defense

By the authority vested in me as President by the Constitution and the laws of the United States of America, including the Federal Vacancies Reform Act of 1998, 5 U.S.C. 3345 *et. seq.*, and notwithstanding the Executive Order I issued today entitled, "Providing an Order of Succession within the Department of Defense" (the order), it is hereby ordered as follows:

(1) Subject to the provisions of paragraphs 2 and 4 of this memorandum, the Acting Deputy Secretary of Defense, as designated by the President, shall act as and perform the functions and duties of the office of the Secretary of Defense (Secretary) during any period when the Secretary has died, resigned, or is otherwise unable to perform functions and duties of the office of the Secretary.

(2) The provisions of paragraph 1 of this memorandum shall only apply if, at the time of the death, resignation, or inability of the Secretary, the Acting Deputy Secretary of Defense meets one or more of the criteria established in section 3345(a)(1)–(3) of title 5, United States Code.

(3) In all other respects, the order shall remain in effect.

(4) The authority of this memorandum shall terminate upon the first appointment by the President of a Deputy Secretary of Defense to occur subsequent to this memorandum, unless sooner terminated by operation of law or by the President.

(5) You are authorized and directed to publish this memorandum in the *Federal Register*.

THE WHITE HOUSE,
Washington, December 22, 2005.

FIGURE 5.13

Presidential Proclamation from the *Federal Register*

Source: Federal Register, Vol. 70, No. 247, December 27, 2005, "Presidential Documents."

The *Federal Register* will be the first place you can review a newly passed rule or regulation in print form. Although the *Federal Register* is "supposed" to be a daily publication, the caveat is that it is not always readily available on a daily basis. Since most agencies have a Web site, check the Web site to locate recently passed or updated rules and regulations. Otherwise, contact the agency directly for the current status of rules and regulations.

Using the *Federal Register* is not always easy. The best place to start is the back of the publication in the section titled "Reader Aids." This section provides information about the *Federal Register* system as compared to the table of contents in the front of the *Federal Register,* which only addresses information in that volume. Also, you can find a list of public laws passed as well as the regulatory code sections affected during that month. Figure 5.14 shows a passage from the *Federal Register.*

FIGURE 5.14 **Passage from the *Federal Register***

Source: Federal Register, Vol. 71, No. 241, December 15, 2006.

Proposed Rules

Federal Register, Vol. 71, No. 241

Friday, December 15, 2006

This section of the FEDERAL REGISTER contains notices to the public of the proposed issuance of rules and regulations. The purpose of these notices is to give interested persons an opportunity to participate in the rule making prior to the adoption of the final rules.

DEPARTMENT OF TRANSPORTATION

Federal Aviation Administration

14 CFR Part 39

[Docket no. FAA—2006–26595; Directorate Identifier 2006–NM–208–AD]

RIN 2120–AA64

Airworthiness Directives; Airbus Model A320 Series Airplanes

AGENCY: Federal Aviation Administration (FAA), Department of Transportation (DOT)

ACTION: Notice of proposed rulemaking (NPRM)

SUMMARY: The FAA proposed to adopt a new airworthiness directive (AD) for certain Airbus Model A320 series airplanes. This proposed AD would require replacing the carbon fiber reinforced plastic (CFRP) actuator fittings of the rudder with aluminum actuator fittings and doing related investigative and corrective actions. This proposed AD results from rupture of a CFRP actuator fitting during maintenance. We are proposing this AD to prevent rupture of a rudder actuator fitting, which could result in reduced controllability of the airplane.

DATES: We must receive comments on this proposed AD by January 16, 2007.

ADDRESSES: Use one of the following addresses to submit comments on this proposed AD.

- *DOT Docket Web site:* Go to *http://dms.dot.gov* and follow the instructions for sending your comments electronically.
- *Government-wide rulemaking Web site:* Go to *http://www.regulations.gov* and follow the instructions for sending your comments electronically.
- *Mail:* Docket Management Facility, U.S. Department of Transportation, 400 Seventh Street, SW., Nassif Building, Room PL–401, Washington, DC 20590.
- *Fax:* (202) 493–2251.
- *Hand Delivery:* Room PL–401 on the plaza level of the Nassif Building, 400 Seventh Street, SW., Washington, DC, between 9 a.m. and 5 p.m., Monday through Friday, except Federal holidays.

Contact Airbus, 1 Rond Point Maurice Belfonte, 31702 Blagnac Cedex, France for service information identified in this proposed AD.

FOR FURTHER INFORMATION CONTACT: Dan Rodina, Aerospace Engineer, International Branch, ANM–116, FAA, Transport Airplane Directorate, 1601 Lind Avenue, SW., Renton, Washington 98057–3356; telephone (425) 227–2125; fax (425) 227–1149.

SUPPLEMENTARY INFORMATION:

Comments Invited

We invite you to submit any relevant written data, views, or arguments regarding this proposed AD. Send your comments to an address listed in the **ADDRESSES** section. Include the docket number "FAA–2006–26595; Directorate Identifier 2006–NM–208–AD" at the beginning of your comments. We specifically invite comments on the overall regulatory economic environmental and energy aspects of the proposed AD. We will consider all comments received by the closing date and may amend the proposed AD in light of those comments.

We will post all comments we receive, without change, to *http://dms.dot.gov,* including any personal information you provide. We will also post a report summarizing each substantive verbal contact with FAA personnel concerning this proposed AD. Using the search

Cont.

FIGURE 5.14 **Passage from the *Federal Register* *Cont.***

function of that Web site, anyone can find and read the comments in any of our dockets, including the name of the individual who sent the comment (or signed the comment on behalf of an association, business, labor union, etc.). You may review the DOS's complete Privacy Act Statement in the **Federal Register** published on April 11, 2000 (65 FR 19477–78), or you may visit *http://dms.dot.gov.*

Examining the Docket

You may examine the AD docket on the Internet at *http://dms.dot.gov,* or in person at the Docket management Facility office between 9 a.m. and 5 p.m., Monday through Friday, except Federal holidays. The Docket Management Facility office (telephone (800) 647-5227) is located on the plaza level of the Nassif Building at the DOT street address stated in the **ADDRESSES** section. Comments will be available in the AD docket shortly after the Docket Management System receives them.

Discussion

The European Aviation Safety Agency (EASA), which is the airworthiness authority for the European Union, notified us that an unsafe condition may exist on certain Airbus Model A320 series airplanes. The EASA advises that a carbon fiber plastic reinforced (DFRP) actuator fitting of the rudder ruptured during incorrect accomplishment of airplane maintenance task 27–21–00–710–001. Investigation revealed that the CFRP actuator fittings cannot sustain limit loads resulting from ground gust conditions due to design of the fitting. Rupture of a rudder actuator fitting, if not corrected, could result in reduced controllability of the airplane.

Relevant Service Information

Airbus has issued Service Bulletin A320–1030, dated March 6, 2006. The service bulletin describes procedures for replacing all three of the CFRP actuator fittings of the rudder with aluminum actuator fittings and doing related investigative and corrective actions. The related investigative action is an inspection of the bushings to ensure that they are not elongated or out of measurement. The corrective action is to replace any damaged bushing with a new bushing. Accomplishing the actions specified in the service information is intended to adequately address the unsafe condition. The EASA mandated the service information and issued airworthiness directive 2006–0262, dated August 25, 2006, to ensure the continued airworthiness of these airplanes in the European Union.

FAA's Determination and Requirements of the Proposed AD

This airplane model is manufactured in France and is type certificated for operation in the United States under the provisions of section 21.29 of the Federal Aviation Regulations (14 CFR 21.29) and the applicable bilateral airworthiness agreement. As described in FAA Order 8100.14A, "Interim Procedures for Working with the European Community on Airworthiness Certification and Continued Airworthiness," dated August 12, 2006, the EASA has kept the FAA informed of the situation described above. We have. . . .

[text omitted]

The Code of Federal Regulations

Published annually, the *Code of Federal Regulations* (cited and often abbreviated as *C.F.R.*) is a compilation of all effective regulations arranged by subject. Similar to the *United States Code, C.F.R.* is segmented into fifty titles and updated annually. However, unlike the statutes, *C.F.R.* volumes are updated quarterly in groups:

- By January 1: Titles 1–16
- By April 1: Titles 17–27
- By July 1: Titles 28–41
- By October 1: Titles 42–50

The titles are divided into chapters, parts, subparts, and sections covering the rules and regulations of that particular federal agency. By checking the current *C.F.R.* and all subsequent issues of the *Federal Register,* you can identify those regulations affected in a given area. Figure 5.15 is an example from the *C.F.R.*

Updates to Code of Federal Regulations *and Agency Actions*

Two publications provide updates in supplement form to agency actions not contained in the main volumes of the *Code of Federal Regulations.* They are the List of Sections Affected (LSA) and CFR Parts Affected.

FIGURE 5.15 Sample Pages from the *Code of Federal Regulations*

CHAPTER XII—TRANSPORTATION SECURITY ADMINISTRATION, DEPARTMENT OF HOMELAND SECURITY

EDITORIAL NOTE: Nomenclature changes to chapter XII appear at 68 FR 49720, Aug. 19, 2003.

[text omitted]
where aircraft operators and foreign air carriers that have a security program under part 1544 or 1546 of this chapter enplane and deplane passengers and sort and load baggage and any adjacent areas that are not separated by adequate security measures.

Security Identification Display Area (SIDA) means a portion of an airport, specified in the airport security program, in which security measures specified in this part are carried out. This area includes the secured area and may include other areas of the airport.

Sterile area means a portion of an airport defined in the airport security program that provides passengers access to boarding aircraft and to which the access generally is controlled by TSA, or by an aircraft operator under part 1544 of this chapter or a foreign air carrier under part 1546 of this chapter, through the screening of persons and property.

Unescorted access authority means the authority granted by an airport operator, an aircraft operator, foreign air carrier, or airport tenant under part 1542, 1544, or 1546 of this chapter, to individuals to gain entry to, and be present without an escort in, secured areas and SIDA's of airports.

[67 FR 8353, Feb. 22, 2002, as amended at 67 FR 8209, Feb. 22, 2002]

Subpart B—Responsibilities of Passengers and Other Individuals and Persons

§1540.101 Applicability of this subpart.

This subpart applies to individuals and other persons.

§1540.103 Fraud and intentional falsification of records.

No person may make, or cause to be made, any of the following:

(a) Any fraudulent or intentionally false statement in any application for any security program, access medium, or identification medium, or any amendment thereto, under this subchapter.

(b) Any fraudulent or intentionally false entry in any record or report that is kept, made, or used to show compliance with this subchapter, or exercise any privileges under this subchapter.

(c) Any reproduction or alteration, for fraudulent purpose, of any report, record, security program, access medium, or identification medium issued under this subchapter.

Cont.

FIGURE 5.15 **Sample Pages from the *Code of Federal Regulations* Cont.**

§ 1540.105 Security responsibilities of employees and other persons.

(a) No person may:

(1) Tamper or interfere with, compromise, modify, attempt to circumvent, or cause a person to tamper or interfere with, compromise, modify, or attempt to circumvent any security system, measure, or procedure implemented under this subchapter.

(2) Enter, or be present within, a secured area, AOA, SIDA or sterile area without complying with the systems, measures, or procedures being applied to control access to, or presence or movement in, such areas.

(3) Use, allow to be used, or cause to be used, any airport-issued or airport-approved access medium or identification medium that authorizes the access, presence, or movement of persons or vehicles in secured areas, AOA's, or SIDA's in any other manner than that for which it was issued by the appropriate authority under this subchapter.

(b) The provisions of paragraph (a) of this section do not apply to conducting inspections or tests to determine compliance with this part or 49 U.S.C. Subtitle VII authorized by:

(1) TSA, or

(2) The airport operator, aircraft operator, or foreign air carrier, when acting in accordance with the procedures described in a security program approved by TSA.

§ 1540.107 Submission to screening and inspection.

No individual may enter a sterile area or board an aircraft without submitting to the screening and inspection of his or her person and accessible property in accordance with the procedures being applied to control access to that area or aircraft under this subchapter.

[67 FR 41639, June 19, 2002]

List of Sections Affected (LSA)

Since *C.F.R.* is issued annually with updates issued quarterly, the List of Sections Affected (LSA) provides a monthly cumulative list of changes to CFR sections. LSA is coordinated to the CFR Parts Affected with such information as its status and the page where that information appears in the *Federal Register.* Consultation with LSA is critical for a comprehensive and accurate review of any administrative rule and regulation. However, the print version of LSA is not nearly as current as one of its electronic versions located at www.gpoaccess.gov. On that site there are three additional LSA supplements, which provide monthly and daily information. They are: List of CFR Parts Affected Today, Current List of CFR Parts Affected, and finally, Last Month's List of CFR Parts Affected. These electronic supplements should be consulted for the most accurate and current administrative information.

PRACTICE TIP

The titles of *Code of Federal Regulations* and the *United States Code* do not match. Do not assume that Title 50 dealing with the Department of Transportation corresponds to Title 50 of the *United States Code.* Check each independently, and if titles happen to correlate, it is only a coincidence.

CFR Parts Affected

Located in the *Federal Register,* the print version of the CFR Parts Affected is issued monthly and only addresses changes in rules and regulations that occurred in that month. As mentioned earlier, in the "Readers Aids" section located in the back of the *Federal Register,* regulations affected will be identified with its *Federal Register* page reference. However, the print version of CFR Parts Affected should not be used to the exclusion of available electronic administrative research sources.

Citing a Federal Rule or Regulation

The two main sources for citing a federal rule or regulation are the *Federal Register* or the *Code of Federal Regulations.* To cite to the *Federal Register,* you need the volume along with the page number where the information you are seeking is located and the date of the volume. Any references to the particular regulation, such as commonly used names or terms, should also be cited. Suppose you needed any recent amendments to the code of business ethics for contractors under the Federal Acquisition Regulation. Information on this topic is located in volume 72, no. 225 of the November 23, 2007 *Federal Register.* Therefore, your citation is: Federal Acquisition

Regulations for Contractor Code of Business Ethics and Conduct, 72 Fed. Reg. 65873 (Nov. 23, 2007) (to be codified at 48 C.F.R. pt.3). Now to cite this provision as it would appear in the *Code of Federal Regulations,* you simply cite it as: 48 C.F.R. § 3.1000, *et seq.* This citation form is similar to the *U.S. Code* except for the name of the legal source.

Agencies' Decisions: Where to Find Them

One of the authorities delegated to agencies is the ability to issue decisions regarding disputes between parties or decisions regarding violations of an administrative rule and regulation. In this capacity, administrative agencies render quasi-judicial decisions and issue orders. As part of this process, administrative agencies can assess fines and penalties relating to violations of its rules and regulations. For example, a company is stockpiling regulated biohazardous material in ordinary trash bags instead of the required "red" bags prescribed in the regulations. The exposure to the public creates a safety issue for which the Environmental Protection Agency has jurisdiction. The EPA can issue a notice of violation and assess a fine or some other type of remedial action to stop the improper disposal of the waste. This function is part of the agency's regulatory and adjudicatory powers.

Unfortunately, there is no single federal publication that gathers all administrative decisions in one place, as the *C.F.R.* does for federal regulations. Rather, every agency publishes its own decisions. For example, the Equal Employment Opportunity Commission publishes its decisions in a series called *EEOC Decisions* published by Wolters Kluwer/Commerce Clearing House (CCH). For more specific information, you can contact the relevant agency directly or check the looseleaf services devoted to the relevant topic (these services include regulations and administrative decisions in their coverage).

State and Local

The systems employed by the states and municipalities to compile administrative regulations and decisions vary widely, although many are based loosely on the federal format already described. Some jurisdictions update their publication of regulations fairly frequently, others only occasionally. For example, Texas and California follow a similar system to the federal administrative process. Rules and regulations are first published in the *Texas Register* and *California Administrative Register* followed by publication in the *Texas Administrative Code* and *California Administrative Code,* which are arranged by title or subject. In many instances you can contact the relevant agency directly in order to identify the current effective regulations. You should learn the system that applies in your state and in any local jurisdiction in which you will be working.

The Good News in Administrative Research

Until recently, researching administrative rules and regulations was a nightmare. That has changed significantly. Most of the administrative agencies have Web sites, which keep up-to-date information on proposed rules and regulations as well as existing ones. You now can follow the process of a proposed rule with relative ease. More importantly, you can find rules and regulations in logical places. Soon the softbound books located in libraries around the country will be obsolete. Web sites such as www.gpoaccess.gov, www.regulations.gov, www.thomas.gov, and www.reinfo.gov provide either information or links to locate administrative agency information. For all practical purposes, the Internet is a better source for administrative information than the print versions.

A Checklist for Locating Administrative Rules and Regulations

There is no one way to conduct administrative research. Much of it depends on what you are looking for. The following is a suggested guide:

- If you know which agency your issue involves, check the Internet to determine whether that agency has a Web site. If it does, let the prompts on the Web site guide you.
- When a statute is involved, check the cross-reference sections at the end of the statute. A corresponding *C.F.R.* section may be cited.
- Review the titles in the *Code of Federal Regulations.* The general titles may lead you to an applicable title. Review the table of contents for that title and determine whether the parts or subparts affect your fact situation.
- If you have located the appropriate *C.F.R.* section, check the LSA and CFR Parts Affected to determine whether your rule or regulation has changed in some manner.
- Check to see if there are secondary authorities on your subject, such as *A.L.R.* annotations, encyclopedia commentaries, treaties, or law review articles on the subject.
- If you need a judicial decision, check a looseleaf service or the agency's Web site for past and present administrative decisions. (In this instance, you may have to consult with a law librarian for direction in finding a looseleaf service on the subject.)
- For state administrative rules and regulations, determine whether the state has an administrative code or whether the state has statutory authority regarding the area you are researching. Check state agency Web sites; contact the agencies directly. They have a wealth of information and can be very helpful.

CYBER TRIP

Explore www.gpoaccess.gov, www.regulations.gov, and www.thomas.gov to determine the content of the Web sites.

Quick Quiz True/False Questions

1. Administrative agencies are considered the "fourth" branch of government.
2. The only type of rulemaking procedure is notice and comment rulemaking.
3. Administrative rules and regulations must be published in the *Federal Register.*
4. The titles in the *Code of Federal Regulations* mirror the *United States Code.*
5. Administrative agencies do not have the power to adjudicate controversies between parties.

THE E-FACTOR

With Internet sources expanding every day, you cannot ignore technology. Hardbound books are not sufficient to adequately perform your research as we have learned, most particularly, in this chapter and will learn throughout this text. If you do not have the Internet available to you, many libraries provide access to online sources. They often are free or have a minimal charge. This all begs the question that in today's day and age, you must have computer skills. The days of avoiding the computer and the Internet are past. Virtually all employers' expectations are that "we" all have a certain level of skill when it comes to the use of computers. Of course each person's level of competency varies, but make no mistake about it, if you intend to practice in today's world, you must be computer literate.

For those who fall behind, many public libraries offer basic computer classes that are free or have a minimal charge. Use these resources to sharpen your skills. You will be expected to have basic comprehension of Microsoft Word or other similar word-processing systems. PowerPoint presentations are becoming the rule and not the exception. Gone are the days when we gawk at the beauty of a PowerPoint presentation and wonder "how they did that." PowerPoints are all too common today. The end result is that as you embark on your career as a paralegal, you must be competent not only in researching the law through conventional means but also in using Internet methods.

PRACTICAL CONSIDERATIONS: THE BENEFITS OF THE INTERNET

Legislative and administrative research is not always easy. Gaining access to the most current versions of statutes and administrative rules and regulations is a challenge. As mentioned throughout this chapter, one of the best and free sources for federal legislative research is a government-sponsored Web site, www.gpoaccess.gov. This Web site provides up-to-date materials for congressional proceedings. Figure 5.16 provides the home page that shows the type of information that is found on the Web site. Another source of legislative information is www.thomas.loc.gov, which was launched in 1995 by the 104th Congress. Mandated by that Congress, federal legislative information is made available to the public free of charge. Some of the current offerings of the Web site are

- Bills and resolutions
- Activity in Congress
- The *Congressional Record*
- Committee information
- Nominations by the president
- Government general resources

This Web site is an invaluable resource when researching statutes and related information. See Figure 5.17 for some of the information that can be found on

FIGURE 5.16
Home Page for www.gpoaccess.gov

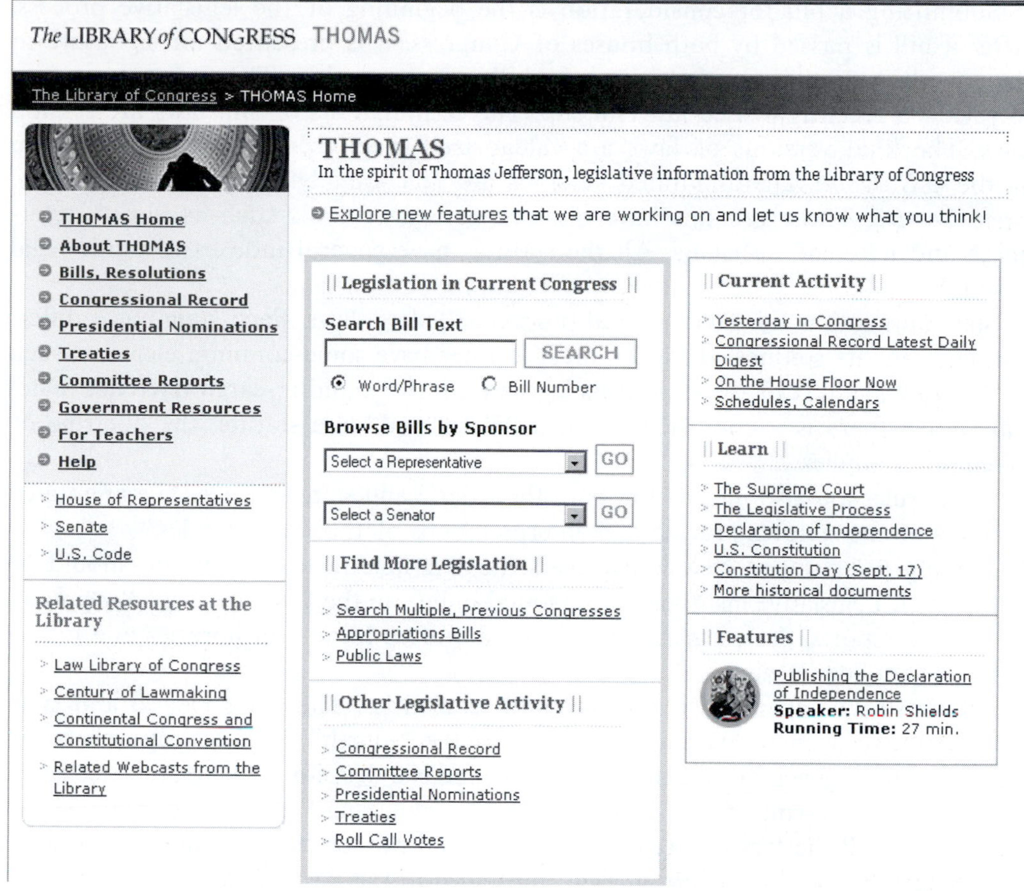

FIGURE 5.17
Home Page for www.thomas.gov

that Web site, which will assist you in providing up-to-date statutory and regulatory information.

And finally, the U.S. House of Representatives has a site, http://uscode.house.gov.usc.htm, which provides legislative material, bills, and the *United States Code.* You can have as little information as the popular name of a statute, and the search will provide all of the relevant statutory entries.

Public domain Web sites make "our jobs" a bit easier amid the confusion of the legislative and administrative process. Many of the administrative agencies have Web sites that provide information about the current and past rules and regulations that have been instituted. In addition to those Web sites, other government Web sites, such as www.regulations.gov and www.archives.gov, provide access to the day-to-day submissions made by the various administrative agencies as well as presidential documents, such as executive orders and proclamations. The abundance of information on the Internet can be overwhelming and daunting. Just focus on what you need and don't get bogged down in the minutia.

PRACTICE TIP

Since researching statutes and administrative rules and regulations can be challenging, be sure you have a plan of action, a strategy for attacking the issue you are assigned. If you need direction from your supervising attorney, remember to ask. Do not stray too far from the assignment by being timid to ask. A simple question may save both you and your attorney hours of wasted time and research.

Summary

The U.S. Constitution is the document that sets forth the structure of the U.S. government. It is the supreme law of the land. The first seven articles establish the framework of the government with the first ten amendments constituting the Bill of Rights. All state constitutions must comport with the strictures of the U.S. Constitution.

Submitting a bill for consideration is the beginning of the legislative process. After a bill is passed by both houses of Congress, it is presented for signature to the president. If the president signs the bill, it becomes law. The first opportunity to review a recently passed law is a slip. The compilations of slip laws are session laws. The final versions of laws are categorized in subject-specific codes known as the *U.S. Code.* The annotated versions are *U.S. Code Annotated* and the *U.S. Code Service.* These versions have research assistance tools such as library references and notes of decisions. All the statutes have general indexes to guide legal research.

State laws follow the same general process as federal laws. Each state has a different name for its statutes. However, most statutes have some common elements such as the complete text of the statute, its legislative history, and research reference material. When there is a conflict between a federal and state statute, the doctrine of preemption applies.

Court rules are also included in both the federal and state statutes. The annotated versions of the statutes provide case interpretations of those court rules.

Finding a legislative history can assist in determining how a statute should be interpreted. Legislative histories can be found online, in the *Congressional Record* and committee reports. State legislative histories are often located in libraries and online through state legislatures.

Administrative agencies create rules and regulations. There are federal and state administrative agencies. Often referred to as the "fourth" branch of government, administrative agencies can legislate and issue judicial decisions. There are three types of rulemaking: formal rulemaking, informal rulemaking, and hybrid rulemaking. Common to all the types of rulemaking is that all proposed and final rules must be published in the *Federal Register.* Once published in the *Federal Register,* the new or amended rule is then added to the *Code of Federal Regulations.* The *Code of Federal Regulations* has fifty titles.

The federal government has created Web sites to assist in locating federal statutes, administrative rules, and regulations and information on the U.S. Constitution. These Web sites contain more organized information than some of the library material.

Key Terms

administrative agencies
administrative decisions or orders
Administrative Procedure Act (APA)
annotated code
bicameral process
charter
code
conference committee
Congressional Record
Constitution
enacted
exhaustion of administrative remedies
general index
injunction proceeding
legislative history
local rules
ordinance
pocket parts
pocket veto
Popular Name Index
preemption
public law number
rule or regulation
rulemaking
rules of court
session laws
slip law
Statutes at Large
sua sponte
supplements
unicameral process
veto

Review Questions

1. What are the articles of the U.S. Constitution that created our three branches of government?
2. Identify the process of how a bill becomes law.
3. What are the three codes that contain U.S. statutes, and do they differ?
4. What are pocket parts and why are they important?
5. Name the two main indexes for the U.S. codes.
6. Define the doctrine of preemption.
7. When and under what circumstances would a legislative history be consulted?
8. What are the three types of rulemaking authority permitted by administrative agencies?
9. Identify the standards of review for administrative decisions.
10. Distinguish between the *Federal Register* and the *Code of Federal Regulations*.

Exercises

1. Locate a copy of the U.S. Constitution and answer the following questions:
   a. Which amendment identifies the right to a speedy trial?
   b. Which amendment provides for religious freedom?
   c. Which article grants the president emergency powers?
   d. Under the Constitution, which branch of government can declare war?
2. Locate a copy of your state's constitution and answer the following:
   a. When was your state constitution formed?
   b. How many amendments does your state constitution have?
   c. Does your state constitution have an "equal rights" provision? If so, what does it state?
   d. Compare your state constitution with the U.S. Constitution. What are the differences and similarities?
3. Identify your state's statute of limitations for the following actions:
   a. Contract action
   b. Negligence action
   c. Medical malpractice action
   d. Assault and battery
   e. Theft
4. Review *Mayer v. Monroe County Community School Corporation,* 474 F.3d 477 (7th Cir. 2007).
   a. What is the constitutional issue in the case?
   b. What are the facts of the case?
5. Review *Engine Manufacturers Association v. South Coast Air Quality Management District,* 541 U.S. 246, 124 S. Ct. 1756, 158 L. Ed. 2d 529 (2004), and answer the following:
   a. What is the statutory provision that the court has to interpret?
   b. Did the court find the statute constitutional? Give an explanation for your answer.
   c. What is the disposition of the case?
6. Choose a bill from the present Congress and determine the following:
   a. In what committee did the bill originate?
   b. What is the bill's number?
   c. Has the bill been passed by both houses of Congress? If the answer is yes, has the president signed the bill into law?
   d. What is the public law number?

7. All you know is that you want to find information on the law No Child Left Behind Act. Locate the title and section of the *U.S. Code* when the law can be found.
8. Locate the titles in the *Code of Federal Regulations* that contain rules and regulations on the following:
   a. Environmental Protection Agency
   b. Transportation Security Administration
   c. Federal Trade Commission
   d. Food and Drug Administration
   e. Federal Communications Commission

PORTFOLIO ASSIGNMENT

It is 4:55 p.m. and your attorney is leaving for a trial in Tennessee in the morning. He has not traveled in a while and wants you to brief him on what he can and cannot bring on the airplane. Specifically, he is concerned about whether he can travel with his favorite cologne and hair gels. Determine whether you need to review a statute, an administrative rule or regulation, or both. Prepare a short e-mail to your attorney with the results of your research.

Quick Quiz True/False Answers

Page 126	Page 149	Page 150	Page 159
1. False	1. False	1. True	1. True
2. True	2. True	2. False	2. False
3. False	3. False	3. True	3. True
4. True	4. False	4. False	4. False
5. True	5. False	5. True	5. False

Part Two

Finding and Updating Tools

Chapter 6

Legal Research Finding Tools: The Traditions and New Trends

After completing this chapter, you will be able to:

- Explain the Key Number System.
- Use a digest.
- Define the use of a headnote in legal research.
- Initiate a key number search online on Westlaw.
- Distinguish between a digest and legal encyclopedia.
- Locate law review articles and legal periodicals.
- Compare *American Law Reports* annotations and encyclopedia commentaries.
- Understand the differences between print-based research and computer-assisted research.
- Learn how to update statutes and regulatory rules and regulations.
- State some general principles about how to begin researching, and how to know when to stop.

You now know the different sources of the law, but how do you find them? The world of legal research provides finding tools to help you locate cases, statutes, and other legal sources to support a client's legal position. You will learn how to use digests, which are one of the primary "searching tools" in the law library. In addition to finding the law through digests, encyclopedias, law reviews, and legal treatises, you will be introduced to Internet legal research. Although Internet research is quickly becoming the dominant force in researching the law, you will learn how to combine print and Internet research for comprehensive legal research. Miss a step in the process and you might make a big "misstep." By following the process methodically, you will ensure success at all levels of your legal research assignment. Let's see how the process works.

CASE FACT PATTERN

Six months ago your firm's client, Mr. Simmons, subleased some excess warehouse space to Mr. Mason (a *sublease* is a lease between a tenant and a subtenant, as opposed to one between the owner-landlord and the original tenant). Under the terms of the sublease, subtenant Mason was to make his payments directly to the landlord. After only two months, however, Mason stopped making his payments, and the landlord has sued Simmons for the back rent. Simmons has come to your supervising attorney, who has requested from you a memorandum outlining the basic law that applies in this situation, namely: What is the liability of the original tenant when a subtenant fails to pay the landlord? You should be asking yourself: "Where do I begin? How do I know which law applies?" Therein lies the "million-dollar" question.

THE DIGEST SYSTEM: A HISTORY OF TRADITION

Finding relevant legal sources could be a paralegal's worst nightmare had the digest system not been invented. Imagine your attorney sending you into a library to research a client's legal issues or find a case decision without a systematic, logical approach to the problem. You can't! It is like looking for a needle in a haystack. The digest system is the backbone of the legal research process; it allows you to methodically locate cases relevant to your research assignment. Let's learn about its origins and how the system works.

The Origins of the American Digest System

Although recording of case decisions dates back as early as the 1600s, no real organized system of categorizing and cataloging the cases was established until 1879 in Minnesota. The founder of West Publishing Company (now ThomsonWest), John West, began publishing Minnesota case opinions without much financial profit. Recognizing a need to have case decisions available for review, he expanded his operations to the neighboring states, creating the first "regional" reporter. However, publishing the cases was only the beginning. As the number of case decisions grew, West developed a system that classified the law into subjects and subtopics. We know this system as West's Key Number System.

Key Number System
A detailed system of classification that currently divides the law into more than 400 separate categories or topics.

Key Numbers and Digests

The **Key Number System** employed in the National Reporter System (and most other West publications) is a detailed system of classification that currently divides the law into more than 400 separate categories or topics (see Figure 6.1 for a sample page

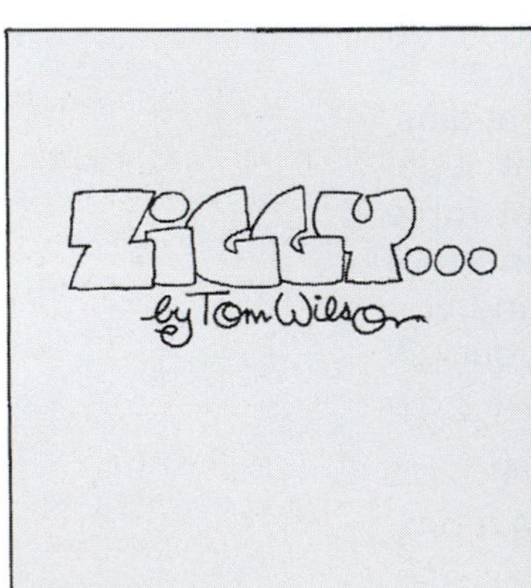

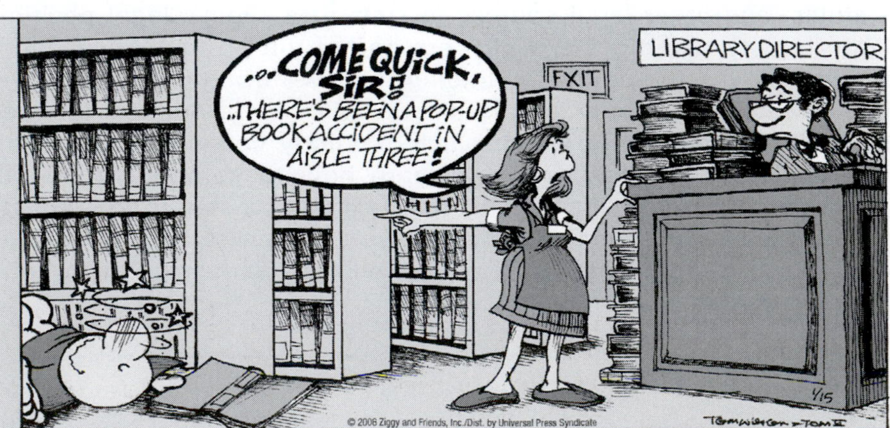

Source: ZIGGY © 2006 ZIGGY AND FRIENDS, INC. Reprinted with permission of UNIVERSAL PRESS SYNDICATE. All rights reserved.

DIGEST TOPICS

See, also, Outline of the Law by Seven Main Divisions of Law preceding this section.

The topic numbers shown below may be used in WESTLAW searches for cases within the topic and within specified key numbers.

1	Abandoned and Lost Property
2	Abatement and Revival
4	Abortion and Birth Control
5	Absentees
6	Abstracts of Title
7	Accession
8	Accord and Satisfaction
9	Account
10	Account, Action on
11	Account Stated
11A	Accountants
12	Acknowledgment
13	Action
14	Action on the Case
15	Adjoining Landowners
15A	Administrative Law and Procedure
16	Admiralty
17	Adoption
18	Adulteration
19	Adultery
20	Adverse Possession
21	Affidavits
23	Agriculture
24	Aliens
25	Alteration of Instruments
26	Ambassadors and Consuls
27	Amicus Curiae
28	Animals
29	Annuities
30	Appeal and Error
31	Appearance
33	Arbitration
34	Armed Services
35	Arrest
36	Arson
37	Assault and Battery
38	Assignments
40	Assistance, Writ of
41	Associations
42	Assumpsit, Action of
43	Asylums
44	Attachment
45	Attorney and Client
46	Attorney General
47	Auctions and Auctioneers
48	Audita Querela
48A	Automobiles
48B	Aviation
49	Bail
50	Bailment
51	Bankruptcy
52	Banks and Banking
54	Beneficial Associations
55	Bigamy
56	Bills and Notes
58	Bonds
59	Boundaries
60	Bounties
61	Breach of Marriage Promise
62	Breach of the Peace
63	Bribery
64	Bridges
65	Brokers
66	Building and Loan Associations
67	Burglary
68	Canals
69	Cancellation of Instruments
70	Carriers
71	Cemeteries
72	Census
73	Certiorari
74	Champerty and Maintenance
75	Charities
76	Chattel Mortgages
76A	Chemical Dependents
76D	Child Custody
76E	Child Support
76H	Children Out-of-Wedlock
77	Citizens
78	Civil Rights
79	Clerks of Courts
80	Clubs
81	Colleges and Universities
82	Collision
83	Commerce
83H	Commodity Futures Trading Regulation
84	Common Lands
85	Common Law
88	Compounding Offenses
89	Compromise and Settlement
89A	Condominium
90	Confusion of Goods
91	Conspiracy
92	Constitutional Law
92B	Consumer Credit
92H	Consumer Protection
93	Contempt
95	Contracts
96	Contribution
96H	Controlled Substances
97	Conversion
98	Convicts
99	Copyrights and Intellectual Property
100	Coroners
101	Corporations
102	Costs
103	Counterfeiting
104	Counties
105	Court Commissioners
106	Courts
107	Covenant, Action of
108	Covenants
108A	Credit Reporting Agencies
110	Criminal Law

XV

FIGURE 6.1
Digest Topics
Source: From *South Eastern Digest, 2nd Series.* Reprinted with permission from ThomsonWest.

PRACTICE TIP

New topics and keys are added slowly. The digest system does not keep up with the changing trends of the law. Therefore, be mindful that a topic that seems logical to you may not be how the ThomsonWest digest system classifies an area of the law.

PRACTICE TIP

Headnotes and associated topics and keys are developed by editors and attorneys at ThomsonWest. *Never* cite headnotes as authority as they are *not* primary authority; they are not the law. Always cite from with the case opinion text.

listing some of these topics). More categories are added as the development of the law requires. Each category is divided into subcategories. With often hundreds or even thousands of subcategories in a given topic, each subcategory is assigned a key number. Using Figure 6.2, notice the topic "Conversion" has only 22 keys and related subtopics. And for example, the topic that comes immediately before it, "Controlled Substances," has 90 keys and related subtopics. Similarly, the topic "Constitutional Law" has more than 300 topics and hundreds of related keys. All these topics, keys, and subkeys form the basis of the digest system and hold the "key" to your successful completion of your research project.

FIGURE 6.2 **Topic and Keys for the Subject "Conversion"**

Source: From *South Eastern Digest, 2nd Series.* Reprinted with permission from ThomsonWest.

97. CONVERSION

SUBJECTS INCLUDED

Changes in the nature of property as real or personal, whether actual, as by exercise of power of eminent domain, sale for partition, foreclosure, etc., investment of funds in land, etc., or constructive, as necessary to carry into effect directions or agreements contained in deeds, wills, settlements, contracts or other instruments in writing

Nature, requisites, incidents, operation and effect of such changes

Reconversion by act of the parties or by operation of law

SUBJECTS EXCLUDED AND COVERED BY OTHER TOPICS

Wrongful conversion of personal property, see TROVER AND CONVERSION

1. Nature and grounds of doctrine.
2. What law governs.
3. Realty into personalty in general.
4. Exercise of power of eminent domain.
5. Sale of land under order of court.
6. ____ In general.
7. ____ Persons under disability.
8. ____ Extent of conversion.
9. ____ Time of conversion.
10. Conveyances and contracts.
11. ____ In general.
12. ____ Extent of conversion.
13. ____ Time of conversion.
14. ____ Directions in will.
15. ____ In general.
    (1). In general.
    (2). Sale for purpose of distribution.
    (3). Void or lapsed bequests and failure of purpose of conversion.
    (4). Actual sale under power.
16. ____ Subject to discretion or option.
    (.5). In general.
    (1). Necessity of imperative direction to sell.
    (2). Intention of testator.
    (3). Sale necessary to fulfill purposes of will.
    (4). Option of beneficiary.
    (5). Discretion as to time and manner of sale.
17. ____ Subject to condition or contingency.
18. ____ Extent of conversion.
19. ____ Time of conversion.
    (1). In general.
    (2). Upon death of testator.
20. Personalty into realty.
21. Operation and effect.
    (1). In general.
    (2). Directions in will.
22. Reconversion.
    (1). In general.
    (2). Election of beneficiary.
    (3). Mode and sufficiency of election.

The Interworkings of the Key Number System and Cases

Each and every case that is to be published in the National Reporter System is analyzed and assigned one or more topics along with key numbers based upon the legal principles addressed in the opinion. This analysis and assignment of key numbers has been taking place continuously since the 1880s.

headnote
A key-numbered paragraph; an editorial feature in unofficial reporters that summarizes a single legal point or issue in the court opinion.

digest
A collection of all the headnotes from an associated series of volumes, arranged alphabetically by topic and by key number or summary of testimony with indexed references of a deposition.

Topics and key numbers are listed near the beginning of an opinion, each followed by a brief paragraph setting forth the corresponding legal principle drawn from the case. A key-numbered paragraph that sets forth a legal principle is called a **headnote.** Headnotes are numbered consecutively, and corresponding reference numbers are inserted into the text of the case, indicating the precise location from which the legal principle in the headnote is drawn. Figure 6.3 shows pages from a typical National Reporter System case, *Young v. District of Columbia,* 752 A.2d 138 (D.C. 2000), and identifies various elements of key numbering.

The key numbers form the basis of the **digest** system. A digest is a collection of all the headnotes from an associated series of volumes, arranged alphabetically by topic and by key number. There is generally a digest for all the jurisdictions in the U.S. judicial system. You will have to determine which one to use. The question is "how do I know which digest to choose?" The answer may be easier to determine than you think.

FIGURE 6.3 **Pages from a Typical National Reporter System Case**

Source: From *Atlantic Reporter, 2nd Series.* Reprinted with permission from ThomsonWest.

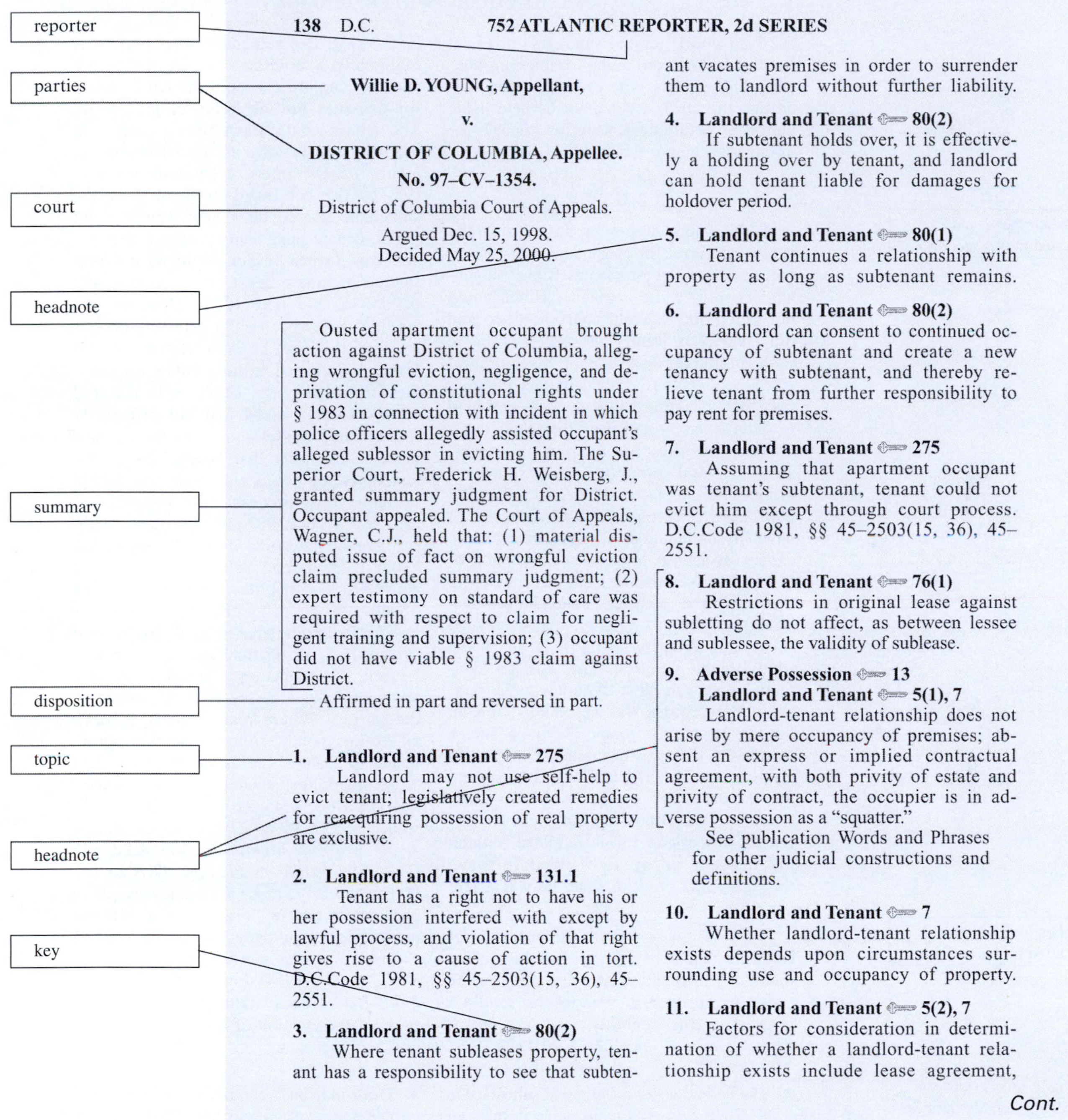

138 D.C. 752 ATLANTIC REPORTER, 2d SERIES

Willie D. YOUNG, Appellant,

v.

DISTRICT OF COLUMBIA, Appellee.

No. 97–CV–1354.

District of Columbia Court of Appeals.

Argued Dec. 15, 1998.
Decided May 25, 2000.

Ousted apartment occupant brought action against District of Columbia, alleging wrongful eviction, negligence, and deprivation of constitutional rights under § 1983 in connection with incident in which police officers allegedly assisted occupant's alleged sublessor in evicting him. The Superior Court, Frederick H. Weisberg, J., granted summary judgment for District. Occupant appealed. The Court of Appeals, Wagner, C.J., held that: (1) material disputed issue of fact on wrongful eviction claim precluded summary judgment; (2) expert testimony on standard of care was required with respect to claim for negligent training and supervision; (3) occupant did not have viable § 1983 claim against District.

Affirmed in part and reversed in part.

1. **Landlord and Tenant 🔑 275**
Landlord may not use self-help to evict tenant; legislatively created remedies for reacquiring possession of real property are exclusive.

2. **Landlord and Tenant 🔑 131.1**
Tenant has a right not to have his or her possession interfered with except by lawful process, and violation of that right gives rise to a cause of action in tort. D.C.Code 1981, §§ 45–2503(15, 36), 45–2551.

3. **Landlord and Tenant 🔑 80(2)**
Where tenant subleases property, tenant has a responsibility to see that subtenant vacates premises in order to surrender them to landlord without further liability.

4. **Landlord and Tenant 🔑 80(2)**
If subtenant holds over, it is effectively a holding over by tenant, and landlord can hold tenant liable for damages for holdover period.

5. **Landlord and Tenant 🔑 80(1)**
Tenant continues a relationship with property as long as subtenant remains.

6. **Landlord and Tenant 🔑 80(2)**
Landlord can consent to continued occupancy of subtenant and create a new tenancy with subtenant, and thereby relieve tenant from further responsibility to pay rent for premises.

7. **Landlord and Tenant 🔑 275**
Assuming that apartment occupant was tenant's subtenant, tenant could not evict him except through court process. D.C.Code 1981, §§ 45–2503(15, 36), 45–2551.

8. **Landlord and Tenant 🔑 76(1)**
Restrictions in original lease against subletting do not affect, as between lessee and sublessee, the validity of sublease.

9. **Adverse Possession 🔑 13**
Landlord and Tenant 🔑 5(1), 7
Landlord-tenant relationship does not arise by mere occupancy of premises; absent an express or implied contractual agreement, with both privity of estate and privity of contract, the occupier is in adverse possession as a "squatter."

See publication Words and Phrases for other judicial constructions and definitions.

10. **Landlord and Tenant 🔑 7**
Whether landlord-tenant relationship exists depends upon circumstances surrounding use and occupancy of property.

11. **Landlord and Tenant 🔑 5(2), 7**
Factors for consideration in determination of whether a landlord-tenant relationship exists include lease agreement,

Cont.

THE AMERICAN DIGEST SYSTEM

We already know that the digest system arranges cases into subjects with associated topics and keys. The digest system also categorizes the subject topics and keys both generally and specifically.

The Decennial Digests

Suppose your research assignment requires you to present an overview of a particular area of the law from all jurisdictions. Rather than check every digest, use

FIGURE 6.3 Pages from a Typical National Reporter System Case *Cont.*

the trial court granted summary judgment for the District on Young's remaining constitutional claims. The court also concluded that the District could not be held liable under a respondeat superior theory for Young's remaining constitutional claims.

II.

headnotes 1 and 2 cited in this section

[1, 2] Young argues on appeal that the trial court erred in concluding that he was not lawfully in possession as Bibbs' subtenant. Therefore, he contends, Bibbs could not evict him without court process, and the District is jointly and severally liable with Bibbs for assisting in his wrongful eviction. It is well settled in this jurisdiction that a landlord may not use self-help to evict a tenant and that "the legislatively created remedies for reacquiring possession [of real property] are exclusive." *Mendes v. Johnson,* 389 A.2d 781, 787 (D.C.1978). "A tenant has a right not to have his or her possession interfered with except by lawful process, and violation of that right gives rise to a cause of action in tort." *Id.* The District acknowledges that Young's wrongful eviction claim may go forward if Young was Bibbs' tenant at the time of the eviction. The District contends, however, that the undisputed facts show that Young was not Bibbs' tenant, but an invitee or roomer who became a trespasser by refusing to leave at the request of the lawful tenant who had surrendered possession to the landlord. Young counters that Bibbs had no right to surrender possession to his landlord without his consent or by first evicting Young through court process, since he was a tenant.

headnotes 3 through 7 cited in this section

[3–7] Where a tenant subleases property, the tenant has a responsibility to see that the subtenant vacates the premises in order to surrender them to the landlord without further liability. *See Sanchez v. Eleven Fourteen, Inc.*, 623 A.2d 1179, 1181 (D.C.1993). If a subtenant holds over, it is effectively a holding over by the tenant and the landlord can hold the tenant liable for damages for the holdover period. *Id.* The tenant continues a relationship with the property as long as the subtenant remains. *Id.* Of course, a landlord can consent to the continued occupancy of the subtenant and create a new tenancy with the subtenant, and thereby relieve the tenant from further responsibility to pay rent for the premises. *See Comedy v. Vito,* 492 A.2d 276, 279 (D.C.1985). However, the landlord here specifically declined Young's request that he be substituted on the lease, and elected to hold Bibbs responsible for the property. Contrary to the trial court's ruling, Bibbs had not effectively relinquished possession when Young was ousted. Assuming that Young was Bibbs' tenant, Bibbs could not evict him except through court process. See *Mendes, supra*, 389 A.2d at 787. We consider whether there was a landlord-tenant relationship between Bibbs and Young which required court process in order for Bibbs to evict Young.

[8] It is undisputed that Bibbs and Young had no written agreement establishing a subtenancy. However, certain tenancies may arise by oral agreement of the parties. Where real property is rented by the month without a written agreement, by statute, the estate created "shall be deemed [an] estate[ ] at sufferance." See D.C.Code § 45–220; *see also Comedy, supra*, 492 A.2d at 279; *Cavalier Apartments Corp. v. McMullen*, 153 A.2d 642 (D.C.1959); *Miller v. Plumley,* 77 A.2d 173 (D.C.1950). "[S]uch a tenancy requires payment of rent or 'hireings' or a 'rate per month' to accompany the estate." *Smith v. Town Ctr. Management Corp.*, 329 A.2d 779, 780 (D.C.1974) (citing D.C.Code 1973, § 45–820).[5] This statute itself does not prohibit the creation of a tenancy at sufferance in a subtenant.[6]

5. The definitions of a tenancy at sufferance in D.C.Code § 45–820 is the same in material respects to the definition in D.C.Code § 45–220.

6. There may be a contractual prohibition to subletting, as there was here. However, "restrictions contained in the original lease against subletting do not affect, as between

Cont.

FIGURE 6.3 **Pages from a Typical National Reporter System Case** *Cont.*

[9-14] The question is whether the undisputed facts showed that Young was not a tenant, as the trial court concluded. "A landlord-tenant relationship does not arise by mere occupancy of the premises; absent an express or implied contractual agreement, with both privity of estate and privity of contract, the occupier is in adverse possession as a 'squatter.'" *Nicholas v. Howard,* 459 A.2d 1039, 1040 (D.C.1983). Whether a landlord-tenant relationship exists depends upon the circumstances surrounding the use and occupancy of the property. *See Anderson v. William J. Davis, Inc.*, 553 A.2d 648, 649 (D.C.1989). Factors for consideration in that determination include a lease agreement, the payment of rent and other conditions of occupancy between the parties. *Id.*[7] While it is undisputed that there was no written lease agreement, other material facts surrounding the nature of the relationship between Bibbs and Young are in dispute which bear upon the issue. According to Bibbs, he simply allowed Young to be a guest in his apartment temporarily while Young was unemployed and homeless, and Young occasionally made token contributions to the household. Such an occupancy arrangement would not give rise to a tenancy. *See Jackson v. United States*, 357 A.2d 409, 410 (D.C.1976) (Where a defendant occupied an apartment rent-free without formal consideration, there was no tenancy at sufferance). Young, however, in a verified response to interrogatories, states that he had an agreement with Bibbs to pay him half the rent ($200) for the premises, which he paid. This disputed issue of fact is material because if Young, in fact, had an oral agreement to occupy the apartment in exchange for regular monthly rental payments as Bibbs' subtenant, a tenancy at sufferance would arise, requiring court process for termination. See D.C.Code §§ 45–1404, –16–1501; *see also Mendes, supra*, 389 A.2d at 787. At least as between Bibbs and Young, assuming a sublessor-sublessee relationship, Young would be entitled to the protections afforded tenants under the Housing Act.[8] The Rental Housing Act of 1985 (Housing Act), which enlarged the protections afforded tenants without leases from sudden evictions, extends to subtenants.[9] *See Anderson, supra*, 553 A.2d at 648. The Act itself includes a subtenant within the definition of "tenant." D.C.Code § 45–2503(36). Similarly, a sublessor is included within the definition of "housing provider."[10] That

headnotes 9 through 14 cited in this section

the lessee and the sublessee, the validity of the sublease." 49 AM. JUR.2d *Landlord and Tenant* § 1162 (1993). *See also* FREEDMAN ON LEASES § 7304d (4th ed.1997).

7. In *Anderson, supra*, the issue under consideration was whether two men who occupied an apartment in partial compensation for performing services in the building were tenants. *Anderson*, 553 A.2d at 648–49. In concluding that the men were not tenants, the court considered that "[t]hey did not pay rent, did not have a lease, and were allowed to occupy the employer-landowner's apartment only as an incident to the services they provided." *Id.* at 649. Therefore, the court determined that they were not entitled to a thirty days' notice to quit as required by D.C.Code § 45–1404.

8. For disposition of this appeal, we need not address the rights of Bibbs' landlord as against any subtenant. *See Sanchez, supra* 623 A.2d at 1181; *Haje's, Inc. v. Wire,* 56 A.2d 158, 159 (D.C.1947).

9. "This court has 'ruled on several occasions that rent control statutes [such as the 1985 [Housing] Act] prevail over provisions adopted earlier that govern evictions, to the extent that the provisions conflict.'" *Anderson, supra*, 553 A.2d at 649 (quoting *Habib v. Thurston*, 517 A.2d 1, 5 n. 3 (D.C. 1985)).

10. D.C.Code § 45–2503(15) and (36) provide respectively that:

> "Housing provider" means a landlord, an owner, lessor, sublessor, assignee, or their agent, or any other person receiving or entitled to receive rents or benefits for the use or occupancy of any rental unit within a housing accommodation within the District.
> "Tenant" includes a tenant, subtenant, lessee, sublessee, or other person entitled to the possession, occupancy, or the benefits of any rental unit owned by another person.

the **Decennial Digest.** The Decennial Digest creates a composite of all the case law on a topic from every jurisdiction. Decennial Digests group cases by time period and subject without regard to jurisdiction. As the name suggests, the Decennial Digests are compiled in ten-year intervals. However, in the mid-70s, the volume of cases increased substantially, causing ThomsonWest to begin publishing the Decennial

Decennial Digests
Digests that group cases by time period and subject without regard to jurisdiction.

Digest in five-year periods with a part one and part two (to maintain the continuity of the decennial concept). Now, in its eleventh series, the Decennial Digest, although comprehensive, is a challenge to use.

General Digest
Digest that supplements the Decennial Digest.

Updating the Decennial Digests is accomplished through the **General Digest.** The General Digest is published annually with the more recent cases and topics updated, more or less, monthly. Cases often are released faster than the General Digests keep pace. Be sure to check the appropriately dated volumes to ensure your research is complete. With all this said, the Decennial and General Digests will not be the digests used more often. The jurisdiction-specific and state-specific digests invariably will be the digests of choice in your legal research. We will begin with the U.S. Supreme Court Digests.

The U.S. Supreme Court Digests

It is probably no surprise that the U.S. Supreme Court has a digest devoted to its opinions. In fact, the U.S. Supreme Court has two digests classifying its cases: *United States Supreme Court Digest* (ThomsonWest) and *United States Supreme Court Reports, Lawyers' Edition* (LexisNexis).

PRACTICE TIP

Decennial Digests are used on a *very* limited basis. Unless you are researching the case law from all jurisdictions, use the appropriate federal, state, or subject-specific digest.

United States Supreme Court Digest: This digest is part of the ThomsonWest system and utilizes the Key Number System to classify its opinions. This digest will refer you to the *Supreme Court Reporter* and other ThomsonWest-related publications. Many believe that this point is significant because of the universality of the Key Number System. When you have found a topic and key within the system, it applies to all jurisdictions in the ThomsonWest system. Convenience is an important factor.

United States Supreme Court Reports, Lawyers' Edition Digest: This digest is specific to the *Lawyers' Edition* only. It is only linked to that reporter and the LexisNexis system of publications. However, this digest does provide references to *American Law Reports* and *American Jurisprudence* (secondary sources), which are discussed later in the chapter. A caveat is important to note here. You still will want to use the ThomsonWest digest system to expand your research in locating topics and keys on the subject. The *Lawyers' Edition* may provide those extra research connections, which is why many attorneys find the digest helpful.

The Federal Digests

All federal cases, whether from the *Federal Reporter, Federal Supplement, Federal Rules Decisions, Bankruptcy Reporter,* or the new *Federal Appendix,* are found in the federal digests. The *Federal Digest* follows the same Key Number System and principles developed by ThomsonWest over one hundred years ago. The *Federal Digest* has evolved over the years and has been supplemented. The federal digest system includes the following:

Federal Digest (1754–1939)
Modern Federal Practice Digest (1939–1960)
West's Federal Practice Digest 2d (1961–1975)
West's Federal Practice Digest 3d (1975–1983)
West's Federal Practice Digest 4th (1984 to Present*)

PRACTICE TIP

There is a separate digest for all bankruptcy cases called the *Bankruptcy Digest.* This digest has incorporated all bankruptcy cases to present.

Locating the newest cases is an important part of legal research. In the federal digests as well as other digests, updates are critical to comprehensive research. The two main ways cases are updated in the digests are through supplements or pocket parts.

*The fourth series incorporates the third series, but some volumes were reprinted at different intervals. Check the volume publication to determine how far back the digest is classified.

FINDING CURRENT INFORMATION: POCKET PARTS AND SUPPLEMENTS

We have learned that the purpose of a multivolume digest—facilitating research—requires that it reference the most recent cases. Each volume, however, is manufactured to last for years. It would be prohibitively expensive to purchase new hardbound volumes every year, so how do these sets stay current?

The answer is through the use of **pocket parts.** Pocket parts are annual (or sometimes more frequent) supplements. Each pocket part corresponds to one volume of the digest set, and is fitted into a pocket inside the back cover of the book. The pocket part contains all the recent headnotes that would have appeared in the main volume had they been available when it went to press. These headnotes are organized in the pocket part as they would have been in the main volume—in the ThomsonWest system, for example, by topic and key number.

pocket parts
Annual supplements to digests.

In addition to annual pocket parts, digests can be supplemented at more frequent intervals by individual paperbound volumes that collect all the material subsequent to the most recent set of pocket parts called **supplements**. In this manner, the content of the digest set is kept current.

supplement
Individual stand-alone paperbound volume that collects all the material subsequent to the most recent set of pocket parts.

As was discussed in this chapter and previous ones, pocket parts are used in many legal publications besides digests, including the *American Law Reports* series, state and federal statutory sets, legal encyclopedias, and even some treatises. When performing legal research, it is absolutely essential that you check for pocket parts! If you haven't assured yourself that you've checked all pocket parts and all paperbound volumes updating pocket parts, then you haven't finished your research. You may even have missed the most recent case on the subject! Get in the habit of checking each resource you use to verify that you've utilized its latest update—be it a pocket part, a paperbound volume, or some other form of update.

A Word about Pocket Parts and Supplements: The Missing Topic and Key

No doubt you know that pocket parts and supplements provide updated information on cases and other sources of the law. You also know that checking these updates is an essential step in your research process. But what does it mean when your topic and key do not appear in the pocket part or supplement? Have you missed a step or done something wrong? Absolutely not! The omission of a topic and key in a pocket part or supplement simply means that no courts have cited that topic and key (point of law) within the time period covered by that pocket part or supplement. So, don't worry if you do not see your topic and key cited in the pocket part or supplement. It's no reflection on your research process.

PRACTICE TIP

Regardless of the source, always check the pocket parts and supplements for current cases and updates.

Regional and State Digests

Each state has either a state-specific or regional digest, which also follows the ThomsonWest Key Number System. When you are researching an assignment, federal or state-specific, locate the digest that applies. Except for Nevada, Delaware, and Utah, there is a corresponding ThomsonWest state digest. The state digests include the federal cases from that jurisdiction as well. Similar to the federal digests, many of the state digests have published different series. Some state digests that are now in their second series are Indiana, Missouri, Texas, Kansas, and Nebraska. Many of the second series completely replace the first; others do not. Be sure you check your state to determine the periods covered by the state digest.

For those states that do not have a state-specific digest, use a regional digest. At one point, all the regional reporters had a corresponding regional digest. However, this is no longer the case. Only the *Atlantic, Pacific, South Eastern,* and *North Western* digests are published. The *North Eastern, South Western,* and *Southern* have not been published for quite some time.

For example, the most recent digest associated with the *Pacific Reporter* includes all the headnotes from all the cases beginning with those from volume 585 of the second series and continuing to the present. (Important note: If you want to search through older cases as well, you have to check through other digests covering earlier periods; a thorough search is not complete until all time periods covering all cases have been checked.) Figure 6.4 shows a partial index page from the topic "Landlord and Tenant," which includes the key number associated with headnote 8 from *Young v. District of Columbia.* Figure 6.5 shows the digest page on which the full text of this headnote appears.

Additionally, digests are now created that are subject-specific. There are digests for bankruptcy, education, and social security. ThomsonWest created these digests in response to the volume of cases decided in those areas. The subject-specific digests cover all jurisdictions and should be used only if you are researching that specific subject. Figure 6.6 presents a comprehensive diagram of the ThomsonWest digest system.

PRACTICE TIP

All the ThomsonWest topics and keys are the same in every digest. Once you have found a topic and key that supports your research topic, you can easily transition from one jurisdiction to another without beginning a search for a new topic and key. That means if you are using the *New York Digest,* topic and key Landlord Tenant Key 80, you will find the same topic and key dealing with the same legal concept in the Texas, Illinois, and Florida digests.

Order of Cases in Digests

The listing of case summaries in the digests follows a specific format. First, the cases are divided between federal and state cases with federal cases cited first. Second, they are then listed from highest court to lowest. And finally, the cases are listed from newest to oldest. Therefore, U.S. Supreme Court cases relating to a topic are listed first. They are followed by the U.S. circuit courts of appeals and then the federal district courts. The cases are listed alphabetically by state. After the federal case listings, any cases from state courts follow. They are listed alphabetically as well with the highest court from the state identified first, newest to oldest case on the topic listed first. Figure 6.7 provides an illustration from a Supreme Court Digest of the order of cases listed under the topic "Elections" and key number 299.

Additional Digest Publications

ThomsonWest is not the exclusive publisher for all the state digests. LexisNexis, Callaghan, and Michie, a LexisNexis publication, publish state digests as well. This suggests that some states have more than one digest in which to find cases. These state digests obviously do not follow the ThomsonWest Key Number System but rather a system unique to that publisher. Conceptually the process is the same. Subject topics are created with a corresponding number system. Any related material by that publisher is usually referenced as a guide to its other research sources. No one digest is better than another. To determine which to use, your attorney will guide you as to the best digest for your jurisdiction or subject matter. The end result is that you want your research to be comprehensive and complete regardless of what digest or sources you use.

FIGURE 6.4 Partial Index Page

Source: From *Atlantic Digest, 2nd Series*. Reprinted with permission from ThomsonWest.

20A Atl D 2d—5 **LANDLORD & TENANT**

III. LANDLORD'S TITLE AND REVERSION.—Continued.

(B) ESTOPPEL OF TENANT.—Continued.

62. Leases and agreements as ground of estoppel.—Continued.
   (3). Tenant in possession at time relation arose.
   (4). Tenant holding over.
63. Operation of estoppel against tenant.
   (1). In general.
   (2). Actions in which estoppel is effective.
   (3). Necessity of surrendering possession to discharge ground of estoppel.
   (4). Sufficiency of surrender.
   (5). Denial of title as to part of property.
   (6). Time as to which estoppel is effective.
64. Persons estopped.
65. As to whom tenant estopped.
66. Adverse possession of tenant.
   (1). In general.
   (2). Necessity of surrender of premises by tenant or repudiation of tenancy and notice.
   (3). Character of tenant's possession.
67. Purchase of tax title.
68. Attornment to third person.
69. Effect of eviction by landlord.

IV. TERMS FOR YEARS.

(A) NATURE AND EXTENT.

70. Nature of estate for years.
71. Commencement of term.
72. Duration of term.
73. Monthly tenancies.

(B) ASSIGNMENT AND SUBLETTING.

74. Assignability and agreements to assign leases and contracts.
75. Right of lessee or tenant to assign or sublet in general.
   (1). In general.
   (2). Statutory prohibition.
   (3). Consent of lessor.
76. Covenants, conditions, and restrictions as to assignment or subletting.
   (1). In general.
   (2). What constitutes breach of covenant.
   (3). Consent of lessor, or waiver of condition.
   (4). Evidence of consent.
   (5). Questions for jury.
77. Parol assignments and sublettings.
78. Requisites and validity of written instrument.
   (1). In general.
   (2). Delivery of assignment.
   (3). Necessity of record.
79. Construction and operation of assignments in general.
   (1). In general.
   (2). Rights and liabilities of assignee.

topic and key from *Young v. Dist. of Columbia*

from headnote 8

FIGURE 6.5 **Digest Page**

Source: From *Atlantic Digest, 2nd Series*. Reprinted with permission from ThomsonWest.

headnote 8

name and citation of case

76(1) **LANDLORD & TENANT** 20A Atl D 2d—142

For later cases see same Topic and Key Number in Pocket Part

D.C. 2000. Restrictions in original lease against subletting do not affect, as between lessee and sublessee, the validity of sublease.

Young v. District of Columbia, 752 A.2d 138.

D.C. 1984. Option clause in lease granting tenant option to lease balance of eighth floor unambiguously entitled tenant to expand demised premises and to utilize all or any part of those premises for any purpose permitted by remaining provisions of lease, and subleasing clause qualified tenant's right to sublet only by requiring landlord's specific consent which was not to be unreasonably withheld; thus, nothing in lease prohibited tenant from exercising option and subleasing entire balance of eighth floor at profit.

1010 Potomac Associates v. Grocery Manufacturers of America, Inc., 485 A.2d 199.

D.C.Mun.App. 1955. A covenant against subletting is for the benefit of the lessor.

Goody's, Inc. v. Stern's Equipment Co., 110 A.2d 311.

D.C.Mun.App. 1952. A covenant against subletting is for benefit of lessor because it is regarded as for his interest to determine who shall be a tenant of his property.

Friedman v. Thomas J. Fisher & Co., 88 A.2d 321, 31 A.L.R.2d 827.

D.C.Mun.App. 1950. Forfeitures of a lease for conditions broken and restrictions upon the right to assign are both looked upon with disfavor.

Burrows Motor Co. v. Davis, 76 A.2d 163.

D.C.Mun.App. 1946. The Emergency Rent Act does not give a tenant by sufferance power to sublet contrary to landlord's expressed will, but landlord's right in that respect, and even an express restriction against subletting in a written lease, may be waived by landlord by accepting rent in advance with knowledge of the subletting. D.C.Code 1940, §§ 45–820, 45–1605(b)(1).

Thompson v. Gray, 50 A.2d 594.

D.C.Mun.App. 1944. A covenant in a lease against assigning or subletting without landlord's consent is for benefit of landlord because it is regarded as for his interest to determine who shall be his tenant. D.C.Code 1940, § 45–820.

Keroes v. Westchester Apartments, 36 A.2d 263.

D.C.Mun.App. 1943. A tenant may not create new tenancy by removing from leased property and placing it completely in charge of sublessees in violation of terms of lease, as Emergency Rent Act protects only actual tenants, not mere middlemen. D.C.Code 1940, § 45–1601.

Hall v. Henry J. Robb, Inc., 32 A.2d 707.

Md. 1990. Contractual restrictions on alienability of leasehold interests are permitted.

Julian v. Christopher, 575 A.2d 735, 320 Md. 1.

If clause in lease is susceptible of two interpretations, public policy favors interpretation least restrictive of right to alienate freely.

Julian v. Christopher, 575 A.2d 735, 320 Md. 1.

Md. 1965. Although landlords agreed that tenants should have right to transfer alcoholic beverage license to any one acquiring all of assets of business should landlords decline to exercise their option to purchase such assets at price offered by prospective purchaser, landlords had right to refuse to assent to removal of one of licensees and substitution of others in absence of provision in lease authorizing such.

Katz v. Williams, 211 A.2d 723, 239 Md. 355.

N.H. 1961. An unequivocal and unqualified restriction against assignment in a lease, freely entered into between the parties, is valid.

Segre v. Ring, 170 A.2d 265, 103 N.H. 278

N.J.Super.A.D. 1976. As a general rule, a restriction against lease transfers contained in an express provision in the lease is viewed as a condition subsequent; therefore, the lessee may transfer despite the restriction, and the transfer is effective until avoided by the lessor.

Xerox Corp. v. Listmark Computer Systems, 361 A.2d 81, 142 N.J.Super. 232.

N.J.Super.A.D. 1954. Covenant in lease against assignment or subletting is personal to lessor and is made for his benefit, and only he or his successors in interest may avail themselves of it.

Stark v. National Research & Design Corp., 110 A.2d 143, 33 N.J.Super. 315.

N.J.Super.A.D. 1952. Assignment of lease without complying with lease requirement that previous written consent of landlord for assignment be endorsed thereon was invalid.

K. & J. Markets v. Martin Packing Corp., 90 A.2d 507, 20 N.J.Super. 515.

Where lease provided that tenant could assign the lease to corporation and that consent for such purpose was given by landlord upon proof of sale of tenant's assets to corporation, assignment by tenant to corporation without knowledge of landlord and without any proof of sale or assets to corporation having been submitted to landlord was invalid and corporation

FIGURE 6.6 **Comprehensive Diagram of the ThomsonWest Digest System**

Source: Retrieved from www.westgroup.com/documentation/westlaw/wlawdoc/wlres/keynumdi.pdf (accessed December 12, 2007). From *ThomsonWest Digest System*. Reprinted with permission from ThomsonWest.

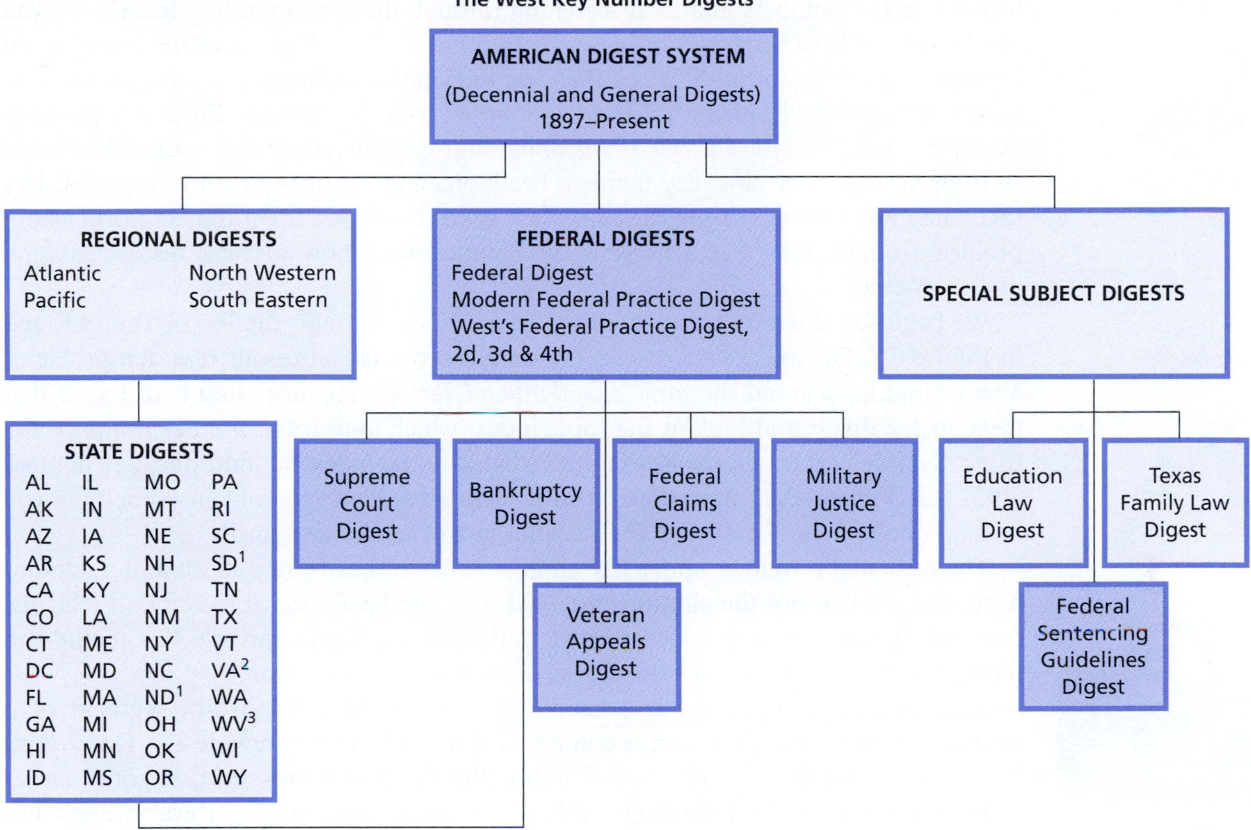

[1]The American Digest System also includes the *Century Digest*, which indexes cases from 1658 to1896. The *Century Digest* does not contain key numbers.

[2]North and South Dakota are combined into one set called *Dakota Digest*.

[3]Virginia and West Virginia are combined into one set called *Virginia and West Virginia Digest*.

FIGURE 6.7 **Order of Cases in a Digest**

Source: From *Federal Practice Digest 4th*. Reprinted with permission from ThomsonWest.

⚷271 ELECTIONS 39 F P D 4th—492

For later cases see same Topic and Key Number in Pocket Part

⚷299.—Re-examination of ballots and recount.

[text omitted]

⚷299(.5). In general.

U.S.Fla. 2000. Manual recounts of ballots on which machines had failed to detect fote for President, as implemented in response to Florida Supreme Court's opinion which ordered that "intent of the voter" be discerned but did not apply specific standards to ensure uniform treatment, did not satisfy minimum requirement for nonarbitrary treatment of voters necessary, under Equal Protection Clause, to secure the fundamental right to vote for President. U.S.C.A. Const.Amend. 14.

[text omitted]

⚷299(4). Proceedings on recount or re-examination.

U.S.Fla. 2000. For state recount in presidential election to be conducted in compliance with requirements of equal protection and due process, it would require adoption of adequate statewide standards for determining what was a legal vote, and practicable procedures to implement them, and also orderly judicial review of any disputed matters that might arise. U.S.C.A. Const. Amend. 14.

Bush v. Gore, 121 S.Ct. 525, 531 U.S. 98, 148 L.Ed.2d 388, on remand Gore v. Harris, 779 So.2d 270, on remand 773 So.2d 524.

A WALK THROUGH A DIGEST: A PRACTICAL EXERCISE

Digests are an excellent place to begin many research projects. By identifying relevant topics and key numbers and then searching through the corresponding headnotes, you will be able to locate citations for cases that appear to be analogous to the issues posed by your research problem. You can then use the citation included with the headnote to review the published opinion in detail as it appears in the reporter. Since our previous example, using *Young v. District of Columbia,* started with a case and worked backward to show you how the case, key number, headnote, and digest topic all fit together, let's take one more example, using the same case cited, but based upon the landlord–tenant problem from the Case Fact Pattern in this chapter, to see how a typical research session might proceed.

We begin by isolating an appropriate topic. Look through the list of topics found in Figure 6.8. Do you see any topics that might prove useful to our research problem? You should have found the topic *Landlord and Tenant.* The next step is to locate that topic in the digest and look at the topic index, which appears at the beginning of the topic. Searching through the key numbers listed in the index, we find one, key number 80(2) (see Figure 6.9), that relates to our Case Fact Pattern problem (which, as you recall, concerns the liability of the original tenant to the landlord).

The next step is to look under key number 80(2) for headnotes. If we find a relevant headnote, we can use the citation provided with the headnote to locate and read the full text of the case as it appears in the reporter. See if you can use this method to locate some relevant cases in the digest of your own jurisdiction.

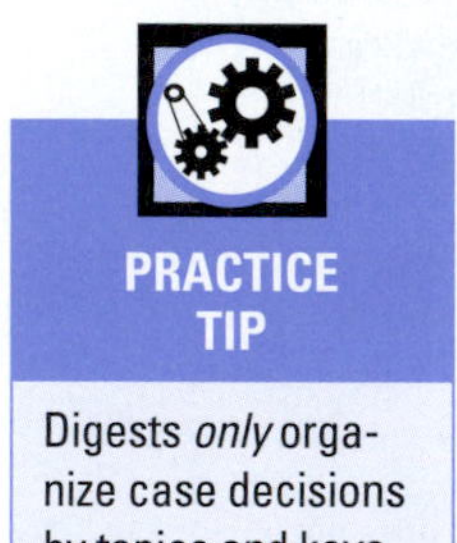

PRACTICE TIP

Digests *only* organize case decisions by topics and keys.

The topics, key numbers, and headnotes are the most important segment of a digest, but there are other useful components as well. These include the Descriptive Word Index, the Words and Phrases Index, the Table of Cases, and, in some earlier instances, the Plaintiff/Defendant Table. (You should note that not every digest has all of these additional sections.) Therefore, beginning your research by searching the digest topics is one way to start your project. We will investigate another approach through the use of indexes.

Indexes to Indexes

Your supervising attorney assigns a client's case to you. The client's case is a puzzle of facts and you want to begin finding cases that will assist in either solving the puzzle, or at least, finding analogous cases that will offer guidance in the matter. What should you do? One of the first places you might search is the Descriptive Word Index of the digest.

Descriptive Word Index
A subject index that provides a researcher with a quick survey of specific key numbers, often from several topics, which apply to a given subject area.

The **Descriptive Word Index** is a subject index that provides a researcher with a quick survey of specific topics and key numbers, often from several topics, that apply to a given subject area. You locate these topics and keys by writing down relevant words that apply to the facts given. The best approach is to think of a combination of broad and specific topics. Often your relevant words are not the same as listed in the digest. Be creative and flexible.

Now, to use the Descriptive Word Index, we would first analyze our legal problem to identify terms that define the issues presented. For our landlord–tenant problem, such terms as "landlord and tenant," "sublease," "nonpayment of rent," and "subletting" might be appropriate. When we look in our Descriptive Word Index under the word "sublease," the entry sends us to the word "subletting" (see Figure 6.10), where we find not only the same key number from the landlord and tenant topic that we found before [that is, key number 80(2)], but also references to key numbers from entirely different topics (see, for example, the reference to key number 16(6) from the topic *Indians,* relating to the subletting of Indian lands). Although these other topics are not relevant to our current landlord–tenant problem, there will be times when the

FIGURE 6.8 **Digest Topics**

Source: From *Atlantic Digest, 2nd Series*. Reprinted with permission from ThomsonWest.

digest topic

DIGEST TOPICS

114	Customs Duties
115	Damages
116	Dead Bodies
117	Death
117G	Debt, Action of
117T	Debtor and Creditor
118A	Declaratory Judgment
119	Dedication
120	Deeds
122A	Deposits and Escrows
123	Deposits in Court
124	Descent and Distribution
125	Detectives
126	Detinue
129	Disorderly Conduct
130	Disorderly House
131	District and Prosecuting Attorneys
132	District of Columbia
133	Disturbance of Public Assemblage
134	Divorce
135	Domicile
135H	Double Jeopardy
136	Dower and Curtesy
137	Drains
138	Drugs and Narcotics
141	Easements
142	Ejectment
143	Election of Remedies
144	Elections
145	Electricity
146	Embezzlement
148	Eminent Domain
148A	Employers' Liability
149	Entry, Writ of
150	Equity
151	Escape
152	Escheat
154	Estates in Property
156	Estoppel
157	Evidence
158	Exceptions, Bill of
159	Exchange of Property
160	Exchanges
161	Execution
162	Executors and Administrators
163	Exemptions
164	Explosives
165	Extortion and Threats
166	Extradition and Detainers
167	Factors
168	False Imprisonment
169	False Personation
170	False Pretenses
170A	Federal Civil Procedure
170B	Federal Courts
171	Fences
172	Ferries
174	Fines
175	Fires
176	Fish
177	Fixtures
178	Food
179	Forcible Entry and Detainer
180	Forfeitures
181	Forgery
183	Franchises
184	Fraud
185	Frauds, Statute of
186	Fraudulent Conveyances
187	Game
188	Gaming
189	Garnishment
190	Gas
191	Gifts
192	Good Will
193	Grand Jury
195	Guaranty
196	Guardian and Ward
197	Habeas Corpus
198	Hawkers and Peddlers
199	Health and Environment
200	Highways
201	Holidays
202	Homestead
203	Homicide
204	Hospitals
205	Husband and Wife
205H	Implied and Constructive Contracts
206	Improvements
207	Incest
208	Indemnity
209	Indians
210	Indictment and Information
211	Infants
212	Injunction
213	Innkeepers
216	Inspection
217	Insurance
218	Insurrection and Sedition
219	Interest
220	Internal Revenue
221	International Law
222	Interpleader
223	Intoxicating Liquors
224	Joint Adventures
225	Joint-Stock Companies and Business Trusts
226	Joint Tenancy
227	Judges
228	Judgment
229	Judicial Sales
230	Jury
231	Justices of the Peace
232	Kidnapping
232A	Labor Relations
233	Landlord and Tenant
234	Larceny
235	Levees and Flood Control
236	Lewdness
237	Libel and Slander
238	Licenses
239	Liens
240	Life Estates
241	Limitation of Actions
242	Lis Pendens
245	Logs and Logging
246	Lost Instruments
247	Lotteries
248	Malicious Mischief
249	Malicious Prosecution
250	Mandamus
251	Manufactures
252	Maritime Liens
253	Marriage
255	Master and Servant
256	Mayhem
257	Mechanics' Liens
257A	Mental Health
258A	Military Justice
259	Militia
260	Mines and Minerals
265	Monopolies
266	Mortgages
267	Motions
268	Municipal Corporations

XVI

Descriptive Word Index will help you find useful key numbers from less than obvious topics. The Descriptive Word Index also enables you to avoid a line-by-line search through hundreds or even thousands of key number entries in the index of a more obvious topic (for example, rather than searching through the many key numbers in the "landlord and tenant" topic index, we were able to quickly find key number 80(2) by scanning Figure 6.10).

The Descriptive Word Index might be thought of as a master index to all the key numbers contained in all the topics in the digest. Thus it is often an excellent place

FIGURE 6.9 **Key Number**

Source: From *Atlantic Digest, 2nd Series*. Reprinted with permission from ThomsonWest.

key number

LANDLORD & TENANT 32C S E D 2d—6

IV. TERMS FOR YEARS.—Continued.

(B) ASSIGNMENT AND SUBLETTING.—Continued.

79. Construction and operation of assignments in general.—Continued.
   (3). Rights and liabilities of assignor.
   (4). Assignment as security.
   (5). Construction as question for jury.

80. Construction and operation of subleases.
   (1). In general.
   (2). Liability of original tenant to landlord.
   (3). Rights and liabilities of subtenants.
   (4). Liability of original lessee to sublessee.

80.5. Evidence of assignment or subletting.

(C) MORTGAGE.

81. Mortgages of leaseholds.
   (1). In general.
   (2). Rights of mortgagee.
   (3). Rights of purchaser at foreclosure sale.
   (4). Recording and filing.

(D) EXTENSIONS AND RENEWALS.

81.5. Nature of right in general.

82. Provisions for extension of term.

83. Covenants for renewal in general.
   (1). In general.
   (2). Conditions precedent to right to renewal.
   (3). Security for renewal.
   (4). Forfeiture of right to renewal.
   (5). Actions for breach of agreement.

84. Persons entitled to renewal.

84.1. _____ In general.

85. _____ Assignees or undertenants.

85.5. Persons bound by agreements to renew.

86. Option to renew and election.
   (1). In general.
   (2). Notice of election.
   (3). Waiver of notice.
   (4). Proceedings to fix amount of rent.

87. Number of renewals.

88. Renewal leases.
   (1). In general.
   (2). Covenants and conditions.
   (3). Evidence of renewal.

89. Extension or renewal by indorsement on lease.

89.5. Implied contracts to extend or renew in general.

90. Extension or renewal by holding over.
   (1). In general.
   (2). Conditions in general.
   (3). Term.
   (4). What constitutes holding over so as to create new tenancy.

FIGURE 6.10 Descriptive Word Index

Source: From *Atlantic Digest, 2nd Series*. Reprinted with permission from ThomsonWest.

STUDENTS 37B Atl D 2d–116

References are to Digest Topics and Key Numbers

STUDENTS

BANKRUPTCY,
Automatic stay, loans and transcripts, **Bankr ⚷ 2403**
Injunction against proceedings, loans and transcripts, **Bankr ⚷ 2372**
Loans. See heading **BANKRUPTCY,** STUDENT loans.

COLLEGES. See heading **COLLEGES AND UNIVERSITIES,** STUDENTS.

SCHOOLS. See heading **SCHOOLS AND SCHOOL DISTRICTS,** generally.

UNEMPLOYMENT compensation. See heading **UNEMPLOYMENT COMPENSATION** STUDENTS, duty to find work.

SUA SPONTE

See heading **COURT'S OWN MOTION,** generally.

SUBAGENTS

See heading **AGENCY,** SUBAGENTS.

SUBCONTRACTORS

INDEMNITY. See heading **INDEMNITY,** CONTRACTORS.

INDEPENDENT contractors. See heading **INDEPENDENT CONTRACTORS,** generally.

MAILS, carriage of, **Postal ⚷ 21(2)**

MECHANICS' liens. See heading **MECHANICS' LIENS,** SUBCONTRACTORS.

PUBLIC contracts, **Pub Contr ⚷ 17**

STATES,
Rights and remedies,
Contracts, **States ⚷ 108.5**

UNITED States, **Pub Contr ⚷ 17, 24**

WORKERS' compensation,
Effect of compensation acts as to other remedies, **Work Comp ⚷ 2166, 2167**
Employees covered, **Work Comp ⚷ 334-361**
Evidence,
Sufficiency, **Work Comp ⚷ 1461**
Persons liable as third persons, **Work Comp ⚷ 2165-2167**
Public officers as employees, **Work Comp ⚷ 389**

SUBDIVISIONS

INCOME tax-federal,
Capital gains and losses, **Int Rev ⚷ 3251**

SUBDIVISIONS—Cont'd

MECHANICS' liens, error in name of subdivision in claim or statement, **Mech Liens ⚷ 136(4)**

MUNICIPAL corporations, **Mun Corp ⚷ 40, 43**

MUNICIPAL employees and officials, Apportionment, **Mun Corp ⚷ 127**

TOWNS, **Towns ⚷ 4**

ZONING approval. See heading **ZONING,** SUBDIVISION approval.

SUBJACENT SUPPORT

MINING, injuries to surface, **Mines ⚷ 122**

SUBJECT OF STATUTE

SINGLE-SUBJECT requirement. See heading **SINGLE-SUBJECT REQUIREMENT**, generally.

TITLES of laws. See heading **TITLES OF LAWS,** generally.

SUBLEASES

See heading **SUBLETTING,** generally.

SUBLETTING

BREACH of covenant or restriction, **Land & Ten ⚷104**

CONSENT, **Land & Ten ⚷ 75(3), 76(3, 4)**

CONSTRUCTION,
Sublease, **Land & Ten ⚷ 80**

CONTRACTS. See heading **SUBCONTRACTORS,** generally.

COOPERATIVE apartments, **Land & Ten ⚷ 360**

COVENANTS,
Generally, **Land & Ten ⚷ 76**
Breach, **Land & Ten ⚷ 104**

DISTINCT from assignments, **Land & Ten ⚷ 79(1)**

EVICTION,
Subtenants, **Land & Ten ⚷ 177.5**

EVIDENCE, **Land & Ten ⚷ 80.5**

INDIAN lands, **Indians ⚷ 16(6)**

INJURIES,
Subtenants, **Land & Ten ⚷ 164(5)**

LEASED premises, **Land & Ten ⚷ 74-81**

LEASES,
Conditions, **Land & Ten ⚷ 76**

Cont.

applicable topic

unrelated reference under topic

FIGURE 6.10 **Descriptive Word Index** *Cont.*

37B Atl D 2d–117 **SUBMERGED**

References are to Digest Topics and Key Numbers

SUBLETTING—Cont'd
LEASES—Cont'd

Consent,
  Assignment or subletting, **Land & Ten 🔑 75(3), 76(3, 4)**
Construction,
  Subleases, **Land & Ten 🔑 80** ← relevant topic and key
Privity, **Land & Ten 🔑 43**

LIABILITIES and rights,
  Subtenant, **Land & Ten 🔑 80(3)**

LIMITATIONS, **Land & Ten 🔑 76**

MOBILE home parks, **Land & Ten 🔑 373**

ORIGINAL tenants,
  Liability to landlord, **Land & Ten 🔑 80(2)**
  Liability to subtenants, **Land & Ten 🔑 80(4)**

PAROL agreements, **Land & Ten 🔑 77**

RECOVERY of possession,
  Suspension,
    Remedies,
      Unauthorized subletting, **Land & Ten 🔑 278.9(1)**

RENT,
  Liability, **Land & Ten 🔑 209**
  Liens,
    Subtenant property, **Land & Ten 🔑 246(4)**

REPAIRS,
  Subtenant rights, **Land & Ten 🔑 150(4), 152(8)**

RESTRICTIVE covenants and conditions, **Land & Ten 🔑 76**

STATUTES, **Land & Ten 🔑 75(2)**

SUSPENSION of rights,
  Reentry and possession recovery,
    Subtenants,
      Regulations, **Land & Ten 🔑 278.4(6)**
      Unauthorized subletting, **Land & Ten 🔑 278.9(1)**

TERMINATION,
  Lease, **Land & Ten 🔑 104**

TRAILER parks or camps, **Land & Ten 🔑 373**

UNDER tenants,
  Right to renewal, **Land & Ten 🔑 85**

USE of premises,
  Subtenants, **Land & Ten 🔑 134(2, 4)**

WAIVER,
  Generally, **Land & Ten 🔑 75(3)**

SUBLETTING—Cont'd
WAIVER—Cont'd

Assignments,
  Leases, **Land & Ten 🔑 75(3), 76(3)**
Covenants, conditions or restrictions, **Land & Ten 🔑 76(3)**

SUBMERGED LANDS

ACTIONS and proceedings,
  Navigable waters, lands under,
    Boundaries, determination of, **Nav Wat 🔑 36(6)**
    Division, **Nav Wat 🔑 36(6)**
    Partition, **Nav Wat 🔑 36(6)**
    Recovery of submerged lands, **Nav Wat 🔑 36(7)**
    Trespass, **Nav Wat 🔑 36(5)**
  Nonnavigable waters, lands under,
    Lakes and ponds, **Waters 🔑 114**
    Water courses, **Waters 🔑 98**

BOUNDARIES, lands under navigable waters, determination of, **Nav Wat 🔑 36(6)**

CONSTRUCTION of grants of lands under navigable waters, **Nav Wat 🔑 37(4)**

CONVEYANCES. See subheading GRANTS under this heading.

COUNTIES, grants of lands under navigable waters to, **Nav Wat 🔑 37(8)**

DIVISION of lands under navigable waters, **Nav Wat 🔑 36(6)**

DREDGING and filling, **Nav Wat 🔑 38**

EQUAL footing doctrine, **Nav Wat 🔑 36(1)**

FLATS,
  Navigable waters, **Nav Wat 🔑 36(2)**
  Nonnavigable water courses, **Waters 🔑 92**

FORFEITURE of grant of land under navigable waters, **Nav Wat 🔑 37(5)**

GRANTS,
  Navigable waters, lands under,
    Generally, **Nav Wat 🔑 37**
    Construction, **Nav Wat 🔑 37(4)**
    Counties, grants to, **Nav Wat 🔑 37(8)**
    Forfeiture, **Nav Wat 🔑 37(5)**
    Grantees, **Nav Wat 🔑 37(3, 4)**
    Leases, **Nav Wat 🔑 37(6)**
    Municipal corporations, grants to, **Nav Wat 🔑 37(8)**
    Power to grant, **Nav Wat 🔑 37(2)**
    Riparian lands, **Nav Wat 🔑 37(7)**
    Towns, grants to, **Nav Wat 🔑 37(8)**

to start your research. You will use the Descriptive Word Index most of the time as it is the most general of the digest indexes.

Words and Phrases Index

The **Words and Phrases Index** of the digest is useful if your research issue turns upon the judicial construction ("construction" in this context is drawn from the verb "construe" and means "interpretation") or interpretation of a specific word or phrase. The words and phrases are arranged alphabetically, with citations to those cases in which the word or phrase is construed.

Words and Phrases Index
An index to a digest that construes a judicial term.

Let's use a new example to demonstrate how the words and phrases section works. Suppose an important issue in a case your office is handling in the U. S. district court in Pennsylvania turns upon interpretation of the term *shrink-wrap.* Turning to the words and phrases index of the *Federal Practice Digest 4th* (see Figure 6.11), you see a listing for the term *shrink-wrap.* Going down the page of cases provided, you'll find that the case of *Peerless Wall and Window Coverings, Inc. v. Synchronics, Inc.* was a Pennsylvania federal court case decided by the Western District. The citation reads "85 F. Supp. 2d [Supp. 2d] 519, affirmed 234 F.3d 1265" and cited in headnote "Copyr[ight] 107."("Copyr" is the key system's abbreviation for the topic copyright.) This tells you that the opinion begins on page 519, and under headnote (number 2) "Copyr 107" of that opinion, there will be a judicial interpretation of the term *shrink-wrap.* See Figure 6.12, which reproduces a page from the case, and find the judicial construction.

PRACTICE TIP

Do not confuse the name of the Words and Phrases Index with the words and phrases you write down to locate a topic and key in the Descriptive Word Index. The Descriptive Word Index is the more general index, with the Words and Phrases Index limited to the legal construction of specific words and phrases in cases. More often than not, you will want to use the Descriptive Word Index rather than the Words and Phrases Index.

In addition to the words and phrases digest index, ThomsonWest also publishes a multivolume set called *Words and Phrases* that includes words and phrases from all jurisdictions for all time periods, and which provides not only citations but also headnotes for each word or phrase. Remember, *Words and Phrases* has a limited purpose and should be not used unless you want a judicial interpretation of a word or phase.

Table of Cases Index

The **Table of Cases Index** of a digest lists all the cases whose text appears in the associated volumes. The cases are listed alphabetically by name of the plaintiff. See Figure 6.13, which shows *Peerless Wall and Window Coverings, Inc. v. Synchronics, Inc.* as it appears in the table of cases in *West's Federal Practice Digest 4th.*

Table of Cases Index
Lists of all the cases whose text appears in the associated volumes.

If you know the name of a case but not the citation, the table of cases will provide you with this information, enabling you to locate the text of the opinion. In addition to the National Reporter citation, you will find the official citation and the procedural history of the case (that is, whether it has been affirmed or reversed on appeal), as well as a list of the key numbers assigned to that case. Locate these elements in Figure 6.13.

Sometimes you only know the name of the defendant in a case. Some digests have a **Defendant/Plaintiff Table** listing the cases alphabetically by the defendant first or a table of cases listing the name of the case both ways. The Defendant/Plaintiff Table contains parallel citations, but not procedural history or key numbers; of course, if you want this information for a case you've found in this table, simply look it up in the table of cases (now that you've learned the plaintiff's name). Figure 6.14 shows the listing for *Peerless Wall and Window Coverings, Inc. v. Synchronics, Inc.* as it appears in the table of cases from the defendant's name.

Defendant/Plaintiff Table
List of the cases alphabetically by the defendant first or a table of cases listing the name of the case both ways.

The Conversion Table

The digest is often reorganized with topics and keys being reclassified. When this occurs, you will be guided to another topic and key that replaces the previous one.

FIGURE 6.11 **Words and Phrases Section**

Source: From *Federal Practice Digest 4th.* Reprinted with permission from ThomsonWest.

case

topic and key

113 F P D 4th—149 **SIGNATORY OPERATOR**

Marasco, 227 F.Supp.2d 322, affirmed in part, reversed in part 318 F.3d 497, on remand 2004 WL 633276.—Arrest 68(4).

SHRINK-WRAP

W.D.Pa. 2000. "Shrink-wrap" software licenses, which the customer impliedly assents to by, for example, opening the envelope enclosing the software distribution media, are generally valid and enforceable.—Peerless Wall and Window Coverings, Inc. v. Synchronics, Inc., 85 F.Supp.2d 519, affirmed 234 F.3d 1265.—Copyr 107.

SHTAR ISKA

Bkrtcy.S.D.N.Y. 2000. "Heter iska" is a type of joint venture designed to avoid Jewish law's prohibition against charging interest, pursuant to which the moneys advanced are treated as a contribution to the venture, and the venturer who advances the funds, that is, the lender, is entitled to an accounting, in lieu of which the parties execute a "shtar iska" which obligates the other venturer, that is, the borrower, to pay a fixed monthly return corresponding to the interest payments called for under the promissory note, and requires the lender to waive any further profits.—In re Venture Mortg Fund, L.P., 245 B.R. 460, subsequently affirmed 282 F.3d 185.—Usury 38.

SICKNESS

C.A.8 (Ark.) 2004. Under Arkansas law, as predicted by Court of Appeals, disabling loss of vision that insured orthopedic surgeon sustained as result of complications from eye surgery constituted "accidental bodily injury" within meaning of disability insurance policies, for which insured was entitled to lifetime benefits, and not "sickness," for which benefits were only payable until age 65; insured's vision loss was not expected, proceeded from unidentified cause, and occurred only by chance.—Kolb v. Paul Revere Life Ins. Co., 355 F.3d 1132.—Insurance 2544(1), 2545(2), 2569.

C.D.Cal. 2002. Neither party's experts, in widow's action against insurer asserting breach of contract claim and seeking declaratory relief arising from insurer's denial of claim under accidental death policy, could testify about whether high-altitude pulmonary edema (HAPE), of which widow's husband died, was a "sickness" within meaning of policy's clause excluding coverage for loss resulting from or caused by physical or mental sickness; the definition of "sickness," not set out in the policy, and the application of that definition to HAPE, were legal, rather than factual, questions, and had to be determined by the Court.—Paulissen v. U.S. Life Ins. Co. in City of New York, 205 F.Supp.2d 1120.—Evid 506, 518.

C.D.Cal. 2002. Although "sickness," "disease," and "illness" have broad, generic definitions, the definitions are narrowly construed in the context of insurance policies.—Paulissen v. U.S. Life Ins. Co. in City of New York, 205 F.Supp.2d 1120.—Insurance 2589(1).

C.D.Cal. 2002. Mountain climber's high-altitude pulmonary edema (HAPE) was not, under California law, a "sickness" for purpose of accidental death policy's sickness exclusion; his HAPE was not a disorder of a somewhat established or settled character, and did not arise from some organic cause, but rather, arose from exposure to high altitudes, and his symptoms would likely have been completely relieved, without medical intervention, if he had reached a lower elevation more quickly.—Paulissen v. U.S. Life Ins. Co. in City of New York, 205 F.Supp.2d 1120.—Insurance 2589(1).

SICKNESS OR DISEASE

E.D.Mich. 2004. Insured's gallstones constituted "sickness or disease," for purposes of exclusion in accidental death and dismemberment policy precluding recovery for loss resulting from sickness or disease; gallstone developed through internal organic functioning of body, and was present in insured's body for almost two years.—Miller v. Hartford Life Ins. Co., 348 F.Supp.2d 815.—Insurance 2589(1).

SIGNALING

N.D.Ga. 2002. In the antitrust context, "signaling" means either that a competitor is inviting all to make a traditional price-fixing agreement, or that there already exists such an agreement and it is being carried out through indirect communications. Sherman Act, § 1, as amended, 15 U.S.C.A. § 1.—Holiday Wholesale Grocery Co. v. Philip Morris Inc., 231 F.Supp.2d 1253, affirmed Williamson Oil Co., Inc. v. Philip Morris USA, 346 F.3d 1287.—Monop 17(1.12).

SIGNAL PICKETING

C.D.Cal. 2003. As used in labor law context; "signal picketing" generally refers to union activity designed to induce employees to strike, not activity designed to inspire consumer boycott.—Kohn v. Southwest Regional Council of Carpenters, 289 F.Supp.2d 1155—Labor & Emp 1379, 1412.

SIGNATORY OPERATOR

U.S. 2002. A "signatory operator" responsible for annual premiums under the Coal Industry Retiree Health Benefit Act is a coal operator that signed any National Bituminous Coal Wage Agreement or any other agreement requiring contributions to the 1950 or 1974 Benefit Plans negotiated between a mine workers' union and various coal operators. 26 U.S.C.A. § 9701(c)(1).—Barnhart v. Sigmon Coal Co., Inc., 122 S.Ct. 941, 534 U.S. 438, 197 A.L.R. Fed. 689, 151 L.Ed.2d 908.—Labor & Emp 529.

FIGURE 6.12 Judicial Construction of Shrink-Wrap

Source: From *Federal Supplement, 2nd Series.* Reprinted with permission from ThomsonWest.

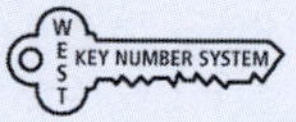

PEERLESS WALL AND WINDOW COVERINGS, INC., Plaintiff,

v.

SYNCHRONICS, INC., a Tennessee Corporation, Defendant.

No. CIV. A. 98–1084.

United States District Court, W.D. Pennsylvania.

Feb. 25, 2000.

Licensee of cash register software which was not year 2000 (Y2K) compliant sued licensor, alleging breach of contract, express and implied warranties, fraud and negligent misrepresentation. Licensor moved for summary judgment. The District Court, D. Brooks Smith, J., held that: (1) possibility of recovering punitive damages satisfied amount in controversy requirement for diversity jurisdiction purposes; (2) implied warranties of merchantability and fitness were disclaimed; (3) 90-day express warranty covered only media containing software, not software itself; (4) integration clause in license precluded fraud claims based on sales literature; (5) under Tennessee law as interpreted by federal court, licensor had duty to disclose that software was not Y2K compliant; (6) fraud claims failed due to lack of showing of reliance; (7) economic loss doctrine precluded recovery for negligent misrepresentation; and (8) nominal damages showing precluded summary judgment based on absence of damages.

Summary judgment for licensor.

1. Federal Courts 🔑 337

Possibility of punitive damages, in putative class action suit by buyer of computer software seeking free upgrade to Y2K compliant software, satisfied amount in controversy requirement for diversity jurisdiction, despite upgrade cost of only $1,500 to $2,000.

2. Copyrights and Intellectual Property 🔑 107

"Shrink-wrap" software licenses, which the customer impliedly assents to by, for example, opening the envelope enclosing the software distribution media, are generally valid and enforceable.

See publication Words and Phrases for other judicial constructions and definitions.

relevant topic and key

topic

3. Copyrights and Intellectual Property 🔑 107

All implied warranties of merchantability and fitness were disclaimed in software license agreement, through disclaimer statement prominently displayed on outside of software container, and by licensee's having signed and returned software registration form including recitation that licensee had read and agreed to software license terms.

4. Copyrights and Intellectual Property 🔑 107

Provision of license agreement covering cash register software, extended express 90-day warranty that software-diskettes and user manual would be free from defects in materials and workmanship read in conjunction with provision that entire risk of performance of software was with licensee, created express warranty of software media, rather than software itself.

5. Evidence 🔑 400(6)

Broad integration clause contained in software license agreement precluded claim that sales literature for software created warranty more extensive than warranty provided in license.

6. Copyrights and Intellectual Property 🔑 107

Statement in sales literature for cash register software, that user would remain up to date, did not commit provider to offer free upgrade to make software Y2K compliant; reference was to ability of software to keep current records of user's business transactions.

7. Evidence 🔑 400(3)

Presence of integration clause in computer software license precluded resort to parol evidence to elaborate upon statement in license making it effective for "useful life" of software.

8. Contracts 🔑 94(4)

Under Pennsylvania law, "fraud in the execution" applies to situations in which parties agree to include certain terms in an agreement, but the terms are not included.

See publication Words and Phrases for other judicial constructions and definitions.

9. Fraud 🔑 3

Under Pennsylvania law, "fraud in the inducement" involves allegations of repre-

Cont.

FIGURE 6.12 **Judicial Construction of Shrink-Wrap** *Cont.*

headnote 2

headnote 2 interpretation of "shrink-wrap"

PEERLESS WALL AND WINDOW COVERINGS v. SYNCHRONICS **527**
Cite as 85 F.Supp.2d 519 (W.D.Pa. 2000)

the existence of every element essential to its case. *Id.* Such evidence must be significantly probative and more than "merely colorable." *Armbruster v. Unisys Corp.,* 32 F.3d 768, 777 (3d Cir.1994).

Once the moving party has satisfied its burden, the nonmoving party is required by Fed.R.Civ.P. 56(e) to establish that there remains a genuine issue of material fact. *Clark v. Clabaugh,* 20 F.3d 1290, 1294 (3d Cir.1994). The nonmovant "may not rest upon mere allegation or denials of [its] pleadings, but must set forth specific facts showing that there is a genuine issue for trial." *Anderson v. Liberty Lobby, Inc.,* 477 U.S. 242, 256, 106 S.Ct. 2505, 91 L.Ed.2d 202 (1986). A fact is material if it "might affect the outcome of the suit under the governing law[,]" *id.* at 248, 106 S.Ct. 2505,[9] and is genuine "if the evidence is such that a reasonable jury could return a verdict for the nonmoving party." *Id.* at 248, 257, 106 S.Ct. 2505.

In determining whether a nonmovant has established the existence of a genuine issue of material fact requiring a jury trial, the evidence of the nonmovant must "be believed and all justifiable inferences are to be drawn in [its] favor." *Id.* at 255, 106 S.Ct. 2505. Whether an inference is justifiable, however, depends on the evidence adduced. *Matsushita Elec. Indus. Co. v. Zenith Radio Corp.,* 475 U.S. 574, 595–96, 106 S.Ct. 1348, 89 L.Ed.2d 538 (1986). An inference based upon speculation or conjecture does not create a material factual dispute sufficient to defeat summary judgment. *Robertson v. Allied Signal, Inc.,* 914 F.2d 360, 382 n. 12 (3d Cir.1990). Likewise, "simply show[ing] that there is some metaphysical doubt as to the material facts" does not establish a genuine issue for trial. *Matsushita,* 475 U.S. at 586, 106 S.Ct. 1348.

III.

A. WARRANTY

[2] As stated *supra,* the software plaintiff acquired was distributed pursuant to a license agreement printed on the diskette envelopes and in the user manuals. The recent weight of authority is that "shrink-wrap" licenses which the customer impliedly assents to by, for example, opening the envelope enclosing the software distribution media, are generally valid and enforceable. *See Hill v. Gateway 2000, Inc.,* 105 F.3d 1147, 1150 (7th Cir.1997) (Easterbrook, J.); *ProCD, Inc. v. Zeidenberg,* 86 F.3d 1447, 1452 (7th Cir.1996) (Easterbrook, J.); *M.A. Mortenson Co. v. Timberline Software Corp.,* 93 Wash.App. 819, 970 P.2d 803, 809–811, *review granted,* 138 Wash.2d 1001, 984 P.2d 1033 (1999); *Paragon Networks Int'l v. Macola, Inc.,* No. 9–99–2, 1999 WL 280385, *4 (Ohio App.Ct. Apr. 28, 1999) (unpublished). *But cf. Step–Saver Data Sys., Inc. v. Wyse Technology,* 939 F.2d 91, 95–106 (3d Cir. 1991) (analyzing enforceability of license under U.C.C. § 2–207 as a "battle of the forms" problem and finding license unenforceable because of prior conduct and manifested expectations of the parties).[10] As Judge Easterbrook insightfully opined:

> Vendors can put the entire terms of a contract on the outside of a box only by using microscopic type, removing other information that buyers might find more useful (such as what the software does, and on which computers it works), or both. . . . Notice on the outside, terms on the inside, and a right to return the software for a refund if the terms are unacceptable . . . may be a means of doing business valuable to buyers and sellers alike. . . . Transactions in which the exchange of money precedes the communication of detailed terms are

9. The parties agree that Tennessee law applies in the case *sub judice,* but disagree whether it differs in any material respect from that of Pennsylvania. I will treat the two bodies of law as interchangeable (especially with respect to the contract claims under the U.C.C.) unless the difference is significant.

10. Neither party contends that *Step–Saver* is controlling here.

FIGURE 6.13 **Table of Cases**

Source: From *Federal Practice Digest 4th.* Reprinted with permission from ThomsonWest.

PEEPER

103 F P D 4th—424

References are to Digest Topics and Key Numbers

Peeper's Sunglasses and Accessories, Inc. peepers; American Eyewear, Inc. v., NDTex, 106 FSupp2d 895.—Const Law 305(5); Fed Cts 76.10; Trademarks 1560.

Peeples v. Bradshaw, CA6 (Ohio), 110 FedAppx 590.—Fed Civ Proc 2734.

Peeples v. Coastal Office Products, Inc., CA4 (Md), 64 FedAppx 860.—Labor & Emp 358.

Peeples v. Coastal Office Products, Inc., DMd, 203 FSupp2d 432, aff 64 FedAppx 860.—Civil R 1018, 1019(2); 1218(6), 1225(1), 1243, 1244, 1252, 1431, 1516, 1540, 1541; Labor & Emp 355.

Peeples; U.S. v., CA11 (Fla), 23 F3d 370.—Sent & Pun 652, 664(6).

Peeples v. Wright Inv. Properties, Inc., MDGa, 36 FSupp2d 1378, aff 204 F3d 1122, reh and sug for reh den 209 F3d 726, cert den 120 SCt 2662, 530 US 1231, 147 LEd2d 276.—Civil R 1217, 1218(4).

Peer; U.S. v., CA4 (SC), 102 FedAppx 777.—Crim Law 1023(11).

Peer; U.S. v., CA10 (Utah), 119 FedAppx 216.—Crim Law 1073.

Peer; Venegas-Hernandez v., DPuerto Rico, 283 FSupp2d 491.—Contracts 147(2), 152, Copyr 33, 47, 47.5; Judgm 540, 584, 713(1), 828.15(2), 828.16(2), 828.16(4).

Peer Bearing Co. v. U.S., CIT, 182 FSupp2d 1285, opinion after remand 2002 WL 1285134, aff 78 FedAppx 718.—Admin Law 416.1; Const Law 318(1); Cust Dut 21.5(1), 21.5(3), 21.5(5), 84(6); Statut 219(1), 219(2), 219(6.1).

Peer Bearing Co.-Changshan v. U.S., CIT, 298 FSupp2d 1328.—Admin Law 330; Cust Dut 21.5(1), 21.5(3), 21.5(5); Statut 217.4, 219(1).

Peer Chain Co. v. U.S., CIT, 316 FSupp2d 1357.—Const Law 286; Cust Dut 21.5(5), 81.

Peer Intern. Corp. v. Latin American Music Corp., DPuerto Rico, 161 FSupp2d 38.—Can of Inst 1; Contracts 316(1); Copyr 33, 44, 46, 47, 47.5, 48, 49, 50.16, 52, 66, 67.2, 75.5, 76, 83(1), 83(3.5), 88.

Peer Intern. Corp.; Venegas Hernandez v., DPuerto Rico, 270 FSupp2d 207.—Copyr 33, 44, 51, 103, 104; Hus & W 249(2.1); Judgm 540, 562, 564(1), 585(1), 668(1), 828.6, 828.20(2).

Peerless Importers, Inc. v. Wine, Liquor & Distillery Workers Union Local One, CA2 (NY), 903 F2d 924.—Labor & Emp 1546(1), 1549(4), 1579.

Peerless Importers, Inc. v. Wine, Liquor & Distillery Workers Union Local One, SDNY, 712 FSupp 346, rev 903 F2d 924.—Labor & Emp 1549(19), 1549(21).

Peerless Ins. Co.; M. Fortunoff of Westbury Corp. v., EDNY, 260 FSupp2d 524.—Insurance 2888, 2889; Statut 184, 190, 208, 212.1, 212.5, 223.5(0.5), 230.

Peerless Ins. Co. v. U.S., EDVa, 674 FSupp 1202.—U S 74.1.

Peerless Motor Car Corp.; Wood v., CCA6 (Ohio), 75 F2d 554.—Pat 16.22, 233.1.

Peerless Plating Co., In re, BkrtcyWDMich, 70 BR 943.—Bankr 2830.5, 2876.5.

Peerless Systems, Corp. Securities Litigation, In re, SDCal, 182 FSupp2d 982.—Fed Civ Proc 1832; Sec Reg 60.15, 60.18, 60.27(6), 60.28(10.1), 60.45(1), 60.51, 60.53.

relevant case listed as plaintive v. defendant

Peerless Wall and Window Coverings, Inc. v. Synchronics, Inc., WDPa, 85 FSupp2d 519, aff 234 F3d 1265.—Contracts 94(4); Copyr 107, Evid 400(3), 400(6), 434(8); Fed Cts 337; Fraud 3, 11(1), 17, 20, 25, 32, 36.

Peer Morton; Ulysses I & Co., Inc. v., CA2 (NY), 11 FedAppx 14, cert den 122 SCt 458, 534 US 992, 151 LEd2d 376.—Civil R 1351(1), 1401; Courts 509; Fed Cts 1142.

Peer Review Systems, Inc.; Whitley v., CA8 (Minn), 221 F3d 1053.—Civil R 1118, 1122, 1137, 1536, 1545; Fed Civ Proc 2497.1; Fed Cts 776.

Peery v. Brakke, CA8 (SD), 826 F2d 740.—Civil R 1448; Judgm 828.7.

Peery; U.S. v., CA8 (Neb), 977 F2d 1230, cert den 113 SCt 1354, 507 US 946, 122 LEd2d 734.—Sent & Pun 765.

Pees; U.S. v., DColo, 645 FSupp 697.—Controlled Subs 6, 9.

Peet; Emmons, Estate of v., DMe, 950 FSupp 15.—Health 699, 703(2); Sent & Pun 1436, 1595.

Peete; U.S. v., CA6 (Tenn), 919 F2d 1168.—Jury 33(5.15); Sent & Pun 1963, 1972(2).

Peets v. U.S., SDNY, 55 FSupp2d 275.—Crim Law 1437, 1438, 1439, 1440(3).

Peffer; Alexander v., CA8 (Neb), 993 F2d 1348.—Civil R 1040, 1304.

Peffley v. Durakool, Inc., NDInd, 669 FSupp 1453.—Civil R 1505(3), 1505(6), 1555; Labor & Emp 806, 1320(14), 1518, 1549(19); Libel 1.

Peffley v. Hermaseal Co., NDInd, 669 FSupp 1453. See Peffley v. Durakool, Inc.

Pegan; Randall v., WDNY, 765 FSupp 793.—Civil R 1457(1), 1457(3).

Pegasus Broadcasting of San Juan, Inc. v. N.L.R.B., CA1, 82 F3d 511.—Labor & Emp 1490(3), 1811, 1860, 1866.

Pegasus Communications of Puerto Rico; Delgado Graulau v., DPuerto Rico, 130 FSupp2d 320.—Admin Law 501; Civil R 1122, 1123, 1168, 1171, 1197, 1505(3), 1505(7), 1711; Fed Civ Proc 2497.1; Lim of Act 95(15), 105(1), 195(3).

Pegasus Gold Corp., In re, CA9 (Nev), 394 F3d 1189.—Bankr 2043(3), 2679, 3570, 3765, 3768, 3782, Fed Civ Proc 776; Fed Cts 14.1, 266.1, 267, 269, 272.

Pegasus Gold Corp., In re, DNev, 296 BR 227, aff in part, rev in part 394 F3d 1189.—Bankr 2043(3), 2056, 2679, 3568(1), 3570, 3782, 3786; Estop 68(2); Judgm 651, 668(1), 713(1), 715(1), 720, 724.

Pegasus Gold Corp., In re, BkrtcyDNev, 275 BR 902, aff 296 BR 227, aff in part, rev in part 394 F3d 1189.—Bankr 2041.1, 2041.5, 2042, 2043(3), 2047, 2056, 2102, 2679, 3568(1), 3570; Const Law 43(1); Fed Cts 5, 14.1, 18, 23, 265, 266.1, 267.

Pegasus Helicopters, Inc. v. United Technologies Corp., CA10 (Colo), 35 F3d 507.—Prod Liab 17.1; Sales 260, 261(6).

Pegasus Petroleum Corp.; Mobil Oil Corp. v., CA2 (NY), 818 F2d 254.—Trademarks 1058, 1081, 1096(3), 1101, 1104, 1111, 1466, 1610, 1630, 1800.

Pegasus Satellite Television, Inc v. DirecTV, Inc., CDCal, 318 FSupp2d 968.—Cons Prot 40; Contracts 187(1); Decl Judgm 301; Fed Civ Proc 103.2, 103.3, 928, 2559; Fed Cts 5, 12.1, 13, 31, 33, 34; Tel 1286; Trade Reg 862.1, 864.

Pegasystems, Inc.; Gelfer v., DMass, 96 FSupp2d 10.—Sec Reg 35.15, 60.45(1).

Pegg v. General Motors Corp., DKan, 785 FSupp 901, on reconsideration 1992 WL 123768.—Civil R 1168, 1204; Labor & Emp 36, 438, 638, 686, 863(1).

Pegg v. U.S., CA11 (Fla), 253 F3d 1274, reh and reh den 273 F3d 395, cert den 122 SCt 1435, 535 US 970, 152 LEd2d 380.—Crim Law 641.5(0.5), 641.13(5), 1517.

Pegg; U.S. v., MDFla, 49 FSupp2d 1322, aff 253 F3d 1274, reh and reh den 273 F3d 395, cert den 122 SC 1435, 535 US 970, 152 LEd2d 380.—Crim Law 1429(2), 1437, 1438, 1451.

For Later Case History Information, see KeyCite on WESTLAW

FIGURE 6.14 Defendant/Plaintiff Table

Source: From *Federal Practice Digest 4th.* Reprinted with permission from ThomsonWest.

SYMANTEC

103C F P D 4th—392

References are to Digest Topics and Key Numbers

141, appeal after remand 29 F3d 630, cert den 115 SCt 638, 513 US 1044; 130 LEd2d 544.—Fed Civ Proc 2493; Fed Cts 947; Trademarks 1428(2).

Symantec Corp. v. CD Micro, Inc., DOr, 286 FSupp2d 1278.—Copyr 87(3.1); Trademarks 1566, 1653, 1656(3), 1658.

Symantec Corp. v. CD Micro, Inc., DOr, 286 FSupp2d 1265.—Copyr 38.5, 48, 51, 75, 77, 80, 83(3.5); Equity 67; Trademarks 1116, 1208, 1299, 1421, 1435, 1565.

Symantec Corp.; Hilgraeve Corp. v., CAFed, 265 F3d 1336, reh and reh den, cert den 122 SCt 1206, 535 US 906, 152 LEd2d 144, on remand 212 FRD 345.—Fed Cts 763.1, 766; Pat 101(2), 206, 211(1), 226.6, 234, 259(1), 312(2), 314(5), 323.2(2), 323.2(3), 324.5, 328(2).

Symantec Corp.; Hilgraeve Corp. v., EDMich, 90 FSupp2d 850, vac 265 F3d 1336, reh and reh den, cert den 122 SCt 1206, 535 US 906, 152 LEd2d 144, on remand 212 FRD 345.—Judgm 634; Pat 101(2), 159, 162, 165(3), 167(1), 167(1.1), 168(2.1), 226.6, 229, 230, 237, 314(5), 327(13), 328(2).

Symantec Corp.; Hilgraeve Corp. v., EDMich, 212 FRD 345.—Fed Cts 13; Pat 310.11.

Symantec Corp.; Hilgraeve, Inc. v., EDMich; 272 FSupp2d 613.—Pat 259(1), 312(1.1), 312(8), 319(1), 323.2(3), 328(2).

Symantec Corp.; Hilgraeve, Inc. v., EDMich, 271 FSupp2d 964.—Pat 16(2), 59, 101(6), 112.5, 226.6, 323.2(3), 323.2(4), 324.60, 328(2).

Symbiotics, L.L.C. v. F.E.R.C., CA10, 110 FedAppx 76. —Electricity 8.4.

Symbol Technologies, Inc.; Datastrip (IOM) Ltd. v., CAFed, 15 FedAppx 843.—Pat 101(2), 235(2).

Symbol Technologies, Inc. v. Lemelson Medical, CA-Fed (Nev), 277 F3d 1361, reh en banc den, cert den Lemelson Medical, Education & Research Foundation v. Symbol Technologies, 123 SCt 113, 537 US 825; 154 LEd2d 36.—Courts 96(5), 96(7); Fed Cts 766; Pat 289(2.1), 328(2).

Symbol Technologies, Inc. v. Lemelson Medical, Educ. & Research Foundation, Ltd. Partnership, DNev, 301 FSupp2d 1147.—Pat 62(3), 66(1.14), 72(1), 97, 99, 110, 159, 160, 161, 165(1), 165(2), 165(3), 167(1), 167(1.1), 168(2.1), 235(2), 289(2.1), 289(4), 325.11(2.1), 328(2).

Symbol Technologies, Inc. v. Metrologic Instruments, Inc., CA2 (NY), 84 FedAppx 112.—Fed Cts 599.

Symbol Technologies, Inc.; Morrissey v., EDNY, 910 FSupp 117.—Civil R 1176, 1537, 1549.

Symbol Technologies, Inc. v. Opticon, Inc., CAFed (NY), 935 F2d 1569, reh den.—Pat 312(1.1), 312(1.2).

Symbol Technologies, Inc., Oye on Behalf of, v. Swartz, EDNY, 762 FSupp 510. See Symbol Technologies Securities Litigation, In re.

Symbol Technologies Securities Litigation, In re, EDNY, 762 FSupp 510.—Trusts 30.5(1).

Syme; U.S. v., CA3 (Del); 276 F3d 131, cert den 123 SCt 619, 537 US 1050, 154 LEd2d 525.—Crim Law 469, 469.1, 881(1), 1030(1), 1032(5), 1038.1(1), 1042, 1043(3), 1144.15, 1167(2), 1167(4), 1172.1(2), 1172.1(3), 1181.5(3.1); Double J 93; Ind & Inf 55, 159(2); Jury 34(1); Postal 35(2); Sent & Pun 2187; Tel 1014(2); U S 121.

Symens v. SmithKline Beecham Corp., CA8 (SD), 152 F3d 1050, appeal after remand 7 FedAppx 534.—Health 107, 322; Prod Liab 46.4.

Symens v. Smithkline Beecham Corp., DSD, 19 FSupp2d 1062, rev in part 152 F3d 1050, appeal after remand 7 FedAppx 534.—Prod Liab 46.4.

Symeonidis v. Paxton Capital Group, Inc., DMd, 220 FSupp2d 478.—Fraud 4; Labor & Emp 256(5), 759, 771, 777, 778, 782, 852.

Symington v. Daisy Mfg. Co., Inc., DND, 360 FSupp2d 1027.—Evid 513(1), 539, 555.2, 555.7; Fed Civ Proc 2515, 2536.1, 2538, 2539, 2545; 2554.

Symington v. Great Western Trucking Co., Inc., SDIowa, 668 FSupp 1278.—Indem 13.1(2.1).

Symington; Parks College v., CA9 (Ariz), 51 F3d 1480. See Parks School of Business, Inc. v. Symington.

Symington; Parks School of Business; Inc. v., CA9 (Ariz), 51 F3d 1480.—Civil R 1027, 1326(4), 1326(5), 1326(6), 1326(7), 1395(1), 1395(2), 1482, 1484.

Symmetricom, Inc.; Shuster, v., CA9 (Cal), 35 FedAppx 705.—Fed Civ Proc 2511; Sec Reg 60.27(1), 60.45(1).

Symms Fruit Ranch, Inc; Chao v., CA9, 242 F3d 894. —Admin Law 413, Labor & Emp 2605, 2611(3); Statut 219(1), 219(6.1).

Symonds; U.S v., CA8 (Iowa), 260 F3d 934.—Consp 51; Crim Law 1158(1); Sent & Pun 66, 94.

Symons; Gould v., EDMich, 275 FSupp2d 843.—Civil R 1376(1), 1376(2), 1376(4).

Symons Corp.; EFCO Corp. v., CA8(Iowa), 219 F3d 734.—Damag 15; Evid 508, 555.2; 555.9; Fed Civ Proc 2339; Fed Cts 415, 715, 763.1, 776, 798, 801, 823, 825.1, 826; Interest 39(2.10), 39(2.20); Torts 215, 241; Trade Reg 870(1), 984, 991, 1002, 1007, 1009.

Symons Corp.; Watson v., NDIll, 121 FRD 351.—Fed Civ Proc 2651.1.

Symorex, Inc v. Siemens Industrial Automation, ED-Mich, 151 FSupp2d 844, vac.—Damag 2, 67; Fed Civ Proc 2774(1), 2828; Interest 22(1), 31, 39(2.6), 39(2.20), 49.

Syms Corp.; Lawrence v., EDMich, 969 FSupp 1014.—Civil R 1118, 1138, 1158, 1159, 1204, 1744.

Syms Corp.; Levine v., NDOhio, 982 FSupp 492.—Civil R 1201, 1203.

Synagro-WWT, Inc v. Rush Tp., Penn., MDPa, 204 FSupp2d 827.—Commerce 13.5, 56; Const Law 48(4.1), 48(6), 115, 154(1), 211(2), 250.5, 251.3, 278.1; Environ Law 346(1); Fed Civ Proc 948, 1788.6; Fed Cts 41, 43, 46; Mines 92.8; Mun Corp 53, 592(1), 621, 956(1), 957(0.5); States 18.3; Tax 2121.

Synagro-WWT, Inc. v. Rush Tp., Pennsylvania, MDPa, 299 FSupp2d 410.—Environ Law 352, 653; Mines 92.8, Mun Corp 111(4), 121, 592(1); Statut 64(1).

Synanon Church v. U.S., CADC, 820 F2d 421, 261 USAppDC 13.—Judgm 828.16(1), 828.21(3).

Synaptic Pharmaceuticals Corp. v. MDS Panlabs, Inc., DNJ, 265 FSupp2d 452.—Pat 165(5), 226, 226.6, 234, 237, 257, 258, 259(1), 259(3), 323.2(3), 328(2); Statut 190, 217.4

Synar v. U S., DDC, 670 FSupp 410.—U S 147(11.1).

Synbiotics Corp. v. Heska Corp., SDCal, 137 FSupp2d 1198—Fed Civ Proc 2544; Pat 52, 57.1, 65, 67.1, 69, 70, 72(1), 165(4), 328(2).

Synchronics, Inc.; Peerless Wall and Window Coverings, Inc. v., WDPa, 85 FSupp2d 519, aff 234 F3d 1265.—Contracts 94(4); Copyr 107, Evid 400(3), 400(6), 434(8); Fed Cts 337; Fraud 3, 11(1), 17, 20, 25, 32, 36.

relevant case listed as defendant v. plaintiff

Synchro-Start Products, Inc.; E.E.O.C. v., NDIll, 29 FSupp2d 911.—Civil R 1118, 1140, 1147, 1536.

Syncor ERISA Litigation, In re, CDCal, 351 FSupp2d 970.—Courts 89; Fed Civ Proc 636, 1832, 1835; Labor & Emp 459, 473, 475, 478, 491(2), 646.

Syncor Erisa Litigation, In re, CDCal, 227 FRD 338. —Fed Civ Proc 172, 184.5.

Syncor Intern. Corp. v. Shalala, CADC, 127 F3d 90, 326 USAppDC 422.—Health 322.

Syncor Intern. Corp. Securities Litigation, In re, CDCal, 327 FSupp2d 1149.—Evid 1, 48; Fed Civ Proc

For Later Case History Information, see KeyCite on WESTLAW

In order to locate the new topic and key, you will have to use the Key Number Translation Table in the front of the digest. The Translation Table does exactly what the name suggests. It translates or converts the old topics and key numbers into a new classification. For example, the topic "bankruptcy" has been revised completely. Figure 6.15 shows the table with the former key number and its corresponding new key numbers. Notice that some keys that were associated with only one key now have multiple keys within the subtopic. Another area significantly overhauled is the topic "civil rights." Don't panic if you look up a topic and key and it appears to have vanished. Check the Key Number Translation Table and you will be led to the new topic and key.

This discussion has focused on the digests in the ThomsonWest system, which are of preeminent importance in legal research. Remember, digests and other finding tools are exactly that—finding tools. They are considered nonauthoritative resources and should not be used or quoted in a legal document. Only cite primary and secondary authority when preparing a formal legal document.

PRACTICE TIP

The Defendant/Plaintiff Table Index has been replaced in a number of digests by the Table of Cases, which lists each party's name regardless of whether they were the plaintiff or the defendant. However, some jurisdictions or older digests still may have a Defendant/Plaintiff Table. Simply be aware that both volumes exist and check the digest set you are using to determine what corresponding indexes are used.

New Trends: Online Digests

Although this chapter focuses on the "print" finding tools, a brief mention of online sources is appropriate. Online digests are available on Westlaw and LexisNexis (discussed in detail in Chapter 9). Both have comprehensive online digest libraries guiding us through the labyrinth of available legal resources. For those of you who believe that print books are obsolete and that the Internet is the "only" comprehensive way to conduct legal research, the only response is "you are wrong." Unless you understand the print-based sources and how to use them and more importantly, know what you are looking for, you will never be sure you have fully accomplished the task assigned. The online sources do not have the filtering mechanism necessary to differentiate sources adequately. Plainly stated, online sources often give you more than you need or nothing you want. (Perhaps this may seem like an overstatement, but the truth is unless you understand the print version of the digests, you will struggle to perform legal research online.) With the hardbound volumes, you can navigate through the digest in a methodical and logical order. So, yes, the trends favor online access, but your success may not depend on the trends but on the traditions of the old reliable "book."

Checklist for Using a Digest

Some suggested methods for using a digest are as follows:

- Write down key words and phrases that pertain to the topic you are researching.
- Locate the Descriptive Word Index and begin looking up the words and phrases.

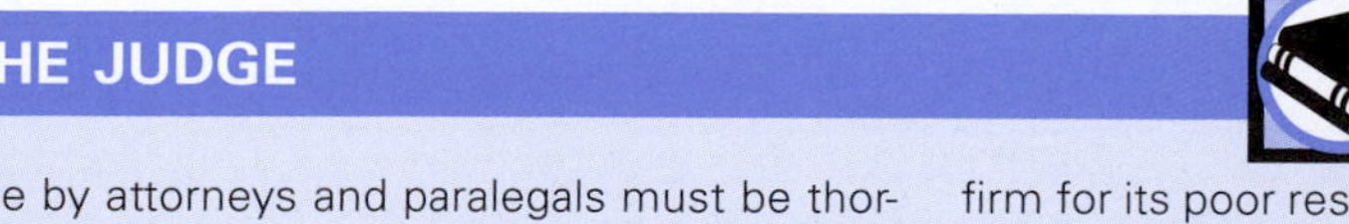

YOU BE THE JUDGE

Research done by attorneys and paralegals must be thorough and complete. Searching digests for headnotes and key numbers is important to the legal research process. Failure to perform these routine tasks can have devastating effects on a client's case. In *Stephens v. Kemp*, 602 F. Supp. 960 (M.D. Ga. 1984), the court admonished a law firm for its poor research in a habeas corpus case. Review the case. What message did the court send to the attorneys in the case? Were the actions of the court warranted? Was the result in the case harsh? Why or why not? Once again, this case shows the importance of proper and complete legal research.

FIGURE 6.15 **Digest Conversion Table**

Source: From *Bankruptcy Digest*. Reprinted with permission from ThomsonWest.

old key

new key

look up old key for conversion to new key

11B Bkrptcy D—41 **BANKRUPTCY**

TABLE 3
KEY NUMBER TRANSLATION TABLE
FORMER KEY NUMBER TO PRESENT KEY NUMBER

The topic BANKRUPTCY has been extensively revised in consideration of the Bankruptcy Reform Act of 1978.

This table indicates the location, in the revised topic, of cases formerly classified to the earlier key numbers.

In many instances there is no one-to-one relation between the key numbers, new and old. This table recognizes only significant correspondence, and the user who has found a particular case classified to an old key number is advised to consult the Table of Cases, where its present classification may be found.

The absence of a key number indicates that there is no useful parallel.

Former Key Number	Present Key Number
1	2012–2018
2, 3	2013.1–2025
4	2001, 2021.1, 2022
5	2023
6	2023–2025
7	2023
8	2026
9	2002, 2513, 2534, 272–2765, 2826
10	2341
11(1)	2001, 2016, 2041.1–2082, 2102, 2104, 2122–2126, 2341
11(2)	2124.1–2126
11(3)	2054, 2084.1, 2121–2133, 2151, 2156, 2203
12–16	2082
17	2131
18(1, 2)	2060.1, 2061
19	2083–2091, 2102–2104
20(1)	2062
21	2058.1
22	2041.1, 2086.1–2089, 2102, 2129–2133
23	2202
24	2127.1
25	2201
27	2321–2325
28	2321
29	2322
30	2323
31	2324
32	2325
33	2127.1
35	2127.1, 2131
36	2133
37	2122
38	2001, 2251
39	2235
41	2222.1–2231
42	2227
43	2224–2228
44	2257, 2311

Former Key Number	Present Key Number
44.5	2255.1, 2256, 2311
47	2258
48	2252.1–2254, 2259.1–2264
49	2264(1)
50	2252.1–2254, 2259.1–2264
51	2251
52	2281, 2293
54	2234
55–64	2281
65	2282, 2284, 2288
67	2222–2231, 2311
68	2229
69	2227
70	2222.1
71	2224–2226
72	2224–2226, 2229
73	2226
74	2222.1
75	2289
76(1)	2283.1–2289
76(2)	2288
76(3)	2283.1
77	2285.1–2289
78	2294
79, 80	2290.1
81	2290.1, 2293
82, 83	2290.1
84(1)	2204.1, 2292
85, 86	2290.1
87	2131
88	2204.1
89	2294
90	2290.1
91	2294
91(1, 2)	2296
92	2282–2289, 2295.1
93	2130; Jury 🔑19(9)
94–96	2295.1
97	3040–3048
98	3761 et seq.
99	2295.1
100	2297
101	3061

- Peruse the various entries until a topic(s) and key(s) that may apply are located.
- Go the digest volume and look up the topic(s) and key(s) found.
- Begin reviewing the entries under the topic and keys for relevant cases.
- Write down cases of interest that pertain to the jurisdiction of your assignment. If cases are not located in your jurisdiction, consult other jurisdictions for guidance. (But remember, that will be persuasive authority and not mandatory authority.)
- Check the pocket parts or supplements for the most recent cases. (Recall that omission of a topic and key means that no recent cases cited that topic and key.)
- Begin retrieving applicable cases from the book shelves (or from an online source).
- Review the cases for relevancy.
- Reshelve case reporters and digests.
- Consider alternative methods, such as reviewing the list of ThomsonWest topics that may apply to your assignment. If a topic is applicable, review the listing of topics and keys under the general topic. Check the pocket parts and supplements for recent cases.
- Once the print version of the digest system is mastered, then consider combining print resources with online sources, such as Westlaw and LexisNexis. Use each source as a check against the other.

Additionally, Figure 6.16 diagrams how to use a digest. Be sure you determine which digest you want to use, such as the *Florida Digest* for a fact problem arising under Florida law.

ETHICS ALERT

Your attorney has asked you to prepare a memorandum of law supporting the Motion for Summary Judgment he filed on behalf of his friend, George Matthews. Matthews hates going through security at airports and constantly showing his identification to every person he meets. He thinks it violates his right to travel and his right to privacy. And anyway, he's not going to do anything to anyone while he is traveling. He is tired of all the harassment and just wants to put some sanity in the system. Who are those TSA people anyway? The case was filed in California and your attorney wants you to research the issue and discuss the status of the law with you. While researching in the digest, you run across a case that was handed down a few months ago, *Gilmore v. Gonzales*. It was decided by the U.S. Court of Appeals for the Ninth Circuit and you believe that case is on point. Should you tell your attorney about the case? Does your attorney need to cite the case in his supporting brief? Is there an obligation to tell the court of the case?

These are all important questions to ask yourself. Attorneys and paralegals have ethical obligations and are guided by the American Bar Association (ABA) Model Code and ABA Model Rules on Ethical Responsibility. Typical ethical responsibilities that confront a paralegal are similar to the hypothetical fact pattern that is posed, especially when the case is contrary to the client's interest. However, this case must be disclosed to your attorney regardless of the effect on the case. The attorney has an ethical and legal obligation to report the case if it is "controlling" law in the jurisdiction. When citing the case in your memorandum, you or your attorney may show how the case can be distinguished or criticized for its result. Perhaps the facts are different. What is important is: do not hide the case from your attorney. You are doing your job by revealing the case to your supervising attorney. Let your attorney decide how to handle the situation. If you do not disclose the case, you run the risk of having the court impose sanctions on your attorney or yourself, which may include monetary or disciplinary action.

FIGURE 6.16
Recap of How to Use a Digest

Researching by Subject → → →	Use the Descriptive Word Index Find applicable topics and keys Look up topics and keys in digest volume Review pocket parts and supplements Review case summaries Retrieve complete cases for review Copy relevant cases Brief relevant cases
Researching by Topic and Key →	Locate digest volume that contains topic Identify applicable key within topic digest Check pocket parts or supplements related to that topic and key to see if recent cases. Review case summaries within topic and key Retrieve complete cases for review Copy relevant cases Brief relevant cases
Researching by Party Name → →	Locate the Table of Cases Index If older case, locate both Table of Cases and Defendant/Plaintiff Table Look up party name in alphabetical index (if too common a name, look up the other party) Narrow party name search by reviewing jurisdiction, federal or state, within citation Write down citation Retrieve case and brief

THE *WORDS AND PHRASES DIGEST*: ITS OWN SET OF BOOKS

PRACTICE TIP

The *Words and Phrases Digest* covers all cases from the National Reporter System. Likewise, the words and phrases index to the subject and jurisdiction-specific digests contain cases for the referenced digest only.

In the previous section, we discussed the Words and Phrases Index as part of the digest indexes. There also is a separate set of volumes known as *Words and Phrases.* You were briefly introduced to it when we reviewed the contents of a reporter. Recall that in many reporters, there is a section devoted to the interpretation of words and phrases construed by courts. The reporter referenced *Words and Phrases.* This is the multivolume set that interprets and construes words and important phrases by various courts. These volumes are separate from the Words and Phrases Index we discussed in the previous section. It is another finding tool and follows the same principles as the Words and Phrases Index. Consequently, if you need the judicial interpretation of a word or phrase and need to know whether your jurisdiction or how many other jurisdictions had a judicial interpretation of a particular word or phrase, you should check the *Words and Phrases Digest.*

Although similar in concept to a "digest," *Words and Phrases* lists the references alphabetically by the word or phrase being interpreted rather than by key number. Headnotes are included from cases in *Words and Phrases* with the pertinent case information listed at the end of the headnote. That is where a key number may be referenced.

Unless you need a judicial interpretation of a word, phrase, or term, the likelihood of using *Words and Phrases* is slim. However, it is useful to know that it exists in the event you do need a case that construes specific words or phrases. Since the main volumes of *Words and Phrases* are nearly twenty-five years old, always review the pocket parts for the newest interpretations.

Quick Quiz True/False Questions

1. There is one digest for the U.S. Supreme Court.
2. All digests have topics and keys.
3. A headnote is a short paragraph summary located in a case with a corresponding topic and key.
4. Every state has a state-specific digest.
5. Digests have only one index, the Words and Phrases Index.

LEGAL ENCYCLOPEDIAS

Next to the digests, **legal encyclopedias** are some of the most valuable finding tools in the library, especially for those unfamiliar with a topic of law. As a secondary source, a legal encyclopedia is a multivolume compilation arranged alphabetically by topic that provides in-depth coverage of every area of the law. Such a purpose is difficult to achieve in practice: Legal encyclopedias are general in nature and are thus rarely cited as authority for a point of law. They should not be disregarded in conducting research, however, since they provide useful general information about a broad range of topics, and can thus be used to obtain background information about an unfamiliar area. They also provide citations to cases and topics and keys, a useful starting point for research. Encyclopedias use footnotes extensively to communicate relevant information. Be sure to review the footnotes when reading a legal encyclopedia.

legal encyclopedia
A multivolume compilation that provides in-depth coverage of every area of the law.

As we mentioned briefly in Chapter 2, there are two primary legal encyclopedias, both now ThomsonWest publications. The first is called *Corpus Juris Secundum* (cited as *C.J.S.*), which is the deep blue set of volumes. And the second set is *American Jurisprudence* (cited as *Am. Jur.*), which is the green set of volumes. Let's examine each set independently.

Corpus Juris Secundum: C.J.S.

Originally published by West, the *C.J.S.* set references the West Key Number System, so that researchers can often go directly from the encyclopedia review to the appropriate digest volume to find relevant case law quickly. (The key system is discussed earlier in the chapter.) Topics are arranged by subject headings with key numbers assigned to the subtopics. Located in the footnotes are cases relevant to the subject topic. In the earlier editions of *C.J.S.*, the footnotes contained virtually all cases relating to the topic. With a shift in philosophy, *C.J.S.* is more selective in the cases it cites in its footnotes, leaning more toward relevance of the decision rather than sheer volume. Subjects are classified differently in *C.J.S.* than in *Am. Jur.* Neither system of classification is better than the other, simply different. At the beginning of each subject, there is a section that tells the reader which topics are covered in the section and which are not. You may be directed to another *C.J.S.* subject that adds to the section you are presently reviewing, or you may determine that another section may be more relevant. The key here is: *read.* The need for critical reading cannot be overstated when performing any legal research. The more you open your eyes, often, the more time you will save researching. Figure 6.17 is an example of a List of Titles in *C.J.S.*

Highlighted in Figure 6.18 is a passage from the section on Landlord & Tenant, again focusing on our example from the Case Fact Pattern. Examine each section carefully and notice the type of information presented. In Figure 6.18, a section in bold is identified directly after the name of the topic covered. This bold information

FIGURE 6.17 List of Titles in *Corpus Juris Secundum*

Source: From *Corpus Juris Secundum*. Reprinted with permission from ThomsonWest.

LIST OF TITLES IN CORPUS JURIS SECUNDUM

Abandonment
Abatement and Revival
Abduction
Abortion and Birth Control; Family Planning
Absentees
Abstracts of Title
Accession
Accord and Satisfaction
Account, Action on
Accountants
Accounting
Account Stated
Acknowledgments
Actions
Adjoining Landowners
Admiralty
Adoption of Persons
Adulteration
Adultery
Adverse Possession
Aeronautics and Aerospace
Affidavits
Affray
Agency
Agriculture
Aliens
Alteration of Instruments
Ambassadors and Consuls
Amicus Curiae
Animals
Annuities
Appeal and Error
Appearances
Apprentices
Arbitration
Architects
Armed Services
Arrest
Arson
Assault and Battery
Assignments
Assistance, Writ of
Associations
Assumpsit, Action of
Asylums and Institutional Care Facilities
Attachment
Attorney and Client
Attorney General
Auctions and Auctioneers
Audita Querela
Bail; Release and Detention Pending Proceedings
Bailments
Bankruptcy
Banks and Banking
Beneficial Associations
Bigamy and Related Offenses
Bills and Notes; Letters of Credit
Bonds
Boundaries
Breach of Marriage Promise
Breach of the Peace
Bribery
Bridges
Brokers
Building and Loan Associations, Savings and Loan Associations, and Credit Unions
Burglary
Business Trusts
Canals
Cancellation of Instruments; Rescission
Carriers
Cemeteries
Census
Certiorari
Champerty and Maintenance; Barratry and Related Matters
Charities
Chemical Dependents
Children Out-of-Wedlock
Citizens
Civil Rights
Clubs
Colleges and Universities
Collision
Commerce
Common Lands
Common Law
Compounding Offenses
Compromise and Settlement
Concealment of Birth or Death
Conflict of Laws
Confusion of Goods
Conspiracy
Constitutional Law
Contempt
Continuances
Contracts
Contribution
Conversion
Convicts
Copyrights and Intellectual Property
Coroners and Medical Examiners
Corporations
Costs
Counterfeiting
Counties
Courts
Covenants
Credit Reporting Agencies; Consumer Protection
Creditor and Debtor
Criminal Law
Crops
Customs and Usages
Customs Duties
Damages
Dead Bodies
Death
Debt, Action of
Declaratory Judgments
Dedication
Deeds
Depositaries
Depositions
Deposits in Court
Descent and Distribution

FIGURE 6.18 **Landlord and Tenant Reference in *Corpus Juris Secundum***

Source: From *Corpus Juris Secundum*. Reprinted with permission from ThomsonWest.

LANDLORD & TENANT — general subject

corresponding west topic and key

§ 60

[text omitted]

privity of contract.[2] However, by merely assigning a lease, the lessee only places the assignee in the same relationship with the lessor as was occupied by the lessee, and nothing else is implied as against the assignor.[3]

Assignee's liability to assignor.

Where an assignee covenants to perform all the covenants in the original lease, he or she is liable to the lessee-assignor in the same manner as the lessee is liable to the original lessor.[4] Where the lessee, after assigning his or her lease, receives a new lease from the landlord to commence on the expiration of the original lease, and the assignee holds over after such expiration, the lessee can recover from the assignee whatever damages are the natural and proximate result of the wrongful trespass of the assignee.[5]

subject of commentary

6. *Construction and Operation of Subleases*

§ 59 Generally

blackletter law

A sublease creates a new estate; the construction and operation of a sublease depend generally on the language of the agreement and the circumstances of the case.

Research References

West's Key Number Digest, Landlord and Tenant ⇐ 80(1)

While an assignment of a lease transfers an existing estate into new hands,[1] a sublease creates a new estate.[2] When a lease is transferred by a sublease, a new lessor-lessee relationship is created between the original lessee and the sublessee, but the original lessee retains both privity of estate and privity of contract with the original lessor and no legal relationship is created between the lessor and sublessee.[3]

The same rules apply to a sublessor-sublessee relationship as are applicable to a lessor-lessee relationship.[4] However, the construction and operation of a particular sublease depend on all the circumstances of the case and on the language of the agreement construed in accordance with the usual rules of construction.[5]

§ 60 Liability of original tenant to landlord

A subletting does not change the relationship of the landlord and the original tenant, or relieve the tenant of liability on the covenants of the lease, unless this is done by the original lease, or by some other transaction or agreement, such as a surrender and a substitution of tenants.

Research References

---

case references

324 Ill. App. 229, 57 N.E.2d 756 (1st Dist. 1944).

Mass.—Maybury Shoe Co. v. Izenstatt, 320 Mass. 397, 69 N.E.2d 666 (1946).

N.J.—Conover v. Solar Oil Co., 14 N.J. Misc. 127, 182 A868 (Sup. Ct. 1936).

[2]Ky.—Entroth Shoe Co. v. Johnson, 260 Ky. 309, 85 S.W.2d 686 (1935).

Minn.—Kostakes v. Daly, 246 Minn. 312, 75 N.W.2d 191 (1956).

[3]Neb.—Beltner v. Carlson, 153 Neb. 797, 46 N.W.2d 153 (1951).

[4]Ariz.—Catalina Groves v. Oliver, 73 Ariz. 38, 236 P.2d 1022 (1951).

Iowa—L. P. Courshon Co. v. Brewer, 215 Iowa 885, 245 N.W. 354 (1932).

[5]Pa.—Taylor v. Kaufhold, 368 Pa. 538, 84 A.2d 347, 32 A.L.R.2d 575 (1951).

[Section 59]

§ 49.

[2]Ark.—Jaber v. Miller, 219 Ark. 59, 239 S.W.2d 760 (1951).

As to distinctions between assignments and subleases, see § 50.

[3]Md.—Italian Fisherman, Inc. v. Middlemas, 313 Md. 156, 545 A.2d 1 (1988).

[4]Neb.—Krance v. Faeh, 215 Neb. 242, 338 N.W.2d 55 (1983).

[5]Cal.—Roadside Rest, Inc. v. Lankershim Estate, 76 Cal. App. 2d 525, 173 P.2d 554 (2d Dist. 1946).

Ill.—Sixty-Third & Halsted Realty Co. v. Goldblatt Bros., 342 Ill. App. 389, 96 N.E.2d 838 (1st Dist. 1951), judgment aff'd, 410 Ill. 468, 102 N.E.2d 749 (1951).

Ind.—Bowers v. Sells, 125 Ind. App. 324, 123 N.E.2d 194 (1954).

Mo.—First Trust Co. v. Downs, 230 S.W.2d 770 (Mo. Ct. App. 1950).

Pa.—McRoberts v. Stadelman, 168 Pa. Super. 489, 79 A.2d 119 (1951).

As to the construction and operation of leases, generally, see §§ 412 to 466.

Contract construction rules applicable

The interpretation and construction of a sublease is governed by the principles of interpretation and construction of contracts generally.

Iowa—Fashion Fabrics of Iowa, Inc. v. Retail Investors Corp., 266 N.W.2d 22 (Iowa 1978).

black letter law
The strict meaning of the law as it is written without concern or interpretation of the reasoning behind its creation.

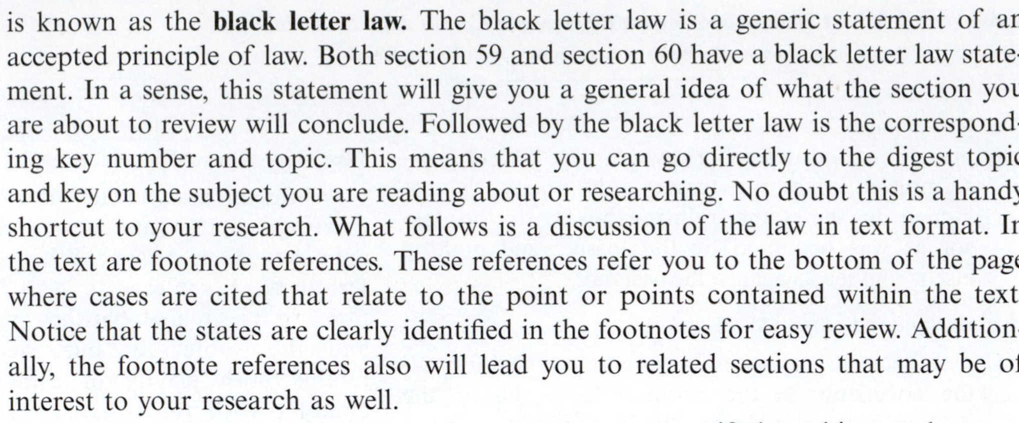

is known as the **black letter law.** The black letter law is a generic statement of an accepted principle of law. Both section 59 and section 60 have a black letter law statement. In a sense, this statement will give you a general idea of what the section you are about to review will conclude. Followed by the black letter law is the corresponding key number and topic. This means that you can go directly to the digest topic and key on the subject you are reading about or researching. No doubt this is a handy shortcut to your research. What follows is a discussion of the law in text format. In the text are footnote references. These references refer you to the bottom of the page where cases are cited that relate to the point or points contained within the text. Notice that the states are clearly identified in the footnotes for easy review. Additionally, the footnote references also will lead you to related sections that may be of interest to your research as well.

PRACTICE TIP

Like the topics in a digest, encyclopedia topics are arranged alphabetically. Unlike a digest, encyclopedias provide their information in a prose style with footnotes containing cases and other valuable information.

Updating of *C.J.S.* is through either a pocket part, or if the subject updates are too voluminous, a stand-alone supplement. Often newer topics are contained in the stand-alone supplements; this practice is common rather than eliminating a complete volume of the encyclopedia.

American Jurisprudence: Am. Jur.

American Jurisprudence is another prominent legal encyclopedia. Its first series was published in 1962; *Am. Jur.* is now in its second series. As with so many legal publications, *Am. Jur.* has had many publishers. Until recently, *Am. Jur.* was owned by Lawyers Cooperative Publishing, but was acquired by ThomsonWest. Now both legal encyclopedias are published by ThomsonWest. Following its previous publishers' reference guides, *Am. Jur. 2d* includes references to *American Law Reports* (*A.L.R.*) annotations as well as cases from all reporters. Like *C.J.S., Am. Jur. 2d* is very useful as a starting place for research and a tool to gain a general understanding of a particular area of the law, but is not looked upon as authoritative. Unlike *C.J.S., Am. Jur. 2d* cites only a select number of cases in the footnotes. Those cited in the footnotes are considered to be the most relevant on the topic rather than a general compilation of all cases on the point. You will find useful information at the beginning of a subject, such as a section telling the reader what is, and what is not, covered in the text. Sometimes a quick scan of the table of contents of the subject topic is helpful as it may suggest areas to review.

Using a page from an *Am. Jur. 2d* as a guide in Figure 6.19, the subject of the topic is landlord–tenant relations just like our *C.J.S.* example. Review Figures 6.18 and 6.19 and notice some of the differences from *C.J.S.* At first sight under the subject section is a "research references" section. This section suggests other research sources that may be helpful on the topic. One key omission is the lack of topics and keys. Even though *Am. Jur. 2d* is now a ThomsonWest publication, topic and keys are not always provided (as books are replaced, topics and keys will be added to *Am. Jur.*). Reference to *A.L.R.* is noted. The footnotes provide cases, *A.L.R.* annotations, formbooks for drafting, and other relevant sections on the topic. *Am. Jur. 2d* also publishes annual pocket supplements to update its text. Review these pocket supplements when performing your research. Compare the *Am. Jur.* and *C.J.S.* texts on the landlord–tenant issue.

PRACTICE TIP

When preparing a brief, a memorandum of law, or any other legal document, limit the use of secondary authority, especially encyclopedias. Never cite a finding tool as your authority for a legal point.

State Encyclopedias

Encyclopedias are also published summarizing the law of some states. These encyclopedias devote their volumes to discussion of a particular state only, and include both state and federal issues from that state. State encyclopedias follow the same format as *C.J.S.* and *Am. Jur.* If the state encyclopedia is a ThomsonWest publication, it will provide topic and key notations and other related research material of that publisher.

FIGURE 6.19 **Page from *American Jurisprudence***

Source: From *American Jurisprudence.* Reprinted with permission from ThomsonWest.

49 Am Jur 2d LANDLORD AND TENANT § 1158

[text omitted]

conveyance to one who is described by a fictitious or assumed name is valid,[18] and accordingly, the reassignment of the term by an assignee although the name of the second assignee is an assumed one, if intended as a bona fide assignment, will be effectual to relieve the assignor of further liability to the lessor, since it effectually destroys the privity of estate.[19]

C. SUBLEASE [§§ 1157–1186]

Research References

ALR Digest: Landlord and Tenant §§ 88 et seq.

ALR Index: Landlord and Tenant

16A Am Jur PI & Pr Forms (Rev), Landlord and Tenant, Forms 421 et seq.

11 Am Jur Legal Forms 2d, Leases of Real Property §§ 161:1241 et seq.

---

1. IN GENERAL [§§ 1157–1161]

§ 1157. Generally

A sublease is a grant by a tenant of an interest in the rented premises less than his or her own, retaining to himself or herself a reversion, and a subtenant is a person who rents all or a portion of leased premises from the lessee for a term less than the original one, leaving a reversionary interest in the first lessee.[20] Where the sublease is for the whole term, it is in law an assignment as between the original lessor and the sublessee, but may be given effect as a contract as between the sublessor and sublessee.[21] An instrument in the form of a sublease is not to be regarded as an assignment so as to transfer the entire interest of the lessee and divest him or her of any reversionary estate or right of re-entry, where the negotiations were for a sublease, the original lessors' consent was to a sublease, the instrument was so designated, the rent was to be paid by the sublessee to the sublessor, the parties were referred to as lessor and lessee, the pleadings referred to the instrument as a sublease, and there were later transactions between the parties with reference to a separate assignment.[22]

§ 1158. Right to sublet

It is well settled that in the absence of restrictions thereon by the parties,[23] or

18. 23 Am Jur 2d, Deeds §§ 33 et seq.

19. Hartman v Thompson, 104 Md 389, 65 A 117.

20. Jackson v Sims (CA8 Okla) 201 F2d 259; Coles Trading Co. v Spiegel, Inc. (CA9 Ariz) 187 F2d 984, 24 ALR2d 702; Haynes v Eagle-Picher Co. (CA10 Kan) 295 F2d 761, 16 OGR 28, cert den 369 US 828, 7 L Ed 2d 794, 82 S Ct 846; Johnson v Moxley, 216 Ala 466, 113 So 656; Cities Service Oil Co. v Taylor, 242 Ky 157, 45 SW2d 1039, 79 ALR 1374; Marcelle, Inc. v Sol. & S. Marcus Co., 274 Mass 469, 175 NE 83, 74 ALR 1012; Davidson v Minnesota Loan & Trust Co., 158 Minn 411, 197 NW 833, 32 ALR 1418.

Restatement 2d, Property § 95.

Forms: Sublease—Office space. 11A Am Jur Legal Forms 2d §§ 161:1251, 161:1252.

—Short form. 11A Am Jur Legal Forms 2d §§ 161:1253.

21. Davidson v Minnesota Loan & Trust Co., 158 Minn 411, 197 NW 833, 32 ALR 1418.

As to assignments, see §§ 1076 et seq.

22. Coles Trading Co. v Spiegel, Inc. (CA9 Ariz) 187 F2d 984, 24 ALR2d 702.

23. §§ 1162 et seq.

Of course, if the encyclopedia is published by another publisher such as LexisNexis, the corresponding research material will be LexisNexis-related. States that presently have legal encyclopedias are shown in the following list:

ThomsonWest Publications
California—*California Jurisprudence 3d*
Florida—*Florida Jurisprudence 2d*
Georgia—*Georgia Jurisprudence*
Illinois—*Illinois Jurisprudence*
Indiana—*West's Indiana Law Encyclopedia*
Maryland—*West's Maryland Law Encyclopedia*
Michigan—*Michigan Civil Jurisprudence*
New York—*New York Jurisprudence 2d*
North Carolina—*Strong's North Carolina Index 4th*
Ohio—*Ohio Jurisprudence 3d*
South Carolina—*South Carolina Jurisprudence*
Texas—*Texas Jurisprudence 3d*

LexisNexis Publications
Illinois—*Illinois Law and Practice*
Michigan—*Michigan Law and Practice Encyclopedia*
Minnesota—*Dunnell Minnesota Digest*
Pennsylvania—*Pennsylvania Law Encyclopedia*
Tennessee—*Tennessee Jurisprudence*
Virginia—*Michie's Jurisprudence of Virginia and West Virginia*
West Virginia—*Michie's Jurisprudence of Virginia and West Virginia*

Using the Indexes to the Encyclopedias

Each encyclopedia has a corresponding general index at the end of its volumes. Encyclopedias also have a subject-specific index at the end of the volume on that topic. Consequently, there are two ways to locate your interested subject in an encyclopedia. If you do not know your subject topic, the general index is the best place to begin. Similar to the approach you took with the digest, write down relevant words and phrases that apply to the area you are researching. Begin looking up the words and phrases until you locate an encyclopedia subject that applies to your research problem. Next to your relevant word or phrase will be the encyclopedia topic followed by the section that pertains to your research. Remember that more than one area may apply to your research assignment. Exhaust all the possibilities before moving on. Once you

YOU BE THE JUDGE

Relying on the court or opposing counsel to point out relevant cases is not an argument to advance—under any circumstances. Nor is an attorney's attempt to convince a court that its own decisions are not controlling. This was not the case in *Schutts v. Bently Nevada Corporation,* 966 F. Supp. 1547 (D. Nev. 1997), however. The court sanctioned an attorney when he tried to tell the court that two cases decided in that jurisdiction, *Newland* and *Collings* (citations omitted), did not apply since the U.S. Supreme Court had not ruled on the issue. As the court stated, "Plaintiff's counsel also advances the truly bizarre argument that although the *Newland* decision 'bind[s] this court, it is not the law of the land until the Supreme Court reconciles it with [a decision by the Second Circuit].' Whether *Newland* and *Collings* are the 'law of the land' or not, they are decisions by the federal court of appeals for this federal judicial district. As such they are the law, here, in this court. End of story." *Id.* at 1563. Doesn't this case boggle the mind! Review the *Schutts* case. Was the judge's action against the attorney warranted and appropriate? What are the facts that the judge relied upon to reach his result? What is the reasoning in the case? What are the lessons learned from the *Schutts* case?

are satisfied that you have located your subject and relevant section, retrieve the book from the shelf and begin reading. As you are reading, you should also be taking notes. Write down additional relevant topics and keys; write down cases from the footnotes; and write down additional sections that the text may suggest to review.

You can use a shortcut to this method when you already know the subject about which you want to review. Retrieve the relevant volume from the shelf and flip to the back of the volume where there is a subject-specific index. This index only has information on the subjects contained within that volume. Focusing on the relevant words and phrases, look them up in the subject-specific index of the encyclopedia. Write down the sections that apply to your subject and begin reviewing the text of that subject.

Although encyclopedias and digests are generally considered the most useful traditional finding tools, there are other sources that can offer a wealth of information to assist in researching a topic, such as *American Law Reports,* treatises, law review journals, and legal texts. These sources provide an alternative to digests and encyclopedias.

Checklist for Using an Encyclopedia

Encyclopedias have an approach similar to that of the digests. Here is a suggested method for tackling an encyclopedia:

- Write down relevant words and phrases from the assignment.
- Retrieve the general index.
- Begin looking up the words and phrases until you have located an applicable subject to review.
- Write down the subject(s) sections.
- Retrieve the relevant encyclopedia volume.
- Begin reviewing the subject by examining the black letter law section, pertinent topics, keys, and footnotes.
- Write down any cases from the footnotes, if applicable.
- Look up the suggested topics and keys or other related legal resources.
- Check the pocket parts or supplements for new additions to the commentary.
- Review any cases.
- Copy relevant cases.
- Reshelve books if appropriate.

Quick Quiz True/False Questions

1. A legal encyclopedia is one of the methods for beginning a legal research project.
2. The two main encyclopedias are *Corpus Juris Secundum* and *American Law Reports.*
3. A legal encyclopedia has an index called the Descriptive Word Index, similar to the digests.
4. Legal encyclopedias use footnotes to alert the reader to relevant cases.
5. State encyclopedias only focus on the laws of the state identified in those volumes.

SECONDARY SOURCES AS FINDING TOOLS: A DIFFERENT APPROACH

You know the basic approach to legal research but you want more than just a listing of the current cases. You want to understand the development of an area of the law and some of the trends that are occurring. Where do you look? Some good starting points include *American Law Reports,* looseleaf services, law review journals, and legal periodicals.

American Law Reports (A.L.R.)

annotation
An in-depth analysis of a specific and important legal issue raised in the accompanying decision, together with an extensive survey of the way the issue is treated in various jurisdictions.

In this section we discuss the *American Law Reports* series more fully. The *A.L.R.* series publishes full texts of only certain state and federal court decisions, which are selected for the level of interest generated by the issues that they address (see Figure 6.20). In earlier editions, each individual case selected was followed by an **annotation,** which provides an in-depth analysis of a specific and important legal issue raised in the accompanying decision, together with an extensive survey of the way the issue is treated in various jurisdictions. Many cases are cited and summarized in these annotations, making them excellent research sources. Beginning with the fifth series, cases are now presented at the end of the volume in their own section. All annotations precede the cases they discuss. An example of the first page of such an annotation is found in Figure 6.21 and an interior page is found in Figure 6.22. The *A.L.R.* volumes are now in their sixth series, cited as *A.L.R. 6th.*

Most of the annotations in the first four series have either been replaced or substantially supplemented by newer annotations. To determine whether an annotation has been replaced (superseded) or supplemented, refer to the Annotation History Table. This table will update the changes that have affected that annotation. Updating of the newer annotations is generally through the pocket parts.

FIGURE 6.20 **Example of an *A.L.R.* Case**

Source: From *Annotated Law Reports.* Reprinted with permission from ThomsonWest.

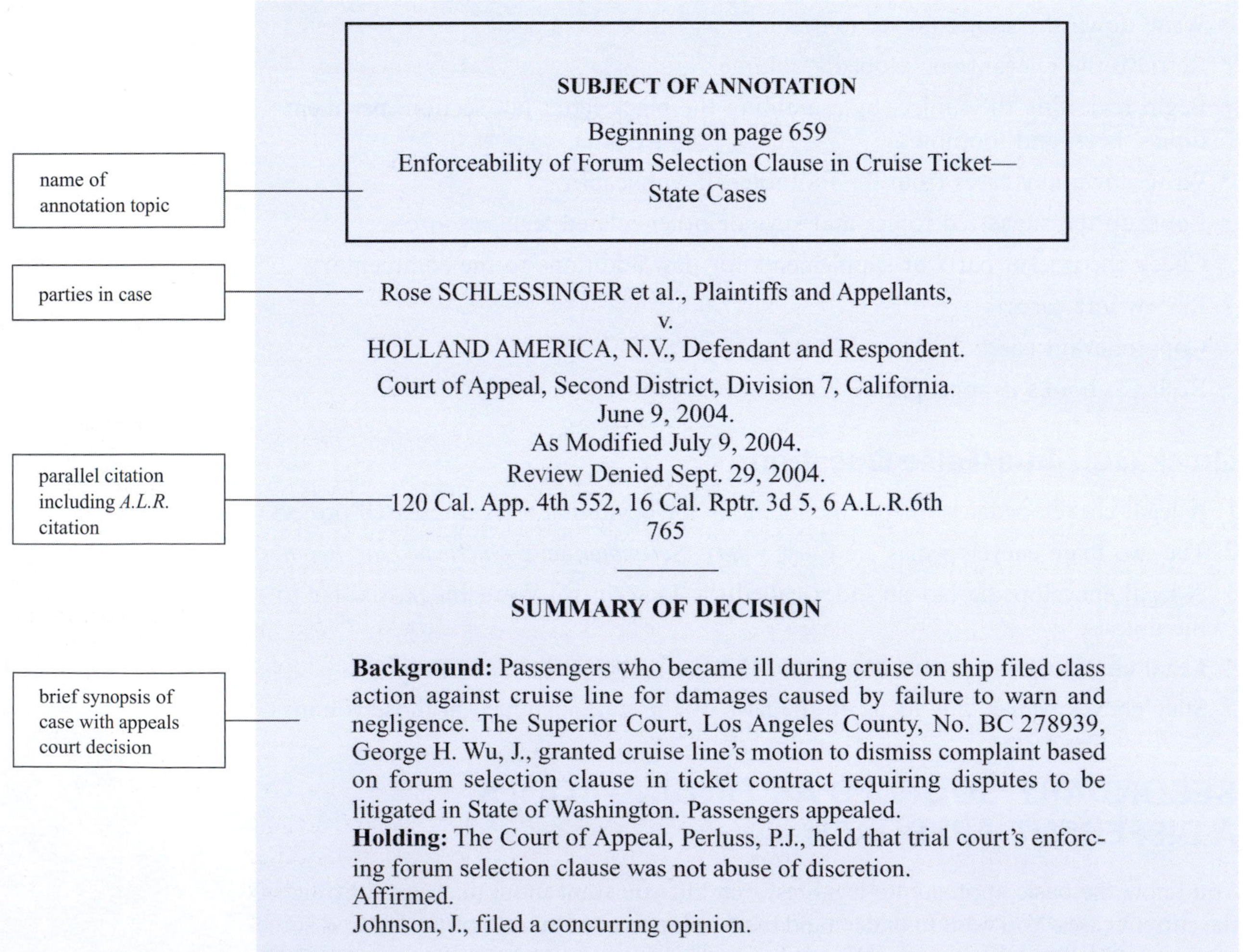

SUBJECT OF ANNOTATION

Beginning on page 659

Enforceability of Forum Selection Clause in Cruise Ticket—State Cases

Rose SCHLESSINGER et al., Plaintiffs and Appellants,

v.

HOLLAND AMERICA, N.V., Defendant and Respondent.

Court of Appeal, Second District, Division 7, California.

June 9, 2004.

As Modified July 9, 2004.

Review Denied Sept. 29, 2004.

120 Cal. App. 4th 552, 16 Cal. Rptr. 3d 5, 6 A.L.R.6th 765

SUMMARY OF DECISION

Background: Passengers who became ill during cruise on ship filed class action against cruise line for damages caused by failure to warn and negligence. The Superior Court, Los Angeles County, No. BC 278939, George H. Wu, J., granted cruise line's motion to dismiss complaint based on forum selection clause in ticket contract requiring disputes to be litigated in State of Washington. Passengers appealed.

Holding: The Court of Appeal, Perluss, P.J., held that trial court's enforcing forum selection clause was not abuse of discretion.

Affirmed.

Johnson, J., filed a concurring opinion.

FIGURE 6.21 First Page of an *A.L.R.* Annotation

Source: From *Annotated Law Reports.* Reprinted with permission from ThomsonWest.

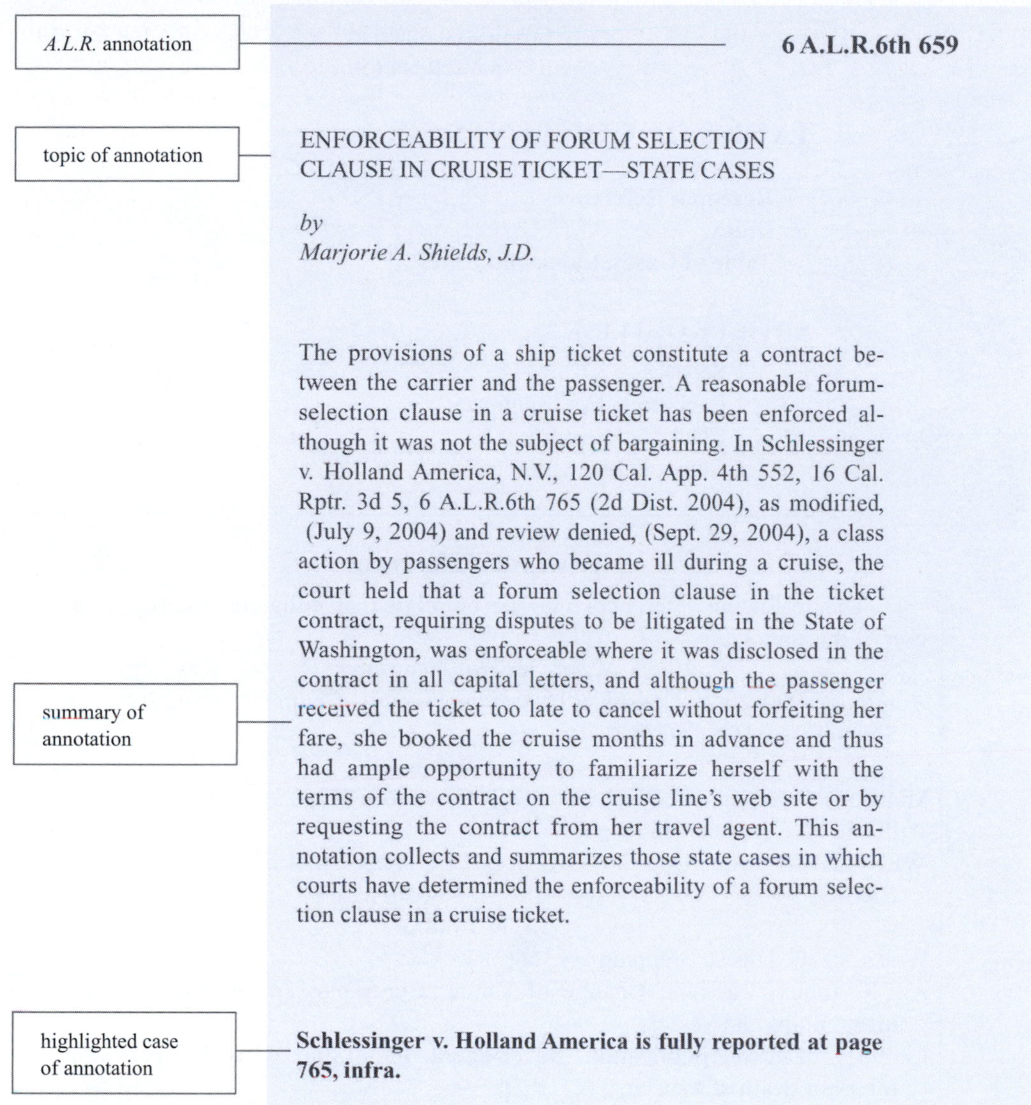

A.L.R. annotation

6 A.L.R.6th 659

topic of annotation

ENFORCEABILITY OF FORUM SELECTION CLAUSE IN CRUISE TICKET—STATE CASES

by
Marjorie A. Shields, J.D.

summary of annotation

The provisions of a ship ticket constitute a contract between the carrier and the passenger. A reasonable forum-selection clause in a cruise ticket has been enforced although it was not the subject of bargaining. In Schlessinger v. Holland America, N.V., 120 Cal. App. 4th 552, 16 Cal. Rptr. 3d 5, 6 A.L.R.6th 765 (2d Dist. 2004), as modified, (July 9, 2004) and review denied, (Sept. 29, 2004), a class action by passengers who became ill during a cruise, the court held that a forum selection clause in the ticket contract, requiring disputes to be litigated in the State of Washington, was enforceable where it was disclosed in the contract in all capital letters, and although the passenger received the ticket too late to cancel without forfeiting her fare, she booked the cruise months in advance and thus had ample opportunity to familiarize herself with the terms of the contract on the cruise line's web site or by requesting the contract from her travel agent. This annotation collects and summarizes those state cases in which courts have determined the enforceability of a forum selection clause in a cruise ticket.

highlighted case of annotation

Schlessinger v. Holland America is fully reported at page 765, infra.

Cases, statutes, and other legal changes are cited to complement and supplement the original annotation.

Beginning in 1969, a second set of *A.L.R.* volumes called *A.L.R. Federal* was created. It is structured identically to the standard *A.L.R.* series, with selected cases (all federal) followed by annotations on the federal issues presented. Like other *A.L.R.* volumes, *A.L.R. Federal* is updated and supplemented through its pocket parts.

There is a digest collecting all the *A.L.R.*, *A.L.R. Federal,* and *Lawyers' Edition* headnotes arranged alphabetically by topic, called the *A.L.R. Digest.* Another useful research aid is the *Index to Annotations,* which indexes all the annotations in *A.L.R. 3d, A.L.R. 4th, A.L.R. 5th, A.L.R. 6th,* and *A.L.R. Federal.*

PRACTICE TIP

When an annotation has been supplemented, review both the original annotation *and* the supplement for completeness.

Using and Finding *A.L.R.* Annotations

Annotations can be a valuable resource tool. They are extensively researched and include all jurisdictions that have dealt with the topic about which the annotation comments. Since *A.L.R.* was purchased by ThomsonWest, the *A.L.R. Digest* now is linked to the Key Number System. Use the same principles learned for using the *American Digest* series. In addition to the topic and key, the *A.L.R. Digest* also provides the relevant annotation.

FIGURE 6.22 Interior Pages of an *A.L.R.* Annotation

Source: From *Annotated Law Reports.* Reprinted with permission from ThomsonWest.

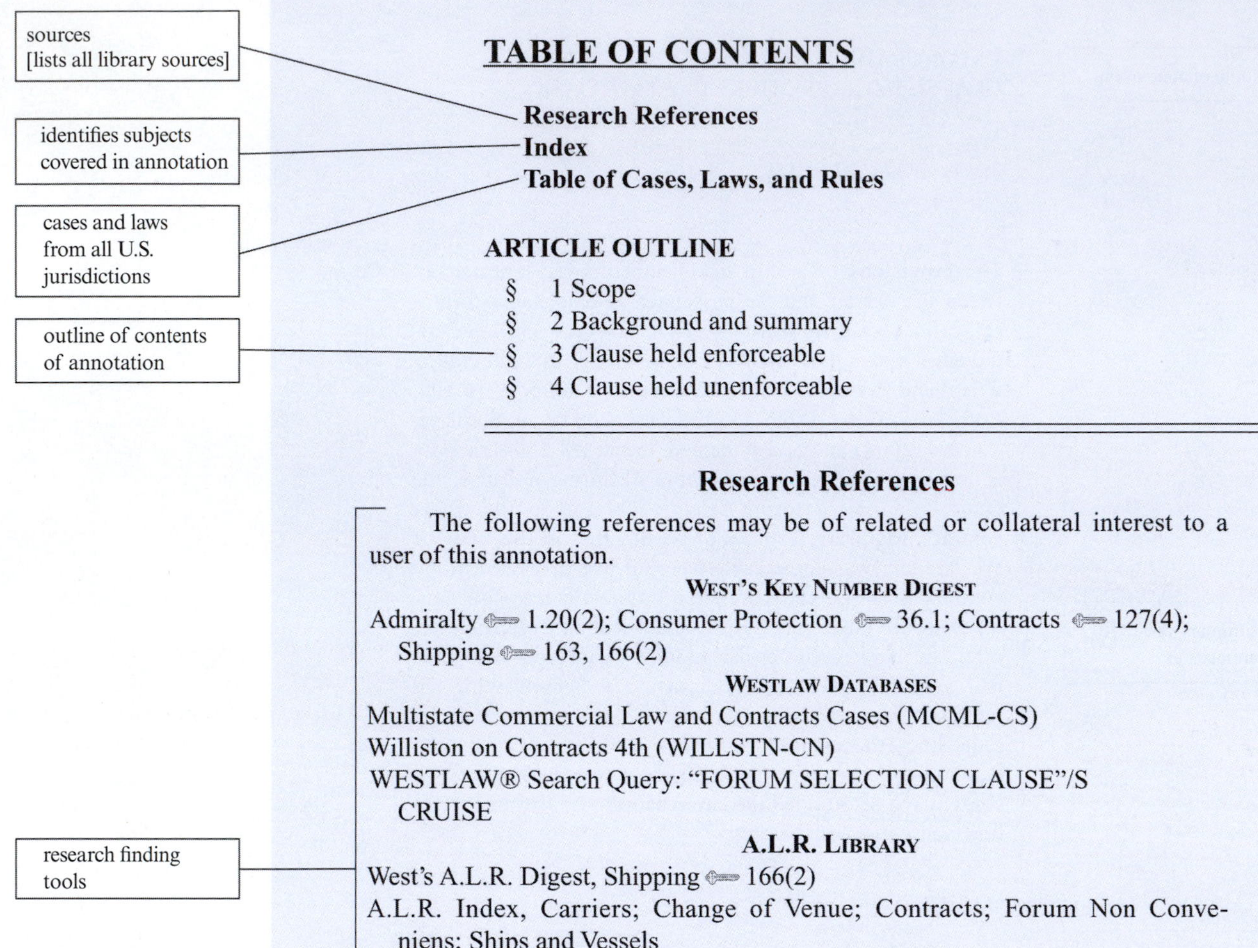

CONTRACTS; SHIPPING 6 A.L.R.6th 659

6 A.L.R.6th 659

TABLE OF CONTENTS

ARTICLE OUTLINE

Research References

The following references may be of related or collateral interest to a user of this annotation.

WEST'S KEY NUMBER DIGEST

Admiralty 1.20(2); Consumer Protection 36.1; Contracts 127(4); Shipping 163, 166(2)

WESTLAW DATABASES

Multistate Commercial Law and Contracts Cases (MCML-CS)
Williston on Contracts 4th (WILLSTN-CN)
WESTLAW® Search Query: "FORUM SELECTION CLAUSE"/S CRUISE

A.L.R. LIBRARY

West's A.L.R. Digest, Shipping 166(2)
A.L.R. Index, Carriers; Change of Venue; Contracts; Forum Non Conveniens; Ships and Vessels
Liability of travel publication, travel agent, or similar party for personal injury or death of traveler, 2 A.L.R.5th 396
Forum non conveniens doctrine in state court as affected by availability of alternative forum, 57 A.L.R.4th 973
Validity of contractual provision limiting place or court in which action may be brought, 31 A.L.R.4th 404
Doctrine of forum non conveniens: assumption or denial of jurisdiction of contract action involving foreign elements, 90 A.L.R.2d 1109
Validity of contractual provision authorizing venue of action in particular place, court, or county, 69 A.L.R.2d 1324
Liability of motor carrier for loss of passenger's baggage or packages, 68 A.L.R.2d 1350

Cont.

FIGURE 6.22 **Interior Pages of an *A.L.R.* Annotation** *Cont.*

CONTRACTS; SHIPPING 6 A.L.R.6th 659
6 A.L.R. 6th 659

FORMS

Am. Jur. Legal Forms 2d, Ships and Shipping §§ 233:131, 233:136
Am. Jur. Pleading and Practice Forms, Carriers § 50

LAW REVIEWS AND OTHER PERIODICALS

periodicals

Dickerson, The Cruise Passenger's Dilemma: Twenty-First Century Ships, Nineteenth-Century Rights, 28 Tul.Mar. L.J. 447 (2004)
O'Hara, The Jurisprudence and Politics of Forum-Selection Clauses, 3 Chi. J. Int'l L. 301 (2002)
Robertson, Recent Developments in Admiralty and Maritime law at the National Level and in the Fifth and Eleventh Circuits, 27 Tul. Mar. L.J. 495 (2003)

ADDITIONAL REFERENCES

briefs of parties from subject case

Appellate Materials, Appellants Reply Brief, 2004 WL 1061992
Appellate Materials, Respondent's Brief, 2004 WL 486057
Appellate Materials, Appellants Opening Brief, 2003 WL 23156187

Westlaw information

KeyCite®: Cases and other legal materials listed in KeyCite Scope can be researched through the KeyCite service on Westlaw®. Use KeyCite to check citations for form, parallel references, prior and later history, and comprehensive citator information, including citations to other decisions and secondary materials.

INDEX

areas discussed in annotation

PRACTICE TIP

Early *A.L.R.* volumes had the cases directly in front of the annotation. Later versions had the cases indexed at the back of the volume.

Once you have located the applicable annotation citation, retrieve the annotation volume for review. The annotation is structured differently than an encyclopedia. Using Figures 6.21 and 6.22, the first substantive piece of information is a summary of the annotation. Review the summary to determine whether the annotation is relevant to the issue you are researching. The summary is followed by the case on which the annotation is based with a reference to its location in the volume. As you begin to examine the annotation, you will observe a table of contents, which lists the contents of the annotation. This section is followed by all the related legal research references. Note that since *A.L.R.* is now a ThomsonWest publication, all related references will be cited. This will include not only the key numbers but also Westlaw data searches and other relevant *A.L.R.* annotations. Coupled with law review articles and periodicals, you will have a wealth of information to assist you in your research.

Annotations list an index at the beginning of the commentary, which is followed by the jurisdictions cited in the annotation. Clearly, the coverage of the subject is extensive and comprehensive just by the number of jurisdictions cited. Then the annotation begins; annotations generally follow a similar format, usually discussing the scope of the annotation in the introductory paragraphs with a summary and comment leading into the annotation analysis.

Now, you can see why many believe that when you locate an applicable *A.L.R.* annotation much of your work is completed. Don't use an *A.L.R.* as your only source of research material. Be sure you check all other finding tools for a comprehensive approach to your assignment.

Looseleaf Services

Chapter 2 introduced looseleaf sources. As you may recall, looseleaf services are often both a primary and secondary source. As a finding tool they are usually subject-specific. A looseleaf service publishes recently decided court cases, statutes with changes, and rules and regulations that pertain to the topic the service covers. With inserts and supplements that are easily interchanged, the looseleaf services are styled as a three-ring binder rather than a bound volume.

There are a large number of looseleaf services spanning a wide variety of topics. Some of the major publishers are the Bureau of National Affairs (BNA); Commerce Clearing House (CCH), a Wolters Kluwer business; and Aspen Publishers. The specific format of each depends upon the publisher, the nature of the material covered, and the scope of the service.

A few generalizations apply to most looseleaf services. Each usually applies to only one topic; for example, the *Immigration Law and Procedure* looseleaf service is published by LexisNexis and relates only to laws and procedures regarding immigration. Weekly updates are usually provided in the form of prepunched supplement or replacement pages to be inserted into the binder in which the service is maintained. Coverage often extends to both state and federal cases relating to the topic, as well as applicable statutes and textual analysis. Looseleaf services are often organized in a complex but extremely effective manner, with numbered paragraphs and topical indexes. For a detailed explanation, refer to the explanatory materials that are included with each service. Often cases are summarized in the text but reprinted in full in companion looseleaf volumes; these companion volumes are organized in a manner similar to reporters, and some looseleaf services ultimately reissue them in permanent bound volumes.

Many of the cases in the looseleaf services are reprinted nowhere else, not even in the reporters of the West system. For this reason, the looseleaf services can be a valuable resource. It is convenient to have textual materials and cases and statutes from many jurisdictions all in one location and with one common system of indexing. Finally, the weekly updates often make the looseleaf services the most current source of information available.

The textual treatment that looseleaf services and annotations provide is a valuable resource. Annotations provide broad analysis and extensive case summaries. The looseleaf services bring together in one topical reporter applicable case texts, statutes, regulations, and independent analysis. A page from a looseleaf service is reproduced in Figure 6.23.

FIGURE 6.23 **Page from a Looseleaf Service**

Source: From *Immigration Law and Procedure.* Reprinted with permission from LexisNexis.

7–21 **SANCTIONS AND DISCRIMINATION** **§ 7.03[2][b]**

§ 7.03 The Prohibition Against Knowingly Hiring, Referring, or Recruiting An Unauthorized Alien; Employment Authorization, Employment Authorization Document ("EAD")

[1]—In General

Just as IRCA's underlying purpose is to discourage unauthorized aliens from immigrating by denying them jobs, its primary method of doing so is to prohibit anyone from hiring them or commercially recruiting or referring them, knowing of their unauthorized status. This prohibition is accompanied by the employment verification requirement, designed to uncover whether a job applicant is an unauthorized alien, and backed up by an enforcement system and penalties. A valid verification gives the employer an affirmative defense of good faith which, however, is rebuttable. Particularly as the term "unauthorized alien" is first introduced by IRCA it warrants close study, as does the "knowing" requirement.

[2]—Unauthorized Alien: Concept and Definition

[a]—In General

In recent decades, more and more attention has been given to sub-rosa immigration, by public figures and journalists who have written with alarm or in explanation of the massive penetration of our borders by "wetbacks" or "illegal aliens." However inappropriate these labels, or inadequate such terms as "undocumented" or "deportable aliens," the issue of terminology is now finessed by IRCA which addresses the alien's status solely in terms of this statute's focus, namely, whether the individual is an alien authorized for the given employment. The statute defines the term only "with respect to the employment of an alien at a particular time" as being "not at that time either (A) an alien lawfully admitted for permanent residence, or (B) authorized to be so employed by this chapter or by the Attorney General."[1]

PLANNING NOTE

The immigration agency has suggested the following language for employers who want to ask potential employees about their work authorization: "Are you currently authorized to work for all employers in the United States on a full-time basis, or only for your current employer?"[1.1]

[b]—Prior Law and Impact of IRCA

Prior to the passage of IRCA, it was clear that an employment relationship was not unlawful simply because the employee was in the United States in violation of law. The taking of a job by an already deportable alien was not criminal or otherwise barred by

[1] INA § 274A(h)(3), 8 U.S.C. § 1324a(h)(3).

[1.1] Letter from OSC Special Counsel (Jun. 24, 1993), *reprinted in* 70 Interpreter Releases 1303–04 (Oct. 4, 1993).

(Rel.108—4/05 Pub.325)

Law Reviews and Periodicals

law review journals
Periodicals edited by the top students at each law school, featuring scholarly articles by leading authorities and notes on various topics written by the law students themselves.

Additional secondary sources that act as finding tools are law review journals and legal periodicals. Law review articles are often exhaustive on a topic and use footnotes to support the propositions cited within the article. Often the footnotes are as long as the article itself! What that should suggest is: pay close attention to the footnotes in law review articles as they will lead you to cases, statutes, books, and other law review articles on the subject. Although the quality of articles may vary, they often provide insight into the trends in a particular subject. Like many other secondary sources, these articles are most valuable as learning tools or sources of citations to relevant primary authorities, and are not often cited in briefs. Nevertheless, an article in a leading law review by a top scholar can have a substantial impact on the profession as well as on your research.

CYBER TRIP

Using www.google.com, find a law review article that discusses the PATRIOT Act.

There are also numerous legal periodicals published by bar associations or private publishers. These periodicals vary in quality from scholarly journals to newsletters. Some are useful as research tools for the profession as a whole; others provide limited information to defined segments of the bar. Articles are usually not scrutinized as thoroughly as a law review article, but do offer commentary on recent cases and trends within the profession.

Finding Law Review Articles and Legal Periodicals

The most familiar method of locating law review and legal periodicals is the *Index to Legal Periodicals and Books* by H.W. Wilson Company. This index has both print and electronic versions of approximately a thousand law review articles and periodicals relating to various legal subjects. The print indexes are arranged by subject and provide the references to the articles, whereas the electronic version is accessed through the "key word search method" and links to those sources.

HeinOnLine provides access to legal periodicals and journals through the Internet. Although a subscription (fee) service, the service offers periodicals that date back to the publication of the periodical. Other services do not provide such a comprehensive database. Additionally, the full text of articles are formatted as PDF files, which makes them easier to read. In addition to the complete texts of law review articles, HeinOnLine also offers access to the *Federal Register,* statutes and session laws, international data such as treaties and journals, and presidential documents, to name just a few.

A DAY IN THE LIFE OF A PARALEGAL

You have been working on a research assignment for over a month. A client is dying of a serious debilitating disease and has been using marijuana to help her cope with the constant pain. She was arrested for the illegal use of drugs and is being prosecuted by the state of California. Your research revealed that no decision has been handed down by your jurisdiction even though you checked the California digests and California law journals since it is such a hot topic in your state. You have placed the final touches on the memorandum of law and your attorney is ready to review and critique it. The best arguments for the client are that the use is for medicinal purposes only and that she has a constitutional right to use the marijuana. The brief has to be filed with the court in 48 hours. While your attorney is driving to the court for his hearing, you happen to look at your e-mail and one of the Web sites you subscribe to has sent an alert. A Ninth Circuit Court of Appeals case just allowed marijuana use but is limited to that one instance. Your attorney is on his way to the courthouse for a pretrial conference with the court and opposing counsel and does not know about the case. You need to get this new information to him immediately. What should you do? This is not an unusual situation. New information and cases are discovered each day. The most important point is to do whatever is necessary to get the information to your attorney as quickly as possible. That may mean driving down to the courthouse yourself if telephones are unavailable. The end result is to get the job done!

YOU BE THE JUDGE

The use of secondary texts and their relevancy was the basis of a U.S. Supreme Court case. In *Kumho Tire Company v. Carmichael*, 526 U.S. 137, 119 S. Ct. 1167, 143 L. Ed. 2d 238 (1999), the court had to decide the relevancy and ultimate reliability of scientific versus expert testimony, and its weight in deciding cases. In the case, tires blew out causing the death of passengers in a car. As part of the lawsuit, the plaintiffs alleged that the tires were defective and had an expert testify to support their premise. The expert's reliability was at issue and the application of another U.S. Supreme Court case, *Daubert v. Merrell Dow Pharmaceuticals, Inc.*, 509 U.S. 579 (1993). Since the case involved the technical expertise and skill of an expert in the tire field, secondary sources were relied upon by the Court. In its opinion, Justice Breyer cited a number of secondary sources upon which an expert witness relied. These sources formed the basis as to whether the Supreme Court accepted the premise behind an expert's testimony. Review the *Kumho* case. What rule of evidence was at issue? List the secondary sources that the U.S. Supreme Court cited in its opinion. What was the holding in the case? What was the basis of the Court's reasoning in arriving at its result?

Another tool for finding legal periodical material is the *Current Law Index* published by ThomsonWest. The online version of this index is called *LegalTrac*. Both indexes provide access or links to over 900 journals and periodicals.

For weekly updated indexes to legal periodicals, the Current Index to Legal Periodicals (CILP) or its sister online version SmartCILP is a good place to start. And of course, the computer-assisted legal research services, such as Westlaw and LexisNexis, provide access to legal periodicals and journals for a fee. Each will be discussed in more detail in this chapter and in Chapter 9.

Sometimes an Internet search will result in finding legal periodicals and law review journals, but they may be difficult to access. Online libraries such as Cornell and the University of Southern California provide access to some of these journals.

treatise
A scholarly study of one area of the law.

texts
One-volume treatises.

hornbooks
Scholarly texts; a series of textbooks that review various fields of law in summary narrative form, as opposed to casebooks, which are designed as primary teaching tools and include many reprints of court opinions.

nutshell
A paperback series of the law; condensed versions of hornbooks.

Treatises and Texts

As discussed in Chapter 2, **treatises** and **texts** are important secondary sources of the law. They also can be another place to begin legal research. Be sure when you choose to review a legal treatise as a finding tool that you are using an accepted scholarly text. Stay away from student guides, such as **hornbooks,** or their condensed versions, **nutshells**, when you are conducting formal legal research. They may not contain the detail that is required for an assignment from a supervising attorney.

Quick Quiz True/False Questions

1. *American Law Reports* is both a primary and secondary source.
2. Looseleaf services only contain secondary material.
3. Similar to encyclopedias, law reviews extensively use footnotes.
4. All treatises and hornbooks are considered scholarly.
5. The only law dictionary is *Black's Law Dictionary.*

PRACTICE TIP

Invest in a law dictionary. Standard dictionaries will not suffice in a law environment.

LAW DICTIONARIES

When you were in grade school, recall your teachers always saying to you, "If you don't know what a word means, look it up in the dictionary." Times haven't changed much. In the area of law, there are specialized dictionaries that define legal terminology called legal dictionaries. The most widely used and cited law dictionary is *Black's Law Dictionary* (8th ed. 2004). In fact, when a court wants to define a legal word, *"Black's"* is often cited as its source. Another commonly used dictionary is *Ballantine's*

Law Dictionary (3rd ed. 1969). Unlike a standard dictionary, which usually only defines words, legal dictionaries define concepts as well. So, if you read a Latin phrase, such as *res ipsa loquitor* (which means "the thing speaks for itself" and is used in negligence cases) and you have no idea what the words mean, check a legal dictionary for guidance.

Legal dictionaries can be found online and can be used for general guidance. Some Web sites that are useful are www.nolo.com, www.jurist.law.pitt.edu/dictionary, and www.dictionary.law.com, to name a few. Be aware that the most authoritative legal dictionary, print or online, continues to be *Black's.*

COMPUTER-ASSISTED LEGAL RESEARCH: A BRIEF INTRODUCTION

PRACTICE TIP

Do not exclude print material in favor of online material as online material may not result in a complete and thorough search for all relevant legal sources. Use print and online sources to complement each other.

The technological explosion that has made this the information age has made available significant new tools for legal research. These tools—computers, online data services—have not yet replaced the traditional primary and secondary sources, but rather have broadened their accessibility and deepened their usefulness. However, the key words here are "not yet." The clear trend is toward more computer-based legal research, whether good or bad. Even though we tend to demand immediate results on just about any topic, always remember that you must understand the print version of legal research to truly be successful at the online versions of legal research. Consequently, although an entire chapter in this text is devoted to computer-assisted legal research, a brief mention of Westlaw and LexisNexis is necessary as they are now becoming two of the most important legal research finding tools.

LexisNexis and Westlaw

The two foremost computer-based legal research systems are LexisNexis and Westlaw. Each contains the full text of an enormous number of documents, from case opinions to statutes to law review articles. Cases on Westlaw also have the West key numbers and headnotes. Like other online data systems, Westlaw and LexisNexis require that you have access to a computer. By linking to these systems you obtain the ability to research in four ways:

- First, by allowing a researcher to obtain the text of a specific known document. For example, suppose you need to look at a specific statute from another state, or a case from a reporter not contained in your firm's library. Enter the appropriate information into LexisNexis or Westlaw, and in a short time the full text will appear on your screen.
- Second, by performing research in the normal sense (online digests or indexes can be reviewed to find applicable materials).
- Third, by searching selected **databases** for key terms or phrases. For example, you could search all the cases from California that use the phrase "strict liability." In addition, because some legal concepts are too complicated to compress to a single word or term, these systems allow you to search for groups of words or terms based upon their proximity—for example, a search for the terms "strict liability" and "ultrahazardous substance" when they appear in the same sentence. Stringing together key terms and words to form a **query** is a skill that takes time and practice to refine.
- Fourth, by some combination of these first three methods. For example, using Westlaw you might want to obtain headnotes under a specific key number (the traditional research method) that contain a specified query term (the third method listed). LexisNexis cases have headnotes linked to its legal publications as well.

database
A collection of information used in computer systems to provide access to related fields of interest.

query
A string of key terms or words used in a computer search.

THE E-FACTOR

An unconventional method of legal research may be the use of "Web logs" or, as they are more commonly known, "blogs." Blogs are Web pages where individuals can share information of any kind in a journal-like format. A developing trend in the legal world is legal blogs. Here, attorneys or paralegals can share information about legal issues and current trends or just plain "talk shop." Often blogs allow legal professionals to share information or even ask questions about a particular set of facts, including those involving actual client cases. But legal professionals must be cognizant of the unique rules that govern the profession. Although blogs are becoming a more popular and informal method of communication, there are ethical issues that legal professionals cannot escape. One clear issue is client confidentiality. When attempting to acquire information or guidance on a client-related issue, be sure that the facts or names are sufficiently different so not to breach the attorney–client confidentiality privilege. With the use of the Internet expanding daily and its limits boundless, those of us in the legal profession must be mindful that our ethical obligations transcend the anonymity of the Internet and its blogs. Do not ever lose sight of what we do as a profession and the ethical obligations associated with that profession.

At first blush, the Internet "appears" to be the more desired form of finding tools for legal research. However, if you don't understand how to use the print material through its step-by-step process, and only use electronic-based sources, you risk missing critical cases as the Internet has no real "checks and balances" on its process. How do you know on the Internet that you have found the leading case(s) or all the relevant cases for that matter? These are tough realities to face. Of course, the Internet is quick and accessible. Let's face it; you don't have to move from your desk to retrieve information from the Internet. But ease and accessibility do not equal accuracy. The best practice is to combine the traditional research methods with electronic methods. Will the Internet replace the traditional print sources? Only time can answer that question. Many libraries are subscribing to fewer and fewer print sources because of the wide use of the Internet and its cost-effectiveness. We are not there yet, however. What that means for you as a paralegal is that you must master both the print and online forms of legal research to be successful at your craft. Print material methods, such as digests and encyclopedias, and online methods go hand in hand in finding the legal sources you need to do your job.

PRACTICE TIP

Unless you understand the basis of the digest system through the print sources, you will have difficulties navigating the online legal research search systems.

PRACTICAL CONSIDERATIONS: HOW TO BEGIN AND WHEN TO STOP

To a great extent one learns how to do legal research by doing it. There is no easy substitute for the benefits of hours of trial and error, nor is there a painless path to satisfying revelation. There are, however, two areas that are fundamental—how to begin your research and when to stop. We'll leave the middle to you.

As we said at the outset of these chapters on legal research, you must isolate your goal and prepare a plan, or risk being overwhelmed by literally millions of pages of materials in the sources we have identified. A legal encyclopedia is a good place to start; it provides a broad overview of the subject area, and might cite to a useful annotation or a case from your jurisdiction. The next stop is probably the index to the relevant annotated statutory code, to see whether a statute governs or affects the issues at hand. If there is a relevant statute, both the text of the statute and the supplemental information provided (case citations, legislative history, references to periodicals) may prove helpful. Next, go to the digest. Using the Descriptive Word Index, the Words and Phrases section, and the topic indexes, search for relevant case law. Finally, look for secondary sources. There may be law review articles, restatement provisions, or treatises that can contribute breadth and depth to your analysis.

CYBER TRIP

Using www.scotusblog.com or www.fourthamendment.com, locate a recent U.S. Supreme Court case or a case from your federal circuit court of appeals that deals with prisoner rights or the Fourth Amendment.

Now assume that you've been researching for some time. You've checked a wide variety of sources; read and photocopied a number of cases, statutes, and secondary sources; taken pages of notes; and found that there is so much material available that you could "go on forever." How do you know when to stop?

There is no easy answer to this question. A definitive reference in a mandatory authority may supply all the information you need. A less tidy research session may be finished when newly explored avenues yield references to the same cases, statutes, and secondary sources. If you have looked in several competing sources (for example, a West digest and an *A.L.R.* annotation) and turned up the same references, your research is probably adequate.

Finding the same references over and over does not guarantee that you are finished; with legal research, like most things in life, absolute certainty is elusive. A thorough search of the most useful references maximizes your coverage within the constraints of the client's problem (you cannot spend $5,000 of research time on a $1,000 case); however, it is reasonable cause to believe that you've found the essential sources.

Once you have completed your legal research, you must review your cases and organize your thoughts to prepare the letter, memorandum of law, or brief you were assigned.

Summary

The digest system is the foundation for finding the law. The system utilizes the Key Number System. The Key Number System was established by West Publishing (now ThomsonWest) to index cases appearing in its unofficial reporters, including the regional reporters of the National Reporter System. Digests collect headnotes, which are points of law drawn from a case and categorized under one or more applicable key numbers, and organize them consecutively by topic and key number. Pocket parts are used to update bound volumes.

A legal encyclopedia is a multivolume compilation purporting to provide in-depth coverage of every area of the law. Restatements are drafted by distinguished panels of legal experts for the purpose of developing and encouraging a uniform approach to various areas of common law. A treatise is a scholarly study of one area of the law, differing from a restatement in that it is usually the work of one author or group of authors, rather than a panel of experts.

American Law Reports provides a unique look at the law through the use of annotations. Annotations are based upon a case of interest and are researched by analyzing the issues from all jurisdictions. With the acquisition of *A.L.R.* by ThomsonWest, an *A.L.R.* digest has been created based upon the Key Number System.

Texts are one-volume treatises. Law reviews are periodicals edited by law students. Looseleaf services and annotations include secondary discussions of legal topics, as well as texts of cases and statutes.

LexisNexis and Westlaw are computer-based legal research systems. A query is a string of key terms or words used in a computer search. Both LexisNexis and Westlaw provide search mechanisms to find cases, statutes, or any other legal document you may need for your research. The Internet also provides Web sites that may be useful in legal research.

A good place to begin legal research is with a legal encyclopedia, followed by a search in the relevant statutory codes, digests, reporters, and secondary sources. When different research techniques and sources begin to turn up references to the same cases and statutes, that may be an indication your research is complete.

Key Terms

annotation
black letter law
database
Decennial Digest
Defendant/Plaintiff Table
Descriptive Word Index
digest
headnote
general Digest
hornbooks
Key Number System
law review journals
legal encyclopedia
nutshell
pocket parts
query
supplement
Table of Cases Index
texts
treatise
Words and Phrases Index

Review Questions

1. Describe the digest system.
2. What is the significance of a case headnote?
3. What is the Key Number System?
4. What is a digest?
5. List the three indexes associated with the digest.
6. Name two legal encyclopedias and identify why they are helpful finding tools.
7. Distinguish the two differences between encyclopedias and *American Law Reports.*
8. Identify the advantages of using either Westlaw or LexisNexis as a finding tool.
9. What secondary sources provide analysis of legal subjects?
10. How should you begin a research project, and once you've begun, how do you know when to stop?

Exercises

1. Using *Federal Practice Digest, 4th Ed.,* find a case that defines "legal assistant" and answer the following questions:
   a. What is the name of the case?
   b. What is the citation for the case?
   c. From which state does the case originate?
   d. What year was the case decided?
   e. How did the case define "legal assistant"?
2. Locate your jurisdiction's state digest and answer the following:
   a. List the indexes that accompany the digest.
   b. How many topics are listed in your state or regional digest?
   c. Does your state digest have topics and keys? If so, where is the general list of topics located in the digest? If not, how are your state digest topics identified and where are they delineated in the digest?
3. Using a legal encyclopedia, locate the volume that discusses sexual discrimination. (Remember to start with an index.)
4. Locate an example of the following finding tools:
   a. A legal treatise
   b. A law review article
   c. An annotation from *American Law Reports*
   d. An article from your state's bar journal

5. Locate a legal treatise from the following areas:
   a. Evidence
   b. Contracts
   c. Criminal law
   d. Real property
   e. Constitutional law
6. Using a U.S. Supreme Court Digest, locate the case that decided the U.S. presidential election in 2000 and provide the complete citation for the case.
7. Find a U.S. Supreme Court case, three federal cases (from your circuit), and three state cases (from your state) that set forth the standards for statutory construction using the "plain meaning" of the language rule.
8. Using the indexes for *American Law Reports,* find an annotation(s) that discusses the "tender years" rule relating to child custody and whether a preference exists for awarding custody to the mother over the father.

PORTFOLIO ASSIGNMENT

Joe Valentine, an avid baseball card collector, went to purchase a Hank Aaron rookie card at Sports Card World in Arlington, Texas. After browsing awhile, he found what he was looking for, the Hank Aaron card. A young clerk approached Valentine asking if he could be of assistance. Valentine pointed to the Aaron card. The clerk quickly looked at the price and said that the card was $100. Valentine was surprised at the low price as he was prepared to go up to $5,000. Wasting no time, Valentine wrote Sports Card World a check and basked in his find. A day later, Valentine received a telephone call from the owner of Sports Card World. The owner was very upset that the clerk had misread the price. The real price for the card was $10,100 not $100. The store owner stated he would refund Valentine's $100 and apologized. Valentine refused the refund and stated they had a contract. Sports Card World sues Valentine. Your attorney, who represents Sports Card World, needs some research on the issues involved. Complete the following tasks:

a. Write down words and phrases that may apply to the fact pattern of the case.
b. Identify the specific procedure you would undertake to accomplish this legal research.

Quick Quiz True/False Answers

Page 195	Page 201	Page 209
1. False	1. True	1. True
2. False	2. False	2. False
3. True	3. False	3. True
4. False	4. True	4. False
5. False	5. True	5. False

Chapter 7

Updating the Law: Shepard's Citations and KeyCite

After completing this chapter, you will be able to:

- Shepardize a case.
- Determine why Shepardizing is important.
- Distinguish between Shepardizing for validation and Shepardizing for legal research.
- Understand how to use Shepard's online.
- Characterize the differences between the online Shepard's and the print version of Shepard's.
- Compare the regional and state versions of the print Shepard's Citations.
- Use the two online versions of case updating: Shepard's Citations and KeyCite.
- Discuss the different signal systems in Shepard's Citations and KeyCite.
- Assess the "treatment" of a case.
- Locate headnotes in Shepard's Citations and use them as research tools.

Now that you have learned about the many sources of the law and how to find them, you may be wondering, "How can I be sure a case I found hasn't been overruled?" This is, in fact, a very important consideration. Just because a case appears as a published opinion in a reporter doesn't mean the principles etablished in the case are still "good law" (that is, still valid precedents). The opinion may have been reversed on appeal, or a later decision by a higher court in a different case may have resolved the same legal issue in a different way, overruling the earlier decision. The solution to this concern is through the use of a **citator.** A citator is a series of print volumes or electronic services that update and validate a case or other legal resources. There is a series of print volumes known as Shepard's Citations and its online versions located on LexisNexis Shepard's online and Westlaw KeyCite. Your research is not complete unless you have checked to determine whether a case is still valid law. Although considered more challenging to use, the print version of Shepard's Citations is discussed first, with the online versions addressed later in the chapter.

citator
A series of books that both update the law and act as finding tools.

CASE FACT PATTERN

The dateline for filing the McAdams brief is tomorrow. You have completed your research and are completing your final check of the cases cited in the brief, which includes Shepardizing all your cases one last time. While Shepardizing the cases from the brief, you learn that one of the cases cited in the brief has been "questioned" by a court in your jurisdiction. You immediately contact your attorney, who is on her way home. She tells you that she is turning around and you should stay in the office. That section of the brief must be rewritten. Your attorney and you will be working through the night to revise the brief so that the case law cited is accurate. Skipping the critical step of Shepardizing can be fatal to an assignment, as our paralegal "almost" experienced. Throughout this chapter, we will explore the different methods of analyzing and validating your legal research.

VALIDATING THE LAW: WHY BOTHER?

Shepardizing
Using Shepard's verification and updating system for cases, statutes, and other legal resources.

Imagine your supervising attorney rigorously arguing a client's case, relying on a case only to learn that the case is no longer valid law. What an embarrassment! There has to be a process whereby attorneys and other legal professionals can have a reliable means to check the history and validity of cases and other sources of the law. The method is through the process of **Shepardizing.** Shepardizing provides a useful method of verifying the validity of a case, statute, or other legal source. Through Shepardizing, you can determine whether a case has been overruled, criticized, or followed by other courts; you can determine whether a statute has been ruled unconstitutional, amended, or repealed; and you can determine whether an administrative regulation is still in force. In short, Shepardizing is *the* means that you will use to confirm the validity of your legal research sources.

PRACTICE TIP

Earlier Shepard's citators did not identify the name of the case when it was first referenced. Therefore, pay close attention to your choice of Shepard's citator volume and make sure you have *all* the volumes necessary to perform a complete search.

SHEPARDIZING A CASE: WHAT IT ACCOMPLISHES

Even though Shepard's is used to validate virtually any legal resource, we will devote much of our energy to understanding Shepard's in the context of case law. The Shepard's system updates every case ever printed in every commonly used reporter. Think about that for a second. Let's say that you found a 1965 case from your jurisdiction that covers our landlord–tenant problem from Chapter 6. Without Shepard's, you would have to search through the text of every subsequent case to see if your 1965 case had been overturned. But with Shepard's, the task is greatly simplified. The Shepard's system lists every reference ever made to your case! Shepard's has two main purposes: (1) a validating tool, and (2) a researching tool. We begin with Shepard's as a validating tool.

Shepard's for Case Validation

parallel citation
A citation of a case text found in two or more reporters.

same case
A Shepard's notation representing the identical case Shepardized but from the lower court.

connected case
A Shepard's notation that either involves the same parties or arises from the same subject matter Shepardized.

The Shepard's system is primarily used to verify the precedential value or validity of a case. Of course, you do not want to reference a case that is no longer valid or whose precedent has been criticized or questioned in some manner. In addition to verification of precedential value, Shepard's can help you find parallel citations, for example, and other cases that are similar in content to the case being Shepardized.

But it is important to remember that Shepard's evaluates how your case was treated by other courts *after* it was decided. You must keep this concept in mind when performing a Shepard's review of a case. Cases dated prior to your case *cannot* mention or give an opinion of your case because your case was not in existence yet. Stop for a moment and think about that statement. Shepard's reviews cases prospectively by using your case as the starting point. To place it in historical context, *Brown v. Board of Education* overturns the precedent set forth in *Plessey v. Ferguson* that separate but equal accommodation for African Americans is acceptable. *Plessey v. Ferguson* cannot reference *Brown v. Board of Education* because it was not decided yet. Therefore, a Shepard's search evaluates your case from the date it is decided and into the future.

Now let's explore the information contained within a Shepard's entry. Not surprisingly, the Shepard's entry provides a multitude of information. We will learn how this system works by using *Bush v. Gore,* 531 U.S. 98, 121 S. Ct. 525, 148 L. Ed. 2d 388 (2000) as our first example; let's identify the different types of information located in the Shepard's citation.

Since it is a U.S. Supreme Court case, we use the Shepard's Citations for the U.S. Supreme Court, the *Supreme Court Reporter Edition.* If we were using a federal case, we could use the Shepard's citator for federal cases. There is a Shepard's citator for all the case reporters (and most other legal sources). The case is located at 121 S. Ct. 525. Shepard's identifies the volume at the top of each page, and the page is located in bold print in between two dashes. (See Figure 7.1.) This is followed by the name of the case. Directly beneath the entry are citations in parentheses. These are the **parallel citations** for the case. (Remember, this is the same case located in a different reporter.)

The parallel citation will appear only the first time the case is cited in Shepard's. This is useful information because if your case has parallel citations and no parallel citation appears beneath the entry, this means there is an earlier Shepard's volume that you missed in your process. Go back to the bookshelves and check to make sure you have the earliest volume that cited the case.

PRACTICE TIP

When you have only one citation for a case and you need to find a parallel citation, use Shepard's Citations to locate the parallel citation. (This exercise is important when your library has only one version of a case. Shepard's will assist you in finding the parallel citation so you can use an alternate reporter to locate your case.)

Following the parallel citations are the citations of the lower court opinions for the case you are Shepardizing. In effect, this is the prior history of the case. The notation "s" will appear in front of the case indicating it is the **same case.** This means that it is the same identical case you are Shepardizing, but only the lower court decision. If a case reaches the U.S. Supreme Court, you would have cases from the federal district court and the federal circuit court of appeals. Since they are the "same" case, just on appeal, an "s" would appear next to the citation. Additionally, you may see the notation "cc," which means **connected case.** This case either involves the same parties or arises from the same subject matter. You may want to examine this case.

The next groups of cases are from the same court (or jurisdiction) that cited your case. In this case, it would be the U.S. Supreme Court. (Notice that the U.S. Supreme Court has not had the occasion to cite the *Bush v. Gore* case, although quite a number of lower courts have cited the case in their decisions.) The next entries are from the federal courts (appeals and district courts) followed by the state courts. Any cases that cited your case will appear in the Shepard's columns. (See Figure 7.1.) As is evident from Figure 7.1, Shepard's separates the different jurisdictions, so if you are looking for a case from the Seventh or Eleventh Circuit Court of Appeals, it will be delineated in the Shepard's entry and labeled with the circuit number. States also are separated individually and listed alphabetically. Notice that a number of the states cited *Bush v. Gore:* Arizona, Illinois, Nevada, and New Hampshire, for example. This makes your research a bit easier as you can directly focus on your state's cases.

PRACTICE TIP

Shepard's cites to the LexisNexis online service of a newly handed-down case, slated for publication, but which has not been assigned a reporter citation. Therefore, you will observe many citations in Shepard's that have the abbreviation "LX." This is the LexisNexis case abbreviation. There will not be an equivalent Westlaw citation in Shepard's Citations, although the case would appear in Westlaw KeyCite with the citation "WL."

Additionally, the citations within the Shepard's column denote the first and second series of a reporter. Within the case citation's letters, you will notice that a small numeral is located near or above the letters (see Figure 7.1). This numeral indicates the second or third series of that reporter. It is important to pay close attention to these numerals because if you want to examine a case more closely, you may retrieve the wrong case if you have not noted the series of the reporter.

Now continue evaluating the Shepard's column and its notations. Notice all the letters next to many of the citations. These entries give you information about the case. They are divided into two main areas: history of the case and treatment of the case. Let's highlight some of the more common notations.

FIGURE 7.1 **A Page from Shepard's Citations, U.S. Supreme Court, the *Supreme Court Reporter Edition***

Source: From *The Supreme Court Reporter Edition*. Reproduced by permission of LexisNexis. Further reproduction of any kind is strictly prohibited.

Callout labels: second series of *Supreme Court Reporter*; volume of reporter; Yale Law Review; headnote 5 from *Bush v. Gore*; page where case begins; parallel citations; circuit citing *Bush v. Gore*; states citing *Bush v. Gore*; *Chicago Law Review*; *California Law Review*; *A.L.R.* entry

SUPREME COURT REPORTER **Vol. 121**

357SoC73
h) 542SE364
586SE584
590SE511
Tenn
f) 63SW63
Tex
52SW754
e) 52SW756
Wash
111WAp452
45P3d598
WVa
211WV565
567SE281
68ChL1459
69ChL1983
70ChL1203
49CLA789
50CLA143
50Geo607
115HLR2066
116HLR16
116HLR1201
117HLR2296
2001IlLR695
86MnL131
88MnL449
98NwL1179
78NYL809
80TxL1255
2001WLR527
2001WLR831

—525—
Bush v Gore
2000
(531US98)
(148LE388)
s) 121SC471
s) 121SC674
s) 772So2d1220
s) 772So2d1243
s) 773So2d524
c) 121SC673
Cir. 1
284F3d46
323F3d[1]141
373F3d227
s) 2004USDist
[LX16380
135FS2d115
156FS2d[5]51
s) 157FS2d159
Cir. 2
265F3d[1]123
336F3d[1]119
24Fed Appx23
2003USDist
[LX21474
160FS2d497
216FS2d186
d) 216FS2d188
217FS2d361
283FS2d607
Cir. 3
j) 241F3d319
d) 2003USDist
[LX25569
Cir. 4
153FS2d789
Cir. 6
259F3d546
17Fed Appx
[273
37Fed Appx
[770
d) 154FS2d
[1202
181FS2d867
Cir. 7
183FS2d1103
f) 209FS2d898
209FS2d[2]898
209FS2d[5]898
Cir. 8
247F3d866
j) 247F3d891
Cir. 9
j) 248F3d873
249F3d951
249F3d[2]953
250F3d709
j) 283F3d996
342F3d[1]1077
342F3d[2]1077
343F3d1203
344F3d894
f) 344F3d895
344F3d917
347F3d1106
174FS2d1067
213FS2d1108
213FS2d[5]1109
215FS2d[5]1116
235FS2d[6]1081
e) 278FS2d1140
284FS2d1245
d) 284FS2d
[1247
Cir. 10
d) 279F3d1213
Ariz
200Az491
28P3d953
Ark
350Ark542
98SW799
Conn
48CS536
Fla
790So2d512
817So2d832
870So2d961
Ill
334IlA1019
d) 334IlA1022
779NE392
d) 779NE395
La
j) 812So2d904
Md
370Md319
850A2d296
Minn
j) 659NW735
Miss
833So2d584
Nev
j) 118NVAdv60
j) 53P3d395
N H
~f) 149NH116
~) 149NH116
~f) 816A2d1031
~) 816A2d1031
N J
19NJT301
N Y
187NYM2d660
722NYS2d717
Okla
d) 51P3d1210
Ore
186OrA256
e) 186OrA257
62P3d845
e) 62P3d846
Pa
j) 839A2d462
Tex
~) 70SW353
80SW660
Utah
54P3d1092
WVa
210WV494
558SE294
Wis
257Wis2d719
d) 257Wis2d
[720
d) 258Wis2d
[482
d) 264Wis2d
[180
652NW432
d) 652NW433
d) 654NW450
d) 667NW329
89CaL1165
89CaL1721
90CaL211
90CaL485
90CaL611
90CaL765
90CaL1541
90CaL1739
91CaL1
91CaL439
91CaL705
91Cal1209
92CaL927
68ChL613
68ChL637
68ChL657
68ChL679
68ChL695
68ChL719
68ChL737
68ChL775
68ChL1089
69ChL1
70ChL55
70ChL159
49CLA1
49CLA1553
51CLA705
86Cor1257
101CR274
101CR1998
101CR2033
102CR237
103CR243
103CR350
103CR1919
104CR837
104CR1150
89Geo2063
89Geo2181
90Geo113
90Geo173
90Geo199
90Geo215
90Geo779
90Geo2087
114HLR1457
114HLR2170
114HLR2502
115HLR1119
115HLR1314
115HLR1939
116HLR16
116HLR163
116HLR593
116HLR649
116HLR684
116HLR2487
117HLR4
117HLR647
117HLR2023
117HLR2731
2001IlLR1135
2001IlLR1159
2003IlLR183
65LCP(3)7
65LCP(3)11
65LCP(3)41
65LCP(3)66
65LCP(3)74
65LCP(3)79
65LCP(3)106
99McL1279
99McL1298
100McL80
100McL1506
100McL2008
101McL80
101McL1733
101McL2084
101McL2103
101McL2341
101McL2409
101McL2565
101McL2677
102McL213
85MnL1729
86MnL131
86MnL227
95NwL907
96NwL191
96NwL283
76NYL750
76NYL1383
77NYL625
77NYL867
78NYL875
149PaL711
149PaL1361
150PaL245
152PaL1697
53StnL1077
54StnL163
56StnL75
56StnL429
56StnL1147
80TxL137
80TxL703
80TxL1057
81TxL1091
81TxL1551
81TxL1985
87VaL1045
87VaL1111
87VaL1619
88VaL789
88VaL951
88VaL1301
89VaL979
89VaL1105
89VaL1463
90VaL551
90VaL1093
2001WLR1493
110YLJ829
110YLJ947
110YLJ1407
111YLJ223
111YLJ399
111YLJ1141
112YLJ153
112YLJ925
113YLJ1801
148LE1089n
1481LE1103n
103A5422n

—675—
Solid Waste
Agency v
United States
Army Crops of
Eng'rs
2001
(531US159)
(148LE576)
s) 191F3d845
s) 248F3d1159
s) 6Fed Appx
[364
s) 998FS946
124SC1212
~) 124SC1643
Cir. 1
322F3d[1]67
257FS2d[4]384
257FS2d[6]384
d) 257FS2d385
257FS2d[5]385
Cir. 2
343F3d86
47Fed Appx67
2004USDist
[LX12273
2004USDist
[LX12816
132FS2d[7]266
136FS2d[3]119
186FS2d[1]240
Cir. 3
182FS2d383
d) 182FS2d384
e) 239FS2d513
f) 239FS2d516
e) 239FS2D[5]516
Cir. 4
281F3d441
332F3d[3]703
e) 332F3d711
344F3d410
e) 344F3d415
39Fed Appx
[871
d) 39Fed Appx
[872
e) 39Fed Appx
[874
f) 152FS2d[3]845
d) 152FS2d848
195FS2d757
195FS2d[1]764
195FS2d[3]764
195FS2d[4]764
195FS2d[5]765
f) 195FS2d768
e) 222FS2D785
222FS2d[1]785
e) 278FS2d670
281FS2d832
Cir. 5
250F3d268
252F3d[7]422
325F3d[5]660
326F3d633
f) 326F3d634
f) 354F3d345
354F3d[7]346
j) 362F3d287
2004USDist
[LX13354
d) 169FS2d659
279BRW517
f) 279BRW[4]518
Cir. 6
2004USApp
[LX15354
339F3d448
339F3d[3]450
c) 339F3d[3]453
369F3d514
16Fed Appx
[345

[text omitted]

History of the Case

As previously mentioned, the history of the case is important to your analysis of the case you are Shepardizing. Figure 7.2 provides the listing of the abbreviations used for the history of a case. For example, a notation of "r" means the case was reversed. Of course, you should reconsider using the case if the court reversed the case you are Shepardizing. Similarly, if you see the notation "v," signifying the court case referenced vacated the decision of the case you are Shepardizing, you should give serious thought to whether to use the case or look for a case that considers the same legal principles you need but has a positive history. If a case is reversed or vacated, you need to pay closer attention to that case, reviewing its content to determine the court's treatment of the case.

Treatment of the Case

The manner in which a court interprets or evaluates your case is important for a number of reasons. You want to locate a case with a **positive treatment.** This means the court that cited your case gave your case favorable analysis. Consequently, if you see an "f" next to a case, the court that cited your case followed its reasoning and used it as authoritative. Cases with an "f' next to them are cases you want to explore further. A case that has a "p" next to it stands for parallel case and may be one to review. These cases may be ones that closely relate to the case you are Shepardizing, as the law and facts are similar to the one in your case. The notations are good to review as these cases may offer support to the issue you are researching. Similarly, notations to pay close attention to are ones with a **negative treatment.** Notations such as "c," criticized; "q," questioned; or worse yet, "o," overruled should give you pause when Shepardizing your case. Simply stated: think twice about using the case. These notations are a warning. Other notations to pay particular attention to are "ca," conflicting authority, and "op," overruled in part. Review the case closely to determine whether you want to reconsider its use. Many notations, such as "e," explained; "d," distinguished;

positive treatment
A treatment suggesting that the case Shepardized is cited as authoritative by a court.

negative treatment
A treatment meaning that the case Shepardized has been criticized, restricted, or overruled in some manner by a court.

FIGURE 7.2
Shepard's Citations Listing of Abbreviations for the History of a Case

Source: From *Shepard's.* Reproduced by permission of LexisNexis. Further reproduction of any kind is strictly prohibited.

CASE ANALYSIS—ABBREVIATIONS

HISTORY OF CASES

cc	(connected case)	The citing case is related to the case you are *Shepardizing,* arising out of the same subject matter or involving the same parties.
m	(modified)	On appeal, reconsideration or rehearing, the citing case modifies or changes in some way, including affirmance in part and reversal in part, the case you are *Shepardizing.*
r	(reversed)	On appeal, reconsideration or rehearing, the citing case reverses the case you are *Shepardizing.*
s	(same case)	The citing case involves the same litigation as the case you are *Shepardizing,* but at a different stage of the proceedings.
S	(superseded)	On appeal, reconsideration or rehearing, the citing case supersedes or is substituted for the case you are *Shepardizing.*
US reh den	(Rehearing Denied)	The citing order by the United States Supreme Court denies rehearing in the case you are *Shepardizing.*
US reh dis	(Rehearing Dismissed)	The citing order by the United States Supreme Court dismisses rehearing in the case you are *Shepardizing.*
v	(vacated)	The citing case vacates or withdraws the case you are Shepardizing.

"h," harmonized; or "L," limited, should be reviewed to determine whether the case will be helpful to your assignment.

Two notations indicate that your case was cited in a dissenting or concurring opinion. They are denoted with a "j" for dissenting opinion. What this actually means varies from opinion to opinion. If you are concerned, pull the case for review. And the notation for a concurring opinion is "~." Again, how this affects your case is determined by how the court treated your case. Once again, simply retrieve the case and read its content if you are interested in the case. Figure 7.3 provides the notations for the treatment of cases in Shepard's Citations.

Learning these notations is helpful as it will make your Shepardizing easier. However, it is a bit daunting to memorize all the notations. Consequently, in the beginning

FIGURE 7.3
Notations in Shepard's Citations for the Treatment of Cases

Source: From *Shepard's*. Reproduced by permission of LexisNexis. Further reproduction of any kind is strictly prohibited.

CASE ANALYSIS—ABBREVIATIONS

TREATMENT OF CASES

c	(Criticized)	The citing opinion disagrees with the reasoning/result of the case you are *Shepardizing,* although the citing court may not have the authority to materially affect its precedential value.
ca	(Conflicting Authorities)	Among conflicting authorities as noted in cited case.
d	(Distinguished)	The citing case differs from the case you are *Shepardizing,* either involving dissimilar facts or requiring a different application of the law.
e	(Explained)	The citing opinion interprets or clarifies the case you are *Shepardizing* in a significant way.
Ex	(Examiner's Decision)	The examiner's decision cites the case you are *Shepardizing.*
f	(Followed)	The citing opinion relies on the case you are *Shepardizing* as controlling or persuasive authority.
h	(Harmonized)	The citing case differs from the case you are *Shepardizing,* but the citing court reconciles the difference or inconsistency in reaching its decision.
j	(Dissenting Opinion)	A dissenting opinion cites the case you are *Shepardizing.*
~	(Concurring Opinion)	A concurring opinion cites the case you are *Shepardizing.*
L	(Limited)	The citing opinion restricts the application of the case you are *Shepardizing,* finding its reasoning applies only in specific limited circumstances.
o	(Overruled)	The citing case expressly overrules or disapproves the case you are *Shepardizing.*
op	(Overruled in Part)	Ruling in the cited case overruled partially or on other grounds or with other qualifications.
p	(Parallel)	The citing case relies on the case you are *Shepardizing* by describing it as "on all fours" or parallel to the citing case.
q	(Questioned)	The citing opinion questions the continuing validity or precedential value of the case you are *Shepardizing* because of intervening circumstances, including judicial or legislative overruling.
su	(Superseded)	Superseded by statute as stated in cited case.

OTHER

#		The citing case is of questionable precedential value because review or rehearing has been granted by the California Supreme Court and/or the citing case has been ordered depublished pursuant to Rule 976 of the California Rules of Court. (Publication status should be verified before use of the citing case in California.)

material of the Shepard's Citations volumes you will find legends that define all the abbreviations used in the volume. Any new notations will be listed there as well. Don't be afraid to explore the front material of the book. It provides helpful hints to better understanding the Shepardizing process.

Remember that in order to perform a complete Shepard's search, you must consult all volumes that contain the case you are Shepardizing. Notice that Figure 7.1 continues the *Bush v. Gore* Shepardizing process. Observe a few things. First, the name of the case is missing. Recall that the name of the case will be cited only the first time it appears in the Shepard's Citations. Second, notice there are no parallel citations. Once again, you will see the parallel citations only in the first volume that cites the citation. And finally, there is a supplement that cited more entries for the *Bush v. Gore* case. At the time of the writing of this text, three volumes were consulted to perform a complete Shepard's search. As years pass and the *Bush v. Gore* decision is cited by the courts, additional entries and volumes will need to be consulted. Therefore, it bears repeating: Check all available Shepard's volumes.

PRACTICE TIP

For those in California, Shepard's lists a notation for cases of "questionable precedential value." The notation to look out for is a number sign, "#." This may mean that the case listed was ordered to be **depublished**. This is unique to California, however.

depublished opinion
Opinion that was originally set for publication by a California court but later ordered unpublished.

Organization of a Shepard's Citations Set: The Colors of Supplements Have Meaning

Shepard's Citations are multivolume sets. The age of your case will dictate how many Shepard's volumes you have to consult. Let's continue with our U.S. Supreme Court case *Bush v. Gore.* (Note: The volumes identified were those at the time of this writing. The editions of Shepard's do change. Simply remember to look for the earliest volume that reports the case you are Shepardizing.) The first time the case appears in a hardbound maroon-colored volume is the eighth edition 2004, where volumes 108 through 124 appear. Then there is a hardbound maroon-colored supplement volume for the years 2004 through 2006, for cases from volumes 1 through 126. At the end of the hardbound volumes are different-colored softbound supplements. These are the most recent additions to that Shepard's set. Each colored supplement represents a period in time. The yellow-colored supplements are the yearly compilations (and sometimes multiple years). The next colors you will see are red-colored supplements, which update the yellow supplements. This is the case with *Bush v. Gore,* at least at the writing of this text. A red softbound volume, dated March 2007, was at the end of the *U.S. Supreme Court Reporter's* Shepard's Citations. It needed to be checked for completeness. And finally, there are light blue supplements, which update the red supplements. Had the Shepard's search commenced in May, there would be a light blue supplement to review as well.

PRACTICE TIP

Shepard's consolidates its supplements regularly. Otherwise you would be reviewing countless paper supplements.

You must be wondering which supplements you need to check to completely Shepardize a case. The answer is *all* the softbound volumes, as each covers a different time period. One of the problems with Shepard's print versions is that they are updated monthly at best, and therefore results may change for a given case that you are Shepardizing. There are a couple of options for completeness. First, there is an 800 telephone number to call for updates. Second, if you have access to an online service at your firm or place of business, use the service. Finally, if you do not have access to the online service through your place of work, you can pay a fee to either LexisNexis or Westlaw to verify and update the case or cases you need.

PRACTICE TIP

Always review the cover of the most recent Shepard's supplement to establish in the "What Your Library Should Contain" section, the listing of the necessary volumes and supplements, to perform a complete Shepard's review.

Now, we will test our understanding of the Shepardizing process, and the easiest way to demonstrate the system is by example. Remember our landlord–tenant case from Chapter 6, *Young v. District of Columbia?* Let's Shepardize it. We won't do a full search, because by the time this book gets to print the search will already be incomplete. But you'll understand the basic principles even through our partial search.

Figure 7.4 is a page from *Shepard's Atlantic Reporter Citations.* Highlighted are the notations for "752," "A.2d," and "138," which correspond to the citation for our case.

FIGURE 7.4 **Page from *Shepard's Atlantic Reporter Citations***

Source: From *Shepard's Atlantic Reporter Citations.* Reproduced by permission of LexisNexis. Further reproduction of any kind is strictly prohibited.

volume of case — **Vol. 752** **ATLANTIC REPORTER, 2d SERIES**

page where case begins — —38—

name of case — Havill v Woodstock Soapstone Co.

case followed — f 733NE151

headnote reference — 807A2d[6]626

[text omitted] **—38—** In re Tucker 2000 (170Vt663) **—38—** Havill v Woodstock Soapstone Co. 2000 (170Vt663) **—38—** In re Green Mt. Power Corp. 2000 (170Vt663) **—38—** In re Towne 2000 (170Vt663) s 749A2d1142	767A2d775 767A2d[11]781 769A2d703 772A2d[2]565 772A2d[3]565 773A2d337 775A2d361 787A2d[12]585 792A2d[12]898 f 804A2d[6]800 820A2d[7]1048 857A2d873 Mass f 733NE151 **—49—** State v Andrews 2000 (253Ct497) s 729A2d232 s 733A2d234 767A2d715 e 767A2d716	851A2d390 **—65—** Fenton v Con- necticut Hosp. Ass'n Workers' Compensation Trust 2000 (58CtA45) **Cert den** 759A2d504 782A2d[12]1285 820A2d[9]290 **—77—** Pender v Matranga 2000 (58CtA19) 759A2d[14]1039 759A2d[15]1039 759A2d[16]1039 783A2d[12]1243 800A2d559 806A2d[11]579	f 857A2d970 **—102—** Decorso v. Watchtower Bible & Tract Soc'y v Watchtower Bible & Tract Soc'y of N.Y. 2000 (46CS386) **—112—** Fike v Ruger 2000 s 754A2d254 f 2002DelCh LX [31 f 2002DelCh LX [118 2002DelCh LX [136 2003DelCh LX [59	[11 2002DelCh LX [21 802A2d[3]291 **—138—** Young v Dis- trict of Colum- bia 2000 829A2d512 f 829A2d515 856A2d1109 **—147—** Flocco v State Farm Mut. Auto. Ins. Co. 2000 cc 520US681 cc 137LE945 cc 117SC1636 cc 161F3d528 cc 990FS657 755A2d[3]1050 779A2d[13]270	f 772A2d862 Cir. 1 2003USDist [LX5377 Wash ~ 29P3d758 **—194—** Largay v Largay 2000 (2000ME108) 778A2d[5]360 778A2d[7]360 j 778A2d363 791A2d[6]109 791A2d[7]110 807A2d[6]626 817A2d[6]870 818A2d[2]1009 818A2d[2]1031 821A2d[9]19 827A2d[1]822 832A2d[2]763 832A2d[5]764

PRACTICE TIP

Shepard's Citations cite to where your case appears in the referenced case. The case identified in 829 A.2d 515 actually begins on page 511. Simply turn to the beginning of the case in the reporter for the correct page, or check the top of the page for the citation.

We've located the correct Shepard's set, found the reference to volume 752 of the second series, and found the reference to page 138 of that volume. Turning to the entry under the 138 notation, we find a citation to another case, 829 A.2d 515. Figure 7.5 is page 515 from volume 829 of the second series of the *Atlantic Reporter*. Sure enough, there is a reference to our case!

A DAY IN THE LIFE OF A PARALEGAL

Assignments and deadlines have piled up. You have to finish the brief you were assigned to prepare for a court hearing tomorrow and jump right into drafting the internal memorandum of law your supervising attorney needs for a client conference the day after. The brief for the hearing is finished except that you do not have the time to Shepardize all the cases cited. That won't matter, because you know that all the cases and statutes you cited are still valid. You are going to chance it as you don't have the time to do everything. At the hearing the next day, the other attorney points out to the judge that the statute that you relied upon in your brief was repealed a year ago. Your attorney has no explanation to the court other than sheer oversight. She is angry because she trusted your research and work. The court reminds your attorney of a quote from a case he likes to cite, *Meadowbrook, LLC v. Flower,* 959 P.2d 115 (Utah 1998), which states in an obscure footnote: "The process of 'Shepardizing' a case is fundamental to legal research and can be completed in a manner of minutes, especially when done with the aid of computer. Though we do not consider counsel's actions to be egregious in this case, we admonish all attorneys to ensure the validity of all cases presented before this court." *Id.* at 120. The judge did not sanction your supervising attorney, but she was embarrassed nonetheless. She calls you from her car and is furious. You lie and tell her you Shepardized the cases and statutes, but you must have missed that one. Since she didn't get sanctioned, she does not fire you, but the damage is done. There will be no next time.

This fact scenario is not unusual. We all get busy and overwhelmed, but there is an obvious lesson to learn. No matter how long it takes, Shepardize all your sources you are citing in any legal document you present to your supervising attorney. If you fail to Shepardize, it may cost your attorney a case, sanctions, embarrassment, and worst of all, it may cost you your job. You should not only take the time, but *make* the time to Shepardize.

FIGURE 7.5 **Citation to Another D.C.-Referenced Case**

Source: From *Shepard's Atlantic Reporter Citations*. Reproduced by permission of LexisNexis. Further reproduction of any kind is strictly prohibited.

page cited in Shepard's

WILSON v. HART D.C. 515

Cite as 829 A.2d 511 (D.C. 2003)

See, e.g., Hogue v. Hopper, supra (arbitrator's determination that Hogue had failed the show error in tax return entitling him to added partnership payout collaterally estoppel claim of such error in action against accountant).[7] Thus, to the extent that appellants' suit in Superior Court against Hart and the District depends upon the establishment of a direct landlord-tenant relationship, we agree with the trial court that collateral estoppel operates to preclude recovery.[8]

Shepardized case cited in opinion

[8] The analysis, however, cannot stop there. In *Young v. District of Columbia, supra,* we held that even where a master lease prohibits the lessee from subleasing or transferring possession of the premises, an unauthorized sublessee has a sufficient interest in the property to prohibit the use of self-help for an eviction, at least by the sublessor.[9] Such a sublessor-sublessee relationship gives rise to a sufficient tenancy to require court process to remove an occupant from the premises. Where there is a genuine issue of material fact as to whether there was a subtenancy, summary judgment is inappropriate as the potential subtenants may have had a right of action arising out of their removal by self-help. *Id.*

Here, appellants and Hart are in sharp dispute as to exactly what transpired in connection with appellants' occupancy of the property and the role of Bey. The hearing examiner apparently considered it sufficient for purposes of the agency proceeding to determine that no direct landlord-tenant relationship existed between appellants and Hart. However this may be in the context of agency relief, *Young* establishes that wrongful eviction may lie in the case of a sublessee. It is true that in the complaint and an affidavit to support the opposition to summary judgment, appellants asserted that their "agreement to rent the subject premises was with Mr. Hart directly and not with Mr. Bey." But in the opposition itself, appellants listed as material matters in dispute "whether plaintiffs entered into a lease agreement with Bey to lease the premises" and "whether the hearing examiner determined in his final decision that no subtenancy was created between plaintiffs and

[text omitted]

7. *Clay v. Faison 583* A.2d 1388 (D.C.1990), relied on by appellants, does not dictate otherwise. There the prior dismissal was determined to be one based on a lack of jurisdiction since the action should have been brought in another division of the court (as contrasted with the alternate ground of failure to state a claim, rather more akin to the ruling of the hearing examiner here).

8. The fact that an issue determination is made in connection with a different underlying claim does not preclude collateral estoppel effect. *Johnson v. Capital City Mortgage Corp.,* 723 A.2d 852, 857 (D.C.1999) (citing Carr v. Rose, supra, 701 A.2d at 1076.)

9. *Young* was an application of the rule in this jurisdiction that a landlord may not use self-help to evict a tenant, first established in *Mendes v. Johnson,* 389 A.2d 781 (D.C.1978) (en banc). In *Young,* the self-help eviction was brought about by the sublessor at the landlord's insistence, even though the master lease had terminated, since the sublessor had the responsibility to see that the sublessee vacated the premises in order to surrender them to the landlord. 752 A.2d at 142. We expressly left open the question as to the master lessor's eviction rights directly against the sublessee. 752 A.2d at 143 n. 8. In the absence of any clear factual determination as to the precise status of appellants' occupancy of the property, we do not address that issue here nor the issue whether a wrongful eviction or breach of quiet enjoyment action may lie even if appellants' occupancy constituted something less than some sort of tenancy. See *Harkins v. WIN Corp.,* 771 A.2d 1025, 1027, *modified and rehearing denied,* 777 A.2d 800 (D.C.2001) (protection against self-help evictions generally not available to roomer or lodger); *Bown v. Hamilton,* 601 A.2d 1074, 1077 (D.C.1992) (quiet enjoyment is a covenant implied in leases).

This reference did not overturn our case. However, suppose a higher court had overturned it? What then? The Shepard's system would place a small "o" in the margin by the entry, which stands for *overruled.* Remember that the Shepard's system employs a whole series of marginal abbreviations (listed in Figures 7.2 and 7.3), which summarize the direct procedural history and subsequent treatment of the case. The absence of a

PRACTICE TIP

If you Shepardize a case through all the available supplements and it does not appear, do not worry. All this means is that the case you are Shepardizing has not been cited by any court recently. Do not read anything into the absence of your case appearing in a supplement.

marginal abbreviation next to the referenced case is an indication that, although the case was cited, it was not cited for any of the significant reasons requiring marginal notation. Our case has an "f" next to it, which means that the court citing the case followed our case. This reference indicates positive treatment, and this is the type of case you may want to review. Scan the page reprinted in Figure 7.4 and find as many marginal notations as you can. Then use Figure 7.3 to find out what each one means.

You might be saying to yourself, "Why bother with the marginal notations? Why not just look up every case in which your case is cited? After all, for *Young v. District of Columbia* there was only one case to look up." For the answer to this question, refer back to our *Bush v. Gore* case that was just decided in 2000 and observe all the references thus far!

Shepardizing for Research

Shepard's can be used as a legal research tool. Within the lists of entries of the case you are Shepardizing, there are a number of entries that can lead you to other related cases. The Shepard's entry may include case headnotes, *American Law Reports* annotations, and law review articles. Each can provide significant information.

Headnotes

The level of specificity provided in the Shepard's entries goes even further. Suppose the case you are Shepardizing has a number of headnotes that identify points of law you are interested in researching. You can narrow your search by focusing on a headnote and locate cases that discussed that point of law. The case you are Shepardizing is our first example, *Bush v. Gore,* with the first pages shown in Figure 7.6; the point of law that interests you is headnote 5 (see Figure 7.1). When you review the Shepard's entries, you notice a small numeral (or a number of superscripts) with the number 5. That's the headnote you are interested in reviewing. Now, you can check each case with the headnote notation 5 to see if any of the cases will be helpful to your research. This point bears repeating—the superscript number is the headnote reference from the case you are Shepardizing. When the superscript is referenced, it is the same point of law found in your case. Retrieve the case and review it. It may be helpful.

PRACTICE TIP

Often the Shepard's entry will cite the same case in multiple circumstances. You can tell if the case cited is the same because the citations are similar (for example, the page numbers are close in proximity). This suggests that the case located in the Shepard's column has multiple entries that may relate to the legal issue you are researching; this case may be one to consider reviewing more closely.

American Law Reports

Recall from Chapter 6 that *American Law Reports* (*A.L.R.*) annotations are exhaustive commentaries on selected areas of the law. Shepard's also identifies *American Law Reports* annotations that have cited your case. This will lead you to annotations that have cited the case you are Shepardizing. Shepard's often will cite the *A.L.R.* with an "n" or an "s" next to the entry. The "n" next to an *A.L.R.* entry signifies that the case has been cited in an annotation, and an "s" signifies the case was cited in the supplement. In our example, the last entry in Figure 7.1 is an *A.L.R.* annotation. The superscript indicates a number 5, which means the annotation is found in the fifth series of *American Law Reports.* If Shepard's cites an *A.L.R.* annotation, chances are this is an annotation you would want to review. But there is a small caveat to keep in mind: The *A.L.R.* citation in Shepard's is where your case appears within the *A.L.R.* annotation and *not* where the annotation begins. You will have to leaf through the pages to locate the beginning of the annotation and then decide whether a close review is warranted.

Other Legal Sources Cited in Shepard's

Depending on the Shepard's citator you are using, you may find sources such as attorney general opinions and law review articles. Attorney general opinions can be useful for state-specific assignments and situations where there is a dearth of case law. But remember that attorney general opinions are secondary sources and subsequent cases will supersede the opinion. Additionally, law review articles can be valuable, since they can lead you to a plethora of sources that cases may not reveal. Notice

FIGURE 7.6 **Case pages from *Bush v. Gore* with Headnote References**

Source: From *Shepard's*. Reproduced by permission of LexisNexis. Further reproduction of any kind is strictly prohibited.

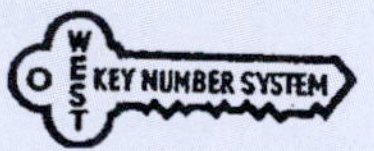

531 U.S. 98, 148 L.Ed.2d 388

⌊98**George W. BUSH, et al., Petitioners,**

v.

Albert GORE, Jr., et al.
No. 00-949.

Dec. 12, 2000.

Democratic candidates for President and Vice President of the United States filed complaint contesting certification of state results in presidential election. The Circuit Court, Leon County, N. Sanders Sauls, J., entered judgment denying all relief, and candidates appealed. The District Court of Appeal certified the matter to the Florida Supreme Court. On review, the Florida Supreme Court, 772 So.2d 1243, ordered manual recounts of ballots on which machines had failed to detect vote for President. Republican candidates filed emergency application for stay of Florida Supreme Court's mandate. The United States Supreme Court, 531 U.S. 1046, 121 S. Ct. 512, 148 L.Ed.2d 553, granted application, treating it as petition for writ of certiorari, and granted certiorari. The Supreme Court held that: (1) manual recounts ordered by Florida Supreme Court, without specific standards to implement its order to discern "intent of the voter," did not satisfy minimum requirement for non-arbitrary treatment of voters necessary, under Equal Protection Clause, to secure fundamental right to vote for President, and (2) remand of case to Florida Supreme Court for it to order constitutionally proper contest would not be appropriate remedy.

Reversed and remanded.

Chief Justice Rehnquist filed concurring opinion in which Justices Scalia and Thomas joined.

Justice Stevens filed dissenting opinion in which Justices Ginsburg and Breyer joined.

Justice Souter filed dissenting opinion in which Justice Breyer joined and Justices Stevens and Ginsburg joined in part.

Justice Ginsburg filed dissenting opinion in which Justice Stevens joined and Justices Souter and Breyer joined in part.

Justice Breyer filed dissenting opinion in which Justices Stevens and Ginsburg joined in part, and in which Justice Souter also joined in part.

1. United States ⚷25

The individual citizen has no federal constitutional right to vote for electors for President of the United States unless· and until state legislature chooses statewide election as means to implement its power to appoint members of Electoral College. U.S.C.A. Const. Art. 2, § 1, cl. 2.

2. Elections ⚷10

When state legislature vests right to vote for President in its people, the right to vote as legislature has prescribed is fundamental, and one source of its fundamental nature lies in the equal weight accorded to each vote and equal dignity owed to each voter. U.S.C.A. Const. Art. 2, § 1; Art. 2, cl. 2.

3. United States ⚷25

The State, after granting individual citizens the right to vote for electors for the President of the United States, can take back the power to appoint electors. U.S.C.A. Const. Art. 2, § 1, cl, 2.

4. Constitutional Law ⚷225.2(1)
Elections ⚷1

The right to vote is protected in more than the initial allocation of the franchise; equal protection applies as well to the manner of its exercise. U.S.C.A. Const. Amend. 14.

5. Constitutional Law ⚷225.3(1) — headnote 5 for figure 7.6

Having once granted the right to vote on equal terms, the State may not, under Equal Protection Clause, value one person's vote over that of another by later arbitrary and disparate treatment. U.S.C.A. Const.Amend. 14.

6. Elections ⚷1

Right of suffrage can be denied by debasement or dilution of weight of citizen's vote just as effectively as by wholly prohibiting free exercise of the franchise.

7. Constitutional Law ⚷225.2(6)
Elections ⚷299(.5)

Manual recounts of ballots on which machines had failed to detect vote for President, as implemented in response to Florida Supreme Court's opinion which or-

[text omitted]

that in the *Bush v. Gore* case, there are a number of law review articles that dealt with the issues in the case. Starting with the *California Law Review,* there are articles from a number of law schools including Harvard, Yale, and the University of Chicago. (See Figure 7.1.) You are asking yourself, "How will I know which school is which?" The

CYBER TRIP

Using *Bush v. Gore,* Shepardize the case and locate either an *A.L.R.* annotation or law review journal that discusses it.

PRACTICE TIP

Shepard's headnote references will not appear in recent cases that have not been published. Recall that headnotes are created by the publishers and not the courts. Newer cases that have not been editorialized do not have their assigned headnotes.

FIGURE 7.7 Shepard's Citations Abbreviations for Legal Periodicals and Journals

Source: From *Shepard's*. Reproduced by permission of LexisNexis. Further reproduction of any kind is strictly prohibited.

TABLES OF ABBREVIATIONS

A2d—Atlantic Reporter, Second Series
ADC—Appeal Cases, District of Columbia Reports
AkA—Arkansas Appellate Reports
Æ5—American Law Reports, Fifth Series
ÆRF—American Law Reports, Federal
ÆRF2d—American Law Reports Federal, Second Series
ÆRF6—American Law Reports, Sixth Series
ApDC—Court of Appeals for the District of Columbia Reports
Ark—Arkansas Reports
Az—Arizona Reports
Bankr LX—United States Bankruptcy Court & United States District Court Bankruptcy Cases LEXIS
BRW—Bankruptcy Reporter
CAAF LX—U.S. Court of Appeals for the Armed Forces LEXIS
C4th—California Supreme Court Reports, Fourth Series
CA4th—California Appellate Reports, Fourth Series
CA4S—California Appellate Reports, Fourth Series, Supplement
CaL—California Law Review
CaR2d—California Reporter, Second Series
CaR3d—California Reporter, Third Series
CCA LX—U.S. Military Courts of Criminal Appeals LEXIS
ChL—University of Chicago Law Review
CIT—United States Court of International Trade
CLA—University of California at Los Angeles Law Review
Cor—Cornell Law Review
CR—Columbia Law Review
CS—Connecticut Supplement
Ct—Connecticut Reports
CtA—Connecticut Appellate Reports
DC4d—Pennsylvania District and County Reports, Fourth Series
DPR—Decisiones de Puerto Rico
F2d—Federal Reporter, Second Series
F3d—Federal Reporter, Third Series
FCCR—Federal Communications Commission Record
Fed Appx—Federal Appendix
FedCl—Federal Claims Reporter
FRD—Federal Rules Decisions
FS—Federal Supplement
FS2d—Federal Supplement, Second Series
Ga—Georgia Reports
GaA—Georgia Appeals Reports
Geo—Georgetown Law Journal
Haw—Hawaii Reports
HLR—Harvard Law Review
Ida—Idaho Reports
Il2d—Illinois Supreme Court Reports Second Series
IlA—Illinois Appellate Court Reports, Third Series
IlCCl—Illinois Court of Claims Reports
IlLR—University of Illinois Law Review
ITS—Jurisprudencia del Tribunal Supremo de Puerto Rico
KA2d—Kansas Court of Appeals Reports, Second Series
Kan—Kansas Reports
LCP—Law and Contemporary Problems
LE—United States Supreme Court Reports, Lawyer's Edition, Second Series
MaA—Massachusetts Appeals Court Reports
MADR—Massachusetts Appellate Division Reports
Mas—Massachusetts Reports
MC—American Maritime Cases
McA—Michigan Court of Appeals Reports
Mch—Michigan Reports
McL—Michigan Law Review
Md—Maryland Reports
MdA—Maryland Appellate Reports
MJ—Military Justice Reporter
MnL—Minnesota Law Review
Mt—Montana Reports
NC—North Carolina Reports
NCA—North Carolina Court of Appeals Reports
NE—Northeastern Reporter, Second Series
Neb—Nebraska Reports
NebA—Nebraska Advance Reports
Nev—Nevada Reports
NH—New Hampshire Reports
NJ—New Jersey Reports
NJS—New Jersey Superior Court Reports
NJT—New Jersey Tax Court Reports

abbreviations of all the law schools and related periodicals are listed in the front of the Shepard's Citations volume. See Figure 7.7 for a sampling of abbreviations. Again, a word of caution is appropriate as Shepard's does not cite every law review article that cited your case. It is selective. If you are led to a law review article, you may want to expand your research to determine whether other articles dealt with your topic, using the *Index to Legal Periodicals* for a start.

ETHICS ALERT

Attorneys and paralegals have certain standards of practice to which they must conform. These standards govern our lives. When the minimum levels of legal research are not performed, the competency of the attorney, and often of the paralegal, is called into question. At best, when competency levels are not met, a court could sanction or admonish the attorney for the gross infraction, or in some cases, ignorance. However, the worst case for an attorney presents itself as malpractice. You must be wondering how incompetent legal research is akin to malpractice. When a client's life, liberty, or property are at stake, missing the obvious or failing to perform the obvious, such as Shepardizing a case, can cause the client harm. The severity of the outcome may depend upon whether a client sues for malpractice. As exhibited by the cases noted in the "You Be the Judge" sections of this chapter, a suit for actual malpractice may not be the remedy. Embarrassment by the court or loss of your job may be the result. None of these outcomes are welcomed or wanted. To avoid these ethics and competency violations, be thorough; be complete; and above all, be zealous in performing your duties as a paralegal.

Comparing the Regional Reporter and State-Specific Shepard's Citations

Many states have two sets of Shepard's Citations that validate case law: a regional reporter and a state-specific reporter. There are differences in the Shepard's citators that are important to note. Shepard's has sets for each state, the regional reporters, the *California Reporter,* and the *New York Supplement.* The state-specific Shepard's cites only that state's opinions that have cited the case as well as federal opinions from that state. Law review articles are cited in the state-specific Shepard's, including articles from that state's law reviews and the nationally recognized top law reviews, such as Harvard, Yale, and Stanford universities. As previously mentioned, state attorney general opinions from that state are included in the Shepard's entries. However, if your purpose is more global than jurisdictional, the better sets of Shepard's to use are the regional Shepard's sets as they include all jurisdictions that have cited the case you are Shepardizing.

PRACTICE TIP

There are Shepard's Citations for every set of reporters in the library. Each case must be Shepardized using the appropriate Shepard's Citations. If you are using a U.S. Supreme Court case and a Federal Reporter case, you must check *both* sets of Shepard's Citations.

There are Shepard's sets for most reporters, as well as for statutes and other publications. Although the basic system is easy to master, you should spend some time looking over the actual sets in your law library. The high volume of opinions generated by the court system has required many Shepard's sets to adopt a multivolume format that can be somewhat confusing. You must be sure you have Shepardized your case in all necessary volumes. All the information you need to assure yourself of this is printed right on the covers or bindings of the applicable Shepard's volumes, so mistakes can

YOU BE THE JUDGE

Shepardizing and validating your research should become a natural part of your research process. Not only do your supervising attorneys expect it, but the courts do as well. By Shepardizing, you will know how other courts view the case you want to cite, and this may alert you to problems with the reasoning in the case. Review *Glassalum Engineering Corp. v. 392208 Ontario Ltd.,* 487 So.2d 87 (Fla. App. 3 Dist. 1986). In this case, the attorney failed to Shepardize and cited a case that had been questioned; the attorney was ostracized by the judge in the case. Judge Pearson observed: "We remind the bar that, as this case dramatically shows, cases must be Shepardized and that when Shepardizing, counsel must mind their p's and q's." *Id.* at 88. What did the court mean by stating that the attorneys must mind their p's and q's? Had the attorneys in the case Shepardized their cases, would the result in the case be different?

TABLE 7.1
A Shepardizing Checklist

Checklist

- Locate the appropriate set of *Shepard's Citations* in the library. (The *Citations* are usually located near the set of reporters of the case you are Shepardizing.)
- Always be sure you are in the correct *Shepard's Citations.* Read the front covers of the volumes and check the time period the volume covers.
- Using your case citation from the case you want to Shepardize, isolate the volume number first in the book. The volume number will appear at the top of the page, or sometimes, within the page itself. (If there is a volume change on that page, it will clearly appear on the page and say "vol. or volume.")
- Find the corresponding page identified in bold.
- Review the citations in the listed column to determine if an "o" (overruled) is in the margin. Continue reviewing the column for other margin references that may be important to your case analysis. (If you forget what the margin references mean, check the front pages of the volume. It has the explanations of all the margin notes and abbreviations.)
- Check *all* paperbound supplements. These supplements have the most recent updates. Do not miss any. (Cautionary note: If your case does not appear in one of the softbound supplements, *do not panic.* It simply means your case has not been recently cited as a court.)

only be the result of sloppiness. Take your time and be thorough—Shepardizing is an important task, often performed by paralegals. In fact, it is inexcusable for attorneys and paralegals not to Shepardize all cited legal references. For some, the omission may be tantamount to legal malpractice. Regardless of the type of legal authority, *always, always* Shepardize. Table 7.1 provides a Shepardizing checklist.

Additional Shepard's Citators; Subject-Specific Citators

There are many other Shepard's citators that are subject-specific. There are Shepard's Citations for areas such as bankruptcy, intellectual property, insurance, immigration, education, and employment law. These sets are classified by cases directly dealing with the subject matter they cover. For example, for cases dealing with labor law issues, the federal labor law citatory is *Shepard's Labor Law Citations.* This citator solely addresses how particular cases were viewed by subsequent labor case decisions and how those decisions have been treated by other labor-related cases, such as those from the National Labor Relations Board (NLRB). These citators follow the same format and principles as other Shepard's volumes, including arranging the citations chronologically as well as updating the case information through multicolored softbound supplements. However, many libraries do not subscribe to the subject-specific Shepard's citators because of the financial costs required to maintain them.

Locating the Shepard's Citators

The Shepard's citators are usually located in three possible places in the law libraries. They are most often found at the end of the set of case reporters. You will find the Shepard's Citations for the *North Eastern Reporter* at the end of the case volumes for the *North Eastern Reporter.* Another place you may find the Shepard's Citations is in a central location in the library. Many libraries house all the Shepard's Citations in one area for easy and quick referencing. You will not have to walk all over the library to find the Shepard's citator at the end of each reporter set. And finally, you may find the Shepard's citator located behind the information or circulation desk. Since the Shepard's volumes are popular and used by everyone, many libraries keep them secluded and require you to ask to use them. They may even require you to give identification to use the volume you need. If you cannot find the Shepard's set you are looking for, remember to ask.

Quick Quiz True/False Questions

1. Shepard's Citations is used only to validate the precedential value of a case.
2. Each regional reporter has a corresponding Shepard's Citations volume.
3. Shepard's Citations updates its volumes annually.
4. Law review journals and *American Law Reports* annotations are never referenced in a Shepard's citator.
5. The Shepard's notations are insignificant when performing a search of a case.

ONLINE UPDATING: SHEPARD'S CITATIONS SERVICE

The Internet has opened the door not only to retrieving cases the day they are decided but also to updating and validating your research. The leading online services are Westlaw and LexisNexis. Both services provide quick updates and validation of your legal research, ensuring reliable coverage of your chosen cases. Each online service is addressed separately.

Shepard's Citations Service Online

Shepard's Citations Service online essentially follows the concept of the Shepard's Citations in print. However, new features have been added to make the process easier and more comprehensive. You can Shepardize a LexisNexis headnote, which assists in finding relevant research topics faster. You can pinpoint cited online references that are relevant by using the FOCUS system. Similar to the Shepard's print version, you can use Shepard's online version as a validating tool or a research tool for most legal sources. Now, let's learn how Shepard's online works.

Using Shepard's Online

Shepard's online is as easy as typing in the case citation and pressing the Enter key. The online Shepard's has two main tracks to follow, like the print version: "validation" or "for research."

Shepard's Online for Case Validation

When your main objective is to determine whether the cases you are Shepardizing are still good law, use an abbreviated process. On LexisNexis all you have to do is enter the case citation and click Shepard's for validation directly under the citation and click the KWIC button. Now, let's use a different case to illustrate our point. Using *U.S. v. Booker,* 543 U.S. 220 (2005) shown in Figure 7.8, Shepard's online reveals a number of important points. Immediately you notice a "yellow" triangle. This means that there is negative treatment about this case. The "caution" signal means just that. Carefully read the case and the cases that may have had negative comments. As you scroll down the page, notice also that many jurisdictions have cited the case and followed its reasoning. If a case has a caution note, the treatments from other courts range from being limited, criticized, modified, corrected, or clarified. You will learn its treatment by reading the case. Notice that nearly 20,000 sources have cited the *Booker* case. That's a lot of cases and secondary sources to read. Consequently, you need a way to narrow your inquiry to the jurisdiction within your research assignment. We can accomplish this through a customized search.

Click the box "Restrictions" and you will be guided through a number of possible queries, which will substantially narrow the extent of your Shepard's search. Where this becomes an important tool and useful is with a case that has a number of Shepard's citations, such as the *Booker* case. Figure 7.9 is an example of a page from LexisNexis showing the custom restriction possibilities.

FIGURE 7.8 Page from Shepard's Online Referencing *U.S. v. Booker*

Source: From Shepard's Citations Services off Shepard's Auto-Cite. Reproduced by permission of LexisNexis. Further reproduction of any kind is strictly prohibited.

Home | Sources | How Do I? | Site Map | What's New | Help

Citation: 543 U.S. 220

Restrictions: Jurisdictions: **U.S. Supreme Court**

Analysis: **Distinguished**

FOCUS™ [ ] Search Within Results

Prin

KWIC | Full

***Shepards®* - 15 Citing References**

All Negative | All Positive | Any Custom | Restrictions | Unrestricted

543 U.S. 220

Single: **Caution** - Possible negative treatment

Citation: ▲ **543 U.S. 220**

Restrictions: Jurisdictions: **U.S. Supreme Court**

Analysis: **Distinguished**

United States v. Booker, 543 U.S. 220, 125 S. Ct. 738, 160 L. Ed. 2d 621, 2005 U.S. LEXIS 628, 73 U.S.L.W 18 Fla. L. Weekly Fed. S 70

PRIOR HISTORY (14 citing references) Hide Prior History

1. United States v. Booker, 2003 U.S. Dist. LEXIS 24609 (W.D. Wis. Sept. 5, 2003)

2. **Subsequent appeal at, Remanded by:**
   United States v. Booker, 375 F.3d 508, 2004 U.S. App. LEXIS 14223 (7th Cir. Wis. 2004)

3. **Later proceeding at:**
   United States v. Booker, 542 U.S. 955, 125 S. Ct. 5, 159 L. Ed. 2d 837, 2004 U.S. LEXIS 4783, 73 U.S.L.W. 3074 (2004)

4. **Writ of certiorari granted, Motion granted by:**
   United States v. Booker, 542 U.S. 956, 125 S. Ct. 11, 159 L. Ed. 2d 838, 2004 U.S. LEXIS 4788, 73 U.S.L.W. 3074 (2004)

5. **Writ of certiorari granted, Motion granted by:**
   United States v. Fanfan, 542 U.S. 956, 125 S. Ct. 12, 159 L. Ed. 2d 838, 2004 U.S. LEXIS 4789, 73 U.S.L.W. 3074 (2004)

6. **Criticized in:**
   United States v. Hammoud, 381 F.3d 316, 2004 U.S. App. LEXIS 19036, 65 Fed. R. Evid. Serv. (CBC) 338 (4th Cir. N.C. 2004)

7. **Motion granted by, Motion denied by:**
   United States v. Booker, 542 U.S. 963, 125 S. Ct. 25, 159 L. Ed. 2d 854, 2004 U.S. LEXIS 4989, 73 U.S.L.W. 3204 (2004)

   Affirmed by, Remanded by (CITATION YOU ENTERED):
   United States v. Booker, 543 U.S. 220, 125 S. Ct. 738, 160 L. Ed. 2d 621, 2005 U.S. LEXIS 628, 73 U.S.L.W. 4056, 18 Fla. L. Weekly Fed. S 70 (2005)

FIGURE 7.9 Page from Shepard's Online with Custom Restrictions

Source: From Shepard's Online. Reproduced by permission of LexisNexis. Further reproduction of any kind is strictly prohibited.

Custom Restrictions: Tips

Citation: ▲ 543 U.S. 220

Type: Analysis, Jurisdictions, HeadNotes, Date

Check restrictions from available options, then select "View Restrictions" button to display your results.

Analyses available in FULL:

Negative:

- ☐ Criticized
- ☐ Distinguished

Positive:

- ☐ Followed

Other:

- ☐ Concurring Opinion
- ☐ Dissenting Op.
- ☐ Harmonized
- ☐ Conflict.Authority
- ☐ Explained

Jurisdictions available in FULL:

Federal:

☐ U.S. Supreme Court	☐ 4th Circuit	☐ 8th Circuit	☐ D.C. Circuit
☐ 1st Circuit	☐ 5th Circuit	☐ 9th Circuit	☐ IRS Agency Materials
☐ 2nd Circuit	☐ 6th Circuit	☐ 10th Circuit	☐ Admin. & Agency Dec.
☐ 3rd Circuit	☐ 7th Circuit	☐ 11th Circuit	☐ U.S. Tax Court

State:

☐ Alaska	☐ Iowa	☐ Montana	☐ Oregon
☐ Alabama	☐ Illinois	☐ North Carolina	☐ Pennsylvania
☐ Arizona	☐ Indiana	☐ Nebraska	☐ Puerto Rico
☐ California	☐ Kansas	☐ New Hampshire	☐ Tennessee
☐ Colorado	☐ Louisiana	☐ New Jersey	☐ Texas
☐ Connecticut	☐ Massachusetts	☐ New Mexico	☐ Utah
☐ Dist. of Columbia	☐ Maryland	☐ N. Mar. I.	☐ Virginia
☐ Delaware	☐ Maine	☐ New York	☐ Vermont
☐ Florida	☐ Michigan	☐ Ohio	☐ Washington
☐ Hawaii	☐ Minnesota	☐ Oklahoma	☐ Wisconsin

Others:

☐ Law Reviews	☐ Statutes	☐ American Law Rpts/Lawyers' Edition Annos
☐ Secondary Sources	☐ Treatises	☐ Court Documents

Headnotes available in FULL:

L. Ed. 2d: ☐ All

☐ 1

Date: No additional date restrictions ☐ 4-digit years

From: ____ To: ____ 4-digit years

View Restrictions **Undo**

Notice you can limit your inquiry to cases that followed or criticized the *Booker* case. You can limit the search further to a specific federal circuit court of appeals and then to a state within that circuit court of appeals. When the Shepard's search is performed, the search will be limited to the jurisdiction chosen and the cases that only followed or criticized the case. If you are interested in additional legal research sources that cited your case, notice at the bottom of the custom restrictions inquiry a section titled "Others," which lists both primary and secondary sources that have cited the case. If you were interested in determining whether any recent law reviews dealt with the issues presented in your case, you could tick the box "Law Reviews" and all law review articles and periodicals that have cited your case will appear.

Recall that the preceding search was a limited search; now click on Full Search and compare the results. Again, the yellow caution sign appears, but observe that the full search shows that nearly 20,000 sources have cited the Booker case. Daunting. Additionally, you can select all cases with "positive" or "negative" treatment about your case. By clicking the "all negative" entry, you will narrow your search to those cases, separated by jurisdiction. Keep in mind that you determine the extent and limitations place on your search. Likewise, if you click "all positive," those cases that gave positive treatment of the case will appear.

Shepard's Signal System

The most significant online tool of Shepard's is the Shepard's Signals. LexisNexis created a "pop-up signal legend" that identifies the type of comments that courts made about your cited case. If your case received negative treatment by a court, it is signaled by a yellow triangular flag or red stop-sign flag, indicating that the case may have been overruled. This is a change from the print version, which indicates the negative treatment of a case through an abbreviation system: o—overruled; c—criticized; q—questioned. Undoubtedly, it is easier and faster to identify the treatment of a case with Shepard's online version. You do not have to wade through volumes of books, and the updating is current. There is no lag time as with the printed version. Most cases are posted on Shepard's online within 48 hours of the case decision.

Cases with a positive treatment are signified by a diamond shape with a cross in the center. Cases with positive treatment have been followed by courts and generally have an approval of the court. And another important signal is the square with a "Q" in the middle. This signifies that the case you are Shepardizing has been questioned by courts. Again, read the case closely and determine how the court's case you are reviewing treated your case. Figure 7.10 illustrates the signal system for Shepard's Citations online.

CYBER TRIP

Shepardize *U.S. v. Booker* and determine whether your jurisdiction, federal or state, has cited the case. Has the treatment of the case been negative or positive?

Headnote Searches

Searching by headnote is available as well on Shepard's online. The headnotes will pop up in the customized search. Simply check the headnotes you are interested in viewing. The custom search will provide the cases that have cited the point in the headnote you have checked. In the *Booker* case, headnote 1 was checked along with limiting the court decisions to the Third Circuit Court of Appeals. See Figure 7.11. Cases citing and discussing headnote 1 appear in your Shepard's inquiry as shown in Figure 7.12.

FOCUS Feature

LexisNexis provides a feature that allows you to highlight search terms and phrases within your search. This feature in LexisNexis is called FOCUS. FOCUS is at the top

FIGURE 7.10 **Signal Legend for Shepard's Citations Service**

Source: From Shepard's Citations Service. Reproduced by permission of LexisNexis. Further reproduction of any kind is strictly prohibited.

Editorial Analysis

The *Shepard's*® results screen lists the citations for cases that cite your case. Each citation is preceded I following indicators:

Positive treatment — Includes the following editorial analyses:
- Affirmed
- Explained
- Followed

Negative treatment — Includes the following editorial analyses:
- Distinguished
- Overruled
- Criticized
- Questioned
- Limited
- Reversed
- Modified

Neutral treatment — Includes the following editorial analyses:
- Connected case at
- Related proceeding at

Cited by — **Cited by** indicates that the editorial staff at *Shepard's*® added no editorial analysis. **Cited by** precedes cases that acknowledge your case as precedent and may cite your case as an authority, but do not expressly revisit your case's reasoning or ruling.

The **Cited by** citing reference does not appear when you click the **Any** link.

See Custom Restrictions for more information on restricting your display to certain editorial analyses.

Shepard's Signal

Warning — Strong negative treatment indicated. Includes:
- Overruled by
- Superseded by
- Revoked
- Obsolete
- Rescinded

Q Questioned — Strong negative treatment indicated. Includes:
- Questioned by

Caution — Possible negative treatment indicated. Includes:
- Limited
- Criticized by
- Clarified
- Modified
- Corrected

Positive — Positive treatment indicated. Includes:
- Followed
- Affirmed
- Approved

A Citing References with Analysis — Other cases cited the case and assigned some analysis that is not considered positive or negative Includes:
- Appeal denied by
- Writ of certiorari denied

I Citation Information — References have not applied any analysis to the citation. For example the case was cited by law reviews, ALR® Annotations, or in other case law not warranting an analysis. Example: Cited By

FIGURE 7.11 **Page from Shepard's Online with Research Restrictions**

Analyses available in FULL: Select All Clear All

Negative: Select All Clear All

☐ Criticized (4) ☐ Distinguished (1455)

Positive:

☐ Followed (2675)

Other: Select All Clear All

☐ Concurring Opinion (98) ☐ Dissenting Op. (152) ☐ Harmonized (4)

☐ Conflict.Authority (1) ☐ Explained (320)

FOCUS Terms:

Return a list of citations to cases that contain your terms.

FOCUS HINT: The FOCUS search will only identify citing l have corresponding documents available in the LexisNexis FOCUS feature is not available if your current results contain 2000 documents.

Jurisdictions available in FULL: Select All Clear All

Federal: Select All Clear All

☐ U.S. Supreme Court (813)	☐ 5th Circuit (2326)	☐ 10th Circuit (1124)	☐ Admin. & Agency Dec. (7)
☐ 1st Circuit (442)	☐ 6th Circuit (1351)	☐ 11th Circuit (1760)	☐ U.S. Tax Court (1)
☐ 2nd Circuit (999)	☐ 7th Circuit (1194)	☐ D.C. Circuit (182)	
☑ 3rd Circuit (1166)	☐ 8th Circuit (1265)	☐ Fed. Circuit (1)	
☐ 4th Circuit (2285)	☐ 9th Circuit (1454)	☐ IRS Agency Materials (1)	

3rd Circuit is checked and will be the focus of the search

State: Select All Clear All

☐ Alaska (24)	☐ Iowa (4)	☐ Montana (2)	☐ Oregon (7)
☐ Alabama (1)	☐ Illinois (1)	☐ North Carolina (4)	☐ Pennsylvania (7)
☐ Arkansas (1)	☐ Indiana (31)	☐ Nebraska (3)	☐ Puerto Rico (4)
☐ Arizona (11)	☐ Kansas (7)	☐ New Hampshire (1)	☐ Rhode Island (1)
☐ California (1545)	☐ Kentucky (1)	☐ New Jersey (10)	☐ Tennessee (78)
☐ Colorado (9)	☐ Louisiana (7)	☐ New Mexico (7)	☐ Texas (12)
☐ Connecticut (3)	☐ Massachusetts (6)	☐ N. Mar. I. (1)	☐ Utah (1)
☐ Dist. of Columbia (2)	☐ Maryland (2)	☐ Nevada (1)	☐ Virginia (8)
☐ Delaware (4)	☐ Maine (8)	☐ New York (12)	☐ Vermont (3)
☐ Florida (13)	☐ Michigan (99)	☐ Ohio (538)	☐ Washington (13)
☐ Hawaii (5)	☐ Minnesota (25)	☐ Oklahoma (1)	☐ Wisconsin (8)

Others: Select All Clear All

☐ Law Reviews (738)	☐ Statutes (53)	☐ Annotations (1)
☐ Secondary Sources (1)	☐ Treatises (196)	☐ Court Documents (135)

cases that have discussed or mentioned headnote 1 will appear

---

Headnotes available in FULL:

number of times headnote referenced

LexisNexis [Show full text of headnotes]: Select All Clear All

☑ *HN1* (2699)	☐ *HN8* (2405)	☐ *HN15* (2696)	☐ *HN22* (1)	☐ *HN29* (163)	☐ *HN36* (9848) ☐
☐ *HN2* (936)	☐ *HN9* (243)	☐ *HN16* (8)	☐ *HN23* (2440)	☐ *HN30* (131)	☐ *HN38* (1860) ☐
☐ *HN3* (54)	☐ *HN10* (447)	☐ *HN17* (263)	☐ *HN24* (6876)	☐ *HN31* (8)	☐ *HN39* (1647)
☐ *HN4* (88)	☐ *HN11* (1077)	☐ *HN18* (44)	☐ *HN25* (8750)	☐ *HN32* (5502)	☐ *HN40* (3877)
☐ *HN5* (709)	☐ *HN12* (7)	☐ *HN19* (10)	☐ *HN26* (7)	☐ *HN33* (4069)	☐ *HN41* (4973)
☐ *HN6* (217)	☐ *HN13* (33)	☐ *HN20* (41)	☐ *HN27* (1)	☐ *HN34* (2706)	☐ *HN42* (6098)
☐ *HN7* (988)	☐ *HN14* (6912)	☐ *HN21* (354)	☐ *HN28* (73)	☐ *HN35* (832)	☐ *HN43* (1128)

L. Ed. 2d: Select All Clear All

☐ 1 ☐ 6 ☐ 10 ☐ 21

Dates: ◉ No additional date restrictions ▾ [ ] (4-digit year)

○ From: [ ] To: [ ] (4-digit years)

FIGURE 7.12 Page from Shepard's Online showing search results with restrictions

Source: From Shepard's Online. Reproduced by permission of LexisNexis. Further reproduction of any kind is strictly prohibited.

LexisNexis *Total Research System*

Switch Client | Preferences | Sign Off | ? Help

My Lexis™ | Search | Research Tasks | Get a Document | *Shepard's*® | Alerts | Total Litigator | Counsel seloc's

Signal. △ Caution. Possible negative treatment
Trail: Unrestricted > Restrict By: 3rd Circuit, LexisNexis HN1 (Edit.)

United States v. Booker, 543 U.S. 220, 125 S. Ct. 738, 160 L. Ed. 2d 621, 2005 U.S. LEXIS 628
73 U.S.L.W. 4056, 18 Fla. L. Weekly Fed. S 70 (2005)

SHEPARD'S SUMMARY Hide Summary

Restricted *Shepard's* Summary: 3rd Circuit; LexisNexis HN1

Subsequent appellate history contains possible negative analysis.

Citing References:

Cautionary Analyses:	**Distinguished (45)**
Positive Analyses:	Followed (39), Concurring Opinion (2)
Neutral Analyses:	Dissenting Op. (7), Explained (13)
LexisNexis Headnotes:	HN1 (164), HN2 (24), HN3 (2), HN4 (1) HN5 (16), HN6 (3), HN7 (30), HN8 (29), HN10 (7), HN11 (32), HN14 (123), HN15 (41), HN1 (14), HN18 (2), HN20 (2), HN21 (4), HN23 (50), HN24 (147), HN25 (130), HN28 (1), HN29 (4), HN30 (3), HN31 (2), HN32 (87), HN33 (58), HN34 (34), HN35 (18), HN36 (106), HN38 (21), HN39 (24), HN40 (78), HN41 (66), HN42 (74), HN43 (14), HN45 (22)

Show All text of headnotes

△ Show Unrestricted Summary

[text omitted]

CITING DECISIONS (164 citing decisions)

3RD CIRCUIT - COURT OF APPEALS

☐ **18. Cited in Dissenting Opinion at:**

United States v. Ricks, 506 F. 3d 281, 2007 U.S. App. LEXIS 24947 (3d Cir. 2007) LexisNexis Headnotes HN1, HN11, HN14, HN24, HN25, HN32, HN33, HN36, HN41, HN42

2007 U.S. App. LEXIS 24742

☐ **19. Cited in Dissenting Opinion at:**

United States v. Ricks, 2007 U.S. App. LEXIS 24742 (3d Cir. Oct. 22, 2007) LexisNexis Headnotes HN1, HN11, HN14, HN24, HN25, HN32, HN33, HN36, HN41, HN42

2007 U.S. App. LEXIS 24742

☐ **20. Cited by:**

United States v. Townsend, 2007 U.S. App. LEXIS 22775 (3d Cir. Pa. Sept. 26, 2007) LexisNexis Headnotes HN1, HN11, HN15, HN24, HN25, HN33, HN41, HN42

2007 U.S. App. LEXIS 22775

☐ **21. Followed by, Followed in Concurring Opinion at, Cited by:**

United States v. Fisher, 502 F. 3d 293, 2007 U.S. App. LEXIS 21649 (3d Cir. Del. 2007) LexisNexis Headnotes HN1, HN24, HN25, HN32, HN33, HN34, HN36, HN38, HN39, HN41, HN41.

Followed by:
502 F.3d 293 p.305

Followed Concurring Opinion at:
502 F.3d 293 p.311

Cited by:
502 F.3d 293 p.295

corner of the page with a corresponding text box. Type in the words, terms, or phrases you want to "focus" on and click. The search will then display the terms you entered in bold if they are present in the case or document on which you are performing a FOCUS search. The more terms highlighted in bold in a document, the more likely the document is one to review. For example, you have a long case that appears to be useful, but you are not sure. Type the key search terms in the FOCUS text box and if those terms appear in your case, they will appear in bold. The more terms highlighted, the better the case.

Alert Feature

A relatively new feature on LexisNexis is Shepard's Alert. With Alert, you can monitor a case (or statute) for changes. This includes changes to how courts treated the case you are monitoring, subsequent cases that cited the case monitored, and any other references that may have cited the case. This feature would probably be used on selected cases that you would want to monitor. Updates are forwarded electronically. In order to monitor a case on Shepard's Alert, your firm or business must subscribe to LexisNexis.

Many of the features on LexisNexis also can be found on Westlaw. We will review Westlaw's KeyCite and compare the features of both online services.

KEYCITE ON WESTLAW: WEST'S VERSION OF SHEPARD'S CITATIONS

KeyCite
The Westlaw case updating and validation system, which is similar to Shepard's Citations Service's system.

Similar to Shepard's Citations Service on LexisNexis, **KeyCite** is the citation research and validation system used on Westlaw. Introduced in 1997, with KeyCite, you can determine whether a case is still considered valid law, check its prior appellate history, and expand your research opportunities. KeyCite validates information not only for cases, but also for statutes and administrative regulations. Like Shepard's, KeyCite provides valuable legal research sources, such as *American Law Reports,* law review articles, and *American Jurisprudence.* Perhaps a highlight of the KeyCite system is its extensive integration of the ThomsonWest Key Number System. We review the KeyCite system as we did the Shepard's Citations online.

Using KeyCite

There are a number of ways to access KeyCite on Westlaw. Simply type in the citation you need to validate in the text box labeled "KeyCite this citation" and click "Go." Additionally, when you have located a case through your research, in the upper-left corner, there is a listing for KeyCite. Click the name and your case will be automatically checked for validation. Once a case is displayed on the computer screen, you have a number of options to select. Under the title "Full History" three choices appear: Direct History, Citing References, and KeyCite Alert.

PRACTICE TIP

The word *Shepardize* has come to represent the process of validating or updating a case, regardless of the publisher's "formal" name of their process. Your attorney may ask you to Shepardize a case or statute, although you may use KeyCite to do it.

The Direct History

The "Direct History" of a case can be displayed in two ways. Within the KeyCite referenced case, the appellate history will appear first in the text. Here you will read the appellate history of the case. A feature of KeyCite is the graphical display of the cases history. Through the use of a schematic diagram, you can visually observe the appellate process of the case you are validating. See Figure 4.12 for a graphic of *U.S. v. Booker* and Figure 7.13 for its direct history.

Citing References

Every case that ever cited your case will be displayed on the screen of the chosen case. Unlike Shepard's, KeyCite uses a symbol system rather than a word notation system to describe the positive or negative treatment of a case. Each system bears discussion.

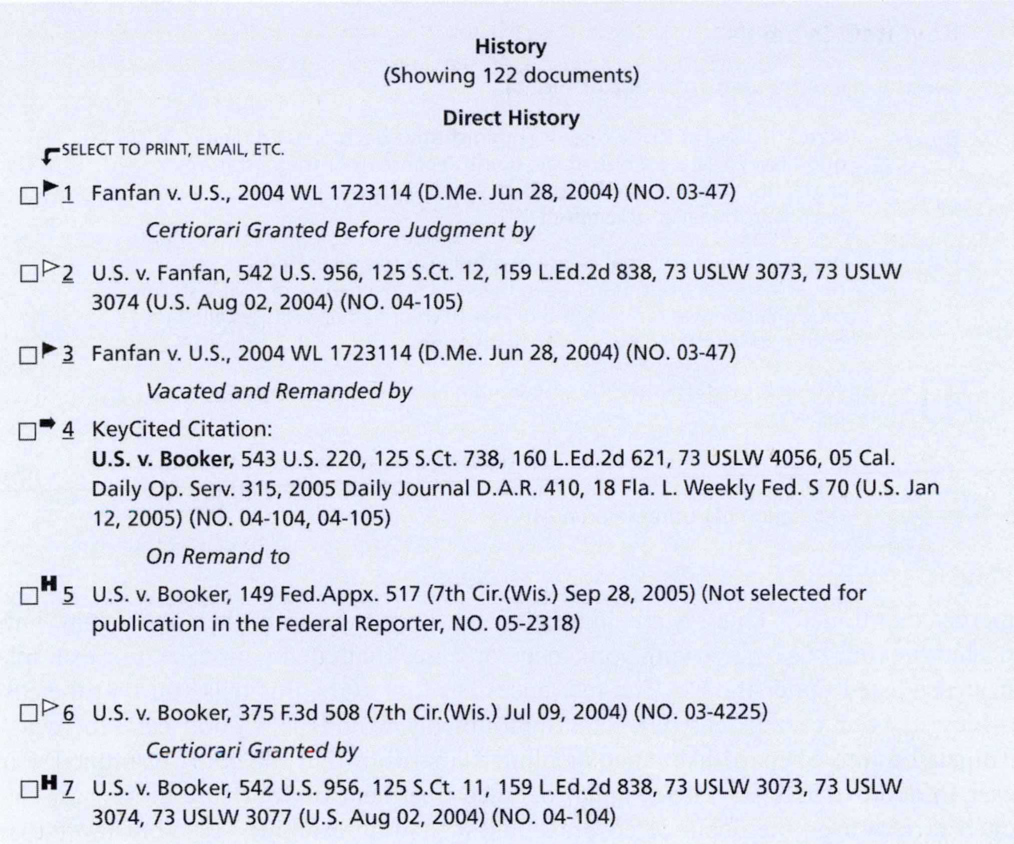
History
(Showing 122 documents)
Direct History
SELECT TO PRINT, EMAIL, ETC.
1 Fanfan v. U.S., 2004 WL 1723114 (D.Me. Jun 28, 2004) (NO. 03-47)
Certiorari Granted Before Judgment by
2 U.S. v. Fanfan, 542 U.S. 956, 125 S.Ct. 12, 159 L.Ed.2d 838, 73 USLW 3073, 73 USLW 3074 (U.S. Aug 02, 2004) (NO. 04-105)
3 Fanfan v. U.S., 2004 WL 1723114 (D.Me. Jun 28, 2004) (NO. 03-47)
Vacated and Remanded by
4 KeyCited Citation:
U.S. v. Booker, 543 U.S. 220, 125 S.Ct. 738, 160 L.Ed.2d 621, 73 USLW 4056, 05 Cal. Daily Op. Serv. 315, 2005 Daily Journal D.A.R. 410, 18 Fla. L. Weekly Fed. S 70 (U.S. Jan 12, 2005) (NO. 04-104, 04-105)
On Remand to
H 5 U.S. v. Booker, 149 Fed.Appx. 517 (7th Cir.(Wis.) Sep 28, 2005) (Not selected for publication in the Federal Reporter, NO. 05-2318)
6 U.S. v. Booker, 375 F.3d 508 (7th Cir.(Wis.) Jul 09, 2004) (NO. 03-4225)
Certiorari Granted by
H 7 U.S. v. Booker, 542 U.S. 956, 125 S.Ct. 11, 159 L.Ed.2d 838, 73 USLW 3073, 73 USLW 3074, 73 USLW 3077 (U.S. Aug 02, 2004) (NO. 04-104)

FIGURE 7.13
Graphic of *U.S. v. Booker* Showing the Direct History
Source: From KeyCite. Reprinted with permission from ThomsonWest.

KeyCite Signal System

KeyCite combines a "status flag" and "star system" to inform the legal researcher of the status and treatment of a case by various courts. As with Shepard's signal system, the flags provide a quick reference regarding the positive or negative treatment of a case you are analyzing. The status flags and star system are the basis of the KeyCite approach.

Status Flags

Using status flags, information is critiqued alerting you to the past and present treatment of a case. For an explanation of the KeyCite status flag system, review Figure 7.14. The most important symbol to watch out for is a red triangular flag, which indicates the case is no longer valid law. When you see this signal, all your instincts should tell you: DANGER ZONE AHEAD. Either immediately read the case and determine why it was assigned a red flag or reconsider using the case in your research assignment. Likewise, a yellow triangular flag, which indicates the case has had some negative comments by courts, should also be viewed with caution—as the color suggests. Although not as significant as a red flag, a yellow flag suggests that the case has been questioned or criticized or received some negative treatment by the court.

Two less problematic symbols are a boldface blue "H," which simply suggests that the case you are reviewing has some history; and a boldface green "C," which suggests that the case has no direct history issues or negative comments from courts. If a flag does not appear next to your case, it suggests that no indirect or direct history exists about that case. Therefore, it is safe to use the case.

Starring System

Another feature of KeyCite is a "star system," which indicates the depth of discussion of your case in a particular case. Has your case been explained, discussed, cited, or

FIGURE 7.14
KeyCite Flag System
Source: From KeyCite. Reprinted with permission from ThomsonWest.

KeyCite® Symbols

See at a glance the status of a case or statute.

A red flag warns that a case or administrative decision is no longer good law for at least one of the points it contains or that a statute or regulation was amended, repealed, superseded, or held unconstitutional or preempted.

A yellow flag warns that a case or administrative decision has some negative history, but hasn't been reversed or overruled, or that a statute or regulation was renumbered or transferred, had its validity called into doubt, or is affected by pending legislation.

A blue H indicates that the case or administrative decision has some history.

A green C indicates that the case or administrative decision has citing references but no direct or negative indirect history, or that a statute or regulation has citing references.

merely mentioned? This system highlights the importance another court may have placed on your case, narrowing your focus on cases that cited your case. For example, if a case listed under the KeyCite references has four stars, this tells you that the case discussed your case extensively. This undoubtedly would be a good case to review. Translated into Shepard-like language, four stars mean that the court examined your case in depth. Three stars also signify detailed treatment of your case in the case that cited it. However, the depth of coverage is less than an examined case but more than a mere indirect citing. This is a case you may want to examine more closely. Cases with one and two stars provide less discussion of your case. Two stars translate into "cited" and one star translates into "mentioned." Consider the treatment of these cases insignificant; these are probably cases that are not worth spending much time reviewing, especially those with one star.

And finally, the last symbol that you will observe in a KeyCite reference is quotation marks (" "). This feature alerts you to the fact that the case you are referencing quoted your case in the decision. This could be significant especially if it is coupled with four or three stars. By learning and understanding the signal system in KeyCite, you can sharpen your research skills and analysis to maximize your time with any project. See Figure 7.15 for a full illustration of the "star system." Many of the general features found on Shepard's Citations Service are found on KeyCite. Both systems provide the critical case validation step in the legal research process as well as citing references to your case.

FIGURE 7.15
KeyCite Starring System
Source: From KeyCite. Reprinted with permission from ThomsonWest.

KeyCite® Symbols

Depth-of-treatment stars tell you how much the citing case discusses the cited case.

EXAMINED - Contains an extended discussion of the cited case, usually more than a printed page of text.

DISCUSSED - Contains a substantial discussion of the cited case, usually more than a paragraph.

CITED - some discussion of the cited case, usually less than a paragraph.

MENTIONED - Contains a brief reference to the cited case, usually in a string citation.

A quotation mark in a citation indicates that the citing case directly quotes the cited case or administrative decision.

Locate Search (Similar to FOCUS)

KeyCite has a feature analogous to Shepard's FOCUS called "Locate." With Locate you can narrow a search result or highlight words, terms, and phrases within a case. The Locate search is usually found in the upper portion of the page. Simply type the words into the text box and press Enter. The search terms will be highlighted within the case, concentrating on the areas of the case that are most relevant to your research. The more terms highlighted, the better the case is to review. This is a feature you will want to use as it will identify which cases are better to use based upon the amount of highlighted words and phrases.

Headnote Search

Since KeyCite is a ThomsonWest product, the Key Number System is integral to a KeyCite search. Any key number and topic that is referenced in a case can be referenced through KeyCite. This is a valuable tool, to say the least. To perform a headnote search on KeyCite, you can type into the text box the topic and key you want to review. Click the Enter button and relevant cases will appear. If you are not interested in a global search of the topic, you can narrow the search by jurisdiction.

Additionally, if you already have a case to review and a topic and key is of particular interest, you can first click "KeyCite Limits" and then click headnotes, which will allow you to focus on the headnote you are interesting in examining. A listing of the topics and keys from the case you are reviewing is displayed with the accompanying text of the headnote. Choose the headnote(s) you want to review; cases that have cited the topic and key will appear.

KeyCite Alert

Suppose you want to monitor a case for future treatment and analysis by different courts around the country. By setting up a KeyCite Alert, you can monitor the case and even statutes for changes, amendments, or other pending matters that may affect the case or statute. This service is similar to the Shepard's Alert feature previously discussed.

To illustrate the online Shepard's Citations Service and KeyCite systems, let's review *United States v. Booker*, 543 U.S. 220, 125 S. Ct. 738, 160 L. Ed. 2d 621 (2005). Figures 7.16 and 7.17 contain a page from Shepard's Citations Service and

YOU BE THE JUDGE

Complete and thorough research is the standard for all attorneys and paralegals. When either of you are remiss in your responsibilities to locate all the appropriate case law, a judge may impose Rule 11 sanctions. Under the Federal Rules of Civil Procedure, an attorney is under a duty to file documents that have a legal basis and are not frivolous. Proper legal research is part of that standard. In *Continental Air Lines, Inc. v. Group Systems International Far East, Ltd.*, 109 F.R.D. 594 (C.D. Cal. 1986), Continental Airlines sought Rule 11 sanctions against Group Systems International because they failed to examine a recently handed-down U.S. Supreme Court case, *Burger King v. Rudzewicz,* that may have made the motion filed frivolous. The defendant acknowledged that it should have found the recent U.S. Supreme Court case that may have been dispositive on one of the issues raised in the motion. Although at the time (1986) the attorney claimed access to Westlaw or LexisNexis was unavailable, the Court was not convinced. In its dicta the Court cites the defendant's claim of "ignorance and neglect—since *Burger King* did not expressly overrule any Ninth Circuit case, his Shepardizing of Ninth Circuit authority did not disclose the existence of the case. By any objective standard, the duty of reasonable inquiry on an issue of constitutional law (here, the due process limits of the exertion of personal jurisdiction) must include, at the least, inquiry to ascertain whether or not and when the United States Supreme Court has ruled on the issue. Here, the U.S. Supreme Court had spoken on the issue four months before the motion was filed." *Id.* at 597. The lesson is clear here and even more so today. In the 1980s, electronic research services were not as prevalent and accessible as they are today. What may not have risen to the level of a Rule 11 sanction then may not be the case today. Under today's standards, the reasoning of the case may have changed. Examine the *Continental Air Lines* case. What are the facts of the case that form the basis for the Court's inquiry? Did the Court order Rule 11 sanctions? Why or why not? What is the basis of the Court's reasoning in the case?

FIGURE 7.16 **Page from Shepard's Citations Service for *U.S. v. Booker***

Source: From Shepard's Citations Services off Shepard's Auto-Cite. Reproduced by permission of LexisNexis. Further reproduction of any kind is strictly prohibited.

Home | Sources | How Do I? | Site Map | What's New | Help

Citation: 543 U.S. 220
Restrictions: Jurisdictions: **U.S. Supreme Court**
Analysis: **Distinguished**

FOCUS™ Search Within Results

Prin

KWIC Full *Shepards®* - **15 Citing References**

All Negative | All Positive | Any Custom | Restrictions | Unrestricted

543 U.S. 220

Single: **Caution** - Possible negative treatment
Citation: **543 U.S. 220**
Restrictions: Jurisdictions: **U.S. Supreme Court**
Analysis: **Distinguished**

United States v. Booker, 543 U.S. 220, 125 S. Ct. 738, 160 L. Ed. 2d 621, 2005 U.S. LEXIS 628, 73 U.S.L.W 18 Fla. L. Weekly Fed. S 70

PRIOR HISTORY (14 citing references) Hide Prior History

1. United States v. Booker, 2003 U.S. Dist. LEXIS 24609 (W.D. Wis. Sept. 5, 2003)

2. **Subsequent appeal at, Remanded by:**
United States v. Booker, 375 F.3d 508, 2004 U.S. App. LEXIS 14223 (7th Cir. Wis. 2004)

3. **Later proceeding at:**
United States v. Booker, 542 U.S. 955, 125 S. Ct. 5, 159 L. Ed. 2d 837, 2004 U.S. LEXIS 4783, 73 U.S.L.W. 3074 (2004)

4. **Writ of certiorari granted, Motion granted by:**
United States v. Booker, 542 U.S. 956, 125 S. Ct. 11, 159 L. Ed. 2d 838, 2004 U.S. LEXIS 4788, 73 U.S.L.W. 3074 (2004)

5. **Writ of certiorari granted, Motion granted by:**
United States v. Fanfan, 542 U.S. 956, 125 S. Ct. 12, 159 L. Ed. 2d 838, 2004 U.S. LEXIS 4789, 73 U.S.L.W. 3074 (2004)

6. **Criticized in:**
United States v. Hammoud, 381 F.3d 316, 2004 U.S. App. LEXIS 19036, 65 Fed. R. Evid. Serv. (CBC) 338 (4th Cir. N.C. 2004)

7. **Motion granted by, Motion denied by:**
United States v. Booker, 542 U.S. 963, 125 S. Ct. 25, 159 L. Ed. 2d 854, 2004 U.S. LEXIS 4989, 73 U.S.L.W. 3204 (2004)

Affirmed by, Remanded by (CITATION YOU ENTERED):
United States v. Booker, 543 U.S. 220, 125 S. Ct. 738, 160 L. Ed. 2d 621, 2005 U.S. LEXIS 628, 73 U.S.L.W. 4056, 18 Fla. L. Weekly Fed. S 70 (2005)

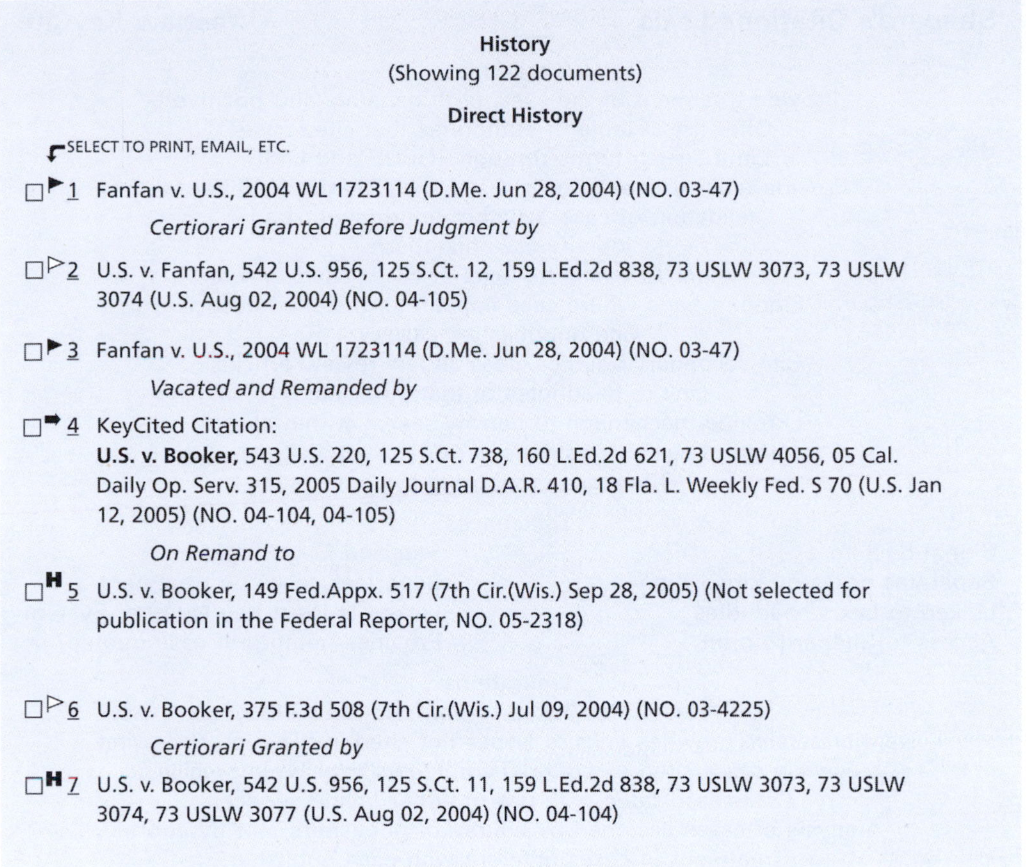

History
(Showing 122 documents)

Direct History

SELECT TO PRINT, EMAIL, ETC.

1 Fanfan v. U.S., 2004 WL 1723114 (D.Me. Jun 28, 2004) (NO. 03-47)

Certiorari Granted Before Judgment by

2 U.S. v. Fanfan, 542 U.S. 956, 125 S.Ct. 12, 159 L.Ed.2d 838, 73 USLW 3073, 73 USLW 3074 (U.S. Aug 02, 2004) (NO. 04-105)

3 Fanfan v. U.S., 2004 WL 1723114 (D.Me. Jun 28, 2004) (NO. 03-47)

Vacated and Remanded by

4 KeyCited Citation:
U.S. v. Booker, 543 U.S. 220, 125 S.Ct. 738, 160 L.Ed.2d 621, 73 USLW 4056, 05 Cal. Daily Op. Serv. 315, 2005 Daily Journal D.A.R. 410, 18 Fla. L. Weekly Fed. S 70 (U.S. Jan 12, 2005) (NO. 04-104, 04-105)

On Remand to

H 5 U.S. v. Booker, 149 Fed.Appx. 517 (7th Cir.(Wis.) Sep 28, 2005) (Not selected for publication in the Federal Reporter, NO. 05-2318)

6 U.S. v. Booker, 375 F.3d 508 (7th Cir.(Wis.) Jul 09, 2004) (NO. 03-4225)

Certiorari Granted by

H 7 U.S. v. Booker, 542 U.S. 956, 125 S.Ct. 11, 159 L.Ed.2d 838, 73 USLW 3073, 73 USLW 3074, 73 USLW 3077 (U.S. Aug 02, 2004) (NO. 04-104)

FIGURE 7.17
Page from KeyCite for *U.S. v. Booker*
Source: From KeyCite. Reprinted with permission from ThomsonWest.

KeyCite, respectively. The pages indicate the treatment of the *Booker* case. When the case is Shepardized, a number of signals appear with cautionary references in both services. Over 600 cases distinguished *Booker* and received negative comment by the United States Supreme Court. Review the prior history of the case and observe that the case was reviewed by the Supreme Court a number of times until a final decision was rendered in 2005. Thus, the importance of Shepardizing cannot be understated, and Shepardizing must be mastered for complete, accurate, and valid citing of the law.

Neither Shepard's Citations online nor KeyCite is better than the other. It often is simply a matter of convenience and availability. Being familiar with both systems provides you with an added advantage: competency and flexibility. Table 7.2 compares the features of Shepard's Citations Online and KeyCite.

Given the speed and ease with which a Shepard's or KeyCite search can be done online, the obvious question is "why would I ever want to use Shepard's print to valid a case?" The answer is twofold. You need to know how to Shepardize using the print version as it may be the only version of the system available to you. And knowing that fact, you need to learn how to Shepardize the print material as you may not have online sources accessible to you when needed.

Quick Quiz True/False Questions

1. Shepard's Citations Service online and KeyCite have the same system of identifying the treatment of a case.
2. KeyCite uses a flagging system to alert the researcher about negative treatment in a case.

TABLE 7.2
Comparison of Shepard's and KeyCite

Shepard's Citations Lexis	Westlaw KeyCite
Similarities	
Provide treatment of the case, both negative and positive	
Offer list of table of authorities that cited case	
Limit search terms through FOCUS and LIMIT	
Provide quick access to new cases, usually within 48 hours	
Validation of case, whether good law or bad	
Identify case histories	
Link to complete texts of cases cited	
Pinpoint page where case appears in the cited case	
Cite unpublished cases	
Cite secondary sources, such as law review articles	
Link to headnotes of that publisher	
Provide mechanism to narrow search within case	
Afford custom restrictions to narrow database	
Offer case monitoring system	
Differences	
Signal System	Star and Flag System
Separates cases by jurisdiction	Separates cases by treatment
Linked to Lexis headnotes	Linked to West Key Number System
Access to Shepard's print	Provides notation if case quoted
Limitations	
Headnotes linked to that publisher	
Neither service provides links to issues not cited in the case reviewing	
Review cases cited as editorial comments may be imprecise	
Costs associated with use of either online service	
Analysis of cases assigned by editors of publishers, not by court	
Treatment of cases different with each publisher	

3. KeyCite provides a detailed schematic of the appeals history of a case.
4. Shepard's online can be used only as a validation and not as a research tool.
5. Shepard's Citations Service online and KeyCite provide a method of verifying the status of a federal or state statute.

CYBER TRIP

Locate the federal Amber Alert statute from a government Web site and establish whether it has been amended or repealed.

UPDATING AND VALIDATING STATUTES AND FEDERAL REGULATIONS

Updating and verifying a statute or federal code of regulations is accomplished in a number of ways. As you might guess, statutes and federal regulations have corresponding Shepard's sets. Statutes should be checked to determine if all or any part of the statute has been repealed or amended. Statutes also should be reviewed to determine whether a court has interpreted the meaning of a statutory provision, especially for constitutionality. This point is significant. When a court interprets and presents a legal evaluation of a statute or a statutory provision, this may affect your legal research. Consequently, when you see the notation "i" next to a statute, it means that the court interpreted the statutory provision you are Shepardizing. Do not ignore cases that have interpreted your case. Review them! Figure 7.18 identifies the notations associated with Shepard's statutes.

Each of the states as well as the federal statutes has a Shepard's citator that provides the history of the statute. A word of caution is that the sets for statutes are only updated annually. Similar to Shepard's for cases, there are softbound volumes that update and report cases that have cited the statute you are reviewing. Now, let's perform a Shepard's search on a statute. The statute we will use is found in Title 30 of the *United States*

FIGURE 7.18 **Page from Shepard's Notations for Statutes**

Source: From *Shepard's Federal Citations.* Used with permission of LexisNexis. Further reproduction of any kind is strictly prohibited.

ANALYSIS OF STATUTES, RULES, REGULATIONS AND ORDERS—ABBREVIATIONS

Legislative

A	(Amended)	The citing reference, typically a session law, amends or alters the statute you are *Shepardizing.*
Ad	(Added)	The citing reference, typically a session law, adds new matter to the statute you are *Shepardizing.*
E	(Extended)	The citing reference extends the scope of, or the time period specified in, the statute you are *Shepardizing.*
L	(Limited)	The citing reference refuses to extend the provisions of the statute you are *Shepardizing.*
R	(Repealed)	The citing reference, typically a session law, repeals or abrogates the statute you are *Shepardizing.*
Re-en	(Re-enacted)	The citing reference, typically a session law, re-enacts the statute you are *Shepardizing.*
Rn	(Renumbered)	The citing reference, typically a session law, renumbers the statute you are *Shepardizing.*
Rp	(Repealed in Part)	The citing reference, typically a session law, repeals ,or abrogates, in part the statute you are *Shepardizing,*
Rs	(Repealed & Superseded)	The citing reference, typically a session law, repeals and supersedes the statute you are *Shepardizing.*
Rv	(Revised)	The citing reference, typically a session law, revises the statute you are *Shepardizing.*
S	(Superseded)	The citing reference, typically a session law, supersedes the statute you are *Shepardizing.*
Sd	(Suspended)	The citing reference, typically a session law, supersedes the statute you are *Shepardizing.*
Sdp	(Suspended in Part)	The citing reference, typically a session law, suspends in part the statute you are *Shepardizing.*
Sg	(Supplementing)	The citing reference, typically a session law, supplements the statute you are *Shepardizing.*
Sp	(Superseded in Part)	The citing reference, typically a session law, supersedes in part the statute you are *Shepardizing.*

Judicial

C	(Constitutional)	The citing case upholds the constitutionality of the statute, rule or regulation you are *Shepardizing.*
cr	(Criticized)	The citing opinion criticizes the statute, rule or regulation you are *Shepardizing* in some significant way, although the citing court may not have the authority to materially affect its precedential value.
DG	(Decision for Gov't)	The citing decision holds for the Government in a dispute concerning the Code section you are *Shepardizing.*

Code, Coal Research and Development, shown in Figure 7.19. The section we want to Shepardize is 30 U.S.C. § 664, which authorizes the Secretary of Energy to hire a Director of Coal Research. We will first review to determine when Congress amended the statute. Although we need to retrieve all volumes of the Shepard's citators for the *United States Code,* let's work backward. Consequently, we will check the corresponding supplements. Checking the most recent supplement, we examine the March 2007 supplement. At the top of the page (Figure 7.18), look for the entry to Title 30. We see an entry for Title 29 followed by the section reference. As we peruse down the page, we see where Title 30 begins. Now, look for section 664 and see if there is an entry. There is. The entry has an "R" next to it. Review Figure 7.18 to determine what is meant by an "R."

FIGURE 7.19

Pages from Title 30 of the *United States Code*

Source: From *Shepard's Federal Citations.* Reproduced by permission of LexisNexis. Further reproduction of any kind is strictly prohibited.

title and section of statute

new title begins

30 *U.S.C.* § 664

TITLE 29 § 2617 UNITED STATES CODE

§ 2617(a)(1)(A)(2)
Cir. 7
2007USDist LX6873 [Δ2007

§ 2617(a)(1)(B)
Cir. 7
2007USDist LX6873 [Δ2007

§ 2617(c)(1)
Cir. 9
2007USDist LX9066 [Δ2007
Cir. 10
2007USDist LX7602 [Δ2007

§ 2617(c)(2)
Cir. 9
2007USDist LX9066 [Δ2007
Cir. 10
2007USDist LX7602 [Δ2007

§ 2654
Cir. 1
472F3d3Δ2006
Cir. 7
472F3d477Δ2006

§ 2801 et seq.
Cir. 6
442FS2d507Δ2006

§§ 2801 to 2945
Cir. 10
2007USDist LX9694 [*2006

§ 2811
Cir. 10
2007USDist LX9694 [Δ2007

§ 2864(d)(3)
Cir. 10
2007USDist LX9694 [Δ2007

TITLE 30

§ 28f
Cir. 9
197Fed Appx709*1994

§ 28i
Cir. 9
197Fed Appx709*1994

§ 28k
Cir. 9
197Fed Appx709Δ2006

§ 181 et seq.
Cir. DC
370FS2d233Δ2005

§ 184
A) 119St714 §352

§ 185
Cir. DC
370FS2d258Δ2005

§ 185(c)(2)
Cir. DC
370FS2d233Δ2005

§ 185(d)
Cir. DC
370FS2d258Δ2005

§ 185(j)
Cir. DC
370FS2d258Δ2005

§ 188
A) 119St734 §371(b)

§ 191
A) 119St725 §365(g)

§ 201
A) 119St762 §436

§ 202a
A) 119St761 §433

§ 203
A) 119St760 §432

§ 207
A) 119St761 §434, 435

§ 226
A) 119St711 §350(a), (b)
A) 119St726 §366
A) 119St730 §369(j)(1)

§ 241
A) 119St731 §369(j)(2)

§ 530
A) 119St673 §236(24)

§ 601
Cir. 4
2007USApp LX2996 [Δ2007

§ 661
R) 119St934 §1009(a) [(1)(A)
Ad) 119St934

§ 662
A) 119St934 §1009(a) [(1)(B)

§ 663
R) 119St934 §1009(a) [(1)(C)

§ 664
R) 119St934 §1009(a) [(1)(C)

§ 665
A) 119St934 §1009(a) [(1)(D)

§ 666
A) 119St934 §1009(a) [(1)(D)

§ 667
R) 119St934 §1009(a) [(1)(C)

§ 668
A) 119St934 §1009(a) [(1)(D)

§ 801 et seq.
Cir. 9
2007USDist LX8390 [Δ2007

§ 811 (a)
Cir. DC
2007USApp LX2886 [Δ2007

§ 811 (a)(6)
Cir. DC
2007USApp LX2886 [Δ2007

§ 811 (a)(6)(A)
Cir. DC
2007USApp LX2886 [Δ2007

§ 811 (a)(7)
Cir. DC
2007USApp LX2886 [Δ2007

§ 814
Cir. 9
2007USDist LX8390 [Δ2007

§ 814(a)
Cir. 2
453FS2d483Δ2006

§ 816
Cir. 2
453FS2d484Δ2006
Cir. 9
2007USDist LX8390 [Δ2007

§ 816(a)(1)
Cir. 2
453FS2d483Δ2006

§ 816(a)(2)
Cir. 2
453FS2d484Δ2006

§ 820(i)
Cir. 2
453FS2d484Δ2006

§ 823
Cir. 9
2007USDist LX8390 [Δ2007

§ 823(d)
Cir. 2
453FS2d483Δ2006

§ 901 et seq.
543US131Δ2004
160LE527Δ2004
125SC568Δ2004
Cir. 4
2007USApp LX2998 [Δ20***

§§ 901 to 945
Cir. 4
199Fed Appx259* 2000

§§ 901 to 944
Cir. 7
2007USApp LX3350 [Δ20***

§ 932(a)
543US131* 1982
160LE527*1982
125SC568*1982
Cir. 4
2007USApp LX2998 [Δ200***

§ 1001
A) 119St671 §236(2)
A) 119St671 §236(5)
A) 119St671 §236(1)

§ 1002
A) 119St672 §236(6)
A) 119St671 §236(1)

§ 1003
Ad) 119St660 §222
A) 119St662 §223(b)

§ 1004
A) 119St661 §223(a)
A) 119St662 §224(a)
A) 119St667 §228
A) 119St668 §230
A) 119St669 §232, 233
A) 119St672 §236(7)

§ 1005
A) 119St668 §231
A) 119St671 §236(1)

§ 1006
A) 119St671 §235

§ 1007
A) 119St668 §229
A) 119St672 §236(8)

§ 1008
A) 119St672 §236(9)

§ 1009
A) 119St672 §236(10)

§ 1010
A) 199St672 §236(11)

Cont.

FIGURE 7.19 **Pages from Title 30 of the *United States Code* *Cont.***

HISTORICAL AND STATUTORY NOTES

Section, Pub.L. 86–599, § 3, July 7, 1960, 74 Stat. 336, related to duties and compensation of advisory committee members.

§ 664. Repealed. Pub.L. 109–58, Title X, § 1009(a)(1)(C), Aug. 8, 2005, 119 Stat. 934

actual notation of repealed section of *U.S.C.*

HISTORICAL AND STATUTORY NOTES

Section, Pub.L. 86–599, § 4 (part), July 7, 1960, 74 Stat. 336, authorized the Secretary of Energy to appoint a Director of Coal Research.

§ 665. Sites for conducting research; availability of personnel and facilities

Research authorized by this chapter may be conducted wherever suitable personnel and facilities are available.

(Pub.L. 86–599, § 3, formerly § 5, July 7, 1960, 74 Stat. 337, renumbered § 3, Pub.L. 109–58, Title X, § 1009(a)(1)(D), Aug. 8, 2005, 119 Stat. 934.)

HISTORICAL AND STATUTORY NOTES

Revision Notes and Legislative Reports

2005 Acts. House Conference Report No. 109–190, see 2005 U.S. Code Cong. and Adm. News, p. 448.

Statement by President, see 2005 U.S. Code Cong. and Adm. News, p. S17.

References in Text

This chapter, referred to in text, originally read "this Act", meaning the Coal Research and Development Act of 1960, which is Pub.L. 86–599, July 7, 1960, 74 Stat. 336, which enacted this chapter. For complete classification, see Short Title note set out under 30 U.S.C.A. § 661 and Tables.

Prior Provisions

A prior section 3 of Pub.L. 86–599, July 7, 1960, 74 Stat. 336, authorizing advisory commit- [text omitted]

We see that the notation means repealed. This means that this section of the statute is no longer in effect. Undoubtedly this is important information if your research centers on who has authority to make decisions relating to research, such as grants. What this exercise will you tell you is that checking the supplements is crucial, and often they may be the place to begin when performing statutory research.

Similarly, federal regulations can be checked in Shepard's Code of Federal Regulations Citations. Simply follow the same basic procedure that you followed for cases and statutes. Shepard's for the Code of Federal Regulations will provide case analysis and treatment of the rule or regulation examined. Remember to review any softbound supplements at the end of the Shepard's volumes. No Shepard's review is complete unless all the softbound volumes are checked as well.

Shepard's online and KeyCite also provide updating and validating processes on their databases. Simply type in the statutory section you are interested in validating in the text box, press Enter, and your search of the statute will appear.

For KeyCite, there are corresponding status flags, like the ones for cases. A red flag indicates some action by a legislature or court, such as an amendment or repeal or being held unconstitutional by a court. Attention should be paid to a red flag, although be mindful of the fact that amending a statute is not necessarily a negative event. Therefore, read the statutory section on which you are performing the search. A yellow flag also presents cause for concern. A statute may have pending legislation affecting it or a case may have provided some negative treatment or may be as simple as

THE E-FACTOR

Although LexisNexis and Westlaw are the most complete method of case and statutory validation, there is a new alternative available on the legal Web site Loislaw, a Wolters Kluwer Company, another online legal research service. Introduced in 2000, GlobalCite is another citator service, although not nearly as comprehensive as LexisNexis and Westlaw. If you are using Loislaw, you can retrieve a case or statute and then perform a GlobalCite check. In a GlobalCite check, a listing of the cases or statutes that have cited the case will appear. Cases are listed in reverse chronological order with statutes and rules and regulations listed by the order of relevance to the search you are performing from your original cited source. To retrieve a case, click on the hypertext link to the citing case. GlobalCite does identify the number of cases that cited your case as well as statutes, treatises, and other documents, but it lists only sources from its database. Within the case or statute that you are reviewing, certain terms such as "reversed," "affirmed," "vacated," and the like are noted in blue. This represents the GlobalCite version of "treatment of the case." Unlike Shepard's and KeyCite, GlobalCite does not analyze the treatment of a case and does not offer advice on how the court case you are reviewing treated the case you are checking. This is a drawback of the service, especially if your case has numerous citations, as does *Bush v. Gore.* It is impractical to review every case to determine how the court treated the case you are validating. For cases with a limited history, GlobalCite offers an alternative to Shepard's and KeyCite. *But do not use GlobalCite as a substitute for Shepard's or KeyCite.* The Loislaw service has not advanced enough to offer a full validation of cases and statutes.

CYBER TRIP

Using www.gpoaccess.gov, determine whether 20 U.S.C. §§ 1681–1688 (Title IX) has had any recent changes.

renumbering. Once again, read the statute in question. KeyCite also enlists its star system to highlight the treatment of a statute.

Shepard's online, too, provides validation of a statute. Utilizing its flag signals, the red stop sign and yellow yield sign suggest either negative treatment or the occurrence of legislative or court action relating to the statute. On LexisNexis, the Shepard's search will supply such information as cases that cited the statute or subsection of the statute, recent session law that affect the statute Shepardized as well as secondary sources that have examined the statute. Don't attempt to read into the signals that LexisNexis or Westlaw assign to a statutory section. Nothing can replace the simple act of reading.

Shepard's and KeyCite are not the only online sites to verify the status of a statute or federal regulation. The government Web site www.gpoaccess.gov updates statutes on a regular basis. Simply enter the statute of interest in the text box. The most recent version will appear, updates and amendments included. (Figure 5.16 shows the process for retrieving a statute from www.gpoaccess.gov.)

Shepardizing State Statutes

Validating state statutes is more challenging. Often state-sponsored Web sites are not updated concurrently with the amending, repealing, or changing of a state statute. In order to have the most current information, check the annotated version of the state statute as well as the most recent session laws for that jurisdiction. If Shepard's or KeyCite is available, use them for the most current version of the statute you are researching. Either one of these services should offer reliable information about the status of a state statute.

Quick Quiz True/False Questions

1. Shepardizing is the only method of updating a statute.
2. When the notation "i" is cited next to a case, you should ignore this reference.
3. In using Shepard's Statutes print version, an "R" next to an entry means the statutory section you are reviewing is repealed.
4. Federal rules and regulations can be validated only on a government Web site.
5. Federal government Web sites provide the current status of U.S. statutes whereas state government Web sites lag behind the updating process.

Source: TANK McNAMARA © Millar/Hinds. Reprinted with permission of UNIVERSAL PRESS SYNDICATE. All rights reserved.

PRACTICAL CONSIDERATIONS: THE FINAL TOUCHES—SHEPARDIZING

We all would prefer to Shepardize using one of the online versions, but the reality is that online Shepard's or KeyCite is not available to all of us. Accredited law schools are required to have the print version of Shepard's available to students and the public. If they do not have the print versions of Shepard's, they may have the online versions available for use. The process, whether by print or online, is a time-consuming, often labor-intensive process, especially with cases that have extensive treatment by courts. As the case in You Be the Judge section indicates, your research is not complete unless you have Shepardized your cases, and the courts expect that your Shepardizing is current either as of the date you file your legal documents or the day you argue your case before a judge. Do not place your supervising attorney or yourself in an embarrassing position by not *completely* and *thoroughly* Shepardizing all your cases. That means every case you are citing in any legal document, whether a brief to the court or a letter to a client, must be checked for its current status. Do not risk sanctions by a court or admonishing from your attorney if you fail to complete the task you were assigned by not Shepardizing your cited cases.

Summary

Updating and validating the law is important in legal research. There are two main systems for validating your legal research: print and electronic. The best-known version of an updating system is Shepard's Citations. Shepard's is available in both print and electronic versions. Through the use of Shepardizing, researchers can determine whether a case has been overruled or cited by other courts. Shepard's also can be used as a research tool. By checking either the Shepard's print column or the Shepard's Citations online service, you can determine whether the case you are Shepardizing has been cited in law review journals or *American Law Reports.*

Both Shepard's print version and the online version use a system that alerts the reader of the treatment of a case. In the print version, a notation system is used. Next to many of the citations of the case you are Shepardizing are letters or symbols that indicate how a court analyzed the case Shepardized. In the electronic version, a signal system is used with a red stop sign and yellow yield sign, indicating that the case you are Shepardizing has received negative treatment. The online version also provides brief notations as to whether the case was followed, distinguished, or other explanations offered by a court.

The counterpart to Shepard's Citations is KeyCite used by Westlaw. This system also reviews the treatment and history of a case as does Shepard's. KeyCite uses a flag and star system to alert you as to the treatment of a case. Red and yellow flags indicate negative treatment of your case. Additionally, the "star" system lets the reader know in what depth a court has reviewed your case. Four stars represent an extensive discussion of your case with one star representing that is was cited only for a general proposition in that case.

Statutes and regulations also can be updated through Shepard's and KeyCite. Government Web sites also provide a method for updating statutes and regulations through sites such as www.gpoaccess.gov and www.thomas.gov.

A new source to check cases is GlobalCite located on Loislaw. This service is not as comprehensive as Shepard's and KeyCite and should not be used to the exclusion of either.

Key Terms

citators
connected case
depublished opinion
KeyCite
negative treatment
parallel citation
positive treatment
same case
Shepardizing

Review Questions

1. What does "Shepardizing" mean?
2. What is the process of Shepardizing a case using the print version of Shepard's Citations?
3. List the different color supplements found in the print version of Shepard's and what each color represents.
4. In the print version of Shepard's, where will you find the parallel citations to a case?
5. Identify two differences between the regional reporter and the state version of Shepard's print version.
6. Name the two primary methods of Shepardizing online.
7. Compare and contrast the signal systems on the LexisNexis and Westlaw updating systems.
8. Other than cases, what other types of legal sources do Shepard's and KeyCite cite?
9. List some of the customized restrictions you can create to tailor your Shepard's inquiry.
10. Identify three other legal sources for which there is a Shepard's citator available.

Exercises

1. Using the Shepard's Federal Cases Citations, locate *U.S. v. McCullough,* 457 F.3d 1150 (10th Cir. 2006), and answer the following questions:
   a. Has the case been appealed to the U.S. Supreme Court? What occurred?
   b. What other federal circuits have cited the *McCullough* case?
   c. Has the *McCullough* case been the subject of an *A.L.R.* annotation?
2. Using Shepard's Citations for U.S. Supreme Court cases, Shepardize *Toyota Motor Manufacturing, Kentucky, Inc. v. Williams,* 122 S. Ct. 681 (2002), and answer the following questions:
   a. What are the parallel citations for the *Toyota Motor* case?
   b. Has the case been questioned? If so, identify the citations.

c. Has the case been cited in a dissenting opinion? If so, identify the case citations.
d. Has the *Toyota Motor* case been the subject of a law review article? If so, list the law review citations.

3. Locate *Elk Grove Unified School District v. Newdow,* 542 U.S. 1, 124 S. Ct. 2301, 159 L. Ed. 2d 98 (2004), and answer the following questions:
   a. What are the facts of the case? The holding?
   b. List the "connected" case to the *Elk Grove* decision.
   c. How many times has headnote 7 been cited by a court?
   d. Has any court explained the *Elk Grove* case? If so, list the citations.
4. Shepardize *Courtroom Television Network v. State,* 5 N.Y.3d 222, 833 N.E.2d 1197, 800 N.Y.S.2d 522 (2005) and answer the following questions. (You can use either the regional reporter version of Shepard's or the state-specific version.)
   a. Has *Courtroom T.V.* been cited by other courts?
   b. Is there law review or *A.L.R.* annotations citing the *Courtroom T.V.* case?
   c. Has the *Courtroom T.V.* case been followed? Explained? Distinguished?
5. Shepardize 181 S.W.3d 292 and answer the following questions:
   a. What is the name of the case?
   b. What year was the case decided and from what state?
   c. Was the case appealed to the U.S. Supreme Court? If so, what action did that Court take?
   d. Has the case been questioned by any jurisdiction?
   e. Has the case been cited in a law review article? If so, identify the law review article(s).
   f. What are the central issues involved in the case you are Shepardizing?
   g. What is the holding of the Court?
   h. What is the name of the judge who decided the opinion?
6. Shepardize *State v. Foster* located at 845 N.E.2d 470 and answer the following questions:
   a. What year was the *Foster* case decided?
   b. Does the *Foster* case have a parallel citation? If so, identify the citation.
   c. Was the case appealed to the U.S. Supreme Court?
   d. Has this case been cited in a dissenting opinion?
   e. Have other jurisdictions cited the *Foster* case?
   f. Has the case been cited in an *American Law Reports* annotation? If so, identify the annotations(s).
   g. What two U.S. Supreme Court cases are cited as dispositive of the *Foster* case?
   h. What constitutional amendment does *Foster* primarily discuss?
   i. How many cases were consolidated into the *Foster* case?
   j. What is the holding in *Foster*?
7. Locate the Shepard's Citations for the federal statutes. The statute you want to Shepardize is 30 U.S.C. sections 662 and 663. Answer the following questions:
   a. Has 30 U.S.C. section 662 been amended? Repealed? Interpreted by a court?
   b. Has 30 U.S.C. section 663 been amended? Repealed?
   c. Retrieve 30 U.S.C. section 662 and identify the title of the section.
8. Locate the Shepard's statutes volume for your jurisdiction. Find the statute that deals with child support or child custody. Shepardize the statute. Has the statute been amended or repealed? (Remember to check the front material to identify the abbreviations for that volume; this question requires you to use skills from previous chapters.)

PORTFOLIO ASSIGNMENT

Your supervising attorney has completed a brief, which will be filed in the court of appeals next week. Before he sends the brief to be bound at the printer's, he wants to make sure that all the cases and statutes cited in the brief are still valid. He requests that you validate and update the legal sources in the following passage:

II. LEGAL STANDARD:

The standards for proving a sexual discrimination case are well established. A *prima facie* case of employment discrimination may be proved under a theory of disparate impact or disparate treatment. *Furnco Construction Corp. v. Waters,* 438 U.S. 457, 581–82 (1978). In order to establish a *prima facie* case of discrimination, Ms. Grant must establish that (1) she is a member of a protected class; (2) she was performing her job satisfactorily; (3) she experienced an adverse employment action; and (4) similarly situated employees were treated more favorably. *Lopez v. Children's Memorial Hospital,* 2002 WL31898188 at *3. (N.D.Ill. 2002) citing *Hoffman-Dombrowski v. Arlington Int'l Racecourse, Inc.* 245 F.3d 644, 650 (7th Cir. 2002).

Once the employee establishes a *prima facie* case of discrimination, the employer must then establish a nondiscriminatory reason for the employment action. *Peele v. Country Mut. Ins. Co.,* 288 F.3d 319, 326 (7th Cir. 2002). If the employer is able to establish a nondiscriminatory reason for the employment action, the plaintiff must then show that the explanation offered is pretextual. *Id.* Prepare an e-mail to the attorney with your results. If newer and better cases appear, report that information as well.

Quick Quiz True/False Answers

Page 229

1. False
2. True
3. False
4. False
5. False

Page 241

1. False
2. True
3. True
4. False
5. True

Page 246

1. False
2. False
3. True
4. False
5. True

Part Three

Planning a Research Project

Chapter 8

Online Search Techniques: Learning the Methods

After completing this chapter, you will be able to:

- Perform a Boolean search.
- Initiate a natural language search on the Internet.
- Understand the use of the "and," "or," and "not" connectors.
- Recognize a "wildcard" search.
- Learn how to group words and phrases through the use of parentheses or quotation marks.
- Eliminate the use of "noise words."
- Limit searches to words within a sentence or paragraph.
- Define the differences between performing a search on LexisNexis or a search on Westlaw.
- Utilize Internet search engines to perform a query.
- Identify the proper and ethical uses of list servers.

Last-minute requests to perform legal research are typical events in the law firm atmosphere. Accurate, fast, and comprehensive research methods are essential. The Internet offers an alternative to print-based research, yet it is not the exclusive alternative to legal research. As you will learn in this chapter and throughout this text, libraries are not quite obsolete despite the rumors of their demise.

CASE FACT PATTERN

You have been assisting your attorney in the Jamison case. You have put in long hours of discovery and interviews, but the case was won at trial. Your attorney needs to present a detailed accounting of the time spent on the case and wants to bill for your services as a paralegal. She believes you have contributed in a meaningful manner to the case, but does not know the legal standards for billing paralegal services. Specifically, in the case you prepared numerous memoranda, drafted pleadings and motions, copied cases, and participated in numerous meetings. A hearing is scheduled next week before the judge to determine the amount of attorney's fees that will be awarded in the case. Your supervising attorney has requested that you research the law regarding billing paralegal services as part of an attorney's fee. You work for a small law firm and presently have access to only the Internet and not a fee-based service. You know there are cases on the subject, but you don't have the time to spend days in the library. A general Internet search engine may be the answer.

OVERVIEW OF PERFORMING AN INTERNET SEARCH

The sky is the limit—literally—on the Internet. Most of us have access to some form of the Internet, and expectations are high of finding the best, most up-to-date information when performing legal research. We have already explored the traditional types of legal research and have been introduced to Westlaw and LexisNexis, but what are the best methods to use for a comprehensive search on the Internet? The answer is searching by using "Boolean" or "natural language" techniques. These techniques are the most used and most common forms on the Internet. However, the results from an Internet search may depend on the technique used. Understanding the "hows" and "whys" of searching the Internet is the focus of this chapter.

Boolean word search
Word search technique using terms and connectors to retrieve information from the Internet.

terms and connectors
Words such as "and," "or," and "not," which link words and concepts to form a searching device on the Internet to retrieve documents and information.

Initiating a Boolean Word Search

When you create a relationship between words and phrases, you are performing the basics of a **Boolean word search.** Boolean searches construct a relationship among and between search terms. The technique is named after George Boole, who perfected the theory that a relationship exists between words and concepts. Basic Boolean searches rely upon the use of **terms and connectors.** These are words and terms that indicate a relationship with each other. The primary Boolean connectors are the words "and," "or," and "not." By using these connectors, you can broaden or limit your search.

PRACTICE TIP

Perfecting a Boolean search on the Internet takes practice. Experiment with different words and combinations of words to maximize your best Internet results.

The Connectors

This following subsections highlight the connectors used in Boolean word searches. The discussion shows that how you use connectors in a search will determine the information you retrieve from your search.

The "And" Connector

Let's consider the connector "and" first. The "and" connector locates concepts and words that are connected in a document. Since you are searching for two related concepts, an "and" search results in fewer documents in a search you create. The more "and" connectors in a search, the fewer documents retrieved. For example, using our facts from the Case Fact Pattern in this chapter, let's assume you are searching for information on the concept of whether attorney's fees include paralegals. Your search could be

attorney fees and paralegal

The result of the search would be documents that contain both words. If a document does not have both words, it would not show up in the search; hence, a more limited search gives a narrower result.

quotation marks
Punctuation used in a search that keeps related words and concepts together.

Source: ZIGGY © 2006 ZIGGY AND FRIENDS, INC. Reprinted with permission of UNIVERSAL PRESS SYNDICATE. All rights reserved.

Some searches could treat the words "attorney" and "fees" separately. A method to prevent this from happening is to place quotation marks around the group of words. If you have a group of words that relate to each other, use **quotation marks** (" "); they will keep the words together in your search. Consequently, if you added quotation marks to your search,

"attorney fees" and paralegal

your search will present results only where the words "attorney fees" appear together and not the words "attorney" and "fees" separately in the document.

Similarly, if you add a **wildcard** character such an **exclamation point** (!) or **asterisk** (*) to the root of the word, you will retrieve all variations of that word. A wildcard character allows the researcher to locate all variations of a word in a search, providing more "hits" in the process. When an exclamation point is used as a wildcard character, it is generally used to replace an unlimited number of letters in a root word. For example, in the preceding search if you placed an exclamation point after "attorney!" and "fee!" your search would produce results containing the words "attorneys fee," "attorneys fees," "attorney fee," and "attorney fees." All variations of the words would be retrieved. Using an exclamation point can be a double-edged sword, however. If the word has a number of root possibilities, your search could produce a number of documents that are unrelated to your search, such as the word "paralegal." If you substitute an exclamation point for "legal" in the word "paralegal,"—"para!"—you may have variations such as these: paragraph, paraprofessional, paraplegic, paranormal, and so on.

When your technique is not precise, you may have what is known as a *false positive* or *false negative* result in your research. A false negative or false positive occurs when more documents are retrieved in a search than either desired or applied. This is an inherent problem in key word searching, especially when using wildcards and root connectors. It is almost inevitable that you will retrieve documents in a key word search that are completely irrelevant to your intended search. You are probably wondering how to avoid false positives and false negatives in your research results. The answer, although seemingly simple in theory, is difficult to achieve: Craft an exacting key word search. Precision, experience, and plain "trial and error" will assist in producing the best results. Just don't give up. Your answer is only a mouse click away!

On the other hand, the asterisk (*) may be used for variations in spelling, such as "chairman" and "chairmen." Using the asterisk, "chairm*n," you will retrieve documents with both spellings. Additionally, if a word has multiple variations in its spelling, you can use an asterisk to retrieve all variations of the name or word. For example, you are searching for the name of the case that has "Greenpeace" as one of its party names. You might find this name spelled either "Greenpeace" or "Greenpiece," or even "Greenpeece." If you replace the common letters with asterisks, "Greenp**ce," all variations of the name will appear. Do not use an asterisk for the first letter of a word or name, however. (See Table 8.1 for a synopsis of the punctuation symbols used in Internet searches.)

wildcard
A character such as an exclamation point or asterisk entered into a search expression that acts as a substitution to retrieve all variations of the expression.

exclamation point
Punctuation used in a search, usually at the root of a search term, to retrieve all variations of the main word.

asterisk
Punctuation used in word searches that allows for variations in spelling when substituted for a letter in the search term.

PRACTICE TIP

Keep reminding yourself that there are no easy answers to performing key word searches on the Internet. The best advice is to have a methodical research plan and back up your research with some time spent in a law library for confirmation of your research results (especially new paralegals).

TABLE 8.1
Table of Punctuation Symbols

Asterisk (*)	Used for variation in spelling of search word. Gives all spelling alternatives. (Root expander)
Exclamation Point (!)	Used at the end of a word as a substitute for word variations. Gives all word variations from the main word. (Root expander)
Quotation Marks ("")	Keeps word phrases together as a group and not separate. The search will not separate words when punctuation is used. Similar to parentheses.
Parentheses ( ) (used later in chapter)	Groups terms and concepts and excludes others. Similar to quotation marks.

PRACTICE TIP

When using an exclamation point (!) as a root word extender, be sure that the exclamation point is used at the end of the word and only once in that word.

PRACTICE TIP

Common sense should not be left at the doorstep. When performing any search, whether print-based or Internet-based, begin by using the terms and connectors that are logical to your topic. Don't try to outguess or out-think the computer or a book.

Therefore, from your search you can retrieve documents that are completely out of the scope of your intended search. The way to avoid a false positive or false negative result is by creating a precise search. But those of us who have experienced searches on the Internet know that creating the "perfect search" is easier said than done! The end result is that, as in print-based research, you should keep trying different combinations until you begin receiving information that makes sense.

The "Or" Connector

The second Boolean connector is "or." Unlike the "and" connector, the "or" connector's results are broader. The "or" connector provides you with synonymous terms and is helpful when similar terms are used in your legal research problem. Synonymous terms would be "attorney" or "lawyer" or "counsel." Any term in that list could be in your document. Continuing with our example, using the "or" connector the search is:

attorney fees or paralegal
or
"attorney fees" or paralegal

The results of this search would contain documents with either the words "attorney's fees" or "paralegal." Sometimes the "or" search may be too general, producing too many documents that prove unhelpful. (Our false positive problem intrudes again.) Now let's try a combination of the "and" and "or" connectors. Adding "legal assistant" to our example, some of the possibilities are:

attorney fees and paralegal or legal assistant
or
"attorney fees" and paralegal or legal assistant
or
"attorney fees" and paralegal or "legal assistant"

With a combination of the connectors, your search results in documents that contain the words "attorney fees" and either "paralegal" or "legal assistant," resulting in more choices. The use of the quotation marks probably will generate more specific but narrower results. Your results also will be more relevant with documents that directly apply to your inquiry. Again, trial and error will determine which search produces the best results.

The "Not" Connector

The third and final Boolean connector is "not." When you use a "not" connector, documents will be excluded from your search. You need to be careful when using the "not" connector, because information you may want may be excluded. For example:

attorney fees and paralegal not legal assistant
or
"attorney fees" and paralegal not "legal assistant"

This search would result in documents that contain the information on paralegals and attorney fees but not documents that use the words "legal assistant." With this result, you may miss important cases on the subject.

A search using "not" is important when you *definitely* want to exclude certain results from your search. For example, often when a search is performed using the term "legal assistant," the term "legal secretary" often appears. By definition a legal secretary is considered different from a paralegal or legal assistant. Yet often searches for "legal assistant" will also retrieve documents containing the words "legal secretary" as a result. Consequently, a search with the "not" connector would be appropriate. Our continuing example is:

attorney fees and paralegal and legal assistant not legal secretary
or
"attorney fees" and paralegal and "legal assistant" not "legal secretary"

The search would exclude all documents that contain the words "legal secretary" in the search. This should substantially narrow your search results.

A WORD ABOUT SEARCH ENGINES

Search engines provide the link to the Internet or World Wide Web. A **search engine** can be either a software program that searches databases to gather information based upon a given set of search terms; or a Web site that searches the Internet for information related to a **query** or **key word search.** A key word search is a technique performed on an Internet search engine that searches the Web for related and relevant documents or Web pages. In response to the search, a list of documents that contain those search words are produced. There are a number of search engines on the Internet, which gather information about a topic queried.

Google.com, yahoo.com, and msn.com are just a few of the available search engines on the Internet. Each produces similar, yet different results when performing a search. Choosing the best search engine is a matter of preference. Each has its own nuances; each has its own methodologies for creating a search on its Web site. Whichever site you choose, review the help link for details of how best to perform a search on that Web site. Google, for example, suggests that the "and" connector is not necessary. It

search engine
A software program that searches databases to gather information based upon a given set of search terms or a Web site that searches the Internet for information related to a query.

query
A string of key terms or words used in a computer search.

key word search
Search technique performed using an Internet search engine to locate relevant documents or Web pages.

THE E-FACTOR

The Internet has broadened everyone's opportunities to find information, both legal and nonlegal resources. Courts are using more nonlegal sources in their decisions; yet with those citations come differences of opinions as to how to use them among the courts. Some courts use secondary sources or statistical information only as guidance and not as mandatory authority. Constitutions, cases, statutes, administrative rules and regulations, and court rules are still the standard for courts as well as attorneys. Statistical information can well be challenged and have no precedential value. Judge Samuel B. Kent, a U.S. district court judge in Texas, expressed concern about the sufficiency of the Internet and its electronic evidence. In *St. Clair v. Johnny's Oyster & Shrimp, Inc.*, 76 F. Supp. 2d 773 (S.D. Tex. 1999), the court made the following comments about the Internet:

> While some look to the Internet as an innovative vehicle for communication, the Court continues to warily and wearily view it largely as one large catalyst for rumor, innuendo, and misinformation. So as to not mince words, the Court reiterates that this so-called Web provides no way of verifying the authenticity of the alleged contentions that Plaintiff wishes to rely upon. . . . There is no way Plaintiff can overcome the presumption that the information he discovered on the Internet is inherently trustworthy. Anyone can put anything on the Internet. No web-site is monitored for accuracy and nothing contained therein is under oath or even subject to independent verification absent underlying documentation. Moreover, the Court holds no illusions that hackers can adulterate the content on any web-site from any location at any time. For these reasons, any evidence procured off the Internet is adequate for almost nothing, even under the most liberal interpretation. *Id.* at 774–75

The Court then concludes by saying that "[i]nstead of relying on the voodoo information taken from the Internet, Plaintiff must hunt for hard copy back-up documentation in admissible form. . . ." *Id.* at 775. Strong language and opinions from the court. Heed the words of the court in this case as his view, although it may seem eccentric on its face, is close to the viewpoint of many courts. The end result is: stick to the standard research plan. Use your primary sources of law and if other sources are helpful, bring them to the attention of your supervising attorney. Regardless of the source, know where you retrieved the information from the Internet. Many times you will find information on the Internet and when it is printed, the Web site is not delineated on the printout.

Therefore, a good practice is to write down on the actual printout, back or front, of the document the Internet source. Too many times we print sources from the Internet in haste and we forget to check whether that source has a reference noted at the bottom. Practice good habits and organizational skills when using the Internet. It will save time in the long run.

also suggests to capitalize the word "OR" in its search. Therefore, review the "help" section of the search engine for tips on its best use.

This point cannot be overemphasized. What works on one search engine may not work on another. Review the "help" pages of your chosen search engine for the best use of its site and, ultimately, the best results. Let's perform an actual search using the preceding example and see what happens.

TESTING THE INTERNET: IMPLEMENTING YOUR SEARCH TECHNIQUES

We will use the search engine Google. After typing www.google.com into the Web address box, enter the words "attorney fees paralegal." The result is over 100,000 entries. (See Figure 8.1.) By perusing the first couple of pages, you observe that a number of organizations, such as the National Federation of Paralegal Association (NFPA), have compiled information on paralegal fees. When you view the article, you will learn that a U.S. Supreme Court case addressed the issue in 1989: *Missouri v. Jenkins,* 491 U.S. 274 (1989). That would be a great start to any research project. Knowing that case, you could Shepardize the case and determine (1) which jurisdictions cited the case, (2) whether your jurisdiction cited the case, and (3) whether there are secondary sources that have reviewed the issue. Not a bad result for a general search. Undoubtedly, the search produced a vast number of results. You have to use your best judgment and common sense as to how many entries you need to review.

Continuing with our Google search, let's add the words "legal assistant" to our search. The results changed, but the Web sites listed are essentially the same. By adding the term "legal assistant," another paralegal organization with a comprehensive article is located. The National Association of Legal Assistants (NALA) has produced a detailed article of the definitions of paralegal and legal assistant as well as some

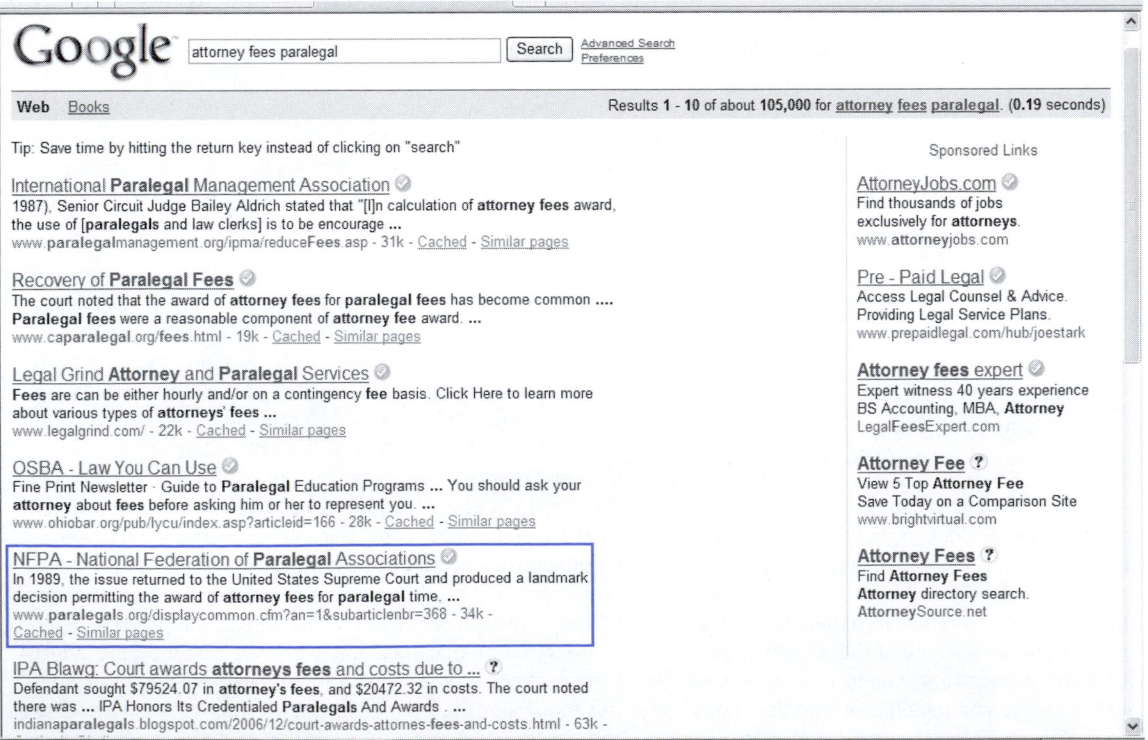

FIGURE 8.1 First Page of Results from Google Search

Source: Copyright © Google. Reprinted with permission.

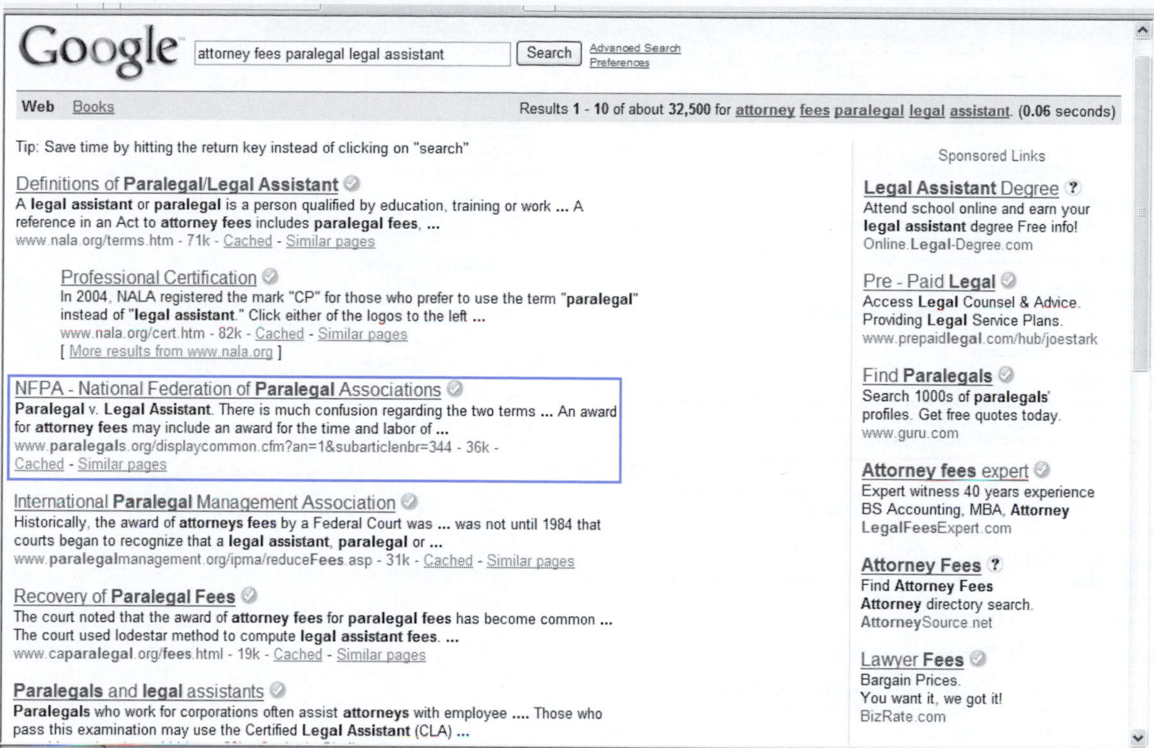

FIGURE 8.2 **First Page of Results from Google Search with Additional Terms and Connectors**

Source: Copyright © Google. Reprinted with permission.

case law, including the U.S. Supreme Court case, which has addressed the paralegal fee issue. Notice that this Web site was the second entry. (See Figure 8.2.) Once again, over 30,000 sites appear. Skim those sites that offer the best resources. The likelihood of reviewing all the sites is slim to none!

Now let's perform a search on www.msn.com. Using the same search criteria, "attorney fees paralegal," results similar to those of the Google search were produced. (See Figure 8.3.) The search provided the same sort of information but in much larger quantities—well over 400,000 entries. A similar search can be conducted at www.yahoo.com. Again, which search engine to use is your choice. No one search engine is better than another. Use the one with which you are most comfortable, but do explore other search engines. Be open to new possibilities.

YOU BE THE JUDGE

A judge admonished an assistant attorney general for not only presenting "bad law" to a court, but being embarrassed by a *pro se* plaintiff who also happened to be incarcerated. Such was the case in *Salahuddin v. Coughlin*, 999 F. Supp. 526 (S.D. N.Y. 1998). Citing a case that had a later precedent that was now controlling, the assistant attorney general failed to competently research and Shepardize his cases. Exasperated with the assistant attorney general's sloppiness, "the court could not fathom how . . ." the attorney could not uncover the controlling case either by Shepardizing, "a keynote search based on keynotes" . . . "or any word search. . . ." *Id.* at 540. Let this case be a warning. Competent research most certainly includes a complete legal search of all sources, including Shepardizing, key word searches, and traditional methods of legal research in order to raise to the level of competency required under the Rules of Professional Responsibility. Locate the case. Determine the facts of the case and what the assistant attorney general failed to do in his legal research. Why did the court admonish the attorney? What is the basis of the court's reasoning in the case?

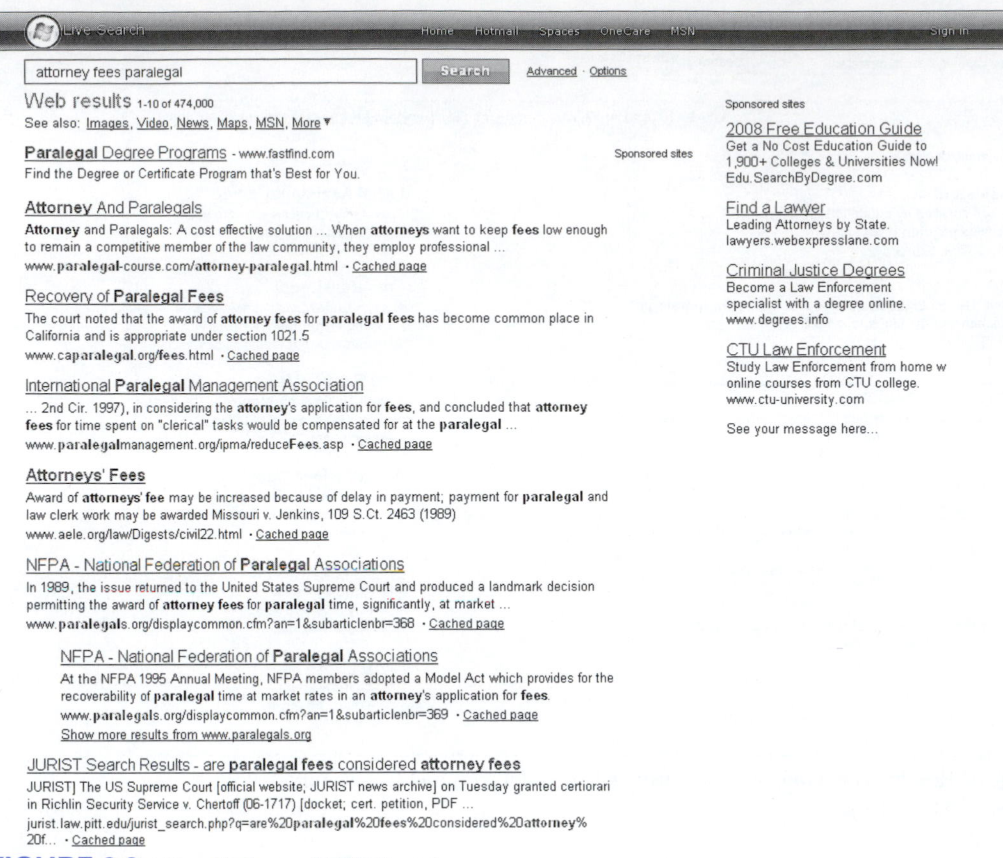

FIGURE 8.3 **Results from a MSN Search**

Source: MSN.com.

Words to Avoid in a Search

noise words
Common everyday words such as "the," "of," and "it," which are eliminated when performing an Internet search.

Some words are considered so common that you should not use them in a search. These words are referred to as **noise words.** Common noise words are listed in Table 8.2.

Some Web sites consider "and" and "or" noise words. Google considers "and" a noise word and does not require you to type in the word. A space between two words is automatically considered "and," at least on Google.com. It does require you to type in the word "or" in capital letters. This is suggested in Google's explanation of its Web site search techniques. Review the information in the Web site for words that it considers "noise words" and for its *best* approach in searching the Web site.

Initiating a Natural Language Search

natural language search
Search technique that uses conversational words to search the Internet.

A **natural language search** uses conversational language and words without the need for special terms and connectors. The words we speak or write are the words used in a natural search. With a natural language search you could search a phrase in quotations such as a famous quote from a U.S. Supreme Court justice: "I know it when I see it." The resulting search would produce all cases that have cited that expression. Suppose we want to know which case the phrase "I know it when I see it" came from. We enter those words on Google.com. The first page of the search results is shown in Figure 8.4.

What we learn from the search is that it comes from a U.S. Supreme Court case about pornography. The phrase is attributed to Justice Potter Stewart, who recognized the difficulty in defining pornography but aptly pronounced "I know it when I see it."

TABLE 8.2
Common Noise Words

Common Noise Words		
the	of	my
when	are	is
a	so	it

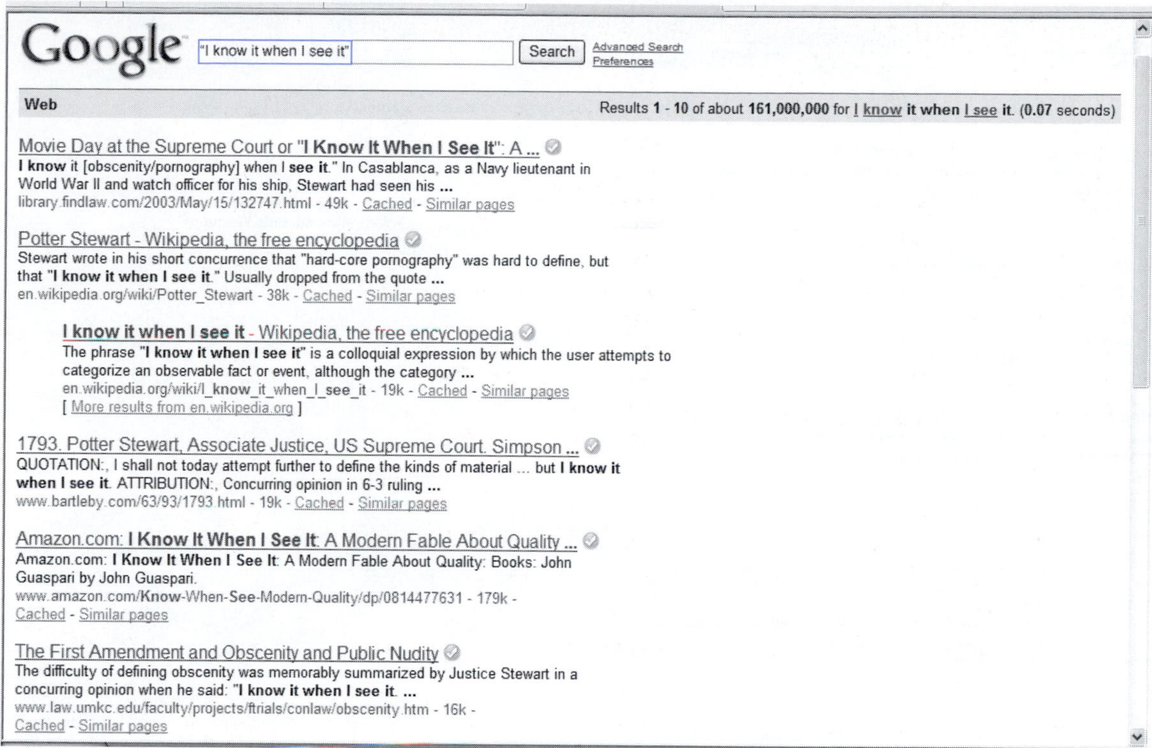

FIGURE 8.4 **Results of Google Search Using Natural Language**

Source: Copyright © Google. Reprinted with permission.

Now suppose we try a legal concept such as "Miranda warnings" and see what happens. We enter the search words "Miranda warnings" in the search box at google.com and press the Enter key. Numerous Web pages appear. Immediately we are led to the 1966 U.S. Supreme Court case, *Miranda v. Arizona,* which set forth the requirements of the warnings when a defendant is arrested or in custody. When we use terms and connectors on www.google.com, we have virtually the same result. (See Figure 8.5.) That should suggest that neither method is better than the other, although natural language searches are more difficult to interpret on a search engine than a Boolean-style search.

CYBER TRIP

Using a general search engine, locate a recent case(s) and commentary on whether reciting the Pledge of Allegiance interferes with the First Amendment right to freedom of religion.

A Web site that uses the natural language techniques is www.ask.com. In the text box, type in a question in natural language and click the Search button. For instance, a natural language search using our paralegal fee example would be:

Can paralegal fees be included in an award for attorneys' fees?

Your search may produce a number of false positive results leading to Web sites for paralegal jobs. You must go far enough into the search (perhaps several pages) to find an entry from the California Alliance of Paralegals. That Web site leads to a summary of many cases, including the leading U.S. Supreme Court case.

Don't limit your search techniques as the possibilities and results are endless. But do limit the words you choose to those that will retrieve the best results for the search requested. Experimenting on the Internet will only enhance your search skills. Practice does make perfect, at least, almost perfect. As you learned from testing a number of the search engines, you were able to locate the leading U.S. Supreme Court case and other cases from other jurisdictions without using a "fee-based" Web site.

Forming a Search Query

At this point, we need to pull all this Internet "gobbledygook" together. One of the first decisions that you need to make and ultimately ask yourself is: "Do I have

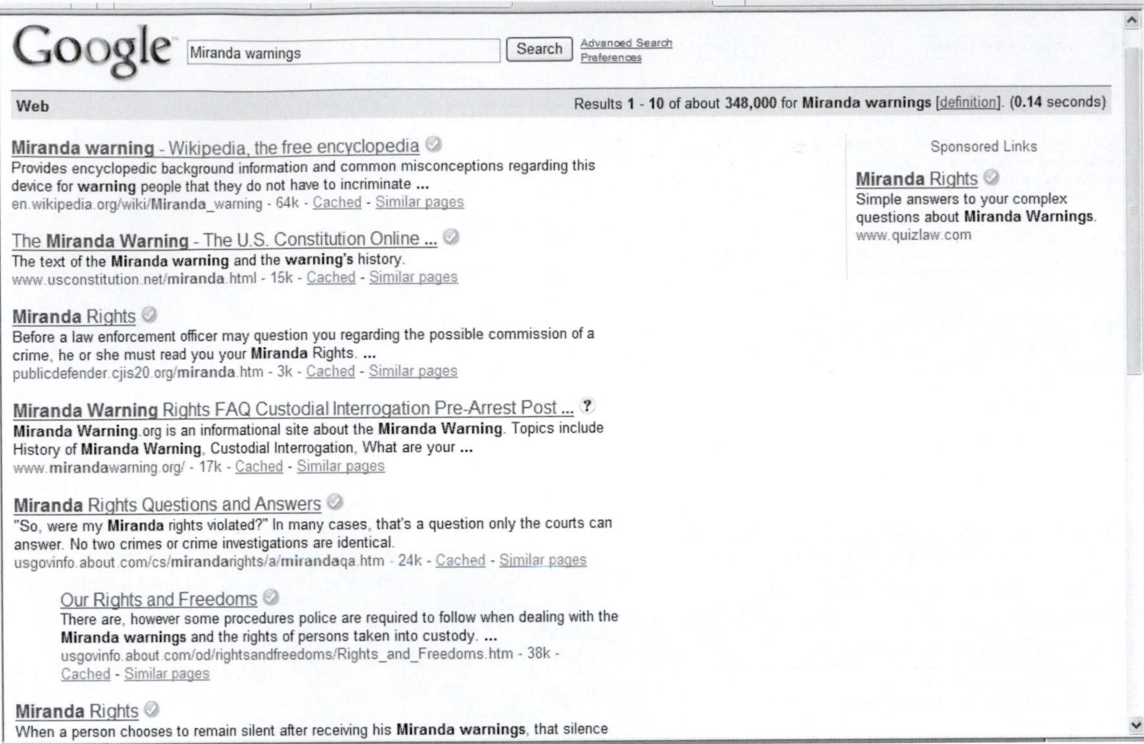

FIGURE 8.5 **Results from Google Search of "Miranda Warnings"**

Source: Copyright © Google. Reprinted with permission.

enough legal knowledge or information to formulate a reasonable inquiry?" If the answer is no, you need to educate yourself. Stop and review a legal encyclopedia for general information about the legal topic you need to research. This will assist you in choosing search words that are more relevant to your topic than jumping in blindly. Once you have educated yourself on the basics of the topic, decide your search mechanism. Are you performing a general Internet search on a search engine, such as Google or Yahoo!, or will you be using a fee-based Web site, such as Westlaw or LexisNexis? Regardless of your choice of Web sites, determine whether your best course of action is a key word/connector search (Boolean) or a natural language search.

If you are performing a key word/connector search, choose relevant words associated with your assignment. Enter those key words or terms in the text box. Press the Enter key and review your results. If your results are too broad or retrieve too many unrelated documents (false positives), begin using search connectors, such as "and" and "or." Do review the help information on the search engine site for its use of connectors. This will save time in the long run. Now, modify your original search query by adding search connectors. Remember, if you want to keep words or concepts together, use quotation marks or parentheses.

Recall that some search engines will allow you to limit your search to a sentence, a paragraph, or within a certain number of words. Use these techniques to focus your search if the search engine permits the technique. Once you are satisfied with the results of the search, begin reviewing the sources by clicking on the various Web sites or sources identified. If you are looking for primary sources of the law, be sure you check that they are still valid law through either a print or electronic medium.

On the other hand, if you are going to conduct a natural language search, construct a sentence that is precise, containing relevant words relating to the assignment. As with the key word search, consult an encyclopedia or some other source to educate yourself on an unfamiliar topic. Isolate the search engine you choose to use and enter in the text box the question or statement you want answered. Press Enter and view the results. If the results do not produce the information you believe is relevant, modify your word choice and begin again. Remember, Internet searches take time just as traditional methods of research do. It all hinges on picking the "right" (or best) search terms. This is not an exact science. There are no right or wrong answers. It is a process of trial and error, which sometimes is quick and easy, other times slow and difficult. Each query is different—just be patient.

Key Word Searches (Boolean)

Here is a checklist to follow for a basic Internet search.

1. Begin by reading a general legal source to provide insight on the topic.
2. Determine key words or phrases that apply to the research problem.
3. Press the Enter key to process the search on the Internet.
4. Review the results to determine relevancy.
5. Click on Web sites that appear relevant.
6. Review the information on the Web site.
7. If the search does not produce the appropriate sources, modify your search by (a) changing word choice, (b) checking spelling of words, (c) using connectors to refine the search, (d) reviewing the help techniques on the Web site, (e) adding punctuation, such as quotation marks or parenthesis, to keep words or concepts together, or (f) adding word limitations using w/n, w/s, or w/p.
8. Explore and exhaust all search combination possibilities within search engine parameters.
9. Repeat steps 2 through 6.
10. Continue modifying your search as suggested in step 7 until you retrieve the information desired.

PRACTICE TIP

If you are performing research on the Internet and you can't seem to find the information or source of law you are looking for, it might simply not be there. Move on or do something else, such as the step-by-step work used in print research.

Natural Language Searches

Here is a checklist for natural language searches:

1. Begin by reading a general legal source to provide insight on the topic.
2. Construct a sentence or question that uses key words relevant to the topic researching.
3. Press the Enter key to process the search on the Internet.
4. Review the results to determine relevancy.
5. Click on Web sites that appear relevant.
6. Review the information on the Web site.
7. If the search does not produce the desired results, modify the query by (a) replacing key words by using synonyms, (b) deleting noise words, or (c) checking spelling of words.
8. Repeat steps 2 through 6.
9. Continue modifying your search as suggested in step 7 until you retrieve the information desired.

CYBER TRIP

Using www.google.com, www.yahoo.com, and www.altavista.com, locate Web sites that provide government statistical information on smoking rates, heart attacks, and colon cancer in the United States.

Quick Quiz True/False Questions

1. A Boolean search is the only method of searching for information on the Internet.
2. An exclamation point can be used as a root word expander, increasing search results.

3. Boolean search techniques use "and," "or," and "not" connectors.
4. An asterisk (*) is always used as a root word expander.
5. Natural language searches and Boolean searches are the same.

LEXISNEXIS AND WESTLAW: THE SAME, YET DIFFERENT

It is no secret that ThomsonWest and LexisNexis are the two main fee-based providers of online legal research sources. Each provides the researcher with vast amounts of legal information from cases and statutes to Shepard's and KeyCite. Choosing the service best suited to your needs is a matter of preference or simple availability; you may not be the one deciding which service to use. Consequently, understanding how each online service works is important to learning online search techniques.

Search Techniques for LexisNexis

LexisNexis provides for both Boolean and natural language searches on its fee-based Web site. Use the search techniques identified in this chapter and add variations. For example, on LexisNexis you can limit a word search to words within a sentence or paragraph using **proximity connectors.** A proximity connector is a term used to limit or specify results within a search inquiry. With proximity connectors, you can tailor your results more closely and eliminate extraneous unrelated terms, or at least, have more applicable results. LexisNexis has a number of proximity connectors available. We will explore some of those connectors.

proximity connector
Term used to limit or specify results within a search inquiry.

Search Connectors on LexisNexis

LexisNexis uses the Boolean connectors "and," "not," and "or" in the same context as we have previously discussed in the first part of this chapter. We will explore the additional search connectors that LexisNexis offers and recommends for a more meaningful and successful search experience.

Finding Words in Close Proximity to Each Other

LexisNexis allows the researcher to link concepts and words by limiting their proximity to the number of words surrounding the main concept you are searching. The symbol that LexisNexis uses is "w/n," which stands for "within" a specified "number" (between 1 and 255) of words. We continue with our Case Fact Pattern example: Suppose you wanted to search for the words "attorney fees" and "paralegal" within ten words of each other. Your search would be:

attorney fees w/10 paralegal

This locates the word "paralegal" within ten words of "attorney fees." You may be thinking, "So what? What type of information does that retrieve? And why place a limit on a word's proximity to another word or phrase?" The reason this is important is that if the words and concepts are close together, there is a higher likelihood that the case or statute retrieved from the search will produce information on the situation you need. The theory is that the further apart the words, the further apart the issues are conceptually. More "hits" with close proximity suggests that the case or statute probably discusses the issue you need: whether an award of attorney fees includes paralegal fees.

Some other variations of the "w/n" connector are "w/s" and "w/p." When these search connectors are used, you are looking for words within the "same sentence" or words within the "same paragraph." In our example, let's create the search query

attorney fees w/s paralegal
or
attorney fees w/p paralegal

Your search would find the words "attorney fees" in a document either in the same sentence or in the same paragraph as "paralegal." Again, the closer the proximity and the more times the combination appears in the document, the higher the likelihood the document is one you would want to review.

You can also combine the preceding techniques with **parentheses** to group terms and concepts and exclude others. Parentheses are used to keep related concepts together in your search similar to the quotation marks. By using parentheses you have better control of the quality of the results. For example,

attorney w/2 fees paralegal or legal w/2 assistant

In this search, you may retrieve documents that have "attorney" within two words of "fees" and "paralegal" or just "attorney" and "fees" or "attorney fees" within two words of legal and not the words "legal assistant." This search would probably produce a number of false positive results. If you group the terms using parentheses, such as (attorney w/2 fees) and paralegal or (legal w/2 assistant), you should retrieve documents that contain either "paralegal" or "legal assistant" in close proximity to "attorney fees." Remember, you can also use the root expanders to enhance your search and quotation marks. There are a multitude of variations for your search.

LexisNexis provides options to search for terms "not" within certain proximity of another word. Suppose you are researching England's involvement in the Iraq War. You do not want to retrieve documents on "New England" in the United States. You could refine your search by inserting the "not" connector. Your search query would be: England NOT w/3 New. This would exclude the word "new" from the search if it is three words or less in proximity of the word "England."

Natural Language Searches on LexisNexis

An alternative search method using natural language is available on LexisNexis as well. In a natural language search on LexisNexis, you can enter descriptive terms and

PRACTICE TIP

Use the "w/n" connector with a low number to locate variations of names. For example, a search for Franklin D. Roosevelt could be "Franklin w/3 Roosevelt." This would produce results for Franklin Roosevelt, Franklin D. Roosevelt, and Franklin Delano Roosevelt.

parentheses
Form of punctuation used to group concepts and terms together in a search inquiry.

PRACTICE TIP

LexisNexis provides detailed "help tools" on its Web site for assisting in Boolean and proximity connector searches. Use these tools to navigate through the site more effectively .

A DAY IN THE LIFE OF A PARALEGAL

As a paralegal, you may work in a small or large law firm. Financial resources often play a role in the availability of your legal research sources. Sometimes you have to improvise, especially when Westlaw and LexisNexis are not available. Performing a general search on Google, Yahoo!, or other search engines may be your only alternative. Thus, you may find a case that is helpful and have a citation for a state case only, but you need a regional reporter citation as you want to review the headnotes. The Internet is not helpful and you are stuck. What can you do? One of the possibilities is to visit a law library and use print-based material to assist your search. If you are faced with a citation to a great case that does not have headnotes or a regional reporter citation, check the Decennial Digest Table of Cases. You can look up the case and locate the regional reporter citation. Retrieve the regional reporter, look up the case, and review the headnotes for the point or points of law that apply to your set of facts. With the topic and key from the regional reporter, you can then use any digest to find cases from your jurisdiction. As you can see, print material is handy when the Internet does not provide all the legal sources you may need. As a paralegal, don't limit yourself to mastering one method of research to the exclusion of the other. Be versatile. Be flexible. Be resourceful. You never know when you may be placed in a situation where the Internet is unavailable and all that's available is a library.

PRACTICE TIP

You can combine the natural language and Boolean search techniques on LexisNexis for an enhanced search.

concepts without focusing on the Boolean-type connectors. Create a search that is in everyday language. A natural language search with our Case Fact Pattern is

Can paralegal fees be included as part of an attorney fee award?

Click the search button and cases will appear in order of their importance. You can also add restrictions in the FOCUS feature. In essence, that is a terms and connector search.

Often individuals use a natural language search when introduced to a new area of the law since they may be unfamiliar with the "key terms" in that area. Or individuals are simply more comfortable using natural language in formulating their search. Regardless of the reasons for using one method over the other, both are available on LexisNexis.

Search Techniques for Westlaw

Like LexisNexis, you can perform both a Boolean-style (terms and connectors) search and a natural language search on Westlaw. Simply select your preferred method of searching and begin.

Terms and Connector Search

Perform a terms and connector search when you looking for a document that contains certain terms or when you are looking for specific information. Remember to connect the relationship between the terms and its connectors. Westlaw's use of terms and connectors is slightly different from LexisNexis. On Westlaw use the connector "and" but use the symbol "&" instead of the words. The term "or" is used by indicating a space and not typing in the word "or," although the search engine will not reject the term. In our example for the terms "paralegal" or "legal assistant," on Westlaw you would only type a space between the words and not the "or" connector.

PRACTICE TIP

Be reminded that not all databases on Westlaw contain the same information or use the same method of document retrieval.

Similarly, the "not" connector is different. Use the symbol "%" rather than the word "not" added to the query.

Westlaw does have numerical and proximity connectors. Add a number to a connector and your search will limit the proximity of the word to within the number of words cited: attorney fees /3 paralegal. The search will look for the term "attorney fees" and "paralegal" within three words of each other.

You also can search terms within the same sentence and same paragraph by using the following combination (as LexisNexis): /s or /p. With these connectors your key words will be in the same sentence or same paragraph, respectively.

Let's continue using our paralegal fees example. The "terms and connectors" search box was selected. First entered was the search: attorney fees and paralegal or legal assistant. The search produced 10,000 documents. That was definitely too many results and too broad. To narrow the search the "w/3" was added to both paralegal and legal assistant. The query was: attorney fees w/3 paralegal or w/3 legal assistant. Although better, that search produced 550 documents—still too many documents to review. Quotation marks were added to the words "attorney fees" and "legal assistant" with the final search query: "attorney fees" & w/3 paralegal or w/3 "legal assistant." That search resulted in 100 documents, which included the U.S. Supreme Court case *Missouri v. Jenkins*. (See Figure 8.6.) Each search highlighted the key words in yellow on the screen (and shown in bold in Figure 8.6) and offered additional words that may have assisted the search. Clearly this exercise was a bit of trial and error, but it also employed the refining search techniques we learned in the chapter and the ones you will use as a paralegal.

Natural Language Searches

Natural language searches are as easy as typing in a question. The key is creating sufficient specificity to either retrieve the cases you need or create a general query and retrieve more cases than you want or may need. A natural language search may be the

QUERY - "ATTORNEY FEES" & PARALEGAL OR "LEGAL ASSISTANT." DATABASES(S) - SCT

1. West Virginia University Hospitals, Inc. v. Casey, 499 U.S. 83, 111 S.Ct. 1138, 1991 WL 34485, 55 Fair Empl. Prac.Cas. (BNA) 353, 55 Empl. Prac. Dec. P 40,606, 113 L.Ed.2d 68, 59 USLW 4180, 67 Ed. Law Rep. 37, Med & Med GD (CCH) P 39,109, , U.S.Pa., March 19, 1991(No. 89-994.89-994)

   . . . statutory authority. 28 U.S.C.A. §§ 1821(b) 1920(3) [2] 102 Costs 102VII Amount, Rate, and Items 102 171 k. **Attorney'sFees.** 102 Costs 102VII Amount, Rate, and Items 102 183 Witnesses' Fees 102 187 k. Experts. **Attorneyfees** and expert fees are separate elements of litigation costs, and statutory authorization for award of **attorneyfees** does not include award of expert fees. [3] 361 Statutes 361VI Construction and Operation 361VI(A) General Rules of Construction . . .

   . . . facile attribution of congressional "forgetfulness" cannot justify such usurpation. [6] 78 Civil Rights 78III Federal Remedies in General 78 1477 **AttorneyFees** 78 1486 k. Services or Activities for Which Fees May Be Awarded. (Formerly 78k301 Fees for services rendered by experts in civil rights litigation may not be shifted to losing party pursuant to Civil Rights **Attorney'sFees** Awards Act, which permits award of "reasonable attorney's fee." 42 U.S.C.A. § 1988 Syllabus FN* The syllabus constitutes no part . . .

   . . . b) Statutory usage before, during, and after 1976 (the date of § 1988 's enactment) did not regard the phrase "**attorney'sfees**" as embracing fees for experts' services. Pp. 1141–1143. (c) At the time of § 1988 's enactment, judicial usage did not regard the phrase "**attorney'sfees**" as including experts' fees. Pp. 1143–1146. (d) Where, as here, a statute contains a phrase that is unambiguous, this . . .

2. Commissioner, I.N.S. v. Jean, 496 U.S. 154, 110 S.Ct. 2316, 1990 WL 71432, 110 L.Ed.2d 134, 20 Envtl. L. Rep. 20,910, Med & Med GD (CCH) P 38,530, Unempl.Ins.Rep. (CCH) P 15427A, , U.S.Fla., June 04, 1990(No. 89-601.89-601)

   . . . hearings and of detaining Haitian refugees during pendency of applications for asylum without any parole. Refugees moved for award of **attorneyfees** and costs under Equal Access to Justice Act (EAJA) after conclusion of underlying litigation. The United States District Court for the Southern District of Florida Eugene P. Spellman, J., awarded **attorneyfees** and costs, and appeal was taken. The Court of Appeals, Eleventh Circuit, 863 F.2d 759, upheld finding that refugees . . .

   . . . fee hearing, however, the Court of Appeals decided that certain errors required that the case "be remanded for recalculation of **attorney'sfees** and expenses." Id., at 780. In view of this holding, we must assume that at least some of the positions . . .

   . . . award of fees for the merits phase of the litigation. But the government should not be required to pay for **attorney'sfees** and expenses incurred in separate litigation over the availability and size of the fee award unless the position of the . . .

3. Missouri v. Jenkins by Agyei, 491 U.S. 274, 109 S.Ct. 2463, 1989 WL 63856, 50 Fair Empl.Prac.Cas. (BNA) 17, 50 Empl. Prac. Dec. P 39,069, 105 L.Ed.2d 229, 57 USLW 4735, 54 Ed. Law Rep. 16, , U.S.Mo., June 19, 1989(No. 88-64.88-64)

   . . . No. 88-64. Argued Feb. 21, 1989. Decided June 19, 1989. Prevailing plaintiffs in school desegregation case sought recovery of **attorneyfees**. The United States District Court for the Western District of Missouri, Russell G. Clark, J., awarded **attorneyfees**, and appeal was taken. The Court of Appeals for the Eighth Circuit, 838 F.2d 260, affirmed. On grant of . . .

   . . . the Supreme Court, Justice Brennan, held that: (1) Eleventh Amendment did not prohibit enhancement of fee award under Civil Rights **Attorney'sFees** Awards Act against state to compensate for delay in payment, and (2) separate compensation award under Civil Rights **Attorney'sFees** Awards Act for paralegals, law clerks, and recent law school graduates at prevailing rates was fully in accord with Act. Affirmed. Justice O'Connor concurred . . .

   . . . on 170BIV(A) In General 170B 264 Suits Against States 170B 265 k. Eleventh Amendment in General; Immunity. Award of **attorneyfees** ancillary to prospective relief in civil rights action is not subject to strictures of Eleventh Amendment. U.S.C.A. Const.Amend. 11 42 . . .

[text omitted]

FIGURE 8.6 **Results from Terms and Connectors Search on Westlaw Using the Paralegal Fee Example**

Source: Reprinted with permission from ThomsonWest.

CYBER TRIP

Locate the *Brown* case used in You Be the Judge through an Internet search using the principles addressed in this chapter.

best direction when your knowledge of a topic is limited. The natural language search does not require that you create a specific query. Again, this has good and bad points. It truly depends on what your search goals are. Now, let's perform a natural language search on Westlaw using the Case Fact Pattern. The query entered in the text box is "Can paralegal fees be included in attorney fees award?" (See Figure 8.7.)

Notice our results produced the leading U.S. Supreme Court case on the issue, *Missouri v. Jenkins*. It also produced a recent 2006 case as well as 99 other documents. Additionally our "key" search terms are highlighted in yellow on the screen (bold in Figure 8.7), allowing you to quickly determine the relevant cases. When reviewing the complete search results from Westlaw, observe at the top of the page suggested words that might refine your results. If you choose, you then can modify your search query question by clicking "Edit Search" and add some of the suggested search terms for more specificity. Your next job is to review the documents for relevancy.

FIGURE 8.7
Results from Natural Language Search on Westlaw Using the Paralegal Fee Example

Source: Reprinted with permission from ThomsonWest.

QUERY - CAN PARALEGAL FEES BE INCLUDED IN ATTORNEY FEES AWARD? DATABASE(S) - ALLFEDS, SCT

1. Richlin Sec. Service Co. v. Chertoff, 472 F.3d 1370 (Fed.Cir., Dec 26, 2006)(NO. 2006-1055)

   paralegal, he could recover at or near the full market rate for **paralegals.** The effect would be to encourage lawyers to refer work to **paralegals** so that full fee recovery could be obtained. This would create a different incentive than the one relied on by the Supreme Court in Jenkins. There the Court concluded that allowing **paralegal fee** recovery would result in the more efficient performance of legal services by allowing lawyers to use **paralegals** at a lower hourly rate in accordance with their normal practice. See Jenkins, 491 U.S. at 288, 109 S.Ct. 2463. Here treating **paralegal fees** as **attorney's fees** would distort the normal allocation of work and result in a less efficient performance of legal services. Finally, there is also no legislative history supporting the **award of paralegal fees** at market rates. Quite the contrary, the legislative history of EAJA supports the conclusion that **paralegal** services are

2. Missouri v. Jenkins by Agyei, 491 U.S. 274, 109 S.Ct. 2463, 105 L.Ed.2d 229, 57 USLW 4735, 50 Fair Empl.Prac.Cas. (BNA) 17, 50 Empl. Prac. Dec. P 39,069, 54 Ed. Law Rep. 16 (U.S.Mo., Jun 19, 1989)(NO. 88-64)

   award of attorney's fees to compensate for delay, it is logical to conclude that § 1988, a more narrowly worded statute, likewise does not allow interest (through the use of current hourly rates) to be tacked on to an **award of attorney's fees** against a State. Compensation for delay in payment was one of the reasons the District Court used current hourly rates in calculating respondents' **attorney's fees.** See App. to Pet. for Cert. A26-A27; 838 F.2d 260, 263, 265 (CA8 1988). I would reverse the **award of attorney's fees** to respondents and remand so that the fees can be calculated without taking compensation for delay into account. Chief Justice REHNQUIST, dissenting. I agree with Justice O'CONNOR that the Eleventh Amendment does not permit an **award of attorney's fees** against a State which includes compensation for delay in payment. Unlike Justice O'CONNOR, however, I do not agree with the Court's

3. Parise v. Riccelli Haulers, Inc., 672 F.Supp. 72 (N.D.N.Y., Nov 03, 1987)(NO. 83-CV-491)

   fee application, plaintiff claims 86.45 hours of **paralegal** work. 82.75 of these hours were performed by two **paralegals** with extensive experience in labor law and ERISA matters. The work performed included the drafting of pleadings, reviewing documents, drafting and engaging in correspondence and calculating delinquencies—all of this work would assuredly have been performed by attorneys had **paralegals** not undertaken it. Given the **paralegals'** experience, it is probable the attorneys would have expended a comparable number of hours at much higher rates if the **paralegals** had not been involved. The court believes such cost saving measures should be encouraged and accordingly **awards** as a component of its **attorneys' fees award paralegals' fees**

LexisNexis	Westlaw
"And" Connector	
Uses "and" connector	Uses the symbol "&"
"Or" Connector	
Uses the "or" connector	Uses a "space" and not "or"
"Not" Connector	
Uses "and not" Uses "not" w/number	Uses symbol "%" Can use words "but not"
Proximity Connectors	
For sentence: w/s For paragraph: w/p For words within word: w/number, i.e. w/5	For sentence: /s For paragraph: /p For words within word: /number, i.e. /5
Wildcards (!) and (*)	
Uses wildcards	Uses wildcards
Quotation Marks	
Uses quotation marks for phrases and closely related terms	Uses quotation marks for phrases and closely related terms

TABLE 8.3
Table Comparing LexisNexis and Westlaw Search Techniques

PRACTICE TIP

Natural language searches are generally not as effective as a well-constructed terms and connector (Boolean-style) search.

LexisNexis and Westlaw have similar features, and both will assist in finding the legal research sources you need to complete a project. Table 8.3 summarizes some of the differences and similarities between LexisNexis and Westlaw.

Quick Quiz True/False Questions

1. Westlaw and LexisNexis both use Boolean and natural language search techniques.
2. To limit a search to within five words of a related word, use the notation "w/s."
3. Quotation marks will separate related words in a search.
4. Both an exclamation point and an asterisk are considered wildcards on LexisNexis and Westlaw.
5. Westlaw has search field restrictions.

judicial notice
When a court acknowledges a fact that is reasonably known in a jurisdiction or is capable of accurate determination and whose source cannot be questioned.

YOU BE THE JUDGE

Use of Internet Web sites caught the attention of a court in Pennsylvania. In *Commonwealth v. Brown,* 839 A.2d 433 (Pa. Super. 2003), an appellate court overturned a lower court's decision because it took **judicial notice** (occurs when a court acknowledges a fact that is reasonably known in a jurisdiction or capable of accurate determination and whose source cannot be questioned. *Id.* at 435) of the Web site "MapQuest." In finding that the lower court erred in giving judicial notice to the Internet site MapQuest, the court unequivocally observed that

> an Internet site such as MapQuest TM, which purports to establish distances between two locations, is not so reliable that its "accuracy cannot reasonably be questioned." An Internet site determining distances does not have the same inherent accuracy as do professionally accepted medical dictionaries, or encyclopedias, or other matters of common knowledge within the community. *Id.* at 436.

Citing the disclaimer of the quality of its information on MapQuest, the court rejected any notion of accuracy on the site. In fact, the court showed how the accuracy of the distances on the Web site could be challenged. The end result was that the Commonwealth, which prosecuted the case, needed to rethink its use of "electronic source data." Review the *Brown* case and draw your own conclusions. Was the result of the court correct? Why or why not? What facts did the court focus on to reach its result? What was the disposition in the case?

list server
An Internet e-mail subscription list that provides a place for multiple computer users to access information common to a group or individual's interest.

PRACTICE TIP

List servers are often referred to as "listservs," after the Listserv software from L-Soft International, which was the first such program.

ETHICS ALERT

Communication through the Internet is common. Today there are chat rooms, blogs, and instant messaging. Information is instant in our virtual world. One of the creations of the Internet age is list servers. By definition, a **list server** provides a place where multiple computer users can access through the Internet information that is common to the group. List servers post such banal items from informational bulletins and meetings to information on the more complex legal issues that arise on a daily basis. The question is: "Can I use a list server as a substitute for performing legal research?" This poses a dangerous question.

List servers often offer advice to their members: some of it good; some of it bad. When you rely upon the information as your "sole source," the problem begins. A criticism of many legal list servers is that attorneys and even paralegals who want a quick answer to a question post the question, wait for the answer, and act. No independent research is commenced. Essentially, the list server member takes the information and runs with it. Bad practice.

There is no doubt that list servers offer multitudes of information for support, guidance, and counseling. But remember, list server information, no matter how tempting, is not a substitute for performing your job. It is an ethics violation for you, the paralegal, as well as for your attorney when competent legal research is not performed. If you get caught trying to shortcut or sidestep your responsibilities, you could get fired or your supervising attorney could get sanctioned if bad information is presented to a court.

When you check the Web, you'll find thousands of list servers: all types and all specialties. Professional list servers exist for every area of the law. The Colorado Bar Association has a Paralegal Committee list server. It states that

> The Paralegal Committee listserv is designed to serve the needs of paralegals who are members of the Colorado Bar Association. Additionally, the listserv will allow for an active and ongoing dialogue between associate members of the Colorado Bar Association Paralegal Committee on issues ranging from the simple to the complex, on many various topics, such as practice-specific issues, and issues regarding the business of law, such as employee issues and job opportunities, law office software and hardware, and ethics considerations. It is hoped that the Committee's more experienced members will assist those less experienced by adding their thoughts to this list. (from www.cobar.org)

Virtually all the bar and paralegal associations have list servers. Their members warn of the lists' limitations especially in the legal area. They are helpful, but you must understand their limitations and purpose. Don't substitute the advice of a list server member for plain, old-fashioned work. Always check your legal sources before you cite them or present them to your attorney. List servers are not the answer to the problem presented in an assignment; they may only be a helpful link.

PRACTICAL CONSIDERATIONS: AN INTEGRATED APPROACH

Courts do not accept information from the Internet as proof of the information's existence or authority. This point is clear from the cases cited in this chapter. Although the Internet opens the "information highway" to limitless bounds, the legal profession has not jumped on the bandwagon. Continue to pay close attention to your primary sources of the law. Primary sources of the law can be located on the Internet, but some sites are not considered the "official source." Be careful when retrieving information from the Internet. Watch where you are retrieving information, and do not eliminate the traditional sources of research from your vocabulary yet. Use a combined approach to legal research and not one of exclusion—traditional books, the Internet, and specialized legal research fee-based sites.

When researching on the Internet, try to use the official court Web sites as your sources when the commercial fee-based sites are unavailable. Stay away from sources that offer "interpretations" of the law and not the law itself. Unless you have a clear understanding of the law you are researching, the Internet can be frustrating and worse yet, provide suspect results. Web sites such as Wikipedia offer information that is useful but unverified. For a paralegal and a lawyer, this could be the "kiss of death."

Therefore, do not disregard the "traditional" legal research tools in favor of exclusive use of the Internet. On the Internet, it is more difficult to perform a step-by-step approach with controlled access and controlled results. Whether we like it or not, books do provide a more controlled approach, but of course, they provide limitations as well. The message to take with you is: use "all" the legal sources available in concert with each other for the more effective results. As is clear from the cases cited in this chapter, in the eyes of many courts, we are still not there yet. Let that be a lesson and a warning to you.

CYBER TRIP

Using any available legal resource, find cases in your jurisdiction discussing the topics of negligence per se and *res ipsa loquitur.*

Summary

Two techniques for searching on the Internet are Boolean searches and natural language searches. A Boolean search uses "terms and connectors" to perform a search. The most common connectors are "and," "or," and "not." There are also wildcard symbols, which allow variations on words used in a search. Wildcards include exclamation points and asterisks. The other common search technique is a natural language search. This search uses everyday conversational language to create a search. Either method is acceptable. Choose the method that either is most comfortable or serves the purpose for which you are researching.

Searches on LexisNexis and Westlaw use proximity connectors. With proximity connectors, you are searching for words or concepts that are within a sentence, a paragraph, or a defined number of words. The symbols used are: /s, /p/, and w/n (w/5).

Searches can also be performed by using a general search engine, such as www.google.com, www.yahoo.com, www.msn.com, or www.ask.com. Each assists the researcher in locating documents and Web pages on the Internet. Search engines help locate cases and information when a fee-based research service is unavailable.

The two main fee-based legal research services are LexisNexis and Westlaw. Both provide for terms and connector and natural language searches. Each also provides different ways to search the sites. Check the Web site help section to determine the best method of effectively using the site.

Key Terms

asterisk
Boolean word search
exclamation point
judicial notice
key word search
list server
natural language search
noise words
parentheses
proximity connector
query
quotation marks
search engine
terms and connectors
wildcard

Review Questions

1. What is a Boolean search?
2. What is a natural language search?
3. Identify why search terms and connectors are necessary in Internet research?
4. What are the advantages of searching online using the connector "and"? The connector "or"?

5. What are noise words?
6. When the terms "w/s" and "w/p" are used in a search, what are the search results?
7. What are the results in a search when a wildcard is used?
8. When an exclamation point (!) is used as part of a word in a search, what is the result?
9. List two differences between a Westlaw and LexisNexis search.
10. What are three advantages and disadvantages of an online legal research inquiry?

Exercises

1. Your attorney has asked you to research the elements needed to prove a case of tortious interference with contract in your state. Perform an Internet search on the issue.
2. A new client retained your law firm to represent him. His wife is presently on life support since she had a stroke after giving birth to their child. The husband wants to disconnect the life support, but his wife's family objects.
   a. What terms and connectors could you use to commence a search?
   b. Begin by entering your search terms on your chosen Web site. What are your results?
   c. Using the results from (b), limit your search to your jurisdiction.
3. Using a general search engine, such as Google, MSN, or Yahoo, locate information on the states that passed legislation requiring school-aged girls to be vaccinated with the cervical cancer vaccine.
4. Using print and electronic information, determine the elements in your state of the following causes of action:
   a. burglary
   b. trespass
   c. consumer fraud/deceptive trade
   d. assault and battery
   e. kidnapping
   f. breach of contract
   g. sexual harassment
5. Perform a search locating the statistics from your state on smoking rates.
6. A client has retained your law firm to prosecute a case against the manufacturer of her 2004 Ford Escape. Her brakes were defective, causing her to run into several parked cars when she attempted to brake. Apparently, she did some research and determined that her model year has been recalled. Research the general issues involved in the case. Prepare a general research plan, using your jurisdiction as the guide.
7. What would be your search query(s) using appropriate search terms and connectors for the following fact pattern:

   The Board for Wireless Computers, Inc. is recommending the purchase of World Telecommunication, LLC. The board votes to purchase the company as it believes World Tel will increase its market share. Both companies are privately held and do not trade on the U.S. stock exchange. After some due diligence from the board's legal counsel, Wireless learns that one of its board members is a silent equity partner in World Tel. The board had a special meeting and questions the validity of the transaction. (Hint: Check a general legal source, such as a legal encyclopedia, to gain insight on the responsibilities of board members before constructing your search query.)

8. Locate the following legal sources on the Internet:
   a. Federal statute on No Child Left Behind
   b. U.S. constitutional amendment that limits the president to two terms in office
   c. State source for powers of governor and legislatures (of your state)
   d. A law review or legal periodical on the issue of employees' privacy rights in the workplace
   e. Federal regulations that monitor air traffic controllers and the number of hours they can work before requiring a break

PORTFOLIO ASSIGNMENT

Read the following and complete the assignment at the end.

FACTS

On April 29, 1985, John Ruiz came to the United States from the Dominican Republic. He began working at the state Department of Health in the Medicaid Department as a clerk preparing customer bills and other related duties. While at the Department, he was supervised by Harry Sanderson, who taught him all the "ins and outs" of patient billing. Ruiz was promoted to a customer service representative in 1996. While Sanderson was on vacation in 1998, Ruiz was asked to assist in the billing of Medicaid patients. Ruiz told the Acting Supervisor, Mr. Steven Marks, that he was too busy working on his own work and could not help. Mr. Marks was not happy and had Ms. Martha Albright do the work. Ms. Albright had worked as a customer service representative since 1979. Mr. Ruiz was written up for being insubordinate.

When Sanderson returned from vacation, it was business as usual. Later that year, Sanderson prepared an evaluation of Ruiz and rated him satisfactorily. He even suggested that he be trained to assume more supervisory acts as Sanderson was thinking of retiring.

Ruiz is a member of a union. As part of the Collective Bargaining Agreement it states that "when a person is placed in an acting position, seniority must be considered when persons of equal title are being considered for the position." Sanderson sent his retirement notice to the Commissioner stating that his last day of work would be December 31, 2000.

Although Sanderson recommended Ruiz for his position, the Department placed Albright as the Acting Supervisor for the Medicaid section. Ms. Albright was from the country of Barbados. Ruiz was not happy. He believed he was most qualified for the job and stated that the reason he was not chosen as the Acting Supervisor was because he was from the Dominican Republic. He believed he was the most qualified person for the position and vowed to "get even." He refused to help Ms. Albright and when the work piled up, he kept calling in sick and disappearing from work. Ms. Albright's initial appointment was from January 1, 2001, through June 30, 2001. She would be paid an additional $5,000 for the additional duties.

In March, 2001, the Human Resources Department of the Department of Health posted a position for Supervisor of the Medicaid Division. The posting listed the qualifications and stated that all interested applicants should apply to the Human Resources Department from March 5 through March 21, 2001.

In January, 2001, Mr. Ruiz applied for leave from March 4 to March 20, 2001. He did not know of the posting for the supervisor's position until he received a telephone call from his coworker who told him about the posting on March 15, 2001. He submitted his resume to the Department and waited to be called for an interview. No one ever called him.

Meanwhile, sometime in July 2001, the Commissioner applied to the Office of Management and Budget (OMB) to clear the position of Supervisor of Medicaid Accounts among other positions. OMB responded with a letter clearing a number of positions, but due to budget constraints, would not approve the position for hiring. The Commissioner received the letter from OMB on August 15, 2001. No one was hired or interviewed for the position. Ultimately, the Department of Health reorganized its billing department and made everyone part of the customer service billing department.

Cont.

PORTFOLIO ASSIGNMENT *Cont.*

Ruiz was not happy. He did not like his new supervisor, Edna Santiago Lineman, who kept piling on the work. She was originally from Puerto Rico. The two fought constantly, with Ms. Lineman writing Ruiz up for insubordination, tardiness, and excessive use of sick leave. In one very public and loud outburst, Lineman said to Ruiz "to go back where he came from." "You know those people from the Dominican Republic have their ways and they just don't fit in with us." Ruiz yelled back at Lineman and walked out. He went to his doctor who gave him a sick leave slip for two weeks because his blood pressure was acting up. Lineman thought it was just a ploy because Ruiz did not want to do his work.

When Ruiz returned he spent the next week in training learning the new computer system and was sent a month later for further training on the new Medicaid rules and regulations. Ruiz was still disgruntled and believed that he should have the job as supervisor of Medicaid. (He did not know that the position was not going to be filled because OMB had not approved it.) Ruiz believed he was being discriminated against because he was from the Dominican Republic. He contacted the EEOC division in the region and filed a complaint against the Department of Health. After an investigation, the EEOC sent a letter stating that it did not reach a conclusion on the matter. The letter also stated that he had 90 days in which to exercise his right to file a lawsuit in the U.S. District Court. Ruiz filed a discrimination action based upon national origin. The Assistant Attorney General representing the Department of Health filed a Summary Judgment against Ruiz stating that he did not have a viable action.

Your attorney has asked you to research the issues involved in this case and prepare an outline by identifying the issues, cases and statutes needed. Brief the cases for your attorney's review as part of this assignment. As part of the Summary Judgment Motion, the Commissioner of Health prepared and signed an affidavit, which follows for your information. If you have any questions, remember you should consult your supervising attorney for clarification. (Research the law based upon your state.)

AFFIDAVIT OF COMMISSIONER JORDAN SPELLMAN, MD

Any County, State of America

BEFORE ME, personally appeared Jordan Spellman, M.D., known to me to be a credible person and of lawful age, who being by me first duly sworn, on her oath, deposes and says:

My name is Jordan Spellman. I am over the age of 18 years old, of sound mind, and am competent to make this affidavit. I reside in Any City, USA, and am a U.S. citizen.

1. I have never been convicted of a crime involving moral turpitude or any other criminal offense. Nor have I been convicted in any court of a misdemeanor crime or domestic violence.
2. I am licensed to practice medicine in the U.S.A.
3. Presently, I am employed with the state Department of Health as the Commissioner.
4. I am familiar with the facts relating to one of the Department's employees, John Ruiz.
5. The Department requested the Office of Management and Budget to approve a position of Supervisor of Medicaid Accounts. Due to budgetary constraints, the position was eliminated from the budget and therefore could not be filled by anyone.
6. The decision to not fill the position was a financial one and was based upon the business judgment of the Director of Office Management and Budget. There were no discriminatory motives behind this decision; the decision was purely financial.
7. Furthermore, Mr. Ruiz was not chosen as the Acting Supervisor of the Medicaid section because the Collective Bargaining Agreement requires that we base our decision not only on qualifications but also on seniority. Again, there was no discriminatory means behind the decision.
8. We have a number of employees from other island countries in the Caribbean as well as other parts of the world. We base our decisions on qualifications and performance.

Cont.

PORTFOLIO ASSIGNMENT *Cont.*

9. Mr. Ruiz was a problem employee and refused to perform tasks when asked. He was consistently insubordinate to his immediate supervisor. He also disappeared for hours without telling his supervisor his whereabouts and consistently called in sick at least once each pay period.
10. Mr. Ruiz was afforded the same opportunities as all Department of Health employees. In fact, other than some of his friends, no one knew he was from the Dominican Republic. The fact that this was Mr. Ruiz's place of origin was irrelevant to any decisions made by the Department.

Affiant Sayeth Not.

____

Jordan Spellman, MD, Commissioner of Health

Subscribed and sworn to before me, this the _____ day of _____, 2008.

Quick Quiz True/False Answers

Page 263

1. False
2. True
3. True
4. False
5. False

Page 269

1. True
2. False
3. False
4. True
5. True

Chapter 9

Internet Sources of the Law: Searching for Reliability

After completing this chapter, you will be able to:

- Choose the best search engines for legal research.
- Locate cases from court Web sites.
- Search the Internet for federal and state statutes.
- Understand the necessity of verifying the accuracy of a Web site.
- List some of the differences between Westlaw and LexisNexis.
- Find alternative sites to Westlaw and LexisNexis.
- Navigate the Internet for the most reliable legal Web sites.
- Determine the most useful Web sites sponsored by law schools.
- Compare the databases of the fee-based Web sites.
- Recognize the importance of integrating print and electronic sources.

In Chapter 8 we set the stage for understanding the different search techniques available on the Internet. You now have a foundation for creating a terms and connectors (Boolean) search and a natural language search. Mastering the search techniques is only part of the equation. You must also have a blueprint for choosing the best and most reliable sites for performing your legal research. That's what this chapter is all about. Of course it is impossible to list all the legal Web sites on the Internet. What this chapter does is introduce you to some of the most utilized and accepted legal Web sites presently available with a brief discussion of their contents. You will be able to use this chapter and Chapter 8 as springboards for most of your legal research projects that involve the Internet. But don't lose sight of the fact that the Internet should always be used in conjunction with the print material we have examined. Your research plan should always contain a check and balance; that is why print and electronic research should complement each other and not be considered mutually exclusive.

CASE FACT PATTERN

Your attorney is irate. He just received a traffic ticket for "texting" while driving. While driving back from a court appearance in neighboring Washington state, he was at a traffic light texting a client on an emergency matter. He doesn't believe there is a law prohibiting texting while driving in the state of Washington. When did the law change? To make matters worse, he was also cited for "distracted driving" and endangering others while driving. He is completely exasperated, not to mention upset about the very expensive ticket he now has to pay. To make matters worse, he intends to fight the ticket. As a result, he wants to know everything about the new law, the relevant cases, and other information he can use to challenge this injustice. Your attorney is determined to "beat" the ticket! Use the Internet, the library; he doesn't care—just get him some ammunition to fight the ticket. And get it by tomorrow. Determining how best to proceed and the best sources to use on the Internet is the focus of our discussion in this chapter; so now you will have the ammunition to complete your assignment.

Source: FOXTROT © 2006 Bill Amend. Reprinted with permission of UNIVERSAL PRESS SYNDICATE. All rights reserved.

UNDERSTANDING THE INTERNET: WHAT IT CAN AND CANNOT DO FOR YOU

Conventional legal wisdom has always assumed print media would remain the main staple for legal research for decades to come with some supplementation by Internet legal research sites, such as Westlaw or LexisNexis. Lawyers, judges, and paralegals have been slower than other professionals to adopt an Internet-based approach to legal research. The reasons for this hesitation are numerous. Law is a relatively conservative profession in many ways. Crazy as it may sound, many attorneys actively practicing law today have not used a computer, do not want to use a computer, and more importantly, have no intention of ever learning how to use a computer. Attorneys trained to handwrite or dictate legal documents might easily anticipate following this practice until they retire. Obviously this is completely at odds with the trends of the present and the future.

However, the law profession is changing and the new techniques are replacing the old because of simple economics. The resources offered by some of the commercial legal research sites are so expensive to replicate that even with the financial resources of an entire courthouse or law school, the library budget cannot compete—never mind the tight budgets of the typical small firm. In fact, most attorneys have adopted digital research methods as part of their typical research practices by sheer necessity. They are not only economical but convenient.

There are some other practical considerations behind a shift to online legal research that anyone considering a career in the law should know. The first is that maintaining a law library is expensive. Although a fully stocked law library has a nice appeal, the annual cost to obtain each newly printed, bound volume, as well as the advance sheets, pocket parts, and other supplements, can easily rise to well into the tens of thousands of dollars depending on the size of the library. There is also the issue of upkeep. As each of these volumes, pamphlets, inserts, and pocket parts arrives, someone must have the responsibility of updating the volumes. Old pocket parts must be removed and discarded. Advance sheets become superfluous when the bound volume is published. For busy law firms, the work of updating the law library often falls to someone who is either too busy to do it correctly or to someone with too little experience to understand exactly what is required.

The Internet solves many of those problems. Online sites, such as Westlaw, LexisNexis, or Loislaw, are always up-to-date. There are no downloads, print media, or CDs to exchange. In fact, online sources are more up-to-date than any print media can ever hope to be. In the best-case scenario, a recent decision by the U.S. Supreme Court can be faxed to various law firms and government agencies within a few hours and can arrive by mail in a few days. However, on the Internet, cases are available from court Web sites the minute they are posted, and the fee-based Web sites often have opinions analyzed and dissected within hours or days of the decision having been handed down. Bound volumes are usually printed annually or semiannually. The same cases contained in that bound volume are available almost instantly online. When an attorney factors in ease of use with the expense of maintaining a print library, the decision is simple: the firm switches to online legal research.

One problem electronic searching does not solve is comfort. Many attorneys were trained using books and other print media; old habits are hard to break. Although electronic media offer many advantages over print media, there are still some advantages to print sources. Many attorneys and paralegals have a research method that is book-centered. How many legal professionals make a habit of looking at the sections immediately before and after the indicated section in a digest or encyclopedia in order to find an answer? It is easy to browse through a book and jump to other sections; it is often difficult and sometimes impossible to simply browse through an online heading. But more important, electronic searching is based upon finding the correct search terms and "buzzwords" to connect you to the relevant material. Unless you "hit" the right words or word combinations, you may be spinning your wheels. And worse yet for the novice, the ever-present problem is not knowing whether the information found is relevant.

Another problem is the abundance of material produced by electronic sources. The filtering methods of the Internet are limiting. Think about it; when you enter a terms and connectors search, every case or legal authority appears without regard to relevancy. If a word appears in a document it is reported in the search. Sometimes the Internet's convenience and immediacy can be its curse. Books often are more manageable and more foolproof. With so much information available, learning what to use, how to use it, and in what combination is the hallmark of a good legal researcher. Therefore, be mindful of all the available sources for legal research, print and electronic. However, since the focus of this chapter is the Internet sources of the law, we begin with learning how to determine the accuracy of Internet sources.

DETERMINING THE ACCURACY OF A WEB SITE

Before we delve into the many types of available legal Web sites on the Internet, we must first spend some time evaluating the information provided by these sites. The most pressing question that needs to be asked and answered is: How can I determine or know that the Web site used provides accurate information? This is not an easy question to answer.

A big problem with the Internet is that there is an overwhelming amount of data available with very few methods to assess the quality or accuracy of the information presented. We all have a tendency to believe what we read, and to a certain extent this basic human response has been bolstered over time by the processes necessary to bring print media into existence. A textbook, for example, is reviewed not only by the authors, but also by other prominent scholars in the field, an editorial advisory board, a copy editor, and additional individuals. These individuals not only check on the accuracy of the various statements made by the authors, but also offer input on a wide variety of topics. All of this occurs long before the book is ever printed and made available. However, anyone with a computer can create a Web site and post any type of information on it that he or she desires. The amount of legal information on the Internet has mushroomed in the last decade, creating the very real problem of deciphering good information from bad. Not all sites that discuss legal issues present accurate and thorough information. Some sites purporting to provide access to legal research materials are nothing more than a platform for extremist viewpoints. The problem for the researcher is to separate out the reliable sources from the unreliable. One method of doing this is to examine the pedigree of the Web site. That examination begins by reviewing the URL.

Examining the URL

uniform resource locator (URL)
Precise location of a specific document retrieved from an electronic source or the Web address for the referenced source.

The **uniform resource locator (URL)** is the basic Web address of a site; it provides an alphabetical reference to the Web address for a particular Web site, which includes its domain name and subdirectories with which it is associated. The most common URL suffixes are .com, .org, .net, .gov, and .edu. By examining the pedigree of the URL suffix, a researcher can learn a great deal about who has provided this information and in turn gain some insight as to the accuracy of information presented on the site. Examine the Web address that follows the abbreviation for the World Wide Web (www). The address can often tell you something about the site. For instance, compare the following URLs:

www.supremecourtus.gov/
www.supremecourt.org

Both of these sites appear to be very similar, but one is the official Web site of the U.S. Supreme Court, and the other appears to list decisions from the court and other information but is sponsored by an independent company. The first URL takes you directly to the U.S. Supreme Court Web site. The second does not. As a general rule, you can rely upon Web sites that end in ".gov" as they are sponsored by the federal government and are usually the "official" Web sites for that agency or federal entity such as a court.

Similar to the federal government, states have official Web sites as well. These Web sites usually contain in their addresses "state.*xx*.us" (the *xx* should be replaced by the state abbreviation) at the end of the Web address. Consequently, if you wanted to locate the official Web site for the supreme court of Texas, its URL is www.supreme.courts.state.tx.us or www.courts.state.tx.us, which is the Web site that links all the Texas state courts. The Web site of the office of the governor of Texas is www.governor.state.tx.us, with the attorney general's Web site located at www.oag.state.tx.us. (In this instance, "oag" stands for office of the attorney general.) Maine's courts can be found at www.courts.state.me.us; Alaska is www.state.ak.us/courts, and so on. When you are searching for information, locate the official Web site, especially for governmental entities, whether federal or state. That's a hallmark for reliability. Of course, there are additional Web sites that provide federal and state information that are reliable, but at least you have a starting point and a basis to compare.

CYBER TRIP

Locate your state's official Web sites for the attorney general, governor, legislature, public safety, and homeland security. For each site, determine the name of the "head" of the department and the length of service in the position.

As you begin to evaluate Web sites by their URL, you can develop a feel for the accuracy of the information presented. As we have discussed in most circumstances, URLs with a .gov extension provide trustworthy information. The same reasoning holds with .edu extensions, which are usually a college or university. Less reliable URLs include .org and .net and some .com extensions. Of course, these rules are not hard and fast. Doubtless there are some government sites that provide inaccurate information and some nonprofit companies that provide impeccable sources. The important point here is not to follow a set rule, but to use your best judgment to evaluate whatever site you locate and to place it in context with others. Although this chapter cannot provide every reliable URL, it does recommend some *safe* Web sites to commence a legal research project. To begin our evaluation of the legal Web sites, we must start with the largest and perhaps the most well known: Westlaw and LexisNexis.

Quick Quiz True/False Questions

1. The Internet is a more precise and economical method of researching.
2. Online sources are updated more often and more quickly than print-based material.
3. Web searches produce only relevant material, especially using the terms and connectors technique.
4. A URL suffix is one of the factors a researcher can use to determine the reliability of a Web site.
5. Reliable Web sites more often than not have a .gov or .edu Web address.

THE PRIMARY FEE-BASED LEGAL SOURCES: WESTLAW AND LEXISNEXIS

Not all Web sites are free. The most widely used legal Web sites are not free but are considered the most comprehensive legal resource sites. They are Westlaw and LexisNexis. Each is discussed separately.

Westlaw

Westlaw is one of the most widely used legal research fee sites and offers an extensive variety and scope of legal sources, both primary and secondary, for the legal researcher. Westlaw's database contains virtually all cases, statutes, and administrative rules and regulations from every state and federal jurisdiction as well as a vast selection of secondary sources, such as *C.J.S., Am. Jur. 2d, A.L.R.*, law review journals, legal periodicals, and many practice-based tools for specialized areas of the law. Chances are if it is not on Westlaw, either it is not available or you do not need it!

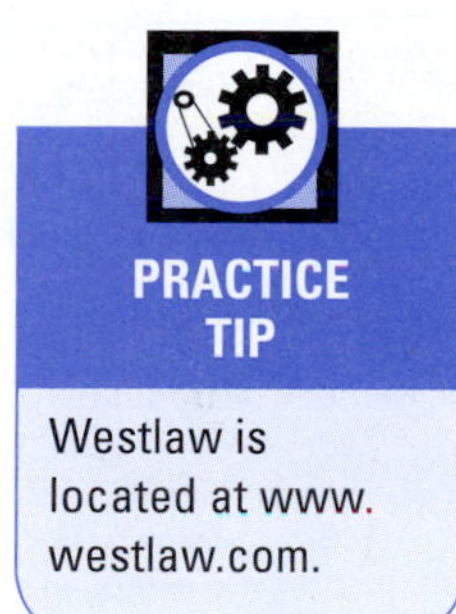

PRACTICE TIP

Westlaw is located at www.westlaw.com.

Links to Westlaw Finding Tools

As we have seen in previous chapters, West was the first company to provide a national reporter system and the Key Number System found in all West digests and publications. One of the biggest advantages to Westlaw is its online version of the West Digest System. Recall from Chapter 6 that we discussed the West Key Number System with its associated topics and keys interconnecting finding tools with West versions of the primary sources, such as cases and statutes. Using Westlaw, the topics and keys associated with digests and the headnotes found in cases are transformed electronically, creating its online system. On Westlaw's site under the search term "KeySearch," a researcher can find cases and secondary sources using West's Key Number System electronically. On Westlaw, there are two different approaches to online searching of the digest. One is through the use of a known topic and key and the other is through the use of searching relevant key words and phrases leading you to topics and keys. We will begin with a known topic and key search.

Online Digest Topic and Key Search: Westlaw

Recall our case from Chapter 4, *Court Television Network, LLC v. State*. In this chapter, the online Westlaw version is provided in Figure 9.1. Looking at the Westlaw version more closely in Figure 9.1, you see that it identifies online topics and keys. Look at headnote 1 and see the topic Constitutional Law, which is assigned the number 92 and key number 90.1(3). This is the print digest reference. Following the print digest reference is the Westlaw (online) digest reference. The numbers represent the following information:

92k90

FIGURE 9.1 **Westlaw Version of *Courtroom Television Network LLC v. State***

Source: From Westlaw. Reprinted with permission from ThomsonWest.

833 N.E.2d 1197
5 N.Y.3d 222, 833 N.E.2d 1197, 800 N.Y.S.2d 522, 33 Media L. Rep. 1887, 2005 N.Y. Slip Op. 05120
(Cite as: 5 N.Y.3d 222, 833 N.E.2d 1197)

Courtroom Television Network LLC v. State N.Y., 2005.
Court of Appeals of New York.
COURTROOM TELEVISION NETWORK LLC,
Appellant,
v.
STATE of New York et al., Respondents.
June 16, 2005.

Background: National cable television network sought declaratory judgment holding unconstitutional Civil Rights Law's prohibition of audiovisual coverage of trial proceedings, and sought order permanently enjoining its enforcement. The Supreme Court, New York County, Shirley Werner Kornreich, J., 1 Misc.3d 328, 769 N.Y.S.2d 70, denied network's motion for summary judgment. The Supreme Court, Appellate Division, 8 A.D.3d 164, 779 N.Y.S.2d 74, affirmed. Network appealed.

Holdings: The Court of Appeals, G.B. Smith, J., held that:

(1) neither First Amendment nor state constitution provides right to televise trials;
(2) even assuming that right to televise courtroom proceedings was equivalent of right of access to trial, prohibition of televised trials comported with First Amendment and state constitution; and
(3) there is no additional or broader protection for press under state constitution than under First Amendment.

Affirmed.

overall topic number

West Headnotes

[1] Constitutional Law 92 ⊶90.1(3)

topic

keynote number

headnote

⊶92 Constitutional Law
⊶92V Personal, Civil and Political Rights
⊶92k90 Freedom of Speech and of the Press
⊶92k90.1 Particular Expressions and Limitations
⊶92k90.1(3) k. Interference with Judicial Proceedings; Contempt; Publicity. Most Cited Cases

Press has no First Amendment right to information about trial superior to that of general public. U.S.C.A. Const.Amend. 1.

[2] Constitutional Law 92 ⊶90.1(3)

overall topic and key

⊶92 Constitutional Law
⊶92V Personal, Civil and Political Rights
⊶92K90 Freedom of Speech and of the Press
⊶92k90.1 Particular Expressions and Limitations
⊶92K90.1(3) k. Interference with Judicial Proceedings; Contempt; Publicity. Most Cited Cases

subtopic under key

First Amendment does not require courtrooms to be open to televise court proceedings. U.S.C.A. Const.Amend. 1.

subtopic under key

[3] Constitutional Law 92 ⊶90.1(3)

⊶92 Constitutional Law
⊶92V Personal, Civil and Political Rights
⊶92k90 Freedom of Speech and of the Press
⊶92k90.1 Particular Expressions and Limitations
⊶92k90.1(3)k. Interference with Judicial Proceedings; Contempt; Publicity. Most Cited Cases

State constitution's free speech provision does not provide right to televise trials. McKinney's Const. Art. 1, § 8.

[4] Constitutional Law 92 ⊶90.1(3)

⊶92 Constitutional Law
⊶92V Personal, Civil and Political Rights
⊶92k90 Freedom of Speech and of the Press
⊶92k90.1 Particular Expressions and Limitations
⊶92k90.1(3) k. Interference with Judicial Proceedings; Contempt; Publicity. Most Cited Cases

Trial 388 ⊶20

⊶388 Trial
⊶388III Course and Conduct of Trial in General
⊶388k20 k. Publicity of Proceedings. Most Cited Cases.

Even assuming that right to televise courtroom proceedings was equivalent of right of access to trial, Civil Rights Law's prohibition of televised trials comported with First Amendment's and state constitution's free speech provisions; governmental interests in right of defendant to have fair trial and in trial court's maintaining integrity of courtroom outweighed any absolute constitutional right of press or public to have access to trials, and, since press's right of access was same as that of public, press could not claim any right or privilege not common to every other citizen. U.S.C.A. Const. Amend. 1; McKinney's Const. Art. 1, § 8; McKinney's Civil Rights Law § 52.

[5] Constitutional Law 92 ⊶90.1(3)

⊶92 Constitutional Law
⊶92V Personal, Civil and Political Rights
⊶92k90 Freedom of Speech and of the Press
⊶92k90.1 Particular Expressions and Limitations
⊶92k90.1(3) k. Interference with Judicial Proceedings; Contempt; Publicity. Most Cited Cases

There is no additional or broader protection for press under state constitution than under First Amendment insofar as access to court proceedings is concerned. U.S.C.A. Const.Amend. 1; McKinney's Const. Art. 1, § 8.

[6] Constitutional Law 92 ⊶50

⊶92 Constitutional Law
⊶92III Distribution of Governmental Powers and Functions
⊶92III(A) Legislative Powers and Delegation Thereof
⊶92k50 k. Nature and Scope in General. Most Cited Cases

Decision whether or not to permit cameras in courtrooms is prerogative of state legislature. McKinney's Const. Art. 1, § 8; McKinney's Civil Rights Law § 52.

***__523__** Boies, Schiller & Flexner LLP, Armonk and Washington, D.C. (David Boies, Jonathan Sherman, David A. Barrett and George F. Carpinello of counsel), and Douglas P. Jacobs, New York City, for appellant.

Eliot Spitzer, Attorney General, New York City (Caitlin Halligan and Gregory Silbert of counsel), for State of New York and others, respondents.

Michael A. Cardozo, Corporation Counsel, New York City (Janet L. Zaleon, Kristin M. Helmers and Jane R. Goldberg of counsel), for Robert Morgenthau, respondent.

***__524__** Mickey H. Osterreicher, Buffalo, and Covington & Burling, Washington, D.C. (Timothy L. Jucovy of counsel), for National Press Photographers Association and others, amici curiae. Chadbourne & Parke LLP, New York City (Thomas E. Riley, Philip Pfeffer and Jennifer Wilson of counsel), for New York State Association of Criminal Defense Lawyers, amicus curiae.

Richard Sexton, New York City, amicus curiae.

Kenneth G. Standard, Albany, Slade R. Metcalf, Kevin W. Goering, Edward J. Klaris and Aimee E. Saginaw for New York State Bar Association, amicus curiae.

Jonathan E. Gradess, Albany, and Stephanie J. Batcheller for New York State Defenders Association, amicus curiae.

McNamee, Lochner, Titus & Williams, P.C., Albany (Michael J. Grygiel and Morgan A. Costello of counsel), for Clear Channel Communications, Inc., amicus curiae.

Patterson, Belknap, Webb & Tyler LLP, New York City (Saul B. Shapiro of counsel), for ABC, Inc. and others, amici curiae.

***227 **1199 OPINION OF THE COURT**

G.B. SMITH, J.

The primary issue on this appeal is whether ***228** Civil Rights Law § 52, which bans audiovisual

[text omitted]

The first number represents the overall topic, Constitutional Law. The "k" is the online equivalent for the West key number symbol, and is coupled with the number "90," which represents the general key number and topic under Constitutional law "Freedom of Speech and of the Press."

Notice that there are other topics and keys, such as 92k90.1, which translates to "Particular Expressions and Limitations." This topic has a subtopic number under the general key number. (Figure 6.1 from Chapter 6 provided the number and topic equivalents.) You must be asking yourself, "How do I find the topic and online number equivalent if I do not have the listing available? The answer is on Westlaw itself. There is a site map at the top of the page with a reference to the Custom Digest or Key Number Digest. This is the same digest as the print version. Refer to Figure 6.1. Therefore, if you already know your topic and key, you can enter that information in the box provided, press the Enter key, and all cases that have referenced that topic and key will appear. Obviously that is not the most efficient way to perform a topic and key search. You then should narrow your search by jurisdiction, such as specific state. By narrowing your search, you will find cases limited to your search parameters. For example, let's assume that you need cases under the topic and key search previously entered, but you want to limit your search to the state of Illinois. In the custom digest box, check the state required, in this case Illinois, and your topic and key search will be limited to Illinois cases.

Headnote Search

Using our example from *Court Television Network,* you could also search relevant cases by focusing on the headnote. Enter "he" (which stands for headnote) and then enter

he(freedom speech and press)

or

he(free! speech and press)

The search will provide headnotes related to free speech cases involving the press. The second inquiry uses the exclamation point (!), which will allow you to have different variations on the word "freedom," such as "free," "freedom (of)," or any other possible variation of the word "free." More search options will be provided, resulting in better research options. (This exercise integrates the information discussed in Chapter 8.)

Similarly, you can search for just a topic. Limit your search query to "to" (which stands for topic) and add the qualifying information.

to(92 & 78)

Recall that all the ThomsonWest topics now have a corresponding number for online search purposes. (Refer back to Figure 6.1 in Chapter 6, which lists the ThomsonWest topics and the assigned numbers.) This means that in our example your topic inquiry will be limited to Constitutional Law, 92, and Civil Rights, 78. A variation on this topic inquiry may be as follows:

to(92 & free! speech & court!)

This inquiry would focus on topic 92, Constitutional Law, but also include information on areas relating to free or freedom of speech and variations on the word "court," which may include courtroom.

General Inquiry

You also can search by using relevant words and phrases to lead you to topics and keys of interest by using ThomsonWest KeySearch. Enter your words and phrases into the field identified as "terms and connectors." For instance, enter "Constitutional law & free! speech & court!" This will provide variations on the words listed and will lead you to topics and keys that may apply to your topic. Or, you could use general words and phrases in the field and request cases that pertain to your search. From the applicable cases you will find topics and keys from which you can now perform a topic and key inquiry. Continuing with our example from the *Court Television Network* case, enter word combinations such as "constitutional law" and "freedom of speech and press." Or try simply "free speech and press." The possibilities and combinations are endless.

Another feature on Westlaw is "locate." You can narrow or expand a search by clicking the Locate button. By using "locate," you can refine your search databases and segments, or add new search terms that may be relevant. This feature is important as it can improve the quality of your research results.

A feature that attorneys and paralegals frequently use is "Find by Citation." This feature allows the researcher to enter a source by citation, press Enter, and retrieve the source identified, such as a case or statute. Analogous to this feature is locating a case source by the name of one of the parties. Once again, enter the name of the party in the case text box, press Enter, and either the case will appear or a list of cases that contain the names of the party searched will appear. The more specific information you have, the better—especially when a case has common names. Knowing the court or year the case was decided will aide the success of your search.

Field Restrictions on Westlaw

field restrictions
A method to limit a search on Westlaw.

Westlaw provides "search field restrictions." In a **field restriction,** you can limit your search to a particular part of document. Two main field restrictions are case law documents and statutory documents. For example, if you don't want to search through an entire document for the information you need, you can limit your search by typing one of the field restrictions noted in Figure 9.2. Combine the field abbreviations and place your search terms in parentheses. If you wanted to locate all opinions by a particular judge you would use: ju(*the judge's name*). All opinions from the judge named would appear. Similarly, suppose you want to locate cases from New York, Connecticut, and Puerto Rico that deal with trademark restrictions. Your field search would begin with co (court) followed by the state abbreviations in parentheses and the term trademarks: co(NY CT PR) & trademarks. Field searches provide specificity to your legal research and are virtually limitless in construction and combination. Figure 9.2 provides some examples of field restrictions on Westlaw.

KeyCite on Westlaw

In Chapter 7, we discussed the methods for updating and verifying the law. The two main sources are Shepard's Citations and KeyCite. Recall that KeyCite is the Westlaw system of updating and verifying the law. It differs from Shepard's in that it uses a starring and signal system to denote the treatment of a case. Refer to Chapter 7 for a more in-depth discussion of the topic, but for our purposes, you simply need to know that KeyCite is part of and available on Westlaw.

Services Offered by Westlaw

The current organization of Westlaw presents users with "tabs" that allow them to customize the information presented on the Web page. In addition to some of the features already mentioned, Westlaw also provides services such as the following:

- KeyCite Alert: This feature allows the researcher to monitor developments in cases, statutes, and other legal sources that are of interest. As new developments occur, Westlaw notifies you automatically and electronically. This is especially important when you are working in a specialty area or when a case you are working on is of particular interest or importance.
- WestCheck: Checking the validity of citations is made easier with this feature. With WestCheck, you can determine the history of a case or verify whether it is

ENTERING YOUR SEARCH

Understanding Field Restrictions

Almost all documents on Westlaw are composed of several parts called *fields*. Each field contains a specific type of information. Use a field restriction in a Terms and Connectors query when you want to restrict your search to a particular portion of a document. The table below provides examples of commonly-used field restrictions in case law documents and statute documents. For information on using the *Fields* list to add field restrictions to your search, refer to page 16.

Case Law Document Field Name	Sample Query
title (ti)	**ti(reno & anti-discrimination)**
judge (ju)	**ju(ginsburg)**
attorney (at)	**at(kuby)**
panel (pa)	**pa(easterbrook & posner)**
concurring (con)	**con(o'connor & abortion)**
dissenting (dis)	**dis(kozinski & "fourth amendment")**
topic (to)	**to(92) /p standing /p air /p quality pollut! emit!**
words-phrases (wp)	**wp("double jeopardy")**
synopsis (sy)	**sy(kimba /2 wood & affirmed)**
digest (di)	**di(standing /p air /p quality pollut! emit!)**
synopsis and digest (sy,di)	**sy,di(standing /p air /p quality pollut! emit!)**

Statute Document Field Name	Sample Query
citation (ci)	**ci(22 +5 2304)**
prelim (pr)	**pr("social security")**
caption (ca)	**ca(oil gas /3 lease)**
prelim and caption (pr,ca)	**pr,ca(marriage & license)**
text (te)	**te(protect! /3 wild-life)**
words-phrases (wp)	**wp(heir)**
historical-notes (hn)	**hn(92-84)**
references (re)	**re(religio! /3 free!)**
annotations (an)	**an("migratory bird treaty act")**

FIGURE 9.2 Examples of Field Restrictions on Westlaw

Source: From Westlaw. Reprinted with permission from ThomsonWest.

PRACTICE TIP

Westlaw offers different packages with varying charges; access may be denied to databases not included in a package. Westlaw charges by time spent on the system. A researcher who does not pay attention to the amount of time spent surfing through the huge quantity of databases might be surprised when a Westlaw session is concluded. Time spent on Westlaw can build up quickly, with a session sometimes costing hundreds of dollars.

still good law. The same is true for statutes. You can check the status of legislation or determine whether a statute has been amended. Administrative regulations can be checked as well on WestCheck.

- StatutesPlus and RegulationPlus: Status updates of both statutes and regulations are provided with these services. Links to virtually everything related to the statute or regulation queried are provided under these services. Locating the history of a statute or regulation is simplified as well.
- ResultsPlus: As a search is commenced on Westlaw, ResultsPlus automatically suggests alternative West-related queries that may be relevant to your search. The material resulting from ResultsPlus ranges from secondary material to state-specific sources that may be applicable to your search. This is a useful tool when performing any search.

Today, Westlaw has over 15,000 databases, with access to more than one billion public records and growing. Each database is searchable, although not all databases are available to all users. That depends on the plan purchased by your company or law firm. Nevertheless, Westlaw offers one of the most comprehensive sources for legal research.

LexisNexis

Like Westlaw, LexisNexis is a fee-based legal research site that allows a user to access federal and state cases, statutes, and administrative rules and regulations along with other secondary materials such as *Am. Jur. 2d,* law review journals, legal periodicals, and specialty areas of practice.

Some sources on Westlaw are not found on LexisNexis. For example, *C.J.S.* and *A.L.R.* are exclusive to Westlaw whereas Shepard's Citations is exclusive to LexisNexis. The West digest system is exclusive to Westlaw; however, LexisNexis does have an equivalent headnote-searching tool on its site. Consequently, although the offerings on these Web sites may be different, each offers extensive databases sufficient to satisfy the research needs for any project assigned. The sections that follow examine some of the features on LexisNexis, including its digest system.

PRACTICE TIP

Both Westlaw and LexisNexis offer terms and connectors (Boolean) searches and natural language searches as options.

General Inquiry on LexisNexis

Performing a general search on LexisNexis is accomplished in a number of ways. When a topic or subject search is required, use the "Search Advisor." This method provides a guide query just like KeySearch on Westlaw. There are different options for using Search Advisor. You can search from a list of legal topics and subtopics provided in LexisNexis, narrow a search by jurisdiction, or commence a search through terms and connectors or natural language. When you use the list of topics located in the drop-down box, after you click "Go" all headnotes related to your topic will appear as well as cases related to the topic. Alternatively, Search Advisor provides a text box for more general searches using one of the standard online techniques. After you enter the query and click the "Search" box, cases related to the topic appear, "usually" sorted by relevancy. Review the case information either generally from the "KWIC" format or its full text.

PRACTICE TIP

LexisNexis is located at www.lexisnexis.com.

Related to a search on Search Advisor is the "FOCUS" search feature. This enables a researcher to narrow results by pinpointing words or phrases within a search. Under the "FOCUS" feature, the words you initially specified can be modified for a more targeted search.

LexisNexis also allows retrieval of a case by citation or the name of the parties. In LexisNexis, the feature is called "Get a Document" by "Citation" or by "party names." Like Westlaw, the more information provided under a party search, the higher likelihood you will retrieve the case desired. When party names are common, all cases using those names will appear; consequently, knowing the year the case was decided or the name of court will assist in narrowing your search results.

Online Digest Searching with LexisNexis

LexisNexis has its own system of headnote search options. The headnotes are linked to cases on LexisNexis and the digest system from the *Lawyers' Edition* of the U.S. Supreme Court reporters. Undoubtedly, LexisNexis's digest/headnote search system is not as comprehensive and advanced as Westlaw's. By clicking on the relevant headnote within the case you are researching—denoted as HN followed by the headnote number—you can review the point of law in the case reference in the headnote. All headnotes in LexisNexis are numbered sequentially. Additionally, headnotes have links to other relevant headnotes from other cases as well. Simply click on the notation "More Like This Headnote" for points of law from other cases similar to the headnote reviewed. Your results are listed in the "Digest View" exhibiting the headnotes and corresponding paragraphs that match your original search. The results are displayed by relevancy and importance. Even though the LexisNexis headnote system is not as elaborate as Westlaw's, its headnote searching system continually develops and expands.

LexisNexis is probably best used through the general "words and phrases" search with limitations applied to the respective jurisdiction. These searches are known as **segment searches,** which are similar to the field search in Westlaw.

segment search
Restricts and narrows a search on LexisNexis. It is equivalent to Westlaw field search.

Segment Restrictions on LexisNexis

To restrict your search, perform a "segment" search on LexisNexis. The most typical segment searches a legal professional will conduct are case and statutory. With a segment search, you can locate judges who authored an opinion, check a disposition within an opinion, and identify parties, to name a few of the available options. To perform a segment search, click the drop-down list from the "Select a Segment" box. Choose a segment from the list. Then enter your selected terms in the text box. Sometimes the drop-down list will not include your topic. With LexisNexis, simply type in your segment with the specific terms contained with the parentheses. For example, if the search revolves around the requirements for a trademark, you could type in the text box: trademark (requirements /5). This query would find sources that have the word "requirements" within five words of the word "trademark."

Finding Tools on LexisNexis

As mentioned, LexisNexis provides finding tools, including *American Jurisprudence 2d* and many law journals and legal periodicals. With the LexisNexis database changing significantly with the elimination of *American Law Reports* (now exclusively on Westlaw), LexisNexis has developed a brand-new feature called "Cases in Brief." Comparable to *A.L.R.* in its treatment and scope, Cases in Brief reviews selected cases of significance and offers a detailed analysis of the issues in the case with updates as future developments occur. Included in this feature are links to LexisNexis's bank of secondary sources. Since this is a new feature, the cases chosen for analysis continue to grow.

Shepard's Citations on LexisNexis

Exclusive to LexisNexis is Shepard's Citations. This is probably the most well-known and recognizable source of legal updating and validating. LexisNexis provides Shepard's for virtually all its legal sources with the corresponding "treatment" and history guides for that source. Chapter 7 focuses on both the print and electronic versions of Shepard's Citations and should be consulted for more detail on the topic. Suffice it to say, Shepard's is an important feature on LexisNexis.

Additional Services Offered on LexisNexis

In addition to the features previously mentioned, LexisNexis offers other features to assist legal researchers. Some of these features are as follows:

- **Courtlink and State Capital Service:** Courtlink provides access to more than a million federal and state court records through a single search interface. The service also provides an automatic update system that notifies clients by e-mail about new cases and other developments that could impact recent research. The "State Capital" service provides access to legislation from all fifty states, as well as pending bills, laws, state constitutions and proposed amendments, state rules and regulations, and even information about state legislatures.
- **Alert:** Changes, updates, and new cases are important to know. A feature of the LexisNexis system is "Alert." Under this feature, a specific area of the law, case, statute, or other source is highlighted. Any developments in the area specified are sent, allowing the attorney or paralegal the most up-to-date information.

The system used by LexisNexis claims to contain in excess of 3.2 billion searchable documents. Although there are similarities between LexisNexis and Westlaw, the differences are large enough to create preferences in the legal community. For your purposes, simply be familiar with both services, and depending on the preferences of the law firm or company with whom you work, you will probably not have a "say-so" in the fee-based system provided.

lexisONE

A low-cost alternative to LexisNexis is lexisONE. This Web site offers both free and fee-based access to electronic legal information. Its free features are extremely limited with access to some cases from the past five years and U.S. Supreme Court cases from 1781. The Web site does provide a listing of what is included in its free database at www.lexisone.com/freecaselaw/coverage. Some access to forms is provided, but the draw for attorneys and legal professionals is that access to LexisNexis is available for as short a period as a day or week at an affordable rate. Be careful of hidden costs; always review the rules for browsing and printing of any legal material.

ADDITIONAL FEE-BASED WEB SITES

Although there are a number of fee-based legal research Web sites in addition to Westlaw and LexisNexis, the most noteworthy are Loislaw, VersusLaw, and Fastcase. One common thread of these Web sites is that they are a more economical alternative but are not as comprehensive as Westlaw and LexisNexis. Depending on the needs of your firm or company, one of these alternative fee-based legal research sites may be a better choice.

Loislaw

Loislaw (www.loislaw.com) is the creation of Wolters Kluwer, another legal publisher. Not until the late 1990s did Loislaw truly become a reality. Through a number of Web site reconstructions and redesigns, Loislaw is emerging as an alternative to Westlaw and LexisNexis. The Web site contains cases, statutes, and administrative rules and regulations from all the jurisdictions as well treatises from its sister publishers Aspen and CCH, Incorporated. You can locate a case through its citation or case name by using "Find A Case" or "SelectCite" or by specific jurisdiction. Similarly, statutes may be located by entering the citation or by narrowing the field of choices to a specific jurisdiction. There are similar tools found on both Westlaw and LexisNexis. But if you are looking for case headnotes or statutory annotations, these finding tools are not located on Loislaw.

As with many legal Web sites, Loislaw has a law alert feature that notifies a user of a case or statute relevant to a predetermined search. This feature is known as LawWatch. When new documents are entered in the Loislaw database that satisfy the search request, an e-mail alert is sent indicating the relevant information.

In its attempt to compete with Shepard's and KeyCite, Loislaw created GlobalCite. Right now, GlobalCite is not nearly as comprehensive as Shepard's or KeyCite as its system is only indexed to its database. This is not extensive enough for a comprehensive review of primary sources. If GlobalCite is your only means of verifying the status of a case or statute, you are best served to head to a library where the print version of Shepard's is available.

VersusLaw

Another more economical fee-based legal Web site is VersusLaw (www.versuslaw.com). With its multilevel approach, VersusLaw offers the basic primary sources of the law with access dependent upon the "package" purchased. For the most comprehensive access on VersusLaw, all the primary sources from both the federal and state governments are provided. On VersusLaw, you can locate a case by citation. But in the query box you must place the citation in parentheses and add the words "cite contains." Consequently, to locate a case on VersusLaw, the information in the text box would be: (cite contains 376 U.S. 254). Use the search tips on its Web site for the best search results for VersusLaw.

V.Cite

VersusLaw has introduced a limited legal validation system known as V.Cite. The premise behind this system is twofold: (1) determine the validity of cited cases, and (2) identify cases with similar issues to the case examined. With V.Cite you can focus a search on a specific jurisdiction, but presently V.Cite does not identify how a case treated the case you are reviewing. You must review each case to determine its applicability and relevancy. This system requires further development to reach the acceptance of Shepard's and KeyCite. Therefore, if VersusLaw is your electronic research database, continue to perform a Shepard's or KeyCite check on all the cases you intend to use in a research project. Your research is not concluded until *all* steps are complete. Don't think you can skip or sidestep an aspect of your research simply because the Web site does not contain a thorough validation or updating tool. You still must conduct comprehensive research regardless of your chosen Internet source. Remember, your supervising attorney or a judge doesn't care what database you had access to, only that your research is accurate and complete. Undoubtedly, VersusLaw has its limitations, which cannot be overlooked.

Fastcase

Yet another low-cost fee-based legal research site is Fastcase (www.fastcase.com). All jurisdictions are represented with access to all the primary sources of the law. Searches range from a general case search to the more specific search known as an "Advanced Case Search." Using the techniques from Chapter 8, you can enter a query into the text box in either Boolean or natural language. These searches can be limited by jurisdiction as well as dates. Simply tick the appropriate boxes to focus your search, which can be multijurisdictional if necessary. Thus, you can customize your results on Fastcase.

FIGURE 9.3 Comparison of Fee-Based Sites

	Westlaw.com	Lexis.com	Loislaw.com	VersusLaw	Fastcase
Database	Extensive database including primary and secondary source material. *C.J.S* and *A.L.R.* exclusive.	Extensive database, including primary and secondary sources. Shepard's exclusive.	Mainly primary source material from all fifty jurisdictions. Linked to Aspen products.	Mainly primary source material from all fifty jurisdictions.	Mainly primary source material from all fifty jurisdictions.
Updating service	KeyCite: Comprehensive system featuring flag and starring system	Shepard's Citations for all sources. Featuring treatment and source histories of cases using notations.	GlobalCite: New system. Not as comprehensive as KeyCite and Shepard's.	V.Cite: Very new system. Not comprehensive.	No system.
Headnote system	West headnote system featuring Key Number System. Print and online.	Lexis headnotes linked to Lexis products.	None.	None.	None.
Retrieve case by citation or name	Available	Available	Available	Available	Available

PRACTICE TIP

Fastcase has an excellent tutorial on its Web site to assist in navigating through the research process on its site.

The resulting searches on Fastcase are listed by most relevant, which is listed first, to the least relevant. The date of the decision is clearly marked in the results. A unique feature is the Advanced Case Search; it also will search and list the number of times a case is cited by other cases. In the "Results" drop-down box, you can narrow relevant cases to the paragraph with the pertinent information and then click onto the case for further evaluation. Again, one of the drawbacks to sites such as Fastcase is that the cases listed do not have headnotes, summaries, or any other finding tools associated with Westlaw and LexisNexis. This also follows for statutes. There are no annotations interpreting the statutes, just the text of the statutes. And, a real challenge with Fastcase is that there is no Shepard's or KeyCite equivalent. Once again, you must locate a source to verify whether the sources used or cited are still valid law. Whether this means a trip to the library or some other means, you must complete all aspects of your legal research plan. Of course, the better the search technique and the more precise it is, the better your results. Figure 9.3 is a limited comparison of some of the basic features on the fee-based Web sites.

YOU BE THE JUDGE

Attorneys often can recover their fees and costs associated with a case. That includes drafting of legal documents, interviews, and legal research. But is computer-assisted legal research recoverable? Is it considered a fee or an expense? These questions seem to have obvious answers, but as the court in *Bruce v. Cascade Collections, Inc.*, 199 Or. App. 59, 110 P.3d 587(Or. App. 2005), recognized, the issue is not a simple one at all. In the *Bruce* case, the Oregon appeals court was faced with the same issues. The problem, the court opined, is that different jurisdictions have different views on the issue. With that said, how did the Oregon court view the debate as to whether computer-assisted legal research fees are recoverable as costs, fees, or not at all? What federal circuit courts of appeals did the Oregon court cite in its opinion and why? What are the facts in the *Bruce* case, which sparked the debate over how to characterize computer-assisted legal research?

Quick Quiz True/False Questions

1. Westlaw and LexisNexis have the same primary and secondary sources.
2. Shepard's is an exclusive source for Westlaw.
3. Both Westlaw and LexisNexis have a headnote system.
4. The equivalent segment search on LexisNexis is a field search on Westlaw.
5. Loislaw, VersusLaw, and Fastcase have equivalent systems to Shepard's Citations.

INTERNET SEARCH ENGINES: WHICH SITES TO USE

Anyone who has spent more than a few minutes on the Internet has come into contact with **search engines.** These are programs that allow a user to search for information, which in turn produces a list of Web sites containing the information for which the search was initiated. As with everything on the Internet, there are varying degrees of quality. The results from a search engine often depend on the information identified in the search. But even the most exacting search can produce less than stellar results. Let's use a simple example. You need a copy of the case from our You Be the Judge example. You have the citation and the name of the case, but you do not have access to a fee-based Web site. So, a general search will have to do—you hope. We decide to use google.com. Enter the *Pacific Reporter* citation as you believe it is more universal. The result is that the case does not appear in the first few pages of the search. You now add the Oregon citation, resulting in even more confusing results. The search engine is breaking up the components of the citation, and unrelated cases appear. Now, you try to place the citation in quotations, limiting your search. The result is that only three entries appear—none of which is the case. Backtracking, you remove the quotations from the citation and begin the search again. Still the *Bruce* case does not appear. At this point, you could try another search engine, locate the case on the Oregon appeals court Web site, or try a free legal Web site. (A free legal Web site, www.findlaw.com, was used.) But you see the problem. Even if you have the exact information you need on a search engine, the information may not be produced as easily and as quickly as you think. That is not to say that the information was not on Google, but since there were over 150,000 entries, the time was better spent determining another method to retrieve the case. With all that said, search engines are invaluable. Determining which search engine to use is clearly a matter of preference. Figure 9.4 lists a number of available

search engine
A software program that searches databases to gather information based upon a given set of search terms or a Web site that searches the Internet for information related to a query.

General Search Engines

www.google.com
General and advanced searches
Extensive database

www.yahoo.com
General and advanced searches
Associated with www.go.com

www.altavista.com
General and advanced searches

www.lycos.com
General and advanced searches
Associated with www.hotbot.com, www.ask.com, and www.msn.com

www.excite.com
General and advanced searches
Associated with numerous other search engines

www.msn.com
General and advanced searches
Associated with lycos.com

Natural Language Searches and Key Word Searches

www.ask.com
Option to conduct search in natural language or key word (Boolean) style
(Formerly www.askjeeves.com)

www.answers.com
Conduct searches in natural language format

FIGURE 9.4 Examples of General Search Engines

YOU BE THE JUDGE

The Internet has catapulted the information highway to new heights. Each day new sites unfold, bringing with them unique legal issues never faced by the courts or legislatures. A phenomenon created on the Internet is myspace.com. Web pages are developed by people of all ages. The question that gnaws at courts is how far is too far when it comes to free speech and the Internet. The Court of Appeals of Indiana had to address these very issues in *A.B. v. State of Indiana,* 863 N.E.2d 1212 (Ind. App. 2007). Since this case involved a minor, only her initials, "A.B.," were used in the case. A.B. created a MySpace page where she made derogatory comments about her school's principal and assistant principal. These comments were quite graphic. The question is what is considered free speech, specifically political speech, and to what extent is speech protected on the Internet under the First Amendment? The result in *A.B.* may surprise you, especially given the graphic language used on the MySpace Web page. Read *A.B. v. State of Indiana.* What are the facts upon which the court based its decision? How did the court rule and why? What is the reasoning in the case, and was the result appropriate? As this case represents, the Internet has brought new challenges for courts—ones that will continue as the Internet becomes a more powerful means of communication.

PRACTICE TIP

It is important for a legal researcher to realize that simply because one site appears higher on a search list does not necessarily mean that it is better than one that appears lower down in the list. Often advertising dollars play a part in where a site is listed on a search. Therefore, you must use your own common sense and critical thinking skills to evaluate the information a search engine provides.

search engines that can be used for a research project. Some of these search engines rely on the key word method while others use natural language. Some instruct you how to create a search on their site. For example, on Google, searches do not use the "and" connector because in Google that is assumed. Other search engines will use the "+" symbol to connect key words or require use of the "and" connector. It is helpful to review the site's information about search methods for the best results.

Another form of search engine is known as **metasearch.** Metasearch engines display the search results from a number of different search engines. A metasearch also may be known as a federated search. The results of a metasearch may be overwhelming and often too broad or general. Therefore, if you choose to use a metasearch engine, be forewarned that the results may be extensive and not necessarily better than a general search engine. Below is a list of the more well-known metasearch engines:

- www.mamma.com
- www.metacrawler.com
- www.alltheweb.com
- www.search.com

metasearch
A global search that displays search results from a number of search engines; less specific.

GOVERNMENT WEB SITES

Under the category of governmental sites, there are enough Web sites to keep a legal researcher busy for weeks. We have already discussed in previous chapters the Web sites for the federal judiciary, such as the U.S. Supreme Court, www.supremecourtus.gov, all federal circuit courts of appeal, and nearly all U.S. district courts, which can be located at www.uscourts.gov and linked to all the federal courts. Additionally, each district court and circuit court of appeals has its own Web sites as well. We know that these sites contain such information as cases, court rules, listing of the judges, briefs, and any other information the court deems relevant to attorneys, litigants, and the public.

But the extent of government sites does not end with the federal judiciary. These days many other federal departments can be found on the Internet, from the Office of the Attorney General to the Federal Bureau of Investigation. These sites offer different types of information. Let's categorize each legal source.

The U.S. Constitution

There are a number of government Web sites that provide information about the U.S. Constitution. Some sites present its history; others offer annotations, and others simply offer copies of the document in varying forms. Sites that can be consulted for the U.S. Constitution are:

- www.gpoaccess.gov: general government Web site
- www.archives.gov: national archives official Web site
- www.senate.gov: U.S. Senate official Web site
- www.loc.gov: Library of Congress official Web site

Legislative Material

The government has a number of Web sites devoted to tracking bills, providing access to legislative histories, and offering reproductions of the *U.S. Code.* Perhaps the two best places to research legislative information are www.gpoaccess.gov and www.thomas.gov. The thomas.gov Web site was created by an act of Congress to provide complete records and access to legislation. Named after Thomas Jefferson (for obvious reasons), this Web site is affiliated with the Library of Congress. Both Web sites contain extensive online libraries of legislative material and are an excellent alternative to fee-based Web sites. Amendments and changes to current statutes are quite current, making these sites reliable sources.

For a complete copy of the *U.S. Code* in addition to the preceding Web sites, www.uscode.house.gov is an excellent source. For convenience, the *U.S. Code* can be downloaded from this Web site.

Information on congressional hearings is located at both www.house.gov and www.senate.gov, which are the official Web sites for the House of Representatives and the U.S. Senate. These Web sites are in addition to the general sites previously mentioned.

Judicial Information

The main Web sites for the federal courts were mentioned previously. However, there are some additional government Web sites that may be helpful to your legal research.

- www.doj.gov: This is the official Web site for the U.S. Department of Justice headed by the attorney general. This site provides access to U.S. Supreme Court briefs as well as U.S. Attorney General Opinions.

Web sites for specialized federal courts are as follows:

- www.uscfc.gov: Official Web site for the United States Court of Federal Claims. This site has cases handed down by this court.
- www.cit.gov: Official Web site for the Court of International Trade along with its case decisions.
- www.armfor.uscourts.gov: Official Web site for the Military Courts of Appeals. Information on its opinions and its rules is located on this site.
- www.ustaxcourt.gov: Official Web site for the tax court of the federal government.

Executive and Administrative Information

Most of the administrative agencies have Web sites containing their case decisions, rules, and regulations. For specific information, visit the Web sites by using one of the search engines listed in this chapter. However, some general Web sites that have information or provide links to administrative information are

- www.regulations.gov: This is a general government Web site dedicated to administrative agencies. Regulations from the different federal agencies are located on this site. It is an excellent resource.
- www.reginfo.gov: A general regulatory Web site.

Along with these two Web sites, www.gpoaccess.gov has a wealth of information on administrative agencies, its rules and regulations, and the process. Consult this site when a search is required on administrative rules and regulations. It is updated daily.

Presidential documents are primarily located at the National Archives, www.archives.gov and www.gpoaccess.gov. And of course, presidential information can be located at www.whitehouse.gov, where orders and proclamations can be reviewed.

The most comprehensive Web site and link to most federal sites is www.gpoaccess.gov. That Web site is always a good springboard for legal research. And www.firstgov.gov is considered the most extensive link to government information and is considered a metalink Web site.

There are other Web sites to retrieve federal information, but the purpose of this section is to identify free government Web sites where information could be located. Generally, these sites are reliable and can be used with minimal concern.

State Government Web Sites

Web sites vary from state to state. Some are extremely comprehensive, others less so. When searching for information about state governments, look for the official Web sites. Many Web sites either end in ".gov" or contain the state abbreviation followed by ".us," which is an indication that this is the official Web site for a state; but this is not always the case. To verify that the site is legitimate, you will have to examine the site for yourself. Some indicators that the Web site is official are the state seal; the official seal of the agency; welcomes by the governor, legislators, judges, or department head; and of course, the words "official Web site." Pay close attention to the sponsors of the Web sites. This is only a guide to follow, as many "unofficial" state sites have accurate and credible information. However, the purpose of this section is to lead you to state-sponsored Web sites.

One Web site that does provide links and access to state and local Web sites is www.usa.gov. This site lists all the states and territories with hyperlinks to the state Web sites. However, some of the links are not comprehensive and official. Be sure you check the source of the Web site and verify the "official" site of the jurisdiction you are researching. Figure 9.5 is the home page from www.usa.gov showing Web links to all the states and territories.

FIGURE 9.5 **Web Page from www.usa.gov**

Source: usa.gov. Web page retrieved from www.usa.gov/Agencies/State_and_Territories.shtml (accessed December 19, 2007).

Quick Quiz True/False Questions

1. Search engines provide guided searches producing only the most relevant information.
2. All search engines provide terms and connectors and natural language searches.
3. A government Web site that links all branches of the federal government is www.gpoacces.gov.
4. Judicial information can be located only at www.uscourts.gov.
5. Official state Web sites only use URLs that end in ".gov."

GENERAL "FREE" LEGAL WEB SITES

In recent years there has been an explosion of free legal research sites. What was once considered a minor curiosity has now blossomed into an industry. Some free sites have been around longer than others and have maintained a consistent Web presence since their inception, while others have skyrocketed to prominence only to fade into obscurity within a few years. Because of this tendency, we will limit our discussion to some of the better known sites. At any given time, it is best to use an Internet search engine to locate the most current legal Web sites. Keep in mind that almost all free sites suffer from the same liabilities: they do not have the breadth of coverage or the time-tested methods to ensure accuracy as the commercial legal research sites, such as Westlaw and LexisNexis. However, there are some free sites that offer an impressive array of resources. They include

- FindLaw.com
- MegaLaw.com

FindLaw

FindLaw (www.findlaw.com) claims to have the highest amount of traffic for a free legal research site. It provides access to cases and statutes; specific practice areas, such as employment law and bankruptcy law; direct access to specific jurisdictions, such as California, New York, and Texas; and it also provides additional biographical information about attorneys. FindLaw also provides a limited number of forms, newsletters, and even an online law dictionary. This site is good for retrieving cases, but it is best to have as much information about the case as possible, such as name, citation, and year. FindLaw has an excellent system of "case alerts," where legal professionals can register to receive by e-mail. The alerts are both subject-specific and jurisdiction-specific. Consequently, if you want to know when a case from the U.S. Supreme Court is handed down or cases from your federal circuit, FindLaw will notify you within twenty-four hours of the decision. It also adds newsworthy issues relating to subject-specific topics. Exploring the wealth of information located on FindLaw is worthwhile.

MegaLaw

Similar in scope to FindLaw, MegaLaw (www.megalaw.com) offers links to both federal and state legal topics, including federal cases, federal rules, and the U.S. Constitution. MegaLaw offers access to statutes of all fifty states and even some international statutes. It also organizes legal topics alphabetically, providing articles and other secondary sources on a myriad of legal topics. Search for forms in many areas of the law, but care should be used as the forms may not conform to the legal requirements in your jurisdiction. In that instance, compare your state statute and the form you may want to use.

CYBER TRIP

Using any Internet source, locate the cases in the You Be the Judge features in this chapter.

THE E-FACTOR

Don't overestimate your computer. Computers don't think; they don't reason; and they don't analyze. Search engines find information based upon your search query—looking for common words and phrases often without regard to relevancy. Of course, you can use different search techniques to narrow your query, but you can't substitute the "human reasoning" process for search engines. Let's face it, the Internet locates information that contains all, some, or none of the factors you delineate. How many times have you attempted a search on the Internet, clicked the Search button, and when you view the results you wonder whether you keyed your search in a different language? It happens to all of us. Another factor in an Internet search is the sheer number of responses to a query. Is it realistic to view one million entries? What about a hundred thousand entries? I don't know many of us who view more than the first five pages of a general search. That's the point. The Internet produces results en masse and does not have the kind of filtering abilities that we possess. We know what works and what doesn't work. The Internet cannot think. Remember that—despite what some Internet purists may argue. However, in a traditional print search, you have more control of the results and can limit the amount of information produced from a search to that which is relevant. The reality is that most of you will lean toward the Internet as your exclusive method of research. But remember, electronic research is more difficult to control, and cyberspace does not offer some of the practical checks traditional print research affords.

LAW SCHOOL WEB SITES

Law school Web sites provide access to an enormous amount of legal information. Often they are geared toward the state in which they are located. This is not good or bad, just a reality of which you should be aware. But some of these law school Web sites produce amazing information apart from the standard primary sources of the law. Many of the professors post guidelines and PowerPoint files they use for students. These can be quite helpful and are worth some exploration. A few well-known law school Web sites are as follows:

- www.law.cornell.edu: Access to all primary sources of law is provided by the Cornell University Law School. Through its Law Information Institute (LLI), the law school provides federal and state information. Topic searches can be performed on the site as well as specific source searches. This is one of the premier law school Web sites.
- www.law.pitt.edu: The University of Pittsburgh has a legal publication called *The Jurist,* which discusses current legal issues. Supported by students, it has become a widely read online legal newsletter. Important cases are linked and provided in full text; the cases are annotated with discussions from law professors and students, who contribute their thoughts about the importance of the case to the overall practice of law. If you are looking for some input on legal subjects from legal scholars, this is an excellent site to visit.
- www.washlaw.edu: Washburn University offers access to an extensive online legal library. With links to virtually every jurisdiction, you can access almost any legal source from the site. Additionally, links to most countries in the world and legal information are located on this site. For general information that is jurisdiction-specific, this is a great site to survey.
- www.law.texas.edu: Search for law review journals using the University of Texas online library. In addition to its general sources, this is a unique feature of this Web site.
- www.law.emory.edu: On this Web site, search for cases from all jurisdictions. Links are provided to federal and many state courts on this online library.

A DAY IN THE LIFE OF A PARALEGAL

A posttrial brief is due in two days. You have almost completed your research except for Shepardizing. It is 5:00 p.m. and all of a sudden, your computer screen turns dark. Panic sets in. Is it just your computer or the entire network? As you race down the hall to another paralegal's office, you notice that all the computers in the firm are dark. The entire network is down. Apparently, there was a power surge and no one knows when the network will be working again. You have to finish your research and Shepardize. The court house library closes at 5:00 p.m. and that's at least a half hour drive away. Luckily, the state university has a law school and you know that library is open until midnight. Shepardizing manually will take a lot of time, but you don't know when the network will be available. You can't take any chances—the case is too important. You are off to the law library to complete your assignment. Scenarios like this one are not uncommon in the world of electronics. Networks fail all the time and you cannot be dependent on one means of research. That's why it is important to master both the print and electronic methods of research. Competency in both forms is essential. In fact, neither form of research is mutually exclusive of the other. Of course, you will always do what it takes to get the job done; but maintain your skills in all the media required to get that job done.

UNIQUE SOURCES OF THE LAW: LIST SERVERS AND BLOGS

The Internet has produced many unique forms of communication. Who ever heard of e-mail fifteen years ago? So much of our communication is electronically generated that it is difficult to escape. Although not your typical Internet source of the law, list servers and blogs are becoming places where opinions are exchanged, questions asked, and information conveyed. Through these electronic sources, its participants learn about new cases and trends and can be a great resource as long as they are not abused and their limitations are recognized. Let's briefly focus on list servers and blogs as an Internet source of the law.

CYBER TRIP

Find paralegal list servers associated with a state bar association. Review a mailing list either in your jurisdiction or from a neighboring state. Detail the type of information offered on the mailing list.

List Servers

It is common for attorneys, paralegals, legal secretaries, and others to join list servers. (They are sometimes referred to as "list servers," after the Listserv software from L-Soft International, which was the first such program.) A list server is group e-mails to approved recipients, discussing narrowly focused issues. The American Association for Paralegal Educators (AAfPE), for instance, maintains a list server for paralegal instructors and educators, which discusses recent changes in the law, technology, and the impact that they have on teaching.

List servers come and go, so many listings placed here would likely be out-of-date by the time the book reaches print. Fortunately, the best way to locate a list server is by using the Internet. Using a standard search engine, such as Yahoo or Google, type "paralegal listserv or "legal listserv." This will produce an up-to-date list of all current list servers focusing on legal issues.

Blogs

blog
An abbreviation for "Web-based log"; an Internet-based daily journal or diary discussing events in an individual's life or providing thoughts and perspectives about contemporary issues.

A **blog,** a contraction of "Web log," is a form of online diary that has become extremely popular in recent years. Blogs cover a dizzying variety of topics and can provide you with an insight into a person's daily cooking regime or the life of a high-powered attorney. Like web sites, blogs vary in quality and require the same level of scrutiny as any other information source. Some blogs can give you valuable information about

YOU BE THE JUDGE

Recently the Delaware Supreme Court had to examine the area of blogs in *John Doe v. Cahill,* 884 A.2d 451 (Del. 2005). In the case, a councilman filed a defamation lawsuit against an anonymous blogger, John Doe. The court was faced with balancing the First Amendment, the councilman's reputation, and the right to disclosure of the blogger. Since the councilman was able to trace the Web site to the provider, Comcast, he wanted to unveil the identity of the blogger. The Court ultimately favored the protection of speech in light of the fact that the councilman could use the same forum to respond to the anonymous blogger's comments. Review the *Cahill* case. What standards did the Court apply in dismissing the case? What are the facts of the case? Was the result justified?

the day-to-day practice of law, even how various paralegals carry out legal research assignments, while others provide nothing more substantial than a vehicle for disgruntled rants.

Quick Quiz True/False Questions

1. An alternative to a fee-based legal research site is www.findlaw.com.
2. Law school Web sites provide a reliable source of many primary and secondary sources of the law.
3. The premier law school Web site is www.lawschool.edu.
4. List servers are Internet forms of communication.
5. The term "blog" is a contraction for "legal Web site log."

ETHICS ALERT

Rendering legal advice to clients is prohibited for a paralegal. There is no argument on that issue. But how is that ethical rule interpreted on the Internet? This question is becoming a common dilemma in many jurisdictions, not just for attorneys but for anyone using the Internet. Since determining the identity of individuals is often difficult on the Internet, knowing who is rendering legal advice is equally difficult. One area that has caught the attention of many bar associations is the "Do It Yourself" and "Self-Help" document and software Web sites that permeate the Internet. You have seen them. How to draft a will? How to prepare documents for a no-fault divorce? How to draft an apartment lease? These sites have become a "source of the law." The sites are not monitored by any legal regulatory authority and according to some, may be a form of the unauthorized practice of law. Sites such as www.nolo.com, www.lawguru.com, www.freeadvice.com, and others skirt the issue of "rendering legal advice." A common concern of both bar associations and courts is not only controlling the practice of law but the quality of the information communicated. Courts and bar associations struggle with the issue of controlling the practice of law on the Internet. Some jurisdictions make the distinction between direct contacts with individuals such as the users of these sites, while others do not. It is a developing area of the law with limited case law as guidance on the subject. In fact, much of the authority dates "pre-Internet" such as *Oregon State Bar v. Gilchrist,* 272 Or 552, 538 P.2d 913 (1975), where the standard was "personal contact." The court stated that contact "in the nature of consultation, explanation, recommendation or advice or other assistance in selecting particular forms, in filling out any part of the forms, or suggesting or advising how the forms should be used in solving the particular customer's . . . problems does constitute the practice of law." *Id.* at 919. In Oregon and the Ninth Circuit Court of Appeals (as exhibited by its decision in *Taub v. Weber,* 366 F.3d 966 (9th Cir. 2004), contacts are a pivotal component of the analysis. Therefore, pay close attention to this developing area of the law as each jurisdiction has its own standards, interpretations, and precedents. Since the Internet poses many unresolved ethical issues, you should be careful how you communicate on the Internet and with whom you communicate. As a paralegal, you need to be acutely aware of the parameters of your job, your ethical obligations, and the limitations imposed by any form of communication.

PRACTICAL CONSIDERATIONS: RELIABILITY COUNTS!

The Internet is boundless. In this chapter, we addressed only a small number of available Internet sites. These are some of the best Web sites available today. Tomorrow it will probably change. As the Internet sources of the law are constantly in flux, you must stay grounded. Use Internet sites that work for you and sites you know are accurate. Of course we are open to new, helpful, and innovative information, but we cannot be aware of every relevant Web site. Be discriminating when researching on the Internet and try not to get overwhelmed, as it is easy to do. When you can limit the scope of your research through Westlaw or LexisNexis, do it. As a general rule, searches through a general search engine do not produce comprehensive legal research. General Internet searches are good for trying to locate a case, a rule, a definition, and sometimes a relevant article. But if you do not have access to Westlaw or LexisNexis, your "real" alternative is a good old-fashioned law library!

Summary

The Internet is quickly replacing print material because of accessibility and costs. Unlike print media, the Internet is updated more easily and in a timelier manner. However, the results of an Internet search can be overwhelming, whether through a general search engine or a fee-based site. Another issue on the Internet is the reliability of the information on a Web site.

One way of determining the reliability of a Web site is through the URL. Web sites ending in ".gov" and ".edu" are generally more reliable than sites with ".net" or ".org" as the URL. Use your best judgment to determine the accuracy and reliability of a Web site.

The two comprehensive legal Web sites are Westlaw and LexisNexis. Both are fee-based sites. Each Web site has similar primary source material, but special features contained within these sites distinguish them from each other. Westlaw contains the West digest system in electronic form using its famous Key Number System. It also contains numerous secondary sources unique to the West family of resources. Both legal encyclopedias as well as *American Law Reports* are accessible from Westlaw. Because Shepard's is exclusive to LexisNexis, West developed KeyCite as its updating and validating system. KeyCite features a starring and flagging system to alert the researcher to the treatment of a case by a court, how often a case was cited by courts, and how closely other cases resemble the legal issues presented in the case you are reviewing.

On the other hand, LexisNexis offers a wide range of features as well. It has a headnote system linked to its publications as well as access to a number of secondary sources. Perhaps one of the most important features of LexisNexis is Shepard's Citations. This is the most recognized and utilized updating and validation system for legal resources. Its online version has a system of symbols and letters signifying how courts treated cases as well as the number of times courts cited the referenced case. Neither Westlaw nor LexisNexis is a better system; it is a matter of preference.

Other fee-based legal Web sites include Loislaw, VersusLaw, and Fastcase. Each provides access to case and statutory law from all fifty jurisdictions. However, none of these fee-based systems provide a comprehensive updating and validating system similar to Shepard's or KeyCite.

Locating information and Web sites on the Internet is made easier with a search engine. Search engines range in quality. However, the most commonly used search engines are Google, Yahoo!, MSN, AltaVista, and Excite. Search engines that offer natural language searches as an alternative are ask.com and answers.com. Some search engines are linked to a number of search engines, known as metasearch engines. Typical metasearch engines are mamma.com, metacrawler.com, alltheweb.com, and search.com.

A safe bet for accuracy is government Web sites, whether federal or state. Government Web sites often provide links to other government sites in specific areas such as the judicial, legislative, and executive branches of government including administrative agencies. As a starting point for government research, www.gpoaccess.gov and www.loc.gov are quite useful. These Web sites provide links to the courts (www.uscourts.gov), Congress (www.thomas.gov), administrative agencies (www.regulations.gov), and the executive (www.archives.gov). State governments have Web sites as well. Locate the official Web sites of a state for reliability and accuracy.

Legal information can be located at sites such as www.findlaw.com and www.megalaw.com. Coupled with these free Web sites are law school Web sites, which provide an alternative to some fee-based sites.

Two unique forms of communication that started on the Internet are list servers and blogs. These are places where ideas and information can be exchanged. Care should be taken when participating in a list server or blog as the quality varies. Additionally, when information borders on "legal advice," paralegals should be mindful of the ethical implications.

Key Terms

blog
field restrictions
metasearch
search engine
segment search
uniform resource locator (URL)

Review Questions

1. Identify three reasons why there is a shift from print sources to electronic sources of the law.
2. What are some of the ways the accuracy of Web sites can be determined?
3. List the different fee-based Web sites and identify two common characteristics among them.
4. Compare and contrast Westlaw and LexisNexis.
5. What is the purpose of an Internet search engine, and which are the most reliable?
6. What is a metasearch?
7. Identify five government Web sites along with some of the legal sources provided on each site.
8. How can a researcher determine whether a state Web site is legitimate?
9. Name two "free" legal Web sites and the information that can be retrieved from those sites.
10. Why can list servers and blogs be a source of legal information? What precautions should be taken when participating in a list server or blog?

Exercises

1. You have located two Web sites that provide contradictory information. One site, with the URL of www.uscourts.gov, states that prosecutors and police must have a search warrant before seeking computer equipment. Another site, www.hatethegovernment.org, states that police and prosecutors are free to seize any information they wish and that the probable cause requirement of the Fourth Amendment has been suspended by the provisions of the USA PATRIOT Act. You are charged with the task of deciding which site is more reliable. Upon which Web site would you rely and why?

2. Locate your own state appellate courts, including your state supreme court (if it goes by that name) and your state court of appeals. Do these sites offer any or all of the following information?
   - Searchable database of current and archived files
   - Biographies of justices
   - Cross-references to other governmental branches, such as the executive or legislative branch
   - Database that can search for cases by name or subject
   - Complete text of decisions
   - Downloadable versions of cases
   - Current court documents
   - Access to briefs and other materials submitted by parties
   - Printable version of appellate rules
   - Ability to file briefs and other materials electronically
3. A client wants to compete with Westlaw and LexisNexis and start a new, low-cost, full-service computer-assisted legal research site. She knows that all the government Web sites are available, but what she really wants is to offer cases with star-paging, summaries, and other finding tools. The client heard about some case from the second or third circuit called *Hyperlaw v. West*—she thinks. Although she is not a lawyer, someone told her that the case allows anyone to use West's cases because their methods are not protected by copyright. Your attorney is skeptical and asks you to locate this *Hyperlaw* case on the Internet. He wants you to verify the case name, citation, year it was decided, and the jurisdiction of origin. Also, he insists that the case be Shepardized, even though your firm does not have access to Westlaw, LexisNexis, or any other pay site. Prepare a summary of your findings and whether the case has precedential value in your jurisdiction. (Answer the exercise based upon the federal appellate circuit of your state.)
4. Using the Internet only, find definitions for the following words:
   a. metadata
   b. cybersquatting
   c. cryptography
   d. spyware
   e. hypertext

   As part of your response, list at least three Web sites you reviewed to determine the accuracy of your definition.
5. You are tired of constantly receiving "spam" (junk e-mail). There must be some statutory authority that regulates spam. Locate statutory authority, both federal and state (if available), that regulates the dissemination of spam. As part of your research, locate both the statutory definition of "spam" and its common use definition.
6. Using the Internet, research which federal administrative agency regulates the National Do Not Call Registry and how you can get on for the list. As part of your research, determine under what statutory authority the list originates.
7. *Citizen Kane* is considered one of the greatest films in our time. When Orson Welles signed the original agreement with RKO and Mercury Productions, no one could ever have anticipated media such as video and DVD. His daughter, Beatrice Welles, sued Turner Entertainment Company, for the home video rights to *Citizen Kane.* Locate the case on the Internet and then prepare a case brief of the issues addressed in the case.
8. The Internet has changed the law in many areas. One area that has received attention is the law of trade secrets (such as the secret formula for Coca-Cola or

Kentucky Fried Chicken). By definition, a trade secret "may consist of any formula, pattern, device, or compilation of information that is used in business and that gives the user an opportunity to obtain an advantage over competitors who do not know or use it." *Restatement of the Law of Torts* (Second) § 757. When trade secrets are posted on the Internet, the owner's rights are often difficult to protect. A number of cases have addressed the issue. Retrieve copies of *Ford Motor Co. v. Lane,* 67 F. Supp. 2d 745 (E.D. Mich. 1999); *DVD Copy Control Assn., Inc. v. Bunner,* 116 Cal. App. 4th 241 (2004); and *Religious Tech. Center v. Netcom On-Line Communications Services,* 907 F. Supp. 1361 (N.D. Cal. 1995). What are the basic arguments from the cases against trade secret protection? Determine whether your state has a statute regarding trade secret protection. If so, identify the citation to the statute and whether your state has any cases regarding trade secret protection and the Internet.

PORTFOLIO ASSIGNMENT

Our attorney from the Case Fact Pattern wants a complete examination of the different cell phone laws within the United States. He still can't believe the state of Washington not only bans cell phones but bans texting as well. What is the world coming to! Therefore, your assignment is to determine the status of cell phone usage not only in your jurisdiction but the other states as well. Do states differentiate between handheld cell phone and hands-free cell phone usage? If a state has banned cell phone usage completely, are there exceptions to the ban and, if so, what are those instances? Create a chart with the results of your research.

Quick Quiz True/False Answers

Page 281	Page 291	Page 295	Page 298
1. False	1. False	1. False	1. True
2. True	2. False	2. False	2. True
3. False	3. True	3. True	3. False
4. True	4. True	4. False	4. True
5. True	5. False	5. False	5. False

Chapter 10

Roadmap for Legal Research: A Guided Plan

After completing this chapter, you will be able to:

- Analyze how best to begin a legal research assignment.
- Use reasoned analysis to determine the best approach to a legal research project.
- Initiate a plan for researching a statute, case law, or other source of the law.
- Determine the type of research plan to develop.
- Perform the necessary steps to begin and complete the research process.
- Incorporate all the basic skills learned from understanding the legal system to knowing which books to review.
- Prepare a plan to locate administrative rules and regulations.
- Develop an outline of a legal research plan.
- Understand the unique issues to consider in commencing a legal research project.
- Combine traditional legal research methods with online legal research.

It is common for paralegals to be tasked to research client issues. The trick to any legal project is knowing where to begin and, equally as important, knowing where to end. Finding the answers to these issues is, to coin an old adage, "easier said than done." Throughout the course of this text, you have learned about the law, where to find it, and how to validate it. But now, we must put theory into practice. As you perform more and more research assignments, you will learn your own shortcuts, sometimes hit a wall, and basically learn what works best for you and your style of research. This chapter gives you some suggested approaches to navigate through the process. So, as some may say, "let's get busy!"

CASE FACT PATTERN

Brooke Dayle, a former professor at State University, has been terminated due to comments she made about the September 11 attacks on the World Trade Center. When her contract was presented to the university board for renewal, it was rejected. Professor Dayle was not tenured nor was she on the tenure track at the university. However, she believes she was effectively terminated due to her comments in violation of her First Amendment rights to free speech. Professor Dayle wants to challenge the university's decision and hires your law firm to prosecute the matter. Prior to the initial client conference, your supervising attorney needs some quick research to gauge the status of the law. The meeting is tomorrow at 11:00 a.m.

Source: NON SEQUITOR © 2005 Wiley Miller. Dist. By UNIVERSAL PRESS SYNDICATE. Reprinted with permission. All rights reserved.

WHERE TO BEGIN YOUR RESEARCH: THE PLAN

In legal research, you need to first think about the assignment presented. Does it involve a statute? Do I need to learn more about the topic through a legal encyclopedia? Can I begin with a digest search to locate cases? Are Internet sources available, such as LexisNexis and Westlaw? All these questions pose different routes you could take in beginning your research project. You must decide the best course based upon the assignment and available resources.

Legal Reasoning and Analysis: Thinking through the Assignment

We have discussed in detail the possible legal research sources to find the law. But, before you can find the law, you need to understand some basic principles underlying the project you are assigned. Am I looking for cases? Statutes? Constitutional provisions? Administrative rules or regulations? Does my assignment encompass more than one source of the law? Do I have any knowledge about the subject I am about to research?

Your first thought, at least in the beginning, is: "I'm new at this and I have no idea what the law is." Or you are thinking, "I don't even understand the terminology the attorney used who gave me the assignment." Relax; we all went through this, whether as an attorney or paralegal.

The first step you should take is to prepare good notes on the assignment presented. If the assignment is presented as a written **internal memorandum of law** or you are taking notes from a meeting or client interview, review the facts; then sit down and write down questions you need to either answer or ask your supervising attorney. ***Rule 1:*** *Never begin an assignment unless you understand it.* A great deal of time is wasted by paralegals and attorneys who either don't understand the assignment or are afraid to ask questions about the assignment.

internal memorandum of law
An internal document that analyzes objectively the legal issues in a client's matter.

Rule 2: *Find out your time constraints on the assignment.* This means know your deadlines. Nothing is worse than thinking you have a month to complete an assignment when in reality it is needed within days. Therefore, get a due date for the assignment.

Rule 3: *Determine the issue or issues you are researching.* Again, more time is wasted when you do not understand the legal concepts you are being asked to research. Here, you must begin to use different methods of legal reasoning. Consider the fact scenario from the Case Fact Pattern.

You have an untenured professor who has been terminated from her job due to comments made about the attacks on the World Trade Center on September 11. She wants her job back and believes her First Amendment rights to free speech were violated.

From the facts, it appears that you may have a constitutional law issue for which you want to find applicable case law. As discussed in Chapter 3, you want to look for cases that support your client's facts. In other words, you want to look for case precedent that will state your client's First Amendment rights were violated and she is entitled to have her job back. What you have just done is to **deductively reason** what you need to prove to assist your supervising attorney in successfully presenting the client's position. You have reasoned that based upon the facts, you will search for supporting authority that finds an untenured professor has rights to her job and can freely express her opinions, without the university's intrusion, as defined in the First Amendment to the U.S. Constitution. What you also have done is to define legal issues from which you can begin cultivating your research plan and reach a conclusion based upon your research.

deductive reasoning
Process of reasoning that draws a conclusion about a specific issue from a general issue in determining how to apply the law to a specific set of facts.

Our next step is to create search terms that apply to our facts. Then, we begin looking up the terms and finding digest topics and keys, encyclopedia sections, and cases that will assist us in finding our answer to the client's problem. By doing this, you will search for cases that either are "on point," similar factually, or provide legal principles that will guide the court in making a decision. In essence, you are trying to find cases that your supervising attorney can argue are analogous to your client's set of facts. This is **reasoning by analogy.** In essence, reasoning by analogy shows a logical relationship between two like or similar concepts that are compared to each other. When you reason by analogy, you are simply relating facts and the law from previous cases that set precedent to your client's case. Arguing by analogy is one of the primary methods attorneys use in presenting information to a court or opposing party. Attorneys always look for as many similarities (or dissimilarities) in the cases they choose for the client they are representing. You will always be searching for "legally relevant" information to present the basis for "why" or "why not" a case, statute, or other legal source is applicable or inapplicable to the set of facts researched. Reasoning by analogy affords attorneys the flexibility and creativity to construct logical relationships between case precedents and the facts of their clients' cases. Consequently, you are always looking for cases from the highest court—precedent—that have facts that are the same as (not likely) or similar to the facts in your case, to show the court why your client's position is best based upon a comparison of the legally relevant information. While you are researching, you make decisions as to which cases to use and not use, which cases represent the best position for the client, and which cases offer the best guidance for a court in deciding the issues before it.

reasoning by analogy
Method of reasoning that compares two similar or like cases, facts, or other legal source law to support the principles presented in your research project.

That brings us to ***Rule 4:*** *Think.* Do not initiate the process of legal research without a direction and without thinking about what you are reading, discarding, and retaining. How can you research an assignment if you are not thinking and reasoning analytically during the process? Know why you are choosing or not choosing a case or source of law. And one of the most important rules is ***Rule 5:*** *Create a legal research plan.* Write down your approach. Do you want to begin with a digest, a statute, or a secondary source for some background information? Will you need to consult a variety of sources, both primary and secondary, to successfully complete your assignment? It is more likely than not that you will use more than one source to research a project. That is your reality. And, perhaps the most important and final rule is ***Rule 6:*** *If you are not finding cases and sources that apply to your project, go back to Rule 1*—get some help from your supervising attorney or another attorney in your firm or company. Don't let precious time slip away from lack of direction or confusion. Stop—pause—ask—regroup.

SELECTING THE BEST SOURCE TO USE IN PLANNING YOUR LEGAL RESEARCH

One point is clear when commencing any legal research project—there is no one way to begin. Much of where to begin depends on what you are looking for and what you want to accomplish. However, there are some basic questions you should ask yourself before beginning an assignment. We will examine some of those questions in this section.

What Are My Time Constraints?

Knowing how much time you have to complete an assignment may play into your source selection and your legal research plan. Most assignments given by your supervising attorney have time constraints—deadlines. Some of the time constraints are court-induced; others are work-induced (requested by the boss). Regardless of the reasons behind the time constraints, you may have to research in a short timeframe. That means you must be economical in managing your research process. To do this, you must prioritize.

Ask when the assignment is due. You may have only a few days to complete a project. In that case, electronic research may be your best solution. This suggests that you need to be or become proficient on the Internet, Westlaw, or LexisNexis. Remember, you can combine both the electronic and traditional print-based research. For example, you may be more comfortable performing the basic legal research using print digests or encyclopedias but Shepardize or KeyCite using an electronic method because it is quicker and more accurate. Think before you act, and know the constraints of the assignment before you begin. The more information you know, the more effective you will be in your work.

What Jurisdiction Applies to My Assignment?

In any assignment you will receive from your attorney, you will always need to know the jurisdiction in which your assignment is based. First you must ask yourself, "Is the matter federal or state?" That is an important question as you must determine whether you will need, for example, the federal digest or state digest. Often, state-specific digests combine federal and state cases for that jurisdiction, so checking your state's specific resources is always a good start.

Knowing what jurisdiction applies also encompasses the court in which your assignment may be located. For instance, if you receive a **complaint,** check the **caption** of the case to identify in which court the case was filed. (Recall Chapter 1, which discusses the court process and general information on legal documents filed with a court.) That will give you an immediate hint as to the scope of your research and which jurisdiction you should be researching. If you are not sure what jurisdiction applies to your assignment, ask your supervising attorney. Don't waste precious time floundering because you either are hesitant to ask or fail to seek guidance when you hit a road block.

complaint
Document that states the allegations and the legal basis of the plaintiff's claims. Also, a charge, preferred before a magistrate having jurisdiction, that a person named has committed a specified offense, with an offer to prove the fact, to the end that a prosecution may be instituted.

caption
The full name of the case, together with the docket number, court, and date of the decision.

What Are the Legal Principles Involved in the Assignment?

Some assignments are subject-specific, which involve certain types of legal resources. Therefore, understand your assignment before rushing off to a digest or encyclopedia. For example, if your assignment is to research the requirements of an appellate brief, you surely are not best served by choosing a digest. If your assignment is to locate certain brief requirements, you may check the court's roles on its Web site; check the statute, which usually has the court rules; or check a looseleaf service that deals with the issue. The point is that every research assignment is different, requiring you to think about which source is best for the assignment. Do not pigeonhole your approach to legal research. Remember, there is not only one way to attack a project. Think about your available legal research sources. Think about what you are trying to accomplish. As much as we all would like to find the "perfect" approach to legal research, there is nothing black and white about researching the law—only shades of gray.

Can Primary Persuasive Authority Be Used in the Assignment?

Using persuasive authority, such as cases from other jurisdictions, wholly depends on whether mandatory authority exists on the topic you are researching. If there is no other legal authority on the issue, then it is appropriate to cite the persuasive authority as long as you are clear in your communications that (1) no authority exists in the jurisdiction you are researching, (2) the state or states cited are used only as persuasive authority as none exists in your jurisdiction, and (3) the authority is presented only as a guide. No one, whether judge or supervising attorney, wants to be told that he or she *must* follow authority from another jurisdiction. Consequently, be frank with the authority you have located when none exists from the jurisdiction where your facts originated.

However, be careful in suggesting to a judge or supervising attorney to follow a state statute from another jurisdiction. This is a bit of a "ticklish" situation. Statutes are unique creatures. They are created by state legislatures usually for a particular purpose. Unless the argument is to suggest a policy point, such as most jurisdictions have laws on responding to an Amber Alert, do not use another jurisdiction's state statute as persuasive authority. If a court wants to create case law to support a particular point where a statute does not exist, the court will evaluate its options, as often courts do not want to substitute their judgment for that of a legislature, unless the statute is deemed unconstitutional.

Consequently, determine your time constraints, your jurisdiction, and the legal principles involved in your assignment; pause for a moment, think about your end result, and then determine your approach. Most people want to determine an approach without thinking about what is to be accomplished in the assignment. Be deliberative and thoughtful.

PRACTICE TIP

New paralegals do not realize the time and thought that an assignment entails. Rarely does an assignment contain only one legal authority. A complete legal research assignment requires sufficient legal sources to present a client's position soundly and adequately.

The sections that follow in this chapter are different legal research plans—roadmaps to assist you in finding the legal sources you will need to complete any assignment that is presented to you by your supervising attorney. No research is carved in stone. Therefore, be flexible and creative. That will lead you on the road to success.

Quick Quiz True/False Questions

1. When performing legal research, refrain from asking your supervising attorney for guidance.
2. Deductive reasoning and reasoning by analogy are the same.
3. Reasoning by analogy is reasoning by example.
4. When researching, always create a detailed plan.
5. One important exercise in research is to determine the issues in the assignment.

PRACTICE TIP

Remember that the annotated code version references the material from only that publisher. Consequently, the *United States Code Annotated* and the *United States Code Service* will have different resources cited in the annotated sections.

ROADMAP FOR STATUTORY RESEARCH: ANNOTATED CODES

Federal Statutes

Recall that there are three basic places to locate federal statutes: *United States Code, United States Code Annotated,* and *United States Code Service.* Although the *United States Code* is the official version of federal statutes, *United States Code Annotated* and *United States Code Service* provide finding tools that assist in performing your legal research. Choose one of the annotated codes when beginning a research project involving a federal statute. The best way to learn how to proceed is by working through the process. Therefore, to thoroughly understand the statutory legal research process, we will begin with a basic set of facts.

Your firm has been hired by Thomas Ballentine, who is accused of accessing information on a protected computer without proper authorization in violation of 18 U.S.C. §§ 1030 (a)(5)(A)(ii) and (B)(i). In the indictment, the statutes and facts upon which Mr. Ballentine is charged are provided.

The first step you should undertake is to locate one of the annotated codes and review the applicable statutes to determine exactly what law Mr. Ballentine may have violated. Use an annotated version of the *United States Code* as this version contains the helping tools you will need to commence your research. Based upon the facts that Mr. Ballentine presented in the initial interview, you will be able to narrow your scope of research. Recall that the annotated codes have sections that provide case interpretation of the statutory section as well as "other" related finding tools such as encyclopedia references, topics, and keys and any other sources the publisher may reference.

Using our example, let's look up 18 U.S.C. §§ 1030 (a)(5)(A)(ii) and (B)(i). (See Figure 10.1.) The section provides a wealth of information. You must determine how to use the information. If the topic is new to you, read the encyclopedia entries to gain insight on the topic. If the topic is familiar, begin reviewing the "notes of decision" section to determine whether any of the cases cited (1) are from your jurisdiction, or (2) apply to your set of facts. Here, you must begin reading and thinking critically. Eliminate cases that do not apply; set aside cases (by writing down the citations) that may help, or hurt, your client. If you are using the print version, check the pocket parts and supplements for changes in the statute, such as amendments or repeals.

PRACTICE TIP

In the early stages of researching a case, you are educating both yourself and your supervising attorney. It is good practice to locate cases that support your position and cases that are adverse to your position. Attorneys who are prepared understand both sides of the argument thoroughly. Therefore, research all aspects of the assignment and let your supervising attorney determine what is needed.

Your next step is to retrieve cases and begin reviewing them for relevancy. In this instance, you have two options available: print or electronic. Although either source is appropriate, remember that often the more helpful source is one with a "topic and key." Use the case as a research source. Review the headnotes, if available. Isolate the headnotes that appear important, and look up the topic and key associated with that headnote in a digest. Allow the headnotes to guide you to other headnotes with relevant topics and keys. Pay attention to how the entire research process intersects with each other. Review the cases cited in the case; follow the analysis of the court for hints as to the "trends" in the law. Make the cases work for you.

Next, you should begin narrowing your cases to the ones that are applicable. Keep a record of the cases reviewed and briefly note why a case was discarded. Organization is important. Most attorneys will question why you chose one case over the other. Be sure you can justify your decisions. Remember that all cases you choose to use as part of your assignment must be validated and updated either through Shepard's Citations, print or electronic, or KeyCite. Do not miss this step, as you do not want to present cases that either have been overruled or have "questionable" comments by a court.

§ 1030. Fraud and related activity in connection with computers

(a) Whoever—
(5)
(A)
(ii) intentionally accesses a protected computer without authorization, and as a result of such conduct, recklessly causes damage; and
(B) by conduct described in clause (i), (ii), or (iii) of subparagraph (A), caused (or, in the case of an attempted offense, would, if completed, have caused)—
(i) loss to 1 or more persons during any 1-year period (and, for purposes of an investigation, prosecution, or other proceeding brought by the United States only, loss resulting from a related course of conduct affecting 1 or more other protected computers) aggregating at least $5,000 in value;
[text omitted]

FIGURE 10.1
U.S. Fraud Code
Source: 18 U.S.C. §§ 1030 (a)(5)(A)(ii) and (B)(i).

Once you have reviewed your cases, copy them for your supervising attorney. Virtually all attorneys will review the cases chosen to assure themselves that the cases are relevant and applicable. Never be offended if an attorney wants to review the cases you present. First, this is required by the rules of ethics as the ultimate decision maker on a case is the attorney. Second, an attorney often reviews with a different critical eye. And finally, the attorney often picks up subtleties that may have been missed and may point you in a new and different direction. This is simply part of the process.

PRACTICE TIP

Cases, either directly from the court or from some electronic sources, will not have the publisher's editorial comments, including headnotes.

Some questions you may be asking yourself now are: "Do I just hand the cases to the attorney for review?" "Do I brief them?" "How should I present the results of my research to the supervising attorney?" That depends on the assignment. The likelihood of you and your supervising attorney having a general discussion without any written component is slim. The form the written component takes will depend upon the needs of the attorney. Usually, if you are researching for general information to assist the attorney in formulating a legal strategy, you will present the results of your research in the form of an **interoffice memorandum.** An interoffice memorandum is an objective document that presents both the positive and negative aspects of a case. This document is usually an internal document used for very limited purposes. (See Chapter 16 for a discussion of an interoffice memorandum and its format.) From that document, additional documents may be drafted such as a **letter, pleading,** or **motion.** These documents will be addressed in the second half of this text on legal writing. Consequently, once you have researched your assignment, you are not finished. You will most likely prepare some type of document for submission.

interoffice memorandum
Objective document that presents all aspects of a case, both negative and positive.

letter
Document that transmits information to a client, opposing counsel, the court, or any other individual or entity.

pleading
Formal documents filed with the court that establish the claims and defenses of the parties to the lawsuit; the complaint, answer to complaint, and reply.

motion
A procedural request or application presented by the attorney in court.

State Statutes

Researching a state statute is similar to that of a federal statute. All states have annotated codes with helpful finding tools. As with the different annotated federal codes, the publisher will dictate the information included in the annotated state codes. A decision to consider in researching a state statute is whether the facts presented are solely a state issue or have federal overtones. For example, states may have statutes on discrimination as well as the federal statutes on the matter. Reviewing the law will dictate how the laws apply and interact with each. Your research may also dictate which court, federal or state, or where an action should be filed. (Recall our discussion of jurisdiction in Chapter 1.) When there are both state and federal issues, a case is usually filed in the federal court. Essentially, the state claims "piggyback" on the federal ones. As you learned in earlier chapters, courts hear cases involving both federal and state claims. When a federal claim has state claims arising out of the same set of facts, the federal court will exercise **pendent jurisdiction.** Here, state claims are "tagged" onto the federal claims and heard in one lawsuit. One of the reasons behind

pendent jurisdiction
Jurisdictional concept where state claims arising out of the same set of facts as a federal claim are heard together.

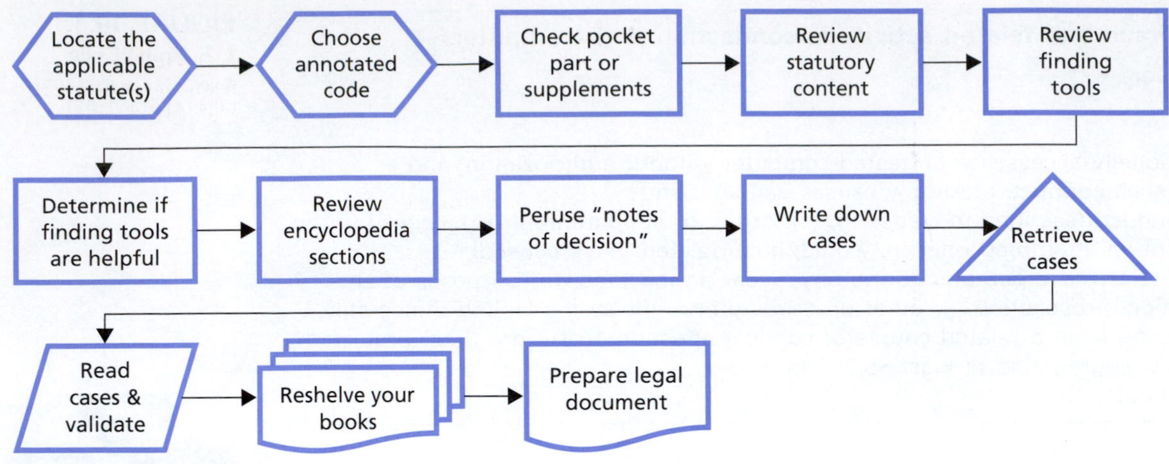

FIGURE 10.2 **Flowchart for Statutory Research: Known Statute**

judicial economy
The overall efficiency a court promotes in hearing its cases, especially when case facts have both state and federal claims.

combining the federal and state claims is for **judicial economy.** Judicial economy refers to the overall efficiency of a court or court system in hearing its cases. For example, if you have 200 persons who have had problems with breast implants leaking fluid, one lawsuit might be filed to address the issues of all the plaintiffs instead of 200. Similarly, when a plaintiff has federal and state claims arise out of the same set of facts, filing the case in two different courts would clog the courts and delay cases, even more than they already are. These are examples of the principle of judicial economy. However, these types of decisions are legal and strategic and will be made by your supervising attorney.

Nevertheless, your research approach should not change. Locate the applicable state statutes; review them; check the pocket parts and supplements; review the cases; choose the cases that apply. Prepare the assignment in the format dictated by your attorney.

A Checklist for Statutory Research

In commencing statutory legal research, determine whether you know or do not know the existing statute. Depending on your information, follow one of the suggested plans.

For a Known Statute

- Locate the applicable statute(s).
- Choose an annotated code, if available.
- Check the pocket part or supplements for amendments or repeals, if print version. Electronic version should be automatically updated in Westlaw, LexisNexis, or a government Web site.
- Review the statute for its content.
- Review the finding tools suggested in the annotated statute.
- Determine whether any of the finding tools would be helpful in your research assignment.
- Review encyclopedia sections, *American Law Reports* annotations, and other legal sources cited in the code, if appropriate.
- Begin perusing the "notes of decision" section in U.S.C.A. or related section of the statute that has cases in U.S.C.S.
- Write down cases that may apply to your assignment.

CYBER TRIP

An Iraqi citizen, who lives in Ohio, claims that he was fired by his company, Soup Supply, Inc., because of his national origin. Locate the federal and Ohio statutes that address discrimination claims based upon national origin. Detail your statutory research plan.

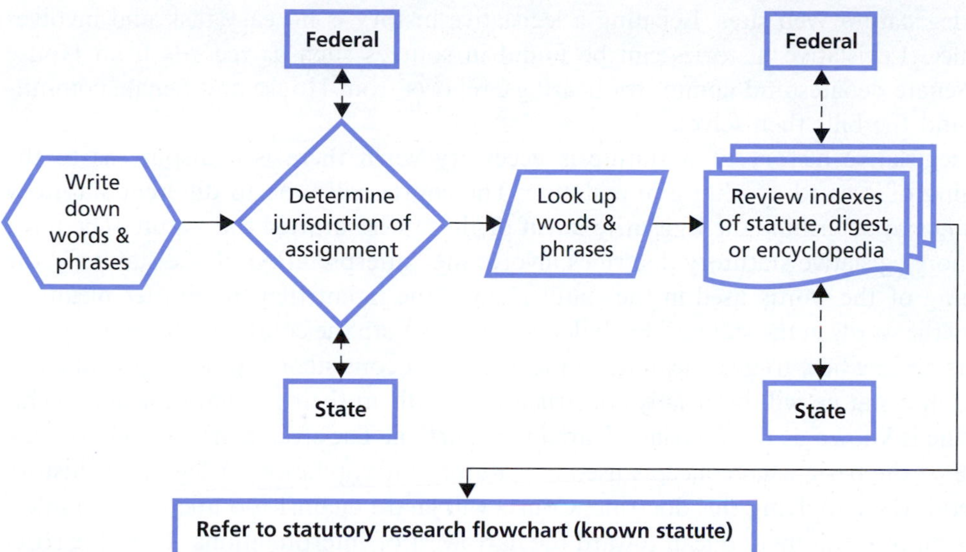

FIGURE 10.3
Flowchart for Statutory Research: Unknown Statute

- Retrieve cases, either print or electronic. Determine which case version is best for your use, although sometimes your choice may be dictated by availability.
- Read the cases chosen and copy those cases that apply to your assignment.
- Validate your cases either through Shepard's Citations or KeyCite.
- Reshelve your books, if appropriate library policy. (Note: Some libraries do not want you to reshelve books. They are concerned about misshelving the books. Check the library's protocols.)
- Prepare the legal document required for the assignment.

See Figure 10.2.

For an Unknown Statute

- Write down words and phrases that may apply to the facts presented for the assignment.
- Determine whether your assignment is federal or state.
- Look up the words and phrases in any digest, encyclopedia, or annotated statute index to start. The indexes should lead you to applicable sections within the source you are using.
- Check the state digest, if available; don't forget the pocket parts.
- Review an encyclopedia or other secondary sources, such as *A.L.R.* treatises or law review journals, for general information and guidance on the subject you are researching. Don't forget to pay attention to the footnotes in encyclopedias for cases.
- Follow the steps for the Known Statute checklist to continue the research assignment.

See Figure 10.3.

ROADMAP FOR LEGISLATIVE HISTORY

On occasion your research will require that you review the legislative history of a case. Federal legislative histories are documented on such Web sites as www.thomas.gov, www.gpoaccess.gov, or www.loc.gov, with state legislative histories often found on the state legislature Web sites. Locating a legislative history is no easy task and involves patience. Legislative histories can be found in sources such as records from House and Senate debates and committee hearings, reports from House and Senate committees, and the bills themselves.

A legislative history of a statute is necessary when there is a dispute as to the meaning of a word or phrase in a statute. The courts will look to different statutory doctrines to determine the **legislative intent** of those who drafted the statute. The most common legislative statutory doctrines involve the "interpretation of the statute," "the meaning of the words used in the statute," and "the intent that the drafter meant to give to the words in the statute." Each doctrine assists both the court and the researcher in understanding how to give meaning to the words in a consistent manner. Consequently, words in a statute will be strictly construed to give them their ordinary meaning. This doctrine is known as the **doctrine of strict construction.** The strict construction doctrine is one of the basic legal concepts used in statutory interpretation. A legislative history is useful when applying this doctrine; Courts will guard against too liberal of an interpretation of a statute and lean toward the narrowest of interpretations. Thus, the strict construction doctrine is born.

legislative intent
Process of interpreting the meaning of the drafters of a statute through legislative history and judicial interpretation doctrines.

doctrine of strict construction
Statutory interpretation doctrine that narrowly interprets a statute's meaning and intent.

Coupled with the strict construction doctrine is the doctrine that words are given their **plain meaning.** This means that words will be interpreted in their ordinary sense. Legislative history can be used to offer insight into "how" and "why" words were chosen over others through reviewing the drafter's comments as he or she participated in the process. Delving into a legislative history can be both a blessing and a curse. It can be a bit like opening up Pandora's box.

plain meaning
Doctrine in statutory interpretation that interprets the words and phrases in a statute in their ordinary sense.

Foremost in a legislative history, you are searching for the intent of the legislators who drafted the statute. Similarly, the court in being presented with statutory interpretation issues will also look to the legislative intent. Courts look for guidance to ensure consistency of their result. What was the context of a legislator's decision to include or exclude a particular word or concept? Essentially, we are attempting to take ourselves back to the time the statute was drafted, to understand the "whys" and "hows" of the development and final version of the statute. To bring ourselves back in history is to understand the true intent of the history of a statute. Faced with this task, follow the suggested plan.

Legislative History Research Plan

- Identify the statute that requires interpretation.
- Review its history in the annotated code, pocket parts, and supplements.
- Locate the original statute at large, public law number, or bill number, if available.
- Isolate the statute's number and search either a government Web site or print material on the statute.
- Review federal or state documents, such as floor debates, committee hearings, reports of committees, and the marked-up bill.
- Check fee-based Web sites, such as Westlaw and LexisNexis, for their databanks of legislative histories.
- Explore other Web sites, such as law school university Web sites.
- Contact the U.S. Congress or state legislatures for recent legislative history material.
- Review the material and isolate the area in the material that is relevant.
- Reduce the information to the format required by your supervising attorney.

Quick Quiz True/False Questions

1. Annotated codes do not have a finding tool.
2. In performing statutory research, do not use Shepard's Citations or KeyCite.
3. When a court exercises pendent jurisdiction, state claims piggyback on federal claims that arise out of the same set of facts.
4. In performing a review of a statute's legislative history, do not examine congressional hearings or committee reports.
5. The strict construction doctrine interprets the words in a statute narrowly to determine its meaning.

ROADMAP FOR CASE RESEARCH

In researching case law, the same basic principles of statutory research apply. Use the lessons learned from the chapters on finding tools and updating the law, and you are on your way to creating a comprehensive roadmap to follow. When presented with a general fact situation and you are not sure where to begin, there are two recommendations: the digest and encyclopedias. Determining which finding tool to use depends on your purpose. If you need a general overview of the law, encyclopedias are an excellent place to start. Otherwise, use a digest, which will lead to cases. The basic process is the same. Use the indexes to the set when presented with a situation where you want to find cases: This will, of course, guide you into the main volumes of the selected books. To begin the process, follow the guidelines in the next two sections.

Using a Digest

- Write down words, phrases, and relevant concepts that may apply to your fact situation.
- Look up the words, phrases, and relevant concepts in a digest or encyclopedia.
- Determine which digest or encyclopedia you want to use: general or specific, state or federal.
- Locate the appropriate volumes of books you want to use.
- Identify which index you need: Descriptive Word Index, Words and Phrases, or Table of Case. Chances are that you will use the Descriptive Word Index as that index is the most general of the indexes.
- Look up the words and phrases you have written down and find applicable topics and keys. (You may have to look up a number of different words or phrases until you locate topics and keys that may apply to your research assignment.)
- Locate the digest volume and retrieve the book from the library shelf once you have a topic and key. (The topics are identified on the outside binding of the digest volumes. Watch for softbound supplements that contain recent information.) When a digest volume has a corresponding softbound supplement, retrieve both volumes for your research.
- Open the volume to the applicable topic and key. (Remember, if the topic and key are not found in the volume, chances are they have been updated. Check the corresponding translation/conversion tables in the front of the digest volume for the current topic and key.)
- Review the digest case summaries to find applicable cases. Watch for cases that apply to the jurisdiction you are researching. Always look for U.S. Supreme Court cases.
- Check the pocket parts and supplements of the digest for new cases under the topic(s) and key(s) you are researching.

- Write down the cases that apply to your assignment.
- Search surrounding keys in the digest for related information. Remember that the surrounding keys relate to the topic you are researching. Take the time to scan the other keys, and you might notice an area that is worth reviewing.
- Retrieve the case reporters from the shelf and begin reading the cases. (Remember to pay attention to the headnotes with corresponding topics and keys. Also, pay attention to the cases cited by the court of the case you are reviewing. New cases may appear in the case that you may not have located from your initial search.)
- Update and validate cases chosen through either Shepard's Citations or KeyCite.
- Copy all cases intended to use for the research assignment.
- Reshelve all case reporters, if appropriate library policy.
- Prepare the requested legal document for your supervising attorney.

PRACTICE TIP

Do not use encyclopedias to the exclusion of other sources. They are not complete enough to be your sole legal research source. Always use them in conjunction with other legal research sources such as a digest, whether print or electronic.

Using an Encyclopedia

- Look up the words and phrases in the general index.
- Through the index, you will be directed to an encyclopedia subject and section.
- Locate the applicable volume and begin reviewing the information in the volume.
- Notice that some encyclopedias offer topics and keys, black letter law, and associated finding tools. The types of finding tools will be dictated by the publisher of the volume.
- As you are reading the text, pay close attention to the footnotes, which contain cases on the subject about which you are reading.
- Write down the citations of any cases that may apply to your research assignment.
- Check the pocket part of the encyclopedia volume as well as any softbound supplements that are related to the main volume you are reviewing.
- Review the cases and copy those that apply for future use.
- Update or validate your cases through Shepard's Citations or KeyCite.
- Reshelve books, if appropriate library policy.
- Consider additional finding tool sources, such as digests, to augment and complement your research in the legal encyclopedias.

CYBER TRIP

Locate cases in support of and opposition to the Case Fact Pattern at the beginning of this chapter and detail your research plan.

State Case Research

To research state case law, follow the general suggested paths identified in the previous sections. It should be recognized that not all states have state-specific encyclopedias; when this is the case, use one of the general encyclopedias, such as *American Jurisprudence* or *Corpus Juris Secundum.* Virtually all states have a state-specific digest, but not all use ThomsonWest. That means that not all state-specific digests will have topics and keys. If this is the case, try a regional digest, if available. If all else fails, use the headnotes from the cases to lead you to the West topics and keys. This method of locating topics and keys is a common approach of attorneys when conducting legal research. By using this approach, you have a clear understanding of how the various legal sources work in concert. Master the system and you will always find a method to accomplish your goals. See Figure 10.4 for a diagram for researching case law.

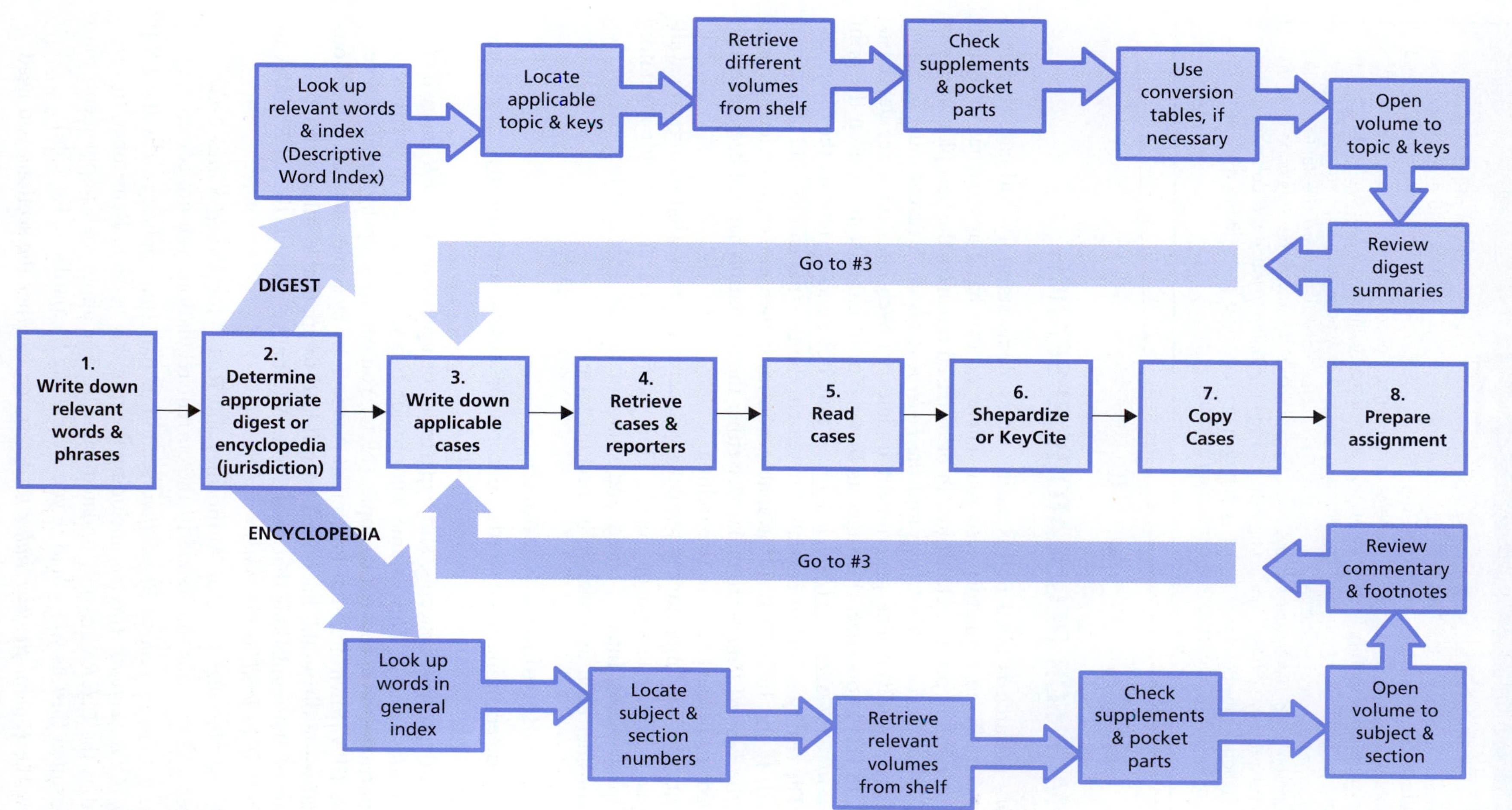

FIGURE 10.4 Case Research

YOU BE THE JUDGE

The competency and adequacy of an attorney's research was the subject in *Baldayaque v. United States,* 338 F.3d 145 (2d Cir. 2003). Ordinarily **statutes of limitations** are strictly followed by courts unless there are some extraordinary circumstances warranting their **equitable tolling.** Such was the case in the **habeas corpus** action of Heriberto Baldayaque. The issue before the court was not only the statute of limitations issues but also the competency of Baldayaque's counsel. As the court observed, the attorney "did no legal research on Baldayaque's case." Additionally, the court noted that the retained attorney did not comply with Connecticut's Rules of Professional Conduct, "which requires a lawyer to 'provide competent representation to a client, [which] requires the legal knowledge, skill, thoroughness and preparation reasonably necessary for the representation.'" *Id.* at 152. As the court ultimately found, the conduct of the attorney was not only egregious but extraordinary. Review the *Baldayaque* case. What are the facts that led the court to its holding? Why was the *Smaldone* case distinguished in the reasoning? Notice the concurring opinion. What was the reasoning of the judge who wrote the concurring opinion?

statute of limitations
Establishes the applicable time limits for filing and responding to certain claims or legal actions.

equitable tolling
Suspending a statute of limitations based upon principles of fairness or an unexpected intervening event.

habeas corpus
A writ employed to bring a person before a court, most frequently to ensure that the party's imprisonment or detention is not illegal.

ROADMAP FOR REGULATORY RESEARCH

Regulatory research is often not as easily accessible as statutory and case research, especially state-based regulatory research. There are two basic approaches to federal regulatory research: print or electronic. In print-based research, the best places to look are the *Code of Federal Regulations* and the *Federal Register.* A caveat must be noted at the outset, however. The government updates its Web sites on a regular basis. Armed with this knowledge, this suggests that the print-based sources, even the print *LSA: List of CFR Sections Affected* sources, may not be as current as the electronic version. The reality is that in regulatory research, the Internet cannot and should not be ignored. If the Internet is not available, you must then entertain reviewing print issues of the *Federal Register* to make sure either the regulation has not been amended or changed to the part you are researching.

Consequently, it is important in regulatory research to know what sources are available as that will dictate your approach. Three basic approaches exist for regulatory research: print-based, Internet-based, and a combination of print and Internet sources. We will consider each approach in a checklist format.

Print-Based Regulatory Research

- Begin by determining basic words, concepts, or specific departments or agencies that may apply to your research project.
- Look up the words, concepts, and department or agency in the *CFR Index and Finding Aids* volume. This volume will provide two ways to research information: by department or agency or by topic. (Note: You can look up by agency name, such as EPA [Environmental Protection Agency], or by topic, such as "hazardous medical waste disposal." Each method will lead to applicable titles, parts, and sections of the regulations that may apply. Alternatively, check the *CFR* (index to the *Code of Federal Regulations*).
- Check the "Parallel Table of Authorities and Rules" for *United States Code* statutes and sections that relate to the current regulations you are researching.
- Locate a *Code of Federal Regulations* section or part that applies; review the *LSA: List of CFR Sections Affected,* including the monthly version. Remember, this is critical as the *C.F.R.*s are only updated annually. The appropriate supplements must be consulted (just as you would if you were using Shepard's or KeyCite).
- Review the *Federal Register Index* to determine whether the sections you need have any proposals or amendments.

PRACTICE TIP

It is highly likely that regulations will have applicable statutory counterparts or enabling legislation. Always check the statutory codes for related information.

Online-Based Regulatory Research

- Determine your concepts or specific agencies that may be applicable.
- Log on to the Internet and go to www.gpoaccess.gov or www.reinfo.gov, for example.
- Search either by topic or agency by entering your query in the text box titled "Search Terms" and press Enter; or review in the list of *Code of Federal Regulations* identified on the Web site. Determine the relevant regulation and check the box(es) of the regulations needed for review.
- Review the *LSA: List of CFR Sections Affected,* which date back to 1997. Be sure to check the monthly lists as well as the *List of CFR Sections Affected Today.* All these queries may be found on the main page. (This Web site is probably one of the only places you can retrieve information on regulations that are or have been affected "today.")
- Search the *Federal Register* main page on www.gpoaccess.gov as well for related information on the area you are researching.
- Check the agency Web site for any new or current information. The agency or department Web sites are full of information that may lead to additional research that may impact your project.

Print- and Online-Based Regulatory Research

- Combine the methods described in the preceding checklists by verifying or expanding the information located in either a print version or an online version. This will act as a check and balance on the information located from both sources.
- Review the sections nearest to the section you are researching. (Often, the few sections before and after may be related to the topic you are researching. This is not necessarily a scientific approach to your research, but the reality of years of experience. Simply leafing through the pages of a *CFR* volume may reveal sections that are either applicable or of interest in your research.) Sometimes the print versions are easier to use because you can scan pages more easily than scanning the Internet version.
- Check the online version of the *LSA: List of Sections Affected* for both today and the current month. Usually the print versions will lag behind.
- Follow up with the *Federal Register* online daily version.
- Check the agency Web site for any additional information that may be helpful.

CYBER TRIP

Determine the federal labeling requirements for wine imported into the United States and whether your state has rules and regulations governing labeling information for wine; if so, what information is required on a wine label used or imported to the United States? Document your research plan.

ROADMAP FOR STATE REGULATIONS

State rules and regulations are not always located in an organized current fashion. The process is getting better, but state agencies and departments have not made the strides that the federal government has in accumulating their regulatory information. Recall that most states do have regulatory codes; most are still in print format. Therefore, determine whether a regulatory code exists for your state and commence your research accordingly. Additionally, many state agencies have Web sites that will assist in locating information on the rules and regulations you need. Check those sites for current information. One area that appears to have regulatory information from all fifty states is the environmental area. The Web site is www.envcap.org and offers information on environmental regulations and related states for all jurisdictions. The best approach is to check your state's Web sites for regulatory information, or try a general Internet search on a search engine for current information. Type the name of your state into the text box with "administrative regulations" and you should find applicable state links.

ETHICS ALERT

The Internet presents uncharted ethics issues. Many of the state bar associations address issues as they arise within their membership. A common theme with most of the bar associations is that the rules of ethics and professional responsibility applied before the Internet and apply equally as the Internet grows in popularity. Issues such as advertising, attorney–client privilege, unauthorized practice of law, and conflicts of interest are just some of the issues facing bar associations with the advent of the Internet. The answers to many questions and issues are unclear and unresolved. One of the most troubling issues is how to monitor the behavior of attorneys and other legal professionals, such as paralegals, on the Internet. So much of the interaction on the Internet is anonymous or with a "pen name." Identities are unknown, and at best, masked.

As a result, you should take care when using the Internet, especially list servers and chat rooms. Do not place yourself in a situation where you may indirectly, or directly for that matter, be rendering legal advice or divulging a client confidence. Although many sites give the appearance of anonymity, remember that much of what you do and say on the Internet can be traced or retrieved. Treat your professional communications on the Internet as though they were public, and do not confuse your personal communications with your professional ones. Attorneys and paralegals have become the subject of newspaper articles and professional ridicule when an innocent communication, for instance, becomes a public nightmare. Never let your guard down, especially when communicating through any means on the Internet. To explore the ethical standards and issues within your jurisdiction and others around the country, you can check www.legalethics.com, which provides links to all the state bar associations' ethical rules. Be aware and be forewarned.

INTERNET RESEARCH

The Internet is both a blessing and a curse. It provides information instantly, but courts still question its accuracy. When researching on the Internet, be aware of the Web sites you are using, and use the "official" sources or the primary sources of law when available. Stay away from Web sites that offer unverified information, such as www.wikipedia.com, or at least be aware of its limitations in legal research. Additionally, the Internet often does not provide all the available sources in one place or often provides too many sources that can be overwhelming, especially in the beginning. Of course, the Internet is an amazing tool; but remember, the Internet still does not eliminate sources like a "thinking human being." When you use either search methods, Boolean or natural language, the Internet often retrieves every time the word or phrase was used in a document without regard to content. Don't forget that! Therefore, the following is a suggested plan for doing research on the Internet, but always keep in the mind the limitations as well as the expansive nature of cyberspace.

YOUR RESEARCH PLAN AND CHECKLIST

Electronic Searches

- Before beginning your electronic search, be sure you are organized, as electronic research is costly.
- Understand your research assignment thoroughly.
- Don't hesitate to ask questions of your supervising attorney.
- Be sure you have notepads, pens, pencils, and Post-it notes to begin the research process. (With time, you will find the tools that work for you. Everyone's method is different.)
- Identify the issues involved.

- Determine the jurisdiction that applies (remember mandatory primary sources over persuasive primary sources).
- Determine whether the Web site you chose uses Boolean or natural language search techniques.
- Write down your search terms (this will help keep track of the words you used in case your initial choice of words does not produce the desired result).
- Review the proper methodology for using connectors (using "or" and "and" to connect your word concepts). Review the Web site's helpful hints section to determine the best search approach on the Web site.
- Enter your search words in the text box provided and click "Go" or "Search."
- If you are using Westlaw or LexisNexis, perform a KWIK (quick) or FOCUS search of the case to determine if you are on the right track.
- Review the results of your research by reading the cases or sources cited from the search.
- Redefine your search, if necessary, by adding, subtracting, or changing your search words. Search within the results provided to narrow the scope.
- Check secondary sources, such as law review articles and online encyclopedias, but be careful of unverified sources.
- Print copies of the relevant cases.
- Shepardize or KeyCite the relevant cases (watch for negative signals).
- Review relevant cases and brief them or take copious notes regarding the important cases intended for use.
- Prepare your assignment in the format dictated by the supervising attorney.

Caveat: In the beginning, if possible, verify your research by performing a manual search in the law library. This method will help verify that the research identified is relevant and complete. Learning the process, whether electronic or manual, takes time. Spend the extra time to validate your work by an alternative means.

Quick Quiz True/False Questions

1. One of the best techniques for commencing research using case law is to use digests and encyclopedias.
2. A method to verify whether a regulation has been changed is to check the *LSA: List of CFR Sections Affected.*
3. To locate current information regarding administrative rules and regulations, review the federal or state agency's Web sites.
4. Creating a research plan for the Internet includes using Boolean and natural language search techniques.
5. A problem with Internet legal research is that Internet searches retrieve every document that includes the search word used without regard to content.

COMBINING PRINT AND INTERNET RESEARCH: AN INTEGRATED APPROACH

As much as we might like to eliminate using print research and exclusively use electronic-based research, you may miss critical cases or information by using one method to the exclusion of the other. Traditional print research allows you to see in one source the applicable cases and legal resources that may apply. And remember, print research is more of a step-by-step approach. Let's say you have a topic and key that applies to your assignment. With print sources you can investigate more easily the surrounding topics and keys to determine whether there may be other topics and keys that apply. This is a bit of a "trolling" method, but by reviewing the surrounding topics and keys, you may see something that catches your attention. Remember, it is the publishers along with their editors who determine which topic and key to assign to a subject. What is logical to them may exclude a legal point that is relevant to you.

Therefore, for the most thorough and accurate legal research plan, combine traditional print and Internet research. Neither method of legal research is mutually exclusive of another. The best approach is a comprehensive integrated approach using all available legal sources and resources to reach the best result in any legal research project.

Each method will be a check on the other. When the same case or information appears from both sources, you can be confident that your research is accurate and probably complete. A suggested approach for integrating both print and Internet sources is the "legal research plan" in Figure 10.5.

CYBER TRIP

Using an integrated approach to legal research, find the leading U.S. Supreme Court cases that developed the parameters of a public employee's First Amendment right to free speech in the workplace.

FIGURE 10.5
Integrated Legal Research Plan

- Understand your research assignment thoroughly.
- Don't hesitate to ask questions of your supervising attorney.
- Determine the jurisdiction that applies. (Remember mandatory primary sources over persuasive primary sources.)
- Identify the issues involved.
- Be sure you have notepads, pens, pencils, and Post-it notes to begin the research process. (With time, you will find the tools that work for you. Everyone's method is different.)
- Start with either a legal encyclopedia or digests. Westlaw and LexisNexis have online versions of both legal encyclopedias and digests. (Many jurisdictions have state-specific encyclopedias and digests. They are a better starting point than the general finding sources but often are not online.)
- Write down words and phrases that apply to your research assignment.
- Look up the words and phases in the digests or other finding tool selected. Or, perform a Boolean or natural language search on Westlaw, LexisNexis, or an Internet search engine. Enter your words and phrases in the text boxes provided.
- Find topics and keys that apply to your problem, whether through a print or online digest, encyclopedia, or other finding source.
- Review the cases under the topics and keys whether in print or online using Westlaw. When using LexisNexis, focus on the headnotes identified within the cases as the ThomsonWest Key Number System is unavailable. With fee-based Internet sources, such as Westlaw and LexisNexis, you can perform field and segment searches, respectively, which will narrow and focus your search.
- Write down the relevant cases. (Search for mandatory primary authority first. Check for U.S. Supreme Court cases. Stay within your jurisdictional parameters. For example, when researching a federal issue, locate cases in your circuit and state federal district court.)
- Avoid other jurisdictions unless no legal authority exists within your jurisdiction. (Remember, other jurisdictions only represent persuasive authority.)
- Retrieve cases either from a library or online, and read them.
- Copy "entire" cases that are pertinent. (When using print materials, many law libraries have copy cards that can be purchased. Be prepared for the copying options in your law library.)
- Shepardize or KeyCite cases chosen for use in your assignment. (Remember, a thorough Shepard's print search requires both hardbound volumes and softbound supplements to be reviewed. Don't skip a softbound volume. You could be courting disaster.)
- Reshelve all your books if in a library or at least determine the library's protocols. That's common courtesy.
- Prepare the assignment in the format designated by your supervising attorney.

AN ALTERNATIVE APPROACH: USING EXISTING SECONDARY SOURCES

Throughout this text we have discussed the traditional print-based sources and the Internet, but there is another approach that uses both print and Internet sources, that is not the traditional approach taught. These sources involve, in a real sense, more practical resources. In this context, we distinguish between a **legal source** and a **legal resource.** We all know the legal sources of the law: cases, statutes, constitutions, administrative rules and regulations, court rules, encyclopedias, and the list goes on and on. But lawyers who are resourceful often revert to "legal resources" to assist them in learning the law in an area. In this context we mean other resources that provide guidance on a topic. These resources may include a brief from your law firm or your opponent's law firm, or a brief posted on the Internet, such as a brief for the U.S. Supreme Court. Here, the research is tested and more than likely quite extensive and thorough, especially briefs submitted to a higher court. In these briefs, cases, statutes, and other sources are cited that can offer guidance on a project for you especially if it is directly related to an area you are researching. For example, all U.S. Supreme Court briefs are posted on the Court's Web site. Anyone can review them. Consequently, if you know that a particular subject has been decided or is about to be decided, chances are the briefs of all the parties involved, including any amicus curiae briefs ("friend of the court" briefs) are posted on the Web site, www.supremecourtus.gov.

legal source
The primary and traditional secondary sources of the law.

legal resource
The practical legal research tools, such as existing briefs, from online and law firm databases, used to assist in performing legal research.

Now, here is the problem with this approach: plagiarism. Don't take a good thing and turn it into an ethical nightmare for yourself. Use the briefs, whether in your office data banks or on the Internet, as guidance and a legal resource finding tool to lead you to the information needed to fulfill the requirements of your research project. As you will read throughout this text, many judges fined attorneys for plagiarism and "poor cut and paste" methods. Don't get trapped. Do your own work. Make the research project your own and not someone else's. But do use the briefs as a legal resource to assist in your own legal research.

Similarly, locate articles from law review journals or legal periodicals that offer current information on a topic. Both sources offer legal analysis that will assist you in better understanding your legal research goals and the project assigned. Use the footnote sections, which provide the basis of the research conclusions in the articles. Pull the cases and statutes or the secondary sources cited within the articles. Again, make the legal resources work for you. Don't just copy the sources and imply that they are your own, or worse, hold them out to be your own. Remember your professional responsibility and rules of ethics.

Other legal resources that we have discussed in this text range from looseleaf reporters to formbooks to seminar articles. Embrace them as do all legal professionals. Just know their limitations and keep remembering our theme throughout this chapter and later chapters: "make them your own." In the later chapters on legal writing, we discuss plagiarism and our professional obligations. So, find the legal resources and use them to your professional advantage, but most importantly, use them appropriately.

There you have it: some alternative approaches to the traditional print-based and Internet research techniques we have learned thus far.

Quick Quiz True/False Questions

1. When researching, you should never combine print books and the Internet.
2. An alternative approach to a typical research plan is to review the briefs written by attorneys, such as those posted on the U.S. Supreme Court Web site.

THE E-FACTOR

Throughout this text, Internet sources have provided alternatives to the traditional print-based legal research methods. What is clear is that there is no single method of doing research. Prior to the Internet, statistics and secondary sources were more difficult to access. With the Internet, most sources are available with just a click of the mouse. However, what should also be clear is that courts have not necessarily kept pace with the abundance of sources the Internet offers. Numerous cases still raise concerns over the reliability of Internet sources and the ability to identify the source itself.

There is no doubt that the Internet has changed the way we conduct legal research; but we must be mindful that although the Internet has broadened the way we perform legal research, the results from the Internet have not necessarily received an unconditional welcome, especially by the courts. Thus, utilize the "accepted" legal research sources and practice an integrated approach to the subject.

Some attorneys attempt to introduce nonlegal or nontraditional sources from the Internet and expect courts to accept those sources as having the same weight as traditional primary sources of the law. Courts have not embraced these approaches. Consequently, when performing your legal research, your approach should include not only the Internet sources but the traditional sources of legal research as well. It appears that courts have lagged behind, but as much of the case law suggests, for good reason—reliability. If an Internet source does not have the appropriate or accepted reliability factor, always have a traditionally accepted source to support a legal concept or contention. Remember, as part of your research plan, use traditional print-based sources along with electronic sources. And be mindful of the source of your electronic legal research. Do not confuse the ease of accessing information from the Internet with its reliability. The two concepts are not inherently related.

YOU BE THE JUDGE

In legal research, one of the constant themes is the requirement that an attorney cite adverse authority to a court. Of course, the attorney can distinguish, explain, or argue why a case should not be followed, but the adverse authority must be presented to the court nevertheless. A New York attorney failed to acknowledge adverse authority and drew the wrath of the court in *Nachbaur v. American Transit Insurance Company,* 752 N.Y.S. 605 (App. Div. 2002). Even more disturbing to the court was the fact that the adverse authority was in one of the attorney's previous cases. As the court harshly wrote, when authority is controlling and especially when counsel is aware of the authority, that authority, "unless and until overruled or disagreed with by this court, is 'controlling' authority that plaintiff's attorney was obligated to bring to the attention of the Court." *Id.* at 608. Read the *Nachbaur* case. What are the facts that led to sanctions of the attorney by the court? What is the holding in the case? What is the main issue in the case and the basis of the appeal?

PRACTICE TIP

Formbooks should have a warning sign printed across their covers. Too many legal professionals use formbooks as the sole basis of the legal document they create rather than the "suggested" guide that they were intended to be. Don't get caught in bad habits.

3. It is not important to determine the jurisdiction that applies to your research.
4. Always know your deadlines and time constraints when commencing a legal research project.
5. Never use persuasive authority in performing your legal research.

A HANDS-ON APPROACH: TRACKING A LEGAL RESEARCH ASSIGNMENT

Let's put all our practical knowledge to good use and track a problem that might be presented to you by your supervising attorney. Your supervising attorney presents the following facts to you in a memorandum:

Our client, Sean Rawlins, who lives in Omaha, Nebraska, has been arrested for possession of an unlicensed firearm. He claims the police entered his apartment unannounced without a warrant and found a "short-barreled shotgun." Rawlins claims the police trapped him and should not have entered his apartment. Upon further investigation, we learned that shots were heard being fired from apartment

7, Rawlins's apartment. Rawlins was seen walking quickly from the apartment to the parking lot toward his car. Officer Townsend stopped Rawlins and asked whether he lived in apartment 7, which he admitted. He did deny that he fired any shots from his apartment. Listening to the story, another officer, Harry Bishops, decided to investigate further. He walked toward apartment 7, where he met Artie Jansen, who had initially made the call to the police.

Jansen told Officer Bishops that he heard the shots come from apartment 7. In Jansen's apartment, looking scared, was Rawlins's girlfriend, Cassandra Mills, who was uncooperative. After checking the surrounding area and finding case shells, Officer Bishops first knocked on the door of Rawlins's apartment and after hearing no answer, decided to enter. He tried to pick the lock, but was later was told to kick in the door. Bishops's concern was that victims might still be in the apartment, constituting an emergency. Once in the apartment, Bishops, along with another officer, Herman, made a protective sweep of the apartment. Although they did not find any victims, they did find shotgun shells and casings in plain view on the floor. At this point, Officer Bishops told Officer Herman to stand guard at the apartment while he obtained a search warrant. Less than two hours later, Officer Bishops arrived with a search warrant for apartment 7 and performed a thorough search. During the search, the officers seized a 12-gauge short-barreled shotgun, expended shell casings, and a spilled box of live shells. Rawlins has been indicted for possession of an unregistered firearm. Your assignment is to locate the law for a motion to suppress, which your attorney wants to file on Rawlins's behalf. The basis for the motion is that all the evidence was obtained through a warrantless search of Rawlins's apartment.

The question is, where should you begin and what is your plan? Based upon the fact pattern, the key to your research is the fact that the evidence was obtained from a warrantless search. It appears that you have a Fourth Amendment search and seizure issue. Before you pull a book off the shelf or touch a computer, you should remember from our facts that the case is set in Omaha, Nebraska. This means you will want to find cases from the Eighth Circuit Court of Appeals where Nebraska is located, cases from the federal district courts in Omaha, and more importantly, U.S. Supreme Court cases. **(Step 1)** Additionally, you would want to check to see whether the indictment that charged Rawlins cited any statutes that may have been violated. If so, you should locate a copy of the statutes, federal and state, and review them. **(Step 2)** Assuming you don't have much knowledge of search and seizure law under the Fourth Amendment, you should gain some insight on the topic. This will aid your research efforts. Therefore, you have a number of places where you could begin: You could start with (a) a legal encyclopedia, (b) a digest, (c) an annotated *United States Code* (recall the amendments are annotated in the *United States Code* volumes), or (d) the Internet, either a general search engine or a fee-based service. **(Step 3)** Your next step, regardless of the source, is to determine what words and phrases to either look up in a print-based source or enter in the appropriate text box on the Internet. In this case, some appropriate words would be: warrantless search, Fourth Amendment, plain view, emergency circumstances, and search and seizures. These are some of the words and concepts you would glean from the fact pattern. **(Step 4)**

Depending upon your chosen source, you should be finding information on warrantless searches and under what circumstances a warrantless search is legal and constitutional. For this exercise, let's choose the Internet and *West's Federal Practice Digest 4th.* Using www.google.com, the phrase "warrantless searches evidence" was entered. The results are shown in Figure 10.6. Not great. Added to that query were the phrase "4th amendment." (See Figure 10.7.) The results were better, such as an article on the Fourth Amendment found on www.gpoaccess.gov, but the results

FIGURE 10.6 Results from Google Search on Warrantless Searches

Google — Web | Images | Groups | News | Scholar | **more »**

warrantless searches evidence — Search — Advanced Search — Preferences

New! View and manage your web history

Web — Results **1 - 10** of about **664,000** for warrantless searches evidence. (**0.17** seconds)

Search and seizure - Wikipedia, the free encyclopedia
The primary remedy in illegal **search** cases is known as the "exclusionary rule". This means that any **evidence** obtained through an illegal **search** is excluded ...
en.wikipedia.org/wiki/Search_and_seizure - 26k - Cached - Similar pages

> **Warrantless searches** in the United States - Wikipedia, the free ...
> **Warrantless searches** have been conducted in America since prior to the ... use of the **warrantless search** to gather **evidence** to use in a criminal trial. ...
> en.wikipedia.org/wiki/**Warrantless_searches**_in_the_United_States - 40k - Cached - Similar pages

WARRANTLESS SEARCH EVIDENCE IS INVALID Crime Control Digest - Find ...
WARRANTLESS SEARCH EVIDENCE IS INVALID from Crime Control Digest in Array provided free by LookSmart Find Articles.
findarticles.com/p/articles/mi_qa4440/is_200405/ai_n16061231 - 26k - Cached - Similar pages

> Montana: **WARRANTLESS SEARCH EVIDENCE** IS INVALID Juvenile Justice ...
> Montana: **WARRANTLESS SEARCH EVIDENCE** IS INVALID from Juvenile Justice Digest in Array provided free by LookSmart Find Articles.
> findarticles.com/p/articles/mi_qa3985/is_200405/ai_n9419599 - 26k - Cached - Similar pages
> [More results from findarticles.com]

Court Strikes Down **Warrantless Searches**
... to electronic surveillance without warrants and based on **evidence** so flimsy that ... Court Strikes Down **Warrantless Searches**: Published: September 27, ...
blogcritics.org/archives/2007/09/27/062351.php - 51k - Cached - Similar pages

www.federalmisconduct.com injustice corrupt harrassment charges ...
injustice corrupt harrassment charges hyping law **evidence** informants perjury snitches crooked civil rights prosecutors **warrantless searches** seizures rats ...
www.federalmisconduct.com/ - 15k - Cached - Similar pages

Az court ruling limits **warrantless** car **searches** | www ...
The ruling said the need for **searches** under officer-safety and **evidence**-preservation exceptions to constitutional protections from **warrantless searches** ...
www.tucsoncitizen.com/ss/local/58540.php - 32k - Cached - Similar pages

Law.com: 3rd Circuit Weighs In on **Warrantless Searches**
It was that decision to conduct a **warrantless** entry and **search** of the room, ... destruction of the **evidence** -- that justified the **warrantless search**. ...
www.law.com/jsp/law/LawArticleFriendly.jsp?id=1139911514164 - 13k - Cached - Similar pages

The Criminal Law Handbook: Know Your Rights, Survive the System - Google Books Result
by Sara J. Berman-Barrett, Paul Bergman - 2006 - Law - 621 pages
Question: Should a judge admit the pieces of jewelry into **evidence**? Answer: No. Exigent circumstances do not justify the **warrantless search**. ...
books.google.com/books?isbn=1413305148...

FIGURE 10.7 **Results from Second Google Search Adding Another Search Term**

Source: Copyright © Google. Reprinted with permission.

Google — Web | Images | Groups | News | Scholar | **more »**

warrantless searches evidence 4th amendmer — Search — Advanced Search | Preferences

New! View and manage your web history

Web Results **1 - 10** of about **374,000** for warrantless searches evidence 4th amendment. (**0.04** seconds)

SSRN-The Fourth **Amendment** Unplugged: Electronic **Evidence** Issues ...
This paper examines Fourth **Amendment** issues regarding **warrantless searches** in crimes committed via wireless networks. Traditionally accepted presumptions ...
papers.ssrn.com/sol3/papers.cfm?abstract_id=630901 - 29k - Cached - Similar pages

Fourth **Amendment** to the United States Constitution - Wikipedia ...
Therefore, government action triggers the **amendment's** protections only when the information or **evidence** at issue was obtained through a **"search"** within the ...
en.wikipedia.org/wiki/Fourth_**Amendment**_to_the_United_States_Constitution - 107k - Cached - Similar pages

Search and seizure - Wikipedia, the free encyclopedia
The Fourth **Amendment** to the United States Constitution ensures citizens' right to "be ...
This means that any **evidence** obtained through an illegal **search** is ...
en.wikipedia.org/wiki/Search_and_seizure - 26k - Cached - Similar pages

FindLaw's Writ - Colb: When Should Fourth **Amendment** Violations ...
When Should Fourth **Amendment** Violations Lead to Suppression of **Evidence**? .... The suppression of the product of a **warrantless search** and seizure is ...
writ.news.findlaw.com/colb/20050713.html - 56k - Cached - Similar pages

Danny Weitzner - Open Internet Policy » **4th Amendment** 'plain view ...
Plain view is the **4th amendment** rule that allows the police to discover and .... a lega system that regards **warrantless searches** as "per se [403 U.S. 443, ...
people.w3.org/~djweitzner/blog/?p=77 - 30k - Cached - Similar pages

FindLaw: U.S. Constitution: Fourth **Amendment**: Annotations pg. 1 of 6
California, 386 U.S. 58 (1967) (**warrantless search** of impounded car was .... **evidence**; violated Fourth **Amendment** in absence of warrant to **search** the home); ...
caselaw.lp.findlaw.com/data/constitution/**amendment**04/01.html - 106k - Cached - Similar pages

Court Strikes Down **Warrantless Searches**
On Wednesday a federal court struck down two provisions of the Patriot Act which allowed **warrantless searches** as violations of the Fourth **Amendment** of the ...
blogcritics.org/archives/2007/09/27/062351.php - 51k - Cached - Similar pages

CRS/LII Annotated Constitution Fourth **Amendment**
United States,14 it approved as "reasonable" the **warrantless search** of a ...... **evidence**; violated Fourth **Amendment** in absence of warrant to **search** the ...
www.law.cornell.edu/anncon/html/amdt4frag1_user.html - 105k - Cached - Similar pages

Warrantless Searches
Note that an exemption from the Fourth **Amendment** restrictions against **warrantless searches** is allowed when "exigent circumstances made that course ...
www.civilliberties.org/ss00**searches**.html - 18k - Cached - Similar pages

The Constitution of the United States of America
28\ The Fourth **Amendment** therefore does not apply to the **search** and ...... of criminal **evidence** found when police conducted a **warrantless search** of an ...
www.gpoaccess.gov/constitution/html/amdt4.html - 253k - Cached - Similar pages

FIGURE 10.8 Natural Language Search Results from LexisNexis

Source: Reprinted with permission of LexisNexis.

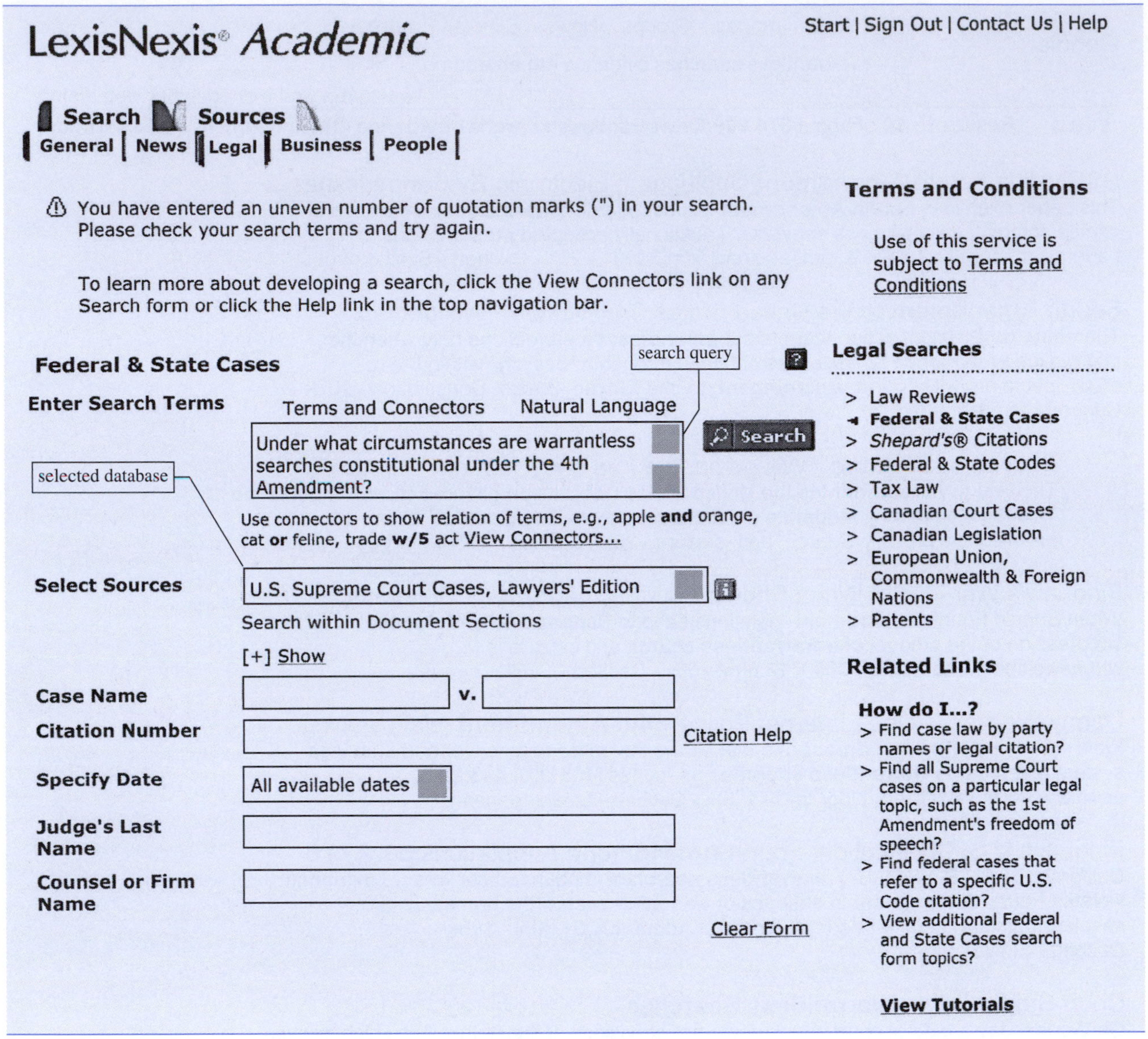

were not very exacting. Wikipedia.com was also tried, but the results were quite general. **(Step 5)** LexisNexis produced better results by using a natural language search. The query entered was "Under what circumstances are warrantless searches constitutional under the 4th Amendment?" (See Figure 10.8.) The results produced 907 cases. Obviously, this is too much to handle. **(Step 6)** In the text box a "focus" search was performed adding "exigent (emergency) circumstances" to our search. Only cases with the words "exigent circumstances" would be produced. The results of that search were 114 cases. **(Step 7)** The cases were then organized by date with the newest cases first. **(Step 8)** (See Figure 10.9.) The first two cases were reviewed, and the second case, *Brigham City v. Stuart,* 126 S. Ct. 1943, 164 L. Ed. 2d 650 (2006), appears promising. Now, you must simply read and review. **(Step 9)** (See Figure 10.10.)

FIGURE 10.9 Results from LexisNexis Search Using Text Box to Narrow Search

Source: Reprinted with permission of LexisNexis.

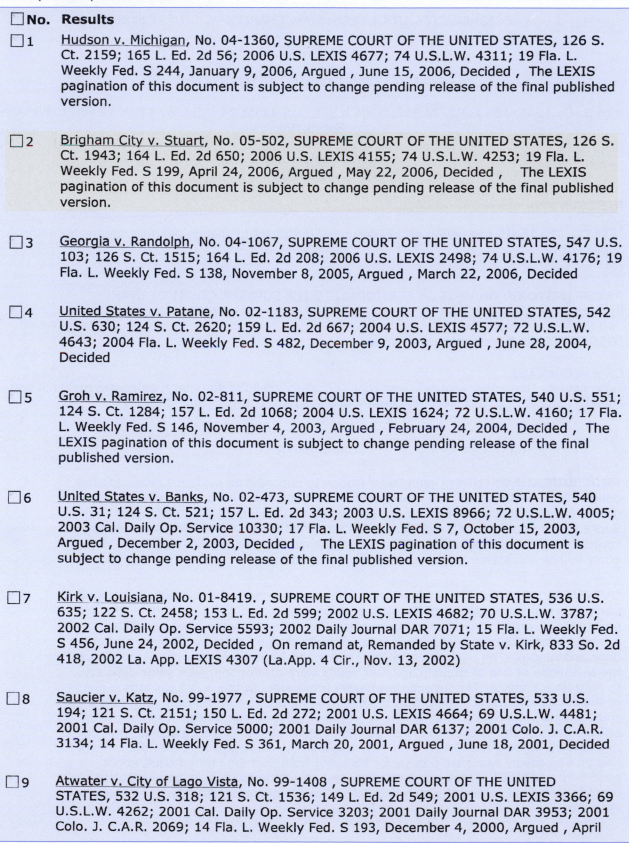

☐No.	Results
☐1	Hudson v. Michigan, No. 04-1360, SUPREME COURT OF THE UNITED STATES, 126 S. Ct. 2159; 165 L. Ed. 2d 56; 2006 U.S. LEXIS 4677; 74 U.S.L.W. 4311; 19 Fla. L. Weekly Fed. S 244, January 9, 2006, Argued , June 15, 2006, Decided , The LEXIS pagination of this document is subject to change pending release of the final published version.
☐2	Brigham City v. Stuart, No. 05-502, SUPREME COURT OF THE UNITED STATES, 126 S. Ct. 1943; 164 L. Ed. 2d 650; 2006 U.S. LEXIS 4155; 74 U.S.L.W. 4253; 19 Fla. L. Weekly Fed. S 199, April 24, 2006, Argued , May 22, 2006, Decided , The LEXIS pagination of this document is subject to change pending release of the final published version.
☐3	Georgia v. Randolph, No. 04-1067, SUPREME COURT OF THE UNITED STATES, 547 U.S. 103; 126 S. Ct. 1515; 164 L. Ed. 2d 208; 2006 U.S. LEXIS 2498; 74 U.S.L.W. 4176; 19 Fla. L. Weekly Fed. S 138, November 8, 2005, Argued , March 22, 2006, Decided
☐4	United States v. Patane, No. 02-1183, SUPREME COURT OF THE UNITED STATES, 542 U.S. 630; 124 S. Ct. 2620; 159 L. Ed. 2d 667; 2004 U.S. LEXIS 4577; 72 U.S.L.W. 4643; 2004 Fla. L. Weekly Fed. S 482, December 9, 2003, Argued , June 28, 2004, Decided
☐5	Groh v. Ramirez, No. 02-811, SUPREME COURT OF THE UNITED STATES, 540 U.S. 551; 124 S. Ct. 1284; 157 L. Ed. 2d 1068; 2004 U.S. LEXIS 1624; 72 U.S.L.W. 4160; 17 Fla. L. Weekly Fed. S 146, November 4, 2003, Argued , February 24, 2004, Decided , The LEXIS pagination of this document is subject to change pending release of the final published version.
☐6	United States v. Banks, No. 02-473, SUPREME COURT OF THE UNITED STATES, 540 U.S. 31; 124 S. Ct. 521; 157 L. Ed. 2d 343; 2003 U.S. LEXIS 8966; 72 U.S.L.W. 4005; 2003 Cal. Daily Op. Service 10330; 17 Fla. L. Weekly Fed. S 7, October 15, 2003, Argued , December 2, 2003, Decided , The LEXIS pagination of this document is subject to change pending release of the final published version.
☐7	Kirk v. Louisiana, No. 01-8419. , SUPREME COURT OF THE UNITED STATES, 536 U.S. 635; 122 S. Ct. 2458; 153 L. Ed. 2d 599; 2002 U.S. LEXIS 4682; 70 U.S.L.W. 3787; 2002 Cal. Daily Op. Service 5593; 2002 Daily Journal DAR 7071; 15 Fla. L. Weekly Fed. S 456, June 24, 2002, Decided , On remand at, Remanded by State v. Kirk, 833 So. 2d 418, 2002 La. App. LEXIS 4307 (La.App. 4 Cir., Nov. 13, 2002)
☐8	Saucier v. Katz, No. 99-1977 , SUPREME COURT OF THE UNITED STATES, 533 U.S. 194; 121 S. Ct. 2151; 150 L. Ed. 2d 272; 2001 U.S. LEXIS 4664; 69 U.S.L.W. 4481; 2001 Cal. Daily Op. Service 5000; 2001 Daily Journal DAR 6137; 2001 Colo. J. C.A.R. 3134; 14 Fla. L. Weekly Fed. S 361, March 20, 2001, Argued , June 18, 2001, Decided
☐9	Atwater v. City of Lago Vista, No. 99-1408 , SUPREME COURT OF THE UNITED STATES, 532 U.S. 318; 121 S. Ct. 1536; 149 L. Ed. 2d 549; 2001 U.S. LEXIS 3366; 69 U.S.L.W. 4262; 2001 Cal. Daily Op. Service 3203; 2001 Daily Journal DAR 3953; 2001 Colo. J. C.A.R. 2069; 14 Fla. L. Weekly Fed. S 193, December 4, 2000, Argued , April

FIGURE 10.10 Excerpts from *Brigham City v. Stuart*

Source: Reprinted with permission of LexisNexis.

BRIGHAM CITY, UTAH, Petitioner v. CHARLES W. STUART et al.

No. 05-502

SUPREME COURT OF THE UNITED STATES

126 S. Ct. 1943; 164 L. Ed. 2d 650; 2006 U.S. LEXIS 4155; 74 U.S.L.W. 4253; 19 Fla. L. Weekly Fed. S 199

April 24, 2006, Argued
May 22, 2006, Decided

NOTICE:

[***1] The LEXIS pagination of this document is subject to change pending release of the final published version.

PRIOR HISTORY: ON WRIT OF CERTIORARI TO THE SUPREME COURT OF UTAH.
Brigham City v. Stuart, 2005 UT 13, 122 P.3d 506, 2005 Utah LEXIS 23 (2005)

DISPOSITION: Reversed and remanded.

Case in Brief **($)**
Time-saving, comprehensive research tool. Includes expanded summary, extensive research and analysis, and links to LexisNexis® content and available court documents.

CASE SUMMARY

PROCEDURAL POSTURE: Defendants' motion to suppress all evidence obtained after police officers entered a home where defendants were restraining a juvenile was granted based on the warrantless entry's violation of the Fourth Amendment. The Supreme Court of Utah affirmed. Certiorari was granted in light of differences among courts concerning the appropriate Fourth Amendment standard governing warrantless entry by law enforcement in an emergency situation.

OVERVIEW: At about 3 a.m., four police officers responded to a call regarding a loud party at a residence. Upon arriving at the house, they heard shouting from inside, and proceeded down the driveway to investigate. There, they observed two juveniles drinking beer in the backyard. They entered the backyard, and saw, through a screen door and windows, an altercation taking place in the kitchen of the home. According to the testimony of one of the officers, four adults were attempting, with some difficulty, to restrain a juvenile. The juvenile eventually broke free, swung a fist and struck one of the adults in the face. The officer testified that he observed the victim of the blow spitting blood into a nearby sink. The court held that it did not matter whether the officers entered the kitchen to arrest defendants and gather evidence against them or to assist the injured and prevent further violence. The court also held that the officers had an objectively reasonable basis for believing both that the injured adult might need help and that the violence in the kitchen was just beginning. Nothing required them to wait until someone was "unconscious" or "semi-conscious" or worse before entering.

Begin making decisions. The *Brigham City* case provides a detailed history of warrantless searches and under what circumstances they are constitutional. This probably would be a good time to begin writing down the cases in *Brigham City* and reviewing the pertinent ones. **(Step 10)** As you begin reviewing your cases you notice that our client, Mr. Rawlins, will have his challenges in getting the evidence suppressed. At this point, you should Shepardize or KeyCite the cases you intend to use. **(Step 11)** Yes, even a 2006 case. Remember, Shepard's or KeyCite may give you additional recent cases that cited the *Brigham City* case and more importantly, cases within the Eighth Circuit Court of Appeals. (See Figures 10.11 and 10.12.) Review the cases from the Eighth Circuit Court of Appeals and you find a case that followed the *Brigham City* case. (See Figure 10.12.) That case, *U.S. v. Valencia,* 499 F.3d 813 (8th Cir. 2007), is similar to your case—with less than positive results. The first page of the case is provided in Figure 10.13, but use your legal researching skills and look up the full text of the case to see exactly what the court had to say. Even though the results are not as you had hoped, you still need to report your findings to your attorney.

But you are clearly on your way. Now, remember this takes time—lots of it. Don't expect to have your answers in an hour. Your analysis must not only be thorough but thoughtful. Once you have completed your research, copy the cases you believe are important and prepare the information for your attorney in the format required. **(Step 12)** The attorney may only want the cases for review or simply briefed. Undoubtedly, that is up to the attorney's discretion.

Now, let's backtrack through our steps and use the print version of *West's Federal Practice Digest 4th*. In these searches we looked up the words and phrases from our original search: search and seizure, warrantless search, emergency or exigent circumstances. Isolating words and phrases in the Descriptive Word Index, we look up "searches and seizures" and "warrantless search." (See Figure 10.14.) That query sends us to "exigent circumstances." We are directed to the topic "Searches" key numbers 42–45, 64 initially. (See Figure 10.15.) We then retrieve the applicable digest volume, 84B Searches and Seizures, key numbers 24–140. We first check the pocket part to determine if there are any recent cases under our "keys." Notice in the pocket part the entry for key number 42 "Emergencies and exigent circumstances; opportunity to obtain warrant." (See Figure 10.16.) Begin reviewing the entries. The first entry is our U.S. Supreme Court case, *Brigham City v. Stuart*. Continue reviewing the entries and focus on "our" jurisdiction—Nebraska and the Eighth Circuit. There are a host of summaries of cases that simply need to be reviewed. There are a couple of different directions that are reasonable. Continue reviewing the entries in the digest or Shepardize or KeyCite the *Brigham City* case. Let's see what happens when we Shepardize the *Brigham City* case. For this exercise, we will use the print version and see the results. Our citation is the *Supreme Court Reporter* citation 126 S. Ct. 1943. In Figure 10.17, we locate our case. Review the Shepard's column for the various notations and then focus on the Eighth Circuit Court of Appeals and Nebraska. Remember, in the print versions all pamphlets must be checked. Therefore, we search the available pamphlets. (See Figures 10.18 and 10.19.) The task now is to read, read, and read. Begin narrowing down your choices to the most relevant cases for the facts presented. (You should encounter the *Valencia* case from your Shepard's search.)

You get the idea that research takes different approaches with different results. Mastering all the legal research techniques is essential to your success. As you saw from our exercise, you have options as to the direction of your research plan—lots of them. Just follow your plan and be flexible. The important lesson to remind yourself is that you can do this!

FIGURE 10.11
Excerpted Pages from Shepard's Citations Online from *Brigham City v. Stuart*
Source: Reprinted with permission of LexisNexis.

Brigham City v. Stuart , 126 S. Ct. 1943, 164 L. Ed. 2d 650, 2006 U.S. LEXIS 4155, 74 U.S.L.W. 4253, 19 Fla. L. Weekly Fed. S 199 (U.S. 2006)

SHEPARD'S SUMMARY Hide Summary

	Unrestricted Shepard's Summary
No subsequent appellate history. Prior history available.	
Citing References:	
△ Cautionary Analyses:	Distinguished (6)
Positive Analyses:	Followed (31)
Neutral Analyses:	Concurring Opinion (1), Dissenting Op. (12), Explained (3)
Other Sources:	Law Reviews (30), Statutes (1), Treatises (33), Court Documents (8)

LexisNexis Headnotes:	HN1 (72), HN2 (30), HN3 (23), HN4 (2)
Show full text of headnotes	

PRIOR HISTORY (7 citing references) Hide Prior History

1. Brigham City v. Stuart, 57 P.3d 1111, 2002 UT App 317, 2002 Utah App. LEXIS 94, 457 Utah Adv. 16 (2002)

    2. Writ of certiorari granted:
    Brigham City v. Stuart, 65 P.3d 1190, 2003 Utah LEXIS 23 (Utah 2003)

    3. Affirmed by:
    Brigham City v. Stuart, 2005 UT 13, 122 P.3d 506, 2005 Utah LEXIS 23, 519 Utah Adv. 17 (2005)

    4. Rehearing denied by:
    Brigham City v. Stuart, 2005 Utah LEXIS 134 (Utah July 18, 2005)

Cont.

5. Writ of certiorari granted:
Brigham City v. Stuart, 546 U.S. 1085, 126 S. Ct. 979, 163 L. Ed. 2d 722, 2006 U.S. LEXIS 7 (2006)

6. Motion granted by:
Brigham City v. Stuart, 547 U.S. 1017, 126 S. Ct. 1607, 164 L. Ed. 2d 297, 2006 U.S. LEXIS 2234, 74 U.S.L.W. 3530 (2006)

7. Motion denied by:
Brigham City v. Stuart, 547 U.S. 1067, 126 S. Ct. 1674, 164 L. Ed. 2d 414, 2006 U.S. LEXIS 2844, 74 U.S.L.W. 3583, 19 Fla. L. Weekly Fed. S 199 (2006)

▶ Reversed by, Remanded by (CITATION YOU ENTERED):
Brigham City v. Stuart, 126 S. Ct. 1943, 164 L. Ed. 2d 650, 2006 U.S. LEXIS 4155, 74 U.S.L.W. 4253, 19 Fla. L. Weekly Fed. S 199 (U.S. 2006)

CITING DECISIONS (152 citing decisions)

U.S. SUPREME COURT

8. Cited in Dissenting Opinion at:
Washington v. Recuenco, 126 S. Ct. 2546, 165 L. Ed. 2d 466, 2006 U.S. LEXIS 5164, 74 U.S.L.W. 4460, 19 Fla. L. Weekly Fed. S 382 (U.S. 2006) LexisNexis Headnotes HN1

126 S. Ct. 2546 p.2553
165 L. Ed. 2d 466 p.477

9. Cited in Dissenting Opinion at:
Kansas v. Marsh, 126 S. Ct. 2516, 165 L. Ed. 2d 429, 2006 U.S. LEXIS 5163, 74 U.S.L.W. 4465, 19 Fla. L. Weekly Fed. S 343 (U.S. 2006) LexisNexis Headnotes HN1

126 S. Ct. 2516 p.2540
165 L. Ed. 2d 429 p.458
1ST CIRCUIT - COURT OF APPEALS

10. Cited by:
United States v. Weikert, 2007 U.S. App. LEXIS 18845 (1st Cir. Mass. Aug. 9, 2007)

2007 U.S. App. LEXIS 18845

FIGURE 10.11
Excerpted Pages from Shepard's Citations Online from *Brigham City v. Stuart* Cont.

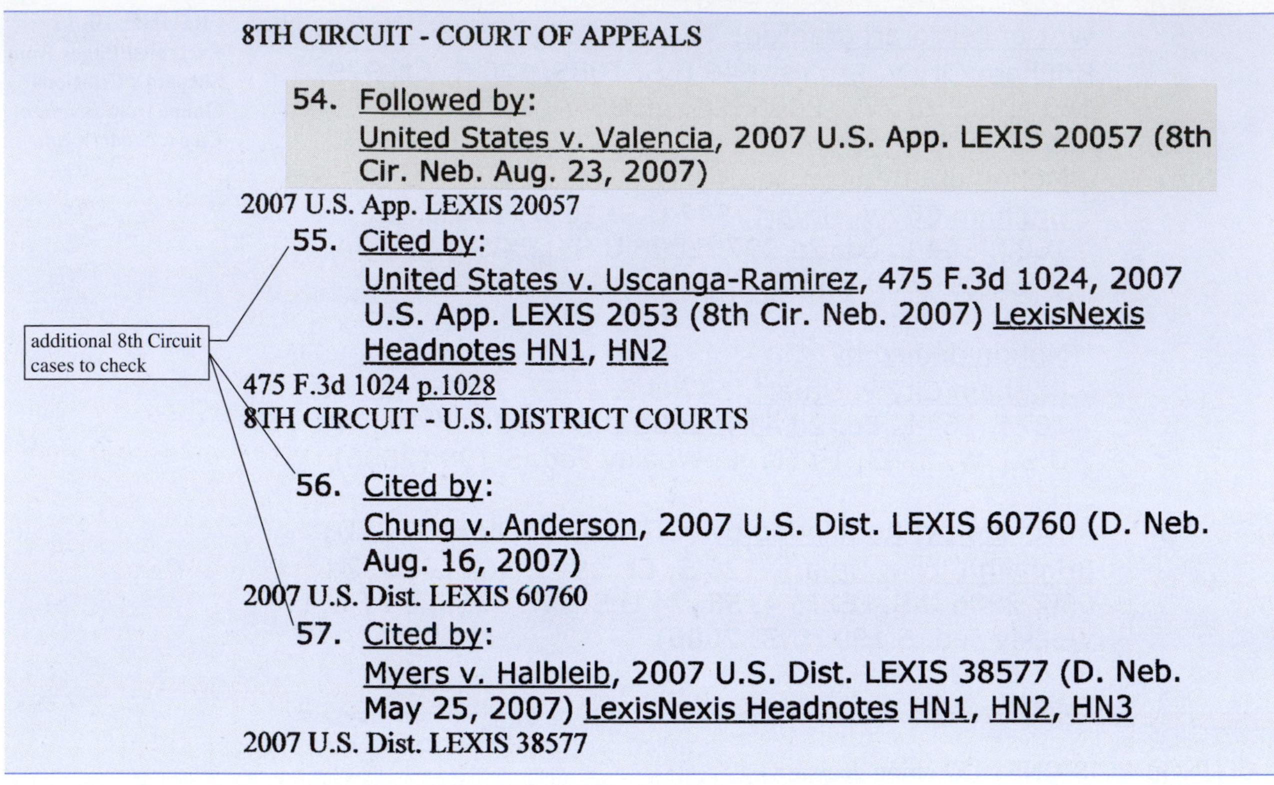
8TH CIRCUIT - COURT OF APPEALS

54. Followed by:
United States v. Valencia, 2007 U.S. App. LEXIS 20057 (8th Cir. Neb. Aug. 23, 2007)

2007 U.S. App. LEXIS 20057

55. Cited by:
United States v. Uscanga-Ramirez, 475 F.3d 1024, 2007 U.S. App. LEXIS 2053 (8th Cir. Neb. 2007) LexisNexis Headnotes HN1, HN2

475 F.3d 1024 p.1028

8TH CIRCUIT - U.S. DISTRICT COURTS

56. Cited by:
Chung v. Anderson, 2007 U.S. Dist. LEXIS 60760 (D. Neb. Aug. 16, 2007)

2007 U.S. Dist. LEXIS 60760

57. Cited by:
Myers v. Halbleib, 2007 U.S. Dist. LEXIS 38577 (D. Neb. May 25, 2007) LexisNexis Headnotes HN1, HN2, HN3

2007 U.S. Dist. LEXIS 38577

FIGURE 10.12 **Eighth Circuit Cases Isolated from Shepard's Citations Online Page**
Source: Reprinted with permission of LexisNexis.

FIGURE 10.13
***U.S. v. Valencia* case from the Eighth Circuit Court of Appeals**
Source: Reprinted with permission of LexisNexis.

United States Court of Appeals
FOR THE EIGHTH CIRCUIT

No. 06-3501

United States of America,	*	
	*	
Appellee,	*	Appeal from the United States
	*	District Court for the District of
v.	*	Nebraska.
	*	
Michael A. Valencia,	*	
	*	
Appellant.	*	

Submitted: June 15, 2007
Filed: August 23, 2007

Before MELLOY, SMITH, and GRUENDER, Circuit Judges.

MELLOY, Circuit Judge.

Police officers entered the apartment of Michael A. Valencia without a warrant, performed a protective sweep, and thereafter obtained a search warrant and recovered a short-barreled shotgun from the home. The government charged Valencia with possession of an unregistered firearm. 26 U.S.C. §§ 5841, 5861(d), and 5871. Valencia claimed that the initial, warrantless entry into his home violated the Fourth Amendment, and he moved to suppress the shotgun as the fruit of the allegedly

[text omitted]

FIGURE 10.14 ***West's Federal Practice Digest 4th,* Descriptive Word Index—Searches and Seizures**

Source: From *West's Federal Practice Digest 4th.* Reprinted with permission from ThomsonWest.

99A F P D 4th—495 **SEARCHES**

References are to Digest Topics and Key Numbers

SEARCHES AND SEIZURES—Cont'd
WARRANTLESS search—Cont'd

Corporate offices and records, **Searches 🔑 76**
Courthouses and courtrooms, **Searches 🔑 79**
DNA testing, **Searches 🔑 78**
Drug testing, **Searches 🔑 78**
Drugs. See heading **DRUGS AND CONTROLLED SUBSTANCES,** SEARCHES and seizures, Warrantless search.
Duration, **Searches 🔑 53**
Emergencies. See subheading EXIGENT circumstances, under this heading.
Entry to make, **Searches 🔑 54**
Exigent circumstances. See subheading EXIGENT circumstances, under this heading.

locate words and phrases

Extraterritorial powers, **Mun Corp 🔑 188**
Identification procedures, **Searches 🔑 78**
Impoundment of motor vehicles, **Searches 🔑 66**
Income tax returns, **Searches 🔑 74**
Information supporting,
  Collective knowledge, **Searches 🔑 38, 39, 41**
  Hearsay, **Searches 🔑 38, 41**
  Nature and source in general, **Searches 🔑 37**
  Suspicion or conjecture, **Searches 🔑 37**
Informers. See subheading INFORMERS, under this heading.
Inventory, **Searches 🔑 58, 66**
Knock-and-announce, **Searches 🔑 54**
Manner of conducting, **Searches 🔑 53–56**
Manner of entry to make, **Searches 🔑 54**
Motor vehicles. See subheading VEHICLES, under this heading.
Plain view. See subheading PLAIN view, under this heading.
Preference for warrant, **Searches 🔑 24**
Probable cause. See subheading PROBABLE cause, under this heading.
Protective searches, **Searches 🔑 70**
Regulated businesses, **Searches 🔑 79**
Safe deposit boxes, **Searches 🔑 77**
Scope and extent, **Searches 🔑 53**
Securing premises while obtaining warrant, **Searches 🔑 42.1**
Security checks, **Searches 🔑 71**
Skin, **Searches 🔑 55**
Standing to object. See subheading STANDING to challenge, under this heading.
Strip searches, **Searches 🔑 55**
Sweeps, protective, **Searches 🔑 71**
Tests, **Searches 🔑 78**
Validity, circumstances affecting, **Searches 🔑 36.1–39**

SEARCHES AND SEIZURES—Cont'd
WARRANTLESS search—Cont'd

Vehicles. See subheading VEHICLES under this heading.
Vessels, **Searches 🔑 59**
Weapons, search for, **Searches 🔑 67–71**
Witnesses, **Searches 🔑 75**

WARRANTS,
Generally, **Searches 🔑 101–150**
Administrative warrants, **Searches 🔑 129**
Affidavits,
  Generally, **Searches 🔑 105–108, 111–120**
  Competency of information, **Searches 🔑 115–120**
  Contents, **Searches 🔑 111–120**
  Form, **Searches 🔑 107**
  Free speech right of access to affidavits, **Const Law 🔑 90.1(3)**
  Persons who may sign, **Searches 🔑 106**
  Unsealing, **Crim Law 🔑 1226(2)**
Anonymous informants, **Searches 🔑 118**
Anticipatory warrants, **Searches 🔑 122**
Application,
  Generally, **Searches 🔑105–108**
Form, **Searches 🔑 107**
Interpretation in general, **Searches 🔑 105.1**
Necessity for writing, **Searches 🔑 107**
Oral presentation or supplementation, **Searches 🔑 108**
Persons who may apply, **Searches 🔑 106**
Staleness, **Searches 🔑 121.1**
  Time for, **Searches 🔑 121.1**
Authority to issue,
  Generally, **Searches 🔑 103, 104**
Impartial magistrate requirement, **Searches 🔑 104**
United States magistrates, **Searches 🔑 103**
Burden of proof, **Searches 🔑 193**
Citizens, information from, **Searches 🔑 119**
Competency of information, **Searches 🔑 115–120**
Complaint. See Application, ante.
Conclusiveness in judicial proceedings, **Searches 🔑 191**
Confidential informants, **Searches 🔑 118**
Corroboration requirement, **Searches 🔑 117**
Credibility of information, **Searches 🔑 117**
Description,
  Misdescription or error, **Searches 🔑 127**

FIGURE 10.15 ***West's Federal Practice Digest 4th,*** **Descriptive Word Index—Searches and Seizures, "Exigent Circumstances"**

Source: From *West's Federal Practice Digest 4th*. Reprinted with permission from ThomsonWest.

SEARCHES 99A F P D 4th—490

References are to Digest Topics and Key Numbers

SEARCHES AND SEIZURES—Cont'd

EVIDENCE obtained, admissibility. See heading **CRIMINAL LAW**, EXCLUSIONARY rule.

EXCLUSION of unlawfully seized evidence. See heading **CRIMINAL LAW**, EXCLUSIONARY rule.

EXECUTION of warrant,
Generally, **Searches** ⚷ **141–150**
Entry to execute, **Searches** ⚷ **143–144**
Evidence, weight and sufficiency, **Searches** ⚷ **196**
Knock-and-announce, **Searches** ⚷ **143.1**
Manner of entry, **Searches** ⚷ **143–144**
Nighttime execution, **Searches** ⚷ **146**
Participants, **Searches** ⚷ **142**
Place of, **Searches** ⚷ **142**
Places, persons and things within scope of warrant, **Searches** ⚷ **148**
Plain view, **Searches** ⚷ **149**
Providing target with copy, **Searches** ⚷ **141**
Scope of search,
Generally, **Searches** ⚷ **147–149**
Inadvertent discovery, **Searches** ⚷ **149**
Places, persons, and things, **Searches** ⚷ **148**
Plain view, **Searches** ⚷ **149**
Time of, **Searches** ⚷ **145–146**

EXIGENT circumstances,
Generally, **Searches** ⚷ **42–45, 64**
Escape or loss of evidence, **Searches** ⚷ **45**
Need for probable cause, **Searches** ⚷ **44**
Pursuit, **Searches** ⚷ **43**
Vehicle searches, **Searches** ⚷ **64**

topic and key from descriptive word index

EXPECTATION of privacy,
Scope of protection in general, **Searches** ⚷ **26–29**
Standing to object to admission of evidence. See heading **CRIMINAL LAW**, EXCLUSIONARY rule.
Standing to object to search, **Searches** ⚷ **162–165**
Vehicles, **Searches** ⚷ **61**

EXPROPRIATION of property by foreign sovereign, **Intern Law** ⚷ **10.12**

EXTENDED border searches**, Cust Dut** ⚷ **126(5)**

EXTRATERRITORIAL powers, warrantless searches, **Mun Corp** ⚷ **188**

FIGURE 10.16 ***West's Federal Practice Digest 4th,*** **Volume 84B, Searches and Seizures (Pocket Part)**

Source: From *West's Federal Practice Digest 4th*. Reprinted with permission from ThomsonWest.

84B F P D 4th—117 **SEARCHES & SEIZURES** ⚷ 42.1

⚷ **42. Emergencies and exigent circumstances; opportunity to obtain warrant.**

See ⚷ 42.1.

⚷ **42.1.—In general.**

recent US Supreme Court case

U.S.Utah 2006. Warrants are generally required to search a person's home or his person unless the exigencies of the situation make the needs of law enforcement so compelling that a warrantless search is objectively reasonable under the Fourth Amendment. U.S.C.A. Const. Amend. 4.—Brigham City, Utah v. Stuart, 126 S.Ct. 1943, 164 L.Ed.2d 650.

One exigency obviating the requirement of a search warrant is the need to assist persons who they noticed blood on his shirt and became suspicious as to whether he had engaged in any foul play in apartment from whose open window he allegedly jumped, was irrelevant to whether exigent circumstances justified officers' warrantless search of apartment, and neither this delay nor the four to five minutes that officers waited for ladder to enable them to peer through apartment's open window belied sincerity of their claims regarding concern for possible crime victims. U.S.C.A. Const.Amend. 4.—U.S. v. Gill, 354 F.3d 963.

Cont.

FIGURE 10.16 ***West's Federal Practice Digest 4th,*** **Volume 84B, Searches and Seizures (Pocket Part)** *Cont.*

Although scope of officer's investigation following entry may be relevant consideration for court in inferring purpose of entry, district court did not have to Infer, merely from fact that a single officer had shined flashlight into cupboard, that officers had entered apartment to look for evidence rather than for crime victims, where circumstances surrounding defendant's arrest in bloody shirt outside apartment from whose open window he had allegedly jumped provided officers with objectively reasonable basis for believing that victims might be present in apartment. U.S.C.A. Const.Amend. 4.—Id.

Even assuming that officers' actions, in using ladder to peer through open window of defendant's apartment, rose to level of search, exigent circumstances justified this limited intrusion, where officers had discovered defendant disoriented and in bloody shirt, present outside apartment, where defendant became agitated when officers questioned him, ran from officers, brandished bar code scanner as if it were a weapon and, when questioned after he was forcibly subdued, provided officers with address different from apartment the last address he had given to police. U.S.C.A. Const.Amend. 4.—Id.

C.A.8 (Mo.) 2003. Not every search without a warrant is unreasonable if an exception, such as the presence of exigent circumstances, exists. U.S.C.A. Const.Amend. 4.—U.S. v. Francis, 327 F.3d 729.

Exigent-circumstances exception to requirement that a search be conducted pursuant to a search warrant justifies immediate police action without a warrant under limited circumstances, such as where lives are threatened, a suspect's escape is imminent, or evidence is about to be destroyed.—Id.

C.A.8 (Mo.) 2003. Exigent circumstances justifying warrantless entry of a house exist where law enforcement officers have a legitimate concern for the safety of themselves or others. U.S.C.A. Const. Amend. 4.—U.S. v. Kuenstler, 325 F.3d 1015, rehearing and rehearing denied, certiorari denied Hill v. U.S., 124 S.Ct. 1037, 540 U.S. 1112, 157 L. Ed.2d 901, certiorari denied 124 S.Ct. 1037, 540 U.S. 1112, 157 L.Ed.2d 901.

8th Circuit case entry in pocket part

The analysis of whether exigent circumstances exception to the warrant requirement has been made out is an objective one focusing on what a reasonable, experienced police officer would believe. U.S.C.A. Const.Amend. 4.—Id.

An ulterior motive 'does not render a search illegal in a situation where officers have objectively reasonable safety concerns. U.S.C.A. Const.Amend. 4.—Id.

†**C.A.9 (Mont.) 2006.** Exigent circumstances justified warrantless entry and protective sweep of defendant's residence, given the bloody rag, damaged door, and broken window that the police officers lawfully observed from outside defendant's house, which supported reasonable belief that residence sheltered victims requiring aid or perpetrators threatening officer safety. U.S.C.A. Const.Amend. 4.—U.S. v. Culkin, 177 Fed.Appx. 675, certiorari denied 127 S.Ct. 143, 166 L.Ed.2d 104.

C.A.9 (Mont.) 2006. Exigent circumstances justify a warrantless intrusion into a home where a reasonable officer would believe that entry was necessary to prevent physical harm to the officers or other persons. U.S.C.A. Const.Amend. 4.—U.S. v. Arellano-Ochoa, 461 F.3d 1142.

†**C.A.9 (Mont.) 2005.** Officers' warrantless search of defendant's trailer was a proper emergency search; and thus was not illegal, even those the officers were in the wrong location; 911 call reporting an overdosing woman at unit 7 gave officers reasonable grounds to believe there was an emergency, search was not primarily motivated by an intent to seize evidence, and mistake of going to trailer 7 rather than cabin 7 was reasonable.—U.S. v. Huebner, 125 Fed.Appx. 767.

C.A.8 (Neb.) 2007. Legitimate concern for the safety of individuals may constitute exigent circumstances justifying warrantless entries. U.S.C.A. Const.Amend. 4.—U.S. v. Uscanga-Ramirez, 475 F.3d 1024.

Law enforcement officers may enter a home without a warrant to protect an occupant from imminent injury. U.S.C.A. Const.Amend. 4.—Id.

The need to protect or preserve life or avoid serious injury is justification for what would be otherwise an illegal warrantless entry absent an exigency or emergency. U.S.C.A. Const.Amend. 4.—Id.

In determining, whether exigent circumstances justified a warrantless entry, the inquiry is objective and focuses, on what a reasonable, experienced police officer would believe. U.S.C.A. Const. Amend. 4.—Id.

Exigent circumstances justified warrantless entry into defendant's home and entry into bedroom; defendant's wife told officers that defendant had locked himself in bedroom with a gun and was very upset over disintegration of marriage. U.S.C.A. Const.Amend. 4.—Id.

†This Case was not selected for publication in the National Reporter System

Cont.

FIGURE 10.16 ***West's Federal Practice Digest 4th,*** **Volume 84B, Searches and Seizures (Pocket Part)** *Cont.*

Exigent circumstances justified warrantless search under pillow in defendant's bedroom; defendant's wife told officers that defendant had locked himself in bedroom with a gun and was very upset over disintegration of marriage, pillow was within defendant's reach and capable of hiding a gun, and pillow was misplaced in middle of bed as opposed to end of bed. U.S.C.A. Const.Amend. 4.—Id.

Law enforcement officers may search a home without a warrant when the exigencies of the situation make the needs of law enforcement so compelling that the warrantless search is objectively reasonable under the Fourth Amendment. U.S.C.A. Const. Amend. 4.—Id.

C.A.9 (Nev.) 2007. Officers' initial warrantless entry into apartment was justified by exigent circumstance of 911 domestic violence call, and thus subsequent seizure of defendant's handgun, after warrant was obtained, did not violate Fourth Amendment; officers reasonably feared that defendant's ex-girlfriend could have been inside apartment, badly injured and in need of medical attention. U.S.C.A. Const.Amend. 4.—U.S. v. Black, 482 F.3d 1035, rehearing and rehearing denied 482 F.3d 1044.

Whether the actions of the police in conducting; a search based on alleged exigent circumstances are objectively reasonable is to be judged by the circumstances known to them at the time. U.S.C.A. Const. Amend. 4.—Id.

Under the "emergency aid doctrine," law enforcement officers may enter a home without a their trail; and (5) ready destructibility of contraband. U.S.C.A. Const.Amend. 4.—Id.

In evaluating whether exigent circumstances justified government agent's warrantless entry, court must look to totality of circumstances surrounding agent's actions,' mindful that review is more akin to examining video tape by instant replay than to examining snapshot. U.S.C.A. Const.Amend. 4.—Id.

To determine whether government agents manufactured exigency to justify warrantless entry, court looks to whether: (1) there was sufficient time to secure warrant, and (2) exigency was created by unreasonable law enforcement tactics. U.S.C.A. Const.Amend. 4.—Id.

Nebraska entries in pocket part

Exigencies deliberately manufactured by government violate Fourth Amendment, especially when government's actions are intentionally taken to avoid warrant requirement. U.S.C.A. Const.Amend. 4.—Id.

Bad faith on part of law enforcement officers is not required to find that government manufactured exigency to avoid warrant requirement. U.S.C.A. Const.Amend. 4.—Id.

S.D.Miss. 2006. Up until point that law enforcement officer prevented defendant from shutting door of his residence by pushing door back toward defendant and pushing his way into residence, officers' warrantless entry into residence was not justified by exigent circumstances consisting of need to ensure officer safety; if officer had permitted defendant to shut door, officer would not have seen defendant run down hallway, and thus, would have had no reason to believe defendant might be running to retrieve weapon, officer on scene had been inside residence earlier that day and had obtained consent from defendant's mother for search of residence, but had decided to wait to search when defendant was present, and mother told officer she did not believe there were weapons in residence. U.S.C.A. Const. Amend. 4.—U.S. v. Sims, 435 F.Supp.2d 542.

When faced with a possible manufactured exigency, for purposes of exigent circumstances exception to search warrant requirement, the court must consider: first, whether the officers deliberately created the exigent circumstances with the bad faith intent to avoid the warrant requirement, and second, even if they did not do so in bad faith, whether their actions creating the exigency were sufficiently unreasonable or improper as to preclude dispensation with the warrant. U.S.C.A. Const.Amend. 4.—Id.

Even if law enforcement officers had reason to fear for their safety at time they entered defendant's house to detain him, any exigent circumstances at that time were created by officers' unreasonable tactics, and thus, did not justify warrantless entry; officer who had been inside house earlier that day to meet with defendant's mother and her caretaker, who had called police to report defendant's use of cocaine in house, testified he believed there was probable cause to obtain warrant, and that impending search of premises was not an emergency, and officer declined to search for weapons on earlier visit to house despite mother's consent to search, and officers knew when defendant was due home from work and could have detained him before he entered house. U.S.C.A. Const.Amend. 4.—Id.

D.Neb. 2003. Law enforcement officials may not enter a house without a search warrant or exigent circumstances, which exist when law enforcement officials have a legitimate concern for the safety of themselves or others. U.S.C.A. Const.Amend. 4.—U.S. v. Custer, 281 F.Supp.2d 1003.

The exigent circumstances exception to the search warrant requirement is narrowly drawn and justifies immediate police action without obtaining a warrant if lives are threatened, a suspect's escape is imminent, or evidence is about to be destroyed. U.S.C.A. Const. Amend. 4.—Id.

FIGURE 10.17 **Results from Print Version of Shepard's Citations—Main Volume**

Source: From *Shepard's United States Citations, Supreme Court Reporter, Part 2.* Copyright 2007. Reprinted with permission of LexisNexis.

Vol. 126 **SUPREME COURT REPORTER**

—1854—
DaimlerChrysler Corp. v Cuno
2006
(164LE589)
US reh den
126SC2961
s) 386F3d738
s) 197Fed Appx [454
2007US LX [8512
~) 2007US LX [8512
j) 2007US LX [8512
f) 126SC2859
j) 127SC1464
Cir. 2
2007USDist [LX19785
2007USDist [LX23218
2007USDist [LX27808
2007USDist [LX42171
d) 470FS2d169
2007Bankr LX [1895
Cir. 3
2007USApp [LX14382
447FS2d424
462FS2d646
f) 466FS2d573
Cir. 4
2007USDist [LX22241
Cir. 5
2007USDist [LX22328
Cir. 7
481F3d980
~) 481F3d988
2006USDist [LX95577
465FS2d883
479FS2d865
Cir. 8
2007USDist [LX42289
Cir. 9
2007USApp [LX8453
2007USApp [LX12628
457F3d950
f) 471F3d1046
477F3d1053
f) 477F3d1063
2007USDist [LX37213
d) 434FS2d967
Cir. 10
479F3d1191
2007USDist [LX198247
435FS2d1156
f) 435FS2d1158
481FS2d1181
Cir. 11
463F3d1169
471FS2d1234
Cir. DC
f) 2007USApp [LX14016
472F3d876
f) 2007USDist [LX22857
448FS2d59
453FS2d5
Cir. Fed.
2007USApp [LX11259
466F3d1029
474F3d1289
476F3d892
CIT
444FS2d1323
ClCt
2007USClaims [LX124
Ariz
158P3d247
Tenn
f) 195SW620
120HLR293
59StnL601
2006WLR1315

—1869—
Sereboff v Mid Atl. Med. Servs.
2006
(164LE612)
s) 407F3d212
s) 303FS2d691
s) 316FS2d265
Cir. 1
470F3d421
477FS2d254
f) 477FS2d257
Cir. 2
f) 457F3d263
193Fed Appx [71
2007USDist [LX25275
467FS2d391
Cir. 3
484F3d655
f) 2007USDist [LX42963
457FS2d540
f) 457FS2d541
d) 457FS2d544
Cir. 4
450F3d574
2006USDist [LX96199
455FS2d480
Cir. 5
f) 2007USDist [LX 17255
2007USDist [LX 19439
481FS2d594
d) 362BRW332
Cir. 6
2007USApp [LX11694
2007USDist [LX26697
2007USDist [LX42294
Cir. 7
e) 467F3d1038
f) 2007USDist [LX18643
e) 2007USDist [LX18643
e) 2007USDist [LX27092
2007USDist [LX28774
f) 2007USDist [LX38617
435FS2d828
435FS2d863
f) 435FS2d866
e) 483FS2d671
Cir. 8
456F3d901
f) 2007USDist [LX24252
f) 465FS2d905
Cir. 9
e) 2007USApp [LX3519
e) 2007USDist [LX30149
d) 2007USDist [LX30149
f) 461FS2d1232
Cir. 11
f) 461F3d1369
e) 461F3d1373
d) 480F3d1224
e) 480F3d1225
d) 2007USDist [LX38130
Cir. DC
ca) 461F3d7
f) 461F3d9
ca) 373ADC194
f) 373ADC196
Okla
d) 157P3d111

—1943—
Brigham City v Stuart
2006
(164LE650)
s) 122P3d506
j) 126SC2540
j) 126SC2553
Cir. 1
454F3d19
469F3d168
2007USDist [LX39631
Cir. 2
2007USApp [LX12138
443FS2d344
Cir. 3
f) 450F3d563
2007USDist [LX36085
Cir. 5
j) 452F3d350
473F3d182
2007USDist [LX39389
Cir. 6
2007USApp [LX7281
2007USApp [LX11959
2007USApp [LX11960
j) 452F3d457
f) 461F3d782
j) 461F3d789
486F3d217
486F3d230
184Fed Appx [474
d) 2007USDist [LX14055
2007USDist [LX14799
445FS2d807
Cir. 7
466F3d1091
2007USDist [LX28517
f) 2007USDist [LX29638
Cir. 8
475F3d1028
2007USDist [LX38577
Cir. 9
2007USApp [LX4039
461F3d1145
466F3d1146
468F3d1189
472F3d1096
j) 475F3d1077
482F3d1041
201Fed Appx [393
216Fed Appx [683
217Fed Appx [627
2007USDist [LX37609
463FS2d1144
Cir. 10
2007USApp [LX4533
2007USApp [LX12294
2007USApp [LX14341
f) 451F3d715
470F3d998
f) 472F3d775
474F3d1252
478F3d1123
478F3d1234
f) 479F3d759
481F3d1248
484F3d1253
f) 209Fed Appx [800
218Fed Appx [773
f) 450FS2d1243
Cir. 11
483F3d1240
~) 483F3d1260
Cir. DC
482F3d543
j) 482F3d552
Calif
38C4th821
j) 38C4th834
f) 143CA4th292
f) 143CA4th1196
43CaR3d757
j) 43CaR3d768
f) 49CaR3d33
49CaR3d840
135P3d8
j) 135P3d18
Fla
934So2d1272
936So2d1221
j) 941So2d443
f) 946So2d1222
f) 953So2d657
Ind
f) 849NE573
La
d) 945So2d813
Minn
f) 726NW788
Nebr
f) 271Neb901
f) 716NW678
NJ
190NJ614
921A2d1086
NY
e) 8NY891
f) 38NYAD915
15NYM1128A
e) 865NE2
e) 832NYS2d [894
Tex
199SW549
Va
e) 639SE223
f) 639SE224
644SE82
120HLR163
120HLR1627
116YLJ1072

US Supreme Court case

8th Circuit entry

Nebraska entries

FIGURE 10.18 **Results for the Print Version of Shepard's Citations for 126 S. Ct. 1943—Pamphlet 1**

Source: From *Shepard's United States Citations, Supreme Court Reporter, Part 2.* Copyright 2007. Reprinted with permission of LexisNexis.

SUPREME COURT REPORTER **Vol. 126**

—1943— Cir. 1 2007USAApp [LX18845 f) 2007USDist [LX52558 Cir. 4 2007USApp [LX15841 Cir. 5 490FS2d775 Cir. 6 486F3d220 486F3d232 222Fed Appx [510	f) 2007USDist [LX54139 2007USDist [LX62465 Cir. 7 f) 2007USApp [LX20964 2007USDist [LX49243 Cir. 8 f) 2007USApp [LX20057 2007USDist [LX60760 Cir. 9	2007USApp [LX17055 216Fed Appx [683 217Fed Appx [627 221Fed Appx [520 Cir. 10 2007USApp [LX16853 f) 2007USApp [LX17978 d) 2007USApp [LX17978 478F3D1123	490F3d1183 218Fed Appx [774 f) 2007USDist [LX58209 Cir. DC 482F3d543 j) 482F3d552 Calif 38C4th820 j) 38C4th834 43CaR3d757 j) 43CaR3d768 135P3d8 j) 135P318 Fla	j) 955So2d627 j) 957So2d7 Mass 449Mas485 869NE614 Minn 732NW336 N J 190NJ614 921A2d1086 N M 162P3d184 N Y e) 8NY891 f) 38NYAD915 39NYAD1051	16NYM1109A e) 865NE2 e) 832NYS2d [894 f) 833NYS2d [561 834NYS2d378 Tex f) 226SW446 Utah 162P3d11113 Vt 924A2d44 Va 49VaA645 644SE82

8th Circuit entries

no new Nebraska cases

FIGURE 10.19 **Results for the Print Version of Shepard's Citations for 126 S. Ct. 1943—Pamphlet 2**

Source: From *Shepard's United States Citations, Supreme Court Reporter, Part 2.* Copyright 2007. Reprinted with permission of LexisNexis.

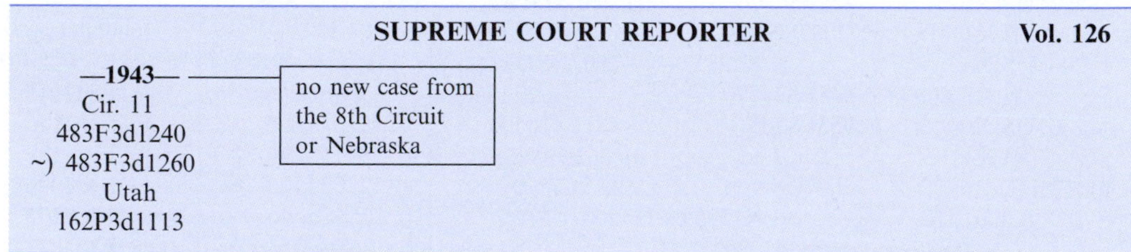

SUPREME COURT REPORTER **Vol. 126**

—1943—
Cir. 11
483F3d1240
~) 483F3d1260
Utah
162P3d1113

no new case from the 8th Circuit or Nebraska

KNOWING WHEN TO END YOUR RESEARCH

The million-dollar question we all ask ourselves is: "How do I know when my legal research is complete?" This is perhaps the most difficult question to answer for anyone who has performed legal research or taught it. There are no easy answers, but as some of the sections of this chapter suggest, you will probably know your research is complete when the same cases keep reappearing. A few suggestions are in order to assist you in reaching a comfort level for this dilemma.

- Follow the steps you have learned. Don't deviate. You know what to do, and you know how to locate the law.
- Shepardize or KeyCite! Or, remember to choose a method to validate the law. Never be caught citing an overruled case or a repealed statute. Do your homework! Don't be lazy and assume a case is still valid, even if it is a new case.
- Try reading a current legal periodical article, if available, to confirm that you are on the right track. Law review or bar journal articles, looseleaf series, and scholarly texts offer an analysis of virtually all the areas of the law. Law review journals, especially recent articles on a topic, can be a gold mine of information. Many times the author of the article does the work, or at least the groundwork, for you. Let the articles work for you. But remember, these articles are only a starting point. Use them with that point in mind and still continue with the plan that you know and whatever cases you use, from whatever source, validate them: Shepardize or KeyCite.

A DAY IN THE LIFE OF A PARALEGAL

You have completed all your research on a very sensitive project for a client. The research contains suggested strategies in the case and, more importantly, you found the "smoking gun" in the case. Apparently, your research showed that the statute the opposing side is relying upon has been amended within the last six months, rendering their claims moot unless they can make a legitimate argument under the **discovery rule.** You found that the discovery rule provides that a statute of limitations is suspended if a party is unable to know about a cause of action because of some hidden information. In this case, you have a document that indicates that the opposing parties in the case knew all the facts and filed their lawsuit in bad faith, hoping to get a quick settlement. As part of your research, you prepared an internal memorandum to your supervising attorney detailing your findings along with all the case law and applicable statutes. Since your attorney is out of town, you decide to e-mail the memorandum with your findings. You send the e-mail to your supervising attorney, the three associates on the case, and you inadvertently add the opposing counsel's name to the e-mail. (One of the associates and the opposing counsel's names are similar.) You do not realize your mistake until the next day. You try to recall the e-mail but it is too late. The damage is done. Now the opposing counsel has all your research with results of your hard work. All you can do is call your supervising attorney, tell her what happened, and seek her advice.

Situations where e-mails are sent to the wrong person are too common. The way these types of headaches and professional disasters can be avoided is to take care in the preparation of any material you prepare or send via the Internet. Had this interoffice memorandum been transmitted through hard copy, you would have had more control over the recipients and any inadvertent "hits" on the computer. Review your e-mails prior to clicking the "Send" button. Make sure the correct individuals are copied. Avoid careless errors and mistakes by taking the extra minute to check your work thoroughly. As wonderful as the immediate nature of the electronic world is, that immediacy gives rise to remorse when improperly sent information is forever gone in cyberspace and cannot be retrieved.

discovery rule
A legal principle that a statute of limitations begins to run when a person discovers, or should have known, that an act of negligence may have been committed.

- Try a different path in your research project. Approach your assignment from a different angle. If you end up with the same legal sources that you already have, you probably have exhausted the subject and are ready to stop.
- Finally, don't leave common sense at home. You know when you are done. You know how to research and you know the steps you have taken to reach your conclusions. Don't underestimate yourself and your skills. And above all, if you believe you haven't "hit" the line of cases that apply and are stuck, ask your supervising attorney for assistance. There is nothing more aggravating to any attorney than wasting time when a simple question would have clarified the subject and set you on the right path.

Therefore, all the signs are there for knowing when you are done. Just don't ignore them. Ultimately, one day you will just *know* when you are finished with a research project, as nothing can be substituted for plain-old experience.

PRACTICE TIP

The importance of Shepardizing and KeyCiting can never be underestimated. Don't ever, ever forget to use one or the other for every legal source that you intend to use in your legal research project.

PRACTICAL CONSIDERATIONS: STICK TO A PLAN!

Some of us feel as though we are between two worlds: the traditional print world and the cyber-world of the Internet. The medium you use may depend on your age, your comfort level with print or Internet resources, availability, or a combination of all the factors. Each method of research requires some basic knowledge of the process and the ability to craft words and phrases relevant to the subject you are researching. The unknown fact in both print and electronic research is whether your chosen words and phrases will retrieve the legal sources needed to successfully complete your research assignment. It should all be a matter of skill, but sometimes it is "sheer luck" the way a case is located. There is nothing magical or intellectual or even deliberate about the method of finding the information; sometimes it just happens. The problem is when you are researching and you believe you have exhausted all possible avenues to learn that you have missed a complete line of cases or a relevant statute. It happens to all of us, but the question is "how can this be avoided or minimized?" The answer is communication. Do not perform your legal research in a vacuum. Articulate how you found the information and why you are relying on the information presented. If your supervising attorney is acting responsibly, he or she should be able to guide you on the right path or be able to ask sufficient questions to find the gaps in the research or the direction that you need to follow. Remember, when you are performing the research, you are responsible for the results. Although your supervising attorney has the "ultimate" responsibility for your research, the more detailed and deliberate you are in the process, the more skilled you will become. Therefore, as this chapter has consistently suggested, follow a plan and create a roadmap to follow when performing your legal research or any assignment that is given to you. Defend what you prepare. One of the ways this is accomplished is through a meticulous research plan. Now that you have the skills needed to perform and complete any research assignment given by your supervising attorney, you must learn how to effectively communicate the information gained in a cohesive and coherent legal document. The remaining chapters of this text will focus on the art of legal writing.

Summary

There are a number of approaches to performing legal research. The common thread is creating a detailed plan to follow. Regardless of the subject of your research, you should follow some basic rules: You must understand the assignment; know the time constraints; determine the issues to be researched; think before you act; and create a research plan.

One method of researching a statute is by using an annotated code. The annotated codes provide finding tools such as topics and keys, secondary sources, and cases to assist in your legal research. Always check the pocket parts and verify the validity of the information through Shepard's or KeyCite. State statutory research follows a similar approach.

Legislative history research focuses on the interpretation of statutory itself. The basic doctrine for statutory interpretation is the strict construction doctrine and the plain meaning of the language rule. In any research conducted, the legislative intent of the drafters is important. Most legislative histories are found in government publications. State legislative histories are not as well organized as their federal counterparts.

Case research is conducted by using digests, encyclopedias, and a variety of secondary sources, which will lead to cases. Case research is both print-based and electronic. When performing case research, it is imperative to validate the cases in either Shepard's or KeyCite.

Performing regulatory research is achieved by using the *Federal Register* and the *Code of Federal Regulations*. Both publications are available in print and electronic versions. Many of the federal regulatory departments and agencies have Web sites, which offer additional information regarding that area. States also have administrative rules and regulations but are not as organized as the federal agencies. Research for state regulatory information will depend upon the state. Each state has different posted information.

Internet research is accomplished in a number of ways. Fee-based services are available, such as Westlaw and LexisNexis. General search engines can be used to locate information on the Internet as well. Searching on the Internet can be initiated through a Boolean search or a natural language search.

Additionally, print and electronic research can be combined for a more comprehensive approach. Neither should ever be used to the exclusion of the other.

A practical approach to legal research is using existing briefs from either a court Web site or your law firm. Secondary sources, such as legal periodicals and law review journals, offer extensive research in their footnotes. Care should be taken when using these "practical" methods, as plagiarism is a common by-product of this approach.

In research you should always consider the jurisdiction involved, the legal principles involved, the time constraints, and whether persuasive authority is appropriate. Moreover, with any research project, you must know when to stop. Often experience will dictate when to stop, but when your research produces the same cases and information, you have probably completed your project.

Key Terms

caption
complaint
deductive reasoning
discovery rule
doctrine of strict construction
equitable tolling
habeas corpus
internal memorandum of law
interoffice memorandum
judicial economy
legal resource
legal source
legislative intent
letter
motion
pendent jurisdiction
plain meaning
pleadings
reasoning by analogy
statute of limitations

Review Questions

1. What distinguishing characteristics do annotated codes have?
2. What are some of the concepts used in legal reasoning?
3. Identify a basic research plan to use when a statute is known to the researcher.
4. What are some of the tools used in case-based legal research?
5. What is a research plan to follow when all that is presented is the client's unique set of facts?
6. What are some of the best methods for researching federal regulations?
7. What are some of the basic research plans for using the Internet?
8. Combining print and Internet research, what is a roadmap that incorporates both methods of research?
9. Identify some of the ways in which a researcher knows that he or she has completed the research assignment.
10. What are some of the pitfalls when using one method of research over another?

Exercises

1. Your attorney has been retained by Harry Johnson who has been indicted for receipt of child pornography in violation of 18 U.S.C. § 2252A(a)(2), and possession of child pornography in violation of 18 U.S.C. § 252A(a)(5)(B). Apparently, Mr. Johnson was viewing child pornography on his work computer. He believes that he had an "expectation of privacy" under the Fourth Amendment. When the

FBI raided his computer at work, they did so without a warrant. The question that your attorney has requested you to research is "whether an employee has an expectation of privacy in the workplace requiring the FBI to procure a search warrant prior to confiscating any information from the computer." Outline your research plan for this assignment.

2. Using the facts from Question 1, what cases would you present to your attorney to argue that Mr. Johnson did have an expectation of privacy and that the information seized from the search should be suppressed?
3. Modifying the facts from Question 1, assume that the computer Mr. Johnson was using was his personal computer that he brought from home. Because the computer at work was slow, Mr. Johnson tied his computer into his work network computer to access company information that he needed to perform his job. Inadvertently, a co-worker happened to access some "private" information on his computer and found child pornography Web sites. Research whether Mr. Johnson has an expectation of privacy in his personal computer that he brings to work and uses for work-related purposes. Limit your assignment to the applicable cases and a short summary of why the case selected would help or harm Johnson's case; identify and track how you found the cases and statutes utilized.
4. For this assignment, use only the Internet. A client has just been cited by the Environmental Protection Agency (EPA) for dumping hazardous waste in the ocean. Your attorney needs the definition of "hazardous waste" under the EPA standards. Locate the statute or regulatory rules and regulations that apply.
5. Your attorney has just received a telephone call from a friend who states he needs to know the requirements and qualifications for granting political asylum to an individual in the United States. Apparently, a talented musician who is touring from either Cuba or Haiti wants to seek political asylum in the United States. Can the musician seek asylum? What are the procedures under the immigration and naturalization statutes and rules and regulations? Identify your research strategy for this assignment.
6. A few months ago Mr. and Mrs. Jonathan Hayes learned that their six-year-old daughter, Melanie, has special needs. After entering first grade, she was having difficulty reading. Melanie was diagnosed with dyslexia. The Hayes have realized that there are certain educational benefits and assistance to which their daughter Melanie is entitled. However, the school is refusing to provide the additional educational assistance for Melanie. Your attorney has requested that you research the statutory requirements in your state for children with special needs. Determine the following:
   a. the applicable state statute;
   b. the statutory requirements of the school system in your jurisdiction to determine who is considered a child with special needs;
   c. the remedies the Hayes have for the school's noncompliance; and
   d. the correct citation for the statute.

   Identify the research plan you utilized to locate your responses.
7. Your attorney needs the requirements for establishing a corporation in your jurisdiction. She wants you to draft the Articles of Incorporation and any statutory documents that are required in your state. Since you are unfamiliar with this process, you need to locate information to assist you. For your assignment, answer the following question:
   a. What sources would you review to assist in the drafting process?
   b. What is the statute in your jurisdiction that delineates the requirements for establishing a corporation?
   c. What are the requirements for incorporation in your jurisdiction?

8. A new client wants to open an adult bookstore in your town. The store will be located approximately two blocks from a high school. Your attorney needs to known whether there are any restrictions or laws prohibiting the bookstore from locating near a school.
   a. Prepare your research plan.
   b. Research your local, state, or federal statutes that may apply.
   c. Present the results of your research.

PORTFOLIO ASSIGNMENT

Your firm represents Global Chemicals Corporation. Global manufactures "polystyrene," which, during the manufacturing process, often releases harmful and hazardous chemicals. On September 5, 2007, Global inadvertently emitted "styrene" into the air and environment in violation of the Clean Air Act and the Comprehensive Environmental Response Compensation and Liability Act (CERCLA). Apparently, when a hazardous chemical is released in the environment, the company must *immediately* notify the Environmental Protection Agency (EPA) and the National Response Center (NRC). Global claims it did immediately notify the appropriate authorities and has claimed its manager, Grant Benjamin, contacted the NRC within 30 minutes of the release of the hazardous chemical. The EPA wants to fine Global Chemicals because it did not *immediately* notify the appropriate authorities pursuant to the law.

Your attorney has requested that you locate the Clean Air Act and the CERCLA. He also wants to know where the notification requirements are located. (Hint: Are the requirements located in a statute? An administrative code?) More importantly, he wants to know whether there is a definition of the word "immediate" in the statute, cases, and administrative rules and regulations, including the *Code of Federal Regulations.* As part of your assignment, detail your research plan and the results of your research.

Quick Quiz True/False Answers

Page 307	Page 313	Page 319	Page 321
1. False	1. False	1. True	1. False
2. False	2. False	2. True	2. True
3. True	3. True	3. True	3. False
4. True	4. False	4. True	4. True
5. True	5. True	5. True	5. False

Part Four

Legal Writing Basics

Chapter 11

Introduction to Legal Writing

After completing this chapter, you will be able to:

- Define "legalese."
- Describe a "term of art."
- List basic techniques for good legal writing.
- Identify the audience for a legal document.
- Describe the difference between an "objective" purpose and an "adversarial" purpose.
- Apply the IRAC method for defining and researching a legal issue.
- Balance time constraints.
- Organize a legal document.
- List several different types of legal documents.
- Identify two different types of pleadings.

We all think legal writing should be filled with complicated words that no one understands and all the legal "gobbledygook." In reality, the opposite is true. The art of writing is communicating complicated subjects and words in a simple, understandable manner. Throw away all those notions you have from movies and television. Wipe the slate clean and focus on the concept that simpler is better. Use "plain English" whenever possible to convey your message regardless of the type of assignment. Less is more; precision and clarity rule the written page. But none of this is accomplished unless you have an organized plan of attack for the assignment. The journey of how to write legalese simply begins now.

CASE FACT PATTERN

On Monday morning you receive a telephone call from a friend who is buying a used car. The language of the contracts, credit agreements, warranties, and disclaimers has left him in a panic—it's too complicated to understand! He wants to make an appointment to have your supervising attorney review and explain the various provisions before he purchases the car. Since your friend is buying a used car, he especially wants to know what it means to buy a car "As Is" and "Without Warranties."

Your supervising attorney suggests you obtain copies of the contracts prior to the meeting for her review. After the meeting, the attorney asks you to prepare a draft of a letter to your friend and new client, explaining the issues in everyday language. Simplifying complicated legal documents is a task you will perform as a paralegal.

TRADITION AND TREND IN LEGAL WRITING

Most people have the same reaction as the friend in our Case Fact Pattern to legal documents—panic. They consider legal writing to be complicated, cumbersome, and incomprehensible. Although some legal writers do, in fact, allow their writing to deteriorate, most are reasonably competent. Why, then, is the image of legal writing so negative? *Nobody knows.*

clarity
Clear and understandable style of communication.

precise
Accuracy of written communication.

One answer, oddly enough, is the importance of precision. As with all writing, good legal writing requires **clarity,** *conciseness, accuracy,* and *simplicity*—but above all else, it must be **precise.** It is essential that every person interpreting a document take the same meaning from the words chosen. This leads to an unwritten rule of law—namely, that once a given usage is agreed to have a given meaning, it should ever after be the accepted method of conveying that meaning. Any change from that usage necessarily implies that an alteration of that meaning is intended.

legal jargon
Legalese.

legalese
Language that is characterized by the frequent use of Latin, French, and Old English terms unfamiliar to most present-day vocabularies in legal writing.

This unwritten rule has led to a reliance on archaic legal language. Terms that originated hundreds of years ago and which sound odd in the context of our modern language are still used in legal documents because their meaning is accepted. **Legal jargon,** often referred to as **legalese,** is characterized by the frequent use of Latin, French, and Old English terms unfamiliar to most present-day vocabularies. You have already seen such Latin terms as *in re* and *ex parte* as they are used in case names (*ex parte* also has another meaning, as we will note). Other terms commonly used include *res ipsa loquitor* (a Latin term from tort law meaning "the thing speaks for itself"), *voir dire* (a French term for the questioning of a potential juror for evidence of prejudice or unfitness), and *writ* (an Old English term for an order of a court, or the first written notice of a lawsuit). These are just a sampling. Other examples of legalese are listed in Table 11.1, but a complete list would be enormous.

Legalese is also characterized by usages rarely seen elsewhere. Such phrases as "Hereof fail not but by these presents make due and proper return" or "Comes now James Jones, Plaintiff in the above-styled and numbered cause, who does by these presents make due complaint" are examples of archaic sentence structure seen in legal documents. Such words as *aforementioned* or *hereinafter,* seldom used in everyday language, clutter legal sentences. These practices are often a holdover from centuries of Anglo-Saxon jurisprudence.

Wordiness is another characteristic of legalese. Lawyers often use a phrase with a combination of synonymous, hence redundant, words. Such phrases as *cease and desist, null and void,* and *give, devise, and bequeath* date back to a time when two or three similar words were used to ensure clarity. Documents had to be interpreted correctly by people of different nationalities, in an era when language lacked the consistency of modern times. Although historically there may have been distinctions between the words used, current legal practice has for the most part erased them and rendered such phrases redundant.

Tradition has been a powerful force in the law, as you might expect from a system in which the concepts of precedent and *stare decisis* play so important a role. Things are done a certain way because that is how they have always been done; certain language is used because it has always been used. Thus, not only for the reason of precision, but also because of institutional custom and perhaps even out of sentiment, the legal profession has clung to traditional language at the expense of broader understanding. Therefore language that is clear to a trained lawyer or paralegal is unclear to the average citizen, leading to the negative image of legalese.

More often than not, legalese is used from habit rather than necessity. The objective of precision can be better achieved by rigorous and exacting use of modern language than by reliance on anachronistic formulas. As Richard Wydick observes in

TABLE 11.1
Examples of Legalese

Legalese	Translation
a fortiori	for a stronger reason
certiorari	discretionary request to the U.S. Supreme Court or other appellate court for review of a case
demurrer	request by defendant for a dismissal of a cause of action
duces tecum	to bring with you; a form of writ or request
ex parte	1. concerning the application of; 2. independent contact with an official, usually the judge, without the presence of the opposing side
inter alia	among other things
laches	principle of equity in which the passage of time prohibits pursuit of a cause of action
remittitur	judicial review and revision of an excessive judgment
res ipsa loquitor	the thing speaks for itself; in tort law, a doctrine that allows a finding of negligence without proof thereof
sua sponte	by the judge's own motion
tort	civil wrongdoing to another person
voir dire	to speak the truth; in practice refers to the examination of prospective jurors
writ	an order of the court, or the first pleading filed in a lawsuit

his book *Plain English for Lawyers, 4th Edition* (Durham, NC: Carolina Academic Press, 1998):

> *We use eight words to say what could be said in two. We use arcane phrases to express commonplace ideas. Seeking to be precise, we become redundant. Seeking to explain, we become verbose. Our sentences twist on, phrase within clause within clause, glazing the eyes and numbing the minds of our readers.*

The modern trend in legal writing is to emphasize broader comprehensibility. Whenever possible, **plain English** should be used. Long, complicated sentences should be the exception, not the rule. Archaic terms and phrases should be replaced by equivalent modern language. When one word is sufficient, avoid redundant combinations.

plain English
The style of writing that uses straightforward, clear, precise language and is generally devoid of legal jargon.

terms of art
Words that are commonly used in the legal profession and have an accepted meaning.

Plain English

Of course, the survival of some legalese is inevitable, and even justifiable. Just as it is easier for doctors to use certain medical terminology, so it is easier for lawyers to use certain shorthand **terms of art** despite their obscurity to the general public. For example, the concise term *voir dire* mentioned previously requires a lengthy explanation in plain English, as does the alternate meaning of *ex parte* (contact with an official of the court in the absence of the opposing party). You must, however, use good judgment when evaluating the desirability of using legalese, and more often than not, there is a better alternative in plain English.

Legal writing needs to be demystified. Many people are under the impression that legal documents must be complicated, and that quality is related to complexity. This

PRACTICE TIP

Do not use the word "said" as an adjective. Replace it with the word "the." It is straightforward and clear.

Frank and Ernest

Source: © 1996 Thaves. Reprinted with permission. Newspaper dist. by NEA, Inc.

is simply not so. Indeed, the best expression of an idea is often the simplest composition that accurately conveys the intended meaning. The use of archaic legal terms and phrases should be minimized and plain English used instead. In the next few chapters we focus on techniques that

- employ short, succinct sentences;
- minimize legalese;
- avoid redundancy;
- emphasize simple language in simple form (subject/verb/object) using accepted rules of grammar; and
- remind us that writing is reading—and good writing will develop only when we reread what we have written.

audience
The person or persons to whom a legal document is directed, such as a client or the court.

PREWRITING CONSIDERATIONS

Now you know why legal language often causes people to panic. You know that eliminating excess legalese can help reduce that panic. You have learned that some legalese remains useful. You have also learned that certain rules that apply to all forms of writing, such as the superiority of short sentences and simple words, apply to legal writing as well. Before you refine your knowledge of legal writing techniques, however, you must address four preliminary considerations: identifying your **audience;** identifying your purpose; defining and researching the issues presented; and evaluating constraints.

PRACTICE TIP

Understanding the assignment is important. As a new paralegal, you may be hesitant to ask questions or ask for clarification. Don't be! If the assignment is unclear to you, let your supervising attorney know. Asking questions in the beginning saves time and avoids the wrong direction in an assignment.

Identifying the Audience

Lawyers prepare a wide range of writings for a diverse group of recipients. Some will be read by highly trained judges; others by less sophisticated clients. Before beginning a writing task, a lawyer or paralegal must determine

- the person to whom the document is directed;
- the level of legal expertise of that person or persons; and
- the degree of that person or persons' familiarity with the subject.

There may be particular problems in a given situation, for example, language barriers or physical or mental disability. As a paralegal, you have to learn how to overcome potential obstacles.

Don't make assumptions when determining the audience. For example, you might think that the audience for a demand letter is easy to identify: the person upon whom your client is making demand, or in other words, the person to whom the letter is addressed. Such an assumption could lead to a critical error if your demand letter must meet statutory requirements in order to be effective. Consider a demand letter to be sent to a physician accused of malpractice. There may be a statute that outlines specific requirements for you to put the physician "on notice" of the claim. In such a case, the demand letter is drafted for two audiences—the physician who is being notified, of course, and, equally important, the court that may eventually have to determine whether the requirements have been met. The court will not appear in the salutation, nor even, quite possibly, in the letter itself—yet the judge who may someday evaluate the letter is a crucial segment of the audience that must be considered.

Identifying the Purpose

In order to draft any effective writing, you must identify your purpose. Do you want to update a client on the status of a lawsuit? Do you want to convince a court that your client's position should prevail in a pending motion? Are you summarizing a deposition transcript? Depending on your purpose, your approach to the task will differ markedly. It is therefore critical that you identify this purpose before you begin drafting.

The purpose of most legal documents falls into one of two broad categories—**objective** or **adversarial.** Objective documents accurately convey information and avoid bias. A letter to your client estimating his chances for success would be an objective document, as would an interoffice memo summarizing the current state of the law that applies to a given set of facts. Adversarial documents, on the other hand, are argumentative, drafted to emphasize the strong points of your client's position and the weaknesses of the opposing party's. They are *not* objective; they are *not* designed to balance both sides. A demand letter written to your client's opponent or a brief submitted to persuade an appellate court are examples of adversarial documents.

objective documents
Documents that convey information and avoid bias.

adversarial documents
Documents that are argumentative, drafted to emphasize the strong points of your client's position and the weaknesses of the opposing party's.

Some documents have both objective and adversarial elements. For example, when drafting a contract proposal you will be seeking to reflect accurately the agreement of the parties (an objective purpose), while at the same time construing all ambiguous aspects of the agreement in your client's favor (an adversarial purpose). By determining your purpose, you establish a focus that will enable you to accomplish your objective in every document you draft. In Table 11.2 we identify some strategies for accomplishing different purposes.

Defining and Researching the Issues

Once you've identified your audience and determined your purpose, are you ready to begin writing? The answer is no. Before you begin writing, you must define the issues presented and conduct the research necessary to address these issues.

For some documents, this last prewriting consideration may be easy. If, for example, you are simply updating a client on recent developments in a case, the issue is identical to the purpose (informing the client), and the research may be as simple as reviewing the file or even relating from memory.

In much legal writing, however, you will have to analyze the issues implied by your purpose and address them to accomplish your objective. A commonly used technique is the **IRAC method:**

IRAC method
A technique used in legal writing that loosely follows the pattern of issue, rule of law, application of the rule of law to the facts and conclusion.

- Identify the *issue* involved.
- Determine the relevant *rule of law.*

TABLE 11.2
Strategies for Different Writing Purposes

Purpose	Strategy
To inform	1. Identify audience 2. Determine extent of audience's knowledge 3. Research relevant information 4. Determine what you desire to communicate
To persuade	1. Identify audience 2. Determine relevant information 3. Research relevant information 4. Emphasize positive information and present in most favorable light 5. Convince audience that your position is the better position
To discover information	1. Identify audience 2. Determine information you need 3. Research relevant sources 4. Determine information that audience may possess 5. Elicit information that is important without revealing your position
To prepare legal documents	1. Identify audience 2. Determine legal requirements 3. Elicit client's needs

- *Apply* the rule of law to the facts of your matter.
- Reach a *conclusion.*

Taking the first letter of the four key items yields the mnemonic (memorizing) device *IRAC.* Let's take a closer look at each of these items.

The Issue

issue
The legal problem presented.

The **issue** is the legal problem presented. Identifying the issue is crucial to preparing your assignment effectively. If the precise legal problem is not identified, how can the problem be solved? Craft your issues so that the reader does not have to guess the subject of the legal document. The following are two issues from the set of facts in our Case Fact Pattern:

1. Can a buyer of a car change the terms in a contract?
2. When a buyer purchases a car "As Is" and "Without Warranties," what is the legal significance of the language in the contract?

Obviously, the second example is crafted more precisely. The language in the issue tells the reader what the subject of the legal discussion is. There is no guessing. The key to drafting the issue precisely is detail and specificity.

For example, the issue in our Case Fact Pattern problem is the meaning of the documents, specifically the "As Is" and "Without Warranties" provisions involved in the purchase of a used car. Through your supervising attorney, you have to inform your friend of several things—what the documents mean, whether they meet all legal requirements, and whether he has any option to negotiate their content.

The Rule of Law

Having determined the issue, you must research the law to identify relevant statutes, regulations, cases, and constitutional provisions. Those sources that apply constitute the **rule of law** controlling the issue. For example, taking our Case Fact Pattern situation, a statute might require certain portions of the contract to be written in plain English or in oversized or boldface typeface, or a case might have held that certain financing disclosures are required.

rule of law
Sources of law that control the issue.

Applying the Law to the Facts

The rule of law is an abstract concept that must be analyzed in the context of the particular facts of your client's matter. Applying the law to the facts enables you to address the issue in a manner meaningful to your client. Suppose, for example, that your research on our Case Fact Pattern problem has shown that a car dealership must identify "As Is" and "Without Warranties" language in conspicuous type, such as boldface, capital letters, or underlined, for the provisions in a sales contract to be enforceable. After you apply this rule of law to the facts of your specific matter, the letter to your friend might read in part as follows:

> *The dealership in an "As Is" purchase is required to inform all prospective purchasers of their rights, to have the "As Is" and "Without Warranties" language conspicuous to draw attention to this provision, and to have the prospective buyer initial the relevant provisions of the contract. Your initials, however, do not appear next to those provisions, nor is the "As Is" language conspicuous as required by the law.*

The letter thus takes the rule (which requires initialing and conspicuous language) and applies it to the facts (your friend did not initial his contract and the language was not conspicuous).

The Conclusion

The result of your analysis is your **conclusion.** Carrying forward the Case Fact Pattern example to this final step, your letter to your friend might conclude

conclusion
Summation of your analysis.

> *The dealership has failed to comply with the requirement that your initial provisions that explain your rights under an "As Is" purchase; nor is the language stating that the purchase is "As Is" and "Without Warranties" conspicuous. This is an important requirement of state law, and the contract is therefore rendered voidable at your discretion.*

The conclusion is the summation of the analysis. It answers the questions raised by the issues.

Evaluating Constraints on Legal Writing

Often legal documents have certain limitations. Those constraints may be as simple as time; length of the document; or, format of the document. Pay close attention to these issues when preparing your legal documents.

Time Constraints

Deadlines are a fact of life in legal practice. Virtually every document filed with a court is governed by a time requirement. In addition, practical considerations often create unofficial deadlines (a client may need certain legal questions answered immediately to gain an edge on his competitors). Finally, as a paralegal you will be expected to complete tasks within the time assigned by your supervising attorney.

An important prewriting consideration is thus to evaluate the time available and allocate your efforts accordingly. A brief due in 48 hours will be prepared in a fashion and on a schedule quite different from one due in four weeks. You must learn to budget your time without affecting the quality of your writing—which can be accomplished by organizing efficiently and taking advantage of all available resources (for example, if an old case involved similar issues, you might use the research from that file as a starting point).

Document Length

Document length may be dictated by your supervising attorney or the court. Rather than read a thesis on a topic, your attorney may limit your assignment to three pages. Often attorneys are pressed for time and need a concise review of a subject. Here economy of word choice is essential. Similarly, courts limit the length of briefs as well. Local rules and appellate rules of court may dictate the length of a brief. Review the rules of court when preparing a court document. Compare the document requirements of the U.S. Supreme Court and the U.S. Court of Appeals for the First Circuit in Figure 11.1.

CYBER TRIP

Locate a rule of procedure in your jurisdiction that sets forth a constraint on a legal document, such as time, document length, and format. The site may be either federal or state based.

Format Style

Your attorney may have a particular way to present certain legal documents, such as a letter or memorandum of law. For example, the attorney may want the date of the correspondence centered; others may want the date justified with the contents of the document. Check with your attorney for their style preferences. Ask for samples of previous documents. Likewise, courts have format requirements. These requirements may be the difference between a court accepting or rejecting a document. Some courts want only twenty-five lines to a page or require a certain size of paper. Do not take any court format requirements for granted; familiarize yourself with the courts in your jurisdiction. If you are working on an assignment in a court with which you have not had experience, get a copy of its rules.

ETHICS ALERT

Writing counts. How you communicate counts. If you produce a substandard product, it is a reflection on you, your supervising attorney, and your firm. Judges pay close attention to the written documents submitted to their courts. Although as a paralegal you may not be directly responsible for the legal documents submitted, the case law is growing on the subject of attorneys and "poor legal writing." Courts are now holding that poor legal writing is a direct reflection on one's competency. The rules of professional responsibility for lawyers, Canon 6 of the Model Code, require that a "lawyer should represent the client competently." Although competency is a standard that we are striving to achieve, it is often undefined. As U.S. Supreme Court Justice Potter Stewart in a case involving the pornography standard stated, "I know it when I see it." *Jacobellis v. Ohio,* 378 U.S. 184, 197 (1964). That has essentially become the standard for judging competency in legal writing. A recent judge in the U.S. District Court for the District of New Jersey sanctioned and admonished a repeat offender for filing sloppy, incomprehensible legal documents. In expressing his disgust with the attorney, Judge Orlofsky observed that "[a]ttorneys may not, consistent with their professional obligations, substitute the 'cut and paste' function of their word processor for the research, contemplation, and draftsmanship that are the necessary elements of responsible legal representation." He further said that an attorney cannot substitute "mouse clicks" for legal judgments. *Mendez v. Draham,* 182 F. Supp. 2d 430, 431 (D. N.J. 2002). This attorney had been admonished three times in eighteen months, and one of his sanctions was to take a class on professional responsibility. As a paralegal you must decide the level of your competency and not be pushed into areas for which you are not competent. Too often attorneys rely, quite heavily, on their paralegals to do their work. Do not get caught in that trap. You should strive for the highest of standards, but you are not the attorney. You did not attend law school or take the bar exam. Paralegals are easy scapegoats. Be mindful that competent and quality representation is the attorney's ethical obligation—that includes competent legal writing as well.

FIGURE 11.1 **Document Requirements of the U.S. Supreme Court and First Circuit Court of Appeals**

Rules of the Supreme Court of the United States

Adopted March 14, 2005
Effective May 2, 2005

Rule 33. Document Preparation: Booklet Format; 8½- by 11-Inch Paper Format

- 1. *Booklet Format:*

(a) Except for a document expressly permitted by these Rules to be submitted on 8½- by 11-inch paper, see, e. g., Rules 21, 22, and 39, every document filed with the Court shall be prepared using using a standard typesetting process (e. g., hot metal, photocomposition, or computer typesetting) to produce text printed in typographic (as opposed to typewriter) characters. The process used must produce a clear, black image on white paper. The text must be reproduced with a clarity that equals or exceeds the output of a laser printer.

(b) The text of every booklet-format document, including any appendix thereto, shall be typeset in Roman 11-point or larger type with 2-point or more leading between lines. The typeface should be similar to that used in current volumes of the United States Reports. Increasing the amount of text by using condensed or thinner typefaces, or by reducing the space between letters, is strictly prohibited. Type size and face shall be consistent throughout. Quotations in excess of 50 words shall be indented. The typeface of footnotes shall be 9-point or larger with 2-point or more leading between lines. The text of the document must appear on both sides of the page.

(c) Every booklet-format document shall be produced on paper that is opaque, unglazed, 6 1/8 by 9 1/4 inches in size, and not less than 60 pounds in weight, and shall have margins of at least three fourths of an inch on all sides. The text field, including footnotes, should be approximately 4 1/8 by 7 1/8 inches. The document shall be bound firmly in at least two places along the left margin (saddle stitch or perfect binding preferred) so as to permit easy opening, and no part of the text should be obscured by the binding. Spiral, plastic, metal, and string bindings may not be used. Copies of patent documents, except opinions, may be duplicated in such size as is necessary in a separate appendix.

(d) Every booklet-format document shall comply with the page limits shown on the chart in subparagraph 1(g) of this Rule. The page limits do not include the pages containing the questions presented, the list of parties and corporate affiliates of the filing party, the table of contents, the table of cited authorities, or any appendix. Verbatim quotations required under Rule 14.1(f), if set out in the text of a brief rather than in the appendix, are also excluded. For good cause, the Court or a Justice may grant leave to file a document in excess of the page limits, but application for such leave is not favored. An application to exceed page limits shall comply with Rule 22 and must be received by the Clerk at least 15 days before the filing date of the document in question, except in the most extraordinary circumstances.

(e) Every booklet-format document shall have a suitable cover consisting of 65-pound weight paper in the color indicated on the chart in subparagraph 1(g) of this Rule. If a separate appendix to any document is filed, the color of its cover shall be the same as that of the cover of the document it supports. The Clerk will furnish a color chart upon request. Counsel shall ensure that there is adequate contrast between the printing and the color of the cover. A document filed by the United States, or by any other federal party represented by the Solicitor General, shall have a gray cover. A joint appendix, answer to a bill of complaint, motion for leave to intervene, and any other document not listed in subparagraph 1(g) of this Rule shall have a tan cover.

Cont.

FIGURE 11.1 **Document Requirements of the U.S. Supreme Court and First Circuit Court of Appeals** *Cont.*

(f) Forty copies of a booklet-format document shall be filed.

(g) Page limits and cover colors for booklet-format documents are as follows:

Type of Document	Page Limits	Color of Cover
i. Petition for a Writ of Certiorari (Rule 14); Motion for Leave to file a Bill of Complaint and Brief in Support (Rule 17.3); Jurisdictional Statement (Rule 18.3); Petition for an Extraordinary Writ (Rule 20.2)	30	white
ii. Brief in Opposition (Rule 15.3); Brief in Opposition to Motion for Leave to file an Original Action (Rule 17.5); Motion to Dismiss or Affirm (Rule 18.6); Brief in Opposition to Mandamus or Prohibition (Rule 20.3) (b)); Response to a Petition for Habeas Corpus (Rule 20.4)	30	orange
iii. Reply to Brief in Opposition (Rules 15.6 and 17.5); Brief Opposing a Motion to Dismiss or Affirm (Rule 18.8)	10	tan
iv. Supplemental Brief (Rules 15.8, 17, 18.10, and 25.5)	10	tan
v. Brief on the Merits by Petitioner or Appellant (Rule 24); Exceptions by Plaintiff to Report of Special Master (Rule 17)	50	light blue
vi. Brief on the Merits by Respondent or Appellee (Rule 24.2); Brief on the Merits for Respondent or Appellee Supporting Petitioner or Appellant (Rule 12.6); Exceptions by Party Other than Plaintiff to Report of Special Master (Rule 17)	50	light red
vii. Reply Brief on the Merits (Rule 24.4)	20	yellow
viii. Reply to Plaintiff's Exceptions to Report of Special Master (Rule 17)	50	orange
ix. Reply to Exceptions by Party Other Than Plaintiff to Report of Special Master (Rule 17)	50	yellow
x. Brief for an *Amicus Curiae* at the Petition Stage (Rule 37.2)	20	cream
xi. Brief for an *Amicus Curiae* in Support of the Plaintiff, Petitioner, or Appellant, or in Support of Neither Party, on the Merits, or in an Original Action at the Exceptions Stage (Rule 37.3)	30	light green
xii. Brief for an *Amicus Curiae* in Support of the Defendant, Respondent, or Appellee, on the Merits or in an Original Action at the Exceptions Stage (Rule 37.3)	30	dark green
xiii. Petition for Rehearing (Rule 44)	10	tan

Cont.

FIGURE 11.1 **Document Requirements of the U.S. Supreme Court and First Circuit Court of Appeals** *Cont.*

- 2. *8½- by 11-Inch Paper Format:*
  - (a) The text of every document, including any appendix thereto, expressly permitted by these Rules to be presented to the Court on 8½- by 11-inch paper shall appear double spaced, except for indented quotations, which shall be single spaced, on opaque, unglazed, white paper. The document shall be stapled or bound at the upper left hand corner. Copies, if required, shall be produced on the same type of paper and shall be legible. The original of any such document (except a motion to dismiss or affirm under Rule 18.6) shall be signed by the party proceeding pro se or by counsel of record who must be a member of the Bar of this Court or an attorney appointed under the Criminal Justice Act of 1964, see 18 U. S. C. §3006A(d)(6), or under any other applicable federal statute. Subparagraph 1(g) of this Rule does not apply to documents prepared under this paragraph.
  - (b) Page limits for documents presented on 8½- by 11-inch paper are: 40 pages for a petition for a writ of certiorari, jurisdictional statement, petition for an extraordinary writ, brief in opposition, or motion to dismiss or affirm; and 15 pages for a reply to a brief in opposition, brief opposing a motion to dismiss or affirm, supplemental brief, or petition for rehearing. The page exclusions specified in subparagraph 1(d) of this Rule apply.

Federal Rules of Appellate Procedure

First Circuit Local Rules

Rule 32. Form of Briefs, Appendices, and Other Papers

(a) **Form of a Brief.**

(1) **Reproduction.**

(A) A brief may be reproduced by any process that yields a clear black image on light paper. The paper must be opaque and unglazed. Only one side of the paper may be used.

(B) Text must be reproduced with a clarity that equals or exceeds the output of a laser printer.

(C) Photographs, illustrations, and tables may be reproduced by any method that results in a good copy of the original; a glossy finish is acceptable if the original is glossy.

(2) **Cover.** Except for filings by unrepresented parties, the cover of the appellant's brief must be blue; the appellee's, red; an intervenor's or amicus curiae's, green; any reply brief, gray; and any supplemental brief, tan. The front cover of a brief must contain:

(A) the number of the case centered at the top;

(B) the name of the court;

(C) the title of the case (see Rule 12(a));

(D) the nature of the proceeding (e.g., Appeal, Petition for Review) and the name of the court, agency, or board below;

Cont.

FIGURE 11.1 **Document Requirements of the U.S. Supreme Court and First Circuit Court of Appeals** *Cont.*

(E) the title of the brief, identifying the party or parties for whom the brief is filed; and

(F) the name, office address, and telephone number of counsel representing the party for whom the brief is filed.

(3) **Binding.** The brief must be bound in any manner that is secure, does not obscure the text, and permits the brief to lie reasonably flat when open.

(4) **Paper Size, Line Spacing, and Margins.** The brief must be on 8 ½ by 11 inch paper. The text must be double-spaced, but quotations more than two lines long may be indented and single-spaced. Headings and footnotes may be single-spaced. Margins must be at least one inch on all four sides. Page numbers may be placed in the margins, but no text may appear there.

(5) **Typeface.** Either a proportionally spaced or a monospaced face may be used.

(A) A proportionally spaced face must include serifs, but sans-serif type may be used in headings
and captions. A proportionally spaced face must be 14-point or larger.

(B) A monospaced face may not contain more than 10½ characters per inch.

(6) **Type Styles.** A brief must be set in a plain, roman style, although italics or boldface may be used for emphasis. Case names must be italicized or underlined.

(7) **Length.**

(A) **Page limitation.** A principal brief may not exceed 30 pages, or a reply brief 15 pages, unless it complies with Rule 32(a)(7)(B) and (C).

(B) **Type-volume limitation.**

(i) A principal brief is acceptable if:

- it contains no more than 14,000 words; or
- it uses a monospaced face and contains no more than 1,300 lines of text.

(ii) A reply brief is acceptable if it contains no more than half of the type volume specified in Rule 32(a)(7)(B)(i).

(iii) Headings, footnotes, and quotations count toward the word and line limitations. The corporate disclosure statement, table of contents, table of citations, statement with respect to oral argument, any addendum containing statutes, rules or regulations, and any certificates of counsel do not count toward the limitation.

(C) **Certificate of compliance.**

(i) A brief submitted under Rules 28.1(e)(2) or 32(a)(7)(B) must include a certificate by the attorney, or an unrepresented party, that the brief complies with the type-volume limitation. The person preparing the certificate may rely on the word or line count of the word-processing system used to prepare the brief. The certificate must state either:

- the number of words in the brief; or
- the number of lines of monospaced type in the brief.

(ii) Form 6 in the Appendix of Forms is a suggested form of a certificate of compliance. Use of Form 6 must be regarded as sufficient to meet the requirements of Rules 28.1(e)(3) and 32(a)(7)(C)(i).

Cont.

FIGURE 11.1 **Document Requirements of the U.S. Supreme Court and First Circuit Court of Appeals** *Cont.*

(b) Form of an Appendix. An appendix must comply with Rule 32(a)(1), (2), (3), and (4), with the following exceptions:

(1) The cover of a separately bound appendix must be white.

(2) An appendix may include a legible photocopy of any document found in the record or of a printed judicial or agency decision.

(3) When necessary to facilitate inclusion of odd-sized documents such as technical drawings, an appendix may be a size other than 8 ½ by 11 inches, and need not lie reasonably flat when opened.

(c) Form of Other Papers.

(1) **Motion.** The form of a motion is governed by Rule 27(d).

(2) **Other Papers.** Any other paper, including a petition for panel rehearing and a petition for hearing or rehearing en banc, and any response to such a petition, must be reproduced in the manner prescribed by Rule 32(a), with the following exceptions:

(A) A cover is not necessary if the caption and signature page of the paper together contain the information required by Rule 32(a)(2). If a cover is used, it must be white.

(B) Rule 32(a)(7) does not apply.

(d) Signature. Every brief, motion, or other paper filed with the court must be signed by the party filing the paper or, if the party is represented, by one of the party's attorneys.

(e) Local Variation. Every court of appeals must accept documents that comply with the form requirements of this rule. By local rule or order in a particular case a court of appeals may accept documents that do not meet all of the form requirements of this rule.

ORGANIZING THE LEGAL DOCUMENT

Organizing the document might be considered your final prewriting consideration, but it is better to think of it as the first consideration in the writing stage itself. Your plan of organization provides the blueprint by which your document will be crafted.

Outlining

The best method of organizing a legal document is by outlining. An **outline** is the skeleton of a legal argument, advancing from the general to the specific. You have no doubt prepared outlines in other contexts in the past. A legal outline differs from these other outlines in content but not concept. It is intended to help you critically examine your approach, leading to a document that flows logically to a conclusion that accomplishes your purpose. An outline will assist you in

outline
The skeleton of a legal argument, advancing from the general to the specific.

- focusing on logical development;
- preventing critical omissions; and
- evaluating how well you accomplish your purpose.

An outline may use a sentence format or a shorthand topic format. When using a topic format, be sure to include enough information to enable you to remember why you included each topic. Unless you are comfortable or familiar with a particular subject area, the fuller sentence format is preferable. An accepted format for an outline is illustrated in Figure 11.2.

FIGURE 11.2 **Example of an Outline**

I. [General Topic]

    a. [Issue]

        1. [Rule of law]
        2. [Application of law to the facts]
        3. [Conclusion]

    b.

        1.
        2.
        3.

II. Requirements of Financing Documents

    a. Disclosure of repossession procedure in event of nonpayment

        1. Purchaser must initial the relevant sections.
        2. Our client did not initial the documents.
        3. Conclusion: the contract is voidable at our client's discretion.

    b.

        1.
        2.
        3.

III. Conclusion

PRACTICE TIP

Do not begin to write until you know what you want to say. Sit down and write; do not procrastinate. Above all, avoid distractions: no telephones, television, or people!

An Alternative to Outlining

An alternative to a written outline is to separate your raw research into categories. This can be accomplished by using file cards or by grouping photocopies of related cases and statutes (for cases and statutes that overlap issues, place a separate copy in each group, or remind yourself with a Post-it note). By ordering the cards or groups of photocopies in a logical sequence, you create in effect an unwritten outline—you have made decisions about organization and development. This method is somewhat unorthodox, but as you gain experience it may be a practical timesaver.

Remember, the purpose of an outline is to help you. If a formal outline does not work for you, don't use it. Find a method of organizing your document that works for you. Some individuals are more visual and may use graphs to organize their work. The point of outlining is to get organized and focused. No matter the form, traditional or not, take the time to think about your assignment and prepare a logical, organized plan before you begin to write.

Quick Quiz True/False Questions

1. Legal writing requires clarity and precision.
2. Terms of art should never be used in legal writing.
3. Most legal documents are either objective or persuasive in nature.
4. The only constraint in preparing a legal writing document is its length.
5. An outline can be prepared only in sentence format.

TYPES OF DOCUMENTS

There are many different types of legal documents, which we discuss in later chapters. Let's consider a few right now.

Letters

Correspondence is essential in virtually every legal matter: letters to the client, to opposing counsel, to the court, to witnesses, to government agencies, the list is endless. Demand letters, opinion letters, retainer letters, settlement letters, update letters advising of case status or court date—some are objective, some are adversarial, all are important. Chapter 15 identifies different types of legal correspondence in greater detail. However, an example of a common letter to a client is illustrated in Figure 11.3.

Internal Memoranda of Law

An **internal memorandum of law,** or interoffice memorandum, explains the law to inform and educate the attorneys. As mentioned, this memo is an objective writing that relates both good news and bad about the law as it applies to the client's case, and it can be used as a basis for strategy, as basic research for a brief, or as background when drafting pleadings or other documents. Chapter 16 focuses on this type of legal document.

internal memoranda of law
An internal document that analyzes objectively the legal issues in a client's matter.

Transactional Documents

Many documents have, as a result of their language and content, legal effects beyond the mere transmission of information. Executed contracts, leases, wills, and deeds are examples of **transactional documents** that lawyers and paralegals draft. Such documents serve to define property rights and performance obligations, and slight alterations in meaning can have great impact on the parties involved. Without minimizing the importance of precision in every document drafted, it is safe to say that you should be doubly attentive to accuracy in transactional documents, especially if drafted to protect or support a client's legal position. Figure 11.4 is a simple employment contract. Notice

transactional documents
Documents that define property rights and performance obligations.

FIGURE 11.3 **Example of a Letter to a Client**

(Letterhead)

December 27, 2008

Clerk of the Court
552 Main St.
Anywhere, TX 75713

Re: Smith v. ABC Corporation,
Case No. 2006-7472

Dear Ms. Anderson:

I am enclosing an original and five copies of the answer in the above referenced matter. Please file stamp the copies and return them in the self-addressed stamped envelope provided with the filing.

By copy of this letter, I am notifying opposing counsel of the filing of this document.

I appreciate your assistance in this matter.

Sincerely,

Drew Emmanuel

cc: Eric Charles, Esq.

FIGURE 11.4 Simple Employment Contract

EMPLOYMENT AGREEMENT

This **EMPLOYMENT AGREEMENT** ("Agreement") is entered into as of this __ day of ____, 2008 by and between the **Law Firm** (the "Law Firm") and Maria Henderson (the "Employee").

WITNESSETH

NOW THEREFORE, the Law Firm and the Employee, intending to be legally bound, agree as follows:

1. Scope of Services

The Employee shall assume the responsibilities and carry out the functions that are specifically outlined in the Job Description for an Executive Assistant for the law firm, which is attached to and incorporated by this reference as a part of this Agreement.

2. Compensation

Salary: The Employee shall be treated as a regular employee and not as an independent contractor. Therefore, the Employee shall be paid on a bi-weekly basis at $19.23 an hour on an annual salary of $40,000. The Employee hereby consents and the Law Firm agrees to deduct applicable local and federal income related taxes specifically including FICA withholding.

3. Employment Standards

The Employee agrees to maintain the standards of conduct and performance consistent with an Executive Assistant in the Law Firm and consistent with its Personnel Policies and Procedures.

4. Fringe Benefits

In addition, the Law Firm agrees to provide to the Employee a package of fringe benefits. The fringe benefits package will include, but not necessarily limited to, medical insurance, workers' compensation, annual leave, sick leave, holidays and retirement benefits and any other benefits provided by the Law Firm's personnel policies.

5. Effective Date

This Agreement is effective for one (1) year as of December 15, 2008 and will continue until December 14, 2009. The parties may extend this contract for a period of six (6) months upon mutual agreement.

6. Termination

The Law Firm may terminate the Employee with or without cause. Further, the assignment of the Employee will be terminated immediately by the Law Firm if it is determined that Employee is incapable of performing the duties of the position, commits acts of professional negligence, is absent from the position without the Law Firm's permission during regular business hours, is insubordinate, engages in substance abuse, violates the Law Firm's express rules or regulations, engages in other unprofessional conduct or breach or neglect of duty, or is repeatedly absent or tardy without good reason and after receiving a written warning. The employee will be on probation for six (6) months in accordance with the Law Firm's policy.

7. Notice

Any notice required to be given by the terms of this Agreement shall be deemed to have been given when sent by certified mail, postage prepaid, express mail, or personally delivered, addressed to the parties involved. Prior to signing this Agreement, Employee will provide the Law Firm with a mailing address, which shall be updated annually or when Employee has a change of address.

Cont.

FIGURE 11.4 **Simple Employment Contract** *Cont.*

8. Governing Law

This Agreement shall be governed by the laws of the state of Texas and jurisdiction is exclusive in Dallas County. The parties agree that venue is proper in Dallas County, Texas.

9. Waivers and Amendments

No waiver, modification, or amendment of any term, condition, or provision of this Contract shall be valid unless made in writing, signed by the parties or their duly authorized representatives, and specifying with particularity the nature and extent of such waiver, modification, or amendment. Any such waiver, modification, or amendment in any instance or instances shall in no event be construed to be a general waiver, modification, or amendment to any of the terms, conditions, or provisions of this contract.

10. Entire Agreement

This constitutes the entire Agreement between the parties and all prior understandings are merged herein.

IN WITNESS WHEREOF, the undersigned have executed this Agreement.

____________	____________	____________	____________
Employee	Date	Law Firm	Date

the termination language in paragraph 6. Clearly the language is drafted in favor of the employer.

A Few Words about Forms

Many types of legal documents, particularly operative documents, incorporate **forms.** Forms are documents that set forth standard language that is the accepted format for accomplishing a given purpose. Recourse to a form is a decision to be made by your supervising attorney, although he or she may delegate some discretion to you.

forms
Documents that set forth standardized language and are used as a drafting guide.

The language in forms may be cumbersome and confusing, with excessive use of legalese and archaic construction. Forms are valuable, however, based upon their widespread acceptance. This is the paradox of precision—that a document confusing on its face due to peculiar language is actually precise as a result of years, even centuries, of accepted meaning.

There are forms for deeds, for wills, and for leases: Indeed, there are multivolume sets of forms covering an enormous range of legal transactions. Most forms provide standard language with blank spaces where specific information from your case can be inserted; others provide the standard language with examples of information from other transactions, which must then be modified to fit your specific situations. The standard language in these forms, often referred to as **boilerplate,** should not be changed unless you are instructed to do so by your supervising attorney. An example of a legal form is the promissory note found in Figure 11.5.

boilerplate
Standard language in a form.

pleadings
Documents filed with the court in a pending lawsuit that define the issues to be decided by the court at trial; the complaint, answer to complaint, and reply.

Pleadings

Pleadings are documents filed with the court in a pending lawsuit that define the issues to be decided by the court at trial. The claims, counterclaims, defenses, and special defenses of the parties constitute the pleadings. The document that initiates a lawsuit is the **complaint,** filed by the plaintiff. The defendant responds to the complaint with an **answer,** replying to the claims of the plaintiff. There can be other pleadings as well. Pleadings are adversarial documents, drafted to place your client's position in the best light, and they must be prepared in the format prescribed by the court's rules of procedure. Chapter 17 addresses the various types of pleadings.

complaint
Document that states the allegations and the legal basis of the plaintiff's claims.

answer
Document that is the defendant's response to the plaintiff's complaint.

FIGURE 11.5 Promissory Note Form

PROMISSORY NOTE

$ 50,000.00 in Dallas, Texas A.D. 200__.

For value received Andrew Mason promises to pay to Paul Johnson on order, the sum of $50,000.00 dollars, with interest from date at the rate of ten percent per annum (10%), both principal and interest payable at the offices of Paul Johnson or a place so designated by the parties.

This note payable in 48 monthly installments of one thousand and forty two dollars ($1,042.00).

All past due principal and interest on this note shall bear interest at the maximum rate permissible under the law.

It is understood and agreed that the failure to pay this note, or any installment as above promised, or any interest hereon, when due, shall at the option of the holder of said note, mature the full amount of said note, and it shall at once become due and payable.

And it is hereby especially agreed that if this note is placed in the hands of an attorney for collection, or collected by suit, or in probate or bankruptcy proceedings, Mason agrees to pay a reasonable amount additional on the principal and interest then due thereon as attorneys' fees.

Address: ______________________________

Phone: ______________________________

____

Signature of Maker

PRACTICE TIP

Form books can be dangerous. They are invaluable as a guide for the unfamiliar; however, they are wrought with tortuous language most practitioners refuse to eliminate. Always be aware of their positive values and their pitfalls.

Motions

A **motion** requests that the court take an action. It can be filed by either the plaintiff or the defendant in a lawsuit. A defendant might file a "motion to strike," asking the court to rule out part of the plaintiff's claim on the grounds that it fails to state a claim supported by the applicable rules of law. Either party might file a "motion *in limine,*" seeking a preliminary ruling on an issue of evidence. Or either party might file a "motion for summary judgment," arguing that there are no disputed questions of fact and that the matter can be decided based on an application of the law to the undisputed facts. This motion is common is a civil lawsuit. Indeed, the number of different motions is high, limited only by the imaginations of counsel. Motions are always adversarial documents, drafted to favor your client's position. Figure 11.6 is an example of a motion to dismiss.

motion
A procedural request or application presented by the attorney in court.

YOU BE THE JUDGE

Form books can be a great help in drafting and they can also be a downfall. Losing sight of a form book's limitations and usefulness can cause attorneys and paralegals the ire of a court. Take a look at *Clement v. Public Service Electric and Gas Co.,* 198 F.R.D. 634 (D. N.J. 2001), where the use of a form book cost an attorney sanctions and public embarrassment. As the judge in the case pointed out: "[a]ttorneys who merely copy form complaints and file them in this court without conducting independent legal research and examining the facts giving rise to a potential claim do so at their peril. Lawyers are not automatons. They are trained professionals who are expected to exercise independent judgment." *Id* at 636. The moral of the story is: watch out for those form books. Copying the boilerplate without any thought or independent legal research can compromise your integrity and reputation. What sanctions did the court impose on the attorney? What are the facts that lead to the attorney's sanctions? Do you believe the judge's disposition was too harsh? Why or why not?

FIGURE 11.6 Motion to Dismiss

IN THE DISTRICT COURT OF THE NEW JERSEY
DIVISION OF CAMDEN

Harry Archer,	)	
	)	
Plaintiff,	)	
v.	)	Civil No. 06 CV 0000
	)	
Franklin Brandson,	)	
	)	
Defendant.	)	
______________________	)	

MOTION TO DISMISS FOR LACK OF PERSONAL JURISDICTION

COMES NOW Defendant, Franklin Brandson, by and through his undersigned attorney, Samantha Daily, Esq., and, pursuant to Rule 12(b)(2) and (3) moves this Honorable Court for the entry of an Order Dismissing this matter with prejudice, for lack of personal jurisdiction. In support of the Motion Defendant incorporates by reference his Memorandum of Law In Support of Motion to Dismiss filed simultaneously herewith.

WHEREFORE, Defendant Franklin Brandson, asks this Honorable Court for the entry of an Order dismissing this matter with prejudice; and, for attorney's fees, expenses, costs and other relief deemed just by this Court.

Law Offices of Samantha Daily LLC
Attorney for Defendant

DATED:

By:______________________
Samantha Daily, Esquire

CERTIFICATE OF SERVICE

I HEREBY CERTIFY that on this ____ day of June, 2008, a true and correct copy of the foregoing MOTION TO DISMISS FOR LACK OF PERSONAL JURISDICTION was caused by me to be served HAND DELIVERY upon: Ethan Donaldsen, Esq., Donaldsen, Anderson and Barone, 500 Oak Avenue, Anytown, Pa. 00000.

____

Briefs

A **brief** is a formal written argument presented to the court, usually countered by a brief written by the opposing party. Note the important difference between a case brief, which you studied in detail in Chapter 4 (an objective document), and the formal brief presented to a court, which is adversarial. A brief filed with the trial court is called a *trial brief;* if filed with an appellate court it is called an *appellate brief.* A close relative of the brief is the *memorandum of law to the court,* which performs exactly the same function as a brief, but is usually filed in support of a less significant motion. The difference between a formal brief and a memorandum of law to the court is more semantic than real. Both types of briefs are discussed in later chapters.

brief
A formal written argument presented to the court.

Discovery Documents

The procedural rules governing lawsuits have liberal provisions that allow for **discovery,** when the opposing parties obtain information in the hands of the other party. Requests

discovery
Process in which the opposing parties obtain information about the case from each other; the process of investigation and collection of evidence by litigants.

interrogatory
Discovery tool in the form of a series of written questions that are answered by the party in writing, to be answered under oath.

for documents or for responses to written questions (called **interrogatories**) are important adversarial documents that enable litigants to learn as much as possible about their opponent's case before trial. Although response to discovery requests must be honestly provided (hence they are objective), in fact an adversarial element often creeps into these responses, which can lead to time-consuming disputes in court. More information on drafting discovery documents is found in Chapter 17.

CYBER TRIP

On the Internet, find an example of a transactional document, a pleading, a motion, and a discovery document.

PRACTICE TIP

To review a document effectively, print it from the computer. Looking at the hard copy adds a different perspective from the computer screen.

POSTWRITING CONSIDERATIONS: REVISING, EDITING, AND PROOFREADING

Good legal writing requires revising, editing, and proofreading. Do not think that one draft of a document is sufficient. Often, two and three drafts still are not enough. Legal writing demands precision and clarity, which does not happen in one try. Prepare yourself to draft, redraft, and revise that draft.

Revising the Document

Revising is rewriting. To revise a legal document does not mean changing a word or two. When revision is necessary, entire sections may be deleted or even moved to a different section of the document. Attack a revision with purpose—to make the document better. Ask yourself:

- Have I effectively communicated the purpose of the document?
- Is the document in the correct format?
- Who is my audience?
- Is the document understandable?
- Have I addressed all the issues?
- Are the rules of the court followed?

These are some of the questions to consider when revising a document. Once a revision is complete, sometimes "fresh eyes" may add a new or different perspective. Ask a colleague to review the document.

Editing the Document

Editing is very different from revising a document. Editing focuses on the more technical aspects of writing, such as grammar, sentence structure, and punctuation. Also, while you edit, review for substantive accuracy of the assignment. During the editing process, you want to make sure the document is understandable. If preparing a brief, check that the headings are presented the same; for example, are they all underlined, in bold, or italics?

When editing, do just that—edit! Strike unnecessary language; correct citations; read for clarity. Certain marks are used for editing and proofreading. Figure 11.7 shows some of the more common marks.

Proofreading the Document

One of the most embarrassing moments for any attorney or paralegal is to find a typographical error in a finished and *submitted* document. Often that shows the level of care devoted to the document. And more importantly, typos look bad and reflect on an individual's attention to detail and professionalism. Documents replete with typos give the wrong impression to your attorney, a client, and a judge. Consequently, one of the most critical stages of writing is proofreading your work. Be sure all words are spelled correctly. Check for mistyping such as inadvertently repeating words or phrases that were not intended, extra spaces, and transposed words or letters. Have someone else proofread your work. Fresh eyes offer a different perspective. Spending

FIGURE 11.7 Common Proofreading Marks

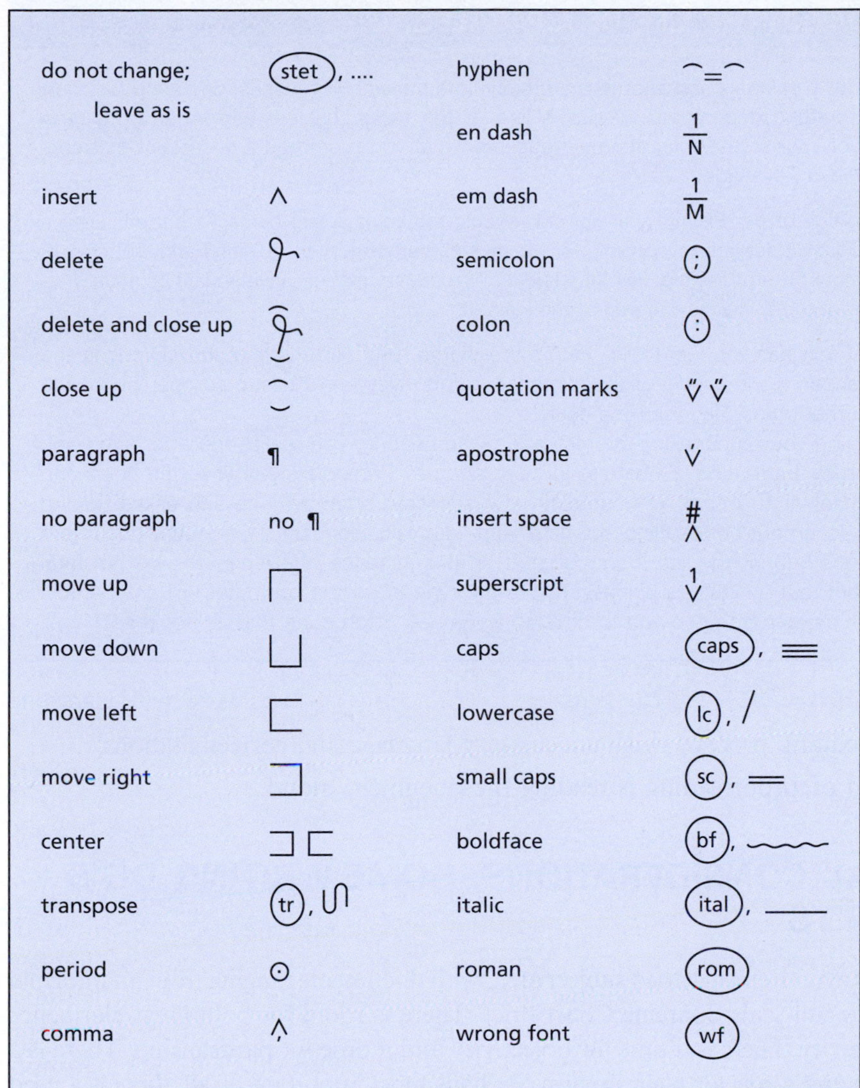

so much time preparing a document clouds our objectivity. After reading a document so many times, the tendency is to miss errors no matter how obvious.

do not change; leave as is
stet, ...
insert
delete
delete and close up
close up
paragraph
¶
no paragraph
no ¶
move up
move down
move left
move right
center
transpose
tr
period
comma
hyphen
en dash
1/N
em dash
1/M
semicolon
colon
quotation marks
apostrophe
insert space
#
superscript
1
caps
caps
lowercase
lc
small caps
sc
boldface
bf
italic
ital
roman
rom
wrong font
wf

Everyone has their own way to proofread, but one common thread to proofing a document is to read slowly. Do not proofread as though you are reading a novel or the newspaper. You cannot proofread effectively by skimming a document. Proofreading requires deliberate, slow review. Sometimes reading the document aloud is another method of proofreading. It forces you to focus on each word. Whatever your method, proofreading is essential to all legal writing. The quality of your document is a reflection on you and your office. Make a professional statement about your work. What you write and how you write it matters.

PRACTICE TIP

Whether you or someone else is correcting the document, draw attention to the needed corrections by placing a "√" at the end of each line requiring correction. This practice reinforces the need for a correction on that line and makes the error stand out. Using a red pen helps the correction stand out as well.

Quick Quiz True/False Questions

1. Examples of types of legal documents are letters, transactional documents, and pleadings.
2. A memorandum of law to the trial court is filed to support a motion.
3. When preparing a legal document, prepare only one complete draft.

A DAY IN THE LIFE OF A PARALEGAL

The lives of both paralegals and attorneys are busy. Interviewing witnesses, preparing for court hearings, and drafting documents are just a few of the tasks that are performed on a daily basis. Last night your supervising attorney requested that you proofread a document that contained the following passage:

> It is the position of the Plaintiff that not only should the court award damages but punitive damages. Both parties are responsible for the injuries suffered by the Plaintiff and [no] one party is immune. Therefore, the Plaintiff respectfully requests that each Defendant be equally responsible for the damages suffered by the Plaintiff.

The original text had the word "no" before the words "one party is immune." Omitting the word "no" changes the meaning of the sentence, but in everyone's haste, no one caught the error. The document was filed with the court.

When you and your supervising attorney are at the hearing, you realize the error and bring it to your attorney's attention. Embarrassed, your attorney immediately notifies the court and opposing counsel of the error. Undoubtedly your attorney is annoyed as she asked you to proofread the document before filing. You have learned a valuable lesson: Check any document slowly and properly prior to filing it with a court. In this instance, the omission was not fatal to the document, but exhibits sloppiness. This is the type of error a computer will *not* identify. Therefore, it is incumbent upon you to develop a method of proofing that is "foolproof."

4. During the editing process, strike unnecessary language and correct citations.
5. One method of proofreading is reading the document aloud.

PRACTICAL CONSIDERATIONS: SOME WRITING DO'S AND DON'TS

Legal writing is an extremely varied subject area, with documents ranging from an informal client letter to a full-scale Supreme Court brief. There is room for both great eloquence and extreme brevity. There is a time for objectivity and a time for partisanship. There is a role for legalese and a role for plain English. Perhaps most important of all, there is a need for precision—a need to communicate ideas in a concise and unambiguous fashion.

A few practical considerations are universal. First, do all necessary background research. This includes the prewriting considerations outlined, as well as checking for technical requirements such as court rules on format.

Second, always make your purpose clear by using a straightforward introduction. Readers do not enjoy guessing. Assuming too much about the expectations or knowledge of your audience can result in a document that confuses rather than enlightens.

THE E-FACTOR

Typographical and spelling errors are a thing of the past. With today's use of spell check in most word processing programs, these types of errors are inexcusable. Programs such as Microsoft Word and Corel WordPerfect highlight the misspelled words, and even offer the correct spelling. Prior to submitting any document for review by your attorney, complete a spell check. This habit is important to acquire. No attorney wants to read a document replete with misspelled words.

Be careful when using spell check programs. Spell check only checks for spelling errors; if a word is mistyped but is still a "proper" word, spell check will not identify the error. For example, if you typed the word "no" but meant "not," spell check will not catch this error. Therefore, spell check is not a substitute for proofreading. It is, however, a mechanism that adds to the final completeness and quality of your legal document.

Third, fully explain your position. Satisfy yourself that your points progress logically. Guide the reader through the subject matter. Avoid arriving at conclusions before exhausting your analysis.

Fourth, prepare a conclusion that concisely ties together the entire document. Again, be straightforward. As the introduction made your intent clear, so your conclusion should make the achievement of that purpose clear.

Finally, reread! Writing is nothing more than creating documents to be read. It is impossible to gauge how another person will read a document unless you read it yourself. By rereading, you can see where your document succeeds and fails and then revise it into a precise, flowing finished product.

Summary

Because of the long-standing and wide acceptance of the meaning of the words of which they are composed, legalese and anachronistic usages persist in legal writing. Although some terms of art remain useful, good legal writing is generally characterized by short, succinct sentences, a minimum of legalese, avoidance of redundancy, emphasis on simple language in simple form, and a recognition of the importance of rereading what you've written.

Prewriting considerations include identifying the audience and recognizing that the sophistication of the audience will affect the nature of the language used; identifying the purpose, which will generally be either objective or adversarial; and making a commitment to properly define and research the issues presented. A good method of analyzing the issues is the IRAC method, in which you identify the *issue* involved, determine the relevant *rule of law, apply* the rule of law to the facts of your matter, and reach a *conclusion.* The final prewriting step is to take into account the time constraints associated with your writing project.

Legal documents are often organized with the help of an outline, which is the framework of the proposed content, advancing from the general to the specific. An alternative to outlining is to group your raw research into categories, either by using file cards or by physically gathering related materials.

There are many different types of legal documents, including letters, internal memoranda of law, operative documents, forms, pleadings, motions, briefs, and discovery documents.

Revising, editing, and proofreading documents is essential to the legal writing process. Revising often requires complete rewriting of portions of the assignment, whereas editing focuses on the mechanics of punctuation and structure. Proofreading is a refining technique that checks for typographical and spelling errors.

Writing is an extremely varied subject area. Keep in mind the following considerations: Do all necessary background research; make your purpose clear with a straightforward introduction; fully explain your position; prepare a concise conclusion that ties your argument together; and finally, reread what you've written to ensure that you've accomplished your purpose.

Key Terms

adversarial documents
answer
audience
boilerplate
brief
clarity
complaint
conclusion
discovery
forms
internal memorandum of law
interrogatories
IRAC method
issue
legal jargon
legalese

motion	precise
objective documents	rule of law
outline	terms of art
plain English	transactional documents
pleadings	

Review Questions

1. What is legalese?
2. What is a term of art?
3. Name some of the basic techniques associated with good legal writing.
4. What is the audience of a legal document?
5. What is the difference between an objective purpose and an adversarial purpose?
6. What is the IRAC method?
7. How can a paralegal effectively balance time constraints?
8. How does a writer go about organizing a legal document?
9. Name several different types of legal documents.
10. What are the three constraints of legal writing?

Exercises

1. Review the promissory note in Figure 11.5.
   a. Determine the purpose of the document and the audience.
   b. Edit out all the legalese and unnecessary words.
2. Obtain a copy of your state's appellate brief requirements and identify all the constraints and legal requirements for filing a brief with your state.
3. Proofread and correct the following paragraph:

   In view of the finding that that respondents conduct did no involve a corrupt motive or morale turpitude and that his disability is remedible, we fund it desireable that and effort be made to remedy the disability.
4. The following is a passage from a recent court decision. Rewrite the paragraph in plain English.

   Finally, Wife points to an oblique reference at the very end of the hearing on the expungement motion in which the court appears to have observed that Husband had the power to expunge the lis pendiens in his own hands, simply by posting a bond for what Wife thought was the amount below market for which the Balboa house was being sold. *Gale v. Superior Court,* 19 Cal. Rptr. 3d 554, 561 (Cal. App. 4 Dist. 2004).
5. Review *In Re Shepperson,* 674 A.2d 1273 (Vt. 1996), and respond to the following questions:
   a. Draft the issue in the case.
   b. What ethical issues are discussed in the case?
   c. What is the reasoning in the case?
6. The following is an excerpt from a legal document. Review the paragraph and redraft it.

   Records shall be uniformly destroyed on a manner determined by the Officer upon the expiration of the retention period. However, prior to the destruction of any records, the Officer shall institute a program of notification whereby the destruction schedule can be interrupted for cause by someone in a position of authority, including the Officer interrupt the destruction process.

7. The following is a provision in a state statute. Rewrite the section so that it is clear and in plain English.

   A food shall be deemed to be adulterated:

   (1) a. If it bears or contains any poisonous or deleterious substance which may render it injurious to health; but in case the substance is not an added substance the food shall not be considered adulterated under this paragraph if the quantity of such substance in such food does not ordinarily render it injurious to health. *Coffer v. Standard Brands, Inc.*, 30 N.C. App. 134, 226 S.E.2d 534 (1976).

8. The following letter is submitted to you for review by another paralegal. Revise, edit, and proofread it.

> Dear Mr. Martin:
>
> Please take notice that on the date of July 15, the warranty of fitness given by you in our Agreemento f July 10 for the purchase and sale of then (10) DVD players was breeched by you and your Company- that with in fifteen (159) days of recieving goods, severn (7 customers have brought back them DVD players because they are fefective.
>
> Unless you remedy thes problems within 10 (10) DAYS of reciept of this Letter, I will tak the appropriate legal acton.
>
> Very truely yours,

PORTFOLIO ASSIGNMENT

Your attorney has a summary judgment hearing next week and needs you to research the standards for that motion. He needs the leading cases on the matter by Friday. Copy and brief the cases on the matter. Draft an outline for the brief your supervising attorney will prepare for the hearing. (Use the techniques learned in the previous chapters. Note: Use your jurisdiction's cases for this assignment.)

Quick Quiz True/False Answers

Page 360	Page 367
1. True	1. True
2. False	2. True
3. True	3. False
4. False	4. True
5. False	5. True

Chapter 12

The Mechanics of Construction

After completing this chapter, you will be able to:

- Set apart a parenthetical phrase.
- Employ commas to provide clarity.
- Identify two methods of combining the clauses of a compound sentence.
- Inject certainty into a series with semicolons.
- Format a block quotation.
- Avoid common spelling and grammar mistakes.
- Learn to distinguish between active and passive voice.
- Distinguish simple, complex, and compound sentences.
- Eliminate sentence fragments and run-ons.
- Draft a paragraph with a topic sentence, a body, and transitional language.

Recall your grammar school days when you thought you learned all you needed to know about the topics of spelling, grammar, and punctuation. Well, they're back! You cannot be an effective legal writer and communicator unless you know and understand the rules of grammar and punctuation. Hopefully, this chapter will be a review of the lessons of the past, but with a twist. The rules of grammar and punctuation in this chapter focus on the nuances used in legal writing, although the basics will be addressed as well. Mastering the basics will provide the foundation for your legal writing. Pay close attention to the practice tips provided and the examples. As painful as spelling, grammar, and punctuation are to learn, a poorly presented document reflects on your standards. So, impress your supervising attorney with your level of professionalism.

CASE FACT PATTERN

You have attended a deposition with your supervising attorney, taking notes on the questions posed and testimony given. Your notes reflect the rapid-fire context—scribbled sentence fragments, abbreviations, and jottings to jog your memory.

Afterward your supervising attorney informs you that, since that transcript is not expected for three weeks, she would like a summary of the deposition. She asks that you translate your notes into a written memorandum.

As you sit at your desk with your notes, you begin to ponder the basic principles of writing—words as the bricks of which a sentence is built, rules as the mortar by which it is held together. Words and rules—language and grammar—provide the foundation from which good writing ascends.

B.C. Johnny Hart

Source: By permission of John L. Hart FLP and Creators Syndicate, Inc.

PUNCTUATION

We affect the meaning of spoken language all the time—with the tone of our voice, by hesitating or speeding up, with facial expressions, hand movements, and the subtleties of body language. All these techniques are physical—and thus unavailable to writers. The writer must learn to re-create in the mind of the reader the impressions left by these embellishments. One way to accomplish this is by the artful use of punctuation. Let's consider some of its more significant aspects.

The Comma

comma
Punctuation used to re-create verbal pauses.

Commas re-create verbal pauses. They separate distinct concepts and eliminate confusion, enabling the writer to establish a rhythm and maintain clarity. Commas often travel in pairs. They surround and set off phrases, as with the parenthetical phrase in Example 12.1.

Example 12.1 Use of Commas

The plaintiff, who performed every act required of her by the terms of the contract, is seeking damages from the defendant.

parenthetical phrase
A phrase that supplements or adds information to a complete thought.

The phrase set apart between commas could have been placed within parentheses, hence the term **parenthetical phrase.** Parenthetical phrases are often placed between commas, although it is not mandatory, as Example 12.2 shows.

Example 12.2 Use of Commas in Parenthetical Phrase

Between commas:
The plaintiff, James Jones, is assisting in the investigation of his case.

Without commas:
The plaintiff James Jones is assisting in the investigation of his case.

Where the parenthetical is short, as with "James Jones," the choice of which to use is largely a matter of personal style. You seek a document that "flows" (more about flow in the next chapter) and must decide whether the commas advance fluidity or impede it. If the parenthetical is long, as in Example 12.1, it should be set off by commas. Remember that you may use two commas to set off a parenthetical, or none, but never use just one. Example 12.3 shows two incorrect uses of commas.

Example 12.3 Incorrect Use of Commas in Parenthetical Phrase

Incorrect:

The plaintiff, who performed every act required of her by the terms of the contract is seeking damages from the defendant.

The plaintiff who performed every act required of her by the terms of the contract, is seeking damages from the defendant.

How can you tell if a phrase is a parenthetical? One way is by reading the sentence without the phrase. If the sentence remains logical and grammatically correct, the phrase is likely a parenthetical. Parenthetical phrases supplement, or add information to, a thought that is already complete. Try reading the sentence in Example 12.1 without the parenthetical phrase—it is less informative, but grammatical and logically complete.

If a phrase is **restrictive** (specifying or restricting the element that it modifies), it is *not* parenthetical, and should not be set apart by commas, as Example 12.4 shows.

restrictive phrase
A phrase that specifies or restricts the application of something.

Example 12.4 Use of Commas in Restrictive Phrase

Correct:

Bankers who violate these statutes should go to jail.

Incorrect:

Bankers, who violate these statutes, should go to jail.

In the correct example, the phrase "who violate these statutes" specifies *which* bankers; it cannot be removed without changing the fundamental meaning of the sentence. The incorrect sentence creates the impression that *all* bankers violate the statutes (try reading it without the phrase).

We have noted that commas often travel in pairs. There are, of course, entirely proper sentences in which you will find only a single comma. A parenthetical, for example, may appear at the beginning of a sentence, as in Example 12.5.

Example 12.5 Parenthetical Phrase at Beginning of Sentence

Having performed every act required of him by the terms of the contract, the plaintiff is seeking damages from the defendant.

A single comma also is seen where a conjunction such as "but" or "and" joins two complete thoughts, as in Example 12.6.

Example 12.6 Use of Commas with Conjunction

The deposition transcript is lengthy, and its contents are fascinating.

or

Her eyesight is failing, but she heard the impact.

A common error in comma usage occurs when dealing with a series. There should be a comma after all but the last item in the series, as shown in Example 12.7.

PRACTICE TIP

Do not place a comma outside a closing quotation mark. "A comma belongs inside the quotation mark," she said.

Example 12.7 Use of Commas in Series

Correct:
The judge, jury, and prosecutor listened intently as defense counsel examined the witness.

Incorrect:
The judge, jury and prosecutor listened intently as defense counsel examined the witness.

This rule, however, does not necessarily apply to law firm names, something which, as a paralegal, you will be dealing with regularly, as in Example 12.8.

Example 12.8 Use of Commas in Law Firm Names

Correct:
Able, Baker & Charlie

Incorrect:
Able, Baker, & Charlie

There are many other specific rules governing the use of commas, some of the more important of which are set forth in Table 12.1. Once you have determined the message you intend, the comma can be a powerful means of avoiding confusion. As a paralegal drafting documents, you should be using commas to maximize clarity first, fluidity second.

The Semicolon

semicolon
A form of punctuation used to indicate a break in thought, though of a different sort than that indicated by a comma.

compound sentence
A sentence in which the clauses could stand separately, each ending with a period.

The **semicolon** is a close cousin of the comma. It is used to indicate a break in thought, though of a different sort than that indicated by a comma. Rather than merely separating two thoughts, a semicolon also suggests a relationship between the two—making it a useful tool for an attorney or paralegal trying to make a point.

Semicolons are often used to join the components of a **compound sentence.** A compound sentence is one in which the clauses could stand separately, each ending with a period. In addition to using a semicolon or a period, a third method of expressing such a compound is with a comma and a conjunction, as we saw in Example 12.6. In Example 12.9 we express the first sentence from Example 12.6 in these three different ways.

Example 12.9 Punctuation of Compound Sentences

With semicolon:
The deposition transcript is lengthy; its contents are fascinating.

As two sentences:
The deposition transcript is lengthy. Its contents are fascinating.

With conjunction and comma:
The deposition transcript is lengthy, and its contents are fascinating.

TABLE 12.1
Some Examples of Common Usage

Use Comma To:	Example:
Set apart transitional language	Indeed, the statute is applicable and controlling.
Set apart quotes	The defendant stated, "I'm innocent."
Indicate an omission	The defendant went to Florida; his brother, New Jersey. (omitted words: "went to")
Clarify a date or number	1,000,000 January 1, 2008
Set apart "yes" and "no"	Is the statute controlling? No, it is not.

In this instance the original choice, with comma and conjunction, is probably the best choice, because the writer probably intended to imply no relationship between the two clauses (*i.e.*, the length of the deposition is not what made it fascinating). Consider, however, the sentence in Example 12.10.

Example 12.10 Strategic Use of Semicolon

The defendant's blood alcohol level was twice the legal limit; his driving was erratic and led to the accident.

The use of the semicolon in this sentence implies the close relationship between the defendant's blood alcohol level and the erratic driving and subsequent accident. Although the two-sentence or comma–conjunction methods would convey the same information, the semicolon method conveys it with more force and is preferable.

A semicolon can also be useful in distinguishing separate elements in a series, particularly when commas are used in describing each individual element, as in Example 12.11.

Example 12.11 Use of Semicolon to Distinguish Separate Elements

Correct:
The witness identified defendant Jones, the butler; defendant Smith, the cook; and defendant Brown, the gardener.

Incorrect:
The witness identified defendant Jones, the butler, defendant Smith, the cook, and defendant Brown, the gardener.

The incorrect example would be correct if the witness had identified five separate people: (1) defendant Jones, (2) the butler, (3) defendant Smith, (4) the cook, and (5) defendant Brown (who was the gardener). However, if three witnesses were identified, the first sentence is clear and the second is confusing and misleading. Indeed, even if the second example were intended because there were five witnesses, it would still be preferable to separate all five by semicolons, so that confusion created by the lack of parallelism among the elements—some identified by name, some by occupation—would be eliminated.

The Colon

Colons have several purposes. They follow the salutation in a letter, are used in expressions of time (for example: 10:48 p.m.), and can lead into a specified list.

colon
A form of punctuation that joins together phrases or explanatory clauses or introduces a block quote.

Example 12.12 Colons Preceding a List

The statutory protection has three prerequisites: adequate notice, sufficient documentation, and a completed application.

Colons can also perform a function similar to a semicolon or period: joining together related phrases, as in this sentence. In general, a colon signifies a closer relationship than does a semicolon or a comma. Explanatory clauses are often preceded by a colon (for example, in Example 12.20 a colon could substitute for the dash). Colons commonly introduce a block quote or a short quotation, such as in Example 12.13 in the next section.

Quotations

The use of quoted materials adds support to memoranda, briefs, letters, and any other legal writing in which the writer is trying to build an argument. Failing to follow the rules with regard to quotation marks, however, may distract the reader and detract from the force of your position.

block quote
A quotation of fifty words or more that is single-spaced and indented in the legal document.

When using a quote, should you include it in the body of the document or set it aside as a **block quote?** Although the context, and your ear for rhythm, will often dictate the better choice, a good rule of thumb is that any quote longer than fifty words (generally about three to five lines) should be set apart. This fifty-word rule is incorporated into *A Uniform System of Citation (The Bluebook)* for briefs and other court documents.

If the block quote format is chosen, the quoted passage is indented and single-spaced. Quotation marks are omitted at the beginning and end, but interior quotation marks should be kept. The citation appears on the line immediately following, at the original left margin. An example is shown in Example 12.13.

Example 12.13 Block Quote

It has been said that the case of *Swift v. Tyson* is based upon a fallacy:

> [t]he fallacy underlying the rule declared in *Swift v. Tyson* is made clear by Mr. Justice Holmes. The doctrine rests upon the assumption that there is "a transcendental body of law outside of any particular state but obligatory within it . . . ," [and] that federal courts have the power to use their judgment as to what the rules of common law are . . . .

Erie Railroad v. Tompkins, 304 U.S. 64, 58 S. Ct. 817, 82 L. Ed. 1188 (1938), quoting from Holmes's dissent in *Black and White Taxicab and Transfer Co. v. Brown and Yellow Taxicab and Transfer Co.*, 276 U.S. 518, 533, 48 S. Ct. 404, 72 L. Ed. 681 (1928).

Note the use of brackets and ellipses (which we discuss further), as well as the use of a period to conclude the citation. Also note that the quote within the quote uses standard double quotation marks, since the outside quotation marks are omitted. If outside quotation marks are included, as when a quoted passage appears in the body of the text rather than in a separate block, the interior quotation marks would be single.

Example 12.14 Interior Quotation

The witness stated, "I heard the defendant shout, 'I didn't mean to kill her!'"

In addition to the standard purpose of attributing words to a specific source, quotation marks can also be used to indicate irony or sarcasm, or to identify or set apart a word or passage.

Example 12.15 Use of Quotation Marks to Indicate Purpose

Irony:
Defendant argues that plaintiff benefited from defendant's partial performance of the obligations of the contract, but this "benefit" is hardly what was intended by the contract or anticipated by the plaintiff.

Sarcasm:
The alleged "witness" was not even present at the scene of the accident.

Identification:
In this contract the word "deliver" means to place in the plaintiff's hands, not send to him in the mail.

Using quotation marks to identify a word or phrase is common and acceptable. Using them for an ironic or sarcastic purpose is generally inappropriate in documents filed with a court, and under any circumstances should be done only after careful reflection.

A common source of confusion with regard to quotation marks is whether concluding punctuation goes inside the final quotation mark, or outside. Table 12.2 lists the rules for different punctuation marks.

TABLE 12.2
Concluding Punctuation

Quotation Mark	Placement of Quotation Mark
The period:	A quotation mark appears *after* a period.
The comma:	A quotation mark appears *after* a comma.
The question mark:	A quotation mark appears *after* a question mark.
The semicolon:	A quotation mark appears *before* a semicolon.
The colon:	A quotation mark appears *before* a colon.

Parentheses, Brackets, and the Ellipsis

Clarity often demands grouping or special identification of text. This can be accomplished with punctuation: **parentheses** ( ) and brackets unite cohesive passages, **brackets** [ ] indicate changes or additions, and an **ellipsis** (...) indicates the elimination of text from an extended quote.

parentheses
A form of punctuation that unites cohesive passages.

brackets
A form of punctuation that indicates changes or additions.

ellipsis
A form of punctuation that indicates the elimination of text from an extended quote.

Parentheses are an alternative to the commas we used in Example 12.1, as shown in Example 12.16.

Example 12.16 Use of Parentheses

The plaintiff (who performed every act required of her by the terms of the contract) is seeking damages from the defendant.

The two examples, 12.1 and 12.16, are identical except that in 12.16 we've replaced the commas with parentheses. Since both are grammatically correct, how do you choose between parentheses and commas? In general, the closer the relationship between the parenthetical clause and the main sentence, the stronger the tendency is to favor the commas. If the relationship is slight, parentheses are the better choice. The relationship in Examples 12.1 and 12.16 probably justifies commas (it is the plaintiff's performance that entitles her to damages), whereas the sentence in Example 12.17 is better expressed with parentheses.

Example 12.17 Use of Parentheses

The plaintiff (who is eighty-five years old) is seeking damages from the defendant.

The choice is, in these instances, simply a matter of degree. When choosing a particular sentence construction, it is often wise to consider balance and variety in your document as a whole. The need for balance and variety or for parallel construction (discussed further in Chapter 13) will often dictate your choice where it would otherwise be a toss-up.

Some confusion may arise over using parentheses with other punctuation marks. As a general rule, you should leave in ending punctuation *within* the parentheses if the parentheses surround the entire sentence; with regard to the remainder of the sentence, punctuate it exactly as you would if the material contained within the parentheses were missing (this means the final punctuation mark should be outside the final parentheses, as you see at the end of this sentence).

In Example 12.13 we saw the word "and" in brackets. What do brackets signify? Generally speaking, brackets appearing in a quote identify some departure from the original text—in Example 12.13 the addition of "and" to the original text makes the quote grammatical without changing the meaning. Brackets are also often used to change capitalization in a quoted passage to conform to the sentence in which it appears, as in Example 12.18.

Example 12.18 Use of Brackets to Identify Departure from Text

The court noted that "[t]he fallacy underlying the rule in *Swift v. Tyson* is made clear by Mr. Justice Holmes."

PRACTICE TIP

Add a period to an ellipsis if the quote ends a sentence (. . . .).

Compare this to the block quote in Example 12.13, and note how the bracketed lowercase "t" here incorporates the quote into the flow of the sentence.

Brackets have other uses as well. They may be used as parentheses within parentheses, and are used to enclose the word "sic", a Latin term used to signify an error of spelling or usage in a quoted passage. For example, in *Kentucky Bar Association v. Brown,* 14 S.W.3d 916, 917 (Ky. 2000), the judge used [sic] because the attorney, Brown, misspelled the word "mandamus."

> *Brown "does admit that the Court of Appeals would have been better served if he had styled his brief as a "Writ of Mandamous [sic]."*

In addition, brackets can be used to insert editorial comments or explanations into quoted materials, as in Example 12.19.

Example 12.19 Use of Brackets to Insert Editorial Comment

The language of the will states, "Any member of the Jones family [there are four surviving members] alive at the time of my death shall be entitled to $1,000 from my estate."

PRACTICE TIP

Periods are regularly used in abbreviations such as "Ltd.," Inc.," or "LLC." (Note that an additional period does not follow an abbreviation at the end of a sentence.)

Another mark used to specially identify text is the ellipsis. Unlike brackets and parentheses, however, an ellipsis indicates the *omission* of text. It is formed by three dots (periods), as we saw in Example 12.13. Punctuation that precedes or follows the omitted text may be included or excluded, depending on the needs of the sentence (the comma, for example, was retained after the ellipsis in Example 12.13). A few simple rules govern the use of the ellipsis. First, there should be a space before the first dot, between each dot, and after the last dot. Second, when the words omitted follow a complete sentence, the sentence should end with the actual period, followed by the three spaced ellipsis points. Finally, when omitting a paragraph or more, the use of a line of dots is sometimes suggested (each spaced several spaces apart), although the three-dot device at the end of the last passage before the omission is also acceptable.

The ellipsis can be a valuable writing tool. Quotes are not always perfectly attuned to the context of your document. By judicious use of the ellipsis, you can eliminate extraneous passages and take your reader right to the heart of the matter. The judge in *In Re Marriage of Jackson,* 136 Cal. App. 4th 980, 39 Cal. Rptr. 3d 365 (Cal. App. 2d Dist. 2006) used the ellipsis to focus on a portion of a statute cited in his opinion.

> *[I]t seems well settled . . . that when a statute authorizes prescribed procedure, and the court acts contrary to the authority conferred, it has exceeded its jurisdiction. . . .*

(Note: Use brackets when the omission of the quote is at the beginning.)

Hyphens and Dashes

hyphen
A form of punctuation used to draw together two or more words to form a single idea.

Hyphens are used to draw together two or more words to form a single idea—"up-to-date" is an example. As language evolves, accepted usage for such combinations often changes, and there is not always a consensus on proper form (for example: closeup/close-up; byproduct/by-product). In addition, although there are some standard rules (for example: hyphenate fractions such as one-half), they often have exceptions (don't hyphenate fractions when used as nouns, as in, "She wrote one half of the brief"). Perhaps it is best to forget the general rules about hyphens and, when in doubt, look it up in a dictionary. Hyphens are also used to divide words at the end of a line. The division must come between syllables, and it is wise to use a dictionary if the division is not obvious.

dash
A punctuation mark longer than a hyphen, which is used for limited purposes, such as separating the segments of a two-part sentence.

Dashes are longer than hyphens and are used for limited purposes. They can substitute for parentheses or parenthetical commas—as in this sentence—and can also be used to separate the segments of a two-part sentence, as in Example 12.20.

Example 12.20 Use of Dashes to Separate a Two-Part Sentence

His testimony was useless—biased, inconsistent, and obviously false.

Dashes are often used to indicate the word "to" when used with page numbers, dates, or other numerical references ("Earl Warren was chief justice during the 1953–1969 period").

The Period

The most common form of punctuation is the period. A period, of course, is used at the end of a sentence. A period is also used at the end of a list that follows an incomplete sentence. For instance:

The constraints in writing are

1. time;
2. length of document; and
3. format.

Question Marks and Exclamation Points

Question marks are used in the ordinary manner in legal writing, with one caveat (warning): Since the purpose of advocacy is to persuade, there is little room for rhetorical questions, hence little use for question marks in briefs or other documents filed with a court, other than formally stating the questions to be addressed.

Likewise, the **exclamation point** carries with it an air of informality that has little, if any, place in formal legal writing. Even if you find a certain fact extraordinary, it is better simply to state the fact than to emphasize it with an exclamation point.

The Apostrophe

Apostrophes arise primarily in two situations—contractions and possessives. As a general rule, contractions should be avoided in legal writing. "Cannot" is better than "can't"; "would not" than "wouldn't"; "it is" than "it's." (Incidentally, it is unforgivable to confuse "it's" with "its"—the former is always a contraction of "it is," the latter always a possessive, as in "Its deadline is next week.")

Possessives are, of course, unavoidable. The general rule is to form a possessive for a singular noun by adding an apostrophe and an *s.* For a plural noun, you can usually simply add an apostrophe. The rule is the same for proper names. Although there are exceptions (*e.g.,* men's, children's), in general you should follow this rule even when the result might seem odd.

Example 12.21 Use of Apostrophe in Possessives

Justice Stevens's opinion was lengthy.

SENTENCE CONSTRUCTION

A sentence uses words, punctuation, and rules of grammar to convey an idea. It is in the sentence that your writing begins to take form. Sentences should carry the reader through your document with a minimum of confusion. Let's turn now to the basics of sentence construction, and then focus on a few things to watch out for.

The Simple Sentence: Subject/Verb/Object

Every sentence has a subject and a verb (also called a *predicate*). On occasion the subject is physically absent but implicit from the context; such usages, although acceptable in literature, have no place in legal writing. The simplest sentence structure is subject/verb.

PRACTICE TIP

Whether to use "its" the possessive or "it's" the contraction is one of the most common errors in writing. Let's make it easy to avoid the mistake. Say the words "it is" in the sentence aloud. If the sentence does not make sense when you read it with the words "it is," then the sentence uses "its" the possessive—no apostrophe. It's that easy! (It is.) "The court's decisions ranked among it's most significant." Now, say "it is" in the sentence: "The court's decisions ranked among it is most significant." It doesn't make sense. Therefore, use "its" for the possessive and do not use an apostrophe.

exclamation point
A form of punctuation used to highlight something extraordinary.

apostrophe
A form of punctuation used to create a contraction or a possessive noun.

PRACTICE TIP

Keep the subject and verb close together. This practice lessens the confusion in conveying your information.

Example 12.22 Subject/Verb Sentence Structure

The plaintiff won.

The subject in the sentence in Example 12.22 is "The plaintiff" and the verb is "won." Most sentences also contain an object that identifies the receiver of the subject's action.

Example 12.23 Simple Sentence

The plaintiff won the trial.

The object in this sentence—which tells what the plaintiff won—is "the trial." This sentence format—subject/verb/object—is the most effective means of conveying ideas, and is known as the **simple sentence.** The further your writing departs from this level of simplicity, the weaker it may become.

simple sentence
A sentence that has a simple format—subject/verb/object.

modifiers
Words that describe a subject, verb, or object in a sentence.

Modifiers: Adjectives and Adverbs

The simple sentence may leave the reader asking questions. What kind of trial was it? How did the plaintiff win? To answer these questions, a writer can use **modifiers**—adjectives and adverbs—to add information. Adjectives modify nouns; adverbs modify other adverbs; and adverbs modify verbs, as in Example 12.24.

Example 12.24 Use of Modifiers

The plaintiff easily won the lengthy trial.

In Example 12.24, "easily" is an adverb describing how the trial was won, and "lengthy" is an adjective describing the trial itself.

Beginning writers often make the mistake of equating lengthy descriptions with good writing. They may think that the more adverbs and adjectives they use, the better their writing will be. This is a false assumption. It is possible to create clear images in the mind of the reader and evoke powerful responses using nothing more than subjects and verbs. Indeed, more often than not, modifiers confuse rather than clarify. The sentence in Example 12.24 may lead the reader to wonder—"lengthy" compared to what? "Easily" as opposed to what? Although it is unfair to evaluate a sentence out of context (perhaps "length" and "ease" are essential to the writer's point), in general you should minimize the use of modifiers.

The Complex Sentence: Clauses

Although the simple subject/verb/object format is generally best, there are often circumstances that justify a departure. The addition of a subordinate clause or clauses creates a **complex sentence,** as in Example 12.25.

complex sentence
A sentence that contains a subordinate clause or clauses in addition to the main clause.

Example 12.25 Complex Sentence

The plaintiff, who had spent a fortune in legal fees, won the trial.

In this sentence the phrase "who had spent a fortune in legal fees" is a **subordinate** (dependent) **clause** describing the subject of the sentence, and the rest of the sentence forms an **independent clause** that could stand on its own (*i.e.,* without the subordinate clause) as a complete sentence.

subordinate clause
A clause that cannot stand on its own as a complete sentence.

independent clause
A clause that can stand on its own as a complete sentence.

Variety in sentence structure tends to create a more readable document, and the use of clauses to combine ideas contained in a succession of simple sentences can improve your writing. Avoid the appearance of a choppy sentence by varying the sentence length. Your goal is to make your point in the simplest manner possible without becoming boring. Complex sentences give readers variety and interest.

The Compound Sentence

Compound sentences have two or more clauses, each of which is independent and could stand alone as a complete sentence. The clauses of a compound sentence are joined by either semicolons or conjunctions and commas to form a new sentence containing closely related ideas.

Example 12.26 Compound Sentences

Comma and conjunction:
The plaintiff won the trial, and her triumph was the result of hard work by her attorney.

Semicolon:
The plaintiff won the trial; her triumph was the result of hard work by her attorney.

In a compound sentence, the semicolon is not generally followed by a coordinate conjunction such as "and" or "but," but can be followed by certain subordinate conjunctions such as "however" or "although." A comma, on the other hand, can never be used to separate independent clauses without a conjunction.

Example 12.27 Separating Independent Clauses

Correct:
The defendant lost the trial; however, since he was thorough in his preparation and argued with eloquence, he should have no regrets.

The defendant lost the trial, but since he was thorough in his preparation and argued with eloquence, he should have no regrets.

Incorrect:
The defendant lost the trial; but since he was thorough in his preparation and argued with eloquence, he should have no regrets.

The defendant lost the trial, since he was thorough in his preparation and argued with eloquence, he should have no regrets.

run-on sentence
A sentence that contains two independent clauses that are not joined by a conjunction.

sentence fragment
A group of words that lacks necessary grammatical information, such as a verb, that would make it a complete sentence.

Compound sentences, together with simple and complex sentences, lend welcome variety to your writing.

The Run-on Sentence and the Sentence Fragment

Run-on sentences have too many clauses for one grammatical sentence, because the independent clauses are not joined by a coordinating conjunction. **Sentence fragments** have too few clauses. This is not the same as saying that run-ons are too long and fragments too short. A sentence can be too long or short stylistically, but grammatically correct. Run-ons and fragments are grammatically incorrect.

PRACTICE TIP

Watch your sentence length. The longer the sentence, the more likely the sentence is difficult to understand or grammatically incorrect. If a sentence runs more than three typed lines, it may be too long, a run-on, a fragment, or simply confusing. Try to create two sentences or eliminate unnecessary words.

Example 12.28 Run-ons and Fragments

Run-on sentence (incorrect):
The plaintiff won the trial was long.

Correct:
The plaintiff won. The trial was long.
The plaintiff won and the trial was long.

Sentence fragment (incorrect):
Testifying in great detail about the contract.

Correct:
The defendant is testifying in great detail about the contract.
The defendant was on the stand for two hours, testifying in great detail about the contract.

The run-on was eliminated by separating it into two sentences, or, alternatively, one grammatical sentence restructured to include two ideas. The fragment was corrected

A DAY IN THE LIFE OF A PARALEGAL

Attorneys are notorious for long, convoluted sentences. Most attorneys subscribe to the writing technique that more is better. Once again, you are presented with a legal document to review. It is a brief in support of a motion that your attorney has prepared. Although you have just been asked to proofread the document for typographical errors and citation form, you notice a number of sentences that are run-ons. They really detract from the argument, but you know your attorney hates to have his writing corrected or edited, especially by a paralegal. You are not sure what to do and how to handle the matter.

There are a number of ways to handle this situation. One is to do nothing and perform the tasks requested. (This should be unacceptable to you.) Another possibility is to offer suggested changes in a separate draft and let the attorney decide which language is preferred. Let the attorney know, through some method of highlighting the rewritten sentences, subtly offering alternative choices. And, there is the direct method. Discuss your suggested changes with your attorney. Any attorney who truly cares about the final work product should appreciate the suggestions especially if the changes enhance the quality of the legal document. Always use your best judgment!

CYBER TRIP

Review and locate on www.archives.gov/federal-register the writing sources suggested to use when drafting a document for a federal agency.

by identifying the subject who performed the action of "testifying." The second correct version is slightly more informative than the first. When choosing among alternative corrections, make sure the result is either a simple, complex, or compound sentence that expresses what the original, incorrect version intended.

Run-ons and fragments are indefensible in legal writing, where clarity is critically important. There is no excuse for allowing errors of sentence construction to muddle your point and confuse the reader.

Active Voice versus Passive Voice

In sentences, the subject and verb relate. One aspect of that relationship is known as "voice." One important element of voice is the active/passive voice. In **active voice,** the subject of the sentence performs the action; in **passive voice,** the subject of the sentence is the object of the action.

active voice
A verb form in which the subject of the sentence performs the action.

passive voice
A verb form in which the subject of the sentence is the object of the action.

Example 12.29 Active versus Passive Voice

Active voice:
The defendant violated the law.

Passive voice:
The law was violated by the defendant.

In the first example, the subject ("defendant") performed the action ("violated"), and the grammatical object ("the law") is also the object of the action. In the second example, "the law" remains the object of the action that the sentence describes, but grammatically it has taken the role of the subject.

Active voice is generally preferable to passive voice. Novice legal writers sometimes adopt passive voice, since it sounds formal, but this usually weakens the power of their words. It is generally better to describe the action than the result. Dull writing can often be enlivened by rewriting passive passages in the active voice.

Passive construction should not be entirely abandoned, however. If the point of the sentence focuses on the object, passive construction may be preferred. In Example 12.30, the active example would be preferable if the writer were discussing the habits of pedestrians, whereas the passive example would be preferable if the writer were discussing the difficulty of enforcing certain laws.

Example 12.30 Active/Passive Preference

Active voice:
Pedestrians have repeatedly violated the jaywalking law, with no enforcement action taken.

Passive voice:
The jaywalking law has been repeatedly violated by pedestrians, with no enforcement action taken.

Quick Quiz True/False Questions

1. A colon is often substituted for a comma.
2. The general rule is not to use a quotation for a block quote.
3. An ellipsis is used to omit language in a quotation.
4. A run-on sentence contains too few clauses.
5. In legal writing, attempt to write in the active voice.

PARAGRAPHING

A paragraph is more than just a group of sentences—it is a group of related sentences. A paragraph uses sentences to convey an idea, which is introduced in the **topic sentence,** usually the first sentence of the paragraph. Having introduced the idea, the paragraph develops it in the **body.** Then, having developed the idea, the paragraph performs a **transitional function** that facilitates orderly progression through the entire document. Let's look at each of these individual areas—topic sentence, body, and transition.

topic sentence
The first sentence of the paragraph, which introduces an idea.

body
The portion of a paragraph that contains the material that you claim supports the contention raised in the topic sentence.

transitional function
Moving the reader though the material in an orderly progression.

The Topic Sentence

The topic sentence of a paragraph is necessary because, quite simply, a paragraph must have a topic. Each sentence in a paragraph must be tied to that topic and must advance it in some way. Sentences must avoid digressions, and even "essential" digressions should be tied somehow to the purpose of the paragraph. Otherwise, the digression belongs in a paragraph of its own.

That being said, let us consider the topic sentence. It generally appears at the beginning of a paragraph and, particularly in legal writing, typically states a proposition, which is then supported in the remainder of the paragraph.

Example 12.31 Topic Sentence at Beginning of Paragraph

<u>The defendant's conduct with regard to the accident constituted negligence and possibly recklessness.</u> She was driving at a speed far beyond the speed limit. She was wearing neither glasses nor contact lenses, though her driver's license requires that she do so. She was weaving from lane to lane as a result of intoxication. Each of these offenses was a violation of her duty to drive with care, and therefore constitutes negligence. Taken together, they represent a blatant disregard for the rights of others that rises to the level of recklessness. In short, she was a threat to any driver unfortunate enough—as was plaintiff—to be on the same road.

The topic sentence in Example 12.31 is underlined and summarizes the argument to come. The sentences that follow support the point established by the topic sentence, culminating in the final two sentences, which repeat the point dramatically.

Topic sentences do not always appear as the first sentence in a paragraph. Sometimes they don't even appear at all—they may be implicit. But the writer who omits the topic sentence is asking a favor of the reader: to store the information provided, sentence by sentence, until the purpose is revealed and the information can be logically fitted into the overall argument. This requires patience on the part of the reader, which constitutes a risk on the part of the writer—a risk that the reader will lose interest before the purpose has been made plain. It may be a risk worth taking—the drama or tension created may add to the overall impact—but it remains a risk nonetheless. In Example 12.32 we see a paragraph with topic sentence at the end.

Example 12.32 Topic Sentence at End of Paragraph

The defendant was driving at a speed far beyond the speed limit. He was wearing neither glasses nor contact lenses, though his driver's license requires that he do so. He was weaving from lane to lane as a result of intoxication. <u>In short, his conduct at the time of the accident constituted negligence and possibly recklessness: He was a threat to any driver unfortunate enough, as was plaintiff, to be on the same road.</u>

The patience required of the reader, and the problems this might pose, should be immediately apparent. In general, then, place your topic sentences at the beginning of each paragraph—and when you depart from this structure, do so with care.

The Body

The body of the paragraph contains the material that you claim supports the contention raised in the topic sentence. In Example 12.31, for example, the sentences describing the defendant's excessive speed, failure to wear corrective lenses, and lane-weaving as a result of intoxication all support the assertion of the topic sentence that defendant was negligent and possibly reckless.

Paragraph development in legal writing often uses basic principles of argumentation. Having stated a proposition in the topic sentence, the writer endeavors to defend or support it in the succeeding sentences using one of several techniques. The proposition can be compared to similar situations; it can be contrasted with, or distinguished from, different situations; it can be explained or illustrated by a straightforward definition or example; it can be demonstrated logically, reasoning from basic principles; or it can be arrived at by some combination of these techniques, or related variants. Whatever technique you use, remember to tie your argument to the topic sentence. In Example 12.31, we show a topic sentence with various alternative follow-ups.

That there is relationship and overlap between and among these techniques is evident. The last two alternatives (explaining and reasoning), for example, are obviously closely related.

You should note that it is possible to use more than one technique in the same paragraph. For example, it is easy to imagine a paragraph that both compares analogous cases and distinguishes dissimilar cases, combining the methods of the first two alternatives.

Example 12.33 Topic Sentence with Follow-up

Topic sentence:
The defendant is not legally responsible for the injuries suffered by the plaintiff, who fell in defendant's store.

Compare and analogize:
Like the storekeeper in the case of *Jones v. Smith* (who was found to have used due care), she had placed large warning signs in prominent positions.

Contrast and distinguish:
Unlike the negligent storekeeper in *Brown v. Blue,* who allowed his employees to leave a freshly washed floor unattended and unidentified, the defendant stationed a clerk by the wet floor to warn customers, and provided a large sign that read "Caution: Wet Floor!"

Explain or illustrate:
Legal responsibility requires a showing of negligence, and negligence requires the existence of a duty owed to the injured party. Because plaintiff was a burglar trespassing on the premises after hours, no duty was owed.

YOU BE THE JUDGE

Grammar plays an important role in writing. There is no argument about that point. Imagine a pleading that is so grammatically offensive that the court orders the attorney to review grammar in a well-known writing textbook. As far-fetched as that may seem, that is exactly what the judge ordered in *Politico v. Promus Hotels, Inc.*, 184 F.R.D. 184 (E.D. N.Y. 1999). Clarity is an important component in writing, which the court recognized. As the court observed, when pleadings are unclear and verbose, it "places an unjustified burden on the court and the party who must respond to it because they are forced to select the relevant material from a mass of verbiage." *Id.* at 233. Was the judge's order appropriate? What is the standard for drafting a pleading? Identify the court's reasoning in reaching its decision.

Reason or demonstrate through logic:
Only the owner of the premises can be held liable under the facts as proven by plaintiff.

Defendant herself was not the owner of the premises in question; the building was owned by a corporation. Therefore defendant cannot be held responsible for the injuries suffered by the plaintiff.

The Closing Sentence

Along with the topic sentence and body, a paragraph should conclude with a **closing sentence.** This sentence summarizes the topic discussed in the body. Often that sentence is your transition into your next paragraph. Example 12.34 provides an example of a closing sentence.

closing sentence
A sentence at the end of a paragraph that summarizes the topic.

Example 12.34 A Closing Sentence

Mr. Goodwynn underwent surgery approximately three months after the automobile collision. The surgery left Mr. Goodwynn with over 300 stitches in and around his eye and forehead area that were removed over a six-month period. He was also left with a significant vision impairment. The nature of his injuries has adversely affected his earning capacity as his profession prior to his injuries was a data entry specialist. Due to the requirements of this type of work, he will never be able to engage in that profession again. <u>Consequently, because of the nature of his injuries, a significant portion of Mr. Goodwynn's damages are economic in nature.</u>

A cautionary note about the closing sentence is in order. All paragraphs do not require a closing sentence. Sometimes a group of paragraphs build to a conclusion, or the closing sentence may be implied. When you review and edit your work, you must decide whether you have communicated your point effectively.

TRANSITIONAL LANGUAGE

Transitional language provides signals to readers about the material they are reading. It reassures readers that there is a relationship between the writer's various points, and it serves to clarify that relationship. It is important, particularly in legal writing, that the reader follow, step-by-step, the progression of the argument. You can accomplish this by, quite simply, telling the reader what the argument is, as we discuss further in Chapter 13. It is this "telling" function that transitional language performs.

Example 12.35 Transitional Language

<u>Next</u>, we will consider the cases that are distinguishable.

<u>Since</u> the cases all support the plaintiff's position, the conclusion is inevitable.

<u>For example</u>, the plaintiff in *Jones v. Smith* was held liable on facts similar to those in the instant matter.

TABLE 12.3
Transitional Words and Phrases

Passing of Time	Contrast or Opinion	Introduction	Summary/ Conclusion	Addition
meanwhile	however	initially	therefore	furthermore
still	notwithstanding	to begin	accordingly	moreover
since	on the contrary	in order that (to)	hence	similarly
ultimately	in contrast	primarily	consequently	additionally
presently	although	first	in conclusion	in addition to
nevertheless		finally		

The transitional language used—"next," "since," and "for example"—ties each sentence to other sentences in the writing, signaling the reader that there is a connection. See Table 12.3 for other examples of transitional language.

The transitional function can also be performed by using parallel construction or repetition, as in Example 12.36.

Example 12.36 Parallel Construction or Repetition

The corporate statutes do not apply because the business is not a corporation; the partnership statutes do not apply because it is not a partnership; and the public utility statutes do not apply because it is not a public utility.

The business is not a corporation because stock has never been sold nor corporate filings completed.

In the first paragraph, the parallel construction using the phrase "do not apply" ties the paragraph together; in the second paragraph, the phrase "The business is not a corporation" repeats a phrase taken from the first paragraph, providing the reader with an implicit indication that the sentences to come will explain the proposition first stated in the first paragraph. Repetition and parallel construction are in many instances (as here) virtually identical concepts. We consider them further in the next chapter.

BASIC GRAMMAR AND SPELLING REMINDERS: THE TROUBLE SPOTS

Let's face it; most of us cringe when the subject of grammar or spelling comes up. We remember with disdain our school days when we sat through those painful lectures on "*i* before *e* except after *c*." Or, when we had to diagram a sentence—nightmares. We hoped that the subject would never rear its ugly head again. But, whether we like it or not, how we write and how we present our work product does matter. So, this section will be a "quick and dirty" review on grammar and spelling.

Common Spelling Mistakes

Plurals

The general rule in forming the plural of a noun is to add an "s." When a word ends in "y," normally you change the "y" to "i" and add "es." Examples are "winery" to "wineries"; "dictionary" to "dictionaries"; and "robbery" to "robberies."

Watch out for words ending in an "f " or "fe," such as "life," "strife," or "shelf." Change the "f " or "fe" to a "v" or "ve." Therefore, the plurals are lives, strives, and shelves. But not all follow that rule: The plural of "belief" is "beliefs." When in doubt, check a dictionary.

Many legal words present difficulties in transitioning from singular to plural. Who can remember if "memorandum" is singular or plural? These confounding problems

TABLE 12.4
Irregular Plural Forms of Commonly Used Terms

Singular	Plural	Incorrect No Matter What You Think!
memorandum	memoranda	memorandums
appendix	appendices	appendixes
index	indices	indexes
syllabus	syllabi	syllabuses
referendum	referenda	referendums

TABLE 12.5
Variations in Spelling

Common Spelling	Variation
canceled	cancelled
criticize	criticise
acknowledgment	acknowledgement
paid	payed
traveled	travelled
color	colour

often derive from Latin or Greek. The best advice is to learn the correct form by memorization or use a dictionary. Some common words you will use are provided in Table 12.4, but these are only some examples of the singular to plural form you will encounter.

Do You Speak English?

A common divide between the British and Americans is not only the way we say things, but how we spell words as well. How do you spell "judgment" or "judgement"? It depends on where you live. Pay close attention to some words that may appear correctly spelled but have an acceptable variation. Table 12.5 provides an example of variations in spelling.

Names

Spelling a client's or judge's name correctly seems like a basic courtesy. Nothing is more offensive or annoying than to have your name spelled incorrectly. Take the extra time to verify the correct spelling of the name of your client, a business, or a judge in a case. There is no louder cry of sloppiness or unprofessionalism than when something as simple as the spelling of someone's name is incorrect.

Capitalize Proper Names and Adjectives

There are some basic rules about when to capitalize a title. Capitalize a title when referring to a specific person or thing; for example, President Bill Clinton, Speaker of

YOU BE THE JUDGE

In *Henderson v. State,* 445 So.2d 1364 (Miss. 1984), the grammar in an indictment was pivotal to its legal sufficiency. Note that the judge in the case referred to the indictment as "grammatically atrocious." *Id.* at 1368. And, the judge in the case began the opinion with the words "[t]he case presents the question whether the rules of English grammar are part of the positive law of this state." *Id.* at 1365. The court castigated the prosecuting attorneys by citing William Shakespeare's *Macbeth*: "It cannot be gainsaid that all the perfumes of Arabia would not eviscerate the grammatical stench emanating from this indictment." *Id.* at 1367, note 1. That sentence catches your attention! Brief the facts and reasoning of the case. What was the court's holding and disposition in the case? Was the result in the case fair? Did the court find in favor of the plaintiff or defendant? Were the grammar errors in the indictment important to the holding? What is the basis of your response?

the House Nancy Pelosi, or Governor Edward Rendell. If referring to the subject generally, do not capitalize the word. For example:

1. The presidents of five major corporations participated in the symposium on global warming.
2. Most federal agencies, such as Federal Trade Commission and Securities and Exchange Commission, perform their regulatory functions through enforcement.
3. Congress passed a number of acts, which included the Fair Labor Standards Act.

CYBER TRIP

Find a Web site that offers grammar tips and pointers for writing legal documents.

Notice that in examples 2 and 3, the words "federal" and "acts" are used generally and are not capitalized.

The bigger question in legal writing is whether to capitalize words such as "plaintiff," "defendant," "court," "appellant," and "appellee." Rather than offer a definitive rule on the subject, the suggestion is to be consistent. If you capitalize the word "Plaintiff" in a legal document, continue capitalizing the word throughout the document. Check with your supervising attorney for his preference.

Grammar Hot Spots

Too often grammar plays a secondary role to getting the work done. Either we are rushed to complete an assignment or, even worse, we simply do not know the proper rules to follow. The end result, regardless of the reason, is poor execution of the basic rules of grammar. This text is not designed to rehash what you should already have learned; rather, this text will highlight common trouble spots encountered while preparing a legal document.

Subject and Verb Agreement

Nothing confuses the reader or undermines a sentence more quickly than failure to use the proper verb form. The verb must always agree with its subject. Consider, for example, the compound subject.

Example 12.37 Subject/Verb Agreement

Incorrect:
The traffic and weather was terrible on the day of the accident.

Correct:
The traffic and weather were terrible on the day of the accident.

Although both traffic and weather are singular, the subject of the sentence is "traffic *and* weather," which has two elements and hence requires a plural verb ("were").

Phrases introduced by certain subordinate conjunctions are not considered part of the subject, despite their obvious relation to the subject, and thus are not taken into consideration when determining verb form.

Example 12.38 Phrases Introduced by Subordinate Conjunctions

Correct:
The judge, as well as plaintiff's counsel, was stunned by the verdict.

Incorrect:
The judge, as well as plaintiff's counsel, were stunned by the verdict.

The subject is "judge" and the verb is "was"; "plaintiff's counsel" is not considered to be part of the subject.

A descriptive prepositional phrase that itself contains a noun can be misleading. Be sure that the verb form agrees with the subject, not the descriptive phrase's noun.

Example 12.39 Prepositional Phrases with Nouns

Incorrect:
The lineup of defendants were a sorry sight.

Correct:
The lineup of defendants was a sorry sight.

The first example is incorrect because the verb was made to agree with the noun "defendants," although that noun is not the subject of the sentence. In the correct example, the verb agrees with the true subject, "lineup." The noun "defendants" is part of the prepositional phrase "of defendants," which merely describes the lineup.

A question often arises with regard to verb usage when the subject is "jury." Is a jury a group of individuals, requiring a plural verb, or a single entity, requiring a singular verb? The answer is, it depends: when a jury is acting in unison, use the singular; when acting individually, use the plural.

Example 12.40 Verb Usage with "Jury"

Correct use of singular:
The jury was unanimous in its verdict of acquittal.

Correct use of plural:
The jury were hopelessly divided on the issue of the defendant's negligence.

The second example is accepted usage, despite the strange sound. It might be better to use the following clearer version.

Example 12.41 Correct Use of Plural

The jurors were hopelessly divided on the issue of the defendant's negligence.

Pronouns

Singular pronouns, such as "he," "she," and "it," use singular verbs. Similarly, plural pronouns, such as "them," "we," or "us," use plural verbs. An **indefinite pronoun** does not refer to a definite person or thing. More often than not, an indefinite pronoun refers to a single indefinite person or thing and uses a singular form of a verb.

indefinite pronoun
A pronoun that does not specify its object.

Everyone waits patiently for the verdict. (singular)
He waits patiently for the verdict. (singular)
They wait patiently for the verdict. (plural)
Each person waits patiently for the verdict. (singular)
All of the individuals wait patiently for the verdict. (plural)

Some examples of indefinite and definite pronouns are:

Indefinite Pronouns	Definite Pronouns
all	I
anybody	them
either	his
everybody	her
neither	it
someone	their

Prepositions

You have heard the statement time and time again: Never end a sentence with a proposition. Well, that may be the statement, but is it truly the rule? No. Grammar rules do permit ending a sentence with a preposition. The problem is that most do not believe the truth and continue to follow the myth. Even though it is not

ETHICS ALERT

The quality of the documents paralegals and attorneys produce is the benchmark of competency in the legal profession. Once a document is circulated in the public domain, it is judged by its sentence structure, word choice, and grammar. Words that do not say what you mean or reflect the client's position can raise the ire of a judge. *In Re Hawkins,* 502 N.W.2d 770 (Minn. 1993), conveys a court's concern over the effect of an attorney's representation in a case. The court observed:

> Hawkins' contention that because there has been "no harm," there is "no foul" is unacceptable. Moreover, harm has occurred: . . . administration of the law and the legal profession have been negatively affected by his conduct. Public confidence in the legal system is shaken when lawyers disregard the rules of court and when a lawyer's correspondence and legal documents are so filled with spelling, grammatical, and typographical errors that they are virtually incomprehensible. *Id.* at 771.

As a paralegal, you may not be disciplined for the quality of a court filing, but the concerns identified by the *Hawkins* court should awaken you to the importance of the work product you create. You may not be an "officer of the court" as an attorney, but your work can and will be judged as a reflection of your supervising attorney. You are an extension of the public confidence and you should be meticulous in the work you produce. Credibility is often all we have, and to lose that creates ineffectiveness. We all know that time constraints and deadlines place undue pressure on us. Cutting corners can lead to mistakes and mistakes can lead to ethical violations, or even worse, the lasting embarrassment a published decision has on an attorney's reputation. In a controversial opinion, a district court judge in Texas wrote these stinging words about the quality of legal writing and credibility of two attorneys: "Take heed and be suitably awed, oh boys and girls—the court was able to state the issue and its resolution in one paragraph . . . despite dozens of pages of gibberish from the parties to the contrary!" *Bradshaw v. Unity Marine Corporation, Inc.,* 147 F. Supp. 2d 668, 672 (S.D. Tex. 2001). Let this be a warning to us all—our reputation and credibility are all we have. Do not compromise them.

grammatically incorrect to end a sentence with a preposition, the better, and more acceptable, practice is to restructure a sentence that ends in a preposition. Therefore, forget the grammarians and the great World War II leader, Winston Churchill, who used those prepositions at the end of a sentence, and follow the crowd: don't end a sentence with a preposition.

Rewriting the sentence is often a simple solution. Sometimes coupling the preposition with the words "that" or "with" or "which" and moving the proposition before a phrase may solve the problem. Let's examine the following:

This style of writing is the kind I am accustomed to. (with preposition)

or

This style of writing is the kind to which I am accustomed. (without preposition)

That speech is just the manner of conduct that the First Amendment protects against. (with preposition)

or

That speech is just the manner of conduct against which the First Amendment protects. (without preposition)

Split Infinitives

Similar to using a preposition at the end of a sentence, splitting infinitives is not improper, but years of indoctrination have drummed the opposite into our heads. A split infinitive occurs when an adverb is placed between the word "to" and the verb. The better practice is to place the adverb after the verb.

THE E-FACTOR

Computers are a wonderful thing. They make our jobs easier and, in many instances, make us look better. One of the many attractions of word processing programs is the grammar check. Similar to the spell check feature, many programs offer grammar suggestions and corrections. The questionable sentence or word is underlined or set off from the rest of the text, alerting the user to the error. You can request an explanation of the error and change it, rework it, or ignore it—your choice. Undoubtedly, if a section of your work is highlighted, it would be imprudent to ignore it. Sometimes the correction is as simple as changing a period to a question mark; other times, an entire sentence or phrase may be highlighted. The prompts offer a detailed explanation of the problem and even suggest a rewritten version or, if a word is improperly used, the correct word choice.

But, sometimes the computer's grammar suggestion is just plain wrong. The suggestions for punctuation, spelling, plurals, and basic grammar are often bizarre. This should tell you to use the spell check with the knowledge that you know more than the computer. If a suggestion does not make any sense, don't use it. You are probably right and the computer is wrong. When the grammar check highlights a "sentence fragment," there is a high likelihood that the sentence can be written better. Take the hint and attempt to rework the sentence. Learn to use this computer program feature to enhance and perfect your work product, but always be mindful of the limitations.

Example 12.42 Split Infinitive

Split infinitive:
The better practice is to completely rewrite the sentence.

Corrected:
The better practice is to rewrite the sentence completely.

Quick Quiz True/False Questions

1. A topic sentence is always at the beginning of a paragraph.
2. A closing sentence summarizes the topic in a paragraph.
3. Always capitalize the words "Plaintiff" and "Defendant" when preparing a legal document.
4. Common grammar errors are splitting an infinitive and failing to have subject and verb agreement.
5. Never end a sentence with a preposition.

PRACTICAL CONSIDERATIONS: READ AND REVIEW

The use of proper punctuation, sentence structure, and paragraphing techniques enables you to communicate ideas clearly. After mastering these basics you can begin to apply more subtle and complicated techniques.

A first draft often contains inconsistencies that will distract the reader and undercut your arguments. The first step in eliminating these problems is to review your draft for errors in the basics. A slight revision to a basic element often leads to dramatic improvement. By eliminating misleading punctuation, or adding punctuation to clarify, you ensure that your sentences accurately convey your ideas. When you vary sentence structure and eliminate run-ons and fragments, your paragraphs combine these ideas into a coherent argument. Finally, by structuring your paragraphs into logical units with clearly defined transitions, you carry the reader along the path to your conclusion.

Summary

Punctuation embellishes writing and removes ambiguity. Commas can be used to set apart parenthetical phrases; semicolons can join the components of a compound sentence or clarify the elements in a list or series. Quotations add support to memoranda and briefs; parentheses, brackets, and ellipses group or identify special passages of text or omitted text. Hyphens draw words together, whereas dashes separate parenthetical clauses or disparate elements of a two-clause sentence. Colons can introduce quotes or lead into specified lists. Question marks and exclamation points are informal usages, and should be used sparingly in formal or legal writing (although question marks are acceptable for use in questions presented sections of memoranda or briefs). Apostrophes indicate contractions (although contractions are generally considered informal and should be avoided in legal writing) and possessives.

Simple sentences contain a subject and verb, and may contain an object and modifiers. Complex sentences contain a subordinate clause, and compound sentences contain at least two clauses that could stand alone as complete grammatical sentences. Simple sentences are preferable, although the need for variety (which prevents writing from becoming monotonous) suggests that complex and compound sentences be used as well. Excessive use of modifiers (adjectives and adverbs) undercuts your writing. A run-on sentence fails to join its component clauses grammatically; a sentence fragment lacks a subject or verb.

A paragraph needs a topic sentence to introduce its subject matter to the reader. The topic sentence is usually at the beginning of the paragraph. The body of the paragraph develops the subject matter introduced by the topic sentence. Transitional language helps guide the reader through the various paragraphs and sections of the document, carrying the reader smoothly from the beginning of the document to the end.

Pay close attention to spelling and grammatical form. In writing, your verbs and subjects should agree; pronouns should refer to a specific subject; and sentences should not end in a preposition.

The first step in eliminating inconsistencies in a first draft is to review the draft for errors in the basics—punctuation, sentence structure, and paragraphing.

Key Terms

active voice
apostrophe
block quote
body
brackets
closing sentence
colon
comma
complex sentence
compound sentence
dash
ellipsis
exclamation point
hyphen
indefinite pronoun
independent clause
modifiers
parenthetical phrase
parentheses
passive voice
restrictive phrase
run-on sentence
semicolon
sentence fragment
simple sentence
subordinate clause
topic sentence
transitional function

Review Questions

1. What is a parenthetical phrase, and how can it be set apart?
2. Describe one way in which commas can bring clarity to a sentence.
3. How can compound clauses be combined?
4. How do semicolons inject clarity into a series?
5. Briefly describe the format for a block quotation.
6. How are parentheses and brackets used to group passages in a sentence?

7. When should a dash be used to separate segments of a sentence?
8. Describe a simple sentence, a complex sentence, and a compound sentence.
9. What is a sentence fragment? What is a run-on sentence?
10. Describe the function of a topic sentence; define *body* in the context of paragraph structure; and explain what is meant by *transitional language.*

Exercises

1. Rewrite the following passage:
   The Supreme Court, held that a "subject to legal documentation" provision in a handwritten document executed by parties after they had agreed on material terms of sale did not establish, as a matter of law, that no sales agreement had been reached.
2. Edit and then proofread the following paragraph:
   I direct that my just and and legal debts and funneral expenses and all federal and state estate and inheratance taxes imposed upon my estate or any beneficiary therof including the portion of any such tax attributable to the proceeds of policies of insurance on my life or other property not constituting a part of my probate estate, be paid in fall out of my residuary estate as soon as convenient. This direction s not obligatory upon my Executrix and he is specifically given the right or renew and extend, in any form that she deems beast, any debt or charge existing at the time of my death, including any mortgage on my home and similarly my Executrix shall have the right and power to incur indebtedness and to borrow money for the purpose of paying any or all of the aforesaid debts, expenses and taxes.
3. Revise and edit the following run-on sentence:
   Data in computerized form is discoverable even if paper "hard copies" of the information have been produced, the producing party can be required to design a computer program to extract the data from its computerized business records.
4. Review the sentences and determine which is correct.
   a. The judge admonished the prosecutor and defense attorney who was distracting the jury from the facts of the case.

      -or-

      The judge admonished the prosecutor and defense attorney who were distracting the jury from the facts of the case.
   b. The judge, who often admonishes attorneys, believes his practice is appropriate.

      -or-

      The judge, who often admonishes attorneys, believe his practice is appropriate.
5. Correct the following passage:
   Patient infommation will not be given to any member of the clergy unless approval and written authorization is obtained from the patient or personnel represenative. Under the privacy rule the hospital only give a one word general discription of the patients condition which will not communicate specific medical inforamtion about the individual patient.
6. Correct the following sentences:
   a. The court state it's position succinctly "the motion is denied".
   b. Mr. Marshall will be finding his accommodation satisfactory.
   c. The judge jury and prosecutor was completely startled by the defense attorneys speech.
   d. Although its critical to the case the attorney failed to completely give the true facts of the case.

7. Review and revise the following paragraph:
After reviewing al the pleadings the underlining records the party arguments; pertinent caselaw and statutes and the other recommendations filed byt eh party's, this court remains of the opinion and view point that the decision is null and void eeven though the attorneys of record attempt to argue otherwise. Because this court has not found no case law directly on the point of the subject before this Coourt, the court will find for the Plaintiffs and not the defendant"s in this matter.
8. Revise the following:
The question is that is facing us with this entire labor crisis iw whether or not this problem will arrest itself (sic; or whether or not in fact lawmakers should now take note and take action to avert this insidious crisis. And I think and I believe that most of us are convincing that in fact something must be done post haste. The one and only singular factor that has not adequately been addressed during these entire crisis is the labor ciris themselves and how do we attempt to properly and adequately education the public.

PORTFOLIO ASSIGNMENT

Your attorney specializes in employment law and was asked to review a job description that his client South Place Hospital plans to post. Please review the job description and revise and edit the document.

Job Description

Title: Head Nurse

Salary: To be Determined

Closing: Until Position Filled

Responable for administration and clinical dutys of the Medical Unit.

Inspects area daily for compliance with policies and procedures and documentation patient teaching/education integrity of medical record.

Assured ongoing Performance Imporvement activites within the Unit./

Assisst with the I mplementing of the corrective action when determined necessary.

Monitors and evaluate the quality/appropriateness of patientcare based on CMS and Standards and other licensing agenies.

Responsible to the assigned (assistant vice president) for the Organization, coordination, and direction of the unit on a 24 (twenty four) hour base.

Maintains a safe comfortable and therapeutic environment for patient/families/relatives in accordance herewith Hospitial Standands.

Oversee the delivery of patientcare to both Medical and Other patients: direct and delegates patientcare assignments to nursing staff; based on acuteness of patientcare; staff availiability. Enhance professional growth, andf development, through participation in educational programs current literature inservice meetings and workshops;

EDUCATIONAL AND EXPERIENCE BSN or associate degree in nursing. Minimum five year(s) recent clinical experiences with demonstrated leadership skills. Current CPR and State License.

Interested individuals should contact Ms. Santiago, Nurse Recruter in her Nursing Office at ext. 6783

Quick Quiz True/False Answers

Page 385	Page 393
1. False	1. False
2. True	2. True
3. True	3. False
4. False	4. True
5. True	5. False

Chapter 13

Effective and Persuasive Legal Writing

After completing this chapter, you will be able to:

- Inject clarity and precision into your writing.
- Define rhythm, flow, and voice.
- Use similes and metaphors to make a colorful point.
- Avoid ambiguity and redundancy.
- Make subjects and verbs agree.
- Use the appropriate tone in your document.
- Compare and contrast periodic sentences and cumulative sentences.
- Differentiate active voice from passive voice, and know when to use each.
- Use structured enumeration to identify the items in a list.
- Develop your arguments logically.

How can you effectively communicate the client's legal position? The answer is through the use of writing techniques such as tone, word choice, and voice, to name a few. Your goal is to communicate your point to the reader, whether you are writing an objective or persuasive document. Don't hide your message in long, complicated sentences or repetitive word combinations. Make your point succinctly and simply and move on. Contrary to what you may think an attorney or judge wants to read, the simple, straightforward approach is preferred. Change the way you think and write, and success is right around the corner. Let's learn some of the "do's" and "don'ts" of legal writing.

CASE FACT PATTERN

Your supervising attorney has asked that you prepare a draft memorandum in support of a motion he will be filing with the trial court. You perform the necessary research and return to your office with pages of notes and a small pile of photocopied cases and statutes. You're now confident in your knowledge of punctuation, sentence structure, and paragraphing, but you want to bring more than just grammatical correctness to this memorandum—you want to prepare a document that will persuade the court. Now that you know the rules, you want to learn to evaluate words—to use language effectively to accomplish your purpose.

WRITING IS READING

A writer strings together words to be read. The audience may be merely the writer himself or herself, as with a diary; one other person, as with a letter; or many thousands, as with a newspaper article or book; but in all cases the words written are intended, ultimately, to be read.

Writing, then, as we noted in Chapter 4, is *reading.* This might seem simplistic. Of course writing is reading, you're saying to yourself. Everybody knows that—what's the big deal? The big deal is simply that, although most people understand the connection, they fail to make use of it to improve their writing.

The point might be clearer if stated this way: "Writing is *re*reading." Too many novice writers fail to understand that to create "good writing," they must reread what they've written—placing themselves in the position of the reader—and improve it through revision. Not even the best writers are above the constant need to refine and perfect their drafts.

This person we've referred to before—"the reader"—is the key to the whole writing process. Good writers get inside the reader's head. They analyze the quality of the words they've chosen by analyzing their impact upon the reader. Only after such analysis can they be sure that their point has been successfully conveyed.

The process of writing is perhaps best illustrated by a comparison. A sculptor starts with a block of granite, which he then chips and shapes until it matches his vision. A writer must *create* her block of granite, called a first draft. Only then can she go about the business of "chipping and shaping" her writing by rereading, **editing,** and revising to match her vision. Let's investigate this process.

editing
To delete, eliminate, or change the text of a legal document.

THE POSSIBILITIES OF LANGUAGE

In Chapter 11 we identified words as the bricks of good writing and rules as the mortar, but we confined our discussion to rules. In this section we turn to words to explore the possibilities of language.

Brevity, Clarity, and Precision

brevity
Strong, tight writing.

Brevity leads to strong, tight writing. To be brief is to be forceful. A writer must be stingy with words; he must be efficient and focused.

Brevity, of course, requires work. An old story is illustrative: When asked why he had composed such a long piece, a writer responded, "I didn't have time to make it shorter." (French author Blaise Pascal, *Lettres provinciales,* Lettre XIV.) Editing takes time; expressing complex concepts in concise packages requires perseverance.

Brevity does not imply the elimination of detail. The writer need not reduce the argument's scope. Rather, the argument must be stated succinctly. This is demonstrated in Example 13.1.

Example 13.1 Being Brief

Correct:
The defendant's negligence is established by his failure to maintain the subject premises and his failure to warn the plaintiff.

Incorrect:
The defendant's conduct was clearly wrong, in that the careless manner in which he maintained the subject premises, combined with the fact that he failed to issue a warning of any kind, certainly violated the duty that he owed to the plaintiff, and hence this court should find that the defendant was negligent.

The two examples convey the same message; the correct version, however, does so with force and brevity.

Clarity is likewise key. Good writing accurately conveys its intended message—no more, no less. Every passage less than clear is a passage over which the reader stumbles, hesitates, or worse, loses interest. The writer must make her message plain.

clarity
The ability to accurately convey the intended message to the reader.

Example 13.2 Being Clear

Correct:
Only on the second day of the trial did the witness testify about the accident.

On the second day of the trial, the witness testified only about the accident.

Incorrect:
The witness testified about the accident only on the second day of the trial.

The incorrect version is imprecise because it can be interpreted as having the meaning of either of the two correct versions.

Closely related to clarity is **precision.** Clarity requires that your writing be open to no more than one interpretation; precision requires that this one interpretation represent the point you seek to convey.

precision
Legal writing that clearly and definitely conveys the point of the document.

Example 13.3 Being Precise

Correct:
The testimony establishes that the defendant had the unusual habit of walking around his block at 3:00 a.m.

Incorrect:
The testimony establishes that the defendant had the unique habit of walking around his block at 3:00 a.m.

It is unlikely that the defendant is the only person ever to demonstrate such a habit (the most common meaning of the word *unique*), and even more unlikely that such a meaning was intended by the writer. Choose your words with care.

Brevity, clarity, and precision are essential characteristics of good writing. By analyzing and editing your writing to ensure that it is succinct, clear, and precise, you gain an added benefit—a deeper, clearer understanding of your own argument.

Voice

Writing **voice,** in general, is a concept that is easy to define but difficult to analyze. It can be defined as the sound heard in the mind of the reader, or the impression created by virtue of the words chosen. Analyzing this sound, the "voice," is challenging because a writer can only "hear" her own mind, not that of the reader.

voice
The sound heard in the mind of the reader, or the impression created by virtue of the words chosen.

Defined more loosely, voice is the poetic aspect of prose writing—the flow and rhythm, the tone, the lyrical quality of the words. Such considerations might seem out of place in legal writing, but not if viewed as means rather than ends. The point is not to create a document that reads like a poem; the point is first to determine the tone you seek, then use voice to help achieve such a tone.

In the last chapter, we touched upon **flow.** A document flows when the reader moves easily through the text from point to point and from argument to argument. The reader's expectations are fulfilled because the writer has provided the elements that the reader needs to understand the content. Establishing flow is the first element of voice.

flow
A quality within or characteristic of the text that moves the reader easily through the text from point to point.

How is flow established? By using effective transitions (which we've touched on before and will discuss further) and by employing logical development (which we also will discuss further), a writer creates a document that carries the reader along. Rereading is once again the key, followed by editing. Improving flow often requires "cutting and pasting": moving paragraphs around. Having placed raw information in a first draft, the writer sets about the task of logical ordering. It also helps to set aside your writing for a time, *then* reread it—the flaws are often readily apparent, since you are not so immersed in the details of your argument.

rhythm
A pattern of writing conveyed through word choice and word placement in the sentence.

Rhythm is an important element of voice as well. A sentence has, so to speak, peaks and valleys and plateaus. A good writer manipulates the terrain, so that major points sit atop the peaks. Suppose you want to emphasize the believable nature of the testimony of an anxious witness. Consider Example 13.4.

Example 13.4 Rhythm in Voice

Correct:
The witness, though nervous, was credible.

Incorrect:
The witness was credible, though nervous.

The high points in a sentence often come at the beginning and at the end, as in this simple example. In the incorrect version the reader is left with the lingering impression that the nervousness undercut the credibility. In the correct version, the impression left is that, despite the nervousness, the witness was credible.

Analysis of rhythm is not as easy as simply making your strongest points first and last in a sentence or paragraph, however. It requires an analysis of style in general, and style in writing is a concept difficult to pin down. Consider the following two examples, both grammatically correct, but one more effective than the other.

Example 13.5 Rhythm to Increase Impact

Ineffective:
The defendant's car had nonfunctional headlights, as well as a barely audible horn and insufficient brakes.

Effective:
The defendant's car had neither functional headlights, nor an audible horn, nor sufficient brakes.

The effective example conveys the same information, but does so with impact. Several techniques can be used to increase impact. In Example 13.5, the power of a series that lists three items is apparent. The rhythm inherent in a list of three is more effective than a series of two or four or any other number.

Example 13.6 Rhythm Inherent in Lists

Two-item series:
The defendant's car had neither functional headlights nor an audible horn.

Four-item series:
The defendant's car had neither functional headlights, nor an audible horn, nor sufficient brakes, nor adequate steering.

The list of two is acceptable, although its abrupt ending is a less powerful construction than a list of three. (Note that this analysis is in terms of *rhythm,* not the fact that the sheer evidentiary weight of three items is superior to two.) The list of four simply goes on too long. If it is essential to pass along all the information, the list of four might have been better stated as in Example 13.7.

Example 13.7 Four-Item List

The defendant's car had neither functional headlights, nor an audible horn, nor sufficient brakes. Indeed, it even lacked adequate steering.

The four-item sentence has been broken into two sentences, the first of which uses the rhythmic power of three.

The effective example from Example 13.5 also works well because it uses **parallel construction.** Parallel construction means repeating usages to make a point, to suggest either a connection or a contrast. Certain word combinations naturally fall into parallel structures—the "neither/nor" combination, for example, or the "former/latter" combination.

parallel construction
Repeating usages to make a point, to suggest either a connection or a contrast.

Example 13.8 Parallel Construction

The judge addressed the accused juvenile in her chambers, then, separately, the juvenile's parents. To the former, she urged the need for maturity; to the latter, the need for discipline.

Parallel construction in Example 13.8 and in the effective sentence from Example 13.5 requires that grammatical usage be consistent. Compare the two examples in Example 13.9.

Example 13.9 Agreement in Parallel Construction

Correct:
Legal writers should communicate clearly, concisely, and effectively.

Incorrect:
Legal writers should communicate in a clear manner, concisely, and be effective.

In the correct example, all three modifiers are adverbs relating back to and agreeing with the verb "communicate." In the incorrect example, the relationship and agreement are muddled. Novice writers often shy away from parallel construction, believing that variety is always better than parallelism. Don't make this mistake—parallel construction has impact.

Under other circumstances, however, variety is an important element of good writing. To give just one such example, consider the following: Although simple sentences (subject/verb/object) are often the most powerful, used exclusively they can lead to a monotonous, droning voice that actually drains the power from your words. A mixture of simple, complex, and compound sentences adds texture to the presentation of your thoughts. Thus, whereas variety should be avoided in parallel comparisons, it is desirable in other contexts.

We have noted that the point of establishing voice is not to make your document read like a poem, but rather to achieve the desired tone. But what is the desired tone? In legal writing, you generally seek to evoke a formal, assertive tone. To achieve such a tone, avoid light, familiar language; be straightforward without being ponderous. Your writing should be neither stuffy nor conversational. Stay away from the flip comment; keep your analysis sharp and your language focused.

A Word about Tone

Closely related to voice in legal writing is the concept of **tone.** Tone focuses on how the writer communicates a point of view. Is the document conveying a strong message? Is the document conveying information to a client? Is the document addressed to the court? Opposing counsel? Tone is established through word choice and sentence structure. For example, a friendly closing is

tone
The way the writer communicates a point of view.

If additional information is required, please do not hesitate to contact me.

Compare this to a closing communicating the importance of a matter, which takes on the following tone:

Your prompt attention to this matter is advised.

The last example leaves no question in the reader's mind about the tone of the letter or the importance of the matter.

Communicating with colleagues, especially through e-mail, requires attention to tone. Observe the tone in the following e-mail:

I received your request to meet regarding the contract issue. The only time I can meet is at 3 p.m. tomorrow. The meeting must start on time since I have a court hearing to prepare for the next day. If you are not there, I will assume you have resolved the matter.

The tone is matter-of-fact. This tone may or may not offend the reader who requested the meeting.

A better, more diplomatic, approach is

I received your request to meet regarding the contract issue. My schedule is tight as I am preparing for a hearing for tomorrow. I do have some time at 3 p.m. if your schedule permits. Otherwise, we can meet after the hearing or early next week. Let me know what works for you.

The second example responds to the same request but in a less offensive tone. Better word choice conveys the message without angering the reader. The words and phrases you choose set the tone of your document.

Often tone is set by the type of legal document you are drafting. A letter may be friendly or tough; a memorandum may be objective or persuasive, depending on the audience. In a brief to the court, your tone is more formal and persuasive. Choose words and phrases that assert the client's position in a clear, concise manner. However, tone in a formal document should avoid the "first person" reference and personal opinions. Nothing is more annoying to a judge than a "preachy" personalized tone.

Writing in the first person often is expected when writing or e-mailing a client. You want to make personal references, as writing in the third person may be construed as cold or pompous. Writing in the first or third person is discussed later in this chapter. Unless your firm does not want to continue representing a client, use a conversational tone in communications relying on longer sentences rather than short, clipped sentences exhibiting a no-nonsense approach. Of course this approach depends on the message you or your supervising attorney are conveying. You may intentionally choose a tone that is direct and to the point for a reason. The point is: know what you want to say; how you want to say it; and who you are saying it to (or, to whom you are saying it!).

Contractions—You Can't Say "Can't"

Do not use contractions in formal legal writing. The tone is too informal and familiar. The legal documents you will be drafting require precision and professionalism. Contractions do not convey that message. However, in a divorce proceeding a California appellate judge was frustrated at a party's lack of understanding of the appellate process after granting the relief requested. In a footnote, Justice Sills expressed the following toward one of the parties:

> *[T]he fact that an appellate court doesn't mention that a litigant didn't raise an argument doesn't mean it wasn't raised, and can't be asserted later if the procedural circumstances warrant.* Gale v. Superior Court, *122 Cal. App. 4th 1388, 1399 note 7, 19 Cal. Rptr. 3d 554, 561 (Cal. App. 4th Dist. 2004).*

Sometimes contractions do make a point and convey a tone.

simile
A direct comparison of dissimilar objects, for the purpose of emphasizing a common characteristic.

metaphor
A figure of speech that links dissimilar objects but is more powerful than a simile in that it equates, rather than compares, the objects.

Similes and Metaphors

Similes and metaphors are figures of speech useful to legal writers. A **simile** is a direct comparison of dissimilar objects, for the purpose of emphasizing a common characteristic. A **metaphor** also links dissimilar objects, but it is more powerful than a simile in that it equates, rather than compares, the objects.

Example 13.10 Simile and Metaphor

Simile:
A good simile is like a good after-dinner speech: short and to the point.

Metaphor:
Metaphors are valuable weapons in the legal writer's arsenal.

When using metaphors, be careful of that entertaining but ineffective species, the mixed metaphor.

Example 13.11 Mixed Metaphor

Metaphors are valuable tools in the legal writer's arsenal.

Until soldiers shower their enemies with hammers and screwdrivers, tools are not to be found in an arsenal! Used selectively, metaphors and similes make a vivid impression in the mind of the reader. Be wary, however, of overuse, which can erode an otherwise effective argument.

PITFALLS IN LANGUAGE

Language presents potential problems, as well as possibilities. When drafting legal documents, there are several pitfalls to avoid.

Ambiguity

Ambiguity exists when a writer has failed in the obligation to provide precision and clarity. In the law, as in perhaps no other subject area, ambiguity can have devastating consequences. At best, ambiguity creates hardships and confusion for the reader; at worst, it can adversely affect your client's essential rights. The legal writer's words must convey her intended message—no more, no less. Consider the following example.

ambiguity
Lack of precision and clarity.

Example 13.12 Pronoun Ambiguity

Neither plaintiff nor defendant knew he had executed the contract without authority.

The sentence in Example 13.12 is ambiguous because the reader is left wondering: Who is "he"? Was it the plaintiff who had executed the contract without authority? Was it the defendant? Did *both* plaintiff and defendant unknowingly execute the contract without authority? Were both plaintiff and defendant unaware that some third party had executed the contract without authority? Because she is left wondering, the reader's inquiry is interrupted and perhaps inhibited. She loses the point of the argument, and she may abandon it altogether. Although the broader context from which this sentence was drawn may clear up some of the confusion, it might have been better stated in one of the alternatives shown in Example 13.13.

Example 13.12 provides an example of **pronoun ambiguity.** Pronoun ambiguity results from an unclear indication about the noun to which the pronoun refers back—in Example 13.12, the pronoun "he."

pronoun ambiguity
Lack of clarity that results from an unclear indication about the noun to which a pronoun refers.

Another form of ambiguity arises when the placement of a modifying clause obscures the object of the modification.

Example 13.13 Unambiguous Alternative

Alternative 1:
Neither plaintiff nor defendant knew that the plaintiff had executed the contract without authority.

Alternative 2:
Neither plaintiff nor defendant knew that the plaintiff's agent had executed the contract without authority.

Alternative 3:
Both plaintiff and defendant were unaware that each had executed the contract without authority.

Example 13.14 Object Ambiguity

The testimony of the accounting expert led to the vindication of the corporation's accounting process as a result of its accuracy.

Was it the testimony in Example 13.14 that was accurate, or the accounting process? Both, we hope, but you see the problem. The placement of the clause obscures the reference of the pronoun "its." Two alternatives appear in Example 13.15.

Example 13.15 Unambiguous Alternative

The accurate testimony of the accounting expert vindicated the corporation's accounting process.

or

The accounting expert vindicated the corporation's accounting process by testifying to its accuracy.

Misplaced Modifiers

modifiers
Words that describe a subject, verb, or object in a sentence.

Along with pronoun ambiguity, misplaced **modifiers** also cause ambiguity in writing. Modifiers describe a subject, a verb, or an object in a sentence. When a modifier is misplaced, a sentence becomes confusing and may mislead the reader. Keep modifiers close to the word described, as shown in Example 13.16.

Example 13.16 Modifier

Correct:
The witness saw a police officer fire while chasing the shooter.

Incorrect:
Chasing the shooter, the witness saw a police officer fire. (Who was chasing the shooter? The witness or the police officer? The sentence is confusing.)

Ambiguity is a common problem that is easily avoided by word choice and careful placement of the modifiers in a sentence.

Sexism

Sexist references and gender-based differentiation, which reinforce sexual stereotypes, have no place in legal writing. Consider the question of sexism when choosing pronouns that relate back to occupational nouns. For example, you should not always use the pronoun "he" when referring to a judge, or "she" when referring to a paralegal. One solution to this problem is to use "he or she," although this can be awkward, particularly when used repeatedly. Another alternative is to make a conscious effort to vary or alternate the pronouns used. This latter alternative has been employed in this book. Another option is to make your original noun plural, enabling you to use a plural (hence gender-neutral) pronoun.

Example 13.17 Relating Back to Occupational Nouns

Gender-specific:
When a judge considers a brief, she reviews form as well as substance.

Gender-neutral:
When judges consider briefs, they review form as well as substance.

TABLE 13.1
Sexist Terminology and Gender-Neutral Alternatives

Sexist Terminology	Gender-Neutral Terminology
mankind	humanity, human race
man-made	hand-crafted, handmade, fabricated
man-power	work force, personnel
man-to-man	face-to-face
chairman	chair, chairperson, executive, businessperson
workers' compensation	workers' compensation
policeman	police officer
spokesman	spokesperson

The use of plurals eliminates the gender differentiation, but, like the "he or she" construction, can also create an awkward feel to the sentence. You will have to use your judgment about the best means of eliminating sexist references. Some examples are given in Table 13.1.

Politically Correct Terminology

Language references change. We might not refer to a group of individuals in the same way that we would have fifty years ago. An obvious goal in legal writing is precision, but another goal is not to offend your reader. The question is, which term should be used: elderly or senior citizen? Handicapped, disabled, or physically challenged? Gay, lesbian, or homosexual? Black or African American? Hispanic or Latino/Latina? Sometimes the law dictates your terminology; however, strive for bias-free language.

Attention should be given when referring to groups. Not all Arabs are Muslim; not all black people are Afro-American as some are from the Caribbean and are referred to as West Indians. Additionally, when the term "Indian" is used, are you referring to people from India or Native Americans? Be sensitive to inappropriate labels. Do attempt to be culturally sensitive in your writing. And, above all, when in doubt, ask.

Clichés, Slang, and Colloquialisms

Clichés are, by definition, overused figures of speech. Legal writing should be crisp and fresh, with points made in clear, logical language that avoids vague references and shopworn phrases. Example 13.18 lists a few of the many clichés to be avoided.

clichés
Overused figures of speech.

Example 13.18 Clichés

Slow as molasses
Kill two birds with one stone
Birds of a feather
The blind leading the blind

If a seasoned writer were to use a cliché to make a point, she would generally set off the cliché with quotation marks. However, after careful reflection, most such usages, although perhaps seeming clever at first, will be seen to be stylistically weak.

Example 13.19 Setting Off the Cliché

To say that defendants are "birds of a feather" is to commit an injustice to birds.

Similarly, **slang** should be avoided. Slang is common to all languages. New forms of expression develop daily and may become acceptable in daily communications. For example, rap, hip-hop, and Ebonics are important culturally, and knowing the terminology may help you communicate with a client. A judge may not know that "bling" is jewelry, but this meaning may be relevant in finding out facts in a case. Unless slang

slang
Informal expressions.

describes a client's circumstance, write in appropriate prose. You may need to define the slang, but do not use it in formal writing.

colloquialisms
Informal language used in everyday conversation.

Likewise, **colloquialisms** are informal phrases used in everyday conversation. For example, defendant did not "rip off" the plaintiff; damages are not "30,000 bucks." There is an appropriate word for "bucks," such as "dollars." Legal documents can be undermined by sloppy, colloquial usages. Stay away from colloquialisms unless they are part of a quote or critical to your facts.

Jargon

legal jargon
Legalese.

Legal jargon or legalese is useful if used in moderation, and if the audience understands it. We discussed some of the problems and benefits of legalese in Chapter 11. To summarize, if you can say it in plain English, say it that way; if your audience is sophisticated legal professionals (as with, for example, an appellate brief), use language that the audience expects and understands, including "terms of art"; and if you feel compelled to use legalese in a document intended for a layperson to read (for example, in a letter explaining a technical legal problem to a client), be sure to explain carefully any terms that the average person might not understand.

Redundancy and Verbosity

Just as ambiguity is the result when clarity and precision are disregarded, so are redundancy and verbosity the result when brevity is lost. That is a slightly verbose way of saying: "Get to the point! And don't repeat yourself!"

redundancy
The repeated use of the same point or concept.

verbosity
The use of an excessive number of words, or excessively complicated words, to make a point.

Redundancy exists when the writer has made the same point over and over. Say it *once.* Say it *forcefully,* but say it *once*. (Is this paragraph now redundant?) Don't underestimate the intelligence of the reader. You have to use your own judgment in particular instances, but generally speaking, repeated hammering on the same point can offend or bore the reader, and actually weaken an otherwise powerful argument.

Verbosity is simply the use of an excessive number of words, or excessively complicated words, to make a point. Some novice writers mistake verbosity for impressive analysis; in fact, it seems pompous and often indicates a lack of command of the subject matter. Keep your sentences as short as possible (given the need for variety) and use the simplest words you can: the defendant was "insensitive," not "obtuse"; the departure was "hasty," not "precipitate"; the road was "slippery," not "lubricious."

CYBER TRIP

Using www.archives.gov/federal-register, locate the listing of the suggested "words and expressions" to avoid in legal writing.

Quick Quiz True/False Questions

1. An important component of voice in legal writing is rhythm.
2. Tone focuses on how the writer communicates a point of view.
3. Contractions are appropriate in formal legal writing.
4. Misplaced modifiers and pronoun ambiguity cause ambiguity in legal writing.
5. When preparing a legal document, use as many colloquial expressions as possible.

YOU BE THE JUDGE

Imagine you are the paralegal on a case where the opposing counsel has filed over 4,000 pages of pleadings. The pleadings fill 18 volumes and require a cart to move them. Does this violate any court rules? The Fifth Circuit Court of Appeals thought so. Read *Gordon v. Green,* 602 F.2d 743 (5th Cir. 1979). What is the standard for filing a pleading? What was the court's disposition in the case? What message was the court sending by stating "Let Thy Speech Be Short, Comprehending Much In Few Words"? *Id.* at 744.

Elegant Variation and the Thesaurus

Somewhere in our early English classes in high school someone must have said: "Don't use the same word twice in a sentence." That couldn't be more wrong. How many times have you rushed to the thesaurus to find another word similar to the one just used in order to avoid repeating a word in a sentence? The problem is the word chosen from the thesaurus does not mean exactly what the word you just used meant. The meaning of the sentence changed; or worse yet, the word means nothing like the word you tried to replace. More embarrassing is choosing a different word that sounds good, but when asked, you have no idea of the meaning of the word. Let's use a simple example: the word "deposit."

Deposit your money in the bank.

We all understand the meaning of the word in this context. Now you intend to use the word again in the next sentence, but want to use a different word because you do not want to repeat yourself. Look up "deposit" in the thesaurus. The entry says

Deposit (submit to a bank) verb

Bank, commit, enter into an account, entrust, invest, keep an account, lay by, present money for safekeeping, put at interest, save. Legal Thesaurus, 4th Ed., William C. Burton (The McGraw-Hill Companies, 1980).

Review the preceding list of words. Do you want to entrust your money into the bank? Save? Commit? Account? No, you want to deposit money. No other word makes sense.

Of course, your goal is to write eloquently and with variety. Do not sacrifice variety for inaccuracy and confusion. It is one issue if you have writer's block and you need a slight nudge to get started. Use a thesaurus. If none of the words convey your point accurately, use the word you know. A thesaurus is not a book of synonyms. Use it sparingly.

Misused Words

A major pitfall in legal writing is misused words. You think what you said is accurate, but it is not. This section is a brief overview of some commonly misused words.

- "Whether." Many issues in briefs, memoranda, and case briefs begin with the words "whether or not. . . ." This use is redundant. The word "whether" implies "not" and is used alone. (This may be a tough sell, since most attorneys use the incorrect variation.)
- "Shall and may." The word "shall" implies mandatory and "may" implies permissive. Know the result you desire and that will determine the correct word.

A DAY IN THE LIFE OF A PARALEGAL

It is common for paralegals to draft standard form letters, such as a collection letter. Usually you are asked to follow the form and simply replace the specifics of one client's facts with another. The form collection letter your firm is using contains a number of redundancies, especially the last sentence of the letter, which states: "We are ready, willing and able to discuss the outstanding past due debt for which you have failed and continue to fail to pay after numerous attempts at collection." You believe the sentence can be simplified without losing the meaning of the sentence. Consequently, you rewrite the sentence to exclude the redundancies, word triplets, and verbosity. Your version of the closing is: "We are willing to discuss the outstanding debt, even though you have failed to respond to our attempts at collection." This sentence is better and conveys the same point. However, as a paralegal, do not rewrite a standard form letter unless you check with your supervising attorney. Sometimes there are reasons attorneys choose particular language. More importantly, some language may appear to be verbose and redundant, but an attorney wants the redundancy for effect. Your job is to suggest an alternative and let the attorney decide which language is best for the document.

CYBER TRIP

Find a sample will and promissory note on the Internet and identify the legal doublets and triplets; identify the legalese and determine whether a common word can be used as a substitute; and locate any terms of art in the documents.

- "Said" (used as an adjective). Replace this word with "this" or "the." Don't use it.
- "Affect" and "effect." "Affect" is a verb, not a noun. It means to influence. "Effect" is either a verb or a noun. As a verb, "effect" means to bring about a result; as noun, it means immediate result. For example: The judge affected the outcome by her comment. The effect of the strobe lights was stunning.
- "And/or." Avoid this construction. Revise the sentence to convey your point. Using and/or creates ambiguity. For example: The fire was caused by arson and/or negligence of the owner. How was the fire started? It is confusing. Revise the sentence as follows: The fire was caused by arson or negligence of the owner, but not both.
- "Etc." Although it is not technically incorrect, do not use the abbreviation for "etcetera" in legal writing.
- The abbreviations *"i.e."* and *"e.g."* The abbreviation *"i.e."* means "that is" or "namely." Limit use of this abbreviation to when you are referring back to what has already been stated. The abbreviation *"e.g."* means "for example" and is commonly used in legal writing with citation and case references.
- "Pled" or "pleaded." "Pled" should not be used. "The attorney pleaded (not pled) his case."
- "Irregardless." This is not a word. The word is "regardless."
- "Whose" and "who's." "Whose" is the possessive pronoun and refers to an object; "who's" is the contraction for "who is" "The court, whose jurisdiction is plenary, has the authority to review the appeal."
- "Principal" and "principle." "Principal" is a noun or an adjective. As a noun, a principal is the head of a school; as an adjective "principal" means highest authority, importance, or degree. "Principle" is a noun meaning settled rule, doctrine, or legal determination.
- "Site" and "cite." "Site" is a location; cite means "to reference." Most likely, you will use "cite" rather than "site" in your work.

PRACTICE TIP

Try not to misspell or misuse the word "counsel," which refers to an attorney; "council" is a group of people. (This is an embarrassing error.)

There are many more examples of misused words in legal writing. The preceding list provides some of the more commonly misused words and is intended only as a quick reference guide.

Writing Fallacies

Misconceptions abound in legal writing. Some of those misconceptions are as follows:

PRACTICE TIP

Do not write the number and then spell it out: $2,200 (two thousand two hundred dollars). Avoid the practice and either write the number or spell it out.

- *Do not begin a sentence with "And" or "But."* Why not? There are no grammatical or stylistic reasons to avoid beginning a sentence with "and" or "but." The key is variation. Do not begin too many sentences with "and" or "but"—that is simple common sense.
- *Always spell out numbers in legal writing.* It depends. Some rules suggest spelling numbers smaller than ten. Others suggest when a number recurs in the text, use numerals. Numbers that begin a sentence are spelled out; larger numbers, such as 10 million, use both numerals and words for clarity; and when referencing a decade, such as the 1960s, do not use an apostrophe—1960's is incorrect.
- *Use variations of the same word for effect.* Doublets and triplets, as they are called, are common in legal writing. Avoid them unless truly a term of art. Usually what

TABLE 13.2
Common Doublets and Triplets

Doublets	Triplets
each and every	give, devise, and bequeath
power and authority	promise, agree, and covenant
cease and desist	right, title, and interest
null and void	ready, willing, and able

TABLE 13.3
Commonly Used Complex Words

Complex Word	Simple Substitute
ameliorate	improve
augment	increase
hide	conceal
stop	discontinue
elucidate	explain
indebtedness	debt
kindly	please
reside	live
surmise	guess

can be stated in one word is sufficient. Attorneys refer to doublets and triplets from habit, and quite simply, because they think it is right. Why use the phrase "liens and encumbrances" when either word will get the point across? Another infamous use is "due and payable." Avoid doublets and triplets and find the best word for communicating your intent (see Table 13.2).

- *Wills are common documents that use doublets and triplets.* A sample of the beginning language in a will is: I give, devise, and bequeath to my wife all my right, title, and interest in all my personal and real property. A simpler way would be to say: I give to my wife all my interest in my personal and real property.
- *Choose complex words rather than the simpler equivalent.* Wrong. When writing, choose "use" over "utilize" or "send" over "forward." Communicate in clear terms; there is no need to show off unless, of course, the assignment requires a more formal tone, and even then simpler words convey as much depth as the complex ones. Table 13.3 offers substitutes for commonly used complex words.

Write in the Third Person

Legal documents are drafted toward a particular audience, as discussed in Chapter 11. The audience, whether judge, opposing counsel, or client, wants to know the law and how it applies to the case. Simply stated: No one cares what you think. Avoid writing in the first person ("I") or giving your opinion. Statements like "I think," "I believe," or "We submit" are inappropriate in legal writing. Let the law speak and not your personal opinions. Do not distract the reader from the strength of your position by interjecting your feelings.

A Word (or Two) about Plagiarism

You know the concept. Plagiarism is borrowing passages from someone else's work without acknowledging the source. Legal writing uses cases, statutes, and other sources to support a legal position. Although it's cumbersome, always cite your source of law. This practice is commonplace in legal writing. Your supervising attorney and judges expect legal sources to be cited in a legal document. In fact, the absence of cited material raises questions. Review the Ethics Alert section of this chapter for a case

YOU BE THE JUDGE

Courts have different views as to what constitutes plagiarism. In drafting documents and preparing briefs, there is often a fine line between what is acceptable and what is not. Review *Frith v. State,* 325 N.E.2d 186 (Ind. 1975) and *Federal Intermediate Credit v. Kentucky Bar Association,* 540 S.W.2d 14 (Ky. 1976), and determine whether these cases can be reconciled. Identify the facts of the cases. What facts distinguish *Frith* from *Federal Intermediate Credit*? Did both cases involve plagiarism allegations? How did each court rule?

where an attorney plagiarized an entire brief from a legal treatise and drew the wrath of the judge. Get in the habit of citing cases and statutes when preparing a memorandum or brief. Chapter 14 will address how to incorporate legal sources into your legal documents. When in doubt, use a source to support your proposition.

ETHICS ALERT

According to a number of case decisions, plagiarism reflects on an individual's level of honesty. Copying material verbatim and claiming it as your own is deceptive. In a recent case, *Iowa Supreme Court Board of Professional Ethics and Conduct v. Lane,* 642 N.W.2d 296 (Iowa 2002), an attorney's license was suspended for plagiarizing. Lane, an attorney, filed a brief plagiarized from a legal treatise without crediting the true author. The court, incensed by the attorney's conduct, believed that "[t]his plagiarism constituted, among other things, a misrepresentation to the court. An attorney may not engage in conduct involving dishonesty, fraud, deceit, or misrepresentation." *Id.* at 299. This language is strong and representative of how courts view this type of conduct. This type of behavior by attorneys only enhances the public mistrust of the legal profession. Adding further insult to the court, Lane requested attorney's fees for his "work." The court, in its stinging discourse, observed that

> [r]ather, the facts show Lane stole all eighteen pages of his legal argument from a single source. Then to justify his request for attorney fees for the eighty hours it took to "write" the brief, Lane submitted a list of over 200 legal sources to the court. In doing so, Lane attempted to have the court believe he researched and relied on each of these sources in writing the brief. These circumstances only support the conclusion Lane endeavored to deceive the court. *Id.* at 300.

Ouch! Obviously, when using legal sources to develop an argument in a brief, memorandum, or legal document, you must credit the source. Although this may seem elementary, attorneys and paralegals, in haste, may omit citing the legal source behind an argument. Don't be the victim of a judge's wrath. Credit all your legal sources or run the risk of a plagiarism charge.

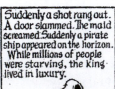

Source: Peanuts: © United Feature Syndicate, Inc.

Tell Them!

A writer begins with an advantage: He knows what he wants to say. But this knowledge can turn into a disadvantage. Why? The reason is simple—because the reader doesn't share the same foreknowledge. The reader doesn't know what the writer wants to say until he says it. And if a writer gets so caught up in the particulars of his argument that he loses touch with this fact, the quality of his writing begins to plummet. He will fail to provide the hints and signals that the reader needs and wants. His message will become obscure.

How do you do away with the obscurity? Often you can cure it by simply telling the reader what you're talking about. Even an excellent writer can become so wrapped up in the details of her argument that she fails to put them in proper perspective. The solution is to step back and review the overall argument for the reader's benefit.

Topic Sentences and Transitions

By rereading an obscure passage, summarizing its importance in your mind, then reintroducing it with the summary, you provide the introduction that the reader needs. In Example 13.20, note the improvement from the addition of a simple sentence that merely states, up front, the intended message.

Example 13.20 Providing an Introduction

Without a lead-in:
In *Jones v. Smith,* the plaintiff claimed that the will was invalid because one of the alleged witnesses had been blind at the time of the will's execution. The court found, however, that the witness had been blind in one eye only. In the present case before the court, the witness in question was blind in both eyes at the time of execution, was partially deaf as well, and hence could not have properly witnessed the testator's signature.

With an informative lead-in:
The case of *Jones v. Smith* is distinguishable, and does not support the plaintiff's contention that the will was properly witnessed. In *Jones v. Smith,* the plaintiff claimed that the will was invalid because one of the alleged witnesses had been blind at the time of the will's execution. The court found, however, that the witness had been blind in one eye only. In the present case before the court, the witness in question was blind in both eyes at the time of execution, was partially deaf as well, and hence could not have properly witnessed the testator's signature.

Simply by telling the reader, at the outset, what will be addressed, the whole passage becomes easier to understand.

This concept of telling the reader what to expect is directly related to the concept of the topic sentence, which we discussed in Chapter 12. Indeed, what we've done in Example 13.20 is nothing more than adding a topic sentence. Our approach in this subsection is different from our previous discussion of topic sentences and transitions, however. In the last chapter, we were building a paragraph from the ground up, that is, drafting. In this subsection, think about it from a different perspective—think about it as *troubleshooting.* You've written a document, and you've reread it, and you know something's wrong. You've corrected all the punctuation and grammatical errors, you've removed the clichés, you've been succinct—and still something's missing. What can it be?

Think back for a moment to our discussion, in Chapter 12 in Example 12.32, of a paragraph that holds back the topic sentence until the end. We noted that such paragraph structure requires patience on the part of the reader, and creates the risk that the reader will lose interest. Now imagine an entire *document* requiring such patience—it's inevitable that the reader will lose interest in such a document. A little of this technique might create useful tension, but a reader should not be kept waiting from beginning to end to find out the writer's point in a brief. Provide topic sentences and transitions to eliminate obscurity—in short, *tell them!*

topic sentence
The first sentence of the paragraph, which introduces an idea.

transition
The writer's ability to move the reader from paragraph to paragraph.

periodic sentence
A sentence that conveys the information at the end of the paragraph.

cumulative sentence
A sentence that conveys the information in a comprehensive manner.

The problem can exist even within an individual sentence. Some sentences, called **periodic sentences,** force the reader to store information until the end (analogous to the paragraph with topic sentence at the end). Contrast such a periodic sentence with the **cumulative sentences** in Example 13.21.

Example 13.21 Periodic and Cumulative Sentences

Periodic sentence:
The treasurer of the corporation, who was elected by unanimous consent of the board of directors, who had been publicly acclaimed by both the corporation's chief executive officer and the local business media, and who in fifteen years of service had never missed a single day of work, has been missing for three weeks, was last seen at the Los Angeles airport, and is believed to have flown to South America with a substantial amount of embezzled funds.

Cumulative sentences:
The treasurer of the corporation is believed to have flown to South America with a substantial amount of embezzled funds. Missing for three weeks and last seen at the Los Angeles airport, he had never missed a day of work in fifteen years of service. He had been elected by the unanimous consent of the board of directors, and had been publicly acclaimed by both the corporation's chief executive officer and the local business media.

The point is obvious. The periodic example makes the reader work, whereas the cumulative example requires the writer to work harder so that the reader need not.

When "something's missing," improving topic sentences and transitions to minimize the work the reader must do will often help cure the problem. But remember, even periodic sentences can have dramatic impact, used sparingly.

Example 13.22 Dramatic Impact of Periodic Sentence

The witness, unruffled in demeanor, untroubled by conscience, and unaffected by the presence of the victim's relatives, testified about her role in the murder.

Like so many other aspects of writing, the final decision on sentence struture is a judgment call. But now you have a foundation on which to base your judgment.

Structured Enumeration

structured enumeration
Identification of each point in a sentence sequentially.

Sequential points are often difficult to follow if not clearly labeled. **Structured enumeration,** which specifically identifies each point, can eliminate the difficulty. Again, the purpose is to tell the reader precisely what is meant.

Example 13.23 Structured Enumeration

Without structured enumeration:
The elements of negligence are all present here. The defendant owed a duty to the plaintiff, and the duty was breached. This breach was the proximate cause of the plaintiff's injury. The plaintiff suffered damage as a result.

With structured enumeration:
The elements of negligence are all present here. First, the defendant owed a duty to the plaintiff. Second, the duty was breached. Third, this breach was the proximate cause of the plaintiff's injury. Fourth, the plaintiff suffered damage as a result.

The structured enumeration makes the paragraph easier to follow and understand. Legal analysis often requires lists of complex factors; structured enumeration helps the reader comprehend such lists.

Take a Positive and Definitive Approach

Positive statements are almost always more forceful than negative ones.

Example 13.24 Negative/Positive Statements

Negative:
The club did not accept his application.

Positive:
The club rejected his application.

If you are trying to make a point, use the positive approach. If you are trying to de-emphasize a point, use the negative approach. For example, suppose the person whose application was rejected in the preceding example sued the club alleging racial discrimination. The club's counsel might use the following sentence in her statement of facts.

Example 13.25 Muting the Negative

Although the plaintiff was not accepted for membership in the club, the club was unbiased in reaching its decision.

This sentence mutes the impact of the rejection, which is the goal of the club's counsel. You should also be definitive when taking a position. There are few words more useless, for example, than "clearly."

Example 13.26 Being Definitive

Correct:
The defendant was negligent.

Incorrect:
The defendant was clearly negligent.

An assumption is built into the incorrect example—an assumption that there are factors to be weighed, and that, based upon these factors, a "clear" conclusion can be reached. Using the word "clearly" in this way actually invites the reader to challenge the main proposition, to weigh the evidence and determine for himself just how "clear" it is that defendant was negligent.

The correct example simply states a proposition: "the defendant was negligent." Period. It assumes no analysis; it simply provides the conclusion. This is the best way to present your points—forthrightly, with confidence, and without qualification. Vague, qualifying words such as "quite," "very," and "rather" have no place in legal writing. The road was not "very slippery," it was "slippery"; the defendant is not "unquestionably guilty," she is "guilty."

This is not to say that you should not support your conclusions with analysis. Such analysis is, of course, essential. By all means, point out the testimony that the road was slippery; by all means, point out that the fingerprints left on the gun were the defendant's. Nor is it to say that no one will challenge your conclusions if you state them forthrightly—they surely will. But in stating the propositions upon which your argument rests, don't undercut them by your own word usage. State them conclusively. You want your audience to know something—so *tell them!*

LOGICAL DEVELOPMENT

It takes more than bricks and mortar to build a house; there must be an architect as well. So it is with good writing: There must be central organizing principles within a document, so that the individual components work together to accomplish the overall objective. There must be structure and a plan.

Source: FOXTROT ©2006 Bill Amend. Reprinted with permission of UNIVERSAL PRESS SYNDICATE. All rights reserved.

The key to organization is logical development. Logical development is present in writing when each point follows naturally from its predecessor. You have learned that you can use topic sentences, transitions, and structured enumeration to ensure that the reader has a reasonable understanding of where the argument is going. In addition to these techniques, you should also analyze your document on a larger scale, as an organic whole.

Several methods can be used to achieve logical development.

IRAC Method

We discussed the IRAC method in Chapter 11. It involves (1) identifying the issue; (2) determining the rule of law; (3) applying the rule of law to the facts of your case; and (4) reaching a conclusion. This structure can be applied to a paragraph or to a series of paragraphs constituting a single argument. If you use the IRAC format, the development of each individual argument will be logical. If your documents involve multiple arguments, you have to order them according to one of the overriding principles that follow.

Strongest Argument First

Writers often place their strongest argument first. By opening with their strength, they can then build on this foundation. Weaker points may be buttressed by association.

Chronological Development

Sometimes arguments are best ordered chronologically, particularly when they fit in a complex factual context, or when the order of events is crucial to the analysis. For example, in a business dispute over the performance of an electronic component built by defendant and purchased by plaintiff, there may be many letters, test reports, and field results that touch upon the knowledge of the parties and the positions taken and the risks assumed by the parties. The legal arguments may build upon the chronological development. In such a case, chronological assessment is essential, particularly with regard to your statement of facts.

When ordering your arguments chronologically, you must take special care that your strongest argument does not get lost. One possible solution is a preliminary summary that emphasizes your important points, followed by the detailed chronological analysis.

outlining
A preliminary step in writing that provides a framework for the assignment.

Outlining and Subheading

Outlining has already been identified as a preliminary step in writing. By starting with an outline, the writer has a framework within which to work. The outline also

THE E-FACTOR

Electronic mail (e-mail) and text messaging are common methods of communication. By their nature, e-mail and text messaging are less formal than other written forms of communication. Do not let the informality fool you. Often the way you say something in an e-mail is completely different than the way you would communicate by letter. When e-mailing, you should think about the tone. To whom are you writing? A colleague? A client? Who could read the e-mail? Do not forget the lessons you have already learned when preparing to write. Who is my audience? What is the purpose of the communication? Will this e-mail be read by my supervising attorney or a partner in the law firm? In the work environment, take a more formal approach to e-mails. Assume the e-mail could be read by a co-worker. What impression is conveyed in the e-mail? Is the tone professional?

The same rules apply to text messaging in the work environment. Assume that your boss will read the text message.

E-mailing and text messaging are representative of the new way business is conducted. Compose your e-mail under the assumption that it is not private. Tone and word choice are important and should be suitable for viewing by anyone.

provides a shorthand format in which the larger argument can be grasped, and against which the logic of its development can be measured.

Subheadings are useful both as transition tools (more will be said about this in future chapters) and as a form of outline. By reviewing your subheadings, you can analyze how the elements of your argument fit into the organic whole. If the progression, as seen through the subheads, does not seem logical, then the body of the argument is probably not logically developed.

subheadings
Headings that identify the subpoints in an argument section.

Quick Quiz True/False Questions

1. Legal writing requires the use of the construction "and/or."
2. Never begin a sentence with the word "and" or "but."
3. In legal writing, it is preferred to use periodic sentences rather than cumulative sentences.
4. IRAC stands for identify, rules, application, and conclusion.
5. Subheadings in legal writing are useful only as transitions.

PRACTICAL CONSIDERATIONS: PRACTICE MAKES PERFECT . . . ALMOST

A novice writes a paragraph. He rereads it. It isn't good. It fails to make the point he wanted to make. The logic doesn't follow from beginning to end. Is he a bad writer?

He might think he is—but he isn't.

He isn't, at least, if he recognized the cardinal rule of writing: almost no one gets it right on the first try.

He isn't a bad writer if he recognizes the weaknesses in his paragraph and then takes out the tools of an editor—a pencil, eraser, scissors, and tape (or their word-processing equivalents)—to begin the task of improving it. Rereading, editing, revising, reworking, shifting paragraphs, substituting words, inserting explanations, deleting redundant elements, eliminating grammatical errors, crossing out, inserting, rereading, rereading, *rereading*—these are the elements that go into good writing.

Nothing you've learned about rules, style, design, and persuasiveness will be of any use if you fail to understand that writing is reading.

Nor is the process easy. "A writer is someone for whom writing is more difficult than it is for other people," said Thomas Mann. Writing is hard work—designed, ironically, to create the appearance of effortlessness and, in the case of legal writing, to persuade.

PRACTICE TIP

Your e-mails, which you might think are private and confidential, are the property of your employer. Think before you hit the "Send" button. Reread all your e-mails for content, tone, and, above all, professionalism. Additionally, distinguish between the "Reply" and the "Reply All" button; you may not want all recipients of the e-mail to receive your response.

Summary

A good writer recognizes that writing is reading and that she must reread what she has written, placing herself in the position of the reader, and improve it through revision.

Good writing requires brevity, clarity, and precision. Include necessary details, but be succinct. Accurately convey your intended message, no more and no less, and make sure the words you have chosen are open to no more than one interpretation. Writing voice is the "sound" that the reader hears in his mind; defined more loosely, it is the poetical or lyrical aspect of writing. Flow is established by combining logical development with a commitment to rereading and editing, so that the reader moves easily from point to point in the finished product. Rhythm in a sentence refers to the varying levels of emphasis of the words—the high points and the low points. Good sentence rhythm can be obtained by employing such techniques as placing the points you wish to emphasize at the beginning or end of a sentence, not hidden in the middle; recognizing the rhythmic power inherent in a series or list of three points; and using parallel construction to emphasize and clarify your points. Similes compare dissimilar objects; metaphors equate them. Both are useful figures of speech that a writer can employ to make a colorful point.

Legal writers must avoid ambiguity. Two things to look out for are pronoun ambiguity and unclear placement of modifying clauses. Sexist references have no place in legal writing, and can be eliminated by using plural forms, by using "he or she," or by alternating male and female pronouns. Misused words are common problems in legal writing. Pay close attention to your word choice in the assignments you prepare. Clichés and slang are overused or excessively informal usages, which are out of place in legal writing. A good writer makes sure verbs agree with their subjects, which requires a careful evaluation of which nouns constitute the subject and which perform some other function in the sentence. Never be redundant, since repetition can undercut, rather than emphasize, your strong points. Don't mistake verbosity for persuasive analysis; it is almost always better to keep your sentences short, your analysis brief, and your words simple.

Obscurity can often be cured simply by telling the reader what you are talking about. Use topic sentences and transitions to make your writing flow easily for the reader. Emphasize the active voice (in which the subject performs the action), but don't eliminate the passive voice entirely. It can be useful where the object of the action is the important point. Structured enumeration enables the reader to follow sequential points easily. Emphasize the strengths of your argument with positive language; de-emphasize the weaknesses by stating them in a negative manner. Always be definitive.

Use the IRAC method as a foundation for logical development. State your strongest arguments first, and use chronological development, preliminary outlining, and explanatory subheadings as devices to improve the manner in which your document develops, so that the reader more easily grasps your arguments.

Almost no one gets writing right on the first try. Reread, revise, and edit until you are satisfied that your points have been presented in the best manner possible.

Key Terms

ambiguity
brevity
clarity
clichés
colloquialisms
cumulative sentence
editing
flow

legal jargon
metaphor
modifiers
outlining
parallel construction
periodic sentence
precision
pronoun ambiguity
redundancy
rhythm
simile
slang
structured enumeration
subheadings
tone
topic sentence
transition
verbosity
voice

Review Questions

1. How can writing be made clear and precise?
2. What do rhythm, flow, and voice mean in the writing context?
3. How are similes and metaphors used?
4. How are ambiguity and redundancy avoided?
5. How are subjects and verbs made to agree?
6. Describe a simple method to eliminate obscurity in your writing.
7. Describe the difference between a periodic sentence and a cumulative sentence.
8. What type of language is inappropriate in a legal document?
9. What is structured enumeration?
10. How can arguments be logically developed?

Exercises

1. Rewrite the following passage from *Cooley v. Board of Wardens* (1851) using proper punctuation and plain English.

   That the power to regulate commerce includes the regulation of navigation, we consider settled. And when we look to the nature of the service performed by pilots, to the relations which that service and its compensations bear to navigation between the several States, and between the ports of the United States and foreign countries, we are brought to the conclusion, that the regulation of the qualifications of pilots, of the modes and times of offering and rendering their services, of the responsibilities which shall rest upon them, of the powers they shall possess, of the compensation they may demand, and of the penalties by which their rights and duties may be enforced, do constitute regulations of navigation, and consequently of commerce, within the just meaning of this clause of the Constitution.

2. Identify the trouble spots in sentence structure in the following passage from *Ranta v. McCarney* (North Dakota, 1986).

   We believe a fair reading of Section 27-1101 and *Christianson* indicate a preference by both the Legislature and our Court of furthering the strong policy consideration underlying the prohibition against the unauthorized practice of law that occurs in this State by barring compensation for any such activities.

3. Rewrite the following passage from *United States v. Nixon* (1974) by simplifying the sentences and word choice.

   [In this case] the traditional contempt avenue to immediate appeal is peculiarly inappropriate due to the unique setting in which the question arises. To require a President of the United States to place himself in the posture of disobeying an order of a court merely to trigger the procedural mechanism for review of the ruling would be unseemly, and would present an unnecessary occasion for constitutional confrontation between two branches of the Government. Similarly, a federal judge should not be placed in the posture of issuing a citation to a President simply in order to invoke the review. The issue whether a President can be cited for contempt could itself engender protracted litigation, and would further delay both review on the merits of his claim of privilege and the ultimate termination of the underlying criminal action for which his evidence is sought. These considerations lead us to conclude that the order of the District Court was an appel;able order. The appeal from that order was therefore properly "in" the Court of Appeals, and the case is now properly before this Court on the writ of certiorari before judgment.

4. Revise the following sentences to be gender neutral:
   a. The judge handed down his decision in the case.
   b. When the attorney files his brief with the court, he must file stamp it.
   c. The spokesman for the paralegal association held a regional meeting in Washington, D.C.
   d. The award for fellowship was presented to the policemen's auxiliary foundation.
5. Identify the mistakes in the following paragraph:

   I believe that the case completely represents the facts and circumstance that the employee violated the employment agreement. What the noncompete clause held was that the employee couldn't work in the industry for six months. Under the law and the cases at bar, the noncompetition agreement is binding and legal. In conclusion, I recommend completely to pursue all your available legal remedies including filing a lawsuit, request injunctive relief and ask for punitive damages.
6. Replace the following legal phrases with one word in plain English:
   a. give, devise, and bequeath
   b. each and every
   c. indemnify and hold harmless
   d. null and void
   e. shall and will
7. Correct the following sentences:
   a. The Chairman of the Board voted to terminate the contract by and between the contractor and the government of Florida.
   b. Finding the legislation unconstitutional, the court ordered the lower court to act accordingly.
   c. Don't send the correspondences out of the office until the corrections completely are made.
   d. Who's case is that in the conference room scattered all over the table.
   e. The messenger delivered the papers, filing the motions and was calling to confirm.
8. A colleague sends you the following e-mail:

   The boss wants to have a meeting on the dead baby case. . . . . again! He wants to talk about discovery and prepping for some depo's. When can you meet. I sure hope he doesn't want to meet on a Friday afternoon. . . . I do have a life! So, let me know. Katy

   Respond to the e-mail.

PORTFOLIO ASSIGNMENT

Your supervising attorney has a new client coming in tomorrow. Based on a brief telephone conversation, she believes the client needs a will. Changes may have occurred in the statute. You receive the following e-mail from the attorney:

Michael,

I have a new client interview tomorrow at 4 p.m. I need you to provide me with an update on the requirements in a will. I think there was a recent change—three witnesses to two. Not sure, but research the legal requirements for wills and e-mail me back by noon tomorrow as to your results. Also, see if there are some updated forms that eliminate some of that awful legalese. Thanks for your help.

Your attorney has asked you to perform three tasks:

- Research the legal requirements on wills in your jurisdiction
- Find updated examples of wills
- E-mail the findings back to the attorney

Prepare the assignment based upon your jurisdiction's law.

Quick Quiz True/False Answers

Page 406

1. True
2. True
3. False
4. True
5. False

Page 415

1. False
2. False
3. False
4. False
5. False

Chapter 14

Citations in Legal Writing

Previous chapters discussed the basics of legal research and writing. Now you are ready to incorporate these concepts into your legal writing. After completing this chapter, you will be able to:

- Understand the differences between *The Bluebook* and *ALWD*.
- Create a proper citation.
- Define a string citation.
- Incorporate citations into legal writing.
- Learn the rules for citing quotations in a legal document.
- Use short form citations.
- Differentiate between the different signals.
- Use *id.* as a short form citation.
- Cite different types of secondary sources properly.
- Verify the accuracy of citations cited in legal documents.

Learning how to research and mastering grammar and punctuation are essential to legal writing. Throughout this text the consequences of poor writing and poor research have been emphasized. You should be wondering how to guard against the mistakes of others. How do I integrate my research into the legal document I prepare? How do I cite a case in a brief? Is there a short form for citing legal authority? How do I cite a quote? All these questions, and more, are answered in this chapter. But before those questions are addressed, some groundwork must be laid, and a foundation set, for understanding the world of legal citations.

CASE FACT PATTERN

A deadline on a trial memorandum approaches. Your supervising attorney has most of the brief written, but was just called out of the office on a personal emergency. He asks you to complete the memorandum since you have worked closely with him on the case. At issue in the case is the interpretation of a statute. Your attorney has asked you to complete the research on the statutory interpretation, write the portion of the memorandum regarding that issue, and cite-check the remaining sections of the memorandum he completed. You have only three days to finish the assignment, which you know will be a challenge. You sit down at your desk, organize your thoughts, prepare a work plan, and begin the assignment.

Source: Peanuts: © United Feature Syndicate, Inc.

IN THE BEGINNING . . . *THE BLUEBOOK*

Remember we discussed *The Bluebook* in Chapter 3. Since 1926, *The Bluebook: A Uniform System of Citation* (18th ed. 2005) was *the* guide to citation form. It dominated the "world of citation form"—there was no other reference book. Albeit difficult and confusing to use, *The Bluebook* provides the accepted approach to citation form and format.

Every few years, *The Bluebook* publishes a new edition, changing, updating, and refining citation form. Sometimes the changes are helpful; other times not. In the sixteenth edition, the publishers changed the way to cite **signals.** Signals are words that introduce additional references to the legal authority cited. They are set off by words such as "see," "see also," and "accord." Although the changes do not seem earth-shattering to the nonacademic community, in the legal academic community it was a significant change. Unfortunately, the victims of all these "academic" changes are often us—the paralegal and practicing attorney. When using *The Bluebook,* especially for the first time, peruse its sections. The preface is particularly significant as it identifies the changes in that edition. More often than not, the changes will not affect your work, but check to be sure. The *Bluebook* format has changed, for the better, with new user-friendly sections.

signals
Words that introduce additional references to the legal authority cited, such as "see," "see also," and "accord."

The new format is as follows:

- **Quick Reference Guide:** The front and back pages of *The Bluebook* provide a "quick reference" guide to citation form in law review footnotes, court documents, and legal memoranda. The back pages are helpful in the practice environment.
- **Preface and Introduction:** The preface introduces the changes to that edition. In the eighteenth edition, the significant change noted is the addition of a section

titled "Bluepages." This section is a practical guide for legal professionals. Another significant addition is the attention to local citation rules. Other changes are always noted in the preface of each edition. The introduction defines the general content and structure of *The Bluebook.* This section discusses three major parts: the Bluepages, the system of citation, and the tables to be used with the citation rules.

- **Bluepages (new):** This section of *The Bluebook* is the newest and is the one you will rely upon in preparing your citations. It is straightforward and geared toward the practicing attorney. The Bluepages section presents a detailed overview and guide for citing all types of legal authority. This section provides examples and discusses all aspects of legal citation. Jurisdiction-specific rules and general style rules of citation are highlighted as well. Take the time to review this section before beginning an assignment.
- **Structure and Use of Citation:** This section is the heart of *The Bluebook* and provides the rules for citing all legal authority. Printed in the white pages of *The Bluebook,* detailed explanations of the rules of citation and style from the general to the specific are provided. Some of the information is geared toward law review articles; therefore, be sure the form you are using is for the correct legal document.
- **Tables:** The section on tables is identified by its blue-bordered pages. The nuances of both federal and state jurisdiction citation rules are noted here along with corresponding Web sites. Also included in this section are proper citation form for foreign jurisdictions, proper case name abbreviation, and periodical citation form.
- **Index:** At the end of *The Bluebook* is an extensive index to locate the information contained with it. The index distinguishes the pages referenced by different-colored ink: (1) black ink references instructions; (2) blue ink references examples.

The Bluebook remains the guide for legal citation, but lurching in the wings are challengers to its rules and form. Publishers of *The Bluebook* never anticipated that the changes to the sixteenth edition would invite a response challenging its dominance.

THE YOUNG UPSTART: *ALWD* CITATION MANUAL

The year was 2000. The twentieth century was coming to a close; Y2K was everyone's fear, and an academic rebellion began in the legal community regarding citation form—enter the *ALWD Citation Manual: A Professional System of Citation* (3d ed., Aspen Publishers, 2006). There are many commentaries hypothesizing what provoked the authors of the *ALWD Manual* to challenge *The Bluebook*. Some suggest the change in citing signals was the culprit; others suggest that the constant, often meritless, changes in form were the trigger. Whatever the reason, the *ALWD Manual* was a "wake-up" call that forced *The Bluebook* publishers to reevaluate their presentation and methodology of citation form. Suffice it to say, the *ALWD Manual* made citation form more accessible. What did *ALWD* accomplish? Simplicity. Directness. Approachability.

For the first time, *ALWD* communicated citation form in a clear, understandable manner. Complaints, from both practitioners and law students, continued because of *The Bluebook*'s difficulty. Tailored for the academician, *The Bluebook* met its challenger—a challenger like no other.

In the past, attempts were made to challenge *The Bluebook*'s authority without much success. (Ever hear of the Maroon book published by the University of Chicago? Probably not. That citation book found only a limited audience.) *ALWD* burst onto the legal market and has never looked back. Now in its third edition, *ALWD* is considered a more practical approach to citation form and a viable competitor for *The Bluebook*. *ALWD* introduces several new concepts:

- It explains citation form in everyday terminology.
- It gives examples of practical usage.
- It illustrates citation formats from all jurisdictions.
- It provides the practitioners' approach to citation form.

ALWD is divided into six parts and appendices, as follows:

- **Part 1, Introductory Material:** This section presents an overview of how to use the *ALWD Manual* and offers some practical word processing advice. Also provided in the introductory material is the organizational material within each part of the manual and a note about local citation rules.
- **Part 2, Citation Basics:** Primarily the "how to" of legal citation, this section discusses typeface, abbreviations, and other technical components of a citation. Format and style components are also highlighted. Among the more significant features of *ALWD* are its Sidebar sections. This feature reinforces important points made within the text and is a useful practice tool.
- **Part 3, Citing Specific Print Sources:** This section is the "guts" of the *ALWD Manual*. Continuing with the Sidebar references, this section also includes Fast Formats, which is a quick reference guide and summary of information contained within the subsection. Another important feature of the manual is its detail regarding punctuation and spacing within citations. Spaces are set off by a small, solid green triangle "▲" (shown here in black), and small, solid green circles "●" (also shown in black) denote the specific citation component. Once again, spend time reviewing this section with its special features.
- **Part 4, Electronic Sources:** *ALWD* devotes an entire section to online and electronic citation formats. Citing Westlaw and LexisNexis are discussed along with other electronic and Internet sources. The Sidebar and Fast Formats are included as well.
- **Part 5, Incorporating Citations into Documents:** In this section, *ALWD* provides explanation of how to integrate citations into legal documents. This section presents the fundamentals of citation placement and use, offering helpful hints.
- **Part 6, Quotations:** Underscoring the importance of quotations, *ALWD* devotes an entire section to them. Considerable time is spent delineating the subtleties of using quotations in legal writing.
- **Part 7, Appendices:** Extensive coverage of all jurisdictional nuances from court rules to abbreviations is provided in this section. Review your jurisdiction's requirements. The treatment of the federal and state court rules is quite extensive.
- **Index:** The index references rule numbers, not pages. Common terms are used for easy access to the material within the text.

Review the structure of the *ALWD* before using it. Even though it is more user-friendly, *ALWD* will introduce you to an unfamiliar world and language. Take the time to carefully peruse the sections and pages for a better understanding of its contents.

THE COMPETITION

ALWD teaches citation form, whereas *The Bluebook* assumes a certain level of familiarity with citation form. The end result is that *ALWD* and *The Bluebook* should be used together and are not mutually exclusive. Some jurisdictions have adopted *ALWD;*

TABLE 14.1
Differences between *The Bluebook* and *ALWD Manual*

Citation Format Topic	The Bluebook	ALWD Manual
United States as a party	Cite as United States (do not abbreviate)	Cite as U.S. (abbreviation accepted)
Use of apostrophes in abbreviation of names	Use apostrophes in name abbreviations: Int'l Gov't	Do not use apostrophes in name abbreviations: Intl Govt
Pinpoint citation	Use only the last two numbers of a reference: Pages 100-03	Use either the last two numbers of a referenced number or all numbers: Pages 100-03 or 100-103
Quotations	More than 50 words, single-space and indent	More than 50 words or more than four lines, single-space and indent
Parallel citations for U.S. Supreme Court	Do not cite parallel citations for U.S. Supreme Court cases	Permits parallel citations for U.S. Supreme Court cases
Information in parentheses for state courts	Provides different information for courts at the appeals level	Provides different information for courts at the appeals level

others remain loyal to *The Bluebook. ALWD* basically parallels *The Bluebook* form as much as possible unless "real life" practice dictates otherwise. For example, the first edition attempted to change the citation for the *Southern Reporter* from "So." to "S." Academic rebellion ensued. The second edition of *ALWD* reverted to the original form. The good news is that the *ALWD Manual*'s apparent wide acceptance forced *The Bluebook* publishers to revisit how they do things. As a result, *The Bluebook* is slowly becoming more accessible and more practice-driven.

The question on your mind should be "which form should I use?" The answer, as always, is "it depends." Your jurisdiction may dictate your format; your supervising attorney may dictate your format. Increasingly the *ALWD* is being taught in law schools and is being adopted by more and more jurisdictions. The *ALWD* Web site tracks the jurisdiction and law school adoptions. Visit the site at www.alwd.org. Also, visit *The Bluebook* site, www.legalbluebook.com, for helpful information as well. Additionally, there are differences between *The Bluebook* and *ALWD Manual*. Table 14.1 summarizes some of the noted differences.

THE OTHER GUIDES

There is a real upheaval in the world of citations. As mentioned in Chapter 3, the *Universal Citation Guide* is yet another citation form. Uniformity is the rule of the day and the American Bar Association (ABA) and American Association of Law Libraries (AALL) are leading the charge. They proposed a universal citation system or **neutral citation** system for adoption. This format departs from both *The Bluebook* and *ALWD* dramatically and is slowly being adopted by some jurisdictions. Approximately ten states, including Maine, Vermont, and Montana, have adopted a neutral citation system. But be careful, as adoption by a state court does not signify that the federal courts of the state adopted the neutral citation system as well. For example, the state of Montana adopted a neutral citation system whereas the Montana federal court system uses *The Bluebook* rules.

neutral citation
Uniform citation system that contains the name of the case, year of decision, court (postal code) abbreviation, opinion number, and paragraph pinpoint for references.

Characteristics of the universal citation system are as follows:

1. The name of the case
2. The year of the decision
3. The court abbreviation (The abbreviation for the state is the name as it appears in its postal [U.S. mail] abbreviation. For lower courts, it is the postal abbreviation along with an additional identifier.)
4. A sequentially assigned opinion number
5. A notation of the letter "U," if an opinion is unpublished or unreported
6. A paragraph number to identify quoted material (This rule is a major departure from present practice. Citation rules require the page number of the quoted material only.)

Will the universal citation concept be the rule and not the exception? Only time will tell. Check your jurisdiction to determine whether the universal system is adopted. A citation in the universal (neutral) format is shown in the following example:

Glidden v. Conley, 2003 VT 12

(Notice the case pages from *Glidden v. Conley* in Figure 14.1. The paragraphs are individually numbered. This corresponds to the neutral citation system format.)

The same citation in *The Bluebook* and *ALWD* format is as follows:

Glidden v. Conley, 2003 VT 12, 820 A.2d 197

CYBER TRIP

Check www.alwd.org and www.legalbluebook.com for any new changes to the rules of citation. Note any changes from the present edition you are using.

And finally, some states have citation and style guides. Texas and California are most notable. They have their own system of citing cases. Many jurisdictions have their own style requirements: Oregon does not place a period after citing its official reporter ("Or" rather than "Or."); Arizona deviates from basic citation form when citing its statutes using West (ThomsonWest); New York cites more specific court information than *The Bluebook* dictates. Check and confirm the citation rules in your jurisdiction; usually these rules are listed in the local rules of court. Most experienced attorneys will know their jurisdictional requirements, but if preparing a legal document for an unfamiliar jurisdiction, do your homework and verify the proper citation form.

The remainder of this chapter will guide you through the process of incorporating citations into your legal writing and erase some of the mystery. Citation format is a learned skill; it is not mastered overnight and takes time to reach a comfort level. Don't get frustrated. Remember, we all began somewhere! Let's start with the basics of legal citation.

A DAY IN THE LIFE OF A PARALEGAL

Citation books offer the "proper" form of legal citations, but often common practice may suggest a different method of citation form. The problem paralegals are faced with every day is "which form should be used?" The first question that needs to be answered is "which form does your jurisdiction follow?" Does your jurisdiction use *The Bluebook* or *ALWD* or something else entirely? You may know the proper form, but the proper form is not always followed. For example, in Oregon, the official citation for *Oregon Reports* uses a period after "Or." whereas in practice the attorneys do not use a period. You have been taught one method but practice dictates another. This is not uncommon.

Unless the court dictates a particular citation format, you should follow the rules of practice in the jurisdiction you are located. Each jurisdiction has its nuances and peculiarities. Your attorney will point out the common practices, and you will gain experience in the jurisdiction. Just remember to be flexible, and even if you believe a format is incorrect, sometimes we must "do as the Romans do" and not question the practice.

FIGURE 14.1 **Pages from a Case with a Neutral Citation System**

Source: From *Atlantic Digest, 2nd Series*. Reprinted with permission from ThomsonWest.

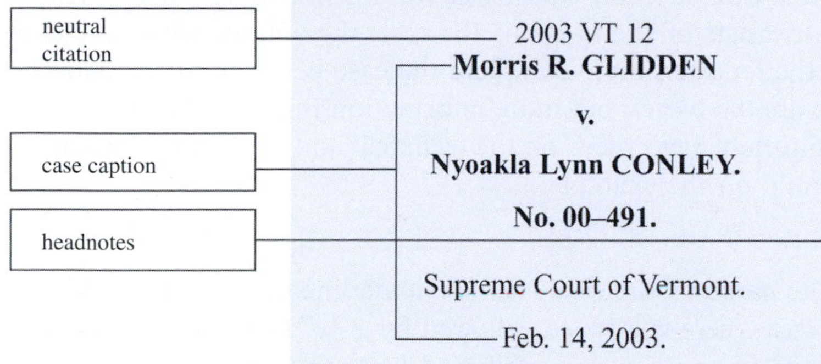

2003 VT 12

Morris R. GLIDDEN

v.

Nyoakla Lynn CONLEY.

No. 00–491.

Supreme Court of Vermont.

Feb. 14, 2003.

Maternal grandmother filed request for visitation. The Windham Family Court, Mary Miles Teachout, J., granted temporary visitation and subsequently denied father's motion for reconsideration of visitation award. Father appealed. The Supreme Court. Skoglund, J., held that: (1) statutory provision governing grandparent visitation was not in violation of a parent's due process rights by not having any absence or consideration to a parent's decision regarding child-grandparent contact, and (2) trial court, in applying statutory provision governing grandparent visitation, impermissibly infringed on father's right to decide what visitation was in his child's best interests by not giving due deference to father's decision regarding grandparent-child contact, and this violated father's right to due process.

Reversed.

1. Child Custody 921(3)

An appellate court reviews an order granting visitation to determine whether the court exercised its discretion on grounds that are clearly unreasonable or untenable.

2. Constitutional Law 48(1)

When considering the constitutionality of a statute, a court begins by presuming that the legislative enactment is constitutional.

3. Constitutional Law 48(1)

In the absence of clear and irrefragable evidence that a statute infringes the paramount law, a court will not strike down a statute as unconstitutional.

4. Constitutional Law 48(1)

If a court can construe the statute in a manner that meets constitutional requirements, it will do so unless the statute's plain language precludes it. [text omitted]

[1–4]. ¶-11. We review an order granting visitation to determine whether the court exercised its discretion on grounds that are clearly unreasonable or untenable. *Cleverly v. Cleverly*, 151 Vt. 351, 355–56, 561 A.2d.99, 102 (1989). When considering the constitutionality of a statute we begin by presuming that the legislative enactment is constitutional. *In re Proceedings Concerning a Neglected Child*, 129 Vt. 234, 240–41, 276 A.2d 14, 18 (1971). In the absence of "clear and irrefragable evidence that [the statute] infringes the paramount law," we will not strike down a statute as unconstitutional. *Id.* Moreover, if we can construe the statute in a manner that meets constitutional requirements, we will do so unless the statute's plain language precludes it. *In re Montpelier & Barre R.R.* 135 Vt. 102, 103–04, 369 A.2d 1379, 1380 (1977). Therefore, we examine Vermont's grandparent visitation statute in the context of the visitation order at issue in this appeal to determine whether the court abused its discretion by applying the statute in a manner that infringes on Glidden's right to raise Amanda without interference by the state.

[5–8] ¶-12. The United States Supreme Court has "long recognized that freedom of personal choice in matters of marriage and family life is one of the liberties protected by the Due Process Clause of the Fourteenth Amendment." *Cleveland Bd. of Educ. v. LaFleur,* 414 U.S. 632, 639–40, 94 S.Ct. 791, 39 L.Ed.2d 52 (1974). The interest of a parent in the custody, care, and control of his child may be the oldest of the fundamental liberty interests our federal constitution protects. *Troxel,* 530 U.S. at 65, 120 S.Ct. 2054; *In re S.B.L.,* 150 Vt. 294, 303, 553 A.2d 1078, 1084 (1988). The state must generally show a compelling interest "before it encroaches upon the private realm of family life." *In re Proceedings Concerning a Neglected Child,* 130 Vt. 525, 530, 296 A.2d 250, 253 (1972). Indeed, there is a "presumption that fit parents act in the best interests of their children." *Troxel,* 530 U.S. at 68, 120 S.Ct. 2054. "[S]o long as a parent adequately cares for his or her children (i.e., is fit), there will normally, be no reason for the State to inject itself into the private realm of the family to further question the ability of that parent to make the best decisions concerning the rearing of that parent's children." *Id.* at 68–69, 120 S.Ct. 2054. [text omitted]

PRACTICE TIP

Some software is programmed to change "2d" to "2nd" and then raise the letters in the abbreviation: "2nd." This feature may have to be disabled in your software as the raised abbreviation (called a superscript) is incorrect. Watch for this feature.

PRACTICE TIP

The correct order for a parallel citation to the U.S. Supreme Court is *U.S. Reports, Supreme Court Reporter,* and then the *Lawyers' Edition.* Whether citing parallel citations is acceptable is dictated by practice and local court rules.

parallel citation
A citation of a case text found in two or more reporters.

THE BASIC CITATION FORM

In Chapter 3, a citation to a U.S. Supreme Court case was illustrated. A quick refresher is warranted. A citation consists of the name of the case, the volume where the case is located, the name of the reporter, the page where the case begins, and the date the case was decided. Those are the basics, but more information is needed to understand proper citation form completely. Let's focus on the technical and practical information of a case citation and build on the example:

PGA Tour, Inc. v. Martin, 532 U.S. 661 (2001)

- Name of the case: The name of the case is either underlined or italicized. After the first name of the case, there is a space, followed by a "v" (standing for versus) with a period. Then add in another space followed by the second named party in the case, followed by a comma.

PGA Tour, Inc. v. Martin,

- Reporter: After the comma in the name, the reporter designation appears. Add a space after the comma, followed by the volume of the reporter, a space, the name of the reporter, a space, and the page number where the case begins:

PGA Tour, Inc. v. Martin, 532 U.S. 661

- Year of the case: The last component is the year the case was decided. After the page where the case begins, there is a space followed by a parenthesis, the year, and a closing parenthesis.

PGA Tour, Inc. v. Martin, 532 U.S. 661 (2001)

Cite only to the official reporter unless directed otherwise by a court or your supervising attorney. However, let's add the **parallel citation** for form purposes.

PGA Tour, Inc. v. Martin, 532 U.S. 661, 121 S. Ct. 1879, 149 L. Ed. 2d 904 (2001) When adding the parallel citations, a comma is inserted between the citations, followed by a space, then the parallel citation.

When a reporter is in its second series or beyond, the series number is placed after the reporter without a space followed by the series abbreviation; for example: 2d (second series), 3d (third series), or 4th (fourth series).

You must be wondering why so much emphasis is placed on spacing, commas, and periods in the citation. Correct spacing and punctuation are as important to the citation form as in a sentence or paragraph. Although a seemingly small detail, incorrect spacing equals sloppiness. Here's how the citation looks when improperly prepared:

PGA Tour, Inc. v. Martin, 532US661 121SCt1879 149LEd2d904(2001)

The citation looks awful and unprofessional. Take pride in your work product and pay close attention to the details of your citation format.

RECENT CASE DECISIONS

Although decisions from unofficial reporters are published quickly, the official reporter text lags behind. When the official reporter is unavailable, use blank lines to delineate its absence followed by the name of the official reporter. For example:

Metro-Goldwyn-Metro v. Grokster Ltd., ___U.S. ___, 125 S. Ct. 2764, 162 L. Ed. 2d 781 (2005)

TABLE 14.2
Selected Subsequent History Notations

affirmed	aff'd
affirmed in part, reversed in part	aff'd in part and rev'd in part
certiorari denied	cert. denied
reversed	rev'd
reversed in part on other grounds	rev'd in part on other grounds
vacated	vacated

SUBSEQUENT HISTORY OF A CASE

Cases proceed through an appellate process. They are appealed to a higher court for review; ultimately these cases are accepted or denied review by an appellate court. When a case opinion is issued after a previous one, this is known as a **subsequent history.** Include a subsequent history in your case citation. For example:

subsequent history
History of a case on appeal.

Hale v. Scott, 252 F. Supp. 2d 728, *aff'd,* 371 F.3d 917 (7th Cir. 2003)

The exception is a **writ of certiorari.** Parties may petition a court of last resort, such as the U.S. Supreme Court, to hear their case. A petition for writ of certiorari is filed. The *writ of certiorari* allows the Court the discretion to accept (grant) a case on appeal or reject (deny) it. Citation rules from *The Bluebook* 10.7 and *ALWD* 12 (8)(a) state that a denial of a *writ of certiorari* should be cited in the case history two years or less after the denial of the *certiorari;* or add the history when a case is particularly relevant to your case discussion. Table 14.2 identifies selected subsequent history notations.

writ of certiorari
Request for appeal where the court has the discretion to grant or deny it; granting of petition, by the U.S. Supreme Court, to review a case.

The subsequent history is placed after the lower court decision, italicized, and followed by the higher court case citation. An example of two cases with a subsequent history is

Cox v. Barber, 275 Ga. 415, 568 S.E.2d 478, *cert. denied,* 537 U.S. 1109, 123 S. Ct. 851, 154 L. Ed. 2d 780 (2003)

Brett v. Jefferson County, Ga., 925 F. Supp. 786, *aff'd in part, vacated in part,* 123 F.3d 1429 (11th Cir. 1997)

PRACTICE TIP

Many attorneys disagree with *The Bluebook* and *ALWD* on when to cite *"cert. denied"* cases. Most believe a notation of *"cert. denied"* is important because it indicates the decision of the lower court is final. This point is significant. Check with your supervising attorney. When in doubt, cite the *"cert. denied"* subsequent history to be safe.

STATE SUBSEQUENT HISTORY GUIDES

A number of states, such as Texas and California, have separate subsequent history table guides. The subsequent histories are required as part of their citations. In Texas, a case citation with a subsequent history or, as it is more commonly known, a "writ history," is illustrated in the following example:

AMR Corp. v. Enlow, 926 S.W.2d 640 (Tex. App. - Fort Worth 1996, no writ)

Check your jurisdiction to determine the rules for citing a subsequent history of a case.

FEDERAL REPORTERS

Recall there are three main federal reporters: the *Federal Reporter, Federal Supplement,* and *Federal Rules Decisions.* Citing these reporters is relatively straightforward.

The *Federal Reporter*

The *Federal Reporter* publishes cases from the circuit courts of appeals. (Refer to Figure 1.5 for the U.S. circuit courts of appeals). The reporter citations are F., F.2d, and F.3d. Along with the name of the case, the reporter, volume, page, and date of the case, include the name of the circuit court of appeals in the parenthetical.

Hargis v. Foster, 312 F.3d 404 (9th Cir. 2002)

The spacing in the parenthetical is

(9th Cir. 2002)

There are no spaces between the numbered circuit and the first parentheses. Place a space between the numbered circuit and the abbreviation for the word "circuit": "Cir." Then add another space followed by the date the case was decided and a closing parenthesis without a space.

The *Federal Supplement*

The *Federal Supplement* publishes cases from the U.S. district courts. (Refer to Figure 1.4 for the district courts.) Presently, the *Federal Supplement* has two series: F. Supp. and F. Supp. 2d. When citing to the *Federal Supplement,* include the district and state of the decision along with the date the case was decided in the parenthetical. The abbreviations of the federal trial courts are as follows:

PRACTICE TIP

Do not cite the *Federal Supplement* as Fed. Supp. This citation form is incorrect.

- N.D.: northern district
- S.D.: southern district
- E.D.: eastern district
- W.D.: western district
- M.D.: middle district
- C.D.: central district
- D.: district (Use this notation for states with only one district court, such as New Jersey, Kansas, and Utah.)

An example of a citation from the *Federal Supplement* is

Philadelphia Gear Corp. v. Swath Int'l, Ltd., 200 F. Supp. 2d 493 (E.D. Pa. 2000)—*The Bluebook* form;

Philadelphia Gear Corp. v. Swath Intl, Ltd, 200 F. Supp. 2d 493 (E.D. Pa. 2000)—*ALWD* form.

(Recall there is a difference in the way the respective citation manuals treat abbreviations: *The Bluebook* uses apostrophes and periods and the *ALWD Manual* does not.)

In the parenthetical include the district court, the state, and the date of the decision. Additionally, the order in the parenthetical is

1. parenthesis, no space;
2. district court designation followed by a period and space;
3. the state of the case decision followed by a period and space; and the date of the case decision, no space, followed by a parenthesis.

Federal Rules Decisions

Federal Rules Decisions publishes cases from the federal district courts on matters involving procedure and evidence. Similar to the *Federal Supplement,* include the district court, state, and date of the decision in the parentheses.

Taylor v. Belger Cartage Service, Inc., 102 F.R.D. 172 (W.D. Mo. 1984)

unpublished case
A case decided by a court that is not published in a reporter because it does not set precedent.

Federal Appendix: A New Reporter

A recent addition in 2001 to the federal reporter system is the *Federal Appendix*. This reporter publishes unreported and **unpublished cases** from many jurisdictions. It is cited as *Fed. Appx.* Be very cautious in using, and even more cautious in citing, this reporter. A number of jurisdictions, such as the fifth and third circuits, forbid citing to unpublished decisions. Mention of this reporter is mainly as an "FYI" (for your information), but do not ever cite to this reporter without alerting your supervising attorney. In fact, many law libraries do not subscribe to this reporter. Consider that a strong warning as to its usefulness. A sample citation to this reporter is

> *Jackson v. Secretary of U.S. Treasury,* 141 Fed. Appx. (2d Cir. 2005) (unpublished)

Notice that the end of the citation adds a parenthetical with the word "unpublished." This notation is required in the citation. Unpublished cases are not selected by a court for publication. They are cases with no new precedential value or cases particular to the parties. When a decision is selected for publication, it is noted on the decision.

CITING STATUTES

As with cases, statutes have official and unofficial publications. Always cite the official version of federal statutes, which is the *U.S. Code.* Include in the citation the following information:

- The title number, followed by a space
- The statutory code, such as the U.S. Code, followed by a space
- The section sign, which is identified by the section "§" symbol, space, and the numbered code section, then a space
- The year the code was published in parentheses

For example:

> 42 *U.S.C.* § 1983 (2000)

Do not cite the unofficial codes, such as *United States Code Annotated* and *United States Code Service.* If the section you need to cite is unavailable in the official code, cite the unofficial code as follows:

> 42 *U.S.C.A.* § 1983 (West 2005)
> Title, code, section (publisher and date)

Citing state statutes varies. Some states cite to a title and section; others cite to named codes such as California, Texas, and New York.

> *Cal. Civ. Pro. Code Ann.* § 977 (West 2000)
> *Tex. Bus. & Com. Code Ann.* § 17.50 (Vernon 2005 Supp.)

Check your jurisdiction for your state's requirements.

ADMINISTRATIVE RULES AND REGULATIONS

Administrative rules and regulations are located in the *Code of Federal Regulations (C.F.R.)* and the *Federal Register (Fed. Reg.).*

Code of Federal Regulations

Similar to the *United States Code, C.F.R.* citations include

- the title of the code, followed by a space;
- the code *(C.F.R.)* followed by a space;
- the section and chapter of the regulation followed by a space; and
- the date (of the most current edition) in parentheses.

An example of a *C.F.R.* citation is

47 *C.F.R.* § 1.333 (2005)

Federal Register

The *Federal Register* contains proposed and final federal rules and regulations, notices, presidential proclamations, and orders. When citing the *Federal Register,* identify the volume number, the *Federal Register,* the page where the material appears, and the date. (Note: The *Federal Register* is printed daily. Indicate the month, day, and year of the cited volume for clarity.) Here is an example:

71 *Fed. Reg.* 17774 (April 7, 2006)

THE CONSTITUTION AND COURT RULES

Constitutions

The U.S. Constitution is cited by identifying the name of the constitution and the article or amendment followed by the specific referenced section. The following is an example of a cite for the U.S. Constitution:

U.S. Const. art. III, § 2
U.S. Const. amend. V

Do not cite a date at the end of the reference.

State constitutions follow the same format as well. The following is an example of a state constitution citation:

TEX. CONST. art. I, § 13

Court Rules

Citations for court rules contain the rule (or code abbreviation) and the rule number; for example:

Fed. R. Civ. P. 56(c)
Fed. R. Evid. 801

SECONDARY SOURCES

Unless you are dealing with a scholarly source, resist citing to a secondary source. Use secondary sources as a legal research tool and seek the primary source material. However, proper citation form for secondary sources is important. The most cited secondary sources are legal treatises. Other secondary sources are books, restatements, law reviews, attorney general opinions, *American Law Reports (A.L.R.)* annotations, and legal dictionaries. Cite secondary sources as shown in the following examples.

Legal treatises and books are cited similarly. Include the following:

- Name of the author
- Name of the publication
- The edition of the publication
- Publisher (if following *ALWD* format)
- Date of publication in parentheses

If you are citing a specific page or section, identify the exact location in the book or treatise where the material is located. An example follows:

John D. Calamari and Joseph M. Perillo, *The Law of Contracts* (5th ed. 2003)
John D. Calamari and Joseph M. Perillo, *The Law of Contracts* (5th ed. West 2003)

Restatements

The restatements are a compilation of the common law. There is a slight difference between *The Bluebook* and *ALWD*. *ALWD* italicizes the name of the restatements; *The Bluebook* does not.

Bluebook: Restatement (Second) of Contracts § 90 (1981)
ALWD: Restatement (Second) of Contracts § 90 (1981)

Law Reviews

Law review citations include

- name of author of article;
- title of article;
- volume of law review journal;
- name of law review journal;
- page of article in journal; and
- year of journal publication.

Robert D. Bills, *Plagiarism in Law Schools: Close Resemblance of the Worst Kind?,* 31 Santa Clara L. Rev. 103 (1990)

Attorney General Opinions

Attorney general opinions are legal opinions issued by an attorney general of a state or the federal government. These opinions represent questions of law usually requested by the different departments or agencies within that state. Opinions are normally state specific and have limited legal authority. An attorney general opinion is cited as follows:

Op. Atty. Gen. Fla. 2006–09 (2006)

A.L.R. Annotations

American Law Reports cites both cases and articles. When citing an *A.L.R.* article, identify

- the author's name;
- annotation title;
- volume number;
- the *A.L.R.* series;
- page number where article begins; and
- date of article.

Benjamin J. Vernia, *State and Local Governmental Liability for Injury or Death of Bicyclist Due to Defect for Obstruction in Public Roadway or Sidewalk,* 12 A.L.R. 6th 645 (2006)

PRACTICE TIP

Do not cite Shepard's or a digest as legal authority. They are updating and finding tools.

Legal Dictionaries

The basic components for citing a legal dictionary acording to *The Bluebook* are

- name of the dictionary;
- page of the definition;
- edition; and
- year of publication.

Black's Law Dictionary 680 (8th ed. 2004)

The *ALWD Manual* adds two more components:

- The name of the editor
- The publisher

> *Black's Law Dictionary 680* (Bryan A. Gardner ed., 8th ed., West 2004)

CYBER TRIP

Locate the citation rules for your jurisdiction for both the federal and state courts. Compare and contrast their differences and similarities.

Quick Quiz True/False Questions

1. The only two books used to explain proper citation format are *The Bluebook* and the *ALWD Manual*.
2. All states now use the universal citation format.
3. Unpublished cases are reported in both the *Federal Reporter* and the *Federal Appendix*.
4. Every jurisdiction has the same format for citing a statute.
5. In preparing a legal document, it is always best to cite secondary sources.

INCORPORATING CITATIONS INTO LEGAL WRITING

Using citations in legal writing is necessary for paralegals and attorneys. Ordinarily, reference material is tucked away in a footnote or at the end in a bibliography. The way you prepared papers in high school or college is not sufficient in the legal setting. The first request is to throw all those preconceived notions of how to do things out the window. The second request is patience. You will learn the way attorneys prepare a document and understand all those subtleties. The third request is: relax. It seems overwhelming at first, but you will master citations and before you know it, your attorney will be asking you how to cite a case. And the final request: read the first three requests again. Everything takes time. Learn one skill at a time and build on those skills. Do not be afraid to look something up in *The Bluebook* or ALWD *Manual*. We all do it.

Citations in Sentences

Let's build on one sentence. The facts surrounding the sentence involve legislative intent. How does a court interpret a statute and determine the legislative intent when the statute is ambiguous? The sentence in your legal document is as follows:

> When interpreting a statute, the court should give effect to the intent of the Legislature as expressed in the statute and begin an interpretation with the statute's language. *Barnhart v. Sigmon Coal Co., Inc.*, 534 U.S. 438 (2002).

The statement requires a legal source to support the legal proposition. You add the case citation directly into the body of the sentence. Notice the case is cited at the end

YOU BE THE JUDGE

Attorneys cite cases to support their legal positions. There is an obligation to cite properly as well as to verify the authorities cited. When attorneys blatantly ignore the law or fail to make reasonable inquiry as to the status of the law, wasting both the court's and opposing counsel's time, courts have something to say. The attorneys in *Smith v. United Transportation Union Local No. 81*, 594 F. Supp. 96 (1984) made the mistake of misleading a district court judge in California, which cost them financially. Review the *Smith* case. What are the facts of the case? What points of law did the attorneys fail to bring to the court's attention? What remedy did the court impose on the attorneys for their misrepresentation of the legal authorities? Undoubtedly, presentation, both oral and written, is essential when appearing before a court.

of the statement. When citing a case at the end of a legal proposition, the case citation is an independent sentence, ending with a period. The sentence can be reworded to have the citation introduce the proposition.

> In *Barnhart v. Sigmon Coal Co., Inc.,* 534 U.S. 438 (2002), the court observed that when interpreting a statute the court should give effect to the intent of the Legislature as expressed in the statute and begin an interpretation with the statute's language.

In the second example, the case is part of the sentence and the entire citation is immersed, or as some refer to it, as an **embedded citation** in the sentence. Which form is correct? It is a matter of preference. Both are correct, although the first sentence is less intrusive. Use placement variations to add sentence variety and minimize monotony.

embedded citation
A citation placed within a sentence.

Continuing with the same example, now let's break up the citation in the sentence.

> In *Barnhart v. Sigmon Coal Co., Inc.,* the court observed that when interpreting a statute the court should give effect to the intent of the Legislature as expressed in the statute and begin an interpretation with the statute's language. 534 U.S. 438 (2002).

Since the citation is close to the case reference, it is proper form to split the citation in two. The key here is that the sentence should not be too long and there should be close proximity between the name of the case and the citation. Again, notice how the citation is considered a sentence ending with a period.

A Shortcut: *Id.* and *Supra*

Using the same example from the previous section, let's assume you cite a proposition from the same case in the next sentence. Do you need to repeat the full citation? No. Use the notation *id* (the abbreviation for the Latin *idem*). ***Id.*** means the same. You have just learned your first **short form citation.** A short citation form is used only after you have cited your legal authority completely once. There are different variations of short forms for citations. For example:

id.
The same.

short form citation
Citation used after the complete citation is used in the legal document.

- *Barnhart,* 534 U.S. at 450. If you cited *Barnhart* completely once and need to reference it again later in the documents, cite the first name of the case followed by the volume and reporter, then the word "at" followed by the exact page reference to the material in the case. This page reference is known as a *pinpoint reference* or *pinpoint cite* or *pincite*. Pinpoint citations direct the reader to the exact page where your material appears. This concept will be discussed as well in the section on quotations. Use the first name of the case, unless this causes confusion or is a government, such as United States; or a state, such as Indiana; or where the notation State or People is used to designate the state. In those instances, use the second name.
- *Barnhart,* 534 U.S. 438. Use this reference if you are referring generally to the case.
- *Barnhart,* 534 U.S. at 450, 122 S. Ct. at 950, 151 L. Ed. 2d at 920. Use this shorthand reference when parallel citations are required. Some jurisdictions may allow citing to the regional reporter only if a state case is involved. Check with your jurisdiction's local rules.
- *Barnhart v. Sigmon Coal Co., Inc.,* 534 U.S. at 450. A longer version of the first example, but acceptable short form.
- 534 U.S. at 450. If you choose this reference, be sure the original citation is close. This reference forces the reader to search the text for the name of the case.

In review, you must cite a full citation before you resort to a short citation form. Remember what you are trying to accomplish: effectively communicating your supporting legal authority to the reader. Ask yourself, "Will the reader understand where the source of information originated?" "Have I supplied sufficient information for the reader to locate the legal source cited?" Our new example follows:

> In *Barnhart v. Sigmon Coal Co., Inc.*, 534 U.S. 438 (2002), the court observed when interpreting a statute the court should give effect to the intent of the Legislature as expressed in the statute and begin an interpretation with the statute's language. The court also must determine whether the language is plain and unambiguous. *Id.*

However, you cannot use *id.* if there is an intervening case citation.

supra
Above.

Although there is a short form citation when a legal source intervenes between another cited source, ***supra*** (meaning "above"), this short form should not be used in court documents. Note that *supra* is used in cases by judges when referring to previously cited cases. However, both *The Bluebook* and *ALWD* advise against using *supra* in formal legal writing, specifically when citing cases, statutes and other legislative related material, constitutions and administrative rules and regulations—the basic primary source material. Whether to use this format is one of those instances where asking your supervising attorney is appropriate. If you use *supra,* use the name of the case, followed by *supra* and the page of your reference. The better approach is a short form citation. For example:

> In *Barnhart v. Sigmon Coal Co., Inc.*, 534 U.S. 438 (2002), the court observed when interpreting a statute the court should give effect to the intent of the Legislature as expressed in the statute and begin an interpretation with the statute's language. The court also must determine whether the language is plain and unambiguous. *Id.* If the language is plain and unambiguous, the language of the statute is conclusive. *Consumer Product Safety Commission v. GTE Sylvania, Inc.*, 447 U.S. 102 (1980). Therefore, the first step in a statutory construction case is determining the meaning of the language. *Barnhart,* at 450.

String Citing

string citation
List of citations in the brief or memorandum of law following a point of law cited.

Suppose more than one case supports your legal point. If you want to communicate to the court that this legal point is well settled, or you want to argue a change in the jurisdiction's position and you need to show all the other jurisdictions that followed the legal position you are presenting, you can use more than one case to illustrate your legal point. This technique is referred to as **string citing.** String citing uses a list of cases to support a legal position. When string citing, separate each case by a semicolon and end the citation string with a period, just like a sentence. Although not improper, string citing is not encouraged. Use the best legal authority that stands for your proposition. Remember, often courts place page limitations on court papers and briefs. Do not waste precious space by restating a point of law by string citing. Say what you have to say and move on! The next example uses string cites to support the legal position from our continuing example:

> When interpreting a statute, the court should give effect to the intent of the Legislature as expressed in the statute and begin an interpretation with the statute's language. *Barnhart v. Sigmon Coal Co., Inc.*, 534 U.S. 438 (2002); *Duncan v. Walker,* 533 U.S. 167 (2001); *Reves v. Ernest & Young,* 507 U.S. 170 (1993); *Mallard v. U.S. District Court of Southern District of Iowa,* 490 U.S. 296 (1989).

If you intend to string cite cases, there is an order of presentation. Use the following as a guide:

- United States Supreme Court: Cases always are cited first in reverse chronological order. That means from the newest to the oldest.
- Federal Circuit Courts of Appeals: These cases are cited next, newest to oldest cases.
- Federal District Court: Cases from this court are cited after the Federal Circuit Court of Appeals, newest to oldest cases.
- State cases: The last group to cite in a string cite are state cases. Always cite from the state's highest court, newest to oldest, followed by the next level of state court.

SIGNALS IN LEGAL WRITING

A signal indicates additional information on a subject or particular point cited in the legal document. Signals can be explanatory, comparative, or informational. Use signals when you are emphasizing a point and not as a method to pepper the legal document with more legal authorities; use signals sparingly but wisely. Signals can have a dramatic effect as they tell the reader you intend to address a significant point. *They are always in italics.* Although there are a number of signals, the most common are as follows:

- *E.g.:* This signal means "for example" and indicates additional authority on the same legal point. This signal represents only some of the legal authorities and is not exhaustive. It is quite common and can be paired with other signals, such as *see* and *generally*.
- *See:* Use *see* when other cases support your legal proposition. This signal indicates that the accompanying cases or authority directly support your statement.
- *See also:* Similar to the signal *see,* but the legal authority, although strong, is not as directly supportive as cases used in with the signal *see*.
- *Compare:* This signal is used for a specific purpose. When you compare legal authorities, you may want your reader to understand the distinctions and different results from other jurisdictions.
- *See generally:* Use this signal when you are referencing helpful background information. This signal will assist your reader in gaining a better understanding of the legal proposition you are presenting.
- *Accord:* This signal is used to show support from other jurisdictions of your legal proposition. It also is used when you are quoting a text and to show additional support for your proposition.

ETHICS ALERT

It is unethical to misrepresent a legal authority in a legal document. The rules of professional responsibility require attorneys and those they supervise to cite legal authority that is reflective of the legal position argued. It is one thing to present a novel argument to the court and the court rejects it. It is quite another to mislead a court on the status of existing law. Zealous representation is the standard required of attorneys in representing their clients. However, there is a fine line between zealousness and misrepresentation. Courts exhibit disdain when attorneys distort court opinions and misquote. A recent case, *Precision Specialty Metal, Inc. v. United States,* 315 F.3d 1346 (Fed. Cir. 2003), took issue with a brief submitted by an attorney who "omitted directly relevant language from what was represented as precedential authority, which effectively changed the meaning of at least one quotation, and which intentionally or negligently misled the court." *Id.* at 1355. Your duties as a paralegal are not to indulge your attorney's whims but rather to act ethically when presented an assignment regardless of the outcome. In every case, there is a winner and a loser. Your responsibility is to communicate the facts and law accurately by citing the cases, statutes, and other legal authority that support the client's position. Review the *Precision Specialty Metal* case. What two rules of procedure did the court compare and analyze? What was the basis of the court's sanctions of the attorney? Where did this case originate, and what were the facts that led it to the Federal Circuit Court of Appeals?

Signals are used to begin an independent citation sentence. Use a capital letter if the signal begins your citation sentence. Using our example, an introductory signal is added to the string cite example:

> *When interpreting a statute, the court should give effect to the intent of the Legislature as expressed in the statute and begin an interpretation with the statute's language.* Barnhart v. Sigmon Coal Co., Inc., *534 U.S. 438 (2002).* See also Duncan v. Walker, *533 U.S. 167 (2001);* Reves v. Ernest & Young, *507 U.S. 170 (1993);* Mallard v. U.S. District Court of Southern District of Iowa, *490 U.S. 296 (1989).*

QUOTATIONS IN LEGAL WRITING

Quotations are commonly used in legal writing. By definition, quotations indicate a reference to a source other than your own and must be attributed to the source or author. Recall the last chapter's discussion on plagiarism; here is your opportunity to guard against plagiarism allegations by learning how to identify the material properly. You may wonder when to use a quote or when to use a general reference, and when are citations or quotations unnecessary. A law review article* sets forth six basic rules to live by:

1. *Cite sources for all direct quotations.* Think of it as copying. You would never consider copying a source without giving credit to the source. No exception exists to this rule.
2. *Cite sources from which language, facts, or ideas have been paraphrased or summarized.* In the examples for using a citation in a sentence, the information was paraphrased, but the court decision was credited for the point of law.
3. *Cite sources for idea(s) or information that could be regarded as common knowledge, but which (a) was not known to the writer before encountering it in a particular source, or (b) the reader might find unfamiliar*. This rule is less definitive, especially given that virtually everything will be a new idea for you in researching the law. If the proposition cited is a general legal point, use a citation. When in doubt, cite a legal source.
4. *Cite sources that add relevant information to the particular topic or argument.* This is the footnote rule. Rather than include explanatory sources in the body of the document, footnote the information. You may also use a parenthetical to introduce the information. The point is to cite a legal source.
5. *Cite sources from and for other kinds of specialized materials.* This rule is limited and focuses on letters and interviews.
6. *Cite sources relied upon for authority to support any legal proposition or rule.* The rule means "when in doubt, use a legal source to support your point." Of course, your work will include many legal sources. It is expected in the legal arena.

These rules are a guide in helping you know when, or when not, to quote or use a legal citation reference in your legal writing.

Returning to the issue of quotations, let's start with two basic rules:

1. Any quote over fifty words is single-spaced and indented into a block, known as a **block quote.** Do *not* use quotation marks at the beginning and end of a block quote.
2. A quote of fifty words or less is kept within the text and *identified with quotation marks.*

block quote
Quotation over fifty words that is single-spaced and indented.

Whether you quote within a paragraph using quotation marks or a block quote, the message is to credit the authority cited.

*Robert D. Bills, "Plagiarism in Law School: Close Resemblance of the Worst Kind" 31 *Santa Clara L. Rev.* 103, 123-30 (1990)

Let's assume certain facts. A golfer who has a walking disability petitions the PGA Tour to use a golf cart rather than walk the tournament as required by the rules. The golfer, Casey Martin, files a lawsuit based upon the American with Disabilities Act (ADA) in that banning the golf cart violates his rights. The U.S. Supreme Court agreed. Using *PGA Tour, Inc. v. Martin,* 532 U.S. 661 (2001), you will learn how to cite a quote in a legal document. You want to quote verbatim a passage from the case. First, you want to introduce the quote with a lead-in sentence. Do not simply state your quote without any connecting or introductory sentence. In previous chapters we discussed transitions; this area is one of those instances when you should use them. This rule applies to quotations.

PRACTICE TIP

ALWD also permits a quote of four lines or less to be embedded in the paragraph using quotation marks. This alleviates the counting method.

Example 14.1

The U.S. Supreme Court in its dicta observed:

> The purpose of the walking rule is therefore not compromised in the slightest by allowing Martin to use a cart. A modification that provides an exception to a peripheral tournament rule without impairing its purpose cannot be said to "fundamentally alter" the tournament. What it can be said to do, on the other hand, is to allow Martin the chance to qualify for, and compete in, the athletic events petitioner offers to those members to enter. That is exactly what the ADA requires.

PGA Tour, Inc. v. Martin, 532 U.S. 661, 690 (2001)

Example 14.2

The U.S. Supreme Court in its dicta observed:

> The purpose of the walking rule is . . . not compromised in the slightest by allowing Martin to use a cart. A modification that provides an exception to a peripheral tournament rule without impairing its purpose cannot be said to "fundamentally alter" the tournament. What it can be said to do, on the other hand, is to allow Martin the chance to qualify for, and compete in, the athletic events petitioner offers to those members to enter. That is exactly what the ADA requires. *PGA Tour, Inc. v. Martin,* 532 U.S. 661, 690 (2001)

The citation of the case is at the end of the quote and is placed on a new line and is not placed directly at the end of the quote as a continuation. Many attorneys follow the second approach, which is incorrect.

Quotes can become complex, and *The Bluebook* and *ALWD* guide us in the proper form. A quick reference for common quotation issues is identified as follows.

- When to use an ellipsis: Recall from Chapter 12 that an ellipsis is used to indicate omitted material. In quoted material, an ellipsis is used to show the omission of material. There are rules to follow when using an ellipsis at the end of the quoted material as well as the middle of quoted material. If you are omitting material at the end of a quote, end with the ellipsis followed by a period (. . . .). There is always space between the periods. Use an ellipsis to indicate omission of material in the middle of quoted material. Do not use an ellipsis at the beginning of a quote. The quote from the previous example is modified, deleting parts of the quotation and using an ellipsis.

YOU BE THE JUDGE

Do not use an ellipsis to mislead your reader. Be complete and accurate when substituting the ellipsis for text. A law firm improperly used ellipses in an appellate court brief to deliberately mislead a court. The judge, angered by the attorneys' dishonesty, sanctioned them in the amount of $71,117.75. Review *Dube v. Eagle Global Logistics,* 314 F.3d 193 (5th Cir. 2002). Were the court's actions appropriate? What was the reasoning behind the sanctions in the case? What was the court's disposition?

PRACTICE TIP

Unless a quotation continues, do not use an ellipsis at the end of quoted material. If the passage quoted ends in a period, then your quotation will end with a single period.

The U.S. Supreme Court in its dicta observed:

> The purpose of the walking rule is therefore not compromised in the slightest by allowing Martin to use a cart. A modification that provides an exception to a peripheral tournament rule without impairing its purpose cannot be said to "fundamentally alter" the tournament. What it can be said to do, on the other hand, is to allow Martin the chance to qualify for, and compete in, the athletic events petitioner offers to those members to enter. . . .
>
> *PGA Tour, Inc. v. Martin,* 532 U.S. 661, 690 (2001)

Using the ellipse signifies to the reader that there is additional information that the writer chose not to include.

- Brackets in a quote: Brackets are used when the letter at the beginning of the quotation changes from lowercase to uppercase and vice versa. Place the first letter in brackets indicating to your reader that the original material was different. Also use brackets when language at the beginning of a quote is omitted. For example:

The U.S. Supreme Court in its *dicta* observed:

> [T]he walking rule is . . . not compromised in the slightest by allowing Martin to use a cart. A modification that provides an exception to a peripheral tournament rule without impairing its purpose cannot be said to *"fundamentally alter"* the tournament. What it can be said to do, on the other hand, is to allow Martin the chance to qualify for, and compete in, the athletic events petitioner offers to those members to enter. That is exactly what the ADA requires.
>
> *PGA Tour, Inc. v. Martin,* 532 U.S. 661, 690 (2001)

- Using "[sic]": When there are mistakes in the original text or grammatical errors, use "[sic]" in the quoted material to indicate that the original was not changed. Recall our example in Chapter 13, where the attorney misspelled mandamus as "mandamous [sic]," the court added "[sic]" to the reference to indicate the misspelling.
- Punctuation in quotations: Periods and commas are placed inside the quotation marks. This mistake is common in citing quotations embedded in the text and is not as problematic with block quotes. Unless part of the quotation, all other punctuation is placed outside the quotation marks. For example:

> The U.S. Supreme Court observed that "[t]he purpose of the walking rule is therefore not compromised in the slightest by allowing Martin to use a cart." *Id.* at 690.

- Emphasis added and emphasis supplied: The words "emphasis added" may be included at the end of a quote if you, the writer, underscored the importance of a particular word or passage in a quote. The quoted material is usually italicized. If "emphasis added" is used, this notation must be added at the end of the quotation in a parenthetical telling the reader that you, not the original author, added the highlighted importance: (emphasis added) If the quoted material already emphasizes a particular point, do not add "emphasis supplied." In our example, we are emphasizing the following and indicating the change.

The U.S. Supreme Court in its dicta observed:

> The purpose of the walking rule is therefore not compromised in the slightest by allowing Martin to use a cart. A modification that provides an exception to a peripheral tournament rule without impairing its purpose cannot be said to *"fundamentally alter"* the tournament. What it can be said to do, on the other hand, is to allow Martin the chance to qualify for, and compete in, the athletic events petitioner offers to those members to enter. That is exactly what the ADA requires.
>
> *PGA Tour, Inc. v. Martin,* 532 U.S. 661, 690 (2001) (emphasis added)

- Quotes within quotes: If there is a quotation within the quote you are citing, keep the quotations in the original if used in a block quote. On the other

THE E-FACTOR

The Internet is posing unique issues for judges and attorneys. Cases are posted almost the moment they are decided. For those attorneys who do not have access to the Internet, LexisNexis, or Westlaw, the disparity can be great. Can an attorney cite a case from Westlaw or LexisNexis without it being available in the printed source? The answer is yes, but the electronic source must be provided to both the court and the opposing attorney. Cite electronic cases as follows:

- Case name
- Docket number
- Database identifier (such as WL for Westlaw and Lexis for LexisNexis)
- Court name
- Complete date of the case (include month, date, and year)
- Pinpoint references (with an asterisk preceding the screen or page number)

To cite to Westlaw or LexisNexis, use the following guide established by *The Bluebook* and *ALWD:*

LEXIS: Irobo v. Martin, No. 16069/03-325D, 2003, ___ N.Y. Misc.2d___LEXIS 1371 (October 20, 2003)

WESTLAW: Irobo v. Martin, 2003. ___N.Y. Misc.2d ___ 2003 WL 17744 (N.Y. October 20, 2003)

When citing from sources other than Westlaw and Lexis-Nexis, which have unique database identifiers, add a parenthetical at the end of the citations indicating the source: (VersusLaw) or (Findlaw).

Local court rules guide the use of electronic case law.

Citing to electronic material also poses new problems. An ever-present problem created by the Internet is the access to unpublished cases. They have no precedential value, but attorneys still attempt to use them as persuasive argument. The new reporter, *Federal Appendix,* previously mentioned in this chapter, adds to the dilemma. When a case is labeled as unpublished, do not cite it. Immediately bring the case to your attorney's attention and allow him or her to decide its value.

Depublished cases pose another problem as well. These cases were scheduled for publication but recalled. California has published a procedure for requesting a case be depublished. Figure 14.2 reproduces the California Rule of Court that identifies the procedure to depublish a case. Stay away from depublished cases if your jurisdiction has the same or similar procedure, as they are not binding authority.

hand, if the quote is fifty words or less, change the original quotation mark to a single mark and add quotation marks to the entire quotation. An example is from the *Barnhart* case from our statutory construction example. Cite the quote as follows:

> The Court in *Barnhart* followed well-settled principles of statutory construction. Specifically, the court opined that they will not substitute their judgment for Congress, and stated:
>
> > This we will not do. "We refrain from concluding here that the differing language in the two subsections has the same meaning in each. We would not presume to ascribe this difference to a simple mistake in draftsmanship." *Id.* at 454.

When a quote is quoting another source, this is signified by referencing the quote in a parenthetical. This often occurs in court cases when a court is quoting a previous case in a newer case. Another example from *Barnhart* illustrates the point:

> The Court in *Barnhart* followed the well-settled general principle on statutory construction that when "Congress includes particular language in one section of a statute but omits it in another section of the same Act, it is generally presumed that Congress acts intentionally and purposely in the disparate inclusion or exclusion.'" *Russello v. United States,* 464 U.S. 16, 23 (1983) (quoting *United States v. Wong Kim Bo,* 472 F.2d 720, 722 C.A. 5 1972). *Id.* at 452.

- Pinpoint citations: Always cite the page number where the quotation begins by using a **pinpoint citation (pincite)** or **jump cite.** This page reference will tell the readers where the cited material is located if they choose to check or reference it. Accuracy is critical when pinpointing your reference. Citing a page reference was discussed in the section on short citation form. There appears to be a difference of opinion when citing multiple pages. *The Bluebook* requires citing two digits of the number and when over three or more digits, omitting the

pinpoint cite (pincite)
The page reference in a citation that directs the reader to the cited material in a case. Also known as jump cite.

jump cite
The page reference in a citation that directs the reader to the cited material in the case. Also called a pinpoint citation or pincite.

FIGURE 14.2
Procedure for Depublishing a Case
Source: 2006 California Rules of Court. Available at www.courtinfo.ca.gov/rules.

Rule 979. Requesting Depublication of Published Opinions

(a) Request

(1) Any person may request the Supreme Court to order that an opinion certified for publication not be published.

(2) The request must not be made as part of a petition for review, but by a separate letter to the Supreme Court not exceeding 10 pages.

(3) The request must concisely state the person's interest and the reason why the opinion should not be published.

(4) The request must be delivered to the Supreme Court within 30 days after the decision is final in the Court of Appeal.

(5) The request must be served on the rendering court and all parties.

(b) Response

(1) Within 10 days after the Supreme Court receives a request under (a), the rendering court or any person may submit a response supporting or opposing the request. A response submitted by anyone other than the rendering court must state the person's interest.

(2) A response must not exceed 10 pages and must be served on the rendering court, all parties, and any person who requested depublication.

(c) Action by Supreme Court

(1) The Supreme Court may order the opinion depublished or deny the request. It must send notice of its action to the rendering court, all parties, and any person who requested depublication.

(2) The Supreme Court may order an opinion depublished on its own motion, notifying the rendering court of its action.

(d) Effect of Supreme Court order to depublish

A Supreme Court order to depublish is not an expression of the court's opinion of the correctness of the result of the decision or of any law stated in the opinion.

Rule 979 repealed and adopted effective January 1, 2005.

Source: 2006 California Rules of Court. Available at: www.courtinfo.ca.gov/rules

repetitive digits, whereas the *ALWD Manual* does not require a minimum number of digits in the pincite.

The Bluebook: Barnhart at 445-46
ALWD: Barnhart at 445-446 or *Barnhart* at 445-46
Neither permit *Barnhart* at 445-6
Multiple page quotations are separated by a (-) hyphen

Quotations have a myriad of rules. Learn the basics and never hesitate to consult *The Bluebook* or *ALWD Manual* for further guidance.

Quick Quiz True/False Questions

1. Always cite a legal source when referencing a legal proposition.
2. String cites are a list of citations that illustrate a legal proposition.
3. It is appropriate to use quotation marks at the beginning and end of a block quote.
4. Use "[sic]" to illustrate mistakes in the original text.
5. A jump cite and pincite are the same.

PRACTICAL CONSIDERATIONS: ACCURACY COUNTS

Another important factor you must master along with citation form is the process of cite checking. As a paralegal, one of your many assignments will be to verify that the material cited in a brief or memorandum is correct. Is the authority still good law? Is the citation in the proper format? Have the local rules been reviewed? Are the cited authorities accurately reflecting the points referenced in the brief or memorandum? Each question requires skill and attention to detail. Let's review the process for each.

1. **Is the authority still good law?** Any authority cited requires verification. Shepardize or KeyCite the authorities cited to ensure the authority is not overruled or questioned. This task is the minimum requirement for cite checking. Bring to your supervising attorney's attention any problematic authorities.
2. **Is the citation in the proper format?** Verify citation form by using either *The Bluebook* or *ALWD Manual* to determine whether the listed legal sources are cited correctly. Check punctuation as well as form. If the citation identifies a pinpoint reference, check the pincite for accuracy.
3. **Have local rules been reviewed?** Many jurisdictions have local rules that dictate how to cite legal authorities. Sometimes they complement *The Bluebook* or *ALWD Manual,* but other times they supersede them. Know the requirements in your jurisdiction.
4. **Are the cited authorities accurately reflecting the points referenced in the brief or memorandum?** Read. Retrieve the cases and review them. Verify they say what they are being cited for. Inaccurately citing an authority may have ethical and professional implications. As tedious as the process may be, it is critical to review all the authority.

Learning how to incorporate citations into legal writing is critical to your work as a paralegal. Care in preparing any legal document is essential to being a successful paralegal. Do take the time to master the detail from the placement of a simple period to selection of a pertinent quote. It may appear overwhelming at first, but practice makes perfect!

Summary

Since 1926, *The Bluebook* has been the authority for citation form. The *ALWD Manual* is another accepted authority for citation form. *ALWD* has a more user-friendly approach to understanding citation form. Another citation approach is the *Universal Citation Guide,* formulating a neutral citation format. Each jurisdiction follows different guides; local rules provide guidance on which format to use.

Case citations fall into a basic format. Cite the name of the case, the volume, the reporter, the page where the case begins, and the date of the decision. Unless dictated by citation form, often information about the court is inserted into the parenthetical with the date of the case. Statutes are cited by identifying the title, code, code section, and the date. This basic format is followed for administrative rules and regulations as well. Whether a primary or secondary source, all legal authority cited must be properly identified according to the rules of citation.

Legal authority must be integrated into legal documents. Citations are placed in sentences to direct a reader as to the basis of the authority relied upon. Short form citations may be used after a complete citation is identified in the text. Signals and string citing provide a method of listing additional authorities in a text. Additionally, when used properly, quotations are a vehicle to cite legal authority.

Cite checking is an important responsibility of a paralegal. Cite checking consists of verifying the law, checking proper citation form, including the local rules, and reviewing the case cited for accuracy in the text.

Key Terms

block quote
embedded citation
id.
jump cite
neutral citation
parallel citation
pinpoint cite (pincite)
short form citation
signals
string citation
subsequent history
supra
unpublished case
writ of certiorari

Review Questions

1. What is *The Bluebook?* What is *ALWD?*
2. List three differences between *The Bluebook* and *ALWD.*
3. What are the basic elements of a case citation?
4. Identify five legal secondary sources.
5. What is the proper order of citing cases in a string cite?
6. What is a subsequent history?
7. What are the criteria for citing a quotation?
8. What are signals and when are they used in legal writing?
9. What is a pinpoint citation and when it is used in a legal document?
10. List the six rules for when to cite a legal authority.

Exercises

1. Prepare the following legal authorities in proper citation form:
   a. State of Florida versus Robert Thomas. The volume of the case is 532 and the page where the case begins is 774. The case is from the U.S. Supreme Court and was decided in 2001.
   b. *Federal Reporter* case from the third series; the volume is 116 and the first page of the case is 310. The parties are Birchem versus Knights of Columbus and the year of the case is 1997 from the eighth circuit.
   c. *North Western Reporter* second series. A Nebraska Supreme Court case decided in 1997 and is found in volume 560 and the case begins on page 157. The parties are the State of Nebraska and Thomas Nissen.
   d. The Plaintiff in the case is John Moore and the Defendant is the Regents of the University of California. The case is located in three reporters.
   West's California Reporter in volume 271 and begins on page 145.
   California Reports third series in volume 51 and begins on page 120.
   Pacific Reporter second series in volume 793 and begins on page 479.
   The case was decided in 1990.
2. Identify the signals used in the passage from *Garcetti v. Ceballos,* __ U.S. __, 126 S. Ct. 1051, 164 L. Ed. 2d 689 (2006):
   At the same time, the Court has recognized that a citizen who works for the government is nonetheless a citizen. The First Amendment limits the ability of a public employer to leverage the employment relationship to restrict, incidentally

or intentionally, the liberties employees enjoy in their capacities as private citizens. *See Perry v. Sindermann,* 408 U.S. 593, 597, 92 S. Ct. 2694, 33 L. Ed. 2d 570 (1972). So long as employees are speaking as citizens about matters of public concern, they must face only those speech restrictions that are necessary for their employers to operate efficiently and effectively. *See, e.g., Connick, supra,* at 147, 103 S. Ct. 1684, 75 L. Ed. 2d 708 ("Our responsibility is to ensure that citizens are not deprived of fundamental rights by virtue of working for the government").

> The Court's employee-speech jurisprudence protects, of course, the constitutional rights of public employees. Yet the First Amendment interests at stake extend beyond the individual speaker. The Court has acknowledged the importance of promoting the public's interest in receiving the well-informed views of government employees engaging in civic discussion. *Pickering* again provides an instructive example. The Court characterized its holding as rejecting the attempt of school administrators to "limi[t] teachers' opportunities to contribute to public debate." 391 U.S., at 573, 88 S. Ct. 1731, 20 L. Ed. 2d 811. It also noted that teachers are "the members of a community most likely to have informed and definite opinions" about school expenditures. *Id.* at 572, 88 S. Ct. 1731, 20 L. Ed. 2d 811. The Court's approach acknowledged the necessity for informed, vibrant dialogue in a democratic society. It suggested, in addition, that widespread costs may arise when dialogue is repressed. The Court's more recent cases have expressed similar concerns. See, *e.g., San Diego v. Roe,* 543 U.S. 77, 82, 125 S. Ct. 521, 160 L. Ed. 2d 410 (2004) *(per curiam)* ("Were [public employees] not able to speak on [the operation of their employers], the community would be deprived of informed opinions on important public issues. The interest at stake is as much the public's interest in receiving informed opinion as it is the employee's own right to disseminate it" (citation omitted)); cf. *Treasury Emples.,* 513 U.S., at 470, 115 S. Ct. 1003, 130 L. Ed. 2d 964 ("The large-scale disincentive to Government employees' expression also imposes a significant burden on the public's right to read and hear what the employees would otherwise have written and said").

Provide an explanation of how and why the Court used the particular signal to introduce a series of cases.

3. Using the passage from question 2, prepare the citations in *ALWD* format.
4. The passage from question 2 has a number of pinpoint citations; locate the cases after each signal and review them to determine the basis for the U.S. Supreme Court references. Why are only U.S. Supreme Court cases cited in the passage?
5. Review the following passage from *Duncan v. Walker,* 533 U.S. 167, 171–172, 121 S. Ct. 2120, 2124, 150 L. Ed. 2d 251 (2001), and answer the questions that follow.

> We granted certiorari, 531 U.S. 991 (2000), to resolve a conflict between the Second Circuit's decision and the decisions of three other Courts of Appeals. *See Jimenez v. Johnson,* 208 F.3d 488 (C.A. 5 1999) *(per curiam); Jones v. Morton,* 195 F.3d 153 (C.A. 3 1999). One other Court of Appeals has since adopted the Second Circuit's view. *Petrick v. Martin,* 236 F.3d 624 (C.A. 10 2001). We now reverse.

   a. What does the Court mean when it states: "We granted certiorari"?
   b. What are the signals referenced in the case excerpt?
   c. What do the words *per curiam* indicate about the Court opinion?
   d. Correct the citations in the excerpt to *The Bluebook* and *ALWD* form.
   e. What did the court signify when it stated: "We now reverse"?
6. Prepare the proper citations for the periodicals listed:
   a. The author is Alex Glashausser and the name of the article is Citation and Representation. The article can be found in the Vanderbilt Law Review Journal in volume 55 and begins on page 59. The article was written in 2002.
   b. The author is Judith D. Fischer and the name of the article is Bareheaded and Barefaced Counsel: Courts React to Unprofessionalism in Lawyers' Papers. The article can be found in the Suffolk University Law Review Journal in volume 31 and begins on page 1. The article was written in 1997.

7. Correct the following citations:
   a. Bruther versus. General Electric Company, 818 Fed. Suppl. 1238 (Southern District of Indiana, 1993).
   b. Lockheed Maring Energy System, Incorporated vs. Slavin, 190 FRD 440 (ED Tennessee: 1999).
   c. Coco Brothers, Inc, vs. Pierce, 741 F2secd. 675 (third circuit 1984).
8. Prepare the short form citation variations as they would appear in *The Bluebook* and *ALWD Manual* for *Carter v. United States,* 530 U.S. 255, 120 S. Ct. 2159, 147 L.E. 2d 203 (2000). The pinpoint reference is page 264 in *U.S. Reports;* 2166 in Supreme *Court Reporter;* 213 in *Lawyers' Edition* 2d.

PORTFOLIO ASSIGNMENT

A brief is due next week and your supervising attorney requested you review the following section of the brief:

> The second issue befor this Court is the interpretation of the statute. When Interpreting a statute, the words should be given their "ordinary common sense Meaning of the words used." *U.S. v. Alvarez-Sanchez,* 114 S.Ct. 1599, 511 U.S. 350 (1994). See also: *C.I.R. v. Brown,* 85 S.Ct. 1162, 380 U.S. 563 (1965). The Court should not be "guided by a single sentence but rather view the entire statute as to its objects and policy. *Zenith Radio Corp. v. Matushita Elect. Industry Co., Ltd.* 402 F. Supp. 244 (E.D. Pa. 1975), *U.S. v. Manache,* 348 US 528 (1955) Therefore, the Court should only not substitute its judgment for that of the Legislature, particularly when the statute is clear and unambiguous. As the U.S. Supreme stated: "(I)n determining the scope of a statute, we look first to its language. If the statutory language is unambiguous, in absence of a clearly expressed legislative intent to the contrary, the language must ordinarily be regarded as conclusive." *U.S. v. Turkett,* 452 U.S. 576, 580 (1981); *United States v. Bay,* 736 F. 2d 891 (3rd Cir. 1984); *Negonsott v. Sanuels,* 113 S,Ct. 1119, 507 U.S. 99, 122 L.Ed.2d 457 (1993); *North Dakata v. U.S.* 103 S,Ct. 1095, 450 U.S, 300, 75 L.Ed.2d 77 (1983).
>
> It is clear that the law is well settled in this area. The court's conclusion regarding the language of the statute can be only one outcome; and that outcome must that the statute is clear and unambiguous.

The assignment includes a complete cite check and spelling and grammar review. Prepare the corrected document for your attorney's review.

Quick Quiz True/False Answers

Page 434	Page 442
1. False	1. True
2. False	2. True
3. False	3. False
4. False	4. True
5. False	5. True

Part Five

Practical Writing Applications

Chapter 15

The Basics of Legal Correspondence

After completing this chapter, you will be able to:

- Identify three functions of legal correspondence.
- Prepare appropriate letters for clients, opposing counsel, and the court.
- Identify the components of a letter.
- Format a letter properly.
- Address a letter to the court and other officials properly.
- Distinguish between a demand letter and an opinion letter.
- Prepare a demand letter.
- Understand the importance of statutory requirements for certain types of letters.
- Draft persuasive letters.
- Understand when paralegals can sign letters.

In this chapter and the remaining chapters, you will practice the skills developed in Parts One and Two of this textbook. Writing legal correspondence requires precision and clarity; proper punctuation and grammar; and above all, effective communication. In this chapter, we discuss different types of legal correspondence and the strategies behind them.

CASE FACT PATTERN

For over three months your client, Electronics, Inc., has been attempting to collect overdue rent from a difficult tenant. Phone calls to the tenant and several meetings have accomplished nothing. A week ago, an officer of the client firm sought your firm's advice. His initial consultation with your supervising attorney was completed shortly thereafter.

As a result of the consultation, a decision was made to take immediate action. You have just been assigned to draft a letter to the tenant on behalf of the client, demanding payment of the overdue rent.

Preparing basic correspondence, including demand letters, is a task often performed by paralegals.

Source: © Tribune Media Services, Inc. All Right Reserved. Reprinted with permission.

THE FUNCTION OF LEGAL CORRESPONDENCE

Although letter writing is something of a lost art in social communication, having been replaced by the telephone call and e-mail, in business and legal matters it remains important. Letters form a permanent written record that can be relied upon later to reconstruct events. Used and drafted correctly, letters help prevent misunderstandings, broken agreements, and missed deadlines.

The legal profession relies on letters for three main purposes—to inform, to advise, and to confirm.

The Informative Letter

informative letter
A letter that transmits information.

Letters that transmit information are known as **informative letters,** also called "for your information" or "FYI" letters. Such a letter might be sent to a client to inform him of the progress of a case, the status of billing and payment, or the need for information to prepare a deposition. An informative letter also might be sent to opposing counsel (for example, to provide dates of availability to schedule a deposition or trial), or anyone to whom the attorney or paralegal needs to provide information.

The Advisory Letter

advisory letter
A formal letter that offers legal opinions or demands.

Advisory letters are more formal than informative letters. They offer legal opinions. This might be in the form of an objective analysis of the case at issue, as a detailed letter to a client. Or it might be written in a persuasive style from an advocate's perspective, as when an attorney writes to opposing counsel proposing settlement. Whatever form it takes, an advisory letter is detailed and formal. Research may be involved, and it must be done with the same care as any other research project. There may be statutory requirements to follow or questions of law that must be resolved. If the letter is incomplete or otherwise flawed, the result may harm your client.

Although the advisory letter is certainly informative, its content goes beyond that of an informative letter. The content and style often resemble more sophisticated legal writing, such as an internal memorandum or a brief, and statutory requirements may apply. Different types of advisory letters are demand letters, letters notifying of intention to litigate, and opinion letters.

The Confirmation Letter

confirmation letter
A letter designed to create a record or restate the content of the original oral communication.

In the course of a legal matter, information is often shared orally, by telephone, or in person. In order to create a permanent record of the passing of such information, a **confirmation letter** is often sent, restating the content of the original oral communication. For example, when an attorney orally advises a client of a court date, a follow-up confirmation letter should be sent immediately. That way, there is no excuse for confusion.

A confirmation letter not only restates orally transmitted information, it also protects the attorney (and the paralegal) from future problems or repercussions. By establishing in writing the date of a court appearance, for example, or the terms of an orally agreed-upon settlement, there is a permanent record, which can be referred to in the event of a disagreement.

EVALUATING THE AUDIENCE: TONE AND STYLE

The tone and style of a letter vary not only with the purpose, but also with the audience. Correspondence with your client, for example, may be less formal than a letter to the court, and less technical than a letter to opposing counsel. A different audience requires a different focus, attention, and style. You create the proper tone by word choice and sentence structure. Depending upon the type of letter you are drafting, your tone may be informal or businesslike. The tone of a letter affects how the reader interprets the letter. Are you communicating to a client? What message do you intend to send? If advice is given on the likelihood of success of a legal claim, the tone is serious and formal. By contrast, if you are communicating a meeting or a court hearing, your tone may be less formal. Think about how you want to be perceived. Do you want to be friends with the client or to be a member of a professional team? As familiar as you may become with a client or opposing counsel, your tone, informal or formal, should remain, above all else, professional. Therefore, consider your audience and ask yourself:

- What is the purpose of the letter I am drafting?
- To whom is the letter directed?
- Should my tone be informal or formal?
- What result do I want to achieve?

By asking yourself these questions, you will be able to tailor your letter to the given assignment successfully.

The Client

Regular contact with your clients is important, both to keep them informed and to minimize the anxiety they may feel because of their unfamiliarity with the legal system. In corresponding with clients, you should keep in mind several considerations.

First, provide concrete answers. Clients dislike lawyers and paralegals who hedge with vague language. This does not mean that you should misrepresent the state of affairs if it really is indefinite, but rather that you explain the indefinite state with concrete, clear language. If the law in your case is subject to several interpretations, say so clearly and identify the possible interpretations.

Second, write to the client's level of understanding. Avoid legalese or, if you must use it, *explain* it. Don't try to impress the client with your technical vocabulary; write in plain English. To do this is not to patronize or condescend—if a client, even an intelligent and educated client, has no legal training, there is no reason to subject her to difficult jargon.

Third, always be respectful and courteous to your clients. They have hired you because they have a legal problem, and it is probably a difficult time for them. Your compassion and understanding in your legal correspondence and face-to-face contacts can help them cope, whereas a harsh or pompous tone would cause more anxiety and ill will.

Finally, choose your words carefully. In litigation, a result is never certain; in a business deal or real estate transaction, the outcome is often unpredictable; in negotiations, the other party is always an uncontrollable factor. Yet clients are always looking for certainties. They want to be told that everything will be all right. You must make it clear that your opinions are not *guarantees.* Avoid the temptation to act like an all-knowing legal forecaster; be accurate and honest, and communicate the uncertainties.

Opposing Counsel

Opposing counsel is not your friend in the case at hand, even if he is your friend in other contexts. Always remember that information shared with opposing counsel will be available to the opposing client (or might even be brought to the court's attention), and can be used against your client. Thus you must choose carefully what you communicate to opposing counsel. Be courteous in your correspondence with opposing counsel, but be cautious as well.

The Court

Correspondence directed to the court usually comes in one of three forms: either a cover letter accompanying documents to be filed; a letter requesting a hearing date or other procedural assistance; or a formal letter to a judge stating a legal position.

cover letter
A standard form letter identifying information such as document filings.

Cover letters accompanying documents are usually standard form letters. They simply identify the documents and the date of filing. Such letters fulfill the confirmation function of correspondence—they provide a written record establishing that the documents were filed, and when. Copies always should be sent to opposing counsel.

clerk of the court
An individual who manages the administrative functions of the court.

A letter requesting a hearing date or other procedural assistance is similarly straightforward in its text—it simply makes a direct request. Whether a letter is addressed to a judge or **clerk of the court,** opposing counsel receives a copy. The clerk of the court is important to the court process. The clerks are the individuals who manage the day-to-day operations of the court. Often they transmit documents from the court to an attorney, or they may acknowledge the filing of a court order. Cover letters normally are transmitted to the clerk of the court for filing of documents, hearing requests, and any other general business with the court. The clerks of courts are integral to the operations of the court and also offer helpful guidance when needed. Unlike a judge, they can communicate directly with you or your attorney.

ex parte
A communication between one party in a lawsuit and the judge.

A letter to a judge stating a legal position is less commonly seen, usually outside the standard course of a lawsuit, and it involves risks. If such a letter is sent, needless to say a copy must be sent to opposing counsel, and must be prepared in a formal manner, as if it were a brief. Be concise, direct, and respectful to judges. Such a communication between one party in a lawsuit and the judge is called an **ex parte** communication (recall this term from our discussion of legalese in Chapter 11). Only under very limited circumstances is such communication acceptable. The problem with ex parte communications is that the other side's opportunity to respond is limited. In any event, no such communication should ever be attempted by you without express authorization from your supervising attorney. (Even then, a fine line is drawn as to the propriety of the communication.)

PRACTICE TIP

Always have a listing of the current clerks of the courts with whom you will deal. Include in the listing the court clerk's name, the name of the court, and the court's address, telephone number, fax, and e-mail, if appropriate.

THE COMPONENTS OF A LETTER

The format of different types of letters varies, and different firms or attorneys may have different preferences, but the following are generally accepted as the standard components of most letters:

- Letterhead
- Date
- Addressee
- Reference line
- Salutation
- Body
- Header
- Closing and signature block

- Referencing initials
- Copy and blind copy

We consider each of these in turn in the following subsections.

letterhead
Standard stationery.

The Letterhead

Most law firms and businesses have standard stationery, called **letterhead,** with the firm or company name, address, telephone number, and other relevant information. Law firm letterhead often lists, just below the firm name, all the attorneys in the firm.

When writing on behalf of your firm, use letterhead. It shows that you are associated with the firm, making the significance of the letter clear. It may even be relevant for professional liability insurance coverage.

Letterhead is used for the first page of a multiple-page letter. The other pages should be on matching paper, but without the letterhead.

PRACTICE TIP

When sending a letter by certified mail, include the certified mail number in the address block under the certified mail designation. Those green cards could get lost or there may be a question as to actual receipt of a letter. If the certified number of the mailing is located on the letter, the confusion is minimized and your record will always be accurate. Verifying receipt of a letter often becomes an issue if a statutory time frame is involved or in case you need a record that the letter was received. This practice may save you and a case from disaster.

The Date

The date appears below the letterhead. It is important for establishing an accurate chronology in a legal matter. Letters often go through several drafts over a period of several days; make sure the date on the letter matches the date of mailing.

The Addressee

The name of the person to whom the letter is written appears at the top left margin, just below the letterhead. If the letter is sent by other than U.S. mail (for example, by fax or overnight delivery), the method of delivery should be indicated above the address block. Use titles, if applicable (for example, "Dr. William Jones"), and note that all attorneys should be addressed with the suffix "Esquire" or its abbreviation, "Esq." (as in "William Jones, Esq."). Do not use the standard "Mr.," "Mrs.," "Miss," or "Ms." in this context. A typical address block is shown in Figure 15.1.

Title of the Addressee

You will correspond with many types of individuals who have different titles. Pay attention to those titles and address them accordingly. The following are examples of the proper method of addressing individuals with whom you may have contact:

- "Mr.," "Mrs.," "Miss," and "Ms.": These are the standard titles used in addressing most individuals. The issue arises whether you address women as "Mrs." or

FIGURE 15.1
Address Block

<u>HAND DELIVERED</u>

Ms. Susan Windsor, President
Electronics Company, Inc.
465 Commerce Blvd.
Lincoln, NE 54321

or

By Fax and U.S. Mail
Ms. Susan Windsor
Chief Operating Officer
Electronics Company, Inc.
465 Commerce Blvd.
Lincoln, NE 54321

or

Certified Mail, Return Receipt Requested
Ms. Susan Windsor,
Chief Operating Officer
Electronics Company, Inc.
465 Commerce Blvd.
Lincoln, NE 54321

PRACTICE TIP

Some states use the term "Justice" for their judges in the highest appellate courts; others simply use "Judge." Check the jurisdiction for the proper protocol. Additionally, do not abbreviate the word Honorable as "Hon."—the abbreviation is inappropriate.

"Ms.": "Miss" or "Ms." When you meet a client, you may want to ask how they want to be addressed. That will set the tone of your communications. Otherwise, use the standard "Mrs." or "Miss," unless directed otherwise.

- Attorney: Some jurisdictions use "Attorney" as a title. This form is a matter of local preference. It is proper etiquette to use "Esq." after an attorney's name if you are not sure of the local usage.
- Judges: It is customary to address a judge as "Honorable" or "The Honorable." For a federal judge, the address block is

Honorable Stanley Brotman
U.S. District Court District of New Jersey
(Address of the court)

For the chief justice of an appellate court, the address block is

The Honorable Craig Enoch
Chief Justice, Texas Supreme Court
(Address of the court)

The address format for other judges follows the same format as the one for a federal court judge.

- Clerk of the court: You will communicate regularly with the clerk of the court. Clerks are addressed as follows:

Name
Clerk of the Court
Name of the Court
Address of the Court

- Political figures: There are protocols for addressing governors, senators, congressional representatives, and other government officials. The common protocol for corresponding with an elected official is as follows:

Honorable Barbara Boxer
United States Senator
Address

Sometimes an elected official dictates the way to address him or her in a formal correspondence. Investigate the proper protocols for addressing an elected official for the jurisdiction with whom you intend to communicate. Some individuals are sensitive as to how they are addressed. Do not invite the wrath of an elected official because your letter addressed them improperly.

- Clergy: Use the proper title of a religious leader if you are corresponding with them. For example:

The Reverend Jesse Jackson
Name of the Congregation
Address

- Individuals with titles: Generally, titles follow the name of the addressee. Be sure you include a person's title when corresponding with them. Again, you do not want to offend anyone.

Name	*Jonathan A. Potts*
Title	*Chief Executive Officer*

FIGURE 15.2
Reference Lines

Prelitigation:
Re: Our Client: Anytime Builders, Inc.
Our File #11-325
Sale of Aacme Service Company, Inc.

Litigation pending:
Re: Anytime Builders, Inc. v. Aacme Service Company, Inc.
Cause No. 08-00576-X
Our File #08-325

Company	*Medical Supply Company, Inc.*
Address	*Address*

The Reference Line

The **reference line** appears below the address block, and identifies the subject matter of the letter. It provides a quick (*very* quick) introduction for the reader, and helps your assistant determine where to file the copy without reading the whole letter.

reference line
A line of text that appears below the address block, and identifies the subject matter of the letter.

The detail in the reference line sometimes depends on the stage of the matter. The parties involved are always identified, along with a brief description of the matter. Some firms also include their internal file number and, if a lawsuit has been filed, the docket number is often included as well. If the parties are involved in several matters, or if only one aspect of a complex matter is addressed in the letter, there may be even more detailed identification. Figure 15.2 shows two examples of reference lines, one prior to litigation and the other afterward.

The Salutation

The **salutation** appears below the reference line. It usually begins with the word "Dear," even in formal correspondence. Use "Mr.," "Ms.," "Mrs.," or "Miss," unless you know the person to whom you are writing, and follow the name with a colon, which is more formal than a comma.

salutation
A greeting that appears below the reference line.

As mentioned in the section titled "The Addressee," knowing how to address titled individuals is important. The following are guidelines based upon the examples:

- Dear Chief Justice Roberts or Dear Mr. Chief Justice
- Dear Justice Souter
- Dear Judge Brotman
- Dear Governor Rendel
- Dear Congressman Rengal
- Dear Reverend Jackson

Unless a specific title such as the above, refer to those with business titles as "Mr.," "Mrs.," "Miss," or "Ms."

The Body

The **body** of a letter contains the information you wish to communicate. It may be as short as one or two sentences (if the purpose, for example, is simply to indicate that you have enclosed documents), or as long as several pages (for an in-depth legal analysis, such as an opinion letter).

body
The text that contains the information you wish to communicate in a letter.

As in most effective legal writing, the opening sentence and paragraph of your letters should summarize what you want to say and why. You should make it clear that you are representing the client, unless you have done this already in prior letters.

FIGURE 15.3
Body of Confirmation Letter

> This letter will confirm our agreement regarding the sale of the Aacme Service Company, Inc., to Anytime Builders, Inc. As a result of our meeting of May 5, 2008, we agreed that Mr. Allen will provide my clients with books and records of the business. Once we have had an opportunity to review the books and records, we will be able to determine whether the sale of the business will be completed.
>
> I have received the weekly installment payment to Mr. Allen in the amount of $1,203.54. As I indicated to you at the meeting, I will be holding all future checks in trust until we can resolve the question of the purchase and sale of the business.
>
> It is my further understanding that some time next week we will meet again to determine whether the business will be sold to my clients, or whether Mr. Allen will reimburse all monies tendered for the purchase of the business to my clients.
>
> I hope we will be able to resolve this matter quickly.

You should use all the writing techniques you've learned—correct sentence structure, parallelism, conciseness, and so on.

Be sure to be complete. Cover all the material you need to communicate, both positive and negative. Avoid a pompous or arrogant tone. In fact, in letters to clients or other friendly parties, you may use a relatively informal tone, although you should be careful that the message is not distorted nor its importance undermined.

When you write an advisory letter, the tone should be formal and authoritative, just as you would write a brief or internal memorandum.

Figure 15.3 shows the body of a letter concerning the resolution of a dispute. In subsequent sections, we discuss the content of other types of letters.

The Header

header
Text that appears at the top left margin of all subsequent pages, and identifies three elements: the person to whom the letter is addressed; the date of the letter; and the page number.

As we stated, letterhead is used only for the first page of multipage letters. However, subsequent pages have identifying information as well, in the form of a **header.** A header appears at the top left margin of all subsequent pages, and identifies three elements: the person to whom the letter is addressed; the date of the letter; and the page number. A practical note: We indicated earlier that the date on the front of the letterhead page should be the date of mailing; this also is obviously true for the date appearing in headers. If the date on your letterhead and headers fails to match the postmark, you will seem disorganized; if different dates appear on the letterhead and headers in the same letter, you will look sloppy and careless. The amount of time it takes to check these details is minor; the impact of an error on your reputation can be great.

The Closing and Signature Block

complimentary closing
The concluding words in the letter just above a signature.

A letter is generally concluded by one or two sentences at the end. A concluding message often contains such courteous statements as, "Please do not hesitate to call if you have any questions." Following the concluding message is the **complimentary closing.** In legal correspondence, the typical closing is "Very truly yours," followed by a comma. Note that the *V* in *Very* is capitalized, but the other words are not. There are other proper closing variations that are also acceptable:

- "Yours truly" or "Yours very truly" (traditional closing).
- "Sincerely" (less formal, but does communicate a tone).
- "Best wishes" or "Best regards" (very informal). Use this closing in a limited setting and only when informality is appropriate.

Stay away from the extremes: very formal and very informal. These types of closing include the following:

- "Respectfully" (usually used in a pleading)
- "Fondly" (do I hear lawsuit?)

FIGURE 15.4
Correct and Incorrect Closings of Letters

Correct closing of letter:
Thank you for your attention to this matter.

Very truly yours,

Anne Simmonds
General Counsel

Incorrect closing of letter:
Thanking you for your attention and courtesies, I remain,

Very truly yours,

Anne Simmonds
General Counsel

FIGURE 15.5
Appropriate Closing by a Paralegal

Very truly yours,

Emily Brady
Legal Assistant or (Paralegal)

or

Very truly yours,

Emily Brady
Paralegal for Marcus Baker

Examples of correct and incorrect concluding messages and closings are seen in Figure 15.4. Note that the correct concluding message ends with a period. It is outdated to end the concluding message with a comma leading into the closing, as in the incorrect example.

Most of the letters you prepare will be for the signature of your supervising attorney. Remember that it is improper, and indeed illegal, for a paralegal to give legal advice. If you do sign a letter, identify yourself as a paralegal or legal assistant (see Figure 15.5).

Referencing Initials

At the end of the letter, initials appear identifying who wrote the letter, and in many instances, who typed the letter. Placing initials at the end of the letter credits the individual who authored the letter, which is ultimately the individual who is responsible for the contents of the letter. In limited number of cases, you may see three sets of initials. This occurs when a partner in a firm signs a letter, an associate prepares the letter and research, and an assistant types the letter. This creates a chain of responsibility. Signify the first set of initials in capital letters followed by a (/) slash and the initials of the preparer of the letter. If there are documents enclosed with the letter, indicate that after the initials of the preparers on a new line. The section will appear as follows:

PRT/prh	*PRT/prh*
Enclosures	*Enc. or Encls.*

ETHICS ALERT

The rules of professional responsibility govern what paralegals can and cannot sign. Paralegals cannot render legal advice. Often clients rely heavily on paralegals for guidance simply because they are more accessible than the attorney. Do not get caught in a trap. You may sign letters transmitting information or setting a meeting. That is not to say that you cannot prepare a letter for the attorney's signature. You can. When the letter is signed, it represents that the letter was read and the contents approved. In some instances when an attorney has not read the contents of a letter or document, they attempt to plead ignorance. Courts definitely do not buy that argument. In *Philadelphia Gear Corp. v. Swath International, Ltd.*, 200 F. Supp. 2d 493 (E.D. Pa. 2002), an attorney reviewed an amended pleading, approved it, and had his secretary print it. She printed and filed the wrong amended pleading. Realizing his error, the attorney wrote opposing counsel a letter stating "I am a victim of sophisticated word-processing, self-editing of documents on the system and my own inattention." *Id.* at 495. The attorney did try to remedy the problem, but the opposing counsel wanted attorney's fees for his time. There was a succession of letters where the issue was not resolved, resulting in the court's involvement. The court observed that there are "no exceptions to the requirement that all reasonable attorneys will read a document before filing it in court.' Attorneys must always keep in mind that computers are not infallible, nor are secretaries, paralegals, or other lawyers." *Id.* at 496 (citations omitted).

Read the case and draw your own conclusions. Do you believe the attorneys acted reasonably in the case? The court? What could have alleviated the problem? What action, if any, did the court take against the attorneys? The moral of the case is: read the letter or document before you sign and file it with a court. A more important point is: pay attention to what you sign. Do not sign a letter that even remotely appears to render legal advice. Ever heard of the unauthorized practice of law?

Copy and Blind Copy (cc and bcc)

cc
Copy.

Copies of correspondence are often sent to parties other than the addressee. The client, for example, is often sent copies of letters to opposing counsel or the court. This fact is denoted at the end of the original letter by the notation **"cc"** (which technically stands for "carbon copy"). But carbon copies are no longer used, and "cc" simply stands for "copy." After the "cc" come the names of any persons to whom the copy is sent. Thus the original addressee also knows who else has received copies. If enclosures are included, note that as well with the designation after the name "with enclosures."

bcc
Blind copy.

Under certain circumstances the author of the letter may want to conceal from the original addressee who else has received a copy. The original letter, then, contains no notation about copies (i.e., no "cc"), but your file copy will contain the notation **"bcc" (blind copy),** followed by the name of the blind-copy recipient. The blind-copy recipient's copy will also have the "bcc" designation, so that she will know it was a blind copy. Proper use of the "cc" and "bcc" designations requires good communication among the attorney, paralegal, and assistant; it is often wise, for example, to clip a note to the original with an instruction such as "bcc John Doe."

FORMATTING THE LETTER

Many word processing systems have programs to assist in preparing letters: Microsoft Word, Corel WordPerfect, and others. They may provide helpful letter templates with a fixed format. The style of your supervising attorney or law firm may dictate the format of a letter. Some possible formatting options are as follows:

- Block style (blocked or left-aligned): With this style all the information contained within the letter is blocked or aligned to the left margin. A blocked style creates

FIGURE 15.6
Transmittal Letters

(a) Transmittal Letter Forwarding Document to Opposing Counsel (block style)

May 15, 2008

Mr. Jeffrey Smith
Attorney at Law
701 Lawnview Avenue
Dallas, TX 78910

Re: Case No. 2008-432-A
O.K. Binding, Inc. v. Southern Paper Co.

Dear Mr. Smith:

Enclosed is a copy of Plaintiff's First Amended Complaint in the above-referenced matter, which has been filed with the Court this date.

Thank you for your attention to this matter.

Very truly yours,

P. R. Hodge
PRH/sst

cc: Client

(b) Transmittal Letter Forwarding Document to Court and Requesting Return of Document (modified block style)

May 15, 2008

Mary Smith
Clerk of the Court
201st District Court
500 Main St.
Dallas, TX 78910

Re: No. 2008-432-A
O.K. Binding, Inc. v. Southern Paper Co.

Dear Ms. Smith:

I enclose the original and two copies of Plaintiff's First Amended Original Petition. Please file the original with the court's records and return a file stamped copy to this office in the enclosed self-addressed, stamped envelope.

Thank you for your cooperation in this matter.

Very truly yours,

Patrick R. Langdon

PRL/sst

the appearance of clean lines. Paragraphs are designated by double-spacing between paragraphs. Although some attorneys choose to center the date, that is still considered block style. An example of block style is shown in Figure 15.6.

- Modified block style: As the name implies, parts of the letter are blocked. Usually with a modified block style, the paragraphs are indented (five spaces) with the remaining parts of the letter in a blocked style. Variations of this style include the date being centered and the signature block being centered or

FIGURE 15.7
Letter Requesting Employment Records

June 1, 2008

CERTIFIED MAIL #P117824932
RETURN RECEIPT REQUESTED
Mr. Martin Banks
Director of Human Resources
Medical Supplies Company, Inc.
603 East 21st Street
Houston, TX 77015

Re: Mrs. Beth Windsor

Dear Mr. Banks:

Enclosed is an authorization for release of employment records signed by my client. At this time, I would request that you forward to my office copies of all employment records in your possession regarding Mrs. Windsor. Please have this information forward to me by July 3, 2008.

Thank you for your cooperation in this matter.

Very truly yours,

Colleen O. Hayward

COH/bng
cc: Client

PRACTICE TIP

There are accepted typefaces for legal letters: Times New Roman, Courier, or Arial. Nonstandard typeface styles convey a lack of professionalism. Stay with the standards unless otherwise directed by your attorney. The point size of the type in the letter is also standardized. Most letters are typed in 12- or 10-point type for readability.

indenting the reference clause with the date and signature block centered. Either style is correct. Figure 15.7 is an example of a modified block style.

Your attorney's preference: This style is probably the one that rules. Many attorneys prefer to block only the left margin, conveying a professional albeit "unstuffy" approach to letter writing. Review existing letters or ask to determine the format to follow.

In addition to signing a document that your attorney has requested you sign on their behalf, prepare a note to the file indicating the instructions you were given by your attorney. If the issue arises later, at least there is a document recording the instructions you were given. You never know who may have selective memory in a crisis.

A DAY IN THE LIFE OF A PARALEGAL

A dilemma that paralegals are constantly faced with is "when should a paralegal sign a letter and when must an attorney sign a letter?" It is abundantly clear that a paralegal may not sign a letter that renders legal advice. But what does a paralegal do when an attorney requests that you sign a letter when he or she is unavailable? First, never, never attempt to "mimic" or more directly, forge an attorney's signature. This practice creates more problems than one can imagine. Second, if a document must be signed, be sure the attorney has reviewed the document. Then sign the attorney's name, but place your initials next to the signature to signify that the document was signed by someone other than the attorney. This is bad practice, and unless you work in a firm with only one attorney, avoid this practice. The point is that attorneys will ask you to sign for them when they are unavailable.

Finally, when other attorneys are available to sign the document, suggest to your supervising attorney that one of his colleagues could sign the document, such as Frederick Cameron for Andrew Scott (the named attorney on the document). This approach is better than you signing the document.

FIGURE 15.8
Letter Requesting Administrative Transcript

June 10, 2008

HAND DELIVERED
Office of the City Secretary
City Hall
Minneapolis, MN 55401

Re: Certified Copy of Transcript of Hearings Held on June 3, 2008, before the Urban Rehabilitation Standards Board Property located at 7042 Rocky Road

Dear Board Members:

I hereby request that a certified transcript of the Urban Rehabilitation Standards Board hearings on June 3, 2008, on the property located at 7042 Rocky Road, Minneapolis, Minnesota, be prepared by the City Secretary of the City of Minneapolis. This transcript is now requested for the purpose of an appeal to the District Court. Please advise when the certified copies of the record will be ready for transmission to the court, and I will have a courier collect them.

Thank you for your prompt attention to this request.

Very truly yours,

Mark O. Walker

MOW/prt
cc: Client

GENERAL LEGAL CORRESPONDENCE

Legal correspondence comes in many forms. As a paralegal, you will draft many different types of general correspondences. Earlier we touched briefly on the **transmittal letter,** a type of confirmation letter that accompanies information sent to a designated party. Sometimes documents sent with a transmittal letter must be signed or filed and returned; if that is the case, a return envelope with proper address and postage should be included, and the transmittal letter should contain instructions about what the receiver should do. Two examples of proper transmittal letters are found in Figure 15.6.

transmittal letter
A type of confirmation letter that accompanies information sent to a designated party.

Another type of correspondence is a letter requesting information. Such requests must be specific. By sending such a letter, you not only obtain information, but also create a record that the request was made. Typically the letter will request medical records, employment records, or other investigative materials. Figure 15.7 shows an example of a letter requesting employment records, and Figure 15.8 shows a letter requesting an administrative transcript.

A **retainer letter** is a form of correspondence important in the practice of law, for it sets forth the agreement and relationship between the attorney and the client. Such things as fees and a description of the matter are included. Figure 15.9 provides an example of a general retainer letter.

retainer letter
A form of correspondence that sets forth the agreement and relationship between the attorney and the client.

In an **authorization letter,** the client provides the attorney with official permission to contact employers, doctors, or other individuals who have records that relate in some way to the matter at hand. The attorney drafts the authorization letter for the client's signature; the client reviews and signs it.

authorization letter
A letter the client provides the attorney granting permission to contact employers, doctors, or other individuals who have records that relate to a case.

The list could go on and on. When preparing general legal correspondence, you should keep the following factors in mind:

- Determine the purpose of your letter.
- Identify to whom your letter is directed.
- Communicate in plain English.
- If you use legalese or terms of art, explain your meaning unless the audience is trained in legal matters.

FIGURE 15.9
General Retainer Letter

LETTERHEAD

July 15, 2008

Mr. Cameron Anderson
CPM Management Company
5177 Oaktree Place
Philadelphia, PA 19105

Re: Retainer Letter Agreement

Dear Mr. Anderson:
This letter will confirm the terms of the engagement of the Law Firm effective July 15, 2008 as counsel for the Company ("Clients") in the matter of CPM Management v. HCCD Enterprises.

a. Professional Services Fee: The Law Firm will bill for its services at an hourly rate of $300.00 per hour for the services of the partner assigned to this case. The partner will be the attorney primarily responsible for this matter. However, the law firm reserves the right to assign other attorneys and staff to assist the partner. The rates for associate attorneys are $200.00 an hour and $75.00 for paralegals. In addition to this hourly rate, the Clients will be responsible for the costs and expenses incurred by the law firm with regard to its representation of Clients in this matter.
b. Costs and Expenses: Law firm will seek reimbursement or request prepayment for all costs incurred and monies expended in connection with this matter. These costs and expenses include, but are not limited to, court costs, transcripts, filing fees, expert witness fees, assessments, investigators, travel expenses, photocopying, telecommunications, computerized research, delivery and courier charges. When substantial or unusual payments to third parties are required, the law firm reserves the right to request an advance of funds to cover these costs or to arrange to have the charge forwarded directly to you for payment.
c. Billing: The law firm will charge an initial retainer of $10,000 toward the professional service fee in this matter. The law firm will bill you monthly and that bill will reflect the number of hours worked times the hourly rate, plus the expenses incurred by the law firm in connection with this matter to be charged against the retainer. Your failure to pay any invoice within thirty days of the billing date shall be the basis of the law firm filing with the Court a motion to withdraw from any further representation.
d. Appeals: Law firm will represent client in the U.S District Court through the disposition of the matter, inclusive of any interlocutory or other appeals based solely upon the issues in this matter. If Clients desire law firm to continue to represent Clients on appeal to the United States Court of Appeals or the United States Supreme Court, Clients shall enter into a separate retainer agreement and shall pay to the law firm a separate retainer.

If the above is your understanding of our legal representation, please sign the two originals of this letter where indicated and return one of the originals to me for my records.

Very truly yours,

David Potter

- Be specific when requesting information.
- Follow the guidelines we've discussed for demand and opinion letters.
- Be polite and courteous.
- Send copies to the appropriate parties.

YOU BE THE JUDGE

Only the attorney can establish the attorney–client relationship, render legal advice, and set fees to the engagement. You may *not* do any of these actions. The rules of professional responsibility for attorneys make this point quite clear. You may interview a client and record information about the interview to pass to your supervising attorney. You may tell a client hourly rates but not set the fee arrangement for the engagement. Case law is well settled on this matter, as is the usage of the respective bar associations around the United States. In a bankruptcy case in Ohio, there was confusion as to the relationship between a nonattorney and a client. Read *In re Ferguson,* 326 B.R. 419 (Bankr. N.D. Ohio 2005), and think about the message the judge conveyed. In the judge's final remarks he warned: "[r]egulations prohibiting the unauthorized practice of law are intended to protect the public from being advised in legal matters by incompetent, untrained, and potentially unreliable persons over whom the judicial branch of government can exercise little control." *Id.* at 424. What acts did the nonattorney commit? What did the nonattorney ask the court to award, and what was the court's response? Do you agree or disagree with the court's actions? Why?

Quick Quiz True/False Questions

1. Legal correspondence is used only to advise the client of important information.
2. All letters should include a date, addressee, salutation, and closing.
3. When corresponding with clients, always refer to them by their first name.
4. A blind copy of a letter conceals the identity of a recipient of the letter.
5. One type of general correspondence is an authorization letter.

letter bank
A depository for firm letters regarding client cases.

SPECIALIZED LEGAL CORRESPONDENCE

Attorneys draft different types of correspondences in their practices. Depending on the nature of the case, specialized correspondences may be required on behalf of the client. The most common specialized legal correspondences are demand letters, consumer protection letters, and letters notifying of intention to litigate. These letters require some legal research as they generally have statutory requirements. Requirements for these letters range from setting forth the contents of the letter to specifying the time period in which the letter must be written and received. If you are asked to draft a specialized correspondence, you must

- research the statutory requirements;
- review the client's file for the pertinent facts;
- request examples from letter banks or other client files of the type of letter to be drafted;
- check form books for suggested standardized language, if available.

demand letter
A letter requesting action on a legal matter.

collection letter
A letter that demands payment of an amount claimed to be owed to a client.

PRACTICE TIP

Most law firms have letter banks. Prior letters on cases are archived and are excellent places to find examples of content and format. If a letter bank is available, ask to review previous files for examples. Do not reinvent the wheel, if possible.

The Demand Letter

Many disputes are resolved through discussion and negotiation, but some are not. As negotiations stall, a client may need to make demands upon the opposing party. Sometimes clients want to make demands even before negotiations have begun. In your role as a paralegal, you will be drafting **demand letters** on behalf of your firm's clients.

The purpose of a demand letter is to motivate a desired response—often, though not exclusively, the payment of a debt. In the following subsections we discuss several categories of demand letter, as well as some guidelines for preparing a response.

The Collection Letter

A **collection letter** demands payment of an amount claimed to be owed to your client. It is not, however, as simple as a "pay up or else" letter—in practice, the concept is more subtle than that. To prepare an effective collection letter, several considerations should be kept in mind.

First, understand your purpose. Again, this is not as simple as it may seem. Are you seeking immediate payment in full? Are you seeking partial payment? Are you seeking to create a written record of the amount claimed due? Are you trying to satisfy statutory notice requirements? Are you trying to accomplish some combination of these? Are you following up earlier client demands, or is your letter the first demand made upon the opposing party? As you can see, there are many factors to consider.

Second, determine whether there are statutory rules or common-law principles that affect your demand letter. If you fail to satisfy any applicable requirements, not only will your letter be faulty, but you may actually undermine your client's ability to collect.

Third, your letter should set forth your client's version of disputed events, and possibly undisputed events as well. State your claim in a concise, authoritative manner, setting forth the amount of the original debt, the date it was incurred, amounts already paid, interest due, the present amount due, and any other relevant terms. In addition, you should probably include supporting evidence, such as invoices, leases, promissory notes, or relevant correspondence.

deadline date
A certain date by which a request or demand should be fulfilled.

Fourth, you should make your demand clear. Do not just demand payment, for example; demand payment by a certain date, called the **deadline date.** Tell the recipient what she can expect if she does not comply by that date, and be prepared to follow through—if your threats are exposed as empty, your credibility is damaged and your future ability to negotiate is undercut.

Finally, if the opposing party is represented by counsel, be sure that you write to the attorney and not to the party. It is a violation of codes of professional responsibility to write directly to a party who you know is represented by a lawyer.

The Fair Debt Collection Statutory Letter

The federal Fair Debt Collection Practices Act, 15 U.S.C. §§ 1692–1692(o), regulates collection of debts owed by consumers. When preparing a collection letter that must comply with this statute's requirements, you should include the following information:

- The amount of the debt.
- The name of the creditor to whom the debt is owed.
- A statement that you assume the debt to be valid, unless the validity is disputed within thirty days.
- A statement that, if the consumer notifies the attorney in writing within the thirty-day period that the debt or any part of it is disputed, verification of the debt will be obtained and sent to the consumer.
- A statement that, upon written request within the thirty-day period, the attorney will provide the consumer with the name and address of the original creditor, if different from the current creditor.
- A statement that the attorney is attempting to collect the debt, and that any information received will be used for that purpose.

Unless the federal statute is complied with, your collection letter may be faulty, and your attempt to collect for your client may fail. You should be familiar with this statute and any similar legislation that is applicable in your state or region.

Figure 15.10 shows a collection letter with a slightly aggressive tone. Figure 15.11 shows a more formal collection letter, written to collect a consumer debt in compliance with the federal Fair Debt Collection Practices Act.

FIGURE 15.10
Example of a Minimally Aggressive Collection Letter

May 24, 2008

Mr. Travis Rande
CD'S UNLIMITED
1617 Concord Street
San Diego, CA 90404

Re: Our Client:
Balance Due and Owing: $5,325.87

Dear Mr. Rande:

The law firm of Helman & Jones represents Productions, Inc. in the above-referenced matter. On or about January 4, 2008, Moulde Productions, Inc. provided you with production services and air time for a commercial advertisement on the "Music Review" television program. For these services and air time, you agreed to pay Moulde Productions, Inc. the total amount of $5,325.87. Presently, there is a balance due and owing of $5,325.87.

In order to alleviate any additional costs and expenses, your prompt attention to this matter is advisable. It is expected that the entire amount will be paid within 30 days. Please contact me to discuss the matter immediately. If we have not received a satisfactory response from you within the time specified above, we will have no alternative but to pursue further action.

Very truly yours,

Jeanne J. Carr

FIGURE 15.11
Collection Letter Prepared in Compliance with the Federal Fair Debt Collection Practices Act

April 28, 2008

CERTIFIED MAIL #P117784262
RETURN RECEIPT REQUESTED
Ms. Linda Starr
Burgers, Etc.
645 Elm Street
Houston, Texas 77204

Re: Our Client: AAA Equipment
Amounts Due on Account: $8,847.58

Dear Ms. Starr:

This law firm has been retained to represent AAA Equipment in the above-referenced matter to effect collection of the amount owed by your company, Burgers, Etc. On or about February 4, 2008, our client provided Burgers, Etc. with restaurant equipment for use in its hamburger business. The cost of the equipment was $9,747.58, for which you paid $1,700 as a down payment, leaving a balance of $8,047.58. As per the contract, the balance was due on or before March 15, 2008. The balance is now past due. If $8,847.58 (constituting the original $8,047.58 plus an additional sum of $800.00 as attorneys' fees) is not received in this office within thirty (30) days from the date of this letter, we will have no alternative but to pursue whatever legal remedies are available to protect our client's interests, including the filing of a lawsuit.

Pursuant to the Fair Debt Collection Practices Act, 15 U.S.C. §§ 1692–1692(o), any such action could subject you to additional liability for attorneys' fees and costs of suit.

If the above amount is not disputed by you within thirty (30) days from the date of this letter, it will be presumed valid. If the debt is disputed, verification of the debt will be provided by my client. Further, any information you provide me will be used in the collection of the debt.

Please be assured this is not the beginning of a series of collection letters. If we have not received a satisfactory response from you within the time specified above, we will have no alternative than to proceed with litigation. In order to alleviate any additional costs and expenses, your prompt attention to this matter is advised.

Very truly yours,

Alex Johnson

FIGURE 15.12
Texas Deceptive Trade Practices Act Basic Requirements for Demand Letter

Source: Texas Business and Commerce Code; Title 2. Competition and Trade Practices; Chapter 17. Deceptive Trade Practices. From TEXAS STATUTES AND CODES ANNOTATED BY LEXISNEXIS. Reprinted with the permission of LexisNexis.

17.505. Notice; Inspection

(a) As a prerequisite to filing a suit seeking damages under Subdivision (1) of Subsection (b) of Section 17.50 of this subchapter against any person, a consumer shall give written notice to the person at least 60 days before filing the suit advising the person in reasonable detail of the consumer's specific complaint and the amount of economic damages, damages for mental anguish, and expenses, including attorneys' fees, if any, reasonably incurred by the consumer in asserting the claim against the defendant. During the 60-day period a written request to inspect, in a reasonable manner and at a reasonable time and place, the goods that are the subject of the consumer's action or claim may be presented to the consumer.

(b) If the giving of 60 days' written notice is rendered impracticable by reason of the necessity of filing suit in order to prevent the expiration of the statute of limitations or if the consumer's claim is asserted by way of counterclaim, the notice provided for in Subsection (a) of this section is not required, but the tender provided for by Subsection (d), Section 17.506 of this subchapter may be made within 60 days after service of the suit or counterclaim.

(c) A person against whom a suit is pending who does not receive written notice, as required by Subsection (a), may file a plea in abatement not later than the 30th day after the date the person files an original answer in the court in which the suit is pending. This subsection does not apply if Subsection (b) applies.

(d) The court shall abate the suit if the court, after a hearing, finds that the person is entitled to an abatement because notice was not provided as required by this section. A suit is automatically abated without the order of the court beginning on the 11th day after the date a plea in abatement is filed under Subsection (c) if the plea in abatement:

(1) is verified and alleges that the person against whom the suit is pending did not receive the written notice as required by Subsection (a); and

(2) is not controverted by an affidavit filed by the consumer before the 11th day after the date on which the plea in abatement is filed.

(e) An abatement under Subsection (d) continues until the 60th day after the date that written notice is served in compliance with Subsection (a).

The Consumer Protection Letter

Many states have created a statutory method for a consumer to file suit against a business that conducts its affairs in a deceptive or unfair manner. When drafting a demand letter setting forth a claim under such a statute, it is important to mention the statute in your letter, and to comply with all its requirements. As with other demand letters, the facts of your claim should be stated, as well as the amount of the demand; indeed, these things may be prerequisites to making a claim for punitive or other damages under the statute.

The basic requirements for a demand letter under the Texas statute appear in Figure 15.12, and a letter drafted to meet these requirements appears in Figure 15.13. If a statute has been passed in your state, you should obtain a copy and review it.

The Letter Notifying of Intention to Litigate

A special type of demand letter is the letter that places an opposing party or counsel on notice that your client intends to initiate a lawsuit. This may be combined with an ordinary letter demanding payment of an unpaid bill, or may relate to a claim where the amount of damage is not immediately quantifiable, as in a personal injury action or an action seeking an injunction.

Most parties, including insurance companies, like to avoid litigation where possible; your intention to go to court, if perceived as realistic, may spur settlement talks. It

FIGURE 15.13
Consumer Demand Letter

April 25, 2008

Mr. Bryan Henley
Office Manager
SMITHTON CHIROPRACTIC CENTER
1487 Orange Grove Blvd.
Galveston, TX 77553

Re: Your letter to Deborah Lee Jones dated March 20, 2008

Dear Mr. Henley:

The undersigned law firm has been retained to represent Ms. Deborah Lee Jones in the matter of her account with Smithton Chiropractic Center. Ms. Jones purchased services from and made use of therapeutic equipment in Smithton Chiropractic Center during the summer of 2008.

This letter is being sent pursuant to Section 17.50 of the Texas Business and Commerce Code, hereinafter referred to as the Deceptive Trade Practices Act ("DTPA"), which requires that such a letter be sent sixty (60) days prior to the initiating of litigation. The DTPA specifically provides that you may tender a written offer of settlement within this sixty (60) day period of time, and further provides that your offer of settlement must include an agreement to reimburse Ms. Jones for her attorneys' fees incurred to date. To date, Ms. Jones has incurred $1,000 in attorneys' fees.

After receiving medical treatment rendered by your clinic on August 26, 2007, Ms. Jones experienced severely painful muscle spasms as a direct result of that treatment. Ms. Jones attempted on several occasions to contact your office without success.

At no time was Ms. Jones informed by your clinic that charges continued to mount even though she no longer subscribed to therapy. Ms. Jones was told that aside from an initial $150.00 charge, she would incur no further cost as a result of her treatment.

Ms. Jones's specific complaints are as follows:

(i) you represented that goods and services had sponsorship, approval, characteristics, ingredients, uses, benefits, or qualities which they did not have;

(ii) you advertised goods and services with no intent to sell them as advertised;

(iii) you failed to disclose information that you knew at the time of the transaction, and such failure to disclose was intended to induce Ms. Jones into a transaction that she would not otherwise have entered into, in that you represented to Ms. Jones that the services would be rendered at no cost to her after payment of an initial $150.00;

(iv) you engaged in an unconscionable action or course of action, by taking advantage of the lack of knowledge, ability, experience, or capacity of Ms. Jones to a grossly unfair degree; and

(v) you charged Ms. Jones for services never rendered.

As a result of your false, misleading, and deceptive acts and practices and unconscionable conduct, Ms. Jones was deceived into executing a purported agreement you now claim obligates her to pay medical fees of $2,000.00. Not only does she not owe this amount, but she has suffered damages in the amount of at least $325.00 and has incurred attorneys' fees in the amount of $1,000.00, as a result of your wrongful acts. We urge you to make a written offer of settlement pursuant to Section 17.50 of the Texas in the amount of $1,000.00, as a result of your wrongful acts. If settlement cannot be reached within sixty (60) days, please take note that my client has authorized me to initiate a lawsuit on her behalf to seek (1) rescission of any agreements procured by your fraud, and (2) the full measure of allowable damages, which can be three times actual damages, plus attorneys' fees and court costs.

As an additional cause of action, Ms. Jones has instructed me to initiate a lawsuit based upon your breach of contract, common law fraud, negligent entrustment, and medical malpractice for misdiagnosing her condition and causing her personal injury. Ms. Jones has instructed me to request rescission of any agreements procured by your fraud, and to seek punitive damages based upon the aforementioned fraudulent representations made knowingly by Smithton Chiropractic Center and its agents.

Very truly yours,

Peter R. Moore

PRM/prh

may also backfire, however, creating a hostile reaction that actually scuttles settlement talks. The risk involved is a matter of concern and interest to you, but the decision on how to proceed will be made by your supervising attorney and the client.

When preparing a letter notifying of intention to litigate, you should

- state the facts accurately;
- state the specific damages you claim, even if the amount is only an estimate (as with a personal injury suit);
- state, if the claim is for other than money damages (as, for example, where the proposed lawsuit seeks an injunction to remove toxic waste), the specific relief sought;
- emphasize your good faith and desire to work out the disagreement, if possible; and
- keep the tone courteous, not belligerent; this is more likely to lead to settlement.

These factors are general considerations; in a specific case, they may or may not apply. Consult with your supervising attorney for your strategy, but keep these things in mind. Figure 15.14 is an example of a letter notifying of intention to take a lawsuit to court.

FIGURE 15.14
Letter Notifying of Intention to Litigate

April 28, 2008

CERTIFIED MAIL #P117784262
RETURN RECEIPT REQUESTED
Ms. Carly Ford
AAA Equipment
645 Elm Street
Houston, TX 77204

Re: Gourmet Services, Inc.

Dear Ms. Ford:

Please be advised that the undersigned has been retained by Gourmet Services, Inc. to represent it concerning its dispute with you on the equipment auctioned from the New Orleans Restaurant.

It is our understanding that you sold equipment owned by Gourmet Services, Inc. without its knowledge or permission. As previously communicated to you in a letter of December 12, 2007, from Gourmet Services, Inc., our client is prepared to settle this matter for the sum of $5,000.12. Demand is hereby made for payment in full of that amount in the form of a cashier's check or money order payable to Gourmet Services, Inc. and sent to me on or before ten (10) days from the date of this letter. Your failure to do so may result in litigation based upon wrongful conversion of the equipment, and other causes of action, which may result in the imposition of court costs, attorneys' fees, and interest. Our client does not desire to pursue this remedy, but is ready to do so if it is made necessary through your failure to comply with this demand.

Unless you dispute the validity of this debt, or any portion thereof within thirty (30) days after receipt of this letter, the debt will be assumed to be valid. Should you dispute the validity of the debt within thirty (30) days from the date of receipt of this communication, a verification of the debt will be obtained and mailed to you.

If you have any questions concerning our client's intention or wish to discuss this matter, please contact me.

Sincerely,

Donna M. Jackson

DMJ/prh
cc: Client

As with other demand letters, an important concern is whether it should be sent under the attorney's name or the client's. If under the attorney's, the recipient may believe that it is too late to settle because the decision to start a lawsuit has already been made. Depending on the circumstances, you may want to send it under the client's name. Consult with your attorney on the proper procedure; and, even if you decide to send it under the client's name, you and your firm should still review (and probably actually draft) the letter.

RESPONDING TO DEMAND LETTERS

When responding to a demand letter, the first step is to review the demand carefully with the client, pointing out the meaning and implications of the offer, and discussing what you believe to be the options for a response. When you begin to draft the response, be careful about reciting details. You should identify your position early, and counter any inaccurate factual claims made by the opposing side. You may want to avoid appearing aggressive, since this may do further harm to what may be a deteriorating situation; again, this is a judgment call.

One option almost always available is to request further information. This may "buy time" while the opposing party decides how to handle your request.

If you deny the claim, identify the reasons for your denial. If there are relevant cases or statutes that favor you, you may want to cite them. If there are documents that aid your cause, you may want to enclose copies. There may be strategic reasons to avoid such disclosure, however—so check with your supervising attorney first.

The best type of response to a demand letter, in general, is one that makes your position clear, but keeps the door open for negotiation. Be firm, though courteous, in your denial, and try to provide a reason for keeping the dialogue open (for example, the request for further documentation). Remember that sometimes a forceful, aggressive approach may be necessary—for example, to threaten a counterclaim.

Figure 15.5 is a letter designed to maintain channels of communication.

CYBER TRIP

Using www.findlaw.com, locate examples of form letters for each of the categories discussed in this chapter. If findlaw.com does not have examples, then perform an Internet search and locate examples of form letters on other Web sites.

FIGURE 15.15
Response to Notice of Litigation

May 4, 2008

CERTIFIED MAIL #P117784265
RETURN RECEIPT REQUESTED
Ms. Lois J. Jackson
Attorney at Law
2350 Alliance Street
Houston, TX 77204

Re: Our Client: AAA Equipment
Your Client: Gourmet Services, Inc.

Dear Ms. Jackson:

The undersigned represents AAA Equipment in the above-referenced matter. The matter that you have addressed in your letter dated April 28, 2008, is disputed. I do not know the basis of your claims or the substance of them. Consequently, pursuant to the Fair Debt Collection Statute, we are hereby placing you on notice that we do dispute the validity of any claims that you are alleging in your letter and request further investigation into this alleged debt.

We appreciate prompt response to this matter.

Very truly yours,

Drew Michaels

cc: Client

ETHICS ALERT

Know the purpose of your letter. If your intent is to harass, intimidate, or act unethically, the courts may just know how to deal with you and your attorney. In a recent Kansas case, *In re Gershater,* 17 P.3d 929 (Kan. 2001), an attorney was suspended "indefinitely" from the practice of law for sending a letter that "was vicious, offensive, and extremely unprofessional. Her letter employed a number of vile and unprintable epithets referring . . . to the attorneys in the case." *Id.* at 931. Not only did the court admonish the attorney for misrepresenting information in her correspondences but also for engaging in professional misconduct. In its observations regarding this particular attorney's conduct, the court emphatically denounced the behavior as one not befitting members of the bar:

> A lawyer should be able to write a letter to an opposing party or a party with an adverse interest and intelligently communicate his or her position without the use of profane, offensive, or derogatory language. "[A]ttorneys are required to act with common courtesy and civility at all times in their dealings with those concerned with the legal process." *In re Vincenti,* 114 N.J. 275, 282, 554 A.2d 470 (1989). "Vilification, intimidation, abuse and threats have no place in the legal arsenal." *In re Mezzacca,* 67 N.J. 387, 389–90, 340 A.2d 658 (1975). "An attorney who exhibits the lack of civility, good manners and common courtesy . . . tarnishes the entire image of what the bar stands for." *In re McAlevy,* 69 N.J. 349, 352, 354 A.2d 289 (1976). *Id.* at 935–36.

Strong language is communicated by the court. Review the case and draw your own conclusions. Was the court justified in its sanctions of the attorney? What acts had the attorney committed for the court to impose an indefinite suspension? What was the court's reasoning and why did it use authority from other jurisdictions?

STATUTORY LETTERS OF INTENT TO LITIGATE: MALPRACTICE CASES

Unfortunate as they are, malpractice cases are common in the litigation world. In most states, intent to litigate a medical malpractice issue has specific statutory requirements. For instance, a number of states require that notification is given to the physician or health care provider sixty or ninety days prior to filing the case. If this requirement is not fulfilled, the injured party may lose her right to pursue the medical malpractice claim. A defective notice of intent to file a malpractice claim may also affect a party's ability to litigate the claim. Are you seeing a pattern here? If you don't get it right, the client may lose the opportunity to sue. The states of New York and Texas present examples of strict statutory requirements for notifying the physician, health care provider, or both. Notice the word "requirements," as deviation may be another form of malpractice—legal. The requirements for both states are identified in Figure 15.16.

YOU BE THE JUDGE

Knowing the statutory requirements, or at least performing the legal research to determine them for a particular cause of action, is the difference between success and failure. In *Toledo v. Ordway,* 576 N.Y.S. 2d 886 (A.D. 2d Dept. 1991), the plaintiff failed to comply with the statutory notice requirements in a medical malpractice case; the court barred the action against the physician. That means whether a claim existed is irrelevant since the statute of limitations expired. What are the facts in Toledo? What statute did the court rely upon to reach its result? What were the requirements of the statute? The case provides two important lessons: (1) obtain accurate dates from the client, and (2) review the applicable law prior to drafting a specialized or statutory letter. This case is not unusual and should be viewed as a warning.

FIGURE 15.16
Statutory Requirements for New York and Texas

Source: Texas Civil Practice and Remedies Code; Title 4. Liability in Tort; Chapter 74. Medical Liability; Subchapter B. Notice and Pleadings. From TEXAS STATUTES AND CODES ANNOTATED BY LEXISNEXIS. New York General Municipal Law; Article 4. Negligence and Malfeasance of Public Officers; Taxpayers' Remedies. From NEW YORK CONSOLIDATED LAW SERVICE.

NEW YORK
50-e. Notice of Claim

1. When service required; time for service; upon whom service required.

(a) In any case founded upon tort where a notice of claim is required by law as a condition precedent to the commencement of an action or special proceeding against a public corporation, as defined in the general construction law, or any officer, appointee, or employee thereof, the notice of claim shall comply with and be served in accordance with the provisions of this section within ninety days after the claim arises; except that in wrongful death actions, the ninety days shall run from the appointment of a representative of the decedent's estate.

(b) Service of the notice of claim upon an officer, appointee, or employee of a public corporation shall not be a condition precedent to the commencement of an action or special proceeding against such person. If an action or special proceeding is commenced against such person, but not against the public corporation, service of the notice of claim upon the public corporation shall be required only if the corporation has a statutory obligation to indemnify such person under this chapter or any other provision of law.

2. Form of notice; contents. The notice shall be in writing, sworn to by or on behalf of the claimant, and shall set forth: (1) the name and post office address of each claimant, and of his attorney, if any; (2) the nature of the claim; (3) the time when, the place where, and the manner in which the claim arose; and (4) the items of damage or injuries claimed to have been sustained so far as then practicable but a notice with respect to a claim against a municipal corporation other than a city with a population of one million or more persons shall not state the amount of damages to which the claimant deems himself entitled, provided, however, that the municipal corporation, other than a city with a population of one million or more persons, may at any time request a supplemental claim setting forth the total damages to which the claimant deems himself entitled. A supplemental claim shall be provided by the claimant within fifteen days of the request. In the event the supplemental demand is not served within fifteen days, the court, on motion, may order that it be provided by the claimant.

TEXAS

74.051. Notice

(a) Any person or his authorized agent asserting a health care liability claim shall give written notice of such claim by certified mail, return receipt requested, to each physician or health care provider against whom such claim is being made at least 60 days before the filing of a suit in any court of this state based upon a health care liability claim. The notice must be accompanied by the authorization form for release of protected health information as required under Section 74.052.

(b) In such pleadings as are subsequently filed in any court, each party shall state that it has fully complied with the provisions of this section and Section 74.052 and shall provide such evidence thereof as the judge of the court may require to determine if the provisions of this chapter have been met.

(c) Notice given as provided in this chapter shall toll the applicable statute of limitations to and including a period of 75 days following the giving of the notice, and this tolling shall apply to all parties and potential parties.

(d) All parties shall be entitled to obtain complete and unaltered copies of the patient's medical records from any other party within 45 days from the date of receipt of a written request for such records; provided, however, that the receipt of a medical authorization in the form required by Section 74.052 executed by the claimant herein shall be considered compliance by the claimant with this subsection.

(e) For the purposes of this section, and notwithstanding Chapter 159, Occupations Code, or any other law, a request for the medical records of a deceased person or a person who is incompetent shall be deemed to be valid if accompanied by an authorization in the form required by Section 74.052 signed by a parent, spouse, or adult child of the deceased or incompetent person.

The prerequisites to filing a lawsuit in both states are stringent and that is why the notice letter must conform completely to the statutory requirements.

General considerations when preparing a letter of intent to litigate a medical malpractice claim are

- the date of client's injury;
- the names of the parties involved in the case; for example, hospital (public or private), physician (hospital staff or private);
- the jurisdiction's statutory requirements; and
- strict compliance with statute's requirements.

Using the Texas statute as our guide, Figure 15.17 is a compliant Notice of Intention to Litigate a Medical Malpractice claim. Included in that figure is a series of letters resulting in the filing of a lawsuit.

FIGURE 15.17
Series of Letters in Medical Malpractice Case

(a) Notice of Claim
February 21, 2008

CERTIFIED MAIL #P117784223
RETURN RECEIPT REQUESTED

Dr. Ned Radcliffe
18015 15th Street, Suite 310
Goodnight, TX 75020

Re: Lynn Murray
Health Care Liability Claim

Dear Dr. Radcliffe:

The undersigned represents Lynn Murray in the above-referenced matter. NOTICE IS HEREBY GIVEN that my client, Lynn Murray, has a "health care liability claim" against you, as the quoted term is defined in Article 4590i, §1.03, Subdivision (a), Paragraph (4) of the Revised Civil Statutes of Texas. This claim is based on the fact that you negligently administered and cared for Ms. Murray upon giving anesthesia on November 12, 2007, in the course of treating her to fill two abscessed teeth. As a result of your negligence, Ms. Murray suffered a sensitivity reaction to the anesthesia, including violent shaking of arms and legs, chattering of teeth, and convulsions.

Due to your negligence, Ms. Murray also contracted a severe skin reaction, triggered by the anesthesia. This condition has caused substantial rashes on her arms and upper body, and could in the future affect her entire body.

As a result of her reaction, Ms. Murray has had to engage the services of medical specialists and undergo and incur expenses for examination and diagnosis of the condition, for psychological consultation and for medication to help her condition, and she will have to continue various treatments, consultations, and medications in the future, and incur expenses.

Prior to your negligence hereinabove referred to, Ms. Murray was twenty-eight (28) years old, in good health, and employed as a representative with MBI Corporation. As a result of your negligence, she has had to miss work at her job and has, therefore, lost wages and will be required in the future to lose further time from her job for an as-yet-undetermined period. As a further result of your negligence, she has suffered severe mental and physical pain and anguish, and in all probability will continue to suffer such mental and physical pain and anguish for the rest of her life, all to her further damage. To date, the amount of damages is $12,587.37, and continues to grow.

YOU ARE FURTHER NOTIFIED that this claim is given pursuant to the provisions of Article 4590i, Section 4.60, Subdivision (a) of the Revised Civil Statutes of Texas, and that, if it is

Cont.

FIGURE 15.17
Series of Letters in Medical Malpractice Case *Cont.*

not settled within sixty (60) days from the date this notice is given, the undersigned will commence an appropriate legal action against you to recover her damages.

Your prompt attention to this matter is advised.

Very truly yours,

Emma M. Costello

(b) Reply from Insurance Carrier

March 10, 2008

Ms. Emma M. Costello
Attorney at Law
6301 Marley Avenue
Anyplace, TX 75311

Re: Lynn Murray vs. Dr. Ned Radcliffe

Dear Ms. Costello:

Your notice letter addressed to Dr. Radcliffe has been referred to us as the professional carrier for the doctor. It is my understanding that Dr. Radcliffe has previously forwarded your client's medical records to you, along with a release executed by your client on December 7, 2007. Thus, not only is there no liability on the part of Dr. Radcliffe, your client has signed a release.

I personally guarantee that if you file a lawsuit with regard to this matter, it will be countered with a lawsuit against your client for breach of contract and a Motion for Sanctions, since the matter is a frivolous claim.

Please address any further correspondence or inquiries to my attention. Do not call or write the doctor with regard to this matter.

Sincerely,

Edward Z. Plant

MEDICAL INSURANCE COVERAGE COMPANY

(c) Response to Insurance Company's Letter

March 18, 2008

Mr. Edward Z. Plant
MEDICAL INSURANCE COVERAGE COMPANY
1601 Ohio Avenue, 5th Floor
Sandy, IL 42930

Re: Lynn Murray vs. Dr. Ned Radcliffe

Dear Mr. Plant:

This is in response to your letter dated March 10, 2008. I do not appreciate the statement in your letter regarding the filing of frivolous lawsuits. Perhaps you should investigate the facts of this matter, as well as the law in Texas.

If you are trying to make threats to me regarding any claims Ms. Murray has against Dr. Radcliffe, those threats are so noted. However, let me assure you that I am well aware of the Texas Rules of Procedure. I can further assure you that I intend to pursue this matter, and will shortly be filing a lawsuit.

Let me encourage you, in the future, to investigate and examine the facts of your cases before you begin threats of Motions for Sanction.

If you choose to discuss this matter in a civil and professional manner, I would be happy to do so. Otherwise, you can expect to be hearing from me with a lawsuit.

Your prompt attention to this matter is advised.

Very truly yours,

Emma M. Costello

NEW STANDARDS FOR REQUESTING MEDICAL INFORMATION

In April 2003, new standards for requesting and acquiring patient information became law. The Health Insurance Portability and Accountability Act, "HIPAA" as it is more commonly known, set forth a host of requirements for accessing patient-protected health information (PHI). Not only does this requirement apply in the medical malpractice setting, but it applies to a personal injury lawsuit, an automobile accident, or any other situation where medical records are required. As a paralegal, you may be asked to draft not only the notice letter, but also a letter requesting medical information, which complies with HIPAA. Texas has included a HIPAA authorization as a statutory requirement in a medical malpractice claim. The authorization requesting patient information must be signed by the client, the client's legal representative, or the client's guardian, if a minor. The authorization required under the Texas law is illustrated in Figure 15.18.

This authorization is a good example of the requirements under HIPAA throughout the United States. Since HIPAA is a federal law, it applies to everyone. Use it as

FIGURE 15.18
Authorization Form for Release of Medical Information
Source: Adapted from *Texas Jurisprudence Pleading and Practice Forms* (ThomsonWest, 2004).

AUTHORIZATION FORM FOR RELEASE OF PROTECTED HEALTH INFORMATION

A. I, Morgan Reilly, hereby authorize Raymond Sullivan, MD, and Memorial Hospital to obtain and disclose, within the parameters set out below, the protected health information, described below for the following specific purposes:
   1. To facilitate the investigation and evaluation of the health care claim described in the accompanying Notice of Health Care Claim; or
   2. Defense of any litigation arising to of the claim made the basis of the accompanying Notice of Health Care Claim.

B. The health information to be obtained, used or disclosed extends to and includes the verbal as well as the written and is specifically described as follows:
   1. The health information in the custody of the following physicians or health care providers who have examined, evaluated, or treated Nathan Reilly in connection with the injuries alleged to have been sustained in connection with the claim asserted in the accompanying Notice of Health Care Claim. _______ [*Listing of names and current addresses of all treating physicians or health care providers.*] This authorization shall extend to any additional physicians or health care providers that may in the future evaluate, examine, or treat Nathan Reilly for injuries alleged in connection with the claim made the basis of the attached Notice of Health Care Claim;
   2. The health information in the custody of the following physicians or health care providers who have examined, evaluated, or treated Nathan Reilly during a period commencing five years prior to the incident made the basis of the accompanying Notice of Health Care Claim. _______ [*List name and current address of such physicians or health care providers, if applicable.*]

C. Excluded Health Information—The following constitutes a list of physicians or health care providers possessing health care information concerning Nathan Reilly to which this authorization does not apply because I contend that such health care information is not relevant to the damages being claimed or to the physical, mental, or emotional condition of Nathan Reilly arising out of the claim made the basis of the accompanying Notice of Health Care Claim:

Cont.

FIGURE 15.18
Authorization Form for Release of Medical Information
Cont.

_______ [*None/listing of names of each physician or health care provider to whom authorization does not extend, and inclusive dates of examination, evaluation, or treatment to be withheld from disclosure.*]

D. The persons or class of persons to whom the health information of Nathan Reilly will be disclosed or who will make use of said information are:
1. Any and all physicians or health care providers providing care or treatment to Nathan Reilly;
2. Any liability insurance entity providing liability insurance coverage or defense to any physician or health care provider to whom Notice of Health Care Claim has been given with regard to the care and treatment of Nathan Reilly;
3. Any consulting or testifying experts employed by or on behalf of Raymond Sullivan, MD, and Memorial Hospital with regard to the matter set out in the Notice of Health Care Claim accompanying this authorization.
4. Any attorneys, including secretarial, clerical, or paralegal staff, employed by or on behalf of Raymond Sullivan, MD, and Memorial Hospital with regard to the matter set out in the Notice of Health Care Claim accompanying this authorization;
5. Any trier of the law or facts relating to any suit filed seeking damages arising out of the medical care or treatment of Nathan Reilly.

E. This authorization expires on resolution of the claim asserted or at the conclusion of any litigation instituted in connection with the subject matter of the Notice of Health Care Claim accompanying this authorization, whichever occurs sooner.

F. I understand that, without exception, I have the right to revoke this authorization in writing. I further understand the consequences of any such revocation as set out in § 74.052 of the Texas Civil Practice and Remedies Code.

G. I understand that the signing of this authorization is not a condition for continued treatment, payment, enrollment, or eligibility for health plan benefits.

H. I understand that information used or disclosed pursuant to this authorization may be subject to redisclosure by the recipient and may no longer be protected by federal HIPAA privacy regulations.

Dated:______ [*date*]

____
Signature of Patient/Representative
Dated:______ [*date*]

____
Name of Patient/Representative
Dated:______ [*date*]

_____ [*Description of Representative's Authority*]

a guide for any case involving medical records, but research your own jurisdiction for its requirements.

THE OPINION LETTER

An **opinion letter** renders legal advice. Based upon specific facts, and applying information gained through research, it analyzes a legal problem and reaches a conclusion about the resolution of the problem. In the subsections that follow, we first discuss

opinion letter
A letter that renders legal advice.

an opinion letter directed to your client, and then address some separate considerations when the opinion letter is directed to a third party.

The Client Opinion Letter

A comprehensive client opinion letter should contain several distinct elements. Let's consider these elements.

Date

The date listed at the top of the letter is important. Your research must be accurate through that date. You cannot be held responsible for changes in the law or new cases or statutes that arise after that date, but you are responsible for all changes in the law *up to* that date.

Introductory Paragraph

disclaimer
A limiting claim or denial.

An introductory paragraph should identify the issue or problem that the letter will address. Included in this paragraph should be a **disclaimer** (limiting claim or denial) indicating that the analysis that follows is based upon the facts as they are set forth in the letter. If a different version of the facts develops, the analysis may change as well. It is important that you emphasize this to protect your firm from liability—and it is important to emphasize to the client the need to provide accurate and complete factual information.

Facts and Background

The next section should set forth the facts and background that have been developed through client conferences and independent investigation. It should again be emphasized that the analysis is based upon these facts. You should take great care in gathering and presenting these facts. Remember that clients' memories may be selective, concentrating on their own strong points and forgetting their weak points. Thus, as with other writing projects, a good client interview is the foundation for a good opinion letter.

Conclusion

A brief statement of your conclusion may precede the analysis. This will help the client, or other reader, follow the arguments to come. The scope of the conclusion should be indicated here, including any limitations or qualifications.

Analysis

This section is like the discussion section of the internal memorandum. In it you analyze the applicable case law, statutes, and other sources. Both strengths and weaknesses of your client's position should be discussed. Remember that you are balancing two goals here—informing the client, and accurately stating the law. This balance requires that you both (1) accurately present complicated legal concepts, and (2) present them in language the client can understand. Don't misrepresent by oversimplifying; take the time and effort necessary to make the document both accurate and understandable. This may, on occasion, require explaining things twice—once using terms of art or other complicated language, and a second time, describing what these terms and language mean in plain and practical language.

Be sure, again, to identify the limitations upon, and qualifications of, the analysis. Define all terms that might create confusion; identify the extent of your investigation; and indicate any and all assumptions on which the analysis is based.

Recommendation

In reaching her conclusion, an attorney rendering an opinion generally makes a recommendation to the client about the best approach to resolving the problem presented. This is perhaps the most important section of the opinion letter—where the attorney takes a position based upon his research. Again, emphasize that the opinion is based upon the facts as they are known to the attorney. If the attorney needs to qualify her position, or indicate problems, she should do so here as well as in earlier sections. Do not use qualifiers to make your position ambiguous, however—use them to describe precisely what you have concluded to be an ambiguous situation.

Directive

Your last paragraph should be an instruction or directive to the client to contact the attorney after reviewing the letter. This contact is important because it will enable you, your supervising attorney, and the client to discuss and clarify any questions that the client has regarding the facts, the conclusion, and the recommendations.

Remember that, as a paralegal, you can *never* sign an opinion letter—only an attorney can render legal advice. However, you may be drafting these letters for an attorney to review. Figure 15.19 shows an example of a client opinion letter.

CYBER TRIP

Using either www.nala.org or www.usdol.gov, find a legal opinion regarding paralegals and the application of Section 13(a)(1) of the Fair Labor Standards Act (FLSA). (Hint: The opinion was issued in 2006.)

FIGURE 15.19
Client Opinion Letter

July 21, 2008

Mr. Neil Crosby
9250 Kingsley Road
Aurora, CO 80011

Re: Evaluation of Insurance Claims

Dear Mr. Crosby:

You have retained me to review the law regarding the responsibility of insurance companies to provide coverage for preexisting medical conditions.

I have reviewed the documentation that you have supplied to me. Based on the medical response from Dr. Stills, it appears that you did not have a preexisting condition at the time you applied for medical insurance. The problem is convincing the insurance company of that fact.

The most logical first step would be to send a letter to the insurance company detailing our position, namely that you did not have a preexisting condition at the time you applied for insurance. However, before a letter is sent, it would be appropriate for us to meet so that I may discuss with you the result of my research on the legal meaning of preexisting condition.

Briefly, the case law on this issue is unsettled. The courts generally look to the definition of "preexisting condition" in your insurance policy, then apply this to your medical history. There is no generally accepted definition of preexisting condition; it is determined by a judge or jury as a question of fact.

This means that estimating our chances for success will be difficult. Unfortunately, unless the insurance company willingly agrees with our position, the most logical next step would be to file a lawsuit against the insurance company for failing to pay your claims.

As we had discussed in our first meeting, this may be quite costly, with the results uncertain. Please call me in the next ten days so we can decide how to pursue this matter: whether to send the letter to the insurance company based on your medicals and my research, or not pursue the matter at all. I look forward to hearing from you.

Thank you for your attention and courtesies.

Very truly yours,

Steven N. Young

THE E-FACTOR

Faxing is a way of life—instant gratification for the parties. Maybe. Using a fax machine to transit letters can be both a blessing and a curse. You fax the document and it is instantaneously received on the other end. You hope. Of course, you have your confirmation, but the attorney, paralegal, or assistant claims they never received the document. Now you are faced with a "he said, she said" situation, where the winner probably is the other side, who claims they never received the document. What are you to do? To guard against this situation, do not assume the fax was received unless you contact the receiving party confirming receipt. Write down the name of the person whom you spoke with and the time you made the contact. Some attorneys may request a return confirmation from the receiver of the fax, avoiding any confusion. Faxing also poses confidentiality problems. Suppose the fax is sent to the wrong number or gets into the wrong hands. Of course we all place warnings on the fax that if the fax is incorrectly received, the recipient should contact the sender immediately. But the damage is already done. Information in the wrong hands can cause a wealth of problems for you, your attorney, and the client. No one is suggesting not using a fax machine; what is being suggested is to be careful in its use and mindful of the consequences for a mis-sent fax.

The Third-Party Opinion Letter

There are occasions when a third party will require that your client provide a legal opinion, so that he can complete a transaction. For example, a client seeking a mortgage may need to provide the bank with a legal opinion regarding a title question. If you are called upon to draft such a letter, there are several points to remember. First, be sure to identify in the letter the firm's relationship with the client. Second, indicate that, despite this relationship, your opinion is based upon honest and unbiased analysis. Third, use language that restricts the applicability of the opinion, for liability purposes—for example, stating: "This opinion has been prepared for the benefit of First National Bank only, and no other party may rely on the representations contained herein." Fourth, identify the reason for the opinion—for example, "This opinion has been requested by First National Bank in connection with a mortgage sought by my client, William Doe." Fifth, be sure that you clearly identify your opinion or conclusion. This can be done with plain, unequivocal language: "Based on the above, it is our opinion that . . ." or "We hereby render the following opinions based upon the preceding analysis. . . ." Finally, clearly identify who is rendering the opinion. For example, on the signature line, the signer (who, as we have noted, will always be an attorney) should probably sign not on his own behalf, but on behalf of his firm.

Most of these points are designed to define clearly the areas, and the limits, of your firm's liability for the opinion rendered, since in the third-party situation, they may not be immediately clear. Figure 15.20 shows an example of a third-party opinion letter.

Quick Quiz True/False Questions

1. One of the tasks required in specialized legal correspondence is legal research on applicable statutory requirements.
2. A collection letter is not considered a form of specialized legal correspondence.
3. When preparing a letter notifying of an intention to litigate, always embellish the facts to the client's advantage.
4. All states have the same requirements for filing a notice of intent to file a malpractice case.
5. A paralegal may sign a client opinion letter.

FIGURE 15.20
Third-Party Opinion Letter

September 18, 2008

Ms. Roberta McMillan, Examiner
Individual Benefit Department
UNITED INSURANCE AGENCY
716 Milton Drive
Richmond, VA 32187

Re: Our Client: Mr. Neil Crosby
Health Coverage Due and Owing Under
Policy number 718465023GB8A dated December 2, 2007

Dear Ms. McMillan:

The undersigned represents Mr. Neil Crosby in the above-referenced matter. You have requested a legal opinion of the law in the state of Texas on preexisting conditions as it relates to my client. A brief synopsis of the facts is necessary.

On December 2, 2007, Mr. Crosby became insured with United Insurance Agency for health insurance with a quarterly premium of $587.60. A copy of the policy is attached hereto as Exhibit A. The policy contained certain contractual obligations, one of which was to pay medical expenses, over and above the noted deductible, for the insured in the event of the occurrence of any health problems. In January 2008, your company failed and refused to pay Mr. Crosby for his health care costs, stating that he had a preexisting condition before the policy was issued and therefore was not covered under your company's policy. A representative contended that Mr. Crosby did not properly and accurately inform your company of his medical history in answers supplied by him on your company's application for insurance. This application, with the responses, is attached hereto as Exhibit B. As noted on the application, Mr. Crosby had not been diagnosed as having any type of disease condition within the five (5) years prior to applying for insurance with United Insurance Agency.

His policy was conditioned upon the information contained within the application being "to the best of my [Mr. Crosby's] knowledge and belief . . . complete and true." Mr. Crosby's information was in fact a truthful representation of his condition.

United Insurance Agency never followed up his application with any type of medical examination by its own physicians. This was a condition that your company would have had to so follow up as a condition precedent to justify any denial of coverage.

The Texas Administrative Code, Section 3.3018 defines preexisting illness as:

> The existence of symptoms which could cause an ordinarily prudent person to seek diagnosis, care, or treatment within a five-year period preceding the effective date of the coverage of the insured person or a condition for which medical advice or treatment was recommended by a physician or received from a physician within a five-year period preceding the effective date of the coverage of the insured person.

My client had no knowledge of any preexisting illness that would preclude coverage as defined in the Texas statute. Further, the law requires knowledge of a preexisting condition, or that the insurer make independent investigation. My client did not have any latent symptoms that were intentionally ignored. Your company had an affirmative duty to investigate independently my client's representation of "good health." Due to your company's failure to investigate my client's health history, my client is not precluded from coverage. Mr. Crosby does fall within the protected class covered under your health insurance application.

United Insurance Agency knew of all medical records pertaining to the medical history of Mr. Crosby, based upon the completed information and history. As a result, you are contractually bound and responsible to pay his health expenses.

Based on my evaluation of the law, it is my opinion that there should be complete reimbursement of all medical expenses of my client from the inception of the policy to the present, as well as the payment of any future medical expenses.

This opinion is based on the present state of the law, as well as the documentation that has been supplied by my client, which included the insurance policy and application. Please contact me at your earliest convenience so that we may discuss this matter.

Thank you for your attention to this matter.

Very truly yours,

Steven N. Young

PRACTICAL CONSIDERATIONS: KEEP THE BALL IN YOUR COURT . . .

We end this chapter with one practical consideration: When framing correspondence, keep the ball in your court!

What does this mean? It's quite simple, and the best way to demonstrate is by example. Assume that your client has a dispute with a customer to whom he has supplied building materials, but from whom he has received no payment. You take the trouble to write a comprehensive demand letter, setting forth the terms on which you would be willing to settle the matter. Figure 15.21 provides two possible closings to your letter, and Figure 15.22 provides comments from letters trying to schedule a deposition.

The point is this: When you leave the ball in your court, you have control over the situation, and inaction on the part of the other party will not impede your ability to take action. When you pass the ball to the other side's court, you place yourself in the position of having to wait for acceptance of an offer, or some other matter. Thus, you needlessly handicap your ability to respond to events as you see fit.

So, in drafting correspondence, use language that keeps your side in control of events. Keep the ball in your court!

FIGURE 15.21
Closings to Your Letter

Closing 1: Ball in *opponent's* court:

Please advise as soon as possible if the enclosed terms are acceptable to you.

Closing 2: Ball in *your* court:

If we have not heard from you by September 1, 2008, we will assume the terms are unacceptable and immediately institute suit.

FIGURE 15.22
Closings to Your Letter: Scheduling a Deposition

Comment 1: Ball in *opponent's* court:

Please advise whether September 1, 2008 is an acceptable date for the deposition of John Doe.

Comment 2: Ball in *your* court:

The deposition will be held on September 1, 2008, unless you advise that this date is unacceptable.

Summary

The legal profession uses correspondence to inform, to advise, and to confirm. Informative letters transmit information; advisory letters are more formal than informative letters and offer legal opinions; and confirmation letters create a permanent record of the oral sharing of information.

The tone of a letter varies with the audience as well as the purpose. Letters to clients should contain concrete answers and be written to the client's level of understanding. They should be drafted to avoid unreasonable expectations in the mind of the client. Letters to opposing counsel should be written with caution, since they may be used against your client. Letters to the court should be written with respect. You should generally send copies to opposing counsel, and be aware of the pitfalls of ex parte communications.

A letter generally contains the following components: a letterhead; the date on which the letter is sent; identification of the addressee; a brief, descriptive reference line; a salutation opening with "Dear" and followed by a colon; a body containing the message of the letter, which may be short or long, but which should always be written clearly; a header, which identifies subsequent pages; and a closing, often "Very truly yours" followed by the signer's name and position. Note that paralegals can *never* sign letters rendering legal advice. Finally, letters show the parties to whom copies have been sent; only your file copy should show those parties to whom blind carbon copies have been sent.

The demand letter is designed to motivate a desired response—often (though not exclusively) the payment of a debt. Demand letters can be in the form of a standard collection letter; a "Fair Debt Collection" letter designed to comply with statutory requirements; a consumer protection letter; or a notice of intention to sue. In drafting a demand letter, you should state your purpose, clarify the action you expect the recipient to take, establish a deadline date, and, under most circumstances, maintain a tone that will keep channels of communication open. In responding to a demand letter, you should review and discuss the situation with your client and identify reasons why you deny the claim. The letter should deny inaccurate factual statements made by the opposition, make your position clear, and, as with a demand letter, keep the channels of communication open.

An opinion letter renders legal advice. In a client opinion letter, work to balance two competing considerations: (1) presenting legal concepts accurately, and (2) presenting them in language the client can understand. Make it clear that your analysis is based upon the facts as you understand them, and make your recommendations clear as well. A third-party opinion letter must indicate your relationship with the client; the purpose of the letter; any limitations for liability purposes; and a clear statement of the bounds of the opinion.

Transmittal letters accompany information, confirming its nature and the fact that it was sent. Letters requesting information should be specific, and serve two purposes: to obtain information and to create a record that the request was made. A retainer letter sets forth the agreement between attorney and client on fees and services to be rendered. An authorization letter enables the attorney to pursue an investigation for the client's benefit into records maintained by third parties.

An important practical point in drafting legal correspondence is to keep the ball in your court, which means that whenever possible, you should maintain control over subsequent events.

Key Terms

advisory letter
authorization letter
bcc
body
cc
clerk of the court
collection letter
complimentary closing
confirmation letter
cover letter
deadline date
demand letter
disclaimer
ex parte
header
informative letter
letter bank
letterhead
opinion letter
reference line
retainer letter
salutation
transmittal letter

Review Questions

1. Name three functions of legal correspondence.
2. List some characteristics of letters addressed to clients, opposing counsel, and the court.
3. What are the components of a letter?
4. What are the appropriate methods of addressing a letter to (a) a judge, (b) a chief executive officer, (c) a governor?
5. How is a reference line prepared?
6. Distinguish between a cc (copy) and a bcc (blind copy).
7. What is the purpose of a demand letter?
8. What is the purpose of a client opinion letter?

9. How does a third-party opinion letter differ from a client opinion letter?
10. List two possible purposes of a letter that requests information, and describe its most important characteristic.

Exercises

1. Your law firm has just been retained to represent a woman who has been injured in an industrial accident. Your attorney has instructed you to request the client's medical history. Draft the letter requesting the information.
2. A client has a claim against an insurance company for nonpayment of medical bills. Draft the representation letter to the insurance company.
3. Prepare a transmittal letter to the court sending the Defendant's Original Answer. (Remember to state that the opposing counsel has been notified of this transmittal.)
4. The issue of universal health care coverage is scheduled for a hearing on Capitol Hill. Draft a letter to your congressional representative requesting a copy of the transcript testimony.
5. Your state attorney general has issued an opinion on your state's Open Records Act regarding the protection of government employees' personnel records. Draft a letter requesting the opinion.
6. Your attorney interviewed a new client who just bought a new car and it is a lemon. You reviewed the attorney's notes and he has asked you to prepare a consumer protection letter based upon your jurisdiction's law. The name of the car company is America's Car, Inc., and it is located at 563 Highway Blvd., your city and state. (Be creative.)
7. You need to file a motion to dismiss in the U.S. district court for your attorney. She forgot to prepare the transmittal letter to the clerk of the court (in your jurisdiction). Prepare the transmittal letter.
8. Your attorney's best friend, Anthony Scott, has a medical malpractice case against his doctor and the hospital. Your attorney requested you research the statutory requirements for a medical malpractice case in your jurisdiction and provide a sample medical malpractice letter. All you know about the case is that the surgeon left a sponge in Scott's stomach after the surgery.

PORTFOLIO ASSIGNMENT

A new client, Apartment Management, Inc., has retained your firm to assist in the collection of an account for past due rent. The tenant was a start-up Internet company, We Search for You, Inc. Its rent was due on the first day of each month in the amount of $1,250.00. Its lease was for two years and it paid only the first six months of the lease. The lease provided for late fees in the amount of $50.00 per month plus interest. Your attorney has requested you prepare the collection letter on behalf of Apartment Management, Inc. The tenant's mailing address is 712 Broad St., Philadelphia, PA. 19106. The president of We Search for You, Inc. is Margaret Mattheson. (Hint: You need to research the jurisdictional requirements.)

Quick Quiz True/False Answers

Page 463	Page 478
1. False	1. True
2. True	2. False
3. False	3. False
4. True	4. False
5. True	5. False

Chapter 16

The Internal Office Memorandum

After completing this chapter, you will be able to:

- Identify different types of internal office memoranda.
- Understand the difference between an interoffice memorandum and the memorandum of law to the trial court.
- Prepare a memorandum summarizing a client or witness interview.
- Describe the objective nature of an internal memorandum of law.
- List several purposes of an internal memorandum of law.
- Identify the information that should be included in the heading section of a memorandum of law.
- Explain the importance of the issues presented section.
- Identify the purpose of the short summary of the conclusion section.
- Prepare an appropriate statement of facts.
- Identify key elements in the discussion and analysis section.

Along with legal correspondence, paralegals draft different types of internal office memoranda. In this chapter, you are introduced to your first assignment integrating both your legal research and writing skills.

CASE FACT PATTERN

Your supervising attorney calls you into her office to tell you about a telephone call she just received from the friend of a client. The friend, whose name is Mr. Giles, has briefly described a problem he is experiencing with regard to a power of attorney document. The problem appears to be urgent, so your supervising attorney immediately schedules an appointment with Mr. Giles to discuss his legal problem.

After the meeting, your attorney requests that you prepare an internal memorandum summarizing the facts of, and law relating to, Mr. Giles's problem.

INTERNAL MEMORANDA: THE BASIC TYPES

Internal office memoranda have different purposes and functions. Some memoranda are used to present an objective analysis of a client's legal issues; others summarize meetings, such as a client's initial interview or witness statements; others may document events, such as a memorandum documenting a telephone call. All these situations conclude with a memorandum. You need to know the purpose of your memorandum to determine the type you will be drafting.

An Internal Memorandum to Summarize Information

A client interview is an important aspect in developing a case. Interviews can be a time to gather information, to evaluate a client's case, or to determine whether the attorney even has the appropriate expertise to handle the matter. If you are either attending an interview or conducting the interview, impressions are important. First, before beginning your investigation into the facts, be sure to identify yourself as a paralegal. You are not someone who is authorized to practice law, and the client should understand this. You are, however, someone whose knowledge of the case is protected under the **attorney–client privilege** (assuming the individual is a client or prospective client; if a nonclient, such as an eyewitness, the privilege does not apply). Privilege is important because it enables the client to speak freely and honestly, without fear of self-incrimination or fear that you could be compelled by subpoena to reveal the information provided. You should also make the client aware that you are trained as a paraprofessional; this should be emphasized to cultivate the client's confidence.

attorney–client privilege
The legal relationship established between attorney and client allowing for free exchange of information without fear of disclosure.

Second, the matter of fees may also arise, particularly if the client is a new or potential client, as in the Case Fact Pattern in this chapter. You should consult your supervising attorney about how to field questions on fee structure. The client is entitled to a precise understanding of this structure, but the responsibility to inform him is ultimately the attorney's.

Finally, you may be asked to prepare documents that will be required during the interview, such as authorization to obtain medical or employment records, and other documents. You should also review any materials already in your firm's file on the matter. If you are aware of any of the details of the client's problem, you should perform some background research to familiarize yourself with the substantive areas of law that seem to be applicable.

During the interview you should be taking comprehensive notes. You will be referring to these notes in the final segment of the interview, when you review the entire account with the client.

After the interview, you should prepare a memorandum summarizing the client's statement in detail. This is not the internal memorandum of law that we discuss in the remainder of this chapter; it is simply a memorandum reviewing the content of the client interview, for the case file. This memorandum should be prepared immediately after the interview, when the details remain fresh in your mind and the references in your notes (including abbreviations and summaries) are still familiar to you. If you wait too long, your own notes may become incomprehensible.

Therefore, one of the tasks you may be asked to undertake is to summarize the facts of an interview or notes from a meeting and present them to your supervising attorney. In a memorandum summarizing facts or notes you should include the following information:

- A standard heading that includes the name of the person to whom the memorandum is directed, the author of the memorandum, the date, and the subject of the memorandum. This information will be discussed in more detail in the next section of this chapter.

- The date and time when the interview or meeting that you are summarizing occurred.
- The objective facts in detail, based upon the interview or meeting.
- Dates that may be critical, such as the date of an automobile accident or filing deadlines.
- A list of assignments that may result from the interview or meeting.
- A summary of any impressions from the interview or meeting.

Often these types of memoranda become an integral part of the file and are an important mechanism for documenting events that occur in a case. Figure 16.1 provides an example of an internal memorandum summarizing information.

PRACTICE TIP

Many law firms or organizations use the individual's title following the name in the heading. Using one's title is a matter of preference and practice. Ask your supervising attorney or review a sample memorandum to determine the attorney's practice.

Memorandum to Document Information

You just received a telephone call from opposing counsel threatening to cancel a settlement meeting. The attorney was rude, shouting obscenities through the phone. Even you know how important the meeting is for the client, but behavior such as that is inappropriate. Since your attorney is out of the office, you want to document the telephone call and have a record of what happened. You should prepare a memorandum to your attorney detailing the substance of the conversation. In a memorandum that documents an occurrence or event, you should

- prepare a heading similar to the one for the memorandum summarizing information;
- specify the date and time of the occurrence;
- summarize the facts leading to the occurrence;
- present a detailed account of the occurrence;
- identify impressions of the occurrence; and
- identify any required action(s).

An example of an internal memorandum documenting information is illustrated in Figure 16.2.

Internal Memorandum of Law

The final type of internal memorandum is an **internal memorandum of law** that provides an objective analysis of the issues presented by the client's matter. Although memoranda differ in completeness, complexity, and the stage of the matter at which they are prepared, the purpose is always the same: to inform, to explain, and to evaluate. Internal memoranda analyze the law as it relates to the client's matter for such purposes as

internal memorandum of law
An internal document that analyzes objectively the legal issues in a client's matter.

- deciding whether to take the case;
- determining how to proceed in the case;
- providing a summary of the facts and the law;
- preparing for a hearing; and
- drafting appropriate legal documents.

The key to understanding the internal memorandum of law is in understanding its point of view—objective.

FIGURE 16.1
Example of an Internal Memorandum Summarizing Information

Memorandum

To: Christine J. Ashton
From: Samantha Daily
Date: July 17, 2008
Re: Interview with Stephen Houseman
Automobile Accident Dated July 4, 2008

This memorandum summarizes the meeting between Stephen Houseman and myself regarding an automobile accident he was involved in the weekend of July 4th. The facts are as follows:

- On July 4, 2008, Mr. Houseman was driving back from the fireworks around 9 p.m. It was dark, but a clear night. As he approached the intersection at Main Street and First Avenue, a black SUV approached quickly and ran through a red light.

- Mr. Houseman was hit on the passenger side close to the left front bumper area. Also in the car at the time were his wife, in the front seat, and his daughter, who was buckled up in the back seat in a booster chair. His daughter, Maddy, is seven years old. She was sitting behind his wife on the passenger side.

- Because of the sudden impact, everyone in the car was pushed forward. All had seat belts on and the airbags activated. Mrs. Houseman suffered injuries of the face and chest due to the impact and the airbags.

- Mr. Houseman suffered face and neck injuries. He also is having back problems, which he never experienced before the accident. The entire family was taken by ambulance to the Community Hospital, where everyone was treated. The little girl, Maddy, was kept overnight for observation and had some head injuries.

- The driver, a young man, Joey Pearson, who is 21 years old was tested for alcohol at the site. He had an alcohol level of 1.9 at the time. The police officer who came to the scene arrested Joey and his friends.

- Mr. Houseman brought a copy of the police report. It is attached.

- Mr. Houseman wants to retain us to represent him and his family.

- I indicated to him that we need to have him sign a retainer agreement and a medical authorization.

- I also indicated to him that you would need to meet with him as soon as possible to discuss the process and what is anticipated.

- I have scheduled an appointment for you on July 20 to meet with Mr. Houseman. I indicated to him that if he had any additional information, such as medical bills and any insurance information, for himself, his family and the driver, he should bring them with him for your review.

I will prepare a draft retainer agreement and medical authorization for your review. If you need any additional documents prepared, let me know.

Memorandum

Date: June 10, 2008

To: Emma Hernandez, Esq.

From: Martha Thompson
Paralegal

Re: Telephone conversation with Rhys Powell
(Singleton case)

On June 10, I received a telephone call from Rhys Powell, one of the attorneys in the Singleton matter. He began shouting at me and kept asking where you were. He said it was urgent that he speak with you and wanted to know where you were. I explained to him that you were at a deposition out of town and would not be available until tomorrow afternoon. I did tell him I would contact you and have you call him as soon as you were free. That was not good enough for him. He then started yelling obscenities at me through the telephone, such as "You women, you think you know it all, well you don't. I am not going to participate in any f***** settlement meetings, even if that pansy a** judge ordered it. Who do you all think you are? The bloody police? I am not showing up with my client and if you f***** don't like it, you can kiss my ***." He then hung up on me.

To say that I was shocked at his outburst is an understatement. I know Mr. Powell has been difficult and abusive, but this was even more abusive than in the past. I immediately told Mr. McKinney, senior partner, about the matter and he instructed me to prepare this memorandum detailing the conversation. I then contacted you to relay the conversation as well. Mr. McKinney asked that I prepare an affidavit, since he thinks the firm will be taking this matter to court.

If you need me to prepare anything else, please let me know.

FIGURE 16.2
Example of an Internal Memorandum Documenting Information

THE INTEROFFICE MEMORANDUM DISTINGUISHED

Unlike a memorandum of law to the trial court, the internal memorandum is not intended to advocate the client's position; it is intended to provide an objective assessment of the client's position. It is thus prepared only for review by the members of your law firm, and perhaps the client's inner circle. In an internal memorandum of law, both sides of the client's matter are analyzed, setting forth the positive and negative aspects of the case. An attorney wants an objective evaluation of the client's case to determine strategy, weaknesses in the case, complete view of the law, and any other legal issues that may be pertinent to the matter. Because all matters often are addressed, this type of memorandum is only used as an in-house tool.

Clearly, this differentiates the internal memorandum from a brief filed with a court, which is written from an advocate's perspective and does not analyze all aspects of the case. In a brief filed with a court, you write to persuade. Your writing style is not objective, but written with a point of view—your client's. The memorandum of law to the trial court is a persuasive document, minimizing the weaker aspects of a client's case. As many cases in our You Be the Judge or Ethics Alert sections indicate, this is not the time to hide the adverse opinion. It is incumbent upon you and your supervising attorney to advocate your client's position zealously but with candor and integrity. However, the remainder of the chapter is devoted to an objective viewpoint—the internal memorandum.

CYBER TRIP

Locate a sample of an interoffice memorandum from a government agency dealing with privacy or security issues. Compare the different information contained in a government interoffice memorandum from that of an interoffice memorandum discussed in this chapter.

PRELIMINARY CONSIDERATIONS

Throughout this textbook, the importance of "getting ready" has been emphasized. Now that you are ready to write, don't forget what to do.

Remember, in preparing to begin an assignment, you will complete the following tasks:

- Determine your audience: To whom is the memorandum directed? Will the memorandum be reviewed by your supervising attorney or the client?
- Determine your purpose: Since the internal memorandum is an objective document, your goal is to present both sides of the law—positive and negative.
- Determine your deadline: Are there time constraints on the assignment? Are there statute-of-limitation issues? Was the client promised an evaluation of their case by a particular date? Check out all this information before you begin your assignment. Make sure your deadline is clear.
- Prepare an outline: An outline will help you organize the assignment. Identify the issues of the case and note what needs to be accomplished.
- Begin your legal research: At this stage of the assignment, you will gather your cases, statutes, and other legal resources that apply to the assignment.
- Verify the status of the law: Shepardize or KeyCite your legal resources. You do not want to cite overruled or questionable legal sources.
- Prepare to write: Determine your format. Does the attorney or law firm have a particular format to follow? Many attorneys or law firms index internal memoranda of law in a **brief bank.** (Recall from Chapter 15 that correspondences are often compiled in one place for future use.) The same is true for internal memoranda of law. Check with your supervising attorney for samples of memoranda to use as a guide in drafting your memorandum. This practice is especially helpful in the beginning when you are just learning how to prepare legal documents or when you begin a new job.

brief bank
A document depository of briefs prepared by a law firm in previous matters.

You are now ready to begin to draft, write, rewrite, redraft, and work toward the completed product: the internal memorandum of law.

Quick Quiz True/False Questions

1. An internal memorandum consists only of an internal memorandum of law.
2. An internal memorandum of law may be used to summarize client information that may be privileged.
3. Internal memoranda include a standard heading identifying the person to whom the memorandum is directed, the author of the memorandum, and the date and subject of the memorandum.
4. Internal memoranda can be used to document information, such as a telephone call.
5. In preparing an internal memorandum of law, the only consideration should be the deadline set by the supervising attorney.

THE INTERNAL MEMORANDUM OF LAW

The format of the internal memorandum may vary from project to project, from firm to firm, and even from lawyer to lawyer (or department to department) within the same firm, depending on personal style preferences. When preparing a memorandum, you should make sure that you understand the format preferred by your

MEMORANDUM OF LAW

TO: Mark Harrison, Senior Partner
FROM: Gregory Johnson, Paralegal
DATE: June 1, 2008
RE: Giles v. Harris

The validity of a transfer of a joint venture interest with a blank power of attorney.

FIGURE 16.3
Example of a Heading

supervising attorney. In general, however, most internal memoranda have the following components:

- Heading
- Statement of issues presented
- Multiple issues presented
- Short summary of the conclusion
- Statement of facts
- Discussion and analysis of the law and facts, with citations to applicable authorities
- IRAC method
- Conclusion

In the next several subsections we discuss each of these components in turn. As we do so, we make reference to figures drawn from an internal memorandum.

heading
A line or more of text that identifies the party for whom the memorandum was prepared; the person by whom it was prepared; the date of preparation; and the subject matter.

The Heading

The **heading** identifies the party for whom the memorandum was prepared; the person by whom it was prepared; the date of preparation; and the subject matter. The heading for our memorandum appears in Figure 16.3.

Begin by identifying the name of the document: Memorandum of Law. Styles vary according to office or attorney preferences. Check a sample to determine your title. The next part of the heading identifies the person to whom the memorandum is directed. The person for whom the memorandum is prepared is usually the attorney who gave you the assignment, and the person actually preparing the memorandum is usually you. This standard scenario may differ in an individual case, however. For example, an associate attorney may ask you to prepare a draft of a memorandum that he will ultimately submit to a partner under his own name (or with both your names). Make sure you understand this circumstance from the outset.

The next element of a heading is the date. If it takes more than one day to prepare a memorandum, do not identify the date when you started the memorandum, nor all the dates on which you worked on it, but rather the date on which you submit it. You should take care that Shepardizing (or other updating) has been completed through that date.

Finally, the heading must identify the subject matter of the memorandum. This usually involves a brief capsule description of the legal issues presented, and possibly identification of the client as well. Although this information may be well known at the time of preparation both to you and the memorandum's recipient, it helps, for future reference, to label it. Such labeling also greatly assists in indexing when the memorandum is placed in the firm's permanent research files, which many firms maintain to avoid duplicating research.

PRACTICE TIP

The date is significant for two reasons: (1) it determines when the memorandum was completed; and (2) if the memorandum is used at a later time, updating of the law may be required. The date of the memorandum determines the starting point for any updating.

A DAY IN THE LIFE OF A PARALEGAL

Unknown to you, a young associate was assigned to prepare an internal memorandum of law by one of the senior partners. The associate is lazy and you know it. She assigns the project to you and you begrudgingly prepare the memorandum. Your heading is styled to the associate, since she is the one who assigned you the project. The associate did not change a word of your interoffice memorandum, except that the heading is changed from the associate to the senior partner. She adopted your work and presented it as her own. You are furious, especially since you were not given credit for a single word of the memorandum. You confront the associate and she reminds you of your place in the firm. What can you do? Shouldn't you be given credit for your work?

This is a common situation in the practice of law. Oftentimes, it is the senior partner who claims the work of a young associate. The difference is that as a paralegal you may not have the opportunity to showcase your work unless *you* create opportunities for yourself. Be careful, though, in the method of letting others know who prepared the work. If you embarrass someone, your life on the job may be difficult. Use your best judgment to determine the appropriate course of action. You need to decide what is most important. Always know that your boss may not acknowledge your work as a paralegal. What is clear is that there always is someone who knows who "really" prepared the work. Sometimes it is simply a matter of time, but eventually everyone finds out.

The Statement of Issues Presented

statement of issues presented
A statement that identifies the legal and factual issues to be discussed in your memorandum.

The **statement of issues presented** or questions presented identifies the legal and factual issues to be discussed in your memorandum. In framing these issues, be concise and direct, and number each issue (unless there is only one). Another key component in drafting the issue for the internal memorandum of law is objectivity. Remember your purpose: to present an objective analysis of the facts and the law. Do not use language that appears to persuade. For example:

> *Objective issue: Can an individual recover for the pain and suffering of a spouse?*
> *Persuasive issue: Can an individual injured by a reckless intoxicated driver recover damages for pain and suffering of an incapacitated spouse?*

The second statement of the issue has a point of view, whereas the first statement is neutral. Additionally, many attorneys pose their issues beginning with the word "Whether." This construction has been discussed in previous chapters. The question is whether to use the word "whether" in presenting the statement of issues. Using the word "whether" is stylistic and clearly a matter of preference of your supervising attorney. This statement of the issues can be redrafted using the "whether" construction.

> *Objective: Whether an individual can recover for the pain and suffering of a spouse. (Notice this construction of the issue ends with a period.)*
> *Persuasive: Whether an individual injured by a reckless intoxicated driver can recover damages for pain and suffering of an incapacitated spouse.*

In determining how to draft your issue, pay attention to word choice. Stay away from emotional language, such as "outrageous," "heinous," or other words that tend to incite a reader. Of course, if the legal standards require the use of expressions such as the "intentional infliction of emotional distress," or "gross negligence," then include them in your issue. Simply remember your audience and your purpose.

You will have an opportunity to test your persuasive drafting skills when you draft the memorandum of law to the trial court or an appellate brief in later chapters.

Under Texas law, is the transfer of a joint venture interest with a blank power of attorney valid?

FIGURE 16.4
Statement of Issue Presented

Figure 16.4 shows an example of appropriate form for a statement of issues presented related to our Case Fact Pattern at the beginning of the Chapter. Each issue should be no longer than one or two sentences, and should generally be drafted to be answerable with a yes or no response.

Although the statement of issues presented is short, the time needed to prepare it may not be. In order to frame the issues properly, you must understand the facts and the relevant substantive law. Often your research will be well under way before you have adequate understanding even to draft a proper statement of issues presented. This may be true even if the ultimate statement amounts to a single short sentence summarizing a single simple issue. Take care in your analysis.

Often your supervising attorney will provide you with a preliminary statement of the issues that she wants investigated, or which she believes are relevant. If that is the case, then your memorandum should be limited to these points. If, however, your research indicates that other areas are more relevant, or at least worthy of consideration, you should consult with your supervising attorney and determine whether further research is warranted. Be careful not to go far afield from the original assignment without authorization; you may waste valuable time and money. Your supervising attorney should provide you with an understanding of the limits of your research; often, as your working relationship is established, you will develop an intuitive understanding of the requirements of a given project. When in doubt, however, ask.

PRACTICE TIP

Prepare your issue after you have completed your legal research and determined your legally significant facts. The two will be combined to create your issue or issues, if more than one, in your memorandum.

Multiple Issues Presented

The client's problems are not singular in nature, and therefore a memorandum of law may have multiple issues. The best approach when presented with multiple issues in a memorandum is to address each issue separately. Think of them as "mini memos" within one document. Each issue should be identified separately with complete legal analysis before you move on to the next issue. As issues are discussed, they should build on each other. Think about your organization. Move from point A to point B. Be logical in your development. This point is important for the clarity of your memorandum. Outlining is crucial when a memorandum of law involves more than one issue, as this will help you remain organized. An outline of a multiple-issue memorandum is presented in Figure 16.5.

Short Summary of the Conclusion

The purpose of the **short summary of the conclusion** is to provide the reader with a quick answer to the yes or no questions raised by the issues. It is always short, but rarely quite as simple in actuality as a mere yes or no. Qualifiers are generally needed to provide a response representative of the analysis and conclusion to follow.

short summary of the conclusion
A summary that provides the reader with a quick answer to the yes or no questions raised by the issues.

The short summary of the conclusion is useful for two purposes. First, to the attorney who is too busy to review the memorandum completely, it provides a capsule summary; second, to those who will study the memorandum in detail, it provides a preview of the end result, helping to place the analysis in perspective. An example is found in Figure 16.6, which relates to our Case Fact Pattern at the beginning of the Chapter.

Statement of Facts

The **statement of facts** sets forth the significant facts obtained in the client interview or provided to you by your supervising attorney, or otherwise present in the client's

statement of facts
A statement that sets forth the significant facts needed to analyze the issues presented in the memorandum of law.

FIGURE 16.5
Outline of a Multiple-Issue Internal Memorandum

Memorandum of Law

Issue I:

A. Identify the issue.

B. Present the law for the issue.

C. Apply the law to the facts of the case.

D. Conclusion for that issue.

Issue II:

A. Identify the issue.

B. Present the law for that issue.

C. Apply the law to the facts of the case. (If there is any overlap of the facts and issues incorporate them, if appropriate.)

D. Conclusion for that issue.

Issue III:

Continue general analysis and format. At the end of the memorandum, prepare a general conclusion with recommendations from your legal research.

FIGURE 16.6
Short Summary of the Conclusion

Yes. Since the power of attorney presented was devoid of any terms, it did not contain the necessary elements to be a valid power of attorney. The acts of the agent exercised under a limited power of attorney are not binding on the principal. However, the cases hold that if the principal received any personal benefits from the transaction, the issue of ratification may be sufficient to validate the acts of the agent.

file. Individual facts are deemed legally significant if they are necessary for an understanding of, or have an impact upon the conclusion drawn regarding, the issues addressed in the memorandum. Although the intended scope and depth of the memorandum is a factor to consider in deciding whether to include specific facts, as a general rule you should lean toward inclusiveness.

Facts should be neither embellished nor downplayed, nor interpreted in the "best light." Rather, they should be objectively and accurately portrayed so that the reader can assess the situation presented. After your review of available materials, you may determine that further investigation is needed for a fair presentation; if so, discuss it with your supervising attorney and proceed if authorized.

A simple, logical, and understandable presentation of the facts is crucial, so that the reader has a clear understanding of the context in which the issues are analyzed

Statement of Facts:
Mr. Giles went to a pre-Thanksgiving party at the home of Mr. Swan. Swan had been his friend and attorney for approximately two years.
At the party, Giles and Swan discussed Giles's desire to purchase a piece of real estate before the end of the year. Giles indicated that he was going out of town for Thanksgiving, and would not be back until January 1. Swan stated that he could close the real estate transaction if Giles would execute a power of attorney. Giles then signed a document entitled "Power of Attorney," which Swan kept. Giles then left the party and departed on his trip.
While Giles was away, Swan was contacted by Giles's partner, Mr. Harris, regarding a joint venture transaction completely unrelated to the real estate transaction. Harris told Swan that Giles was supposed to assume all of Harris's interest in the joint venture before January 1. Swan told Harris he had a power of attorney to close a real estate transaction, but did not know how he could help Harris out. Harris suggested to Swan that he could use the power of attorney to facilitate the transfer of the joint venture interest. Swan hesitated, but Harris indicated that Giles would not receive the tax benefits attendant to the transfer if he did not close the deal before December 31. Swan finally agreed to execute the transfer of the joint venture interest using the power of attorney, and shortly thereafter the deal was completed.
When Giles came back to town, he was furious, and told Swan that he did not want to assume the entire joint venture interest and wanted the transaction voided.

FIGURE 16.7
Statement of Facts Section

PRACTICE TIP

Unless directly dispositive of your results, do not cite legal authority in your conclusion. Legal authority is cited in your discussion section.

and the conclusion reached. Chronological development is often best; sometimes it may be useful to emphasize crucial facts first, and then demonstrate how they fit into the chronological whole. Using the Case Fact Pattern, Figure 16.7 illustrates a clear, concise statement of facts.

In presenting your statement of facts for a memorandum of law, you should strive to complete these goals:

- Be objective: Remember the purpose of the document. Do not let your opinions creep into your work.
- Be complete: Do not leave out relevant facts, whether they support your client's position or not. State the disputed facts as they may have bearing on your legal analysis.

YOU BE THE JUDGE

Substantiating the truthfulness of facts is a responsibility of an attorney. When an attorney knowingly misrepresents facts to a court, a violation of the rules of professional responsibility occurs. Such was the case in Nebraska when an attorney decided to represent his brother in his divorce. In *State Ex. Rel. Bar Association v. Zakrzewski,* 560 N.W.2d 150 (Neb. 1997), an attorney filed an affidavit that contained false claims about the attorney representing his sister-in-law. The issue centered on child abuse allegations of the wife/mother of a child (his nephew), which the attorney stated in his affidavit she was directed to file by her attorney. Because of this directive, the parties were trying to "vilify" and "interfere" with his brother's rights of visitation. *Id.* at 153. The plain facts were that his sister-in-law's attorney never directed her to do anything claimed. In fact, the facts established the opposite conclusion.

The court's investigation showed that the attorney possessed no knowledge to support his assertions in the affidavit and conducted no investigation to substantiate his claims. *Id.* at 155. Because the attorney's actions were maliciously motivated, and his behavior toward the disciplinary committee investigating the allegations was unprofessional, the court ordered suspension for eighteen months. The court believed the conduct so serious that in its reasoning it opined that "[t]he making of false statements by an attorney obviously reflects negatively on both that attorney's ability to practice law and the reputation of the entire bar in general. Such a practice must be deterred by this court." *Id.* at 156. Review the case. Which rule of professional responsibility did the court cite? What are the facts that led to the suspension of the attorney? What is the court's reasoning in the case?

legally significant facts
Facts that are critical to the analysis of a case.

- Identify **legally significant facts:** Your legal analysis may turn on a fact in the case. Be sure you include the legally significant facts in your statement of facts. Certain facts set the tone and background; other facts are so critical to the analysis that they are integral to the case.
- Be clear: The order of presentation of the facts guides the reader. Do not confuse facts with analysis or facts with conclusions. Present a road map for the reader to follow that is decisive.
- Be accurate: Do not embellish the facts; do not hide facts; do not create facts. The law directly relates to the facts. If you misstate the facts, you could create a domino effect in which your analysis becomes flawed.

Discussion and Analysis

discussion and analysis
The heart of the memorandum, which presents the legal analysis with supporting citations.

The **discussion and analysis** section is the heart of the memorandum. In this section you will be

- identifying points of law and supporting them with citations;
- quoting from relevant cases, statutes, and other sources; and
- relating your research to the facts of your matter.

Always remember that your purpose is to discuss objectively the strengths and the weaknesses of your case. You must view the issues not only from your client's perspective, but also from that of your opponent. The negative side of your client's position will surface eventually; the internal memorandum prepares your firm to deal with such weaknesses. Discuss both those points that operate to your client's advantage and those likely to be cited against him; identify counterpoints to your own strong arguments and counterpoints to the opponent's. The reader should get a sense of how an objective observer might look at the matter.

PRACTICE TIP

Do not state legal conclusions in the statement of facts. Remember, state "just the facts."

As with the statement of facts, and indeed the other components of a memorandum as well, the scope and depth of your discussion will vary with the intended use. In some cases, your assignment will be to prepare an exhaustive survey of the law in a given area, citing all possibly relevant cases and statutes, and perhaps even providing separate copies or abstracts of these primary sources. In other cases, the assignment will be to obtain a quick answer, citing only the most relevant cases. Know your assignment, and hence your goal, from the outset.

Quotations from cases can be as useful in a memorandum as they are in other projects (and they are often incorporated into later briefs), and references to secondary sources can give added support to your arguments. All these possibilities should be discussed with your supervising attorney, and you should be sure that you understand her expectations before you begin.

CYBER TRIP

Using the Internet, locate two examples of an inter-office memorandum of law. (Hint: Check court Web sites as well as law firm sites with document banks.)

Discuss the cases, statutes, and other material *favoring* your client first. Describe how they support your argument, and how they may be attacked. Then discuss the materials that go *against* your client's position, stating how they are harmful, and whether and how they can be distinguished.

Emphasize primary sources over secondary and mandatory precedents over merely persuasive precedents. If the issues involved are state law issues, emphasize research in state law sources; if federal issues, emphasize federal sources.

You should constantly integrate the law and the facts. Don't do this at the expense of an extended discussion of a complicated legal concept, however; by all means, make the status and meaning of the law clear. But make sure the reader understands throughout the discussion, and particularly at the end, how the law affects the specific facts of the client's matter. A means to communicate this information is by using the IRAC method.

The IRAC Method

In the previous chapters, the IRAC method of legal analysis was discussed. To review, IRAC is the acronym for issue, rule of law, analysis or application of law (to the facts), and conclusion. Although this method appears restrictive, it provides a good guide, especially in the beginning when writing an internal memorandum of law is unfamiliar. Let's review each letter of IRAC:

Issue: The issue is analogous to your topic sentence. This sentence will tell the reader what the paragraph or succeeding paragraphs will discuss. Recall that paragraphs should have a lead-in sentence, a topic sentence, or a transitional sentence. If the issue is your topic sentence, it will identify to the reader the topic that you are to cover. The issue is your starting point in the paragraph or the paragraphs that follow.

Rule of Law: Present your legal research in this part of the analysis. This is where you cite your relevant cases, statutes, and other legal authority that will ultimately support your analysis. Incorporate your cases into your sentences. Quote your legal authority. Use the information you mastered in Chapter 14 in this section. Remember, you must cite legal authority for a legal proposition. Support a legal statement by a legal source.

Analysis or Application: Together with the facts and law of your case, you must now analyze how the law affects your facts. Does the law support the client's position or the opposing party? Your analysis sets the stage for the conclusion, so be thorough. Do not forget to relate your legal research to the facts; otherwise, the exercise becomes a report on the law. Remember why you are preparing the memorandum—for the client. Unless you incorporate the primary objective, your client's problem, into your analysis, you have not accomplished your goal.

As part of your analysis, you must present the opposing party's position. What will the other side argue? Consider this the "yes, but . . ." section of the analysis. You need to present the counterarguments so that a true picture of the client's problem can be analyzed. You know there are three sides to an argument: my view, your view, and the right view! Therefore, take a broader approach in your analysis and look at all sides of the issue.

Conclusion: The conclusion is the summation sentence of your analysis of the law and facts of the case. This section should be no more than one or two sentences and should succinctly state your conclusions based upon your research for that issue. This section, after reviewing the law and facts, tells the reader the reasons for the possible legal outcome in the case. This section differs from the conclusion section in that "this" conclusion is a sentence that summarizes the paragraphs that preceded it. The conclusion section summarizes the entire memorandum of law and recommends strategies based upon the legal research.

An example of a proper discussion section appears in Figure 16.8. Note that *The Bluebook* citation form is used. You should not deviate from proper citation form, regardless of whether it is *The Bluebook* or *ALWD,* just because the memorandum is to be used internally, rather than filed with a court. Your text may someday be incorporated into a brief; the more accurate its form and substance, the more valuable the memorandum will be.

Conclusion

Although the discussion section forms the heart of your memorandum, the **conclusion** is the culmination. In a paragraph or two, you summarize what your research has shown about the law relating to your client's problem. You may even recommend a course of action, if that was part of your assignment.

conclusion
The summary of your analysis in a memorandum.

Though coming to a conclusion generally means stating your opinion about how the legal issues will be resolved, it does not imply that you should become an advocate when

FIGURE 16.8
Discussion Section

Discussion:

Before a thorough analysis can be completed, a power of attorney must be defined. Under the law, a power of attorney creates an agency relationship whereby one person, the principal, appoints another person, the agent, to act on the principal's behalf. *Lawler v. Federal Deposit Insurance Corp.,* 538 S.W. 2d 245 (Tex. Civ. App.–Dallas 1976, writ ref'd n.r.e.). The relationship is consensual. *Texas Processed Plastics, Inc. v. Gray Enterprises, Inc.,* 592 S.W. 2d 412 (Tex. Civ. App.–Tyler 1979, no writ); *Green v. Hanon,* 367 S.W. 2d 853 (Tex. Civ. App., Texarkana 1963, no writ). The law specifically defines a power of attorney as "[a]n instrument by which the authority of one person to act in the place and stead of another as attorney in fact is set forth." *Olive-Sternberg Lumber Co. v. Gordon,* 143 S.W. 2d 694 (Tex. Civ. App.–Beaumont 1940, no writ). The document in this case identified neither the principal, nor the agent, nor the extent of the authority of the agent. The document's validity is thus questionable.

However, before the validity of the document is determined, it must be interpreted using the current standards of the law. Under Texas law, certain rules of construction and interpretation must be followed. The rules of construing a document date back as far as 1889, to the leading case of *Gouldy v. Metcalf,* 75 Tex. 455, 12 S.W. 830 (1889). In *Gouldy*, the Texas Supreme Court set out the rules of construction for a power of attorney:

> [w]hen an authority is conferred upon an agent by a formal instrument, as by a power of attorney, there are two rules of construction to be carefully adhered to:
>
> 1. The meaning of general words in the instrument will be restricted by the context, and construed accordingly.
>
> 2. The authority will be construed strictly, so as to exclude the exercise of any power which is not warranted, either by the actual terms used or as a necessary means of executing the authority with effect. *Id.* at 245.

Expanding the guidelines set forth in *Gouldy*, case law establishes that "all powers conferred upon an agent by a formal instrument are to receive a strict interpretation, and the authority is never extended by intendment or construction beyond that which is given in terms, or is necessary for carrying the authority into effect, and the authority must be strictly pursued." *Bean v. Bean*, 79 S.W. 2d 652 (Tex. Civ. App.–Texarkana 1935, writ ref'd); *See, Dockstader v. Brown*, 204 S.W. 2d 352 (Tex. Civ. App.–Fort Worth 1947, writ ref'd n.r.e.).

In applying the rules of construction, for a power of attorney to be valid certain elements must be contained within the document. The necessary elements are the name of the principal, the name of the agent, and the nature and extent of the authority granted. *Sun Appliance and Electric, Inc. v. Klein*, 363 S.W. 2d 293 (Tex. Civ. App.–Eastland 1962, no writ).

The power of attorney in the present matter contained only the signature of the principal, and nothing else. In analyzing the power of attorney under the strict considerations, the essential terms of the power of attorney were missing. As such, it appears that the document does not comply with the legal definition of a power of attorney.

The facts further indicate that the power of attorney was executed for a specific purpose, although not stated. Giles had orally instructed Swan to use the power of attorney to consummate a real estate transaction only. As stated in *Giddings, Neiman-Marcus v. Estes*, 440 S.W. 2d 90 (Tex. Civ. App.–Eastland 1969, no writ):

Cont.

FIGURE 16.8
Discussion Section
Cont.

> The authority will be construed strictly, so as to exclude the exercise of any power which is not warranted either by the actual terms used or as a necessary means of executing the authority with effect.

Since no authority was conferred to Swan by the document, he could not have acted on Giles's behalf. Consequently, any acts performed by Swan for Giles under the power of attorney are invalid.

However, the facts reveal that Swan had acted as Giles's attorney on a number of occasions. This fact may give rise to an implication that Swan was acting with apparent authority. This is defined as "such authority as a reasonably prudent man, using diligence and discretion in view of the principal's conduct, would naturally and reasonably suppose the agent to possess." *Great American Casualty Company v. Eichelberger*, 37 S.W. 2d 1050 (Tex. Civ. App.–Waco 1931, writ ref'd). Thus, as the Houston Court of Civil Appeals stated in its dicta:

> [a]n agency may arise with respect to third persons if acts or appearances reasonably lead third persons to believe that an agency in fact has been created. And . . . apparent authority of an agent to bind a principal, by want of ordinary care, clothes the agent with such indicia of authority as to lead a reasonably prudent person to believe that he actually has such authority. *Hall v. Hallamicek*, 669 S.W. 2d 368 (Tex. App.–Houston [14th Dist.] 1984, no writ).

Because of the standard in the *Hall* case, Harris may try to use apparent authority as a means to validate the transfer, as Giles has the burden of proof that Swan did not have the authority to act on Giles's behalf. *Dockstader v. Brown*, 204 S.W. 2d 352 (Tex. Civ. App.–Fort Worth 1947, writ ref'd n.r.e.).

There is a problem with the apparent authority argument, however. Harris knew that the power of attorney was for a specific purpose: to close the real estate transaction. The law is very clear that a third party has a duty to inquire into the scope and fact of the agency and the burden is on the third party to "ascertain at his peril the nature and scope of the authority of such agent." *Lawrie v. Miller*, 2 S.W. 2d 561 (Tex. Civ. App.–Texarkana 1928, no writ); *Eliot Valve Repair v. Valve*, 675 S.W. 2d 555 (Tex. App.–Houston [1st Dist.] 1984, no writ); *Boucher v. City Paint & Supply*, 398 S.W. 2d 352 (Tex. Civ. App.–Tyler 1966, no writ).

The facts of our case indicate that Mr. Harris neither investigated nor examined the extent of Swan's authority. As such, Giles cannot be held responsible for the acts of Swan and their effect.

In analyzing the facts and the law, it is apparent that the document which purports to be a power of attorney is not a valid one; and that Swan did not have the authority to act on Giles's behalf under any circumstance. Consequently, the power of attorney is valueless and any action resulting from the use of the document is void.

Although the case law appears to be in our client's favor, there is an issue that may be raised by the defense which weakens our case substantially. The issue is the principal's ratification of the transaction. Ratification requires that the principal have full and complete knowledge of all material facts pertaining to the transaction prior to any affirmation of the act. *Leonard v. Hare*, 161 Tex. 28, 336 S.W. 2d 619 (1960). For ratification to occur, the principal must retain the benefits and "the critical factor in determining whether a principal has ratified an unauthorized act by his agent is the

Cont.

FIGURE 16.8
Discussion Section
Cont.

principal's knowledge of the transaction and his actions in light of such knowledge." *Land Title Company of Dallas, Inc. v. Stigler,* 609 S.W. 2d 754, 756 (Tex. 1980); *First National Bank in Dallas v. Kinnabrew,* 589 S.W. 2d 137 (Tex. Civ. App.–Tyler 1979, writ ref'd n.r.e.). In the event that it is determined that Giles took benefits from Swan's actions, specifically tax benefits, the transaction may be valid, regardless of whether the initial power of attorney was legally insufficient.

FIGURE 16.9
Conclusion Section

Conclusion:
Since the power of attorney did not grant specific authority to the agent, the power of attorney is void. Based upon the strict construction doctrine, one cannot construe a grant of authority which is nonexistent. The power of attorney did not contain the name of the agent, the purpose of the agency, or the grant of authority to the agent, and therefore could not confer any powers upon the agent. The acts of the agent were improper and the principal is not legally responsible for the effects of those acts. However, as noted, if the principal received any benefits from the transaction, the acts of the agent may be ratified, which would validate any acts of the agent. This act could make the transaction valid.

drafting your conclusion. If you have strong reservations about your conclusion, or believe that a court could easily justify a different ruling, say so. Once again, you must keep in mind the most important rule of the internal memorandum of law—*objectivity*!

An example of a good conclusion is found in Figure 16.9.

A sample of a complete memorandum of law is provided in Figure 16.10.

POSTWRITING CONSIDERATIONS

Do not forget to practice what you learned in previous chapters. Before you present your internal memorandum of law to your supervising attorney, be sure you have completed the following postwriting exercises:

- Reread your work.
- Redraft your work.
- Proofread for spelling, grammar, and punctuation.
- Cite-check your legal sources for correctness and accuracy.
- Edit.
- Proofread, again.
- Edit one last time.

FIGURE 16.10
Sample Memorandum of Law: The Validity of a Transfer of a Joint Venture Interest with a Blank Power of Attorney

Memorandum

TO: Mark Harrison, Senior Partner
FROM: Gregory Johnson, Paralegal
DATE: June 1, 2008
RE: Giles v. Harris

Cont.

FIGURE 16.10
Sample Memorandum of Law *Cont.*

Issue Presented:

Under Texas law, is the transfer of a joint venture interest with a blank power of attorney valid?

Answer to the Issue:

Yes. Since the power of attorney presented was devoid of any terms, it did not contain the necessary elements to be a valid power of attorney. The acts of the agent exercised under a limited power of attorney are not binding on the principal. However, the cases hold that if the principal received any personal benefits from the transaction, the issue of ratification may be sufficient to validate the acts of the agent.

Statement of Facts:

Mr. Giles went to a pre-Thanksgiving party at the home of Mr. Swan. Swan had been his friend and attorney for approximately two years.

At the party, Giles and Swan discussed Giles's desire to purchase a piece of real estate before the end of the year. Giles indicated that he was going out of town for Thanksgiving, and would not be back until January 1. Swan stated that he could close the real estate transaction if Giles would execute a power of attorney. Giles then signed a document entitled "Power of Attorney," which Swan kept. Giles then left the party and departed on his trip.

While Giles was away, Swan was contacted by Giles's partner, Mr. Harris, regarding a joint venture transaction completely unrelated to the real estate transaction. Harris told Swan that Giles was supposed to assume all of Harris's interest in the joint venture before January 1. Swan told Harris he had a power of attorney to close a real estate transaction, but did not know how he could help Harris out. Harris suggested to Swan that he could use the power of attorney to facilitate the transfer of the joint venture interest. Swan hesitated, but Harris indicated that Giles would not receive the tax benefits attendant to the transfer if he did not close the deal before December 31. Swan finally agreed to execute the transfer of the joint venture interest using the power of attorney, and shortly thereafter the deal was completed.

When Giles came back to town he was furious, and told Swan that he did not want to assume the entire joint venture interest, and wanted the transaction voided.

Discussion:

The basic question to address is can a blank power of attorney be used to transfer a joint venture interest. Before a thorough analysis can be completed, a power of attorney must be defined. Under the law, a power of attorney creates an agency relationship whereby one person, the principal, appoints another person, the agent, to act on the principal's behalf. *Lawler v. Federal Deposit Insurance Corp.,* 538 S.W. 2d 245 (Tex. Civ. App.–Dallas 1976, writ ref'd n.r.e.). The relationship is consensual. *Texas Processed Plastics, Inc. v. Gray Enterprises, Inc.*, 592 S.W. 2d 412 (Tex. Civ. App.–Tyler 1979, no writ); *Green v. Hanon*, 367 S.W. 2d 853 (Tex. Civ. App. Texarkana 1963, no writ). The law specifically defines a power of attorney as "[a]n instrument by which the authority of one person to act in the place and stead of another as attorney in fact is set forth." *Olive-Sternberg Lumber Co. v. Gordon*, 143 S.W. 2d 694 (Tex. Civ. App.–Beaumont 1940, no

Cont.

FIGURE 16.10
Sample Memorandum of Law *Cont.*

writ). The document in this case identified neither the principal, nor the agent, nor the extent of the authority of the agent. The document's validity is thus questionable.

However, before the validity of the document is determined, it must be interpreted using the current standards of the law. Under Texas law, certain rules of construction and interpretation must be followed. The rules of construing a document date back as far as 1889, to the leading case of *Gouldy v. Metcalf*, 75 Tex. 455, 12 S.W. 830 (1889). In *Gouldy*, the Texas Supreme Court set out the rules of construction for a power of attorney:

> [w]hen an authority is conferred upon an agent by a formal instrument, as by a power of attorney, there are two rules of construction to be carefully adhered to:
>
> 1. The meaning of general words in the instrument will be restricted by the context, and construed accordingly.
>
> 2. The authority will be construed strictly, so as to exclude the exercise of any power which is not warranted, either by the actual terms used or as a necessary means of executing the authority with effect. *Id.* at 245.

Expanding the guidelines set forth in *Gouldy*, case law establishes that "all powers conferred upon an agent by a formal instrument are to receive a strict interpretation, and the authority is never extended by intendment or construction beyond that which is given in terms, or is necessary for carrying the authority into effect, and the authority must be strictly pursued." *Bean v. Bean*, 79 S.W. 2d 652 (Tex. Civ. App.–Texarkana 1935, writ ref'd); *See, Dockstader v. Brown*, 204 S.W. 2d 352 (Tex. Civ. App.–Fort Worth 1947, writ ref'd n.r.e.).

In applying the rules of construction, for a power of attorney to be valid certain elements must be contained within the document. The necessary elements are the name of the principal, the name of the agent, and the nature and extent of the authority granted. *Sun Appliance and Electric, Inc. v. Klein*, 363 S.W. 2d 293 (Tex. Civ. App.–Eastland 1962, no writ).

The power of attorney in the present matter contained only the signature of the principal, and nothing else. In analyzing the power of attorney under the strict considerations, the essential terms of the power of attorney were missing. As such, it appears that the document does not comply with the legal definition of a power of attorney.

The facts further indicate that the power of attorney was executed for a specific purpose, although not stated. Giles had orally instructed Swan to use the power of attorney to consummate a real estate transaction only. As stated in *Giddings, Neiman-Marcus v. Estes*, 440 S.W. 2d 90 (Tex. Civ. App.–Eastland 1969, no writ):

> The authority will be construed strictly, so as to exclude the exercise of any power which is not warranted either by the actual terms used or as a necessary means of executing the authority with effect.

Since no authority was conferred to Swan by the document, he could not have acted on Giles's behalf. Consequently, any acts performed by Swan for Giles under the power of attorney are invalid.

Cont.

FIGURE 16.10
Sample Memorandum of Law *Cont.*

However, the facts reveal that Swan had acted as Giles's attorney on a number of occasions. This fact may give rise to an implication that Swan was acting with apparent authority. This is defined as "such authority as a reasonably prudent man, using diligence and discretion in view of the principal's conduct, would naturally and reasonably suppose the agent to possess." *Great American Casualty Company v. Eichelberger*, 37 S.W. 2d 1050 (Tex. Civ. App.–Waco 1931, writ ref'd). Thus, as the Houston Court of Civil Appeals stated in its dicta:

> [a]n agency may arise with respect to third persons if acts or appearances reasonably lead third persons to believe that an agency in fact has been created. And . . . apparent authority of an agent to bind a principal, by want of ordinary care, clothes the agent with such indicia of authority as to lead a reasonably prudent person to believe that he actually has such authority. *Hall v. Hallamicek*, 669 S.W. 2d 368 (Tex. App.–Houston [14th Dist.] 1984, no writ).

Because of the standard in the *Hall* case, Harris may try to use apparent authority as a means to validate the transfer, as Giles has the burden of proof that Swan did not have the authority to act on Giles's behalf. *Dockstader v. Brown*, 204 S.W. 2d 352 (Tex. Civ. App.–Fort Worth 1947, writ ref'd n.r.e.).

There is a problem with the apparent authority argument, however. Harris knew that the power of attorney was for a specific purpose: to close the real estate transaction. The law is very clear that a third party has a duty to inquire into the scope and fact of the agency and the burden is on the third party to "ascertain at his peril the nature and scope of the authority of such agent." *Lawrie v. Miller*, 2 S.W. 2d 561 (Tex. Civ. App.–Texarkana 1928, no writ); *Eliot Valve Repair v. Valve*, 675 S.W. 2d 555 (Tex. App.–Houston [1st Dist.] 1984, no writ); *Boucher v. City Paint & Supply*, 398 S.W. 2d 352 (Tex. Civ. App.–Tyler 1966, no writ).

The facts of our case indicate that Mr. Harris neither investigated nor examined the extent of Swan's authority. As such, Giles cannot be held responsible for the acts of Swan and their effect.

In analyzing the facts and the law, it is apparent that the document which purports to be a power of attorney is not a valid one, and that Swan did not have the authority to act on Giles's behalf under any circumstance. Consequently, the power of attorney is valueless and any action resulting from the use of the document is void.

Although the case law appears to be in our client's favor, there is an issue that may be raised by the defense which weakens our case substantially. The issue is the principal's ratification of the transaction. Ratification requires that the principal have full and complete knowledge of all material facts pertaining to the transaction prior to any affirmation of the act. *Leonard v. Hare*, 161 Tex. 28, 336 S.W. 2d 619 (1960). For ratification to occur the principal must retain the benefits and "the critical factor in determining whether a principal has ratified an unauthorized act by his agent is the principal's knowledge of the transaction and his actions in light of such knowledge." *Land Title Company of Dallas, Inc. v. Stigler,* 609 S.W. 2d 754, 756 (Tex. 1980); *First National Bank in Dallas v. Kinnabrew,* 589 S.W. 2d 137 (Tex. Civ. App.–Tyler 1979, writ ref'd n.r.e.). In the event that it is determined that Giles took benefits from Swan's actions, specifically tax benefits, the transaction may be valid, regardless of whether the initial power of attorney was legally insufficient.

Cont.

FIGURE 16.10
Sample Memorandum of Law *Cont.*

Conclusion:

Since the power of attorney did not grant specific authority to the agent, the power of attorney is void. Based upon the strict construction doctrine, one cannot construe a grant of authority which is nonexistent. The power of attorney did not contain the name of the agent, the purpose of the agency, or the grant of authority to the agent and therefore the document could not confer any powers upon the agent. The acts of the agent were improper, and the principal is not legally responsible for the effects of those acts. However, as noted, if the principal received any benefits from the transaction, the acts of the agent may be ratified, which would validate any acts of the agent. This act could make the transaction valid.

ETHICS ALERT

Care must be taken when eliciting information from clients, as your attorney may be relying on you to verify the accuracy of the facts presented. Therefore, you have the same duty as an attorney in investigating the validity of facts. If you are interviewing a client, be sure to write down an accurate account of the facts. Do not accept the client's word as the only source of the "truth." Sometimes clients have improper motives for pursuing legal actions and their claims may be unfounded in law. Sometimes their memories are selective or skewed. The rules of professional responsibility require a good-faith basis for a claim. Relying on the client's version of the facts is insufficient.

Remember our attorney from New Jersey in Chapter 11 who filed incomprehensible pleadings in *Mendez v. Draham,* 182 F. Supp. 2d 430 (D. N.J. 2002)? Well, he managed to incite the wrath of the court on another occasion as well. In this case, *Carlino v. Gloucester City High School,* 57 F. Supp. 2d 1 (D. N.J. 1999), the court sanctioned Mr. Malat again for not investigating the facts of his case prior to filing a lawsuit. In the case, some students became intoxicated on a class trip and were prohibited from participating in graduation exercises. Mr. Malat filed a lawsuit claiming violations of constitutional rights and other causes of action. The court publicly admonished the attorney for his "flagrant failure to conduct any legal research." *Id.* at 38. The court pointed out that even the most minimal investigation would have showed that the claims of the students were barred by statute. *Id.* at 38. He was fined again and ordered "to attend two continuing legal education courses." *Id.* at 39.

Although this attorney's practice is the exception and not the rule, the message from the court is undeniable: Investigate and make reasonable inquiry to determine the validity of the facts in a case. This inquiry involves not only independent verification of the facts but also verification of the law. No matter what the assignment is, diligence on your part is directly linked to your performance and integrity as a professional. Do not squander the confidence your supervising attorney instills in you.

Quick Quiz True/False Questions

1. There is only one format that should be followed when preparing an internal memorandum of law.
2. An internal memorandum of law is considered a persuasive document.
3. The statement of facts in an internal memorandum of law should be persuasive and presented in the most favorable manner that supports the client's position.
4. The discussion and analysis section presents the relevant legal points with supporting citations.
5. The conclusion section should never recommend a course of action.

THE E-FACTOR

Everybody has one; everybody uses them. Cellular telephones. But should you be using them to discuss sensitive client matters? Cell phones have become a way of life; however, their level of security is questionable. If client matters are overheard by a third party, are those communications still privileged? Many of the bar associations around the country have issued opinions on the cell phone security, and with the different opinions come varying conclusions. Some opinions recognize that cell phones are so common that even if a conversation is intercepted, the privilege continues. Others suggest gaining authorization from the client to communicate by cell phone because of the possible interception or crossing of lines. Whatever your jurisdiction's position on the issue, cell phones are not a safe mode of communication with a client. If a cell phone must be used, keep the conversations brief and delay sensitive matters for a secure telephone. You do not want to test the waters if information is inadvertently released and it gets into the hands of the opposing party. Some courts view the risk as "your risk," and if the information is improperly intercepted, it may be your supervising attorney's burden to show why the information is still protected by attorney/client privilege. Do not place yourself in that situation—limit the circumstances in which you use cell phones with clients.

PRACTICAL CONSIDERATIONS: DON'T FORGET WHAT YOU'VE LEARNED

An internal memorandum will inevitably involve at least some of your own opinions, since you must reach a conclusion based upon your research. It is important, however, that you let neither your opinions nor your conclusion color your analysis; that is, you must also include in your memorandum those portions of your research that go against your conclusion. The memorandum is designed to *inform* your supervising attorney, so that he is prepared to advocate on behalf of your client; the memorandum itself should not advocate a position.

In drafting your memorandum, remember the many basic rules you've learned in previous chapters. Use punctuation, sentence structure, and paragraphing to make your points clear; write with precision and forcefulness; avoid ambiguity, use logical development; and be sure your writing tells the reader what you want her to know.

Source: © 2005 Thaves. Reprinted with permission. Newspaper dist, by NEA, Inc.

Summary

Prepare all necessary documents ahead of time, and do preliminary background research. Before commencing the initial client interview, be sure to identify yourself as a paralegal. Be prepared to discuss fees. In the interview itself, establish a positive relationship with the client, and proceed in stages to gather the facts. Ask focused questions after the client has told his story, and review the entire fact pattern before he leaves. Then immediately prepare a postinterview memorandum.

The internal memorandum of law is designed to inform, to explain, and to evaluate. It is intended to assist with such things as deciding whether to take a case or determining how to proceed on a case. Its purpose is objective. The heading identifies the parties preparing and receiving the memorandum, the date of submission, and the subject matter covered. The statement of issues presented identifies the legal and factual issues to be discussed. The short summary of the conclusion provides a quick answer to the questions raised by the statement of issues presented. The statement of facts presents an accurate picture of the facts. The discussion and analysis section identifies applicable points of law and supports them with citations to, and quotes from, relevant cases, statutes, and other sources, always relating the research to the facts of the specific matter. The conclusion is the culmination of the research, summarizing the implications of your analysis and possibly including a recommended course of action.

Although an internal memorandum of law necessarily involves some of the writer's own opinions (since she must reach a conclusion), these opinions should not be allowed to color the analysis. The writer must remain objective, including in the text both those references that support her conclusions and those which go against it.

Key Terms

attorney–client privilege
brief bank
conclusion
discussion and analysis
heading
internal memorandum of law
legally significant facts
short summary of the conclusion
statement of facts
statement of issues presented

Review Questions

1. Identify the different types of memoranda.
2. What is the difference between an interoffice memorandum and a memorandum of law to the trial court?
3. What are three prewriting considerations in preparing an interoffice memorandum of law?
4. What does it mean when we describe an internal memorandum of law as "objective"?
5. What are some of the purposes of an internal memorandum of law?
6. List the information that should be included in the heading section of an internal memorandum of law.
7. What is the importance of the issues presented section?
8. What is the purpose of the short summary of the conclusion section?

9. What factors should be considered in preparing an appropriate statement of facts?
10. What are the key elements of the discussion section?

Exercises

1. Read *American Heritage Life Insurance Company v. Koch,* 721 S.W.2d 611 (Tex. App., Tyler 1986, no writ), and draft the issue presented.
2. Draft the statement of facts from the memorandum in Figure 16.1.
3. Prepare a memorandum of law on the status of law in your state regarding the comparative negligence statute.
4. A new client interview was completed by your supervising attorney. She wants you to prepare an interoffice memorandum based on the following facts:

   Mr. Hunter is a forty-five-year-old man who was fired from his job on May 10, 2008. The company claims that he was terminated because of his performance, but Mr. Hunter was never disciplined and does not have any negative evaluations in his personnel file. He believes he was fired because the company wants to hire a younger person for less money. He believes the company discriminated against him and he wants to file a lawsuit. What are the procedures, if any, that we must follow prior to filing the lawsuit? Do we need to have a determination by the EEOC (Equal Employment Opportunity Commission)? What is the status of the laws and how do they relate to our client?
5. Your office represents Community Hospital. It has just been sued by a visitor who slipped on a wet floor on the second floor. There was a sign posted stating that the floor was wet. What is the hospital's liability to the visitor? Does the liability change if the hospital is a government hospital or private hospital? Prepare an interoffice memorandum of law discussing all issues.
6. Your supervising attorney just discovered some new information on a case and wants to prepare an interoffice memorandum of the status of the law on whether admissions of liability in settlement discussions can later be used at trial against the person who made the statement. (This memorandum will be limited to mainly a discussion on the law.)
7. The now-defunct Enron and WorldCom companies created a new corporate environment. Your attorney was retained by a nonprofit hospital and is concerned about the new standards created under the Sarbanes-Oxley Act. He believes Section 404 of the statute is critical in advising his client. The hospital wants to know what is required to comply with Sarbanes-Oxley, even though it knows it is not a legal requirement now; because it is a nonprofit corporation, it still wants guidance on the compliance issue. Prepare an internal memorandum of law on the general requirements of the "best practices standard" under Sarbanes-Oxley.
8. A new client has arrived quite upset. Her husband just emptied all their joint accounts and canceled the credit cards; he has left her penniless. Her husband is a wealthy businessman and he wants revenge. The client says she has been a loyal wife and has not cheated on her husband. They have two minor children who both attend private school. The wife wants to know if she can get immediate spousal support and begin divorce proceedings today. Prepare the memorandum of law on the issues based upon your jurisdiction's requirements.

PORTFOLIO ASSIGNMENT

Your attorney wants to bill for your services as a paralegal. She believes that you have contributed in a meaningful manner to the case, but does not know the legal standards for billing paralegal services. In the case you prepared numerous memoranda, drafted pleadings and motions, copied cases, and participated in numerous meetings. A hearing on attorney's fees is scheduled for next week. Your assignment from your supervising attorney is

a. research the law regarding billing a paralegal's services as part of an attorney's fee;

b. prepare an internal memorandum for your attorney's review.

Quick Quiz True/False Answers

Page 488	Page 502
1. False	1. False
2. True	2. False
3. True	3. False
4. True	4. True
5. False	5. False

Chapter 17

Court Documents: Pleadings, Discovery, and Motions

After completing this chapter, you will be able to:

- Explain why preliminary research is important to the proper drafting of a complaint.
- Describe the difference between a complaint and an answer.
- Identify the benefits and pitfalls of using form books and models to assist in the preparation of pleadings.
- Explain why the discovery process is needed.
- List the different types of discovery.
- Explain the usefulness of a request for admissions and a production of documents.
- Draft a motion for summary judgment.
- Understand the difference between a motion for protective order and a motion to compel discovery.
- Learn the importance of reviewing and understanding the rules of procedure before drafting a court document.
- Build on the skills learned from basic legal writing to prepare court documents.

Court documents encompass a broad category of legal documents. Generally, they include pleadings, discovery, and motions. All are drafted with a persuasive point of view with an eye toward convincing a judge of a client's particular position. Crafting a well-drafted court document is no easy task. This chapter will highlight only some of the court documents you will draft as a paralegal. But whatever court document you will draft, keep in mind the importance of precision, brevity, and clarity—the lessons learned in our previous chapters.

CASE FACT PATTERN

Your firm's client, Mary Mackey, is fifty-one years old. After thirty years of continuous employment with XYZ Corporation, and despite a personnel file that contains exceptional performance reviews and no hint of misconduct, she was recently fired with no explanation and for no apparent reason. Based on conversations she had with former co-workers, she believes that she was replaced by a thirty-three-year-old woman who came in at a higher salary despite minimal qualifications.

Your supervising attorney believes that Mrs. Mackey's termination constitutes age discrimination. He has written to XYZ Corporation, demanding that Mrs. Mackey be reinstated and that she be reimbursed for the weeks of salary missed since the firing. The corporation has rejected this demand, and refuses to discuss the situation further.

Your supervising attorney has decided that litigation can no longer be avoided. You have been assigned to draft a complaint and some preliminary discovery on behalf of Mrs. Mackey.

AN OVERVIEW OF THE COURT PROCESS

In earlier chapters we discussed the court process and the basic legal documents that are filed. Recall that a complaint commences a lawsuit and is filed by a plaintiff; it sets forth the claims and issues between the parties. Responding to the complaint is the defendant, who files an answer to the complaint. To learn more about the claims and defenses of the parties to a lawsuit, each party will conduct discovery. This process allows the parties to investigate information each side has regarding the issues in a case. Discovery often is a complicated process; each party serves discovery documents such as interrogatories, request for admissions, production of documents, and notices of depositions. Likewise, each party must respond to the discovery or risk a motion being filed against them, such as a motion for sanctions. Other motions are common in the litigation process, but perhaps the most common motion used by attorneys to attempt to end a lawsuit is a motion for summary judgment. If granted by a judge, this document may end the legal process between the parties. As a paralegal, you will assist your supervising attorney in all aspects of the court process. With the process unfolding, you must understand how to draft the basic court documents and why it is important to carefully craft those documents. Let's now start with pleadings.

PLEADINGS IN GENERAL

When a lawsuit is begun, it is important for the court and the litigants—the competing parties—to identify the issues in dispute. If the issues are unclear, the plaintiff will be unable to prepare for trial; the defendant will be unable to prepare a defense; and the court will be unable to evaluate the competing positions. The problem is solved by the filing of pleadings. **Pleadings** are formal documents filed with the court that establish the claims and defenses of the parties to the lawsuit.

pleadings
Formal documents filed with the court that establish the claims and defenses of the parties to the lawsuit; the complaint, answer to complaint, and reply.

Although pleadings are filed with a court, they are not necessarily drafted with only the court in mind. Pleadings are drafted for two audiences: the court and the parties to the case. Know that your purpose is twofold and think about the message you want to convey. For the court, you want to comply with the legal requirements as well as communicate your client's problem effectively. On the other hand, you need to convey to the opposing party the claims you are pursuing. As discussed in Chapter 13, "tell them"—create a story that leaves the reader wanting to right a wrong or correct an injustice. The pleadings are not objective documents and are drafted from either the plaintiff's or defendant's perspective. Word choice is important; writing in plain English is important; but communicating in a precise, clear fashion is most important. You will use all the tools you have developed in previous chapters to draft pleadings.

Types of Pleadings

There are several different types of pleadings. They are filed in sequence, in a manner specified by procedural rules. Some are filed by a plaintiff, some by a defendant.

The **complaint** is the first pleading filed by any party to a lawsuit. It is the filing of the complaint that actually commences the lawsuit; before the complaint reaches the court, no lawsuit is pending. The complaint tells the defendant who is suing him and why and also identifies the nature and extent of the damages claimed.

The **answer** is filed by the defendant in response to the complaint. It generally denies the plaintiff's claim, sets forth the reasons for the denial, and identifies affirmative defenses that the defendant asserts.

A **counterclaim** or **cross-claim** may also be included in the pleadings in a particular case. A counterclaim is made by the defendant against the plaintiff—not a defense, but a new claim for damages, as if the defendant were the plaintiff in a separate suit. A cross-claim is made in a suit where there are two or more defendants, one of whom also acts like a plaintiff in a separate suit. But rather than making her claim against the plaintiff (as in the counterclaim), she makes it against another defendant. (Think of it as a lawsuit within a lawsuit.) Figure 17.1 diagrams the different countersuits and the relationship of the parties.

In this chapter we use the complaint and the answer as a backdrop for exploring the drafting of pleadings and discovery by the legal writer. We then briefly consider the other types of pleadings followed by discovery documents and then explore drafting of some basic motions. Where procedural rules are mentioned, we often discuss the Federal Rules of Civil Procedure (FRCP), since they are uniform throughout the United States. Remember, however, that our purpose is to teach you how to draft a pleading, discovery, and motions, as opposed to mastering the rules.

We cannot, however, overemphasize the importance of learning the rules. Even when the FRCP are applicable, for example, there will be additional local rules that

complaint
Document that states the allegations and the legal basis of the plaintiff's claims. Also, a charge, preferred before a magistrate having jurisdiction, that a person named has committed a specified offense, with an offer to prove the fact, to the end that a prosecution may be instituted.

answer
The defendant's response to the plaintiff's complaint.

counterclaim
A claim made by the defendant against the plaintiff—not a defense, but a new claim for damages, as if the defendant were the plaintiff in a separate suit; a countersuit brought by the defendant against the plaintiff.

cross-claim lawsuit
A lawsuit against a party of the same side; plaintiffs or defendants suing each other (defendant versus defendant or plaintiff versus plaintiff).

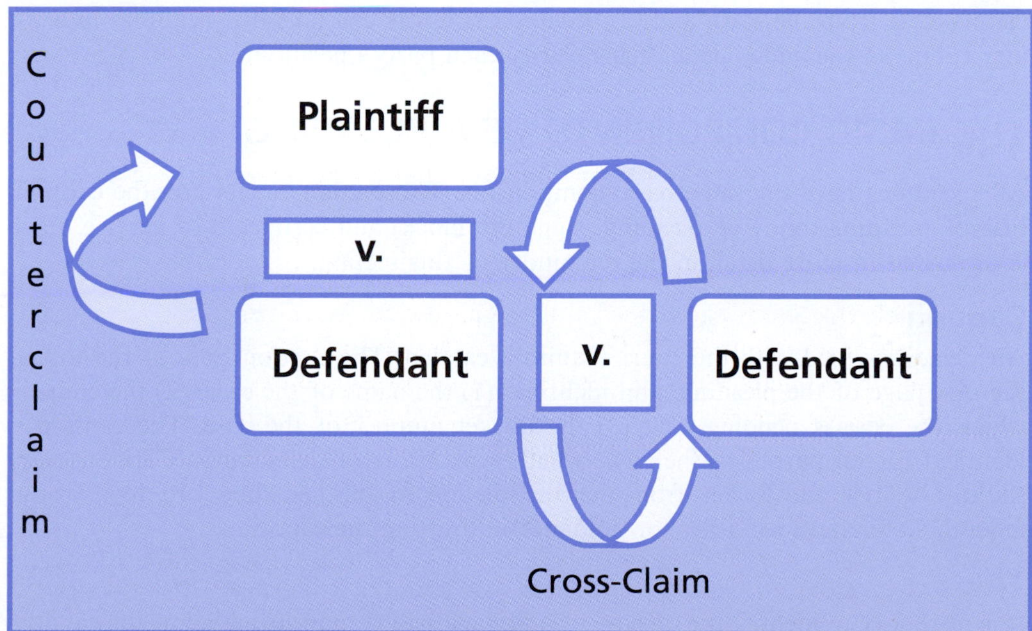

FIGURE 17.1 Diagram of Different Countersuits

YOU BE THE JUDGE

Imprecise drafting in a securities fraud case was the focus in *Gardner v. Investors Diversified Capital, Inc.*, 805 F. Supp. 874 (D. Colo. 1992). The plaintiff in the case was alleging fraud in the purchase of some securities. Numerous opportunities were given to the plaintiff to properly plead a securities fraud case; but in the end, the plaintiff's complaint was not only insufficient but replete with grammatical and typographical errors. Additionally, the judge, apparently unhappy with the quality of the pleadings, noted a T. S. Eliot poem in a footnote. The poem was cited in a tongue-in-cheek gibing of the "obtuse" nature of the plaintiff's pleadings, and the judge ultimately dismissed the case. Review the *Gardner* case. Were the actions of the court harsh? Explain your response. What were the facts that supported the court's decision? What was the holding in the case? Once again, we see the melding of legal research and legal writing and the importance of precise drafting.

govern certain technical matters. Failure to follow *all* applicable rules and to file pleadings in the manner and in the order that the rules require can waive (forfeit) your clients' rights and lead to a disastrous result.

Fact Pleading and Notice Pleading Distinguished

There are two broad styles of pleading—fact pleading and notice pleading. You should always determine which style is required in the jurisdiction in which your lawsuit is pending.

fact pleading
A style of pleading that requires you to identify all the facts necessary to allege a valid cause of action.

Fact pleading requires that you identify all the facts necessary to allege a valid cause of action. In other words, the pleading must include, at a minimum, those facts which must be proved in order to win on the claims made.

notice pleading
A short and plain statement of the allegations in a lawsuit.

Notice pleading, which has been incorporated into the FRCP, requires only a short, plain statement of the grounds on which a party is basing her claim, and a showing of why the party is entitled to relief. The party need not allege all the facts needed to support the claim, but only such facts as are needed to put the opposing party on notice of the claim.

discovery
The pretrial investigation process authorized and governed by the rules of civil procedure; the process of investigation and collection of evidence by litigants; the process in which the opposing parties obtain information about the case from each other; the process of investigation and collection of evidence by litigants.

The rationale behind the less strict requirements of notice pleading is that the facts will be developed by the parties through **discovery,** which is the investigation aspect of pretrial procedure (which we discuss later in this chapter). However, parties often include significant detail in their pleadings anyway, for two reasons: (1) to make their claims clear from the start, and (2) because the jurors can take the pleadings into the jury room, so the added detail helps clarify each party's position.

THE BASIC COMPONENTS OF A PLEADING

All pleadings have the same basic components. Those components are: the caption, title of pleading, body of pleading, signature block, and certificate of service. Each is discussed in more detail in the remainder of this section.

Caption

caption
The full name of the case, together with the docket number, court, and date of the decision.

All pleadings filed with the court require a **caption.** The caption goes at the top of the first page of the pleading, and identifies (1) the name of the case, (2) the court in which the case is pending, and (3) the docket number of the case. The caption is identical for all parties in the case, whether plaintiffs or defendants. Captions vary slightly in style and format from one jurisdiction to another; therefore, review your federal, state, and local rules for guidance in drafting the caption.

Title

It is necessary to identify the type of pleading with a title appearing below the caption; or as in some jurisdictions, the title is placed to the right of the identity of the parties.

The rules for your jurisdiction determine how the title is styled. With multiple parties it is often helpful to include enough information in the title to clearly differentiate the pleading from other, potentially similar pleadings (for example, "Defendant Johnson's Answer and Affirmative Defenses").

PRACTICE TIP

As discussed in the context of letters, paralegals cannot sign pleadings. Only an attorney can sign a pleading or any document filed with a court. Signing a pleading is considered the unauthorized practice of law.

Body

Consider the body of the pleading the section that conveys the substantive information to the reader. The body of the pleading states the party's problem. With sufficient detail, the party, plaintiff or defendant, sets forth the claims it has against another party in the lawsuit. Using all the skills you learned in previous chapters is critical to drafting a proper pleading. In the body of the pleading, you set out your claims or defenses, your legal theories, and your relief. Be complete yet precise in your presentation. Do not plead facts unless you have a reasonable basis for believing them to be true. As you will see throughout this chapter and the ones that follow, unless you file a pleading or court document in good faith, the court can impose sanctions. Therefore, in the body of a pleading

- know your purpose;
- understand the law;
- check the court rules; and
- draft with sufficient specificity to communicate your claim or legal issue.

PRACTICE TIP

Some jurisdictions require the attorney to sign the certificate of service; others allow the paralegal or executive assistant to sign. Check your jurisdiction for the rule or standard of practice.

Signature Block

Someone must sign all pleadings, usually the attorney for the party filing the pleading. The signature constitutes a pledge by the person signing that the contents have been prepared in good faith. If it can be shown that this is not the case, a lawyer can be sanctioned under FRCP 11.

The Significance of Rule 11

Rule 11 of the Federal Rules of Civil Procedure requires a pleading to be filed in good faith and not for purposes of harassment or delay. Pleadings cannot be frivolous or without legal foundation. That is the standard. Throughout this text, case examples are given where attorneys filed groundless, incomprehensible pleadings and were severely sanctioned by a court. Rule 11 is not to be taken lightly. By signing a pleading, the attorney makes certain representations. The representations are as follows:

- The case has a legal basis.
- Legal research was performed to determine the law.
- The facts are verified.
- The pleading is filed in good faith.

Courts review Rule 11 claims with great care. It is serious when a Rule 11 claim is raised and even more serious when sanctions are assessed. Be sure all clients' claims are properly verified and researched before a case is filed, as the legal ramifications are significant.

Most states have a Rule 11 equivalent. Review your state's requirements for filing a pleading and the sanctions for violations of the rule.

CYBER TRIP

Locate on the Internet your jurisdiction's equivalent to FRCP Rule 11. What are the differences and similarities in the rules?

Certificate of Service

Almost every jurisdiction requires some form of certification or guarantee by an attorney (or a party, if the party does not have an attorney) that copies of the pleading

certificate of service
Verification by an attorney that pleadings or court documents were sent to the opposing counsel in a case.

have been sent to all other parties. The certification is called a **certificate of service.** This certification is very important, because unless the other parties are aware that the pleading has been filed, they cannot make appropriate responses in accordance with the applicable rules and deadlines.

Quick Quiz True/False Questions

1. Pleadings, answers, counterclaims, and cross-claims are considered types of pleadings.
2. All pleadings have a caption.
3. Pleadings do not need to have a legal basis.
4. A certificate of service must be signed by an attorney.
5. Counterclaims and cross-claims are the same type of pleadings.

THE COMPLAINT

As noted, the complaint is the pleading that commences the lawsuit. A complaint prepared in accordance with the FRCP includes an introduction; a body (an identification of the parties, a statement of the basis for jurisdiction, numbered paragraphs containing the allegations [including damages], and causes of action; a prayer for relief; and a signature block and verification. It does *not* include an ordinary certificate of service, because a complaint must be served according to its own special rules. Let's take a look at each of these areas.

Caption

The caption that appears on the complaint includes the same information that appears on every other caption, with the exception of the docket number. The court clerk assigns the docket number after the filing of the complaint; subsequent pleadings will show it, but the complaint cannot show the docket number until the clerk assigns it (more about the sequence of events later). The only time the docket number is left blank is when the initial complaint is filed.

Introduction

Although the trend is to eliminate the introductory paragraph of pleadings, it is still used in many jurisdictions. The introductory paragraph identifies the party filing the pleading and the nature of the pleading.

Body

allegations
Facts forming the basis of a party's complaint.

The body of the complaint consists of the identification of the parties, the basis for jurisdiction, and the numbered paragraphs containing the **allegations** and cause of action.

The parties are identified by name and status (*i.e.,* whether an individual, corporation, or some other status), state of citizenship, and street address. These characteristics can be important; their significance is discussed in the subsection titled "Service of Process." Figure 17.2 shows examples of paragraphs identifying various parties.

Complaints prepared under the FRCP must also identify the basis for the alleged jurisdiction of the federal court. This usually requires identifying the substantive federal statutes that apply to the facts to form the basis of the jurisdiction, or, if no substantive statute is the basis for the jurisdiction, then the applicable federal jurisdictional statute (usually relating to diversity of citizenship) is cited, with a statement showing that its requirements have been satisfied.

FIGURE 17.2
Examples of Paragraphs Identifying the Parties in a Lawsuit

Natural Persons—Single Parties

Plaintiff is a citizen of the State of Montana, and resides in the City of Billings. Defendant is a citizen of the State of Minnesota and resides in the City of International Falls and may be served with process at (address of Defendant). The matter in controversy, exclusive of interest and costs, exceeds seventy-five thousand dollars ($75,000.00).

Multiple Plaintiffs

Plaintiff, ALBERT CROSS, is a citizen of the State of Rhode Island, Plaintiff, SANDRA CROSS, is a citizen of the State of Rhode Island, and Defendant, CHRISTOPHER VAIL, is a citizen of the State of Rhode Island and may be served with process at (address). The matter in controversy exceeds, exclusive of interest and costs, the sum of one hundred thousand dollars ($100,000.00).

Corporations

Plaintiff is a corporation incorporated under the laws of the State of Delaware, having its principal place of business in the State of New Hampshire, and Defendant is a corporation incorporated under the laws of the State of New Hampshire, having its principal place of business in a State other than the State of New Hampshire. Defendant may be served with process by serving its registered agent at (name of agent and address). The matter in controversy exceeds, exclusive of interest and costs, the sum of fifty thousand dollars ($50,000.00).

Following the identifying and jurisdictional paragraphs are the allegations of the plaintiff. The allegations set forth the claims of the party. Asserted as a group, they form the plaintiff's cause of action, which is the particular legal theory upon which plaintiff claims a right to judicial relief, or recovery of damages, against the defendant. The complaint should include all claims that the plaintiff has against the defendant that arise from the same facts and circumstances. If there is more than one claim, each separate claim or cause of action is set forth in a separate **count.**

count
The cause of action in the complaint.

The allegations are the substantive heart of the complaint. It is here that legal writing considerations come into play. The drafter cannot simply state facts and claim damages. Preliminary research must be conducted to determine what elements the law requires the plaintiff to prove. All such elements must then be pleaded, or else the plaintiff has "failed to state a claim" on which relief can be granted, leaving himself open to the motion to dismiss (discussed in this chapter), which is filed by the defendant. Careful drafting often requires that certain specific language be used to comply with statutory or common law requirements; the sufficiency of the complaint depends on it. The extent of detail required varies, of course, depending on whether the jurisdiction requires fact pleading or notice pleading.

Case law is never cited in the complaint, but statutes and regulations relied upon are generally identified. For example, the complaint based on the facts in the Case Fact Pattern to this chapter would identify the federal age-discrimination statute on which the claim is based.

The allegations are contained in consecutively numbered paragraphs. Sometimes the identification of the parties is included in these numbered paragraphs. Each paragraph should be limited to one concise idea or statement. The language used should be accurate but adversarial—telling the plaintiff's story from the plaintiff's perspective, and sympathetic to the plaintiff for the wrong allegedly committed against her. The writer should strike a balance between mundane, unemotional language and

FIGURE 17.3
Example of Statement in Complaint Avoiding Redundancy

Second Count

1. Paragraphs 1–8 of the First Count are hereby set forth as paragraphs 1–8 of this, the Second Count.

excessively expressive language; the reader should be able to visualize events without sensing that they have been exaggerated or embellished.

Often a later count requires a restatement of allegations already set forth as paragraphs in an earlier count. If this is the case, it is not only acceptable but indeed important to eliminate redundancy by using a phrase such as the one shown in Figure 17.3.

By thus eliminating redundancy, the writer minimizes the risk that the reader will become bored or miss the significant points as a result of wading through repetitions.

The allegations should also identify the damages suffered by the plaintiff. The recovery of damages in the form of money is a **legal remedy.** On the other hand, if the remedy sought is **equitable relief** (which resolves a lawsuit by directing the wrongdoer either to perform a certain act, or to refrain from performing a certain act), the specific nature of the equitable remedy sought should be identified as well.

legal remedy
Relief provided by the court to a party to redress a wrong perpetrated by another party; the recovery of money damages in a lawsuit.

equitable relief
A remedy that is other than money damages, such as refraining from or performing a certain act; nonmonetary remedies fashioned by the court using standards of fairness and justice. Injunction and specific performance are types of equitable relief.

When you begin drafting complaints, and even when you are more experienced, it is often helpful to refer to form books and models. **Form books** are publications that contain complete or partial sample complaints, with sample factual situations and various alternative methods of stating the legal basis for the cause of action. **Models** are copies of actual complaints, obtained from your firm's files, that have a similar factual foundation. These sources are useful in that they give you a basic framework within which to begin drafting your complaint. In the case of a model, you have an actual complaint that has withstood scrutiny; in the case of a form book, a sample complaint that has withstood editorial scrutiny by a panel of experts. You must be careful, however, when using models and form books. Problems can arise. If the law has changed since the model or form book was prepared, for example, or if you fail to recognize the significance of a twist in your particular factual situation, you may make critical drafting errors. Thus, you should use models and form books to supplement your research, not in place of it.

form books
Publications that contain complete or partial sample documents, often with sample factual situations and various alternative methods of stating that legal document.

models
Copies of actual complaints, obtained from your firm's files, that have a similar factual foundation.

In general, when drafting the body of the complaint you should keep in mind the many factors we've discussed in previous chapters about effective legal writing—concise sentences, a minimum of legalese, and good punctuation and grammar. (See Figure 17.4 for an example of the body of a complaint.)

Prayer for Relief

The **prayer for relief** sets out the specific demands that the plaintiff has against the defendant. In essence, the plaintiff is telling the court what he seeks to gain from the lawsuit.

prayer for relief
A summation at the end of a pleading, which sets forth the demands by a party in the lawsuit.

Since the prayer for relief often begins with the phrase "Wherefore, the plaintiff claims . . . ," followed by a statement of the relief sought, it is often called the "wherefore clause." The current trend toward simplifying pleadings has streamlined the language in some jurisdictions, however, eliminating the archaic term "wherefore."

Almost all prayers for relief have a "catch-all" provision, which states that the plaintiff also seeks "such other and further relief as the court may deem proper or

FIGURE 17.4
Example of the Body of a Complaint

TO THE HONORABLE JUDGE OF SAID COURT:

1. Plaintiff Robert Andrews is an individual residing in Travis County, Texas, and is the natural parent of Francis Andrews, the minor Plaintiff. Defendant George Peters is an individual residing in Any Town, Oklahoma, and service of process may be had at 8362 Longhorn Drive, Any Town, Oklahoma. Defendant D.C. Computers, Inc. is a corporation duly formed and existing under the laws of the State of Texas and may be served with process by serving its agent for service, David Clark at 287 South Main, Austin, Texas 75853.

2. On the 4th day of June, 2008, Plaintiff Francis Andrews was a passenger in a vehicle driven by Plaintiff Robert Andrews, which was traveling eastbound in the 8700 block of Elm Street in Austin, Travis County, Texas.

3. Defendant Peters attempted to make a left turn in front of the Andrews vehicle. As a result, the Andrews vehicle and the vehicle driven by Defendant Peters collided, causing injuries to Plaintiff, Francis Andrews. At the time of the collision, the vehicle driven by Defendant Peters was owned by Defendant D.C. Computers, Inc.

4. As a result of the negligent conduct of Defendant Peters, Plaintiff Francis Andrews suffered the damages and injuries set out hereinafter.

5. Plaintiffs would show that Defendant Peters was guilty of the following acts and omissions of negligence, each of which, separately or concurrently, was a proximate cause of the damages and injuries sustained by the Plaintiff, Francis Andrews:

a) Failure to yield right of way;

b) Failure to keep a proper lookout;

c) Failure to take proper evasive action;

d) Failure to apply brakes.

6. At the time of the collision described above, Defendant Peters was the agent, servant, and employee of Defendant D.C. Computers, Inc. and was acting within the scope of his authority as such agent, servant, and employee.

7. Defendant Peters was incompetent and unfit to safely operate a motor vehicle on the public streets and highways.

8. Defendant D.C. Computers, Inc. knew, or in the exercise of due care should have known, that Defendant Peters was an incompetent and unfit driver and would create an unreasonable risk of danger to persons and property on the public streets and highways of Texas.

9. Plaintiff Francis Andrews was severely injured as a proximate result of the negligent conduct of the Defendants. Plaintiff Francis Andrews has suffered physical pain and mental anguish in the past and in reasonable probability will suffer from such in the future. Plaintiff Francis Andrews has sustained physical impairment and in reasonable probability will sustain such impairment in the future.

10. Plaintiffs have sustained reasonable medical expenses in the amount of $52,000.00 as a result of the Defendants' negligence in the past and in reasonable probability will sustain additional medical expenses in the future.

11. At the time of this collision, Defendant Peters was under the influence of an alcoholic beverage. The conduct of Defendant Peters in driving the vehicle while under the influence of an alcoholic beverage constitutes gross negligence. As a result of such conduct, the Plaintiffs are entitled to recover exemplary damages.

appropriate." By using this or a similar catch-all clause, the plaintiff gives the court discretion on the relief it may grant, even allowing it to go beyond the plaintiff's specified requests.

Signature Block and Verification

The attorney preparing the complaint must sign it. As we noted earlier, Rule 11 of the FRCP states that the signature constitutes a written affirmation that she has a good-faith basis for filing it (protecting against frivolous or harassing suits). Usually the attorney's name, address, fax number, and telephone number are typed below the signature. Many jurisdictions have attorney identification numbers, called bar card numbers, which are required with all court submissions; check the rules in your jurisdiction for the requirements of a signature block, or review a sample block from a pleading from your law firm or company. Figure 17.5 shows sample signature blocks.

verification
Acknowledgment by a party of the truthfulness of the information contained within a document.

service of process
The procedure by which a defendant is notified by a process server of a lawsuit.

process server
A person statutorily authorized to serve legal documents such as complaints.

Some complaints require a brief affidavit, called a **verification,** in which the plaintiff swears to the truth of the contents. This requirement is usually dictated by statute or court rule. By signing the verification, the plaintiff (1) shows that he has read the complaint, (2) shows that he understands the contents, and (3) pledges that, to the best of his personal knowledge, the allegations are true. The purpose of the verification is to protect further against false claims. An example of a verification appears as Figure 17.6.

Service of Process

The certificate of service is not needed in a complaint; since the complaint is the first notice of a lawsuit that a defendant receives, the service requirements are actually much stricter than merely requiring a certificate of service. **Service of process** is the procedure by which a defendant is notified by a **process server** (a person

FIGURE 17.5
Sample Signature Blocks

Respectfully submitted,

____

Andrea Boxman
Attorney Bar No. or Identification No.
Address
City, State and zip code
Telephone number
Fax number
E-mail address
(Party Representing)

If a law firm

Respectfully submitted,
(Name of Law Firm)

____

Name of Attorney in Charge of Case or Signing Pleading
Address
Bar No. or Identification
Telephone number
Fax number
E-mail address
(Party Representing)

FIGURE 17.6
Sample Verification

STATE OF NEW JERSEY §
COUNTY OF CUMBERLAND §

BEFORE the undersigned Notary Public for the State of New Jersey, at large personally appeared, ROBERT ANDREWS, Plaintiff in the above-styled cause, who, being by me first duly sworn, deposes and says that the averments contained in the foregoing Complaint are true and correct.

This the ___ day of August, 2008.

____
ROBERT ANDREWS

Sworn to and subscribed before me, this ___ day of August, 2008

____
NOTARY PUBLIC IN AND FOR THE STATE OF NEW JERSEY
My Commission Expires: __________

OR

STATE OF ____________
____________ COUNTY

On this day, Cameron Chapman appeared before me, the undersigned notary public. After I administered an oath to him and upon his oath he stated that he read the Complaint and that the facts stated in it are within his personal knowledge and are true and correct.

____
Cameron Chapman

SWORN TO and SUBSCRIBED before me
Cameron Chapman on _______, 2008.

____
Notary Public in and for the State
Of____________________

statutorily authorized to serve legal documents such as complaints) that she is being sued. Among the papers that a defendant receives is a summons, ordering her to appear in court at a certain time or suffer the consequences. Service of process is accomplished by delivery of the complaint and **summons;** the procedure has many technical requirements, which vary from one jurisdiction to another. The *status* of the defendants is also significant for the purpose of service of process. Rules of service differ depending on whether the defendant is an individual, a corporation, or of some other status.

summons
The notice to appear in court, notifying the defendant of the plaintiff's complaint.

Checklist

The full text of a complaint appears in Figure 17.7. The following is a checklist for preparation of a complaint:

- Determine the parties who will be sued.
- Identify the court in which suit will be filed, and verify that the court has jurisdiction.
- Research and determine the necessary elements for the causes of action you intend to allege, including the applicable statutes.
- Identify the necessary and useful facts, and determine whether yours is a fact- or notice-pleading jurisdiction.

- Identify the damages suffered and the relief sought.
- Check the applicable procedural rules, form books, and models to determine the proper style of pleading.
- Prepare the caption and the introduction.
- Draft concise, effective statements that establish the cause of action in a light that favors your client.
- Draft the prayer for relief.
- Prepare the summons and determine the proper procedure to complete service of process. Review and edit your drafts.

Quick Quiz True/False Questions

1. When a complaint is filed, it contains a caption with a docket number.
2. The body of a complaint contains the allegations.
3. Case law should be cited in a complaint.
4. The prayer for relief sets forth the demands that the plaintiff has against the defendant.
5. An attorney must sign a complaint prior to filing.

FIGURE 17.7
Sample Complaint

UNITED STATES DISTRICT COURT FOR THE SOUTHERN DISTRICT OF CALIFORNIA SAN DIEGO DIVISION

MELANIE COLEMAN,	§	
Plaintiff	§	
	§	COMPLAINT
vs.	§	Civil Action, File Number _____
	§	
PRODUCTS OF AMERICA, INC.	§	
Defendant	§	

Plaintiff alleges:

1. Defendant is a Delaware corporation, donig business in the State of California. The address of its principal place of business is San Diego, California.

2. At all times relevant, Defendant was an "employer" as defined by 29 U.S.C. § 640(b) and is thus covered by and subject to the Age Discrimination in Employment Act of 1967 ("ADEA"), 29 U.S.C. § 621 *et seq.* This court has jurisdiction under 29 U.S.C. 640 (b).

3. As of July 15, 2008, Plaintiff was fifty-five years and two months of age and is an individual protected by the ADEA.

4. As of December 1, 2008, Plaintiff was employed by Defendant in the capacity of "project manager."

5. Plaintiff had been employed in various positions by Defendant from approximately October, 1982 until December, 2008.

Cont.

FIGURE 17.7
Sample Complaint
Cont.

6. Plaintiff was discharged by Defendant on December 2, 2008.

7. Plaintiff's discharge was because of Plaintiff's age in violation of the ADEA.

8. Defendant's violation of the ADEA was willful.

9. Plaintiff has satisfied all of the procedural and administrative requirements set forth in 29 U.S.C.§ 626.

a. Plaintiff has filed a timely charge with the appropriate state fair employment practice office.

b. Plaintiff has filed a timely charge with the Equal Employment Opportunity Commission.

c. These charges were filed more than sixty (60) days prior to the filing of this action.

10. Proper venue is in this court as the unlawful action occurred within this jurisdiction where Defendant is doing business.

11. Plaintiff has suffered, is now suffering, and will continue to suffer irreparable injury as a result of Defendant's actions.

WHEREFORE, Plaintiff hereby demands a trial by jury and prays for the following legal and equitable remedies:

a. Defendant be ordered to employ and reemploy the Plaintiff to the position from which she was discharged, together with all benefits incident thereto, including but not limited to wages, benefits, training, and seniority.

b. Defendant be required to compensate Plaintiff for the full value of wages and benefits that Plaintiff would have received had it not been for Defendant's unlawful treatment of the Plaintiff, with interest thereon, until the date Plaintiff is offered reemployment into a position substantially equivalent to the one Plaintiff occupied on December 2, 2008.

c. That a final judgment in favor of Plaintiff and against Defendant be entered for liquidated damages in an amount equal to the amount of wages due and owing Plaintiff as provided by 29 U.S.C. §§ 626(b) and 216(b).

d. That defendant be enjoined from discriminating against Plaintiff in any manner that violates the Age Discrimination in Employment Act.

e. That Plaintiff be awarded against the Defendant the costs and expenses of this litigation and reasonable attorneys' fees.

f. That Plaintiff be granted such other and further legal and equitable relief as the court may deem just and proper.

Respectfully submitted,

KEATCH AND WYNN

By_______________

Cynthia Goodman
Attorney for Plaintiff
1801 S. Main St., Suite 104
Any Town, State
Telephone Number
Fax Number
E-mail address
Attorney Identification Number

THE ANSWER

The complaint has been correctly served. Under FRCP 12(a), the defendant must file a response within twenty days of receipt of the complaint; you should always check the rules of your jurisdiction to verify such a deadline.

If the defendant believes that some aspect of the plaintiff's allegations is inadequate, he may file one of the motions described in the next section. If, however, no such motion is filed, then the defendant files his response, called an *answer.*

The Components of an Answer

An answer is the defendant's response to the plaintiff's complaint and comprises several distinct parts. First, it contains a section responding specifically to the plaintiff's numbered paragraphs. It either admits an allegation, denies it, or pleads that the defendant "lacks sufficient knowledge or information to form a belief as to the truth or falsity" of the allegation. This last category would apply to those of the plaintiff's allegations that relate to issues of her own status or conduct, necessarily outside the knowledge of the defendant. Each and every allegation must be addressed and responded to by the defendant; failure to respond can be taken as an admission.

Rule 8 of the FRCP does not allow for a "general denial" disputing all of the plaintiff's claims in one generalized statement; rather, each allegation must be identified and responded to. Most jurisdictions follow this rule; Texas and California are two notable exceptions.

general defenses
Specific responses by the defendant to the plaintiff's complaint.

affirmative defense
An "excuse" by the opposing party that does not just simply negate the allegation, but puts forth a legal reason to avoid enforcement. These defenses are waived if not pleaded.

special defenses
Affirmative defenses.

Second, **general defenses** are sometimes included in the answer. These are items that, under the FRCP, can also be made by motion; we discuss them further in the section "Additional Pleadings." They cover such things as an assertion that the court lacks jurisdiction, or that the plaintiff has failed to state a claim on which relief can be granted.

The next section of the answer contains the **affirmative defenses,** which are also called **special defenses.** Affirmative defenses are those which go beyond mere denial of the plaintiff's claims; because of a separate affirmative fact, the defendant asserts that a defense exists even if plaintiff's allegations are true. Such defenses are usually waived unless specifically pleaded, which means that the defendant can introduce evidence to prove an affirmative defense only if he has included it in his answer. The affirmative or special defenses that must be included in the pleadings are often identified by statute or rule, as with Rule 8(c) of the FRCP. Figure 17.8 is an example of an answer with general and affirmative defenses.

PRACTICE TIP

Take great care in reviewing your state and local rules, because state and local terminology can vary dramatically. In California, for example, what we have just described as a "counterclaim" is referred to as a "cross-complaint."

Under some circumstances, the defendant includes a counterclaim after her defenses. A counterclaim may be filed with the answer or separately. It may arise out of the same facts as the complaint or be unrelated. Whatever the context, a counterclaim can be thought of as a separate lawsuit within a lawsuit, in which the defendant sues the plaintiff. The drafting considerations are similar to those for a complaint.

To complicate matters even more, a cross-claim (which we discussed as a type of pleading) can be brought within the original lawsuit. A cross-claim is filed against a co-party, almost always by one defendant against another defendant, and must relate to the cause of action in the main complaint.

Checklist

The following is a checklist that you can use in drafting an answer:

- Check the rules to verify the deadline for filing the answer.
- Review the law and perform any legal research necessary to substantiate your response.

FIGURE 17.8
Answer with General and Affirmative Defenses

DEFENDANT'S ORIGINAL ANSWER

1. Defendant admits the allegations of Paragraph 1 of the complaint.

2. Defendant denies the allegations of Paragraph 2 of the complaint.

3. Defendant denies the allegations of Paragraph 3 of the complaint, but has no knowledge of information sufficient to form a belief regarding the ownership of the vehicle.

4. Defendant denies the allegations of Paragraph 4 of the complaint.

5. Defendant denies the allegations of Paragraph 5 of the complaint.

6. Defendant admits the allegations of Paragraph 6 of the complaint.

7. Defendant denies the allegations of Paragraph 7 of the complaint.

8. Defendant D.C. Computers, Inc. has no knowledge or information sufficient to form a belief regarding the truth of the allegations of Paragraph 8 of the complaint.

9. Defendant D.C. Computers, Inc. has no knowledge or information sufficient to form a belief regarding the truth of the allegations of Paragraph 9 of the complaint.

10. Defendant D.C. Computers, Inc. has no knowledge or information sufficient to form a belief regarding the truth of the allegations of Paragraph 10 of the complaint.

11. Defendant denies the allegations of Paragraph 11 of the complaint.

GENERAL DEFENSES

12. This court lacks personal jurisdiction pursuant to Federal Rule 12(b).

13. Plaintiff has failed to state a claim upon which relief can be granted.

AFFIRMATIVE DEFENSES

14. Plaintiff was contributorially negligent in operating his automobile and is barred from recovery.

15. Plaintiff was traveling at an excessive speed and the alleged accident was unavoidable due to Plaintiff's negligence.

Defendant requests that this matter be dismissed and that Defendant be reimbursed its costs and attorneys' fees expended in the defense of this matter.

- Admit or deny each allegation of the complaint, or allege that you have insufficient information to respond.
- Check to be sure that every paragraph and allegation of the complaint have been responded to.
- Allege any affirmative or general defenses that apply.
- Set forth any applicable counterclaim or cross-claim.
- Review and edit your draft.

ADDITIONAL PLEADINGS

motion for more definite statement
A request by a defendant for additional specificity of plaintiff's complaint.

motion to dismiss
A motion that dispenses with the lawsuit because of a legal defense.

In addition to the complaint, answer, counterclaim, and cross-claim, there are also several motions considered to be pleadings. For example, a party who believes that the claims made in the pleadings of another party are unclear can file a **motion for more definite statement.** A party who believes his opponent has "failed to state a claim" for which the court can grant relief can file a **motion to dismiss,** which, if granted by the court, dismisses the claim. Other motions may be available with other names, or similar motions with variant names, depending on the rules of your jurisdiction; you should become familiar with the rules that apply in your area.

AMENDING AND SUPPLEMENTING PLEADINGS

Although pleadings must be prepared in good faith, and hence should be prepared fully and to the best of the drafter's knowledge and ability, often information arises after filing that a party may wish to add. In addition, a party may be *required* to add information when a motion for more definite statement is granted. A drafter may also have forgotten to include some information. Such additions (or analogous deletions) are made by filing amended or supplemented pleadings.

Amended Pleadings

amended pleading
A pleading that changes, corrects, revises, or deletes information from a prior pleading.

An **amended pleading** changes, corrects, revises, or deletes information from a prior pleading. Information from the original pleading that is not changed remains in force, but information that is superseded is no longer in force. It is critically important to distinguish that which is changed from that which remains as before—your skills of writing with clarity become important in this regard. It is generally best to file an entirely new pleading, identifying it as "amended" in the title (for example, "Amended Complaint"), incorporating all the old and new provisions in one place.

Supplemental Pleadings

supplemental pleading
A pleading that adds to a pleading without deleting prior information.

A **supplemental pleading** adds to a pleading without deleting prior information. The prior pleading remains intact and is read in conjunction with the supplement. A supplemental pleading is usually filed when additional facts become known after the filing of the original pleading, perhaps after information is learned through a deposition or other discovery procedure. Court permission may also be required prior to the filing of a supplemental pleading.

That's it. You now know how to draft some basic pleadings in a lawsuit. Once the lawsuit has begun, you must learn more about the case and the parties' claims and defenses. This task is accomplished through the discovery process.

YOU BE THE JUDGE

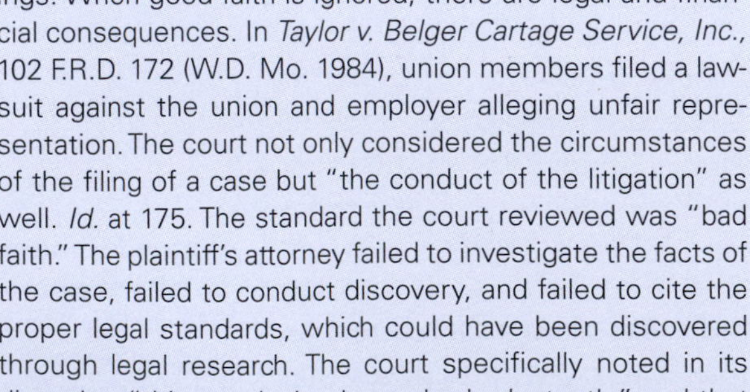

We now know that good faith is inherent in filing of pleadings. When good faith is ignored, there are legal and financial consequences. In *Taylor v. Belger Cartage Service, Inc.*, 102 F.R.D. 172 (W.D. Mo. 1984), union members filed a lawsuit against the union and employer alleging unfair representation. The court not only considered the circumstances of the filing of a case but "the conduct of the litigation" as well. *Id.* at 175. The standard the court reviewed was "bad faith." The plaintiff's attorney failed to investigate the facts of the case, failed to conduct discovery, and failed to cite the proper legal standards, which could have been discovered through legal research. The court specifically noted in its dicta that "this conclusion is reached reluctantly" and that the plaintiff's attorney failed to meet the "liberal threshold standards for initiating litigation." *Id.* at 180. As the court warned: "At the very least, trained attorneys who are licensed by the state owe their clients, the judicial system and the public a duty to analyze problems brought to them in light of easily ascertainable legal standards and to render detached, unemotional, rational advice on whether a wrong recognized by the law has been done. Attorneys should file and pursue on behalf of their clients only those cases which they reasonably believe are well grounded in fact, are warranted by existing law or a good faith argument for the extension, modification or reversal of existing law." *Id.* at 181. Read the *Taylor* case. Was the attorney wrong in pursuing the case? Were the sanctions by the court reasonable? Why? What was the court's reasoning in the case for awarding attorney's fees? Pleadings cannot be filed simply because you "feel" a wrong has been or may have been committed. Facts, real facts, must substantiate the claims prior to filing a pleading with a court.

Quick Quiz True/False Questions

1. An answer is the defendant's response to the plaintiff's complaint.
2. An answer contains only general defenses.
3. A permissive counterclaim must be filed with an answer.
4. A motion to dismiss can be filed by a defendant and, if granted by a court, dismisses all claims.
5. Pleadings may be amended and supplemented.

DISCOVERY IN GENERAL

The "surprise witness" who arrives to testify at the eleventh hour of a trial, turning certain defeat into stunning victory, is a character still seen in television or movie courtrooms, but not in reality. The days of "trial by ambush," where one side or the other held back key information until unleashing it in front of a jury, have been replaced by the era of discovery. Rule changes in FRCP 26(a)(1) now require litigants in federal court to voluntarily disclose information to the other party such as

- the names of individuals who may have discoverable information and the nature of that information;
- a copy of, or description of, documents in the possession of the party;
- a computation of, or description of, any category of damages; and
- a copy of any insurance agreement, if at issue.

As with any rule, exceptions are listed. The rule should be reviewed to determine whether any of the exceptions apply to the initial disclosure of information. The point is that discovery has changed, and the days of *Perry Mason* are long gone. But what is discovery and what is its purpose? These questions and the methods of discovery will be examined in the sections that follow. The focus will be on the "drafting" of discovery.

Discovery is the pretrial investigation process, authorized and governed by the rules of civil procedure. Discovery rules are broad, so that parties have the ability to pursue information in the hands of other parties to a lawsuit.

Earlier in this chapter we discussed the motion for more definite statement. You may now ask: "If more information about a party's claim is needed, why not simply file that motion?" The reason that a distinct and separate discovery process is needed, at least in part, is this: There are limits on the detail that a party can be required to place in her pleadings. Indeed, a court will often deny a motion for more definite statement on the grounds that the detail requested is more appropriately sought through the discovery process, and goes beyond the requirements of even a fact-pleading jurisdiction. Pleadings are intended to be straightforward summaries, not all-inclusive tracts. Furthermore, there may be strategic reasons why one party wishes to learn information about another *without* having it placed in the pleadings. Finally, such forms of discovery as a deposition are of a character entirely different from mere written information—a deposition supplies not just words, but also the personal characteristics or condition of the person deposed.

There are four main types of discovery: interrogatories; requests for admission; requests for production of documents and things; and depositions. Some aspects are common to all; some are unique to each. In the sections that follow, we discuss each form in turn, highlighting format, drafting, and strategy requirements.

INTERROGATORIES

interrogatory
A discovery tool in the form of a series of written questions that are answered by the party in writing, to be answered under oath.

PRACTICE TIP

Many jurisdictions have limitations on the number of interrogatories a party can send. This limitation applies to an interrogatory with subsections. If you draft an interrogatory with four subsections, many jurisdictions consider these four separate answers and therefore four questions. Be very mindful of the requirements in your jurisdiction and carefully review the restrictions and requirements. FRCP 33 limits the responses to twenty-five including subsections.

instructions and definitions
A section in many forms of discovery requests that defines terms in the document to avoid confusion.

An **interrogatory** is a written question submitted by one party to another, to be answered under oath. Rule 33 of the FRCP sets out the requirements governing the use of interrogatories in the federal courts. Most states have adopted a similar rule; check the rules that apply in your jurisdiction.

By following certain preliminary procedures, you will be able to prepare more effective interrogatories. First, review the case file and pleadings to become thoroughly familiar with the facts and allegations. Identify the information you need to fill in gaps or increase your understanding. Make lists of areas of appropriate inquiry. Next, as with pleadings, you can use form books and models for assistance. Again, be wary of relying on them exclusively. Also, consult the rules, and review any questions you have with your supervising attorney. Form books and models will also be helpful in drafting documents associated with the other discovery methods to be discussed.

When you draft your interrogatories, use specific and detailed language that precisely identifies the information you seek. Use short sentences in simple language. Avoid the phrase "and/or," or a large number of colons and semicolons, which can confuse the reader and lead to an unsatisfactory response. Avoid multiple subtopics and sections in the interrogatory, which can also cause confusion. Such subtopics may even be prohibited in some jurisdictions, or each subtopic may be counted as a separate interrogatory in a jurisdiction that limits the total number of interrogatories allowed.

Take care in choosing verb tenses. If an interrogatory is phrased in the present tense, the information received may be different than if worded in the past tense. Who *has* possession of the records of Wellington Company, for example, may be a different party than who *had* those records.

Interrogatories should also be drafted to avoid a response of yes or no. The request should require the respondent to present additional information. If all that is desired is a yes or no response, another form of discovery, such as the request for admissions, might be the better method.

Certain interrogatories are common to many different types of cases, seeking such information as identification of the person responding to the interrogatories (if the party to whom the request is directed is a corporation or other form of business); the names of witnesses and experts who will testify; and identification of documents that are relevant, such as correspondence or contracts. The format of such questions is often similar, even for different types of cases. Other interrogatories must be tailored to reflect the peculiar circumstances of the particular case at hand.

To add to the precision of individual interrogatories, the drafter often includes **instructions** and **definitions** that precede the interrogatories and define terms to avoid confusion. The drafter can often anticipate and eliminate potential problems by clarifying ambiguous terms with precise definitions. Instructions often serve to eliminate evasive answers, as, for example, an instruction that if a party objects to one subpart of a question, he should still respond to the remaining subparts.

Although you should be sure to check the rules of your jurisdiction for specific guidance in the drafting of interrogatories, the following subsections discuss elements common to all sets of interrogatories.

Components of the Interrogatory Document

When drafting an interrogatory, you should include the caption of the case with the identification to whom the document is addressed. After the caption, you will draft a general introductory paragraph that identifies the procedural rule that grants the

6. Identify all employees of Wellington Company with whom Henry Wellington has discussed his meeting of March 15, 2008, with John Ascot.

7. Identify all correspondence in the possession of Wellington Company, including copies of correspondence, which in any way references, describes, or relates to the meeting of March 15, 2008, at which Henry Wellington and John Ascot were present.

8. List the dates of every in-person meeting between Henry Wellington and John Ascot between January 1, 2008, and April 30, 2008.

9. Provide the date and time of day of every phone call between Henry Wellington and John Ascot that occurred between January 1, 2008, and April 30, 2008.

FIGURE 17.9
Examples of Interrogatories

authority for the discovery. The next sections are the definition and instruction sections. These sections are important as they will provide specificity for your document as well as providing parameters for the opposing party responses. Carefully crafted definitions and instructions will lead to fewer objections by the opposing counsel, providing your client with the information they desire.

PRACTICE TIP

Checking the rules of procedure is important. Do not assume that your current practice conforms to the rules. For example, there are a number of rule changes for discovery effective December 1, 2006. They mainly relate to electronic data. This change will affect you, so always take the extra time to verify the current obligations under the rules of discovery.

Interrogatories

After the definitions come the interrogatories themselves. They are numbered, and enough space is generally left between interrogatories for the party responding to type in her response. The detail in the questions should be enough to make them clear and precise, and will vary depending on the detail already set forth in the instructions and definitions. For example, if the term "identify" is defined to mean "provide the full name, residence address and phone number, business address and phone number, age, and marital status of," then a proper interrogatory designed to elicit all this information would simply state: "Identify Mr. Wellington." If no such definition is provided, then the information must be requested specifically. Figure 17.9 provides some examples of interrogatories.

Signature Block and Certificate of Service

In most jurisdictions the interrogatories are signed by the attorney preparing them, but not by the party she represents (in contrast to the *responses,* which must be signed not only by the attorney but also by the party responding; more about that later). To verify the date when the interrogatories were sent to opposing counsel, a certificate of service is required.

Responses to Interrogatories

Responses to interrogatories must be prepared within the time established by the applicable procedural rules. Under Rule 33 of the FRCP, the time limit is thirty days. Extensions can be requested by motion; at least in the early stages of the discovery process, the court will probably be lenient about granting such requests, and few opposing counsel will object to reasonable extensions.

Responses must be signed and verified by the client. The attorney preparing them signs them as well, but the client must attest to their accuracy. Figure 17.10 shows an example of **verification.** The response can be either a presentation of the information requested, or an objection. Objections should be addressed to individual interrogatories; it is not proper to object to *all* the interrogatories, and it remains necessary to provide responses for all those interrogatories not objected to (which is to say that the presence of one or more objectionable interrogatories does not negate the entire set of interrogatories).

verification
Acknowledgment by a party of the truthfulness of the information contained within a document.

FIGURE 17.10
Example of Verification to Interrogatory Response

THE STATE OF____________________ §

§

COUNTY OF ____________________ §

NED RADCLIFFE, being duly sworn upon his oath deposes and says: I am the Defendant in the above-entitled action and have read the interrogatories served upon me by the Plaintiff, Gilda Murray; and the foregoing answers to those interrogatories are true according to the best of my knowledge, information, and belief.

____

NED RADCLIFFE

SUBSCRIBED AND SWORN to before me

this ___ day of December, 2008__________

____

NOTARY PUBLIC IN AND FOR THE

STATE OF ___________

My Commission Expires:____________

PRACTICE TIP

Some jurisdictions do not require discovery requests to be filed with the court. Because of this, the certificate of service is important as a verification of when the opposing party received the discovery document. Deadlines will flow from the date of receipt. Certified mail is a recommended method of transmitting discovery requests.

REQUESTS FOR ADMISSION

The **request for admission,** authorized under Rule 36 of the FRCP, provides the drafter with the opportunity to conclusively establish selected facts prior to trial. A proposition is presented to the opposing party for admission or denial; if admitted, no further evidence need be presented on the point; the trial court accepts it as fact, at least with regard to the party who admitted it. Admissions serve to limit the complexity and expense of trials.

request for admission
A document that provides the drafter with the opportunity to conclusively establish selected facts prior to trial.

The caption, signature of the preparing attorney, and certificate of service are the same for a request for admissions as for a set of interrogatories. The introductory paragraph and the text of the requests are discussed in the next subsections, followed by a few words about preparing responses.

The Introduction of a Request for Admission

The introductory paragraph of a request for admissions is similar to a request for interrogatory; it includes an identification of the party to whom the request is directed, the rule providing for the request, and the time period allowed for response.

Text of a Request for Admission

The requests themselves consist of statements that are to be admitted or denied by the recipient. The statements are numbered sequentially.

An effective technique for drafting the requests is to move through the case point by point, from general points to those more specific. Alternative versions can appear as different numbered statements, and consecutive questions can feature finely drawn distinctions; the responses to such a pattern of requests can assist the drafter in reaching an understanding about the nuances of the other party's position. An example of this technique is shown in Figure 17.11.

Alternative requests for admission:

Admit or deny the following:

1. On June 1, 2008, defendant Jones executed the contract that is attached as Exhibit A.

2. On June 2, 2008, defendant Jones executed the contract that is attached as Exhibit A.

3. On June 3, 2008, defendant Jones executed the contract that is attached as Exhibit A.

Requests for admission with finely drawn distinctions:

1. On March 15, 2008, defendant Jones attended a meeting at which were discussed the terms of a contract with Mr. Smith.

2. On March 15, 2008, defendant Jones and plaintiff Smith attended a meeting at which were discussed the terms of a contract with Mr. Smith.

3. On March 15, 2008, defendant Jones and plaintiff Smith attended a meeting at which they executed the contract that is attached hereto as Exhibit A.

FIGURE 17.11
Sample Technique Used in Requests for Admission

PRACTICE TIP

Most law firms have systems to keep track of when discovery responses are due. Learn the system in your office. If your office does not have a formal diary or "tickle" system, be sure you have a methodology to track when discovery is received and when it is due. Do not leave discovery responses to the last minute, as poorly drafted responses can have long-lasting effects on a case.

Several different formats are acceptable for requests for admission, four of which appear in Figure 17.12. The most important consideration in drafting requests for production is that they be so straightforward that they avoid an evasive response. The more detail added to the sentence, the greater the tendency to elicit a qualified response.

A common use of requests for admission is to establish the authenticity of documents. A copy of a document can be appended to the set of requests, and the requests can ask for an admission or denial that the copy is an exact copy of the original. Figure 17.13 shows an example of a request for admission inquiring into the genuineness of a document.

Responses to Requests for Admission

Requests for admission must be answered with great care because of the impact of an admission. If a request is impossible to respond to with a flat admission or denial, but is not otherwise objectionable, a qualified response is acceptable. A qualified response should not be used for the purpose of evading, however.

(a) Admit or deny that you requested a refund on March 6, 2008, for the car repairs performed by Defendant.

(b) Do you admit or deny that you requested a refund on March 6, 2008, for the car repairs performed by Defendant?

(c) Do you admit that you requested a refund on March 6, 2008, for the car repairs performed by Defendant?

(d) Admit or deny the following facts:

(1) That you requested a refund on March 6, 2008, for the car repairs performed by Defendant.

FIGURE 17.12
Formats for Requests for Admission

Admit or deny that the document marked "Exhibit A" and attached hereto is a true and genuine copy of the Lease dated June 17, 2008.

FIGURE 17.13
Request for Admission Regarding Genuineness of Document

PRACTICE TIP

Review the law for your jurisdiction on the requirements and parameters of discovery of computerized data. This area of the law is relatively new and continually developing.

A DAY IN THE LIFE OF A PARALEGAL

Deadlines are a way of life for attorneys and paralegals who litigate. What happens when a deadline is missed responding to discovery? More importantly, what happens when the deadline for filing responses to request for admissions is missed? We all get busy and sometimes we just plain "mess up." You realize that a set of request for admissions were due last week and a sense of panic runs through your body. What do you do? The first piece of advice is: "don't hide it from your attorney." You will only make it worse. As soon as you realize the error, immediately bring it to your attorney's attention. Although admissions that are not responded to in a timely manner are deemed admitted, your attorney may be able to file a motion to the court to have the deemed admissions set aside. As long as the mistake was not intentional and deliberate, usually an attorney can file a motion to attempt to fix the problem. That is not to say that you want to rely on the possibility that your attorney may be able to file a motion. The attorney still has to present the motion to the court for a ruling and overcome the objections of opposing counsel. It is not an easy task. What you should simply be aware of is: (1) you must tell your attorney immediately, and (2) there may be a way to fix the problem. Remember, the problem cannot be fixed if no one knows, and each day that goes by makes the problem worse. So, as hard as it is, admit a missed deadline quickly as there may be a way to fix the error.

REQUESTS FOR PRODUCTION OF DOCUMENTS AND THINGS

request for production of documents and things
A discovery device that requests the production of certain items, such as photographs, papers, reports, and physical evidence; must specify the document sought.

Under Rule 34 of the FRCP, a party can request the other side to produce for inspection documents or objects in its possession. The materials requested need not be specifically identified, nor need they even be known to exist; but the description in the request should be sufficiently specific that the opposing party can reasonably determine whether a document is responsive. It would not, for example, be acceptable to ask the other side to produce "all relevant documents"; it *would,* however, be acceptable to request "all correspondence between Henry Wellington and John Ascot." The request for production allows for the evaluation and assessment of the physical evidence that is available for presentation at trial.

As with other forms of discovery, the request for production has a caption, title, introductory paragraphs, the requests themselves, the signature of the attorney making the request, and a certificate of service. In preparing requests, the drafter should take care that all relevant documents have been requested; this generally requires a review of the pleadings and facts of the case. In responding, you must take care that all requests not objected to are fully complied with; failure to produce a document requested is grounds for excluding that document, even if otherwise admissible, at trial.

An example of the body of a request for production of documents and things is located in Figure 17.14.

FIGURE 17.14
Example of a General Request for Production of Documents and Things

1. All documents pertaining to or reflecting any damages for which you are seeking recovery in this suit.

2. All correspondence, notes, memoranda, recordings, or other documents evidencing or reflecting any communication, conversation, transaction, or dealing between Plaintiff and this Defendant (including Defendant's agents, employees, or representatives), or between the Plaintiff's family and Defendant (including Defendant's agents, employees, and representatives).

3. All documents and tangible things prepared by any person whose work product forms a basis, in whole or in part, of the opinions of the expert witness.

4. The expert's entire file pertaining to this case.

THE DEPOSITION

In a deposition, a party or witness is placed under oath and questioned by attorneys, and the content of the examination is recorded in a transcript prepared by a certified court reporter. The party or witness who is questioned is referred to as a **deponent.**

There are three types of deposition: the oral deposition; the deposition on written questions; and the video deposition. The nature of each varies somewhat.

The **oral deposition,** in which the witness responds to questions from an attorney, is by far the most common. Depending on the answers to the questions, the attorney generally frames follow-up questions that explore an area in detail.

In the **deposition on written questions,** questions are submitted in advance; only those questions are answered, with no follow-up questions allowed. Often, no attorney is even present; the court reporter swears the witness in and records the responses to the prepackaged questions. This type of deposition has very limited use.

Video depositions are simply videotaped versions of the oral deposition; the videotape serves as an additional method of preserving the testimony, in addition to the transcript. If a witness is going to be unavailable for trial because he is beyond the subpoena power of the court (more about subpoenas later) or is aged or ill, a video deposition is a good means of preserving the immediacy of real testimony for trial.

deponent
The party or witness who is questioned in a deposition.

oral deposition
A discovery tool in a question-and-answer format in which the attorney verbally questions a party or witness under oath.

deposition on written questions
A deposition based on written questions submitted in advance to a party; only those questions are answered, with no follow-up questions allowed.

video deposition
Videotaped version of the oral deposition; the videotape serves as an additional method of preserving the testimony, in addition to the transcript.

Notice of Intention to Take Oral Deposition

A formal document must be drafted to notify all parties that a deposition is to be taken. This is called a notice of intention to take oral deposition (or often simply notice of deposition). In addition to a caption, title, and introductory information, the notice identifies the deponent, the location of the deposition, often the rule under which the deposition is authorized, and the fact that it will be taken before a certified court reporter or official authorized to administer oaths. An example of the body of a deposition notice appears in Figure 17.15.

Applicability of a Subpoena

If a *party* is identified as the deponent, the party is required to appear at the time and place identified, unless a motion for protective order is filed (more about such a motion later). The deponent need not necessarily be a party, however—she may be merely a witness. A witness has not submitted to nor been brought under the control of the court; a witness might simply refuse or neglect to appear for the deposition.

The solution to this potential problem is the subpoena. A **subpoena** is a document similar to a summons, in that it is served upon an individual under authority of the court, and orders the person to appear at a certain place and certain time, or suffer the consequences. Subpoenas are often used to ensure the presence of a witness at a deposition; the subpoena and deposition notices are served simultaneously.

subpoena
A document that is served upon an individual under authority of the court, and orders the person to appear at a certain place and certain time for a deposition, or suffer the consequences; an order issued by the court clerk directing a person to appear in court.

FIGURE 17.15
Sample Body of a Deposition Notice

TO: Dr. Ned Radcliffe, by and through his attorney of record, Matthew Brockton, Suite 850, 3265 Montclaire Avenue, Waco, Texas 75683

PLEASE TAKE NOTICE that on October 12, 2008, at ten o'clock (10:00) a.m. at the law office of Emma M. Costello, 6301 Marley Avenue, Waco, Texas 75204, Plaintiff, GILDA MURRAY will take the deposition of DR. NED RADCLIFFE. The deposition will be taken on oral examination pursuant to Rule 200 of the Texas Rules of Civil Procedure before an officer authorized to administer oaths, and will continue from day to day until completed.

Production of Documents in Conjunction with a Deposition

duces tecum
A deposition notice requiring the deponent/witness to "bring with him" specified documents or things.

It is possible to combine a request for production of documents and things with a deposition notice. In this case, the deposition notice contains an additional sentence, referring to the request for production attached to the notice. The Latin term ***duces tecum*** signifies a deposition notice or subpoena requiring the deponent/witness to "bring with him" specified documents or things.

There you are; an abbreviated introduction to discovery. Like all types of legal writing, practice makes the process and task easier. However, the process is always a little easier with a checklist. The following is a checklist of items to keep in mind when formulating discovery requests and responses:

CYBER TRIP

Find different examples on the Internet of discovery documents. Be sure they conform to the requirements of your jurisdictions. If your examples do not comply with your jurisdiction's rules, adapt the examples.

- Review the rules of procedure to determine the applicable bounds of discovery.
- Make a point of identifying and remaining alert to all applicable deadlines. Review your client's file and make notes about the areas of the case in which discovery is desirable or necessary.
- Prepare discovery requests that are detailed and specific.
- Draft requests that will survive the opposition's efforts to object.
- Organize materials so that confusion is minimized and access maximized.
- Coordinate with your supervising attorney at every step.
- Analyze your client's position and determine whether objections to discovery requests are in order.
- Evaluate discovery responses to determine whether they are in compliance with the requirements of the rules and fully responsive to the corresponding requests. Evaluate both responses that you receive from the other side and responses that you prepare.
- If the discovery process breaks down, prepare all necessary motions.

Quick Quiz True/False Questions

1. Discovery is the pretrial investigative process.
2. There are no limits to the number of interrogatories a party can serve on the opposing party.
3. Requests for admission serve a limited purpose and are best for document identification.
4. Failure to produce a document pursuant to a request may be grounds to exclude a document at trial.
5. A notice of deposition may include a request for production of documents.

DISCOVERY MOTIONS

motion for protective order
A motion filed by a party upon whom a discovery request has been made to protect the disclosure of information.

motion to compel discovery
A motion filed by a party seeking to force compliance with a discovery request.

motion for sanctions
A motion filed by any party to counter alleged violations by another party in the case.

Parties often try to evade in the discovery process by making indefensible requests, failing to respond to reasonable requests, or otherwise abusing the process. This may lead to the filing of motions designed to resolve disputed issues. The three principal motions seen in discovery practice are the **motion for protective order,** filed by a party upon whom a discovery request has been made; the **motion to compel discovery,** filed by a party seeking to force compliance with a discovery request; and the **motion for sanctions,** filed by any party to counter alleged violations by another. Each of these motions generally includes attachments consisting of the discovery requests objected to or sought to be enforced; check the rules for format and special requirements. Each is discussed in the subsections that follow.

(Caption of the Case)

Defendant, Dr. Ned Radcliffe, in the above-entitled and numbered cause, files this his Motion for Protective Order, and in support of this Motion would show unto the Honorable Court as follows:

1. On or about September 17, 2008, Plaintiff issued upon this Defendant Plaintiff's First Set of Written Interrogatories and Request for Production of Documents. In responding to the discovery requests, this Defendant objected to Interrogatory Nos. 4, 11, 13, and 15 and Request for Production Nos. 1, 2, and 4, as well as making general objections. The objections are attached hereto and incorporated herein as Exhibit A.

WHEREFORE, Defendant hereby requests that upon final hearing and trial hereof, that the Court enter an Order sustaining his objections to the discovery requests of the Plaintiff, and for such other and further relief, in law or in equity, to which this Defendant may show himself to be justly entitled.

(Signature block)

FIGURE 17.16
Motion for Protective Order

The Motion for Protective Order

When the party upon whom a discovery request has been filed contends that the request oversteps the bounds of the rules, she can file a motion for protective order. Such a motion argues that the information sought is irrelevant or privileged, or that the request is unduly burdensome or overly broad or ambiguous. It may argue that a deposition is inappropriate at the location suggested. Whatever the argument, the purpose is to obstruct the other side. Figure 17.16 shows an example of a motion for protective order opposing certain interrogatories and a request for production of documents.

The Motion to Compel Discovery

The motion to compel discovery is the reverse of the motion for protective order—it seeks not to obstruct discovery, but to force it.

Simply because a party chooses not to disclose information, or has objected to its disclosure, does not mean it isn't discoverable. The party seeking the information must notify the court of the failure to respond, and the need to have the court rule on the dispute. This can be done through a motion to compel discovery, which identifies the information sought; notes that it is relevant, unprivileged, and not otherwise subject to protection; and argues that it should be supplied. Such a motion can also be supported by a brief. A motion to compel discovery is often filed in response to a motion for protective order, or sometimes simply as a means of prodding a party who has allowed the deadline for discovery response to pass without having filed the response. An example of a typical motion to compel discovery is found in Figure 17.17.

The Motion for Sanctions

A motion for sanctions is filed when there have been attempts to force cooperation, but based upon alleged deliberate inaction or gross indifference of one party, discovery has been stalled. Failure to appear at a duly noticed deposition, without making an objection or indicating the intention not to attend, would be an example of behavior that might justify a motion for sanctions, since time and resources were wasted (a court reporter had to be paid to attend) with no justification. Another example

FIGURE 17.17
Motion to Compel Discovery

(Caption of the Case)

Defendant by her attorney and moves the Court as follows:

1. On October 14, 2008, Defendant, after commencement of the above-entitled action, served on the Plaintiff in this cause ten interrogatories in writing pursuant to Rule 33 of the Federal Rules of Civil Procedure, which interrogatories are attached hereto.

2. Plaintiff answered Interrogatories 1, 2, 3, 4, 5, and 10, but did not answer such interrogatories under oath as required by Rule 33 of the Federal Rules of Civil Procedure.

3. Plaintiff failed to answer Interrogatories 6, 7, 8, and 9.

Defendant moves that this Court enter an order directing and requiring Plaintiff to answer all of said interrogatories under oath.

Defendant further moves the Court for an order awarding Defendant the reasonable expenses, including attorneys' fees incurred in this motion.

(Signature block)

ETHICS ALERT

Throughout this chapter and Chapter 15, the message is that paralegals cannot sign certain documents that render legal advice. That is clear. Another ethical concept also related to the filing of pleadings is the requirement under the Federal Rules of Civil Procedure, Rule 8, that filed pleadings are not frivolous. What the rule requires is due diligence in investigating the claims upon which the attorney bases a lawsuit. Not only must a claim be investigated, but there also must be a "good faith" basis for filing of the pleading. In *Yankee Candle Company, Inc. v. Bridgewater Candle Company, LLC,* 140 F. Supp. 2d 111 (D. Mass. 2001), the court awarded over $1 million in legal fees and court costs because of the behavior of the plaintiff, the Yankee Candle Company. The case was disguised as a copyright infringement case, but the court determined that the case was filed primarily to harass and intimidate the defendant, damaging the company financially. The court noted that "Yankee's handball conduct in pursuing this litigation provides evidence of an improper motivation: to drain as much profit as possible out of a far smaller competitor." *Id.* at 118. In reviewing the cases, the court examined such components as the plaintiff's conduct and oppressive actions, economic coercion, and groundless arguments. *Id.* at 121. Review the case. Were the actions of the court appropriate? Why or why not? How did the court calculate the award of attorney's fees? What fees were included in the calculation? What is the message the court is communicating in its decision? The *Yankee Candle Company* case's message is quite clear. Filing pleadings in a court has legal significance and ethical responsibilities. Courts will not hesitate to sanction a party for inappropriate conduct that constitutes bad faith and harassment.

would be a failure to follow the order of the court on a motion to compel discovery. The granting of a motion for sanctions often includes an award of attorney's fees and expenses incurred in its preparation.

motion for summary judgment
A request by a party for a decision from a court that is based upon legal arguments only; the standard is that there are no genuine issues of material fact and the moving party is entitled to judgment as a matter of law.

A METHOD OF CULMINATING THE CASE: THE MOTION FOR SUMMARY JUDGMENT

At some point either during discovery or after it is completed, an attorney may recognize that there are no factual issues in dispute and the case can be decided as a matter of law through a motion. That motion is a **motion for summary judgment.**

Either party may file a motion for summary judgment. The standard in a motion for summary judgment is that one party asserts (1) that there is "no genuine issue of material fact," and (2) that it is entitled to judgment in its favor "as a matter of law" (see Rule 56 of the FRCP). If the motion is granted by the court, the case ends. To explain these concepts fully, a brief discussion is in order.

There are two aspects to every legal controversy—the *facts* and the controlling *law*. When a lawsuit is filed, the parties involved are in essence saying to the court, "We will each present our version of the facts and our interpretation of the law; you decide who is right." The presentation of evidence in the form of documents, exhibits, and witness testimony is designed to enable the trier of fact (the jury or the judge) to weigh the competing positions and determine whose version of the facts is accurate. Once the facts have been established by the trier of fact, the judge applies the controlling law and renders a decision.

Sometimes there is no dispute as to the facts, or at least one party *asserts* that there is no significant and genuine controversy over important facts. If the court finds this assertion to be true, no trial is necessary. The only matter left for the court is to apply the controlling law to these facts. When one party files a motion for summary judgment, the other party can contest it by asserting (1) that there *is* a genuine factual dispute that needs to be decided by the court, or (2) that, although there is no factual dispute, the court should nevertheless find against the moving party based on the controlling law. In a summary judgment motion, no witnesses appear. A determination is made based upon the pleadings, discovery, affidavits submitted, and other documentary "paper" information submitted by the parties.

The motion for summary judgment should include a brief statement of the basis for the motion, and you should attach all documentary evidence and deposition passages that support your position. A brief in support of the motion, arguing that there is no contested factual issue and developing the filing party's legal position, is generally filed as well (and sometimes the attachments are appended to this brief rather than to the motion). This brief is styled as a memorandum to the trial court, which is discussed in the next chapter. Unlike the interoffice memorandum, a brief in support of a motion for summary judgment is persuasive.

Rule 56 of the FRCP, quoted previously, governs the procedure for motions for summary judgment filed in federal court. You should check your local jurisdiction for its requirements. The body of a motion for summary judgment is shown in Figure 17.18.

Source: © Tribune Media Services, Inc. All Rights Reserved. Reprinted with permission.

FIGURE 17.18
Body of Motion for Summary Judgment

Body of Motion for Summary Judgment

1. Plaintiff's Complaint has been filed and served on Defendant VICTRONIC, INC. Defendant has appeared and answered herein. Plaintiff's action is based upon a lease agreement.

2. The pleadings on file herein, together with all the pretrial discovery documents on file herein, the official records of the Court, and the Affidavits of Victor Brennan and Amelia Johnson, attached hereto, all show that there is no genuine issue to any material fact and that the Defendant, as moving party herein, is entitled to judgment in its favor as a matter of law.

3. Defendant asks the Court that, on hearing of this Motion, judgment be entered against Plaintiff.

4. If the Court grants this Motion for Summary Judgment, Defendant requests that immediately after hearing of the Motion, the Court shall award Defendant its attorney fees and costs of suit.

Quick Quiz True/False Questions

1. Either party can file a motion for protective order.
2. A motion to compel discovery is filed to force a party to comply with a discovery request.
3. A motion for summary judgment is not a method to end a lawsuit.
4. The standard for a motion for summary judgment is that there are no genuine issues of material fact and the moving party is entitled to judgment as a matter of law.
5. A brief may not be filed in support of a motion for summary judgment.

THE E-FACTOR

Two important issues arise in the electronic age: amending pleadings and filing pleadings. With computers comes an ease in adding, changing, and deleting information. Usually the information we choose to change in the computer document is changed; the problems occur when a program fails or human error intervenes. In *Philadelphia Gear Corp. v. Swath International,* we examined the case for the proposition "read before you sign." But that case also addressed another issue: human error. In the case, a pleading was supposed to be amended. Something happened. The attorney inadvertently filed the original pleading without the changes. The attorney acknowledged the error but the opposing counsel was not so cooperative. All this could have been averted if the attorney had checked his work. The moral is: "what you think you prepared and changed may not be changed at all." Computers are not infallible. Remember to take the extra time to check your work and ensure its correctness.

The other important issue, apart from the word processing function of the computer, is the electronic filing of pleadings and how to address some of its inherent problems.

Many courts offer electronic filing of pleadings. E-filing, as it is known, allows parties to a lawsuit to file court documents electronically instead of filing paper pleadings. With a push of a key on a keyboard, pleadings are filed with courts, eliminating the need to personally serve court papers to the court clerks. Although this is the wave of the future, all courts have not subscribed to e-filings. Obviously, money is an issue forcing many jurisdictions to invest millions of dollars to upgrade their infrastructure to accommodate e-filings. There is debate as to "how" e-filings should be implemented. Concerns over privacy exist; concerns over bad faith and harassing tactics exist. Since e-filing access is virtually instantaneous, issues arise regarding how to best protect litigants in sensitive situations.

The philosophical debates will continue among attorneys, judges, and academicians, but for you, the paralegal, your role is to understand and comply with the protocols of the courts in which you will practice. What are the rules of practice for filing e-pleadings? They vary, of course, among the courts and jurisdictions around the country. What is considered acceptable practice for one court may be taboo for another. Some courts have instituted a Case Management/Electronic Case Files (CF/ECF) system. Others are still in the process of determining how they will implement e-filings and under what conditions they will be permitted. Before you file a pleading electronically, be clear on the procedures for e-filing. Do not place yourself in a compromising situation by violating court rules and having an e-pleading rejected for filing. Not all courts' rules are the same. You have learned this time and time again throughout this textbook. Filings in a state court, and even a county or parish within a state, may differ dramatically; differences exist for filings among the federal district courts as well. Appropriate procedures in the northern district of California, for example, and the southern district of California for the federal courts may differ, and you need to know the difference before you file the pleading. Read your court rules!

PRACTICAL CONSIDERATIONS: RULES, RULES, RULES

Drafting court documents and discovery is both a science and an art. It is a science in that specific rules must be strictly followed, or the document fails on technical grounds. It is an art in that the drafter must use creative skills to plot a strategic course and draft documents that assist in reaching the intended destination.

It is difficult to separate the science from the art, and this chapter has talked as much about rules as about writing. Mastering the rules is essential to mastering the drafting of court documents, hence you should take the time to thoroughly review both the Federal Rules of Civil Procedure and the state and local rules applicable in your jurisdiction. We have only touched on these considerations; you should go much further.

Additionally, the role of paralegals in discovery is often an important one. Complex cases may involve hundreds or thousands of documents, which must be tracked, reviewed, evaluated, disclosed, requested, and cataloged. Numerous depositions and interrogatories may be needed; multiple medical examinations may be necessary; and lengthy medical records may require interpretation. Much time-consuming work is involved—work that can be tedious, but that requires a sharp and trained mind nevertheless. By refining your skills at organizing the discovery process, you can heighten your value as an essential member of your firm's litigation team.

Summary

Pleadings are formal documents filed with the court that establish the claims and defenses of the parties. The complaint is filed by the plaintiff, and commences the lawsuit. The answer is filed by the defendant in response to the complaint. There may also be counterclaims and cross-claims, and motions directed to the content of the pleadings. In filing pleadings, it is critical to know and understand the applicable procedural rules. Fact-pleading jurisdictions require more detail in their pleadings than notice-pleading jurisdictions. The caption, title, body, signature block, and certificate of service are common components of pleadings.

The complaint begins with a caption and an introduction followed by the body of the complaint, with a statement of the jurisdiction of the court (if in federal court), identification of the parties, and numbered paragraphs containing the allegations of the plaintiff. The language of the complaint is adversarial; the story it tells is sympathetic to the plaintiff. Each cause of action is stated in a separate count. The prayer for relief identifies the remedy sought by the plaintiff. A complaint must be signed, and sometimes verification is required. Rather than a certificate of service, delivery of the complaint is made by the more complicated procedure of service of process.

The answer responds to the allegations of the complaint by admitting them, denying them, or pleading insufficient information to respond. General defenses, affirmative defenses, counterclaims, and cross-claims are also often included. A general defense can be made by motion as well as in the answer; an affirmative defense must be stated in the answer, or is waived. A counterclaim is filed by a defendant against a plaintiff; a cross-claim is filed by one co-party against another, usually by a defendant against another defendant.

A motion to dismiss is a means to assert certain specified defenses, including (in a federal lawsuit) an assertion that the plaintiff has failed to state a claim on which relief can be granted. A motion for more definite statement seeks more information from the other party about the details of their pleading, as a means of pinning down vague allegations; it can set the stage for other defenses.

An amended pleading changes, corrects, revises, or deletes information from a prior pleading. A supplemental pleading adds to a pleading without deleting prior information. Court permission may be required for amended and supplemental pleadings.

Discovery is the pretrial investigatory process authorized and governed by the rules of civil procedure. To be discoverable, information requested must be reasonably calculated to lead to the discovery of admissible evidence.

An interrogatory is a written question submitted by one party to another to be answered under oath. Interrogatories should be specific and precise. Definitions and instructions can be included to reduce ambiguity. Basic background information can be sought with interrogatories, as well as specific information about the case at hand, information about experts consulted, and information about the content of the pleadings. The truth of the responses must be attested to by the signature of the party on whose behalf the responses are filed.

The request for admission allows the filing party to conclusively establish contested issues prior to trial. This serves to limit the complexity and expense of the ensuing trial. A common use of requests for admission is to authenticate documents.

A request for production of documents and things enables one party to inspect the physical and documentary evidence of the other party. The responding party must be reasonably able to determine whether a given document or thing is responsive.

In a deposition, the deponent (who can be a party or a witness) provides testimony that is transcribed by a court reporter. The deposition can be taken in response to oral or written questions, and can also be videotaped. The opportunity for follow-up questions makes the oral deposition a useful form of discovery. A document request can be combined with a deposition notice.

A motion for protective order can be filed by a party in opposition to a discovery request that the party believes oversteps the acceptable bounds of the discovery rules. The motion to compel discovery is filed by a party seeking to force compliance with a discovery request. A motion for sanctions can be filed by a party who believes that the opposing party's discovery conduct is particularly uncooperative or unlawful.

Key Terms

affirmative defenses
allegations
amended pleading
answer
caption
certificate of service
complaint
count
counterclaim
cross-claim lawsuit
deponent
deposition on written questions
discovery
duces tecum
equitable relief
fact pleading
form books
general defenses
instructions and definitions
interrogatory
legal remedy
models
motion for more definite statement
motion for protective order
motion for sanctions
motion for summary judgment
motion to compel discovery
motion to dismiss
notice pleading
oral deposition
pleadings
prayer for relief
process server
request for admission
request for production of documents and things
service of process
special defenses
subpoena
summons
supplemental pleading
verification
video deposition

Review Questions

1. What is the difference between fact pleading and notice pleading?
2. Why is preliminary research important to the proper drafting of a complaint?
3. Describe a benefit and a pitfall of using form books and models to assist in the preparation of pleadings and discovery.
4. Why can an attorney sign a pleading and a paralegal cannot?
5. What is the difference between a counterclaim and a cross-claim?
6. Why is the discovery process needed?
7. What are some of the characteristics of a properly drafted interrogatory and a request for admission?
8. Why are instructions and definitions important to include with discovery requests?
9. What is a motion for summary judgment?
10. What is the difference between a motion for protective order and a motion to compel discovery?

Exercises

1. Mr. and Mrs. Crandall are from Bangor, Maine, and were traveling cross-country in their new automobile on August 3, 2008. While en route to their destination of Cheyenne, Wyoming, they traveled through Illinois. Harry Hart of New Town, Illinois, was crossing through the town square in New Town and hit the Crandalls' car. Mrs. Crandall was thrown against the windshield, and Mr. Crandall hit the steering wheel. Mr. Hart was barely scratched because his car had airbags, but his car was completely destroyed. The medical and hospital expenses for the Crandalls were $78,000, and repairs to their car were $6,000.
   a. Draft a complaint on behalf of the Crandalls, based on these facts.
   b. Using the same set of facts, draft the answer of Mr. Hart.
   c. Go to the library and find your state's procedural requirements for complaints, answers, and defenses, and draft your documents accordingly.
2. Dr. Evan Potter just received a complaint for medical malpractice from a former patient, April Dawson. He performed surgery on her right arm over three years ago and he is now receiving the complaint. The doctor has not heard from April since her surgery. He believes the statute of limitations is two years; but he also thinks that since April never paid her medical bill, she is trying to find a way out of paying him. Dr. Potter has hired your law firm to represent him.
   a. Prepare the motion to dismiss for your supervising attorney's review. (Assume for purposes of this exercise that Dr. Potter has been sued in your state's trial court. Determine the appropriate court in which the lawsuit should be filed. Check the rules of court for compliance with any rules, both state and local.)
   b. Assume that April Dawson wants to file an amended complaint. Using the facts from this question, what are the procedures in your jurisdiction for filing an amended complaint?
   c. Determine the rules in your state and federal courts for filing of e-pleadings.

3. Drew Michelson bought a new computer from Computers R Us, Inc., on September 5, 2008. When he went home to set up the new desktop, there was a dent in the hard drive and a big scratch on the screen. Upset, Drew went back to Computers R Us and asked for his money back. The salesperson told Drew all sales were final, as they were a discount retailer. Drew lives in Chicago, Illinois. Drew paid cash for the computer, so he was stuck with the damaged equipment. Drew decided to sue Computers R Us and wants your law firm to represent him. Prepare the appropriate documents that will be needed to pursue Computers R Us.
4. Arts of the World, Inc., receive the following letter from its lead actress:

   Dear Mr. Weston:
   I realize that there are five weeks left until the show closes, but I cannot continue. Mary Jean Warner, the director, is abusive and unprofessional. I cannot work under these conditions. You will have to find a replacement for me. My notice is effective today. I am sorry I could not continue, but Ms. Warner's behavior is causing me emotional distress.
   Sincerely,
   Adele Taylor

   Mr. Weston is furious. He will have to put the understudy on for tonight's show. He wants his lawyers on the telephone now. Ms. Taylor has a contract. The contract states that she is committed to the show until October 31, 2009. She cannot quit the show. He wants to sue Adele. Prepare the questions that you and your supervising attorney would ask Mr. Weston, prior to filing the lawsuit.
5. Check your state rules of procedure and compare and contrast your rules with the federal rules for interrogatories, admissions, and production of documents and things. Determine the differences or similarities with the federal rules in your jurisdiction's discovery requirements.
6. Andrew Goddard is James Lewiston's landlord. James signed a one-year lease from January 14, 2008, to January 13, 2009, for an apartment located at 674 Brandy Lane, Dallas, Texas. He stopped paying rent nine months into the lease and the landlord sued for the back rent. Prepare the motion for summary judgment in the case.
7. Denise Bailey went to the hair stylist to have her hair colored. Color Cuts, Inc., employed William Tonbridge as a stylist. He has worked for Color Cuts for approximately six months. When William was applying the color, Denise's scalp began to tingle. She told William and he said that it was normal. While she was waiting for the color to set, her scalp began to burn. William quickly washed the color out, but it was too late. Denise's scalp was badly burned. She went to the emergency room where they determined she had second-degree burns on her scalp. Most of her hair fell out. She had to wear scarves until her scalp was less sensitive. Denise sued Color Cuts and William. Draft the interrogatories and requests for admission in the case.
8. The defendant's counsel, David Fredericks, has made a request for production of documents and things in *Software Corporation v. Data Information Systems Inc.* He has requested all electronic documents, including but not limited to, invoices, accounting records, e-mails, letters, and memoranda from 1990 to present between software corporation and data information systems. This request is overly broad and burdensome.
   a. Prepare the motion for protective order for your client, Software Corporation.
   b. Data Information Systems has filed a motion for sanctions against Software Corporation for filing the motion for protective order. Prepare the response to the motion for sanctions.

PORTFOLIO ASSIGNMENT

Your firm has been retained to represent Dana Marsh in her suit against A1 Delivery Service, Inc., a New Jersey corporation. On April 20, 2008, A1 delivered Mrs. Marsh's new refrigerator to her house located at 323 Garfield Lane, Haddonfield, New Jersey. While backing out of the driveway, the deliveryperson, Herbert Killington, drove over Mrs. Marsh's cat, Buttons. Mrs. Marsh, who is seventy-five years old, had the cat for fifteen years and was quite upset over its death. She wants to sue A1 and collect as much in damages as she can. Mrs. Marsh says she still cannot get over how her "poor Buttons" looked and cannot get the blood out of her driveway.

1. Draft the complaint for your supervising attorney's review. Include in your complaint the method of service of process. Check the New Jersey laws for service of process on a corporate defendant.
2. As part of your assignment, draft the answer of A1 Delivery Service, Inc. (A1 is not happy with its employee, Herb; seems as though he was drinking on the job again. A1 wants to file a cross-claim against Herb.)
3. Draft the answer for Herb. (Herb claims the brakes on his truck were faulty again. He says he couldn't stop the truck when he saw Buttons.)

Mrs. Marsh wants to proceed with discovery in her case against A1 Delivery Service, Inc., and Herbert Killington. Using the facts from the Portfolio Assignment, prepare the following discovery:

1. Draft interrogatories to A1 Delivery Service and Herbert Killington.
2. Draft a request for admissions for A1 and Herbert Killington.
3. Draft the request for production of documents and things for A1.

Remember to use models and form books to prepare your discovery. Also, research the status of the law on the liability of an employer for the negligence of an employee. Does the employer have any legal defenses to the lawsuit?

Quick Quiz True/False Answers

Page 512	Page 518	Page 523	Page 530	Page 534
1. True	1. False	1. True	1. True	1. True
2. True	2. True	2. False	2. False	2. True
3. False	3. False	3. False	3. True	3. False
4. False	4. True	4. True	4. True	4. True
5. False	5. True	5. True	5. True	5. False

Part Six

Persuasive Writing

Chapter 18

The Memorandum of Law to the Trial Court

After you have completed this chapter, you will be able to:

- Identify the two audiences for a trial memorandum.
- Explain how to prepare a trial memorandum to assist the trial judge.
- Draft your trial memorandum to minimize the impact of the attack of opposing counsel.
- Describe the characteristics of a trial memorandum in regard to a motion.
- Identify the reasons why a judge might request a trial memorandum.
- Explain the potential importance of an unsolicited trial memorandum that anticipates issues.
- Understand the importance of the caption and the title of a trial memorandum.
- Explain the perspective from which the issues presented section is drafted.
- List four objectives of a statement of facts.
- Describe the difference between the discussion section of an internal memorandum and the argument section of a trial memorandum.

The memorandum of law to the trial court is an important document in the litigation process, commonly seen and often instrumental in defining the scope and nature of the trial and its outcome. In your role as a paralegal, you will likely be called upon to participate in the preparation of such memoranda. This chapter focuses on the components and the skills needed to draft the memorandum of law to the trial court.

CASE FACT PATTERN

Your firm's client, Dr. Williams, has been served with a subpoena *duces tecum*, commanding her to testify at a deposition and to produce all medical records of an identified patient. Neither Dr. Williams nor her patient wishes to disclose these records.

The doctor has consulted with your supervising attorney, and a decision has been made to file a motion for protective order asserting the existence of a patient–physician privilege. Since the law on this point in your state is not entirely clear, a supporting memorandum that argues in favor of the motion must be prepared. You have been assigned the task of drafting this memorandum.

The Wizard of Id

Brant Parker and Johnny Hart

Source: By permission of John L. Hart FLP and Creators Syndicate, Inc.

THE NATURE AND PURPOSE OF THE MEMORANDUM OF LAW TO THE TRIAL COURT

memorandum of law to the trial court
An adversarial document filed with the trial court and written to persuade the trial court of a party's position on a disputed point of law.

The **memorandum of law to the trial court** (which we also will refer to as a *trial memorandum*) is an adversarial document filed with the trial court and written to persuade the trial court that one party's position on a disputed point of law is superior to the opposing party's position. It may be written in support of or in opposition to a motion; it may be written at the request of a judge to assist her in rendering a decision; or it may be an unsolicited memorandum filed at trial in order to persuade the judge on anticipated legal questions. Whatever the reason, the content should be one-sided, or *partisan.*

We have already used two names, trial memorandum and memorandum of law to the trial court, for this. There are still other names that refer to the same type of document: memorandum of points and authorities, memorandum in opposition to motion, brief in support of motion, trial brief in opposition to motion, and others. These titles all refer to the same basic document—an adversarial document setting forth legal arguments to the trial court. The title depends upon the jurisdiction, and even on individual attorneys and judges. Different courts and individuals have different styles. It is important to remember that, regardless of the name applied, the factors to take into account are essentially the same.

One potential area of confusion should, however, be cleared up at the outset. In some areas, the term *trial brief* refers to the materials that an attorney prepares, not for filing with the court, but rather to assist him with the conduct of the trial—such things as witness lists, summaries of pleadings, an outline of his opening statement, copies of important cases, possible jury instructions, and so on. Such preparatory materials will be called a *trial notebook,* to distinguish it from a trial brief. Thus, we consider a trial brief to be the same as a trial memorandum.

Although some trial courts have specific requirements for the format of a trial memorandum, in general these requirements are less formal than those for an appellate brief (which we discuss in Chapter 19). You should learn your jurisdiction's requirements for a trial memorandum.

It is important to take into consideration the audience for the trial memorandum. Although your client may read your trial memorandum, and should certainly be consulted about the factual background, she is *not* part of the audience for whom the trial memorandum is written. The audience is composed of two segments—the judge, whom you must convince, and the opposing counsel, whom you must refute and whose attack your arguments must survive. Let's take a moment and consider these two audiences.

First, the judge. Unlike appellate judges, who sit in judgment only on appeals, trial judges handle varied responsibilities, from overseeing courtroom personnel, to deciding motions, to conducting trials. Often their schedules are busy, and time is short. Whereas an appellate judge may have the time and the responsibility to read and research enough to render appropriate decisions (which have broad impact), a trial judge generally only needs to know how the higher courts have dealt with the issues presented, or analogous situations. This is not to say that trial judges are not thoughtful, or do not take their responsibilities seriously; they are and they do. It is simply a warning that a trial memorandum needs to get to the point. Tell the judge what you want, why you want it, and why you are legally entitled to it, as concisely as you can. If you must make a complicated argument, by all means make it—but if it can be done more simply, it is a mistake to write a lengthy explanation. Keep your memoranda short, concise, and direct.

Opposing counsel are the second audience. Unlike judges, who will give your arguments a fair reading, opposing counsel are the enemy. They scour your arguments looking for logical holes and unjustified analytical leaps, in an effort to refute your arguments and prove that your client's position is not supported by law. You must, therefore, write *accurately*. Do not overstate your arguments, and never misstate or misrepresent the law. If you are honest in your interpretations (partisan, yes, but nevertheless honest), and if you Shepardize or KeyCite with care, your arguments should survive the attack of opposing counsel. Indeed, by recognizing the threat posed by opposing counsel, you may well be saved from making the type of borderline argument that, if read and rejected by a judge, might tend to poison your other, more logical arguments in the eyes of the court.

TYPES OF TRIAL MEMORANDA

All legal memoranda argue a point of law in an adversarial manner. Each of the three broad categories we identified earlier, however—a **memorandum in regard to a motion,** a **memorandum at the request of a judge,** and an **unsolicited memorandum anticipating legal issues**—presents its own unique considerations for the drafter. Let's take a look at each.

memorandum in regard to a motion
A persuasive memorandum supporting the points and authorities in a motion.

memorandum at the request of a judge
A persuasive memorandum of legal points requested by the trial court judge.

unsolicited memorandum anticipating legal issues
A memorandum of law prepared by one of the parties to the case in support of an anticipated legal issue.

Memorandum in Regard to a Motion

Many issues arise in the course of a lawsuit—issues about the content of the pleadings, the propriety of discovery requests, the sufficiency of responses, the right of a party to file amendments, and on and on. Such issues must be resolved before the case is ready for trial. Sometimes they are resolved by mutual agreement of the parties, but often they are not. When agreement is not possible, a motion is generally made to the court in which one party requests that the court resolve the dispute in its favor, so that the case can move to trial. The motion itself generally identifies the nature of the dispute and the order or relief that the filing party seeks, but typically does *not* contain any legal analysis or arguments. These analyses and arguments are reserved for the trial memoranda filed in regard to the motion.

The trial memorandum of the party that filed the motion is drafted, of course, in support of it, whereas the opposing party files a trial memorandum in opposition. For example, in conjunction with the motion for protective order filed on behalf of Dr. Williams from our Case Fact Pattern problem, a supporting trial memorandum would discuss the issues of physician–patient privilege that are posed by the motion and argue that they justify withholding the information requested; a trial memorandum in opposition, arguing for disclosure, would be filed by the party that requested the deposition. The issues discussed in the two memoranda are limited to the issues raised by the motion.

During the course of a lawsuit, there may be several motions pending, hence several trial memoranda in regard to these motions. Each should have a title that identifies the party filing it and the motion to which it relates. We discuss format further in the following subsections. Perhaps one of the most common motions where a memorandum of law in support of the motion is prepared is the motion for summary judgment. (See Figure 17.22.) A typical brief in support of a motion for summary judgment is exhibited at the end of this chapter.

Memorandum at the Request of a Judge

Contested issues continually arise during the course of a lawsuit, both during the pretrial stage and during the trial itself. During oral argument on a motion, for example, the judge may raise a point that the parties had not anticipated or addressed in their trial memoranda. Or an objection to the introduction of a piece of evidence at trial may present a novel legal problem that neither the judge nor the parties have ever considered. Under such circumstances the judge, rather than ruling immediately on the issue at hand, may request that the parties submit trial memoranda setting forth their positions on the disputed issue before he makes his decision.

The response of the attorneys is the memorandum at the request of the judge. This memorandum will be adversarial, like a memorandum in regard to a motion, and will be limited to the issue that the judge raised. It is designed to provide the judge with guidance on the issue presented, in the form of legal support for the position favoring your client. Your goal is to predispose the judge to your client's position, and downplay the opponent's position. The memorandum should be direct and concise, particularly at trial, where time is short.

The judge may even request an additional memorandum on a given point after the trial is completed, but before her decision is rendered. Again, you will be emphasizing the superiority of your client's position on the issue raised.

Unsolicited Memorandum Anticipating Legal Issues

By the conclusion of a trial, the legal issues that control the trial's outcome are clear. It is often useful to prepare a trial memorandum that identifies these issues, then argue in favor of a resolution that benefits your client. By clarifying the issues and identifying your strongest arguments at the conclusion of the trial and for the benefit of the judge, you can establish a foundation on which the judge can render a decision in which your client prevails.

An unsolicited trial memorandum should be straightforward, identifying the issues at the outset and presenting arguments that are clear and direct. You should highlight the issues that are most important to you, and include every issue that you believe has bearing on the result. In other words, if you are going to file an unsolicited memorandum, you should be thorough; prepare it correctly. If, for strategic reasons, you want to emphasize only a particular aspect of the contested issues, then make that absolutely clear. Otherwise, you may leave the impression that you are conceding on the points left unaddressed. An example of a situation where an unsolicited memorandum may occur is when the attorney wants to include paralegal fees as part of an attorney's fees in a case. To ensure proper consideration of the issue, the attorney may file a brief in support of this request. (Recall your portfolio assignment in Chapter 16. The interoffice memorandum could easily be converted into a memorandum of law to the trial court in support of inclusion of paralegal fees as part of an award for attorney's fees.)

GETTING READY TO WRITE: THE PREWRITING CONSIDERATIONS

Don't forget what you have learned in previous chapters. Incorporate all your prewriting skills to begin composing a concise, persuasive trial memorandum. Remember to

- get organized;
- outline;
- research the law;

- validate the law through Shepard's or KeyCite;
- determine your audience;
- choose appropriate words for a persuasive document;
- check all court rules: state and local or federal and local;
- review requirements for specific judges;
- reference attachments or evidence in brief as required;
- check your time constraints; and
- ask your supervising attorney any questions needed for clarification.

Regardless of the assignment, you must always perform the basic preparatory work. If you skip a step, you may risk having a brief rejected, information stricken, or worse yet, having the opposing counsel identify improperly cited authority, embarrassing both yourself and your supervising attorney. So, don't get complacent—always stick to your game plan. Prepare, prepare, prepare.

Quick Quiz True/False Questions

1. The trial memorandum is an objective document.
2. The only audience in trial memorandum is the judge.
3. One type of trial memorandum is a memorandum in support of a motion.
4. A judge may request a memorandum of law on a contested issue.
5. A trial memorandum does not require the validation of the law nor any legal research.

THE COMPONENTS OF A MEMORANDUM OF LAW TO THE TRIAL COURT

The format of trial memoranda varies from jurisdiction to jurisdiction, and from judge to judge. The following comments are offered as a general frame of reference; you should check the rules applicable in your jurisdiction for more specific guidance. Note that some courts lean toward a more formal presentation of memorandum of law or brief than others. Many courts have page limitations similar to those identified in the appellate rules of procedure. Pay attention to the trial court's requirements. Some judges refuse to accept the brief, or they simply stop reading. An example of trial court brief requirements is identified in Figure 18.1, which is an excerpt from Local Civil Rule 7.1 Affidavits and Briefs in the U.S. District Court for the Northern District of Illinois.

The Caption or Heading

As with pleadings and discovery requests, trial memoranda must have captions identifying the court, parties, and docket number. The title of the pleading may be included as well. Figure 18.2 shows two alternative captions.

Neither a brief in support of or in opposition to any motion nor objections to a report and recommendation or order of a magistrate judge or special master shall exceed 15 pages without prior approval of the court. Briefs that exceed the 15-page limit must have a table of contents with the pages noted and a table of cases. Any brief or objection that does not comply with this rule shall be subject to being stricken by the court.

FIGURE 18.1
Excerpt from Local Civil Rule 7.1 Affidavits and Briefs in the U.S. District Court for the Northern District of Illinois

YOU BE THE JUDGE

Often the court and not the rules of procedure set limitations on briefs and memoranda of law. The judge in *Insulated Panel Company v. The Industrial Commission,* 318 Ill. App.3d 100, 743 N.E.2d 1038 (Ill. 2001), set page limitations on trial briefs. On appeal, one of the issues was whether the judge abused his discretion by limiting the briefs to 10 pages and "considering only the first 10 pages of respondent's" 50-page brief. *Id.* at 1040. The court reviewed the arguments of counsel and held that the "court has the inherent power to control its own docket, and the ruling limiting briefs to 10 pages was not an abuse of discretion." *Id.* at 1040. The case represents the importance of complying with court rules and court orders. They are indistinguishable. Read the case. Identify the facts and issues on appeal. What was the court's reasoning in the case? What is the rule of law for the case?

Title

If the title of the pleading is not included in the caption, it must appear below it. As mentioned earlier, the title should be specific enough to identify the party filing it and, if in regard to a motion, the title of the motion. If not in regard to a motion, it should identify the context—for example, "Plaintiff's Memorandum Regarding Admissibility of Plaintiff's Psychotherapy Records" or "Plaintiff's Trial Brief" (if an unsolicited summary of the issues after trial).

FIGURE 18.2
Examples of Caption Setup

Ⓐ IN THE DISTRICT COURT OF DALLAS COUNTY, TEXAS

101st JUDICIAL DISTRICT

STEPHEN GILES, Plaintiff	§ § §	
	§	
vs.	§	No. 12344
	§	
GEORGE HARRIS, Defendant	§ § §	

Plaintiff's Memorandum in Support of Motion for Summary Judgment

—or—

Ⓑ IN THE UNITED STATES DISTRICT COURT FOR

THE NORTHERN DISTRICT OF TEXAS

STEPHEN GILES, Plaintiff	§ § §	
	§	
vs.	§	CIVIL ACTION NO. 2008-12387
	§	Plaintiff's Memorandum in Support of Motion for Summary Judgment
GEORGE HARRIS, Defendant	§ §	

(1)
TO THE HONORABLE JUDGE OF SAID COURT:

COMES NOW, STEPHEN GILES, Plaintiff, and files this Memorandum of Law to the Trial Court in Support of Plaintiff's Motion for Summary Judgment and would show unto the Court as follows:

—or—

(2)
Plaintiff STEPHEN GILES submits this Memorandum of Law in Support of this Motion for Summary Judgment in this matter:

FIGURE 18.3
Introduction to the Court

PRACTICE TIP

After the introduction of a party, you may want to use a shorthand reference. Long names often lend themselves toward using this technique. Refer to the full name first, such as the United States Government, and then in a parenthetical state your shorthand reference: (hereinafter referred to as "the Government"). You can use this technique for all parties or long names that may be repeated throughout a document, such as Community Memorial Hospital (hereinafter referred to as "Hospital"). Use this technique in pleadings and discovery documents as well.

Introduction to the Court

A formal introductory section is still required in some jurisdictions, although others, such as California, have done away with the requirement. The introduction seen in Figure 18.3 illustrates the formal tone associated with a document filed with a court. For example, the opening phrase, "To the Honorable Judge . . . ," is a means of showing respect to the court. The trend today, however, is toward the elimination of such introductions.

Issues or Questions Presented

Although similar to the analogous section of an internal memorandum, the **issues or questions presented** section of a trial memorandum should be slanted toward your client's position. The issues should be stated accurately, but the outcome you seek should be implied in the questions.

Several styles for this section are commonly seen. The issue can be stated commencing with the word "Whether," followed by a statement of your client's position. The issue can also be drafted as a positive statement, or as an ordinary question. Figure 18.4 shows three numbered alternative formats for stating the issue presented; the (A) section of each alternative is drafted from a plaintiff's perspective, and the (B) section from the defendant's perspective. The best method of drafting the issue may be dictated by the court or your supervising attorney's preference. This situation is one where not only checking court rules is appropriate but reviewing models from other cases as well.

issues or questions presented
A section that identifies the legal issues presented in the memorandum of law to the trial court.

Statement of Facts

The trial memorandum, like the internal memorandum, contains a **statement of facts** that relates the factual context of the issue posed. The critical difference between the facts as stated in an internal memorandum and those stated in a trial memorandum, however, is in the point of view of the drafter. In the internal memorandum (which is drafted to be objective), the facts are set out in straightforward fashion. In a trial memorandum, the facts should be set out accurately, but drafted to favor your client's position.

Facts should be presented chronologically. You seek to develop sympathy for your client's position, using descriptive words and emotional facts to predispose the court toward accepting your client's position. You have four objectives in drafting a statement of facts:

1. Introduce your client's case to the court.
2. Provide an accurate presentation of the events.
3. Minimize those facts which favor your opponent.
4. Paint a memorable picture of your client's position.

statement of facts
Section of a brief that sets forth the significant facts and information needed to analyze the issues presented.

FIGURE 18.4
Forms of the Issues Presented Section

Alternative 1

(A)

Issue Presented. Whether there exists a genuine issue of material fact when a blank power of attorney is used by an agent who was not authorized to act on behalf of Plaintiff, the principal.

(B)

Issue Presented. Whether an issue of fact exists if Plaintiff accepts tax benefits ratifying the actions of an agent where a blank power of attorney was used.

Alternative 2

(A)

Issue Presented. No issues of fact exist in a transaction where an unauthorized agent used a blank power of attorney to act on behalf of the Plaintiff, the principal.

(B)

Issue Presented. No issue of fact exists in a transaction where an agent using a blank power of attorney attempts to create a valid transaction through ratification by the principal.

Alternative 3

(A)

Issue Presented. Are there issues of material fact in a transaction where an agent using a blank power of attorney creates an agency relationship to validly act on behalf of the Plaintiff, the principal?

(B)

Issue Presented. Are there issues of material fact when the principal ratifies the unauthorized acts of his agent?

Although you are writing from your client's perspective, do not misstate, misrepresent, or ignore key facts that are detrimental to your case. A misrepresentation of damaging facts will be pointed out to the court by the opposition; ignoring them allows the other side an unchallenged opportunity to emphasize their importance. Rather, identify them, attempt to minimize their importance in your statement of facts, and then, in your argument section, show why you contend that they are unimportant.

Figure 18.5 shows a statement of facts written from the plaintiff's perspective.

Courts and judges may determine the format of the statement of facts. For example, in the U.S. District Court for the Western District of Wisconsin, two district court judges have completely different requirements for preparing the statement of facts in a motion for summary judgment. The requirements are so specific that the judge

PRACTICE TIP

Do not overlook the rules of procedure of your jurisdiction as well as the local rules. Sometimes the rules for motions and briefs are tailored to a particular judge's court requirements. For example, in the U.S. District Court for the Western District of Wisconsin, two district court judges have completely different requirements for filing a motion for summary judgment. The requirements are so specific that the judge indicates that a fact must be identified in a numbered paragraph followed by the supporting evidentiary reference, such as an interrogatory response, request for admission, page of deposition testimony, or an affidavit. Pay close attention to all the rules of court, especially the local rules. Check the Web sites of the courts for updates and changes to the rules. Failure to follow the rules of a court or local rules may result in the pleading, motion, or brief being stricken from filing or the record.

FIGURE 18.5
Statement of Facts

The facts in the case are undisputed. Mr. Giles went to a holiday party on November 20, at the home of Mr. Swan, a business associate. Mr. Swan had been Mr. Giles's friend and attorney for some time. Giles was going out of town for Thanksgiving and would not be back until the first of the new year. Giles wanted to purchase a piece of real estate before the end of the year, but was going out of town. The only business discussion that evening concerned the real estate transaction.

Swan suggested that Giles could execute a power of attorney, with Swan as Giles's representative. The gentlemen went into Swan's study and Giles signed a document entitled "Power of Attorney." Neither man filled in any information in the document. Swan's name did not appear anywhere on the document. Swan kept the Power of Attorney in his top desk drawer. Giles went on his trip.

While Giles was on his trip, one of his partners, Mr. Harris, contacted Swan regarding a joint venture transaction completely unrelated to the real estate transaction. Giles and Harris had been discussing dissolving the joint venture, with Giles acquiring Harris's interest. Swan knew nothing about this transaction.

Harris stated to Swan that Giles was supposed to assume all Harris's interest in the joint venture before January 1. Harris inquired whether Swan could help him. Swan told Harris that he had a power of attorney to close a real estate transaction, but did not know how he could help Harris out.

Harris asked Swan to use the power of attorney to transfer the joint venture interest. Harris told Swan this would save his friend some money. Swan continued to tell Harris that he only had authority to close a real estate transaction. Harris, however, was able to persuade Swan to execute the transfer of the joint venture interest, using the power of attorney on December 29.

When Giles came back to town, Swan informed him of the transfer from Harris and told him that he had used the power of attorney. Giles was enraged and told Swan he had no authority to transfer the interest. Giles wanted the transaction rescinded.

indicates that a fact must be identified in a numbered paragraph followed by the supporting evidentiary reference, such as an interrogatory response, request for admission, page of deposition testimony, or an affidavit. Pay close attention to all the rules of court, especially the local rules. Judge Crabb offered the following requirements reproduced in Figure 18.6.

The requirements of Judge Shabaz were decidedly different. And yes, both judges were from the same district court in Wisconsin. Compare the statement of facts from Judge Shabaz in Figure 18.7 with that of Judge Crabb.

CYBER TRIP

Determine whether your jurisdiction, federal and state, has specific requirements for drafting a motion for summary judgment.

The Argument

The **argument** of a legal memorandum presents your client's position; it is the heart of the memorandum. You present the results of your research in an adversarial form intended to persuade the court of the superiority of your client's contentions. The partisan purpose and slant of the argument section differentiate it from the discussion section of an internal memorandum, where the legal analysis is objective, not adversarial. In the trial memorandum, your purpose is to have your position prevail.

argument
The section of the brief where the issues are analyzed through citation of legal authorities.

Effective writing techniques are essential for this section. Outline for logical organization. Be definitive. Write to convince, not simply to inform. Use language that is positive and forceful. Make the court believe that your position is correct.

Move from general points to those more specific, applying the law to the facts and using the IRAC model as your guide. A method of guiding the judge through your brief when multiple issues are involved is by using **point headings** and **subheadings.** They act as an outline of the memorandum of law. A point heading identifies the argument in a section of the brief. A subheading presents subpoints of the point

point headings
Headings that outline and identify the argument in the section.

subheadings
Headings that identify the subpoints in an argument section.

heading. Like the issue, they are drafted with a persuasive slant. The practice of using point headings helps the judge in two ways: First, they highlight your arguments in a precise form; and second, judges who do not have lots of extra time can scan the brief and focus on the pinpoint and subheadings in the brief. Using these headings streamlines your brief and organizes the argument.

FIGURE 18.6
Summary Judgment Requirements of Judge Crabb
Source: Guides and Procedures for the U.S. District Court for the Western District of Wisconsin, available at www.wiwd.uscourts.gov/rules/guidproc/html.

HELPFUL TIPS FOR FILING
A SUMMARY JUDGMENT MOTION
IN CASES ASSIGNED TO JUDGE BARBARA B. CRABB

Please read the attached directions carefully – doing so will save your time and the court's.

REMEMBER:

1. All facts necessary to sustain a party's position on a motion for summary judgment must be explicitly proposed as findings of fact. This includes facts establishing jurisdiction. (Think of your proposed findings of fact as telling a story to someone who knows nothing of the controversy.)
2. The court will not search the record for factual evidence. Even if there is evidence in the record to support your position on summary judgment, if you do not propose a finding of fact with the proper citation, the court will not consider that evidence when deciding the motion.
3. A fact properly proposed by one side will be accepted by the court as undisputed unless the other side properly responds to the proposed fact and establishes that it is in dispute.
4. Your brief is the place to make your legal argument, not to restate the facts. When you finish it, check it over with a fine-tooth comb to be sure you haven't relied upon or assumed any facts in making your legal argument that you failed to include in the separate document setting out your proposed findings of fact.
5. A chart listing the documents to be filed by the deadlines set by the court for briefing motions for summary judgment or cross-motions for summary judgment is printed on the reverse side of this tip sheet.

IN THE UNITED STATES DISTRICT COURT
FOR THE WESTERN DISTRICT OF WISCONSIN

PROCEDURE TO BE FOLLOWED ON MOTIONS FOR SUMMARY JUDGMENT

I. MOTION FOR SUMMARY JUDGMENT

A. Contents:

1. A motion, together with such materials permitted by Rule 56(e) as the movant may elect to serve and file; and

2. In a separate document, a statement of proposed findings of fact or a stipulation of fact between or among the parties to the action, or both; and

3. Evidentiary materials (see I.C.); and

4. A supporting brief.

B. Rules Regarding Proposed Findings of Fact:

1. Each fact should be proposed in a separate, numbered paragraph.

2. Each factual proposition must be followed by a reference to evidence supporting the proposed fact. For example,

> "1. Plaintiff Smith bought six Holstein calves on July 11, 2001.
> Harold Smith Affidavit, Jan. 6, 2002, p.1, ¶ 3."

3. The statement of proposed findings of fact shall include ALL factual propositions the moving party considers necessary for judgment in the party's

Cont.

favor. For example, the proposed findings shall include factual statements relating to jurisdiction, the identity of the parties, the dispute, and the context of the dispute.

4. The court will not consider facts contained only in a brief.

C. Evidence

1. As noted in I.B. above, each proposed finding must be supported by admissible evidence. The court will not search the record for evidence. To support a proposed fact, you may use:

a. Depositions. Give the name of the witness, the date of the deposition, and page of the transcript of cited deposition testimony;

b. Answers to Interrogatories. State the number of the interrogatory and the party answering it;

c. Admissions made pursuant to Fed. R. Civ. P. 36. (State the number of the requested admission and the identity of the parties to whom it was directed); or

d. Other Admissions. The identity of the document, the number of the page, and paragraph of the document in which that admission is made.

e. Affidavits. The page and paragraph number, the name of the affiant, and the date of the affidavit. (Affidavits must be made by persons who have first-hand knowledge and must show that the person making the affidavit is in a position to testify about those facts.)

f. Documentary evidence that is shown to be true and correct, either by an affidavit or by stipulation of the parties. (State exhibit number, page and paragraph.)

[text omitted]

FIGURE 18.6
Summary Judgment Requirements of Judge Crabb *Cont.*

IN THE UNITED STATES DISTRICT COURT
FOR THE WESTERN DISTRICT OF WISCONSIN

PROCEDURE TO BE FOLLOWED ON MOTIONS FOR SUMMARY JUDGMENT

I. A motion for summary judgment made pursuant to Rule 56 of the Federal Rules of Civil procedure shall be served and filed in the following form:

A. The motion itself together with such materials permitted by Rule 56(e) as the movant may elect to serve and file; and

B. Either (1) a stipulation of facts between or among all the parties to the action, or (2) a statement of the findings of fact proposed by movant, or (3) a combination of (1) and (2).

1. Whether a movant elects a stipulation or a statement of proposed findings, or both, it is movant's obligation to present no more and no less than the set of factual propositions which movant considers necessary to judgment in movant's favor, and as to which movant considers there is no genuine issue.

2. Such factual propositions shall be set forth in numbered paragraphs, the contents of each of which shall limited as far as practicable to the statement of single factual proposition.

3. At the close of each numbered paragraph shall be set forth one or more references to the PLEADINGS, DEPOSITION TRANSCRIPTS, ANSWERS TO INTERROGATORIES, ADMISSIONS on file or AFFIDAVITS supporting movant's contention there is no genuine issue as to that factual proposition.

Cont.

FIGURE 18.7
Summary Judgment Requirements of Judge Shabaz

FIGURE 18.7
Summary Judgment Requirements of Judge Shabaz *Cont.*

4. References to the record shall include:

   a. in the case of pleading, the numbered paragraph of that pleading;
   b. in the case of a deposition transcript, the name of the witness and the page of the transcript;
   c. in the case of an answer to an interrogatory, the number of that interrogatory and the identity of the party to whom it was directed;
   d. in the case of an admission in response to, or resulting from a failure to respond to, a request for admission made pursuant to Rule 36, Federal Rules of Civil Procedure, the number of the requested admission and the identity of the party to whom it was directed;
   e. in the case of an admission on file which is not in response to, or resulting from a failure to respond to, a request for admission made pursuant to Rule 36, the form such admission takes and the page or paragraph of the document in which that admission is made. Admissions made solely for the purpose of the motion for summary judgment should be so designated.

C. A statement of the conclusions of law proposed by movant, in numbered paragraphs.

D. A motion for summary judgement in the form required by I., above, shall be served and filed together with a supporting brief.

[text omitted]

PRACTICE TIP

Since subheadings follow the rules of outlining, you must use more than one subheading within a point heading. Otherwise, limit yourself to one general point heading for each argument section within the memorandum of law. The point heading is typed in capital letters with the subheadings in regular type. Present your strongest arguments and points first. By doing this, you set the tone of your brief. Guide the judge logically and methodically through the argument.

Therefore, in your brief emphasize your strong points and facts; de-emphasize and attack the opposition's strong points and facts. Most of all, avoid obscurity—tell the court your position clearly and effectively. However, do not misstate or mislead the court. When a point is not favorable, distinguish it, but do not lose credibility by ignoring adverse authority. Integrity in your presentation goes a long way in gaining the confidence of the court. An example of an argument section is provided in Figure 18.8.

Another reason to state your legal position clearly and effectively is that the issues raised in the trial court may determine the issues on appeal. In most circumstances, the issues argued at the trial court level are the same legal issues on appeal. If issues are not raised in the pleadings and briefs before the trial court, there is no record identifying those issues existed. Appellate courts frown upon attorneys attempting to use an appeal as the first time to raise issues that should have been raised at the trial court. Often the result is either dismissal of the appeal or refusal to hear the "new" issue on appeal. Consequently, you and your supervising attorney should take care in addressing all the issues at the trial court level or face having them forever waived at the appellate level. That means you should be thinking strategically from the moment the complaint and answer are filed in a case. Every document in a trial-level case has legal significance. Thus the information and evidence used at the trial court are the building blocks that set the foundation for the record on appeal.

Conclusion

The conclusion section is a summary of the legal position taken in the trial memorandum. It informs the court of the finding and relief sought. Although a one-sentence conclusion

FIGURE 18.8
Argument Section

This case presents a unique question of law which is what is the authority granted a principal by an agent when the power of attorney is blank. The answer is none. Any acts performed by a principal with a blank power of attorney are void. It is clear that a power of attorney must set forth the authority and the name of the principal and agent. The document before this court does neither.

The law on this matter is well settled in Texas and dates back to the 1880s. To determine the validity of the power of attorney and the extent of the authority granted, certain rules of construction and interpretation must be addressed. The leading case of *Gouldy v. Metcalf, 75* Tex. 455, 12 S.W. 830 (1889), sets out the rules of construction for a power of attorney, which are:

> [w]hen an authority is conferred upon an agent by a formal instrument, as by a power of attorney, there are two rules of construction to be carefully adhered to:
>
> 1. The meaning of general words in the instrument will be restricted by the context, and construed accordingly.
> 2. The authority will be construed strictly, so as to exclude the exercise of any power which is not warranted, either by the actual terms used or as a necessary means of executing the authority with effect.
>
> *Id.* at 458.

Expanding the guidelines set forth in *Gouldy*, case law establishes that "all powers conferred upon an agent by a formal instrument are to receive a strict interpretation, and the authority is never extended by intendment or construction beyond that which is given in terms, or is necessary for carrying the authority into effect, and the authority must be strictly pursued." *Bean v. Bean*, 79 S.W. 2d 652 (Tex. Civ. App.–Texarkana 1935, writ ref'd); *Dockstader v. Brown*, 204 S.W. 2d 352 (Tex. Civ. App.–Fort Worth 1947, writ ref'd n.r.e.).

Giles and Swan had a specific conversation about Swan closing a real estate transaction. No mention of a joint venture ever took place. Swan did not have the authority to use the power of attorney for the joint venture transfer. As stated in *Giddings, Neiman-Marcus v. Estes*, 440 S.W. 2d 90 (Tex. Civ. App.–Eastland 1969, no writ), "[t]he authority will be construed strictly, so as to exclude the exercise of any power which is not warranted either by the actual terms used or as a necessary means of effecting the authority with effect." Since no authority was conferred on Swan by the document, he could not have acted on Giles's behalf. Consequently, any acts performed by Swan for Giles under the power of attorney are invalid, especially ones (like the joint venture transfer) not anticipated.

Swan told Harris that the power of attorney was for a specific purpose, which was to close the real estate transaction. The law is clear that a third party has a duty to inquire into the scope and fact of the agency, and the burden is on the third party to "ascertain at his peril the nature and scope of the authority of such agent." *Lawrie v. Miller*, 2. S.W. 2d 561 (Tex. Civ. App.–Texarkana 1928, no writ). *See also, Eliot Valve Repair v. Valve*, 675 S.W. 2d 555 (Tex. App.–Houston [1st Dist.] 1984, no writ); *Boucher v. City Paint & Supply*, 398 S.W. 2d 352 (Tex. Civ. App.–Tyler 1966, no writ). It was Harris's responsibility to investigate the extent of Swan's authority. Harris indeed knew the purpose of the power of attorney, but chose to coerce Swan to sign the document under the guise of "friendship." Any acts resulting from Harris's coercion and Swan's misuse of his authority cannot be imputed to Giles, and thus cannot be his responsibility.

The document that Harris is relying upon to effectuate the transfer of the joint venture interest is useless and invalid. The power of attorney does not comply with the requirements for a valid power of attorney, and Swan's actions violated Giles's instructions and interests.

The standard for a summary judgment is that there are no genuine issues of material fact and the moving party is entited to judgment as a matter of law. *Lear Siegler, Inc. v. Perez*, 819 S.W. 2d 470 (Tex. 1991). The facts are undisputed. The power of attorney is blank. It did not, nor could not, confer authority to anyone much less Swan. The law is clear on this point and the court must find for Giles.

YOU BE THE JUDGE

In one case, an appellate court judge refused a motion to file a "fat brief" as he called it. Obviously, the judge was not convinced that the request had merit. In *United States v. Molina-Tarzon,* 285 F.3d 807 (9th Cir. 2002), the attorney represented that he did everything possible to edit his brief to meet the court's page limits. His original brief was thirty pages when the limit was fifteen pages. He submitted a nineteen-page brief with the accompanying motion. The judge chastised the attorney by saying "[c]ounsel's belief that he has exhausted his ability to edit the brief is not a showing of 'diligence and substantial need.' To satisfy the standard, counsel must show that the additional space is justified by something unusual about the issues presented, the record, the applicable case law or some other aspect of the case. Counsel has shown nothing of the sort; nor is it self-evident what this something might be." *Id.* at 808. This case is typical of most judges' disdain for verbose, inarticulate, and often unfounded briefs and motions. Review the case. Why did the judge deny the motion? What are the facts of the case? Were the judge's actions reasonable? Why or why not?

CYBER TRIP

Using your jurisdiction as a guide, determine whether there are page limitations for filing of motions.

requesting relief is sometimes acceptable, particularly for a short trial memorandum, a better approach summarizes the entire argument, crystallizing the legal contentions. Figure 18.9 shows a conclusion that summarizes the argument, and identifies the relief requested.

Signature Block and Certificate of Service

As with all other documents filed with a court, the trial memorandum must be signed by the responsible attorney. As we have noted before, you as a paralegal are not authorized to sign a court document on behalf of a client. The name of the attorney and firm name, address, telephone number, fax, and sometimes a state bar identification number are among the items to be included in a signature block. Figure 18.10 shows an example of an acceptable signature block.

FIGURE 18.9
Conclusion and Requested Relief

Since the purported power of attorney from Giles to Swan did not contain specific authority granted to the agent, the power of attorney is void. Based upon the strict construction doctrine, one cannot construe a grant of authority that is nonexistent. The power of attorney contained neither the name of the agent, the purpose of the agency, nor the authority of the agent; therefore, it could not confer any powers upon the agent. Swan's acts were improper, and Giles is not legally responsible for the effects of those acts. Giles requests that the Motion for Summary Judgment be granted upon the court's finding, as a matter of law, that the transfer of the joint venture interest was invalid and the power of attorney void.

FIGURE 18.10
Signature Block

Respectfully submitted,

____
Nicholas Barron
State Bar #12344567
1234 Main Street, #10030
Dallas, TX 75202
(214) 555-1212
Attorney for Plaintiff

ETHICS ALERT

Throughout this text, you have been consistently reminded of the prohibition of signing pleadings and certain types of letters. Electronic filings present some unique ethical issues that were never considered in the past. The U.S. Court for the Eastern District of Michigan has a section on its Web site that discusses electronic case filing. There is a Frequently Asked Questions section that poses some interesting ethical issues for attorneys and paralegals. One question posed was: "Can an attorney authorize someone in the attorney's office (such as a paralegal) to use the attorney's login name and password to file documents in CM/ECF?" (case management/electronic case filing). The answer from the court's Web site was: "Yes, but access should be limited and controlled since whatever is filed under that login and password is deemed to have the attorney's signature on it." A follow-up question was: "Can any member of the public register to e-file documents with the court?" The response was "No. Only eligible attorneys can register to e-file."

Interesting ethical issues are posed by electronic filings of documents. The assumption for e-filings is that the attorney read the document, filed the document, and is responsible for its content. Recall some of our cases where these issues were addressed. The ultimate responsibility was the attorney's. Since e-filing is a relatively new practice, rules are being developed and the case law is sparse on the issue. As problems arise, the rules behind e-filings will be refined. The advice to you is to pay close attention to the rules of the courts in which you practice; read the case law as it develops on e-filings; and never forget that, as a paralegal, you *do* have restrictions as to what you can and cannot do. Do not allow attorneys to compromise your integrity or ethics. Most bar associations have ethics hotlines for sensitive questions, or you can check with courts' written protocols to determine the parameters of practice.

If a brief or pleading is filed electronically, the courts have rules for the signature block. A typical example of a rule for filing an electronic document and signature is shown in Figure 18.11 from the U.S. District Court for the District of New Jersey. This rule provides for multiple as well as nonattorney signatures.

Likewise, a certificate of service attesting to the fact that copies of the trial memorandum have been sent to other attorneys of record (or parties) must be included. The method of service—ordinary mail, certified mail, hand delivery, or other accepted means—is identified. A simple statement certifying delivery is adequate for the purposes of the certificate; remember, if service ever comes into question, proof will become important. Hence the certified mail option (with a return receipt proving delivery) is better than, say, ordinary mail. Check the rules and practices of your jurisdiction to determine applicable rules and requirements. A typical certificate of service is seen in Figure 18.12.

Since many courts are requiring that documents are filed electronically, the certificate of service must conform to the court's requirements. Review Figure 18.13 for the requirements in the District Court for the Northern District of Ohio.

POSTWRITING REVIEW

As with the prewriting considerations that were discussed earlier in the chapter, the postwriting considerations must be performed as well. Never forget the lessons learned in presenting a final polished document. Your postwriting review should include

- checking for punctuation, spelling, and grammatical errors;
- paying attention to transition and topic sentences;
- reviewing citations for correct format;

FIGURE 18.11
Example of a Rule for Filing an Electronic Document and Signature
Source: U.S. District Court for the District of New Jersey.

14. Signatures.
(a) **Attorney Signatures.** The user login and password required to submit documents to the Electronic Filing System serve as the Filing User's signature on all electronic documents filed with the court. They serve as the signature for purposes of Federal Rules of Civil Procedure 11, all other Federal Rules of Civil Procedure, Federal Rules of Criminal Procedure, and the Local Rules of this court, and any other purpose for which a signature is required in connection with proceedings before the court.

An electronically filed document, or a document submitted on disk or CD-ROM, and in compliance with Local Civil Rules 10.1 and 11.1, must include a signature line with "s/," as shown below.

s/ Jennifer Doe

No Filing User or other person may knowingly permit or cause to permit a Filing User's password to be used by anyone other than an authorized agent of the Filing User.

(b) **Multiple Signatures.** A document requiring signatures of more than one party must be filed electronically either by: (1) submitting a scanned document containing all necessary signatures; or (2) in any other manner approved by the court.

(c) **Non-Attorney Signatures.** A document requiring the signature of a non-attorney must be filed electronically by: (1) submitting a scanned document containing all necessary signatures; or (2) in any other manner approved by the court.

15. Retention Requirements.
A document that is electronically filed and requires an original signature other than that of the Filing User must be maintained in paper form by the ECF Filing User and/or the firm representing the party on whose behalf the document was filed until one year after all periods for appeals expire. On request of the court, the ECF Filing User or law firm must provide the original document.

PRACTICE TIP

Remember from Chapters 3 and 14 that many courts dictate the correct form for citations. Do not assume a court follows *The Bluebook* or *ALWD*. Remember that a number of jurisdictions have adopted the universal citation format. Citations should conform to the local rules of the court in which you intend to file your brief.

- checking that quotations are properly cited;
- incorporating the facts with the law;
- editing the document for conciseness and precision;
- reviewing the redraft and re-editing the document;
- revising the final draft;
- complying with court rules for preparing briefs and submitting attachments;
- checking length, font size, and margins of brief; and
- filing deadlines with court.

FIGURE 18.12
Certificate of Service
Source: U.S. District Court for the District of New Jersey.

CERTIFICATE OF SERVICE

I certify that a true copy of the Memorandum of Law in Support of Plaintiff's Motion for Summary Judgment was served on Jane Smith, Attorney for Defendant, at 111 Main Street, Suite 123, Ft. Worth, Texas, by certified mail, return receipt requested, in accordance with the Texas Rules of Civil Procedure on May 12, 2008.

____
Nicholas Barron

The following is a suggested certificate of service for electronic filing:

Certificate of Service

I hereby certify that on [date], a copy of foregoing [name of document] was filed electronically. Notice of this filing will be sent by operation of the Court's electronic filing system to all parties indicated on the electronic filing receipt. All other parties will be served by regular U.S. mail. Parties may access this filing through the Court's system.

s/ [Name of Password Registrant]
Name of Password Registrant
Address
City, State, Zip Code
Phone: (xxx) xxx-xxxx
Fax: (xxx) xxx-xxxx
E-mail: xxx@xxx.xxx
[attorney bar number, if applicable]

It is the responsibility of the filing party to ensure that all other parties are properly served. Fed. R. Civ. P. 5(b)(3) notes that service by electronic means is not effective if the party making service learns that the attempted service did not reach the person to be served. If a party requiring service is not listed on the electronic filing receipt as having been sent an electronic notice of the filing, the filing party must serve that party by other appropriate means.

FIGURE 18.13
Certificate of Service Requirements for Electronic Filings in the Northern District of Ohio

Source: U.S. District Court Northern District of Ohio, available at www.ohnd.uscourts.gov/Clerk_s_Office/Local_Rules/Civil_Rules06_05_06.pdf.

Quick Quiz True/False Questions

1. A trial memorandum contains a caption.
2. All jurisdictions require an introduction to the court section.
3. The statement of facts in a trial memorandum is persuasive.
4. A method of guiding a judge through an argument section is through the use of point headings.
5. A trial memorandum contains a signature block and certificate of service.

A DAY IN THE LIFE OF A PARALEGAL

Most motions and memoranda of law in support of a motion have attachments, such as affidavits or exhibits. It is usually the function of the paralegal to prepare the final motion and brief with the accompanying attachments. You prepare the motion, brief, and attachments for filing with the court. The documents are messengered to the court clerk for filing, but you failed to hole-punch the documents as well as **bates stamp** the exhibits. The court rejects your document for filing and the messenger does not bring them back until after 5:00 p.m. You have missed your filing deadline. What are you to do?

There are two lessons to be learned here. The first lesson is when a deadline is missed, you must immediately notify your supervising attorney. He will handle the situation. Do not handle the matter yourself as you could make it worse.

The second lesson is that many courts have rules for submitting motions with briefs and attachments. Always check the rules of court, including the local rules for filing requirements. With the filing requirements changing with the advent of electronic filing of legal documents, it is imperative to stay current regarding the filing requirements for each court in which one of your cases may be filed. To miss a deadline could be tantamount to malpractice. Read, read, and reread those court rules.

bates stamp
A self-inking stamp system that sequentially numbers documents.

THE E-FACTOR

Electronic filing of briefs presents unique issues for the paralegal and attorney. Many courts have limitations on the size of the electronic file. If your brief and supporting documents exceed the megabytes requirement, then the document must be filed manually. Often you will need to file a notice of manual filing when you file a document manually. Most courts provide an example of this document. Figure 18.14 is a sample notice of manual filing. The courts make it quite clear that a document filed manually does not excuse untimely filing of the entire submission. Since e-filing is becoming mandatory in most federal courts, stay current on your jurisdiction's requirements.

Another e-filing issue requiring attention is privacy. As so many individuals have been victims of identity theft, personal information about parties to a case should be **redacted,** when possible. Redacted is the fancy way of saying "taken out." Balancing the public's rights to know against the privacy and security of litigants is a fine line. Courts warn attorneys not to include sensitive information in documents filed with the court. Courts suggest redacting "personal data identifiers" such as

- Social Security numbers;
- financial account numbers;
- dates of birth;
- names of minor children; and
- (in criminal cases only) home addresses.

(See U.S. District Court Northern District of Ohio Electronic Filing Policies and Procedures Manual, January 1, 2006.)

Although e-filing has many attributes, such as twenty-four-hour, seven-day-a-week filing capabilities, reduced use of paper clutter in court files, and instantaneous access to court documents, the technical glitches we all experience are not eliminated. There are help desks and trainings for use of the "new" e-filing systems. Understanding the process and how that process interacts with the rules of court will take time for those just introduced to the world of law and legalese. Do not get frustrated. Ask questions, review the court Web sites, and get trained. E-filings are here to stay, so learn the process and rules.

FIGURE 18.14
Sample Notice of Manual Filing
Source: U.S. District Court Northern District of Ohio, available at www.ohnd.uscourts.gov/Clerk_s_ Office/Local_Rules/Civil_Rules06_05_06.pdf.

redacted
Eliminated from a legal document due to privacy and security matters.

<u>**Appendix C**</u>

UNITED STATES DISTRICT COURT
NORTHERN DISTRICT OF OHIO

	)	
	)	
Plaintiff	)	Case No.
	)	
v.	)	Judge
	)	
Defendant	)	Notice of Manual Filing
	)	
	)	

Please take notice that [Plaintiff/Defendant, Name of Party] has manually filed the following document or thing

[Title of Document or Thing]

This document has not been filed electronically because

the document or thing cannot be converted to an electronic format; the electronic file size of the document exceeds 1.5 megabytes (about 15 scanned pages).
[Plaintiff/Defendant] is excused from filing this document or thing by court order.

The document or thing has been manually served on all parties.

Respectfully submitted,
s/ [Name of Password Registrant]
Name of Password Registrant
Address
City, State, Zip Code
Phone: (xxx) xxx-xxxx
Fax: (xxx) xxx-xxxx
E-mail: xxx@xxx.xxx
[attorney bar number, if applicable]

PRACTICAL CONSIDERATIONS: SOME FINAL TIPS

A trial memorandum is an important document in the litigation process, because if properly drafted it can resolve issues in your favor and begin to turn the lawsuit toward your client. Furthermore, since the amount at issue in many cases will not justify the expense of an extended appeals process, prevailing at the trial level is often the guarantee of prevailing once and for all.

An example of a completed trial memorandum appears as Figure 18.15. In general, you should keep in mind the following points when preparing a trial memorandum:

- Check for local jurisdictional requirements about format or content.
- Identify your purpose.
- Aways draft from your client's perspective.
- Present the law honestly and accurately, but with a partisan slant.
- Identify all significant facts, and present them in a manner that minimizes the opposition's strong points and paints a memorable picture of your client's position.
- Write convincingly, using effective and persuasive writing techniques.
- Be clear, precise, and concise.
- Tell the judge what result and relief you seek.

FIGURE 18.15
Memorandum of Law to the Trial Court

IN THE DISTRICT COURT OF DALLAS COUNTY, TEXAS
101st JUDICIAL DISTRICT

STEPHEN GILES	§	
	§	
Plaintiff	§	
	§	
vs.	§	No. 12344
	§	
GEORGE HARRIS	§	
	§	
Defendant	§	

MEMORANDUM OF LAW IN SUPPORT OF PLAINTIFF'S MOTION FOR SUMMARY JUDGMENT

TO THE HONORABLE JUDGE OF SAID COURT:

STEPHEN GILES, Plaintiff, files this Memorandum of Law to the Trial Court in Support of Plaintiff's Motion for Summary Judgment and would show unto the Court as follows:

Issue Presented

No issues of fact exist in a transaction where an unauthorized agent used a blank power of attorney to act on behalf of the Plaintiff, the principal.

Cont.

FIGURE 18.15
Memorandum of Law to the Trial Court
Cont.

Statement of Facts

The facts in the case are undisputed. Mr. Giles went to a holiday party on November 20, at the home of Mr. Swan, a business associate. Mr. Swan had been Mr. Giles's friend and attorney for some time. Giles was going out of town for Thanksgiving and would not be back until the first of the new year. Giles wanted to purchase a piece of real estate before the end of the year, but was going out of town. The only business discussion that evening concerned the real estate transaction.

Swan suggested that Giles could execute a power of attorney, with Swan as Giles's representative. The gentlemen went into Swan's study and Giles signed a document entitled "Power of Attorney." Neither man filled in any information in the document. Swan's name did not appear anywhere on the document. Swan kept the Power of Attorney in his top desk drawer. Giles went on his trip.

While Giles was on his trip, one of his partners, Mr. Harris, contacted Swan regarding a joint venture transaction completely unrelated to the real estate transaction. Giles and Harris had been discussing dissolving the joint venture, with Giles acquiring Harris's interest. Swan knew nothing about this transaction.

Harris stated to Swan that Giles was supposed to assume all Harris's interest in the joint venture before January 1. Harris inquired whether Swan could help him. Swan told Harris that he had a power of attorney to close a real estate transaction, but did not know how he could help Harris out.

Harris asked Swan to use the power of attorney to transfer the joint venture interest. Harris told Swan this would save his friend some money. Swan continued to tell Harris that he only had authority to close a real estate transaction. Harris, however, was able to persuade Swan to execute the transfer of the joint venture interest, using the power of attorney on December 29.

When Giles came back to town, Swan informed him of the transfer from Harris and told him that he had used the power of attorney. Giles was enraged and told Swan he had no authority to transfer the interest. Giles wanted the transaction rescinded.

Argument

This case presents a unique question of law which is what is the authority granted a principal by an agent when the power of attorney is blank. The answer is none. Any acts performed by a principal with a blank power of attorney are void. It is clear that a power of attorney must set forth the authority and the name of the principal and agent. The document before this court does neither.

The law on this matter is well settled in Texas and dates back to the 1880s. To determine the validity of the power of attorney and the extent of the authority granted, certain rules of construction and interpretation must be addressed. The leading case of *Gouldy v. Metcalf*, 75 Tex. 455, 12 S.W. 830 (1889), sets out the rules of construction for a power of attorney, which are:

> [w]hen an authority is conferred upon an agent by a formal instrument, as by a power of attorney, there are two rules of construction to be carefully adhered to:
>
> 1. The meaning of general words in the instrument will be restricted by the context, and construed accordingly.
> 2. The authority will be construed strictly, so as to exclude the exercise of any power which is not warranted, either by the actual terms used or as a necessary means of executing the authority with effect.
> *Id.* at 458.

Expanding the guidelines set forth in *Gouldy*, case law establishes that "all powers conferred upon an agent by a formal instrument are to receive a strict interpretation, and the authority is never extended by intendment or construction beyond that which is given in terms, or is necessary for carrying the authority into effect, and the authority must be strictly pursued." *Bean v. Bean,* 79 S.W. 2d 652 (Tex. Civ. App.–Texarkana 1935, writ ref'd); *Dockstader v. Brown,* 204 S.W. 2d 352 (Tex. Civ. App.–Fort Worth 1947, writ ref'd n.r.e.).

Cont.

FIGURE 18.15
Memorandum of Law to the Trial Court
Cont.

Giles and Swan had a specific conversation about Swan closing a real estate transaction. No mention of a joint venture ever took place. Swan did not have the authority to use the power of attorney for the joint venture transfer. As stated in *Giddings, Neiman-Marcus v. Estes*, 440 S.W. 2d 90 (Tex. Civ. App.–Eastland 1969, no writ), "[t]he authority will be construed strictly, so as to exclude the exercise of any power which is not warranted either by the actual terms used or as a necessary means of effecting the authority with effect." Since no authority was conferred on Swan by the document, he could not have acted on Giles's behalf. Consequently, any acts performed by Swan for Giles under the power of attorney are invalid, especially ones (like the joint venture transfer) not anticipated.

Swan told Harris that the power of attorney was for a specific purpose, which was to close the real estate transaction. The law is clear that a third party has a duty to inquire into the scope and fact of the agency, and the burden is on the third party to "ascertain at his peril the nature and scope of the authority of such agent." *Lawrie v. Miller*, 2 S.W. 2d 561 (Tex. Civ. App.–Texarkana 1928, no writ). *See also, Eliot Valve Repair v. Valve*, 675 S.W. 2d 555 (Tex. App.–Houston [1st Dist.] 1984, no writ); *Boucher v. City Paint & Supply*, 398 S.W. 2d 352 (Tex. Civ. App.–Tyler 1966, no writ). It was Harris's responsibility to investigate the extent of Swan's authority. Harris indeed knew the purpose of the power of attorney, but chose to coerce Swan to sign the document under the guise of "friendship." Any acts resulting from Harris's coercion and Swan's misuse of his authority cannot be imputed to Giles, and thus cannot be his responsibility.

The document that Harris is relying upon to effectuate the transfer of the joint venture interest is useless and invalid. The power of attorney does not comply with the requirements for a valid power of attorney, and Swan's actions violated Giles's instructions and interests.

The standard for a summary judgment is that there are no genuine issues of material fact and the moving party is entited to judgment as a matter of law. *Lear Siegler, Inc. v. Perez*, 819 S.W. 2d 470 (Tex. 1991). The facts are undisputed. The power of attorney is blank. It did not, nor could not, confer authority to anyone much less Swan. The law is clear on this point and the court must find for Giles.

Conclusion and Requested Relief

Since the purported power of attorney from Giles to Swan did not contain any specific authority granted to the agent, the power of attorney is void. Based upon the strict construction doctrine, one cannot construe a grant of authority that is nonexistent. The power of attorney contained neither the name of the agent, the purpose of the agency, nor the authority of the agent, and therefore it could not confer any powers upon the agent. Swan's acts were therefore improper, and Giles is not legally responsible for the effects of those acts. Giles requests that the Motion for Summary Judgment be granted upon the court's finding, as a matter of law, that the transfer of the joint venture interest was invalid and the power of attorney void.

Respectfully submitted,

____

Nicholas Barron
State Bar #12344567
1234 Main Street, #10030
Dallas, Texas 75202
(214) 555-1212
Attorney for Plaintiff

CERTIFICATE OF SERVICE

I certify that a true copy of the Memorandum of Law in Support of Plaintiff's Motion for Summary Judgment was served on Jane Smith, Attorney for Defendant, at 111 Main Street, Suite 123, Fort Worth, Texas, by certified mail, return receipt requested, in accordance with the Texas Rules of Civil Procedure on May 12, 2008.

____

Nicholas Barron, Esq.

Summary

The memorandum of law to the trial court is an adversarial document written to persuade a trial court on a disputed issue of law. It is also known as a trial memorandum, and other similar names, depending on the jurisdiction. The audience for a trial memorandum consists of the judge, who will read it fairly but must be convinced, and opposing counsel, who will read it looking to attack logical holes and unjustified analytical leaps. Be accurate but partisan in drafting a trial memorandum.

There are three broad categories of trial memoranda: the memorandum in regard to a motion; the memorandum prepared at the request of a judge; and the unsolicited memorandum that anticipates and addresses key legal issues. All are drafted with an adversarial purpose, designed to persuade a judge that a disputed question of law should be resolved in favor of a particular party.

There are several components to a trial memorandum. First come the caption, title, and introduction to the court. Next, in the issues presented section, the drafter presents the legal questions raised in a manner that suggests a resolution in favor of the client on whose behalf the drafter is working. Similarly, the statement of facts should state all events accurately, but with a slant toward the position of the client. The argument is the heart of the trial memorandum, presenting the results of the drafter's research in an adversarial argument designed to persuade the court of the superiority of the client's contentions. The conclusion summarizes the argument and identifies the relief sought. It is followed by a signature block and a certificate of service.

A properly drafted trial memorandum is an important part of the litigation process. Indeed, since appeals are often too expensive for clients to pursue, drafting effective trial memoranda can lead to a victory in the trial court that stands once and for all.

Key Terms

arguments
bates stamp
issues or questions presented
memorandum at the request of a judge
memorandum in regard to a motion
memorandum of law to the trial court
point headings
redacted
statement of facts
subheadings
unsolicited memorandum anticipating legal issues

Review Questions

1. Who are the two audiences for a trial memorandum?
2. How should a trial memorandum be prepared to assist a judge?
3. How should a trial memorandum be drafted to minimize the impact of the attack of opposing counsel?
4. What are the characteristics of a trial memorandum prepared in regard to a motion?
5. Why might a judge request a trial memorandum?
6. What is the potential importance of an unsolicited trial memorandum that anticipates issues?
7. What is the importance to a trial memorandum of the caption and the title?
8. From what perspective is the issues or questions presented section of a trial memorandum prepared?

9. What are the four objectives of a statement of facts?
10. What is the difference between the discussion section of an internal memorandum and the argument section of a trial memorandum?

Exercises

1. Assume that your attorney has been served with a request to produce tax returns in a personal injury case in your jurisdiction. Go to the library and research whether the tax returns are protected information. Then prepare the argument section of the memorandum of law to the trial court, requesting an order that the documents not be produced.
2. Determine for your jurisdiction the format for a trial memorandum. Check both the state and federal requirements.
3. Louis Harris is a resident of Florida and files a lawsuit against George Hillary of Miami, Florida, in the U.S. District Court in Miami, Florida, based upon diversity jurisdiction. Mr. Harris claims that on July 31, 2008, Mr. Hillary negligently hit Harris's Airstream trailer, damaging it in the amount of $75,000. Mr. Hillary's attorney, Jonathan Lineman, files a motion to dismiss based upon lack of diversity jurisdiction. Prepare the motion to dismiss and brief in support of the motion.
4. Laura Coleman filed an age and sexual discrimination lawsuit against her employer, Designers Corporation. She claimed in an affidavit that she was over forty-five years old and that on May 12, 2008, her supervisor, Carlton Peterson, made sexual advances, which she rejected, and on June 15, 2008, Mr. Petersen kissed Coleman on the cheek. Through investigation, Designers determined that Coleman is really forty years old. Coleman deliberately lied on her affidavit. Had the attorney performed minimum investigation, Coleman's attorney would have known that the allegation in the affidavit was untruthful. Designers' attorney wants to file a motion for sanctions against coleman. Prepare the motion for sanctions and brief in support of the motion.
5. The time has passed for responses to interrogatories in *Paradise Paving Company v. Discount Wholesalers, Inc.* Prepare the motion to compel and brief on behalf of Paradise. Assume the case is filed in the U.S. district court in Rhode Island.
6. Paradise Paving Company (from exercise 5) notices the president of Discount Wholesalers, Avery Pennington, for a deposition on May 27, 2008. Mr. Pennington is very busy and cannot attend the deposition. The case involves nonpayment for paving services on a parking lot in one of Discount's Providence stores. Prepare the motion for protective order and brief in support of the motion.
7. Community Nursing Home has not paid its utility bill for electricity and water in six months. It now owes $275,000. Revenues have been down at the nursing home. South Carolina Water Power Authority sent Community a demand letter dated August 15, 2008, requesting payment of the outstanding balance signed by the chief financial officer (CFO) Harvey Buckman. Assume the Authority sued the nursing home. Prepare the interrogatories and requests for admission on behalf of the utility company.
8. Using the facts from exercise 7, prepare the motion for summary judgment, affidavit of Harvey Buckman, CFO, and the brief in support of the motion. (Hint: Determine what you need to prove to support the case, such as the outstanding balance.)

PORTFOLIO ASSIGNMENT

Using the facts from the Portfolio Assignment in Chapter 17, Mrs. Dana Marsh has requested that your office bring this matter to a close. Your supervising attorney has assigned you to complete the following tasks:

1. Prepare a motion for summary judgment, supporting affidavits and memorandum of law in support of plaintiff's motion for summary judgment against A1 Delivery Service, Inc., and Herbert Killington.

   Assume that A1 and Killington have received the motion and must now file a reply as part of this assignment.

2. Prepare the response to the motion and brief in opposition to the summary judgment. Remember, you must submit evidence to support your motion, such as interrogatory and admission responses. Affidavits are important as well. An opposition also must have evidence, such as an affidavit of Herb Killington or a representative of A1. Get creative.

Quick Quiz True/False Answers

Page 547

1. False
2. False
3. True
4. True
5. False

Page 559

1. True
2. False
3. True
4. True
5. True

Chapter 19

The Appellate Brief

After completing this chapter, you will be able to:

- Explain the importance of following the appellate rules.
- Explain the function of the appellate brief.
- Identify the components of the record on appeal.
- Differentiate errors of fact from errors of law.
- Describe the jurisdictional statement section of an appellate brief.
- Explain the "road map" function of the table of contents.
- Identify two key points to remember in drafting the statement of facts section.
- Use point headings to divide the body of your brief into distinct segments.
- Draft a persuasive appellate argument.
- Distinguish between an appellant's brief, an appellee's brief, a reply brief, and an amicus curiae brief.

Writing an appellate brief is an art. Learning how to frame issues and write with just the right amount of passion and persuasiveness requires time and patience. In appellate brief writing, the record must be mastered, the legal standards researched, and the rules of the court followed to the letter. You will participate in all aspects of the preparation of an appellate brief whether your firm represents the appellant or the appellee. As a paralegal, it is your job to assist your supervising attorney in this process. This final chapter concludes with the last stage of the legal process and incorporates all the skills learned in this textbook. Let's begin the final stage of the process.

CASE FACT PATTERN

Closing arguments have concluded in a court trial in which you have been the assisting paralegal, and the judge informs counsel that a decision will be rendered after trial briefs are submitted. Briefs are then filed and both sides nervously await the result.

Within a week the decision arrives in your office mail. The judge has denied the permanent injunction sought by your supervising attorney—in short, your client has lost. The supervising attorney reviews the opinion, determines that there are valid reasons to question the judge's reasoning, consults with the client, and decides that she will file an appeal.

The next morning there is a memorandum on your desk. You have been assigned to assist in the legal research and preparation of the appellate brief.

Source: © King Features Syndicate.

A PRELIMINARY NOTE ABOUT PROCEDURAL RULES

Although this chapter addresses the preparation of the appellate brief, a proper examination of that subject requires that we consider two preliminary steps essential to *all* phases of an appeal, from its initiation through the briefing phase, and even beyond. These preliminary steps relate to the content of the rules of your specific jurisdiction.

Appealing the decision of a trial court is a complicated process. It involves extensive technical requirements. Before the appellate court will review your client's arguments, it must be satisfied that post trial motions, briefs, and other filings comply with specific, detailed criteria. This is true in every appellate court, state and federal. Figure 19.1 provides a diagram of the appellate process in the federal court system.

appellate rules
Procedures set forth by the appeals court in processing an appeal.

Fortunately, these criteria are spelled out in the **appellate rules** of each jurisdiction. Although there are many broad similarities among the rules of various appellate courts, a word of caution is in order. There are often significant differences in specific formats, filing deadlines, and other particulars. Furthermore, the rules can be strict in their requirements (see Figure 19.2, which reproduces a section of the federal circuit requirements of Rule 32). Failure to follow with precision the rules that apply to your jurisdiction can be fatal to your appeal. Never assume anything; check to make sure.

The *first step* in pursuing an appeal, then, is to obtain a copy of the applicable rules of your jurisdiction, and to verify that they are current.

The *second step,* having obtained the current rules, is obvious but commonly disregarded. Simply stated, you must read the rules, and make sure you understand them.

The importance of the two steps cannot be overemphasized for the preparation of the appellate brief as well as every other aspect of an appeal. They are critical. Although the attorney for whom you work is ultimately responsible for compliance with the rules, your value as an assisting paralegal is directly related to your ability to follow the detailed requirements that govern the appeal process.

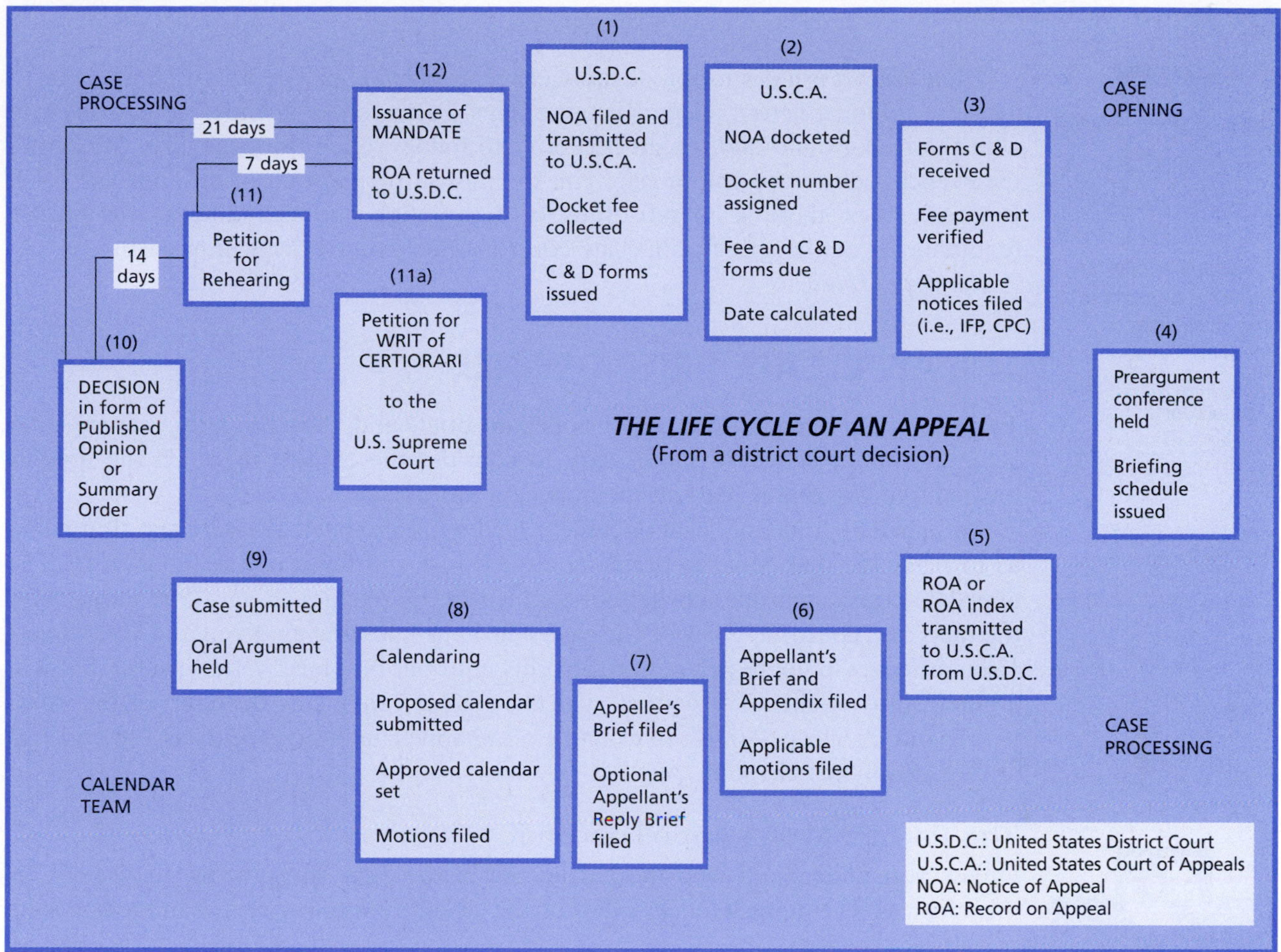

FIGURE 19.1 **Diagram of Appellate Process in the Federal Court System**

Source: U.S. Court of Appeals for the Seventh Circuit.

FIGURE 19.2 **Appellate Brief Requirements**

<u>**Federal Rules of Appellate Procedure**</u>

Rule 32. Form of Briefs, the Appendix, and Other Papers

(a) Form of Briefs and the Appendix. Briefs and appendices may be produced by standard typographic printing or by any duplicating or copying process which produces a clear black image on white paper. Carbon copies of briefs and appendices may not be submitted without permission of the court, except in behalf of parties allowed to proceed in forma pauperis. All printed matter must appear in at least 11 point type on opaque, unglazed paper. Briefs and appendices produced by the standard typographic process shall be bound in volumes having pages 6 1/8 by 9 1/4 inches and type matter 4 1/6 by 7 1/6 inches. Those produced by any other process shall be bound in volumes having pages not exceeding 8 1/2 by 11 inches and type matter not exceeding 6 1/2 by 9 1/2 inches, with double spacing between each line of text. In patent cases the pages of briefs and appendices may be of such size as is necessary to utilize copies of patent documents. Copies of the reporter's transcript and other papers reproduced in a manner authorized by this rule may be inserted in the appendix; such pages may be informally renumbered if necessary.

If briefs are produced by commercial printing or duplicating firms, or, if produced otherwise and the covers to be described are available, the cover of the brief of the appellant should be blue; that of the appellee, red; that of an intervenor or *amicus curiae*, green; that of any reply brief, gray. The cover of the appendix, if separately printed, should be white. The front covers of the briefs and of appendices, if separately printed, shall contain: (1) the name of the court and the number of the case; (2) the title of the case (see Rule 12(a)); (3) the nature of the proceeding in the court (e.g., Appeal; Petition for Review) and the name of the court, agency, or board below; (4) the title of the document (e.g., Brief for Appellant, Appendix); and (5) the names and addresses of counsel representing the party on whose behalf the document is filed.

CYBER TRIP

Locate the appellate rules of procedure for filing an appellate brief in both your federal and state courts.

What follows is a discussion of those elements of an appellate brief that are in large measure uniform across all jurisdictions. This discussion is intended to provide you with the background and insight necessary to follow your own local rules. Mastering the elements described will prepare you to assist in preparation of an appellate brief. But remember: there is no substitute for a thorough understanding of the precise requirements of the specific appellate court in which your brief will be filed.

Know the rules!

THE APPELLATE BRIEF DEFINED

To understand the purpose of an appellate brief, and thus properly prepare it to achieve your objective, it is necessary to consider the context in which the brief is drafted and the role it plays in the appellate process.

appellate brief
Brief filed in an appeals court.

An **appellate brief** is a legal document filed with an appellate court and drafted so as to persuade that court to decide contested issues in favor of the filing party. The appellate court uses the appellate briefs filed by the parties to gain familiarity with the facts and controlling law of the case. The appellate brief that you and your supervising attorney prepare will not present this information objectively, however, but will argue from your client's viewpoint, with the goal of convincing the court of the validity of your client's position. An example of an appellate brief appears as Figure 19.12 at the end of this chapter.

The Parties to the Appellate Brief

Unless you understand who the parties are in the appellate process, the process is meaningless. Therefore, a quick review of the labels given to the parties in the appellate process is necessary.

PRACTICE TIP

The notice of appeal is normally filed with the trial court clerk and not the appellate court unless court rules dictate otherwise.

The Appellant

The appellant is the party who is dissatisfied with the lower court's decision and begins the process by filing a request for appeal or Notice of Appeal. This notice informs the parties and the trial court of the appeal. An example of a notice of appeal is presented in Figure 19.3. The notice begins the appellate process. When the notice of appeal is properly filed, the succession of deadline dates begins. A deadline missed by an appellant could risk dismissal of the appeal. This point reinforces what was stated earlier in the chapter: "Know the rules!"

The Appellee

The appellee is the party responding to the appeal. The appellee is satisfied with the decision of the lower court, and for all practical purposes, doesn't want to be involved. Although critical, the appellee does not drive the process like the appellant. The appellee wants the result of the lower court to be affirmed; remember, she already has a favorable decision.

Petitioner and Respondent

petitioner
Name designation of the party filing an appeal.

respondent
Name designation of the party responding to an appeal.

Many appellate courts designate the parties by the terms **petitioner** and **respondent.** The petitioner is the party appealing the lower court's decision, whereas the respondent is, as the name suggests, responding to the appeal. The rules of the particular appellate court tell you the proper party designation. Review the appellate court rules in your jurisdiction for the proper terms.

After reviewing the arguments set forth in the briefs, the appellate court often allows the parties to elaborate on their positions in oral argument. The attorneys appear before the court and verbally present their competing positions, emphasizing

Form 1. Notice of Appeal to the United States Court of Appeals for the Federal Circuit from a Judgment or Order of a United States District Court

Name of United States District Court for the____________________

Case Number____________________

__________________________, Plaintiff,

v. **NOTICE OF APPEAL**

__________________________, Defendant.

Notice is hereby given that __________________________ (name all parties* taking the appeal) in the above named case hereby appeal to the United States Court of Appeals for the Federal Circuit from the ______________________________ (from the final judgment) ((from an order) (describe the order)) entered in this action on _____________, _____ (date).

____
(Signature of appellant or attorney)

____
(Address of appellant or attorney)

FIGURE 19.3
Notice of Appeal
**See* Fed. R. App. P. 3(c) for permissible ways of identifying appellants.

the strong points and clarifying any complex or confusing points. The oral argument stage also enables the appellate judges to directly question the attorneys on specific points that require further explanation.

The appellate court will not always allow oral argument, however. Thus, you must prepare the appellate brief as if it is your only opportunity to present your client's position. Use skill and care; each word must count.

There are two key elements of the context in which the appellate brief is filed: (1) the record and (2) the standard of review.

The Record

At trial, having defined the disputed issues in the pleadings, the parties began the presentation of evidence with a blank slate. They could bring to the attention of the court any and all facts that were relevant and material, and were free to cite to any and all legal authorities deemed applicable. With a few technical exceptions, such as failure to disclose information during the discovery stage (which need not concern us here), there were generally no prior restraints on the introduction of evidence, nor was there any limitation on the right to formulate legal arguments.

The situation is quite different on appeal. The parties do not start with a blank slate in an appellate court. *No* new evidence is presented on appeal. The appellate court considers only whether, based upon the evidence and legal arguments already offered in the trial court, the trial court in fact reached the correct conclusion. If a particular piece of evidence or legal argument was not at least offered in the trial court, as a rule it will not be considered by the appellate court.

PRACTICE TIP

When a litigant is unrepresented by an attorney, you will see the term *pro se* used. According to *Black's Law Dictionary,* fifth edition, page 1099 (West Publishing 1979), *pro se* means for himself or in his own behalf. Either party may be represented *pro se. Pro se* parties are often seen in the criminal setting at the appellate level. In *Fischer v. Cingular Wireless, LLC,* 446 F.3d 663 (7th Cir. 2006) U.S. App. LEXIS 10790, decided May 1, 2006 (7th Cir. 2006), the plaintiff was *pro se* and is identified by the court with that label by stating "Donna Fischer filed a suit *pro se* against her former employer, Cingular, charging age and sex discrimination." *Id.* at *1.

record
Documentation of the trial court, including pleadings, physical evidence, transcript, and decision of the trial court.

This brings us to consideration of the **record.** The record is the documentation of the trial, including pleadings; briefs; physical evidence introduced; a transcript of the proceedings, including all witness testimony and judge's rulings on admissibility of evidence and testimony, and the decision of the trial court. It is the record on which the appellate court will rely in evaluating the appeal. A consideration of the individual components of the record is worthwhile.

Pleadings

pleadings
Formal documents filed with the court that establish the claims and defenses of the parties to the lawsuit; the complaint, answer to complaint, and reply.

The **pleadings** appearing in the record include the complaint, which defines the underlying claim; the answer and special defenses, which define the response to the complaint; and all cross-claims and responses thereto. The pleadings establish the bounds of the lawsuit.

Briefs

The briefs filed by the parties in the lower court are often part of the record as well, and can set the stage for the legal arguments addressed in the appellate court.

Discovery

Interrogatories, requests for admission, and deposition testimony may be included as part of the record. This information is of particular importance in appeals of motions for summary judgment when the only evidence consists of affidavits, responses to interrogatories, admissions, and deposition testimony.

Physical Evidence

All exhibits admitted into evidence by the trial court, as well as those exhibits offered into evidence but denied admission by the trial court, are part of the record. The issues on appeal often result from the trial court's rulings on admissibility of the physical evidence.

Transcript

transcript
Written account of a trial court proceeding or deposition.

court reporter
Individual who transcribes the court proceedings and certifies their authenticity.

The **transcript** is a written account of all proceedings in the trial court, including questions and comments of the attorneys; witness testimony; and the judge's rulings and comments. The transcript is usually a stenographic record created by a **court reporter** (who is a court employee certified to record and transcribe court proceedings).

Decision of the Trial Court

The decision of the trial court, and any written opinion of the judge explaining her reasoning, is always a part of the record.

Motion Practice in the Court of Appeals

Unlike the trial courts, motion practice is limited in the court of appeals. There are, however, specific procedures to follow if a motion is filed. The following motions are typical in the court of appeals:

- Motions to accelerate appeal. This motion is only used in limited circumstances, such as in an injunction situation where one party may suffer harm if the process is prolonged.
- Motion to dismiss. Either party may file a motion to dismiss. Issues may change; the appeal may be untimely; the court may not have jurisdiction.

YOU BE THE JUDGE  **Hypothetical 19.2**

In *Independent Towers of Washington v. State of Washington,* 350 F.3d 925 (9th Cir. 2003), the judge ripped into the attorneys for their poorly written brief as well as their failure to articulate well-defined legal arguments. The court refused to search through the briefs to find the arguments. The judge's stinging comments regarding Independent Towers of Washington's (ITOW) brief were: "[w]hen reading ITOW's brief, one wonders if ITOW, in its own version of the 'spaghetti approach,' has heaved the entire contents of a pot against the wall in hopes that something would stick. We decline, however, to sort through the noodles in search of ITOW's claim." *Id.* at 929. The court continued its comments by citing a Seventh Circuit case "in its now familiar maxim, 'judges are not like pigs, hunting for truffles buried in briefs.'" *Id.* at 929 citing *United States v. Dunkel,* 927 F.2d 955, 956 (7th Cir. 1991). The court continued its comments by observing, "[t]he art of advocacy is not one of mystery. Our adversarial system relies on the advocates to inform the discussion and raise the issues to the court. Particularly on appeal, we have held firm against considering arguments that are not briefed. But the term 'briefed' in the appellate context does not mean opaque nor is it an exercise in issue spotting. However much we may importune lawyers to be brief and get to the point, we have never suggested that they skip the substance of their argument in order to do so." *Id.* at 929-30. Review the case. What was the court's disposition in the case? Were all the issues raised by the attorneys decided on appeal? What was the court's reasoning in the case? Be sure all issues are articulated not only at the trial level but in the appellate brief as well.

- Motion to supplement the record. Additional information may be required to be filed. You cannot file additional information without permission of the court.
- Motion to file a longer brief. If the brief is anticipated to be longer than the rules permit, a motion requesting permission to file a longer brief is required, or the party risks sanctions being imposed by the court.

PRACTICE TIP

A motion must be filed under particular rules of the court and may have a special color cover sheet to identify it as a motion. Do not risk rejection of a motion for failure to comply with the rules.

The Standard of Review

As stated, the issue on appeal is whether, based on the evidence and legal arguments presented at trial, the trial court decided the case correctly. You and your supervising attorney will be scouring the record to determine whether the lower court made any errors in reaching its conclusion.

If errors are found and an appeal taken, the appellate court must then evaluate these alleged errors and determine whether reversal of the lower court's decision is justified or, rather, that the lower court be upheld. The guideline that the court applies in evaluating the alleged errors is called the **standard of review.**

standard of review
Guideline the court applies in evaluating the errors on appeal.

There are two types of error to which a standard of review must be applied: errors of fact and errors of law.

Errors of Fact

The parties at trial often present competing versions of the facts. The trial court must sift through the evidence and decide which version of the facts is correct. The party whose version was not accepted by the trial court has the right to appeal the decision, on the ground that the facts as found by the trial court are not supported by the evidence that was admitted—in other words, that there was an **error of fact.** The standard of review by which the appellate court evaluates such an appeal, however, is extremely difficult to satisfy. In general, an appellate court shows great deference to the trial court's judgment with regard to fact finding. Only if the facts found by the court are wholly unsupported by the record can a decision be overturned based on errors of fact. For example, a trial court's factual findings with regard to an injunction application (as in our Case Fact Pattern) will be overturned in most jurisdictions only if the appellate court finds that the trial court's interpretation of the facts constituted an **abuse of discretion,** meaning that it was completely unreasonable and not logically based upon the facts.

error of fact
Legal standard on appeal alleging the facts accepted by the trial court judge are incorrect.

abuse of discretion
Standard of review on appeal that a judge's decision is unreasonable and not logically based upon the facts.

Errors of Law

error of law
Standard of review on appeal alleging error of the court in applying the standards of the law.

The more common basis of appeal is an **error of law.** Errors of law include procedural errors, in which the trial court allowed the lawsuit to proceed in a manner not authorized by the rules; evidentiary errors, where the court admitted evidence that should have been excluded, or excluded evidence that should have been admitted; and substantive errors, where the court incorrectly interpreted the specific rules of law applicable to the facts of the case. Procedural or evidentiary errors must be shown to have caused harm to the appellant's position for a reversal to be granted (another term for this is that the appellant was "prejudiced" by the error). Otherwise it is considered to be **harmless error,** and the original decision is allowed to stand. Where errors are substantive, the appellate court will generally reverse if its interpretation of the law differs from that of the trial court.

harmless error
Standard of review that has not caused legal error requiring reversal of the trial court's decision.

De Novo *Review*

de novo
Standard appellate review where the appellate court reviews the facts and law independent of the trial court's decision.

Another standard of review is ***de novo.*** This word means "a new." When a court reviews an appeal *de novo,* the appeals court reviews the record independent of the trial court's decision. No deference or consideration is given to the trial court's decision. The reviewing appellate court exercises judgment completely separate from the trial court, and makes its own conclusions regarding the facts and law of the case.

Determining the Standard of Review

The question you should ask yourself is, "How do I know which standard of review applies?" The answer is "legal research." Case law, through its many precedents, sets forth the standard of review. The cases often actually say "the standard of review for this action is. . . ." You must locate a case that identifies the standard of review for your case and cite that standard and case in your appellate brief. For example, the standard of review for overturning a denial of a temporary injunction is abuse of discretion. The following example is from *Dallas Anesthesiology Associates, P.A. v. Texas Anesthesia Group, P.A.,* 2006 Tex. App. LEXIS 3630, May 1, 2006:

> A. Standard of Review
> Section 51.014(a)(4) of the Texas Civil Practice and Remedies Code permits an interlocutory appeal of a district court's grant or denial of an application for a temporary injunction. TEX. CIV. PRAC.& REM. CODE ANN. § 51.014(a)(4) (Vernon Supp. 2005). The decision to grant or deny an application for a temporary injunction is within the sound discretion of the trial court. *See, e.g., Butnaru v. Ford Motor Co.,* 84 S.W.3d 198, 204, 45 Tex. Sup. Ct. J. 916 (Tex. 2002); *Walling v. Metcalfe,* 863 S.W.2d 56, 57, 37 Tex. Sup. Ct. J. 18 (Tex. 1993) *(per curiam); Wilson N. Jones Mem'l Hosp. v. Huff,* No. 05-03-00596-CV, 2003 Tex. App. LEXIS 8769, 2003 WL 22332387, at *2 (Tex. App.-Dallas, Oct. 14, 2003, pet. [*9] denied) (published, but not yet reported in S.W.3d). An appellate court will not reverse a trial court's decision to deny an application for a temporary injunction absent an abuse of discretion. *See, e.g., Butnaru,* 84 S.W.3d at 204; *Walling,* 863 S.W.2d at 58; *Wilson N. Jones Mem'l Hosp.,* 2003 Tex. App. LEXIS 8769, 2003 WL 22332387 at *2.

This excerpt is directly from the case. The case guides you to the standard of review. Similarly, in *Crawford v. Dammann,* 277 Ga. App. 440, 444 626 S.E.2d 632, the standard of review is clearly identified:

> Restrictive covenants on real estate run with the title to the land and are specialized contracts that inure to the benefit of all property owners affected. n2 'The [***7] construction, interpretation and legal effect of [such] a contract . . . is an issue of law' to which the appellate court applies the plain legal error standard of review. n3 Accordingly, we determine de novo whether the trial court correctly ruled that all of the fees at issue were permitted by the Covenants. *Id.* at 444.

And finally, we present a case from a Nebraska Supreme Court showing the same concept. Again, the standard of review is clearly delineated in *Pony Lake School*

District 30 v. State Committee for the Reorganization of School Districts, 271 Neb. 173, 179-180, 710 N.W.2d 609 (2006):

> IV. STANDARD OF REVIEW
>
> [1] An action for injunction sounds in equity. In an appeal of an equity action, an appellate court tries the factual questions de novo on the record and reaches a conclusion independent of [*180] the findings of the trial court. *Denny Wiekhorst Equip. v. Tri-State Outdoor Media,* 269 Neb. 354, 693 N.W.2d 506 (2005).
>
> [2] The constitutionality of a statute is a question of law, and this court is [***10] obligated to reach a conclusion independent of the decision reached by the trial court. *State v. Diaz,* 266 Neb. 966, 670 N.W.2d 794 (2003).
>
> [3] Constitutional interpretation is a question of law on which the Nebraska Supreme Court is obligated to reach a conclusion independent of the decision by the trial court. *Hall v. Progress Pig, Inc.,* 259 Neb. 407, 610 N.W.2d 420 (2000).

Format Requirements

Assume that every appeals court has different format requirements for briefs; in doing this, you will always check the rules of court before proceeding in the appeal. The federal appeals are different from the state appeals; state appeals differ among the fifty-plus jurisdictions in the country. Many appeals courts, both federal and state, have local appellate rules that supplement the primary appellate rules of that jurisdiction. The slightest misstep can jeopardize a case resulting in dismissal—starting to get the "big" picture? Appeals are complex and the rules only add to the complexity. The rules dictate the spacing, the font, the margins, and the paper, to name just a few requirements. And, the judges *do* notice the presentation of your brief. Also, notice the rules even provide instruction on how to assemble the brief, such as the type of binding. Never use staples, paper clips, or other improper fasteners. Do not overlook even the smallest detail. The court will notice. Appellate courts are notorious and particular about following their rules to the letter. Review Figure 19.4, which sets forth the appellate rules for the state of Oregon. Notice the rules detail. Strict compliance is the rule of the day.

Quick Quiz True/False Questions

1. An appellate brief is filed with an appeals court and drafted objectively.
2. The only party designation at the appeals level is appellant and appellee.
3. The record on appeal consists of the trial transcript and pleadings only.
4. The best way to determine the standard of review for an appeal is to perform legal research.
5. All appeals courts have the same format requirements.

FIGURE 19.4
Appellate Court Rules for the State of Oregon
Source: Oregon Rules Of Appellate Procedure, amended January 1, 2005.

Rule 5.05
SPECIFICATIONS FOR BRIEFS

(1) Briefs, including petitions for review or reconsideration in the Supreme Court, shall be reproduced by any duplicating process that makes a clear, legible, black image; the Administrator will not accept carbon copies, copies on slick paper, or copies darkened by the duplicating process.

(2) (a) No opening, answering, or combined brief shall exceed 50 pages. That limitation does not include the index, excerpt of record, or appendix.

(b) A party's excerpt of record or appendix or combined excerpt of record and appendix shall not exceed 50 pages.

(c) No reply brief shall exceed 15 pages.

(d) Unless the court orders otherwise, no supplemental brief shall exceed five pages.

Cont.

FIGURE 19.4
Appellate Court Rules for the State of Oregon *Cont.*

[text omitted]

(4) All briefs shall conform to these requirements:

(a) Front and back covers shall be paper of at least 65-pound weight. The cover of the brief shall be:
(i) For an opening brief, blue;
(ii) For an answering brief, red;
(iii) For a combined answering and cross-opening brief, violet;
(iv) For a reply or combined reply and answering brief on cross-appeal, or an answering brief to a cross-assignment of error under Rule 5.57, gray;
(v) For the brief of an intervenor, the color of the brief of the party on whose side the intervenor is appearing;
(vi) For the brief of *amicus curiae*, green;
(vii) For a supplemental brief, the same color as the primary brief.
(viii) For a petition for review or reconsideration in the Supreme Court, yellow;
(ix) For a response to a petition for review or reconsideration in the Supreme Court, orange;
(x) For a brief on the merits of a petitioner on review in the Supreme Court, white;
(xi) For a brief on the merits of a respondent on review in the Supreme Court, tan.

(b) The front cover shall set forth the full title of the case, the appropriate party designations as the parties appeared below and as they appear on appeal, the case number assigned below, the case number assigned in the appellate court, designation of the party on whose behalf the brief is filed, the court from which the appeal is taken, the name of the judge thereof, and the names, bar numbers, addresses, and telephone numbers of counsel for the parties and the name, address, and telephone number of a party appearing pro se. The lower right corner of the brief shall state the month and year in which the brief was filed.

(c) Pages and covers shall be a uniform size of 8-1/2 x 11 inches.

(d) Paper for the text of the brief shall be white bond, regular finish without glaze, and at least 20-pound weight with surface suitable for both pen and pencil notation. If both sides of the paper are used for text, the paper shall be sufficiently opaque to prevent the material on one side from showing through on the other.

(e) Printed or used area on a page shall not exceed 6-1/4 x 9-1/2 inches, exclusive of page numbers, with inside margin 1-1/4 inches, outside margin 1 inch, top and bottom margins 3/4 inch.

(f) Briefs shall be legible and capable of being read without difficulty. Briefs may be prepared using either uniformly spaced type (such as produced by typewriters) or proportionally spaced type (such as produced by commercial printers and many computer printers). Uniformly spaced type shall not exceed 10 characters per inch (cpi). If proportionally spaced type is used, it shall not be smaller than 12 point for both the text of the brief and footnotes. Reducing or condensing the typeface in a manner that would increase the number of words in a brief is not permitted. Briefs printed entirely or substantially in uppercase are not acceptable. All briefs shall be double-spaced with double space above and below each paragraph of quotation.

(g) The last page of the brief shall contain the name and signature of the author of the brief, the name of the law firm or firms, if any, representing the party, and the name of the party or parties on whose behalf the brief is filed.

(h) Pages shall be consecutively numbered at the top of the page within 3/8 inch from the top of the page. Pages of the excerpt of record shall be numbered independently of the body of the brief, and each page number shall be preceded by "ER," *e.g.*, ER-1, ER-2, ER-3. Pages of appendices shall be preceded by "App," *e.g.*, App-1, App-2, App-3.

(i) A brief shall be bound in a manner that allows the pages of the brief to lie flat when the brief is open, as provided in this paragraph. Regardless of whether a brief is prepared with text on one or both sides of the pages, the brief may be bound with a plastic comb binding, with the binding to be within 3/8 inch of the left edge of the brief. A brief also

Cont.

may be bound by stapling if the brief is prepared with text only on one side of each page or if the brief is prepared with text on both sides of the pages and does not exceed 20 pages (10 pieces of paper), excluding the cover but including the index, the excerpt of record and any appendix. A brief bound by stapling shall be secured by a single staple placed as close to the upper left-hand corner as is consistent with securely binding the brief.

(5) The court on its own motion may strike any brief that does not comply with this rule.

[Footnotes omitted]

FIGURE 19.4
Appellate Court Rules for the State of Oregon *Cont.*

THE SECTIONS OF AN APPELLATE BRIEF

Several basic sections to an appellate brief are required by the rules of virtually all appellate courts. Though the precise title of each section, as well as its order of appearance in the finished brief, may differ between jurisdictions, the substantive content is universal. Keeping in mind, then, that you should refer to your own local rules for specific guidance, what follows is a general discussion of the sections:

- Title or Cover Page
- Certificate of Interested Parties
- Table of Contents
- Table of Authorities
- Jurisdictional Statement
- Statement of the Case
- Questions Presented
- Statement of Facts
- Summary of the Argument
- Argument
- Conclusion
- Signature Block
- Certificate of Compliance with Length Requirements
- Certificate of Service
- Appendix

YOU BE THE JUDGE

Another attorney on appeal earned the wrath of a judge for failing to comply with the format and substantive requirements of the rules of that jurisdiction. In *Catellier v. Depco, Inc.*, 696 N.E.2d 75 (Ind. App. 1998), the attorney was sanctioned and had to pay attorney's fees to the other party for his failure to conform to the rules. The court found that the attorney committed bad faith. In its dicta, the court found "[p]rocedural bad faith 'is present when a party flagrantly disregards the form and content requirements of the Rules of Appellate Procedure, omits and misstates relevant facts appearing in the record, and files briefs appearing to have been written in a manner calculated to require the maximum expenditure of time both by the opposing party and the reviewing court.' Conduct can be classified as procedural bad faith even if it falls short of being deliberate or by design.'" *Id.* at 79. This case is yet another of an attorney falling short in his professional responsibilities. Review the case. What are the facts of the case? What facts led the court to impose sanctions on the attorney? What rules did the attorney violate?

Title or Cover Page

title page
Cover page of the brief.

The first page of an appellate brief is called the **title page** or the cover page. The title page identifies

- the court in which the appeal is pending;
- the lower court in which the case originated;
- the names of the parties involved in the appeal;
- the docket number of the case;
- the name of the party on whose behalf the brief is being filed;
- the name of the attorney or law firm filing the brief; and
- the date of filing.

Some courts also require that, if oral argument is desired, it be requested on the title page. If your appeal is pending in such a court, failure to include this request may waive your client's right to demand oral argument at a later stage. This can damage the outcome of the appeal. Part of your responsibility as a paralegal, then, is to know your jurisdiction's rule for requesting oral argument.

When the list of parties involved in an appeal is long, some jurisdictions allow the use of the abbreviation "et al.," which means "and others," to substitute for a full listing. Again, check your local rules.

A question always arises as to the order in which parties are listed in the appellate caption. In the past, the party making the appeal was generally listed first. This could lead to confusion when a defendant was making the appeal, however, since a case known as *Smith v. Jones* in the trial court (with Smith being the plaintiff and Jones the defendant) would become *Jones v. Smith* in the appellate court. The modern practice is to retain the caption order as it appeared in the lower court and simply identify the parties as appellant or appellee. Of course, you must check your own local rules on this point.

amicus curiae
Brief filed by a nonparty known as a "friend of the court."

Some courts require that the color of the title page correspond to the status of the filing party. Thus, an appellant might have a light blue title page, an appellee a red title page, and an **amicus curiae** (literally, "friend of the court," discussed later in the chapter) a green title page. Jurisdictions are not consistent on this practice, so again you must check.

A title page of an appellant's brief appears in Figure 19.5, with various components identified.

Certificate of Interested Parties or Disclosure Statement

certificate of interested parties
Statement in a brief identifying parties who have an interest in the outcome and financial affiliations.

The **certificate of interested parties** or **disclosure statement** identifies all those parties to the case who have an interest in the outcome. It appears immediately after the title page (see Figure 19.11 at the end of this chapter) and is intended to provide the appellate judge with an opportunity to determine the existence of a conflict between her own financial and personal interests and those of a party to the appeal.

recusal
Voluntary disqualification by a judge due to a conflict of interest or the appearance of one.

If the judge determines that a conflict exists, she will exercise the **recusal** option. A recusal occurs when the judge voluntarily disqualifies herself from further participation in the disposition of the case.

Some jurisdictions do not require the certificate of interested parties. Check your local rules.

Table of Contents

table of contents
Road map of the appellate brief, which includes the section headings and corresponding page numbers in the brief.

Although the **table of contents** exists primarily to identify section headings with corresponding page numbers, it is far more than just an index. It is, rather, a concise outline of your client's contentions, the "road map" by which the court will follow the path of your argument.

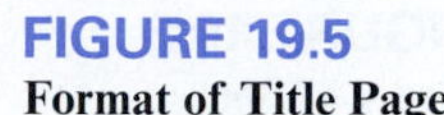

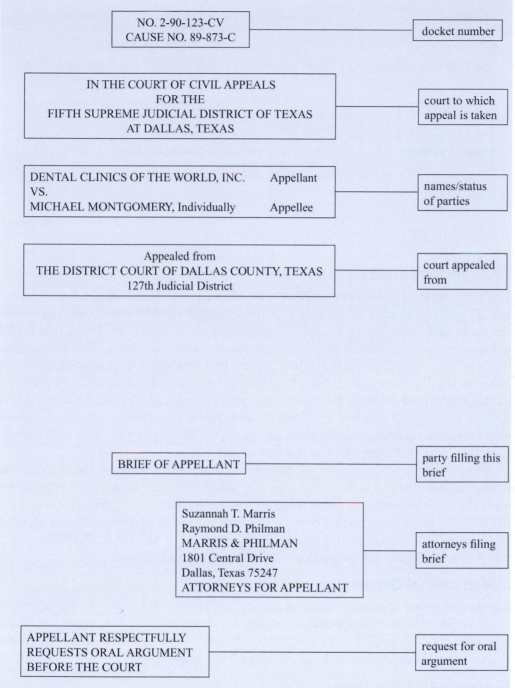

FIGURE 19.5
Format of Title Page

NO. 2-90-123-CV
CAUSE NO. 89-873-C — docket number

IN THE COURT OF CIVIL APPEALS
FOR THE
FIFTH SUPREME JUDICIAL DISTRICT OF TEXAS
AT DALLAS, TEXAS — court to which appeal is taken

DENTAL CLINICS OF THE WORLD, INC. Appellant
VS.
MICHAEL MONTGOMERY, Individually Appellee — names/status of parties

Appealed from
THE DISTRICT COURT OF DALLAS COUNTY, TEXAS
127th Judicial District — court appealed from

BRIEF OF APPELLANT — party filling this brief

Suzannah T. Marris
Raymond D. Philman
MARRIS & PHILMAN
1801 Central Drive
Dallas, Texas 75247
ATTORNEYS FOR APPELLANT — attorneys filing brief

APPELLANT RESPECTFULLY
REQUESTS ORAL ARGUMENT
BEFORE THE COURT — request for oral argument

The road map objective is achieved through expanded reference to the argument section. As will be discussed further, point headings and subpoint headings in the argument section identify, in an orderly and logical fashion, the rationale behind your client's position on appeal. In the table of contents, the complete text of each of these headings is set forth. Thus, simply by referring to the table of contents the court will be able to learn the broad parameters of your argument before exploring the details. Review the table of contents that appears in Figure 19.11 at the end of the chapter.

Although the table of contents is one of the first sections to appear in your brief, it is one of the last sections you will draft. This is because page numbers, and perhaps even the text of the point headings, will not be finalized until you approach completion of the project.

FIGURE 19.6
Order of Source Material in Table of Authorities

Case opinions	Judicial decisions are listed first and *alphabetically* (some states require cases ranked by court: The U.S. Supreme Court, the U.S. courts of appeals, etc.). List each page number where case appears.
Constitutional provisions	Federal constitutional provisions are listed first, with state constitutional provisions to follow. List the provisions in descending numerical order.
Statutory provisions	Federal statutory provisions are listed after constitutional provisions; state statutes follow. As with the constitutional provisions, list in descending numerical order.
Secondary authority	Secondary authorities are listed last, alphabetically by author. Secondary authorities range from legal periodicals to treatises, and include all other sources that are neither case decisions, constitutional provisions, nor statutes.

Table of Authorities

table of authorities
Section of the appellate brief that identifies the cases, statutes, constitutional provisions, and all other primary and secondary authority contained within the brief.

The term **table of authorities** refers to the cases, statutes, constitutional provisions, and all other primary and secondary sources that are cited in your brief. Since both the court and opposing parties will be examining these sources in detail, it is useful to have an easily referenced list. Although the requirements for the table of authorities may vary in different jurisdictions, Figure 19.6 provides a common listing of the order of legal sources in the table of authorities. References appearing in the table of authorities should be drafted in conformity with the rules of *The Bluebook* or *ALWD Manual* unless your appellate court has its own special requirements. The table should also reference every page on which each authority appears in the brief. (See sample appellate brief in Figure 19.11 at the end of this chapter.)

Along with the table of contents, the table of authorities is one of the last sections prepared. Accuracy in both is important. If inaccurate and sloppy, they will undermine the court's confidence in the credibility of your arguments. Figure 19.7 sets forth the rules in the First Circuit Court of Appeals for citing cases, law review articles, and unpublished cases. Notice the strict requirements of the court. Preparing these tables is a task often left to paralegals. Great care should be taken.

Jurisdictional Statement

jurisdictional statement
Section of the brief that identifies the legal authority that grants the appellate court the right to hear the case.

The **jurisdictional statement** identifies the legal authority that grants to the appellate court jurisdiction over the appeal. It usually makes reference to the statute establishing the right of appeal. The jurisdiction conferred by such a statute is a prerequisite to the appeal. (See Figure 19.11 at the end of this chapter.)

Statement of the Case

statement of the case
Section of the appellate brief that sets forth the procedural history of the case.

The **statement of the case** sets forth the procedural history of the case. It identifies the lower court or courts in which the case has been heard and the decision of each. It is analogous to the "prior proceedings" section of a case brief. (See Figure 19.11 at the end of this chapter.)

There are several different titles in use for this section besides "statement of the case." Others include "preliminary statement," "nature of the action," or "nature of the case." The case history information is also frequently incorporated into the statement of facts. Your statement of the case should include the following items:

- A concise statement of the nature of the cause of action (one or two sentences), not to be confused with the detailed statement of facts.
- Whether the appeal is from a court trial, a jury trial, or a hearing.

FIGURE 19.7
Citation Requirements of the First Circuit Court of Appeals

Local Rule 32.2 Citation of State Decisions and Law Review Articles
All citations to State or Commonwealth Courts must include both the official state court citation and the National Reporter System citation when such decisions have been published in both reports; e.g., Coney v. Commonwealth, 364 Mass. 137, 301 N.E.2d 450 (1973). Law review or other articles unpublished at the time a brief or memorandum is filed may not be cited therein, except with permission of the court.

Local Rule 32.3 Citation of Unpublished Opinions
(a) An unpublished opinion of this court may be cited in this court only in the following circumstances:
(1) **When the earlier opinion is relevant to establish a fact about the case.** An unpublished opinion of this court may be cited to establish a fact about the case before the court (for example, its procedural history) or when the binding or preclusive effect of the opinion, rather than its quality as precedent, is relevant to support a claim of res judicata, collateral estoppel, law of the case, double jeopardy, abuse of the writ, or other similar doctrine.
(2) **Other circumstances.** Citation of an unpublished opinion of this court is disfavored. Such an opinion may be cited only if (1) the party believes that the opinion persuasively addresses a material issue in the appeal; and (2) there is no published opinion from this court that adequately addresses the issue. The court will consider such opinions for their persuasive value but not as binding precedent.
(3) **Procedure.** A party must note in its brief or other pleading that the opinion is unpublished, and a copy of the opinion or disposition must be included in an accompanying addendum or appendix.
(4) **Definition.** Almost all new opinions of this court are published in some form, whether in print or electronic medium. The phrase "unpublished opinion of this court" as used in this subsection and Local Rule 36(c) refers to an opinion (in the case of older opinions) that has not been published in the West Federal Reporter series, e.g., F., F.2d, and F.3d, or (in the case of recent opinions) bears the legend "not for publication" or some comparable phraseology indicating that citation is prohibited or limited.
(b) Unpublished or non-precedential opinions of other courts, as defined or understood by those courts, may be cited in the circumstances set forth in subsection (a)(1) above. Such opinions may also be cited in circumstances analogous to those set forth in subsection (a)(2) above, unless prohibited by the rules of the issuing court. If an unpublished or non-precedential opinion of another court is cited, the party must comply with the procedure set forth in subsection (a)(3) above.

- The name of the court whose decision is being appealed.
- The name of other courts that have had jurisdiction over the case, and the nature of their disposition.
- The name of the party bringing the appeal.

Questions Presented

In the **questions presented** section of the brief, you provide the appellate court with a convenient, concise statement of the grounds upon which the decision of the trial court is being questioned. For each ground, there should be a separately numbered question.

questions presented
Section of the appellate brief that identifies the grounds upon which the decision of the trial court is questioned.

Although at first glance it might appear that drafting these questions is an objective task, in fact, you should be applying your persuasive skills. The questions should be framed so as to suggest an answer that favors your client. Useful techniques include

- identifying the erroneous ruling of the lower court and suggesting, in question form, the result you seek;
- keeping the questions short, clear, and succinct;
- presenting separate issues in separate questions; and
- identifying the applicable standard of review.

FIGURE 19.8
Examples of Contrasting Versions of a "Question Presented"

From the appellant's perspective:
Did the District Court err and abuse its discretion by denying appellant's application for a temporary injunction, since appellant proved a probable right and probable injury and established sufficient grounds to impose an injunction and preserve the status quo?

From the appellee's perspective:
Was the District Court correct in denying plaintiff's request for an injunction?

The questions presented section is sometimes referred to as "points of error," "issues presented," or "assignments of error." As always, check your local rules.

In Figure 19.9, two questions are set forth that were drafted by opposing sides on the same appeal. Note the manner in which the appellant and appellee have stated the same basic issue in a contrasting, and partisan, fashion.

Statement of Facts

statement of facts
Section of a brief that sets forth the significant facts and information needed to analyze the issues presented.

The **statement of facts** is the first of the two major sections of the appellate brief, the other being the argument. In it you set forth the background information and significant facts of your client's case, so that the appellate court has a clear factual framework within which to consider the legal questions presented. (See Figure 19.12 at the end of this chapter.)

The statement of facts is not based upon your memory of events in the case, nor is it based upon those facts which you believe you can prove, since there is no opportunity to "prove" facts on appeal. It is based, rather, on the record of the case. If a fact is not contained in the record of the case, then, for the purposes of the appellate court, that fact simply doesn't exist.

There are two key points to remember in drafting your statement of facts:

- Every fact set forth should be followed by a reference in parentheses to that portion of the record in which the fact appears.
- The statement of facts should be drafted in a persuasive fashion, setting forth the facts in a light most favorable to your client, while at the same time remaining accurate, straightforward, and faithful to the record.

The first of these points, making reference to the record, is easy to understand but often difficult to accomplish. The record of a trial court can be bulky. Many trials are lengthy, and the transcript can run to hundreds of pages or more, with a large number of exhibits. Sometimes the exhibits themselves are lengthy and complicated documents, the meaning of which is disputed by the parties.

There is no magic solution to mastering the record. Simply stated, you must study the transcript and exhibits until you develop a full understanding of their content. It is likely that, in your role as a paralegal, you will be responsible for having a good working knowledge of the record. You will be expected to locate references quickly. Your supervising attorney may draft a statement of facts without parenthetical references, and then expect you to provide the missing information.

indexing method
Referencing method of the record to assist in identifying the important pieces of information, such as the transcript excerpts and pleadings, which will be used in the various parts of the appellate brief.

One method that is useful for mastering the record is the **indexing method.** By preparing an index to the transcript—for example, identifying (1) the party testifying, (2) the attorney conducting the examination, (3) the content of the testimony, and (4) the transcript page on which the testimony appears, you will have a useful shorthand reference enabling you to locate specific items quickly. An index can also be used to summarize documentary exhibits.

Indexes are sometimes also called "digests." Although some might say that a digest suggests a summary more detailed than an index, the difference is largely semantic, and the purpose of each is identical—namely, to summarize a lengthier document.

Different appellate courts have different rules with regard to referencing the record. For example, references to the transcript might be identified by "(T-78)," meaning "page 78 of the transcript," or a variation such as "(R-78)," meaning "page 78 of the record." You should check your local rules for the appropriate style in your jurisdiction.

Though a tedious task, providing comprehensive parenthetical references is very important to the success of your brief. By identifying all those portions of the record that support your factual claims, you not only provide a useful summary of the record but also establish credibility in the eyes of the court. A thorough and well-referenced statement of facts provides the foundation on which you build your arguments and persuade the appellate court.

The second point requires that your statement of facts be not only honest and accurate but also partisan. Although on the face of it this might seem to be inconsistent, in fact it goes to the essence of persuasive legal writing. In order to set the stage for your legal arguments, you want the court to interpret the facts in a light most favorable to your client. At the same time, you do not want the court to think that you are distorting the record. To accomplish these objectives, you should employ several techniques:

- Set forth the facts in chronological order, which is the easiest and most logical to follow.
- Emphasize those facts which support your client's position.
- When negative facts are essential to an accurate presentation, resist the temptation to omit them, since this will erode your credibility in the eyes of the court (you can be sure that the other side will draw such facts to the court's attention anyway). You should address these negative facts in such a way that their impact is minimized.

PRACTICE TIP

As a general rule, every sentence should have record reference in the statement of facts.

Summary of the Argument

A concise summary of the argument is required prior to the argument section of the brief. In this section, those arguments presented in the body of the argument are summarized for the court. This section should not be merely a restatement of the issues, but a well-thought-out, accurate account of the legal argument in the brief. This section is your "snapshot" of the brief. Treat this section as if this were the only section the court was going to read. Be precise. Choose your words carefully. Don't restate what you have already stated in the main argument section. This section should be no more than a paragraph or two.

Argument

The most important section of the appellate brief is known as the **argument.** In this section you analyze the legal issues raised by the questions presented section and interpret the applicable cases and statutes to demonstrate that your client's position should prevail on appeal.

argument
Section of the brief where the issues are analyzed through citation of legal authorities.

YOU BE THE JUDGE

Proper referencing of the facts in your appellate brief is important. The attorney in *Hurlbert v. Gordon,* 824 P.2d 1238 (Wash. App. 1992), learned the hard way that failure to cite specific references to the record is inexcusable, resulting in sanctions by the appeals court. Apparently, in *Hurlbert,* the record on appeal was voluminous—some 6,000 pages. The rules, like all appellate rules, require reference to the record when establishing facts on appeal. The judge cited the purpose behind the rule and admonished the attorney for forcing the court and opposing counsel to wade through the mass of court pages. As the court warned: "[s]everal references were made to 20- or 50- or 100-page documents rather than to specific pages of the record relating to the particular factual statements made." *Id.* at 1245. Opposing counsel was forced to request permission to file a 95-page responding brief because of the complexity of the issues and lack of references in the case. Because of the attorney's behavior, the judge ordered a fine. Read the case. Identify the facts of the case. What are the ethical issues addressed in the case? What rules of appellate procedure were violated?

The argument section of an appellate brief is the highest point of persuasive legal writing. Its preparation represents the climax of all your training in written advocacy. The success or failure of your appeal will turn in large measure on your ability to state logically and forcefully, in writing, your client's position. Every stylistic decision has an impact; every substantive choice a consequence; every word an effect.

The argument section comprises two components, the point headings and the body. (See Figure 19.11 at the end of this chapter.)

Point Headings

Recall from Chapter 18 that point headings are brief synopses of the argument to follow, set apart from the body of the brief by underlines or type style. (See Figure 19.11 at the end of this chapter.) They perform both a stylistic function, in that they divide the brief into distinct sections for easier reading, and a substantive function, in that they separate the argument into logical components. They provide concise answers to the questions posed in the questions presented section, thus giving the court a preview of the detailed argument, and in general, introduce the complex reasoning to follow.

The level of complexity of the brief determines the number of point headings. Isolate the distinct legal issues presented, and begin the discussion of each separate issue with a new point heading.

If the discussion of a given legal issue is complex, you may need subpoint headings as well. In deciding whether subpoint headings are needed, you must keep in mind that too many subpoint headings may actually confuse the reader. If you decide that subpoint headings are justified, choose a format or type style that clearly distinguishes subpoint headings from point headings, so as to maintain clarity.

The brief in Figure 19.11 shows both point headings and subpoint headings. In reviewing this brief, note both the substantive content of the headings and the manner in which capitalization, indenting, spacing, and underlining are used to differentiate headings from the body, and point headings from subpoint headings.

Body

body
Main text of the argument section of the appellate brief.

The **body** of the argument is the section in which the main text is set forth. (See Figure 19.11 at the end of this chapter.) It is here that you inform the court of the detailed arguments that support your client's position.

The sole purpose of the body of the brief is to present the law to persuade the court. Although this purpose may appear obvious, many attorneys and paralegals lose sight of this consideration when drafting a brief. The problem arises as a result of the interpretation that the drafter attaches to the term "detailed argument." Appellate courts often see briefs that exhaustively document the issue presented, but fail to persuade. You must keep in mind that your job is not to draft a treatise on the issues raised, but rather to persuade the court to resolve the issues in favor of your client. This requires that you cite essential sources and discuss relevant concepts, hence the word "detailed." It does not require that you cite every source, nor discuss every concept, that might arguably be deemed relevant to your brief. Say what you have to say and move on. A former judge, Ruggero J. Aldisert, senior U.S. circuit judge of the Court of Appeals for the Third Circuit, in his book *Winning on Appeal, Second Edition* (National Institute for Trial Advocacy, 2003) quoted a University of Vermont professor Robert Huber who taught debate. He explained to his debate students a "schematic N-E-P-C," which means "NAME IT, EXPLAIN IT, PROVE IT, CONCLUDE IT." *Ibid.* at p. 23. These are words to remember and live by when writing an appellate or trial brief. Judges want you to get to the point and tell them what you want. They do not want to scour through your brief trying to figure out the issues and the arguments. Before you begin to write, think about the result you want and how best to achieve that result. Place yourself in the shoes of the judge, who has to read hundreds of briefs over the course of a year. You would want the writer to present the legal argument in as few words as possible.

If the issue presented is not complex (or even in many cases where it is complex), it is possible that one or two controlling cases and one or two applicable statutes may adequately define and support your argument. If you address such a context in an excessively complicated manner, you dilute the impact of these essential authorities.

Remember that deciding upon the final content of a brief is often a balancing act between simplifying the issues for ease of understanding on the one hand, and accurately reflecting the state of the law on the other. Your goal is a brief that is easy to understand, thorough, and an accurate and defensible representation of the law—in a word, *persuasive.* In achieving this goal, you should follow the basic rules and techniques of writing that we addressed in previous chapters, including clarity and brevity. In addition, keep in mind the following points:

- Place your strongest point first. Write in a manner that is easily understood. Do not pontificate. Remember keep your reader's interest and attention.
- The court will be relying on precedent, not your personal theories. When the law is on your side, tell the court. When it is not, distinguish the precedents by pointing out factual or other differences between their context and that of your appeal. It is almost always advisable to avoid the temptation to improvise theory.
- Where the case law is against you, argue that "justice and fair play" compel the court to find for your client and reverse the precedents. This is the so-called equitable argument.
- Never misrepresent facts or case law to the court.
- A court is often persuaded by "public policy arguments." Whether your case is supported by precedent or not, it is always useful to show the court how a decision in your favor will benefit the public interest.
- String citations (long lists of cases that you claim support your point) may actually undercut your argument, if the significance of the most important precedent is diluted. The trend is to cite the one best and most recent case for your point.

string citations
List of citations in the brief following a point of law cited.

Conclusion

The **conclusion** is a brief statement appearing after the argument section. It does not summarize your argument, but rather "respectfully submits" that, based upon the logic of your argument, the court must grant the relief you desire. All the sections of your brief lead to the conclusion, which convinces the court to grant the relief requested, for example, to reverse, vacate, or affirm the lower court's decision. In other words, the appellant concludes that the trial court should be reversed, whereas the appellee concludes that it should be upheld.

conclusion
Short statement at the end of the brief telling the appeals court the relief requested.

The key here is to be specific. Do not leave the court to guess at the relief you seek—*tell* the court. (See Figure 19.11 at the end of this chapter.)

Signature Block

The **signature block** provides a line for the signature of the attorney who is ultimately responsible for the brief. His name, bar card identification number, address, fax, and telephone number are typed below the signature. The client on whose behalf the brief is filed is also identified and sometimes other information as well. (See Figure 19.11 at the end of this chapter.) Check your local rules for the specific requirements in your jurisdiction.

signature block
Section of the brief for attorney's signature that includes the name, address, bar card identification, fax, and telephone number.

Certificate of Compliance with Length Requirements

It will come as no surprise that all briefs have page limitations. Now, the federal courts of appeal require a **certificate of compliance** at the end of a brief that attests to the

certificate of compliance
Attorney certification at the end of an appellate brief attesting to compliance with the page limitations set forth by that court's rules.

FIGURE 19.9
Certificate of Compliance with Length Requirements
Source: U.S. Eleventh Circuit Court of Appeals.

SAMPLE CERTIFICATE OF COMPLIANCE REQUIRED BY FRAP 32(A)(7)(C)
If your principal brief exceeds 30 pages or your reply exceeds 15 pages, you must include a certificate of compliance within the brief, immediately preceding the certificate of service. You may use the following certificate:

CERTIFICATE OF COMPLIANCE

I certify that this brief complies with the type-volume limitation set forth in FRAP 32(a)(7)(B). This brief contains ____ words.

Or, if you are using a monospaced face, you may instead use the following certificate:

CERTIFICATE OF COMPLIANCE

I certify that this brief complies with the type-volume limitation set forth in FRAP 32(a)(7)(B). This brief uses a monospaced face and contains ____ lines of text.

With either certificate, you must fill in the blank line; you may rely on the word or line count of the word-processing system used to prepare the brief.

PRACTICE TIP

Most courts require a "joint appendix." This is often a requirement of the rules of the court. Each of the parties to the appeal must confer regarding the portions of the trial court record that should be included for review by the appellate court. When the appellant refuses to include some portion of the trial court record requested by the appellee, a supplemental appendix may be filed, usually through a motion.

page limits. This requirement is set out in Federal Rules of Appellate Procedure Rule 32(A)(7). The certification tells the court that not only the page limits are met, but also that footnotes were not used to undercut the page limitations. See Figure 19.10 for an example of a Certificate of Compliance. Check state appellate rules for similar requirements.

Certificate of Service

Discussed in previous chapters, the **certificate of service** is an acknowledgment at the end of any court-filed document, including an appellate brief, verifying delivery of the document to all persons entitled to a copy, and identifying the date and type of service. (See Figure 19.11 at the end of this chapter.) Mail delivery is usually sufficient.

Those entitled to service generally include the attorneys in the case, as well as parties who represent themselves without the assistance of an attorney. Sometimes the certification must also verify that a copy was served upon the court.

The certificate of service is attested to by the attorney filing the brief. Your local rules will provide specific guidance.

certificate of service
Verification by attorney that pleadings or court documents were sent to the opposing counsel in a case.

Appendix

Appellate briefs often contain an **appendix,** which is a supplementary collection of primary source materials. Most of these materials are taken from the record. In many jurisdictions it is mandatory to include certain portions of the record in the appendix, for example, those pages from the transcript that are referenced in the text of the appellate brief.

The appendix appears as the last section in the brief. In addition to transcript pages, it often contains relevant passages from pleadings, evidentiary exhibits introduced at trial, and the lower court's judgment and opinion.

appendix
Contains the supplementary collection of the sources from the trial court.

Quick Quiz True/False Questions

1. In most cover pages of appellate briefs, the name of the court from which the appeal is taken is identified.
2. The table of authorities identifies the sections and section headings in the brief.

3. The statement of the case sets forth the procedural history of the case.
4. The statement of facts and argument sections of the brief contain legal authorities that support the arguments on appeal.
5. The signature block is signed by the attorney only.

THE FOUR CATEGORIES OF APPELLATE BRIEFS

All appellate briefs share the same basic characteristics outlined. The approach to drafting a specific appellate brief, however, varies somewhat with the procedural status of your client. An appellant, for example, takes a different approach than an appellee, whereas the brief filed by an amicus curiae has its own unique emphasis. The stage at which a brief is filed also affects its content, a reply brief being a different creature altogether from an opening brief. It is worthwhile to take a moment and review the differences in emphasis among the four categories of appellate brief: appellant's; appellee's; the reply brief; and that of the amicus curiae.

Appellant's Brief

The appellant, as you recall, is the party making the appeal. It is the appellant who asserts that the decision of the trial court must be overturned. Almost without exception, the **appellant's brief** will be filed first. Thus the appellant has the opportunity to set the tone of the appeal and define the issues that will be brought before the appellate court. Although this might appear to be an advantage, any edge inferred is offset by the fact that the appellant is seeking to overturn the judgment of a trial court that has carefully considered the issues and found for the other side. The burden of proving the trial court wrong is on the appellant.

appellant's brief
Brief of the party filing the appeal.

Appellee's Brief

The **appellee's brief** is filed in response to the appellant's brief. Thus the appellee has the appellant's brief in hand as the response is prepared. This enables the appellee to review and attack the specific arguments made by the appellant. In addition to attacking the arguments of the appellant, the appellee should also set forth independent reasons that demonstrate why the lower court should be upheld.

appellee's brief
Brief of the party responding to the appeal.

Reply Brief

The term **reply brief** could be attached to any brief filed by a party in response to an earlier brief filed by an opposing party. The appellee's opening brief is thus technically a reply brief, since it is filed after, and in response to, the appellant's brief. In general, however, the term reply brief refers to a brief filed by the appellant in response to the appellee's opening brief.

reply brief
Short responsive brief of the appellant to the appellee's brief.

The justification for allowing such a reply brief is simple. It would be unfair to deny the appellant an opportunity to respond to the arguments of the appellee, since the appellee had the opportunity to review and attack the arguments set forth in the appellant's first brief. Hence the appellant is authorized to file a reply brief.

When preparing a reply brief, the appellant should resist the temptation to restate arguments already set forth in the first brief. The court will not forget these earlier arguments. Rather, the appellant should concentrate on addressing issues raised for the first time in the appellee's brief. It is similarly inappropriate (although probably prudent) for the appellant to raise points in the reply brief that it failed, through negligence or oversight, to address in the opening brief. If such points are raised in the reply brief, the court may allow the appellee another chance to respond, or disregard the new points entirely.

CYBER TRIP

Choose a recent case from the U.S. Supreme Court and review the appellate briefs of the parties to the case. If amicus curiae briefs were submitted, review those briefs and list any format changes between those briefs filed by the parties and the *amicus* parties.

Amicus Curiae Brief

Amicus curiae is a person or organization that was not directly involved in the lawsuit between the parties, but which has an interest in the outcome of the appeal and has succeeded in petitioning the court for the right to file a brief on the issues presented. An **amicus brief** (as it is often called) may correspond to any of the other three categories of brief, depending on whose interest the amicus brief mirrors and what stage the appeal has reached. One difference between the amicus brief and others is that the amicus brief argues from a public policy viewpoint. This type of brief is most common in the U.S. Supreme Court, where significant legal and public policy issues arise that often change the course of history. Recall *Brown v. Board of Education* (separate is not equal—segregation), *Roe v. Wade* (abortion), *U.S. v. Nixon* (Watergate), and *Bakke v. California Board of Regents* (reverse discrimination), to name a few.

amicus brief
Brief filed by a nonparty to an appeal who has an interest, whether political, social, or otherwise, in the outcome of the case.

WRITING THE BRIEF

Regardless of whether your client is appellant or appellee, the writing process does not change. You must be vigilant in both your preparatory work as well as your concluding review. Practice what you have learned by performing these tasks:

- Analyze the issues on appeal with your supervising attorney; this preliminary step in an appeal is critical to determine whether an appealable issue exists.
- Review the current appellate rules of court and any local appellate rules; check the court's Web site, if one is available, to determine any recent changes.
- Determine your timetable and time limitations; appellate cases have specific time constraints, such as when to file a notice of appeal, the briefs of the parties, and the record. Prepare a graph, diagram, or schematic to help you keep track of the court-imposed deadlines. Check the deadline schedule daily.
- Research the law; identify the standard of review, which is one of the first critical steps in beginning the appeals process. Choose cases that best represent the legal position forwarded on the client's behalf. But do not gloss over adverse authority. Confront it directly, exhibiting integrity to the court.
- Update the law through Shepard's Citators or KeyCite; do not cite overruled cases or cases whose history is highly suspect.
- Determine your audience; remember, you are writing to the court and the opposing counsel, but mainly to the court.
- Identify the components for that court's appellate brief; remember that not all appellate courts have the same components. Conform your brief to the requirements of the court.
- Organize your document; prepare an outline to assist you in organizing the sections of the brief, especially the statement of facts and argument and authorities sections.
- Write succinctly; say what you have to say and move on. Craft your issues, statement of facts, and argument in a persuasive tone. An appellate brief is no time to be objective. You do have a point of view. Communicate it. State your strongest arguments first and build on that argument. Use point and subpoint headings for organizing the flow of the brief.
- Redraft and revise your brief; remember, you and your supervising attorney will prepare a number of drafts before everyone is satisfied with the final product.
- Check punctuation, grammar, and spelling; do not rely solely on word processing programs because they will not pick up properly spelled words used incorrectly, such as typing "of " when you mean "or."

- Edit the final draft; recheck for proper citation format and review the final draft for clarity, precision, and accuracy.
- Format the brief; conform the brief to the court's font specifications and word and page limitations. Be sure you have the correct color cover page and correct size of paper.
- Prepare the table of authorities; this section will be one of the last sections you complete since you will not know the authorities cited until the brief is completed. It is a good practice to begin compiling the table of authorities as you prepare the brief. Keep a separate tablet to list the legal sources cited in the brief. When the brief is completed, compare the cited authorities with the list. This should ease the preparation of this section. Remember to cite the corresponding page numbers where the case appears in the brief in the Table of Authorities.
- Prepare the table of contents; along with the table of authorities, this will be one of the last sections prepared in the brief.
- Check your word count; if required, prepare your certificate of compliance.
- Assemble the final product; one last check.
- File your brief with the court; be sure the required copies are prepared, or if e-filing is required, check the rules for verification of filing. Transmit the brief to opposing counsel.

That's it! You have completed your appellate brief and can breathe a sigh of relief. It is on to the next project. (See Figure 19.11 at the end of this chapter for a sample appellate brief.)

ETHICS ALERT

During the pendency of a case, an attorney and a paralegal are prohibited from contacting a represented person. Simply stated, you cannot directly contact a plaintiff in a case if your office is representing the defendant. Attorneys may use "you" to contact a represented person under the guise that either you do not know any better or you are not the attorney. Both situations are unethical. This anti-contact rule, as it is commonly known, continues through the appellate process as well. Do not have direct conversations or contact with someone you know is represented by an attorney in a matter your firm is handling against that party. In short, you are held to the same standard as an attorney.

If individuals are not represented by an attorney, you may contact them directly. Be careful to ask whether they are represented by an attorney, and document that inquiry. You should also identify yourself, your position, whom you represent, and the reason for the contact. Often individuals think you are acting in a friendly manner or they twist the conversation to suggest an inappropriate contact. Or, they may attempt to glean legal advice or information from you. Make your position clear and avoid creating any misunderstanding between yourself and the unrepresented party. More importantly, you do not want to give an unrepresented person the impression you are rendering legal advice, partaking in the unauthorized practice of law. Undoubtedly, contacting unrepresented parties poses unique issues, especially when representing themselves *pro se*. Proceed with caution when speaking with unrepresented parties in whatever stage of the proceeding you are in.

There are *very limited* situations when contact is appropriate, but emphasis is on the words "very limited," and you should consult your attorney before making the contact. Communications may be permitted with a public entity or large corporation when the communication with the represented party is unrelated to the litigation between the parties. Often this situation occurs between government agencies. For example, your law firm has a lawsuit against the government in an eminent domain action for which contact is inappropriate, but may contact the government on an unrelated licensing issue. The situation is tricky, and probably the best approach is to not only identify yourself as a paralegal acting on behalf of your law firm, but also disclose to the person the pending litigation. These are difficult areas of the law—think before you speak.

THE E-FACTOR

Courts are keenly aware that attorneys will manipulate the system to skirt the rules of appellate procedure when it comes to the formatting requirements. In fact the Seventh Circuit Court of Appeals in *DeSilva v. DiLeonardi,* 185 F.3d 815 (7th Cir. 1999), investigated an attorney's certification of the "type-volume limit." In that case, the court discussed the 14,000-word limits for briefs. The attorney certified his brief was 176 words short of that limit—13,824. After review of the contents of the brief, the court was skeptical and performed its own count. The court's count included the main text and the twenty footnotes for a total of 15,056, making the brief over the limit. According to the court, the problem was with the word processing program, and the opinion concludes that the "Appellants' brief was prepared with Microsoft Word 97, and an unfortunate interaction occurred between that software and the terms of Rule 32." *Id.* at 815. The court determined that "Microsoft Word does not offer a way to count words in those footnotes attached to the selected text." *Id.* at 815. Amazing as all this sounds, the court determined that other word processing systems did not have the design problem of Microsoft Word and "flagged" briefs using Microsoft Word. In the final paragraph of the opinion, the court noted that "[w]e will send copies of this opinion to those responsible for such design decisions. In the meantime, we will flag this issue in the court's Practitioner's Guide and in materials distributed to counsel when an appeal is docketed. Law firms should alert their staffs to the issue pending resolution at the software level. Our clerk's office will spot-check briefs that have been prepared on Microsoft Word, are close to the word limit, and contain footnotes." *Id.* at 817. True to their word, the Seventh Circuit Checklist does caution attorneys who use Microsoft Word about the "word counting flaw." See Figure 19.10.

The obvious point of all the attention paid to formats, word counts, spacing, margins, and all the other requirements of the Appellate Rules is read those rules. And read those rules again. Many of the courts have checklists to follow. Use them. Take the process seriously and do not deviate from the process or the rule. Do not try to manipulate the word processing system and attempt to outsmart the system and the court. You may not get caught the first time, but it will, at some point, catch up with you. Remember, the attorney has to sign a certification of compliance with the page limitations. Your attorney is held accountable and could be sanctioned for filing a false certification. If you believe a brief borders on the word limit or some other rule limitation, tell your attorney and either edit the brief or prepare a motion for your supervising attorney to file with the court.

FIGURE 19.10
Seventh Circuit Checklist about Word-Counting Programs

<u>**Seventh Circuit Brief Filing Checklist**</u>

13. Fed. R. App. P. 32(a)(7) requires principal briefs not exceed 30 pages unless it contains no more than the greater of 14,000 words or 1,300 lines of text if a monospaced face is used. Reply briefs must contain no more than half of the type volume specified in Rule 32(a)(7)(B)(i). In cross-appeals the appellants' principle [sic] brief - 30 pages or 14,000 words; appellees' combined principle brief/response brief - 35 pages or 16,500 words; appellants' combined reply brief responsive brief - 30 pages or 14,000 words; appellees' reply brief in cross appeal - 15 pages or 7000 words. Fed. R. App. P. 28.1(e). Briefs submitted under the word count sections of the rules require a certificate of compliance that the brief complies with the volume limitations. **NOTE TO USERS OF MICROSOFT WORD** – Be advised that the word counting feature of some early versions of Microsoft Word may not properly count words in footnotes. Counsel must assure [sic] that they count all words in the brief before certifying compliance with Rule 32 or 28.1. *See DeSilva v. DiLeonardi*, 185 F.3d 815 (7th Cir. 1999). Briefs less than 30 pages do not require a certificate of compliance. Fed. R. App. P. 32(a)(7)(C).

Quick Quiz True/False Questions

1. The appellant's brief has the burden of proving the lower court reached the wrong conclusion.
2. Parties may file an amicus curiae brief if they have an interest in the outcome of a case.
3. In preparing an appellate brief always check the timetables and timelines for the filing requirements.
4. Always prepare the table of contents and table of authorities first when drafting the appellate brief.
5. All appellate briefs use the same size paper.

A DAY IN THE LIFE OF A PARALEGAL

Virtually all appellate briefs have requirements. They have page and word limitations as well as font requirements, to name a few. Your attorney is a bit long-winded and has used the footnotes in his brief to advance his appellate argument. He has asked you to check the number of words he has used in the brief, which has a limitation of 15,000 words. You check the rules to verify the limitation, but while reviewing the rules you notice that the rules require a 12-point font for both text and footnotes. Your attorney used an 8-point font so he could stay within the page limitations. Should you tell your attorney of the requirements in the rules? The answer is absolutely yes.

Communicating this information is important, especially since your attorney may not have known of the font requirements. At this juncture, the ball is in your attorney's court. He can either change the font to conform to the rules, which would probably require him to edit his brief. Or he could ignore the information, take his chances, and run the risk of either the court rejecting the submission or the opposing counsel objecting to the font size. Whatever approach the attorney takes, you have fulfilled your obligation by letting the attorney know of the rule requirements.

PRACTICAL CONSIDERATIONS: MANAGING YOUR TIME

An appellate brief is not prepared in a day. Unlike briefing schedules in the trial court, often characterized by tight deadlines imposed by the trial judge, an appellate briefing schedule is generally established by specific rules that set reasonable minimum time periods.

Thus there are two important practical considerations in preparing an appellate brief: First, you have ample time to polish your brief; second, because of this, appellate judges expect a polished product. You must schedule sufficient time to perform the tasks that go into every appellate brief—reviewing the record; researching the issues; writing a draft; editing; finalizing your draft; preparing the tables of contents and authorities, as well as all other supplements; and reviewing the final version to ensure that it is as polished as you can make it. It's easy to delude yourself into thinking, "The brief's not due for four weeks—I'll do other things first." If you fall into this trap, you'll end up with a major headache—a brief due in a week or less, and insufficient time to prepare it correctly.

There is one other important practical consideration. Remember that this chapter is only an *introduction* to writing the appellate brief, and is not the final word. There are as many opinions on appellate advocacy, briefing strategies, and brief writing as there are on trial advocacy. But all good briefs have a few common characteristics—they are thorough, yet concise; accurate, yet partisan; and most of all, they are *persuasive.*

A FINAL WORD

You have acquired the skills to become a top-rate paralegal. But as with all things, unless you practice the skills learned, you get rusty. Keep writing and refining those skills. You are an invaluable contributor to the legal process, and this is only the beginning. Attorneys often forget how accomplished and important you are to the process of successful lawyering. Don't let lawyers overpower you and compromise your integrity. This textbook has combined legal writing and legal ethics for a reason. They are the backbone of our profession. Learn your craft well, but above all else, be professional and ethical in your practice.

FIGURE 19.11 Sample Appellate Brief*

1

No. 2-06-123-CV
CAUSE NO. 05-873-C
IN THE COURT OF CIVIL APPEALS
FOR THE FIFTH SUPREME JUDICIAL DISTRICT OF TEXAS
AT DALLAS, TEXAS

DENTAL CLINICS OF THE WORLD, INC. Appellant
vs.
MICHAEL MONTGOMERY, Individually Appellee

Appealed from
THE DISTRICT COURT OF DALLAS COUNTY, TEXAS
127th Judicial District

BRIEF OF APPELLANT

Suzannah T. Marris
Raymond D. Philman
MARRIS & PHILMAN
1801 Central Drive
Dallas, Texas 75247

ATTORNEYS FOR APPELLANT

APPELLANT RESPECTFULLY
REQUESTS ORAL ARGUMENT
BEFORE THE COURT

Refer to the corresponding key numbers to identify each element of this Brief.

❶ — Title or Cover Page
❷ — Certificate of Interested Parties
❸ — Table of Contents
❹ — Table of Authorities
❺ — Jurisdictional Statement
❻ — Statement of the Case
❼ — Questions Presented
❽ — Statement of Facts
❾ — Summary of the Argument
❿ — Argument and Authorities
⓫ — Point Heading
⓬ — Body
⓭ — Conclusion
⓮ — Signature Block
⓯ — Certificate of Service

Cont.

*Normally each component of the appellate brief begins on a separate page indicated by the white space in this figure.

FIGURE 19.11 **Sample Appellate Brief** *Cont.*

CERTIFICATE OF INTERESTED PARTIES

2

The following are all the interested parties in this Appeal:
1. Dental Clinics of the World, Inc.
2. Michael Montgomery
3. Joseph Dean

3

Table of Contents

4

Table of Authorities

Cases

Cont.

FIGURE 19.11 **Sample Appellate Brief** *Cont.*

JURISDICTIONAL STATEMENT

5

This court has jurisdiction of this appeal pursuant to the Texas Constitution Art. 5 § 6 and Tex. Civ. Prac. & Rem. Code Ann. § 51.014 (Vernon 1986).

STATEMENT OF THE CASE

6

This case is an appeal from the denial of a temporary injunction. Dental Clinics of the World, Inc. ("Dental Clinic" or "Appellant") filed suit against Michael Montgomery ("Montgomery" or "Appellee") alleging that Appellee used Appellant's confidential and proprietary information and trade secrets. Montgomery used information that he gained through his employment with Dental Clinic to bid on a servicing contract with Health Care, Inc., Dallas, Texas. The information was Dental Clinic's proprietary, confidential information and trade secrets, which Montgomery acquired and used in violation of his obligations to Dental Clinic. Montgomery also contacted other persons to attempt to establish a business that would compete with Appellant, using Dental Clinic's information. A temporary injunction hearing was held by the 127th Judicial District Court, Dallas, Texas. On June 20, 2005, the Court entered an Order denying the temporary injunction.

QUESTION PRESENTED

7

Did the District Court err and abuse its discretion by denying appellant's application for a temporary injunction, since appellant proved a probable right and probable injury establishing sufficient grounds to impose an injunction and preserve the status quo?

STATEMENT OF FACTS

8

Dental Clinic is a Texas corporation specializing in dental clinic services. It offers personnel and equipment (for example, drills, x-ray machines, and other equipment) to dental clinics in Texas. (Tr. 47)

In 2000, Dental Clinic employed Montgomery as a salesperson. Montgomery became Vice President of the company in 2004. (Tr. 36) While Vice President, Montgomery had many responsibilities, including hiring employees, purchasing equipment, compiling marketing data, selling the company's services, and dealing with customers. (Tr. 38) Throughout his tenure with the company, Montgomery gained confidential knowledge and information, which he would not have gained but for his employment with Dental Clinic. As a service-oriented business, Dental Clinic develops business relationships with its customers. (Tr. 44) Through contracts with its customers, Dental Clinic provides equipment and personnel. The customers are normally small clinics or health centers. (Tr. 45) Dental Clinic installs the equipment and provides the technicians as well. Only three other companies provided a similar service in Texas. (Tr. 31)

To determine whether an area is appropriate for a dental clinic, a sizable amount of research and development takes place. This research and development takes years. (Tr. 51) If competitors obtained this information, thousands of research dollars could be saved, as well as the time spent researching. Having this information would allow a competitor to set up a clinic in an area or forego an area based on Dental Clinic's research.

Dental Clinic treated this information as confidential, proprietary data and trade secrets. This information was kept from employees unless needed in their job functions. (Tr. 55) Montgomery was one of the few employees of Dental Clinic who had access to <u>all</u> Company information. (Tr. 55) This information included, but was not limited to, customer lists, supplier lists, pricing lists, clinics, and manufacturers. As an employee and fiduciary of the Company, Montgomery knew this information was confidential and proprietary. (Tr. 56)

Montgomery worked directly with Dental Clinic's customers. In fact, Montgomery worked with clinic administrators and found out that one of Dental Clinic's customers had received a bid from another company. Montgomery was asked to revise Dental Clinic's prior contract and gave the information to the President of the company. (Tr. 71) The new bid was resubmitted to the clinic with Montgomery's new prices. (Tr. 72) Montgomery gained all this information while employed with the Company and he only could have gained this information because of his employment with Dental Clinic.

On November 17, 2004, Montgomery resigned and terminated his employment with Dental Clinic. (Tr. 95) Not more than one month after he left Dental Clinic, Montgomery formed his own company, Dental Health Care. This company offered the same services as Dental Clinic. (Tr. 98)

Cont.

FIGURE 19.11 **Sample Appellate Brief** *Cont.*

8

Montgomery contacted one of Dental Clinic's customers regarding a dental services contract. (Tr. 101) The clinic turned out to be the same clinic Montgomery had revised the pricing for while employed with Dental Clinic. Montgomery did not contact anyone for pricing information. In fact, Montgomery knew his bid would be lower than Dental Clinic's since he had access to the information while employed with Dental Clinic. (Tr. 107) Months later, in January 2005, Dental Clinic was notified that its contract with the clinic would be cancelled and that Montgomery's company would receive the contract. (Tr. 158) Montgomery also contacted other customers of Dental Clinic and attempted to gain their contracts. Clearly, Montgomery knew all Dental Clinic customers, the services performed for them, and the prices charged. This information could only be gained from Montgomery's employment. Dental Clinic sued Montgomery for misappropriation of trade secrets and confidential proprietary information and requested a temporary injunction. This injunction was denied, and the denial has been appealed.

9

SUMMARY OF THE ARGUMENT

A former Vice President of Dental Clinic misappropriated confidential and proprietary and trade secret information. This information was a compilation of years of work and finanical investment which Montogomery had access to because of his fiduciary relationship with Dental Clinic. While Dental Clinic was negotiating a contract for which Montgomery prepared the financial data, he resigned his employment and began his own business using the confidential and proprietary information he gained through his employment with Dental Clinic. Montgomery's actions caused immediate and irreparable injury for which Dental Clinic requested a temporary injunction to preserve the status quo pending a trial on the merits.

10

ARGUMENT AND AUTHORITIES

11

I. THE TRIAL COURT ABUSED ITS DISCRETION BY NOT GRANTING THE TEMPORARY INJUNCTION.

12

The trial court refused to grant the temporary injunction in this case and abused its discretion because the facts clearly established the elements of a temporary injunction. Under the Texas Civil Practice and Remedies Code, section 51.014 (a) (4), an interlocutory appeal is proper when a district court grants or denies an application for temporary injunction. TEX.CIV.PRAC.& REM. CODE ANN. section 51.014 (a) (4) (Vernon Supp. 2005) The standard of review for an appeal in a temporary injunction hearing is whether the trial court abused its discretion in granting or denying the temporary injunction. *Butnaru v. Ford Motor Co.*, 84 S.W.3d 198, 204 (Tex. 2002); *City of Spring v. Southwestern Bell Telephone Company*, 484 S.W.2d 579 (Tex. 1974). In determining whether the granting or denial of a temporary injunction is proper, this Court must look to the record in the trial court and determine whether the party requesting relief is entitled to preservation of status quo of the subject matter pending trial on the merits. *Green v. Stratoflex, Inc.*, 596 S.W. 2d 305 (Tex. Civ. App.–Ft. Worth 1980, no writ). In evaluating whether the trial court abused its discretion in granting or denying a temporary injunction, this Court must consider whether the trial court erroneously applied the law to undisputed facts, where pleadings and evidence presented a probable right and probable injury. *Southland Life Insurance Co. v. Egan*, 126 Tex. 160, 86 S.W. 2d 722 (1935); *Plagge v. Gambino*, 570 S.W.2d 106 (Tex. Civ. App.–Houston [1st Dist.] 1978, no writ); *Morgan v. City of Humble*, 598 S.W.2d 364 (Tex. Civ. App.–Houston [14th Dist.] 1980, no writ).

The purpose of the temporary injunction is to preserve the status quo of a matter in controversy until final hearing on the merits of the case. For a temporary injunction to be issued by a trial court, a party need show only a probable right and a probable injury, and is not required to establish that he will finally prevail in the litigation. Therefore, the burden in a temporary injunction hearing is substantially different than it is in a trial on the merits. The movant has to prove there is a probable right to recovery at a trial on merits, but does not have the burden to prove that he would ultimately prevail at a final hearing. *Transport Co. of Texas v. Robertson Transports,* 152 Tex. 551, 261 S.W.2d 549 (1953).

At the temporary injunction hearing, Dental Clinic proved a probable injury was suffered and Dental Clinic had a probable right to recovery. Montgomery stole information from his employer, Dental Clinic, and, in turn, used the information to injure the company. The misappropriation of this information was wrongful, for which Dental Clinic was entitled to relief in the form of a temporary injunction. The trial court abused its discretion by failing to properly apply the law to the facts. Dental Clinic made a proper showing to meet the standards necessary for issuance of an injunction.

Cont.

FIGURE 19.11 **Sample Appellate Brief** *Cont.*

Dental Clinic did have a probable right to recovery and clearly sustained an injury by losing an established contract with one of its customers.

11 II. TEXAS PROHIBITS THE USE OF TRADE SECRETS AND CONFIDENTIAL PROPRIETARY INFORMATION WHEN MISAPPROPRIATED BY A CORPORATE OFFICER.

Montgomery was a Vice President of Dental Clinic. The Supreme Court of Texas has held that corporate officers are fiduciaries of the corporation. *International Bankers Life Ins. Co. v. Holloway*, 368 S.W.2d 567 (Tex. 1963). Not only do the courts impose a general fiduciary obligation on officers, but additionally, the courts have articulated a specific rule that an employee has a duty *not* to disclose the confidential matters of its employer. *Lamons Metal Gasket Co. v. Traylor,* 361 S.W.2d 211 (Tex. Civ. App.–Houston 1962, writ ref'd n.r.e.); *Jeter v. Associated Rack Corp.*, 607 S.W.2d 272 (Tex. Civ. App.–Texarkana 1980, writ ref'd n.r.e.), *cert. denied*, 454 U.S. 965 (1980). Certain information was considered confidential by Dental Clinic. The undisputed testimony of the President shows that Dental Clinic considered customer lists, renewal dates, and pricing as confidential. (Tr. 57-59) Montgomery intentionally disregarded his fiduciary responsibilities to further his own personal endeavors. But for Montgomery's relationship to Dental Clinic, he would not have known the trade secrets and confidential and proprietary information. The law is clear that Texas prohibits the use of confidential information by a former corporate officer, which Montgomery clearly was in this case. *Weed Eater v. Dowling*, 562 S.W.2d 898 (Tex. Civ. App.–Houston [1st Dist.] 1978, writ ref'd n.r.e.)

A. A TRADE SECRET BY DEFINITION MAY BE A COMPILATION OF INFORMATION, INCLUDING A CUSTOMER LIST.

In defining a trade secret, the Texas Supreme Court has adopted the Restatement of Torts,
12 2nd § 757, which defines a trade secret as follows:

> A trade secret may consist of any formula, pattern, device, or *compilation of information which is used in one's business and which gives him an opportunity to obtain an advantage over competitors who do not know or use it.* It may be a formula for a chemical compound, a process of manufacturing, treating, or preserving materials, a pattern for a machine, or other device, or *a list of customers*.* * * Trade secret is a process or device for continuous use in the operation of the business. *See, Hyde Corp. v. Huffines*, 158 Tex. 566, 314 S.W.2d 763, 776 (1958) (emphasis added).
> The Restatement of Torts § 757 further states that:

> One who discloses or uses another's trade secrets, without a privilege to do so, is liable to the other if (a) he discloses the secret by improper means, or (b) his disclosure or use constitutes a breach of confidence reposed in him by the other in disclosing the secret to him. *Hyde Corp*. at 769 (emphasis supplied).

Dental Clinic had developed confidential and proprietary information that it used in its business. This information gave it an advantage over competitors. For years Dental Clinic compiled information. The information included but was not limited to customer lists, contact persons at clinics, pricing information, financial information, and market planning strategies. (Tr. 57) Information had been exclusively developed through Dental Clinic's financial investment and research and was not readily accessible to outsiders of the company without substantial monetary and time investment. This compilation of information is Dental Clinic's trade secrets and proprietary and confidential information, which it uses in the development of its business activities.

It is undisputed Montgomery had access to trade secrets and confidential and proprietary information of Dental Clinic by virtue of his position of confidence and trust with the President, Joseph Dean. As the testimony showed, Dean and Montgomery worked together in the development of Dental Clinic. Montgomery had access to all the information regarding Dental Clinic. The information Montgomery acquired is a valuable asset of Dental Clinic. A temporary injunction is the only remedy that will protect Dental Clinic's investment. A temporary injunction will preserve the status quo pending a trial on the merits. Without the injunction, Dental Clinic will continue to suffer harm and injury.

In the temporary injunction hearing, Montgomery admitted he took information he gained while employed with Dental Clinic to contact other dental clinics. He made offers and submitted proposals to the clinics. (Tr. 88) Specifically, Montgomery contacted Dental Resources of the Southwest, with whom Dental Clinic had been negotiating a renewal of its contract. Montgomery breached his fiduciary relationship with Dental Clinic by using its proprietary and confidential information and trade secrets. When a vice president breaches his fiduciary duty, it is proper under Texas law to grant

Cont.

FIGURE 19.11 **Sample Appellate Brief** *Cont.*

a temporary injunction. *Weed Eater v. Dowling*, 562 S.W.2d 898 (Tex. Civ. App.–Houston [1st Dist.] 1978, writ ref'd n.r.e.). The trial court should have granted the temporary injunction to protect Dental Clinic's proprietary and confidential information and trade secrets. Now, Dental Clinic is left without a viable remedy as it continues to suffer due to its former Vice President's actions.

More importantly, in any analysis of trade secrets and confidential and proprietary information, the Court must evaluate how the information was acquired. Although it may be argued by Montgomery the information was generally available for someone with time and money to accumulate the information, the fact is clear that the data which Montgomery utilized to compete with his former employer came from Dental Clinic's investment of hundreds of hours and substantial sums of money to accumulate and develop the data. Even if Montgomery could acquire the information that does not mean he is entitled, through a breach of confidence, to gain the "information in usable form and escape the efforts of inspection and analysis." *K & G Oil Tool & Service Co. v. G & G Fishing Tool Service*, 158 Tex. 594, 314 S.W.2d 782 (1958). The law in Texas imposed equitable measures against an individual who has breached a fiduciary relationship through a temporary injunction. As the court in its dicta in *Weed Eater* recognized,

> [W]here an employee will acquire trade secrets by virtue of his employment, the law permits greater restrictions to be imposed on the employee than in other contracts of employment.
>
> *Confidential business information* is not given protection merely as a reward to its accumulator. The courts condemn employment of improper means to procure trade secrets. *The fact that a trade secret is of such a nature that it can be discovered by experimentation or other fair and lawful means does not deprive its owner of the right to protection from those who would secure possession by unfair means.* (emphasis added). 562 S.W. *Id.* at 901.

12

Texas law clearly imposes a responsibility on a corporate officer such as Montgomery not to disclose information gained during employment. The responsibility of the corporate fiduciary is implied and is part of a contract of employment.

Although Montgomery would suggest that liability can be imposed only if a written contract existed, this is not the law. In confidential and proprietary information actions, a contract of employment is not necessary to create the right. As *Texas Shop Towel, Inc. v. Haine* points out:

> [a]n owner may protect a trade secret even in the total absence of any contract with his employees, and the agents and employees who learn of the trade secret or secret formula are prohibited from its use. *In the case of a trade secret, a contract does not create the right, for the right exists by reason of the confidence.* It will exist in the total absence of a contract. A contract may be additional evidence of the existence of the trade secret but an owner's rights in his secrets do not depend upon a contract (emphasis added). *Texas Shop Towel* at 485 (Tex. Civ. App.–San Antonio 1952, no writ).

No employment contract is necessary to hold Montgomery legally responsible for his actions. The testimony and the evidence before this Court are undisputed:

- Montgomery received Dental Clinic's confidential, proprietary, and trade secret information in confidence as Dental Clinic's employee
- Montgomery was an officer of Dental Clinic and as such was a fiduciary of the corporation.

In *E.I. DuPont De Nemours Power Co. v. Masland*, 244 U.S. 100 (1917), the Supreme Court of the United States recognized the importance of a fiduciary duty and the consequence of a breach of that duty. The Supreme Court in its dicta made the following observation:

> [w]hether the Plaintiffs have any valuable secret or not, the Defendant knows the facts, whatever they are, through a special confidence that he accepted. The property may be denied, but the confidence cannot be. Therefore, the starting point for the present matter is not property or due process of law, but that the Defendant stood in confidential relations with the Plaintiff, or one of them. These have given place to hostility, and the first thing to be made sure of is that the Defendant shall not fraudulently abuse the trust reposed in him. It is the usual incident of confidential relations. If there is any disadvantage in the fact that he knew the Plaintiff's secrets, he must take the burden with the good. *Id.* at 102.

The U.S. Supreme Court recognized the rights of an employer over fifty years ago. It is a right that continues today. The only remedy Dental Clinic has is a temporary injunction.

B. AN INJUNCTION IS AN APPROPRIATE REMEDY FOR MISAPPROPRIATION OF TRADE SECRETS AND FOR THE BREACH OF A FIDUCIARY RELATIONSHIP.

The evidence is clear that Montgomery acquired trade secrets and confidential and proprie-

Cont.

FIGURE 19.11 **Sample Appellate Brief** *Cont.*

tary information from Dental Clinic while an employee. After his resignation, Montgomery used the trade secrets and confidential and proprietary information of Dental Clinic to his own benefit. Though the information may have been available to a competitor, that availability did not give Montgomery the right to violate his confidential relationship with Dental Clinic. *See generally, Texas Shop Towel, Inc. v. Haine*, 246 S.W.2d 482 (Tex.Civ.App.-San Antonio 1952, no writ). By not issuing a temporary injunction and preserving the status quo, the trial judge abused his discretion. The facts in this case are undisputed by the evidence and the testimony.

By applying the undisputed facts to the law, Dental Clinic is entitled to a temporary injunction to preserve the status quo. Dental Clinic proved through the testimony and evidence that it
12 had a probable injury, which would result from (1) Montgomery's utilizing information to undercut Dental Clinic's contract bid, and (2) Montgomery's contacting users of Dental Clinic services.
Dental Clinic also showed that there was a probable right to recovery since the information was admittedly gained through Montgomery's employment with Dental Clinic. Montgomery admitted that he learned the information that he utilized to prepare the clinic's contract from his employment with Dental Clinic. Therefore, clearly the trial court abused its discretion by not granting the temporary injunction as the court did not properly apply the law to the undisputed facts. In *Weed Eater*, the Houston Court of Appeals recognized that a temporary injunction is a proper remedy when there is a breach of confidence and a misuse of proprietary information and trade secrets. 562 S.W. *Id* at 901. The facts in this case support such a conclusion of probable injury and probable right and the law dictates the issuance of an injunction.

CONCLUSION

In a temporary injunction hearing, Dental Clinic had to show only a probable right to recovery
and a probable injury and that there was not an adequate remedy at law. In applying the law to the facts,
Dental Clinic showed an injury, Montgomery's interference with a business contract, and a right to
recovery arising from Montgomery's use of information gained while employed with Dental Clinic. As
a matter of law, this information was confidential and proprietary and trade secrets of Dental Clinic. By
13 not granting the temporary injunction, the trial court erred and abused its discretion by misapplying the
law to the facts. Dental Clinic requests that this court instruct the trial court to issue and enter a temporary injunction to preserve the status quo in this case until a final trial on the merits can be heard.

Dental Clinic requests this Honorable Court instruct the trial court to issue and enter a temporary injunction against Montgomery to preserve the status quo until a final trial on the merits by ordering Montgomery not to contact any customers or dentists who are customers of Dental Clinic during the pendency of the litigation.

Respectfully submitted,

____

SUZANNAH T. MARRIS
State Bar #18769283
RAYMOND D. PHILMAN
14 State Bar #27619317
MARRIS & PHILMAN
1801 Central Drive
Dallas, Texas 75247
(214) 512-0927

ATTORNEYS FOR APPELLANT

CERTIFICATE OF SERVICE

I certify that a true and correct copy of the foregoing Brief of Appellant has been
forwarded to Appellee, by and through their attorney of record, C. J. Coldaway at
15 617 LBJ Freeway, Dallas, Texas, 76202, by certified mail, return receipt requested, on
this _____ day of _____, 2006.

____

Suzannah T. Marris

Summary

The first step in pursuing an appeal is to obtain a copy of the current appellate rules applicable in your jurisdiction. The second step is to read and understand them.

An appellate brief is a legal document filed with an appellate court and drafted to persuade that court to decide contested issues in favor of the filing litigant. An appeal is based on the record, which is the written documentation of the trial. The guideline that the court applies in evaluating an appeal is called the standard of review. There are two types of errors to which a standard of review is applied: errors of fact and errors of law.

There are several basic sections to an appellate brief, which may vary slightly in designation or content from one jurisdiction to the next, but are otherwise always required. The title page identifies the parties and court, and usually also contains the request for oral argument. The certificate of interested parties identifies those parties with a direct interest in the outcome of the case. The table of contents provides section headings with corresponding page numbers, and performs a "road map" function. The table of authorities identifies references cited. The jurisdictional statement identifies the legal authority that grants the appellate court authority over the appeal. The statement of the case sets forth the procedural history of the case. The questions presented section provides a convenient and concise statement of the grounds of the appeal. The statement of facts is based upon the record, and should be both accurate and partisan. The argument is the most important section of an appellate brief, composed of point headings and the main text or body, and containing the legal and factual positions of the party preparing it. The conclusion identifies the relief sought. A signature block and certificate of service are also included, as well as an appendix containing source materials from the record.

An appellant's brief is filed first, and sets the tone and defines the issues. The appellee's brief is filed in response to the appellant's brief, and both attacks the appellant's arguments and makes its own arguments. The reply brief is filed by the appellant in response to the appellee's brief. An amicus curiae brief is filed by a nonparty presenting public policy arguments.

Because of the nature of appellate briefing schedules, you have ample time to prepare an appellate brief. However, this means that judges expect a polished product, so make sure that you leave yourself adequate time to do your best work.

Key Terms

abuse of discretion
amicus brief
amicus curiae
appellant's brief
appellate brief
appellate rules
appellee's brief
appendix
argument
body
certificate of compliance
certificate of interested parties
certificate of service
conclusion
court reporter
de novo
error of fact
error of law
harmless error
indexing method
jurisdictional statement
petitioner
pleadings
questions presented
record
recusal
reply brief
respondent
signature block
standard of review
statement of facts
statement of the case
string citations
table of authorities
table of contents
title page
transcript

Review Questions

1. Why is it important to follow the applicable appellate rules?
2. What is the function of the appellate brief?
3. What are the components of the record on appeal?
4. Explain the difference between errors of fact and errors of law.
5. What is a jurisdictional statement?
6. What is the road map function of the table of contents?
7. What are two key points to remember when drafting the statement of facts?
8. What are point headings?
9. What is the significance of a certificate of compliance?
10. Describe the different characteristics of the appellant's brief, the appellee's brief, the reply brief, and the amicus curiae brief.

Exercises

1. Check the federal, state, and local appellate court rules for your jurisdiction and answer the following questions:
   a. When must an appeal be filed?
   b. When must the record be filed? The transcript?
   c. How much time does the appellant have to prepare and file the appellant's brief? The appellee?
   d. List the page length, paper size, color of cover page, and binding requirements.
2. Compare your state rules of appellate procedure and the Federal Rules of Appellate Procedure, and list the differences in the rules.
3. Using the memorandum of law in Chapter 18, create the table of authorities based upon the rules of the court in your state's appeals court.
4. Based upon the facts of the memorandum of law in Chapter 18, prepare a motion to the state appellate court to file a longer brief.
   a. Determine the rules for filing the motion.
   b. Determine the color of the cover page and the requirements. Prepare the cover page according to the rules of the court.
5. Ms. Liann Wang sought political asylum in the United States because of alleged political persecution by the government of China. Ms. Wang entered the United States illegally. Because of her illegal entry, the U.S. government sought removal proceedings against Ms. Wang in case number INS No. A99-000-098. The immigration judge denied Ms. Wang's petition for asylum because her testimony did not support her claims of political persecution. Ms. Wang requested her removal hearing be reopened. The immigration judge denied the request. Ms. Wang appealed to the Board of Immigration Appeals. The board issued an order denying the request. Ms. Wang appeals the case to the Third Circuit Court of Appeals under Local Appellate Rule (LAR) 34.1(a). What is the standard of review to reopen a removal case in an immigration matter? Research the law in the Third Circuit and the U.S. Supreme Court. Find the cases with the highest precedential value on the issue.
6. Using the facts in exercise 5, prepare the cover sheet and title page for appeal to the Third Circuit Court of Appeals. The case number for the Third Circuit Court of Appeals is No. 08-10000. The attorney representing Ms. Wang is Charles Reese, 111 Market St., Philadelphia, PA. 19103. Oral argument is requested.

7. Historical Preservation Society of America, Inc. seeks a temporary injunction against Demolition R Us, Co. It seems that Demolition has been hired by Property Management Inc. to demolish a historic hotel in downtown Miami, Florida, on October 15, 2008. The historic hotel was built in 1912 and is certified as a landmark. Unfortunately, the building was abandoned years ago and Property Management Inc. wants to build a five-story parking lot on the site. Property Management owns the land and building. Historical Preservation files a request for temporary restraining order and temporary injunction requesting the demolition cease and the building remain in tact. The judge denies the temporary restraining order and temporary injunction on October 5, 2008. Property Management intends to begin the demolition in ten days. Historical Preservation files a notice of appeal in the trial court in Miami. The appeal is properly perfected and your law firm has been hired to prepare the appellate brief. Determine the proper appeals court to file the appeal. Review the rules of the court.
   a. What motion should be filed with the appeals court in this case?
   b. Prepare the motion from your response to the set of facts in exercise 7(a).
8. Using the facts from exercise 7, prepare the following:
   a. standard of review for the case
   b. statement of facts
   c. argument and authorities section
   d. conclusion

   Use your best persuasive writing skills to "save" the historic site. Be creative.

PORTFOLIO ASSIGNMENT

Continuing with our Mrs. Marsh and "Buttons" facts from the Portfolio Assignment from chapters 17 and 18, Mrs. Marsh was granted a summary judgment against A1 and Herbert Killington. Both parties want to appeal.

1. Choose one of the parties to represent and prepare the appellate brief on behalf of one of the appellants. (Remember, the standard of review is for a summary judgment.)
2. Prepare the appellee's brief on behalf of Mrs. Marsh. (Hint: Stay focused on the fact that there are no genuine issues of material fact. If the appellant can create one, the judgment may be overturned.)

Be sure your brief complies with the rules of the jurisdiction. Check to see if the appellate court has any local rules to follow.

Quick Quiz True/False Answers

Page 575
1. False
2. False
3. False
4. True
5. False

Page 586
1. True
2. False
3. True
4. False
5. True

Page 590
1. True
2. True
3. True
4. False
5. False

Glossary

12(b)(6) motion A motion under the provisions of Rule 12 of the Rules of Civil Procedure that challenges the basis of the complaint for failure to state a claim upon which relief can be granted.

A

abandoned property Personal property that the owner has intentionally discarded and to which the owner has relinquished ownership rights.

abandonment Quitting the use by the adverse user, which terminates the tolling of time.

abatement Doctrine in which will bequests may fail due to insufficient estate funds at the time of testator's death.

ability to cure A breaching party may be able to fix the defective performance.

absolute sale The title transfers upon delivery and payment.

abuse of discretion Standard of review on appeal that judge's decision is unreasonable and not logically based upon the facts.

abuse of process Using the threat of resorting to the legal system to extract agreement to terms against the other party's will.

acceptance The offeree's clear manifestation of agreement to the exact terms of the offer in the manner specified in the offer.

acceptance of services or goods Where an offeree has taken possession of the goods or received the benefit of the conferred services, he is deemed to have accepted the offer.

accessory after the fact A person who, knowing a felony to have been committed by another, receives, relieves, comforts, or assists the felon in order to enable him to escape from punishment, or the like.

accessory before the fact One who orders, counsels, encourages, or otherwise aids and abets another to commit a felony and who is not present at the commission of the offense.

accomplice One who knowingly, voluntarily, and with common intent unites with the principal offender in the commission of a crime.

accord Agreement, but it must be agreement to substitute.

accord and satisfaction An agreement to accept imperfectly proffered performance as a fulfillment of the contractual obligations.

acquittal The legal and formal certification of the innocence of a person who has been charged with a crime.

actions inconsistent with rejection A buyer must not do anything that is contrary to her previous refusal of the goods.

active concealment Knowingly hiding a situation that another party has the right to know and, being hidden from her, assumes that it does not exist.

active voice A verb form in which the subject of the sentence performs the action.

actus reus The guilty act.

ademption Failed bequest in a will because the property no longer exists.

adequacy of consideration Sufficient under the circumstances to support the contract.

adequacy of performance An obligation meets the minimum or completeness test.

adequate assurances Either party may request the other to provide further guarantees that performance will be forthcoming if the requesting party has reasonable suspicion that the other may default. Under the UCC, merchants may request of each other further promises that performance will be tendered.

adequate compensation A party denied the benefit of his bargain may be paid or otherwise put in a position equivalent to where he would have been if performance had been in compliance with the contractual terms.

adequate consideration Exchanges that are fair and reasonable as a result of equal bargaining for things of relatively equal value.

administrative agencies Statutorily created departments that have the authority to legislate, adjudicate, and investigate matters between parties or violations of rules or regulations.

administrative agency regulations and rules (administrative codes) Processes and guidelines established under the particular administrative sections that describe acceptable conduct for persons and situations under the control of the respective agency.

administrative decisions or orders The judicial-like decisions of an administrative agency.

administrative law The body of law governing administrative agencies, that is, those agencies created by Congress or state legislatures, such as the Social Security Administration.

Administrative Procedure Act (APA) A statute that lays the foundation as to how administrative agencies function, create rules and regulations, and adjudicate violations of those regulations.

admissibility A ruling on whether the jury will be allowed to view proffered evidence.

admission Acknowledgement of the facts as true.

admit To agree or stipulate to the allegations presented in a complaint.

adoption The taking of a child into the family, creating a parent–child relationship where the biological relationship does not exist.

advance sheets Softcover pamphlets containing the most recent cases.

adversarial documents Documents that are argumentative, drafted to emphasize the strong points of your client's position and the weaknesses of the opposing party's.

adverse possession The legal taking of another's property by meeting the requirements of the state statute, typically open and continuous use for a period of five years.

advisory letter A formal letter that offers legal opinions or demands.

advisory opinion Statement of potential interpretation of law in a future opinion made without real case facts at issue.

affiant The person who makes and subscribes an affidavit.

affidavit A sworn statement.

affirm(ed) Disposition in which the appellate court agrees with the trial court.

affirmative acts Knowing and conscious efforts by a party to the contract that are inconsistent with the terms of the agreement and that make contractual obligations impossible to perform.

affirmative defense An "excuse" by the opposing party that does not just simply negate the allegation, but puts forth a legal reason to avoid enforcement. These defenses are waived if not pleaded.

affirmative duty The law requires that certain parties positively act in a circumstance and do not have to wait until they are asked to do that which they are required to do.

against the drafter Imprecise terms and/or ambiguous wording is held against the party who wrote the document as he was the party most able to avoid the problem.

agency adoption Using an agency, either government or private, but government-regulated, to facilitate the process.

aggravated assault Criminal assault accompanied with circumstances that make it more severe such as the intent to commit another crime or the intent to cause serious bodily injury.

aggravated battery A criminal battery accompanied by circumstances that make it more severe such as the use of a deadly weapon or the fact that the battery resulted in serious bodily harm.

aggravated robbery Robbery committed by a person who either carries a dangerous weapon or inflicts bodily harm on someone during the robbery.

aggravating Enhancing.

aggravating factor A fact or circumstance that increases the degree of liability or culpability for a criminal act.

aid and abet Help, assist, or facilitate the commission of a crime; promote the accomplishment thereof; help in advancing or bringing it about; or encourage, counsel, or incite as to its commission.

Alert The case-clipping system used by LexisNexis to monitor legal developments.

alimony Court-ordered money paid to support a former spouse after termination of a marriage.

alimony pendente lite Temporary order for payments of a set amount monthly while the litigation continues.

allegations Facts forming the basis of a party's complaint.

alter ego doctrine A business set up to cover or be a shield for the person actually controlling the corporation, and thus the court may treat the owners as if they were partners or a sole proprietor.

alternative dispute resolution (ADR) Method of settling a dispute before trial in order to conserve the court's time.

ALWD Citation Manual A legal citation resource, published by the Association of Legal Writing Directors, that contains local and state sources that may not be found in *The Bluebook*.

ambiguity Lack of precision and clarity.

amended pleading A pleading that changes, corrects, revises, or deletes information from a prior pleading.

American Bar Association (ABA) A national organization of lawyers, providing support and continuing legal education to the profession.

American Jurisprudence (Am. Jur. and Am. Jur. 2d) Legal encyclopedia organized by topics and subheadings presenting law and scholarly discussion from multiple jurisdictions.

American Law Institute A nongovernmental organization composed of distinguished judges and lawyers in the United States.

American Law Reports Set of books known for its annotations, which contain both primary and secondary sources of the law.

American rule of attorney fees and costs Expenses incurred by the parties to maintain or defend an action for the breach of contract are generally not recoverable as damages.

amicus brief Brief filed by a nonparty to an appeal who has an interest, whether political, social, or otherwise, in the outcome of the case.

amicus curiae Translated from the Latin as a "friend of the court."

analysis Applied after finding the law and interpreting the application to the facts to formulate a persuasive argument supporting your position.

annotated code A code that provides, in addition to the text of the codified statutes, such information as cases that have construed the statute; law review articles that have discussed it; the procedural history of the statute (amendments or antecedents); cross-references to superseded codifications; cross-references to related statutes; and other information.

annotated version Presents the law as enacted or case opinion as stated along with discussion and commentary.

annotation An in-depth analysis of a specific and important legal issue raised in the accompanying decision, together with an extensive survey of the way the issue is treated in various jurisdictions.

annulment Court procedure dissolving a marriage, treating it as if it never happened.

answer The defendant's response to the plaintiff 's complaint.

anticipation An expectation of things to come that has reasonable basis for the conclusion.

anticipatory breach Party provides notice, or it otherwise becomes known, that the anticipated performance will not be completed.

anticipatory repudiation Words or acts from a party to the contract that clearly and unquestionably state the intent not to honor his contractual obligations before the time for performance has arrived.

apostrophe A form of punctuation used to create a contraction or a possessive noun.

appeal Tests the sufficiency of the verdict under the legal parameters or rules.

appellant The party filing the appeal; that is, bringing the case to the appeals court.

appellant's brief Brief of the party filing the appeal.

appellate brief Brief filed in an appeals court.

appellate court The court of appeals that reviews a trial court's record for errors.

appellate jurisdiction Power of a court to hear challenges from a lower court.

appellate rules Procedures set forth by the appeals court in processing an appeal.

appellee The prevailing party in the lower court, who will respond to the appellant's argument.

appellee's brief Brief of the party responding to the appeal.

appendix Contains the supplementary collection of the sources from the trial court.

appraisal The evaluation by an expert of the cash value of a contest item.

arbitration Alternative dispute resolution method mediated or supervised by a neutral third party who imposes a recommendation for resolution, after hearing evidence from both parties and the parties participated in reaching, that is fully enforceable and treated in the courts the same as a judicial order.

arbitrator Individual who imposes a solution on the parties based on the evidence from both parties.

argument Section of the brief where the issues are analyzed through citation of legal authorities.

arraignment A court hearing where the information contained in an indictment is read to the defendant.

arrest The formal taking of a person, usually by a police officer, to answer criminal charges.

arson At common law, arson had four requisites. First, there must be some actual burning (though this requirement did not include destruction of the building or even of any substantial part of the building). Second, the burning must be malicious (negligence is not sufficient). Third, the object burned must be a dwelling house. Fourth and finally, the house burned must be the habitation of another.

articles of incorporation The basic charter of an organization, written and filed in accordance with state laws.

articles of partnership Written agreement to form a partnership.

Articles of the Constitution Establish government form and function.

asportation The act of carrying away or removing property or a person.

assault Intentional voluntary movement that creates fear or apprehension of an immediate unwanted touching; the threat or attempt to cause a touching, whether successful or not, provided the victim is aware of the danger.

assertion of defenses Either the original parties or a third-party beneficiary has the right to claim any legal defenses or excuses that they may have as against each other. They are not extinguished by a third party.

assignee The party to whom the right to receive contractual performance is transferred.

assignment The transfer of the rights to receive the benefit of contractual performance under the contract.

assignor The party who assigns his rights away and relinquishes his rights to collect the benefit of contractual performance.

assisted suicide The intentional act of providing a person with the medical means or the medical knowledge to commit suicide.

associate attorney An attorney who is an employee of an attorney partnership.

assumption of the risk The doctrine that releases another person from liability for the person who chooses to assume a known risk of harm.

asterisk Punctuation used in word searches that allows for variations in spelling when substituted for a letter in the search term.

attempt To actually try to commit a crime and have the actual ability to do so.

attestation clause The section of the will where the witnesses observe the act of the testator signing the will.

attorney general opinions Legal opinions given by the highest-ranking legal officer in the federal government or a state.

attorney–client privilege The legal relationship established between attorney and client allowing for free exchange of information without fear of disclosure.

attractive nuisance doctrine The doctrine that holds a landowner to a higher duty of care even when the children are trespassers, because the potentially harmful condition is so inviting to a child.

audience The person or persons to whom a legal document is directed, such as a client or the court.

authentication Proof by an officer, witness, or certifying document that evidence is what it is claimed to be.

authorization letter A letter the client provides the attorney granting permission to contact employers, doctors, or other individuals who have records that relate to a case.

avoid The power of a minor to stop performance under a contract.

avoid the contract Legally sufficient excuse for failure to complete performance under the contract.

B

bad faith Intentional misrepresentation, wanton disregard for truth, or fraudulent activity that can be the basis for an additional award of damages to the party that can establish such activity occurred.

bail Court-mandated surety or guarantee that the defendant will appear at a future date if released from custody prior to trial.

bailee The recipient of the property, temporarily taking possession.

bailment The delivery of personal property from one person to another to be held temporarily.

bailor The owner of the property transferring possession.

bankruptcy appellate panel Panel that hears an initial bankruptcy appeal.

bankruptcy courts Federal courts of exclusive jurisdiction to hear cases regarding debtors.

bar examination A test administered to graduates from approved law schools that determines the applicant's knowledge of the law and suitability to practice in the state.

bates stamp A self-inking stamp system that sequentially numbers documents.

battery An intentional and unwanted harmful or offensive contact with the person of another; the actual intentional touching of someone with intent to cause harm, no matter how slight the harm.

battle of the forms An evaluation of commercial writings whose terms conflict with each other in order to determine what terms actually control the performances due from the parties.

bcc Blind copy.

bench trial A case heard and decided by a judge.

bench warrant The process issued by the court itself for the attachment or arrest of a person.

beneficiaries The persons named in a will to receive the testator's assets.

benefit Gain acquired by a party or parties to a contract.

benefit conferred The exchange that bestows value upon the other party to the contract.

bequest Gift by will of personal property.

best interest of the child Premier concern in every family law matter.

beyond a reasonable doubt The requirement for the level of proof in a criminal matter in order to convict or find the defendant guilty. It is a substantially higher and more-difficult-to-prove criminal matter standard.

bicameral process One of the types of legislative bodies that has two separate houses required to pass a bill, such as the House and Senate of the U.S. Congress.

bifurcated Separated from other issues.

bigamy One spouse knowingly enters a second marriage while the first remains valid.

bilateral Affecting or obligating both parties.

bilateral contract A contract in which the parties exchange a promise for a promise.

Bill of Rights Sets forth the fundamental individual rights that government and law function to preserve and protect; the first ten amendments to the Constitution of the United States.

billing Record keeping of time and tasks performed by a paralegal for each client and the legal task performed on behalf of the client.

bills Laws proposed by a legislature; the formal introduction to a piece of legislation.

binding authority (mandatory authority) A source of law that a court must follow in deciding a case, such as a statute or federal regulations.

black letter law The strict meaning of the law as it is written without concern or interpretation of the reasoning behind its creation.

Black's Law Dictionary Dictionary of legal terminology and word usage.

blackmail The extortion of payment based on a threat of exposing the victim's secrets.

block quote A quotation over fifty words that is single-spaced and indented.

blog An abbreviation for "web-based log"; an Internet-based daily journal or diary discussing events in an individual's life or providing thoughts and perspectives about contemporary issues.

board of directors Policy managers of a corporation, elected by the shareholders, who in turn chose the officers of the corporation.

bodily injury Physical damage to a person's body.

body Main text of the argument section of the appellate brief.

body (writing) The portion of a paragraph that contains the material that you claim supports the contention raised in the topic sentence; the text that contains the information you wish to communicate in a letter.

boilerplate Standard language in a form.

booking Administrative step taken after an arrested person is brought to the police station that involves entry of the person's name, the crime for which the arrest was made, and other relevant facts on the police blotter.

Boolean word search Word search technique using terms and connectors to retrieve information from the Internet.

brackets A form of punctuation that indicates changes or additions.

brain death When the body shows no response to external stimuli, no spontaneous movements, no breathing, no reflexes, and a flat reading on a machine that measures the brain's electrical activity.

breach of contract A party's performance that deviates from the required performance obligations under the contract; a violation of an obligation under a contract for which a party may seek recourse to the court.

breach of duty The failure to maintain a reasonable degree of care toward another person to whom a duty is owed.

breaking In the law of burglary, the act of entering a building without permission.

brevity Strong, tight writing.

bribery The offering, giving, receiving, or soliciting of something of value for the purpose of influencing the action of an official in the discharge of his or her public or legal duties.

brief A formal written argument presented to the court.

brief bank A document depository of briefs prepared by a law firm in previous matters.

briefing a case Summarizing a court opinion.

briefing schedule Timetable for various required filings by both parties throughout the appeal process.

bright line rules A legal standard resolves issues in a simple, formulaic manner that is easy in application although it may not always be equitable.

bulk sale Agreement to transfer all or substantially all the goods to the buyer.

burden of proof Standard for assessing the weight of the evidence.

burglary Breaking and entering into a structure for the purpose of committing a crime.

business judgment rule The rule that protects corporate officers and directors from liability for bad business decisions.

business organization A form of conducting business.

"but for" test If the complained-of act had not occurred, no injury would have resulted.

by a preponderance of evidence The weight or level of persuasion of evidence needed to find the defendant liable as alleged by the plaintiff in a civil matter.

bylaws Corporate provisions detailing management structure and operating rules.

C

calendar call A mandatory court hearing in which the judge inquires about the readiness of the parties to go to trial; also known as a docket call.

calendaring System of tracking dates, appointments, filing deadlines for documents, and events throughout the case file for both the attorney and the paralegal.

cancel the contract The aggrieved party has the right to terminate the contractual relationship with no repercussions.

cap on damages Limit established by statutes.

capacity The ability to understand the nature and significance of a contract; to understand or comprehend specific acts or reasoning.

caption The full name of the case, together with the docket number, court, and date of the decision.

Cardozo test Zone of foreseeability and proximate cause analysis as a test of the scope of damages.

carjacking The crime of stealing a motor vehicle while the vehicle is occupied.

case brief An objective summary of the important points of a single case; a summary of a court opinion.

case evaluation The process of investigating the facts, issues, and legal implications of a proposed lawsuit before it is ever filed.

case holding The statement of law the case opinion supports.

case law Published court opinions of federal and state appellate courts; judge-created law in deciding cases, set forth in court opinions.

case management Keeping track of the progress or status of the file and proactively organizing the work of both the attorney and the paralegal.

case of first impression A case in which no previous court decision with similar facts or legal issue has arisen before; a case with a legal issue that has not been heard by the court before in a specific jurisdiction.

case on all fours A case in which facts, issues, parties, and remedies are analogous to the present case.

case on point A case involving similar facts and issues to the present case.

case opinions Explanations of how and why the court interpreted the law as it did under the specific facts and applicable law of the individual case.

case reporters Sets of books that contain copies of appellate court opinions from every case heard and published within the relevant jurisdiction.

causation Intentional act resulted in harm or injury to the complaining plaintiff.

cause of action A personal, financial, or other injury for which the law gives a person the right to receive compensation.

cc Copy.

certainty The ability for a term to be determined and evaluated by a party outside of the contract; the ability to rely on objective assurances to make a determination without doubt.

certificate of compliance Attorney certification at the end of an appellate brief attesting to compliance with the page limitations set forth by that court's rules.

certificate of interested parties Statement in a brief identifying parties who have an interest in the outcome and financial affiliations.

certificate of marriage Completed when the official completes the ceremony confirming the ceremony took place and is recognized by the state.

certificate of service Verification by attorney that pleadings or court documents were sent to the opposing counsel in a case.

certification The recognition of the attainment of a degree of academic and practical knowledge by a professional.

Certified Legal Assistant (CLA) Standardized test based primarily on general concepts and federal law administered in connection with paralegal certification.

certiorari (Cert) (Latin) "To make sure." An appellate court's authority to decide which cases it will hear on appeal.

chain conspiracy A single conspiracy in which each person is responsible for a distinct act within the overall plan.

challenge An attorney's objection, during *voir dire,* to the inclusion of a specific person on the jury.

charter Local constitution.

chattel Tangible personal property or goods.

checks and balances Mechanism designed into the Constitution that prevents one branch from overreaching and abusing its power.

child custody Arrangement between the parties for residential and custodial care of the minor children.

child support The right of a child to financial support and the obligation of a parent to provide it.

Chinese wall The shielding, or walling off, of a new employee from a client in the new firm with whom there may be a conflict of interest.

circuit One of several courts in a specific jurisdiction.

circumstantial evidence Evidence that suggests a conclusion.

citation Information about a legal source directing you to the volume and page in which the legal source appears.

citators A series of books that both update the law and act as finding tools.

civil cause of action A claim for damages that is based on the relevant substantive area of law and has facts that support a judicial resolution.

civil law The legal rules regarding offenses committed against the person.

civil liability Finding that the defendant acted or failed to act, resulting in damages or harm. It cannot be punished by incarceration.

civil verdict Finds liability.

clarity The ability to accurately convey the intended message to the reader in a clear, precise manner.

class action A lawsuit involving a large group of plaintiffs who have been certified by a court as having mutual interests, common claims, and a representative plaintiff who will pursue the action on the basis of the entire group.

clean hands doctrine A plaintiff at fault is barred from seeking redress from the courts.

clear and convincing Evidence that indicates that a thing to be proved is highly probable or reasonably certain.

clear and convincing evidence Having a high probability of truthfulness, a higher standard being preponderance of the evidence.

clerk A government official responsible for maintaining public records.

clerk of the court An individual who manages the administrative functions of the court.

clichés Overused figures of speech.

client intake Basic demographic and case-specific information developed in the first meeting with the client following the formal engagement.

closely held corporation A business that is incorporated with limited members, typically related family members.

closing sentence A sentence at the end of a paragraph that summarizes the topic; the concluding message in a letter.

closing statements (closing arguments) A statement by a party's attorney that summarizes that party's case and reviews what that party promised to prove during trial.

***Code of Federal Regulations* (*C.F.R.*)** Federal statutory law collection.

Code of Hammurabi First formalized legal system (1792–1750 B.C.).

code A multivolume compilation that groups statutes by subject matter and is well indexed, in order to make the statutes more accessible for research purposes.

codicil A provision that amends or modifies an existing will.

cohabitation agreement A contract setting forth the rights of two people who live together without the benefit of marriage.

collateral source rule A rule of evidence that allows the jury to be informed about the plaintiff's other sources of compensation, such as insurance, worker's compensation, and so forth.

collection letter A letter that demands payment of an amount claimed to be owed to a client.

colloquialisms Informal language used in everyday conversation.

collusion Illegally created agreement of the parties.

colon A form of punctuation that joins together phrases or explanatory clauses or introduces a block quote.

comity Federal government respect for state government power and authority results in federal refusal to intervene in matters clearly within the sole jurisdiction of the state government.

comma Punctuation used to re-create verbal pauses.

commencement of action The formal document filed in the court describing the plaintiff, the party bringing the action, and the wrongdoing alleged by the plaintiff against the defendant, or the party against whom the claim is made.

Commerce Clause Statement in the Constitution that the federal government has absolute authority in matters affecting citizens of all states.

commercial impracticability Impossibility of performance in a commercial context and contracts governed by UCC Article 2.

commercial unit A batch of goods packaged or sold together in the normal course of the relevant industry.

commingling A term for mixing a client's funds with the attorney's personal funds without permission; an ethical violation.

common law Judge-made law; the ruling in a judicial opinion.

common law marriage A form of marriage that is legally recognized in certain states, if the two people have been living together for a long period of time, have represented themselves as being married, and have the intent to be married.

community property All property acquired during marriage in a community property state, owned in equal shares.

community service A criminal sentence requiring that the offender perform some specific service to the community for some specified period of time.

comparative negligence Applies when the evidence shows that both the plaintiff and the defendant acted negligently.

compensatory damages A payment to make up for a wrong committed and return the nonbreaching party to a position where the effect or the breach has been neutralized.

competence The ability and possession of expertise and skill in a field that is necessary to do the job.

competent jurisdiction The power of a court to determine the outcome of the dispute presented.

complaint Document that states the allegations and the legal basis of the plaintiff 's claims. Also, a charge, preferred before a magistrate having jurisdiction, that a person named has committed a specified offense, with an offer to prove the fact, to the end that a prosecution may be instituted.

complete defense The individual entered the relationship knowingly with legal capacity.

complete integration A document that contains all the terms of the agreement and the parties have agreed that there are no other terms outside the contract.

complex sentence A sentence that contains a subordinate clause or clauses in addition to the main clause.

complicity A state of being an accomplice; participation in guilt.

complimentary closing The concluding words in the letter just above a signature.

compound sentence A sentence in which the clauses could stand separately, each ending with a period.

compulsory counterclaim A counterclaim that is required to be pleaded because the facts relate to the same transaction as that set forth in the original complaint.

computer-assisted legal research (CALR) Research method using electronically retrieved source materials.

conclusion Summation of your analysis in a memorandum or relief requested in a brief.

concur To agree with the majority opinion.

concurrence Another view or analysis written by a member of the same reviewing panel. Also, a meeting or coming together of a guilty act and a guilty mind.

concurrent condition An event that happens at the same time as the parties' performance obligations.

concurrent jurisdiction Jurisdiction over the subject matter exists in both state and federal court, unless statutorily prohibited.

concurrent ownership More than one individual shares the rights of ownership.

concurrent sentences Two or more sentences of jail time to be served simultaneously.

concurring opinion An opinion in which a judge who agrees with the ultimate result wishes to apply different reasoning from that in the majority opinion.

condemnation proceedings The process by which state or federal government obtains property.

condition An event that may or may not happen upon which the rest of the performance of the contract rests.

condition precedent An event that happens beforehand and gives rise to the parties' performance obligations. If the condition is not satisfied, the parties do not have a duty to perform.

condition subsequent An event that, if it happens after the parties' performance obligations, negates the duty to perform. If the condition is satisfied, the parties can "undo" their actions.

conditional acceptance A refusal to accept the stated terms of an offer by adding restrictions or requirements to the terms of the offer by the offeree.

conditional sale Terms other than delivery and payment must be met to transfer title of the goods.

conditional transfer Conditions stated at the time of the conveyance; the original owner, despite the conveyance, retains an interest.

conference committee A committee made up of members of both houses of Congress who review a bill, iron out the differences, and present it for approval to their respective bodies.

confidentiality Lawyer's duty not to disclose information concerning a client.

confirmation letter A letter designed to create a record or restate the content of the original oral communication.

conflict check A procedure to verify potential adverse interests before accepting a new client.

conflict letter A letter sent by an attorney to the judge explaining that the attorney has several different appearances scheduled for the same date and detailing which courts the attorney will go to first.

conflict of interest Clash between private and professional interests or competing professional interests that makes impartiality difficult and creates an unfair advantage.

Confrontation Clause Sixth Amendment guarantee that the accused has the absolute right to confront his accusers and all evidence.

Congressional Record Contains the official records of proceedings and debates of Congress.

connected case A Shepard's notation that either involves the same parties or arises from the same subject matter Shepardized.

consanguinity The relationship between blood relatives, such as brothers and sisters.

consecutive sentences Two or more sentences of jail time to be served in sequence.

consent All parties to a novation must knowingly assent to the substitution of either the obligations or parties to the agreement. Also, voluntarily yielding the will to another.

consequential damages Damages resulting from the breach that are natural and foreseeable results of the breaching party's actions.

consideration Parol evidence is permitted to show that the subject matter of the contract as received was not as it was bargained for.

conspicuous limitation or exclusion of warranties A seller may specifically deny any warranties as long as the limitation or exclusion of the warranties is set forth in language that is understandable and noticeable by the buyer.

conspiracy By agreement, parties work together to create an illegal result, to achieve an unlawful end.

constitution The organic and fundamental law of a nation or state, which may be written or unwritten, establishing the character and conception of its government, laying out the basic principles to which its internal life is to be conformed, organizing the government, regulating functions of departments, and prescribing the extent to which a nation or state can exercise its powers.

constitutional law Based on the federal Constitution and arising from interpretations of the intent and scope of constitutional provisions.

consular marriage Conducted by a diplomat of the U.S. government.

contempt A willful disregard for or disobedience of a public authority.

contingency fee The attorney's fee calculated as a percentage of the final award in a civil case.

continuing consideration Extends over time.

continuing legal education (CLE) Continued legal competence and skills training required of practicing professionals.

contraband Commodity that cannot be legally possessed.

contract A legally binding agreement between two or more parties.

contract of adhesion An agreement wherein one party has total control over the bargaining process and therefore the other party has no power to negotiate and no choice but to enter into the contract.

contractual capacity Legal capability to enter a contract.

contractual good faith See *good faith*.

contradictory Evidence that is in conflict with the terms of the contract and inadmissible under the parol evidence rule.

contributory negligence The plaintiff played a large part in causing the injury; thus, fundamental fairness precludes assigning liability to the defendant.

conversion An overt act to deprive the owner of possession of personal property with no intention of returning the property, thereby causing injury or harm.

conveyance A transfer.

conviction Results from a guilty finding by the jury in a criminal trial.

corporation An organization formed with state government approval to act as an artificial person to carry on business and issue stock.

corpus delicti Latin: "body of the crime." The fact of the transgression or the physical evidence of a crime such as the body of a murder victim.

***Corpus Juris Secundum* (*Cor. Jur. 2d*)** Legal encyclopedia organized by topics and subheadings presenting law and scholarly discussion from multiple jurisdictions.

count The cause of action in the complaint.

counterclaim A claim made by the defendant against the plaintiff—not a defense, but a new claim for damages, as if the defendant were the plaintiff in a separate suit; a countersuit brought by the defendant against the plaintiff.

counterfeiting Forging, copying, or imitating without a right to do so and with the purpose of deceiving or defrauding.

counteroffer A refusal to accept the stated terms of an offer by proposing alternate terms.

course of dealing The parties' actions taken in similar previous transactions.

course of performance The parties' actions taken in reliance on the particular transaction in question.

court Place where parties have problems resolved.

Court of International Trade Part of the federal lower-court level authorized to hear matters related to international trade agreements and disputes.

court reporter Individual who transcribes the court proceedings and certifies their authenticity.

court rules Regulations with the force of law governing practice and procedure in the various courts.

covenant The promise upon which the contract rests.

covenant marriage The couples make an affirmative undertaking to get counseling prior to the marriage and to seek counseling if contemplating divorce.

covenant not to compete An employment clause that prohibits an employee from leaving his job and going to work for a competitor for a specified period of time in a particular area.

covenant not to sue An agreement by the parties to relinquish their right to commence a lawsuit based on the original and currently existing cause of action under the contract.

cover The buyer can mitigate her losses from the seller's breach by purchasing substitute goods on the open market; the nonbreaching party's attempt to mitigate damages may require that he purchase alternate goods on the open market to replace those never delivered by the breaching party.

cover letter A standard form letter identifying information such as document filings.

creditor A party to whom a debt is owed.

crime Any act done in violation of those duties that an individual owes to the community, and for the breach of which the law has provided that the offender shall make satisfaction to the public.

criminal law The legal rules regarding wrongs committed against society.

criminal trespass The offense committed by one who, without license or privilege to do so, enters or surreptitiously remains in any building or occupied structure.

criminal verdict Finds the defendant guilty or not guilty of the criminal offense charged and tried.

criticism An opinion.

critique A position that is presented with supporting evidence.

cross-claim lawsuit A lawsuit against a party of the same side; plaintiffs or defendants suing each other (defendant versus defendant or plaintiff versus plaintiff).

cross-examination Occurs when the opposing attorney asks the witness questions.

cumulative sentence A sentence that conveys the information in a comprehensive manner.

cure The seller is given a reasonable opportunity to fix the defects in the goods found by the buyer.

curtilage Outbuildings that are directly and intimately connected with the habitation and in proximity thereto and the land or grounds surrounding the dwelling that are necessary and convenient and habitually used for family purposes and carrying on domestic employment.

custodial parent Parent with whom the child(ren) resides primarily following dissolution of the marriage.

custody The legal authority to make decisions concerning a child's interests. Also, the care and control of a thing or person.

damage Detriment, harm, or injury.

damages Money paid to compensate for loss or injury.

dash A punctuation mark longer than a hyphen, which is used for limited purposes, such as separating the segments of a two-part sentence.

database A collection of information used in computer systems to provide access to related fields of interest.

de novo Standard appellate review where the appellate court reviews the facts and law independent of the trial court's decision.

deadline date A certain date by which a request or demand should be fulfilled.

deadly force Defense available in cases involving the defense of persons, oneself, or another. It is a violent action known to create a substantial risk of causing death or serious bodily harm.

deadly weapon Any firearm or other device, instrument, material, or substance that, from the manner in which it is used or is intended to be used, is calculated or likely to produce death.

death or incapacity of a party An excuse for performance on a contract due to the inability of the party to fulfill his obligation.

debtor One of the parties in a bankruptcy action who owes money to creditors.

Decennial Digest Digest that groups cases by time period and subject without regard to jurisdiction.

Declaration of Independence Statement, preceding the U.S. Constitution, giving the intention to form a new government in the colonies and including general principles guiding the form of that new government.

declaratory judgment The court's determination of the rights and responsibilities of a party with respect to the subject matter of the controversy.

decree nisi The divorce and all related issues are finalized pending passage of the statutorily prescribed period.

deductive reasoning Process of reasoning that draws a conclusion about a specific issue from a general issue in determining how to apply the law to a specific set of facts.

deed The written document transferring title, or an ownership interest in real property, to another person.

defamation An act of communication involving a false and unprivileged statement about another person, causing harm.

default judgment A judgment entered by the court against the defendant for failure to respond to the plaintiff's complaint.

defects in formation Errors or omissions made during the negotiations that function as a bar to creating a valid contract.

defendant The party against whom a lawsuit is brought.

Defendant/Plaintiff Table List of the cases alphabetically by the defendant first or a table of cases listing the name of the case both ways.

defense Legally sufficient reason to excuse the complained-of behavior.

defense of arrest In situations involving police officers or, rarely, private citizens with evidence that the arrest was in furtherance of the reasonable duties of the officer.

defense of consent The plaintiff consented fully, knowingly, and willingly to the act or acts.

defense of discipline Requires the discipline be reasonable under the circumstances.

defense of necessity Available with invasion of property when such occurs in an emergency.

defense of others A justification defense available if one harms or threatens another while defending a third person.

delegant/delegator The party who transfers his obligation to perform his contractual obligations.

delegate/delegatee The party to whom the obligation to perform the contractual obligations is transferred.

delegation The transfer of the duties/obligations to perform under the contract.

delivery In commercial contracts, delivery may be accomplished by transferring actual possession of the goods, or putting the goods at the disposal of the buyer, or by a negotiable instrument giving the buyer the right to the goods.

demand letter A letter requesting action on a legal matter.

democracy Government form characterized by rule of and by the people or, if more practical, by elected representatives of the people.

demonstrative evidence Any object, visual aid, model, scale drawing, or other exhibit designed to help clarify points in the trial.

deny (denial) To disagree with or contest the allegations presented in a complaint

deponent The party or witness who is questioned in a deposition.

deposition A discovery tool in a question-and-answer format in which the attorney verbally questions a party or a witness under oath.

deposition digest A summary of deposition testimony of a witness.

deposition on written questions A deposition based on written questions submitted in advance to a party; only those questions are answered, with no follow-up questions allowed.

depraved heart murder A murder resulting from an act so reckless and careless of the safety of others that it demonstrates the perpetrator's complete lack of regard for human life.

deprived of expected benefit A party can reasonably expect to receive that for which he bargained; if he does not receive it, the breach is considered material.

depublished opinion Opinion that was originally set for publication by a California court but later ordered unpublished.

Descriptive Word Index A subject index that provides a researcher with a quick survey of specific key numbers, often from several topics, which apply to a given subject area.

desist To cease an activity.

destruction or loss of subject matter The nonexistence of the subject matter of the contract, which renders it legally valueless and unable to be exchanged according to the terms of the contract; excuse of performance is based on the unforeseeable and unavoidable loss of the subject matter.

detain To restrain, arrest, check, delay, hinder, hold, keep, or retain in custody.

detention The act of keeping back, restraining, or withholding, either accidentally or by design, a person or thing.

deter To turn aside, discourage, or prevent from acting.

determinate sentence A sentence for a fixed length of time rather than for an unspecified duration.

deterrent effect The authority to assess excessive fines on a breaching party often can dissuade a party from committing an act that would subject him to these punitive damages.

detriment A loss or burden incurred because of contract formation.

detriment incurred The exchange that burdens the party in giving the consideration to the other party to the contract.

detrimental effect A party's worsening of his position due to his dependence on the terms of the contract.

detrimental reliance An offeree has depended upon the assertions of the offeror and made a change for the worse in his position depending on those assertions.

devise A disposition of real property by will.

dictum (plural: **dicta**) A statement made by the court in a case that is beyond what is necessary to reach the final decision.

digest A collection of all the headnotes from an associated series of volumes, arranged alphabetically by topic and by key number or summary of testimony with indexed references of a deposition.

diminished capacity The doctrine that recognizes that an accused does not have to be suffering from a mental disease to have impaired mental capacities at the time the offense was committed.

direct evidence Evidence that establishes a particular fact without resort to other testimony or evidence.

direct examination Occurs when the attorney questions his or her own witness.

disaffirm Renounce, as in a contract.

disavowal A step taken by a formerly incapacitated person that denies and cancels the voidable contract and thereby makes it unenforceable.

disbarment Temporary suspension or permanent revocation of an individual's license to practice law.

discharge of duties Recognition by both parties that contract obligations are completed whether by performance or by agreement of the parties.

discharged Contract completion as to every requirement; that is, completed and terminated.

disclaimer A term which limits claim or denial.

discovery The pretrial investigation process authorized and governed by the rules of civil procedure; the process of investigation and collection of evidence by litigants; process in which the opposing parties obtain information about the case from each other; the process of investigation and collection of evidence by litigants.

discovery rule A legal principle that a statute of limitations begins to run when a person discovers, or should have known, that an act of negligence may have been committed.

discussion and analysis The heart of the memorandum, which presents the legal analysis with supporting citations.

dismissal An order or judgment finally disposing of an action, suit, motion, or other without trial of the issues involved.

disorderly conduct Behavior that tends to disturb the public peace, offend public morals, or undermine public safety.

disposition Appears at the end of the opinion and tells the reader how the court handled the lower court decision.

dispositive motion A motion that terminates some or all of the pending issues in a case.

dissent (dissenting opinion) Opinion in which a judge disagrees with the result reached by the majority; an opinion outlining the reasons for the dissent, which often critiques the majority and any concurring opinions.

dissipating Wasting the marital estate.

dissolution of marriage Process resulting in termination of the marital union.

distinguishing Explaining why the factual differences call for a decision differing from established law.

distinguishing facts Facts that establish the different analysis and application of settled law.

diversity jurisdiction Authority of the federal court to hear a case if the parties are citizens of different states and the amount at issue is over $75,000.

diversity of citizenship jurisdiction Federal jurisdiction conferred when the case involves citizens of different states.

dividends Portion of profits, usually based on the number of shares owned.

divisibility/severability A contract may be able to be compartmentalized into separate parts and seen as a series of independent transactions between the parties.

divorce/dissolution The legal termination of a marriage.

docket A court's caseload.

docket number The number assigned by the court to the case for its own administrative purposes.

doctrine of strict construction Statutory interpretation doctrine that narrowly interprets a statute's meaning and intent.

doctrine of unclean hands A party seeking equitable remedies must have acted justly and in good faith in the transaction in question; otherwise, equitable remedies will not be available to a wrongdoer.

documentary evidence Any evidence represented on paper that contributes to supporting the legal position and/or verbal testimony of witnesses, for example, medical billing records, physician treatment notes, bank statements, and canceled checks.

do-gooder arguments Appeals to the save-the-world attitude.

domicile The place where a person maintains a physical residence with the intent to permanently remain in that place; citizenship; the permanent home of the party.

donee A party to whom a gift is given.

donor The person making a gift.

double jeopardy Being tried twice for the same act or acts.

duces tecum A deposition notice requiring the deponent/witness to "bring with him" specified documents or things.

due process Ensures the appropriateness and adequacy of government action in circumstances infringing on fundamental individual rights.

due process clause Refers to two aspects of the law: procedural, in which a person is guaranteed fair procedures, and substantive, which protects a person's property from unfair governmental interference or taking.

duress Unreasonable and unscrupulous manipulation of a person to force him to agree to terms of an agreement that he would otherwise not agree to. Also, any unlawful threat or coercion used by a person to induce another to act (or to refrain from acting) in a manner that he otherwise would not do.

duty A legal obligation that is required to be performed.

duty to resell The UCC requires commercial sellers to try to resell the goods that have not been accepted by the original buyer.

duty to warn See *landowner's duty.*

dwelling A house or other structure that is used or intended for use as a residence.

E

earning capacity The ability to earn based on objective evidence.

easement A right to use another's property for a specific purpose, such as a right of way across the land.

economic duress The threat of harm to a party's financial resources unless demands are met.

editing To delete, eliminate, or change the text of a legal document.

eggshell skull theory A plaintiff with a preexisting condition does not change or diminish the defendant's liability.

elements of the crime Those constituent parts of a crime that must be proved by the prosecution to sustain a conviction.

ellipsis A form of punctuation that indicates the elimination of text from an extended quote.

embedded citation A citation placed within a sentence.

embezzlement The fraudulent appropriation of property by one lawfully entrusted with its possession.

eminent domain The government can take land through the process of condemnation when the taking is for public use.

empty promise A promise that has neither a legal nor a practical value.

en banc Appellate review by the entire circuit appeals judiciary after review by the intermediate panel.

en banc decisions Decisions made by the court as a whole because of their legal significance.

enacted A bill that is in effect.

enhancements Added factors to a criminal charge that make the charge carry greater weight.

entrapment An act of a law enforcement official to induce or encourage a person to commit a crime when the defendant expresses no desire to proceed with the illegal act.

enumerated powers Powers listed in the Constitution or the jobs of the particular office, for example, the president, or the branch, for example, the judicial.

equal bargaining power Both parties have the same position in terms of strengths and weaknesses.

equitable distribution Divides the assets acquired during the marriage between the parties.

equitable relief A remedy that is other than money damages, such as refraining from or performing a certain act; nonmonetary remedies fashioned by the court using standards of fairness and justice. Injunction and specific performance are types of equitable relief.

equitable remedy Nonmonetary damages, such as an injunction.

equitable tolling Suspending a statute of limitations based upon principles of fairness or an unexpected intervening event.

equity The doctrine of fairness and justice; the process of making things balance or be equal between parties.

error of fact Legal standard on appeal alleging the facts accepted by the trial court judge are incorrect.

error of law Standard of review on appeal alleging error of the court in applying the standards of the law.

escheat To pass property to the state, as is done with the assets of a person who dies without a will and without heirs.

espionage Spying or the gathering, transmitting, or losing of information respecting the national defense with intent or reason to believe that the information is to be used to the injury of the United States, or to the advantage of any foreign nation.

estate in land An ownership interest in real property; the compilation of all a deceased's assets and debts.

ethics Standards by which conduct is measured.

evidence Any fact, testimony, or physical object that tends to prove or disprove allegations raised in a case; must be reasonably calculated to lead to the discovery of admissible evidence.

ex parte A communication between one party in a lawsuit and the judge.

exceptions to contract enforceability Legally adequate reasons for nonperformance of contract obligations.

excessive and unreasonable cost A court will only consider excusing performance based on impracticality if the additional expense is extreme and disproportionate to the bargain.

excited utterance An exception to the hearsay rule that allows a statement made spontaneously after a shocking event to be admissible at trial.

exclamation point A form of punctuation used to highlight something extraordinary. Also, punctuation used in an Internet search, usually at the root of a search term, to retrieve all variations of the main word.

exclusionary rule Circumstances surrounding the seizure do not meet warrant requirements or exceptions; items seized deemed *fruit of the poisonous tree* are excluded from trial evidence.

exclusive jurisdiction Only one court has the authority to hear the specific case; for example, only a federal court can decide a bankruptcy case.

exculpatory evidence Supports the possibility of the defendant's innocence.

excuse A reason alleged for doing or not doing a thing.

excused for cause Process of excusing jurors for bias, prejudices, and legitimate reasons as well, such as sickness, job commitment, or others.

excused from performance The nonbreaching party is released from her obligations to perform due to the other party's breach.

executed The parties' performance obligations under the contract are complete.

executed contract The parties' performance obligations under the contract are complete.

executive order Order issued by the U.S. president having the force of law but without going through the typical process for enacting legislation.

executive privilege Special protection afforded communications of the president.

executor/executrix The administrator of the estate.

executory The parties' performances under the contract have yet to occur.

executory consideration An exchange of value completed over time.

executory interest Following the termination of the life tenant's possession, other conditions or circumstances become complete at some designated future date or occurrence.

exemplary damages Punitive damages, awarded as a punishment and a deterrent.

exhaustion of administrative remedies Provision that a nonlitigation process to informally resolve disputes must be attempted prior to filing a complaint.

exhibit A document attached to a pleading that is incorporated by reference into the body of the pleading.

exigent circumstances Compelling reason to believe the evidence may be destroyed or otherwise removed.

existence of the subject matter The goods to be transferred must exist at the time of the making of the contract.

expectation damages A monetary amount that makes up for the losses incurred as a result of the breach that puts the nonbreaching party in as good a position as he would have been had the contract been fully performed.

expectation-of-privacy test See *Katz expectation-of-privacy test.*

explanatory Oral testimony is permitted to clarify the terms of the contract.

express acceptance Stated or, if applicable, written statement from the offeree that mirrors the offer; that is, it is precisely the same as the offer.

express conditions Requirements stated in words, either orally or written, in the contract.

express consideration Stated clearly and unambiguously.

express contracts An agreement whose terms have been communicated in words, either in writing or orally.

express warranty A written representation by the seller as to the nature of the goods to be sold.

extinguishment of liability Once a novation has occurred, the party exiting the agreement is no longer obligated under the contract.

extortion The obtaining of property from another induced by wrongful use of actual or threatened force, violence, or fear, or under color of official right.

F

fact pleading A style of pleading that requires you to identify all the facts necessary to allege a valid cause of action.

facts Significant objective information in a case.

fair market value The amount that a willing buyer would pay for an item that a willing seller would accept.

false imprisonment Any deprivation of a person's freedom of movement without that person's consent and against his or her will, whether done by actual violence or threats.

false pretenses False representations of material past or present facts, known by the wrongdoer to be false, made with the intent to defraud a victim into passing title in property to the wrongdoer.

family court Court of limited jurisdiction that hears cases such as divorce, custody, and child support.

federal question jurisdiction The jurisdiction given to federal courts in cases involving the interpretation and application of the U.S. Constitution or acts of Congress.

Federal Register Pamphlet service that records the daily activity of the Congress.

Federal Rules Decisions (F.R.D.) Contains decisions of the federal district courts relating to the rules of civil and criminal procedure.

Federal Rules Digest Digest of opinions related to rules of procedure in the federal court system.

Federal Rules of Civil Procedure (Fed. R. Civ. P.) The specific set of rules followed in the federal courts.

Federal Rules of Criminal Procedure (Fed. R. Crim. P.) Rules governing the procedural issues in criminal prosecutions.

Federal Rules of Evidence The procedure for the introduction of evidence in a federal legal proceeding.

federalism Balanced system of national and state government in the U.S. Constitution; the federal government has jurisdiction over all matters related equally to all citizens of all states and the state governments have specific authority in matters affecting only the citizens of the respective state entity.

fee simple absolute A property interest in which the owner has full and exclusive use and enjoyment of the entire property.

fee simple defeasible An interest in land in which the owner has all the benefits of a fee simple estate, except that property is taken away if a certain event or condition occurs.

felony A crime punishable by more than a year in prison or death.

felony murder rule The doctrine holding that any death resulting from the commission or attempted commission of a dangerous felony is murder.

fiduciary One who owes to another the duties of good faith, trust, confidence, and candor.

fiduciary relationship A relationship based on close personal trust that the other party is looking out for one's best interests.

Field Code The forerunner to our present code of procedure; developed in New York in 1848.

field restrictions A method to limit a search on Westlaw.

final judgment The last possible order or judgment entered in the lower court; the required threshold for filing a notice of appeal.

finding tool Legal resource that assists in locating primary and secondary sources of the law.

fine A pecuniary punishment or penalty imposed by lawful tribunal upon a person convicted of a crime or misdemeanor.

finish or scrap The seller has the option to either finish producing the partially manufactured goods or stop production and scrap the materials for their recycled value.

firm offer An option contract to keep the offer open between merchants that does not have to be supported by separate consideration in order to be valid; an agreement made by a merchant-offeror, and governed by the Uniform Commercial Code, that he will not revoke the offer for a certain time period. A firm offer is not supported by separate consideration.

first pleading Complaint.

fixtures Personal property that has become permanently attached or associated with the real property.

flow A quality within or characteristic of the text that moves the reader easily through the text from point to point.

forbearance of a legal right Consideration that requires a party to refrain from doing something that he has the legal right to do.

force majeure An event that is neither foreseeable nor preventable by either party that has a devastating effect on the performance obligations of the parties.

foreign corporation A business that is incorporated under the laws of a different state, doing business in multiple states.

foreseeability The capacity for a party to reasonably anticipate a future event.

forfeiture A loss caused by a party's inability to perform; an unreasonable loss.

forgery The process of making or adapting objects or documents with the intention to deceive.

form books Publications that contain complete or partial sample documents, often with sample factual situations and various alternative methods of stating that legal document.

formal contract An agreement made that follows a certain prescribed form like negotiable instruments.

forms Documents that set forth standardized language and are used as a drafting guide.

forum The proper legal site or location.

forum *non conveniens* Venue is inconvenient despite the otherwise appropriateness of a jurisdiction choice.

forum shopping Plaintiff attempts to choose a state with favorable rules in which to file suit.

four corners doctrine A principle of contract law that directs the court to interpret a contract by the terms contained within the pages of the document.

fragile class Group considered particularly susceptible to harm such as the very old or the very young.

fraud A knowing and intentional misstatement of the truth in order to induce a desired action from another person.

freedom of contract The doctrine that permits parties to make agreements on whatever terms they wish with few exceptions.

freehold estate An estate interest that includes both ownership and possessory interests.

freelancer Paralegal in business for herself who contracts with an attorney or law firm to perform specific tasks for a designated fee.

fruit of the poisonous tree Evidence tainted based on illegal seizure; may not be used in a trial.

frustration of purpose Changes in the circumstances surrounding the contract may render the performance of the terms useless in relation to the reasons for entering into the contract.

full performance Completed exactly as set forth in the contract.

fundamental individual rights Contained in the first Ten Amendments to the Constitution, which spell out the individual rights the government functions to preserve and protect; those rights essential to ensuring liberty and justice.

future interest Right to property that can be enforced in the future.

G

gambling Making a bet when there is a chance for profit if a player is skillful and lucky.

general damages Those that normally would be anticipated in a similar action.

general defenses Specific responses by defendant to plaintiff's complaint.

General Demurrer A responsive pleading filed by a party attacking the legal sufficiency of a complaint.

General Digest Digest that supplements the Decennial Digest.

general gift Gift of property that is not exactly identified, as in furniture.

general index The index at the end of the statutes that provides a guide to locating relevant statutes.

general intent An unjustifiable act; reckless conduct.

general jurisdiction The court is empowered to hear any civil or criminal case.

gift Bestowing a benefit without any expectation on the part of the giver to receive something in return and the absence of any obligation on the part of the receiver to do anything in return.

gift *causa mortis* A gift made by the donor in contemplation of death.

gift *inter vivos* Gift made during the lifetime of the donor.

good consideration An exchange made based on love and affection, which have no legal value.

good faith The ability, competence, and intent to perform under the contract; the legal obligations to enter and perform a contract with honest and real intentions to complete performance and other conditions; fair dealing, integrity, and commitment to perform under the contract in an appropriate, timely, and responsible manner.

good faith dealing Doing the best possible to complete the contractual obligations.

good faith obligation Both buyers and sellers must deal with each other in a reasonable and fair manner without trying to avoid legitimate performance obligations.

goods Movable items under the UCC definition.

grand jury A jury of inquiry who are summoned and returned by the sheriff to each session of the criminal courts and whose duty is to receive complaints and accusations in criminal cases, hear evidence, and decide if the defendant should stand for trial.

grantee The person receiving the property.

grantor The person transferring the property.

gratuitous promise A promise in exchange for nothing.

gratuitous undertaking An act undertaken for reasons other than duty and measured with the same legal standard reasonably attributable to those with appropriate training.

guarantee An agreement in which a third party assures the repayment of a debt owed by another party.

guarantor A party who assumes secondary liability for the payment of another's debt. The guarantor is liable to the creditor only if the original debtor does not make payment.

guardian ad litem A person appointed by the court to represent the best interests of the child in a custody determination.

guilty A verdict only available in criminal cases in which the jury determines that the defendant is responsible for committing a crime.

H

habeas corpus A writ employed to bring a person before a court, most frequently to ensure that the party's imprisonment or detention is not illegal.

habitation Place of abode; dwelling place; residence.

harmful error An error by the court that has an identifiable negative impact on the trial to such a degree that the constitutional rights of a party are compromised.

harmless error Standard of review that has not caused legal error requiring reversal of the trial court's decision.

hate crime A crime motivated by the victim's race, color, ethnicity, religion, or national origin.

header Text that appears at the top left margin of all pages in a letter except the first page, and identifies three elements: the person to whom the letter is addressed; the date of the letter; and the page number.

heading A line or more of text that identifies the party for whom the memorandum was prepared; the person by whom it was prepared; the date of preparation; and the subject matter.

headnote A key-numbered paragraph; an editorial feature in unofficial reporters that summarizes a single legal point or issue in the court opinion.

hearsay An out-of-court statement offered to prove a matter in contention in the lawsuit.

heat of passion Rage, terror, or furious hatred suddenly aroused by some immediate provocation.

heirs Persons entitled to receive property based on intestate succession.

holding That aspect of a court opinion which directly affects the outcome of the case; it is composed of the reasoning necessary and sufficient to reach the disposition.

holographic will A will entirely written and signed by the testator in that person's own handwriting.

homicide The killing of a human being by the act or omission of another.

hornbooks Scholarly texts; a series of textbooks that review various fields of law in summary narrative form, as opposed to casebooks, which are designed as primary teaching tools and include many reprints of court opinions.

hyphen A form of punctuation used to draw together two or more words to form a single idea.

I

id. The same.

identification of the goods to the contract Once a seller has designated specific goods as the ones that will be delivered to the buyer, the buyer has a protectable interest in them.

identity or quality of the subject matter The goods to be transferred must be described with sufficient clarity to allow an outside third party to recognize them.

ignore the repudiation If the repudiating party has not permanently made his performance impossible, the aggrieved party can wait to see if the repudiator changes his mind and does perform.

illegal contract A contract that is unenforceable because the subject matter of the agreement is prohibited by state or federal statutory law and thus void.

illegal scheme A plan that uses legal steps to achieve an illegal result.

illusory promise A statement that appears to be a promise but actually enforces no obligation upon the promisor because he retains the subjective option whether or not to perform on it.

immaterial fact A fact that is unimportant to the case and its holding.

immediate right to commence a lawsuit The aggrieved party does not have to wait until the time when performance would be due under the contract term where there has been an anticipatory repudiation.

impartial jury A jury that is unbiased and does not favor one party or the other.

impasse The declaration by the mediator that the parties are unable to reach an agreement.

impleader The involuntary addition of a new party to the litigation; a party without whom all issues raised in the case could not be resolved.

implied acceptance Acceptance of the offeror's terms and conditions by actions or words indicating clearly the intention to accept.

implied contract An agreement whose terms have not been communicated in words, but rather by conduct or actions of the parties.

implied in fact Conditions that are not expressed in words but that must exist in order for the terms of the contract to make sense and are assumed by the parties to the contract.

implied in law Conditions that are not expressed in words but are imposed by the court to ensure fairness and justice as a result of its determination.

implied warranty An unwritten representation that is normally and naturally included by operation of law that applies to the goods to be sold.

impossibility of performance An excuse for performance based upon an absolute inability to perform the act required under the contract.

impracticality An excuse for performance based upon uselessness or excessive cost of the act required under the contract.

in loco parentis In the place of the parent.

***in personam* jurisdiction** A court's authority over a party personally.

***in rem* jurisdiction** A court's authority over claims affecting property.

incapacitation Punishment by imprisonment, mutilation, or death.

incapacity The inability to act or understand the actions that would create a binding legal agreement.

inchoate crime An incipient crime; an act that generally leads to a crime.

inchoate offenses Uncompleted crimes.

incidental beneficiaries Persons who may derive some benefit from the performance of a contract but who were not intended to directly benefit from the performance.

incidental or nominal damages Damages resulting from the breach that are related to the breach but not necessarily directly foreseeable by the breaching party.

indefinite pronoun A pronoun that does not specify its object.

independent clause A clause that can stand on its own as a complete sentence.

indeterminate sentence A sentence of an unspecified duration such as one for a term of five to ten years.

indexing method Referencing method of the record to assist in identifying the important pieces of information, such as the transcript excerpts and pleadings, which will be used in the various parts of the appellate brief.

indictment A written list of charges issued by a grand jury against a defendant in a criminal case.

indigent One who is needy and poor, or one who does not have sufficient property to furnish him a living or anyone able to support him or to whom he is entitled to look for support.

inducement The act or process of enticing or persuading another person to take a certain course of action.

infancy The state of a person who is under the age of legal majority.

inference A conclusion reached by considering other facts and deducing a logical consequence.

informal contract Can be oral or written and executed in any style acceptable to the parties.

information States that the magistrate determines there is sufficient cause to make an arrest and also sets forth the formal charges sought by the prosecution.

informative letter A letter that transmits information.

infraction A violation of a statute for which the only sentence authorized is a fine and for which violation is expressly designated as an infraction.

infringement An act that interferes with an exclusive right.

initial client meeting The first meeting with a prospective client in which information will be gathered, additional information requested, and the attorney–client relationship formed.

injunction A court order that requires a party to refrain from acting in a certain way to prevent harm to the requesting party.

injunction proceeding A judicial proceeding where an order may be issued requiring a party to cease an act or perform an act.

injunctive relief Court order to cease or commence an action following a petition to enter such an order upon showing of irreparable harm resulting from the failure to enforce the relief requested.

INS Immigration and Naturalization Service, which has been reorganized into part of the Department of Homeland Security.

insanity defense A defendant's claim that she was insane when the crime was committed, even if temporarily insane.

insolvency A party's inability to pay his debts, which may result in a declaration of bankruptcy and put all contractual obligations on hold or terminate them.

inspect The buyer must take steps to examine the goods to ensure they are of the type indicated in the contract. The seller must make the goods available for this purpose.

instructions and definitions A section in many forms of discovery requests that defines terms in the document to avoid confusion.

instrumentality of crime Used in committing a crime.

insufficient consideration Inadequate value exchanged to form a enforceable contract.

intangible property Personal property that has no physical presence but is represented by a certificate or some other instrument, such as stocks or trademarks.

intent Having the knowledge and desire that a specific consequence will result from an action.

intent of the parties Almost always the controlling factor in determining the terms and performance of an agreement.

intent to deceive The party making the questionable statement must plan on the innocent party's reliance on the first party's untruthfulness.

intentional Voluntarily and knowingly undertaken.

intentional infliction of emotional distress Intentional act involving extreme and outrageous conduct resulting in severe mental anguish.

intentional torts An intentional civil wrong that injures another person or property.

interference with business relations Overt act causing disruption or interruption to a business done with the intent to harm the business.

interlocutory appeal Appeal entered prior to entry of a final order by the trial court judge.

internal memorandum of law An internal document that analyzes objectively the legal issues in a client's matter.

interoffice memorandum Objective document that presents all aspects of a case, both negative and positive.

interpleader The deposit of contested funds with the court, followed by the removal of the filing party from other action in the suit.

interrogation The process of questions propounded by police to a person arrested or suspected to seek solution of crime.

interrogatory A discovery tool in the form of a series of written questions that are answered by the party in writing, to be answered under oath.

intervention The voluntary insertion of a third party into a pending civil action, often to resolve issues directly related to the third party's interests.

intestate The state of having died without a will.

intoxication Under the influence of alcohol or drugs, which may, depending on the degree of inebriation, render a party incapable of entering into a contractual relationship or of acting in the manner in which an ordinarily prudent and cautious person would have acted under similar circumstances.

invitation to treat A person is expressing willingness to enter into negotiations, inviting another to make an offer.

invitees People wanted on the premises for a specific purpose known by the landowner.

involuntary manslaughter Homicide in which there is no intention to kill or do grievous bodily harm but that is committed with criminal negligence or during the commission of a crime not included within the felony murder rule.

IRAC method A technique used in legal writing that loosely follows the pattern of issue, rule of law, application of the rule of law to the facts, and conclusion.

irreparable harm The requesting party must show that the actions of the defendant will cause a type of damage that cannot be remedied by any later award of the court.

irresistible impulse An impulse to commit an unlawful or criminal act that cannot be resisted or overcome because mental disease has destroyed the freedom of will, the power of self-control, and the choice of actions.

irrevocable offers Those offers that cannot be terminated by the offeror during a certain time period.

issue The legal problem presented or point of law or fact on which the appeal is based; questions presented; a section that identifies the legal issues presented in the memorandum of law to the trial court.

J

joint and several liability Shared responsibility, apportioned between all of the defendants, but in no case can the plaintiff recover more than 100 percent of the damages awarded.

joint custodial arrangements Detail the scope of the shared parental responsibility, whether legal, physical, or both.

joint stipulation States agreement of the parties to implement the change or other mutual agreement.

joint tenancy The shared ownership of property, giving the other owner the right of survivorship if one owner dies.

judge Trier of law.

judgment The court's final decision regarding the rights and claims of the parties.

judgment notwithstanding the verdict (judgment N.O.V.) Asks the judge to reverse the jury verdict based on the inadequacy of the evidence presented to support the law and the verdict.

judgment on the pleadings A motion that alleges that if all of the allegations raised in the pleadings are true and correct, the movant would still be entitled to a ruling in his favor and a dismissal of the opposition's pleadings.

judicial economy The overall efficiency a court promotes in hearing its cases, especially when case facts have both state and federal claims.

judicial notice A request that a court accept evidence as fact without the necessity of further proof.

judicial opinions Analysis of a decision issued by an appellate court panel.

judicial precedent A court decision in which similar facts are presented; provides authority for deciding a subsequent case.

judicial review The power of a court to determine the constitutionality of actions of the executive and legislative branches of government.

jump cite Same as a pinpoint citation.

jurisdiction The power or authority of the court to hear a particular classification of case. Also, the place or court that may hear a case, based on subject matter and/or geographic area.

jurisdictional clause Establishes that the court in which the action is filed is empowered to hear the case and has jurisdiction over the parties.

jurisdictional statement Section of the brief that identifies the legal authority that grants the appellate court the right to hear the case.

jurors Those people who have been selected to sit on a jury; they will consider the evidence and reach a verdict in the case.

jury Trier of fact.

jury instructions (jury charge) Directions for the jury regarding what law applies and how it applies to the facts of a case; also known as *points of charge*.

jury panel Group of people called to court from which a jury is chosen.

jury strike The removal of a jury panel member, also known as a jury challenge.

jury trial Case is decided by a jury.

justiciable content Genuine issue of law and fact within the power of the court to decide.

juvenile court Court of limited jurisdiction that hears cases involving minors.

K

Katz expectation-of-privacy test Two prongs: (1) reasonableness of the expectation of privacy—the subjective prong; (2) efficacy of the expectation asserted based on community standards—the objective prong.

Key Number System A detailed system of classification that currently divides the law into more than 400 separate categories or topics.

key search terms Words or phrases used in legal research to help focus the research.

key word search Search technique performed using an Internet search engine to locate relevant documents or webpages.

key words Terms used in legal research to identify the law related to your case facts and legal issues.

KeyCite The Westlaw case updating and validation system, which is similar to Shepard's Citations system.

kidnapping The unlawful confinement, removal, or hiding of a person against his/her will for the purpose of holding the person to obtain a ransom, to serve as a hostage, to facilitate the commission of a felony, to inflict harm or terrorize the victim, or to interfere with the performance of a governmental or political function.

knowing and intentional A party must be aware of and plan on the outcome of his words or actions in order to be held accountable for the result.

knowledge of the offer An offeree must be aware of the terms of the offer in order to accept it.

L

landlord The lessor of property.

landmark cases Interpretation of the applicable rule is overruled or changed substantially and intentionally.

landowner's duty To warn of known unsafe artificial conditions on the property.

lapse of time An interval of time that has been long enough to affect a termination of the offer.

larceny The common law crime of taking property of another without permission.

larceny by trick Larceny in which the taker misleads the rightful possessor, by a misrepresentation of fact, into giving up possession of the property in question.

"last in time = first in right" A principle in law that favors the most current activity or change with respect to the transaction as it is most likely the most reflective of the intent of the parties.

law A set of rules and principles that govern any society.

law review journals Periodicals edited by the top students at each law school, featuring scholarly articles by leading authorities and notes on various topics written by the law students themselves.

lawsuit A legal mechanism to resolve disputes between parties.

lay the foundation To present sufficient background material to establish the relevancy and competency of a particular piece of evidence.

leading Attorney objection based on the question creating the desired answer.

legal analysis The process of examining prior case law and comparing it to your case.

legal argument A well-reasoned presentation of your position.

legal assistant Individual qualified to assist an attorney in the delivery of legal services.

legal citation Unique identifier of all legal sources.

legal custody The right and obligation to make major decisions regarding the child, including, but not limited to, educational and religious issues.

legal document assistant A specialized type of paralegal, legally able to provide assistance to clients in preparing forms.

legal encyclopedia A multivolume compilation that provides in-depth coverage of every area of the law.

legal issue The point in dispute between two or more parties in a lawsuit.

legal jargon *See* legalese.

legal memorandum Summary of the case facts, the legal question asked, the research findings, the analysis, and the legal conclusion drawn from the law applied to the case facts.

legal remedy Relief provided by the court to a party to redress a wrong perpetrated by another party; the recovery of money damages in a lawsuit.

legal resource The practical legal research tools, such as existing briefs, from online and law firm databases, used to assist in performing legal research.

legal secretary A secretary trained to perform specialized tasks directly related to the practice of law.

legal source The primary and traditional secondary sources of the law.

legal value Having an objectively determinable benefit that is recognized by the court.

legalese Language that is characterized by the frequent use of Latin, French, and Old English terms unfamiliar to most present-day vocabularies in legal writing; jargon.

legally significant facts Facts that are critical to the analysis of a case.

legislation Regulations codified into laws by Congress.

legislative history The transcripts of the legislative debates leading up to the passage of the bill that became the law or statute.

legislative intent Process of interpreting the meaning of the drafters of a statute through legislative history and judicial interpretation doctrines.

letter Document that transmits information to a client, opposing counsel, the court, or any other individual or entity.

letter bank A depository for firm letters regarding client cases.

letter of intent/nonbinding offer A statement that details the preliminary negotiations and understanding of the terms of the agreement but does not create a binding obligation between parties.

letterhead Standard stationery.

LexisNexis Commercial electronic law database service.

liability A jury's determination that one party is responsible for injuries to another party; the basis for an award of damages.

libel Oral defamatory statements.

license The original owner and the grantor retain the right to revoke or withdraw the rights conferred.

licensee One known to be on the premises but whose presence gives no benefit to the property owner.

licensure The requirement of governmental approval before a person can practice a specific profession.

life estate An ownership interest in property for a designated period of time, based on the life of another person.

limitation of acceptance A commercial offeror may specifically state that the offeree must accept all terms as set forth in the offer with no deviations.

limitation of damages An amount of money agreed upon in the original contract as the maximum recovery the nonbreaching party will be entitled to in the event of a breach.

limited jurisdiction The court is empowered to hear only specified types of cases.

limited liability company A hybrid business formed under state acts, representing both corporation and partnership characteristics.

limited partnership A partnership of two or more persons, consisting of limited partners, who provide only financial backing, and general partners, who manage the business and have unlimited liability.

limiting physical conditions Class considered for purposes of the standard of care to be reasonable for an ordinary person with those limiting physical conditions, for example, blindness or deafness.

liquidated damages An amount of money agreed upon in the original contract as a reasonable estimation of the damages to be recovered by the nonbreaching party. This amount is set forth in the contract so the parties have a clear idea of the risk of breach.

list server An Internet subscription list that provides a place for multiple computer users to access information common to a group or individual's interest. Also known as an *electronic mailing list.*

litigants A party to a lawsuit.

litigation process Adversarial process in which parties use the courts for formal dispute resolution.

local rules Individual rules for a particular court that supplement the other rules of court.

loitering To stand around or move about slowly; to linger or spend time idly.

looseleaf service A service that publishes recently decided court decisions in looseleaf binders, such as *U.S. Law Week;* provides for information to be easily updated. The loose pages are used to replace the existing pages in the notebook to ensure that the most current information is available.

loss of consortium A claim filed made by the plaintiff's spouse for the loss of companionship in the marriage caused by the injuries.

lost profits A calculable amount of money that the nonbreaching party would have made after the execution of performance under the agreement but that has not been realized due to the breach.

lost property Personal property with which a person has involuntarily parted possession.

M

M'Naghten Rule The defendant alleges he lacked capacity to form criminal intent.

magistrate judge A public civil officer, possessing such power—legislative, executive, or judicial—as the government appointing him may ordain.

Magna Carta British document (originally issued in 1215) describing the system and form of government and law upon which the U.S. Constitution was modeled.

mailbox rule A principle of contract law that sets the time of acceptance of an offer at the time it is posted and the time of rejection of an offer at the time it is received.

majority opinion An opinion where more than half of the justices agree with the decision. This opinion is precedent.

malice Person's doing of any act in reckless disregard of another person.

malice aforethought The prior intention to kill the victim or anyone else if likely to occur as a result of the actions or omissions.

malicious mischief The act of willfully damaging or destroying the personal property of another; sometimes referred to as criminal mischief.

malum in se An act that is prohibited because it is "evil in itself."

malum prohibitum An act that is prohibited by a rule of law.

mandatory authority Authority that is binding upon the court considering the issue—a statute or regulation from the relevant jurisdiction that applies directly; a case from a higher court in the same jurisdiction that is directly on point; or a constitutional provision that is applicable and controlling.

mandatory sentence A sentence set by law with no discretion for the judge to individualize punishment.

manslaughter The unlawful killing of a human being without premeditation.

marital estates (marital property) The property accumulated by a couple during marriage, called community property in some states.

marital privilege An evidentiary protection that permits married individuals to refuse to testify against one another.

market price The amount of money that another neutral party would pay for the goods on the open market.

marketable title The title transfers full ownership rights to the buyer.

marriage A union between a man and a woman.

material A term is material if it is important to a party's decision whether or not to enter into the contract; an element or term that is significant or important and relates to the basis for the agreement.

material alteration A change in the terms that would surprise or impose hardship on the other party if allowed to become a part of the agreement.

material breach Substantial and essential nonperformance.

material fact A fact that is essential to the case and its holding; a fact that, if different, might alter the entire outcome of the case.

mayhem The maiming, dismembering, disabling, or disfigurement of the body part of another with the intent to harm or cause permanent injury.

mediation A dispute resolution method in which a neutral third party meets with the opposing parties to help them achieve a mutually satisfactory solution without court intervention.

mediator Individual who facilitates a resolution by the parties using methods designed to facilitate the parties' reaching a negotiated resolution.

mediation The process of submitting a claim to a neutral third party who then makes a determination about the ultimate liability and award in a civil case.

medical authorization A form, signed by the client, that allows the legal team to review and obtain copies of the client's medical records.

medicinal side effects Under the influence of over-the-counter or prescription drugs having an impact on a person's mental capacity that may render a party incapable of entering into a contractual relationship.

meeting of the minds A legal concept requiring that both parties understand and ascribe the same meaning to the terms of the contract; a theory holding that both parties must both objectively and subjectively intend to enter into the agreement on the same terms.

memorandum at the request of a judge A persuasive memorandum of legal points requested by the trial court judge.

memorandum in regard to a motion A persuasive memorandum supporting the points and authorities in a motion.

memorandum of law Analysis and application of existing law setting forth the basis for filing the motion.

memorandum of law to the trial court An adversarial document filed with the trial court and written to persuade the trial court of a party's position on a disputed point of law.

mens rea "A guilty mind"; criminal intent in committing the act.

mental duress The threat of harm to a party's overall well-being or a threat of harm to loved ones that induces stress and action on the party of the threatened party.

mentally infirm Persons not having the capacity to understand a transaction due to a defect in their ability to reason and, therefore, who do not have the requisite mental intent to enter into a contract.

merchantable Goods must meet certain standards that are required in the relevant industry.

merchants Businesspersons who have a certain level of expertise dealing in commercial transactions regarding the goods they sell; persons who regularly deal in goods of the kind specified in the agreement. They hold themselves out as having special knowledge in their area.

mere request for a change A party's interest in renegotiating the terms of the contract does not amount to anticipatory repudiation.

merger Combining previous obligations into a new agreement.

merger clause Language of a contract that indicates that the parties intend to exclude all outside evidence relating to the terms of the contract because it has been agreed that all relevant terms have been incorporated in the document.

metaphor A figure of speech that links dissimilar objects but is more powerful than a simile in that it equates, rather than compares, the objects.

metasearch A global search that displays search results from a number of search engines; less specific.

minimum contacts The test, based on the case *International Shoe v. Washington,* that courts use to ascertain if a defendant has some contact with the state of which he is not a resident.

minors Persons under the age of eighteen; once a person has reached eighteen, she has reached the age of majority.

Miranda warnings Mandatory notice given detainees specifically advising that anything said while in custody can be used subsequently as trial evidence.

mirror image rule A requirement that the acceptance of an offer must exactly match the terms of the original offer.

misdemeanor A lesser crime punishable by less than a year in jail and/or a fine.

mislaid property Personal property that the owner has intentionally placed somewhere and then forgot about.

misrepresentation A reckless disregard for the truth in making a statement to another in order to induce a desired action.

mistake in fact An error in assessing the facts, causing a defendant to act in a certain way.

mistrial A trial that has been terminated prior to a normal conclusion.

mitigate To lessen in intensity or amount.

mitigate damages (mitigation of damages) The obligation to offset or otherwise engage in curative measures to stop accrual of unreasonable economic damages; that is, to minimize the damage incurred through affirmative actions.

mitigating circumstance (mitigating factor) A fact or situation that does not justify or excuse a wrongful act or offense but that reduces the degree of culpability and thus may reduce the damages in a civil case or the punishment in a criminal case.

mitigating factor See *mitigating circumstance.*

Model Penal Code (MPC) A comprehensive body of criminal law, adopted in whole or in part by most states.

models Copies of actual complaints, obtained from your firm's files, that have a similar factual foundation.

modification A change or addition in contractual terms that does not extinguish the underlying agreement.

modifiers Words that describe a subject, verb, or object in a sentence.

monetary remedy Money damages.

moral obligation A social goal or personal aspiration that induces a party to act without any expectation of a return performance from the recipient.

moral turpitude An act or behavior that gravely violates the sentiment or accepted standard of the community.

motion A procedural request or application presented by the attorney in court.

motion for a directed verdict A request by a party for a judgment because the other side has not met its burden of proof.

motion for a new trial Post-trial relief that requests a new trial on the same issues for specific reasons that must be clearly explained and argued in the motion.

motion for more definite statement A request by a defendant for additional specificity of plaintiff's complaint.

motion for protective order A motion filed by a party upon whom a discovery request has been made to protect the disclosure of information.

motion for sanctions A motion filed by any party to counter alleged violations by another party in the case.

motion for summary judgment A motion by either party for judgment based on all court documents.

motion *in limine* A request that certain evidence not be raised at trial, as it is arguably prejudicial, irrelevant, or legally inadmissible evidence.

motion to compel Request for the production of information or testimony for use at trial.

motion to compel discovery A motion filed by a party seeking to force compliance with a discovery request.

motion to dismiss A motion that dispenses with the lawsuit because of a legal defense.

motion to suppress Asks the court to eliminate allegedly tainted evidence.

motive Something such as willful desire that causes an individual to act.

municipal court City court of limited jurisdiction that hears cases such as traffic violations and violations of city ordinances.

murder The killing of a human being with intent.

mutual assent Concurrence by both parties to all terms.

mutual benefit bailment A bailment created for the benefit of both parties.

mutual mistake An error made by both parties to the transaction; therefore, neither party had the same idea of the terms of the agreement. The contract is avoidable by either party.

mutual release (mutual rescission) An agreement by mutual assent of both parties to terminate the contractual relationship and return to the pre-contract status quo.

mutual will Joint wills executed by two or more persons.

mutuality of assent Both parties must objectively manifest their intention to enter into a binding contract by accepting all of the terms.

mutuality of contract (mutuality of obligation) A doctrine that requires both parties to be bound to the terms of the agreement.

N

Napoleonic Code French code of law and government influencing certain aspects of our system. It serves as the model for the government and law in the State of Louisiana.

National Association of Legal Assistants (NALA) A legal professional group that lends support and continuing education for legal assistants.

National Federation of Paralegal Associations (NFPA) National paralegal professional association providing professional career information, support, and information on unauthorized practice of law.

natural language search Search technique that uses conversational words to search the Internet.

necessaries of life Generally legally considered to be food, clothing, and shelter; necessities; goods and services that are required; basic elements of living and employment.

necessity A justification defense for a person who acts in an emergency and commits a crime that is less harmful than the harm that would have occurred but for the person's actions.

negative treatment Treatment meaning that the case Shepardized has been criticized, restricted, or overruled in some manner by a court.

negligence The failure to use reasonable care to avoid harm to another person or to do that which a reasonable person might do in similar circumstances.

negligence *per se* Results from statutes establishing that certain actions or omissions are impermissible under any and all circumstances; the failure to use reasonable care to avoid harm to another person or to do that which a reasonable person might do in similar circumstances.

negligent Careless or unintentional act or omission.

neutral citation Uniform citation system that contains the name of the case, year of decision, court (postal code) abbreviation, opinion number, and paragraph pinpoint for references.

new law A novel interpretation of established law.

no-fault divorce A divorce in which one spouse does not need to allege wrongdoing by the other spouse as grounds for the divorce.

noise words Common everyday words, such as "the," "of," and "it," which are eliminated when performing an Internet search.

nolo contendere Latin for "I do not wish to contend"; to plead no contest.

nominal consideration The value of the things exchanged are grossly disproportionate to each other so that very little is given in exchange for something of great value.

nominal damages A small amount of money given to the nonbreaching party as a token award to acknowledge the fact of the breach.

nonconforming Goods that are not in reasonable compliance with the specifications in the contract.

noncustodial parent Parent with whom the child(ren) stays or visits some of the time but not as primary residence.

nondisclosure The intentional omission of the truth.

non-freehold estate A lease agreement.

nonpossessory interests The holder does not have per se possession of the property but may have use interests such as easements, profits, and licenses.

nonprivileged information Discoverable information not protected by confidentiality provisions even when exchanged between parties who may enjoy privileged communications in certain circumstances.

notice of appeal Puts the trial court, the appeals court, and the opposing party on notice that the judgment entered is challenged.

notice pleading A short and plain statement of the allegations in a lawsuit.

novation An agreement that replaces previous contractual obligations with new obligations and/or different parties.

nuncupative will An oral will, usually made by the testator near death.

nutshell A paperback series of the law; condensed versions of hornbooks.

oath Any form of attestation by which a person signifies that she is bound in conscience to perform an act faithfully and truthfully.

objection for cause The attorney making the objection states the reason, which must be such as to impair the juror's ability to rule impartially on the evidence.

objection to terms A merchant must state her disapproval of the offeree's new or different terms within a reasonable time, or else they are considered accepted by her.

objective Impartial and disinterested in the outcome of the dispute.

objective documents Documents that convey information and avoid bias.

objective impracticality A party's performance is excused only when the circumstances surrounding the contract become so burdensome that any reasonable person in the same situation would excuse performance.

objectively determinable The ability of the price to be ascertained by a party outside of the contract.

objectively reasonable A standard of behavior that the majority of persons would agree with or how most persons in a community generally act.

obligor The original party to the contract who remains obligated to perform under the contract.

obscenity The quality or state of being morally abhorrent or socially taboo, especially as a result of referring to or depicting sexual or excretory functions.

offer A promise made by the offeror to do (or not to do) something provided that the offeree, by accepting, promises or does something in exchange.

offeree The person to whom the offer is made.

offeror The person making the offer to another party.

official reporters Government publications of court decisions (for example, 325 Ill.3d 50).

open-fields doctrine The personal residence per se is protected from unreasonable search; the open fields surrounding the property are not equally protected.

opening statement An initial statement by a party's attorney explaining what the case is about and what that party's side expects to prove during the trial.

opinion Analysis supported by emotion; a formal statement by a court or other adjudicative body of the legal reasons and principles for the conclusion of the court.

opinion letter A letter that renders legal advice.

option contracts A separate and legally enforceable agreement included in the contract stating that the offer cannot be revoked for a certain time period. An option contract is supported by separate consideration.

oral argument Oral presentation by attorney of key issues and points of law presented in the appeals documents and written legal argument.

oral deposition A discovery tool in a question-and-answer format in which the attorney verbally questions a party or witness under oath.

Order *Nunc Pro Tunc* An entry made by a court now of an event that previously happened and made to have the effect of the former date.

ordinance A law passed by a local government, such as a town council or city government.

ordinary person standard The reasonable behavior for an ordinary individual in a similar situation.

original jurisdiction Authority of a court to review and try a case first.

outline (outlining) The skeleton of a legal argument, advancing from the general to the specific; a preliminary step in writing that provides a framework for the assignment.

output contract An agreement wherein the quantity that the offeror desires to purchase is all that the offeree can produce.

outrageous conduct Exceeding all bounds of decency and propriety.

overrule A judge's ruling in disagreement with the party who raised the objection.

overt act Identifiable commission or omission, an intentional tort requirement.

owner One who has the right to possess, use, and convey something.

P

PACE Two-tiered paralegal certification program requiring a bachelor's degree, completion of a paralegal program, and practical experience to qualify for the proficiency examination leading to certification.

PACER Federal court online document system. Stands for Public Access to Court Electronic Records.

palimony A division of property between two unmarried parties after they separate or the paying of support by one party to the other.

panel A group of people who have been called for jury duty; the final jury will be selected from this group; also known as venire.

paralegal A person qualified to assist an attorney, under direct supervision, in all substantive legal matters with the exception of appearing in court and rendering legal advice.

parallel citation A citation of a case text found in two or more reporters.

parallel construction Repeating usages to make a point, to suggest either a connection or a contrast.

parental kidnapping The kidnapping of a child by one parent in violation of the other parent's custody or visitation rights.

Parental Kidnapping Prevention Act (PKPA) An act related to jurisdictional issues in applying and enforcing child custody decrees in other states.

parentheses A form of punctuation that unites cohesive passages.

parenthetical phrase A phrase that supplements or adds information to a complete thought.

parol evidence Oral testimony offered as proof regarding the terms of a written contract.

parol evidence rule A court evidentiary doctrine that excludes certain types of outside oral testimony offered as proof of the terms of the contract.

parolee Ex-prisoner who has been released from jail, prison, or other confinement after having served part of a criminal sentence.

partial breach A failure of performance that has little, if any, effect on the expectations of the parties.

partial integration A document that contains the essential terms of the contract but not all the terms that the parties may have or need to agree upon.

partial performance doctrine The court's determination that a party's actions taken in reliance on the oral agreement "substitutes" for the writing and takes the transaction out of the scope of the Statute of Frauds and, thus, can be enforced.

partial performance/substantial beginning An offeree has made conscientious efforts to start performing according to the terms of the contract. The performance need not be complete nor exactly as specified, but only an attempt at significant compliance.

parties The persons involved in the making of the contract.

partners Attorneys who own the law firm and split the profits and losses.

partnership Business enterprise owned by more than one person, entered into for profit.

partnership agreement The contract between the partners that creates duties, establishes responsibilities, and details benefits of the attorneys involved in the partnership.

passive voice A verb form in which the subject of the sentence is the object of the action.

past consideration A benefit conferred in a previous transaction between the parties before the present promise was made.

paternalism One person looked out for another; companies took care of their employees.

paternity action A lawsuit to identify the father of a child born outside of marriage.

pen register Records telephone numbers for outgoing calls.

pendent jurisdiction Jurisdictional concept where state claims arising out of the same set of facts as a federal claim are heard together.

per capita distribution The equal division of assets according to the number of surviving heirs with the nearest degree of kinship.

per curiam A phrase used to distinguish an opinion of the whole court from an opinion written by any one judge.

***per curiam* decision** A decision that reflects agreement of all the judges on the correct disposition of the case.

per diem (Latin) "by the day" or daily.

per stirpes distribution The division of assets according to rights of representation.

peremptory challenge (peremptory jury strike) An attorney's elimination of a prospective juror without giving a reason; limited to a specific number of strikes.

performance prevented If a party takes steps to preclude the other party's performance, then the performance is excused due to that interference.

periodic sentence A sentence that conveys the information at the end of the paragraph.

periodic tenancy Tenancy in which the tenant is a holdover after the expiration of a tenancy for years.

perjury The willful assertion as to a matter of fact, opinion, belief, or knowledge, made by a witness in a judicial proceeding as part of his/her evidence, either upon oath or in any form allowed by law to be substituted for an oath, whether such evidence is given in open court, in an affidavit, or otherwise, such assertion being material to the issue or point of inquiry and known to such witness to be false.

permanent injunction A court order that prohibits a party from acting in a certain way for an indefinite and perpetual period of time.

permissive counterclaim A counterclaim that is not required to be filed with a complaint because the facts do not arise out of the same set of circumstances as the complaint.

personal jurisdiction A court's power over the individuals involved in the case; when a court has personal jurisdiction, it can compel attendance at court hearings and enter judgments against the parties.

personal property Movable or intangible thing not attached to real property.

persuasive authority A source of law or legal authority that is not binding on the court in deciding a case but may be used by the court for guidance, such as law review articles; all nonmandatory primary authority.

petition for dissolution of marriage Request for an order dissolving the marriage of the petitioner and spouse.

petitioner Name designation of a party filing an appeal.

physical custody Child living with one parent or visiting with the noncustodial parent.

physical duress The threat of bodily harm unless the aggressor's demands are met.

piercing the corporate veil To show that a corporation exists as an alter ego for a person or group of individuals to avoid liability.

pinpoint citation (pincite or jump cite) The page reference in a citation that directs the reader to the cited material in the case.

plagiarism Taking the thoughts of another and presenting them as one's own without properly crediting or citing the source.

plain English The style of legal writing that uses straightforward, clear, precise language and is generally devoid of legal jargon.

plain error A decision or action by the court that appears to a reviewing court to have been unquestionably erroneous.

plain meaning Doctrine in statutory interpretation that interprets the word and phrases in a statute in their ordinary sense.

plain meaning rule Courts will use the traditional definition of terms used if those terms are not otherwise defined.

plaintiff The party initiating legal action.

plea bargain The process whereby the accused and the prosecutor in a criminal case work out a mutually satisfactory disposition of the case subject to court approval.

pleadings Formal documents filed with the court that establish the claims and defenses of the parties to the lawsuit; the complaint, answer to complaint, and reply.

pledge to charity A legally enforceable gift to a qualifying institution.

pocket parts Annual supplements to digests.

pocket veto A veto of a bill when Congress is not in session or has adjourned before the expiration of the ten-day time limit. An indirect rejection of a bill as no action occurs by the president or governor.

point headings Headings that outline and identify the argument in the section.

points of charge See *jury instructions.*

political asylum Immigration status available under some circumstances when the party seeking asylum claims political persecution. Not commonly and broadly available without a clear showing of oppression.

polygamy Multiple marital relationships are entered while others remain intact.

poor judgment Contract law does not allow avoidance of performance obligations due to a mistake that was simply a bad decision on the part of one party.

Popular Name Index An index located at the end of the statutes that provides the common name for a statute.

position Analysis supported by fact.

positive treatment Treatment suggesting that the case Shepardized is cited as authoritative by a court.

positively and unequivocally In order to treat a party's statement as an anticipatory repudiation, the statements or actions from the potential repudiator must clearly and unquestionably communicate that intent not to perform.

possession Having or holding property in one's power; controlling something to the exclusion of others.

prayer for relief A summation at the end of a pleading, which sets forth the demands by a party in the lawsuit.

precedent The holding of past court decisions that are followed in future judicial cases where similar facts and legal issues are present.

precedential value The force that a cited authority exerts upon the judge's reasoning.

precise Accuracy of written communication.

precision Legal writing that clearly and definitely conveys the point of the document.

predominant factor test An examination of a transaction to determine whether the primary purpose of the contract is the procurement of goods or services.

preemption Right of the federal government to exclusive governance in matters concerning all citizens equally.

preexisting duty An obligation to perform an act that existed before the current promise was made that requires the same performance presently sought.

preliminary hearing An appearance by both parties before the court to assess the circumstances and validity of the restraining application. Also, a hearing by a judge to determine whether a person charged with a crime should be held for trial.

preliminary matters Determining the legal issues, parties, venue, and jurisdiction.

premeditation Conscious consideration and planning that precedes some act.

prenuptial agreement An agreement made by parties before marriage that controls certain aspects of the relationship, such as management and ownership of property.

preponderance of the evidence The weight or level of persuasion of evidence needed to find the defendant liable as alleged by the plaintiff in a civil matter.

present obligation The performances under the contract must not have been carried out but must still be executory in order to be available for a novation.

pretrial conference The meeting between the parties and the judge to identify legal issues, stipulate to uncontested matters, and encourage settlement.

pretrial memo Outlining the legal and factual issues, as well as the recommended jury instructions, and other matters related to trial conduct.

pretrial motions Used to challenge the sufficiency of evidence or the suppression of allegedly tainted evidence or other matters that could impact the focus, the length, and even the need for trial.

pretrial order An order, prepared by the trial judge with the input of the parties, that summarizes key issues in the case, including witness order, evidence, and other critical concerns

pretrial phase (pretrial stage) The steps in the litigation process before trial, to accomplish discovery and encourage settlement.

price The monetary value ascribed by the parties to the exchange involved in the contract.

price under the contract The seller has the right to collect the agreed-upon price for the goods where the buyer has possession, despite the market conditions at the time.

prima facie (Latin) "At first sight." A case with the required proof of elements in a tort cause of action; the elements of the plaintiff's (or prosecutor's) cause of action; what the plaintiff must prove; accepted on its face, but not indisputable.

primary authority The original text of the sources of law, such as constitutions, court opinions, statutes, and administrative rules and regulations.

primary sources of law State the law in the state or federal system and can be found in statutes, constitutions, rules of procedure, codes, and case law; that is, the most fundamental place in which law was established.

principal in the first degree The criminal actor; the one who actually commits the crime, either by her own hand, by an inanimate agency, or by an innocent human agent.

principal in the second degree The one who is present at the commission of a criminal offense and aids, counsels, commands, or encourages the principal in the first degree in the commission of that offense.

prior or contemporaneous agreements These negotiations and resulting potential terms are governed by the principles of the parol evidence rule.

prior proceedings The procedural history of a case.

private adoption Parents acting on their own behalf or with the assistance of a third-party intermediary.

private necessity Invasion into property of another was for purposes of protecting the property.

private reprimand The minimum censure for an attorney who commits an ethical violation; the attorney is informed privately about a potential violation, but no official entry is made.

private sale A sale between the buyer and the seller without notice or advertisement.

privilege Reasonable expectation of privacy and confidentiality for communications in furtherance of the relationship such as attorney–client, doctor–patient, husband–wife, psychotherapist–patient, and priest–penitent.

privity A relationship between the parties to the contract who have rights and obligations to each other through the terms of the agreement.

probable cause The totality of circumstances leads one to believe certain facts or circumstances exist; applies to arrests, searches, and seizures.

probable cause for a search Thing(s) sought and assertions as to location, date, and time are correctly represented and researched prior to a search.

probate The court process of determining will validity, settling estate debts, and distributing assets.

probate court The court empowered to settle estates for those individuals who have died with or without a will.

probation A court-imposed criminal sentence that, subject to stated conditions, releases a convicted person into the community instead of sending the criminal to prison.

probative evidence Evidence that tends to or actually proves the fact.

procedural due process These requirements mandate scrupulous adherence to the method or mechanism applied. Notice and fair hearing are the cornerstones of due process, though certainly not the only consideration.

procedural law The set of rules that are used to enforce the substantive law.

process server A person statutorily authorized to serve legal documents such as complaints.

product liability theory The manufacturer and the seller are held strictly liable for product defects unknown to consumers that make the product unreasonably dangerous for its intended purpose.

professional corporation Business form organized as a closely held group of professional intellectual employees such as doctors.

professional duty Exercising a reasonable level of skill, knowledge, training, and understanding related to the specific profession.

profit interest The grantee has the right to enter the property of another and remove a specified thing or things from the premises.

promisee The party to whom the promise of performance is made.

promisor The party who makes a promise to perform under the contract.

promissory estoppel A legal doctrine that makes some promises enforceable even though they are not compliant with the technical requirements of a contract.

promissory reliance A party's dependence and actions taken upon another's representations that he will carry out his promise.

promoter A person, typically a principal shareholder, who organizes a business.

pronoun ambiguity Lack of clarity that results from an unclear indication about the noun to which the pronoun refers.

proper dispatch An approved method of transmitting the acceptance to the offeror.

property Rights a person may own or be entitled to own, including personal and real property.

prosecutor Attorney representing the people or plaintiff in criminal matters.

Prosser on Torts Legal treatise or discussion on the law of torts.

prostitution The act of performing, or offering or agreeing to perform, a sexual act for hire.

protection defense Includes self-defense, defending another, and defending one's own property.

protective frisk A pat-down search of a suspect by police, designed to discover weapons for the purpose of ensuring the safety of the officer and others nearby.

province of the jury An issue that is exclusively the responsibility of the jury to determine.

proximate cause The defendant's actions are the nearest cause of the plaintiff 's injuries.

proximity connector Term used to limit or specify results within a search inquiry.

proxy marriage An agent for the parties arranges the marriage for the couple.

prurient interest Characterized by or arousing inordinate or unusual sexual desire.

public law number The number assigned a bill after it is signed into law.

public necessity defense The invasion is necessary to protect the community and therefore is a complete bar to recovery.

public reprimand A published censure of an attorney for an ethical violation.

public sale A sale advertised to the public and subject to UCC provisions.

publicly held corporation A business held by a large number of shareholders.

puffing The use of an exaggerated opinion—as opposed to a false statement—with the intent to sell a good or service.

punitive damages An amount of money awarded to a nonbreaching party that is not based on the actual losses incurred by that party, but as a punishment to the breaching party for the commission of an intentional wrong.

putative marriage The couple completes the requirements in good faith, but an unknown impediment prevents the marriage from being valid.

Q

qualified domestic relations order (QDRO) Retirement account distributions' legal documentation requirement for ultimate distribution.

quantum meruit A Latin term referring to the determination of the earned value of services provided by a party.

quantum valebant A Latin term referring to the determination of the market worth assignable to the benefit conferred.

quasi-contract (pseudo-contract, implied-in-law contract) Where no technical contract exists, the court can create an obligation in the name of justice to promote fairness and afford a remedy to an innocent party and prevent unearned benefits to be conferred on the other party.

quasi *in rem* jurisdiction The court takes authority over property to gain authority over the person.

query A string of key terms or words used in a computer search.

question of fact An issue that has not been predetermined and authoritatively answered by the law; a disputed issue to be resolved by the jury in a jury trial or by the judge in a bench trial.

question of law An issue to be decided by the judge concerning the application or interpretation of the law.

questions presented Section of the appellate brief that identifies the grounds upon which the decision of the trial court is questioned.

quitclaim deed A deed transferring only the interest in property of the grantor, without guarantees.

quotation marks Punctuation used in a search that keeps related words and concepts together.

R

rape Unlawful sexual intercourse with a person without consent.

ratification A step taken by a formerly incapacitated person that confirms and endorses the voidable contract and thereby makes it enforceable.

real property Land and all property permanently attached to it, such as buildings.

real property ownership Legally recognized interest in land, fixtures attached thereto, and right to possession, transfer, or sale.

reasonable Comporting with normally accepted modes of behavior in a particular instance.

reasonable assignment A transfer of performance obligations may only be made where an objective third party would find that the transfer was acceptable under normal circumstances and did not alter the rights and obligations of the original parties.

reasonable person standard The standard of conduct of a person in the community in similar circumstances; when objectively assessed, a reasonable person would consider the complained-of activity both unwanted and the cause of harm.

reasonable suspicion Such suspicion that will justify an officer, for Fourth Amendment purposes, in stopping a defendant in a public place, as having knowledge sufficient to induce an ordinarily prudent and cautious man under the circumstances to believe that criminal activity is at hand.

reasoning The court's rationale that sets forth the legal principles the court relied upon in reaching its decision.

reasoning by analogy Method of reasoning that compares two similar or like cases, facts, or other legal source law to support the principles presented in your research project.

rebuttal witness Refutes or contradicts evidence presented by the opposing side.

receiving stolen property The crime of acquiring or controlling property known to have been stolen by another person.

reciprocal will Wills in which testators name each other as beneficiaries under similar plans.

reckless(ness) Lack of concern for the results or applicable standards of decency and reasonableness.

record Documentation of the trial court, including pleadings, physical evidence, transcript, and decision of the trial court.

recuse (recusal) Voluntary disqualification by a judge due to a conflict of interest or the appearance of one.

redacted Eliminated information or material from a legal document due to privacy and security matters.

redirect examination The attorney who originally called the witness asks more questions.

redundancy The repeated use of the same point or concept.

reference line A line of text that appears below the address block, and identifies the subject matter of the letter.

reformation An order of the court that "rewrites" the agreement to reflect the actual performances of the parties where there has been some deviation from the contractual obligation; changed or modified by agreement; that is, the contracting parties mutually agree to restructure a material element of the original agreement.

regional reporters Reporters that contain the cases of all the states in a particular geographical area.

regulatory law Laws passed by administrative agencies and court interpretations.

rehabilitation Restoring a person to his or her former capacity.

rejection A refusal to accept the terms of an offer.

release A discharge from the parties' performance obligations that acknowledges the dispute but forgoes contractual remedies.

relevance Reasonably related or associated with the ultimate facts and legal theories.

relevant evidence Evidence that makes the existence of any fact more probable or less probable than it would be without the evidence.

relevant fact A fact that is significant to a case and its holding.

reliability Confidence of soundness.

reliance A party's dependence and actions based on the assertions of another party.

reliance damages A monetary amount that "reimburses" the nonbreaching party for expenses incurred while preparing to perform her obligations under the agreement but lost due to the breach.

remainder Right to receive property interest at some point in the future.

remainder interest The original owner transfers the remaining portion of the interest and property upon termination of the life estate.

remand(ed) Disposition in which the appellate court sends the case back to the lower court for further action.

removal Moving a case from the state court to the federal court system.

renunciation Abandonment of effort to commit a crime.

reply The responsive pleading provided in Rule 7 to a counterclaim.

reply brief Short responsive brief of the appellant to the appellee's brief.

reporters Hardbound volumes containing judicial decisions.

request for admission (request to admit) A document that provides the drafter with the opportunity to conclusively establish selected facts prior to trial.

request for medical examination Form of discovery that requests a medical examination of an opposing party in a lawsuit.

request for production of documents and things (request to produce) A discovery device that requests the production of certain items, such as photographs, papers, reports, and physical evidence; must specify the document sought.

requirements contract An agreement wherein the quantity that the offeror desires to purchase is all that the offeror needs.

res ipsa loquitur Doctrine in which it is assumed that a person's injuries were caused by the negligent act of another person as the harmful act ordinarily would not occur but for negligence.

res judicata (Latin) "The thing has been adjudicated." The principle that a court's decision on a particular matter is binding on future litigation between the parties; sometimes referred to as "res adjudicata."

resale value The nonbreaching party's attempt to mitigate damages may require that he sell the unaccepted goods on the open market. The nonbreaching party can recover the difference in price between the market price and the contract price.

rescission and restitution A decision by the court that renders the contract null and void and requires the parties to return to the wronged party any benefits received under the agreement.

rescission Mutual agreement to early discharge or termination of remaining duties.

rescue doctrine Doctrine in which a tortfeasor is liable for harm caused to a person who is injured while rescuing the original victim.

research Process of locating law.

research memorandum Reviews case facts, presents the research question, summarizes the research findings, and answers the research question with a legal analysis of the applicable law.

residence The permanent home of the party.

residuary gift Gift of the remaining property of an estate after expenses and specific gifts have been satisfied.

respondent Name designation of the party responding to an appeal.

restatement A recitation of the common law in a particular legal subject; a series of volumes authored by the American Law Institute that tell what the law in a general area is, how it is changing, and what direction the authors think this change is headed in.

Restatement of the Law of Torts, Second An authoritative treatise that is a compilation of the key principles of tort law.

restitution Returns the injured party to the same position enjoyed prior to the breach.

restitution damages A monetary amount that requires the breaching party to return any benefits received under the contract to the nonbreaching party to ensure that the breaching party does not profit from the breach.

restrictive phrase A phrase that specifies or restricts the application of something.

retainer letter A form of correspondence that sets forth the agreement and relationship between the attorney and client.

retract the repudiation Until the aggrieved party notifies the repudiator or takes some action in reliance on the repudiation, the repudiator has the right to "take it back" and perform on the contract.

retreat rule The doctrine holding that the victim of a crime must choose to retreat instead of using deadly force if certain circumstances exist.

retribution Punishment based on just deserts.

reversal The act of the appellate court that overturns the decision of a lower court.

reverse(d) (reversal) Disposition in which the appellate court disagrees with trial court.

reversible error An error that affects a party's substantive rights or the case's outcome, and thus is grounds for reversal if the party properly objected.

reversionary future interest Upon completion of the life estate, the property, in its entirety, passes back again to the original owner.

reversionary interest Upon completion of the terms under the conditional estate, the remainder of the real property reverts to the original owner, or his or her estate, as appropriate and consistent with the type of ownership originally vested in the owner.

revert (reversion) Right to receive back property in the event of the happening of a certain condition.

revocation of a previous acceptance A buyer has the right to refuse to accept the seller's attempts at a cure if those attempts are still not in conformance with the contract requirements.

revoke (revocation) To take back, as in to retract an offer at any time prior to it being accepted; the offeror's cancellation of the right of the offeree to accept an offer.

rhythm A pattern of writing conveyed through word choice and word placement in the sentence.

right of survivorship The right of a surviving joint tenant to take ownership of a deceased joint tenant's share of the property.

right to transfer The party supplying the goods must have the legal title (ownership) or legal ability to give it to the receiving party.

riot An unlawful disturbance of the peace by an assembly of usually three or more persons acting with a common purpose in a violent or tumultuous manner that threatens or terrorizes the public.

risk management Prospectively evaluating potential problems or legal challenges in a particular situation and implementing avoidance strategies in advance to limit potential liability.

robbery The direct taking of property from another through force or threat.

Rule 11 One of the major rules under the Rules of Civil Procedure; it requires an attorney to investigate an action before bringing it.

rule of law Sources of law that control the issue.

rule or regulation Similar to a statute; the agency's protocols that govern the behavior of citizens and businesses.

rulemaking The agency process of developing its rules and regulations.

rules of construction The rules that control the judicial interpretation of statutes.

rules of court The rules that govern the litigation process in civil and criminal proceedings.

run-on sentence A sentence that contains two independent clauses that are not joined by a conjunction.

S

sale on approval The agreement may provide that the contract for sale is not consummated until the buyer receives and approves of the goods.

sale or return The agreement provides that if the buyer is unable to resell the goods, she is permitted to return the unsold goods to the original seller.

sales contract The transfer of title to goods for a set price governed by the UCC rules.

salutation A greeting that appears below the reference line.

same case A Shepard's notation representing the identical case Shepardized but from the lower court.

sanctions Penalty against a party in the form of an order to compel, a monetary fine, a contempt-of-court citation, or a court order with specific description of the individualized remedy.

satisfaction Changed agreement resulting from agreed discharge of obligations.

scienter A degree of knowledge that makes a person legally responsible for his or her act or omission.

search engine A software program that searches databases to gather information based upon a given set of search terms or a Web site that searches the Internet for information related to a query.

search warrant Issued after presentation of an affidavit stating clearly the probable cause on which the request is based. In particular, it is an order in writing, issued by a justice or other magistrate, in the name of the state, and directed to a sheriff, constable, or other officer authorizing him to search for and seize any property that constitutes evidence of the commission of a crime, contraband, or the fruits of the crime.

secondary authority Authority that analyzes the law such as a treatise, encyclopedia, or law review article.

segment search Restricts and narrows a search on LexisNexis. It is equivalent to Westlaw field search.

seizure Personal exercise of the possessory right to particular property is interrupted or denied by virtue of government action.

self-authenticating document A document that is authorized by statute and that can be used without additional offer of proof.

self-defense A defendant's legal excuse that the use of force was justified.

self-incrimination Acts or declarations either as testimony at trial or prior to trial by which one implicates himself in a crime.

semicolon A form of punctuation used to indicate a break in thought, though of a different sort than that indicated by a comma.

seminal Most important, fundamental.

sentence The judgment formally pronounced by the court or judge upon the defendant after his/her conviction in a criminal prosecution, imposing the punishment to be inflicted, usually in the form of a fine, incarceration, or probation.

sentence fragment A group of words that lacks necessary grammatical information, such as a verb, that would make it a complete sentence.

sentencing The post-conviction stage of the criminal justice process in which the defendant is brought before the court for imposition of sentence.

separate property One spouse is the exclusive owner.

separation Legally requires continuously living separate and apart for the statutorily set period.

separation agreements Contract between husband and wife to live apart; the document outlines the terms of the separation.

separation of powers A form of checks and balances to ensure that one branch does not become dominant; the doctrine that divides the powers of government among the three branches established under the U.S. Constitution.

serious bodily injury Serious physical impairment of the human body; especially, bodily injury that creates a substantial risk of death or that causes serious, permanent disfigurement or protracted loss or impairment.

service of process The procedure by which a defendant is notified by a process server of a lawsuit.

session laws The second format in which new statutes appear as a compilation of the slip laws; a bill or joint resolution that has become law during a particular session of the legislature.

settled law Established law.

settlement A negotiated termination of a case prior to a trial or jury verdict.

severability of contract The ability of a court to choose to separate and discard those clauses in a contract that are unenforceable and retain those that are.

sham consideration An unspecified and indeterminable recitation of consideration that cannot support an exchange.

shareholder The owner of one or more shares of stock in a corporation.

Shepard's Citations Reference system that reports the legal authority referring to the legal position of the case and making reference to the case opinion.

Shepardizing (Shepardize) Using Shepard's verification and updating system for cases, statutes, and other legal resources.

short form citation Citation used after the complete citation is used in the legal document.

short summary of the conclusion A summary that provides the reader with a quick answer to the "yes or no" questions raised by the issues.

signals Words that introduce additional references to the legal authority cited, such as see, see also, and accord .

signatory A party that signs a document, becoming a party to an agreement.

signature block Section of the brief for attorney's signature that includes the name, address, bar card identification, fax number, and telephone number.

signed by the party to be charged The writing that purports to satisfy the Statute of Frauds must be signed by the party against whom enforcement is sought.

silence In certain circumstances, no response may be necessary to properly accept an offer.

simile A direct comparison of dissimilar objects, for the purpose of emphasizing a common characteristic.

simple sentence A sentence that has a simple format—subject/verb/object.

Sixth Amendment Protections include a speedy trial, the right to confront the accuser, a jury trial, and the assistance of counsel.

skip tracing A general term for tracking a person who has absconded or is attempting to avoid legal process.

slander Written defamatory statements.

slang Informal expressions.

slip law The first format in which a newly signed statute appears; a copy of a particular law passed during a session of legislature.

slip opinion The first format in which a judicial opinion appears.

small claims court Court whose jurisdiction is generally limited by monetary ceilings.

social guest licensee Property owner derives no benefit or economic gain from the individual's presence and legal use of the property.

Socratic method Analysis and teaching tool based on questioning and discussion.

sodomy Oral or anal copulation between humans.

sole custody Only one of the divorcing spouses has both legal and physical custody, but the noncustodial parent may have visitation rights.

sole proprietorship A business owned by one person.

solemnization A formalization of a marriage, as in for example a marriage ceremony.

solicitation The crime of inducing or encouraging another to commit a crime.

solicited offer An invitation for members of a group to whom it is sent (potential offerors) to make an offer to the party sending the information (the potential offeree).

special appearance A term describing a defendant's contest of jurisdiction; the defendant enters the court for the limited purpose of contesting the case, but does not submit to the court's jurisdiction for other purposes.

special damages Those damages incurred beyond and in addition to the general damages suffered and expected in similar cases.

special defenses Affirmative defenses.

special prosecutor Specially appointed government attorney.

specialized goods A product made for a particular buyer with specifications unique to that buyer so that it could not be sold on the general market.

specific gift A gift of a particular described item.

specific intent The mental desire and will to act in a particular way.

specific performance A court order that requires a party to perform a certain act in order to prevent harm to the requesting party.

specific reasons for rejection The buyer is under an obligation to notify the seller within a reasonable time not only that the goods have been rejected but also the reasons for the refusal to accept the goods.

speculative damages Harm incurred by the nonbreaching party that is not susceptible to valuation or determination with any reasonable certainty.

split sentence A sentence where part of the time is served in confinement and the rest is spent on probation.

spot sale A purchase on the open market in that particular place at that particular time.

spousal payment See *alimony, support.*

stalking The act or offense of following or loitering near another with the purpose of annoying or harassing that person or committing a further crime.

standard of care Criteria for measuring appropriateness of behavior.

standard of review Guideline the court applies in evaluating the errors on appeal.

standards of good faith and fair dealing A party's performance will be judged in light of the normal or acceptable behavior displayed generally by others in a similar position.

standing Legally sufficient reason and right to object.

stare decisis (Latin) "Stand by the decision." Decisions from a court with substantially the same set of facts should be followed by that court and all lower courts under it; the judicial process of adhering to prior case decisions; the doctrine of precedent whereby once a court has decided a specific issue one way in the past, it and other courts in the same jurisdiction are obligated to follow that earlier decision in deciding cases with similar issues in the future.

star-paging A practice that enables the reader to identify the page breaks in one reporter by reviewing the decision as reprinted in another reporter.

state bar The organization that licenses and oversees the practice of law and the conduct of attorneys in the state. An attorney must be a member of the state bar before she will be allowed to practice in that state.

state or federal rules of civil procedure (rules of the court) Rules related to all aspects of the legal process from the proper court and judicial system for a particular dispute through each aspect, including appeals and agency proceedings.

state rights Constitutionally defined rights of individual state governments to preserve and protect individual rights of citizens of the state, providing there is no conflict with the federal Constitution.

state supremacy Constitutional principle that the individual states have sole governmental authority over matters related to only state citizens without influencing or negatively impacting federal rights and privileges.

state supreme court The final and highest court in many states.

statement of facts Section of a brief that sets forth the significant facts and information needed to analyze the issues presented.

statement of issues presented A statement that identifies the legal and factual issues to be discussed in your memorandum.

statement of the case Section of the appellate brief that sets forth the procedural history of the case.

Statute of Frauds Rule that specifies which contracts must be in writing to be enforceable.

statute of limitations Establishes the applicable time limits for filing and responding to certain claims or legal actions.

statute Written law enacted by the legislative branches of both federal and state governments.

Statutes at Large Official permanent collection of the laws passed by each session of Congress.

statutory authority The legislature of a jurisdiction may codify certain actions as subject to punitive damages if they occur in conjunction with a contractual breach.

statutory law Derived from the Constitution in statutes enacted by the legislative branch of state or federal government; primary source of law consisting of the body of legislative law.

statutory rape The sexual intercourse with a female who is under a certain age (usually fourteen to eighteen, depending on the state). The minor child is considered legally incapable of consenting.

stay(ed) Extraordinary relief suspending the process in one court while the appellate court reviews the legal issue, which may result in dismissal of the case from the lower court.

stipulation An agreement between attorneys and parties in a case about a procedural or factual issue.

stop and frisk The situation where police officers who are suspicious of an individual run their hands lightly over the suspect's outer garments to determine if the person is carrying a concealed weapon.

strict liability The defendant is liable without the plaintiff having to prove fault. Also, liability that is based on the breach of an absolute duty rather than negligence or intent.

strict scrutiny standard Most exacting and precise legal analysis because fundamental constitutional rights may have been unconstitutionally restricted or revoked.

string citation List of citations in the brief following a point of law cited.

structure Fundamental principle of law and social order in any government system.

structured enumeration Identification of each point in a sentence sequentially.

style Also known as caption; the heading or title used in all legal pleadings.

sua sponte On his or her own motion; rarely exercised right of the judge to make a motion and ruling without an underlying request from either party.

subheadings Headings that identify the subpoints in an argument section.

subject matter The bargained-for exchange that forms the basis for the contract.

subject matter jurisdiction A court's authority over the res, the subject of the case.

submission The agreement to arbitrate a specific matter or issue raised between the parties.

subordinate clause A clause that cannot stand on its own as a complete sentence.

subpoena A document that is served upon an individual under authority of the court, and orders the person to appear at a certain place and certain time for a deposition, or suffer the consequences; an order issued by the court clerk directing a person to appear in court.

subpoena *duces tecum* A type of subpoena that requests a witness to produce documents.

subrogation The right to sue in the name of another.

subsequent agreements Negotiations and potential terms that are discussed after the agreement has been memorialized are not covered by the parol evidence rule.

subsequent history History of a case on appeal.

substantial beginning An offeree has made conscientious efforts to start performing according to the terms of the contract. The performance need not be complete nor exactly as specified, but only an attempt at significant compliance.

substantial capacity The term used in the definition of legal insanity proposed by the Model Penal Code.

substantial compliance A legal doctrine that permits close approximations of perfect performance to satisfy the contractual terms.

substantial detriment The change in a party's position in reliance upon another's representations that, if unanswered, will work a hardship on that party.

substantial performance Most of the contracted performance is complete.

substantial-cause test Analysis of which of the possible factors was the real cause.

substantive due process Requires that legislation be reasonable in scope and limitations, and further that the statute serve a legitimate purpose, including equal impact on all citizens.

substantive law Legal rules that are the content or substance of the law, defining rights and duties of citizens.

substituted agreement A replacement of a previous agreement with a new contract with additional but not inconsistent obligations.

substituted goods The products purchased on the open market that replace those not delivered by the breaching party.

sufficiency Adequacy.

sufficient consideration The exchanges have recognizable legal value and are capable of supporting an enforceable contract. The actual values are irrelevant.

summary judgment A method of ending a court case without a formal trial. The case must have no genuine issues of material fact and the moving party must be entitled to judgment as a matter of law.

summons The notice to appear in court, notifying the defendant of the plaintiff's complaint.

supervening illegality An agreement whose terms at the time it was made were legal but, due to a change in the law during the time in which the contract was executory, that has since become illegal; a change in the law governing the subject matter of the contract that renders a previously legal and enforceable contract void and therefore excusable.

supplement Individual stand-alone paperbound volume that collects all the material subsequent to the most recent set of pocket parts.

"supplemental evidence which adds to, but does not contradict, the original agreement is admissible under the parol evidence rule" Agreements of the parties that naturally add to, but do not conflict with, the original terms of the partially integrated contract.

supplemental pleading A pleading that adds to a pleading without deleting prior information.

supplemental response Additional response to previously filed discovery because of newly found information.

support Periodic payments extending over time.

suppression hearing A pretrial proceeding in criminal cases in which a defendant seeks to prevent the introduction of evidence alleged to have been seized illegally.

supra Above.

Supremacy Clause Sets forth the principle and unambiguously reinforces that the Constitution is the supreme law of the land.

surety A party who assumes primary liability for the payment of another's debt.

survey A description of the boundaries of a piece of property.

suspended sentence A sentence postponed so that the defendant is not required to serve time in the absence of certain circumstances.

sustain A judge's ruling in agreement with the party who raised the objection.

syllabus A short paragraph summary in the official reporter identifying issue, procedural history, and ruling of the court; an editorial feature in unofficial reporters that summarizes the court's decision.

synopsis A short paragraph summary prepared by the publisher in unofficial reporters that identifies the issue, the procedural history, and the ruling of the court in the instant case.

T

table of authorities Section of the appellate brief that identifies the cases, statutes, constitutional provisions, and all other primary and secondary authorities contained within the brief.

Table of Cases Index Lists of all the cases whose text appears in the associated volumes.

table of contents Roadmap of the appellate brief, which includes the section headings and corresponding page numbers in the brief.

tangible evidence Evidence that can be touched, picked up.

tangible property Personal property that can be held or touched, such as furniture or jewelry.

technical terms, specifications, or **trade/business custom** Parol evidence is permitted to explain the meaning of special language in the contract as the parties understood it if the plain ordinary meaning of the language was not intended or was ambiguous.

temporary injunction A court order that prohibits a party from acting in a certain way for a limited period of time.

temporary restraining order A court order barring a person from harassing or harming another.

temporary suspension A punishment for an ethical violation; an attorney is temporarily prohibited from practicing law or representing clients

tenancy by the entirety A form of ownership for married couples, similar to joint tenancy, where the spouse has right of survivorship.

tenancy for years A lease with fixed beginning and ending dates; for example, a lease may be for one year.

tenancy in common A form of ownership between two or more people where each owner's interest upon death goes to his or her heirs.

tenant A person, or corporation, who rents real property from an owner; also called a lessee.

tender of delivery The seller is ready to transfer the goods to the buyer and the goods are at the disposal of the buyer.

tender of performance Acts in furtherance of performance; the offeree's act of proffering the start of his contractual obligations. The offeree stands ready, willing, and able to perform.

terminated Performance is complete and the contract is discharged.

tendering The process of admitting evidence in a trial by asking the court to rule on relevance.

terms and connectors Words such as "and," "or," and "not," which link words and concepts to form a searching device on the Internet to retrieve documents and information.

terms of art Words that are commonly used in the legal profession and have an accepted meaning.

terrorism The use or threat of violence to intimidate or cause panic, especially as a means of affecting political conduct.

testamentary capacity The ability to understand and have the legal capacity to make a will.

testimonial evidence Oral statements made by a witness under oath.

testate The state of having died with a valid will.

testator/testatrix The person who writes a will.

texts One-volume treatises.

The Bluebook: A Uniform System of Citation, 17th ed. Widely used legal citation resource, published by the Harvard Law Review Association, that is regularly revised and updated.

theft The taking of property without the owner's consent.

third-party beneficiary A person, not a party to the contract, who stands to receive the benefit of performance of the contract.

third-party claim A suit filed by the defendant against a party not originally named in the plaintiff's complaint.

tickler file System of tracking dates and reminding what is due on any given day or in any given week, month, or year.

time for performance A condition that requires each party be given a reasonable time to complete performance.

time of the essence A term in a contract that indicates that no extensions for the required performance will be permitted. The performance must occur on or before the specified date.

timekeeping Records of the time spent and the nature of the work done for each client; a legal task for both paralegals and attorneys.

title The legal link between a person who owns property and the property itself; legal evidence of a person's ownership rights.

title insurance policy The insurance provided by a title company; it protects the lender and buyer in case it is discovered that the title is imperfect.

title page Cover page of the brief.

title search A search of the abstract of title; the short history of a piece of property including ownership interests and liens.

tone Language and style used to present an argument; the way a writer communicates a point of view.

topic sentence The first sentence of the paragraph, which introduces an idea.

tort A civil wrongful act, committed against a person or property, either intentional or negligent.

tort reform law Limiting or capping the monetary awards juries can make for specific classes of tort actions such as personal injury or automobile liability.

tortfeasor Actor committing the wrong, whether intentional, negligent, or strict liability.

tortious A private civil wrong committed by one person as against another that the law considers to be punishable.

torts against property Trespass to land and chattel, interference with business relations, and conversion.

torts against the person Assault and battery; false imprisonment; defamation, either libel or slander; and intentional infliction of emotional distress.

total breach A failure of performance that has a substantial effect on the expectations of the parties.

totality of circumstances test Evidence offered must be sufficient in terms of quantity or comprehensiveness.

totality of the circumstances A legal standard that requires focus on the entire situation and not on one specific factor.

trade fixtures Pieces of equipment on or attached to the property being used in a trade or business.

trade secret Property that is protected from misappropriation such as formulas, patterns, and compilations of information.

traditional (manual) legal research Uses libraries, books, and other materials in paper format.

transactional documents Documents that define property rights and performance obligations.

transactions in goods A sale or other transfer of title to identifiable, tangible, movable things from a merchant to a buyer.

transcript Written account of a trial court proceeding or deposition.

transfer of interest In a purchase agreement, a preliminary requirement is that the seller has legal title to the subject matter and authority to transfer it to the seller. If the seller transfers his interest to a third party, this preliminary requirement can no longer be met.

transferred intent doctrine The doctrine that holds a person liable for the unintended result to another person not contemplated by the defendant's actions.

transition The writer's ability to move the reader from paragraph to paragraph.

transitional function Moving the reader though the material in an orderly progression.

transmittal letter A type of confirmation letter that accompanies information sent to a designated party.

treason A breach of allegiance to one's government, usually committed through levying war against such government or by giving aid or comfort to the enemy.

treatise A scholarly study of one area of the law.

trespass to chattel Interfering with the right to freedom of possession of chattel, or personal property, rightly owned and possessed.

trespass to land Intentional and unlawful entry onto or interference with the land of another person without consent.

trespassers Uninvited guests on the property of the landowner.

trespassory taking The act of seizing an article from the possession of the rightful owner.

trial courts Courts that hear all cases and are courts of general jurisdiction.

trial notebook Started and organized prior to the pretrial conference, it contains all documentary and other tangible evidence or materials used by the attorney in trial.

trial order Also called a trial schedule order; issued by the judge assigned to the case.

trial The forum for the presenting of evidence and testimony and the deliberation of guilt.

trier of fact Jury.

trier of law Judge.

TRO A temporary restraining order that is issued prior to any hearing in the court.

unauthorized means The offeree accepts the offer by a method that is not the same as specified by the offeror.

umpire A person with greater authority than an arbitrator; this person has the authority to make a final and binding decision when an arbitrator has been unable to do so.

unauthorized practice of law (UPL) Practicing law without proper authorization to do so.

unconscionable contract A contract so completely unreasonable and irrational that it shocks the conscience.

unconscionable So completely unreasonable and irrational that it shocks the conscience.

uncontested dissolution Following the waiting period prescribed by statute, parties jointly file the documents required by law to dissolve the marriage, based on voluntary agreement.

under the influence Persons who do not have the capacity to understand a transaction due to overconsumption of alcohol or the use of drugs, either legal or illegal, and, therefore, who do not have the requisite mental intent to enter into a contract.

undue enrichment Gain experienced without related duty or obligation of performance.

undue influence Persons who do not have the capacity to understand a transaction due to overconsumption of alcohol or the use of drugs, either legal or illegal, and, therefore, who do not have the requisite mental intent to enter into a contract.

undue influence Using a close personal or fiduciary relationship to one's advantage to gain assent to terms that the party otherwise would not have agreed to.

unfair detriment A burden incurred for which there is no compensation.

unforeseen circumstances Occurrences that could not be reasonably forecast to happen.

unicameral process A legislature that only has one body required to pass a bill, such as Nebraska.

Uniform Child Custody Jurisdiction Act (UCCJA) An act that resolves jurisdictional issues related to child custody.

uniform laws Proposed standardized statutes that may be adopted by a state

Uniform Parentage Act An act defining legal parentage and establishing parental rights.

uniform resource locator (URL) Precise location of a specific document retrieved from an electronic source or the Web address for the referenced source.

uniform statute Model legislation drafted by the National Conference of Commissioners on Uniform State Laws, dealing with areas of the law such as sales transactions.

unilateral One-sided; relating to only one of two or more persons or things.

unilateral contract A contract in which the parties exchange a promise for an act.

unilateral mistake An error made by only one party to the transaction. The contract may be avoided only if the error is detectable or obvious to the other party.

United States Code Federal statutes currently in force in the United States.

United States Code Annotated Federal code published by ThomsonWest that contains finding tools.

United States Code Service Federal code published by LexisNexis that contains finding tools.

United States Constitution The fundamental law of the United States of America, which became the law of the land in March of 1789.

unjust enrichment The retention by a party of unearned and undeserved benefits derived from his own wrongful actions regarding an agreement.

unlimited liability A finding that a business owner's personal assets may be used to satisfy a judgment against the business.

unofficial reporters Private publications of court decisions (for example, 525 N.E.2d 90).

unpublished case A case decided by a court that is not published in a reporter because it does not set precedent.

unsolicited memorandum anticipating legal issues Memorandum of law prepared by one of the parties to the case in support of an anticipated legal issue.

usage of the trade Actions generally taken by similarly situated parties in similar transactions in the same business field.

U.S. Bankruptcy Code Defines the rules related to bankruptcy filing, process, and adjudication.

U.S. circuit courts of appeals Appeals courts in the federal system.

U.S. Constitution The fundamental law of the United States of America, which became the law of the land in March of 1789.

U.S. Court of Federal Claims Part of the lower or trial court level of the federal court system in which disputes with the U.S. government are heard.

U.S. courts of appeals Intermediate review level of the federal court system that reviews the decisions of the district or trial court level.

U.S. district courts Trial or lower court level in the federal system.

uttering The crime of presenting a false or worthless document with the intent to harm or defraud.

V

vacate(d) Disposition in which an appellate court voids the decision of the lower court.

vagrancy The act of going about from place to place by a person without visible means of support, who is idle, and who, though able to work for his/her maintenance, refuses to do so, but lives without labor or on the charity of others.

value The objective worth placed on the subject matter in a transaction.

value of the goods as accepted The buyer is entitled to a "set-off " for the difference between the price of the goods as specified in the contract and the actual price those goods would garner on the open market.

vandalism Such willful or malicious acts are intended to damage or destroy property.

vehicular homicide The killing of another person by one's unlawful or negligent operation of a motor vehicle.

venue County in which the facts are alleged to have occurred and in which the trial will take place.

veracity test Meets truth or strict correctness in process and content.

verbosity The use of an excessive number of words, or excessively complicated words, to make a point.

verdict Decision of the jury following presentation of facts and application of relevant law as they relate to the law presented in the jury instructions.

verification Acknowledgment by a party of the truthfulness of the information contained within a document.

vested Having a present right to receive the benefit of the performance when it becomes due.

veto Rejection of a bill by the president or governor.

vicarious liability (*respondeat superior*) One person, or a third party, may be found liable for the act of another or shares liability with the actor.

video deposition Videotaped version of the oral deposition; the videotape serves as an additional method of preserving the testimony, in addition to the transcript.

visitation rights The right to legally see a child, where physical custody is not awarded.

voice The sound heard in the mind of the reader, or the impression created by virtue of the words chosen.

void A transaction that is impossible to be enforced because it is invalid.

void ab initio Marriages that are void from the inception.

void contract Agreement that does not meet the required elements and therefore is unenforceable under contract law.

void marriage The marriage fails to meet the legal requirements.

voidable Having the possibility of avoidance of performance at the option of the incapacitated party.

voidable contract Apparently fully enforceable contract with a defect unknown by one party.

voidable marriage Valid in all legal respects until the union is dissolved by order of the court.

voidable obligation A duty imposed under a contract that may be either ratified (approved) or avoided (rejected) at the option of one or both of the parties.

voir dire The process of selecting a jury for trial.

voluntary destruction If a party destroys the subject matter of the contract, thereby rendering performance impossible, the other party is excused from his performance obligations due to that termination.

voluntary disablement If a party takes steps to preclude his own performance, then the performance due from the other party is excused due to that refusal/inability to perform.

voluntary manslaughter An act of murder reduced to manslaughter because of extenuating circumstances such as adequate provocation or diminished capacity.

voluntary repayment of debt An agreement to pay back a debt that cannot be collected upon using legal means because the obligation to make payments has been discharged.

waiver A party may knowingly and intentionally forgive the other party's breach and continue her performance obligations under the contract.

warrant Issued after presentation of an affidavit stating clearly the probable cause on which the request is based.

warrantless search Compelling reasons support search without a written warrant.

warranty A promise or representation by the seller that the goods in question meet certain standards.

warranty deed A deed guaranteeing clear title to real property

warranty of title The seller promises the buyer that the seller has the right to transfer the title free and clear of encumbrances to the buyer.

waste Deterioration of the property.

Westclip An electronic clipping service used on Westlaw that monitors legal developments.

Westlaw Commercial electronic law database service.

Wharton's rule The doctrine that an agreement by two or more persons to commit a particular crime cannot be prosecuted as a conspiracy if the crime could not be committed except by the actual number of participants involved.

wheel conspiracy A conspiracy in which a single member or group separately agrees with two or more other members or groups.

wildcard A character such as an exclamation point or asterisk entered into a search expression that acts as a substitution to retrieve all variations of the expression.

will A document representing the formal declaration of a person's wishes for the manner and distribution of his or her property upon death.

witness locator service A company that provides information about a witness's former addresses, telephone numbers, employment, and current location.

Words and Phrases Index An index to a digest that construes a judicial term.

work product An attorney's written notes, impressions, charts, diagrams, and other material used by her to prepare strategy and tactics for trial.

writ A written order of a judge requiring specific action by the person or entity to whom the writ is directed.

writ of certiorari Granting of petition, by the U.S. Supreme Court, to review a case; request for appeal where the Court has the discretion to grant or deny it.

writ of habeas corpus Literally "bring the body"; application for extraordinary relief or a petition for rehearing of the issue on the basis of unusual facts unknown at the time of the trial.

writing to satisfy the Statute of Frauds A document or compilation of documents containing the essential terms of the agreement.

Index

A

B

C

D

E

F

G

H

I

J

K

L

S

T

U

V

W

Y